THE BUILDINGS OF ENGLAND

FOUNDING EDITOR: NIKOLAUS PEVSNER
JOINT EDITORS: BRIDGET CHERRY
AND JUDY NAIRN
ADVISORY EDITOR: JOHN NEWMAN

LONDON 3: NORTH WEST

BRIDGET CHERRY AND NIKOLAUS PEVSNER

Essex

London 4:
North and
North East

N

WALTHAM
FOREST
(WF)

REDBRIDGE
(Re)

HAVERING
(Hv)

NEY
(Hc)

TOWER
HAMLETS
(TH)

NEWHAM
(Ne)

BARKING
(Bk)

GREENWICH
(Gr)

BEXLEY
(Bx)

R. Thames

LEWISHAM
(Le)

Kent

BROMLEY
(Bm)

D ON

/////// Shaded areas are described in *London I:
The Cities of London and Westminster*
········· London County Council Boundary 1888–1965
— — — Greater London Council Boundary from 1965

| 0 | 5 | 10 | 15 km |
| 0 | | 5 | 10 miles |

The publishers and authors gratefully acknowledge
a grant received from the Greater London Council
to cover the costs of research

London
3
NORTH WEST

BY

BRIDGET CHERRY

AND

NIKOLAUS PEVSNER

THE BUILDINGS OF ENGLAND

PENGUIN BOOKS

PENGUIN BOOKS
Published by the Penguin Group
27 Wrights Lane, London W8 5TZ, England

Viking Penguin, a division of Penguin Books USA Inc.,
375 Hudson Street, New York, New York 10014, USA
Penguin Books Australia Ltd, Ringwood, Victoria, Australia
Penguin Books Canada Ltd, 10 Alcorn Avenue, Toronto, Ontario, Canada M4V 3B2
Penguin Books (NZ) Ltd, 182–190 Wairau Road, Auckland 10, New Zealand

Penguin Books Ltd, Registered Offices: Harmondsworth, Middlesex, England

First published 1991

ISBN 0 14 071048 5

Made and printed in Great Britain
by Butler & Tanner Ltd, Frome and London
Set in Monotype Plantin

In memory of
ALLEN LANE
founder of Penguin Books
and instigator of
The Buildings of England
to whom
BE3 *Middlesex*
was dedicated in 1951
and of
JUDY NAIRN
editor of
The Buildings of England
1955–1991

CONTENTS

CONTENTS

FOREWORD

BY BRIDGET CHERRY

Like its predecessor, London 2: South, *this volume is divided according to the boroughs created by the Greater London Council on its formation in 1965:* London 3: North West *deals with Brent, Ealing, Harrow, Hillingdon, and Hounslow from the former county of Middlesex, and Kensington and Chelsea, Hammersmith and Fulham, and outer Westminster (i.e. St Marylebone and Paddington) from the area of the former London County Council. The old City of Westminster and the City of London are covered by* London 1: the Cities of London and Westminster *(3rd ed., 1973); the northern and north-eastern boroughs will be dealt with in* London 4: North and North East *(in preparation). Thames Crossings are described in* London 2: South.

The territory covered here previously formed part of two very early Buildings of England *volumes, Nikolaus Pevsner's* Middlesex *(1951) and* London except the Cities of London and Westminster *(1952), both invaluable landmarks in their time, particularly in their appreciation of buildings in the C 19. The progress of research, however, the broadening of architectural appreciation, and building developments of the last forty years have necessitated extensive revision and expansion.*

Disparity between the size and density of different areas has dictated some flexibility of arrangement. The inner boroughs are subdivided into their pre-1965 administrative areas, broadly coinciding with the ancient parishes and reflected in the dual names retained by Kensington and Chelsea, Hammersmith and Fulham. In the outer areas, which are composed of larger numbers of districts and parishes, the main places are listed alphabetically. Within each subdivision, the arrangement follows established Buildings of England *practice: Churches (Anglican, Roman Catholic, Nonconformist, and places of worship for other religions, each section strictly alphabetically by name) and Cemeteries; Public Buildings*; and Perambulations (divided into reasonably brief and, it is hoped, manageable itineraries). The exception is southern St Marylebone, where streets are listed alphabetically. No arrangement will satisfy all users, but it is hoped that with the help of the map on pp. 2–3 (which shows the boundaries of the other London volumes and the abbreviations used for all boroughs), the borough maps,*

---

*Public buildings are in the following order where possible:
 1. Town hall and municipal buildings.
 2. Other official buildings (law court, police station, fire station, ambulance headquarters, post office, prison).
 3. Other local authority buildings (library, museum, baths, sports centre, community centre).
 4. Educational buildings.
 5. Medical buildings.
 6. Parks.
 7. Utilities (market, gasworks, power station, waterworks, sewerage).
 8. Transport (railways, docks and canals, bridges).

the indexes of streets and buildings and of boroughs and localities, and the indexes which precede each borough, as well as the separate introductions which deal with the development of individual boroughs and point to some of their architectural highlights, readers will be able to find their way around this sprawling mass of suburban building. Two exceptions have been made to the boundary divisions: the outlying part of Westminster s of Hyde Park is treated with the neighbouring part of Kensington; and the E strip of Regents Park (which is in Camden) is included together with the rest of Regents Park under St Marylebone.

The general introduction provides a broad chronological conspectus of architectural development in the area of the gazetteer. For the C 19 and C 20 it is arranged by building types rather than according to the achievements of individual architects, as these can be pursued through the separate index. The introductions to geology and industrial archaeology also relate to North West London. The other specialist introductions cover the whole of Greater London.

Some further elucidatory notes must be added. It must be stated firmly that mention of houses or other buildings in no way implies that they are open to the public. Where a pair of dates is quoted, the first is generally for the acceptance of the design, the second for the completion, in so far as these are known to the compilers. For modern buildings the names of job architects or architects in charge have been included in addition to the name of the firm, when that information has been available. In the case of buildings by local authorities, to save repetition, the names of heads of departments are not mentioned on each occasion, but are given in the borough introductions or, in the case of the L.C.C., G.L.C., and M.C.C., on p. 20. The general principles on which the gazetteer is based follow those of previous Buildings of England volumes. On churches prior to c. 1830 and secular buildings of more than local interest up to around the same period information ought to be as complete as recent research makes possible, and as the space of the volume permits; the exceptions to the rule are that certain church furnishings are omitted (bells, hatchments, chests, chairs, plain fonts, altar tables, and plate) or included only occasionally (royal arms, coffin lids with foliate crosses). Movable furnishings in secular buildings are not mentioned. For buildings after 1830, which bulk so large in Greater London, space demands that the traditional Buildings of England approach of greater selectivity has had to be followed. However, it will be found that much more is included and more positively appreciated than in early volumes in this series, reflecting the expanding interest in all types of nineteenth- and twentieth-century architecture and the more sympathetic eye that develops when survivals begin to have a rarity value. Information on these buildings, however, despite recent research, is still patchy, and it will be seen that there is still plenty of scope for further research here, as on earlier periods.

I have attempted to keep track of new research and current architectural developments up to c. 1990–1, but change has been so rapid during the last few years that there may well be some recent demolitions, discoveries, or alterations that have been overlooked. By the time this book is in print there will certainly be new buildings completed which it has not yet been possible to assess here. So this foreword must end with the usual request to readers for information on errors and omissions, and with a plea for tolerance over the inevitable problem that some areas of the book may be partly out of date by the time of publication.

ACKNOWLEDGEMENTS

The core of this book owes much to those who helped with the creation of its forbears of 1951 and 1952: Middlesex, *for which the research was carried out by Dr Gertrude Bondi, and* London except the Cities of London and Westminster, *which was prepared by Mrs Katharine Michaelson. The books also benefited greatly from the help given by the librarians and staff of the London public libraries, from the photograph collections of the National Buildings Record, from the then as yet unpublished statutory lists of historic buildings prepared by the Ministry of Local Government and Planning, and from much information collected by J. H. Farrar of the Historical Records Department of the L.C.C. Furthermore, access was kindly given to H. S. Goodhart-Rendel's notes on Victorian churches and to Sir Thomas Kendrick's index of Victorian glass. Others from those years whose help should be recorded are Miss Darlington at the Members' Library, County Hall, Mr Stonebridge at the St Marylebone Public Library, Mr Wesencroft at the University Library, Mr Rayne Smith at the Guildhall Library, the Jewish Historical Society of London, the Public Relations Department of the London Transport Executive, and the many rectors and vicars, local historians and occupiers of houses, who went to much trouble in providing answers to written questions.*

As for the present volume, the second in the trio designed to cover suburban London, my first debt is to the late Sir Nikolaus Pevsner, who encouraged me to take on the foolhardy task of bringing the Greater London area up to date, and the second to Penguin Books, who have tolerated the fact that the enterprise has proceeded less rapidly than I had hoped. This volume, like its predecessor on South London, has benefited from the specialists who have contributed: Joanna Bird, who, in addition to the introduction on prehistoric and Roman archaeology, provided me with geological and archaeological notes for the borough introductions, as well as gazetteer entries; Eric Robinson, who has contributed the introduction on geology and building materials; Malcolm Airs, who made available his expert knowledge of timber-framed building in the London area; and Malcolm Tucker, who, as well as writing an informative introduction on industrial archaeology, contributed a very large number of gazetteer entries on industrial structures.

The maps are the work of Reginald and Marjorie Piggott, many of the line drawings are by Richard Andrews, the photographs were assembled by Susan Rose-Smith with her usual efficiency and enthusiasm. Among the multitude of people who have helped in various ways, my first thanks must go to the staff of the Historic Buildings Division of the Greater London Council, under Ashley Barker, and of its successor, the London Division of English Heritage, under Sophie Andreae. I have been given generous access to their records, and much friendly help and advice from both past and present staff. I must thank

*in particular Andrew Saint and Robert Thorne, who have improved
so many entries in this book by their wide-ranging research and careful
scrutiny. I am also grateful for information from David Atwell, Susie
Barson, the late Susan Beattie, Victor Belcher, Roger Bowden,
Stephen Brindle, Neil Burton, John Earl, Elain Harwood, Frank
Kelsall, Mike Kilburn, Anthony Quiney, Anne Riches, Catherine
Steeves, and Philip Whitbourne. I have been helped also by the staff
of the Survey of London under Hermione Hobhouse, and by John
Phillips at the Greater London Record map room. On churches I
benefited from advice from the late B.F.L. Clarke, and from dis-
cussions with Donald Findlay and Michael Gillingham. On English
Heritage buildings Juliet West and Richard Hewlings were also most
constructive. Anthony Quiney was a valuable guide to the buildings of
the outer boroughs. As usual, the willing cooperation of the staff of
local libraries has been invaluable, and borough planning departments
have also been extremely cooperative. Our debts to these and to the
numerous local organizations and individuals who have assisted over
different areas, and to the specialists who have given us information
on particular buildings, are more fully acknowledged at the ends of the
borough introductions.*

*The Further Reading (p. 113) can give only a partial indication of
the extent of recent research. I gratefully acknowledge here several
unpublished London University theses which have been consulted:*
Christopher Monkhouse, The Station Hotel in Nineteenth-Century
England *(M.A. 1970); Lynne Walker, E.S. Prior (Ph.D. 1978);
Roger Dixon, James Brooks (Ph.D. 1976). It is a pleasure to be
able to thank many other scholars who have contributed entries or
information in advance of fuller publication elsewhere. I am particularly grateful to Denis Evinson DE, who provided long lists of
Roman Catholic churches; Adam White and Geoffrey Fisher (C 17
and C 18 monuments); Peter Cormack (PC) who provided much
on early C 20 stained glass; James Stevens Curl and Hugh Meller,
who both supplied information on cemeteries; Christopher Stell, who answered questions on Nonconformist churches; Susie Barson (buildings
of the Metropolitan Police); H.G.D. Gibson and Oliver Green (details
on London Transport stations); Hilary Grainger (the work of Ernest
George); Alison Kelly (lists of Coade stone); Alan Powers (buildings
of the 1930s); Matthew Saunders (the work of Teulon); Mark Swenarton (contributions on early C 20 public housing); Andrew Saint (the
work of R. Norman Shaw and much else); T. Rory Spence (the work
of Leonard Stokes); A.G. Stavridi (the work of Kempe's firm); and
Alexandra Wedgwood (the work of Pugin). For the entries on industrial
archaeology we have been grateful for information and other help
from J. Yates (Kew Bridge Waterworks), P. Calvocoressi and other
members of the staff of the G.L.C. Historic Buildings Division (now
London Division), and members of the Greater London Industrial
Archaeology Society. Michael Robbins (from whose book on Middlesex I have benefited greatly) provided invaluable assistance in
checking maps. Among others who contributed information I must
acknowledge H.M. Colvin, Dennis Corble, the late Alec Clifton
Taylor, W.H.H. van Sickle, and Gavin Stamp, and collectively the
work of the Victorian Society and the Thirties Society, which together
have put so many unknown buildings on the architectural historian's
map.*

Our consultant editor, John Newman, was an unfailing source of wise advice on tricky subjects, and much needed encouragement was provided by John Cherry and by my colleague Elizabeth Williamson. In the office my greatest debt is to my research assistant Tye Blackshaw, who took much of the load of Kensington from my shoulders, and helped constructively in many other ways. Valuable office help was given by Kathryn Penn-Simkins, Sara Eaton, and Kerrie Bowie; Stephany Ungless solved many tricky problems in the last hectic stages. The appearance of the book owes much to the careful attention to detail given to it by Gerald Cinamon and Tony Kitzinger. Finally, as always, I have to thank my indomitable co-editor Judy Nairn for her immaculate and tactful editing, and for undertaking the formidable task of the compilation of the indices. The mistakes and omissions that remain are my own.

PHOTOGRAPHIC ACKNOWLEDGEMENTS

We are grateful to the following for permission to reproduce photographs:

Arcaid/Richard Einzig: 109

Architectural Press: 103

James Austin: 11, 29, 34, 44, 48, 67, 72

Martin Charles: 3, 4, 5, 6, 14, 17, 19, 26, 43, 57, 58, 63, 68, 73, 74, 82, 94, 96, 99, 100, 102, 113, 114, 116, 117

Eric de Maré: 64

John Donat: 1, 25, 36, 37, 38, 47, 49, 50, 52, 54, 65, 70, 75, 84, 85, 92, 95, 101, 104, 108, 112

Greater London Record Office and History Library: 45, 53, 59, 62, 76, 91, 97, 98

Peter R. Keen: 33, 88

A. F. Kersting: 2, 7, 8, 13, 16, 20, 21, 27, 28, 30, 31, 32, 35, 39, 40, 41, 42, 46, 51, 55, 56, 60, 66, 71, 78, 79, 80, 81, 83, 87

Sam Lambert: 110a and b

Sir Denys Lasdun: 105, 111

John Novis: 10, 93

Jo Reid and John Peck: 115

RMJM Ltd: 106

Rogue Images/Mary Ann Kennedy: 69, 77

Royal Commission on Historical Monuments (England): 9, 12, 18, 22, 23, 24, 61, 86, 89, 90

Henk Snoek: 107

G. F. Stanley: 15

The plates are indexed in the indexes of artists, of streets and buildings, and of boroughs and localities on pp. 735 ff.

LIST OF LINE ILLUSTRATIONS,
MAPS, DIAGRAMS AND TABLES

Borough, town, and other plans marked RP are by Reginald Piggott. Other plans not reproduced direct from source were redrawn by Richard Andrews.

ABBREVIATIONS
AND LIST OF COUNTY COUNCIL ARCHITECTS

Area Authorities

M.B.W.	Metropolitan Board of Works (1855–88)
L.C.C.	London County Council (1888–1965)
G.L.C.	Greater London Council (1965–86)
I.L.E.A.	Inner London Education Authority (1965–90, covering the area of the former L.C.C.)
M.C.C.	Middlesex County Council (1889–1986)

Boroughs

See map on pp. 2–3.

Other Abbreviations

DoE	Department of the Environment
NMR	National Monuments Record
R.C.H.M.E.	Royal Commission on Historical Monuments of England
R.I.B.A.	Royal Institute of British Architects
V and A	Victoria and Albert Museum
V.C.H.	*Victoria County History*

In order to avoid repetition, chief architects of public authorities are not mentioned on every occasion in the gazetteer. Borough architects are listed under individual boroughs. The chief County Council architects are as follows:

Architects to the Metropolitan Board of Works, the London County Council and the Greater London Council

Superintending Architects
Frederick Marrable 1856–61
George Vulliamy 1861–87
Thomas Blashill 1887–99
W. E. Riley 1899–1919
G. Topham Forrest 1919–35
E. P. Wheeler 1935–39
F. R. Hiorns 1939–41
J. H. Forshaw 1941–46
(Sir) Robert Matthew 1946–53
(Sir) Leslie Martin 1953–6
(Sir) Hubert Bennett 1956–71
(Sir) Roger Walters 1971–8

F. B. Pooley 1978–80
P. E. Jones 1980–

Fire Brigade Branch
Edward Cresy 1866–70
Alfred Mott 1871–9
Robert Pearsall 1879–99
Owen Fleming 1900–

Housing of the Working Classes Branch
Owen Fleming 1893–1900
John Briggs 1900–2

Rob Robertson 1902–10

Education Branch (until 1904 architects to the School Board for London)
E. R. Robson 1871–84
T. J. Bailey 1884–1910
Rob Robertson 1910–

The Constructional Division (absorbed the Fire Brigade Branch and the Housing of the Working Classes Branch from 1910, and the Education Branch from 1920. Housing was placed under the Valuers Department from 1946 until 1950, when the whole of the Architect's Department was reorganized under Sir Robert Matthew, with separate heads of department for housing and education.)

Housing
H. J. Whitfield Lewis 1950–9

K. J. Campbell 1959–74
G. H. Wigglesworth 1974–80

Education
S. Howard 1950–5
M. C. L. Powell 1956–65
Schools: C. E. Hartland 1965–72
Education: M. C. L. Powell 1965–71
G. H. Wigglesworth 1972–4
P. E. Jones 1974–80

Special Works (a separate department responsible for fire and ambulance stations, magistrates' courts, civic buildings, etc.)
G. Horsfall 1960–76 (also senior architect Civic Design, 1965–70, and Thamesmead Manager from 1970)
R. A. Michelmore 1977–80 (from 1980, principal Construction Architect)

Surveyors to the Metropolitan Police

Charles Reeves 1842–66
Thomas Charles Sorby 1867–8
Frederick Caiger 1868–81
John Butler Sen. 1881–95
John Dixon Butler 1895–1920

G. Mackenzie Trench 1921–47
J. Innes–Elliot 1947–74
M. Belchamber 1974–88
T. Lawrence 1988–

Architects to the Middlesex County Council

H. T. Wakelam (County Surveyor from 1898)
H. G. Crothall (Surveyor of Schools from 1903, then architect to the Education Committee; County Architect from 1908)

W. T. Curtis (County Architect 1930–46)
C. G. Stillman (County Architect 1946–59)
H. J. Whitfield Lewis (County Architect 1959–65)

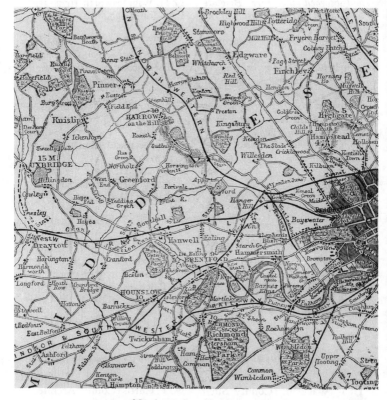

Northwest London *c.* 1850

INTRODUCTION

BY BRIDGET CHERRY

The wedge of London covered by this book extends some fifteen miles west of Charing Cross. On the outer fringes of the built-up area, beyond the highways lined with sleek new hotels and warehouses, lie the winding roads of the dormitory suburbs of the first forty years of the C20 – the Middlesex 'Metroland' built for 3 owner occupiers of modest means, made possible by the progress of electric transport. Further in, where trams and suburban railways arrived a little earlier, the prim tiled roofs of the C20 lap up against colonies of more spacious Edwardian villas and taller late Victorian terraces. These are the buildings which dominate the arc four to five miles from London, where the turn-of-the-century suburbs expanded around the old villages of Chiswick and Ealing, Acton 2 and Willesden. Here one may still find an occasional older park or mansion; discoveries that become rarer among the denser inner suburbs built in the era of horse-drawn transport – the tightly packed brick terraces of Hammersmith and Fulham, and the long stucco stretches of Chelsea, Kensington, and Paddington. These predominantly Victorian areas, crisscrossed by canal and railway lines, punctuated by national institutions, major termini, and C20 4 tower blocks, now offer few hints of the uneventful Middlesex 1 countryside which existed until the C19.

Two centuries ago the experience would have been very different. Georgian London extended no farther than Hyde Park. Further west the C18 traveller would have encountered only two major market towns: Uxbridge at the Middlesex boundary on the road to Oxford, or the straggling line of Old and New Brentford on the route to the south-west, before crossing the river Brent to brave the desolate wastelands of Hounslow Heath. The flat fertile stretches of Chelsea and Fulham near the Thames were covered by market gardens supplying the city. The gentle hills rising further north on the edge of the London Basin, once heavily wooded (as the names Northwood and Harrow Weald indicate), were by the C18 mostly pasture and arable land scattered with small villages, hamlets, and farms. But even Uxbridge was only a day's ride from London, and already in the C16 and C17 courtiers and City men were building mansions and villas in the Middlesex countryside. The banks of the Thames were especially favoured for such summer retreats, and by the C18 the brick terrace house so fashionable in London was beginning to give an urban gloss to the villages of Chelsea, Hammersmith, and Chiswick, presaging their future absorption into the 2 metropolis.

The first significant intrusion into this leisurely rural pattern came around 1800, with the construction of the Grand Union Canal

from Uxbridge to Brentford, with a branch to Paddington, Regents Park, and the Docks. The swathe of industrial activity which it generated can still be traced through Yiewsley, Southall, Hanwell, Hayes, and Greenford towards Paddington, although the brick-yards, gasworks, and other anti-social industries that once inter-mittently bordered the banks have given way to warehouses and offices, and much of the canal itself, once a busy route for the transport of goods, has been given over to secluded recreation. C 19 industries also grew up along the Thames, although they were not as continuous as they were to the east of London. But now, the newly made walks beside the river offer few reminders of the once industrial character of Fulham Reach or Old Brentford. In the C 20 similar patterns were created by new roads: ribbon developments
94 of show factories of between the wars along the North Circular Road and Western Avenue and along the Great West Road north of Brentford, and, still more recently, warehouses and offices around Heathrow Airport, the principal agent for change in outer west London over the last forty years.

Around and beyond these industrial and commercial arteries the residential suburbs expanded relentlessly from the early C 19 onwards, but in the outer areas they have not entirely overwhelmed the buildings of the old rural Middlesex, and even in the most heavily built up inner suburbs, clues to an older past can be found

LONDON'S POPULATION 1801–1981

| | Greater London 1951 Conurbation Area | |
| | L.C.C. Area (thousands*) | G.L.C. Area (thousands*) |
Census Date		
1801	959	1,117
1811	1,139	1,137
1821	1,380	1,600
1831	1,656	1,907
1841	1,949	2,239
1851	2,363	2,685
1861	2,808	3,227
1871	3,261	3,890
1881	3,830	4,770
1891	4,228	5,638
1901	4,536	6,586
1911	4,522	7,256
1921	4,485	7,488
1931	4,397	8,216
1939 (est.)	4,013	8,728
1951	3,348	8,348
1961	3,200	8,183
1971	2,772	7,452‡
1981	2,497	6,696‡

* All figures are approximations due to slight differences in the definition of areas.
‡ The Greater London figures for 1971 and 1981 are those for the (slightly smaller) G.L.C. area.

in the erratic courses of old roads and the survival of greens and commons, and even the occasional older building. However, the surviving evidence is weighted heavily towards the C 19 and C 20, and this introduction to the buildings of what are suburbs of north-west London is inevitably unbalanced, for it covers only a part of a county, a section of a torso without a head; an area which has no ancient cathedral or great church, no centre of county admin-istration.

Originally London was part of Middlesex (rather than the other way round) – indeed, the county council continued to meet in Westminster until it was subsumed into the Greater London Council in 1965. In 1855 the Metropolitan Board of Works (con-cerned principally with the construction of sewers) was formed to cater for the special needs of the new urban areas, to be succeeded in 1888 by the London County Council, which was granted wider powers within the same boundaries. Then in 1965, in belated recognition that built-up London had for long extended far beyond the London County Council border, the Greater London Council was established; its abolition in 1986 has meant that there is now no central administration either for inner or for outer London, and that local government is in the hands of the boroughs. These were a creation of the G.L.C., formed by amalgamating the former administrative areas, themselves based on the old parishes. Today's borough boundaries (which form the main subdivisions of this book), arbitrary though some may seem in a modern urban context, thus perpetuate some of Greater London's most ancient divisions.

The Middle Ages

It is difficult nowadays to envisage a time when the parish church was the only ambitious stone building in most Middlesex villages. There were very few MONASTIC HOUSES compared with the number concentrated in and immediately around medieval London; the only remains are those of a late medieval undercroft from the royal foundation of the Bridgettine Syon Abbey (founded on its present site near Isleworth in 1431), now incorporated within the courtyard house created in the C 16. From the small Augustinian Bentley Priory, founded in 1171, only the name remains attached to a later house; the Knights Hospitallers had a camera at Harefield, from which a C 13 building survived until the 1950s; and the Tri-nitarian Friars had a chapel at Hounslow, to which the present parish church can trace its origins but none of its fabric. Hazier records exist of small hospitals at Hammersmith and Brentford. One reason for the dearth of significant monastic buildings may be the close control exercised by leading secular ecclesiastics. The Bishop of London held numerous manors in Middlesex, among them Acton, Ealing, and Fulham (his principal country seat); the Dean and Chapter of St Paul's had property at Chiswick, Willesden, West Drayton, and Twyford; and Harrow and Hayes, with their dependent chapels of Pinner and Norwood, were 'peculiars' of the Archbishop of Canterbury.

We know almost nothing of the very early history of PARISH CHURCHES anywhere in Middlesex, although evidence from else-where (for example that produced by the excavations at St Mary

Barnes (Ri), s of the Thames) may go to suggest that the earlier churches were simple buildings of timber. In the area covered by this volume, out of nearly forty ancient parishes which had medieval churches or chapels (about half the number in the whole of pre-c 19 Middlesex), around twenty buildings preserve some old fabric, but none that can with certainty be dated earlier than the c 12.

The site most suggestive of an important early history is Harrow-on-the-Hill, where the place name points to a pagan religious centre on this prominent eminence, and the early significance of the church is suggested not only by the fact that the Archbishop owned it, but by the cruciform plan which it possessed before its later medieval enlargement. The sturdy w tower is certainly a survival from the c 12. Pinner also has a cruciform plan, with transepts still visible, perhaps of the c 13. These are exceptions. Most early village churches consisted simply of a nave and a chancel. Enough remains to show that stone buildings of this kind were widespread by the c 12. Kingsbury is a simple rectangle; the more common two-cell arrangement is illustrated by Cowley, Bedfont, and Harlington, all with recognizable c 12 features, and by Perivale, perhaps also of this period. The survival of this two-cell type in later buildings such as Ickenham, Northolt, Greenford, and Norwood suggests how small and remote some Middlesex settlements remained throughout the Middle Ages. The detail of these buildings varies, presumably depending on the generosity of their patrons. The small church of Cowley is completely plain, East Bedfont has a handsome chancel arch and s doorway, both with chevron
5 ornament, and Harlington an exceptionally elaborate s doorway of three orders whose decoration includes an unusual form of beak-head paralleled only at Lincoln Cathedral. Harmondsworth has a similarly decorated doorway, probably reset, and also a s aisle of
6 the c 12, an early example of the type of enlargement that becomes standard from the c 13 onwards.

Middlesex is not a good county for building stone (*see* Intro-duction to Geology, below). The varied texture of older walls is frequently made up of a mixture of the local rust-coloured gravel conglomerate with chalk and flint (the last often an indicator of heavy c 19 restoration). Dressed stone had to be brought from elsewhere. The doorways at Harlington and Harmondsworth make use of oolitic limestone, but the most frequently imported worked stone was the friable greensand from Reigate, whose poor weather-ing quality accounts for the restored appearance of so many exteriors, and may partly explain the lack of good surviving c 13 work. That it could be of high quality is proved by a fine stiff-leaf capital at Hillingdon, sedilia and piscina at Hayes, and a piscina at West Drayton – all evidence of the general fashion for enlarging chancels at this time. Geometric windows of *c.* 1300 in the small
9 church at Northolt show an up-to-date awareness of new designs. Elsewhere there is the usual pattern of enlargement by means of aisles. They are not easy to date precisely, as capitals and mouldings are very plain. Generally circular columns are the earlier type (Harrow, Harmondsworth N aisle, Willesden s aisle, c 13). Octag-onal columns are popular from the c 14, becoming slenderer in the
6 c 15 (Pinner, c 14; Hayes, West Drayton, c 15; Harmondsworth N chapel, *c.* 1500). Only Ruislip has the more ambitious arrangement

of the two types in alternation (probably late C 13), while the Perp
quatrefoil pier common in other areas makes a single appearance at
Harefield. These west Middlesex churches were never as grand as
for example St Dunstan Stepney (TH), which served the early
suburbs E of London; the largest are Ruislip with a nave of six bays,
Pinner and Harrow with five. There are no total rebuildings of the
Perp period, as one finds in other richer counties – only piecemeal
modernizations. Harmondsworth chancel was remodelled in 1396–
8 with a new E window in the latest fashion, at the expense of the
patrons, Winchester College. Harrow was given a clerestory in the
C15, as were Pinner and West Drayton. Such heightenings required
new roofs; Harrow and West Drayton still have their original ones
with the typical shallow pitch of the late Middle Ages, the Harrow
example with especially fine moulded beams and carved bosses.
Other churches preserve earlier types. Collar-beam and crown-
post roofs (which originated by the C 12, although the dates of the
Middlesex examples are uncertain) are to be found at Cowley,
Harmondsworth nave, and Greenford. The chancel at Hayes has a 8
wagon roof with close-set rafters, perhaps C 14; Ruislip chancel has
an arch-braced roof of the type common in the C 15; Hayes nave
has a ceiled roof, seven-sided with carved bosses, also probably
C 15. The most ambitious late medieval type, the hammerbeam, is
used grandly at Uxbridge, for the large mid C 15 guild aisle, an
addition swamping the older town chapel, and on a miniature scale
for the N chapel at Harmondsworth remodelled in the early C 16.
Roofs were not the only feature to exhibit accomplished carpentry;
at Ruislip the well detailed late medieval woodwork includes doors
as well as the aisle ceilings. Willesden has a traceried door of the
C 14. As in much of SE England, decorative timber porches were
popular; the survivors at Hayes, Heston, and Harlington (all much 7
restored) are probably of the early C 16. Hayes and Heston also
have timber lychgates. Greenford and Perivale both have sturdily
framed W belfries attached to their stone naves; East Bedfont had
a similar structure until the C 19.

Timber belfries may once have been more common, although
not universal. At Twyford in 1297 two bells were hung from trees
in the churchyard. But by the end of the Middle Ages a stone W
tower adequate for a peal of bells had become the most familiar
feature of Middlesex churches, giving a superficial impression of
uniformity to these buildings of diverse ages. Available dates
suggest that the Middlesex tower is a development of the early
C 15 (although some were completed later). At Fulham (perhaps 10
significantly, the manor of the Bishop of London) work on the
tower was in progress c. 1440; at Chiswick the tower was built
during the time of a vicar who died in 1435. (Both these towers had
five bells in 1547, a number matched at this time only by six other
Middlesex churches.) Most Middlesex towers are fairly short but
well-proportioned structures of four stages, with battlements and
a taller corner stair-turret. There are over a dozen in this volume;
the type is also found further afield, spreading beyond Middlesex
and the Thames valley into Buckinghamshire and Hertfordshire,
and east into Kent. The somewhat stumpy irregular battlemented profile – so different from the soaring symmetry of the great
towers of East Anglian and Somerset churches – perhaps owes its

inspiration to the smart gatehouses of royal and episcopal foundations (cf. e.g. New College Oxford), and beyond that to traditions
7 of military buildings. The simplest towers are unbuttressed (Hayes,
West Drayton), although whether this proves they are earlier than
the rest is uncertain. Most have diagonal w buttresses, as became
common from the c 14. Heston, with an unusually tall transomed
belfry, is a specially handsome example, graced by a fine square-
headed Perp w door with matching small water stoup.

MEDIEVAL CHURCH FURNISHINGS are too few to need a long
account. The oldest are Purbeck marble FONTS of the late c 12, at
Willesden and Ruislip, both square on corner columns, and
Harrow, circular with scalloped decoration. (Their occurrence in
the largest parishes may be some measure of the significance of
these places.) The Harmondsworth font is square, with the type
of simple arcading common c. 1200; the circular font at Hayes of
similar date is decorated with lively foliage patterns. Liturgical
fittings of c 13 chancels have already been mentioned; from the c 15
the most notable work in stone is the elaborately carved octagonal
font at West Drayton. Unostentatious wooden PEWS begin to
appear in the c 15 and c 16. Harmondsworth has the best; others
are at Ruislip and West Drayton. WALL PAINTINGS are few but
11 interesting. At East Bedfont there are two exceptionally fine panels
of the late c 13, a Crucifixion and a Christ in Majesty. At Ruislip
are larger but more fragmentary late medieval series including the
Seven Deadly Sins and the Acts of Mercy. STAINED GLASS is
limited to a medley of late medieval fragments assembled at Greenford, said to come from King's College Cambridge.

The earliest MONUMENTS are brasses. There are half-figures of
priests at Hayes (c. 1370), Harlington (1419), and Greenford (c.
1450). Among the miscellaneous surviving fragments and inscriptions which show how numerous such memorials were in the c 15
and c 16, only a few complete figures remain, among them two
knights of the Flambard family at Harrow, late c 14; a knight at
Hayes, Walter Grene, 1456; and a priest at Greenford, Thomas
Symons, 1521. The most remarkable brass is at Hillingdon, to Lord
Strange, his wife and daughter, of 1509, a surprising date for such
very large figures. In a totally different tradition is the lozenge-
shaped brass with half-figure in a shroud, to Margaret Hornbolt,
c. 1529, at Fulham, probably Flemish work.

No medieval stone effigies survive. The most common form of
late medieval monument is the canopied altar tomb with four-
centred or flattened arch, popular from the later c 15 as a setting
for brasses. Such tombs were often of Purbeck marble: Harefield
has two simple examples, and the remains of the more elaborate
canopied tomb-chest to the Duchess of Northumberland at Chelsea
(1555) show that there was still a demand for this traditional type
in the mid c 16. In general the surviving evidence suggests that
ostentatious monuments were not erected in Middlesex parish
churches at this time. Indeed, the trend in the opposite direction is
expressed in extreme form by the low, very modest wall-monument
erected in the chancel at Chelsea by no less a person than Sir
Thomas More. The Cheeseman monument at Norwood, which
doubles as an Easter Sepulchre, is a related type, of the more
sophisticated design which was used for a number of early c 16

tombs in the London area, e.g. at Hackney (Hc), Edmonton (En), and Lambeth (La). The popularity at this time of the Easter Sepulchre combined with a personal tomb is demonstrated also by the monument to Gregory Lovell at Harlington (1545), whose curious form is most likely attributable to its being a reworking of older material. Its brasses are indeed palimpsests (as are some at Harefield), perhaps spoil from monastic houses – indicators of the disturbance both to existing monuments and to their production that resulted from the Reformation.

Few MEDIEVAL SECULAR BUILDINGS of any importance remain. Occasionally one can glimpse evidence of a settlement with the manor and church closely related. At Ruislip the church lies just outside the bounds of a CASTLE of C11 origin, from which some earthworks remain around the manor farm which succeeded it. The remains of a moated manor house are still visible close to the church at Northolt, where excavations have shown that there were stone buildings by the C14. But moated enclosures were not always close to churches, as is shown by the spectacularly large one (now filled in) which surrounded the Bishop of London's manor at Fulham, or by the Archbishop of Canterbury's manor at Headstone, between Pinner and Harrow, where, remarkably, a fragment of the C14 timber-aisled hall is encapsulated within the picturesque later house standing within the moat. The most elaborate medieval timber roof in this volume, however, is an importation from the City of London: it belongs to the supremely grand City mansion of the C15 merchant John Crosby, whose great hall was rebuilt in Chelsea in the late C19. Its ceremonial space, with stone bay-window, and timberwork with intricate cusping and pendants, underlines the contrast that existed at this time between the wealthiest City houses and those of the countryside.

In Middlesex the dominant material for secular work in the Middle Ages remained timber. Hidden in the outer suburbs, scattered especially thickly around the former fields and commons of Harefield and Ruislip, a surprising number of timber-framed houses survive. They date mostly from the C15 to the C17; their 14 development is discussed in the separate introduction to timber-framed buildings, below. The majority are relatively modest, the houses of yeoman farmers; somewhat grander exceptions are Ickenham Manor, with a main wing with ground-floor hall of the early 15 C16, and the much restored Southall Manor House, built in 1588, although no doubt other timber-framed houses of superior status once existed. They have the close-set uprights characteristic of much timber building of south-east England.

Farm buildings naturally were also of timber; the outstanding example is the vast aisled barn at Harmondsworth, exceptional for 13 its double-framed construction, which can be identified with the barn known to have been built by Winchester College in 1427. Large and small barns also survive at both Headstone and Ruislip.

Architectural Developments c. *1500–1680*

By the C16 brick had become the accepted building material for the houses of the upper classes. The major example in this volume

16 is Fulham Palace. The oldest standing part of this courtyard house
   of the Bishops of London consists of the diapered brick hall range,
   probably of *c.* 1480, which according to the most recent research
   had the progressive arrangement of a ground-floor hall with great
   chamber above. The existing hall porch and ranges of lodgings
   around the W courtyard were added in the early C16. The more
   important E court, with the private apartments of the bishop and
   (presumably) the main entrance, was rebuilt later, so we do not
   know how it appeared. Conversely, the sole survival from the great
   mid C16 mansion of the Pagets at West Drayton is the tantalizing
   fragment of the lower part of the robust brick gatehouse, its twin
   turrets reminiscent of Hampton Court. The Thames-side royal
   palaces W of London – Hampton Court and Richmond – lie only
   just outside the bounds of this volume, and their impact must have
   been considerable. But from other major estates there are only
   suggestive fragmentary survivals, such as the fine early C16 brick
17 dovecote at Breakspears, Harefield. The only significant relics at a
   royal possession, the former hunting lodge at Hanworth, are two
   reset early C16 terracotta roundels of the type found at Hampton
   Court (possibly brought here later), and some foundations of
   service buildings. The other early indication of Renaissance influ-
12 ence is the pair of exquisite capitals of 1528 from the More chapel
   at Chelsea parish church, which are of a quality that likewise
   suggests foreign, probably French, workmanship.
       The evidence for MAJOR HOUSES of the later C16 is sparse. We
   know almost nothing about the early phases of the Northumberland
   conversion of the monastery at Syon, and have only the vaguest
   details about Sir Thomas Gresham's brick courtyard house at
   Osterley. Otherwise there are only a few fragments – such as a
   range with a row of chimneystacks from the Crown and Treaty
   (formerly The Place), Uxbridge, and part of Walpole House, Chiswick Mall – to show that there were substantial brick houses of the
   C16 and early C17. Among the lesser buildings of this time the
18 most interesting survivals are the original schoolroom of Harrow
19 School (1608–15), and the Countess of Derby's Almshouses at
   Harefield of after 1637, with a proud display of clustered chimneystacks. The brick chimneystack at this time also becomes the dominant up-to-date showpiece of many timber-framed farmhouses.
       By the end of the C16 along the river at Chelsea there was already
   a string of handsome country retreats – among them Chelsea Manor
   House, a favourite haunt of Henry VIII, and Sir Thomas More's
   house, later known as Beaufort House – as we know from Thorpe's
   surveys and other evidence. Such lost precedents must be borne in
   mind as we turn to the survivals of EARLY C17 COUNTRY HOUSES.
   The rising ground to the N of Kensington village was a favourite
   location. Here the rich merchant Sir Baptist Hicks built Campden
   House (demolished in the 1890s), the courtier Sir Walter Cope
   built Cope Castle (later Holland House), and Sir George Coppin
   built what was later called Nottingham House, the core of the future
   Kensington Palace. Cope's and Coppin's houses (both drawn, and
   perhaps planned, by *Thorpe*) did not have ranges around courtyards
   in the medieval tradition, but were compact creations designed to
   make an outward show. The fragment of Holland House that
   survived the Second World War still stands in its park, although

Kensington, Holland House, *c.* 1606–7 (burnt 1941)

one wing and a part of the ground floor are barely enough to recall the fanciful outline of the original building with its loggia heavily encrusted with Netherlandish strapwork, and its skyline of gables and turrets. The decorative tradition established by such buildings, in direct contrast to the more austere Italian forms promoted among more limited court circles by Inigo Jones, was continued in later country houses built in the London neighbourhood. There is a well-known group of the 1630s, characterized by the accomplished use of cut and rubbed brick associated with City of London brick-layers, which includes Cromwell House Highgate (Hy) and Kew Palace (Ri). The most interesting example in this volume is Swake-leys of 1638, with its lively roof-line of Dutch gables, its contrasts 26 of red brick and feigned stonework, and a plan which combines the progressive double pile (found already at Cope Castle and Nottingham House) with projecting wings and a traditional great hall entered at one end. It is interesting to compare the great chamber over the hall at Swakeleys with the one at Boston Manor Brentford, which, although considerably altered externally, is another house of this period with a compact double-pile plan. The Boston Manor great chamber has an exceptionally elaborate overmantel and plaster ceiling dated 1623, with erudite iconography 27 drawn from late c 16 Flemish sources; the later great chamber at Swakeleys has a plaster ceiling with bold wreathed framing of the type introduced by Inigo Jones. Otherwise the purer classicism of *Jones* is demonstrated only by a garden gateway built for Lord 25 Cranford in 1621 at Beaufort House Chelsea, piously removed to Chiswick House by Lord Burlington a century later.

Before considering the later c 17, we should return to churches, and more particularly to their monuments of the early c 16 to *c.* 1650. About CHURCH BUILDING there is less to note. Brick is the normal material: the upper part of Harmondsworth tower, most of All Saints Chelsea (where not rebuilt), both early c 16; Ickenham N aisle, later c 16. Ickenham also has an eccentric little N chapel of the mid c 17, with niches for upright coffins (a feature found also in the c 17 remodelling of the crypt at West Drayton). At Hillingdon the w tower is dated 1629, an entirely traditional rebuilding in stone, a reminder that there may be more work of this date than has generally been recognized. In contrast, at the old church at Great Stanmore (now a ruin), rebuilt in 1632 by the patron, Sir John Wolstenholme, the w tower is attached to a plain brick rectangular preaching box with Venetian e window, an early expression of the new classical principles of Jones, probably channelled through his assistant *Nicholas Stone*, who was paid both for work on the porch and for the fine Wolstenholme monument.

The MONUMENTS of this period are a good indication of the number and wealth of the principal inhabitants about whose houses we know so little. The most evocative ensembles are at Harefield and Cranford, squeezed huggermugger into chancels no longer required for elaborate liturgy. The wall-monument with carved kneeling figures, a recurrent type of the c 16 and early c 17 which carries on the tradition established by late medieval brasses, makes an early appearance in the mid c 16 at the Windsor tomb at Hounslow (only fragments remain), set in a heavy classical frame. More ambitious classical compositions are the triumphal arch at Chelsea commemorating Richard Jervoise † 1563, and the wall-monument, also at Chelsea, to Lord and Lady Dacre, 1594–5, with recumbent figures under a coffered arch decorated with the ribbonwork typical of the Netherlandish carvers associated with Southwark workshops. The high point comes in the early c 17, an inventive period for London tomb-makers. A more flamboyant version of the Dacre tomb is found at Hayes, where the effigy of Sir Edward Fenner † 1611–12 reclines stiffly below a superstructure thickly decorated with strapwork and allegorical figures. Still more
21 ambitious is the tomb of Sir Roger Aston at Cranford, by *William Cure II*, 1611–13, where the finely carved figures kneel beneath a tripartite composition with central coffered arch, based on the Cure family's Westminster Abbey tomb of Mary Queen of Scots (1605–
20 13). At Harefield the remarkable monument to Alice Spencer, Countess of Derby, † 1637 is a late example of the four-poster tomb. She lies beneath a Baroque-looking baldacchino complete with feigned curtains, a dramatically realistic framing device that also appears on other tombs. On the large monument at Hillingdon to
22 Sir Edward Carr † 1636, the touchingly realistic figures of the kneeling family are framed by knotted curtains hanging from an extraordinarily mannered arch, a curved shape thrust up into a stepped gable flanked by languid allegorical ladies. Curtains occur also on smaller wall-monuments with kneeling figures: Sir Thomas Chaloner † 1615, Chiswick; Sir Robert Aston † 1617, Harefield. The more wayward iconography popular in the 1630s is illustrated by the monument at Greenford (signed by *Humfrey Moyer*) to Bridget Coston † 1637, kneeling with her children in front of the half-figure of her husband in a niche, with allegorical figures above, and by the monument to Leonora Bennet † 1638 at Uxbridge, possibly by *John & Matthias Christmas*, with its charnel-house theme below the reclining figure. Among the new motifs of this time are the seated figure, e.g. Margaret Leigh † 1605 at Fulham (a type that appears first in the Westminster Abbey monument to

Elizabeth Russell of 1602–3), and the frontal half-figure, e.g. Edward Fenner † 1615 at Hayes; at Chelsea, the theme of Sara Colville † 1632, eloquently rising in her shroud, is similar to that of Stone's monument to Donne in St Paul's Cathedral. *Nicholas Stone*'s own work is represented by the recumbent effigy set up in 1641 to Sir John Wolstenholme † 1639 at Great Stanmore, and by 24 the restrained tomb to Elizabeth Lady Berkeley at Cranford (1635), both distinguished by their use of unpainted black and white marble, in contrast to the polychromy popular in the early c 17.

The courtly patronage which favoured the classicism of Nicholas Stone and Inigo Jones was disrupted by the Civil War. The new type of formal classical VILLA introduced by Jones at the Queen's House, Greenwich (Gr), had few immediate successors. One of them, an important prototype in our area, was John Webb's Gunnersbury House of *c.* 1658, which existed until 1801. But elsewhere the occasional survival, such as Sandford Manor Chelsea of *c.* 1660 (the outside altered, but the interior well preserved), shows that for middle-sized houses, plain brick elevations with gabled roof-lines remained a familiar type. The humble Ingram Almshouses at Isleworth of 1664, however, have a row of pediments, an indication that such detail was beginning to infiltrate the vernacular tradition.

After the Restoration the legacy of Jones and Webb began to be assimilated more thoroughly, combined with new French and Dutch influences. Chelsea Hospital is a prime monument of this 28 period. Begun for Charles II in 1682 by *Sir Christopher Wren*, its plain yet noble classicism is far distant from the busy Artisan Mannerism of the mid century. Restrained brick elevations owing much to contemporary Dutch fashion are also characteristic of William and Mary's additions to Kensington House (the former Nottingham House) of 1689 onwards. This homely but dignified domestic manner rapidly became the accepted form for lesser

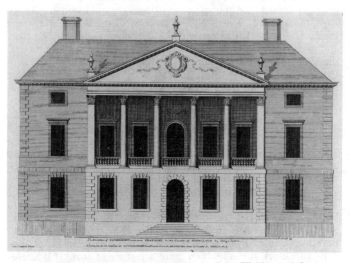

Gunnersbury House (demolished), by John Webb, *c.* 1658

country houses. Its hallmark is a regular brick front, occasionally
embellished by brick pilasters, with tall sash windows below a
modillion cornice and hipped roof. Lindsey House Chelsea (c. 1674,
but much altered) is the largest survival; Stanley House Chelsea
(before 1691) and the more modest Grange at Harmondsworth
(dated 1675) are more typical of the smaller post-Restoration brick
house. There were once many others of this type in and around
London; *Hugh May*'s house for Sir Stephen Fox at Chiswick of
1682 (demolished in the early C 19) was an especially distinguished
example. At the same time older houses were modernized: the later
C 17 wing added to Breakspears, Harefield, is typical, still with
mullion-and-cross rather than sash windows; the remodelling of
the early C 17 Boston Manor Brentford more unusual, its gabled
frontages brought up to date by windows with heavy classical
surrounds. By the end of the century speculative builders were
adopting the style for houses further down the social scale, as at
35 The Butts Brentford, which was gradually developed from c. 1685
with a combination of short terraces and single and paired houses
(cf. The Grove Highgate, Hy), half urban and half rural.

The appearance at The Butts of the brick terrace house is a
reflection of what was happening in London, where such houses
had become the standard type after the Great Fire of 1666, and
were beginning to appear in formal arrangements on the fringes of
the City and Westminster (St James's Square, Bloomsbury Square,
Red Lion Square, etc., on the pattern of Jones's earlier Covent
Garden). The earliest development completely in the urban spirit
to invade a Middlesex village appeared at Kensington in the late
1680s, when John Young laid out Kensington Square. The group
of houses around a courtyard at Chiswick, called Chiswick Square,
originated around the same time. Cheyne Row Chelsea dates from
1708. The trend gathered momentum between c. 1715 and 1730,
when an increasing number of urban-looking terraces indicate that
landowners and speculative builders were taking advantage of the
growing demand for houses in the villages around London. Church
Row Hampstead, North Side Clapham Common, Wandsworth
Plain, Croom's Hill Greenwich, Montpelier Row Twickenham,
and in this volume Holland Street Kensington (1724), all illustrate
the type. The most monumentally Baroque of such groups is at
Cheyne Walk Chelsea, built in 1717–20. Broad, generously scaled
frontages overlook the river, not yet entirely uniform, and (like
Kensington Square) with considerable diversity of internal layouts.
Lesser terraces followed, in Chelsea, Chiswick, Hammersmith,
2 and Kensington, often replacing the older mansions in their own
grounds. Older houses that remained were disguised by new frontages, as can be seen at Walpole House Chiswick. One fragment of
this time of especially high quality is the festive garden façade of c.
1700 preserved from Bradmore House Hammersmith, perhaps by
Thomas Archer, with brickwork of great delicacy and refinement.

In the City of London the late C 17 was also a great church-
building period, but the impact of the post-Fire City CHURCHES
was felt only distantly in the countryside. The influence of Wren's
Baroque steeples is perhaps reflected in the charmingly rustic little
bell- and clock-turrets which were a feature of many Middlesex
towers during the C 18: survivors are at Harlington, Harmonds-

worth, and Uxbridge, and until the c19 there were others, for example at Kensington and Ealing. In several cases the body of the church was completely rebuilt – Kensington in the late c17, Isleworth in 1705 by *John James*, Cranford in 1710, Ealing in 1735–30 (*J. Horne*), Brentford in 1764 (*T. Hardwick*) – but none retains its Georgian fittings, and only at Isleworth, Cranford, and Ealing is some of the c18 fabric visible. None rivalled St Lawrence Little Stanmore, which will be mentioned shortly.

MONUMENTS continued to proliferate. Some traditional types continued, such as the rather clumsy four-poster to John Wolstenholme at Great Stanmore († 1669), and the more elegant example at Harefield to Mary Newdigate († 1692). The most ambitious setting is that provided for Charles Cheyne and his family at Chelsea († 1672), designed by the younger *Bernini*, where Mrs Cheyne's reclining effigy is set in a very Italian manner in a toplit recess, framed by a heavy Baroque curved aedicule. Other monuments concentrated on realistic portraiture, ranging from the infant Robert Clayton at Ickenham († 1665) to increasingly 23 accomplished busts, for example Sir John Bennet and wives at Harlington († 1686) and Sir Orlando Gee † 1705 at Isleworth, a demi-figure by *Francis Bird*. This also was the period for elaborate cartouches and tablets in architectural frames; the most notable is the festooned urn to Sir Christopher Clitherow by *William Stanton* at Pinner († 1685). Other good examples of the second half of the c17 can be found at Acton, Harefield, Heston, Ruislip, and elsewhere.

BAROQUE ARCHITECTURE in the grand manner is represented in this book by Queen Anne's garden buildings at Kensington: the admirably bold orangery of 1704, probably by *Hawksmoor*, and the 30 large summer house of 1706–7. The royal interiors of late c17 Kensington, with their simple panelled rooms and a little carving by *Gibbons*, did not aim to rival the splendour of William and Mary's main seat at Hampton Court, but the more elaborate interior decoration of the period can be seen at Chelsea Hospital. Here the council chamber is splendidly adorned with carving by *Emmett* and 29 plasterwork by *Grove*, and here too the tradition of Baroque wall painting in the Italian manner was introduced: the dining hall has a vast allegorical portrait of Charles II, begun in 1687 by *Antonio Verrio*, completed in 1690 by *Henry Cooke*; another Italian, *Sebastiano Ricci*, in England from 1711 to 1716, painted the dome of the chapel.

For a short period such royal endeavours were rivalled by a presumptuous Middlesex mansion of extravagant splendour, the notorious Canons at Little Stanmore, rebuilt for the Duke of Chandos from 1713 to 1720 by *Talman*, *James*, and *Gibbs*. The house was given two grand fronts, and lavishly decorated inside by a series of foreign craftsmen and painters. The only survival of Chandos's patronage is the church of St Lawrence on the edge of the park, rebuilt by *James* in 1715, with an interior which makes a 34 unique attempt to emulate the bravura of continental Baroque: an artfully lit altar with paintings by *Antonio Bellucci*, a vault by *Laguerre*, and walls by *Sleter*. In the attached mausoleum added 32 by *Gibbs* in 1735–6, entirely covered with fictive architectural painting by *Sleter* and *Brunetti*, *Gibbons*'s lordly figure of Chandos reigns over the family monuments. N of the church the lines of the great avenues can still be traced through the park and the encroaching suburban housing.

The flamboyance of Canons was exceptional; rural simplicity was the avowed aim of Viscount Bolingbroke's 'farm' at Dawley, Harlington, a substantial but short-lived building designed by *N. Dubois* and improved by *Gibbs c.* 1725, whose rustic nature was emphasized by a hall painted with arcadian scenes in which (as a poem of 1731 described) 'Young winged cupids smiling guide the plough, And peasants elegantly reap and sow'. Different again in 40 concept is Osterley House, whose romantic brick corner turrets belong to an earlier c 18 remodelling for the wealthy bankers, the Childs. These deliberately historicizing features were probably intended as a conscious echo of the Elizabethan Osterley of Sir Thomas Gresham (an approach which recalls Vanbrugh's castellated houses at Greenwich, Gr). The first signs of more conventional Gothic revival appear *c.* 1750, with *Sanderson Miller's* battlemented stables at Hanworth, contemporary with Horace Walpole's nearby Strawberry Hill at Twickenham (Ri).

Most houses in the London countryside built at this time were more modest villas for successful professional men. Despite later enlargements, the compact early c 18 forms of Gumley House and Gordon House, both at Isleworth, can still be recognized. Another is The Elms at Acton (now Twyford C. of E. High School) of *c.* 1735. In all three, the staircases are showpieces of fine joinery, taking up a good quarter of the total ground floor, a reminder of the attention given to grand circulation spaces at this time even in houses of lesser rank. A more austere mode, in the tradition of Vanbrugh, is represented by the stepped brick front of Fulham House of *c.* 1730; more elaborate is Argyll House in King's Road Chelsea, with a small but elegant five-bay front of 1723 by *Leoni*.

A major turning-point in the move towards a more rigorous 31 classicism is represented by Lord Burlington's villa at Chiswick. Designed from 1724 as an annexe to an older house which was later demolished, Chiswick villa was an expression of *Burlington's* personal vision of antiquity, inspired not only by the examples of his mentors, Jones and Palladio, but also by his own collection of drawings of Roman buildings. Its chaste, precise elevations and its intricately planned, richly coloured suites of rooms set new standards of taste for both town and country buildings. *William Kent*, Burlington's protégé who worked on the interiors at Chiswick, was also employed to decorate the remodelled Kensington Palace. Here, in 1724–5, he combined allegorical and illusionist painting in the Italian manner with more novel ideas: a precocious imitation of Etruscan–Pompeian decoration in the King's Presence Chamber and a coffered dome *à la* antique in the Cupola Room, still somewhat experimental and uncertain in its effect.

The remodelling of the grounds of Chiswick House and Kensington Palace were also influential enterprises. At Chiswick, Burlington experimented first with formal vistas leading to classical garden buildings. When he extended the grounds in the 1730s these were supplemented by a more relaxed, picturesque layout, with a wilderness and a winding river with rocky cascade. At Kensington similar effects were pursued, but on a more heroic scale, cul-minating in the creation of the Serpentine, the broad curving lake between Kensington Gardens and Hyde Park. These schemes had a wide legacy outside the London area. In this volume the only notable survival is Gunnersbury Park, which still has a mid C18 temple from the time of Princess Amelia.

The Chiswick villa was much admired, but had no direct imitators. It was the parallel prototype of Marble Hill, Twickenham (Ri), that was a more direct influence on the neat white villas that sprang up in the later C18 in the London countryside. Most of these were concentrated around the fashionable riverside settlements of Twickenham and Richmond, others were scattered among the villages s of the Thames (*see London 2: South*), but in our area the only noteworthy survivor is the house built after 1747 as successor to Canons (now much altered).

Eighteenth-century Urban Expansion

Meanwhile London itself was growing, and it is to the buildings of its new suburbs that we must now turn. The spread of the built-up area N of Oxford Street into the parish of St Marylebone began with the laying out of Cavendish Square and its surrounding streets on the estate of Edward Harley from c. 1719. His development took off only slowly, and the Duke of Chandos's grand town house on the N side of the square never materialized. Nothing from the earliest period remains apart from *Gibbs*'s delightful little estate chapel of 1721–4 (now St Peter Vere Street), with its exuberant Baroque interior. The earliest remaining domestic work is part of the interior of No. 20 (preserved within the College of Nursing), its fine staircase with bold illusionistic paintings of c. 1735 by the scene-painter *John Devoto* demonstrating the superior standards to which the square aspired. Otherwise the earliest surviving houses are a restrained pair, Nos. 17–18 Cavendish Square, 1756–7 by the Palladian *Henry Keene*. More extensive stretches of plain terrace houses of the later C18 remain in the grid of streets which spread out around the square and continued up to the Marylebone Road, the New Road constructed in 1756 to run eastward to the City, and which defined the northern boundary of built-up London until the end of the C18. The long, severe terraces of these later streets adopted the new principles introduced under Palladian influence: the use of the grey-yellow London stocks in place of the 'hot' red brick of the earlier C18, and the introduction of rusticated or channelled stucco for the ground floor, to create the impression of a stone basement supporting the *piano nobile* with the main reception rooms. Stone was an extravagance, and is found only occasionally, as in the case of the unusually formal pair which were eventually built on the N side of Cavendish Square in the 1770s. In streets where the original buildings have been least disturbed one can still appreciate the efforts to design blocks as a whole, 'palace fashion', with end and centre houses set forward or made slightly taller. From the 1770s the availability of new materials encouraged a taste for greater enrichment, and façades began to be embellished by *Coade* stone keystones, occasional all-over stucco work, and delicate

38 fanlights and iron balconies (see for example Nos. 61–63 New
Cavendish Street).

The Later Eighteenth Century – Town and Country

A prime influence in this development away from the severity of
early Palladianism was the work of the Scottish-born *Robert Adam*,
whose HOUSES are well represented in our area. Adam settled in
London in 1757 after three years in Italy. Fascinated like Burlington
before him by the remains of antiquity, he interpreted them with
an unprecedented lightness and elegance that immediately became
popular. His first work in England was an addition of 1758–9 to
Gordon House Isleworth: a wing with a dining room whose ceiling
already displays elements of his characteristic style. Among the
numerous country-house commissions that followed, the remodelling of the interiors of Syon House began in 1762, those of
Osterley in the following year. At Syon he created within the shell
of the old house some of his most powerful interiors, a hall and
39 antechamber of heroic grandeur, in startling contrast to the more
frivolous but carefully controlled delicacy of the long gallery. At
40 Osterley he lightened the red-brick exterior by the addition of an
airy portico, as well as creating a series of rooms notable for their
perfectly integrated decoration and furnishings.

At the same time he began to be employed on town houses in
London. Those in this volume date from the 1770s. His entrée to
St Marylebone began with a house in Duchess Street for General
Robert Clerk in 1768 (demolished), followed by the stone-fronted
Chandos House nearby in Queen Anne Street, built in 1770–1 for
the 3rd Duke of Chandos. Speculative development followed in
Mansfield Street from 1770, and, with his brothers *William* and
James Adam, in Portland Place from 1773. Here they created a
calmly elegant streetscape with groups of stuccoed houses embellished with central pediments, the general effect sadly disrupted
in the C20, although a few good individual houses and interiors
remain. Robert Adam's most remarkable surviving town house is
Home House, Portman Square, 1773–6 for the Duchess of Home,
41 a *tour de force* of ingenious planning, with a spectacular toplit
staircase, and differently shaped rooms decorated with great inventiveness and finesse.

Only a few other country houses of the mid to later C18 need be
mentioned. At Osterley and also at Fulham Palace, which was
extensively remodelled for the Bishops of London from the mid
C18, there are rooms with good mid-century Rococo plasterwork.
Pitshanger, Ealing, has a wing of 1768 by *George Dance*, with
attractive plasterwork in a slightly later style. Harefield House
Ickenham (much altered) was built for Sir Roger Newdigate of
Harefield by *Henry Couchman* in 1786, an unassuming stucco
replacement of the old Newdigate mansion at Harefield. More
fragmentary later C18 work remains at Feltham House and Ealing
Park, both conversions of older buildings. Worton Hall Isleworth
is a dignified design perhaps by its owners, the masons *John Devall*
and his son. Such buildings still stood on their own in the countryside. The banks of the Thames, however, were becoming increas-

ingly thickly populated with houses. Along Cheyne Walk Chelsea one can still see how terraces and individual houses jostled for the riverside sites as they replaced the older mansions or were squeezed into their grounds. At Fulham and Hammersmith, more spaciously sited houses spread along the river bank, but only one major example survives, Hurlingham House Fulham, with its tall pedimented river front of 1797–8 by *George Byfield*.

The landscaped GROUNDS that once surrounded such houses rarely survive. Syon and Osterley are the only substantial examples, both with garden buildings by *Adam* and picturesque landscaping with serpentine lakes of the types popularized by *Capability Brown*. On a lesser scale are Walpole Park, once the grounds of Pitshanger Manor Ealing, laid out by *John Haverfield*, Ravenscourt Park Hammersmith, perhaps by *Repton*, and Harefield Grove Hillingdon.

The elegant restraint of which late Georgian Neo-classicism was capable is eloquently demonstrated among CHURCHES by St Mary Paddington, rebuilt in 1788–91 by *John Plaw*, an architect fas- 46 cinated by the possibilities of the central layout. It is exceptional not only because of its regular Greek plan, but also because the late C18 was not a significant time for Anglican church building. The new suburbs were served only by small private chapels, and these, like the early Nonconformist chapels, were almost invariably rebuilt in the C19. The earliest survivals lie outside C18 London: the simple Friends' Meeting Houses at Isleworth (1785) and Uxbridge (1817). The only village church rebuilt at this time was the modest Feltham of 1802. The older churches, however, continued to be the repositories for MONUMENTS, although these rarely compete with the pomp and circumstance of the earlier C18. The most elaborate are to Henry Pagett, Earl of Uxbridge, † 1743 at Hilling- 33 don, a finely carved reclining figure in Roman dress, and to Robert Child † 1782 at Heston, a graceful urn with putti by *Adam* and *Vangelder*. A good example of the popular motif of the mourning female figure is the monument to John Dalton † 1791 at Great Stanmore, by *Bacon*. Elsewhere there are numerous Neo-classical urns, obelisks, and tablets, memorable among them the chaste urns to the Newdigate ladies at Harefield († 1765, 1774, 1810), and the monument at West Drayton to Fysh de Burgh † 1793, by *Bacon*, with an urn and relief. Not all the best monuments are indoors, for the C18 is also the time when the antique spirit is evoked by increasingly elaborate churchyard memorials. The Bishops of London have a fine sequence of monuments at Fulham, including one by *Vardy*; Chiswick also has a churchyard rewardingly crammed with fine tombs, among them one by *Kent* to Lord Burlington's bricklayer Richard Wright † 1734, and an urn to Hogarth † 1764; Chelsea has an urn to Sir Hans Sloane † 1763, by *Wilton*. The tradition of antique sarcophagi is continued by later examples by *Soane* at Kensington and Norwood.

While church monuments are unrelievedly classical, the Gothic style began to attract adherents among those who were attracted by the romance of MEDIEVAL TRADITIONS. Fulham Palace was given a castellated wing already in 1764–5 by *Stiff Leadbetter*, but the castle style never caught on in the London area, and Fulham's Gothic detail, too frivolous for later episcopal taste, was removed by 1814. A few small country houses around London at the turn

of the century exhibited similar interests; the only survival in our
area is Twyford Abbey, *c.* 1807 by *William Atkinson*; until recently
there was also Berrymead Priory, Acton (their monastic names in
both cases entirely historical fantasies). There were also occasional
cottages ornés with charmingly playful Gothic detail still unaffected
by the rise of antiquarian accuracy; one of the most famous was
45 Craven Cottage Fulham. The best surviving example is at Hanwell.
   The outstanding architect of the turn of the century is *John
Soane*. His earliest work in Middlesex is his additions of 1788–98
44 for the Marquess of Abercorn at Bentley Priory (a genuine monastic
site in a remote position on Harrow Weald). Behind the c19 disguise one can still recognize much of Soane's plan, with its large
central rotunda, and some characteristic Grecian detail. In 1800
Soane settled in Ealing, having acquired Pitshanger Manor, to
42 which he added a small but grand centrepiece in an intensely
antique spirit, through which one enters a series of intimate, idio-
43 syncratic rooms whose eclectic detail and unusual colour schemes
(recently restored to striking effect) provide a parallel to his town
house in Lincoln's Inn Fields. The triumphal-arch theme of the
Pitshanger front was echoed by his contemporary Norwood Hall of
1801–3 (now much altered), while at Chelsea Hospital his surviving
work includes a brick stable block (1809–17) whose exquisitely
minimal detail recalls the classic austerity of Dulwich Picture
Gallery (Sk). Soane was also responsible for Holy Trinity, one of
the most elegant and expensive of the Neo-classical churches of
Marylebone. But by the time this was built in 1828 much else had
happened in the London suburbs, and to these we must now return.

Urban Developments from the Late Eighteenth Century

The period from the late c18 to around 1850 is one of the most
interesting in the history of English URBAN PLANNING. It is at
this time that the traditional grid of squares and streets, familiar
from the mid c17, begins to be leavened by the bolder forms of
crescents, circles, and ovals. The first example of the introduction
into London of such Neo-classical concepts, the small circus and
crescent – a tiny echo of Bath – off the Minories to the E of the
City, was built by *George Dance* in 1767. s of the river *Robert Mylne*
laid out St George's Circus in 1769. In west London the first steps
in this direction were *Henry Holland*'s Hans Town, begun in 1777
on the Knightsbridge estate of Lord Cadogan, with a series of
bevelled squares of different sizes; and *Novosielski*'s now vanished
speculative development in Brompton of 1786, which included a
crescent. The only late c18 survival in this spirit in our area is the
half-completed circus in Great Cumberland Place Marylebone of
c. 1790. In south London there were similar schemes by *Michael
Searles*, of which the most notable survival is his Paragon at
Blackheath (Gr) begun in 1794, a crescent composed of pairs of
houses. Other ideas too were in the air: a plan for the development
of the Eyre estate, covering part of what is now St John's Wood,
published in 1794, proposed not only a grand double circus, but
the novelty of a suburb built up with detached and semi-detached
villas in their own gardens.

Such schemes were the prelude to London's most ambitious and enjoyable piece of town planning, *John Nash*'s creation of the select suburb of Regents Park on the royal estate of Marylebone Park, and its connection to the heart of the west end by the stately new thoroughfare of Regent Street. His first plans for the park, developed from around 1812, included as a centrepiece a double circus of houses, perhaps influenced by the Eyre plan, but what was built in the end, mostly during the 1820s–30s, was much less urban – a spacious landscape scattered with a small number of chaste classical villas, the best of them designed by *Decimus Burton*. The park, however, was surrounded by terraces of houses disguised by grandiose stuccoed frontages. They are of an unparalleled length 50 (the longest is nearly 1,100 ft) – comparable in size to the vast contemporary military buildings of Woolwich or the warehouses of the docks. Behind them to the E were market squares of cottage terraces, and the two Park Villages, picturesque groups of small gabled or Italianate villas, not completed until the 1840s.

The influence both of the picturesque villas and of the palatial terraces of Regents Park can be traced in subsequent SUBURBAN DEVELOPMENT, although in one respect Nash's scheme marks an end rather than a beginning; from the early C 19 the most fashionable suburbs lay not to the N, but to the W. The march W took the form of two pincer movements of the 1820s–30s. The southern arm consisted of Thomas Cubitt's Belgravia, which linked Westminster with Knightsbridge, Chelsea, and Brompton. Meanwhile, N of Hyde Park, the squares and crescents of Tyburnia were laid out on the Bishop of London's Paddington estate, inspired by a master plan of 1824 by *S. P. Cockerell*. The development of Bayswater and much of Kensington followed in the 1840s and 50s. The advance was by no means regular; it was preceded by ribbon development along the main roads, and by early outposts which sprang up on the edges of the old villages: the large but unambitious Edwardes Square from 1811, on Lord Kensington's land at the W end of Kensington High Street, and even further out, St Peter's Square Hammersmith, an elegant layout of the 1820s with which *J. C. Loudon* may have been associated. This consisted of houses grouped in threes, instead of the usual terraces. Loudon's own house in Porchester Terrace Bayswater of 1823–5 was a declaration of belief 53 in the virtues of the semi-detached villa, and it is at this time that the villa in either classical or Gothic dress becomes popular as a suburban alternative to the terrace house. In St John's Wood, where 52 villas mushroomed in the 1830s–40s, the picturesque opportunities offered by a mixture of styles are exploited in a similar way as in Nash's Park Villages. Elsewhere there were select developments of villas alone (Campden Hill Kensington, as early as 1814), or villas mixed with terraces (Hyde Park Gate off Kensington Gore, of the 1830s), while semi-detached pairs of neat stuccoed houses for the less wealthy lined the roads out of town (see e.g. Goldhawk Road and Stamford Brook Road Hammersmith).

The distinctive characters of these various developments depended on the ambitions of the landowners and the abilities of the architects and surveyors they employed. Some of the buildings of the 1830s–40s have a crisply restrained elegance still in the tradition of the late C 18; there are some especially distinguished

51 examples in Brompton, South Kensington: *Basevi*'s Pelham and
Egerton Crescents (1833, 1840s); *John Blore*'s Brompton Square
and Hereford Square (1834, 1845); and – an outlier to the NW –
Robert Cantwell's Royal Crescent and Norland Square (1837).
Tyburnia is a different matter, its theatrical accents of giant
columns and curvaceous bows representing a more urban rendering
of elements of Nash's Regents Park terraces. Yet Tyburnia also has
its open spaces. Its speciality was the secluded communal garden
immediately accessible from an adjacent terrace – an idea copied in
parts of Bayswater and North Kensington, most notably in the
Ladbroke estate on Notting Hill. Here the concept of the circus re-
emerges, proposed first in a plan of 1823 by *Thomas Allason*, but
realized only in the 1840s in the form of grand sweeps of concentric
crescents.

  While there is a family resemblance between the planning of the
squares and crescents of the earlier C19 and those of the 1840s–
50s, the most ambitious HOUSES of the mid century are easily
distinguished by their greater height, their more lavish interiors,
and their rich encrustations of Italianate ornament. There is a
telling contrast between the demure terraces and squares which
developed off Brompton Road or the King's Road Chelsea during
the 1830s–40s, and the developments of the 1840s onwards. The
most ambitious of these followed Nash in exploiting prime positions
overlooking the royal parks; in 1845 *Cubitt*'s lofty pair of mansions
rose at Albert Gate Knightsbridge, on the edge of Hyde Park
(*see London: 1*); in Kensington the trailblazers were the palatial
mansions built on the Crown land along Kensington Palace
Gardens, laid out in 1843. They were designed by some of the most
eminent architects of the day – the office of *Charles Barry*, *James
Knowles*, *T. H. Wyatt*, *David Brandon*, *Sydney Smirke*, *Owen Jones*
(who perversely introduced some Moorish detail). The speculative
builders of the 1850s took up the mood, as can be seen by developments all over Kensington, too many and too diverse to enumerate
54 here in detail: *Thomas Allom*'s grandiose terraces E of Ladbroke
55 Grove, the *Godwins*' sumptuous villas in The Boltons, and the tall
terraces along Queen's Gate – the principal boulevard of newly
fashionable South Kensington – are among the most sumptuous
examples. Behind such buildings lay private stables or more often
57 rows of mews, originally built for the wealthy residents' servants
and carriages, and sometimes still concealed by the grand entrance
arches of the type first introduced by Nash at Regents Park.

  The patterns set in Paddington, Kensington, and Chelsea began
to be imitated further afield: Ravenscourt Park Hammersmith is
ringed by mid C19 streets of genteel villas and terraces; The Park,
Ealing, built up from 1847, has a handsome row of Italianate villas
by *Sydney Smirke*. In other places beyond the limits of built-up
London a few larger estates of ambitious detached or semi-detached
mansions were begun. The pattern for such development was set
by Cubitt's Clapham Park in south London (built up slowly from
1825). In west London the success of such enterprises was limited,
and in most cases only the street plan and a few battered original
houses remain as melancholy evidence of their developers' grandiose intentions, stranded among the denser suburban building
that arrived with the improved transport of the later C19. Spring

Grove Isleworth was begun in the 1850s by *John Taylor*, who made use of his own patented cement render for his tall, dour, classical houses; Woodridings at Hatch End was advertised in 1855, a surprisingly far-flung outlier, explained by its early railway connections. At Castlebar Ealing, broad streets were lavishly laid out in 1860, but the developer went bankrupt in 1872. The more successful riverside development of Grove Park Chiswick was built up from 1867 in a mixture of styles characteristic of its time, although as late as the mid 1870s the villas of Stonebridge Park Harlesden were planned in a picturesque rustic Italianate.

In general stucco Italianate prevailed for respectable urban developments through the 1860s and into the 70s, doggedly main- 56 tained by builders aiming to profit from the cramped, repetitive terraces filling the smaller streets on the fringes of outer Kensington and Paddington. It was, however, only one among a variety of styles being practised, and by this time the success of the Gothic Revival for churches (*see* below) was beginning to have an impact on other building types. A surprisingly early and consistent example of Ruskinian Gothic taste by a speculative builder is Randolph Avenue Maida Vale Paddington of 1862; the most extreme is the group of intensely Gothic boarding houses built by Harrow School (1863 onwards by *C.F. Hayward*), which, together with the other new school buildings, stamped Harrow-on-the-Hill with a High Victorian Gothic atmosphere somewhat like north Oxford, but unparalleled elsewhere in the London area. Even in Kensington the more enterprising developers began to experiment with eclectic novelties – the *Godwins* introduced a lush mix of classical and Gothic in Redcliffe Square (1869–76), while in 1877–9 at Cornwall Gardens two vast and ornate French Second Empire mansions (a style introduced on the Grosvenor estate in Westminster already in 1860) provide a diversion among the familiar rhythms of the stucco terraces of ten years earlier. For the terrace houses which so rapidly filled the less fashionable suburbs expanding on the fringes of west London, from Fulham and Hammersmith to Acton and Willesden, the standard adornment from *c.* 1860 to *c.* 1880 was a more economical mixture of classical and Gothic trimmings (the latter gradually ousting the former) applied to doorways and bay-windows, with roofs and eaves now exposed instead of hidden by 'dishonest' parapets.

The BUILDINGS OF THE COUNTRYSIDE of after 1815 need only brief notice. Middlesex was now too close to London to appeal to those with extensive landed ambitions. The riverside remained an attraction: *Blore*'s Isleworth (now Nazareth) House of 1832 is a good example of neo-classical turning Italianate, in the manner of Nash, with interior features to match. The move towards more ornate interiors is demonstrated by the enlargement and decoration of Gunnersbury Park (a building of *c.* 1802 which had replaced Webb's mansion) for the Rothschilds in 1838, by *Sydney Smirke*; the grand staircase and the main reception rooms are an early example of the taste for a lavish French Empire style. Also in the French manner, although more Rococo, are the interiors of Hillingdon Court (now American Community School), a country house in its own grounds, built by *P.C. Hardwick* in 1854–8 for the banker Charles Mills. Other large C19 houses were built on the still attractively rural high ground of Stanmore Common and Harrow Weald, although few survive. The romantic profile of Stanmore Hall remains (begun in 1847 by *McDuff Derick*, enlarged by *Brightwen Binyon*), although its *Morris & Co.* decoration has gone. Not far off is Bentley Priory, where Soane's work is encased in a Italianate extravaganza created after 1852 for the railway engineer Sir John Kelk. Mid C19 Pinner was dominated by the eccentric local landowner A. W. Tooke, who in the 1860s indulged in a burst of building activity, adding a new front to his house on Pinner Hill (now golf club), building a Gothic fantasy, Woodhall Towers (now demolished), and adding to his estate whimsical folly-like farm buildings and cottages, some of which remain.

There is an earlier, more rational reminder that this NW part of Middlesex was still an agricultural area. Engulfed by the C20 suburbia of Wealdstone is the model farm in Kenton Lane designed *c.* 1810 by *Robert Abraham* for William Loudon, the father of J. C. Loudon. It was one of the younger Loudon's first campaigns of improvement (the energetic Scotsman had been shocked by the lazy habits of rustic Middlesex farmers) before he turned his attention to suburban buildings (*see* above). Loudon's influential journalism covered a wide range of interests, and the improvement of the design of conservatories was another of his passions. There are two major examples in west London which excited his interest. He criticized *Samuel Ware*'s conservatory of 1813, built on the extended grounds of Chiswick House (a nevertheless innovative building, with a dome of cast iron), while the design of the conservatory at Syon House, an admirable work of 1827–30 by the inventive *Charles Fowler*, has a dome with a steeper profile designed to accord with Loudon's theories about the need to transmit the sun's rays directly. It was in part due to Loudon that conservatories became a favourite Victorian adjunct to houses of all sizes; a good middle-of-the-range survival is the attractive one at Bishopshalt Hillingdon, a substantial neo-Jacobean villa of 1858 (now a school).

From around 1870 a new approach became evident in the design of country houses, as ponderous Gothic or Italianate was abandoned in favour of the relaxed tilehung and half-timbered 'Old English' inspired by the vernacular of Surrey and Sussex and vigorously promoted by the work of *Norman Shaw*. At Harrow Weald a prime example of this consciously picturesque manner, 60 Grim's Dyke, was built in 1870–2 for the artist Frederick Goodall, designed as a skilful combination of studio house and country mansion. The influence of the style was far-reaching, and had an immediate effect on such architects as *Ernest George* (who indeed himself was responsible for additions to Grim's Dyke in 1890) – as is shown by his estate cottages of 1879–80 at Eastcote – but also in the longer term on a more popular level, as is evident from the suburban reflections of the style which continued into the 1920s. But that is to anticipate. Here we are still concerned with the 1870s, and at this point it is apposite to return to what was happening in the London suburbs.

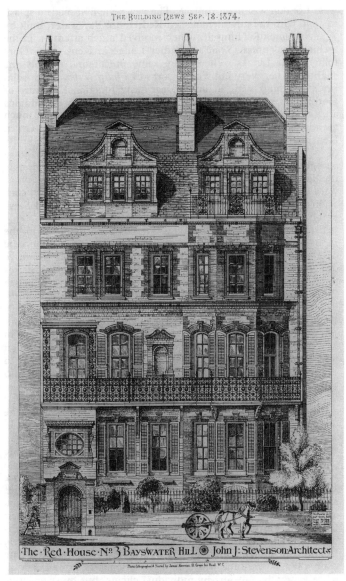

THE BUILDING NEWS SEP. 18. 1874.

·The·Red·House·Nº 3 Bayswater Hill ◉ John J: Stevenson Architect

Bayswater, The Red House (demolished), by J. J. Stevenson, 1870

Urban and Suburban Housing from 1870 to 1910

In the early 1870s a new type of urban domestic architecture burst upon the London scene. Its cheerful, lively red brick manner was derived chiefly from c 17 English and Dutch precedents, although it was rather confusingly labelled 'Queen Anne' by contemporaries. Its chief protagonists were *Norman Shaw* and his associates, and west London was its birthplace. The new style first made a splash in 1870 with the now-demolished Red House Bayswater, built by *J. J. Stevenson* for himself, which received much attention in the architectural press. *Shaw*'s Lowther Lodge in Kensington Gore followed in 1872–5. There were some precursors, notably the slightly earlier, very individual works of *Philip Webb*, plain, solid brick buildings with an unselfconsciously functional mixture of Gothic and vernacular elements. Webb's west London buildings 59 are a studio house at Glebe Place Chelsea of 1868–71, and the much grander studio mansion built for George Howard at Palace Green Kensington in 1872–6. Next door on Palace Green was the house of W. M. Thackeray, who as early as 1860–2 had insisted on a straightforward red brick frontage in the early c 18 manner, despite the disapproval of the Crown Commissioners. But such buildings were too plain to have a wide appeal, and it was the pretty, consciously artistic detail and picturesque gables of Shaw and Stevenson that caught popular attention.

From *c.* 1874 both *Shaw* and *Stevenson* participated in the 58 rebuilding of the Cadogan estate Chelsea, where it can at once be seen that Shaw was by far the more interesting and inventive designer. His ingenuity in devising a series of quite different houses for rich individual clients is also demonstrated along the Chelsea Embankment, where plots were let from 1874. Other equally original red brick houses began to disrupt the stucco reaches of Queen's Gate, notably Shaw's No. 196 of 1874. Shaw's houses are significant not only for the variety of their façades, but also for the way in which they abandoned the conventional planning of the London terrace house, ingeniously redisposing the main staircase so as to create large, well-lit rooms at both front and back. Shaw also showed how such aims could be achieved on a lesser scale when from 1877 he became involved in Bedford Park, Jonathan Carr's artistic suburb on the fringes of Acton and Chiswick. Here he 73 designed both the church (*see* below), and the pub and stores, in an engaging style reminiscent of a traditional English market town, and devised a range of small, carefully planned houses which made play with trim white woodwork, sited to create a picturesque streetscape. At Bedford Park he was abetted by *E. J. May* and *Maurice Adams* (both local residents); in Chelsea and Kensington a host of architects soon jumped on the bandwagon, too many to discuss individually here. Among them the exuberant houses of *Ernest George* are particularly enjoyable, revelling in their broad, flamboyant Netherlandish Baroque gables (Cadogan Square Chelsea; Collingham and Harrington Gardens Kensington). The latter date from 1882–8, the time when the new style starts to be taken up more generally, not just by individual clients, but by speculative builders, as can be seen if one pursues the perambulations of southwest Kensington, and the adjoining parts of Hammersmith.

As will be already clear, the new style was closely allied with the aspirations of the artistic community, and ARTISTS' HOUSES of this period developed as a distinctive genre, their special requirements – a well lit studio which would accommodate and impress the visiting public – stimulating fresh and original approaches to planning and design. The most celebrated group was built in the neighbourhood of Val Prinsep's house on the edge of Holland

Park: Lord Leighton's house in 1866, plain without, but riotously 61
colourful and exotic within; then, in the new Queen Anne manner,
Shaw's houses for Marcus Stone (1875) and Luke Fildes (1876).
Here, too, also designed in 1876, is *William Burges*'s own forcefully
romantic castle with its intensely personal medievalizing interiors. 62
In Chelsea the most famous group was in Tite Street, built up from
1877 behind the Chelsea Embankment. The street gained notoriety
through *E. W. Godwin*'s provocatively austere White House,
designed for Whistler. This has disappeared, but other studio
houses remain to show how radically the type defied the conventions
of the regular terrace.

Other artists settled further out on what was still the fringe of
London. Among the unusually high quota of studios at Bedford
Park *Voysey*'s Tower House of 1891 in South Parade struck a new
note of calculated simplicity. There are other individual artists'
houses of the 1890s worth hunting out: in north Fulham they range
from *James MacLaren*'s free classical composition in Avonmore
Road to *Voysey*'s homely cottage in St Dunstan's Road, while in
Talgarth Road *Frederick Wheeler* contributed a striking terracotta- 63
trimmed terrace for bachelor artists, with an array of tall arched
studio windows which now cheer the traveller on the approach to
the M4. *Voysey*'s inventiveness can be seen yet again in his two
houses tucked away beside Harrods in Hans Road Chelsea (1891),
where there is a third house by *Mackmurdo*, also responsible for
No. 25 Cadogan Gardens Chelsea, an elegant frontage with elongated oriels in tribute to Shaw. Even in heavily built up Kensington,
studios and small houses began to spring up in back streets and
mews (see e.g. around Stratford Road) as improvements in public
transport led to a decline in demand for stables.

The AESTHETIC MOVEMENT had a wider effect on the appearance of London, for by the 1890s there was a concern not only with
the design of individual buildings, but with their settings, and
with the development of forms of building that were considered
appropriate for different parts of London. In the lesser streets of
the most urban areas, much effort was devoted to exploring new
forms for the narrow street front of the traditional flat Georgian
terrace house. This can be studied especially well in the rebuilding
activity which took place from the 1890s on the Howard de Walden
estate N of Oxford Street. Mixtures of red brick, terracotta, and
stone, shaped gables, and shallow projecting bows and oriels were
favourite devices: Harley Street is especially rich in examples.
Frank Elgood was one of the most active architects here; another
was the more original *Beresford Pite*, whose special interests were
layered brickwork (former Y.W.C.A. Mortimer Street, 1903) and
the use of architectural sculpture (No. 37 Harley Street, 1899– 77
1900). The inventiveness of this period is further demonstrated by
H. Fuller Clark's original and colourful free-style compositions
around Candover Street, in the same neighbourhood.

The modest charm of the older parts of Chelsea was particularly
cherished at this time; *C. R. Ashbee* strove to enhance its character
with a series of original, tautly designed houses in a consciously
old-world spirit (of which the only survivors are Nos. 38–39 Cheyne 72
Walk, of 1898–9); the tradition continued in more subdued form
elsewhere in Chelsea during the early C 20. Other architects became

similarly involved in enhancing their home ground. At Ealing *Leonard Shuffrey* demonstrated his allegiance to Shaw's Old English manner with his own house of 1888; at Harrow-on-the-Hill *E. S. Prior* also was an early champion of this style, contributing in the 1880s a number of attractive tile-hung, gabled houses for members of his family, but also other buildings, such as the extraordinary Byzantine-inspired billiard room in Mount Park Avenue (1889), which reveal his quirkily original approach. *Arnold Mitchell*, another Harrow resident, scattered the still sylvan slopes of Harrow Hill with a series of houses of 1891 onwards (including two for himself) in his distinctive, comfortably homely free classical style.

The outer reaches of our area, especially the still pleasantly rural higher ground of the NW, continued to attract the comfortably off. The development on these heavy clay uplands was too expensive to make smaller houses profitable. Northwood, well connected by train, became a particularly superior suburb, reminiscent of parts of Surrey developed at the same time, although its good assortment of large houses has been considerably diminished since the 1960s. A good example of this half-country, half-suburban type is *Cecil Brewer*'s restrained Fives Court Pinner of 1900–8, built for the son of Ambrose Heal, who lived in the area too (his house, also by Brewer, has been demolished). A more flamboyant case was the transformation of the late C18 Canons (now North London Collegiate School) in 1910 by *C. E. Mallows* into a mansion for the rubber magnate Arthur Ducros.

Store owners were among the most wealthy patrons. Ernest Debenham could afford a substantial new house with large grounds 76 on the edge of Holland Park (No. 8 Addison Road, 1905). Here *Halsey Ricardo* was able to indulge his enthusiasm for colourful ceramic facing for his monumental Renaissance-inspired exterior; the lavish interior with its mosaic-clad domed central hall and its wealth of *William de Morgan* tiles is equally impressive. Similar in taste but on a smaller scale are the rich Art Workers' Guild interiors created in 1904–13 for the banker Montagu Norman at Thorpe Lodge (now part of Holland Park School Kensington). Quite different in spirit is the spare and original manner of *Voysey*, illustrated by his refitting at No. 13 Chelsea Embankment for Emslie Horniman in 1906.

In inner London by the turn of the century the large new house was exceptional. Pressure from developers was coupled with growing demand for convenient smaller establishments, and increasingly almost all the prime frontages of the main roads in the inner west London suburbs were given over to large blocks of superior MANSION FLATS. The shift is marked most acutely in the juxtaposition of Lowther Lodge by *Shaw*, begun in 1872, and Albert Hall Mansions, the towering blocks of flats which Shaw helped to design next door five years later. The later examples range from *Worley*'s highly decorated piles around the Albert Hall of 1894 onwards, continuing what had been begun by Shaw, *Balfour & Turner*'s Campden House Chambers in Kensington, 1894, much praised at the time, to some attractive free classical blocks of the early C20 (*Gordon & Gunton*'s Manor House Marylebone Road of 1907, *F. S. Chesterton*'s developments in Hornton Street and High Street Kensington of 1905 etc.). The fashion spread in a less distinguished manner up Edgware Road, over the yet unbuilt parts of Maida Vale, and gradually swamped much of St John's Wood.

Urban Improvements

The western suburbs were not exclusively the preserve of the rich and respectable, although our area had little to compare with the vast expanses of teeming slums stretching E of the City towards the docks, and S of the industries along the Thames. Yet by the mid C19 the back lanes and alleys of St Marylebone also contained overcrowded pockets of extreme squalor, while on the fringes of built-up London a series of insalubrious shanty towns led a brief, scandalous existence before being swept away by more permanent suburbs – Tomlins New Town in Paddington, Portman Town at St John's Wood. Even Chiswick had its 'New Town' of workmen's dwellings by the mid C19. The most notorious of these was the area of North Kensington known as the Potteries and Piggeries, the 'West End avernus' of later C19 journalists.

Attempts to improve such conditions were at first very piecemeal, unassisted by any statutory obligation on the part of the local authorities. At first the chief role was taken by the philanthropic organizations set up from the 1840s onwards, whose solution was the building of tenement blocks for the better-off artisan classes, and most of whose efforts were understandably concentrated in south and east London. However, Octavia Hill's pioneer efforts at housing management began in St Marylebone in the 1860s, with a policy of gradually repairing or replacing some of the worst pockets of overcrowded buildings; an early case was St Christopher's Place, between Oxford Street and Wigmore Street, where the old houses were replaced in 1877 and 1882 by slightly Gothic tenements by *Elijah Hoole*. Hoole was responsible for other improvements of this kind – at Old Church Street Chelsea (Hereford Buildings, 1878), in King's Road Chelsea, 1885, and in Racton Street off Lisson Grove St Marylebone, 1885–6 (cf. also in south London Red Cross Cottages Southwark (Sk), 1887). His later buildings display a deliberately picturesque and cottagey style in intentional contrast to the grimmer tenements of workmen's dwellings being built at the same time by the philanthropic trusts. There are relatively few of these in west London, although some characteristic examples can be found E of Lisson Grove.

Around the same time an alternative type of workers' housing was developed by the Artizans, Labourers and General Dwellings Company, a self-help organization founded in 1867 whose policy was to build neat grids of low-rental cottage terraces on cheap land on the suburban fringes. Their first estate was in south London (Battersea (Ww), 1872–7), the second at Queen's Park Harrow Road, on the edge of outer Paddington (1875 onwards), where their architect was *Rowland Plumbe* (also responsible for later Artizans' flats of 1890 in St Marylebone in Chiltern Street and Dorset Street). An organization with similar aims, the Co-Partnership Tenants, was responsible for the Brentham Garden estate at north Ealing, 74 begun in 1901. This is an instructive case of how an initial rather uninspired layout was transformed from c. 1907 through the involvement of *Raymond Unwin* and *Barry Parker*. Parker & Unwin's debut in the application of picturesque Arts and Crafts principles to the planning of housing estates was in 1903, with their plan for Letchworth Garden City, Herts, followed closely by their work at Hampstead Garden Suburb (Bn). Their influence was to be widespread, not only in local authority housing (*see* below) but in smaller schemes such as the buildings for the Ruislip Manor Cottage Society (1911 onwards, largely by architects involved at Hampstead Garden Suburb), an enterprise which aimed to provide the expanding Metroland suburb with a socially balanced population. C19 housing provided by employers is rare in London: exceptions are the Imperial Gas Company's Imperial Square Fulham, its grand name a curious contrast to its modest cottage terraces, and a few streets of late C19 railway workers' housing at Neasden.

In the inner districts wholesale clearance of overcrowded areas became possible after the Housing Act of 1890, although the local authorities could only build for themselves on such sites after 1901. The effects of such activity can be seen in Chelsea, where the slum cottages which had grown up around Chelsea Common were in the early C20 replaced by the serried rows of Samuel Lewis Housing Trust and Sutton Trust flats flanking Ixworth Street. Chelsea's own early efforts were the St Thomas More estate in Beaufort Street of 1903–4, and Pond House Pond Place of 1906 (both by *Joseph & Smithem*), blocks of flats cheered by quite jolly details, rather in the manner of private mansion flats. Other boroughs were less enterprising; indeed in north Kensington improvements in the notorious Potteries area continued very largely to be carried out by private organizations.

The *L.C.C.*, which in other parts of London took the lead in building early working-class housing, also did little in the western boroughs. A change came only in the early C20 with the new policy of building cottage estates outside built-up London. Most of these are to the north, south, or east, where land was cheaper, but west London has one of the most attractive of these L.C.C. schemes, the Old Oak estate at East Acton, on the northern fringe of Hammersmith. Begun in 1911, this is a mature expression of Parker & Unwin principles, with its picturesque groups of houses interspersed with small greens and generous front gardens, compact enough to avoid the amorphous character of some of the more spread-out cottage estates built after 1918.

The importance of PARKS and OPEN SPACES as an element in London improvements had been recognized from the mid C19, with the government's creation of Battersea Park (Ww) and Victoria Park (TH). The existence of Regents Park, of Hyde Park and Kensington Gardens – the latter enhanced in 1860 by formal Italian water gardens at the head of the Serpentine – together with numerous private squares and gardens precluded the need for large new parks in the wealthier western suburbs. However, fragments of ancient greens and commons were preserved from development as a result of the campaigns of the Commons Preservation Society and the Act passed in 1866. Shepherds Bush and Brook Green Hammersmith, Parsons Green and Eel Brook Common Fulham, are examples, important not only as precious green oases in built-up areas, but also for the way in which they provided some historic identity and individuality for the expanding suburbs. Towards the end of the century there was a widespread movement to open private grounds to the public – Ravenscourt Park Hammersmith in 1887, Bishop's Park Fulham in 1893, Walpole Park Ealing in 1901. Occasionally, too, deliberate efforts were made to make new parks in overcrowded areas: Avondale Park in the Potteries north Kensington dates from 1892, while the park at Bosworth Road Kensal New Town has the surprising feature of a 'Pleasance', a pretty enclosure designed by *Voysey*, given in 1911 by Emslie Horniman (Voysey's patron at Chelsea Embankment, *see* above).

Churches: 1815–1914

In 1818 a parliamentary Act cut through the labyrinthine ecclesiastical procedures of the C 18 and established a commission to select sites and grant funds for new churches. In the uncertain years after the Napoleonic wars Anglican churches were seen as an essential means of promoting social stability in expanding towns, and the aim was to build quickly and cheaply. The respectable western suburbs of London, well provided with private chapels, were perhaps less in need of this attention than other areas, but benefited nonetheless. In expanding St Marylebone, churches were given key positions. A precedent had already been established by the siting of the new parish church (of 1813–17 by *Thomas Hardwick*) as a focal point in *Nash*'s layout around Regents Park. Hardwick's building combines a galleried preaching box with a festive Corinthian portico and tower, an elaboration of the tradition established by Gibbs's St Martin in the Fields, which continued to be the norm for the classical church of this period (see for example St Peter Hammersmith by *Lapidge*, 1827–9, and, as late as 1852, *Allom*'s St Peter Kensington Park Road). *Nash* himself adopted a more daring design for All Souls Langham Place (1821–2), the first Commissioners' church in St Marylebone: its w end ingeniously pivots on the curve linking Regent Street and Portland Place, with a wayward steeple ringed by a circlet of classical columns, which aroused much contemporary disdain. Elsewhere, maximum impact was achieved by a flexible approach to entrances, regardless of liturgical arrangement – an E portico at *Hardwick*'s Christ Church Cosway Street (1822–4), a s one to *Smirke*'s St Mary (1831–3), satisfyingly sited on the axis of Wyndham Place. The details here are cautiously Grecian. Grecian detail had been pioneered for churches a few years earlier by the Inwoods' St Pancras (Ca), and was used also with great elegance by *Soane* for Holy Trinity Marylebone Road (1826–7), one of the most expensive of all Commissioners' churches.

The Gothic Revival

For C 19 churches, the style of the future was not classical but Gothic. It was used with precocious seriousness for one of the first of the Commissioners' churches, St Luke Chelsea by *James Savage* 79

(1820–4), an even more expensive building than Soane's Holy Trinity. Its firmly buttressed Perp W tower and genuine stone vaults distinguish it from its thinner and cheaper Gothic successors of the same decade such as St John Walham Green Fulham by *J. H. Taylor*, 1827, Holy Trinity Brompton by *Donaldson*, 1826–9 (whose simplicity in disguised by later embellishments, as so often happened), and St John Hyde Park Crescent by *Fowler*, 1829–32, whose mild Perp seems disappointingly bland in the grandiose setting of Tyburnia (Cockerell had originally planned a classical building for the site). St Barnabas Addiston Road Kensington, 1827–9 by *Vulliamy*, likewise is a Perp building with corner turrets in the manner of King's College Cambridge. This was an idea perhaps borrowed from *Poynter*'s St Katharine's Hospital Regents Park of 1826, whose bare brick comes as a boldly abrupt innovation at the end of Nash's stucco terraces.

Capacious galleried churches in plain versions of Commissioners' Gothic, with E.E. lancets or Perp tracery, continued to rise in the new suburbs, by architects for whom Gothic was only one among a variety of styles in which they were prepared to build (Christ Church Chelsea by *Blore*, 1838, St Saviour Chelsea by *Basevi*, 1840, St Mark St John's Wood by *Thomas Cundy II*, 1846–7, St James Norlands Kensington by *Vulliamy*, 1848–9, etc.). An early case of more accomplished handling of the lancet style is *Scoles*'s R.C. church of Our Lady Lisson Grove St Marylebone (1833–6). But generally it was in the 1840s that a more earnest and single-minded approach developed. Fuelled by increasing antiquarian research, the chief inspiration was Pugin's advocacy of Gothic as the only truly religious way of building, allied to the Cambridge Camden (later Ecclesiological) Society's enthusiasm for more elaborate liturgy. From then on a distinct breed of church architects began to emerge. The effect of such ideas can be pursued in the development of *G. G. Scott*'s work in the expanding villages around London, from his first efforts in partnership with *Moffatt* – Christ Church Turnham Green Chiswick, 1841–3, and St Mary Hanwell, 1841, tall galleried buildings in the lancet style, but robustly flint-faced – to St John Camberwell (Sk) in south London of 1844, the turning point in his approach to Gothic, and thence to St John Wembley (1846), the restoration of St Mary Harrow (1846–9), St Matthew Yiewsley (1858–9), unusually bold, in coloured brick, and Christ Church Harrow (1862), a mature rendering of the flint-faced village church tradition.

Some of the more solid and serious Gothic churches of the 1840s – for example *Daukes & Hamilton*'s St Andrew, built in Wells Street St Marylebone, but now transplanted to Kingsbury (Brent) – were still in the Perp style, but this was not *Pugin*'s ideal. He favoured 'Second Pointed', the decorative and inventive English Gothic of the late C13 to early C14, and put his ideas into practice at the R.C. St Thomas Fulham (1847–8), his only complete parish church in London. His pupils continued the work: *Benjamin Ferrey* at Christ Church Victoria Road Kensington, and *William Wardell* at the R.C. Holy Trinity Brook Green Hammersmith (both 1851). St Stephen Hammersmith by *Salvin* (1849–50) is another early example of ecclesiological principles. These are modest buildings compared with *Scott*'s triumphant proclamations a few years later:

Christ the Saviour Ealing (1852), Harrow School Chapel (1854–7), St Andrew Uxbridge (1865), and then, most flamboyantly of all, the rebuilding in 1869–79 of St Mary Abbots, which provided fashionable Kensington with the tallest spire in London.

By this time spires and towers were providing confident new landmarks all over the suburbs: Christ Church Lancaster Gate, 1854–5 by *Francis*, is a typical early example, still rather spindly; the spire of *J. L. Pearson*'s St Augustine Kilburn, completed only in 81 1898, is one of the most mature and accomplished. The townscape qualities of Gothic churches could be developed further, for in contrast to classical buildings with a single important façade, the Gothic church could exploit the picturesque massing of tower and steep roofs seen from a variety of angles. Such buildings were not only suitable for prominent island sites in new suburbs – see *George Godwin*'s St Mary The Boltons Kensington (1849–50), St Stephen Paddington (1855–6 by *Francis*), St Stephen Ealing (1875 etc.) – but in the hands of the most skilful architects could make the best even of cramped settings in the slums.

Churches in the Puginian tradition – ragstone-faced, with Dec tracery, lofty naves and roomy chancels, and lush stone carving if funds allowed – remained a reliable if somewhat uninspired conservative ideal for respectable suburban areas, pursued in the 1860s–70s by lesser architects such as the *Francis* brothers (St Mary Acton, St Paul Brentford), and retaining their appeal even in the Edwardian years, as can be seen from the popularity of *J. S. Alder*'s work in north London. However this style was only one among the varied interpretations of Gothic that were developed by the most original architects during the second half of the C 19. They are well represented in this volume. *William Butterfield* made his name with All Saints Margaret Street St Marylebone (1849–59). It was built 82, as an exemplar of the principles of the Camden Society, with a large 83 raised chancel, rich decoration, and provision of accommodation for the clergy, but its architectural significance was much wider: this was a truly urban church cleverly squeezed into a narrow space, which daringly exploited the aesthetic potential of coloured brick for its exterior, and likewise depended on the 'structural polychromy' of its building materials for its insistently abundant interior ornament. Butterfield developed these principles in later churches: St John Hammersmith (1856), with its powerfully gaunt tower; St Augustine Kensington (1870–7), which flaunts its brickwork at its stucco neighbours; and – in the still semi-rural outer districts – the quieter but still recognizably Butterfieldian All Saints Harrow Weald (1845 and 1889–92) and Holy Innocents Kingsbury (1883–4). The influence of Butterfield can be seen in the striped brick and angular towers of some of *A. W. Blomfield*'s churches – for example St Matthew and St Simon, both in Hammersmith. Also allied to Butterfield in his use of structural polychromy, although with very different results, is *William White*, whose All Saints north Kensington (1852–61) has a lofty tower which is an early case of the influence of continental Gothic. *G. E. Street*, who was inspired by a similarly wide range of sources, has one major work in this book, St Mary Magdalene Paddington (1865–78), ingeniously planned on an awkward site, its spare banded tower intended as a landmark among the now vanished canalside slums.

Street's skill at producing interiors with carefully integrated sculpture and furnishings can be seen both here and in his remodelling of St James Paddington (1881–2). His inventive ironwork takes pride of place among the notable fittings of the 1860s which embel-
86 lished St Andrew Wells Street. *J. L. Pearson*, the master of sophisticated Gothic elevations, is also well represented by some of his
81 best buildings: St Augustine Kilburn and the Catholic Apostolic Church Paddington, noble vaulted spaces of the 1870s; an impressive successor in a similar spirit is the fine interior of the R.C. St James Spanish Place St Marylebone by *Edward Goldie* (1885 onwards).

There were alternatives to the refinement of the Gothic tradition based on precise medieval sources. A perverse elaboration of angular detail was a speciality of some of the more wilful of the mid C19 architects – St Simon Zelotes Chelsea (*Peacock*, 1858) and St George Kensington (*Bassett Keeling*, 1864). *E. B. Lamb* was responsible for the even more eccentric chapel of Brompton Hospital Kensington (1849–50), full of his typically emphatic timbering. Those who defied the standards laid down by High Church ecclesiologists produced buildings which have their own distinctive flavour: *George Godwin's* low church St Jude Kensington (1867–70), with its iron columns, wide nave, and galleries, is typical. In a similar spirit, but expressed much more flamboyantly, is *S. S.*
87 *Teulon's* idiosyncratic recasting of the C18 classical St Mary Ealing (1866–74), flaunting its ironwork within a notched brick Byzantine carapace. A quite different mood is expressed by the great brooding brick Gothic basilicas of *James Brooks*, an impressive but relatively cheap building type first developed to spread High Church ideals in poor areas, but also adopted in better-class suburbs – St John Kensington (1872–89) and Holy Innocents Hammersmith (1887), and the more elaborately detailed St Andrew Willesden Green (1886–7). Brooks's influence can be seen in many of the impractically large and not very distinguished churches of the 1880s–90s that sprang up in the outer suburbs (St Matthew Ealing, St Alban Acton, etc.). A daunting scale, with long naves hopefully anticipating massed congregations, is a general characteristic of churches of the 1880s – see for example those by *H. Roumieu Gough*: St Paul Hammersmith (with *Seddon*) and St Cuthbert Kensington.

Victorian Church Furnishings

Buildings such as those just discussed were ideally envisaged as envelopes for rich furnishings, and indeed St Cuthbert is the supreme example of such ambitions; these, however, were mostly completed later, and so must be referred to again below. This is indeed typical of most of the major churches of the western suburbs. It was only gradually, after building expenses were paid off and – often – intended towers abandoned, that funds could accumulate for the adornment of interiors; earlier Victorian fittings were often replaced or eclipsed by later improvements. Exceptions are the commissions from the wealthy patrons who favoured Butterfield and Street, both of whom paid much attention to the design of appropriate furnishings. For an overview of ecclesiological taste of

c. 1850–80 the most rewarding collection of furnishings is at St
Andrew Kingsbury (*see* above), a showpiece of the ecclesiologists, 86
but in most of the churches in the more prosperous suburbs there
is something worthwhile to discover, from *Butterfield*'s splendid
font of coloured marbles at All Saints Margaret Street to *Teulon*'s 83
inventive marine pupit at St Mary Ealing. Elaborate MONUMENTS
are few (effigies at St Peter and Paul Harlington by *R. C. Lucas*, at
St John the Evangelist Great Stanmore by *Boehm*, 1875, and at St
Andrew Kingsbury – intensely medieval – 1862 by *Nicholl* in a
setting by *Burges*). Instead the favoured form of memorial became
the STAINED GLASS window. Among much excellent work by the
leading artists and workshops of the time there is space only to
mention a selection. Early examples of the rediscovery of this art
form, which became so significant for Victorian churches, are the
window by *Wailes* at All Saints Fulham (1840) and work by
Hardman at St Thomas Fulham (1850). A high point comes in the
1860s, when *Clayton & Bell* developed their medallion windows
inspired by the rich tones of C 13 glass (see e.g. St Mary Acton, St
Mary Abbots Kensington, St James Paddington). The lively
designs of *Heaton, Butler & Bayne* occur frequently (St Mary
Acton, St John Pinner, St Mary Ealing, All Saints Harrow Weald,
and – especially good – in the 1880s at All Saints Fulham). *William
Burges* probably designed the forceful chancel window at St Nicholas Chiswick (1867). Among windows by the best designers
working a little later, there are examples by *Henry Holiday* at St
Mary Magdalene Paddington and Holy Trinity Hammersmith, and
by *William Morris*'s firm at St Peter Vere Street (1881, an early
case of a pictorial work), Holy Trinity Northwood, All Saints
Harrow Weald (both of the 1880s), Holy Trinity Chelsea, and
Christ Church Fulham.

Non-Anglican Religious Buildings: Other Styles

The character of ROMAN CATHOLIC churches also owes much to
their furnishings: the most distinguished are the Gothic additions
and fittings of the 1860s onwards by *J. F. Bentley* at St Francis
north Kensington (his earliest work), St Mary Chelsea, and St
Mary Paddington. The fervent brand of Gothic of another R.C.
architect, *Hansom*, is illustrated by the ornate interior of Our Lady
of Dolours Kensington (1874–6). However, the summit of R.C.
ambitions in west London, the Brompton Oratory in Kensington, 84
was built not in the Gothic style but in an accomplished and
convincing Roman Baroque, designed in 1878 by *Herbert Gribble*,
although the lavish fittings were completed only in the 1930s. 85
Successors in the same mode were *Goldie*'s Most Holy Redeemer
Chelsea (1895) and Our Lady Acton (1902), and *Kelly & Birchall*'s
Our Lady Chiswick (1904).

  Although Gothic was the general rule for C 19 churches, it will
already be clear that it was not quite universal. An early Anglican
exception was *Vulliamy*'s engaging All Saints Ennismore Gardens
(now Russian Orthodox) of 1848–9, a rare example of Lombard
Romanesque (another rather clumsier effort is *Kendall*'s St John
Kensal Green, 1844). Like Wild's Early Christian Christ Church

Streatham in south London of 1840-2, these represent a brave attempt at establishing an alternative tradition to Gothic. But such an approach did not flower until the last quarter of the century, when the round-arched Romanesque, Byzantine, or Early Christian styles were explored as part of a more eclectic and wide-ranging approach to sources. The result was some buildings of striking 88 originality. The Rhineland Romanesque exterior of *Tarver's* All Souls Harlesden (1875-6) encloses a remarkable octagonal centre dominated by its bold roof-timbers. Alternatives to Gothic are however more common among non-Anglican buildings; Bentley's Byzantine Westminster Cathedral is of course the major example of the end of the century. Byzantine was used already in 1877, most appropriately, by *Oldrid Scott* for the Greek Orthodox St Sophia Paddington, while *Audsley & Joseph's* monumental New West 92 End Synagogue Paddington (1877-9) is an intriguing blend of Romanesque, Moorish, and Gothic. Other synagogues of this period are similarly inventive (New London Synagogue St Marylebone, 1882 by *Collins*, Romanesque and classical; Spanish and Portuguese Synagogue Paddington, 1896 by *Davis & Emmanuel*, Byzantine).

Ambitious NONCONFORMIST churches could also be innovative – see for example the former Talbot Tabernacle north Kensington (terracotta Romanesque, 1887 by *Habershon & Fawkner*). However the story of the bulk of Nonconformist buildings is of a slow shift from classical façades to Gothic exteriors inspired by Anglican developments. Inside, however, the tradition was maintained of handsome galleried interiors focused on the pulpit. For such buildings classical porticos remained acceptable for fifty years – former Congregational Chapel St John's Wood, 1830s, Kensington Congregational Allen Street (now United Reformed), 1854-5 (very grand), St Marylebone Methodist Church and St Marylebone Welsh Baptist Chapel (both of the 1880s and both rather quirky). The Gothic strand appears as early as 1848-9 with Horbury Congregational Chapel (Kensington Temple) by *John Tarring*, one of the best Nonconformist architects, and grows in strength in the following decades; good examples among many are Ealing Green Church (former Congregational), 1859-60 by the Ealing architect *Charles Jones*; the former Ealing Broadway Methodist Church, by *Tarring* and *Jones* together, with a fine spire (1867); Rivercourt Methodist Hammersmith, by *Charles Bell*, 1875; and the impressively noble remains of West Kensington Congregational Church, 1882 by *James Cubitt*.

Churches after 1880

What novelties could the Anglicans offer towards the end of the century? The west London suburbs boast some of their most enterprising buildings. A new note was struck by *Norman Shaw's* fresh and lively St Michael (1879-80) for the progressively artistic suburb of Bedford Park (*see* above), a successful integration of late Gothic and C17 domestic detail. His church (now a youth club) for the Harrow Mission in the slums of north Hammersmith (1887-9), with its large, strongly mullioned W window, is equally original.

Its influence can be seen at Holy Trinity Sloane Street Chelsea
(1888–90), one of the most important churches by Street's gifted
pupil *J. D. Sedding*, who developed here a free version of late Gothic
expressed with remarkable organic fluency. St Peter, in the affluent
suburb of north Ealing, designed by Sedding in 1889 and completed
after his death by his pupil *Henry Wilson*, is in a similar spirit. One
of the most original interpretations of free Gothic in an art nouveau
mood, combined with the 'new sculpture' of the age, is *Frederick
Wheeler*'s forceful little hospital chapel at Mount Vernon Northwood (1902–4), while a refreshingly free style of a more domestic
character is demonstrated by *Arnold Mitchell*'s church hall at St
Andrew Sudbury (1904–5).

At Holy Trinity Chelsea, Sedding drew together a team of tal-
ented designers to make the church a treasure house of spirited,
although hardly unified, furnishings, in an invigorating mixture of   89
Gothic, Renaissance, and free Arts and Crafts. No other London
church of this time has such a range of inventive work, although
some good individual pieces are to be found elsewhere, such as
Heywood Sumner's 1890s art nouveau decoration of All Saints
Ennismore Gardens, *Bainbridge Reynolds*'s lectern at St Cuthbert
Kensington (1897), *Moira* and *Wood*'s monument to George Shaw
† 1901 at St Barnabas Kensington, and *Nelson Dawson*'s lectern and
pulpit at All Saints Ealing (1903–5). In church furnishings the
radical, exploratory mood of the Arts and Crafts movement of the
end of the C19 had its most interesting legacy in the STAINED
GLASS of the early C20. The leading master was *Christopher Whall*
(clerestory of Holy Trinity Chelsea, 1904–23). From 1906 Whall
and his fellow-workers had their workshops at Lettice Street
Fulham, and this may help to account for an assortment of good
though isolated windows in west London churches; names to look
out for include *Martin Travers, Louis Davis, Paul Woodroffe, Karl
Parsons*, and *Leonard Walker*.

Sedding is an exception. Generally Edwardian High Anglican
taste was more conventional, favouring a refined, delicately detailed
distillation of late Gothic, seen at its best in the late works of *George
Bodley*: Holy Trinity Kensington, 1901–6, St Faith Brentford,
1906–7 (with *Hare*), and in the noble interior of the Annunciation
St Marylebone (1912–14) by Bodley's former assistant *Walter
Tapper*. An intensely felt, richly colourful expression of this spirit
is also to be found in the early buildings and furnishings of another
Bodley pupil, *Ninian Comper* (crypt of St Mary Magdalene Pad-   90
dington, 1895; St Cyprian St Marylebone, 1902–3). In such buildings FITTINGS become all-important; the propriety of reredoses
and screens was no longer questioned, as it had been in the mid
Victorian years when some considered them dangerously Popish
(although Comper still had some problems with his High Church
fittings at St Mary Magdalene). In the richer parishes much effort
was expended on furnishing and adorning buildings, to the extent
that many are now dominated by fittings added after 1890 – St
Augustine Kilburn received its ornate carved screen by *Nicholls* in
1896, Christ the Saviour Ealing its attractive painted organ cases
and pupit by *Bodley* in 1906, to mention only two important
examples. The most ambitious date from *c.* 1910–14: *Ernest Geldart*'s colossal Spanish Gothic reredos at St Cuthbert Kensington,

and the baldacchino and screen at Holy Innocents Hammersmith; *Tapper*'s screen at the Annunciation St Marylebone is on a similarly overwhelming scale. The bravura of monumental continental furnishings – but in Baroque rather than Gothic – continued to appeal after 1918; *Martin Travers* was the chief exponent (reredos at St Augustine Kensington, 1928).

These works are only the High Church cream. The outer suburbs made do with less exciting churches, conventional ragstone Dec by *Alder* (e.g. St Michael Cricklewood, 1909–10), or sparsely furnished brick rectangles, long-naved and narrow-aisled, their exteriors articulated by a little fancy buttressing and brightened by some free Perp detail. The interiors can be more impressive than the usually towerless profiles. The prolific *Cutts* brothers produced many examples in outer London, as did the more original *W. D. Caröe*, architect to the Church Commissioners. Among the more rewarding examples in this volume are *Caröe*'s St Michael Chiswick (1908–9) and *Fellowes Prynne*'s St Peter Harrow (1911–13). The Nonconformist churches building so busily at this time in the new Edwardian suburbs, often on prominent high street sites rather than in the residential areas, frequently made more positive contributions to the townscape. Here the innovations of Shaw and Sedding were readily adopted, with façades, corner towers, and turrets which exploit the playful flamboyance of free late Gothic detail. Good exponents are *Gordon & Gunton* – see their Methodist churches at Hanwell (1904) and Acton (1907). Wealdstone Baptist Church (1905 by *Wills*) and Cricklewood Congregational (1901 by *Wallis*) both display the turn-of-the-century enthusiasm for
91 colourful materials. Cricklewood Baptist Church of 1907–8 by Shaw's pupil *Arthur Keen* is in an unusually bold Baroque, while *Frederick Rowntree*'s Presbyterian Church at Northwood of 1914 is in a well detailed domestic manner reminiscent of Lutyens's Free Church at Hampstead Garden Suburb. In a category all on its own is *R. F. Chisholm*'s First Church of Christ Scientist Chelsea (1908), a grand, exotic blend of free Byzantine and eastern influences accomplished in an Arts and Crafts spirit.

Secular Building: Late Eighteenth to Early Twentieth Century

Before London took over Middlesex, the old settlements had few buildings for community use apart from churches. The towns had market houses, of which the one at Uxbridge still stands, a spare, pedimented late Georgian structure of 1788, with the traditional arrangement of open ground floor below upper rooms. The precursor of the village hall was the church house; at Pinner a timber-framed building near the church may have had this function. SCHOOLS depended on private benefactors. Harrow has the only
18 considerable one; its original schoolroom of 1608–15 has already been mentioned, a very modest space compared with what surrounded it in the C19 and C20. The even humbler domestic character of C18 village schools can be seen at Norwood (1767) and Greenford (1780).

In the C17 and C18 the London countryside was scattered with private schools for the children of London residents, but few were purpose-built, most occupying (and thus preserving) older country houses whose appeal as private homes diminished as London expanded. Even at Harrow, new building began only in 1819–21, when the original schoolhouse was enlarged by *Cockerell*. But with the development of national organizations to promote education, village schools were more frequent by the mid C19, and several remain to show how the type was developed as a picturesque as well as an educational asset. Tudor Gothic was the favoured style: Isleworth, 1846; Broomhouse Lane Fulham, 1854–5 by *Francis*; former National Society School Harrow, 1851–4 by *Habershon*. In the new suburbs a few schools of the earlier C19 adopted the prevailing classicism of their neighbours – see the handsome urban building in Wyndham Place St Marylebone (1824 probably by 47 *Edward Tilbury*), and the pure Grecian front of the former Western Grammar School in North Terrace Kensington (1835 by *W.F.* 49 *Pocock*). An unusual, more ambitious group is *Edward Blore*'s former College of St Mark and St Luke Chelsea, established in 1840 as one of the first teacher training colleges. It was designed in the austere but not unattractive stock brick *Rundbogenstil* that was briefly popular at this time (*see also* churches) and includes a chapel and octagonal schoolroom. By the 1850s, just as with churches, Gothic had taken over in the suburbs as well as in the country; St Marylebone Philological College (later Grammar School) was rebuilt in Marylebone Road – a charming little polygonal Gothic building in coloured brick (1856–7 by *Habershon*) is all that remains – while Harrow, now expanding rapidly as one of the nation's leading public schools, acquired a series of buildings by famous names: a large, earnestly Gothic chapel and library by *Scott* (1854–7 and 1861–3), and a more eccentrically medievalizing Speech Hall by *Burges* (1874–7). They were followed over the next twenty years by others equally in the van of fashion – by then no longer Gothic – by *Champneys* and *Prior*, but that is to anticipate. At Isleworth, an impressive building was erected in 1866 by *Norton & Massey* (now part of the West London Institute of Higher Education) by an organization called the International College, its decoration redolent of its ambitious but shortlived aims.

ALMSHOUSES also have a long history before the C19 (see the examples at Harefield and Isleworth, already mentioned). However, most surviving London almshouses date from after 1800. At this time the City foundations began to rebuild on the cheap land on the fringes of built-up London, as their valuable central sites became too noisy and crowded to accommodate the elderly in comfort. Most of the City Company almshouses lie N, S, and E of the City, rather than in the more distant western areas, but Acton has one of the most attractive of such groups, the Goldsmiths' 48 Almshouses of 1811 by *Charles Beazley*. Just as with churches, one can contrast its elegantly up-to-date stuccoed Neo-classicism with the trim Perp popular a little later, illustrated by *Ambrose Poynter*'s St Katharine's Precinct at Regents Park of 1826 (not an almshouse, but comparable in its layout), and with the more earnest and self-conscious Gothic which was adopted for good works of this kind in the later C19. *J.P. Seddon*'s Powell Almshouses at Fulham of 1869, still in the spirit of Pugin's *Contrasts*, illustrates the type to perfection. The lead taken by the churches in the provision of social welfare in the later C 19 is demonstrated by other communal buildings: the CONVENTS and CLERGY HOUSES often associated with a church school, hospital, or old people's home. Only a few now survive of the many that were established either in older houses (Isleworth: Nazareth House, Gumley House) or in purpose-built premises; the groups by *Butterfield* around All Saints Margaret Street, and by *Shaw* at the Harrow Mission Hammersmith, show that in the hands of the best architects such buildings could make eloquent contributions to their tight urban settings. The most distinguished and spacious of such groups is *J. F. Bentley's* Sacred Heart Convent Hammersmith (originally planned as an R.C. seminary) of 1876–84, with forcefully detailed brick ranges around a cloister (a luxury rarely possible on urban sites). A later example, in a more playful free Gothic, is the convent at Chiswick of 1896 by *C. F. Whitcombe*.

Almshouses and convents, however, could not on their own solve the social problems of Victorian London, and the prevailing trend by the 1860s was for the much larger official establishments, as will be seen shortly. The new scale that characterized Victorian institutions was foreshadowed by the MILITARY BUILDINGS of the C 18. West London has nothing quite as ambitious as the military establishments at Woolwich in south London, but the Hounslow cavalry barracks, set up on Hounslow Heath in 1793 in preparation for Napoleon, still retain some early buildings among the later additions: an orderly group around the original parade ground. At St John's Wood there is a riding school of the Royal Engineers of 1824–5.

HOSPITALS, a favourite concern of C 18 philanthropists, could also be on a considerable scale. Guy's, established in Southwark in 1721, was followed by a rash of foundations N of the Thames in the 1740s–50s – St Luke's, St George's, the Westminster, the Foundling Hospital, and by the London Hospital in the East End (the only one of this group to retain any original buildings). The example in our area, the Middlesex (St Marylebone), was established in 1745, but its lively composition of Palladian buildings of 1755 onwards by James Paine was replaced in the early C 20. The oldest surviving west London example of a philanthropic institution on a grand scale (other than Chelsea Hospital) is therefore the former military orphanage at Chelsea (now Duke of York's Headquarters), a straightforward formal classical design of 1801–5 by *Sanders*.

Throughout the C 19 the cheap land beyond the London suburbs was utilized for the large INSTITUTIONS for the poor, the sick, the insane, and the criminal, set up in consequence of the campaigns of the humanitarian reformers and the parliamentary Acts which followed. Such establishments were characterized by the orderly, symmetrical planning that was a legacy of the classical tradition, and by an enthusiasm for innovative materials and ingenious organization of functions that was typical of the C 19. However, overcrowding and haphazard additions too often soon obscured the merits of the original buildings, and changing attitudes to social reform have ensured that few survive in anything like their complete state. In west London the only major relatively unaltered example still in use is the late one of Wormwood Scrubs Prison, an array of suitably forbidding pavilions on the northern fringe of Hammersmith, of 1876 by *Edward Du Cane*. The best earlier group, also still virtually complete (but with a future uncertain at the time of writing), is the former Middlesex Lunatic Asylum at Southall (later St Bernard's Hospital), 1829–31 by *William Alderson*. This was one of the first examples of a progressively planned asylum, designed as a vast, self-sufficient establishment, with plain well-organized buildings, its monumental scale heralded by a grand classical entrance. Not far off at Hanwell were the equally huge London Poor Law Residential Schools of 1856–7, of which the only reminder is the central building, now a community centre. *Banks & Barry's* Industrial Schools (i.e. reformatory) of 1857–9 at Feltham have also disappeared, replaced by a modern establishment with similar aims, but less dominant in the landscape.

WORKHOUSES were put up by the various Boards of Guardians established after 1834. At Kensington one wing of the building of 1848 by *Thomas Allom* remains in Marloes Road, Kensington, preserved as part of the St Mary Abbots Hospital and now incorporated in new housing. Contemporary with it, and more complete, is the Brompton Hospital (1844–6 by *Francis*) built for consumptive patients, the new type of specialist hospital characteristic of the C 19, although still with a traditional layout of ranges around courtyards. Both these institutions, like many of the schools of the period, are in quite a cheerful brick Tudor, which no doubt helped to make them acceptable in what were rapidly becoming built-up areas.

Other HOSPITALS which expanded and multiplied during the C 19, often on sites which were cramped and unsuitable, have since been much extended and rebuilt – the case of St Mary's Paddington of 1843 onwards is typical. Many developed haphazardly from workhouse infirmaries; one of the more coherent is the formidable pile of St Charles Hospital north Kensington, 1879–81 by *Saxon Snell*, which adopted the Nightingale system of separate pavilions (first introduced at the Royal Herbert Hospital, Woolwich (Gr), in 1865). It was not surprising that there was a movement from the 1890s in favour of smaller and more homely establishments, demonstrated by the growth of cottage hospitals in the outer areas – see Willesden Green (1892–9 by *Newman & Newman*) and, especially attractive, Harrow-on-the-Hill (1905–6 by *Arnold Mitchell*).

The most permanent architectural legacy of the reformers of the earlier C 19 was the CEMETERIES. The scandal of the overcrowded city graveyards with their stenches, decomposing corpses, drunken gravediggers and resurrectionists was exposed by journalists including Dickens. The London Cemetery Company was formed in 1830; the cholera epidemic of two years later spurred it into action. Kensal Green was the first and largest cemetery to be 80 laid out, in 1833, and has the most ambitious landscaping. It was followed in the next ten years by Brompton (1837) and by those on other fringes of London – Norwood and Nunhead to the south, Highgate and Abney Park to the north. From the mid C 19 the private cemeteries were supplemented by others laid out by the local authorities. The chapels and lodges reflect the general development of church architecture (*see* above) – classical or skimpy Perp for the early private cemeteries, an almost ubiquitous ragstone Gothic for the later ones. In the early cemeteries, so evocative of the diversity and earnestness of Victorian endeavour, classical and Egyptian mausolea and sarcophagi mingle with Gothic shrines, angels, and obelisks in haphazard, melancholy disarray. Among the medievalizing tombs the finest are those to Commander Ricketts by *Burges* (1867) at Kensal Green, and to Frederic Leighton by *Burne-Jones* (1892) at Brompton.

The supreme example of the Victorian Gothic MEMORIAL is however not in a cemetery but in Kensington Gardens – the elab-
64 orate shrine to Prince Albert erected to designs by *G. G. Scott* (1863–72). Prince Albert's association with Kensington began with the London public building which achieved the greatest fame in the mid C 19: the Crystal Palace, erected for the Great Exhibition held in Hyde Park in 1851. Although it had only a short life on this site before being rebuilt at Sydenham, the exhibition focused the attention of the government, and more particularly of Prince Albert, on the desirability of a cultural and educational centre in west London. From 1856 onwards a mulifarious collection of MUSEUMS and educational establishments sprang up north of the newly laid out Cromwell Road, stretching from Brompton up to Kensington Gardens, helping to establish 'South Kensington' (the name had a superior cachet to Brompton) as the most interesting and fashionable new suburb in London. Architecturally, they started modestly with the utilitarian glass and iron exhibition building nicknamed the 'Brompton Boilers' (later removed to Bethnal Green), but in the 1860s, under the aegis of *Sir Henry Cole* and the architectural direction of *Francis Fowke* of the Royal Engineers, the new building materials – iron and glass – were innovatively combined with the Italian early Renaissance ornament promoted by Cole and his circle. The South Kensington Museums (the later Victoria and Albert Museum) became a testing ground for experiments in a whole variety of media, as can still be seen in some of the inner reaches of the museum today. For exterior ornament, moulded terracotta, sgraffito, and mosaic were the most significant, and they were taken up enthusiastically for the later buildings at South Kensington: the
65 lofty Royal School of Naval Architects ornamented with terracotta (now Henry Cole wing of the V. and A.), 1868–73, the Albert Hall
66 of 1867–71 by *Fowke* and his successor *H. Y. D. Scott*, its swelling oval bulk boldly girdled by a giant mosaic frieze, and next door the Royal College of Organists (1875–6), the building by *H. H. Cole Jun.*, its fresh and charming all-over sgraffito by *F. Moody*. *Water-*
67 *house*'s Natural History Museum of 1872–81 rejected the Renaissance in favour of Romanesque, but successfully developed the potential of terracotta on an unprecedented scale, both for the exterior and for the monumental great hall and galleries.

Such buildings set new challenges to their designers both in their plans and in their construction. The dual requirements of public display and scholarly study, a perennial problem for museums, were met at the Natural History Museum by a supremely rational and well-organized plan, which was in complete contrast to the haphazardly *ad hoc* expansion of the South Kensington Museums and art schools across the road. The influence of Waterhouse's plan can indeed be seen in *Aston Webb*'s front ranges added in 1900–9 to what was by then the Victoria and Albert Museum. In both museums the advantages of toplighting encouraged experiments with glass roofs, though none was quite as daring as the huge glass and wrought-iron dome of the Albert Hall, one of the major engineering achievements of the c 19. Just as the South Kensington Museums can be seen as one line of descent from the Crystal Palace, another can be traced in the development of the great glass and iron structures used for the major RAILWAY TERMINI and EXHI-BITION HALLS (*see also* Introduction to Industrial Archaeology). West London has one of the earliest and most important of these, the Great Western Railway's Paddington Station of 1850–4, by 4 *Brunel* and *M. D. Wyatt*. A later example is the National Agri-cultural Hall of 1885 by *H. E. Coe*, now part of Olympia, Ham-mersmith.

Compared with these buildings of national significance, the mid c 19 CIVIC BUILDINGS of the suburban local authorities were still quite small and modest. The old vestry hall of Kensington, now a bank in Kensington High Street, 1851 by *Broadbridge*, is typical, its pretty Jacobean detail perhaps a deferential allusion to the local great mansions, Holland House and Campden House. Increasing civic consciousness, together with expanding bureaucracy, is seen in the more ambitious town halls which followed, as their vestries became urban districts and then boroughs in their own right. Ealing grew so rapidly that its first municipal buildings of 1877 (now a bank) had to be replaced by a new town hall already in 1886 (both by the local architect *Charles Jones*). Jones built in Gothic, but more often a grandiose Italianate was preferred, somewhat on the model of London clubs (town halls of Chiswick, 1876 by *Trehearne*, and Fulham, 1888–9 by *G. Edwards*), a style suitable for the grand staircases and meeting rooms required for civic pomp. Chelsea broke new ground in 1885 with a design by *Brydon* in a quieter Wrenish Baroque, the manner that was to be developed with such enthusiasm for public buildings of the early c 20.

The local authorities were also responsible for LIBRARIES and PUBLIC BATHS. These are often more playful in their details, at first combining the decorative repertoire of South Kensington with fanciful motifs of the 'Queen Anne' movement, then developing the eclectic versions of Baroque which became popular from the later 1890s. Early and pretty west London LIBRARIES are at Notting Hill Kensington, 1891–4 by *H. Wilson* and *T. Phillips Figgis*, and at Queen's Park Paddington, 1890 by *Karslake & Mortimer*; *Maurice Adams* made use of an inventive free classical at Acton and at Shepherds Bush Hammersmith (1894, 1898–9), as did *Edmeston & Gabriel* at Kilburn (1894); *Henry Hare* practised a more full-blown Edwardian Baroque at both Hammersmith and Fulham (1904–9). While such libraries are still valued (at least by 68 their users), changing social conditions have swept away many of the PUBLIC BATHS that were once so necessary in poor areas, including one of the most lavish and well appointed groups, the buildings by *Verity* at Silchester Road north Kensington (1886–8). Others have survived as swimming baths (Chelsea, Acton); else-where only stately frontages remain to demonstrate the pride felt in such buildings. The St Marylebone Baths of 1897 are dignified enough to convince as Magistrates Courts, their present use. More adventurous is the appealing free classical façade preserved from the Fulham Baths at North End Road (*E. Deighton Pearson*, 1902).

More ubiquitous than baths or libraries were the SCHOOLS that sprang up in response to the Education Act of 1870. In what was to become the L.C.C. area (i.e. the parishes at that time under the Metropolitan Board of Works), elementary schools were the responsibility of the elected School Board for London. Proud of its independence from the religious bodies that had hitherto dominated education, the board rejected traditional Tudor or Gothic in favour of the radically secular and domestic manner of the budding Queen Anne style. Shaped gables, sash windows, and sparing decoration in the form of carved or terracotta panels were already features of schools of *c*. 1872–3 (now demolished) by *J. J. Stevenson* and *Basil Champneys*, and of many others built in the first decade by the board's architect *E. R. Robson* (see e.g. Latimer Road Hammersmith, 1879–80; Park Walk Chelsea, 1880). The classic type for tight urban sites was developed by Robson's successor from 1884, *T. J. Bailey*: skilfully planned towering 'three-deckers' superimposing the separate establishments of Infants, Boys, and Girls, each with their separate entrances and staircases, and each by the 1890s requiring an assembly hall in addition to well-lit classrooms. Their romantic profiles of hipped roofs flanked by cupola-topped stair-turrets became prominent landmarks all over the London suburbs; Fulham is an especially rich hunting ground. Their symmetrical elevations lent themselves easily to the introduction of more formal classical elements from the 1890s, and then gradually to less dramatic neo-Georgian forms in the early C20.

In the more rural areas, school boards took longer to become established. An exception is Harrow, interesting for its early introduction of the Queen Anne style for rural schools (by *Ernest George* at Alperton and Sudbury, 1877–8 and 1879). In the more populous boroughs further in to London, the local boards became very active in the 1890s, stamping their neighbourhoods with their own brand of schools derived from the T. J. Bailey type: notable among them are the sequence in Acton by *Monson* culminating in Acton Green (1891), and the slightly later series in Willesden by *G. E. S. Laurence*, from Kensal Green (1896) to the proud terracotta-trimmed Chamberlayne Wood Kensal Rise (1902–4) and Cricklewood (1905).

The Bailey type was adapted for London secondary schools of after 1904: Hortensia Road Chelsea and Fulham Cross (both 1908) are early examples, dressed in an exceptionally flamboyant and mannered Baroque. The Middlesex County Council, which had likewise taken over the responsibilities of local school boards, also produced a series of secondary schools at this time. With more space available, London School Board precedents could be disregarded; the first showpieces of 1910, by *H. G. Crothall* (Surveyor of Schools from 1903, County Architect from 1910), had long wings of classrooms extending at angles from a formal central block given presence by rather jerky Baroque features (Harrow County Boys, now Gayton High; Western County Girls, now Featherstone High, Southall). A few years later solid buildings in a decent, quiet Wrenian manner became the norm (Ealing County Boys, now Ealing Green High, 1913).

PRIVATE SCHOOLS did not of course aim to look like board schools. *Waterhouse*'s now demolished buildings of 1881 for St

Paul's Boys' School Hammersmith were still earnestly Gothic (as can still be seen from the Head Master's house in Hammersmith Road). But Harrow maintained its enthusiasm for progressive architectural fashions with *Champneys'* Museum Schools in an 71 eclectic Renaissance-cum-Queen Anne (1884–6) and *E. S. Prior's* Music School of 1890, an early case of a refreshingly free and bold handling of classical elements. St Paul's Girls' School Ham- 70 mersmith of 1904–7 by *Gerald Horsley* is one of the best examples anywhere of a mature version of free classical, with a well composed group of buildings enhanced by much sculpture. Others preferred to stick to well tried formulas, as in the case of the Tudor Gothic great hall built in 1904 by *H. O. Cresswell* for the Commercial Travellers' School, Hatch End.

The London board schools were one way in which the disparate Victorian suburbs were given a tangible common identity. Other London-wide authorities added their contributions. The L.C.C.'s FIRE STATIONS progressed from picturesque Gothic (St Mary- 69 lebone 1889, Fulham 1896) to the varied and inventive free style practised in the early C20 by the Fire Brigade Branch led by *Owen Fleming* and *C. C. Winmill* (Kensington 1905, Hammersmith 1913–14). The POLICE STATIONS, mostly by *J. Dixon Butler*, are also a distinctive breed, found over a wider area, for the Metropolitan Police authority extended beyond the L.C.C. into Middlesex. Their standard style was a slightly mannered free classical with some Tudor elements (e.g. Wealdstone 1905), although they sometimes branched into other styles in sympathy with the neighbourhood (tactful Old English at Northwood, 1910). In the Middlesex areas other familiar landmarks are the series of early C20 LAW COURTS built by the county architect *H. T. Wakelam* in the cheerful free Baroque of the period (Acton 1907, Uxbridge 1906–7, Ealing 1914).

Among buildings for communal use, some – like those intended for ENTERTAINMENT – were a matter not for public but for private initiative. Because such buildings had to fulfil complicated requirements, they gradually became the preserves of specialist architects. This was not yet the case with the earliest C19 examples in our area, the structures for the ZOO in Regents Park. The first buildings of the 1820s by *Decimus Burton* were still in the tradition of decorative garden adjuncts; the later ones place greater emphasis on the needs of the animals and on requirements for scientific study. Regents Park, a favourite place of recreation in the C19, catered for other forms of entertainment, e.g. *Decimus Burton's* Colosseum of 1823–7 (demolished 1875), and the Diorama of 1823, an early precursor of the cinema, designed by *A. C. Pugin* and *James Morgan*, whose shell remains although its ingenious movable interior has gone.

Such novelties waned in popularity in the later C19, as the lure of the THEATRES increased. They were concentrated in the West End, but were once more common in the suburbs than they are today. The best example in our area of a late C19 auditorium still in use is the Lyric Hammersmith (even though it is a reconstruction of the 1970s), preserving *Frank Matcham's* typically exuberant Rococo decoration. Also by Matcham is the Empire Hammersmith of 1903, now used as television studios, but with an exterior that is still a striking free classical landmark at Shepherds Bush Green. The Royal Court in Sloane Square Chelsea is by *Bertie Crewe*, 1888; the Coronet Notting Hill of 1898, by another major theatre architect of the period, *W. G. R. Sprague*, is a cinema at the time of writing, but retains its prettily decorated interior. SPORTS BUILDINGS, another structural type that developed in the later C 19, rarely aimed at architectural show – see the plain functional buildings of the Queen's Club, Fulham (1887 etc.). The exception is *Verity*'s cheerful, quite flamboyant Pavilion at Lord's of 1889–90. The football stand at Craven Cottage Fulham of 1905, a rare survival of an early work by *Archibald Leitch*, the Scots engineer who specialized in these structures, has a plain iron frame with a minimally decorated street front in red brick.

More architectural attention was lavished on C 19 PUBLIC HOUSES, designed to attract passing trade, and so deliberately made more showy and prominent than their neighbours. The progression from variations in mid C 19 Italianate to the more exuberant front-ages produced by end-of-the-century rebuilding can be studied well in old thoroughfares such as Marylebone High Street or King Street Hammersmith. Kilburn High Road is the place to explore the most atmospheric examples of the palatial drinking halls of *c.* 1900; glittering, cavernous interiors extravagantly enriched with tiles and engraved glass. The stricter licensing laws of the 1870s, designed to combat the alcoholism rife at the time, resulted in fewer but larger pubs; further reforming zeal led to a quieter, more demure type considered suitable for family use, which flourished especially in the outer suburbs. The west London architect *Nowell Parr* specialized in such buildings: good examples in his free dom-estic style are the Beehive at Brentford (1907) and the Forester at Northfields, Ealing (1909). More extreme reformers preferred radical alternatives: at Pinner *Ernest George*'s delightfully pic-turesque former Cocoa Tree Tavern of 1878 is an early witness to the efforts of the Temperance Movement.

The C 19 trend towards larger buildings comprehensively cater-ing for all needs is demonstrated by two other building types: hotels and department stores. The story of HOTELS is closely bound up with the railways. West London has one of the first really ambitious railway hotels, the Great Western at Paddington, 1851–4 by *P. C. Hardwick*, an early introduction to London of a French Second Empire frontage (cf. the slightly later Grosvenor at Victoria). Even grander, daringly intruding into a residential area away from a railway terminus, is the Langham in Portland Place St Marylebone, a vast Italianate palazzo of 1863 by *Giles & Murray*, which set new standards of luxurious comfort for its aristocratic guests. The other major hotel in our area is the Great Central (1897–8 by *Edis*), built to serve St Marylebone station, with lavish terracotta ornament typical of its decade and equally sumptuous public rooms (which, like those of the Langham, after long neglect were restored to hotel use in 1990–1).

DEPARTMENT STORES reached their zenith in the early years of the C 20. West London has two supremely self-confident creations of those years: Harrods, rebuilt from 1894 onwards by *C. W. Stephens*, flamboyantly parading its long terracotta frontage along Knightsbridge; and Whiteleys at Queensway, Bayswater, with a grandiose Baroque front of 1908–12 by *Belcher & Joass* as a prelude to a sumptuous staircase and toplit galleries (reincarnated as a shopping mall in 1989). Most of the department stores congregated along Oxford Street (*see London 1*), with an outlier – the former Debenham's store – in Wigmore Street, 1907–8 by *Wallace & Gibson*, lavishly faced in *Doulton*'s Carrara tiles.

As the outer suburbs grew, their identity was expressed by the SHOPPING CENTRES that grew up around the new stations. The most prestigious buildings were generally the BANKS: those at Willesden Green by *Maurice B. Adams*, 1892–3, Wealdstone by *Horace Field & Simmons*, 1907, and Harrow by *Banister Fletcher*, 1915, were clearly intended to lend tone to their neighbourhoods. SHOPPING PARADES could also be designed with panache: Fulham has a good late Victorian sequence along Fulham Road, St John's Wood High Street is typical of the flamboyant red brick gabled approach of the turn of the century, while King's Parade Acton (1904 by *A. H. Sykes*) is a more unusual example of an artistic composition in a free style. A concern to integrate the suburban STATION with its surroundings is also apparent at this time – at High Street Kensington and South Kensington, the underground passenger emerges into pretty glazed shopping arcades (by *George Sherrin*, 1903–7), while the new outer suburbs of Hatch End and Wealdstone were provided with delightful individually designed stations by *Gerald Horsley* (1911). These were exceptions, however; the more general trend was towards neat standardization. The glazed-tile frontages of the Edwardian Metropolitan and District line stations, many of them by *Leslie Green*, are still familiar landmarks throughout the inner suburbs.

Around the turn of the century a few architects practising in a free style responded to the challenge of COMMERCIAL AND INDUSTRIAL BUILDINGS (for these *see* also the Introduction to Industrial Archaeology). Some admirably original and experimental solutions were produced. Especially memorable is *Voysey*'s design for Sanderson's factory at Chiswick (1902), with its crisp 75 play of curves and cleancut vertical lines; less well known is *Walter Cave*'s Aeolian factory at Hayes (1912), with its concrete vaults and layered brickwork. New inventions and new attitudes could stimulate some novel architecture. The Michelin Building in 93 Fulham Road, Chelsea, of 1909–11 by *F. Espinasse*, is another concrete structure, hidden entirely by its enjoyably flamboyant coloured tiles celebrating the triumph of the motor car, a precocious forerunner of the self-advertisement of art deco two decades later. The Metropolitan Railway's Selbie House at Baker Street Station (1911 by *C. W. Clark*) is in a similar spirit. Equally well disguised is the Piranesian concrete framework of *Belcher*'s Mappin Terraces at the Zoo (1913), conceived as a new type of natural, free-ranging animal enclosure. The POWER STATIONS required at this time for electric transport inspired an interestingly varied approach: the outstanding example is *Curtis Green*'s heroically monumental tramways power station at Chiswick (1899–1901), one of the first of its kind. The vast power station for the District Railway at Lots Road Chelsea (1902–4) is more starkly functional; the Metropolitan line's substation at Baker Street (1904–5) hides behind an elegantly classical frontage.

Developments from 1910 to 1939

In the early years of the c 20 the loose eclecticism of the turn of the century was replaced by a grandiose Baroque or classical manner, considered especially appropriate for major public buildings. *Aston Webb*'s Victoria and Albert Museum frontage of 1899–1901, and his more bombastic Royal School of Mines of 1909–13, illustrate the shift in emphasis. Baroque on a grand scale was likewise the choice for *Ernest George*'s quite jolly Royal Academy of Music in Marylebone Road of 1910–11 and for *Edwin Cooper*'s more sober stone-faced St Marylebone Town Hall of 1912–18, buildings comparable in mood and scale to those lining the new Kingsway and to the rebuilding of Regent Street (*see London: 1*). From around 1910 a drier, more rigorous classicism influenced by French Beaux-Arts ideals began to make headway, particularly for institutional buildings. St Marylebone has a good range of early examples: *Belcher*'s dignified neo-Grec Royal Society of Medicine, 1910–12; *Eustace Frere*'s elegant General Medical Council Hallam Street, 1915; *Claude Ferrier*'s Royal National Institute for the Blind Great Portland Street, 1909–14; and *Verity*'s Polytechnic Regent Street (1911). Domestic buildings in the same area exhibit similar trends, from *Sydney Tatchell*'s individual houses (e.g. No. 12 Devonshire Street, 1912) to the overweening stone-faced blocks of flats in the Parisian manner, by *Wills & Kaula* among others, which began to take over Portland Place in the 1920s. A more tactful approach of the same period is *Cooper*'s skilfully designed classical frontages for the Royal College of Nursing and Cowdray Club (1926 onwards) at the corner of Cavendish Square. The general move towards a curbing of excessive ornament is seen also in *Office of Works* buildings such as the Science Museum of 1913–28 by *Sir R. Allison*, with its severe frontage of giant columns, and even more dramatically in the vast, austerely functional offices built at Bromyard Avenue Acton for the Ministry of Pensions in 1914–22 (by *J. West*).

Domestic Building up to 1939

The classical tradition was not the only one to be drawn upon during the period up to *c*. 1930. Arts and Crafts buildings continued to go up, especially when the style appeared historically appropriate, as in the case of *Godfrey*'s free Tudor college buildings attached to Crosby Hall Chelsea (1926); it was used, too, for a few large individual private houses (a relatively rare type in the London area after 1918), such as *F. L. Pearson*'s Heriots at Stanmore (1925). In the outer areas the anti-urban vernacular tradition also maintained a strong hold on PUBLIC HOUSING, following the precedents set by Parker & Unwin before 1914 (*see* above). Suburban cottage housing was continued by the government's munition workers' estates of the war years, designed by *Frank Baines*; the west London example is Roe Green Kingsbury, aesthetically a little disappointing in comparison with his highly picturesque contemporary Well Hall estate at Eltham in south London. From 1916 *Raymond Unwin* became one of the chief government advisers on working-class housing. His principles of low-density development (twelve houses to the acre), together with improved standards (such as the inclusion of baths), became the rule in the cottage housing built after the Town and Country Planning Act of 1919, through which the government gave financial assistance to the local authorities' building programmes. The first Homes for Heroes campaigns – see the Long Drive, north Acton, whose cottages include some experimental types in concrete – was followed by a flurry of activity by local councils (Willesden's Brentfield estate, Harlesden, begun in 1919, is an early example) until subsidies were withdrawn in 1933.

It was, however, the L.C.C. that took the lead. Its relatively small Wormholt estate in north Hammersmith (1919 onwards) maintained the high standards set before the war by the neighbouring Old Oak estate. However the merits of such planning were diluted in the ambitious and only partially realized programme of cottage estates beyond the L.C.C. boundaries that was devised in the 1920s in an attempt to solve London's housing problems. The largest of these 'out-county' estates – Downham (Le), Bellingham (Le), Becontree (Bk) – were on the cheap land to the south and east; to the west there are fewer (north Greenford is typical), pleasantly laid out but incohesive, with houses generally in the pared-down neo-Georgian favoured by the L.C.C. Architect's Department under *G. Topham Forrest*. The L.C.C. housing in inner London at first also followed a neo-Georgian formula: solid blocks of neat but anonymous four- or five-storey walk-up flats. Few of these were built in our area until the 1930s, when a shift in policy led to the creation of the deadening utilitarian ranks of the vast White City estate in Hammersmith (1938–9), built (like the out-county cottage estates) with a singular lack of amenities for the residents. The housing activities of the inner boroughs at this time produced little that was architecturally outstanding, although the start of slum clearance programmes established patterns that were to be continued after the Second World War, radically transforming some of the poorer neighbourhoods, as in the case of St Marylebone's activities around Lisson Green, or Kensington's at Notting Hill. The most adventurous new housing was Kensal House North Kensington, sleekly curved blocks of working-class flats intended to be the last word in modern technology, designed in 1936, together with a nursery school, by a team led by *Maxwell Fry* for the Gas, Light & Coke Company.

Occasionally in the outer areas social housing on a humane scale was produced by private or communal enterprise, following traditions established before 1914 (*see* above) – the privately funded Fairholme estate East Bedfont, picturesquely laid out around a formal green, of 1934 by *T. Cecil Howitt*, the Co-Partnership G.W.R. garden village at north Acton, designed in 1923–5 by *Alwyn Lloyd*, and the Artizans' very attractive Pinner Wood Park (1931–9, for middle-class rather than working-class tenants) – but such developments were exceptional.

Between 1919 and 1938 nearly three quarters of a million new houses and flats were built in Greater London, but only about one fifth of these were by the local authorities (*c.* 76,000 by the L.C.C., about the same figure by the other local councils together). In many of the outer areas the populations doubled within ten years – in

Harrow U.D.C. the figure jumped to 49,020 in 1921, to 95,656 in 1931, and reached 190,200 in 1939. For Wembley the comparable figures are 18,239, 65,799, 121,600. These are the highest totals in the outer areas, but even the less densely developed U.D.C. of Hayes and Harlington had reached over 50,000 by 1939, while Uxbridge, right out on the Middlesex county boundary, stood at 45,150.*

Thus in the outer suburbs, and particularly in west London, it is PRIVATE HOUSING that dominates the scene, carried out by a large number of builders and speculators exploiting the opportunities offered by the new suburban railways. Only rarely were layouts of streets and house types controlled by thorough planning which took public amenities into consideration. The local authority of Ruislip–Northwood was an exception, basing its plan of 1914 on a scheme by *A. S. Soutar*, and intending a balanced mix of houses of different sizes, although this was not carried through as planned, and achieved little in the way of distinguished architecture. The Harrow Garden Village at Rayners Lane, Pinner, developed by the Metropolitan Railway from 1926, is more appealing, with its layout of houses around little greens. But generally the private housing of these years, like that of the Victorian speculative builders fifty years earlier, was an arbitrary and opportunist exercise. The chief difference was in the image promoted, which now was essentially one of rural nostalgia. The Metroland commuter worked in the city, but maintained the illusion of living in the country. So the old village centres were cherished, and patches of old woodland preserved and surrounded by long, winding suburban roads lined with repetitive semi-detached villas with front and back gardens. Their details were derived from Shaw and Voysey's turn-of-the-century country houses, with just enough ornament – half-timbered gables, tile-hung bows, stained-glass landing windows – to make sure that they could not be mistaken for council housing.

The most extreme examples of the nostalgic style indulged in lavish half-timbering and other whimsical detail, sometimes incorporating old materials. *Blunden Shadbolt* specialized in such buildings; his work can be found among the superior detached houses on Pinner Hill. The heavily picturesque houses begun along Canons Drive Little Stanmore in 1926 by *A. J. Butcher* are other examples, typical in that they were too expensive to sell well, so that the style was not maintained for further developments in the area. A more successful scheme, with its careful mixture of trim 97 half-timbered flats and houses, was the Hanger Hill garden estate at Ealing (1928–36 by *Douglas Smith & Barley*). Superficially similar to these enterprises, although in a rather special category, are the houses of the eccentric Swedenborgian architect *E. G. Trobridge* (the best group is in Slough Lane Kingsbury, from 1921); his buildings were inspired less by commercial profit than by deeply held beliefs in the worth of timber construction and the symbolic value of traditional roofs and hearths.

These were only one facet of private housing. Other houses (chiefly those where architects as well as builders were involved)

---

*For general London population figures *see* p. 24. A. Jackson, *Semi-Detached London* (1973), Appendix 1, gives further details on suburban expansion.

were in the quieter neo-Georgian or late c 17 traditions inherited from the Edwardian period; good examples are *Oliver Hill's* Oakington Manor Drive Wembley (1924) and *Avray Tipping's* houses at Harefield (1934). Neo-Georgian was also the style favoured for the few infill schemes for which room could occasionally be found in inner London; *Williams & Cox* were particularly accomplished practitioners in this manner in the 1920s (see Melbury Road and Drayton Gardens, Kensington). The rebuilding of Tyburnia begun in the 1930s (by *Septimus Warwick*) is rather less successful, but serves to underline the reaction that had set in against the grand stucco palazzi of the c 19. The classical tradition produced a few fine individual buildings, such as the two houses by *Hill* in Chelsea Square, and *Giles G. Scott's* Chester House Clarendon Place Paddington (1925–6). Yet the craze for rustic old-world detail invaded even Chelsea and Kensington at this time, as will be apparent from the quaintly incongruous additions to be found in some of the back streets and mews.

So much for tradition. What of the new architectural ideas that began to gain currency around 1930? The earliest domestic group in west London to adopt the principles of the modern movement were the houses and flats of 1933 on the Warren estate around Kerry Avenue Stanmore by *Douglas T. Wood, Gerald Lacoste,* and *Owen Williams*. A few speculative builders tried out the flat roofs and streamlined windows that were the most recognizable attributes of the new manner: the Haymills housing at Wembley, 1933–4, and Hanger Hill Ealing, 1934, both with houses by *Welch, Cachemaille-Day & Lander*, were the most consistent efforts of this kind. At Ruislip there is a small but inventively composed group of three 98 by *Connell, Ward & Lucas*, 1936, but in general the outer suburbs were resistant to innovation, and only isolated private commissions raised the flag for the plain walls, cubic massing, and open planning that were a part of the progressive new ideas imported from the continent: at Hatch End in 1934, at Kerry Avenue Stanmore by *R. Uren*, at Halsbury Close Stanmore by *R. Frankel*, at South Parade Bedford Park by *F. Ruhemann* (all built in 1938). The last two architects were among the new émigrés whose influx provided a significant boost to the modern movement in England. Others were *Mendelsohn* and *Chermayeff*, responsible for No. 64 Old Church Street Chelsea (1935), and *Walter Gropius*, who in partnership with *Maxwell Fry* designed the neighbouring No. 66 Old Church Street (now much altered), also in 1935. In inner London there were however few chances to build detached houses of this kind – *Denys Lasdun's* own house, No. 10 Newton Road Paddington (1937–8), is one of the rare exceptions.

Modern FLATS also had little success in the face of general hostility from the architectural establishment. The two most radical blocks in our area, both dating from 1938, are the somewhat gaunt but interestingly planned No. 10 Palace Gate Kensington, by *Wells Coates*, and *Maxwell Fry's* airier composition in Ladbroke Grove. There were however a few hybrid efforts at a modern look, such as *T. P. Bennett's* Dorset House Marylebone Road and *Collcutt & Hamp's* The Grampians Shepherds Bush Road Hammersmith, where period detail is abandoned in favour of the stepped profiles and busy ironwork of art deco, while in the outer suburbs two engagingly flashy groups in Pinner of 1936 (Pinner Court by *H. J. Mark*, Elm Park Court by *H. F. Webb*) flirt with the neo-colonial fashion for white walls and glazed green roof tiles.

Churches and Public Buildings: 1918–39

The community buildings erected to serve the new suburbs were in general less ambitious architecturally than those of the period up to 1914. CHURCHES remained the traditional social centres for the new areas. The tradition of careful craftsmanship which had characterized Edwardian church building of all types was shattered by the First World War. Church design remained the province of specialized architects but was radically simplified. None of the Anglican churches of between the wars was remotely innovative in liturgical planning, sticking to the safe, well-tried formula of the chancel with long aisled nave and one or two more intimate side chapels, although sometimes experimenting with novel lighting effects, such as toplit chancels.

From the 1920s the only buildings of note are the exceptional, exquisite little Armenian church in Kensington, by *Mewès & Davis*, a conscientious piece of historicism, and *Edward Maufe*'s church for the deaf, St Saviour Acton (1924–7), an early pointer in the move toward the angular simplification of Gothic detail. Maufe carried this further at St Thomas Hanwell (1934), its austerely effective concrete-vaulted interior a significant precursor of his Guildford Cathedral, Surrey. St Thomas is the place to study the most up-to-date taste in Anglican fittings and furnishings of the time, including sculpture by *Eric Gill* and *Vernon Hill* and glass by *Moira Forsyth* – bland in comparison with Edwardian work, yet not without a restrained charm. Generally the furnishings of this period are traditional and of indifferent quality; the one interesting exception is the screen with forceful stylized ornament at St Andrew Uxbridge, a late work by *W. R. Lethaby* of 1927. Among the more conservative church architects *J. H. Gibbons* was one of the most successful, building in competent Early Christian at St Francis Dollis Hill, domestic vernacular at St Jerome Harlington (both 1933), and in a minimal yet well-detailed brick Gothic at St Mary Kenton, 1936, and St Barnabas Northolt, 1939–54. Another subdued but skilful Gothic essay is *Adrian Scott*'s R.C. St Joseph Wealdstone of 1931. More exceptional is the passionate Mediterranean Gothic favoured by *E. C. Shearman*. His earliest west London work is St Barnabas Ealing, 1914–16; to continue the manner uncompromisingly into the 1930s (St Gabriel Acton, St Francis Osterley) was decidedly eccentric, although rather more fun than the worthy, plain, blocky Romanesque used by *Cyril Farey* (St Michael Wembley, 1932, All Hallows Greenford, 1940–1). The uncertainty about the right way forward for church building can be sensed by the experiments with other styles as well – classical details for *Charles Nicholson*'s accomplished small church of St Lawrence Eastcote (1932–3), a more eclectic mixture for his All Saints Hillingdon (1932). One of the most attractive and unclassifiable buildings is *Albert Richardson*'s Holy Cross Greenford of 1939, which is in a vaguely Scandinavian timber vernacular, without any obviously period detail. *Seely & Paget*'s Ascension at Ealing (1938–9), although with some classical details outside, has a plain, almost styleless interior. The breakthrough to a more innovative approach in fact came already in the mid 1930s with *A. W. Kenyon*'s St Alban north Harrow (1936–7), whose stylish if slightly mannered blend of Early Christian and Swedish modernism was much fêted at the time. Recognition of the potency of continental expressionism for church building had arrived a little earlier in south London, with *N. F. Cachemaille-Day*'s St Saviour Eltham (1932–3). His west London churches are not so extreme in mood, but are all interesting in their efforts to convey the spirit of the Gothic tradition by modern means: St Anselm Wealdstone, 1935–41 (an exception re-using parts of an older church), St Paul Ruislip, 1936, St Paul Harrow, 1937–8 (an abrupt cubist composition reminiscent of Eltham, but with rendered walls instead of exposed brick), and the austere concrete-vaulted St Paul Dollis Hill of 1939. Far more ruthlessly modern than any of these is the entirely concrete Dollis Hill Synagogue of 1937–8 by *Owen Williams*.

The community buildings for which there was the most pressing need in the new suburbs were SCHOOLS for the rising youthful population. These were the responsibility of the Middlesex County Council (*W. T. Curtis*, County Architect from 1930, with *H. W. Burchett* assistant architect for educational buildings). The Middlesex schools of before 1914 had been in a free Edwardian Baroque (*see* above); the first ones built after 1918 are quietly classical. The change to modern-utilitarian came after a financial crisis of 1931, when it was decided to cut costs by 30 per cent by adopting new constructional methods – at first steel framing (Oakington Manor Wembley, 1934), then concrete slab floors – supported on piers, which had the advantage of allowing flexibility of internal planning, although the traditional courtyard layout continued. The flat roofs and the wider windows resulting from lower ceilings produced a strong horizontal emphasis. Pinner Park (1934) was an early example. Some effort was made to exploit these new elements visually, and the most striking examples have effectively composed entrance fronts in the manner of the Dutch architect W. M. Dudok, just then becoming popular in England. The horizontals were countered by effective cubic massing of the austere brickwork, with a vertical accent provided by a stair-tower. The larger secondary schools lent themselves better to compositions of this kind than the primary schools. Good examples are Greenford High School and Pinner County (now Heathfield) of 1937. Occasionally a little leavening appeared in the form of stone fins to the windows (Belmont Secondary, Wealdstone, 1935), two colours of bricks (Lady Bankes, Ruislip, 1936–7), or bands of tiles (Evelyns, Yiewsley, 1936).

In inner London, thanks to the earlier energetic activity of the London School Board and the L.C.C., very few new schools were needed, especially as by the 1930s the population of the inner areas was beginning to fall. The only school comparable to the Middlesex efforts is Burlington Danes, Hammersmith, of 1936 by *Burnet, Tait & Lorne*, a skilful street composition on a tight site in the Dudok manner, with classrooms in a long wing behind – an arrangement reflecting the general disillusion with the compact planning and consequent inadequate lighting and ventilation of the earlier Board Schools. It was this firm (and probably chiefly *Francis Lorne*, who joined it in 1930) that was responsible for the Royal Masonic 101 Hospital Hammersmith of 1931, one of the first buildings in England in a modern brick style, combining a formal symmetrical plan with curved streamlined wings and nautical-looking balconies. The M.C.C.'s Harefield County Sanatorium of 1933–7 adopted similar principles for its more modest buildings, and a number of minor Middlesex public buildings also adopted an unadorned brick style making use of occasional curves (e.g. Isleworth Library, 1936). However, the most famous trailblazers for a new, modern image for public works were *Charles Holden*'s UNDERGROUND STA-TIONS for the Piccadilly line extensions, inspired by the patronage of Frank Pick. Holden's firm, *Adams, Holden & Pearson*, had been employed for the stations on the 1926 Northern line extension to Morden (*see London 2: South*) which were in a stone-faced, stripped classical style. The new stations with their uncluttered brickwork and simple geometric massing were designed after Holden visited Scandinavia and Holland. They represent a high point of pro-gressive planning in England, providing a clear and rational cor-porate image for the newly united London underground. The 99 prototype was Sudbury Town, designed in 1930–1; its successors followed rapidly (Ealing Common 1931, Sudbury Hill 1932, Acton Town 1932–3, Alperton 1933, etc.), usually drawn up from an initial sketch by Holden and worked up by his assistants, or by the underground's own architects headed by *Stanley A. Heaps*. In a few cases, because of pressure of work, other architects were brought in (*Welch & Lander* at Park Royal, *Uren* at Rayners Lane, *L. H. Bucknall* at Uxbridge). Holden's booking halls are pleasingly varied, their different identities expressed by a range of simple shapes, but united by their cleancut brick detailing and careful functional planning, with signing and furnishings admirably inte-grated into the total design.

The battle between the modernists and the traditionalists in the 1930s was fought on a number of fronts, most prominently over the design of PUBLIC BUILDINGS AND INSTITUTIONS. Broadcasting House Portland Place (St Marylebone) of 1931 incorporated within its lumpily neutral stone envelope some daringly modern (and alas ephemeral) interiors by a team led by *Raymond McGrath*. Just up 103 the road the Royal Institute of British Architects selected a design by *Grey Wornum* for its generously planned headquarters (1932–4) which skilfully blended classical proportions with boldly conceived interconnecting spaces around the grand staircase, with much emphasis on novel forms of architectural ornament and fine materials. Among the civic buildings of this period Wembley Town Hall (*Clifford Strange*, 1935–40) is a plain functional demonstration of modern movement principles, Hammersmith Town Hall (*E. Berry Webber*, 1938–9) a rather clumsier traditional building with some modern trimmings, while *Cooper*'s St Marylebone Library (1938–9) and *McMorran*'s Hammersmith Police Station (1938) look back to classical and neo-Georgian precedents. Different again is the Institut Français in Kensington, 1939 by *P. Bonnet*, in a curi-ously angular form of brick art nouveau.

Commercial, Exhibition, and Entertainment Buildings

While St Marylebone has the most interesting institutions, Kensington is the place to study the evolution of the SHOWROOM AND DEPARTMENT STORE, from the dignified neo-Wren of *H. Austen Hall*'s former Gas Light & Coke Co. showrooms in Kensington Church Street (1926) to the series of massive buildings created by Barkers and its subsidiaries along the High Street: *Blomfield and Cabuche*'s florid Baroque of 1924, the ornamented neo-Grec of the former Derry & Toms of 1929–31, and finally the main store of 1933 with its exuberantly flashy glazed stair-towers (the last two 96 by *B. George*). A year or two later Peter Jones at Sloane Square 95 Chelsea (1935–7 by *Slater & Moberly*, with *Crabtree* and *Reilly*) demonstrated that a neatly detailed, well proportioned exterior – the first example in London of a curtain wall – could impress without the assistance of any decorative elements; but this was an exceptional approach among commercial building of this time. More popular for stores which wanted to convey an up-to-date image was a streamlined frontage with ribbon windows and faience tiles (see e.g. the former British Home Stores in King Street Hammersmith, and Randalls, Uxbridge, of 1937–8).

An important potential forum for the display of the new materials and methods which became a part of the modern movement canon was in the realm of EXHIBITION BUILDINGS. In 1924 reinforced concrete was used by *Simpson & Ayrton* for the buildings of the Empire Exhibition at Wembley, although they were given a classical dress, and arranged with Beaux-Arts formality. The Wembley Arena added ten years later by *Owen Williams*, with its wide hinged concrete arches, is a more straightforward demonstration of an engineer's approach (cf. his later Synagogue at Dollis Hill – *see* above). At the same time the firm of *Tecton*, led by *Berthold Lubetkin*, one of the most interesting of the émigré architects, showed that reinforced concrete could be used in a much more lighthearted fashion, in some lively and original creations for the London Zoo – among them the Penguin Pool of 1934. Display (rather than the 102 comfort of the animals) was the prime purpose, so such a structure can be classed most easily with exhibition buildings. However, other larger enterprises in this category lack any such wit – *Emberton*'s Olympia of 1929–30 is only a façade with modernist trappings (although his multi-storey garage added in 1936 is interesting as a prototype for this post-war urban phenomenon), while Earls Court (1936–7 by *C. Howard Crane*) impresses only by size.

While the austerity favoured by the adherents of the modern movement was found appropriate for certain types of building, particularly those in the cost-conscious public sector, it had much less appeal for clients who wanted to make a splash in order to attract commercial attention. The development of the CINEMA is a prime example, as can be seen from the wide range offered by the west London suburbs (of which only a selection can be mentioned here). This new building type starts with an early surviving purpose-built cinema, the Electric in Portobello Road Kensington (1910 by *G. S. Valentin*), a small hall with pretty classical decoration. *Frank Verity*'s much larger Pavilion Shepherds Bush of 1923 was the first cinema to win architectural acclaim, its vast brick bulk leavened by sparse but powerful classical detail. *Leathart & Granger*'s Odeon Kensington of 1926 likewise has a strong classical front, with the currently fashionable neo-grec trimmings. However, later cinemas, especially those in the suburban areas, abandon sober classicism for more colourful and exotic glazed tile frontages inspired by American precedent. Their variety is impressive. *E. Norman Bailey*'s Regal Uxbridge of 1932 has one of the best and most inventive displays of art deco detail, both outside and in (complete, although no longer used as a cinema). In 1929 the versatile *George Coles* produced both the Chinese-inspired Palace (later Liberty) at Southall, of which only the frontage remains, and the faience-clad but still fairly classical Commodore Stamford Brook Hammersmith; his last work was the monumental Gaumont State Kilburn (1937), with streamlined faience front, tall tower, and vast Renaissance auditorium. *F. E. Bromige*'s original frontages at Rayners Lane Pinner (1936) and Acton (1937) demonstrate his fascination with Baroque forms and curved glass, while the escapist 'atmospheric' interiors of the time are best represented by the former Avenue at Northfields, Ealing, by *Cecil Massey*, 1932, a Moorish extravaganza with tented auditorium probably by *Theodore Komisarjevsky*. In contrast to the exoticism of the suburban cinema, the SUBURBAN PUBLIC HOUSE played a much safer game, often adopting a trim, slightly formal composition for the new type of 'roadhouse' along the main arterial routes. *E. B. Musman*'s slightly neo-Georgian Myllett Arms at Perivale and his Scottish Baronial Berkeley Arms at Cranford (1932) are characteristic types.

New FACTORIES on prominent sites also sought to advertise themselves by eyecatching frontages – usually a long two-storey building with central entrance feature, concealing more utilitarian factory floors behind. The chief competition was along the new Great West Road N of Brentford, which had an especial attraction for firms producing motor accessories. The first to introduce colourful art deco features was Firestone (alas, demolished) in 1928. This was by *Wallis, Gilbert & Partners*, the chief firm specializing in factory design at this time – an earlier work, plainer but constructionally interesting, is their Wrigley factory at Wembley of 1926–8. They were responsible for the most stylish of the bypass factories of the 1930s, among them Pyrene on the Great West Road (1930), Hoover on the A40 at Perivale (1931–5), with a particularly striking combination of white glazing and green trim, and Glaxo at Greenford (1936), with a long streamlined front with rather Odeonesque cream and black details. Only a few industries turned to traditionalists for an alternative image: the Guinness Brewery at Park Royal is a model layout in a landscaped setting, with a well composed group of brick buildings by *Giles Gilbert Scott*, 1933–5; Gillette on the Great West Road, by *Banister Fletcher*, 1937, adopts the usual bypass composition but in sober brick, with a monumental tower.

After 1945

The architectural scene in west London immediately after 1945 was considerably less interesting than it had been before the war. Up to 1954, when building restrictions were lifted, HOUSING was the main concern, but the major post-war reconstruction efforts were concentrated not in west London but on the areas where bomb damage had been greatest – predominantly in and E of the City of London; moreover most of early comprehensive development areas advocated by *Forshaw* and *Abercrombie*'s *County of London Plan* of 1943, and confirmed by the official County of London plan of 1951, were concentrated in the poorer parts, chiefly in the S and E.* But the inner western suburbs also had their slum clearance programmes, the most interesting among them at Paddington, where an early showpiece was the conventional but pleasantly laid out Fleming Court at Paddington Green (1948); much more daring was the Hallfield estate, designed by *Tecton* in 1947 and carried out by two Tecton members, *Drake* and *Lasdun*, after the firm broke up in 1948. Hallfield, together with the Tecton estates for Finsbury (Is), represents a radical departure from the traditional walk-up flats of the pre-war years. The layout avoided the conventional grid pattern; the blocks were of mixed heights, their elevations were intended to be aesthetic, not purely utilitarian, and an impressive range of amenities was provided, including *Lasdun*'s delightful child-scaled school of 1955, whose curved plan recalls the pre-war nursery school at Kensal House. 105

The rejection of the traditional street frontage in favour of the idyll of tall flats in parkland – an idea which owed much to Le Corbusier – became almost universal among postwar housing authorities, and the *L.C.C.* laid much stress on it after the reorganization of its architect's department in 1950: one of the more successful examples is their well-detailed Maida Vale estate (1959–64). There was however – generally on relatively small urban sites – a tendency to pack in too much and to economize on the landscaping. Fulham's Clem Attlee estate (1955), with its three bold Y-shaped point blocks, is a characteristic example of a decline in quality when compared with the same borough's earlier, less ostentatious Sulivan estate (1949–56), where the grouping of slab blocks is more spacious and informal.

One justification put forward for building towers or tall slabs of flats was the density rule prescribed by the County of London Plan. This specified 200 persons per acre for the inner areas (i.e. Westminster, Knightsbridge, Tyburnia, and southern St Marylebone), 136 for the middle range suburbs (Kensington and Chelsea, the rest of Paddington and St Marylebone), and 70 for further out. The objective was to prevent the unplanned urban sprawl of the pre-war years, and to contain London within the green belt established already before the war. The *L.C.C.*'s solution for the 136-density range was 'mixed development', i.e. a mixture of dwellings of different sizes in blocks of different heights. But the architects and engineers responding to the challenges presented by the construction of towers were pressurized further by government incentives in the 1960s encouraging the use of industralized building techniques. So towers got taller, planning became more repetitive and mechanical, intended landscaping and amenities were omitted, and maintenance was forgotten. Late results of these

*For more details on post-war planning and on the work of the L.C.C. see the Introduction to *London 2: South*, pp. 84 ff.

trends can be seen at the *G.L.C.*'s Elgin estate in Paddington, with
its sleek steel-framed white-clad towers of 1966–9, twenty-two
storeys high (the first to be covered in glass-reinforced plastic), and
also, rather poignantly, at the Cheltenham estate North Kensington, where *Ernö Goldfinger*'s Trellick Tower, completed as late as
1972, rears its striking concrete silhouette beside the Grand Union
Canal. By this time general disillusion with this type of development
had set in, and it had become clear that in any event there were
other forms of building that could achieve high densities. As the
fact sank in that London's population was continuing to decline
(see adjoining table), the density rules began to seem more and
more irrelevant.

Here and there the L.C.C. had already shown its flexibility in
dealing with sensitive areas. The curved crescent at the Warwick
estate at Little Venice, Paddington (1966), inadequate though its
detail may now seem, was intended as a response to the stuccoed
terraces of the neighbourhood. Likewise, the county council's
decision in the 1960s to rehabilitate rather than demolish the dilapidated Porchester Square (also in Paddington) set an important
precedent, taken up more widely as government money became

GREATER LONDON'S

	Area (hectares)	Population 1961	1971	1981
GREATER LONDON	157,946	7,992,443	7,452,346	6,696,008
City of London	274	4,767	4,245	5,893
Inner NW (*old L.C.C. area*):				
City of Westminster	2,158	271,703	239,748	190,661
Kensington and Chelsea	1,195	218,528	188,227	138,759
Hammersmith and Fulham	1,617	222,124	187,195	148,054
Outer NW:				
Brent	4,421	295,899	280,657	251,257
Ealing	5,547	301,646	301,108	280,042
Harrow	5,082	209,083	203,215	195,999
Hillingdon	11,036	228,361	234,888	229,183
Hounslow	5,852	208,893	206,956	199,782
Inner N *and* NE (*old L.C.C. area*):				
Camden	2,171	245,707	206,737	171,563
Hackney	1,948	257,522	220,279	180,237
Islington	1,489	261,232	201,874	159,754
Tower Hamlets	1,973	205,682	165,776	142,975
Outer N *and* NE:				
Barking and Dagenham	3,419	177,092	160,800	150,175

available for such projects in the 1970s. The s side of Porchester Square indeed became one of the boldest reconstruction schemes of the 1970s, a daring blend of old and new by *Farrell & Grimshaw* (1973–81).

Meanwhile, after the G.L.C. reorganization of 1965, the boroughs had become larger and more financially powerful. The BOROUGH HOUSING initiatives increased, those of the 1960s–70s heavily influenced by the requirements of industrialized building systems. Perhaps through a desire to be different from county council housing, some adopted the type of large estate with linked slab blocks which had made an early appearance at Park Hill Sheffield, and which was soon – but not soon enough – recognized to be so disastrous socially. Hence the dour and dismal ranges of Brent's Chalkhill estate at Wembley, St Marylebone's (later Westminster's) Lisson Green and Paddington's (later Westminster's) Brunel estate. Others continued with mixed development with towers, generally very poorly laid out (Hounslow's Haverfield estate, Hammersmith's Edward Woods estate). More interesting than these were a number of experiments with alternative forms of housing which began in the 1960s. Chelsea's World's End, the final 112

POPULATION 1961–81

	Area (hectares)	Population		
		1961	1971	1981
Barnet	8,953	318,373	306,560	292,331
Enfield	8,115	273,857	268,004	258,825
Haringey	3,031	259,156	240,078	203,175
Havering	11,776	245,598	249,696	240,318
Newham	3,637	265,388	237,390	209,290
Redbridge	5,647	250,080	239,889	225,019
Waltham Forest	3,966	248,591	234,680	215,092
Inner s (*old L.C.C. area*):				
Lambeth	2,727	341,624	307,516	245,739
Lewisham	3,473	290,582	268,474	233,225
Southwark	2,880	313,413	262,138	211,708
Wandsworth	3,492	335,451	302,258	255,723
Outer s:				
Bexley	6,065	209,893	217,076	214,818
Bromley	15,179	293,394	305,377	294,451
Croydon	8,658	323,927	333,870	316,557
Greenwich	4,744	229,810	217,644	211,806
Kingston-upon-Thames	3,756	146,010	140,525	132,411
Merton	3,796	189,013	177,324	164,912
Richmond-upon-Thames	5,525	180,949	174,628	157,867
Sutton	4,342	169,095	169,484	168,407

stage of a large redevelopment area, planned in 1961 although
built only in 1967–77 (by *Eric Lyons, Cadbury-Brown, Metcalfe &
Cunningham*), was a well-intentioned if not entirely successful effort
to humanize a high-density, high-rise estate by means of friendly
materials (brick) and plentiful amenities. Reporton Road Fulham
was an early experimental low-rise scheme planned from 1964 (built
1966–8) by *Higgins & Ney*, with garages below an upper 'street' –
part of the general concern at this time over how to cope with the
car. Pedestrian segregation could become an obsession and led
to some notoriously over-complex multi-layered schemes such as
Westminster's Mozart estate at Queen's Park (1971–7), although
other Westminster housing of the 1970s (Cato Street, Broadley
Street) demonstrated the merits of simple infilling on a small scale.
One of the most telling reactions against both high-rise and comprehensive redevelopment took place from *c.* 1970 in north Kensington, in the overcrowded and run-down neighbourhood of the
new elevated Westway. In place of the clean sweep which had
produced such unhappy results in the Silchester Road area a little
further W, a gradual programme of reconstruction was undertaken
(carried out jointly by the G.L.C. and Kensington), involving both
rehabilitation and new building in the form of unassuming low-
rise terraces, shielded from the motorway and railway by carefully
planned barrier blocks.

The outer boroughs created in 1965 consistently resisted the
G.L.C.'s proposals that pressure on the inner areas should be
relieved by county council housing spread over their territories,
so there are relatively few *G.L.C.* estates in these areas: among
the more ambitious ones are Smith's Farm Northolt of *c.* 1974 (an
early but rather dull case of neo-vernacular), and the large but uninspired Tiber estate at Brentford Dock of 1970–9. Among the
outer boroughs Hillingdon Borough Architect's Department
(under *Thurston Williams*) produced the most interesting work
in the early 1970s, experimenting with a great variety of new
types ranging from expandable homes to single persons' flats,
scattering select outer suburbia with small pockets of unusual
(and sometimes controversial) developments, such as *Cullinan*'s
wide-frontage back-to-back blue-roofed terrace houses at
Eastcote (1974–7).

By the mid 1970s there was not only a universal move in favour
of low rise (or at least of nothing over four storeys) but a desire to
produce housing with a traditional and more friendly image –
conveyed principally by the use of brick and the inclusion of pitched
roofs. Well-thought-out examples of this urban neo-vernacular,
before the concept became a cliché, are by *Darbourne & Darke* at
South Africa Road for Hammersmith and Fulham (1975–8), by
H. M. Grellier & Son for the Octavia Hill and Rowe Housing Trust
in north Kensington (1973–9), and by *Hutchison, Locke & Monk*
at south Acton for Ealing (1978–9), all imaginatively planned with
pedestrian routes and enclosed private spaces.

In the later 1970s, as, increasingly, Victorian terraces were
rehabilitated rather than replaced, the concern to build in a humane
fashion began to go hand in hand with an appreciation of local
character. The desire to fit in tactfully was expressed most often
by the use of materials traditional to the locality – most frequently

yellow stock brick and grey slate roofs. While such parameters
could produce dull results, they could also inspire imaginative
designs. One of the most interesting and influential schemes of this
time was *Jeremy Dixon*'s terraces at St Mark's Road Kensington 113
(1976–80), two brick gabled rows enlivened by subtle touches of
colour, not in any way pastiche, yet fitting comfortably into the
neighbourhood. This was a convincing and confident return to
street architecture, combined with a sensitive appreciation of the
need for clear definition of individual entrances and private spaces
(so often neglected in earlier public housing). The client was the
Kensington Housing Trust; such organizations (funded at this time
by the government) were often more sensitive to the needs of
tenants than larger, more impersonal bureaucracies, and did much
to stimulate this kind of small-scale development. The Notting
Hill Housing Trust was a similar sponsor; its schemes by *Pollard
Thomas Edwards & Associates* also demonstrate the desire to
provide inexpensive low housing with a distinctive, quite decorative
character, first demonstrated at Norland Road Hammersmith
(1977–9); the same firm's nearby group in Bramley Road for a
housing cooperative (1983 etc.) has similar aims. However in the
later 1980s this type of building became rarer, as subsidies for low-
rental housing disappeared, replaced by the government's 'right to
buy' policy for council tenants. Two further crisply individual
groups by *Dixon* can be noted, both built for Westminster: in
Lanark Road Maida Vale (1983), flats (intended for sale) are
arranged in a series of villas – the reminiscences are now more
overtly classical – while in Ashmill Street Lisson Green is a tiny,
more eclectic terrace of 1983. Its materials are brick and render –
like those of the more self-effacing neighbouring group by *Lazenby
& Smith* of 1987, in deliberate response to the early c 20 character
of much of the area. The dominant architectural concern here was
to weld together a homogeneous neighbourhood from a century of
disparate rebuilding programmes. In contrast are the more self-
contained groups of SHELTERED HOUSING and housing for old
people, which often provoked a specially sympathetic response to
the need for a humane and friendly scale of building. Worth seeking
out are *Edward Jones*'s Lovat Walk Cranford (1977), the conversion
of the former c 19 barracks in Pears Road Hounslow (*Hounslow
Architect's Department*, 1978–9), Benjamin Court Hanwell (*Ealing
Architect's Department*, 1983), and *Hammersmith and Fulham*'s
delightful Rosewood Square on the Wormholt estate (1984) and
the low terraces s of Bagley's Lane Fulham.

The tally of interesting PRIVATE HOUSING since 1945 is in
inverse proportion to the public works just discussed. Immediately
post-war traditionalist and modernist approaches are represented
respectively by *Raymond Erith*'s restrained neo-Regency group at
Aubrey Walk Kensington (1950), and some provocatively non-
period bomb-damage infilling among Kensington stucco work:
Ovington Square by *Walter Segal*, 1957, and Hereford Square,
1956–8 by *Colin Wilson* and *Arthur Baker*. A few intriguing private
houses of the 1960s–70s can be found cleverly squeezed into tight
sites: by *Timothy Rendle* at Strand on the Green Chiswick (1966);
by *Tom Kay* at Kensington Place (1967–8); and by *Jeremy Lever*
at Lansdowne Crescent Kensington (1973), all in a spare modernist

spirit. Post-modern fantasy is represented by *Charles Jencks*'s conversion in Lansdowne Walk (1978–83).

Among speculative groups there is little that needs mention from
the 1960s. The most interesting are those which gave some thought
to their settings. In Paddington, the three rather clumsy tall towers
of the Water Gardens, by *Trehearne & Norman, Preston & Partners*
(1961–6), were given a well-intentioned surrounding of hard landscaping, like the contemporary Barbican flats, but they were nevertheless an unprepossessing flagship for the Church Commissioners'
intended high-class redevelopment of Tyburnia. Rather better are
two *Wates* developments: Lakeside at Castlebar, Ealing (1966),
with a landscaped setting not imitated by the other
flats which invaded this area, and *Fry, Drew & Partners*' intricately
planned low-rise Woodsford Square Kensington (1968–74), its
straightforward detail a refreshing contrast to the feeble versions
of neo-Georgian favoured for so many of the more affluent housing
developments of the time. A good small group at Brook Green
Hammersmith by *John Melvin & Partners*, 1982–3, a thoughtful
design in local materials, with classical undertones, comparable
in aim to the contemporary public housing discussed above.

As the demand for prime sites by the local authorities declined,
a much greater quantity of private housing was built in the 1970s
and 80s in both the inner and outer boroughs, but very little that
is architecturally memorable. Some of the most ambitious groups
are along the Thames, on the sites made available by the departure
of riverside industries. At Fulham Reach, where the borough
pursued a policy of freeing the riverside, at first mostly for public
housing, an early example of luxury waterside flats is the forceful
brick stepped composition by *Ted Levy, Benjamin & Partners*
(1974–7). The 1980s schemes tend to be multi-functional packages.
Speyhawk's rapid redevelopment at Isleworth (1986–8, for both
residential and commercial use), by *Broadway Malyan* and others,
is mostly in the pastiche warehouse vernacular of the type much
favoured in Docklands. Chelsea Harbour, Fulham (1986–9), is
larger, brasher, and more eclectic, with housing, hotel, offices,
and shops gathered around a former dock, developed from a plan
devised by *Ray Moxley* and *Peter Bedford*. Far more distinguished
architecturally is the north end of Fulham Reach, where *Richard
Rogers*'s crisp high tech flats (1985–8) form a group with his own
offices (a conversion by *Lifschutz Davidson*), with more to come
by *Foster Associates*. Elsewhere increasing numbers of exclusive,
inward-looking clusters of expensive flats and houses appeared
during the 1980s. They are generally dressed in bright post-modern
trappings – see for example the groups by *Phippen Randall Parkes*
(Lisson Grove; Carlton Gate, Harrow Road; Sudbury Hill,
Harrow-on-the-Hill), all with shallow stepped pitched roofs and
coloured trim, and the fanciful elevations by *David Landaw &
Partners* at Brook Green Hammersmith. But such buildings are
perhaps a little more enterprising than the predictable classical
pastiche of *Quinlan Terry*'s villas in Regents Park (1989–90).

It will already be obvious that during the 1980s it becomes
difficult to separate out different building types, as residential,
commercial, and community elements are enclosed in a single developer's package, which may adopt more or less any stylistic

wrapping. However, some effort must now be made to investigate
the PUBLIC WORKS AND OTHER BUILDINGS of the 1950s
onwards, or rather of the period 1950–80, for little in the way
of public works has been built since. First, TRANSPORT and its
architectural effects. The most significant government enterprise
immediately after the war was the creation of Heathrow Airport.
The expansion of air traffic was far more rapid than had been
anticipated, and the early, gently elegant red brick buildings of the 104
1950s by *Frederick Gibberd & Partners* were soon enveloped in
extensions. A fourth terminal on a new site to the south, more
satisfactorily related to earthbound transport, was added only in
1982–6 (*Scott, Brownrigg & Partners*). The airport gradually
spawned a ring of largely undistinguished hotels, warehouses, and
offices (*see* below), totally transforming this area of once quite
rural outer suburbia. In inner London, the concentric series of
motorways proposed in the County of London plan was never
carried out, and the only major roadworks to produce a significant
effect on the inner western suburbs date from the 1960s: the Hammersmith flyover (a particularly elegant piece of engineering) and
the elevated Westway bringing the A40 to Marylebone Road. In
both cases the havoc wrought on their surroundings was only slowly
put to rights, rather imaginatively in the case of Westway, where
in the north Kensington area an ingenious number of activities
were tucked beneath the road from the later 1970s. As with the
airport, a more prominent visual consequence was the rash of tall
buildings – in the inner suburbs chiefly for offices – in the immediate
neighbourhood; especially noticeable was the transformation of the
region around Edgware Road in this way during the 1960s. The
only major work in public transport was the extension of the Piccadilly line to Heathrow.

  PUBLIC BUILDINGS of the 1950s are few. One of the first to go
up after the lifting of restrictions was Kensington Library, 1955 by
Vincent Harris, which stalwartly maintained a monumental
Wrenaissance tradition. In total contrast to this conservative
approach, in 1955–7, in nearby Holland Park (now taken over as a
public amenity), the *L.C.C.* erected a brusquely modern youth
hostel as a foil to the remains of the Jacobean Holland House, and
the government built the Commonwealth Institute (planned from 106
1958, built in 1960–2, by *Robert Matthew, Johnson-Marshall &
Partners*). This was the second major public building in London
(the Festival Hall being the first), a 'tent in the park' with a daring
concrete roof and impressive free-flowing spaces, although not
entirely satisfying in its exterior detail.

  Holland Park was indeed a testing place for new architecture,
for on its edge was also one of the L.C.C.'s new comprehensive
SCHOOLS (Holland Park, by *D. Rogers Stark* of the *L.C.C.*, 1958–
61). The energy put into school design was one of the most impressive achievements of the post-war L.C.C. The London School Plan,
drawn up in 1944–7, had included in its ambitious programme the
total reorganization of secondary education in the L.C.C. area on
comprehensive lines. To achieve a balanced mix it was at first
thought essential to have at least twelve-form entry schools (i.e.
over 2,000 pupils). So the first new comprehensives were large, and
visibly revelled in their scale, and in the use of modern ideas such

as curtain walling and open ground floors. Holland Park, despite its size, is a pleasantly compact yet airy design, only four storeys high (unlike some of the larger early schools in south London). The early secondary schools in the western suburbs are of considerable variety: Hammersmith (1954–8 by *Edward Hollamby* of the *L.C.C.*) is an attractively laid out brick group (originally two linked schools) with ingenious timber roofs (to solve the shortage of building materials at the time) and decorative tiles to add some visual enjoyment. Hurlingham, Fulham, is a neat, compact layout of 1956 by *Sheppard Robson & Partners*, also brightened by coloured tiles. Quintin Kynaston, St Marylebone, 1958 by *E. D. Mills*, is another example of linked schools, using curtain-walled blocks of different heights. The former Sarah Siddons, Paddington, by the *L.C.C.* (1958–61), is a well composed group of more sober brickwork with some colourful detail, and the former Rutherford, St Marylebone, 1960–1 by *Leonard Manasseh & Partners*, is given character by its intriguing roof shapes (the last two now linked as North Westminster Community School). Numerous low, friendly PRIMARY SCHOOLS were also built at this time, in reaction against the formality of the old board schools. They were often of standardized components in imitation of the Hertfordshire experiments (see e.g. Sulivan, Fulham), but there were also some more individual designs

105 before ideas became stereotyped: *Lasdun*'s at Hallfield, Paddington, has already been mentioned; another with a strong character of its own is *Ernö Goldfinger*'s concrete-framed Westville Road Hammersmith (1950–3), and a third is *Chamberlin, Powell & Bon*'s attractively colourful curtain-walled Bousfield, Kensington (1954–6). Immediately after the war the Middlesex County Council also produced some lively primary schools, such as Fairholme East Bedfont (1952), more lighthearted than their pre-war standard types.

West London has fewer outstanding secondary school buildings of the 1960s onwards. Worth a mention as examples of later developments are the American School St John's Wood by *Shaver & Co.* of 1969–70, an early introduction to England of open planning for secondary education, and The London Oratory Fulham, by *David Stokes & Partners* (1970), a tight design on a small site, in contrast to the space available in the outer boroughs for such schools as Heathlands at Hounslow (1972). This has the tough brutalist image still popular for public buildings at this time; Hounslow's Cranford (1972–6) is not much more attractive, but interesting for its inclusion of community amenities, an early example of this principle. A general trend in the 1960s–70s was the creation of more flexibly used spaces instead of formal classrooms – a concept adopted first for primary schools (after the Plowden report of 1967) and later by secondaries. The friendlier face of school design of the 1980s is well illustrated by St Clement and St James Kensington, a primary school by *Green, Lloyd & Adams* (1986), and by several schools at Southall by Ealing, e.g. Blair Peach, 1988–9. Another trend of the times is demonstrated by the smart transformation of a 1950s M.C.C. school at Acton into a private Muslim school, the King Fahad Academy, complete with mosque, by the *Carnell Green Partnership* (1988–9).

While the 1950s was the decade for schools, the most important

FURTHER EDUCATION BUILDINGS went up about ten years later.
Precursors are some early works by the Middlesex County Council
under *C. G. Stillman*, such as Ealing College, 1953, cheerfully
detailed in the Festival spirit. A major enterprise was begun in
1958, when the decision was taken to provide new buildings for
Imperial College on the site of the Imperial Institute at South
Kensington, but although the plan is quite interesting – an early
example of a raised pedestrian spine – the buildings by *Norman &
Dawbarn* are disappointingly bland and confusing. More impressive is the very Corbusian concrete crate of students' lodgings in 108
Prince's Gardens, of 1960–3 by *Sheppard Robson & Partners*. The
same firm was responsible for the master plan of Brunel University
(Hi); here the main college buildings of 1965–71, forceful, well-
composed groups in dark brick, are complemented by *Stillman &
Eastwick-Field*'s laboratories and engineering buildings (1965–7), 107
which likewise exploit the aesthetic of exposed concrete and plain
brickwork. A similarly brutalist approach is illustrated by the strikingly tall, functional frontage of the Royal College of Art in Kensington Gore, 1959–64 by *H. T. Cadbury-Brown*, and by the School
of Engineering and Science of the Polytechnic at Marylebone,
1965–8 by *Lyons Israel Ellis*, an effective composition with concrete
lecture theatre jutting out over the entrance. These are the best
examples; handled with less confidence and skill (see e.g. the Polytechnic buildings by I.L.E.A. in Marylebone Road), large concrete
building could easily alienate both user and beholder. The move in
the 1970s away from such uncompromising forms and materials
led to an enthusiasm for brick as the universal panacea. The unmiti-
gated red brick cladding of the Hammersmith and West London
College (by *Bob Giles* of *I.L.E.A.*, completed 1977) demonstrates
the change.

The tradition which had established St Marylebone as the area
for PROFESSIONAL INSTITUTIONS was carried on by one distinguished post-war example, the Royal College of Physicians in 111
Regents Park, 1961–4 by *Sir Denys Lasdun*, an original and subtle
building, particularly enjoyable for its skilful handling of internal
spaces. Contemporary but rather different Regents Park com-
panions which demonstrate the versatility of the 1960s can be found
at the Zoo: *Casson & Conder*'s chunky Elephant and Rhino House
(1962–5), and the light but powerful Aviary (by *Cedric Price* and
others, 1961–5), a precursor of later interest in tensile engineering
structures.

With the reorganization of the boroughs in 1965 came aspirations
towards new CIVIC BUILDINGS, although only four of the west
London boroughs started from scratch to cater for their enlarged
bureaucracies. Hounslow was the first, with a sensible but not very
exciting modern building in pleasant parkland (1965–75 by *G. A.
Trevett*). Harrow produced at Wealdstone an uninspired, compact
civic centre with regular ranges around a courtyard (*Eric Broughton*,
1972). Kensington commissioned a more interesting plan from
Sir Basil Spence in 1965 (executed by the *John S. Bonnington
Partnership* in 1972–6), with halls and offices grouped irregularly
around a polygonal courtyard, and large expanses of plain wall in
the red brick that was *de rigueur* in the mid 1970s. But all these
suddenly seemed out of date as Hillingdon proceeded in 1973–8 at

110 Uxbridge with its novel design by *Andrew Derbyshire* of *Robert Matthew, Johnson-Marshall & Partners*. Its remarkable achievement was the translation of the homely vernacular imagery – red brick and pitched roofs – that was beginning to be exploited for small-scale housing (*see* above) into a cladding for deep-plan offices on a monumental scale. It marked a turning point in recognizing the popular demand for buildings that were, at least superficially, traditional in their form and detail – a trend that was to be pursued in other building types (*see* shopping centres, below).

Now for briefer mention of the most interesting examples among some miscellaneous building types. Some original solutions for UTILITIES were produced in the 1960s–70s. The neat curved forms 109 of Paddington Maintenance Depot, 1968 by *Bicknell & Hamilton*, provided an interesting foil beside the new Westway. Brentford Refuse Transfer Station, by the *G.L.C. Special Works*, 1978, makes a cheerful show near the M4, while the Kensington Depot by *Arup Associates* of 1970–6 is an ingenious construction with rooftop housing over a wide-span working area. HOSPITALS on the other hand are dispiriting; a series of huge, impersonal enterprises of the 1960s, generally with wards stacked in towers, surrounded by anonymous lower buildings (Northwick Park Kenton by *Llewelyn-Davies & Weeks*; Hillingdon by *Gollins, Melvin, Ward & Partners*; Ealing by *John R. Harris*). Only Charing Cross at Fulham, by *Ralph Tubbs*, 1969–73, with its distinctive cross-shaped tower with a grid of balconies, and a chapel with some good glass, has more individuality. At Ealing some lively additions of the 1980s by *Hutchison, Locke & Monk* have helped to leaven the lump. A comparable change in the image of POLICE STATIONS is demonstrated by the contrast between the severe building at Harrow Road Paddington, 1966–71, and the jazzily post-modern one at Uxbridge, 1987–8 by *Jeff Rutt*.

CULTURAL, COMMUNITY, AND LEISURE BUILDINGS form a mixed and overlapping collection. Baden Powell House, Queen's Gate, Kensington, by *Ralph Tubbs*, 1959–61, is a good example of the free planning and straightforward modern materials of the time. An early post-war example of an entirely new type of building was the B.B.C. Television Centre at Hammersmith, planned from 1950 by *Norman & Dawbarn*, an ingenious if rather cluttered circular arrangement of studios. Otherwise there is not much to note for the performing arts in west London: a tiny experimental theatre by *Edward Mendelsohn* of the *G.L.C. Education Branch* at Gateforth Street St Marylebone (1969–70), and a few economical conversions such as the Riverside Hammersmith (1975) and the Tricycle Kilburn (Br) (1980 by *Tim Foster*). In the outer boroughs multi-purpose cultural centres began to be provided in the 1970s: the ever-enterprising Hillingdon built the Alfred Beck Centre at Hayes (1972–5) in the new vernacular manner and Brentford was provided with the more utilitarian Waterman's Centre as part of a developer's package (1982–4 by *O. Garry & Partners*). A rather better deal produced an excellent library for Uxbridge (by *Gibberd, Coombes Partnership*, 1985–7). Museum buildings are represented only by the bold but successful concrete-and-glass extension to the Natural History Museum, Kensington, by the *P.S.A.*, 1972–5.

Among SPORTS BUILDINGS, Harrow's Centre at Wealdstone of

1975 and Ealing's Bromyard Centre at Acton of 1988–9 (which incorporates a library) both try quite hard to be appealing. The outstanding success in this category, however, is the Mound Stand 117 at Lords by *Michael Hopkins*, 1985–7, an enjoyable application of high tech expertise to the traditional forms of a grandstand and awning.

CHURCHES were the traditional social centres of the suburbs, but remarkable post-war buildings are few. Most of the early post-war churches were by older architects who continued with more pallid versions of 1930s eclecticism. One of the more original ones is *Cachemaille-Day*'s centrally planned All Saints Hanworth of 1951, a solitary example until this type of plan became fashionable in the 1960s. The only novelties were contributed by artists trained outside England: *Hans Feibusch*'s Baroque-expressionist mural paintings (Ascension Wembley, St Michael Harrow Weald, 1957–8) and some forceful stained glass by *Max Nauta* (St Andrew Pinner, 1956). The first west London buildings to echo the challenge of the postwar modernist approach of Coventry Cathedral were St Etheldreda Fulham (1955–8 by *Guy Biscoe*) and St Mary Ruislip (1958–9 by *Laurence King*), both straightforward portal-framed constructions, St Mary enlivened by glass by *Keith New*. *Ansell & Bailey*'s Westbourne Park Baptist Chapel of 1961 is the Nonconformist equivalent (generally Nonconformist churches of both before and after the war are too minor to be mentioned here). R.C. churches at first continued in a simplified Romanesque, the style made popular between the wars by *F. X. Velarde* and used by him for St Luke Pinner in 1957. A new approach came with St Aidan Hammersmith of 1958, another portal-frame, but more notable for its enterprising collection of interesting furnishings, including an altar painting by *Graham Sutherland*. The Immaculate Heart of Mary at Hayes of 1961 has a comparable collection, although not of the same quality. Both buildings are by *Burles, Newton & Partners*, R.C. architects prolific in the London suburbs. St Anselm Southall, 1967, is one of their more interesting churches.

It was the liturgical reforms of the 1960s, placing a new emphasis on an altar accessible to the congregation instead of distanced in a remote chancel, which provided the impetus for several more radically modern buildings which, although in an entirely different mode, recapture something of the fervour of Victorian church building. The pioneer in London was *Maguire & Murray*'s St Paul, Bow Common, Stepney (TH), of 1958–60. St Joseph Northolt by the same firm, 1967–9, and *Gerard Goalen*'s R.C. St Gregory Ruislip (1966–7), with glass by *Reyntiens*, are the west London examples – arresting, fortress-like buildings of unconventional shape, with airy, well lit, and imaginatively laid out interiors. From the same period is *Michael Blee*'s bold rebuilding of All Saints Isleworth (1967–70), a dynamic building with quite brutalist external details forcefully intermeshed with the remains of the burnt-out C18 church. That is nearly the end of the story as far as Anglican buildings are concerned in the outer suburbs, although one interesting building is in progress at the time of writing: the remodelling and extension of St Paul Brentford, also by *Michael Blee*. In inner London it has been a matter of demolition or conversion of redundant churches rather than building anew, although occasionally modest new churches have arisen on parts of the old sites. *Biscoe & Stanton*'s St Saviour and St Peter in Paddington (both of the early 1970s and both rather mean replacements of their Victorian predecessors) and *A.J. Monk*'s St Luke Hammersmith (1976–8) are examples; defensively reticent exteriors concealing austere spaces with plain walls of exposed brick. Liturgical and other changes made to older interiors are rarely of much aesthetic interest, although among the many churches subdivided for a variety of uses, *Michael Reardon*'s alterations to St Margaret Uxbridge (1987–9) can be singled out as unusually careful and sympathetic. The most ambitious religious buildings of the last twenty years have been those for non-Christian groups: *Frederick Gibberd*'s Mosque of 1972–8, whose large golden dome makes an exotic contribution to the Regents Park skyline, and the richly finished Ismaili Centre at South Kensington by *Casson & Conder*, 1978–83.

Now to COMMERCIAL AND INDUSTRIAL BUILDINGS. Early post-war offices include two prestige headquarters outside central London, both by *T.P. Bennett & Son*, 1957–8: Taylor Woodrow at Western Avenue Ealing and McDermotts at Wembley, brick buildings in the reticent modern manner of the 1950s. *Tayler & Green*'s Imhofs factory of 1961 at Uxbridge is a rare example of good, quiet detailing and landscaping in an indifferent industrial setting. The sleeker, more sophisticated image of the American office arrived in England in 1955–60 with Castrol House in Marylebone Road, by *Gollins, Melvin, Ward & Partners*, a curtain-walled slab and podium inspired by Lever House, New York. The same firm built the first curtain-walled offices in London, in New Cavendish Street, Marylebone, two low, unassuming buildings of the 1950s, of which one survives, although transformed by recladding. The type rapidly became too frequent to excite comment. However, Sanderson's long curtain-walled showrooms in nearby Berners Street, 1960 by *Slater, Moberly & Uren*, deserve a mention because of their enterprising inclusion of artwork in different media, including stained glass by *Piper & Reyntiens*. The British Gas offices at Peterborough Road Fulham (1961–3) are likewise interesting for the external *Piper* mural, commissioned in an effort to brighten a drab area. But such sensitive approaches are exceptional among the generally indifferent offices and commercial buildings that multiplied at this time.

In the 1960s came the switch from Miesian reticence to a more sculptural treatment of elevations, exploiting the expressive qualities of concrete, although brutalism was rarely used for office blocks with the same confidence as for public buildings (*see* Further Education, above). An exception is the work of *Owen Luder & Partners* in many of the outer suburbs at this time; a west London example is at Hayes (Colman House). The latest American fashion – tapering concrete piers – was used by the eminent American firm of *Skidmore Owings & Merrill* for the Heinz headquarters at Hayes Park already in 1961, and the influence of such mannerisms can be seen in the work of *R. Seifert & Partners*, for example in the Royal Garden Hotel Kensington of 1965, better than many of the later hotels, if one can forgive its siting on the edge of Kensington Gardens. A good, quieter example (an early case of a hotel tower) is the Carlton Tower Hotel in Sloane Street, Chelsea, by *M.*

Rosenauer, 1961. Among industrial buildings of the 1960s, Watneys Brewery Isleworth, by *S. Hutchings*, is an impressive piece of engineering, while a rather elegant version of brutalism is to be found in the concrete and glass offices and warehouses for Penguin at Harmondsworth by *Arup Associates*, 1968–72.

The search for a friendly 'vernacular' image in the 1970s, noted already in both housing and public buildings, can be paralleled in the development of the SHOPPING CENTRE at this time. Most 1960s pedestrian shopping centres were uninspiring affairs, as were the covered malls that began to succeed them in the 1970s (see e.g. Kings Mall Hammersmith). The breakthrough to something different came with the development of the Ealing Broadway Centre by *B.D.P.*, 1978–85, a massive complex including offices and public library as well as shops. As a result of public demand, its bulk was disguised by a deliberately picturesque design, with an open pedestrian square, and a series of eclectically detailed street front-ages in brick, while the multi-storey car park, so often one of the ugliest and least considered aspects of such developments, was also given decorative trimmings and ingeniously made a focal point of the composition. The shopping malls, however, are still low and unexciting. *B.D.P.*'s later Lancer Square, on the site of Kensington Barracks in Kensington Church Street (1987–9), carries on with decorative brick detailing but reverts to open-air pedestrian walks. Other centres adopted the American form of the glazed atrium – exhilarating at its best, but soon to become a repetitive cliché. Examples are the Treaty Centre at Hounslow (another package incorporating a library), 1984–7 by *Fitzroy, Robinson & Partners*, and the St Ann's Centre at Harrow (*Bernard Engle & Partners*, 1986–7). Glazed roofs were introduced too by *Fitch & Co.* at The Pavilions, Uxbridge, a clever 1980s revamping of a dull 1960s pedestrian centre, with some witty new centrepieces. During this period of the retail boom, when any style became permissible, the consumer could be wooed by a whole range of novelties, from jokey Egyptian quotations (by *Ian Pollard* at Sainsbury's Homebase in Warwick Road Kensington) to a forceful version of high tech engin-eering (*Nicholas Grimshaw*'s building for the same firm at Brent-ford).

From the later 1970s OFFICES AND WAREHOUSES began to spring up in ever greater numbers in the neighbourhood of Heath-row and the western motorways. Most are without aesthetic merit, although there are two handsome exceptions: *Foster Associates*' warehouse group for IBM at Greenford (1978–9), and *Aukett*'s 114 factory for Landis & Gyr at North Acton (1979), both with the minimalist transparency and immaculate detailing characteristic of the most elegant forms of high tech. This is an act that it is not easy to imitate well, as can be seen from the vast, sleek, anonymous offices that disastrously dominate Hammersmith Road between the Broadway and Olympia, and have taken over much of Uxbridge – a transformation almost as rapid and brutal as that of Croydon in the 1960s. However, Uxbridge does have at least one good office group, Charter Place, a light and airy atrium composition by *Gibberd, Coombes & Partners* (1985–8). HOTELS, generally an undistinguished type of C20 building, have also adopted the atrium, most impressively at the Sterling Hotel Heathrow (1988–90 by

Manser Associates). In the inner areas, where new sites are scarce, refurbishment is often more common than total rebuilding; the best efforts of this kind can produce a distinguished combination of old and new, as in the case of the restoration and additions to the Michelin Building Fulham by *Y.R.M.* and *Conran Roche* (1985–6).

In the 1980s an alternative to the urban office was developed: the BUSINESS PARK, with offices for a variety of firms arranged in a landscaped setting with ample amenities. The prime west London example is Stockley Park (Hi), conveniently close to Heathrow, created on waste land from 1985 following a master plan by *Arup Associates*. Its reticently elegant pavilions are admirably combined with thoughtful landscaping. The early buildings by *Arup Associates* were followed by some larger, more flamboyant ones by other architects, outstanding among them *Foster Associates'* refined yet monumental stepped block supported by Y-shaped piers. Others are by *Ian Ritchie* and *Troughton McAslan*. Another rural development, although with a formal layout, is at Bedfont Lakes (master plan by *Michael Hopkins & Partners*, phase 1 by *Hopkins* and *Edward Cullinan*, 1990–1). A more urban group at Chiswick Park was under discussion in 1990–1 (*Terry Farrell & Co.*).

Transparent high tech was only one among a number of possibilities employed for commercial and industrial buildings in the 1980s. An alternative was a more solid and decorative approach of which an early and very convincing example is *John Outram's* McKay Trading Estate of 1981 in Kensal Road, Kensington. Outram's buildings reinterpret familiar, classical forms – pediments and columns – to good functional effect. Others borrow more eclectically, as in the case of *Terry Farrell's* playful Egyptian revival and aeroplane trimmings in the art deco spirit at Penfold Street and Hatton Street, St Marylebone. During the 1980s one can detect a growing taste for more dynamic and colourful façades, some of the most original among them by *Piers Gough* of *CZWG* (the studios in Lancaster Road North Kensington represent his work in west London), while an entirely novel approach to three-dimensional design is demonstrated by the curved glass forms of *Ralph Erskine's* Hammersmith Landmark, planned in 1989.

And so this introduction ends, with a survey of the opportunist pluralism of private enterprise architecture of the 1980s, and with an open question as to where these diverse strands will lead in the more stringent economic climate forecast for the 1990s. It is a world far removed from that of the 1950s, when the only post-war buildings to be mentioned in *London except the Cities of London and Westminster* were a few blocks of council flats and the Royal Festival Hall.

GEOLOGY AND BUILDING MATERIALS

BY ERIC ROBINSON

The geology of Middlesex and north London, like its topography, is uncharacteristically subdued and almost subtle. It consists of two simple elements, a foundation of *solid* rock, and a *superficial* cover of sands and gravels principally found in the valleys.

Beneath the entire area, the Chalk forms a solid basement which rises to a surface outcrop to the west of the Colne Valley, to the north of Watford, and the line of the Great North Road beyond Potters Bar. Within this curving arc, the Chalk dips below the surface to form a shallow basin below Greater London so that its top surface lies some 200 ft below Camden Town (Ca), overlain by a thickness of Tertiary sands and clays. In the past, the Chalk has provided building material in the form of hard chalk ('clunch'), but more especially the hard and irregularly shaped flints which occur as discontinuous seams throughout its thickness. At one time, flint was worked from shallow mine shafts around Pinner and Hatch End (Hw), but has always been more readily available from the weathered top surface of the Chalk ('clay-with-flints') or from the river gravels within the basin.

The Tertiary rocks which fill the basin consist of Thanet Sands (up to 20 ft in thickness), Reading Beds (again up to 20 ft), London Clay (as much as 200 ft in places), and finally Bagshot Sands of up to 30 ft in thickness capping the Middlesex heathlands. Before human activities took a hand, these Tertiary rocks must have given rise to well-wooded sandy heaths (the Reading Beds), or heavy-clay-floored valleys (the London Clay), while the isolated higher hill cappings of heathland correspond with the Bagshot Sands outcrop.

Of the Tertiary beds, the Reading Beds were ancient river deposits and so consist of sands and gravels, mainly flints derived from the Chalk below, with less frequent bands of clay. Locally, patches of flint gravel have been cemented by siliceous springs to produce the distinctive pebble rock known as Hertfordshire Puddingstone, used as building material in the St Albans area. A speciality of south Hertfordshire, rocks of a similar kind and origin could occur in the Colne Valley and have provided the dark brown pebbly sandstone seen in Pinner church (Hw), or the sarsen-type green sandstone seen in the tower of the church at Harlington (Hi). Such rocks can develop patchily in beds of unconsolidated sand as groundwaters rich in silica or iron salts permeate and bond together the sand grains and create an extremely hard rock. The type is referred to as 'ferricrete' in this volume.

The London Clay is a marine mud deposit which had a great influence upon topography and buildings in Middlesex, for as a rock type, this clay has both a high plasticity and a dynamic response to weathering. (Exposed to air, sulphide minerals within the fresh clay oxidize and expand, producing a visible upheaval of the ground.) Hot summers produce drying out and deep cracking of the surface, allowing penetration of moisture in succeeding wetter periods. So is initiated a continuing cycle of ground movement which, even in the more modest hill slopes of north London, can produce worrying landslip and subsidence. In Middlesex, the London Clay was always a prime source of brick-making clay (Hampstead Heath, Copenhagen Fields, Edgware).

The *superficial* rocks of Middlesex and north London are principally a legacy of the Ice Age. Roughly 150,000 years ago, glaciers from the north came to a halt in the Vale of St Albans, with a southernmost lobe pushing down the Dollis Brook into Finchley (Bn). The ice left behind a sticky, pebbly clay ('chalky boulder clay') which runs through Finchley to end beyond the North Circular Road in the cemeteries of East Finchley. Further N a well-marked ridge of pebbly gravel extending from Chipping Barnet through Arkley (Bn), which we can project westwards to Brockley Hill, Stanmore (Hw), and Bushey (Herts), represents a water-washed moraine of the same pebbly clay and the same ice sheet.

The melt waters of these great ice sheets were responsible for the second category of superficial rocks, the sands and gravels of the Thames drainage, spread out as broad, flat surfaced terraces extending beneath Uxbridge, Heathrow, Hayes (all Hi), Ealing (Ea), and Kensington (KC). The deposits of ancient Thames watercourses, the principal materials of the gravels are flints either washed from the Chalk outcrops of the Chilterns and the North Downs, or derived from the older gravels and sands of the Tertiary solid geology described above. Undoubtedly the terrace deposits have long been the source of the flints used in medieval churches and grander buildings, just as they are the continuing source of bulk material for foundation work, ballast, and readi-mix concrete in the present age.

It follows from what has been said of the geology of Middlesex and the London Basin that the area is lamentably short of good quality building stone. For this reason, Norman masons naturally looked to the Caen Stone from Normandy which they had been accustomed to use for work of importance. Later, they made do with the gritty limestone collectively known as 'Kentish Rag', limestones ranging from shelly ragstone from Kent through to stone of freestone quality, Reigate Stone from north Surrey. Easy to work and dress into all forms of mouldings, Reigate often proved too readily weathering for external use and has often been replaced by other stone. No such weakness characterizes the limestones from Lincolnshire, originally brought into London by the Romans and used also in the well-known c 12 carved doorways of Harlington and Harmondsworth churches (both Hi). The shelly Jurassic oolite stone in both cases is thought to be Barnack Rag quarried from the area a few miles south of Stamford.

Much later, Bath Stone and Cotswold and Oxfordshire oolite arrived by canal from the West Country for c 18 and early c 19 work, mainly the stone dressings to churches. Later still, when the Great Western Railway made the same stone still cheaper to procure, more and more of the deep orange freestone appeared in large houses, municipal halls, and offices as well as newer parish churches in London suburbs.

It remains to be said that sand and gravel aggregate and the ubiquitous flint derived from the Chalk have always been the available material for London and Chiltern builders. The aggregate forms a brown puddingstone in the s of the area (*see* East Bedfont, Ho) and can occur in quite large lumps (see the base courses to the great barn at Harmondsworth, Hi). Further N it takes the form of a darker and denser carstone, harder enough to be used for quoins, as in Pinner church (Hw). The local builders' handling of the materials produced fabric and styles just a shade different from those found a short distance away in Buckinghamshire, Hertfordshire, Suffolk, and Essex where in all respects builders started with the same disadvantages.

PREHISTORIC AND ROMAN ARCHAEOLOGY

BY JOANNA BIRD

The founding of London shortly after the Roman invasion of A.D. 43 established a focus for trade, government, and general human activity which has been growing and changing almost continuously ever since. This growth has obscured much of the natural landscape of the area, and it is difficult now to see that Greater London actually incorporates parts of several distinct regions. Earlier patterns of settlement have been largely destroyed, and much of our knowledge of London's archaeology is dependent on chance finds and imprecise records, and on comparison with more fortunate areas. Even those parts – mainly in the outer boroughs – where information does survive are under constant threat from building, and modern archaeological effort is almost completely devoted to 'rescue' work.

Despite the problems, however, it is still possible to draw some general conclusions about the occupation of the area during prehistoric and Roman times from the distribution of finds and settlement sites. During the Palaeolithic and Mesolithic periods, light woodland and river banks were favoured for their game, fowl, fish, and fresh water; the presence of flint for tools may also have had an influence. From the Neolithic onwards, the need was for soils that could be easily cleared and farmed using primitive implements, with good drainage and abundant water supply: the light soils over gravels (notably in West London) and along the springline of the North Downs were consistently chosen, while the intractable and densely forested London Clay was as consistently avoided.

Several features of London's archaeology are of particular importance, and are discussed in more detail below. Briefly, they include the wealth of Lower Palaeolithic material, the complex of Neolithic monuments in the Heathrow area, the presence of what must have been a major Late Bronze Age industrial centre, and the evidence for some of the earliest Saxon settlements in England; while the Thames in West London has produced a range and quantity of Bronze and Iron Age metalwork that is without parallel.

Now for GEOLOGY. The basic shape of Greater London's landscape is formed by a fold in the Chalk, which has produced ridges to N (the Chilterns) and S (the North Downs), and left a wide basin in the centre through which the Thames now flows. Much of the Chalk has been subsequently covered by later geological deposits, producing a variety of soils and surface cover. The first, consisting of a series of sand, clay, and pebble beds, which provide relatively light soils of varying utility where they reach the surface, occur mainly in SE London, and there is a springline at the junction with the Chalk. The London Clay, deposited subsequently by a warm sea, forms much of the land surface, notably in N Middlesex and across the centre of the southern portion. It is heavy and impermeable, and naturally carries dense forest. In places it is overlain by sands mixed with clay and pebbles, which form a dry light soil with springs at the junction with the clay: Hampstead and Highgate in North London are instances of this. The most recent geological deposits consist of gravels, mainly laid down during the later Ice Ages. In particular, the wanderings of the Thames have deposited a complex series of gravel terraces, forming a broad band beside the modern course of the river. Springs occur at the junction with the Clay, and light, easily worked soils are produced; the upper levels of the gravels are often a clay-like loam ('brick-earth'), naturally wooded but not difficult to clear.

The area is roughly divided by the Thames, and a major feature is the number of smaller rivers draining into it from N and S; those in the central area, such as the Fleet, have now been led into the artificial drainage system. The presence of these rivers and the flatness of the river basin has meant that much of the area bordering the Thames is naturally marshy: places such as Southwark, Lambeth, and Westminster, and large tracts of East London, would not have been habitable until relatively recently. In these areas, the river gravels are overlain by silts. Southwark was first drained during the Roman period, and the problem of securing London from flooding continues to exercise the authorities today.

The earliest traces of human activity in Greater London belong to the PALAEOLITHIC (Old Stone Age), ranging from 450,000 to 12,000 B.C. This was also the period of the later Ice Ages, and it is unlikely that the area was continuously habitable. The wide variations of climate during and between the glaciations are reflected in the animal remains: those of cave bear, mammoth, and reindeer bear witness to arctic and sub-arctic conditions, those of the hippopotamus to hot conditions. The archaeology of this immense period is complicated by the contemporary geology. The course and depth of the Thames varied considerably, and a series of gravel terraces was laid down by the river: their number, sequence, and chronology are not yet fully understood, and it is from them that most of the Palaeolithic finds have come.

The Palaeolithic can be broadly divided into three phases, distinguished by the types of tools in use: they are the Lower (450,000–100,000 B.C.), with flint axes and crude flint flakes; the Middle

(100,000–40,000 B.C.), with more advanced flake tools; and the Upper (40,000–12,000 B.C.), with fine flint blades (it is to this last phase that the painted caves of France and Spain belong). Almost all the material in Greater London comes from the Lower Palaeolithic; the few Middle and Upper Palaeolithic finds probably represent the debris of brief hunting sorties. The Upper Palaeolithic coincided with the last Ice Age, and it is probable that the area, lacking natural shelters such as caves, was largely uninhabitable.

Some of the most important Lower Palaeolithic sites in Europe lie along the Lower Thames Valley, and some of the richest are within Greater London: at Yiewsley–West Drayton (Hi), Ealing–Acton (Ea), Stoke Newington (Hc), and Crayford (Bx). Other concentrations occur in the West End, at Wandsworth, and along the springline of the North Downs. These sites would have been the camps of small hunting communities, and animal remains have been found with tools at Southall (Ea), Kings Cross (Ca), and Stoke Newington (Hc). Acton, Stoke Newington, and Crayford have produced evidence, in the form of flint waste, for the manufacture of implements. Other evidence is fragmentary and tantalizing: a few birch stakes woven with clematis and fern, perhaps a shelter, from Stoke Newington, and burnt stones, possibly from a hearth, at West Drayton.

The MESOLITHIC (Middle Stone Age), c. 12,000–4,000 B.C., followed the last glaciation, and for much of the period Britain was still joined to the Continent. Initial sub-arctic or tundra conditions were succeeded by forest, and the climate became warmer and wetter; arctic fauna were replaced by forest animals such as boar and deer. The typical tools of the period are small neatly worked flint 'microliths', made to be mounted in bone or wooden shafts as hunting and fishing weapons, saws, and scrapers. Heavy flint axes ('Thames picks'), antler hammers, and tools of bone (e.g. harpoons) were also produced. There are a number of known settlements where hunters and fishers had their camps, including sites where flint waste indicates working, and one site, at Twickenham (Ri), where a midden of shells and tools was found. The main areas of occupation lie beside rivers, on the less heavily wooded soils, and along the springline of the North Downs, including Hampstead Heath (Ca), Harefield Moor (Hi), Ham Fields (Ri), Wimbledon Common (Me), and Putney Heath (Ww).

The NEOLITHIC (New Stone Age), c. 4,000–1,800 B.C., saw the introduction of agriculture and pastoralism, which spread gradually from the Near East and the Balkans and reached Britain during the fourth millennium. The process must have been slow, with a considerable overlap between old hunter-gatherer and new farmer. Some at least of the Neolithic settlements would have been the permanent homes of farmers, who would for the first time have begun to change their environment by clearance and by sowing and stock-rearing. In the London area, most of the known Neolithic settlement is concentrated on easily drained and worked soils, the gravels of West London and the sands along the springline of the Downs, where water and flint were abundant. Settlements include Putney (Ww), Harmondsworth (Hi), Twickenham (Ri), Brentford (Ho), Rainham (Hv), and Baston Manor (near Hayes, Bm); some have also produced flint-working debris. Flint tools were modified to new needs (e.g. sickles), and a characteristic axe type, of polished stone or flint, was in use: some of these were traded considerable distances, and the London area has produced axes originating in the Lake District and the Alps. A further innovation at this period was pottery; despite its technical crudity – it was hand-made, and probably fired in bonfires – distinct forms and decorative styles can be recognized. A quantity of Neolithic pottery indicates a further settlement at Kingston (Ki).

In addition to settlements, there are more substantial monuments of the Neolithic, of which there was clearly an important complex in the Heathrow area and westwards beyond the Greater London boundary in the areas of Staines, Runnymede, Stanwell, and Shepperton. Henges, roughly circular ritual enclosures marked by a ditch within a bank (and sometimes containing rings of stone or wooden uprights), are the most famous Neolithic monuments, and there are remains of hengiform enclosures at Heathrow and East Bedfont. Earlier Neolithic causewayed camps (ditched enclosures with access causeways) probably served a social and religious purpose; none have so far been identified within Greater London, but there is at least one nearby, at Yeoveney (Middlesex). Another typical Neolithic monument was the cursus – a long, straight earthwork distinguished by two parallel banks and ditches – for which a ritual use is generally suggested. Part of a cursus has been identified running northwards across the western end of Heathrow (Hi); it was at least 3.6 km long, and there is probably a second one crossing it. Another long earthwork traced at Heathrow was probably a mortuary enclosure. The characteristic burial rite was inhumation beneath a long, gently wedge-shaped 'long barrow': this might contain galleries, chambers, or simple burials, of considerable variety, and was normally flanked by a ditch from which the mound had been excavated. Only the Queen's Butt, on Wimbledon Common (Me), is a serious candidate for a long barrow in London, and must, if genuine, have been altered in more recent times.

The main feature of the BRONZE AGE, c. 1800–600 B.C., was the introduction of metals, first copper and later bronze. The metals had to be imported, copper from Wales or Ireland and tin from Cornwall, and implements were made by casting in clay or stone moulds. Imports of metal objects bear witness to trade with the Continent, probably carried along the Thames. Flint and stone continued to be of importance, particularly for heavy agricultural tools for which bronze was unsuitable. Few settlement sites are known – e.g. Hayes Common (Bm), Upminster (Hv), and Heathrow and Harmondsworth (Hi) – but concentrations of finds indicate a similar pattern to that of the Neolithic. A group of stone hut circles once visible on Wimbledon Common may have been of this date. Bronze Age burials were placed beneath a round barrow, one of which has been excavated at Teddington (Ri); there are a number of other possibilities, notably the mound on Parliament Hill (Ca) and King Henry VIII Mount in Richmond Park. Later Bronze Age cremations, placed in a pottery urn, were sometimes buried in a stone chest beneath a barrow or inserted (like the secondary burial at Teddington) in an older barrow. The latest rite was to bury groups of urns together, and some evidence for such urnfields comes from Yiewsley (Hi), Acton (Ea), Kingsbury (Br),

Coombe (Ki), Upminster (Hv), Ilford (Re), and Ham Common (Ri).

Two features of the Bronze Age in the London area are of outstanding interest. One is the high number of Late Bronze Age smiths' hoards (broken implements, copper ingots) found along the edge of the North Downs; these indicate a major metalworking industry in the area, probably trading its goods over considerable distances. The second is the enormous quantity of Middle and Late Bronze Age metalwork recovered from the Thames, mainly in West London. This cannot at present be accounted for as debris from riverside settlements: although there are very likely to be unknown sites – notably in the area of Old England, Brentford (Ho) – much of this metalwork is likely to represent ritual or funerary offerings to the river deity.

The IRON AGE, c. 600 B.C.–A.D. 43, saw the introduction of iron, a metal more easily obtainable (e.g. from the Weald) and worked than bronze, and with wider uses. Another innovation, later in the period, was currency, in the form both of metal bars and of coinage. Continuing trade with the Continent is shown by imported goods, including fine wheel-made and kiln-fired pottery and Mediterranean luxury items such as wine and silverware. The most notable monuments of the period are its 'hill-forts' (not necessarily on hills), some at least of which were probably first constructed in the Late Bronze Age. They were enclosed in single or multiple bank and ditch defences, and vary widely in complexity and sophistication. The best surviving examples in Greater London are the two 'Caesar's Camps', at Keston (Bm) and Wimbledon (Me); more fragmentary ones are known at Enfield (Bush Hill), Carshalton (Su) (Queen Mary's Hospital), and Hadley Wood (Bn). Uphall Camp Ilford (Re) contains a number of round houses, rectangular buildings, including granaries, and internal enclosures. Settlement sites follow the pattern of preceding periods, with concentrations along the North Downs (e.g. Beddington, Su) and in the w (notably at Harmondsworth, Hi, and East Bedfont, Ho). The site of Heathrow Airport (Hi) included a temple, and there may also have been a shrine at Hounslow (Ho). Many settlements formerly classed as Iron Age have now been reassessed as Romano-British: the distinction is often difficult with small rural sites of the first centuries B.C./A.D., in the absence of distinctive pottery. To this group belong the sites at Charlton (Gr) and Old Malden (Ki), and a number in the Cray valley, as well as the only surviving ancient field system, on Farthing Down (Cr). As in the Bronze Age, there is a concentration of metalwork from the Thames in West London, and it includes some of the finest from Britain: the Battersea shield and the Waterloo helmet, both now in the British Museum, are among the best known pieces.

The ROMAN invasion of A.D. 43 and the founding of Londinium shortly afterwards affected the settlement pattern of the area considerably. A system of major roads radiating from the city to the military and civil centres of the province attracted new villages, and there is some evidence for activity in the areas of the London Clay, although the main ritual pattern continued to follow that of earlier periods. Apart from Londinium, there was an important suburb at Southwark, and there must have been a bridge across the

Thames on the approximate site of Old London Bridge. Southwark began as a settlement of small clay and timber buildings laid beside the road to the bridgehead, but was later occupied by more spacious stone buildings, including one beneath the cathedral. Another, with finely painted wall plaster and part of an inscription, lay on the site of Winchester Palace, Southwark, and may have had some official function. A well preserved wooden warehouse has also been found close to the Roman waterfront. There is evidence for at least two stone buildings at Westminster, including the abbey site. Large cemeteries lay outside these centres, notably in Bloomsbury (Ca) and Aldgate (*London 1*), and along the roads to the SE. Settlements include Brentford (Ho) on the Silchester road, Brockley Hill (Bn) (possibly the Sulloniacae named in the later Roman Antonine Itinerary) on the Verulamium (St Albans) road, Enfield and Edmonton (En) on the Lincoln road, Old Ford (TH) where the Colchester road crossed the Lea, and Crayford (Bx) (probably Noviomagus) on the Dover road, with further probable sites at Croydon on the Lewes road and Merton on the Chichester road. Settlements at Putney (Ww) and Fulham (HF) must have served a river crossing, and many smaller roads with farms and villages must have lain between the major routes; the most densely occupied areas seem to have been the Cray valley, the 'brick earths' to the W, and the edge of the Downs. There is not a great deal of evidence for villas, in the sense of large country houses with estates, but there is some, notably at Keston (Bm), Beddington (Su), Orpington (Bm), Wanstead (Re), and perhaps Leyton (WF). A large building in Greenwich Park has produced a number of fragmentary inscriptions, and was probably a temple of some importance. A late Roman signal station, consisting of a square stone tower within a ditched enclosure, has been excavated at Shadwell (TH); it was probably part of the coastal defence system of the C3 and C4. Another Late Roman military-style structure has been found at Uphall Camp Ilford (Re). Industrial activity is represented by two pottery sites, one at Brockley Hill (Bn) on a large scale, exporting its wares as far as the military sites in Scotland and Wales, and a more local one in Highgate Wood.

The earliest SAXON settlers (early C5 onwards) were probably mercenary soldier-farmers, and their sites ring London to the S, combining a reasonable closeness to the city with good agricultural land. No actual settlements are known, but cemeteries have been found at Mitcham (Me), Beddington (Su), Croydon (Cr), and Orpington (Bm). At the Battle of Crecganford (probably Crayford, Bx), of A.D. 457, described in the Anglo-Saxon Chronicle, the Britons, officially abandoned by the Roman authorities after A.D. 410, were defeated by the Saxons. Later (C6–7) pagan barrows can still be seen in Greenwich Park and on Farthing Down (Cr), and pagan settlements are also indicated in Middlesex by place-name evidence. The linear earthwork known as Grim's Ditch, which runs across the borough of Harrow, is probably Saxon, and may be a defence against invaders from the north.

TIMBER-FRAMED BUILDINGS

BY MALCOLM AIRS

Given the lack of suitable building stone and the comparatively late exploitation of local brick earths, the vernacular or minor domestic architecture of the Greater London area (of which a surprising amount survives) is predominantly timber-framed. The carpentry traditions are those of south-eastern England, so that there is no evidence for fully cruck-framed buildings; moreover the decorative possibilities provided by the timbers of the wall-framing are discreetly observed, and – with the notable exception of the late C 16 manor house at Southall (Ea) – there are none of the exuberant virtuoso displays characteristic of the western counties.

Apart from the handful of very early examples, the majority of surviving timber-framed buildings are comparatively modest in size and were built for the 'yeoman' class. The flimsier structures of their economic and social inferiors do not appear to have survived from before the C 17 at the earliest, and similarly, the houses of most of their superiors are mainly represented by post-medieval buildings of brick.*

As to CARPENTRY TECHNIQUES, it is generally within the roof space that vernacular buildings have been least altered, and it is possible to follow the development of roof trusses in Greater London from about 1300 onwards. The earliest type so far identified can be reconstructed from the much-altered large barn at Manor Farm, Ruislip (Hi). All the main timbers are of uniform scantling and it originally had passing-braces with minimally jowled principal uprights. Of about the same date was the sole example of semi-base cruck construction, at Moor Hall Harefield (Hi), destroyed by fire in 1922 but recorded at the time by Sir John Summerson and identified by S. E. Rigold in a paper published in 1965. Base crucks were an expensive and high-class device to clear the open hall of inconvenient aisle-posts, and an alternative method of achieving the same end can be seen at Headstone Manor House (Hw), where two massive parallel arch-braces rose from each principal post to support the tie-beam, which in turn supported the wall-plates in the position known as 'reversed assembly'.

*The dating of timber-framed buildings at a vernacular level is notoriously difficult and is more reliant on intuitive experience in the field than many investigators are prepared to admit. The relatively new scientific techniques of dendrochronology and radio-carbon dating have hardly been tested in the area and, consequently, it must be stressed that the dates that will be suggested are in many cases tentative and are largely based on theoretical concepts founded on the evolution of plan forms, roof trusses, and joinery details. Fortunately, the combined documentary and structural research carried out by the Historic Buildings Division of the Greater London Council in the late 1960s and early 1970s has established a corpus of firmly dated buildings to give greater evidence to such regional typological sequences than is often the case elsewhere.

Headstone, built shortly after 1344 as the principal Middlesex residence of the Archbishop of Canterbury, contains the earliest crown-post roof so far discovered in the region. By 1399 this roof form had filtered sufficiently down the social scale to be employed by New College, Oxford, when they built a chaplain's house at Hornchurch (Hv) (demolished in 1970 following a fire; part of the framework has been preserved in the Passmore Edwards Museum), and throughout the following century it was the most common roof truss at yeoman level. Examples abound throughout the region and
14 include East End Farm Cottage Pinner (Hw); the Cross Keys Dagenham (Bk); The Tudors and No. 33 Halfway Street Sidcup (Bx); and No. 161 Crofton Lane Orpington (Bm). In an urban context, crown-post roofs survive at No. 39 High Street Kingston (Ki) and the Church House in Romford Market Place (Hv), and a particularly majestic and plain version is preserved in the important barn attached to Upminster Hall (Hv).

The only form of longitudinal stability above wall-plate level in a crown-post roof was supplied by the central collar-plate, and the next step in the refinement of carpentry techniques, at least on the w and NW edges of the London area, seems to have been the transference of that strength to either side of the roof by means of side-purlins. Such a device was economical of timber and labour in that it was no longer necessary to provide collars for all the common rafters, yet at the same time it opened up a new area for decorative effect, with curving wind-braces rising from the principal rafters to triangulate and support the purlins. It first
13 appears at the great barn of 1427 at Manor Farm, Harmondsworth (Hi), which was built by carpenters imported from Winchester. The central post of each truss, devoid of its collar-plate, is here known as a lower king-strut, and the side-purlins are butted into the principal rafters (fig. 1). Although other examples exist in comparatively modest hall-houses in Edgware High Street (Hw), it was never widespread throughout the region, and the crown-post roof retained its popularity into the c 16.

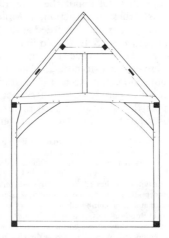

Fig. 1. Lower king-strut with through-purlins

The roof truss which superseded it and which was destined to remain the most common type until the disappearance of indigenous carpentry traditions in Greater London was the queen-strut roof with through-purlins clasped in the angles between the collar and the principal rafters. This was a logical development from the lower king-strut roof and, similarly, first seems to appear in one of the larger barns in Middlesex, which again could well have been constructed by carpenters who came from outside the county. The barn at Headstone Manor (Hw) was built before 1514 and has arch-braced tie-beams and queen-struts rising to the collars. It differed from the developed form of the truss only in the use of a double row of butt-purlins on each side of the roof. By the second half of the c16, through-purlins had become the adopted norm, and the dated examples include the modest three-bay barn at Smith's Farm Northolt (Ea) of 1595* and the curiously hybrid trusses at No. 2 Bickley Road Bromley (Bm), which are almost certainly contemporary with its brick gateway dated 1599. Queen-strut roofs were almost universal in the area in the c17 and c18 and examples are too numerous to mention individually. Towards the end of the tradition the queen-struts tended to be set at an angle rather than on a vertical plane, and dated examples include the barn at Orange Court, Downe (Bm), with much re-used medieval timber and joggled butt-purlins, of 1779, and the demolished barn of 1809 at Coldharbour Farm, Hayes (Hi). The introduction of softwood roof trusses with king-posts and straight raking braces joined by metal straps of the types familiar from such contemporary pattern books as William Salmon's *Palladio Londinensis* (1734), Peter Nicholson's *The Carpenter's New Guide* (1792), and Batty Langley's *The City and Country Builder's and Workman's Treasury of Designs* (1745), marked the beginning of the end for local craft traditions in roof carpentry.

The earliest surviving MEDIEVAL PLAN FORM in English vernacular achitecture is the aisled hall. A few examples are known from the Greater London area, albeit in a fairly fragmentary state. At the highest social level the form was already obsolete by the mid c14; thus the Archbishop of Canterbury's manor house at Headstone (Hw) was exploring ways of liberating the hall space from aisle-posts whilst incorporating conventional aisled construction in the closed trusses in *c.* 1345. Elucidation of the complete original form of this building awaits archaeological investigation, but the two-storeyed service wing aligned at right-angles to the hall and containing the entrance passage survives intact. At Hornchurch Chaplaincy (Hv) in 1399, at what might be termed 'gentry' level, the aisled hall was still a principal feature of the building. Here, only the cross-wing at the upper end of the hall survived, but there was sufficient structural evidence left to identify the aisled form of the hall trusses.

Neither of these two c14 houses was complete at the time of investigation, but by the c15 hall-houses survive in increasing numbers, and it is possible to categorize them according to their original form. Many are comparatively modest yeomen houses with

*Now taken down and re-erected at the Chiltern Open Air Museum, Chalfont St Giles, Bucks.

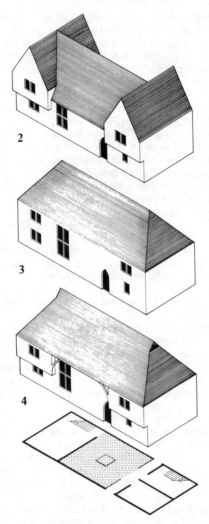

Figs. 2–4. Medieval house-types: hall with flanking cross wings;
unitary plan; Wealden type

two-bay halls and ancillary accommodation arranged in a variety
of ways. The grander examples, concentrated mainly in the E, have
a central hall flanked by two-storeyed wings roofed at right-angles
to the hall and with the upper storeys on the entrance front
invariably jettied (fig. 2). They include the Cross Keys public house
in Crown Street Dagenham (Bk); Great Tomkyns, Upminster (Hv);
Turpingtons, Southborough Lane, Southborough (Bm); The
Ancient House, Church Lane, Walthamstow (WF); and another
public house, the Spotted Dog, No. 212 Upton Lane, Forest Gate
(Ne). A slightly smaller variation on this theme was provided with
only a single cross-wing, as at No. 161 Crofton Lane Orpington

(Bm). But at the typically yeoman level, the accommodation of open hall, screens passage, service rooms, parlour, and two upper chambers were all neatly arranged under a single unitary roof in a form common throughout south-eastern England (fig. 3). Good examples can be seen in Sidcup (Bx) (The Tudors, with a hall of only one bay, and No. 33 Halfway Street), Pinner (Hw) (East End 14 Farm Cottage), and Harmondsworth (Hi) (the King William IV public house, Sipson Road). When the upper-storey 'wings' of the unitary hall-house were jettied, the centre of the building defining the hall inevitably gave the appearance of being recessed behind the common wall-plate; there are examples of this so-called 'Wealden' type both s (Nos. 1–4 Tudor Cottages, Foots Cray High Street, Bx) and N (The Old Cottage, Cowley Road, Cowley, Hi) of the river Thames (fig. 4). Other 'Wealdens' are known to have existed closer to the centre of London, as at the corner of Clayton Road and High Street, Peckham (Sk), pulled down in 1850, and it is possible that the origins of the design should be sought in the metropolis.

The declining importance of the open hall as the dominant and principal room in the house seems to have begun early in the c16. The initial impetus apparently came from a desire for a greater number of smaller rooms and, perhaps, a changing emphasis towards making better use of the upper storey, rather than from any great dissatisfaction with the smoke and inconvenience of the open hearth. Certainly, in a number of cases the first stage in modernizing an existing medieval house in conformity with the changed social circumstances of the c16 involved the flooring-over of only part of the hall and the retention of the open hearth in the remainder of the space. Usually, one bay was floored over to provide an extra upper-storey room and a gallery was contrived over the open bay, thus providing full circulation between all the first-floor rooms for the first time. The gallery and the new chamber over part of the hall were protected from the infiltration of smoke by partitions, thus effectively forming a smoke bay from the open hearth on the ground floor up into the rafters of the roof. The arrangement is best seen at East End Farm Cottage Pinner (Hw), where the partitions still survive for their full height and the upper part of the smoke bay has never been converted into a room. The obvious advantages of inserted brick chimneystacks to heat the house meant that the smoke bay was a fairly short-lived feature. However, innate conservatism ensured that new houses with smoke bays were being constructed as late as the end of the c16 (No. 20A Waxwell Lane Pinner, Hw), and at No. 161 Crofton Lane Orpington (Bm) the open hearth in the partially floored-over hall was not finally abandoned until 1671. Conversely, the continuous-jettied Whitehall at Cheam (Su) appears to have been built with a chimneystack as an integral part of the design as early as c. 1500.

Now for POST-MEDIEVAL PLANS. With the exception of Headstone Manor House (Hw), all the medieval hall-houses in the area were fully floored-over and had had chimneystacks inserted during the course of the c16 and c17. And, of course, the same domestic pressures which had led to such radical alterations of existing buildings had evolved brand-new house types in the same period. As with the converted medieval houses, the basic requirement was

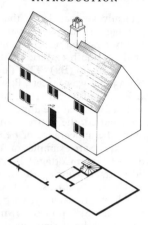

Fig. 5. Lobby entry

to devise a way of providing a larger number of more specialized rooms with ease of access to the upper storeys and greater comfort in the form of heated rooms with enclosed fireplaces. The devastatingly simple answer was to put all the new service functions in a narrow bay at the centre of the house, leaving the remainder of the rectangular structure free for uncluttered domestic use. With a large chimneystack of four flues placed in the centre of the building, it was possible to heat the rooms individually on either side and on both floors, while still leaving sufficient space in the same bay to accommodate a staircase winding round the back of the stack and a small, draught-free entrance lobby at the front of the stack (fig. 5).

These lobby-entry houses – a common post-medieval type throughout lowland England – are represented in the Greater London area in substantial numbers. In their larger form they are generally asymmetrical, with a single bay to one side of the entrance stack and two bays beyond, as at Sweetman's Hall Pinner (Hw). This meant that the rooms in the far bay were either unheated or required a separate chimneystack such as seems to be an original feature at No. 2 Bickley Road Bromley (Bm). This house can be dated to 1599, but it seems likely that the type had been established in the area for at least a generation before that. So effective was the concept that, particularly in its smaller two-bay symmetrical form with all the principal living rooms heated from a common stack, it remained a viable house design right down until the advent of central heating in the present century rendered its basic feature obsolete. Typical examples in Greater London include the three-bay vicarage in Crown Street Dagenham (Bk), dated 1665; the two-bay Maygoods Farm Cowley (Hi) of the early c 18; and the appealingly Gothick No. 25 Corkscrew Hill West Wickham (Bm) of about a hundred years later. Examples in the part of Surrey near London can be seen at Nos. 1 and 2 Church Road Cheam (incorporating the crown-post wing of an earlier structure) and at No. 210 Coulsdon Road Coulsdon (Cr).

Since the basic theme flourished over such a time-span, it is

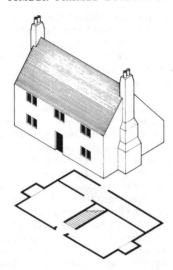

Fig. 6. Central entry with gable-end stacks and rear outshot

hardly surprising that there were a number of minor variations. Some of the early examples incorporated a porch with a small chamber above as an entrance feature, and by the late C 17 a lean-to scullery along the rear elevation had become an inevitable addition. Although the relationship between the axial chimneystack and the entrance was implicit in the definition of the design, the staircase was sometimes placed in front of the stack and opened directly onto the lobby, as at the Manor House in Manor Road Merton (Me); in other examples it was housed in a separate turret at the rear of the stack. Moreover, on a few occasions greater emphasis was placed on the principal ground-floor room by giving the bay that accommodated it the form of a cross-wing at right-angles to the remainder of the house, such as seems to have been the case at Nos. 33–35 Pinner High Street (Hw) and No. 226 Southborough Lane Southborough (Bm).

Of course, the lobby-entry plan was not the only house type that emerged in response to the changed domestic requirements of the post-medieval period, but none of the other types seems to me to have provided quite such a brilliantly simple response to the demand for draught-free warmth and comfort and first-floor bedrooms. Instead of an enclosed axial chimneystack generating radiant heat, the principal alternative plan had a chimneystack in each gable-end, similarly heating the four principal rooms, but with a certain amount of heat-loss through the outside walls and providing no structural support for the staircase (fig. 6). As a type, it seems to have evolved slightly later than the lobby-entrance house and was possibly inspired by a conscious desire for a fashionably symmetrical façade. At a time when brick was beginning to supersede timber, it had the advantage of integrating the stacks with the shell of the house. The staircase was invariably centrally placed in line with the entrance and was often of more generous proportions than the lobby-entry stair. Rear outshots, like that at Ashgrove Cottage,

Chevening Lane, Knockholt (Kent) (just outside our area), and staircase-turrets, as at Windmill Farm, Stites Hill Road, Coulsdon Common (Cr), were common refinements. Humbler examples, such as No. 164 Sidcup Hill Foots Cray (Bx) and the Ramblers Rest public house in Chislehurst (Bm), had only a single gable-end chimneystack, leaving the bay on the opposite side of the central entrance unheated.

In form, the single gable-end stack house is identical to the true peasant cottage, one and a half storeys in height, surviving from the C17 and C18 elsewhere in the country, but few of the London examples seem to be small enough to postulate a direct link. Instead, the study of the housing of the vast mass of the population needs to be directed towards the lightly framed and weatherboarded buildings which survive in increasing numbers from the late C17 onwards. They are found in most of the London boroughs and range in social stature from small, detached farmhouses, such as No. 5 Pike Lane Cranham, near Upminster (Hv) (with an interesting attached barn), through groups of semi-detached houses like those in Anglesea Road St Mary Cray (Bm), to the rows of humble terraces familiar in many of the outer suburbs. Some of them have aspirations of grandeur expressed by simple classical architectural detailing or the sham of a fashionable brick façade (Nos. 1–3 and 5–7 High Street Bexley and the imposing three-storeyed terrace dated 1737 at Nos. 4–8 Church Road, Foots Cray, Bx), but the majority are the genuine vernacular of the C18 and C19. They lie outside the hardwood carpentry traditions which have interested scholars over the past thirty years, but they are urgently in need of systematic investigation before their original arrangements irrevocably disappear under the heavy hand of the improver.

In a survey of this nature, it is only possible to draw attention briefly to the overall picture of timber-framing in Greater London. Limitations of space preclude any detailed analysis of the regional differences apparent in the areas N and S of the river or the effect of London itself as a source of innovation. Specialized aspects, such as the magnificent late medieval barns in what were Middlesex (Ruislip, Hi, Harmondsworth, Hi, Headstone, Hw) and Essex (Upminster, Hv), or the imposing inns on the roads out of London (for example the Golden Lion Romford, Hv, and the White Hart Edgware, Hw) can only be mentioned in passing, while recognition of the problems of interpretation attached to buildings like the long jettied row at Nos. 57–65 Stanmore Broadway (Hw) must be sought in the gazetteer.*

*I would like to acknowledge my debt to John Ashdown, who first taught me the importance of London's vernacular architecture; to J. T. Smith, who over the years has discussed a number of individual buildings with me; to Frank Kelsall, who has always been prepared to pass on his unrivalled knowledge of London's buildings; and to Anthony Quiney and Bob Weston, in whose stimulating company much of the fieldwork was carried out.

INDUSTRIAL ARCHAEOLOGY

BY MALCOLM TUCKER

For 1900 years, London owed its commercial pre-eminence to the tidal Thames bringing ocean-going ships forty miles inland. West London, however, is oriented to the inland arteries of transport – the Thames as a major river but crossed by bridges, the canals connecting to it, the railways and roads that radiate from the capital, and recently the international airport at Heathrow.

The RIVER THAMES had substantial traffic from early times. Yet the lower river, from Staines down to Putney, was wholly unimproved until the provision of towing paths, training works, and dredging in the 1770s, and the construction of locks and weirs from 1811. The river is now tidal below Teddington Weir, and the tidal range and scour have increased considerably since the removal of old London Bridge in 1832, affecting the character of the riverside villages. Salmon were netted in the Thames until the 1820s, when the river became too polluted. Wharves and industry spread upstream as far as Hammersmith and Fulham in the C19, but much has been redeveloped for housing since the 1960s. The eyots and backwaters provided sites for boatbuilding yards, particularly around Brentford, where the canal and railway systems met the river, but there is little activity now.

The increasing engineering and financial capabilities of the C18 and early C19 produced a remarkable flourish of bridges across the Thames, described in *London 2: South*. Timber decay, tidal scour, and increasing traffic have required the replacement of virtually all of them since the mid C19. The bridges which abut the area of the present volume include arched railway bridges of cast iron between Barnes and Chiswick (1846–9, disused) and wrought iron between Battersea and Chelsea (1861–3), two suspension bridges at Chelsea (Chelsea Bridge, 1934–7, and Albert Bridge, 1871–3) and one at Hammersmith (1883–7), and the handsome granite arches of Kew (1903). Away from the river, there is a unique wrought-iron arched bridge of 1790 across a lake at Syon Park.

CANALS arrived fairly late in the London area, and they were generally 'broad', to accommodate the smaller river barges. The Grand Junction Canal, connecting Brentford and Paddington to the Midlands, was opened in stages from 1796. The Regent's Canal (1812–20) is of special character, passing the inner suburbs of Westminster, Camden, and Islington, to link the Grand Junction Canal with the Docks. It has good tunnels and bridges, particularly Macclesfield Bridge in Regents Park (1816, on Doric columns). The Grand Junction has a fine roving bridge (1820) above Brentford, and the three-level Windmill Bridge (1859) above Hanwell locks. The Grosvenor Canal (1825) and the Kensington Canal

(1828) were relatively short-lived branches from the Thames. Water was scarce, and canal reservoirs were built at Aldenham (1795), Ruislip (c. 1810), and the Welsh Harp (1835, enlarged 1854).

Much industrial development was attracted to the canal banks in the later C 19 and early C 20, with arms and docks formerly abounding in the Hayes and Southall areas, notably Maypole Dock (Ea) of 1913. The Slough Arm (Hi) (1888) was the last significant canal built in southern England.

Steam-hauled RAILWAYS came to London in four phases – an early flurry in the 1830s with several trunk lines (see table), a period of consolidation in the 1840s and early 50s, a boom (especially s of the Thames) in the late 50s and 60s, and a culminating spread of suburban branches. Early stations remain on the London & South Western Railway's loop via Chiswick and Kew Bridge to Feltham, in Sir William Tite's simple classical style of 1849. *I. K. Brunel*'s Great Western Railway, the most heroic of the early lines, has the splendid and individualistic viaduct at Hanwell (1838), the iron-arched terminal station at Paddington (1854), and suburban stations from Hanwell (1877) onwards. *Robert Stephenson*'s London and Birmingham line (1837) made little architectural impact on the fields of Middlesex until the suburban period, when nice buildings were erected at Harrow and Wealdstone (1912), Hatch End (1911), and Stanmore L.N.W.R. (1890, demolished). The latecomer Great Central Railway chose Marylebone (1899) for its terracotta-faced London terminus and hotel. Extensive colonies of industrial

STEAM RAILWAYS IN LONDON TO 1840

Company	Principal Act of Parliament	First section completed	Line completed
London & Greenwich	1833	1836	1838
London & Birmingham	1833	1837	1838
London & Southampton	1834	1838	1840
Great Western	1835	1838	1841 (to Bristol)
London & Croydon	1835	1839	1839
Eastern Counties	1836	1839	1849 (to Norwich)
Northern & Eastern	1836	1840	1845 (to Cambridge)
London & Blackwall	1836	1840	1841 (Fenchurch St)
London & Brighton	1837	1841	1841
West London (Birmingham, Bristol & Thames Junction)	1836	1844	(Willesden to Kensington)
South Eastern	1836	(used the Greenwich/ Croydon/Brighton line into London)	

housing were built by the railways near their marshalling yards and depots at Willesden, Neasden, and Cricklewood (just over the Barnet boundary; *see London 4: North East*).

A parliamentary commission in 1846 decided that surface railways should not enter the central area, a policy slightly relaxed around 1860 when railways crossed the Thames from the s. The passenger termini therefore lie in a ring, linked by a circumferential UNDERGROUND RAILWAY at shallow depth (now called the Circle line) of which the first section, the Metropolitan from Paddington to Farringdon Street, opened in 1863. It was engineered by (Sir) *John Fowler*. The stations at Paddington (Praed Street), Bayswater, and Notting Hill Gate still carry parts of their overall roofs with wrought-iron arches, between the heavily buttressed retaining walls, while Baker Street and the two stations eastward are fully underground, with arcaded openings that formerly let the smoke out and the light in. It was mainly the early underground railway companies, the Metropolitan and the Metropolitan District, which expanded overground through Middlesex in the 1870s, their frequent train services facilitating suburban growth, and actually promoting it in the early C20, as 'Metroland'. Penetration of central London awaited the development of a rapid tunnelling method, deep in the London clay, and electric traction, and with these the core of the deep 'tube' network, of constricted loading gauge, was completed between 1890 and 1914. Between the World Wars, these lines in their turn were extended above ground to the extremities of North West London. Terracotta-clad surface buildings distinguished the Edwardian tube lines, notably those in ruby red by *Leslie Green* for the Underground group, which also used colourful tiles on the platform walls. Modernism was fostered by the Underground group, tentatively with *Charles Holden*'s work on the Morden extension in South London (1926) and demonstratively with his high clerestoried booking halls on the Piccadilly line extensions (1932 onwards). The London Passenger Transport Board* was established in 1933, and pursued these ideals beyond the Second World War. The ELECTRIC TRAMWAY systems, which finally closed down in 1952, may be remembered by the ornamental power station building of 1899–1901 at Chiswick High Road (it supplied trolley-buses till the early 1960s).

The Roman and medieval pattern of MAIN ROADS radiating W and NW towards Staines, Bath, Oxford, Aylesbury, and St Albans remained unaltered in the turnpike period, but the New Road of 1756, from Paddington to Islington and the City, was a very early bypass to the urban congestion of Holborn. The arterial roads programme of 1919–39 created the Great Chertsey Road, Great West Road, Western Avenue, and North Circular Road, narrowly in advance of the great building-over of Middlesex and attracting residential and industrial ribbon developments along their length. Their usually generous corridors permitted later widening to dual carriageways.

Aviation and AIRFIELDS have been prominent in Middlesex. Hendon (*London 4: North East*) started as a 200-acre public flying ground and manufacturing centre in 1911, Hanworth served air-

*London Transport Executive from 1948, after nationalization.

craft factories in the First World War, Heston opened in 1929 and
became a commercial airport from which a reinforced concrete
hangar remains, the wartime R.A.F. station at Northolt was used
by civilian traffic after the Second World War, and Heathrow
Airport was started in 1946. The first customs airport was a short-
lived airstrip at Hounslow Heath in 1919, superseded by Croydon
(*London 2: South*) in 1920.

Since the war, there have been some impressive motorway
viaducts, particularly Hammersmith flyover (1961) and the
Western Avenue extension (1970), and some modest extensions of
tube lines. Heathrow has expanded voraciously. But otherwise,
with Greater London largely built up, transport improvements
have not regained their former momentum.

In the provision of services, WATER SUPPLY was the earliest
concern. Conduits and wells served the urban area inadequately
until the New River was cut from Hertfordshire, a remarkable
endeavour of 1609–13 (*London 4: North East and East*). Early
private supplies included those to Hampton Court (Ri). The Duke
of Northumberland's River in Hounslow (early c16, for water
power) and the Longford River (1638, for ornamental waters at
Hampton Court, Ri) may also be noted. From 1581, an increasing
proportion of London's water was pumped mechanically from the
Thames; one of the earliest steam pumping stations (by *Savery*)
was erected in the Strand in 1712. Filtration was developed at the
Chelsea waterworks in 1826–9. In the c19 increasing river pollution
drove the water companies up-stream, e.g. to Kew Bridge, Brentford, in 1837. All abstraction from the tidal waters below Teddington Weir was forbidden by the Metropolis Water Act of 1852,
which also required filtration and the roofing of service reservoirs.
This and the rapid expansion of the supply network prompted
major new works in the 1850s and 1860s, particularly at Hampton
(Ri). Under the Metropolitan Water Board (established 1903) there
was further major investment, especially in south-west Middlesex,
as at Kempton Park. Major recent schemes have been the 19-mile-
long Thames–Lee Raw Water Tunnel (1955–61), and the similar
Tunnel Ring Main under construction from 1986 for treated water,
deep in the London Clay.

Waterworks ENGINE HOUSES are among the capital's most
notable industrial buildings. At Kew Bridge, staid sub-Georgian
of 1837 is followed by masculine Italianate of 1845. The manometer
tower there (1867) is unmatched in size, as is the largest of the
Cornish beam engines in the Kew steam museum. Kempton Park
has two giant triple-expansion steam engines of 1928. Cricklewood
of 1905 and later is representative of smaller stations on the trunk
distribution network.

The MAIN DRAINAGE works of the 1860s were the foremost
achievements of *Sir Joseph Bazalgette*, engineer of the Metropolitan
Board of Works created in 1855 after the public health crises of the
previous two decades. Interceptor sewers were dug from W to E to
discharge to the estuary via pumping stations well downstream of
London. To house the interceptor sewers along the shores of the
Thames, the Victoria, the Albert, and Chelsea EMBANKMENTS
were created. Relief sewers and storm pumping stations were added
by the L.C.C. in the early c20, while newly-built-over Middlesex

was drained to the large and advanced sewage treatment works at Mogden (Ho) (1931–5).

GASWORKS manufacturing from coal began in 1810 and thrived from the 1820s until 1970. Its masculine architecture of the C19 has mostly vanished; West London has an early gasholder (c. 1830) at Fulham, while others, more modern, are prominent landmarks.

ELECTRICITY supply started in 1878 in London, for the first electric-arc street lights, and grew rapidly in the 1890s. The prosperous West End districts were early customers for the electric light companies, such as the Grosvenor Gallery station of 1883 in Mayfair. The earliest building surviving is at Kensington Court (1886). On the much larger scale of the new century, the power station for electric traction remains at Lots Road Chelsea (1902–5). Combined heat and power plant was a feature of the enlarged Harrod's department store in Kensington of 1904. Kensington Court also had its own HYDRAULIC POWER station, for working the lifts in the mansion blocks. This function was more generally served in central areas from the extensive mains of the London Hydraulic Power Company, established in 1883 and closed down in 1977.*

Architectural evidence of former EXTRACTIVE INDUSTRIES includes chalk mines at Pinner, tile and pottery kilns preserved at Harrow Weald, North Kensington, and Fulham, and brick-kiln debris used decoratively for garden walls. More permanent have been products such as *Coade* stone, *Doulton* terracotta, general sanitary ware, and the ubiquitous pink or yellow London stock bricks. In parts of Middlesex, vast tracts of land were worked over during the C19 for brickmaking. Some workings were quickly built upon, others were filled with town refuse brought as return loads by canal barges or rail, and left derelict. But these also are now giving way to redevelopment, notably at Stockley Park.

Early industry in western Middlesex was on the medium-sized rivers, the Colne and the Crane, where there was WATER POWER. The distributaries of the Colne still abound in the sites of cornmills and later adaptations, as at West Drayton. The Duke of Northumberland's River was first cut in the mid C16 to divert these waters to mills at Isleworth, but along its course are the sites of the famous Hounslow gunpowder mills, at Bedfont and Whitton (Ri/Ho), with a few surviving wheelpits, machine bases, and blast mounds.

There were MALTINGS at Chiswick and Strand on the Green, their grain formerly brought downstream by barge. There is still a working BREWERY at Chiswick.

Industrial sites on the outskirts of C19 London were numerous and diverse. They were concentrated particularly near navigable waterways and railways and away from the desirable residential districts. FACTORIES were mostly characterized by plain stock-brick walls, iron window-frames, wooden floors, and slate roofs, with cast-iron columns and an increasing amount of other ironwork as the century wore on. Around the turn of the century there were some efforts to give factories more architectural treatment, often by the use of colourful engineering bricks or glazed bricks. The

*The grandest power station of all, Grove Road (Lodge Road) St John's Wood of 1902–4 by *Peach* and *Reilly*, has been demolished.

Monsted Margarine factory at Southall (1893 onwards) was particularly exuberant in its combination of Dutch and free Renaissance motifs, while *Voysey*'s extension to Sanderson's wallpaper
75 factory at Chiswick (1902) is an original application of a free style.

Interesting structural features are more commonly found in other
buildings. IRON ROOFS, originating in the early 1810s, were
applied where there was a risk of fire, and the unsophisticated
trusses of wrought-iron flats at Kew Bridge Waterworks (1837) are
an excellent example of this genre. More generally they were used
for long spans, and a fairly early iron roof covers the riding school
at Syon Park, next to *Charles Fowler*'s splendid conservatory of
1827–30.

The curvilinear GLASSHOUSE, with a web of thin metal glazing-
bars to maximize the sun's penetration, was developed by *J. C.
Loudon* in 1816 in a prototype at Bayswater, and one survives at
Nuffield Lodge, Regents Park (1823–4). The climax of this style
was achieved just outside the area of this volume at the Kew Palm
House (1844–8) (*London 2: South*). Rolled wrought-iron I-beams
were also used there for the first time in building. The Crystal
Palace of 1851 demonstrated the wholly rectilinear, multi-storey
iron framing recently developed in the naval dockyards, and the
principles of mass production. It was immediately followed by the
4 great wrought-iron arched train sheds, of which Paddington (1854)
is architecturally the finest. The roofs of the Albert Hall (1871) and
of Olympia (1886) deserve mention for their size.

At the end of the century, STEEL framed buildings were appearing. Harrod's department store in Kensington made extensive use
of structural steel from 1901 onwards, while the Ritz Hotel (1903–
6; *London: 1*) is accredited as the first in Britain not to depend on
stabilizing masonry for carrying some of the loads. CONCRETE,
made with lime mortar, had first been used in quantity in 1817 by
Sir Robert Smirke, for the foundations of the Millbank Penitentiary
(*London 1;* demolished). Fireproof floors of concrete on iron joists
appeared in the 1840s, and by the 1860s improvements in the
manufacture of Portland cement allowed concrete to be exposed
externally without facings of brick or stucco, in particular for the
first mass-concrete bridge in Britain, on *John Fowler*'s District
Railway, near Earls Court (1867, demolished 1873). REINFORCED
CONCRETE was used as early as 1899 for a railway warehouse at
Brentford Dock (demolished), but it gained ground slowly at first.
In inner London it was hampered by building regulations until
1916. The use of reinforced concrete permitted the stark external
exposure of the structural frame, as in the early part of the EMI
factory at Hayes (1912–14), now much altered. However, as with
polite buildings, factories of the early C20 often concealed their
reinforced concrete construction behind quite ambitious architectural frontages, as in the case of the Clement-Talbot motorworks
in Barlby Road North Kensington (1903), which has an urbane
stone-faced front, and the Piano Factory at Hayes (1909) and the
Ford Service building at Brook Green Hammersmith (1915–16),
both of which have decorative brick detailing. Flat slab construction
with mushroom column-heads, and the edge columns set back
behind uninterrupted bands of glass, was introduced from America
in 1927 at the Wrigley factory, Wembley, and used in 1931 at EMI.

The architects for these were *Wallis, Gilbert & Partners*, the leading exponents of the flamboyant art deco 'Great West Road Style', as at Firestone, Brentford (1928, demolished), Pyrene, Brentford, and Hoover, Perivale (1932). A more functional form of expression, 94 with arched frames and haunched cantilevers, was a hallmark of *Sir Owen Williams*, e.g. the interior of the Palace of Industry at the Wembley Exhibition (1924, demolished), the Arena at Wembley (1934, with a remarkable three-pin portal frame of 236 ft span), and the great BOAC maintenance hangars at Heathrow (1950–5).

The postwar period has been a disappointment in terms of industrial building and architecture. Until recently, the depletion of traditional manufacturing in the congested and expensive inner areas was encouraged by planning policies, while clean-air legislation helped to eliminate the factory chimneys which once dominated some eastern, down-wind parts of London. The biggest changes of the 1970s were the development of huge storage buildings and other facilities in West London to serve the expanding Heathrow Airport, which re-emphasized the relative decline of the other industrial areas of London.

FURTHER READING

There is no space to do more than provide some indication of the wealth of literature. The Greater London History Library has comprehensive, up-to-date indices arranged topographically and by subjects, for those who wish to delve further. Older books are listed in their published catalogue (*L.C.C. Members Library*, 1939). A more recent compilation, *The London Region, An Annotated Geographical Bibliography*, by P. Dolphin, E. Grant, and E. Lewis (1981), includes a section on historical patterns of growth and development and lists the public libraries holding local collections. The following notes concern general books: some of the most useful works on individual areas and buildings are listed at the end of each borough introduction.

On the Prehistoric and Roman periods the most useful recent books are N. Merriman, *Prehistoric London* (1991); R. Merrifield, *The Archaeology of London* (London, 1975); D. Collins *et al.*, *The Archaeology of the London Area: Current Knowledge and Problems* (Special Paper No. 1, London and Middlesex Archaeological Society) (London, 1976); *Time on our Side? A Survey of Archaeological Needs in Greater London* (Department of the Environment, Greater London Council, and Museum of London) (London, 1976); and R. Merrifield, *Roman London* (London, 1969). *The Archaeology of Surrey to 1540*, ed. J. Bird and D. G. Bird (Surrey Archaeological Society, 1987), covers the sw boroughs, with reference also to material beyond the Greater London boundary. Recent discoveries are reported in *The London Archaeologist*, published quarterly. The county journal is the *Transactions of the London and Middlesex Archaeological Society*. There are major collections of the archaeological material in the British Museum and the Museum of London.

The general background for much of Middlesex, including parts of the old L.C.C. area, is now provided by the *Victoria County History*. Vol. 1 (1969) is useful on ecclesiastical organization, vols. 11–1x (1962–89) deal with the development of individual parishes (*see* borough introductions for further details). For the areas outside the L.C.C. there is the still invaluable survey by Michael Robbins, *Middlesex* (1953), which has an excellent bibliography, and the same author's compilation on churches in vol. 18 (1955) of the *Transactions of the London and Middlesex Archaeological Society*. Older county books are D. Lysons, *Parishes of Middlesex* (1800), the *Little Guide* by J. B. Fish (1906), and M. J. Briggs, *Middlesex Old and New* (1934). *Memorials of Old Middlesex*, ed. J. Tavernor-Perry (1909), is especially useful for its chapters on churches and their furnishings (by Charles Cox and Aymer Vallance). On the same subject, J. Sperling's *Church Walks in Middlesex* (1849) is a valuable account by a critical ecclesiologist of buildings on the eve of Victorian restoration.

From the later C18 onwards topographical surveys and guides appeared which provide a mixture of historical notes and contemporary descriptions about the neighbourhood of London. The source used by many later guides was Daniel Lysons' invaluable *Environs of London* (1795). James Thorne's *Handbook to the Environs of London* (1876, reprinted 1970) is an especially comprehensive gazetteer to the area within twenty miles of London. His elegiac comments on the retreating countryside swallowed by the *Suburban Homes of London* contrasts with W. Clarke's amusingly enthusiastic eulogy of these in his book of that name (1881). The flavour of Middlesex at the turn of the century is given by such books as C. G. Harper's *Rural Nooks round London* (1907). The most useful recent guide is Ann Saunders, *Art and Architecture of London* (1984), which covers the whole of Greater London in a single volume.

Topographical illustrations up to 1850 are listed in the admirable survey by Bernard Adams, *London Illustrated, 1604–1851* (1983), while the maps that chart the expansion and development of London have been usefully catalogued by J. Howgego, *Printed Maps of London c. 1553–1850* (2nd ed., 1978) and R. Hyde, *Printed Maps of Victorian London 1851–1910* (1975). To bring them vividly to life one should look at the contemporary social investigations: Mayhew's *London Labour and the London Poor* (1851); Charles Booth's *Life and Labour of the People of London* (1902); and *The New Survey of London Life and Labour* (1934).

Among general histories, C. Trent's *Greater London, A History through 2000 Years* (1965) is a concise one-volume account. The two series published by Cassell and Secker & Warburg concentrate on central London, but the C19 volumes in both include much that is relevant to the suburbs: they are Francis Sheppard's *London 1808–1870, the Infernal Wen* (1971), and Priscilla Metcalf's *Victorian London* (1972). The architectural historian of the suburbs can also learn from contributions made by geographers and social and economic historians to the relatively new discipline of urban history. H. J. Dyos's pioneer investigation, *Victorian Suburb: A Study of the Growth of Camberwell* (1961), has had numerous progeny: see e.g. the *Studies in Greater London* edited by J. T.

Coppock and H. Prince (1964); D. A. Reeder, 'A Theatre of Suburbs, Some Patterns of Development in West London, 1801–1911', in *The Study of Urban History*, ed. H. J. Dyos (1968); F. M. L. Thompson (ed.), *The Rise of Suburbia* (1982); and on C 20 suburbs, Alan A. Jackson, *Semi-Detached London, Suburban Life and Transport, 1900–1939* (1979). On the political and administrative background the basic reference book is K. Young and P. Garside, *Metropolitan London, Politics and Urban Change 1837–1981* (1982).

Working-class housing is another subject where the interests of architectural, social and economic historians overlap. Among studies which must be mentioned are those by J. N. Tarn, especially *Five Per Cent Philanthropy* (1973), and the Peabody Donation Fund (*Victorian Studies*, 1966), and A. S. Wohl, *The Eternal Slum: Housing and Social Policy in Victorian London* (1977). The early role of the L.C.C. is admirably dealt with by S. Beattie in *A Revolution in London Housing, L.C.C. Housing Architects and their Work, 1893–1914* (1980) and the next phase of public housing by Mark Swenarton in *Homes Fit for Heroes* (1981). The story of the county council's housing efforts is carried on more summarily up to 1975 by the G.L.C.'s *Home Sweet Home* (1976), and by the contemporary records: the L.C.C.'s *Housing* (1928), *Housing 1928–30* (1931), *Housing ... 1945–9* (1949). *G.L.C. Architecture 1965–70* and *G.L.C. Architect's Reviews* (1974, 1975, 1976) also cover other types of building. For the county council's early schools see D. Gregory-Jones, 'The London Board Schools, E. R. Robson', in A. Service (ed.), *Edwardian Architecture; The Schools of the London School Board and the L.C.C. Education Department* (G.L.C. Department of Architecture and Civic Design, typescript); and for later ones as well, R. Ringshall *et al.*, *The Urban School* (The Greater London Council, 1983). On public works in Middlesex there is much less; a general account is C. W. Radcliffe, *Middlesex, the Jubilee of the County Council, 1889–1939* (1939).

For after the Second World War the essential background books are the planning documents: Forshaw and Abercrombie's clear and attractively illustrated *County of London Plan* (1943) and Abercrombie's complementary *Greater London Plan* (1944), which describe London as it was then, and the proposals for post-war reconstruction and decentralization. These formed the basis for the official *County Development Plan* of 1951. *The London Plan, First Review* (1960) summarized the uneven progress made in the first few years. The next stage comes with the formation of the G.L.C. in 1965, and the *Greater London Development Plan* (2 vols: *Statement* and *Report of Studies* 1969) and the numerous documents emanating from the lengthy inquiry that followed. More recent social and economic trends are considered briefly in *Changing London*, edited by Hugh Clout (1978).

On industrial archaeology the pioneer study was Ashdown, Bussell, and Carter's *Industrial Monuments of Greater London* (1969). *London's Industrial Heritage* by A. Wilson (1967) discusses selected items in greater detail. For general coverage of individual aspects see J. Dredge, *Thames Bridges* (1897), the London County Council's *Bridges* (1914), and Geoffrey Phillips, *Thames Crossings* (1981); parts of three regional volumes in the *Canals of the British*

Isles series and M. Denney, *London's Waterways* (1977); H.W. Dickinson, *Water Supply of Greater London* (1954), and publications of the former Metropolitan Water Board (1953, 1961, etc.); S. Everard, *History of the Gas Light and Coke Company* (1949) and the North Thames Gas Board's *Historical Index of Gas Works* (1957); Farries and Mason's *Windmills of Surrey and Inner London* (1966). P. G. Hall, *Industries of London since 1861* (1962), gives a geographical background to manufacturing. An important more specialized study is A. W. Skempton, 'Engineering in the Port of London, 1789–1808 and 1808–1834', *Transactions of the Newcomen Society*, 50 (1978–9) and 53 (1981–2). Much technical information can be found in the *Minutes of Proceedings of the Institution of Civil Engineers* and other contemporary publications; recent fieldwork is published by the Greater London Industrial Archaeology Society. Railway history, so significant for the development of outer London, is covered by T. C. Barker and M. R. Robbins, *A History of London Transport*, 2 vols (1963, 1974); H. P. White, *A Regional History of the Railways of Great Britain*, vol. 3, *Greater London* (2nd ed., 1971); A. Jackson, *London's Termini* (1969); and H. V. Borley, *Chronology of London Railways* (1982).

A list of specifically architectural publications can start with the Royal Commission on Historical Monuments, whose volumes on *Middlesex* (1937) and *West London* (1925) deal with buildings up to 1714. The latter can be supplemented by the publications of the Survey of London: early selective volumes on *Chelsea* (3 vols., 1909, 1913, 1921) and *Hammersmith* (1915), and the much more exhaustive ones on *Kensington* (4 vols., 1973–86). There are also early Survey of London monographs on Sandford Manor (HF), Swakeleys (Hi), and Crosby Place (KC). For buildings up to and including selected C 20 examples, one can consult the Department of the Environment's *Lists of Buildings of Historic and Architectural Interest* (*see* borough introductions). The main landmarks of architectural history, in which the London area is so rich, are of course included in the general histories of architecture, John Summerson's *Architecture in Britain 1530–1830* (revised 1991), *Victorian Architecture* by R. Dixon and S. Muthesius (1978), and *Edwardian Architecture* by A. Service (1977). Other essential tools are *The King's Works* (H.M.S.O., 1963 onwards) for Kensington Palace and other royal buildings; H. M. Colvin's *Biographical Dictionary of British Architects 1600–1840* (1978); Stuart Gray's *Edwardian Architecture, a Biographical Dictionary* (1985), excellently illustrated with London subjects; and the *Catalogues* of the Drawings Collection of the Royal Institute of British Architects. For contemporary accounts of C 19 buildings the *Illustrated London News*, *The Builder*, *Building News* (later the *Architect and Building News*), and *London* (later the *Municipal Journal*) are invaluable; for the C 20 the *Architectural Review*, the *Architects Journal*, *Official Architecture and Planning*, and the *London Architect* must also be mentioned. The publications of the London Topographical Society have much of interest on older buildings; the *London Journal* and *Country Life* also include articles on London architecture.

Two books on which this volume has leant heavily must be singled out: John Summerson's lucid account of *Georgian London*, which first appeared in 1945 (latest revised edition 1988), and

B. F. L. Clarke's *Parish Churches of London* (1966), which covers all Anglican churches in the old L.C.C. area. Research on individual periods and topics has multiplied fast in the last forty years, particularly on C 19 subjects; only a sample of relevant work can be indicated here (*see also* borough introductions). General books and articles on architectural history relevant for this and other *Buildings of England* volumes are listed in *The Buildings of England Further Reading, A Select Bibliography*, compiled by T. Blackshaw, B. Cherry and E. Williamson (1990). Recent illuminating studies concerned wholly or partly with buildings and monuments in the London suburbs include *Good and Proper Materials, The Fabric of London since the Great Fire* (London Topographical Soc. 40), ed. A. Saunders (1989); A. White, 'Westminster Abbey in the Early Seventeenth Century, A Power House of Ideas', *Church Monuments*, I V (1989); D. Cruikshank and N. Burton, *Life in the Georgian City* (1990); D. Cruikshank and P. Wyld, *London, The Art of Georgian Building* (1975); and M. Port, *600 New Churches, 1818–1856* (1961).

On C 19 building activity much has been published, although only in Kensington has the work of the speculative builders been investigated exhaustively (see the Survey of London volumes). For one particularly energetic and far-flung firm see David Prout, 'Willett Built', *Victorian Society Annual* (1989), 21–46. In addition there are John Summerson, *The London Building World of the 1860s* (1973); D. J. Olsen, *The Growth of Victorian London* (1976); Mark Girouard, *Victorian Pubs* (1975) and *Sweetness and Light, the Queen Anne Movement 1860–1900* (1977); John Summerson, 'The London Suburban Villa', *Architectural Review*, vol. 104 (August 1948) (reprinted 1990 in his collected essays, *The Unromantic Castle*); and S. Muthesius, *The English Terraced House* (1982). On other subjects there are Hugh Meller, *London Cemeteries* (1981); on theatres of 1900–1914 *Curtains!!!* (published by John Offord, Eastbourne, 1982) and on cinemas David Atwell, *Cathedrals of the Movies* (1980), both with comprehensive gazetteers.

Among monographs on architects and builders especially relevant for this volume are John Harris, *William Chambers* (1970), J. Summerson, *John Nash* (1980), Priscilla Metcalf, *James Knowles, Victorian Editor and Architect* (1980), Hermione Hobhouse, *Thomas Cubitt* (1971), Andrew Saint, *Richard Norman Shaw* (1976), A. P. Quiney, *John Loughborough Pearson* (1979), and A. Crawford, *C. R. Ashbee* (1985). Well illustrated London anthologies include G. Stamp and C. Amery's *Victorian Buildings of London 1837–1887: An Illustrated Guide* (1980), A. Service, *London 1900* (1979), and G. Stamp (ed.), *London 1900* (*Architectural Design*, vol. 48, nos. 5–6, 1978). David Dean, *The Thirties: Recalling the Architectural Scene* (1983), is relevant for many London buildings.

For the last fifty years an adequate synthesis is lacking. Contemporary periodicals and local authority plans and brochures remain the most useful sources. Lionel Esher's *A Broken Wave, the Rebuilding of England 1940–1980* (1981) has a chapter on London, and one building type is discussed by A. Saint: *Towards a Social Architecture, the Role of School Building in Post War England* (1987). Otherwise there are a number of brief guide books, one retrospective (*Battle of Styles: A Guide to Selected Buildings in the London Region of the 1914–39 Period,* R.I.B.A. London region, 1975), the others recording buildings of their time: Hugh Casson, *New Sights of London* (London Transport, 1938); Ian Nairn, *Modern Buildings in London* (London Transport, 1964); Charles McKean and Tom Jestico, *Guide to Modern Buildings in London 1965–75* (R.I.B.A., 1976). Finally, for those who do not want all this detail, this list should end by recommending two personal responses to London that have stood the test of time: S. E. Rasmussen's *London: The Unique City* (first published in 1934, revised in 1948) and *Nairn's London* by Ian Nairn (1966, revised 1988).

BRENT

INTRODUCTION

The river Brent which gives the borough its name cuts through the London Clay from NE to SW, a natural division between Willesden, mostly built up by the end of the C19, and the uplands of Wembley and Kingsbury, which became suburban only between the two world wars. The areas on either side of the river are therefore now quite distinct in architectural character, whereas before the C19 all was countryside scattered with small, remote settlements. The only important road was the Roman Watling Street along the W boundary.* The former metropolitan borough of Willesden began as a large medieval parish with several scattered settlements. Lanes and paths linked the church at Church End to farms and hamlets that later developed into the suburban centres of Harlesden, Brondesbury, Willesden Green, and Neasden. As late as 1881 the area could be described as 'a charming locality still, abounding in rural attractions' (Clarke's *Suburban Homes*), but between 1881 and 1901 the population grew from 27,000 to 115,000, and by 1931 it had reached 184,000, as the northern fringes of Neasden and Dollis Hill filled up with houses. By this time nearly all the older buildings had been swept away. The only pre-mid-C19 remains worth mention are the much restored medieval church isolated in the indifferent industrial area of Church End, Willesden; a timber-framed farmhouse stranded amidst factories near the North Circular Road at Dollis Hill; the outbuildings of a late Georgian house, The Grange (converted to a local history museum), marooned on

---

*Early settlement remains include some Palaeolithic finds, and a Bronze Age urn from Brent reservoir, perhaps indicating a nearby urnfield. There was probably a Roman building at Kingsbury, where Roman tile is incorporated in St Andrew's church.

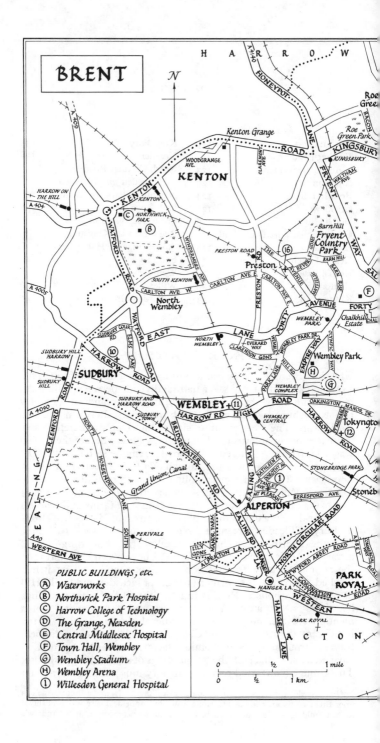

BRENT

N

PUBLIC BUILDINGS, etc.

(A) Waterworks
(B) Northwick Park Hospital
(C) Harrow College of Technology
(D) The Grange, Neasden
(E) Central Middlesex Hospital
(F) Town Hall, Wembley
(G) Wembley Stadium
(H) Wembley Arena
(I) Willesden General Hospital

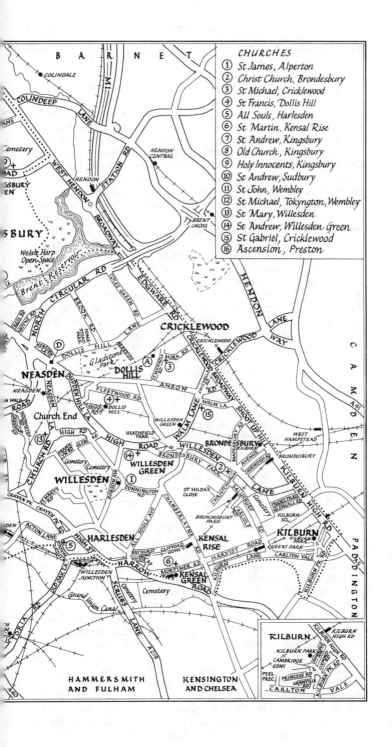

CHURCHES
1. St James, Alperton
2. Christ Church, Brondesbury
3. St Michael, Cricklewood
4. St Francis, Dollis Hill
5. All Souls, Harlesden
6. St Martin, Kensal Rise
7. St Andrew, Kingsbury
8. Old Church, Kingsbury
9. Holy Innocents, Kingsbury
10. St Andrew, Sudbury
11. St John, Wembley
12. St Michael, Tokyngton, Wembley
13. St Mary, Willesden
14. St Andrew, Willesden Green
15. St Gabriel, Cricklewood
16. Ascension, Preston

a roundabout at Neasden; and a pretty early C19 country villa, still thankfully in its own grounds (now Gladstone Park), at Dollis Hill.

Those intrigued by suburban development, however, will find plenty to interest them: elegant stucco terraces of the 1860s at Kilburn (slummy by the mid C20, remnants now rehabilitated), fragments of an exclusive suburb of villas of the 1870s at Stonebridge (Harlesden), the spacious avenues of Brondesbury (the large houses now giving way to flats) leading N to Willesden Green and Cricklewood, and, between these once sought after suburbs, the more monotonous lower-class districts of Harlesden, Willesden, and Kensal Rise. By the early C20 the main shopping centres were Kilburn High Road, Willesden Green, and Harlesden, all still today with minor late Victorian buildings of character. Harlesden also has the most distinguished church of these years, *Tarver*'s All Souls, on an octagonal plan. *Brooks*'s St Andrew Willesden Green is more conventional, but on an impressive scale inside, and with nicely grouped accompanying buildings. As landmarks, the façades of the many Nonconformist chapels (see e.g. Cricklewood) are often more effective than the incomplete, towerless Anglican churches. There is also a sprinkling of attractive little libraries (Willesden Green, Kilburn), the contribution of the Willesden Local Board (formed 1894), as well as large schools of the same period by *G. E. S. Laurence*, mostly variations on London School Board types, with striking silhouettes.

To the N and W of Willesden the architectural character is blander. Historically, Kingsbury was a small medieval parish, and Wembley a prosperous hamlet in the parish of Harrow. In 1934 they were united to form an urban district, along with a number of outlying hamlets (Alperton, Sudbury, Kenton) by then part of the outer suburbs. Amidst its maze of winding suburban roads, Kingsbury's tiny, simple C12 church remains beside its more spectacular replacement, a richly furnished High Victorian building moved here from Wells Street St Marylebone in 1934. Wembley lost its old character when it achieved fame as the site of the exhibition of 1924–5, and only a lodge and some fragments of a *Repton* landscape recall its once pleasant rural surroundings. The most memorable domestic C20 buildings are at Kingsbury: the simple but attractive First World War munitions housing at Roe Green, and, around Slough Lane, *E. G. Trobridge*'s wonderfully eccentric timber-framed houses and eclectic flats. The formal Wembley exhibition buildings represent an opposite, neo-classical tradition, paradoxically combined with the exploration of the new possibilities of concrete, demonstrated still more forcibly in *Sir Owen Williams*'s later Wembley Arena, and also by the earlier Wrigley factory. But for the most part architectural innovation was not encouraged in suburbs whose appeal lay in their association with a vanishing idyll of rural Middlesex, and their uneventful domesticity was disrupted between the wars by only a few notable buildings in a different idiom: the dignified, reticent group of the Guinness Brewery at Park Royal (by *Giles Gilbert Scott*), the austerely progressive Wembley Town Hall (by *Clifford Strange*), the folded concrete synagogue at Dollis Hill (*Sir Owen Williams*), and the underground stations at Sudbury Hill, Sudbury Town, and Alperton, among the first to be built in the clean-cut Scandinavian style pioneered by *Charles Holden*.

Since the mid C20, nothing of architectural consequence has been built in Brent. The council housing estates of the 1960s–70s include some of the least appealing examples of industrialized building; the commercial and industrial areas redeveloped from the 1970s (chiefly the Wembley exhibition area and stretches of the dismally traffic-beset North Circular Road) are slicker but inchoate. The population of the borough was 253,275 in 1981 – a decrease of over 40,000 since 1961.

FURTHER READING AND ACKNOWLEDGEMENTS

The area is well covered by the *Middlesex V.C.H.* vols. IV (Wembley), V (Kingsbury), and VII (Willesden). The *Willesden Survey* of 1949 is an exceptionally informative planning document. Useful local studies include I. R Dowse and R. Egan (eds.), *A Short Guide to the Parish Churches in the Rural Deanery of Brent* (Wembley History Society, 1970), G. Hewlett (ed.), *A History of Wembley* (1979), and K. J. Valentine, *Neasden, a Historical Study* (1989). On the work of E. G. Trobridge see the exhibition catalogue (Oxford Polytechnic) by G. P. Smith, *Ernest George Trobridge 1884–1942, Architect Extraordinary* (1982). The local history museum at The Grange, Neasden, has much useful material, including the plans deposited with the Willesden Urban District from the 1890s. I am especially grateful to Valerie Bott and to G. Hewlett, who provided much information and advice.

ALPERTON

A suburb which developed at the turn of the century from a hamlet on the road from Wembley to Ealing.

St James Church Centre, Stanley Avenue. On part of the site of a church of 1911 by *W. A. Pite*. 1990 by *Anthony Rouse* of *K. C. White & Partners*. Functional barn-shaped building of yellow brick with red brick trimmings, a big side entrance, and a slightly projecting gable to the road with a circular window. This lights the third of the building used for worship, and has stained glass by *Michael Coles*. Hidden immersion font; otherwise liturgically conventional, with raised altar at one end. Adjoining halls linked by folding doors.

Baptist Church, Ealing Road. In the style of its time, 1937. Brick, with concrete windows and a modish doorway with curved jambs.

Teachers' Centre, Ealing Road. 1877–8 by *Ernest George*. An early school put up by the Harrow School Board. A pioneering application of the Queen Anne style for rural schools. A pretty composition with details in the Shaw manner: end gables with decorative tile-hanging, and wooden oriels flanking the entrance. Extended with large *M.C.C.* additions, 1911.

HIGH SCHOOL, Stanley Avenue. 1922, built as Wembley County
   School on the site of Alperton Hall, the main house of the old
   hamlet. Yellow brick with pedimented centre, from the pre-
   modern phase of the *M.C.C.*
VICARS GREEN SCHOOL, Lily Gardens. An M.C.C. school of
   1938 by *Curtis* and *Burchett*, quadrangular, with asymmetrically
   placed entrance tower.
ALPERTON UNDERGROUND STATION, Ealing Road. By *Charles
   Holden*, 1933, one of the excellent group derived from Sudbury
   Town, Br (q.v.). Functional, yet not without elegance, they
   were among the first buildings to introduce the principles of
   contemporary continental design to Britain. The same motifs
   (metal-framed windows, projecting flat roofs) recur throughout
   the group, but every time subtly modified to suit the requirements of the particular site. Here the entrances are without the
   brick piers of Sudbury Town, and the booking hall is flanked by
   low wings with shops.
The best suburban buildings are near the junction of EALING
   ROAD and Stanley Avenue. At the corner, THE CHEQUERS, a
   big pub with steep tiled roof. STANLEY AVENUE starts with
   Nos. 1–3, humble Victorian brick cottages in polychrome brick,
   but continues with more ample and ornate suburban housing of
   the end of the century: Nos. 2–4 are a low pair with nicely detailed
   terracotta trim, others on the N side and along Ealing Road have
   pargetting and half-timbering. Later more modest streets (e.g.
   KATHLEEN AVENUE and DOROTHY AVENUE, named after
   the builder's daughters) stretch N towards Wembley.

BRONDESBURY

A generously laid out late Victorian suburb on the slopes above
Kilburn, much rebuilt, but still with a recognizable character.

CHRIST CHURCH with St Laurence, Willesden Lane and Christchurch Avenue. By G. G. Scott's pupil *Charles R. Baker King*,
   1866 with later additions: s aisle and s transept 1899, choir vestry
   1909. The stately Northamptonshire-Early-Gothic NE tower and
   spire make a good landmark. The tower now forms the entrance
   to the reduced church occupying the choir and transepts, remodelled in 1990 by *Aron Sloma* of *Integrated Design & Development;*
   the nave and aisles were divided into flats by *Ram Brand*. The
   domestication is discreet; apart from a few roof-lights, windows
   are within the original openings. The bonus is the cleaning and
   repair of the whole building, so that the crisp Dec and E.E.
   limestone detail stands out against gleaming white surfaces, ragstone externally, limewashed inside the E end. The T-shaped area
   used for the church was given a level floor and a simple gallery
   across the former chancel arch, allowing for maximum liturgical
   flexibility. Attractive C19 painted boarded ceiling to the
   chancel. – The only older furnishings retained are some STAINED
   GLASS windows: three tall lancets at the E end with medallions
   of the Life of Christ, 1867, of good quality, perhaps by *Lavers,
   Barraud & Westlake*, and a N window (miraculous draught of

fishes) of *c.*1950 by *Lilian Pocock* (in store at the time of writing). – Well organized ancillary rooms fitted into former organ chamber and vestries.

ST ANNE, Salusbury Road. 1904–5 by *J.E.K. & J.P. Cutts.* Predictable red brick, Dec, no tower. Long nave; bell-gable over the chancel. – (Small FONT of 1711 from West Meon, Hampshire. – Some C19 SEATING from St James Marylebone.)

SHREE SWAMINARAYAN TEMPLE, Willesden Lane. 1986–8 by *Ian Pattie Associates.* A rarity, a purpose built Hindu temple. A substantial building in brown brick with stone bands and colourful decoration of traditional Indian form. Three domed porches with filigree spandrels; roof with two domes and central spire with curved profile.

PADDINGTON CEMETERY, Willesden Lane. Ragstone chapels by *Thomas Little,* 1855, connected by carriage porches and central bellcote.

BRONDESBURY AND KILBURN HIGH SCHOOL, Salusbury Road. The main buildings were for the Maria Gray Training College (founded 1878, now at Isleworth, Ho), a tall, austere, gabled block of 1892 by *J. Osborne Smith,* an unusual combination of college with demonstration girls' school. Kindergarten on the ground floor, classrooms and hall on the first floor, with observation gallery and students' rooms above. The part of the school on the E side of Salusbury Road was built as the Kilburn Boys' School, a pleasant asymmetrical essay in the free style, by *G.B. Carvill,* 1899, rather in the manner of Champneys. Wide flat-hooded entrance up steps, flanked by a big roughcast gable on the l. and a powerful chimneystack on the r. N elevation with full-height bay-windows lighting the first-floor hall. To the S, extensions of 1927 in a plainer but sympathetic idiom. The Stone Hall at the corner of Carlisle Road is the former Brondesbury Synagogue, 1904 by *F.N. Marks.* W front on a grand scale, with twin copper-domed towers flanking three Moorish entrance arches. First-floor hall with gallery on iron columns; Moorish arches.

In KILBURN HIGH ROAD some simple late Georgian to early Victorian terrace houses remain, Nos. 261–267 and opposite Nos. 164 etc., including the SIR COLIN CAMPBELL. The heart of the Victorian suburb lay further W around WILLESDEN LANE, an old road winding gently uphill, but only a few large plain detached villas survive to the S of Christ Church. To the N the former VICARAGE (No. 173), a handsome, reticent gabled front of striped brick and stone. A few more Victorian villas of the 1860s onwards remain in BRONDESBURY PARK and CHRISTCHURCH AVENUE. MAPESBURY ROAD to the N, with gables and pargetting, is a good representative of the 1890s. Among the replacements of the 1970s the most appealing is JOHN BARKER COURT in Brondesbury Park near Christchurch Avenue, sheltered old people's housing by *Andrews Downie & Kelly,* 1978, a symmetrical composition to the road with passageway through to an informal courtyard. Attractive surfaces with much use of wood; boarded gables and balconies in a homely neo-vernacular mode. N of Christchurch Avenue two other developments worth a look (once one has passed the disappointing utilitarian parking area between them): ROSEDENE, low flats, simply detailed, with bands of plum-coloured brick, approached through intimate courtyards and surrounded by generous gardens buffered by garages; and ST HILDA'S CLOSE, a pedestrian enclave of houses with a more restless pattern of gables.

CRICKLEWOOD

An indeterminate district on the E fringe of the borough, mostly in Hendon (Bn); chiefly housing and light industry of the end of the C19 onwards. No trace now of the woods which gave the area its name, or of the farmland which replaced them in the C17 and C18. During the early C19 houses spread along the main road (now Cricklewood Broadway) near a farm at the junction with Cricklewood Lane. Extensive building started only after the arrival of the Metropolitan line in 1879, when leafy Edwardian streets began to spread W towards Willesden Green; the best houses are in the neighbourhood of St Gabriel.

ST GABRIEL, Walm Lane. 1896–7 by *W. Bassett Smith* and *R. P. Day*, W end completed 1902–3. Well sited, with a slightly Butterfieldian saddleback-topped W tower which makes the most of a bend in the road. The tower is the most original feature inside, doubling as a baptistery, with a lofty brick and stone vault divided from the nave by a very tall slender quatrefoil pier. The rest is standard Dec, buff limestone outside, red brick within, with stone columns. Five-bay nave, generous chancel, apsed Lady Chapel to the N. – Rich fittings: huge carved REREDOS with painted wings, by *Coates Carter*, c. 1912, contemporary with the E window by *Powell* of *Whitefriars*. – In the Lady Chapel another REREDOS, also by *Carter*. – STAINED GLASS. In the apse lancets small scenes of the life of the Virgin of c. 1897–1907. – Large window over the NE door by *Kempe & Co.*, 1919: Crucifixion. – N aisle third from E by *M. Travers*, 1927: Carrying of the Cross, in a crisp, clear drawing style. – Fourth from E by *Osmund Caine*, 1951, in a style verging on caricature.

ST MICHAEL, Mora Road. 1909–10 by *J. S. Alder*. Future uncertain. Tucked away in a curious backwater by the waterworks. Impressive stone exterior in Alder's conventional rather fussy Dec, with a polygonal bay for the baptistery projecting at the W end. The intended tower was not built. The interior, well lit by fine large E and W windows with Dec tracery, is also of stone, with quatrefoil piers and clerestory. – Elaborate, well-crafted WOODWORK, mostly of between the wars, wholly traditional: carved REREDOS with Transfiguration and Gothic canopy-work; carved STALLS, 1910; SCREEN 1928, delicately Dec, LECTERN 1929, both by *F. E. Howard*. – STAINED GLASS. A notable E window, a lively scene of the Blessed in Paradise, much purple and pink.

91 BAPTIST CHAPEL, Anson Road. 1907–8 by *Arthur Keen*, a grand Baroque front, an unusual style for a Baptist church. Red brick and stone. Broad doorway within a rusticated surround, with a

window in a pedimented aedicule above. Large brick campanile
at the side, ending in four gables.

MOSQUE AND ISLAMIC CENTRE, Chichele Road. A former Congregational church, 1901–2 by *Walter Wallis*. Ambitious orange
terracotta façade in free Gothic, with two towers; schools in the
basement below.

MORA ROAD SCHOOL. A good group of 1905 by *G.E.S.
Laurence*, in his later style. Shaped and scrolled gables with very
red terracotta trim (cf. Chamberlayne Wood, Kensal Rise, Br),
but with infants and juniors in separate buildings in place of the
densely packed three-deckers of the previous decade.

WATERWORKS, W of St Michael's Road. A handsome group built
for the New River Company in 1901–5. Large stock brick Italianate tower and PUMPING STATION, tall arched windows with
stone keystones, and a projecting porch with heavy corbels. Later
red brick buildings for the Metropolitan Waterworks 1909–12.

DOLLIS HILL

Rising land N of Willesden Green, still pleasant countryside in the
C19, now largely inter-war suburbia with patches of public housing,
enclosed on the N by a dismally indifferent array of industry and
offices along the North Circular Road. Gladstone Park is a welcome
respite to the C20 monotony.

DOLLIS HILL HOUSE, Gladstone Park, is a modest Regency
house built in 1825 by the Finch family, stock brick, two storeys,
with stucco porch. In the later C19 it was occupied by the Earl
of Aberdeen and much visited by Gladstone; his name was given
to the grounds which became a public park in 1901. Nos. 112–
114 DOLLIS HILL LANE, two cottages of *c.* 1860, were built
for the Earl of Aberdeen's servants.

MONUMENT, Gladstone Park, to victims of concentration camps.
Five figures on a platform, by *Kotis, c.* 1968.

A few of the buildings for the new suburbs are worth seeking out.

ST FRANCIS, Fleetwood Road. 1933 by *J. Harold Gibbons*. Buff
brick with pantiled roofs, simply but carefully detailed, with
round-headed entrance and circular W window, inspired by the
lower church at Assisi. Low central tower, transepts, and,
unusually for this date, a central altar beneath the crossing. –
STAINED GLASS. E window 1933 by *M.E. Aldrich Rope*.

ST MARY AND ST ANDREW (R.C.), Dollis Hill Lane. Italianate,
of brick, with a strong pedimental gable. Basilican interior;
arcades with green marble columns, barrel-vault and apse. Presbytery dated 1911.

MAHARASHTA MANDAL LONDON, No. 306 Dollis Hill Lane.
Built as ST PAUL, 1939 by *N.F. Cachemaille-Day*. An austere,
fortress-like brown brick W front high above the road, with a
stone cross against slit windows, approached up a formal flight
of steps. They lead to N and S porches within the ends of the
aisles. Airy whitewashed concrete interior with broad flat-headed
arches with rounded corners and small rectangular clerestory

windows. No medieval detail, although the concrete net vault on
angular piers (the intermediate ribs springing from above the
arches) has general late Gothic affinities (cf. the architect's contemporary St Barnabas Gloucester), so that the effect is less
revolutionary in spirit than his earlier St Saviour Eltham (Gr).
Large E window, a grid of small panes with thick centre mullion,
the contemporary STAINED GLASS, a stylized Te Deum in bright
colours with much red, designed by *Cachemaille-Day*.

SYNAGOGUE, Gladstone Park. 1937–8 by *Sir Owen Williams*.
Uncompromisingly modern, an early example of reinforced concrete used in folded slabs. Zigzagging side walls, hexagonal and
shield-shaped windows in two tiers punched starkly into the flat
surfaces. Cantilevered galleries inside, panelled later.

SCHWEPPES INTERNATIONAL, Brook Road. Dominating the
hill-top, a large neo-Georgian range with thin Swedish turret,
1933 by *A. R. Myers*, originally for the Post Office.

HOMESTEAD PARK, N of Dollis Hill Lane, 1926 by *W. E. Sandars*,
is the one out-of-the-ordinary development in suburban housing:
Y-shaped clusters with shared service cores, a progressive idea
expressed in entirely traditional picturesque form.

Finally, one older survival, a rarity in Brent; OXGATE FARM,
Coles Green Road, just S of the North Circular Road amidst
industry. Two timber-framed storeyed ranges, now rendered,
with gables to the road. The C16 N part may be a fragment of a
larger building. Ground-floor room with unusually elaborate
double-hollow-chamfered beams and brought-in panelling; a
smaller room to its W. Roof of collar-beam–queen-strut type, of
three bays plus a puzzling half-bay at the W end. The two E bays
have regular wind-braces below the purlins. The S part of the
house is unusual in being built parallel with the older building,
thus creating a primitive double-pile plan. It has the two-room
lobby-entrance plan typical of the C17, with the entrance on the
S, in line with the central brick stack. Windows all altered.

HARLESDEN

In the later C19 the old settlement was transformed (population of
All Souls parish 2,390 in 1881, 9,929 in 1891) into a flourishing
commuter suburb served by Willesden Junction (opened in 1866)
and Harlesden Green on the North London line. From this era of
dramatic change a lively variety of buildings remains in and around
the High Street. NW from this centre C20 council building has
largely replaced the suburbs that developed from the mid C19 at
Stonebridge, near the railway line.

ALL SOULS, Station Road and High Street. A remarkable building
of 1875–6 by *E. J. Tarver*, an architect of greater interest than is
usually recognized. The church is a large brick octagon – a plan
associated more often at this date with Nonconformist churches.
The three-bay nave, extended to five in 1890, was demolished in
1978 (the screen wall behind the car park is part of the aisle
wall). Exterior as well as plan derive from the Rhineland late
Romanesque, not then a common source. Sanctuary with canted

apse, with a dwarf gallery flanked by two turrets, the windows a mixture of round and pointed forms. The centre is stressed only by a conical little open iron lantern. The interior is still more exceptional: indeed the exciting timber construction of its roof 88 is worth a special visit. There are no internal supports; the huge tie-beams meet in a centre star supported by arched braces springing from corbels. The beams are clasped by pairs of straight braces bearing the lantern. – Low brass SANCTUARY RAILS project into the centre space. – FONT COVER. A small traceried spire. – STATIONS OF THE CROSS. Naturalistic low reliefs against mosaic. – STAINED GLASS. Much of the 1880s, especially good the pictorial panels set in quarries with coloured borders in C13 style. – E windows of 1900: Crucifixion, Nativity, and Resurrection beneath Renaissance canopies. – Contemporary VICARAGE.

ST MATTHEW, St Mary's Road. 1900–6 by *W. D. Caröe*; one of his numerous suburban churches. The usual long red brick exterior; stepped buttresses and two small shingled spirelets over the porch are the memorable details. Standard Caröe features inside: a broad and spacious nave with passage aisles; panelled piers supporting wooden transverse arches which effectively articulate the ceiled wagon roof. White plastered walls contrast sharply with red brick arches. – Notable FONT and PULPIT of 1901: conventional Perp detail, but applied to curvaceous and tapering art nouveau shapes. – SCULPTURE. Oak figure of St Matthew, about 75 cm. high, late medieval, with generously draped robes. Allegedly from Glastonbury; given in the 1930s. – STAINED GLASS. Tiny N aisle windows with prophets, 1904 etc.

ST MICHAEL AND ALL ANGELS, Hillside, Stonebridge Park. By *Goldie & Child,* nave 1890–1, chancel 1894. Unexciting exterior of red brick, lancet style, with Dec windows to the aisles. – (STAINED GLASS. Two lights with St Faith and St Michael by *Morris & Co.*)

FIVE PRECIOUS WOUNDS (R.C.), Brentfield Road. 1967. A large, blocky building of small red bricks neatly laid, with a few brutalist touches of the 1960s (projecting beam ends over the church hall below). Plain campanile over the entrance. – Narrow windows with abstract STAINED GLASS.

OUR LADY OF WILLESDEN (R.C.), Acton Lane. 1930–1 by *W. C. Mangan.* Massive steep-roofed Early-Christian–Romanesque brick basilica, the W entrance within a giant arch, a meagre campanile over the SE porch. Whitewashed interior, an impressive, huge, chilly, aisleless space divided only by broad concrete transverse arches. Clerestory with small lancets. Sanctuary with much marble, austerely detailed.

BAPTIST CHURCH, Acton Lane. 1890. The usual quite effective mixture of E.E. and Dec, the W wall with a rose window, a tower with spire on the side.

ST MARGARET AND ST GEORGE (United Reformed and Moravian), Craven Park Road. Built as a Presbyterian church in 1876 by *Thomas Arnold,* enlarged in 1884. Brick, Dec, with transepts and polygonal E end. An eclectic mixture: spherical triangles in the clerestory, domestic timber porch.

CROWN COURT, No. 41 Craven Park Road. 1880. Projecting bays, quite pretty Tudor detail.

MAGISTRATES COURT, St Mary's Road. 1899 by *H. T. Wakelam* of the Middlesex County Council. Routine free Tudor.

POLICE STATION, Craven Park. 1911–13. Impressive in scale, a successful hybrid of mid C17 domestic forms: brick mullioned windows, gabled dormers, and a steep hipped roof.

TELEPHONE EXCHANGE, Station Road. Large, in a competent, quiet neo-Georgian of 1938, with extensions of 1968 onwards. The antithesis of the crowded classical and Arts and Crafts frontages of the little SORTING OFFICE opposite (1887 and Edwardian).

LIBRARY, Craven Park Road. 1893 by *John Cash*. Very plain. One large and two small shaped gables.

THE SHRINE COMMUNITY CENTRE, St Mary's Road. Fussy Queen Anne of 1893.

COMMUNITY ARTS WORKSHOP, Harrow Road (corner of Victor Road). A former Primitive Methodist school, 1897 by *Howdill & Howdill* of Leeds. A charming little Flemish Baroque gable to the road, a porch on either side.

BOARD SCHOOLS. STONEBRIDGE SCHOOL, Hillside, of 1898, is one of *G. E. S. Laurence*'s nicely detailed three-deckers; scrolly gables with arched windows and polygonal excrescences (cf. Kensal Green, Br). His later (much altered) DOG LANE SCHOOL, Brentfield Road, 1907, is on a large site and to a more spreading plan: two storeys only.

BRENT VIADUCT. 1838 by *Robert Stephenson* for the London and Birmingham Railway, carrying the main line from Euston, originally over the Brent valley, now also over the North Circular Road. Large central arch, smaller side arches; E side widened.

The pivot of Victorian Harlesden is the junction of Station Road and the HIGH STREET, marked by the JUBILEE CLOCK of 1887, a pretty little affair on an iron column, now without its lamps, and too spindly to dominate the traffic that flows round it. The run-down shopping parades of the 1890s extend E to the ROYAL OAK with its stumpy turret at the corner of Park Parade, 1891 by *Tinker & Morewood* (some interiors with mosaics), and further on along the High Street to where the GREEN MAN is set back from the road, a decisive composition of 1908, designed, together with the shops on the l., by *Harrison & Ward*. Ground floor with a series of sturdy depressed arches and a rather Dutch skyline with alternating shaped and crowstepped gables.

S from the clock, beyond All Souls, STATION ROAD, with the WILLESDEN JUNCTION near the stations, a big-boned, debased Italianate pub of *c.* 1870, with some terraces of the same date, in a dismal semi-industrial setting. To the NW the HIGH STREET follows the line of the old Harrow Road. The most eye-catching buildings are the frontages of FUTTERS, a former pub of the turn of the century, and further on (in CRAVEN PARK ROAD) the ROYAL BANK OF SCOTLAND at the corner of St Mary's Road, built as the National Bank in 1882, only one storey, but with a sumptuous classical corner entrance.

W of the shopping centre the remains of select late Victorian neighbourhoods. In CRAVEN PARK, whose southern stretch was laid

out in 1855 as a short cut to the winding Harrow Road, from No.
15 onwards a few villas of the 1870s–80s (stock brick, Gothic
detail) and later (tile-hanging). STONEBRIDGE PARK was a more
ambitious venture by *H. E. Kendall Jun.,* laid out *c.* 1876, when
it was advertised as 'three miles from Victoria Gate, Hyde Park',
and conveniently served by a direct railway line to the City
(station now closed). From it remain only two houses (Conservative Club and Services Rendered Club), both much altered
but once very handsome – capacious, rustic Italianate villas with
belvedere towers – and a hotel, the STONEBRIDGE PARK, Hillside, with two shallow Italianate gables and a covered balcony as a
decorative centrepiece. The rest of Stonebridge is now straggling
council housing, ranging from the sub-Georgian pre-war cottages of FAWOOD AVENUE to the horrifically ugly industrialized
buildings of the 1960s, towers and lower linked slabs in grey and
brown concrete (first phase completed 1967).

To the N there is yet more PUBLIC HOUSING. The BRENTFIELD
ESTATE, around Conduit Way and the North Circular Road, was
Willesden's first council housing, 1919 onwards by the council
engineer *F. Wilkinson.* Its roughcast cottages in groups of four,
laid out in the Parker & Unwin manner, are now sadly compromised by the widened North Circular. N of the bypass, around
BESANT WAY, *Brent's* ST RAPHAEL'S ESTATE of the 1960s,
away from the traffic, but less enticingly planned: three- and
four-storey brick terraces with access galleries canted out from
the upper floors. In DORMAN WALK more intimate yellow brick
houses of the 1970s.

NORTH CIRCULAR ROAD. Opened in 1921. Along the Stonebridge stretch office buildings began to replace factories in the
1970s. The best is the group by the junction with the M1
(SPERRY-UNIVAC), two elegantly curving slabs of tinted glass
with a central link, 1973–5 by *R. Seifert & Partners.* For the
North Circular Road *see also* Neasden (Br).

KENSAL GREEN

Kensal Green lies on Brent's southern boundary, beside the railway
line. The most rewarding monument, the cemetery, is in North
Kensington (KC), and the C19 church of St John built for Kensal
New Town is in Paddington (Wm outer). The chief reminder of
the pre-suburban hamlet which grew up after the enclosure of
the green in 1823 is an early C19 domestic group along HARROW
ROAD, facing the cemetery wall: the humble Nos. 822–834 date
from 1822–4. No. 842, a detached villa, was built after the
cemetery. The second terrace, with stucco trim, marks the transition to more metropolitan tastes. The GEORGIAN HOUSE
dated 1922 is a surprise in this setting: self-conscious period
revival of a type more at home in the later parts of Hampstead
Garden Suburb.

KENSAL GREEN STATION, further W, is a neat little neo-vernacular shed of 1975–9 by *James Wyatt* in trim contrast to its
drab surroundings of railwayside industry, among which a few

former houses can be spotted: a simple terrace of 1864, and a badly mauled villa (No. 703) with *Coade* stone keystone.

KENSAL GREEN SCHOOL, Harvist Road. 1896–8 by *G. E. S. Laurence*. A huge three-decker, with romantically battlemented stair-turrets projecting from the ends of the wings as its special feature.

KENSAL RISE

An unremarkable, respectable late Victorian suburb, covering the slopes above Kensal Green, developed on land belonging to All Souls College Oxford. CLIFFORD GARDENS of the 1890s, near the station, is a little out of the ordinary: gables decorated with pictorial scenes.

ST MARK, Bathurst Gardens and All Souls Avenue. 1914 by *J. S. Alder*, in his usual competent but dull Dec; the w end was finished off only in 1968, a bleakly utilitarian red brick façade by *Riley & Glanfield*, with long rectangular windows. – (PULPIT, FONT, and LECTERN from St Olave Whitechapel.)

ST MARTIN, Mortimer Road. 1899 by *J. E. K. & J. P. Cutts*. The usual long nave of red brick, with lancets, the intended tower over the porch never completed. Built as a memorial to C. J. Vaughan, headmaster of Harrow, † 1897, who is commemorated by a bronze relief. – (STAINED GLASS. E window by *Henry Payne*, 1910. – S aisle and W windows by *Payne* and assistants, *c.* 1910–30.)

CHURCH OF THE TRANSFIGURATION (R.C.), Chamberlayne Road. Built as a Wesleyan church by *W. G. Morley* of Bradford, 1899. Robust Dec, brick and stone, with tower and spire on one side. Contemporary schools next door, now the Methodist church.

LIBRARY, Bathurst Gardens. 1899–1900 by *Done Hunter & Co.* of Cricklewood, extended 1903–4. An attractive mixture of Baroque and Tudor.

CHAMBERLAYNE WOOD SCHOOL, Chamberlayne Road. 1902–4, one of the best of *G. E. S. Laurence*'s many schools for the Willesden School Board. Splendidly pompous in every detail, from the symmetrical yellow terracotta-trimmed three-storey front with shaped gables down to the self-important lettering of the lower adjuncts, the 'caretaker's residence' and the building for 'manual instruction'.

KENTON

Partly in the borough of Harrow (q.v.). Once a small settlement along Kenton Road.

ALL SAINTS, Claremont Avenue. 1963 by *J. E. Sterret & B. D. Kaye*; steeply pitched roof and detached campanile.

ANNUNCIATION, Windermere Avenue, South Kenton. 1961 by

Riley & Glanfield. – (WALL PAINTING and STAINED GLASS by *John Hayward.*)

KENTON GRANGE. A cottage orné built (as Kenton Lodge) for John Lambert in 1803–7 on the S side of Kenton Green, extended between 1865 and 1896. Staircase and much interior woodwork of *c.* 1914; also a brought-in C17 fireplace surround. Now an old people's home. Picturesque later C19 STABLES with clock tower (now Parks Department Depot); two LODGES of *c.* 1900 in WOODGRANGE AVENUE (formerly the main road).

NORTHWICK PARK HOSPITAL, Watford Road. By *Llewelyn-Davies & Weeks.* A large and prominent landmark of the 1960s onwards, including a clinical research centre, built on open land E of Harrow School playing fields. Main wards of seven to eight storeys surrounded by lower buildings.

CENTRAL LONDON POLYTECHNIC (built as Harrow College of Technology), Watford Road, immediately N of the hospital. By the *M.C.C.* (*Whitfield Lewis* in succession to *C. G. Stillman*), 1959–61. The main building is an eight-storey slab of classrooms, in a clearly expressed concrete egg-crate frame, the regular pattern broken at the back by the projecting window of the photographic studio. One-storey workshops with powerful half-barrel-vaults and north lights.

KILBURN

The SE edge of the borough, around Kilburn High Road, the N continuation of Maida Vale. The most important monument, the church of St Augustine, lies just over the border in Paddington (Wm outer), the most historic site, that of the medieval nunnery of Kilburn (founded 1139 in place of an earlier hermitage), lay near Kilburn High Road Station on the Camden side of the borough boundary. That leaves very little to single out here; the S end of the down-at-heel shopping street retains no reminiscences of the spa that existed in the C18, the mid Victorian residential areas have mostly been replaced by council flats.

WEST KILBURN BAPTIST CHURCH, Kilburn Lane. 1865. Handsome semi-classical front with pedimented gable broken into by an arched recess framing two tiers of round-headed windows. (Good cast-iron galleries inside.) Minor alterations (new vestry, lobby, and classroom) 1896 by *J. Wallis Chapman.*

TELEPHONE HOUSE, Shoot Up Hill. A large five-storey T-shaped building by *Eric Bedford* of the Ministry of Works, 1953. Cautious official recognition of the modern movement is marked by the off-centre porch within a tapering frame, the back wing on stilts, and the contrast between the vertically linked windows in a framed panel and the large expanses of plain walling of small bricks.

KILBURN LIBRARY, Salusbury Road. 1894 by *Edmeston & Gabriel,* enlarged in 1908. One of the attractive small libraries put up by the new Willesden U.D.C. Brick and stone stripes, a canted bay rising to a turret, Baroque porch, and pargetted gable with the motto 'Knowledge is Power'. Originally part of a little civic group, next to contemporary local board offices and police station.

KILBURN POLYTECHNIC. Established in 1896 in the buildings of St Lawrence's Institute (1891 by *Arthur Lett*). The oldest surviving part in Glengall Road is of 1902–4 by *H. T. Wakelam* of the *M.C.C.* Brick and terracotta stripes with a gable on the l. and a tower over the entrance porch. Backing on to it in Priory Park Road an inter-war extension, vertical windows between fancy modernistic brick piers, and an equally dated post-war addition of the 1950s, with a flamboyant angular hooded basement window. Further extension 1970.

BOARD SCHOOLS. Characteristic examples of massive three-deckers, both by *G. E. S. Laurence* and both somewhat altered, are SALUSBURY Junior Mixed and Infant School, Salusbury Road, 1901, symmetrical gables with round-headed windows, and CARLTON VALE (now Carlton Centre), 1911, plainer, with a small central bell-turret. Carlton Vale was for girls and infants only, with a laundry centre in the big hipped roof.

ST AUGUSTINE'S SCHOOL. *See* Paddington (Wm outer).

The most rewarding residential area is around OXFORD ROAD and CAMBRIDGE AVENUE and the stretch of High Road between them, the relics of a respectable neighbourhood created by the builder-developer *James Bailey* on the Ecclesiastical Commissioners' estate from 1857 until 1866, when he went bankrupt. Brick and stucco terraces and pairs, their special features enriched arched first-floor windows. The two roads lead to the wedge shape at CAMBRIDGE GARDENS (now deprived of its focal point, St John, 1871 by *Francis*), from where the more modest PRINCESS ROAD (rehabilitated 1982) leads E to PEEL PRECINCT. This touch of post-war new town utopia by Willesden borough council is the only executed part of an ambitious slum clearance scheme (see *The Willesden Survey*, 1949). The centre is a pedestrian shopping parade, a low terrace with Festival trappings (cylindrical advertisement hoardings in the continental manner), surrounded by tall slabs of flats in windswept public gardens.

KILBURN HIGH ROAD's post-war innovation is KILBURN SQUARE, council housing in towers (first stage completed 1964), with a two-level shopping precinct facing the main road, sleekly faced with unbonded tiles (1967–71 by *Ardin & Brookes*). Its success could be gauged by the state of the outdoor escalator at one end, disused and moss-grown by the 1980s. The perennial survivals in this vigorously Irish part of north London are the numerous turn-of-the-century pubs, several still with a rich display of engraved glass screens, coloured tiles, etc. Examples are the COCK, 1899–1900 by *Bird & Walters*, with massive Baroque portal; the EARL DERBY, the earlier type of *c.* 1870, with much notched brickwork and sgraffito lintels; the NORTH LONDON TAVERN (Cavendish Road corner), with stained glass of railway engines; and further N (on the Camden side) the BLACK LION (1898) with corner turret and especially well-preserved interior. For the N end of Kilburn High Road *see* Brondesbury (Br).

CINEMAS are the other special feature of this area. The GAUMONT (former Kilburn State) in Kilburn High Road, 1937, is *George Coles*'s last major work, a monumental corner piece to Willesden Lane in cream and black faience, with a tower. Lavish Renaissance interiors, the foyer still complete; the auditorium (planned to seat 4,000) was altered in 1960 but has been refurbished since, and is used for bingo at the time of writing. The organ survives. Opposite, the former GRANGE CINEMA, with domed corner entrance and a good foyer, by *E. A. Stone*, 1914. In total contrast is the TRICYCLE THEATRE, an intimate scaffolded auditorium built within an older hall by *Tim Foster*, 1980, and reconstructed after a fire in 1987, with minor alterations to increase seating.

KINGSBURY

Uneventful hilly early C20 suburbia stretches N from the Brent reservoir by the North Circular Road, enveloping a tiny ancient church, the sole relic of an old hamlet, and various scattered settlements: Roe Green, Slough Lane, and Kingsbury Green on Kingsbury Road, the last important enough in the later C19 to have its own church. The area had developed sufficiently to become an urban district in 1900; it was combined with Wembley in 1934. The most rapid growth took place between the wars (population 1,856 in 1921, 16,636 in 1931). Kingsbury and Queensbury Stations opened in 1932 and 1934.

ALL SAINTS, Waltham Avenue. 1954 by *Romilly B. Craze*; brick.

HOLY INNOCENTS, Kingsbury Road, Kingsbury Green. By *Butterfield*, 1883–4, decidedly a minor work, with only a small polygonal W turret. Stock brick with coloured patterns. The interior is plastered with occasional tile effects. Chancel screen of timber with a tiled reredos, 'quaint and characteristic, though ugly enough', according to Goodhart-Rendel. Narthex, N aisle, and vestries added in 1957.

ST ANDREW, Church Lane. The OLD CHURCH in Old Church Lane (now disused and maintained by Wembley History Society), secret in its overgrown churchyard, consists of a simple rectangle, its rubble construction unappealingly roughcast, with a wooden bell-turret of rustic Middlesex type (rebuilt 1870). Much re-used Roman material (tiles and hypocaust flues). W quoins similar to long and short work, but more likely C12 than Saxon. S door, some way from the W end, of simple C12 type, uncovered in 1888 and much restored; a single order with chamfered hoodmould. Small C13 priest's door; Perp E window. The 1888 restoration was by *Newman & Newman*. The church has the oldest bell in Middlesex, dating from 1349.

   The present church stands proudly on a prominent site adjoining the old churchyard. For reasons unconnected with Kingsbury it is of greater historical note than the medieval church: originally erected in 1847 in Wells Street, St Marylebone (outer Wm), by *S. W. Daukes & Hamilton*, it became famous as a centre of early Victorian Anglo-Catholicism. The vicar from 1862 to 1885,

Benjamin Webb, was co-founder of the Cambridge Camden Society and editor of *The Ecclesiologist*, and he it was who was largely responsible for involving so many leading artists and architects of the Anglo-Catholic movement in the improvement of the interior. The church was re-erected at Kingsbury in 1934 by *W. A. Forsyth*, complete with its furnishings, as part of the drive to make use of redundant urban churches in the new suburbs – an interesting proof of the respect still felt then for such interiors.

The building is one of the first to deserve the description neo-Gothic; it is solid, knowledgeable, and a little stodgy, with nothing left of the thinness of the Commissioners' style. The Perp front, with substantial NW tower and spire, is big and earnest, the interior spacious with five tall Perp arches, clerestory, and aisles. The interior arrangements were an ingenious solution to the problems posed by the awkward Marylebone site. All the same, the *Ecclesiologist* objected because the style was Perp, and Eastlake, in his *Gothic Revival* of 1872, still found 'the selection of so late a type of Gothic a mistake'. The very shallow sanctuary and the absence of a proper chancel are also still in the tradition of the early C19. After Benjamin Webb became vicar, steps were taken to rectify these failings. The sanctuary was enclosed by a low CHANCEL SCREEN, extending one bay into the nave, a delicate piece of ironwork by *Street*, who was also responsible for the very original openwork metal PULPIT. The space was further defined by a painted CEILING with square panels with angels. Behind the ALTAR (by *Pugin*), a sumptuous REREDOS was added, also designed by *Street*, in memory of Webb's brother, with an alabaster Crucifixion by Webb's protégé *H. Redfern*, and with three tiers of carved figures extending upward to embrace the E window. The sanctuary arcading and SEDILIA by *Pearson* were added later as a memorial to Benjamin Webb. The monument in the S aisle to Webb's predecessor John Murray † 1862 is more boldly detailed, as one would expect from its designer, *William Burges*: a cusped niche embellished with vigorous animal stops and hefty crockets, containing a recumbent effigy (by *W. Nicholl*), all painted. Beneath the tower the BAPTISTERY, with wooden fan-vault. The octagonal FONT of coloured marbles with foliage panels is by *Street*, 1878 (replacing an earlier font by Pugin), enclosed by good railings, and surmounted by an elaborate pinnacled wooden FONT COVER by *Pearson* (after 1885). WALL PAINTING of the Baptism of Christ by *Clayton & Bell*. The GALLERY, now confined to the W end, formerly (in pre-ecclesiological fashion) ran round three sides of the church. It is decorated with delicate paintings of saints by *Alfred Bell*. The handsome two-sided brass LECTERN was made for Murray in 1847 by *Butterfield*.* BRASS to V. Knox † 1852 with medievalizing figure. Green and white marble TILES by *Farmer & Brindley*. The STAINED GLASS in the E windows by *Goddard & Gibbs* replaces Hardman glass designed by Pugin destroyed in the Second World War. By *Clayton & Bell* the NW

*The LITANY DESK by *William Burges* (1867) is now in the Victoria and Albert Museum. The church also possesses some notable altar plate by *Burges*, and a missal designed by the architect *Birch*.

and SW windows of 1868 and 1877, especially charming in their chaste design and reticent colouring; the W window, of the Te Deum, has a more vivid display of reds.

(ST SEBASTIAN AND ST PANCRAS (R.C.), Hay Lane. Begun in 1926, completed in 1959 by *T. G. Birchall Scott*. – In the Sacred Heart Chapel, STATUES by *Michael Clark*. – STAINED GLASS by *Theodore Kern*.)

SYNAGOGUE, Kingsbury Green. By *David Stern & Partners*, 1965–8. Polygonal, with central roof-light and exposed brick walls.

KINGSBURY HIGH SCHOOL (annexe), Bacon Lane. Typical neat post-war work by the *M.C.C.* under *C. G. Stillman, c.* 1955.

BRENT RESERVOIR. Created in 1835 by *William Hoof* for the Grand Junction Canal (enlarged 1854), partly in Barnet.

SLOUGH LANE is memorable for the best collection of the eccentric houses of *E. G. Trobridge* (1884–1942), who used the vernacular idiom of the Arts and Crafts tradition not just for picturesque old-world effect (although that is how the houses may first strike the spectator) but with a gritty determination to demonstrate his Swedenborgian belief in symbolism. Hence the exaggerated emphasis on the sheltering roof, the focal hearth, and the entrances. The houses were all designed for individual clients and were built of green elm, the method of construction patented by Trobridge, designed for mass construction and to combat shortage of building materials. Roofs are tiled or thatched, and the standardized metal windows have leaded lights. The best examples are the irregular group of Nos. 152 of 1921, 154 (Midcot) of 1928, and 156 (Hayland) of 1921 (built for the architect's father-in-law and later lived in by Trobridge himself). Also by Trobridge are Nos. 134, 142, and 148, all of *c.* 1921. N of Kingsbury Road in BUCK LANE is another group: Nos. 3–5, *c.* 1926 (especially good), and Nos. 43 and 45, *c.* 1929–30. Here also are several groups of highly peculiar Trobridge flats of 1934–7, of brick and stone, for by then his patent system of construction was no longer economical, and he decided to experiment in brick and stone. TUDOR GATES (1934) has twisted chimneys; ROCHESTER COURT (1935) stone facings inspired by Rochester Castle; WHITECASTLE MANSIONS (1935) and STONEGATE COURT and HIGHFORT COURT (both 1936) are all fancifully crenellated with chimneys disguised as turrets, and 'drawbridge' entrances. Other examples, in a parody of mock Tudor, are MONTAIRE COURT (1935–8), in HIGHFIELD AVENUE, and ASH TREE DELL. Further N some more of his houses in STAG LANE (Nos. 345–351, 1922–4).

FERNDENE in Slough Lane is housing association flats of 1965 by *Clifford Wearden & Associates*, a small-scale version of the intricate housing-above-cars scheme popular with architects in the 1960s, in the typical, rather forbidding dark brick and concrete of the period. On the entrance side the upper deck is approached by a grand flight of steps and a prominent concrete ramp; the garden side is pleasantly informal, with stepping-back balconies.

In ROE GREEN PARK, KINGSBURY MANOR, a picturesque half-timbered affair with tall chimneys, 1899 by *W. West Neve*, a pupil of Norman Shaw, for the Dowager Duchess of Sutherland. The former COACH HOUSE (Kingsbury Veterans Club) was used in 1928 for pioneering television work by John Logie Baird (foundations of masts remain).

ROE GREEN VILLAGE, Stag Lane. Built in 1917–19 by *Frank Baines,* principal architect of the *Office of Works,* to house munitions workers at the Aircraft Manufacturing Company's factory at The Hyde (Bn). The scheme continued the 'virtuoso-picturesque' mode established at Well Hall Eltham (Gr) in 1915, albeit in a rather more restrained manner. 250 dwellings, planned at garden-suburb densities (about eleven to the acre) and laid out around the village green. Forty per cent were not houses but 'cottage flats', built in two-storey blocks resembling ordinary cottages in appearance, but economizing on circulation spaces and staircases (one staircase to four flats).*

In KINGSBURY ROAD, opposite Holy Innocents, the former premises of HARRY NEALE, a progressive 1930s factory by *Brian O'Rorke.*

NEASDEN

N of Willesden, not fully built up until between the wars, sliced through by the North Circular Road of 1921 and by the underpasses beneath it created in the 1970s. *Private Eye* did it less than justice in singling it out as the archetypal undistinguished suburb, for it has a little more of interest than some of its neighbours.

ST CATHERINE, Dudden Hill Lane. 1916 by *J. S. Alder,* Dec, with a dreary W front of 1954 by *E. B. Glanfield.*

THE GRANGE (local history museum), Neasden Lane. Former outbuildings of The Grove (demolished), unhappily stranded on a roundabout just S of the North Circular Road. A picturesque two-storey rambling composition, rendered, with Gothic sash-windows. The details date from 1806–17, when the buildings were converted to a house for James Hall. Interior entirely remodelled in 1975.

WICKHAM SCHOOL, Aboyne Road. 1930 by *F. W. Wilkinson.* Tidy minimal Georgian, pantile roofs, Baroque doorway, around courtyards. Front repaired and SW wing added in 1949 (*G. F. Rowe*).

DUDDENHILL SCHOOLS (now part of Kilburn Polytechnic), Dudden Hill Lane and Cooper Road. *See* Willesden.

The earlier housing includes two very modest sets of railway workers' cottages of the turn of the century: for the Great Central Railway, 1899 by *A. R. Stenning,* in WOODHEYES ROAD and GRESHAM ROAD (S of the North Circular Road), each house only one window wide; and, more regularly laid out by the Metropolitan Railway in 1882 and 1904, QUAINTON STREET, VERNEY STREET and AYLESBURY STREET, a neat little enclave off the N end of Neasden Lane.

The NORTH CIRCULAR ROAD (*see also* Harlesden, Br) attracted

*This entry is by Mark Swenarton.

bypass factories between the wars, though none with the panache of those along the Great West Road (*see* Brentford, Ho). The much altered survivors are now interspersed with taller, more forceful buildings of the 1960s on (*see also* Harlesden, Br). The herald of the new style was RADIATION HOUSE, a thirteen-storey tower of reinforced concrete, 1960 by *Dennis E. Pugh* (consultants *Yorke, Rosenberg & Mardall*). Its original appearance, with emphatic white bands between continuous windows, was transformed in 1989 by shrieking yellow trimmings for the Swedish furniture firm Ikea. Its vast retail warehouse behind is one among many which demonstrate the trend towards out-of-town shopping that developed during the 1980s. Other prestige office blocks were also short-lived: in PRESS ROAD, the neat slab-and-podium group (also with white bands) built for the Oxford University Press, 1965 by *Searle, Row & Smith*, was converted to a hostel in 1985, with additional family housing in a domestic idiom, by the *Borough of Brent*.

PARK ROYAL

Park Royal owes its name to the Royal Agricultural Society's short-lived efforts of 1901–5 to establish a permanent site for its annual show between the canal and the railway line at East Twyford. The name was taken over for the larger industrial estate which grew up at Twyford between the wars, spilling over the Ealing boundary. Architecturally it is largely mediocre, although ambitious plans for rebuilding are under discussion at the time of writing.

GUINNESS BREWERY, Coronation Road. The one distinguished contribution to the area, set off by a generous sports ground in front of the main buildings. A good design by *Sir Giles Gilbert Scott* (consultant architect) with *Sir Alexander Gibb & Partners* (consultant engineers), 1933–5. Careful brickwork, with decorative brick cornices as the only ornament – a restrained approach, comparable to his treatment of Battersea power station (Ww), in direct contrast with the exuberance of contemporary bypass Art Deco. Along James's Way, N of Coronation Road, the impressive array of large, rectangular buildings of different sizes consists of (from S to N) malt store, brewhouse, storehouse, central offices, and storage vat house; and behind these the larger racking and cleansing shed. All are part of the original design, and survive little altered in front (top floor of the brewhouse converted from a hop store to offices, with a new row of windows; central offices with penthouse of 1959). At the back there are more extensive additions, including the E part of the racking and cleansing shed of the late 1950s and other rear extensions mostly of the 1970s by *John Laing Design Associates*. To the N the group has been extended by the north block (*John Laing Design Associates*, 1969) and club (*C. W. Hutton*, 1960).

In COMMERCIAL WAY, off Abbey Road, a cul-de-sac of WARE-HOUSES of *c.* 1980 makes a cheerful splash in the dull neighbourhood: colourful paintwork and some circular and arched windows to add variety; landscaped parking areas.

CENTRAL MIDDLESEX HOSPITAL, Acton Lane. 1900–3 by *A. Saxon Snell*. Future uncertain. Built as the Willesden workhouse infirmary, a spreading, symmetrical composition with plain ward blocks linked by quite pretty free Jacobean detail. The effect is spoilt by clumsy C20 yellow brick extensions. Additions of 1908 (further wards and dining hall) and 1914 (separate buildings for old people and infants by *Saxon Snell*, and children's homes by *John Cash*).

TWYFORD ABBEY and WEST TWYFORD. *See* Twyford (Ea).

PARK ROYAL STATION. *See* Ealing (Ea).

SUDBURY

Once a hamlet within the parish of Harrow. Developed at the turn of the century, an outlier of the more affluent area of Sudbury Hill, Hw (q.v.).

ST ANDREW, Harrow Road. 1925–6 by *W. Charles Waymouth*, a late and rather awkwardly detailed example of free Gothic. Brick arches dying into stone piers; no tower.

CHURCH HALL, behind St Andrew. Built as a mission church, 1904–5 by *Arnold Mitchell*, who did much work in Harrow at this time. An attractive Arts and Crafts exterior, with a large tiled roof sweeping down over little domestic windows, and a stumpy bell-turret in the centre – an idiom comparable to Norman Shaw's at St Michael Bedford Park Chiswick (Ho). – STAINED GLASS. An angel with flaming sword, over the entrance, designed and given by *Mitchell*.

ST GEORGE (R.C.), Harrow Road. 1926 by *Leonard Williams*, completed by *J. Eustace Salisbury*. Traditional Perp, grey brick and stone. – Iron GATES from a former house on the site.

SUDBURY SCHOOL, Watford Road. The original part is *Ernest George*'s second school for the Harrow School Board, 1879–80 (cf. Alperton, Br). Two simple brick gables to the road; much extended.

SUDBURY AND HARROW ROAD STATION. 1905. Original weather-boarded buildings.

SUDBURY TOWN STATION, Station Approach. At the end of the line when built. By *Charles Holden*, 1930–1, the prototype for his later Piccadilly line stations at neighbouring Alperton (q.v.) and Sudbury Hill (*see* below) and those on the Cockfosters extension in Enfield and Haringey. It was inspired by the modern buildings seen by Holden and Frank Pick of London Transport when they visited Scandinavia. The tall, rectangular brick ticket hall, of elemental simplicity, is capped by a flat concrete roof with projecting eaves, and the spacious, airy interior is lit by long metal-framed windows. Cantilevered platform canopies. A footbridge of exposed concrete over the tracks. An outstanding example of how satisfying such unpretentious buildings can be, purely through the use of careful details and good proportions. The similar booking hall on the W side of the tracks is now disused.

SUDBURY HILL STATION, Greenford Road, of 1932, derives its elements from Sudbury Town but combines them differently – see the variations in canopies and fenestration.

BARHAM PARK, Harrow Road. Within the public park, terracotta terrace balustrading and a pergola remain from the demolished Victorian mansion of the local benefactor Titus Barham (of Express Dairies); also some red brick garden walls and gates from the time of its C18 predecessor, Crabs House, part of which survives as the PUBLIC LIBRARY.

Along HARROW ROAD a few pre-suburban brick cottages of c. 1820, Nos. 971–977, with a carriage arch through, and the BLACK HORSE, altered, but still recognizable as a country inn. To the N, in ELMS LANE, a rare survival, an early C16 brick building of unknown function which survived as a farm outbuilding. Two storeys, three-light arched windows, with straight moulded hoodmoulds, all the details in brick. Three windows on the ground floor with two (later?) doors in between, two windows above. At the back, windows on the first floor only. A five-light window in the end gable. The farmhouse is a neat brick villa of c. 1840, with a hipped roof with overhanging eaves. Further on, in SUDBURY COURT ROAD, a modest C18 pair, Nos. 96–98.

WEMBLEY

Wembley was until the C20 a hamlet on the main road to Harrow, with open countryside to the N. 'As quiet and retired at seven miles distance [from London] as if it could have been seventy,' said Repton in 1795, when he was planning improvements for Sir Richard Page of Wembley Park. The village centre lay on Wembley Hill, around the High Street at the SW corner of the green, but was much rebuilt c. 1880. It was the British Empire Exhibition of 1924–5 that made Wembley famous. Between the wars, unremarkable respectable suburban housing covered the areas to the N, merging with the expanded older settlements of Kingsbury and Kenton, Br (qq.v.). The main buildings of interest are in the neighbourhoods of the three Wembley stations: Wembley Central serves the architecturally indifferent shopping centre along the High Road and Harrow Road; Wembley Park and Wembley Stadium lie to the N and s of the site of the exhibition centre.

ASCENSION, The Avenue, Preston. 1957 by J. Harold Gibbons. Well sited at an angle to the road. Carefully detailed in Gibbons's pre-war manner: yellow brick with tiled eaves, stepped stone plinth, and a recessed w entrance (cf. St Mary Kenton, Br). E bell-turret. – WALL PAINTING on the E wall by Hans Feibusch. – STAINED GLASS by Walker and Carter Shapland.

ST CUTHBERT, Watford Road and Carlton Avenue West. 1958–9 by Romilly B. Craze. Brick, with a little eaves decoration below the shallow pitched roof. Trusses boldly pierced with circles, a motif repeated in the leading of the tall, thin windows. – E wall with MURALS by Harper & Hendra.

ST JOHN, High Road. A smallish, somewhat rustic building of

flint, with fancy tiled roofs and a shingled w bell-turret, set back
from the main road in a large churchyard. By *G. G. Scott &
Moffatt,* 1846, the gift of the Misses Copland of Crabs House
(now Barham Park Library), Sudbury. N aisle 1859, with plate
tracery; s aisle 1900 by *H. R. Brakspear*; baptistery and choir
vestry 1935 by *G. P. Pratt.* A very odd design for the piers. –
STAINED GLASS. E window by *J. E. Nuttgens,* 1949.

ST ANDREW'S CHURCH OF THE FIRST BORN (formerly Presbyterian), Ealing Road. 1904. In a robust free style, roughcast
above red brick, with a tapering tower topped by a timber cupola.
Flank walls with large lunettes. – CHURCH HALL to the N, 1898
in similar style, with two striped corner turrets.

ST MICHAEL TOKYNGTON, St Michael's Avenue. Named after
a medieval chapel which existed in this area until the C18. A plain
brick church by *Cyril Farey,* 1932, elementary Romanesque, with
a circular w window. Whitewashed interior with passage aisles
with transverse arches. E end rebuilt in 1966 after war damage.
Contemporary neo-Georgian VICARAGE.

ENGLISH MARTYRS (R.C.), Chalkhill Road. 1971 by *B. D. Kaye.*
Circular, with a low ambulatory, clerestory, and a laminated
timber ceiling rising up to a central lantern.

ST JOSEPH (R.C.), High Road, Wembley Hill. 1956–7 by *Reynolds
Scott,* large and stodgy; a big westwork with hipped roof instead
of a tower.

WEMBLEY PARK FREE CHURCH, Beverley Gardens. By *Smee &
Houchin,* 1938, with slightly modernistic angular window-heads.

TOWN HALL, Forty Lane. 1935–40 by *Clifford Strange,* who had
worked with T. S. Tait. The best of the pre-war modern town
halls around London, neither fanciful nor drab. The long front
has no conspicuous climax but not one detail either that could
jar. It is given dignity by its position above the road, a serene
composition of overlapping brick planes, with slightly recessed
ground-floor windows enlivened by curved tiled mullions. The
main building was planned with offices to the E and a self-
contained library to the w. Inside, the main staircase is also far
from spectacular, but airy and sensible, like the great hall at the
back. This lies on the main axis, but can also be approached from
the E, through a well planted garden whose trees provide just the
right foil to the plain brickwork behind.

EDWARD VII PARK, Park Lane. Opened 1914. LODGE and other
buildings by the council engineer and surveyor, *Cecil R. W.
Chapman.*

WEMBLEY COMPLEX STATION (formerly Wembley Hill). 1905
for the Great Central Railway. Original weatherboarded buildings.

WEMBLEY HILL CUTTING, by Park Lane. 1905; approaching 20
metres deep in London Clay.

The perambulation falls into two parts. First, w of Empire Way
and N of Forty Avenue.

WEMBLEY PARK. Of the grounds laid out by *Repton* in 1793 for
Richard Page (†1803), whose house, demolished in 1908, stood
near Wembley Green, only a delightful little thatched LODGE
(with later additions) remains at the junction of Wembley Hill
Road and Wembley Park Drive. Most of the grounds were sold

in 1889 to Sir Edward Watkin, who in 1892 laid the foundations for a crazily ambitious and unsuccessful venture: a copy of the Eiffel Tower. The incomplete structure was demolished after the Wembley Park Estate Company laid out the W part of the grounds for housing in 1907.

In WEMBLEY PARK DRIVE an enjoyable assortment reflecting the changing tastes of suburban builders. Among the earlier houses, the usual variations on Norman Shaw and Baillie Scott themes are supplemented by a few more eccentric efforts, for example Nos. 73–75, Voyseyesque roughcast with some lancets, by *T. Merrison Garrood*, 1908. To the N, off Forty Avenue, a scatter of early modern features appear among the Haymills houses of the 1930s: in BARN RISE, Nos. 54–60 by *Welch, Cachemaille-Day & Lander*, 1932, and others in THE AVENUE and MAYFIELDS by *Welch & Lander*, 1933–4.

FRYENT COUNTRY PARK, Wembley Park and Kingsbury. There was once on Barn Hill a prospect house called Page's Folly. The surviving landscaping, together with the mature trees scattered among the suburbs on the S slopes, dates from the late C18, the time of Richard Page of Wembley Park (*see* above), and is probably by *Repton*.

N of the railway bridge at Wembley Park is FORTY LANE, with the town hall (q.v.) and, opposite, the borough's awful mistake, the vast system-built CHALKHILL ESTATE, planned in 1963, built in 1966–70, a repelling maze of linked high-rise concrete slabs housing five thousand people. Demolition of the links was under way in 1990–1. Further W, in NORTH WEMBLEY, to the S of East Lane, tucked in among high-class inter-war suburbia, *Brent*'s EVERARD WAY ESTATE in CLARENDON GARDENS, completed *c.* 1980 (chief architect *Kenneth Morris*), demonstrates the change of approach typical of later council housing: 139 houses and flats on a pleasant domestic scale, with front doors opening on to pedestrian routes. N of East Lane JOHN PERRIN PLACE, Preston Hill, old people's housing of 1963–5 by the *Borough of Wembley*, on the site of Lyon farmhouse, one of the few rural buildings that survived into the C20.

On the N side of EAST LANE an industrial area near the railway, where the most prominent building is WRIGLEYS FACTORY by *Wallis, Gilbert & Partners*, 1926–8, with long horizontal bands of glazing. It is one of the first in Britain of reinforced concrete flat slab construction, with mushroom column-heads.

The second part of the perambulation is the area E of Empire Way.

WEMBLEY EXHIBITION SITE. The E part of Wembley Park, with its lake, became pleasure grounds, and then in 1924 was taken over for the EMPIRE EXHIBITION, mounted to 'display the Natural Resources of the various countries of the Empire, and the activities, industrial and social of their people'. The main axis, EMPIRE (now OLYMPIC) WAY, led s from Wembley Park station, with low exhibition buildings on either side, passed over a series of lakes, and rose up to the climax of the stadium on a slight eminence. The formal layout and architectural detail of the main buildings, by *Sir John Simpson* and *Maxwell Ayrton* with *Sir Owen Williams*, evoked the permanence of the imperial glories of antiquity (a doubtful rationale for a temporary exhi-

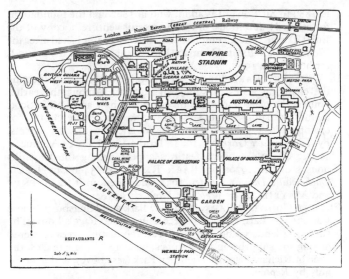

Wembley Exhibition Centre, from a plan of 1924

bition). Their novelty lay not in their appearance, but in their construction in reinforced concrete (chosen for speed and cheapness). Concrete was also used for minor details such as fountains, lamps, and bridges, and even for the lions outside the British Government building. The more exotic contributions scattered in between, including a domed Indian pavilion, a Burmese pagoda, and a native African village, have vanished, but the main buildings were taken over by Wembley Trading Estate in 1928, and the stadium was developed as a sports centre, supplemented in 1934 by the arena. Some of the formal buildings remained into the 1970s, amid squalor and decay, but haphazard rebuilding since has ignored the scale and logic of the original arrangement. The exhibition buildings E of Olympic Way (including the Palace of Engineering) were swept away in the late 1970s in favour of large, anonymous industrial sheds neatly clad in ribbed aluminium, sheltering behind a motley group of taller offices along the main route. The chief older survivals are described below, from N to S.

WEMBLEY PARK STATION. 1923 by the Metropolitan Railway Co., in quite a showy colonial style (pantile roofs), with self-effacing brick extensions in the Holden manner.

PALACE OF INDUSTRY, Olympic Way, w side. The largest surviving exhibition space, now government warehouses. Steel-trussed roof, partly glazed, not as daring as the larger Palace of Engineering (which included concrete arches of 23 metre span). Windowless concrete walls with a little channelled decoration and lion-head corbels.

PALACE OF ARTS, w of the above. A smaller version, with more overtly Egyptian allusions. Walls with a pronounced batter; central pediment. Inside were period rooms designed by, among others, *Sir Albert Richardson* and *Goodhart-Rendel,* and modern

rooms by *Palmer-Jones, Gerald Wellesley,* and *Trenwith Wells.*
Facsimile rebuilding of the much eroded outer walls around new
exhibition spaces was under discussion in 1991, retaining the
small apsed basilica projecting to the W, which had housed
examples of ecclesiastical art. Unlike the rest of the building, it
is of rendered breeze-blocks, with the exception of the concrete
windows: they project outward, so that their splays inside give
the illusion of a thick-walled building.

STADIUM. A concrete oval, in area twice the size of the Colosseum,
planned for 120,000 spectators. The superstructure is supported
by large semicircular arches. Twin domes face down Olympic
Way (the vista now interrupted by the later raising of the
approach). Quite a romantic piece of neo-classicism when seen
from the S rising behind trees.

ARENA AND EMPIRE POOL. By *Sir Owen Williams,* 1934. Ten
years later than the stadium, and without classical reminiscences.
An impressive demonstration of the power of reinforced
concrete. Three hinged arches spanning over 70 metres (240 ft),
the largest concrete span in the world when built. Roof-lights in
between, and further lighting from the rectangular end windows
stepping up into the gables. A bold show of concrete buttresses
at the sides, cantilevered out above the basement. There were
originally sun-bathing terraces at the E end.

Around the fringes of the site are a muddle of large buildings of
the 1970s, built on the land left over from the exhibition. Among
the most prominent: WEMBLEY CONFERENCE CENTRE,
Empire Way, a very large, slickly detailed circular building with
tinted glazing, by *R. Seifert & Partners,* 1977, the first purpose-
built conference centre to be completed in Britain. Nearby, the
HILTON NATIONAL HOTEL, an eleven-storey slab, also by *R.
Seifert & Partners,* 1971–2.

In WEMBLEY PARK DRIVE Nos. 151–169 (BASF), a brash
mirror-glazed slab, 1978–80 by *Halpern & Partners,* its facile
anonymity shown up by McDERMOTT HOUSE by *T. P. Bennett
& Son,* 1957–8, prestige offices near the former exhibition
entrance, a long curved frontage of mottled brick, with a sunken
water garden in front – a better than average effort for its date.

S of Wembley Complex station, around OAKINGTON MANOR
DRIVE and St Michael's church (q.v.), WEMBLEY HILL
GARDEN SUBURB, spaciously laid out traditional suburban
housing of *c.* 1924, partly by *Oliver Hill* for the builders Callow
& Wright.

In HARROW ROAD, S of Oakington Manor Drive, THE GREY-
HOUND, a 1930s pub by *E. B. Musman,** a demure curved front
with eclectic brick detail. Further W, WEMBLEY HIGH ROAD,
the main shopping area, has nothing to single out except for the
church of St John (q.v.) and the VILLAGE INN at the corner of
Ealing Road, a characteristic pub of 1897.

WILLESDEN

Only the medieval church recalls the old village; the rest is a dismally incoherent muddle. In the early C 19 there were two distinct settlements: Church End by the church, and Willesden Green (*see* below) along the road leading E to Edgware Road and Cricklewood. Church End grew scrappily, a mixture of industry and poor housing linking it to Harlesden by the turn of the century, although the cemeteries and Roundwood Park remained as green oases to the S. The character of the area around the church was drastically altered in the 1960s by road widening and indifferent rebuilding.

ST MARY, Neasden Lane, Church End. The old grey church stands in its large churchyard as a lonely survivor, cut off by busy roads from the Victorian shopping street to the S. The medieval parts are the nave, chancel, and S aisle with SW tower, all much restored by *Thomas Little* in 1852, when the tracery was completely renewed and a W bay added. The N aisle was rebuilt in 1872 by *E. J. Tarver*, and further restoration followed in 1895 (nave roof), 1917 (SE chapel), and 1960–4. The best views are from the SW and SE, where the rough walls of ragstone rubble with a little flint and local ferricrete retain some of their original texture.* The tower of *c.* 1400 is low, with no string course; angle buttresses, and a NW stair-turret truncated in the later C18. The interior, also low, is on a homely scale. Two S piers are typical C13, circular, with simple capitals and arches; the contrast to the tower arch next to them, with its polygonal responds, is instructive of the development from the C13 to the C14. The SE chapel and the rebuilt chancel arch are late Perp. The westernmost column of the N aisle was discovered in the churchyard and re-used in the C19 rebuilding. Medieval SOUTH DOOR, rehung, with C14 blank tracery – a rarity in the London area. – FONT. Also rare in the London area: a Norman survival. It is of Purbeck, a tall, square tapering bowl on a thick central shaft with four slender subsidiary shafts; elementary abstract ornament. – Good Elizabethan COMMUNION TABLE with bulbous legs. – Charming simple IRON RAILINGS of the C17(?) now used to guard the weights of the clock; the uprights end in sunflowers. – SCULPTURE. In the SE chapel a black Virgin, 1972 by *Catherine Stern*, recalling a statue and shrine for which Willesden was famous before the Reformation. – BRASSES. Six, ranging in size and in date (from 1494 to 1609). – MONUMENTS. Quatrefoiled tomb-chest in a low recess in the S wall of the S chapel. – Richard Payne † 1606 and wife † 1595. Wall-monument with small kneeling figures below a double arch; obelisks and arms above. – John Barne † 1615 and Francis Roberts † 1631, a pair; coloured marbles and alabaster. – Richard Francklyn † 1615, another small wall-monument, with a pediment. – John Francklyn † 1647. Bold architectural tablet of black and white marble with scrolled open pediment. – Many good late C17–18 LEDGER STONES.

UNITED REFORMED CHURCH (former), Church Road. 1899 by

---

*Traces of two C12 windows found in 1872 were destroyed.

Spalding & Spalding, a robust landmark in a dull road; red brick with terracotta battlements to a tapering tower topped by a timber cupola.

CEMETERIES. The two cemeteries adjoin. WILLESDEN CEMETERY, Franklyn Road, of 1891, originally had unique Pont Street Dutch red brick chapels by *C. H. Worley*, now demolished. More rewarding is the JEWISH CEMETERY, Glebe Road, 1873 by *N. Joseph*, with three ragstone Gothic buildings and many elaborate marble and granite MONUMENTS, e.g. to the Roths- childs. The Samuel family has an enclosure of white marble Corinthian columns.

MAGISTRATES COURT, High Road. 1989. A large red brick build- ing, straightforward at the back, but with a front dressed up in feeble classical detail. Spacious entrance hall with curving staircase.

KILBURN POLYTECHNIC, Dudden Hill Lane (for the original buildings *see* Kilburn, Br). By the *M.C.C. Architect's Depart- ment*, the earliest part 1934 (*W. T. Curtis*), utilitarian-modern buildings (brick with ribbon windows) around a courtyard. Extensions of 1950–3 (*C. G. Stillman*), with four floors on con- crete piers. Additions of 1971, with sloping roof-lights. The former DUDDENHILL SCHOOLS, Dudden Hill Lane and Cooper Road, now part of the polytechnic, are of 1895 by *G. E. S. Laurence*, one of his three-deckers of quite picturesque outline (stairs in polygonal end turrets), but to an old-fashioned plan (classrooms both sides of the hall).

WILLESDEN GREEN

The hamlet on the high road developed into a suburb after the station opened in 1879, its residential streets merging into the northern parts of Brondesbury and the western parts of Crickle- wood (qq.v.).

ST ANDREW, High Road, Willesden Green. 1886–7 by *James Brooks*. A most typical contrast to the old village church of Willesden. Impressive in scale, and more elaborately detailed than his East End churches. Large and ambitious, with crossing and transepts. It displays a stately if somewhat dull E.E. Long four-bay chancel, its straight E end with a group of five lancets; transepts and nave with simple wagon roofs but vaulted aisles. Brick and stone interior, with pointed arcades of medium height, galleries, and lancet windows in the clerestory. Most unusual for Brooks are the robust stone tracery screens dividing each of the E chapels from the transepts. The NE chapel is vaulted. – Lavish furnishings, especially a spectacular high altar with REREDOS (paintings by *Westlake*, in gilded Gothic frames) in the Flemish Renaissance manner. – FONT. 1897; a handsome chunky geo- metric composition of coloured marbles. – Low iron SCREEN with a pair of semicircular AMBONES for pulpit and lectern. – The painted STATIONS OF THE CROSS of *c.* 1911 on the aisle walls and the STAINED GLASS in the E, N, and S chapel windows

all by *Lavers, Barraud & Westlake*. – The aisle windows of 1963
(Life of Christ, in an angular figure style) are by *John Hayward*. –
NE porch window by *Kempe*.

The VICARAGE to the S, linked by a little cloister, and the
PARISH HALL and SCHOOLS across the road, all by *Brooks,*
make a good group with the church.

NEW TESTAMENT CHURCH OF GOD, High Road. Free Italianate
with octagonal tower. Built in 1904 for the Primitive Methodists.

SYNAGOGUE, Heathfield Park. 1936–8 by *Fritz Landauer.*

LIBRARY CENTRE, High Road and Brondesbury Park. The original building, now a flagship on the High Road for the larger
centre behind, is of 1893 by *Newman & Newman.* An ingenious
plan on a corner site. Two wings (for reading room and lending
library) open at an angle off a central hall. The entrance was
stressed by a shell-hooded doorway with a pretty conical roofed
turret above. *Brent*'s bulky complex of 1990 zigzags down Brondesbury Park, its windows lighting two deep-plan library floors.
The rest of the building enterprisingly incorporates an exhibition
hall, studio theatre, restaurant, and bookshop, all opening on to
an informal central mall.

WILLESDEN GENERAL HOSPITAL, Robson Avenue. Built as a
Passmore Edwards cottage hospital, a pretty design with par-
getted and tile-hung gables, 1892–9 by *Newman & Newman.*
Many later additions.

WILLESDEN SPORTS CENTRE, Donnington Road. The stadium
by the athletics track is by *Emberton, Tardrew & Partners,* 1966,
a forceful design in reinforced concrete making good use of a
split level site. Seating for 500 with training and restaurant areas
below.

The HIGH ROAD is the main shopping street, retaining a solid late
Victorian and Edwardian atmosphere, punctuated by its church
and chapels and a series of pubs, of which the best is the dignified
stuccoed SPOTTED DOG. The best of the commercial buildings
are at the junction with WILLESDEN LANE. The former London
and South Western BANK is of 1892–3 by *Maurice B. Adams,*
gable flanked by two turrets, ground floor with a broad arch and
Loire valley motifs, a good contrast with the white 30s-modern
ELECTRICITY SHOWROOMS in Willesden Lane.

EALING

INTRODUCTION

The borough of Ealing is pleasingly varied. A broad tract of open land still remains along the valley of the river Brent, which meanders through the centre of the borough from Perivale in the N to Hanwell in the S, where it is crossed by *Brunel*'s Wharncliffe Viaduct for the Great Western Railway, the borough's most impressive industrial monument. Acton, on the E edge, was already London-over-the-border by the end of the C19; at Northolt on the Hillingdon boundary, rural Middlesex remained undisturbed until Western Avenue was cut through in the 1930s. The heart of the modern borough is Ealing itself, once a large, prosperous village close to the Uxbridge road, the old main route NW out of London. Well served by railways, it developed during the later C19 into a comfortably spacious, well-run middle-class suburb, with winding streets of superior houses extending N over the rising ground of Castle Bar and Hanger Hill.

The uneventful C20 residential suburbs in the outer areas of the borough are interspersed with sizeable patches of industry, located according to the C19 and C20 lines of transport. The earliest developed around the Grand Union Canal and its Paddington branch, especially where the two arms meet at Southall, although the area became urban only at the end of the C19. This end of the borough, with a character all its own on account of its concentration

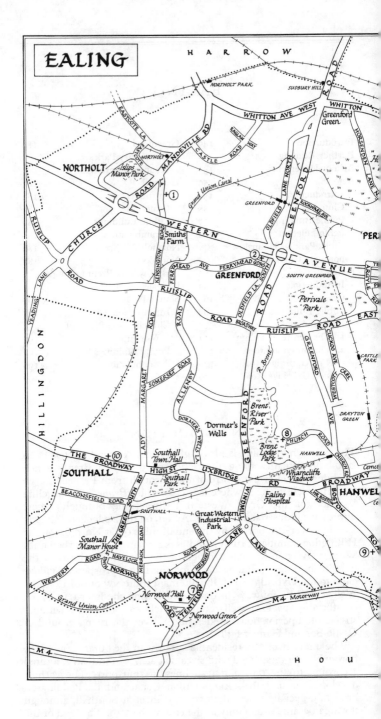

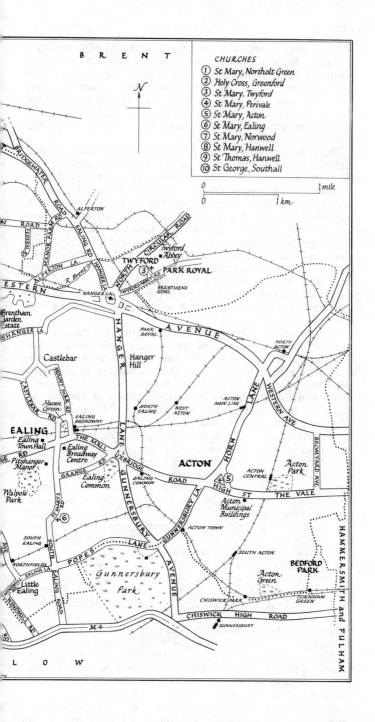

CHURCHES
1. St Mary, Northolt Green
2. Holy Cross, Greenford
3. St Mary, Twyford
4. St Mary, Perivale
5. St Mary, Acton
6. St Mary, Ealing
7. St Mary, Norwood
8. St Mary, Hanwell
9. St Thomas, Hanwell
10. St George, Southall

0   1 mile
0   1 km

BRENT

N

ALPERTON

BRIDGEWATER ROAD
EALING MANOR FARM RD
ALPERTON LA

TWYFORD
Twyford Abbey
NORTH CIRCULAR ROAD
PARK ROYAL
TWYFORD ABBEY RD
BRENTMEAD GDNS

R. Brent
HANGER LA

ESTERN

HANGER LA

Brentham garden estate

SHANGER LA

Castlebar

Hanger Hill

PARK ROYAL

AVENUE

NORTH ACTON

CASTLEBAR

MOUNT PARK RD

Haven Green

NORTH EALING

WEST ACTON

ACTON MAIN LINE

HANGER LANE

WESTERN AVE

BROMYARD AVE

EALING
Ealing Town Hall
RD
Pitshanger Manor

EALING BROADWAY

THE MALL

UXBRIDGE LANE

Ealing Broadway Centre

GRANGE RD

Ealing Common

EALING COMMON

UXBRIDGE ROAD

ACTON

ACTON CENTRAL

Acton Park

HIGH ST

HORN LANE

ST MARY'S RD

Walpole Park

6

Acton Municipal Buildings

THE VALE

5

GUNNERSBURY LA

SOUTH EALING

POPES

LANE

ACTON TOWN

GUNNERSBURY AVENUE

SOUTH ACTON

BEDFORD PARK

NORTHFIELDS

EALING LA

Little Ealing

SOUTH EALING RD

Gunnersbury Park

Acton Green

HAMMERSMITH and FULHAM

WINDMILL RD

CHISWICK PARK

TURNHAM GREEN

CHISWICK HIGH ROAD

M 4

GUNNERSBURY

LOW

of Asian immigrants, is the part that is changing most rapidly in the later C20. South Acton, once an area of small late C19 streets crammed with service industries for the growing metropolis, was extensively and for the most part uninspiringly rebuilt after 1950. Industrial areas also grew up from the 1930s around Western Avenue on the northern edge; here the monotony is leavened by some flamboyant landmarks – 1930s art deco at Perivale, 1970s high tech at Greenford and North Acton.

The other architectural riches are not spectacular but are nevertheless enjoyable. In the places which did not grow until the C20 – Northolt, Norwood, Perivale, and Greenford – modest medieval village churches remain, relatively unspoilt, in quiet settings. Of country houses there is less to see, but at Southall there is the surprising survival of a large C16 timber-framed manor house. Ealing Green, moreover, is graced by a building of national interest: Pitshanger Manor, *John Soane*'s own house, which he rebuilt with a memorably idiosyncratic neo-classical centre attached to an earlier wing by *George Dance*; the interiors here have been excellently restored. There is another, much altered house by *Soane* at Norwood, and two other lesser houses with interesting C18 parts, now converted to schools, remain at South Ealing (Ealing Park) and Acton (The Elms).

The *forte* of Ealing is the variety of good suburban building. The churches erected to cater for the expanding population range from the confident but very different Victorian efforts by *Scott, Teulon,* and *Sedding* in Ealing, through the gradual but by no means immediate waning of the Gothic tradition in the C20 (*Shearman* at Acton and Ealing, *Gibbons* at Northolt, *Maufe* at Hanwell and Acton), to the more innovative approaches of *Cachemaille-Day* or *Maguire & Murray* (Twyford, Northolt). The Middlesex County Council and the various local authorities responded well to the challenge of rising populations, as can be gauged by looking at their school buildings, from the late C19 examples at Acton to the late C20 ones at Southall. The dichotomy of suburban life between the wars is illustrated by the contrast between the trim functional stations of the Piccadilly line extension and the exotic escapist cinemas of Northfields (South Ealing) and Southall. As for housing, there is plenty to study, from the Victorian spaciousness of Ealing's hilly Castle Bar suburbs and the happy intimacy of the CoPartnership tenants' Edwardian Brentham Garden Estate to the experimental Homes for Heroes at Acton of the 1920s and the lusher varieties of inter-war styles around Hanger Lane.

The older suburbs were in general unsympathetically treated in the 1950s and 1960s: many greedy blocks of flats went up (*see* Castle Bar, Ealing), while drab council estates replaced the artisan terraces of South Acton and spread over the open land remaining on the western fringes. Developers' greed has not abated, but from the later 1970s onwards a trend towards a more sensitive approach has become apparent. The imaginative re-use of redundant buildings is demonstrated in different ways by the churches of St Mark Hanwell and St Mary Perivale. For new buildings there has been a return to friendly materials and more tactful grouping and landscaping, as is shown by *BDP*'s Ealing Broadway Centre, the late 1970s housing of South Acton, and the most recent additions at

Ealing Hospital, Southall. Here the c 20 approach to hospital design can be instructively compared with that of the vast c 19 asylum on the adjacent site which awaits a new role at the time of writing.

FURTHER READING

The area of the present borough is well covered by the V.C.H.: Greenford and Hanwell in vol. III (1962); Norwood, Southall, Perivale, and Northolt in vol. IV (1971); Acton, Ealing, and West Twyford in vol. VII (1982). The most useful older history is T. Faulkner, *The History and Antiquities of Brentford, Ealing and Chiswick* (1845). On Ealing in the c 19 there is the contemporary account by the borough engineer, Charles Jones, *Ealing, from Village to Corporate Town* (1902). A broader modern survey is M. Jahn, 'Suburban Development in Outer West London 1850–1900', *The Rise of Suburbia*, ed. F. M. L. Thompson (1982). There is a useful survey of the borough's churches and their contents in Ealing Museum's Art and History Society's *Art, Architecture and History of Ealing Churches* (1978). Current local history research is published in *Acton Past and Present* and the *Ealing Local History Society Papers*. K. McEwan, *Ealing Walkabout* (1983), is a useful popular summary. On particular topics: R. N. G. Rowland, *The Street Names of Acton* (1977); R. Hayes, *New and Old. A History of St Peter's Church, Mount Park, Ealing* (1985); B. Johnson, *Brentham, Ealing's Garden Suburb*; M. Tims, Ealing Tenants Ltd, *Ealing Local History Society Papers*, 8 (1966) (also on Brentham); D. Stroud, 'Sir John Soane and the Rebuilding of Pitshanger Manor', *In Search of Modern Architecture, A Tribute to H.-R. Hitchcock* (1982); E. Leary, *Pitshanger Manor* (1986); Alan Powers, *The Heights of Ealing* (Thirties Society notes on Hanger Hill) (1985); P. Guillery, 'Norwood Hall and Micklefield Hall', *Architectural History*, 30 (1967). The DoE list dates from 1981.

ACKNOWLEDGEMENTS

Ealing is full of architectural enthusiasts. For information, comments and advice we are most grateful to Maureen Gooding and the staff of Ealing Library, and to Brian Rayment and John Templeton of Ealing Planning Department, who were most helpful and informative on both old and new buildings. Among many others who provided information we must especially thank T. and A. Harper Smith and R. N. G. Rowlands (Acton), John Foster White, whose Victorian Society notes on Ealing were most instructive, I. Khan (Ealing Park), Emmeline Leary (Pitshanger Manor and Norwood), R. C. Gurd of the Ealing Civic Society (especially for details of the Hanger Hill estate and Northfields cinema), and K. Fitzherbert of the Hanwell Preservation Society.

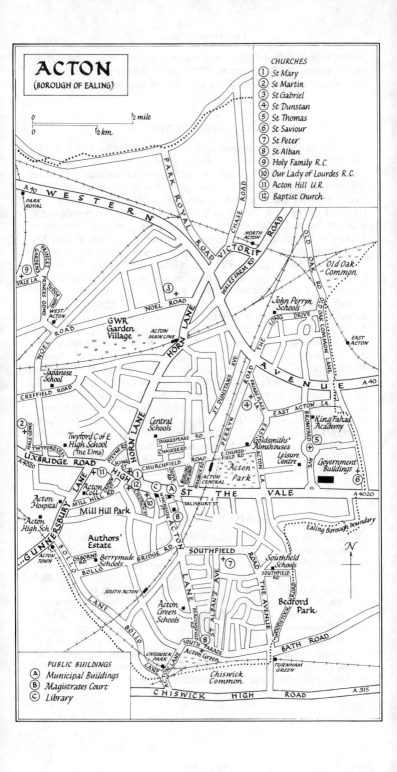

ACTON
(BOROUGH OF EALING)

0 ____ ½ mile
0 ____ ½ km

CHURCHES
1. St Mary
2. St Martin
3. St Gabriel
4. St Dunstan
5. St Thomas
6. St Saviour
7. St Peter
8. St Alban
9. Holy Family R.C.
10. Our Lady of Lourdes R.C.
11. Acton Hill U.R.
12. Baptist Church

PUBLIC BUILDINGS
Ⓐ Municipal Buildings
Ⓑ Magistrates Court
Ⓒ Library

ACTON

INTRODUCTION

The parish of Acton had 1,425 inhabitants in 1801, 3,150 in 1861, 17,000 in 1881, 37,000 in 1901, 71,000 in 1931. Up to the early C19 there was simply the village around St Mary's church on one of the main roads out of London, with some settlement extending N up Horn Lane, and a separate hamlet known as East Acton. Further N were scattered houses and farms, for example at Acton Wells, Old Oak Common, one of London's minor spas in the late C17 to C18, and at Friars Place Green. After the coming of the railways (Acton had five stations by 1880) London swamped Acton and converted it into a suburb, although it remained just outside the London County Council. South Acton became industrial, with dense working-class terraces (mostly replaced since the Second World War) interspersed with laundries serving inner west London, covering the area down to Acton Green. Here, on the boundary with Chiswick, the garden suburb of Bedford Park was begun in the 1870s (described under Hounslow). The northern part of the old parish was still largely open land in the 1920s, when it was sliced through by Western Avenue; by 1939 it was built up.

CHURCHES

St ALBAN, South Parade, Acton Green. 1887–8 by *E. Monson*. A large raw red basilica on the edge of the green. Nave with lancets, apsed E end with Dec tracery. – (STAINED GLASS. E window by *F. Hamilton Jackson*, c. 1887. PC)

St DUNSTAN, Friars Place Lane, East Acton. 1878–9 by *R. Hesketh* (architect to the Goldsmiths' Company, which paid for the building). Tower with broach-spire over the porch, a good landmark. The interior reordered and partly subdivided in 1983 by *Ian Goldsmid*.

St GABRIEL, Noel Road. 1929–31 by *E. C. Shearman*. A large church, of dark brick with stone bands, derived from Shearman's earlier St Barnabas, North Ealing (Ea), and with similarly wild Dec tracery. Shallow S transept with an especially prominent rose window. Austere red brick interior with narrow pointed arcade arches, as at St Barnabas. Unfinished W end. – SCULPTURE. Two low-relief terracotta plaques by *George Tinworth*, given in 1930; one exhibited in the 1878 Paris exhibition, the other of 1883, formerly in Sandringham church, Norfolk.

St MARTIN, Hale Gardens, West Acton. 1906 by *E. Monson & Sons*. Old-fashioned for its date. Lofty and ambitious, but incomplete. Red brick, the transept gables with chequerwork flanked by turrets. Nave with stone quatrefoil columns. Church hall on the site of the unbuilt chancel.

St MARY, King Street. The parish church existed by 1228, was much rebuilt and enlarged in 1837, and then entirely reconstructed in 1865–7 by *H. Francis* on the much larger scale needed by the new suburban population. W tower replaced in 1875–6, a heightened version of the Middlesex type with turret projecting above the battlements. Red brick with stone dressings, quite a lively exterior, appropriate for its prominent island site above the High Street. Tall Dec windows below gables on the N side, but to the S the composition varied by low S aisle windows between the baptistery gable and the projecting SE chapel. The N aisle formerly had a gallery. Inside, arcades with capitals very lushly carved by *E. G. Anstey* with realistic foliage and birds; brick walls with modest polychromy. – ALTAR SLAB. Pre-Reformation, black Derbyshire marble. – FONTS. A small bowl on a column, 1805. – An octagonal Gothic font, of mahogany, carved in New Zealand for the Wembley exhibition. – CURIOSA. Carved wheatsheaves from a bread charity table; *c.* 1700. – Some excellent STAINED GLASS, especially the windows at the E end contemporary with the church: chancel E and N, and N aisle E, 1866, all by *Clayton & Bell*. Small scenes below canopies, glowing colours. – By the same firm the W window, 1871, N aisle NE, 1874, S aisle windows above the organ, 1882. – In three S windows of the nave, animated Old and New Testament subjects representing Faith, Hope, and Charity, by *Heaton, Butler & Bayne*, 1870–80. – The more stridently coloured windows in the S transept are by *Alexander Gibbs*, 1866. – MONUMENTS. Many minor wall-monuments preserved from the old church, gathered together at the W end of the church. – Brass to Humphrey Cavell † 1558, kneeling figure. – Lady Conway † 1637. Inscription flanked by two standing allegorical figures in niches. – Several cartouches. Catherine Henshaw † 1680. – Frances Thomas † 1698. An unusually handsome scrolly example with angels' heads. – Daniel Wait † 1707, with drapery. – Lady Caroline Adair † 1769, with a portrait profile in a circle of leaves above a sarcophagus. – Rev. William Antrobus † 1853. A bust on a column. – Several neat tablets made *c.* 1866 to commemorate older lost monuments. – Outside the S vestry, John Way † 1804 by *John Bacon Jun.*; obelisk with urn. – CHURCH HALL to the S planned 1989, by *Norman Haines Design Partnership*.

St Peter, Southfield Road, Acton Green. 1914–15 by *W. A. Pite*. Plain and reasonable, an Early Christian basilica. Stock brick with red brick dressings. W front embellished by a stone doorway with tiles and mosaic. Simple basilican interior with apse and narrow aisles, the arcades carried across the two transeptal chapels. – In the S chapel a SCREEN from the Quebec Chapel, Marylebone, of 1788. It has elegantly light open arches, the larger centre one crowned by a pediment. – The ORGAN comes from St Alphege London Wall. – The church replaced a domestic-looking temporary building of 1907 by *Morley Horder*, now the church hall, hidden behind the vicarage of 1952.

St Saviour (Centre for Deaf People), Old Oak Road. 1924–7 by *E. Maufe*. Built to replace a church of 1873 by *Blomfield*, in Oxford Street. Reticent brick exterior, a two-tier arrangement, with social centre on the ground floor, and the church reached by a double flight of rather steep stairs from the W door. W window under reticulated tracery below a shallow gable. A pleasantly intimate interior with pale painted brick walls, nave roof with boldly patterned tie-beams, and some minimally Gothic detail such as the unmoulded arches to the side chapel. Typically Maufian gently curved tops to altar surround and chancel wood-work. Techniques to increase visual impact include the raked nave floor, and the chancel treated rather like a stage, with two ambones instead of a pulpit, and side lighting instead of an E window. Attractive sun-shaped shields to the hanging lamps in the nave to throw the light forward. – FONT. 1893, coloured marbles, from the Oxford Street church. – STAINED GLASS. W window 1925.

ST THOMAS, Bromyard Avenue, Acton Vale. Disused at the time of writing. A cruciform church with an E apse, on a prominent island site. 1915 by *A. Blomfield Jun.*, the nave completed in a plainer Perp in 1937–9 by *Lester Richard*. Brick with stone dressings. – Small CHURCH CENTRE to the N by *Hutchison, Locke & Monk*, 1973.

HOLY FAMILY (R.C.), Vale Lane, West Acton. 1967 by *P. J. Mabley*. An irregular pentagon of ungainly profile. Attractive interior, brick with boarded ceilings. – CRUCIFIX by *Michael Clark*.

OUR LADY OF LOURDES (R.C.), High Street. 1902 by *E. Goldie*. Italian Romanesque in style, with a circular W window, and a concrete dome over the crossing.

ACTON HILL CHURCH (Methodist and United Reformed), High Street and Gunnersbury Lane. 1907 by *Gordon & Gunton*, with a characteristic tower with a marked batter to the corner buttresses, and Gothic detail of the free style typical of Nonconformist churches of *c.* 1900. (Long nave with galleries, transepts, apse containing organ.)

BAPTIST CHURCH, Church Road. 1864 by *W. Mumford*. Pleasant debased classical front with a pediment. Round-headed windows with curious lamp-brackets above.

PUBLIC BUILDINGS

MUNICIPAL BUILDINGS. A large assemblage, including the town hall, between the High Street, Winchester Street, and Salisbury Street, built in the grounds of Berrymede Priory (which survived behind until demolished *c.* 1985). Facing Winchester Street the MUNICIPAL OFFICES of 1908–10 by *Raffles & Gridley*, a classi-cal brick and stone palazzo on a fairly modest scale, as required by the local ratepayers' association. Five broad bays with pro-jecting end pavilions; windows generously pedimented. The top floor is treated more freely: striped brick and stone, triplet windows below a rich cornice. Council chamber with large arched window to Salisbury Street. Tactfully extended in 1939 in similar style along the High Street to provide assembly and concert hall by *R. Atkinson* and the borough surveyor, *W. G. Cross*. Recess with carved coving over the entrance. The plain entrance and stair hall are more recognizably of the 1930s. Restored 1990. Further E, behind offices added in 1926, the PUBLIC BATHS of 1904 by *D. J. Ebbets*, with decorative pedimented gable to Salisbury Street; interiors, complete with slipper baths, restored to their former glory in 1989–90.

MAGISTRATES COURT, Winchester Street. 1907 by the county architect, *H. T. Wakelam*, small but dignified. Brick, with channelled pilasters and elaborate stone cornice. Courtroom with arched windows, flanked by lower offices with hipped roofs.

PASSMORE EDWARDS LIBRARY, High Street. 1898–9 by *M. Adams*, in his typical rather bulging Baroque paraphrase of the accepted Tudor of the late Victorian decades.

GOVERNMENT BUILDINGS, Bromyard Avenue, Acton Vale. Built for the Ministry of Pensions, 1914–22 by *Sir J. West*. Impressive by sheer size. An ultra-austere interpretation of the Georgian tradition, five storeys, with a far-projecting plain cornice on paired brackets, its only ornaments the rustication of the ground floor, emphatic quoins, and large entrance archways. The carefully proportioned sash-windows deplorably renewed in plastic in 1988.

BROMYARD LEISURE CENTRE, Bromyard Avenue. 1988–9 by the *Borough Architect's Department*. A cheerful cluster in pale brick and grey-and-white cladding, set off by yellow trimmings; the usual rectangular outline softened by the low curved BRANCH LIBRARY by the entrance. The two sports halls behind are overlooked by a central top-lit cafeteria on the upper floor.

ACTON COLLEGE, Mill Hill Road. Opened in 1928 in the High Street as one of the first further education colleges built by the county council. The science department moved to Mill Hill Road in 1951, and then on to Hillingdon to become Brunel University (q.v.). The main older buildings on the site between Mill Hill and Crown Street are those of the first county school built by the *M.C.C.* and opened in 1906; red brick with Gothic detail and a pretty ventilator-flèche on the hall roof. They face a long, straightforward, five-storey range with exposed concrete frame and brick-faced ends, completed in 1958 (by the *M.C.C. Architect's Department* under *C. G. Stillman*).

ACTON HIGH SCHOOL, Gunnersbury Lane. 1939 by the *M.C.C.*, as new buildings for the county grammar school, with the usual plain brick tower over the entrance. Many later extensions, the most prominent the REYNOLDS SPORTS CENTRE, neat but dull, of dark brick with yellow ribbed cladding, 1978 (*V. Sargin*, architect in charge; *Martin Gardiner*, borough architect).

TWYFORD C. OF E. HIGH SCHOOL, Twyford Crescent. The centre is THE ELMS, a compact Baroque country villa rather in the style of *John James*. Probably built *c.* 1735* by Charles Morren, a gentleman from Covent Garden, and owned from 1737 to 1749 by Sir Joseph Ayloffe, lawyer, antiquary, and Keeper of State Papers. Two storeys above a tall basement, five bays wide, with four giant Doric pilasters carrying a central pediment. (This looks weak in comparison with the handsome heavy cornice, and has perhaps been rebuilt.) Brown brick with good red brick dressings and stone keystones to the windows. The back elevation has giant angle pilasters, and a plainer projecting centre, its former door with segmental hood on lush brackets. Grand entrance-cum-staircase hall in the E three bays; stairs rising in

---

*The date is known from a paper found in the house during repairs, which also recorded the name of a builder, *James Cole* (information from R. N. G. Rowland). For the history of the house, see T. and A. Harper Smith, *Acton Past and Present*, 5 (1985).

three flights with Corinthian column newels, matching dado
panelling, spiral balusters, carved tread-ends. Pretty carved band
below the landing balusters. Square saloon to the w, formerly
with a painted ceiling attributed to *Sleter*. The centre panel
with the Judgement of Paris is now in the Victoria and Albert
Museum, the corner paintings of cupids in Gunnersbury Park
Museum. On the garden side were a 'fore parlour' and a smaller
'back parlour' next to the service stairs (inventory of 1749).
Samuel Wegg, another lawyer, added lower E and W wings after
1758. The E wing is one-storeyed with a canted end, the w
wing two-storeyed and much altered; the present cloister on the
ground floor was created in the 1980s.

The Elms is now a sixth form centre; the rest of the school lies
to the E. The *M.C.C.* acquired the house in 1954 and added a
three-storey classroom block and a lower wing around a small
courtyard in 1957. Technical block to the s, 1967–8, on the site
of a factory which replaced the farm building sold off in the
1890s. Adjoining this is the sports hall of 1988–9 by *Smith &
Barron* (also responsible for refurbishing the other buildings,
1981–8). Red and yellow brick, angled away from the house and
so not as tactless as many buildings of this type. Slate roof
sweeping down towards a green glazed public entrance on the s
side.

JAPANESE SCHOOL, Creffield Road. Large, plain Jacobean of
1901, with N extension of 1910, built for Haberdashers' Aske's
Girls' School (at Elstree since 1974) by *H. W. Stock*, surveyor to
the Haberdashers. Extended 1989.

KING FAHAD ACADEMY (Boys' School), Bromyard Avenue and
East Acton Lane. Formerly Faraday High School, 1955 by the
M.C.C., transformed and extended in 1988–9 by the *Carnell
Green Partnership*. It is now a crisply elegant post-modern group,
with a mixture of brick, rendered, and glazed exteriors with
colourful trimmings, unified by careful hard landscaping and
well detailed railings. At the back a MOSQUE with minaret.

BOARD SCHOOLS. Three remain in South Acton, all by *E. Monson*
(who was a district councillor). They illustrate the increasing
confidence with which this type of building was handled. The
earliest are the BERRYMEDE SCHOOLS, Osborn Road, 1880,
enlarged 1897–8, with boys' school of 1903 across the road to
the N. All in the same style, tall, gaunt institutional-domestic,
softened by bands of local brick and wooden bargeboards to the
half-hipped roofs. The former PRIORY SCHOOL, at the N end
of Acton Lane, 1882, extended 1896, has lower two-storey buildings, busy frontages of yellow brick with red brick dressings.
The triumph is the stately group of ACTON GREEN SCHOOLS
(formerly Beaumont Park), at the s end of Acton Lane. Main
building of 1891, lower infants' range to the l. 1891, addition to
the r. 1898. Well composed elevations in red brick with lavish
use of red terracotta for bands, window heads, and ornamental
plaques; gables with ball finials. The main building also with
diapered brickwork. The planning nevertheless not progressive;
built without the assembly halls that were general in London
Board Schools by this time. Also by *Monson*'s firm (by then *H. C.
& E. C. P. Monson*) are the schools built for Acton after 1903:

SOUTHFIELD ROAD, 1906, and the former CENTRAL
SCHOOLS, Shakespeare Road, 1905, with pedimented central
gable.

JOHN PERRYN FIRST AND MIDDLE SCHOOL, The Long Drive.
1931 for the Homes for Heroes estate (*see* Perambulation). Two
storeys, with simplified classical centrepiece, by *W. G. Cross*,
borough surveyor, and *W. L. Leicester*.

WEST ACTON SCHOOL, Noel Road. 1937 by *W. G. Cross*, on the
veranda principle.

ACTON HOSPITAL, Gunnersbury Lane. Originally the Passmore
Edwards Cottage Hospital, 1897–8 by *Charles Bell*. Three-bay
centre with steep hipped roof, and pretty decoration in early C18
style in stone and red brick. Dull 1920s extensions.

ACTON CENTRAL STATION, Churchfield Road. The first station
in Acton, opened in 1853. The line was extended to provide a
commuters' route to Broad Street in the City in 1865, and the
station rebuilt in 1876. One of the few C19 examples left on the
North London line, the platforms still with their pretty ironwork
and fringed canopies. The handsome station building is now
Acton Park Wine Bar.

LONDON TRANSPORT STATIONS. ACTON TOWN of 1932–3 is
one of the first of *Charles Holden*'s excellent station buildings,
functional yet not without elegance. Lofty booking hall straddling the tracks, with three large windows below a projecting flat
roof – cf. Sudbury Hill and Sudbury Town (Br) and Northfields
(Ealing, Ea) – and a long curved ground-floor canopy. CHIS-
WICK PARK, also on the District line, is likewise of 1932 by
Holden, and similarly detailed, but with a canopy on axis with
the curved ticket hall, and a tower at the side. Platforms with
original fittings and cantilevered concrete canopies. In contrast,
EAST ACTON and NORTH ACTON, on the Central line, still
have little wooden platform shelters in the tradition of C19 minor
stations. For Park Royal, *see* Ealing (Ea).

PERAMBULATION

In the HIGH STREET, as a reminder of the old village, the GEORGE
AND DRAGON and the adjacent No. 135, much altered but early
C17, with a jetty and projecting bay-windows. The rest is typical
of a once prosperous turn-of-the-century suburban centre, with
banks and pubs providing the focal points around the small green
in front of the church. The best is BARCLAYS, close to the
church, built for the London and South Western Bank and dated
1884, with a fancy crowstepped end-gable and unusually lavish
Jacobean detail in brilliant red terracotta. On the S side of the
High Street, No. 199, the MIDLAND BANK, *c.* 1900 with pretty
carved oriel, and the SIX BELLS, with shaped gables, looking
across to the KINGS HEAD with its corner turret. All rather
down-at-heel by 1989, when the area was on the verge of transformation. A large SAFEWAYS by *Miller, Bourne & Partners*, to
the N of a pedestrianized King Street, was begun in 1991. Its
style takes its cue from the former FIRE STATION of 1899,
further W along the High Street, with picturesque half-timbered

gable (converted to an old people's centre in 1990–1). A little further on, KING'S PARADE on the s side, an appealingly 'artistic' shopping parade of 1904 by *A. H. Sykes*, climbs uphill with decorative upper bow-windows and steep gables alternating with tall attic lunettes with art nouveau balconies. To the s, the humble scale of CROWN STREET, with its one-storey shops, was challenged in 1989 by a prominent five-storey block on the E side by *Lanchester & Lodge* for the Notting Hill Housing Trust, stock brick with red brick window heads, gabled end pieces. On the w side the entrance to THE WOODLANDS, a small park, where an ICE HOUSE survives from the house demolished in 1903.

E from the church the main landmarks are the turn-of-the-century public buildings (*see* above). N of the High Street, CHURCHFIELD ROAD has a few modest early to mid C19 cottages and villas (Nos. 48–50, 52, 68) among the later C19 shopping terraces which sprang up to serve the Victorian streets close to Acton Central station. The optimistically named BURLINGTON GARDENS is a little enclave with urban stucco-trimmed terraces on each side, but most of the other roads were developed in more piecemeal fashion; Acton never became a smart suburb like Ealing, although the mixture of small villas and terraces in GROVE ROAD and BIRKBECK ROAD is quite appealing.

To the N, some early C18 railings, gatepiers, and garden walls along back gardens at the w end of CHAUCER ROAD, all that remain from the large older houses and grounds in this area (they belonged either to Acton House, demolished 1904, or Derwentwater House, rebuilt 1804, demolished 1909). E of the railway line is ACTON PARK (created 1888, mostly on Goldsmiths' Company land), with an OBELISK probably from the grounds of one of the older houses.

Overlooking the park is the most attractive group in Acton, the GOLDSMITHS ALMSHOUSES in East Churchfield Road, 1811 48 by *Charles Beazley*, a long, two-storey yellow brick building with two wings coming forward towards the street. At their ends and in the centre modest Ionic features, stuccoed. The centre has a semicircular porch and pediment.

One can return w along the HIGH STREET, where there is little to single out apart from the late Victorian RAILWAY HOTEL, a few elaborately detailed C19 terraces on the s side (Nos. 1–11, a tall terracotta-trimmed block, then Nos. 13–21 with much cut brickwork), and on the N side the GRANADA SOCIAL CLUB, the former DOMINION CINEMA of 1937 by *F. E. Bromige*. Exterior with confidently gross bulgy brick curves (cf. Rayners Lane, Pinner, Hw). (Curvaceous auditorium with concealed lighting.)

Now the outlying areas, roughly clockwise from the NE. In EAST ACTON LANE, running N from Acton Park towards the former hamlet of East Acton, one corner worth a look: Nos. 102–112a, near Friars Place, an attractive, irregular, cottagey close with terraces of re-used stock brick, by *Rosenberg & Gentle*, 1975–7, for a housing association. N from here the land was not built up until the 1920s. Beyond Western Avenue is a large area of council housing, in which the most interesting groups are in THE LONG DRIVE and THE BYE, attractively laid out around little greens and closes: experimental cottages built for the Ministry of Health in 1920–1 to encourage the flagging 'Homes for Heroes' campaign. Most used concrete (blocks, poured, or post-and-slab), but one pair (near the corner of The Long Drive and Old Oak Common Lane) was built to a patent system of interlocking hollow terracotta blocks, much approved by the Ministry and widely adopted by local authorities.* As a further reminder of the diversity of styles and materials of the 1920s, one can return s down BROMYARD AVENUE past PERRYN HOUSE, 1926–7 by *A. Burnett Brown*, surveyor to the Goldsmiths' Company, unusually robust neo-Georgian working-class flats around three sides of a court, an interesting contrast to the more austere government buildings nearby (*see* Public Buildings). Along THE VALE, attractive old people's housing, *c.* 1988 by the *Borough Architect's Department*.

SOUTH ACTON was once a territory of dense working-class housing, factories, and laundries, built up rapidly from the 1860s. Immediately s of THE VALE all is industrial, with much indifferent rebuilding of the C20. Around ACTON LANE something of the old character of the area remains, a haphazard muddle of low housing and backyard industry, its modest bustle and variety considerably more agreeable than the soulless wastes of the AUTHORS ESTATE further w, N of Bollo Bridge Road. This is an inchoate sprawl of council housing of the 1950s and 1960s, in slab blocks of different heights, with a Board School group in Osborn Road (*see* Public Buildings) and a couple of older pubs as the only humane survivals. The reaction against this type of redevelopment is decisively expressed by the housing at the s end of ACTON LANE by *Hutchison, Locke & Monk*, 1978–9 for the borough of Ealing, tall, tough red brick terraces with picturesquely grouped roof-lines, compactly set out amid carefully designed hard landscaping. Acton Lane continues as Beaconsfield Road to ACTON GREEN, overlooked on the s side by a few demure early C19 villas. In SOUTH PARADE, the elaborately decorated DUKE OF SUSSEX, 1898, is by the pub architects *Shoebridge & Rising*, stuccoed and tilehung. To the E Bedford Park begins, partly within the borough of Ealing, but all described under Chiswick (Ho), Perambulation 3.

E of Gunnersbury Lane MILL HILL PARK was developed slowly from 1877 by the builder *William Willett* as Acton's first select suburban estate, close to the station, on winding roads around AVENUE ROAD. They were laid out in the grounds of an older house (of which a fragment remains at No. 11 Avenue Crescent).

WEST ACTON developed only from the early C20, when the area became one with the eastern fringes of Ealing. In UXBRIDGE ROAD only one older building, No. 407, WEST LODGE, dating from 1795–6, a tall house of painted brick, with a bow on one side, rather hemmed in. The flat area N of the Uxbridge Road is covered by a grid of genteel Edwardian streets around the larger landmarks of the former Haberdashers' Aske's School and St Martin (qq.v), Further N, over the main railway line, the G.W.R.'s garden village around NOEL ROAD, a large CoPart-

*Information from Mark Swenarton.

nership housing estate for railway workers, 1923–5 by *T. Alwyn Lloyd*, a former assistant of Raymond Unwin. Attractively simple paired cottages, brick or rendered (too many, alas, with their Georgian sashes replaced), set behind low privet hedges. A little variety achieved by angling corner houses, and by a few groups with gables instead of hipped roofs.

NORTH ACTON, split off by Western Avenue, is largely industrial, like the neighbouring area of Park Royal (*see* Brent). The one old survival was demolished in 1989 (THE FRIARS, later Leamington Park Hospital, Wales Farm Road, a tall, much altered mansion probably built *c.* 1785). Among the factories the only distinguised example is LANDIS & GYR in Chase Road, making the best of its show position next to the railway line. 1979 by *Michael Aukett & Partners*, a crisp, compact high tech box in the Foster tradition, with walls partly clad in ribbed aluminium and partly with mirror glass framed in blue. The building takes advantage of the sloping site, with offices and canteen on the s side beneath the factory, opening on to a landscaped patio.

EALING

INTRODUCTION

Ealing, the centre of the modern borough, the 'queen of the suburbs' in the late c 19, was already a large village a century earlier, stretching from the old centre around the parish church N towards the hamlet of Haven Green close to the main Uxbridge Road. To the sw was a smaller settlement known as Little Ealing, to the NW the hamlet of Drayton Green, and on the rising ground to the N isolated farms and country houses. Only a few of the once numerous country seats survive: *Soane's* Pitshanger Manor in the village centre is the most notable. Ealing Park at Little Ealing has some good interiors. (For Gunnersbury Park on the s border *see* Hounslow.) Ealing throughout the c 19 maintained a reputation for respectability. The suburban development that followed the arrival of the railways (the G.W.R. in 1838, the District line in 1879) was generous in scale, especially around Castle Bar to the N where the tone had been set by Castle Hill Lodge, the country house of Queen Victoria's father, the Duke of Kent.

The transformation of the village to a proud and successful Victorian suburb (U.D.C. in 1894, borough in 1901) owed much to the local surveyor and architect *Charles Jones*, who was responsible not only for the layout of the streets and their services but for all the major civic buildings (see his *Ealing, from Village to Corporate Town*, 1902). Ealing is still a pleasant place, with enough remaining of the older houses and open spaces to give it a distinctive character, and with plenty of comfortable, well-cared-for Victorian suburbs. The largest houses have been replaced by flats, and the w end of the Broadway has suffered from indifferent commercial rebuilding, but the civic centrepieces of the late c 19 survive, complemented now by a shopping centre whose design forcibly

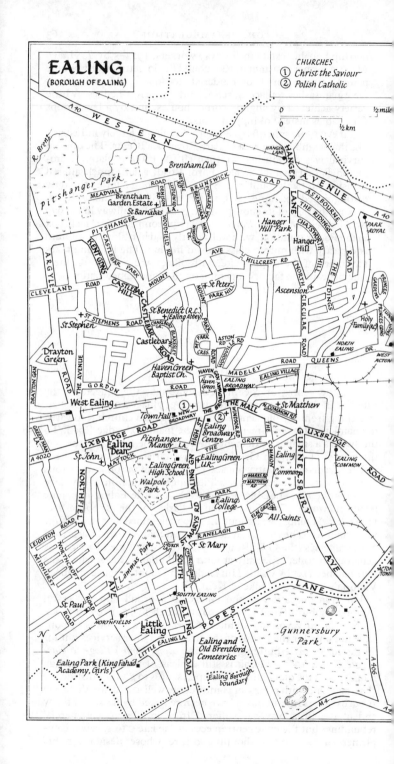

EALING
(BOROUGH OF EALING)

CHURCHES
① Christ the Saviour
② Polish Catholic

½ mile
½ km

A 40 WESTERN
HANGER LANE
HANGER AVENUE

R. Brent
Pitshanger Park
Brentham Club
MEADVALE ROAD
Brentham Garden Estate
St Barnabas
DENISON
LUDLOW
NEVIL
FOWLERS WK
BRENTHAM WAY
BRUNSWICK
WINDSOR
WOODFIELD RD
ROAD
THE RIDINGS
ASHBOURNE ROAD
CHATSWORTH
PARK ROYAL
A 40

PITSHANGER
Hanger Hill Park
Hanger Hill
KENT GDNS
CASTLEBAR PARK
MOUNT
AVE
HILLCREST RD
NORTH CIRCULAR ROAD
THE RIDINGS
THE RIDINGS
PRINCES GARDENS
PRINCES
TUDOR
ARGYLE
CLEVELAND ROAD
CASTLEBAR HILL
CASTLEBAR
St Peter
MOUNT PARK HILL
Ascension
PARK ROAD
Holy Family (R.C.)
NORTH EALING
WEST ACTON
DR

+ ST STEPHENS ROAD
St Stephen
CHARLBURY GR
CASTLEBAR ROAD
BLAKESLEY
St Benedict (R.C.)
(Ealing Abbey)
Castlebar
ASTON RD
GOODWILL RD
MT PARK CRES
MADELEY ROAD
QUEENS

Drayton Green
DRAYTON GDN
THE AVENUE
GORDON ROAD
Haven Green Baptist Ch.
HAVEN GREEN
Haven Green
EALING BROADWAY
EALING VILLAGE

West Ealing
Town Hall ①+
NEW BROADWAY
②+
Ealing Broadway Centre
THE MALL
N. COMMON RD
+ St Matthew

UXBRIDGE ROAD
A 4020
St John +
Ealing Dean
MATTOCK
Pitshanger Manor
EALING GREEN LA.
THE GROVE
WINDSOR RD
Ealing Common
EALING COMMON
UXBRIDGE ROAD

NORTHFIELD AVE
GREEN MAN LA.
Ealing Green U.R.
Ealing Green High School
Walpole Park
ST MARKS RD
ST MATTHEWS RD
GUNNERSBURY
ELM GROVE RD

THE PARK
Ealing College
RANELAGH RD
All Saints
ACTON TOWN
A 406

LEIGHTON ROAD
NORTHCROFT
MIDHURST
Lammas Park
CHURCH GDNS
St Mary
SOUTH GDNS

St Paul
NORTHFIELDS
Little Ealing
SOUTH EALING
LITTLE EALING LA.
POPES LANE
Gunnersbury Park

Ealing Park (King Fahad Academy, Girls)
SOUTH EALING ROAD
LITTLE EALING ROAD
Ealing and Old Brentford Cemeteries
Ealing Borough boundary
M 4
A 4

N

demonstrates the local concern that the new should be in harmony
with the existing character of the area.

CHURCHES

ALL SAINTS, Elm Grove Road, Ealing Common. 1903–5 by *W. A.
Pite*. Built as a memorial to Spencer Perceval, the prime minister
assassinated in 1812, with money bequeathed by his youngest
daughter. Conventional stone Gothic, apart from the E end,
where lancets are visible through an open arched reredos. – Much
carved WOODWORK, and a memorable LECTERN and PULPIT
of brass and iron, with art nouveau allusions, by *Nelson Dawson*.
ASCENSION, Hanger Hill. 1938–9 by *Seely & Paget*. A classical
pediment over the entrance, but otherwise without period detail.
Concrete frame hidden by grey brick; a tower over the chancel,
canted barrel-vault over the nave. Passage aisles divided off by
square piers. – Simple, unmoulded striped FURNISHINGS of
different woods by *George R. Hammer*.
CHRIST THE SAVIOUR, New Broadway. A proud design of 1852
by *G. G. Scott* for the Victorian centre of Ealing. Kentish rag
and Bath stone, in correct Second Pointed style, that is with
geometric tracery and plenty of naturalistic carving of capitals
and corbels inside. An impressively tall, rather busy W tower,
with an octagonal top, corner pinnacles, and spire. Lofty interior
with tall arcades and clerestory, the general effect not helped by
the standard type of post-war STAINED GLASS in the E windows
(by *Hugh Easton*, 1952) and clear windows elsewhere. – The best
fittings are the ORGAN CASES (chancel and W end) with Gothic
cresting and angels in relief. They are of 1906 by *Bodley*, who
also added the PULPIT and other woodwork, the pretty painting
to the roofs, and the sacristies.
ST BARNABAS, Pitshanger Lane. 1914–16 by *E. C. Shearman* and
Ernest A. Tyler of Ealing, the ambitious scale a surprising contrast with the neighbouring cottages of the Brentham estate for
which the church was built. The first of Shearman's three West
London churches to express his characteristic personal version
of Mediterranean Gothic, which he had tried out already at St
Silas, Kentish Town (Ca). Dramatic flowing window tracery
offset by austere dark purple brick walls with stone bands. Spacious interior with broad arch-braced roof; passage aisles behind
plain painted brick arches. The width of the nave embraces both
the chancel and the narrow ambulatory around the apse. Tall
clerestory, and a large W rose window with cruciform mullion
and transom. The most wayward effects are found in the small S
chapel. This has its own tiny W gallery, and a canted-out E bay
with narrow lancets, all dominated by a stunningly colossal,
excellently leaded E rose with flowing tracery. Original plans
included a N nave chapel, never built, and a parish room below
the W gallery flanked by a W tower. In the unfinished SW tower
paired entrance archways with flattened ogee heads: the STATUE
above, designed by *Shearman*, was added as a memorial to the
first vicar († 1926). – WALL PAINTING. Last Judgement, with
a host of angels around the sanctuary, by *James Clark*. – STAINED

GLASS. Two five-light windows in the S aisle by *Clayton & Bell*, installed 1922, Nativity with saints and elders, good colours.

ST JOHN, Mattock Lane, West Ealing. 1875 by *E. H. Horne*, in a ponderous stock brick lancet style. Battlemented tower over the chancel – quite an effective composition from the E. Formerly with a spire, demolished after a fire in 1920. Alterations to the W end 1970; liturgical reordering 1984 by *I. Goldsmid*.

ST MARY, St Mary's Road. The medieval parish church was rebuilt in 1735–40 by *J. Horne* and drastically enlarged and remodelled in 1866–74 by *S. S. Teulon*. Its C18 form is just recognizable from the SE, where the pedimented E end rises above Teulon's apse. Now, instead of Horne's modest preaching box at the end of this quiet backwater of modern Ealing, one has the overweening landmark of Teulon's eccentrically elephantine W tower. From the W a mighty composition builds up: low narthex, two low polygonal towers, and then the top-heavy tower with its tall belfry windows and emphatic machicolation. The recessed pyramid roof of 1871 is in place of the intended spire. The stair-turret which gives the tower its lopsided outline was an addition of 1874. The body of the Georgian church is thoroughly disguised by much notched brickwork, striped buttresses, and other wayward decoration. Archbishop Tait called the alterations 'the conversion of a Georgian monstrosity into the semblance of a Constantinopolitan basilica', but this hardly prepares one for the piling on of effects inside: the exotic horseshoe arches of the E end, the notched brickwork of the arcades dimly visible beyond the iron stovepipe columns supporting the pierced wooden gallery, and the riot of coarse punched-out tracery spandrels beneath the shallow pitched roof. The iron columns were originally painted with spirals and diapers. A later unsuitable muted blue and cream colour scheme was provided in a redecoration of 1955 by *Goodhart-Rendel*. Plenty of confidently large pieces of carving by *Earp* (gallery-level corbels and chancel angels) and *Blomfield* (chancel capitals); lively IRONWORK and WOOD-WORK. The liturgical re-ordering by *I. Goldsmid* (first phase 1980) has not disturbed the main fittings. – REREDOS of marble and Caen stone, with a *Salviati* mosaic. – PULPIT. A splendidly inventive piece by *Teulon*: a drum on barley-sugar columns, above a splayed stone base carved with fishes. It was given by *Thomas Boddington* of Gunnersbury Lodge, who also designed much of the STAINED GLASS which fills the whole church. It was made by *Heaton, Butler & Bayne*, with the exception of the angels in the small E roses of the transepts by *Morris & Co.*, 1866, and the curious sepia and yellow windows of the baptistery on the S side, made by *Lavers & Barraud*, probably to the design of *Teulon*. – MONUMENTS. Many minor tablets, prominent among them those to the Walpole and Spencer Perceval families. – Henry Beaufoy † 1795 by *R. Westmacott Sen.* – Charles Hutchinson † 1828 by *Sir Richard Westmacott*. – BRASSES. Nave W wall: Richard Amondesham, in civilian dress, and wife, *c.* 1490, small kneeling figures. – Baptistery: W. W. Jackson, bishop of Antigua, † 1895, with effigy. – S of the church, THE POLYGON, a yellow brick church room with hexagonal windows, 1959, enlarged to the W by more sober multi-purpose rooms in a darker

brick, 1978 by *K. C. White & Partners*. – In the churchyard
some good TABLE TOMBS; also a festive LYCHGATE by *Teulon*
with patterned slates and decorative ridge tiles.

ST MATTHEW, North Common Road. 1883–4 by *Alfred Jowers*.
The usual late C19 capacious red brick basilica with apsed E end;
w gable with Dec tracery (also in brick) facing Ealing Common. –
Late C19 FITTINGS: Munich REREDOS, 1889, canopied CHOIR
STALLS of carved oak, 1892 by *T. W. Cutler*. – Italian marble
FONT, 1913. – Much STAINED GLASS, the most unusual two N
aisle windows by *Reginald Hallward*, 1919 and 1924, in a loose
drawing style; typical post-war Arts and Crafts sentimental
figures.

ST PAUL, Northcroft Road. 1906. Stock brick, simple tracery.
N transept. Apsed S chapel 1906 by *F. Hall-Jones* and *E. S.
Cummings*.

ST PETER, Mount Park Road. Designed in 1889 by *J. D. Sedding*,
who died in 1891; executed in 1892–3 by his partner, *Henry
Wilson*. An admirable demonstration of the use of Gothic forms –
especially the curvaceous forms of late Gothic – to produce a
building of great originality. The aim was 'a thoroughly congregational town church which though simple in general effect
shall attain picturesqueness and breadth of effect by arrangement
of simple masses, thickness of walls and variety of arched forms'.
The picturesqueness is achieved externally by the treatment of
the long nave roof, enlivened by two chains of shallow stone
arches linking small turrets (the larger of these are the tops of
the nave piers). The intended N transeptal tower was never built.
The W front has two tall turrets (as at Holy Trinity Sloane
Street Chelsea, KC) flanking a huge deeply recessed curvilinear
window. This is half concealed by flying buttresses in the form
of free-standing mullions linked to the window by openwork
tracery. The side doors in the W front are later additions. Inside,
the generously proportioned nave of four bays combines simple
wooden panelled piers with a more conventional Gothic
triforium, its dark openings contrasting to good effect with the
gloriously light W window with its lively leading patterns. The
chancel has an E wall with circular E window, a less elaborate
arrangement than the thicker wall with internal tracery that was
originally intended. Also unexecuted was the intended surface
enrichment by sculpture (life-size apostles in niches on the nave
piers) and painting on the cove of the roof. S chapel added 1913
by *E. J. May*; painted framed ceiling. – Fittings mostly of the
early C20, and less exciting than the church, except for the inner
WEST DOORS with art nouveau metalwork obviously by *Wilson*. –
ALTAR. Alabaster, 1912, converted from the reredos in 1958. –
Curved COMMUNION RAILS also 1912. – SCREEN. Low, originally curving inwards, cut back for *Bodley & Hare*'s conventional but well carved STALLS of 1932. – REREDOS in the S
chapel, a war memorial, elaborately carved Gothic by *C. G. Hare*,
1920. – PULPIT. 1910, accomplished ogee Gothic, in memory of
the first vicar, W. Petty. – STAINED GLASS. By *Kempe* the four-
light windows of the nativity in the S chapel. – Brass ornamented
CROSS to Mary Petty † 1894, by *T. Pratt & Sons*. – CHURCH
HALL to the N by *Laurence King & Partners*, 1981.

St Stephen, The Avenue. A proud c19 ragstone church with the usual E.E. detail. Converted to twenty-two flats by *Berkeley House plc* in 1985–7. It is a composite creation on a fine island site, designed as a prominent centrepiece for the smart suburb of Castle Bar (*see* Perambulation 2a). Chancel, nave, s aisle 1875–6 by *J. Ashdown*; continued by *A. Rovedino* (s aisle, s transept, 1880) and by *A. Blomfield*, who added the tower with its elaborate spire in 1891. – The c20 CHURCH CENTRE across the road, 1986 by *I. Goldsmid*, equally typical of its date, is a minimal brick box with pyramid roof, attached to an older hall now used for worship.

St Benedict (Ealing Abbey) (R.C.), Charlbury Grove. Remarkable both for its medieval scale and for length of building time. Two bays were completed in 1895–7 by *F. A. Walters*; the w end of the nave followed in 1905 (by *E. J. Walters*). Damaged in the war, the building was restored and enlarged in 1962 by *S. Kerr Bate*, who completed the transepts and continued the central tower. The chancel is not yet built. Dull stone Perp w front with gable between two turrets *à la* King's College chapel. Eight-bay nave on a parish church rather than monastic scale (no gallery or clerestory). Hammerbeam roof. No furnishing of interest except for a PAINTING of St Peter by *Ribera* (N aisle). The priory became an abbey in 1955. Monastic buildings 1903–4 by *Walters*; later school buildings.

Ealing Green Church (since 1972 Methodist and United Reformed). Built for the Congregationalists in 1859–60 by *Charles Jones*. Competent Kentish rag Gothic front with canted gabled sides. Interior modernized in 1929. Adjoining former manse of 1860 in the same materials. The rear addition to the church was rebuilt in 1981. The LITTLE CHURCH behind, now used for storage, was added as a children's church in 1926 by *P. Morley Horder*. It has an attractive whitewashed interior with round-headed arcades on wooden columns, and a barrel-vault.

Haven Green Baptist Church. 1880–1 by *J. Wallis Chapman*. Large, with polygonal end to the road. Red brick, Gothic. Chancel 1928. c20 glazed lobby (but original pews and galleries inside).

Polish Catholic Church (formerly Ealing Broadway Methodist Church), Windsor Road. 1867 by *Charles Jones* and *John Tarring*, unusually ambitious for a Nonconformist church of that date. Ragstone cruciform plan, early Dec detail. Tall spire, modelled on Tarring's church at Clapham Common (La). Former school buildings 1893 by *C. Ashby Lean*. Memorial hall 1925.

St Andrew (United Reformed), Mount Park Road. 1886–7 by *Wallace*, enlarged 1892. Gothic, red brick with stone stripes. Small tower over the porch.

Welsh Presbyterian Church, Ealing Green. *See* Perambulation 1.

West Ealing Baptist Chapel, Chapel Road. 1864–5 by *William Mumford*; stuccoed front with pediment. Porch 1927.

Ealing and Old Brentford Cemeteries, South Ealing Road. A well planned layout: corner lodges; two ragstone Gothic chapels linked by a ceremonial archway. 1861 by *Charles Jones*.

PUBLIC BUILDINGS

Town Hall, New Broadway. 1888 by the local board surveyor, *Charles Jones*. Ragstone Gothic with asymmetrically placed tower with spirelet; considerably more ambitious than its predecessor in the Mall (*see* Perambulation 1) of only fourteen years earlier, an indication of the expanding size and ambition of the new suburb. Originally it housed library as well as offices, and a public hall which is reached from the half-landing of a sumptuous imperial stair with iron balustrades. To the E an extension of 1930 by *Prynne & Johnstone*, still Gothic, with a second entrance and another grand staircase. Internal alterations 1988–9.

Civic Centre, New Broadway, dwarfing the town hall. A demonstration both of insensitive urban design and of expanding bureaucracy: built as speculative offices in 1980–3 by *Sidney Kaye, Eric Firmin & Partners*, and occupied by the council from 1987. Curious spanner-shaped plan. Seven storeys, with top-heavy polygonal corners emphasized by heavy imitation-brick balcony bands. The entrance is in Longfield Avenue. Opposite this is the Old Fire Station of 1888, a picturesque gabled composition, renovated in 1989 as offices and the borough's printing department.

Magistrates Courts, Green Man Lane. Free Baroque of 1914 by *H.T. Wakelam* of the M.C.C.; two storeys, with striped quoins, two dentilled gables, and a stone centrepiece.

Fire Station, Uxbridge Road. 1932–3 by *Evan E. Morgan*, chief architectural assistant to the borough surveyor, *W.R. Hicks*. Neat thirties-modern symmetrical stone front.

Pitshanger Manor, Mattock Lane and Ealing Green. The most interesting house in Ealing, used as a library from 1901, admirably restored from 1985 as a museum. In the C18 the estate belonged to a City merchant, Thomas Gurnell, for whom *George Dance Jun.* designed a S extension with two spacious reception rooms in 1768. At the time *John Soane* was a junior assistant in his office. In 1800, Soane, by then well established in his career and looking both for a country retreat for his family and for a place to develop his collections, bought the house, retained the plain brick Dance wing, and in 1801–3 replaced the rest by a new centre.

It is on a grandiose scale of which he alone in England was 42 capable. The contrast between the actual size of a small villa of only three bays and the scale of the design is surprising every time one compares an illustration of the house with the original. Also typical of Soane is the contrast between the bare walls and the grand Ionic order of Portland stone set in front of it like a screen. The idea of the detached order with strongly projecting entablature over each column is found earlier in Adam's S front at Kedleston, Derbyshire (1765), but of course comes originally from the Arch of Constantine in Rome. Soane had himself used it just before in the Lothbury Court of the Bank of England. The decoration was also intended as quotations from the antique. The entablatures carry standing statues (as at the Bank of England) placed against a windowless attic half the height of the ground floor. Between them, two roundels with the Medici lion, and a

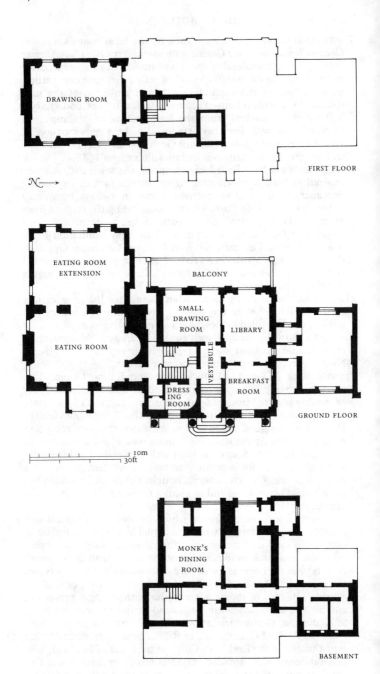

FIRST FLOOR

DRAWING ROOM

N→

EATING ROOM
EXTENSION

BALCONY

SMALL
DRAWING
ROOM

LIBRARY

EATING ROOM

VESTIBULE

DRESS
ING
ROOM

BREAKFAST
ROOM

GROUND FLOOR

10m
30ft

MONK'S
DINING
ROOM

BASEMENT

Ealing, Pitshanger Manor,
plans of first floor, ground floor, and basement

central square panel with a putto; below the windows, panels with eagles in wreaths. The figures are all of *Coade* stone. The centre is raised higher than the rest. No roof shows. Balustrades emphasize the severe rectangularity of the design. On the garden side to the w instead of columns there are flat strips with incised lines without bases or capitals. The basement and raised ground floor were originally hidden by a conservatory.

Inside, Soane's spaces are comparable to the interiors of his town house at No. 12 Lincoln's Inn Fields: small and intimate, but with plenty of characteristic detail. Narrow ENTRANCE HALL, tiny, but full of interest, with its sequence of a tunnel-vault, raised lantern, and another tunnel-vault at the level of the *piano nobile*. Over two doorways reliefs representing the sun and moon, copies of terracottas by *Banks*, based on the medallions of the Arch of Constantine. Originally the lower walls were marbled, and all the plaster reliefs were bronzed. The inner hall leads to a small DRAWING ROOM formerly opening into the conservatory which overlooked the garden, now plain apart from an original fireplace and ceiling with incised lines around the edges. N of this room is the LIBRARY, its shallow groined vault with a recessed central rosette. The original delicate ceiling dec-oration of trellising and flowers was painted over in the c19 but is known from Gandy's view; the present similar scheme painted by *Alan Powers* in 1986 is based on paint analysis, aided by the similar ceiling in the breakfast room of No. 12 Lincoln's Inn Fields of 1792. In the walls, mirror-lined niches for Soane's urns and vases, with bookcases below; at the E end a shallow coffered arch. Beyond is the BREAKFAST ROOM, repainted with its orig- 43 inal rich and powerful colour scheme (established by scrapes, and noticeably different from Gandy's perspective preserved in the Soane Museum, which shows Soane's earliest ideas). A very shallow dome is supported at the corners by four *Coade* stone Egyptian caryatids painted copper bronze. They stand flat against the wall, and the elegant segmental arches with their spandrels touching the corners in a point have all the brittle thinness and precision so typical of Soane. The centre of the vault is painted with cloud effects; the pale surround has a raised fret pattern with silver-bronze plaster winged figures in relief on the pen-dentives. The walls are marbled in slate blue-green and porphyry colour around niches (recreated in the restoration). They orig-inally held antique sculptures. Marble fireplace inlaid with Greek key patterns.

To the l. of the entrance hall is a small LOBBY or dressing room, with curved end and tiny fireplace and mirror, and the STAIRCASE, a curious construction of cast iron with inset stone treads (possibly a reworking of older material), lit by an oval roof-light. In a recess a figure of Minerva above two large ox skulls; in another niche an early c19 bust of Spencer Perceval (after *Nollekens*). Perceval's five daughters lived here from 1844; the last survivor died in 1900. The ground-floor EATING ROOM in the Dance wing, redecorated in late Georgian blues and greens, has a strongly geometric ceiling decorated with arabesques and rosettes, and a serving niche at one end flanked by roundels. The arched windows and niche all have thick fluted surrounds.

Original fireplace. The room was tactfully doubled in depth towards the garden in 1901 by *Charles Jones*, repeating the ceiling decoration. The first-floor DRAWING ROOM is delicately ornamented with composite pilasters framing the windows; ceiling with arabeques and fans, and two roundels with harvest trophies. The blue and green colouring is based on paint analysis, and shown in a view by Richardson of 1832; the Chinese wallpaper is an addition of 1986, based on the Richardson view. In the basement of the Soane block the MONK'S DINING ROOM was originally used for Soane's collections, a foretaste of his later 'monk's rooms' at Lincoln's Inn Fields. It has a curious, presumably deliberate, mixture of plasterwork styles. Soane's kitchen was in a separate block to the N, replaced by the lending library of 1940. Beyond it to the N lay an even more eccentric creation: a collection of half-buried mock ruins to hoodwink antiquarian visitors. There were indeed many visitors, but Soane's two sons, whom the house was intended to inspire, showed no interest in pursuing an architectural profession, and the disappointed father sold the estate in 1810, removing his collections to Lincoln's Inn Fields.

In the C19 addition to the N is displayed a collection of Martinware pottery (produced at Southall from 1877 to 1923), including a fireplace designed by *W. A. Berry* in 1891 for Buscot Park, Oxfordshire. N of the house the extension for the lending library (now offices) was rebuilt in 1940, muted classical, yellow brick, with three roof-lights, the middle one with a shallow dome in a slightly Soanic spirit.

The grounds behind the house are now WALPOLE PARK, opened to the public in 1901. The cedars on the W lawn go back to the C18, as does the walled kitchen garden which now shelters a rose garden. The ornamental gardens were landscaped in 1800 by *John Haverfield* of Kew. The earlier serpentine lake NW of the house was replanted as a sunken garden in the 1920s. It is bounded at the N end by a picturesque three-arched BRIDGE designed by Soane in 1802, of flint and cyclopean masonry, the show front to the S incorporating re-used fragments. Soane's NE GATEWAY also has an eccentric mixture of materials: rubbed red brick, with pilaster strips of knapped flint, and stone top hampers of typical Soanic outline. (An early scheme for the house proposed a mixture of flint and brick.) Small NE LODGE, also by Soane, now incorporating the coach house. The more conventional main E gates to the house are a post-1918 WAR MEMORIAL by *Leonard A. Shuffrey*. In the park, near the bridge, a MONUMENT to the Ealing borough surveyor Charles Jones † 1913, a bronze portrait bust by *Frank Bowcher*, made for the town hall.

EALING COLLEGE OF HIGHER EDUCATION, St Mary's Road. On this site from 1929. Main buildings of 1953 by *C. G. Stillman* of the *M.C.C.*, a quietly modern front of the Festival era: four storeys, brick-faced, with ground floor recessed behind columns. The concrete frame is exposed in the long classroom range behind. Later extensions. The college incorporates the buildings of the former Girls' County School in The Park.

EALING GREEN HIGH SCHOOL, Ealing Green. Original build-

ings of 1913, for Ealing County Boys, by *H. G. Crothall*, architect
to the *M.C.C.*: facing the green a dignified front in early C 18 style,
red brick, with a stone centrepiece with pediment. Extensions of
1936, 1961, 1964.

NOTTING HILL AND EALING HIGH SCHOOL, Cleveland Road.
The centre is a tall stuccoed house of *c.* 1870, one of the few
survivals of its date in the Castle Bar area.

EALING PARK (King Fahad Academy Girls' Upper School), Little
Ealing Lane. Ealing Park was famous in the C 19 for its grounds,
landscaped by *Repton* and planted and improved by William
Lawrence and his wife, who lived there from 1838. Until the
estate was sold for building to the British Land Company in
1882, the house stood in a park with lakes and fine trees extending
E as far as South Ealing Road, and with flower gardens, formal
pool, aviary, etc., to the W. The house survived in a sadly constricted setting as a convent and school; it was sympathetically
restored for its present use in 1988–9 by the *Carnell Green
Partnership*. Restrained C 18 entrance front, facing E, of 3–3–3
bays, two storeys, with central pediment and stone quoins. The
red brick walls have been covered by later stucco. Four-column
Tuscan porch. But the core of the house goes back at least to the
C 17: timber-framing including a curved brace was revealed in
the spine wall between front and back rooms during conservation
work in 1988. Entrance hall with stone paved floor and good late
C 18 cornice, another in the room to the N; the smaller room to
the S has an elaborate fitted bookcase with lead-patterned glazing.
These later C 18 improvements may date from 1789–92, when
the land tax returns show that the house increased in value. In
the SW (staff) room, niches flanking the fireplace, and another
cornice with deep Greek-key frieze. Here, and in the adjoining
stair hall, the colours are based on evidence of the original
schemes. Fine C 18 staircase with iron balustrade; its awkward
siting suggests that the flight may have been reversed later. The
NW rooms form a double drawing room, with florid ceiling
decoration of the later C 19, and French windows opening on to
an Ionic loggia of 2–4–2 bays along the W front. These improvements may date from the time of the Lawrences; likewise the SW
bedroom upstairs, which has plausibly been associated with a
visit by the young Queen Victoria. It has charmingly lighthearted painted decoration: on the walls, foliage trails and arabesques; on the partially preserved shallow domed ceiling, small
figures in medallions. The centre, formerly with a mirror, now
has a painting of clouds and birds. A C 19 account describes the
room draped in muslin.

S of the main house lower C 19 service buildings. To the SE a
tall, octagonal garden building with arched windows, rendered
over red brick, traditionally said to be a dairy.

HEALTH CENTRE, Mattock Lane. 1983–5 by *Kemble Croft* (North
West Thames Regional Health Authority), on the site of a former
hospital. Large glazed porch, otherwise discreetly unassuming:
one and two storeys, brown brick, with domestic pitched roof.

STATIONS. The most interesting are the Piccadilly extension line
stations of the 1930s. EALING COMMON, by *Charles Holden*,
1931, resembles the stations of the Northern line extension to

Morden. Its non-period bare concrete forms are a little bleak compared with NORTHFIELDS, 1932–3 by *Charles Holden* with *S. A. Heaps*. This is of the Sudbury Hill type (*see* Sudbury, Br), elegant without being fussy, with a straight ground-floor canopy and a higher ticket-hall block at right angles to it, straddling the tracks, with one large, wide window. PARK ROYAL, opened in 1901, was rebuilt in 1935–6 by *Welch & Lander* as part of their development at Hanger Hill (*see* Perambulation 2a). It is a picturesquely stepped group, building up from the railway to a circular booking hall and tower, neatly tied in with the curving shopping parade at street level. SOUTH EALING, originally of 1932, was rebuilt in 1988 on the N side of the railway; NORTH EALING, for the Metropolitan District Railway, is of 1903. EALING BROADWAY (main line) was rebuilt in 1965, with an ugly tower block above.

PERAMBULATIONS

1. The centre of Ealing, from the old village to the Common and the Broadway

Starting from St Mary's church, the broad tree-lined stretches of ST MARY'S ROAD and EALING GREEN still have a leisurely atmosphere and a few buildings to recall the period up to the mid C19 when Ealing was simply a large village with some comfortable small country houses on its fringes, and only a little tentative suburban development. Near the church a scatter of attractive small houses remains: a short C19 stuccoed terrace in RANELAGH ROAD contrasts with older, lower cottages opposite in CHURCH LANE (Nos. 1, 15–17) and in ST MARY'S ROAD (Nos. 72–74, detached, set-back houses, with steep gables to the road, once part of the old workhouse built *c.* 1700). On two sides of the little ST MARY'S SQUARE are humble Georgian terraces; also the very modest OLD FIRE HOUSE of 1888. Opposite, at the bend in the main road, WESTFIELD HOUSE, No. 94, a grander late Georgian house of three bays with Ionic porch, large arched window above, and lunette on the top floor. A diversion S can take in ST MARY'S HOUSE at the end of CHURCH GARDENS, two-storey almshouses of 1902–3 by *W. A. Pite*, in free Tudor, half-timbered, with stone centrepiece (a replacement for earlier almshouses in The Mall).

Now to the N up ST MARY'S ROAD. On the W side EALING COURT MANSIONS, built in 1867 as an industrial school, in conservative late Georgian style, five bays, three storeys, much added to. On the E side Ealing College of Higher Education (q.v.) and behind an older garden wall from the former vicarage, a Y.M.C.A. hostel, large but quite tactful, in traditional brick, with corner tower; 1982–5 by *Hurley, Porte & Duell*. A single early Victorian villa and a taller pair follow, all with nice neo-Grecian gateposts. Off to the E THE PARK, a side street laid out by *Sydney Smirke* from *c.* 1847, with five pairs of large stuccoed Italianate paired villas, somewhat reminiscent of grander developments in Kensington (KC). Entrances set back in side bays, the central pair (Nos. 21–22) with towers.

After this, St Mary's Road widens to become EALING GREEN, with a good varied sequence along the W side. The celebrated C20 EALING FILM STUDIOS, partly by *R. Atkinson*, 1931, incorporate an older house. THE LAWN is early Victorian stock brick, 1–3–1 bays, with arched ground-floor windows, a parapet with faintly Jacobean raised centre, and coach house to match. Assorted small houses of *c.* 1840 and earlier follow, then the WELSH PRESBYTERIAN CHURCH of 1908, hidden down an alley, with pretty iron overthrow, and the charming former GIRLS' SCHOOL of 1861 (now Kingdom Hall), a small, gabled, U-shaped group in polychrome brick, with patterned tiled roofs. Then, in a deplorably messy setting (for which British Telecom are responsible), ST MARY'S, a good five-bay C18 house with central dentilled pediment, followed by Ealing School, and the best house of all, Pitshanger Manor (for both, *see* Public Buildings).

On the E side THE GROVE now starts as the access road to the C20 shopping centre (*see* below), but continues with demure Victorian villas along the S side. Opposite, ST SAVIOUR'S CLERGY HOUSE (once close to a now-demolished church), 1909 by *G. H. Fellowes Prynne*, a substantial group, coloured brickwork, free Gothic detail, with stepped gable over the entrance. Past the KING'S ARMS of 1897, with jolly corner turret, one arrives at EALING COMMON, still a large, pleasant open area with plenty of trees, despite the North Circular Road traffic thundering along the E side. The surrounding streets were built up only gradually from the C19. At the N end of the W side, a few quite grand mid C19 stucco-trimmed terraces. The best (No. 8 etc.) is of *c.* 1840; all stuccoed. To their S two pretty artisan cul-de-sacs of *c.* 1880 which replaced older cottages: ST MARK'S ROAD and ST MATTHEW'S ROAD. The N side, with its ambitious gabled and turreted houses flanking St Matthew's church in NORTH COMMON ROAD, was developed only from the 1880s; the S side has an early C20 assortment built in the grounds of Elm Grove, the house which belonged to Spencer Perceval in the early C19.

THE MALL leads W from the Common into the Victorian centre. Near the start, Nos. 42–43, a handsome mid C19 stuccoed pair of villas with giant pilasters. The scale changes in WINDSOR ROAD to the S, with its larger, more urban stucco-trimmed houses, built by *c.* 1870. On the N side of The Mall, the NATIONAL WESTMINSTER BANK, built in 1874 as offices for the U.D.C. by its enterprising surveyor *Charles Jones* (*see* Public Buildings: Town Hall). Kentish rag, chunky French Gothic detail, with a tower; more daring than most suburban municipal buildings of this date. N of The Mall HAVEN GREEN, an open space surviving from a former hamlet, now buffers the commercial centre from the residential areas of the N. Its highlight is No. 36 on the E side, D.L. LEWIS, a chemist's shop with complete art-nouveau frontage of 1924 and fittings of 1902 and 1924. On the N side, the domineering HAVEN GREEN COURT, flats of 1937–8 which replaced a house called The Haven.

EALING BROADWAY CENTRE is now the hub of the Victorian

shopping area. The comprehensive redevelopment of the area s
of The Mall, much discussed from the 1960s, was finally carried
out in 1979–85, after plans for a destructive bypass to the Broadway had been dropped and the site reduced in size. Winners of
the competition were the *Building Design Partnership* (partner in
charge *Keith Scott*; design architect *Frank Roberts*). Historically
the centre is important as one of the first cases where, as a result
of local pressure, the usual package of covered shopping malls,
lucrative offices, and multi-storey car parks was designed to make
a deliberately picturesque contribution to the town centre. The
use of brick and of pitched roofs, and the attention paid to public
open space, is paralleled by the other West London revival of
traditional forms, Hillingdon Civic Centre, Uxbridge (Hi), but
here the allusions are both more exotic and more urban. The
brick towers and turrets evoke a continental medieval walled city,
as parts of Hampstead Garden Suburb tried to do sixty years
earlier. The machine-made textures lack the appeal of early C20
craftsmanship, but the variety of inventive detail is impressive.
The planning is also ingenious, with all servicing from the basement. The main focus is the TOWN SQUARE, a pedestrian area
open to the sky, rather cluttered, but a humane breathing-space
after the indoor shopping areas. Glazed arcades on three sides.
The ornamental metalwork is by *Giuseppe Lund*. On the w side
a backdrop is provided by tall neo-Victorian offices (their glossy
modern atrium inside is entirely concealed). On the E are the
seven-storey car parks, exploited here remarkably successfully as
a visual asset: the gaping holes are masked by decorative grilles,
and the whole is effectively prefaced by a grand staircase flanked
by two frankly romantic lift towers with pointed roofs. The
stairs also lead to the LIBRARY, tucked into the centre as an
afterthought, and disappointingly cramped inside. The pretty
timbered fantasy overlooking the square from the s is used by a
sports club. On the exterior frontages red brick provides a uni-
fying feature, but varied detail expresses the different functions:
to the s the triangular oriels of the library; to the High Street a
lofty covered arcade beneath the offices (of brick with eclectic
stone dressings, in a vaguely classical spirit); above the shops in
The Broadway, a flashier vertical rhythm of faceted mirror glass
between brick fins. At the opposite end, the housing in CARIL-
LON COURT, off Oxford Road, looks appropriately domestic,
behind an entrance archway by *Giuseppe Lund*.

2. *The outlying areas: roughly clockwise from the* N

2a. N *of Uxbridge Road*

CASTLE BAR. The high ground N of Uxbridge Road was in the
   early C19 occupied by farmland and a few large houses. The
   most illustrious resident was the Duke of Kent, the father of
   Queen Victoria. His house, Castle Hill Lodge, was demolished
   in 1827, but the neighbourhood retained its superior status when
   it was developed later. Indifferent C20 flats now dominate many
   of the broad roads, but there are still mature trees recalling

former large gardens, and some enjoyable older survivals, mostly of the end of the C19. The houses from the ambitious mid Victorian scheme of 1860 have all gone. They were built by the owner of the successor to Castle Hill Lodge, Henry de Bruno Austin, who began to lay out a large estate of detached villas along a grid of roads around rectangular pleasure gardens (cf. Isleworth, Ho). Only twenty houses were built (in Kent Gardens and Cleveland Road) before he went bankrupt in 1872.

Starting from Haven Green, CASTLEBAR ROAD begins with a few early and mid C19 villas (the best group facing a small green opposite Carlton Road). Later houses in the side streets: in BLAKESLEY AVENUE to the r., No. 2 by *E. R. Barrow*, c. 1906, a well crafted corner house with angled wing, Ipswich window, and half-timbered gables. In CHARLBURY GROVE tall late C19 houses in the style of Shaw, opposite Ealing Abbey (*see* Churches: St Benedict). The abbey precincts cover the site of Castlehill House, an C18 house which belonged to General Wetherall, a friend of the Duke of Kent. Halfway along CASTLEBAR HILL, ST DAVID'S HOMES for ex-servicemen, incorporating the remains of Austin's house on the site of Castle Hill Lodge, and still surrounded by large grounds. Low stuccoed buildings, with Doric arched loggia to the garden; many additions. CHAPEL of 1919 by *A. S. G. Butler*, classical, rather French, with rusticated pilasters, broken pediment, and a central dome. Stained glass of 1866. To the N, in CASTLEBAR PARK, a detour to take in two groups of almshouses: the former Victorian Homes of 1898 and, further W, the Wheeler Homes (Nos. 69–73) of 1909, three modest roughcast cottages. Back on Castlebar Hill the most prominent late Victorian survival is WYKE HOUSE, 1891 by *J. Kershaw*, with tall octagonal viewing tower. To the S, in EDGEHILL ROAD, *Leonard Shuffrey* demonstrated the variety of picturesque 'Old English' traditions with his own house, THORNCOTE, of 1888, which has two shaped gables and a big hooded porch, and the neighbouring INGLESIDE (much altered), with crowstepped end gable. The COACH HOUSE with pretty turret, set back across the road, is also by him. At the corner with ST STEPHEN'S ROAD, LAKESIDE, 1966, one of the best of the C20 redevelopments, unfortunately little imitated. *Wates* tilehung houses and a tall block of flats, in a carefully landscaped setting, with lake (preserved from The Grange), clearly much influenced by contemporary Span estates. The second tower was a later addition. Opposite, No. 30, a trim textbook-modern children's home of 1968–9 by *Yorke, Rosenberg & Mardall*; pale brick ground floor, flat roof, the oversailing timber-framed upper floor clad with glazed sheeting. At the junction of St Stephen's Road and The Avenue, the focal point is ST STEPHEN'S COURT, now flats, but so obviously a former church that it must be included under churches (q.v.). THE AVENUE continues S, built up less ambitiously, down to West Ealing station, where the main landmark is the DRAYTON COURT HOTEL, heavy-handed High Victorian, white brick with two turrets. Further W, DRAYTON GREEN, still with a green as a reminder of the former hamlet.

A second excursion from Haven Green leads N up MOUNT PARK

ROAD, an area which epitomizes Ealing's reputation as 'Queen of the Suburbs'. The boldly ornamental lamp posts at the corner of Aston Road and Woodville Road and of Mount Park Road and Park Hill, dated 1895, were converted from early electricity transformers. Some of the late Victorian and Edwardian houses along the winding roads in this area have been replaced, but MOUNT PARK CRESCENT and PARK HILL are virtually intact, and St Peter's church (q.v.) remains, with an appealing VIC- ARAGE next door, 1910 by *Morley Horder*, an Arts and Crafts design with projecting gable, mullioned windows, and coved eaves. To the w, in EATON RISE, CHESTERTON COURT, shel- tered flats for the elderly, by *Edward Cullinan Architects*, 1990, a crisp five-storey block enlivened by patterned brickwork, with a generous deep-eaved porch flanking a projecting common room.

Further N, WOODFIELD ROAD begins with Nos. 2–14 by *W. G. Wilson*, with quiet Queen Anne detail. The N end is something different, the start of the BRENTHAM GARDEN ESTATE,* West London's answer to Hampstead Garden Suburb, a development of 1901–15 for Ealing Tenants Ltd, pioneers of the Co-Part- nership movement. It was built on what was then just still open country. The earliest houses indeed predate the Hampstead suburb: they are Nos. 71–87 Woodfield Road, 1901, named Vivian Terrace after Henry Vivian M.P., the guiding light in the enterprise. Fifty houses had been completed by 1905, small terraces along straight roads, stylistically unremarkable. The change came after 1907, when further land was acquired (the total came to 60.5 acres), and *Raymond Unwin* and *Barry Parker* (by then busy at Hampstead) were invited to lay out the estate. By 1914 there were about 650 houses. As at Hampstead, the Parker & Unwin layout achieves variety by winding roads, by the creation of cul-de-sacs, by staggering frontages, and by skilfully angling buildings across corners so that each road junction is a model of picturesquely composed simple vernacular forms: hipped tiled roofs, gables, rendered walls, casement windows of various sizes – all lessons that were to be spelt out in Unwin's later reports and publications. Parker & Unwin themselves designed Nos. 1–7 Winscombe Crescent, and Widecombe in Brentham Way. The other architects involved were *F. Cavendish Pearson* (Ludlow Road, Meadvale Road, Neville Road, Ruskin Gardens, upper end of Brentham Way) and, later on, *G. Lister Sutcliffe* (w end of Brentham Way, Fowler's Walk, Denison Road). Low hedges, playing fields, and neighbouring allotments, together helped to foster the rural image. The social centre was provided by the excellent INSTITUTE, now the Brentham Club, in Meadvale Road, 1911, with its bold, rather Germanic-looking red brick corner tower with pyramid roof looking down Denison Road. (Its prototype was the now destroyed Hampstead Tenants' Club.) An intended extension with cloister and second hall was never built. The estate was less comprehensive in its social pro- vision than Hampstead, although school and church were soon provided nearby in PITSHANGER LANE, where there is also a

74

---

*The following account owes much to the Brentham Society's publication, *Brentham, Ealing's Garden Suburb*, compiled by B. Johnson (1977), and to notes by Mervyn Miller.

small but flamboyant contemporary shopping arcade with much yellow terracotta, 1909 by *S. H. Burdward*.

In WESTERN AVENUE, W of the roundabout, the head offices of the construction firm TAYLOR WOODROW, by *T. P. Bennett & Partners*, 1957–8, a typical but well handled design of its date: a brick-faced six-storey front with long bands of windows and boxed-out centrepiece. In front of the entrance, 'Teamwork', a massive granite SCULPTURE by *David Wynne*, 1958, inspired by the firm's logo of four men pulling together.

The area around Hanger Lane S of the roundabout is a good hunting-ground for the thirties enthusiast. To the E is HANGER HILL, superior suburbia built up between the wars, largely by Haymills Ltd, whose architects were *Welch, Cachemaille-Day & Lander*. A series of concentric crescents was laid out on a former golf course, starting with No. 1 THE RIDINGS, 1934 (an individual commission: the client was inspired by the architect's earlier estate in Hendon). It is a flagship for progressive modern design: flat-roofed, with a curved balcony over the entrance, smooth rendered upper walls, and originally with blue-painted metal windows. Streamlined interior, including a sweeping steel stair rail and plenty of fitted cupboards. Several other versions of the same image (Nos. 7, 11a, 15, 19), but other houses are in safer, more traditional styles. Park Royal Station (q.v.), rebuilt at the same time, is the focus for one of the few 1930s suburban centres which sought to escape from a cosy garden city image. The PARK ROYAL HOTEL makes a show with twisted brick columns. It was intended also as a social centre for the estate. 1936 by *Welch & Lander*. Nearby, in WESTERN AVENUE, HANGER COURT FLATS, by the same firm, 1935, an angular composition of brick in a slightly awkward hybrid style: flat projecting eaves, corner windows, and roof pergola.

Between North Ealing and West Acton Stations is the different world of the HANGER HILL GARDEN ESTATE, the beau ideal 97 of romantic rural Metroland. Immaculate half-timbered houses and flats of 1928–36 by *Douglas Smith & Barley*. Unusually well landscaped: the large blocks of flats stand in spacious lawns off QUEENS DRIVE, the houses are set off by attractive planting in PRINCES GARDENS. More glamorous aspirations of the inter-war period are represented by the Dutch-Colonial–Baroque frontages of EALING VILLAGE, tucked away N of the railway line W of Hanger Lane, 1934–6 by *R. Toms & Partners*. Five blocks of flats, with clubroom and swimming pool.

2b. S of Uxbridge Road

Buildings of interest are more scattered here than in the northern parts of Ealing. S of Ealing Common the main road leads to Gunnersbury (*see* Hounslow). POPES LANE skirts the N edge of Gunnersbury Park. Further S in SOUTH EALING ROAD the EALING PARK TAVERN, 1886 by *F. W. Lacey*, a flamboyant Old English cornerpiece. To the W in LITTLE EALING LANE two substantial houses remain from the old hamlet of Little Ealing: Ealing Park, now a school (*see* Public Buildings), and

across the road to the N, ROCHESTER HOUSE, now Institute of
Production Engineers. This has an attractive early C18 three-
storey N front of brown brick with six (formerly seven) bays of
segment-headed windows with rubbed red brick heads. The
range backing on to this has a later C18 stock brick front with
five more broadly spaced straight-headed windows, the central
one with eared surround. Also on the N side, CONVENT of the
Order of the Sacred Heart of Mercy, 1976 by *Francis Weal
Associates*. Three-storey residential wing, quite bold, with a high
splayed plinth and two free-standing brick piers. Lower range
ending in a top-lit lozenge-shaped chapel. In NORTHFIELD
AVENUE the most notable buildings are Northfields Station (*see*
Public Buildings) and the former AVENUE CINEMA (now Top
Hat Club) opposite, of 1932 by *Cecil Massey*, an original exterior:
an oblong of white roughcast topped by a cornice of glazed tiles,
with elaborate wall lamps. Known as 'Spanish City' from its
luxurious interior, possibly by *Theodore Komisarjevsky*. Miniature
Moorish village scenery (cf. the former Odeon Finsbury Park,
Hy); exotic tented auditorium. Further N, minor well preserved
Edwardiana. Shopping parade of 1904; a forceful design with
much yellow terracotta. To the W a grid of small respectable
contemporary terraces, still with their corner shops, centred on
NORTHCROFT ROAD. In LEIGHTON ROAD, a good 'reformed'
pub, THE FORESTER, by *Nowell Parr*, 1909, a handsome corner
composition with roughcast gables on heavy carved brackets, art
nouveau glass, and Parr's favourite dark green tiles and polished
granite. Well preserved interior.

WEST EALING is another former hamlet, also known as Ealing
Dean, built up modestly from the mid C19. Near the old centre,
at the W end of MATTOCK LANE, a few small stucco-trimmed
houses remain around the Baptist church and St John's church
(qq.v.). Further E, No. 86, haphazardly enlarged, but with an
early C19 centre with Greek Doric porch. On the N side, looking
out over Walpole Park, larger, more ambitious villas and pairs of
the 1860s onwards (the later ones with coloured brick and tile
trim instead of stucco). Near the E end, the QUESTORS
THEATRE, 1963–4 by *N. Bransom*, with later additions, and the
colourful fascia re-erected from the demolished Walpole Picture
Theatre of 1912.

Finally, the NEW BROADWAY and UXBRIDGE ROAD. The C19
residential ribbon development has been replaced by indifferent
commercial building. One cheering note: the HALFWAY
HOUSE, 1905, with jolly Jacobean detail.

GREENFORD

Amidst the C20 suburban roads a few traces of the old village
remain near the parish church in Oldfield Lane, just S of Western
Avenue. The industry and warehousing further N, towards Greenford Green, carries on a tradition established by C19 development around the transport provided by canal and railway, and
reinforced by the arrival of Western Avenue in 1934. To the W,

much characterless later C20 council housing stretches towards Northolt.

ALL HALLOWS, Horsenden Lane North, Greenford Green. 1940–1 by *C. A. Farey*. Lumpy brick exterior. The interior more appealing; simple whitewashed Romanesque, with altar beneath the crossing tower. – (Circular E window by *Wilhelmina M. Geddes*, 1952. PC)

HOLY CROSS, Ferrymead Gardens and Oldfield Lane South. The old church, only 60 ft long, was left standing next to the new church built in 1939. Flint-faced with lumps of ferricrete, apart from the weatherboarded tower (cf. Perivale, Ea), which rests on an interesting timber structure visible from inside; tie-beam with cross-braces at different levels. The tower was much restored in 1913 by *W. Braxton Sinclair*, but the staircase and W gallery seem to be early C17. The chancel roof is C15, with octagonal crownpost with four-way struts (cf. Perivale). The lateral struts support subsidiary braces beneath the collar-beam. The nave windows have tracery (much restored); the chancel windows are square-headed. Good S door, Perp, with quatrefoils in spandrels. – FONT. Small bowl on four-sided baluster, 1638. The cover (stolen in 1990) was possibly of the same date, although still with four crocketed volutes. – COMMUNION RAILS. Late C17; twisted balusters. – STAINED GLASS. A noteworthy collection of pieces. Panels of *c.* 1500 said to have come from King's College Cambridge (patron of the living). They are mostly heraldic and display in the E window the arms of Henry VIII and Catherine of Aragon, in the SE window the same and those of Eton College. There are also other motifs, the initials T.P., T.B., and T.H., the arms of the Grocers' Company, a little windmill, etc. – BRASSES. Demi-figure of a priest, the same mid C15 type as at Hayes (Hi), Stanwell (Surrey), Harlington (Hi), etc. – Thomas Symons, rector, small figure, *c.* 1520. – Inscription, 1544. – William Henry Ogle-Skan † 1915. Well executed kneeling figure in C16 style, made in 1928. – MONUMENTS. Rev. Michael Gardiner † 1630 and wife, the usual type with the two figures kneeling opposite each other. Almost certainly a documented work by *Nicholas Stone*, contracted for in 1632. – Bridget Coston † 1637, a curious combination of the kneeling family type and the type with portrait bust in niche. Mrs Coston kneels to the l. holding the infant John, and behind her kneel her daughters, labelled Frances, Mary, Jane, Anne, and Philadelphia. Behind the group, a little further up, appears the mourning husband, as if he were looking out of a window, with his cheek resting on his hand. At the sides of the pediment figures of Faith and Hope hold up curtains. A figure of Charity above, and two flaming balls. Signed by *Humfrey Moyer*, who was one of Nicholas Stone's assistants. – John Castell † 1695. Architectural tablet with portrait bust supported by putti; flaming urn above.

HOLY CROSS NEW CHURCH, Ferrymead Gardens. 1939 by *Sir Albert Richardson*. An unusual but successful building, largely of timber. The front has a projecting foyer and a huge hipped roof behind, broken by a tall oriel window with a little spirelet poking through, a rather Scandinavian effect. Aisles with sloping buttresses linked by arches. The interior is large and long, with

a very high open timber roof, sturdy wooden posts to separate
the passage aisles, and complex cross-bracing. At the E end stairs
to a former upper Lady Chapel.

OUR LADY OF THE VISITATION (R.C.), Greenford Road.
1960–1 by *D. Stokes*. Large, red brick, with concrete buttresses
and vault. Thin campanile.

Apart from the churches, the best building of the old village is
Greenford Hall, now the COMMUNITY CENTRE, Oldfield Lane
South, opposite the parish church. A tall, much altered house of
C18 origin with a crazy display of Venetian windows (renewed
in the C19). The S wing of three storeys and the lower part of
the N wing are late C18; the top storeys of the latter an addition
of *c*. 1890. Further S No. 168, late C18, a pretty, low stuccoed
house, five windows wide, formerly a school (see inscription with
the date 1780). The C19 BETHAM'S SCHOOLS are close by,
with an engagingly quirky small late C19 clock tower.

The old E–W route is RUISLIP ROAD further S. The only notable
pre-C20 survival is the roughcast HARE AND HOUNDS, late
C18, quite low and rural. The alterations of 1902 by *Nowell Parr
& A.E. Kates* added a hunting scene in the gable. Nearby,
GREENFORD SCHOOL, an *M.C.C.* secondary of 1937, a confident example of the bold cubist massing in plain brickwork
used for the cost-conscious schools of this era. Symmetrical, with
far-projecting central porch with curved ends, and tall stair-
tower behind.

WESTERN AVENUE crosses the N part of Greenford with a flyover
of 1979, a slim ribbon of prestressed concrete on circular piers.
Among the inter-war factories along Western Avenue the most
prominent is the former ALADDIN works, with a central tower
like an Italian campanile; 1932 by *Nicholas & Dixon Spain*.

In the industrial area to the N the pre-war building with the most
presence is GLAXO, 1936 by *Wallis, Gilbert & Partners*, a formal
brick frontage along Greenford Road, with blocky stepped-up
centre flanked by long wings smartened by black glass pilaster
strips between the windows. (Stylish double-height entrance hall
with curved corners.) The most ambitious and elegant among
more recent arrivals is the IBM WAREHOUSE AND DIS-
TRIBUTION CENTRE, Rockware Avenue, 1978–9 by *Foster
Associates*, symptomatic of its time both in its purpose – the
display and warehousing of computers – and in its cool, crisp
high-tech style. The prelude is a huge car park with diagonal
lines of trees leading the eye to the main entrance between two
cubic masses. On the r. is the distribution centre, five storeys
high; the smaller block has an elegant double-height machine
hall for demonstrating large computers, lit by a glazed N wall. At
the back a sunken road for lorry access is skilfully arranged so
as not to disturb the pristine geometry. The exterior surfaces
alternate between blank areas of ribbed aluminium and sheer
glass walls of unusually large rectangular panes. Behind them
shimmers the internal steel structure, painted in the architect's
favourite brilliant green.

HANWELL

INTRODUCTION

In the mid C 19 Hanwell was famous for its gargantuan institutions: the London poor law schools, the county lunatic asylum (just over the Southall border, but called Hanwell Asylum), and the cemeteries, prospects which did not encourage respectable Victorian expansion in the area, although Hanwell had grown sufficiently to become an urban district in 1885. The schools have gone, but along the busy Uxbridge Road the main landmarks are still the cemeteries and the hospital (*see* Southall, Ea). To the N is the splendid vista of the railway viaduct over the Brent valley, providing a perfect screen for the remains of the village in Church Road, which comes as a great surprise after the mediocre C 19 main-road development. Extensive suburban expansion to N and S came only in the early C 20.

CHURCHES

St MARK, Lower Boston Road. *See* Perambulation.

St MARY, Church Road. 1841 by *Scott & Moffatt*. One of Scott's earliest churches, contemporary with Christ Church Turnham Green, Chiswick (Ho). Flint with London stock dressings and a broach-spire; in the detail still with something of the thinness and prim rectangularity of the Commissioners' style. It replaced a Georgian preaching box of 1781–2 by *Thomas Hardwick*, which was a rebuilding of a small thatched medieval church. Scott's pre-ecclesiological phase is apparent from the galleries set behind the octagonal piers and from the originally very shallow chancel (lengthened in 1897–8 by *William Pywell*, re-using the three E lancets). The walls, formerly with murals and foliage patterns, were whitewashed in 1958. – REREDOS and ALTAR. 1965. – STAINED GLASS. In the E lancets, Crucifixion, Nativity, and Resurrection of *c.* 1841, quite notable for their date, using hard, bright colours. – MONUMENTS. All post-1782, a minor catalogue of changing fashion. Margaret Emma Orde † 1790, made in 1796 by *Vangelder* (also responsible for the Child monument at Heston, Ho): modest but quite original, a plain slim urn against a back plate flanked by fluted demi-columns with unorthodox bases and capitals, and supported by a kind of gable with convex sides; a touch of Chinese in the Grecian chastity of the rest. – Ann Graeme † 1812. Oval tablet with urn. – Martin Wolsey † 1837. Neo-classical tablet with urn. – Rev. T.T. Walmesley † 1847, builder of the church. A Gothic tablet. – Rev. Alec Field † 1915, missionary, bronze bust with spectacles and laurel wreath, an odd combination, by *Hal Ludlow*. – Pleasant CHURCHYARD overlooking the Brent valley.

St MELLITUS with St Mark, Church Road. 1909–10 by *A. Blomfield & Sons*. Red brick, lancet style, with buttressed W turret.

ST THOMAS, Boston Road. By *Edward Maufe*, 1934. Important
both as a precursor of Maufe's Guildford Cathedral, and for its
contemporary sculpture and furnishings representing the best
efforts of English religious art of the 1930s. The street runs along
the E side, which displays a Crucifixion by *Eric Gill* against and
below a round E window beside a tall square NE tower with a
green copper cap. All the other windows are narrow lancets, the
largest the one at the centre of the W side. Over the N door, doves
carved by *Vernon Hill*. The exterior is of brown brick with paler
bands, but inside the concrete is exposed in the walls and the plain
unribbed cross-vaults. Passage aisles, pointed arches without
capitals (the minimal Gothic of Guildford), tiny clerestory
windows. The austere and lofty main space contrasts with the
intimacy of the two low side chapels. – REREDOS (by *Cecil Hare*),
a large Gothic tabernacle, and ORGAN, both from St Thomas
Portman Square, whose demolition provided funds for the building. – FONT. By *Vernon Hill*. – Oak ORGAN SCREEN by *James
Woodford*, a bold open grid with stylized carved angels on top. –
STAINED GLASS. Small panels at the W end, by the font, by
Moira Forsyth: Suffer Little Children, in the pale colours of the
Arts and Crafts movement, but a livelier figure style. – In the
children's chapel on the N side, more glass by *Forsyth*, and WALL
PAINTINGS by *E. Starling*. – In the Lady Chapel an English
ALTAR (cross and candlesticks by *Edward Spencer*) and stone
Virgin and Child by *Vernon Hill*, in a sentimental elongated
Romanesque. The colours here all blue and white and silver, with
angels and stars outlined on the ceiling, and lighting concealed by
the beams. – Elsewhere, very effective ELECTROLIERS.

OUR LADY AND ST JOSEPH (R.C.), Uxbridge Road. 1964–7 by
Reynolds & Scott; purple brick with aluminium-clad roof, and
a horrible jagged outline of concrete dormers. E tower over the
sanctuary. – W front SCULPTURE by *A. K. Brobowski*. – STAINED
GLASS by *Goddard & Gibbs*.

HANWELL METHODIST CHURCH, Church Road. 1904 by
Gordon & Gunton. Free late Gothic: red brick and stone, with a
thickly mullioned W window between Gothic pinnacles.

CEMETERIES. N of the Broadway, KENSINGTON CEMETERY,
1855 by *Thomas Allom*, ragstone Gothic lodges and chapels. S of
the Broadway the CITY OF WESTMINSTER CEMETERY, 1854
by *Robert Jerrard*, with a very substantial lodge and Gothic
gatepiers, and a cedar avenue leading to the chapels.

PUBLIC BUILDINGS

COMMUNITY CENTRE, Cuckoo Avenue. The administrative
block of the once vast London and District Residential Schools,
built in 1856–7 in the grounds of Hanwell Park by *Tress &
Chambers*. It was designed for over a thousand poor law pupils.
Converted to a community centre after the school closed in 1933.
Three-storey, nine-bay centre with small clock tower, arched
windows, and a ground-floor arcade on bulbous columns. Seven-
bay wings, originally much longer. Brick and stucco.

DRAYTON MANOR SCHOOL, Drayton Bridge Road. The dull buildings of 1930 stand on the site of Hanwell Park, an early C19 neo-classical house demolished *c.* 1928.

ST ANN'S SCHOOL, Springfield Road. 1902; a good example of the Board School period.

ST MARK'S CHURCH SCHOOLS, Lower Boston Road. *See* Perambulation.

HOBBAYNE SCHOOL, Greenford Avenue. 1911 by *H. G. Crothall* of the *M.C.C.* Symmetrical, hipped roof, Queen Anne detail.

HEALTH CENTRE, Church Road. A composition of angular concrete boxes with gun-slit windows.

HANWELL STATION. Rebuilt 1875–7. Polychrome brick with very pretty wooden platform canopies and cast-iron work.

WHARNCLIFFE VIADUCT. 1835–8 by *Brunel*, to carry the G.W.R. over the Brent valley. Doubled in width in 1877. An impressive stretch of eight elliptical brick arches of 21-metre span and 5.3-metre rise, on stocky brick piers in the Egyptian style. The capitals and cornice are in finely dressed sandstone; at the centre, the arms of Lord Wharncliffe. Few viaducts have such architectural panache. This was Brunel's first major structure; he used the elliptical form for several other bridges on the line, notably at Maidenhead across the Thames.

BRENT BRIDGE. A fine road bridge across the Brent valley; C19 balustraded stone parapet. On the W side three C18 brick arches (said to incorporate two arches from a medieval bridge).

CANALS. At Hanwell the Grand Union Canal (1794) rises from the valley of the Brent by a flight of six locks, and a further two at Norwood. Attractive cottages at locks 92 and 93. *See also* Southall (Ea).

THREE BRIDGES, Windmill Lane. *See* Southall (Ea).

PERAMBULATION

The remains of the old village (somewhat diminished over the last thirty years) lie along CHURCH ROAD. By the little green, No. 134, CROSSWAY, a simple C18 five-bay rendered front, and a one-storey LODGE to the former Hanwell Park, white brick with Gothic windows. SPRING COTTAGE opposite also has some Gothic detail, but the gem is THE HERMITAGE, a peach of an early C19 Gothic thatched cottage with two pointed windows, a quatrefoil, and an ogee-arched door, all on a minute scale. Inside, an octagonal hall and reception room. RECTORY COTTAGE, S of the church, also has two little pointed windows of the early C19, and pretty trellis porches. Further S, in Brent Lodge Park, a STABLE BLOCK of *c.* 1800, nine bays with central pediment, now the Brent River Park Environmental Centre. BRENT RIVER PARK, a green swathe following the flood plain of the river Brent, extends all the way from the canal at Boston Manor, Brentford (Ho) to Perivale and Hanger Lane. It was created by Ealing in the 1970s following proposals by the Brent River and Canal Society. N of the old village, suburban expansion towards Greenford; the CUCKOO ESTATE is pleasantly laid out housing in the

garden suburb tradition, by the *L.C.C.*, mostly of 1933–9, built
on the land attached to the former poor law schools. The main
axis is CUCKOO AVENUE, the former drive leading to the schools
(now a community centre, *see* Public Buildings).

Just to the S of Uxbridge Road, in LOWER BOSTON ROAD, traces
of a hamlet with some mid C19 cottages around a small green;
also ST MARK'S CHURCH SCHOOLS, established on this site
in 1855, with many extensions (1871, 1884, 1895, etc.). The
earlier parts simple Gothic. Nearby is ST MARK'S COURT, a
transformation of St Mark's church, built in 1879 by *William
White*, a tall, cruciform building with clerestory and apsed
chancel. Coloured brick with Dec stone detail. The nave was
completed in 1883; the intended tower and spire were not built.
The conversion to flats (1989) has created a building of interest
in its own right, the attic dormers fitting happily into the steep
tiled roof, and the square-headed lower windows with moulded
stone lintels sympathetically complementing the Dec tracery
above. (The interior had brick arches on stone columns and roof
with alternate hammerbeam trusses.) In Uxbridge Road THE
VIADUCT, a jolly tiled Edwardian pub, and Nos. 168–174, a plain
terrace dated 1844. In Westminster Road, S of the Broadway,
BENJAMIN COURT, sheltered housing by *Ealing Architect's
Department*, *c.* 1983, sensitively detailed three-storey brick
ranges around a courtyard with a walnut tree.

NORTHOLT

Northolt remained a retired rural parish, a small village with a few
outlying hamlets, until it was sliced in half by Western Avenue in
the 1930s. Yet the village centre just N of the road still preserves
its rural feel, with its little church isolated on an eminence above
the green. The flat fields to the S disappeared under council housing
after the Second World War; to the W there is still open land around
Northolt airport.

ST BARNABAS, Raglan Way. 1939 by *J. H. Gibbons*, completed
1954. The end of the free Gothic tradition (cf. the same architect's
St Mary, Kenton, Hw). Pale brick, with quiet but well crafted
detail – see the tiles above the windows and under the eaves. The
W front is more mannered; slim Dec window anchored by an
oddly random stone base whose irregular horizontal courses turn
the corner to link up with the thin SW tower with bell under an
elongated open arch. Deep S porch. Interior with round-arched
arcade; E chapel.

ST JOSEPH THE WORKER, Yeading Lane. 1967–9 by *Maguire &
Murray*. A forceful interpretation of Early Christian traditions
for the liturgical movement, like the architects' earlier St Paul,
Bow Common (TH). Free-standing cylindrical campanile of concrete blocks; square church, the lower part also of blockwork,
the slightly recessed upper part zinc-clad. After the fortress-like
exterior, the spatial handling inside is the more exciting. Low

foyer, continued as a baptistery, contrasting with the lofty main space with thin columns up to the roof. Lighting concealed behind white boarding. Blocky concrete FONT, and boarded PULPIT, echoing the building materials.

ST MARY, Northolt Green. A little medieval village church in an attractive setting, spared later enlargement. White rendered walls, steep tiled roofs and weatherboarded W turret glimpsed through trees. The body of the church is essentially of c. 1300, aisleless, and only 13 by 8 metres. An interesting variety of windows of high quality (disastrously repaired in 1913 with Roman cement). The western ones have geometric tracery, the eastern ones the more advanced Dec forms which are gaining ground c. 1300: an elongated quatrefoil instead of a circle above the two lights. Chancel added in 1521, brick outside, stone within (the exterior rendered in 1940), built in line with the N wall of the nave. On the S side of the nave a blocked E window and Perp piscina with cusped arch below a square head. Nave roof early C16: sturdy tie-beams and crown-posts. W gallery on Tuscan columns, said to be erected in 1703. The chancel was cleared of furnishings in the 1970s. – FONT. Octagonal, C14, with foiled panels and arms possibly of Nicholas Brembre († 1388). – Pretty braced FONT COVER, 1624. – ROOD. In Byzantine style; from the 1951 Festival of Britain. – SCULPTURE (S chapel). Statue by M. Travers. – PAINTING (formerly over the altar). Copy of a Flemish or Dutch Adoration of the Magi, C18. – ROYAL ARMS. Stuart, late C17. – BRASSES. H. Rowdell † 1452, small, in armour; John Gyfforde † 1596 and wife † 1560, with twelve children (palimpsests of C15 brasses). – I. Bures † 1610, with kneeling cleric. – In the chancel, two good LEDGER STONES (1697, 1749).

ST BERNARD (R.C.), Mandeville Road. 1964–5 by Scott & Jacques, portal-framed, with copper roof and tower.

ST HUGH OF LINCOLN (R.C.), Kensington Road. 1970 by I. Nellist. Low, of red brick. – STAINED GLASS by P. Fourmaintreaux behind the altar.

BELVUE SCHOOL, Rowdell Road, close to Western Avenue. Special School of 1966 by Austin-Smith, Salmon, Lord Partnership. Low yellow brick group with monopitch roofs.

ISLIP MANOR, Eastcote Lane. Now a clinic. Picturesque bargeboarded house of 1865, rebuilt on a medieval site by the antiquary George Harris. C19 Tudor lodge. The grounds are now a park.

Close to the old church is a former SCHOOL (now parish hall) of 1868, enlarged in 1881. Boldly angular polychrome brick windows. Around the green a few cottages and C19 villas. To the N is the site of a moated medieval manor house.*

SMITH'S FARM, off Kensington Road. 396 houses and flats, c. 1974 by the G.L.C. The most enterprising of the housing estates scattered over the amorphous flat area S of Western Avenue. In the vernacular mode just becoming popular at the time. Tight pitched-roofed clusters (taller flats at the corners) to give the place some identity. Well organized minor spaces with little paths compensate for the dull rectangular street plan. The adjoining housing near the canal, built for British European Airways, is of

*Excavated in 1967. The moat was dug in the early C14. Timber buildings were replaced in stone in the late C14.

similar materials but with fussier garaging. The old FARMHOUSE survives further N, three bays, two storeys. Close to the new housing a BARN of three bays with queen-strut roof, dated 1595, survived until vandalism made necessary its re-erection at the Chiltern Open Air Museum in 1989. It was perhaps built to serve the common field which existed here.

In KITTIWAKE ROAD, off Ruislip Road, a low courtyard layout intended for old people. 1976 by *Julian Sofaer*. A deliberate contrast to the neighbouring G.L.C. tower blocks.

NORWOOD

Until 1859 Norwood was within the parish of Hayes; soon after, it was eclipsed by its subsidiary settlement of Southall, Ea (q.v.). The unusually large village green with the church close by is attractive, although only a few old houses remain.

ST MARY, Tentelow Lane. The C12 to C13 date of the S, W, and E walls is evident only to the student. The exterior was refaced rather gaudily with black flint and multi-coloured bricks in 1864; the tower is later still (1896), replacing a boarded W bell-turret. A restored C13 lancet can still be seen in the chancel S wall, and another in the nave S wall. C15 roofs: moulded wall-plates in both nave and chancel; nave roof with crownposts. S porch probably of the same date, but heavily restored. The present N arcade with its florid French Gothic capitals is mostly of 1864, but replaced an earlier one – see the late C12 W arch and respond and the E respond – which had been altered in 1824 and 1849. – FONT. Plain, octagonal C15. – STAINED GLASS. E window, St Michael and St George, by *Karl Parsons*, 1911. – Chancel S by *Oswald Fleuss*, 1901. – W window with old foreign roundel reset in 1864, 'the gift of the tradesmen'; S window with new roundel, 'the gift of the working class'. – BRASSES. Francis Awsiter † 1614 and Matthew Hunsley † 1618; small figures. – MONUMENTS. A good collection. In the N chancel wall monument to Edward Cheeseman of Dormer's Wells, cofferer to Henry VII, and his son Robert † 1556, probably made *c.* 1530. Niche with panelled jambs and four-centred arch above a quatrefoiled tomb-chest. Renewed inscription on the back plate. The same design as several London tombs of *c.* 1510–40 (cf. examples at St Mary Lambeth, La; St John Hackney, Hc; All Saints Edmonton, En, etc.), many of which were intended also as Easter Sepulchres. Above the tomb a HELM of *c.* 1600, and a short sword. – Francis Merrick † 1702. Fictive drapery against white and grey marble, flanked by putti. – John Merrick † 1749. Standing wall-monument with life-size semi-reclining figure on sarcophagus with straight tapering sides, supported by lions' feet; the whole against an obelisk background. – Joseph Biscoe of Norwood Hall † 1760. Tablet with egg and dart. – Isabella Norton † 1769. Inscription on bowed front, with urns and putto. – J. Robins of Regent Street and Norwood Hall, 1831. Very unpretentious, with a little sarcophagus in relief above an inscription tablet, but generous branches of weeping willow hanging down to the l. and r. – In the churchyard, the Robins family sarcophagus, neo-classical, with tapering sides and shallow urn on top, perhaps by *Soane* (*see* below).

NORWOOD HALL, next to the church, in Tentelow Lane. Now a horticultural institute. Horribly pebbledashed, with large late C19 extension, but the W part still recognizable as the house built in 1801–3 by *John Soane* for his business associate, the auctioneer and estate agent John Robins.* The S front is remarkable as a minor echo of the triumphal arch elevation of Pitshanger (*see* Ealing, Ea), distorted now by inserted windows, added attic floor, and the loss of the original entrance, but still recognizable. On each side of the arch a simple niche below a blind oculus, part of the original design. Soane's drawing shows within the triumphal arch a pedimented Roman Doric portico with segmental-headed window above. The central balustrade was formerly lower, with lantern to the attic floor visible behind. The plan also is reminiscent of Pitshanger. The entrance led up to the raised main floor; a further flight of steps (now covered over) continued within the entrance hall, where two original shallow groin-vaults remain. To the E was the main staircase (since rebuilt), to the N the dining room. In the closet adjoining the room to the W, a ball cornice and window shutters remain from Soane's time; upstairs, several incised doors, also perhaps original. In the former kitchen below the dining room, a re-used C18 door enriched with egg and dart; the irregular basement plan suggests that old foundations were incorporated. To the W are the late C19 extensions for the Unwin family, consisting chiefly of a large stair hall, approached by a new porch on the N side.

Opposite Norwood Hall in Tentelow Lane, VINE COTTAGE, formerly several cottages, possibly built by Robins, with good early C19 rubbed brick window-heads. Further E the former FREE SCHOOL, with the date 1767, established by Elisha Biscoe of Spring Grove, Isleworth, a pretty example of what small village schools were like in the C18. Brown brick with Gothic glazing in arched windows. (Above the ground-floor fireplace an appealing contemporary painted plaster overmantel of the Three Ages of Man, discovered in 1990; three figures against Gothic ruins.) Nearby, the PLOUGH INN, low, early C17, a timber-framed building of four bays, with end chimneystack, and NORWOOD LODGE, a nice early C19 two-bay house. Further E, facing the green, FRIARS LAWN and THE GRANGE, a pair of tall late C18 houses with emphasized quoins. In NORWOOD ROAD Nos. 196–198, an early C19 pair, and THE WOLF, a simple village pub of two storeys, with stables next to it.

WOLF FIELDS FIRST AND MIDDLE SCHOOL, Melbury Avenue, is a new school of 1989 by the *Borough Architect's Department* (cf. Southall, Ea).

In POPLAR AVENUE and GLADE LANE, good canalscape (*see* Southall and Hanwell, Ea) with the British Waterways Board Sanitary Station, a simple mid C19 brick villa.

*See P. Guillery, *Architectural History*, 30 (1967), 181–9.

PERIVALE

There is a poignant contrast between the tiny church close to the
river Brent, its isolated rural setting maintained by playing fields
and golf course, and Western Avenue with its factories and suburban development immediately to the N.

St Mary, Perivale Lane. Since 1981, the West London Arts
Centre, established by the Friends of St Mary's Perivale. The
building has been maintained intact, together with its fittings.
Its distinguishing feature is the little c16 weatherboarded W
tower, very unusual in Middlesex (but cf. Greenford, Ea, 1 m.
w), its roughly chamfered curved braces on two levels visible
inside. On the S face a sundial dated 1818. The white-rendered
body of the church is less than 15 metres long, aisleless, with
Perp windows and W door probably inserted into older fabric.
c15 crownpost roof; tall posts with four-way struts. The chancel
is c13, with a low-side window in its S wall. Restored by *Robert
Willey* from 1868 (E wall rebuilt, new chancel arch, roofs
exposed), and again by *Laurence King* in 1964, when much of
the Victorian character of the interior was eliminated. – FONT.
Plain, octagonal c15, with handsome cover of 1665, a pinecone
finial on four volutes. – Painted ROOD, COMMUNION RAIL, and
CEILING over the altar all of 1965. – Also of 1965 the feeble
STAINED GLASS by *F. Stephens* in the c19 E window. – Medieval
fragments reset in the chancel N window. – Nave SW, 1871 by
Lavers, Barraud & Westlake. – Former ALTAR (now at the W
end of the nave) with frontal with painted figures attributed to
Comper. – MONUMENTS. Tiny brass in the nave floor to Henry
Myllett † 1500 and his two wives, with their fifteen children. –
Joane Shelbery † 1623. Tablet with skulls and ribbons; small
shrouded figure in a 'predella' below a long inscription. – Lane
Harrison † 1740 by *Thomas Adye*. Large plump putto holding a
shield, placed against a pyramid. – Ellen Nicholas † 1818 by *R.
Westmacott*. Fine interlaced group of a young woman on a couch,
supported by an angel, against a plain pointed back plate. – Many
other minor monuments. – CHURCHYARD with many c18 and
c19 monuments; it was used for burials of Londoners until
1906. – The bold LYCHGATE with scissor-braced trusses dates
from 1904.

St Mary with St Nicholas, Federal Road. 1963 by *Laurence King*.
Centrally planned, with altar below clerestory-lit crossing. A
good straightforward design rather cluttered by furnishings. –
CORONA and large ROOD above the altar.

St John Fisher (R.C.), Langdale Gardens. 1970–3 by *B.D.
Kaye*, with an aluminium roof sloping up to a central tower.

Perivale United Reformed Church, Medway Drive. 1936
by *J.P. Blake*. Blocky brick exterior with S tower-porch.

Apart from the church, Perivale (or Little Greenford) had in the
c18 nothing but rectory, manor house, and a few farmhouses. All
these have gone. With Western Avenue came the Hoover
94   Factory of 1931–5 by *Wallis, Gilbert & Partners* (job architect

F. Button), the most striking of all their West London buildings, especially now that the Firestone factory on the Great West Road has gone. 'Perhaps the most offensive of the modernistic atrocities along this road of typical bypass factories,' was Pevsner's verdict in 1951. Such a judgement rests on the premise that a factory should be functional and not show off to passers-by with a frontage which has nothing to do with the production floor behind. Forty years on one can enjoy the brash confidence of the façade with more detachment. The symmetrical, monumental front is indeed still in the tradition of many Victorian and Edwardian commercial buildings. But while those wooed the pedestrian with busy detail, this is designed to flash upon the eye of the passing motorist. The sparkling white glazing and crisp and colourful art deco detail aptly advertise the factory's modern aids to hygiene. The ends are neatly punctuated by recessed stair-towers; their eye-catching quadrant-shaped corner windows with green glazing-bars have a distinct and perhaps not coincidental affinity with post modern work of the 1980s. Inside the front block the mood is continued by the main staircase with stylish iron rail. Excellent contemporary gatepiers and railings, also with art deco Egyptian motifs, moved back for road widening in the 1980s. To the w the canteen of 1938 (job architect *J. Macgregor*), also white-glazed (although steel-framed, not reinforced concrete like the main building). Ribbon windows, contrasting with the angular vertical window of the staircase. The factory closed in 1982; at the time of writing the buildings still await a sympathetic new use.

To the w, a row of contemporary bank and shops, appropriately clad in glazed tiles with green trimmings. Opposite, the MYLLETT ARMS, 1935 by *E. B. Musman*, hipped pantiled roofs and arched windows, not daringly modern like his later pubs.

In PERIVALE INDUSTRIAL ESTATE, off Horsenden Lane South, No. 12 (High Street Transport), 1978 by *Covell Matthews, John Wheatley Partnership*. Crisp blue corrugated-clad portal frames, a fairly early example of the type.

Further N HORSENDEN LANE NORTH still crosses the Paddington branch of the Grand Junction Canal by a narrow bridge and becomes for a short while a rural lane climbing up Horsenden Hill, a patch of countryside preserved between Perivale and Wembley.

SOUTHALL

INTRODUCTION

Southall began as a hamlet within the parish of Hayes, an outlier of the once more important settlement of Norwood. It became a centre of industry after the construction of the canal (1794) and the Great Western Railway (1839). The population grew fast only from the end of the c 19, encouraged by the arrival of electric trams in

1901; by 1936 Southall was urban enough to become a borough (the population in 1901 was 13,200, in 1921, 30,165). The old centre with the manor house lies at The Green, s of the railway, from where South Road continues N to meet the High Street and The Broadway on the line of the Uxbridge Road. Coming from the sw, from the still semi-rural centre of Norwood, the change is dramatic. Up to the 1980s the lively and colourful character of the area owed more to its population than to its mostly mean and scruffy buildings; extensive commercial and industrial redevelopment began to make an impact from 1989.

CHURCHES AND PLACES OF WORSHIP

EMMANUEL, Fleming Road. 1974. Square dual-purpose church and community hall for the Golf Links estate. A curved corner for the sanctuary.

HOLY TRINITY, Uxbridge Road. 1890 by *J. Lee*. Exterior of brick and stone, interior polychrome brick. Aisles, apsidal baptistery.

ST GEORGE, Lancaster Road. 1908 by *A. Blomfield*. Large, of red and yellow brick, with a shingled turret at the end of its sweeping roof. One of the suburban churches endowed from the sale of City church sites. – (ORGAN CASE from St George Botolph Lane in the City, by *R. Bridge*, 1753.)

ST JOHN, King Street. Disused. Inexpensive London stock brick chapel of 1838, given by the owner of the local vitriol factory. Succeeded by a church in Cheam Road (1910 by *C. G. Miller*).

CHRIST THE REDEEMER (R.C.), Allenby Road. 1964 by *M. Farey*. A prominent open bellcage over the crossing. Nearly symmetrical to the road; central sanctuary with large bowed window, flanked on the l. by the nave with syncopated pattern of coloured glass windows and on the r. by the church hall (movable screens inside). – Stone FONT, with fibreglass cover, by *E. J. Clack*. – LAMP STANDARDS and PROCESSIONAL CROSS by *Michael Murray*. – STAINED GLASS in the lantern over the crossing by *M. Trahearne*.

ST ANSELM (R.C.), South Road, 1967 by *J. Newton* of *Burles, Newton & Partners*. Brick-faced, a large ovoid with two projecting chapels and a tiny baptistery with concave walls divided by coloured glass. Restrained interior with shallow curved concrete arches to aisles and clerestory. – The STAINED GLASS is by *Patrick Reyntiens*, 1971.

METHODIST CHURCH, South Road. High, semicircular meeting room with conical slated roof, behind a crowded brick and stone classical front of 1916 by *Sir Alfred Gelder*.

GURU RAVIDASS TEMPLE, Western Road. Built *c.* 1980. Square, with polygonal corner turrets and central and corner domes.

PUBLIC BUILDINGS

SOUTHALL MANOR HOUSE, The Green. Now offices. The one notable ancient building of Southall, a major timber-framed manor house of the later C16, unique in the London area. Built (or reconstructed) by Richard Awsiter in 1587. Facing the road the hall with gabled cross-wings; facing the public garden to the N a wing added in the early C17 and extended W in the C18. Much restored in 1847–8 and in the 1920s. The C18 addition is confusingly faced with half-timbering. The original house is of close-studded timbers, much restored. The composition is irregular yet no doubt far from haphazard – the designer must have deliberately used the greatest variety of heights, widths, and depths for his various gabled bays: from l. to r. first a wide bay with a large gable, a slight projection on the first floor, and one pedimented oriel on the ground floor and a second on the first; then a polygonal bay-window projecting a little further and with a smaller and lower gable; then the porch, still further advancing and with a gable of the same dimensions as the previous one; finally the r. bay, with a bay-window identical with the other but farther away from the porch, so that a semblance of symmetry between porch and bays is avoided. Also this bay-window is not crowned by a small gable but has a strongly projecting large one, as high as the gable on the l. Contemporary fireplace in the entrance hall.

TOWN HALL, High Street. 1897 by *T. Newell*. Debased classical with a central pediment. White brick with stone dressings. Former fire station next door with a scrolly pediment.

POLICE STATION, High Street. Fearsome purple brick; 1975 by *Brewer, Smith & Brewer*.

LIBRARY, Osterley Park Road. A Carnegie building, opened in 1905, with nice art nouveau lettering and triple-arched entrance.

SOUTHALL COLLEGE OF TECHNOLOGY, Beaconsfield Road. Opened 1928. A mixture with ingredients typical of their various dates; *M.C.C.* 1920s roughcast gabled range to the road, with extensions of 1934 and 1937; 1950s-modern blocks behind, red brick with boxed-out windows; bolder brick and concrete additions of the 1970s.

The SCHOOLS are among the best buildings of Southall, good indicators of its various stages of growth. There follows a selection of the various types.

FEATHERSTONE FIRST SCHOOL, Western Road. 1890, one-storeyed, in a Gothic idiom, old-fashioned for Board Schools of this date. The JUNIOR SCHOOL of 1901 much jollier, with a busy three-gabled Baroque front; arched windows with prominent keystones, bold lettering.

FEATHERSTONE HIGH SCHOOL (former), Western Road. Built as the Western County Secondary Girls' School, 1910 by *H. G. Crothall*. Unusual half-butterfly plan with domed turrets in the angles, and a centre with recessed canted bay (cf. the contemporary boys' school in Gayton Road, Harrow, Hw).

BEACONSFIELD FIRST AND MIDDLE SCHOOLS, Beaconsfield Road. Similar to the first phase of the technical college; 1920, quite homely brick and roughcast, with gables. Nicely detailed entrance.

BLAIR PEACH FIRST AND MIDDLE SCHOOLS, Beaconsfield Road. At the W end, in quite a rural setting close to the canal. A friendly, domestic-looking cluster of one and two storeys, dark red mottled brick with cheerful green trimmings. Top-lit upper hall in the centre. By the *Borough Architect's Department*, 1988–9, built in response to the expanding local population (likewise the contemporary DAIRY MEADOW FIRST AND MIDDLE SCHOOL, Merrick Road).

PATHWAY FURTHER EDUCATION CENTRE AND HAVELOCK SCHOOLS, Havelock Road. A pleasant campus of low, reticent brick buildings with deep eaves to their tiled roofs. By the *Borough Architect's Department*, c. 1989.

EALING HOSPITAL, Uxbridge Road. C20 buildings planned from 1967. There is a telling contrast between the buildings of the first phase (1967 onwards by *John R. Harris* for the North West Metropolitan Hospital Board) and those added from the late 1980s. First impressions are of the usual oppressively impersonal and utilitarian blocks on a large scale, grouped around a tall slab with exposed concrete frame, set in a sea of parked cars – a complex as forbidding as any Victorian institution, and without the mitigating order and grandeur that these often possessed (*see* below). But the slab has been brightened up by blue cladding, and behind, the livelier approach of the later phases is demonstrated by the MATERNITY UNIT, by *Hutchison, Locke & Monk*, completed in 1988, a pleasantly humane building, with its cheerful variety of window shapes, textures, and colours. Striped stone cladding alternates with white render below shallow blue pitched roofs.* Further s, more buildings in the same materials (1989 onwards) are beginning to create a ring around the older ones. Near the canal, the quieter, well detailed THREE BRIDGES REGIONAL SECURE CENTRE of 1987, russet-brown brick with pantiled roofs, also by *Hutchison, Locke & Monk*.

The C19 buildings further w, later known as ST BERNARD'S HOSPITAL, were built as Middlesex County Lunatic Asylum; a dignified and rational design of 1829–31 by *William Alderson*, an early example of the carefully planned C19 institution on a grand scale. It was intended for 300 patients but soon had to be enlarged: the wings of 1838 in a similar style are by *William Moseley*; later alterations, including an attic floor, 1854 and 1857 by *J. Harris*. Still recognizable as an impressive formal composition, despite the clutter of later C19 and C20 accretions. The original building is on a U-plan with an octagonal centre originally with a chapel. From this, a wing (with another chapel and ballroom), added in 1854–7, projects forward, dividing the men's quarters on the l. from the women's on the r. At the end of each of the main wings is an octagonal end pavilion, from which the 1838 extension projects outward. All of plain stock brick, originally only two storeys above basements, distinguished by a firm rhythm of stone floor bands and round-arched windows of cast iron; to avoid the danger of open windows they have distinctive circular ventilators instead of sashes or casements. The highly decorative iron fire escapes were added from 1860. Behind the wings are airing courts, and around them to the s, close to the canal, the extensive stores and workshops that made the institution virtually self-sufficient. The central octagon originally contained the superintendent's apartment; the first-floor

*In the hospital are twelve tile panels by Carter's Poole Pottery Company (1934), transferred from the King Edward Memorial Hospital, Ealing.

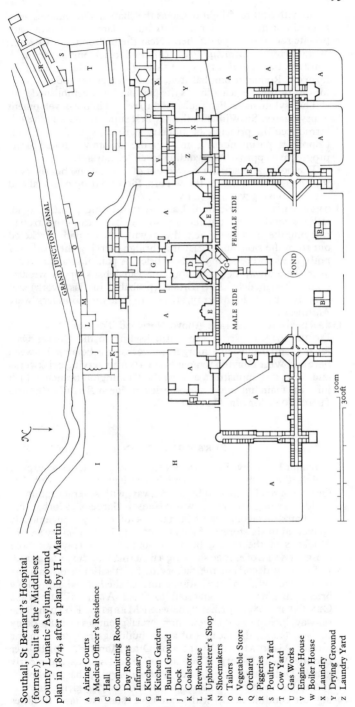

Southall, St Bernard's Hospital (former), built as the Middlesex County Lunatic Asylum, ground plan in 1874, after a plan by H. Martin

A Airing Courts
B Medical Officer's Residence
C Hall
D Committing Room
E Day Rooms
F Infirmary
G Kitchen
H Kitchen Garden
I Burial Ground
J Dock
K Coalstore
L Brewhouse
M Upholsterer's Shop
N Shoemakers
O Tailors
P Vegetable Store
Q Orchard
R Piggeries
S Poultry Yard
T Cow Yard
U Gas Works
V Engine House
W Boiler House
X Laundry
Y Drying Ground
Z Laundry Yard

GRAND JUNCTION CANAL

FEMALE SIDE

MALE SIDE

POND

100m
300ft

room with oval roof-light began as the chapel. The inmates were housed not in conventional wards but in large day rooms with private rooms opening off them. Near the ballroom the CHAPEL of 1881 by *H. Martin*, E.E., coloured brick inside; three w windows by *Westlake*, 1885. GATEWAY to Uxbridge Road in the form of a Roman triumphal arch; beside it, a house added *c.* 1860 for one of the medical officers (its pair has been demolished).

The asylum has a distinguished C19 record in the development of psychiatry. Sir William Ellis, the first superintendent († 1839), introduced the principle of industry as therapy; under Dr John Conolly, superintendent from 1839, the asylum was noted for its progressive approach in avoiding forcible restraint.

The hospital gradually moved out of most of the buildings in the 1980s; conversion of the w parts for a mixture of social and private housing was agreed by 1991.

THREE BRIDGES, Windmill Lane. The meeting point of road, railway, and canal, ingeniously solved by a cast-iron trough carrying the canal over the railway (with towing path bracketed out from the side) and a cast-iron bridge carrying the road over both. Piers and retaining walls of brick. A pair of strainer arches over the railway helps to abut the canal bank at its weakest point. Designed by *I. K. Brunel* (probably his last work) and executed by *E. F. Murray*, 1855–61. The ironfounders were *Matthew T. Shaw*.

GRAND UNION CANAL. Above Norwood Toplock, MAYPOLE DOCK, 1913, a narrow canal arm leading to the Quaker Oats factory and Monsted's margarine works (*see* below). Between here and West Drayton remnants of C19 arms serving brickworks and other C19 industries; also on the Paddington branch, which joins the main line under a good brick bridge at BULL'S BRIDGE JUNCTION. *See also* Hanwell (Ea).

PERAMBULATION

The manor house by THE GREEN (*see* above) comes as a surprise among the seedy Victorian and Edwardian parades. N of The Green the road is crossed by the railway, with several prominent buildings alongside. To the w (off Hanson Gardens), a forbidding castellated octagonal WATER TOWER of *c.* 1895, ingeniously converted to six storeys of flats in 1979–83 by *F. Vickery* and *E. Moffet*. S of the tracks, between Southall and Hayes, a bold mosaic PANEL of *c.* 1906 showing a fisherman holding a large rod. It formerly decorated the factory of Scott's Emulsion (makers of cod liver oil). E of the station a former shed of red and yellow brick, imaginatively converted to THE ARCHES BUSINESS CENTRE in 1989. Further E, between MERRICK ROAD and the railway, incorporated in new commercial premises of 1989–90 by *Steven Adams*, the façades of a few buildings remain from the former MARGARINE WORKS of Otto Monsted, which later became Walls factory. They are of 1894 onwards, in a curly gabled Dutch style (by *Bird & Whittensbury*), of hard red brick and yellow terracotta. This was a model factory, hygienic (including air-conditioning), with extensive staff welfare facilities including the COMMUNITY CENTRE on the E side of Merrick Road, built as a recreation hall in a self-conscious Beaux Arts style in 1910 by *A. Marshall Mackenzie*.

N of the railway SOUTH ROAD is cheered by one unforgettable building on the W side, as colourfully exotic as the contents of the surrounding Asian shops: THE LIBERTY SHOPPING HALL, built as a Gaumont cinema in 1929 by *George Coles*. A unique example of a Chinese cinema exterior, with much coloured faience; tiled pagoda roofs with bold gilded dragons. The mediocre E side of South Road was earmarked for ambitious redevelopment at the time of writing (shopping centre, library, and other amenities, by *BDP*).

The HIGH STREET and THE BROADWAY at the N end of Southall developed only from the turn of the century. Very low key, apart from the town hall (q.v.) and the nearby GEORGE AND DRAGON, 1914–15 by *Frank J. Fisher*, with elaborately half-timbered gables. At the corner of South Road, the THREE HORSESHOES, 1922 by *Nowell Parr*. Jettied first floor with leaded casements. (Good unaltered interior.) Further E a few older buildings: the RED LION, three storeys, C18 but much altered, and, up NORTH ROAD, GROVE HOUSE, an early C18 house of five bays with segment-headed windows and a hooded porch (much restored) on one side of a little green with the low, gabled PLOUGH INN opposite, a timber-framed building in disguise. Further E, in DORMER'S WELLS LANE, traces of the moat from the manor house of the Cheesemans (*see* Norwood church, Ea). SOUTHALL PARK, S of the High Street, was formed from the grounds of a C19 private asylum of Sir William Ellis, one of several such institutions in the area, encouraged by the existence of the county asylum (*see* Ealing Hospital, above).

Further W, off The Broadway, the NORTHCOTE ARMS in Northcote Avenue, 1907 by *Nowell Parr*, half-timbered and green faience.

GREAT WESTERN INDUSTRIAL PARK, Windmill Lane. Developed from the 1980s. ELEMETA has one of the firm's first English examples of structural silicone glazing, with a double-height atrium behind. By *Bell, Daniels, Slater Partnership*, 1984.

TWYFORD

An ancient parish, although in the C17 and C18 with nothing but manor house and church. Surprisingly, both survive, the house even with some land around it, sandwiched between the North Circular Road and the industrial area of Park Royal which lies partly in Ealing and partly in Brent (*see* Brent: Park Royal).

ST MARY, Brentmead Gardens, close to Twyford Abbey. Much enlarged in 1958 by *N. F. Cachemaille-Day*, when the small chapel rebuilt in 1808 by *William Atkinson* for Thomas Willan of Twyford Abbey (*see* below) became a Lady Chapel. It has an E window with ogee hoodmould and headstops in Roman cement. The nave is quite boldly non-period, of brick, with tapering concrete columns. W wall with small rectangular windows with

coloured glass. W tower over the porch. – STAINED GLASS. E
window 1958 by *A. E. Buss.* – MONUMENTS. Two to the Moyles:
Robert † 1638, erected 1657, and Walter † 1660. Both are wall-
monuments with a bust in an oval niche, pilasters to r. and l., an
inscription tablet below and pediment above, yet the earlier still
has the restraint of the Commonwealth, the later – in costume,
pediment, and all details – goes Baroque.

TWYFORD ABBEY. Thomas Willan, the dairy farmer who had the
lease of the land which became Regents Park, acquired the
manor house around 1807 and employed *William Atkinson* to
transform it into a romantic castellated abbey. It is one of the
few survivals of the type around London; its cement-rendered
exterior, Gothic windows, and little octagonal turrets still
impress as one approaches from the low SW lodge up the drive,
as the early C20 additions, although substantial, were remarkably
sympathetic. The SE part of the house may be early C18 or older,
but this is only apparent in various odd changes of level. The
neat villa-like SW part is Willan's addition. W entrance lobby
with ribbed vault; hall cornice with rose and portcullis; simple
Gothic fireplace in the room to the N. The large S-facing drawing
room has an elaborate ceiling with the novelty of light-bulb
fittings in wooden rosettes. It dates from the time of A.H.
Alhusen, who bought the house in 1890 and spent nearly £6,000
on it. E of this, in front of the older range, was a conservatory,
subdivided and heightened in 1914, with a tower at the end (also
heightened in 1914). The main addition, when the house became
a nursing home run by the Alexian brothers, was the wing to the
N of 1904–5, a discreet copy of Willan's house, linked to the main
building by a less tactful addition of 1962. To the N the former
stable court, and walled kitchen gardens. CHAPEL in the W stable
block, originally lavishly furnished. The altar and reredos (now
separated) are of 1916 by *Earp* and *Hobbs*, alabaster and marble,
with a delicate relief of the Holy Family; the ceiling painting,
1906 by *Brother Adolph*, was part of a once more extensive
scheme of the seven works of mercy. Brass to J.E. Prestage
† 1914, with an angel. The future of both buildings and grounds
is uncertain at the time of writing.

HAMMERSMITH AND FULHAM

INTRODUCTION

The creation in 1965 of the borough of Hammersmith and Fulham reunited two L.C.C. boroughs which had once been joined in the single large parish of Fulham, a long strip of land between the Thames and Old Oak Common near Willesden Junction. The retention of the two names acknowledged the characters which each had developed during the C19, and which demand separate treatment here. One aspect common to both areas should however be mentioned: the borough's creation of small parks, and especially the opening up of the riverside for public enjoyment, as industry was replaced in the 1970s–80s by a mixture of social and private housing. Borough architects from 1965: *E. G. Sames*; *Denis Browne* (from 1970); *Richard A. Michelmore* (from 1972); *S. Campbell* (from 1977); *Anthony Wood* (from 1980); *Peter Ackhurst* (from 1985).

FURTHER READING

The Fulham and Hammersmith Historical Society's *Buildings to See in Fulham and Hammersmith* (1972) is a brief but useful list, wider in its scope, although less detailed, than the DOE list (1985). The very few buildings of before 1714 are included in R.C.H.M. *West London* (1925). Hammersmith is covered by an early *Survey of London* volume (1915); Sandford Manor, Fulham, by a *Survey* monograph of 1907. On Fulham Palace there is a very detailed archaeological and architectural appraisal made for the borough by Warwick Rodwell in 1988. The most useful older local reference books are T. Faulkner, *Historical and Topographical Account of Fulham, including the Hamlet of Hammersmith* (1813), and C. J. Fèret, *Fulham Old and New*, 3 vols. (1900). More recent general histories are *Hammersmith* (1965) and *Fulham* (1970), both edited by P. D. Whitting.

ACKNOWLEDGEMENTS

For amplification of the published information I am much indebted to the resources of the Borough Libraries' Local History Departments, and especially to Christine Bayliss at Fulham and to Elizabeth Aquilino at Hammersmith, both of whom read and commented on draft texts and provided further details. Tom West and Barbara Woda of the Planning Department did likewise, and were especially helpful in bringing me up to date with recent developments. Among others who kindly supplied information I must thank the Hammersmith and Fulham Historic Buildings Group, and in particular Maya Donelan, Charles Tylee, and Keith Whitehouse.

HAMMERSMITH

INTRODUCTION

The bustle of Hammersmith Broadway today is difficult to reconcile with its countrified pre-Victorian past. Before 1834, Hammersmith was a rural appendage of the large parish of Fulham. It had few buildings of importance: no church or chapel of ease before the C17, no religious houses, and only two manor houses worth the name. Of one of them, Bradmore House, a façade has been preserved (*see* Perambulation 1); of the other, Palingswick, destroyed during the Second World War, the grounds survive as Ravenscourt Park. When Rocque's map appeared in 1745, the centre of the village was at Broadway with ribbons running W along King Street and S down Queen Caroline Street towards the river, where the Lower and Upper Malls were built up with houses overlooking the Thames, continuing without a break into Chiswick. They remain the best places to appreciate C18 Hammersmith. At Brook Green to the N there was a small cluster of houses. Round about there were market gardens, as at Fulham, and agricultural land stretched further N to Wormholt and Old Oak Commons. Even in maps of 1853 there is still plenty of open land everywhere between the main roads. The population was *c.* 6,000 in 1801, *c.* 13,000 in 1841, and *c.* 25,000 in 1861. Then between 1861 and 1881, as the suburban transport system improved, it rose to 72,000, reaching 112,000 in 1901, and in 1931 136,000. Since then, the usual decline has set in: 1951, 119,000; 1961, 110,333; 1981, 73,196.

The pattern of growth from s to n can be traced in the change from the Georgian riverside to the surviving C19 stuccoed villas and terraces between King Street and Goldhawk Road, to Edwardian and later streets further n, and so to the cosy early C20 L.C.C. cottage estates beyond Uxbridge Road, an area then right on the fringe of London. To their n, part of the ancient common land of Old Oak Common and Wormwood Scrubs still survives between the prison and the railway wastes of Willesden Junction.

The C19 residential streets of Hammersmith still have much appeal, ranging from formal 1820s groups around St Peter's Square – a surprisingly urban outlier right at the w end of the parish – to the mid C19 hotchpotch of artisan cottages n of Brook Green. There is much less of interest from after 1918 (with the exception of some good public buildings, especially schools). A drab monotony and an inhuman scale alike characterize the huge L.C.C. estate of the 1930s on the 1908 exhibition site at White City, the borough's 1960s tower blocks on the Kensington border, and most of the commercial buildings that transformed King Street and Hammersmith Road in the 1970s–80s. In compensation one can single out the borough's imaginative use of the riverside, beginning in the 1960s; the reconstruction of the Lyric Theatre (*see* Perambulation 2); and the pockets of friendly new housing in north Hammersmith (*see* Perambulations 5 and 6). These have had to compete with two powerful and disruptive C20 agents of change: the construction of the flyover at Hammersmith Broadway, and Westway and its feeder road n of Shepherds Bush. Easy access both from the w and to inner London has provided the impetus for major new developments of the 1980s in both these areas, still in progress at the time of writing, of which one of the most spectacular is likely to be *Ralph Erskine*'s remarkable office tower s of the flyover.

CHURCHES

There is no medieval church. Hammersmith village, as part of the large parish of Fulham, had a chapel of ease from the C17, rebuilt in the later C19 as St Paul. The earliest surviving church is the neo-classical St Peter of the 1820s. Changing Victorian ecclesiastical taste can be traced through the most notable of the later ones: *Wardell*'s Puginian R.C. Holy Trinity (1851–3), *Butterfield*'s tougher St John (1857–8), and *Brooks*'s Holy Innocents (1887 etc.), its noble interior now sadly altered.

HARROW MISSION, Freston Road. *See* Harrow Club, Perambulation 6.

HOLY INNOCENTS, Paddenswick Road. Designed by *James Brooks* in 1887; e parts and one bay of the nave 1889–90; nave and aisles 1891; W wing 1901; divided up in 1989. Red brick of harsh colour, no tower. Both E and W ends have small corner turrets, and the aisles are articulated by tall gabled buttresses. Before the drastic subdivision, this was a typical Brooks interior, austere and lofty, with a wide and tall nave, low passage aisles with low stone piers without capitals, and tall lancets in the clerestory. The nave has now been divided off, the deep W choir gallery removed, and the Lady Chapel destroyed. What remains are the impressive transepts, high and two-aisled, with groups of twice three windows at the N and S ends. The chancel is separated from the crossing by a low pointed arch with three openings above, through which one sees the chancel roof. – BALDACCHINO. Huge, Gothic, with carved angels, possibly by *Ernest Geldart.* – PULPIT. 1896, elaborately carved in Perp style. – ROOD SCREEN. A vast wooden structure with openwork tracery, by *Charles Spooner,* on a dado of a screen begun by *Geldart.* – Inappropriate large curved STALLS in a Baroque style, made for the Chapel of St Michael and St George in St Paul's Cathedral by *G. Somers Clarke Jun.,* given in 1904; the N transept panelling is probably from the same source. – TRIPTYCH (formerly in the Lady Chapel) with painting of the Nativity and carved wings, 1902 by *Ernest Geldart.* – The excellent STAINED GLASS from the Lady Chapel, by *Henry Holiday,* 1891 (Suffer Little Children), is now in the S transept.

ST JOHN THE EVANGELIST, Glenthorne Road. 1857–9 by *Butterfield.* Large and rather grim; yellow brick banded with red, stone dressings. Tall SW tower (1879–82) with saddleback roof standing S of the aisle. A spire was intended. Low, narrow lean-to aisles; arcades with a simple chamfer; as harsh as Butterfield liked to be. Exposed brick in the nave (the lower walls plastered later); the chancel lofty, with an E wall tiled and gilt, also very Butterfieldian. Good FLOOR TILES as well. – *Butterfield* FONT of coloured marbles, octagonal with sunk quatrefoils, and WOODWORK (the screen has been removed). – ORGAN CASE by *Bentley,* 1899, colourful and lovely. – *Bentley*'s matching interior

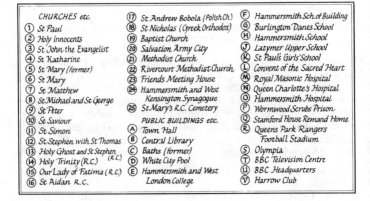

CHURCHES etc.
1 St Paul
2 Holy Innocents
3 St John the Evangelist
4 St Katharine
5 St Mary (former)
6 St Mary
7 St Matthew
8 St Michael and St George
9 St Peter
10 St Saviour
11 St Simon
12 St Stephen with St Thomas
13 Holy Ghost and St Stephen
14 Holy Trinity (R.C.)   (R.C.)
15 Our Lady of Fatima (R.C.)
16 St Aidan R.C.

17 St Andrew Bobola (Polish Ch.)
18 St Nicholas (Greek Orthodox)
19 Baptist Church
20 Salvation Army City
21 Methodist Church
22 Rivercourt Methodist Church
23 Friends Meeting House
24 Hammersmith and West
     Kensington Synagogue
25 St Mary's R.C. Cemetery

PUBLIC BUILDINGS etc.
A Town Hall
B Central Library
C Baths (former)
D White City Pool
E Hammersmith and West
     London College

F Hammersmith Sch. of Building
G Burlington Danes School
H Hammersmith School
J Latymer Upper School
K St Paul's Girls' School
L Convent of the Sacred Heart
M Royal Masonic Hospital
N Queen Charlotte's Hospital
O Hammersmith Hospital
P Wormwood Scrubs Prison
Q Stamford House Remand Home
R Queens Park Rangers
     Football Stadium
S Olympia
T BBC Television Centre
U BBC Headquarters
V Harrow Club

HAMMERSMITH

N

0   ½ mile
0   ½ km

BRENT

HARROW ROAD

SCRUBS LANE

WILLESDEN JUNCTION

College Park

All Souls Cemetery (Kensal Green)

Grand Union Canal

Wormwood Scrubs

Old Oak Common

Old Oak Estate

WULFSTAN STREET

FITZNEAL ST

EAST ACTON

ERCONWALD ST

OLD OAK COMMON LANE

OLD OAK LANE

A 40(M)

EALING

DU CANE ROAD

WOOD LANE

SCRUBS LANE

KENSINGTON

WESTWAY

WESTWAY

White City

Wormholt Estate

Cleverley Estate

Viola Sq.

HEALLOCK

BLOEMFONTEIN RD

AUSTRALIA RD

COMMONWEALTH AVE

NEW ZEALAND

SOUTH AFRICA RD

BRYONY ROAD

Wormholt Park

STEVENTON RD

SAWLEY

WORMHOLT RD

ADELAIDE GROVE

BOSCOMBE RD

Hammersmith Park

WHITE CITY ROAD

WOOD LANE

White City

BRAMLEY RD

LATIMER ROAD

Sch

M41

NORLAND ROAD

QUEENSDALE RD

Edward Woods Estate

HOLLAND PK RD

UXBRIDGE ROAD

ASKEW ROAD

COBBOLD ROAD

GOLDHAWK ROAD

STAMFORD BROOK RD

LOFTUS RD

COVERDALE RD

RYLETT RD

TRUSSLEY RD

CATHNOR RD

LIME GROVE

Shepherd's Bush

SHEPHERD'S BUSH

STERNE ST

Shepherd's Bush Green

ROCKLEY RD

BLYTHE

LAKESIDE RD

MASBRO RD

SINCLAIR ROAD

BLYTHE ROAD

Sch

MACLISE RD

KENSINGTON (OLYMPIA)

GOLDHAWK

STARCH GREEN

Sch

GOLDHAWK RD

HAMMERSMITH

IFFLEY RD

CAMBRIDGE GROVE

RAVENSCOURT PARK

PADDENSWICK RD

WELLESLEY AVE

DALLING RD

GLENTHORNE ROAD

Brook Green

MERCERS PL

Pol.

Fire Stn.

HAMMERSMITH BROADWAY

BROOK GREEN

ROAD

HOUNSLOW

STAMFORD BROOK

RAVENSCOURT GDNS

KING STREET

RAVENSCOURT PK

ST PETERS RD

ST PETERS GROVE

ST PETERS SQUARE

BRITISH GROVE

CHISWICK MALL

HAMMERSMITH TERR.

WEST

GREAT

Pumping Station

OIL MILL LA.

S. BLACK LION LA.

UPPER MALL

R. Thames

Barnes

HAMMERSMITH BRIDGE

RICHMOND

KINGS MALL

GLENTHORNE ROAD

CAMBRIDGE GROVE

BEADON RD

QUEEN CAROLINE ST

HAMMERSMITH FLYOVER

TALGARTH RD

CHANCELLORS RD

BARONS COURT

FULHAM

decoration of the chancel has disappeared, but his remodelled s
chapel of 1898, in a spirit very different from Butterfield's,
remains complete. It was extended one bay E, given a stone vault
and new windows with ogee-headed lights, and richly furnished
with a *Bentley* REREDOS with well painted Virgin and Child (by
Innes Fripp), an ALTAR by Bentley's assistant *J. A. Marshall*,
1902, and STAINED GLASS in s and E windows by *Kempe*, with
much delicate canopy work. The earlier stained glass of the
1860s–70s was designed by *Butterfield* and made by *Lavers &
Barraud*; six windows by *A. Gibbs* remain in the N aisle, single
figures under canopies, 1863–73. – VICARAGE to the NE also by
Butterfield, 1864–6. – MISSION HALL in Iffley Road, 1883–4 by
H. Roumieu Gough.

ST KATHARINE, Westway and Primula Street. 1958–9 by *J. R.
Atkinson*, on the foundations of St Katherine Coleman of 1922
by his father *Robert Atkinson*, which was destroyed in the war.
The apse was omitted. Steel-framed, with the roof supported on
piers between brick panels. The nave is top-lit, without side
windows; the exterior sculpture is by *A. W. Banks*. The w end
of the nave was divided off in 1975. – FITTINGS of the 1960s
by *Colin Shewring*. – Enormous CRUCIFIX behind the altar by
Michael Clark. – In the Blessed Sacrament Chapel to the SE,
COMMUNION RAILS, the only survival of the fittings brought
from the City church of St Katherine Coleman.

ST LUKE, Uxbridge Road. 1976–8 by *A. J. Monk* of *Hutchison,
Locke & Monk*, a small but forceful building, with vicarage to
the E and housing in Wormholt Road, all on the site of a church
of 1871–2 by *A. Evers* and *C. H. M. Mileham*. The main accents
of the brick composition are a bell-tower of two thin brick piers
attached to the hall at the w end of the church, an E roof rising
up sharply to provide a clerestory lighting the altar (which is
conventionally placed in a chancel), and a drum-shaped SE baptistery. Lofty interior, very plainly detailed, with exposed brickwork and boarded roofs. – Tall E window with STAINED GLASS
by *John Hayward*, incorporating glass from the old church.

ST MARY, Stamford Brook Road. 1886 by *Charles J. Gladman*.
Red brick, lancet style. Unsympathetically converted into flats in
1986. Low-church plan, with a wide nave; small apsidal chancel
added later. N apsidal baptistery. – (STAINED GLASS. In the s
aisle window, three lights by *Veronica Whall*, 1930.)

ST MATTHEW, Sinclair Road. 1870–1 by *A. Blomfield*. Still Butterfieldian, that is, hard and not accommodating. Streaky brick,
with streaky slate roof. No tower; only a bellcote over the chancel
arch. w porch with gable jutting up into the zone of the windows.
Renovated 1888 by *R. Aylmer*, chancel altered 1897, restored
1956–7.

ST MICHAEL AND ST GEORGE, Commonwealth Avenue. 1952–
3 by *Seely & Paget*, a humble, quietly modern L-shaped group
of church and church hall, with shallow curved roofs. Exterior
tympanum with naive paintings. – (WALL PAINTING above the
altar by *Brian Thomas*.)

ST PAUL, Queen Caroline Street. On the site of a C17 chapel of
ease in what was once the centre of the old village. Rebuilt in
1882 by *H. Roumieu Gough* and *J. P. Seddon*, replacing a C17

chapel of ease. Large and well-mannered, if dull. Not a building
which it would be easy to grow fond of (thought Pevsner in
1952), but now one of the few landmarks of character in the area.
The church is painfully close to the flyover, and the windows
have been made bland by double glazing. Tall NE tower (completed 1889) with tall pinnacles, tall nave with lancet windows
and clerestory. Pale brick with stone dressings. The interior also
very reticent, E.E., with moulded capitals on polished black
octofoil piers and wooden cross-ribbed barrel-vault. The chancel
is elaborated by dogtooth and carved corbels. – FONT. Simple,
late C17, but surrounded by a ring of gargantuan C19 columns. –
PULPIT. From All Hallows, Thames Street, presented in 1900.
An elegant piece of the Wren period, octagonal, on a column
with a rich capital. Oval marquetry panels in frames of deeply
undercut flower garlands; angles with foliage and cherubs'
heads. – CHAIRS in the chancel, late C17. – Much STAINED
GLASS, mostly of indifferent quality. – MONUMENTS. Close to
the N porch, Sir Nicholas Crisp † 1665, erected by him during
his lifetime to commemorate 'that Glorious Martyr King Charles
the First of blessed memory'. Attributed to *Jasper Latham*. Black
and white marble. A tall black shaft against the wall with segmental pediment holding a bronze bust of the king, probably by
Le Sueur; in front of the shaft on a bracket a shorter column with
an urn. – Earl of Mulgrave † 1646 (chancel N). A sophisticated
tablet.– James Smith † 1667 and his wife † 1681, a striking wall-
monument of black and white marble, with a heavily moulded
sarcophagus on a plinth, heavier still, over-decorated with acanthus. On the top a steep pediment with two little allegorical figures, and between them the bust of the alderman. – Many minor
early C19 tablets. – W. Tierney Clark, civil engineer, † 1852.
Tablet with suspension bridge, signed *Westminster Marble Co.*
ST PETER, Black Lion Lane. A Commissioners' church of 1827–
9 by *E. Lapidge,* the oldest church in Hammersmith and the only
lovable one, although cheaply built. Yellow stock brick, attached
Ionic portico, W tower above it, octagonal, then circular with
attached angle pilasters. Low but wide plain room with a gallery
on three sides, on Tuscan columns. The W end has been divided
off, quite tactfully, to make a rather dismal foyer below the W
gallery (1968 by *H. Norman Haines*). Original pewing. Columns
are painted white and gold. – Wooden panelled REREDOS by
Horsley, 1906, very restrained. – SCULPTURE. Virgin and Child
by *Alan Howes*, showing the influence of Gill and Romanesque
art. – WALL PAINTINGS on the E wall, 1932 by *Winifred
Hardman* and *Dorothy Cohen*. – STAINED GLASS. E window by
Clayton & Bell, the Risen Christ, flanked by decoration by
Richmond, and two PAINTINGS of 1928–30, Fishers of Men and
St Peter Preaching, in pale fresco colours.
ST SAVIOUR, Cobbold Road. 1888–9 by *C.N. Tudor* and *J.S.
Alder;* chancel 1894; subdivided and reordered in 1970 by *N.
Haines*. Red brick. – (STAINED GLASS. A series by *Percy Bacon*,
1910–30.)
ST SIMON, Rockley Road. 1879–85 by *A.W. Blomfield*. Lancet
windows, and the distinguishing feature of an odd NW hexagonal
tower and spire (completed 1886).

St Stephen with St Thomas, Uxbridge Road. 1849–50 by *Salvin*, paid for by the Bishop of London. An early example of a Dec ragstone building, with quite delicate tracery; 'on the whole a very pretty and ecclesiastical looking structure', said the *Ecclesiologist*. Originally with a spire (removed after war damage). Restoration and new vestry 1909. Cleaned and restored to good effect in 1987–8. – stained glass. Post-war e window by *Goddard & Gibbs*, replacing one by *Wailes*. – The parsonage in Coverdale Road, brick and gabled, is contemporary and by the same architect.

Holy Ghost and St Stephen (R.C.), Ashchurch Grove. 1904 by *Scoles & Raymond*. – (stained glass. n chapel n window by *Veronica Whall*, 1948. pc)

Holy Trinity (R.C.), Brook Green. 1851–3 by *W. W. Wardell*. The site was presented by Cardinal Wiseman. Confident and ambitious; ragstone, in Puginian c14 style, with a big Dec e window. The tall spire is of 1867 by *C. F. Hansom*, fussier than Wardell had intended. w porch by *Scoles*, 1872. Spacious, lofty interior with a bold roof of hammerbeam type (the carved angels an afterthought), built-in confessionals in the aisles, and a chancel enriched by foliage capitals. – ne (Blessed Sacrament) chapel with ceiled roof with bosses, divided off by good iron screens. In the chapel carved reredos of 1854 by *J. J. Scoles* and stained glass by *Hardman*, likewise in the s chapel. – Other furnishings (diminished by a 1970s reordering): stone reredos in the chancel; font with ornate wooden cover designed by *Wilberfoss*, made by *T. Orr;* rood by *P. P. Pugin*, 1892. – In the e window good stained glass by *Hardman*, 1853; other windows, of less note, by *Mayer* of Munich, who also provided the stations of the cross. – brass to the founder, Joseph Butt, † 1861.

Our Lady of Fatima (R.C.), Commonwealth Avenue. 1965–6 by *Wilfrid Cassidy*. Minor domestic Romanesque, with s w tower.

St Aidan (R.C.), Old Oak Common Lane. 1958–61 by *John Newton* of *Burles, Newton & Partners*. In the middle of a shopping parade on the border with Acton (Ea). Brick and concrete, with large w window and open campanile. The building is a simple envelope for the exceptionally rich collection of works by contemporary artists, commissioned by the parish priest, Father James Etherington,* a notable achievement for a suburban R.C. church of this date. – sculpture. Many statues. St Aidan (on exterior), St Theresa (*K. Parbury*), St Joseph (*G. Campbell*), St Anthony (*Lindsey Clark*), St Gerard Majella (*A. J. Ayres*). – Frieze with stations of the cross (figures in concrete against mosaic), by *A. Fleischmann*; also by him the perspex panels with Evangelists in the porch. – painting over the altar, Crucifixion by *Graham Sutherland*, his first commission for an R.C. church, planned 1958, executed 1963 (cf. his earlier Crucifixion at St Matthew Northampton). – Two painted triptychs (Sacred Heart and Our Lady of Walsingham), both flanked by saints, by *Roy le Maistre*. – ceramics in the baptistery by *A. Kossowski*. – stained glass. By *P. Four-*

---

*I am grateful to J. C. M. Nolan for details about these.

maintreaux (Whitefriars Studios), symbols of the Catholic faith in the porch, and six panels with saints and martyrs in the sanctuary. – Nave windows by *Arthur Buss* of *Goddard & Gibbs*.

ST ANDREW BOBOLA (R.C.) (Polish church), Leysfield Road. Built as St Andrew's Presbyterian church, 1870 by *Edmund Woodthorpe*, converted 1961 by *A.P. Klecki*. Uneventful ragstone exterior, the w tower with pinnacles, but the interior daringly modernized. The w foyer looks into a church with whitened walls, light seating made from the old pews, and a striking sanctuary. All the fittings are by *Klecki*: E wall with bronzed cast cement panel with the martyrdom of St Andrew Bobola, in sketchy, angular relief; STATIONS OF THE CROSS in the same style and materials; aluminium CROSS with Christ the King over the altar, and a large circular window above with STAINED GLASS with stylized star shapes.

BAPTIST CHURCH, Shepherds Bush Road. 1907 by *P.W. Hawkins*, in the cheerful Perp of the period. Brick and stone dressings, with a funny little spire on the SW tower.

FRIENDS MEETING HOUSE, Nigel Playfair Avenue. 1954–5 by *Hubert Lidbetter*, a modest brick meeting room with lower surrounding parts. It replaces the C18 meeting house by Hammersmith Creek, lost in the war.

METHODIST CHURCH, Askew Road. 1953–4 by *Sir Guy Dawber, Fox & Robinson*, completed 1968.

METHODIST CHURCH, Shepherds Bush Road. 1879 by *Charles Bell*. Large, ragstone Gothic, jacked up over a tall basement. A prominent landmark; the gabled aisles and transept create quite a lively profile. Future uncertain.

RIVERCOURT METHODIST CHURCH, King Street. By *Charles Bell*, 1875, renovated 1975. Ragstone; quite florid Dec tracery to the gabled aisles; NW tower and spire.

ST NICHOLAS (Greek Orthodox Cathedral), Godolphin Road. Built as St Thomas, 1882 by *A.W. Blomfield*, chancel added 1887. Brick, very plain. Tall clerestory; w buttresses carried up to a bell-turret. – (The Greek Orthodox furnishings incorporate the large Baroque ALTAR added in 1932, and the PULPIT and RAILS brought from Belgium. – Greek WALL PAINTINGS.)

SALVATION ARMY CITADEL, Dalling Road. Formerly Albion Congregational Church. 1891–2 by *F.W. Stocking*. Grand pedimented front with giant pilasters and rusticated basement. – SCHOOL and HALL 1905–6 by *T.E. Davidson*.

HAMMERSMITH AND WEST KENSINGTON SYNAGOGUE, Brook Green. 1890 by *Delissa Joseph*, enlarged in 1896. Schoolrooms 1894, also by *Joseph*; classrooms of 1927 and 1956–7. Gabled red brick front; interior with iron columns.

ST MARY'S R.C. CEMETERY, Harrow Road. Immediately w of Kensal Green Cemetery (KC, q.v.). Gothic buildings of 1859–60 by *S.J. Nicholl*. Several grand MAUSOLEA, including those to the Marqués de Misa, elaborate late C19 Gothic, and to the Campbell family, neo-Byzantine, 1904 by *C.H.B. Quennell*. – Belgian WAR MEMORIAL of *c.* 1920, Portland stone, with a sculpture of the Pietà between columns with Byzantine capitals.

PUBLIC BUILDINGS

TOWN HALL, King Street. 1938–9 by *E. Berry Webber*. An unfortunate building, both in the way it destroyed the picturesque
character of the area around the former creek, and in what has
happened to it since. It is a large, symmetrical rectangle with
inner courtyard, of ungainly bulk, although well detailed in a
somewhat Swedish hybrid style, classical with modern touches.
Exterior of raked red brick above a channelled stone ground
floor, the courtyard walls of yellow brick and so less oppressive.
On the s side a tall central brick arch marks the former entrance
to the council chamber; the doorway is now blocked, leaving a
meaningless grand double stair facing the busy Great West Road.
On the N side the three large coffered arches leading to the public
hall are obscured by an ill judged series of decks and stairs serving
the overbearing extension towards King Street. This is of 1971–
5 by the *Borough Architect's Department* and makes no attempt
to harmonize with the older building. Five storeys and a recessed
mezzanine high up on piers above a bleak concrete plaza (a garden
was intended). Four widely spaced uprights stand in front of
the window bands; typically 1970s steep mansard. In the older
building there is a generous foyer to the public hall, a lofty
space lit by the three large arches on the N side, decorated with
attractive wall paintings of Hammersmith riverside scenes, 1956
by *Alfred Daniels* and *John Titchell*. In the s range, the mayor's
parlour looks out over the river, the council chamber (with original furnishings) projects into the courtyard, lit by upper
windows. Between these rooms is a handsome top-lit antechamber with attractive ornamental gallery grilles and original
light fittings. w of the main building a little REGISTRY OFFICE
of 1971 by *M. J. Gleeson* of the Borough Architect's Department:
two linked octagons, windows with lunettes above and below,
and an outside staircase.
POLICE STATION, Shepherds Bush Road. 1938 by *Donald
McMorran* (of *Farquharson & McMorran*), in the restrained but
slightly quirky classical style typical of the architect. Granite with
brick above; attic windows not in line with the lower windows.
FIRE STATION, Shepherds Bush Road. 1913–14, from the classic
phase of the Fire Brigade Branch of the *L.C.C. Architect's
Department*. Five storeys, red brick above a stone ground floor,
enlivened by original free classical features: a giant arcade linking
ground and first floors, two cornices above, and two little projecting stone pavilions with circular windows.
POST OFFICE, Blythe Road. *See* Perambulation 4.
TELEPHONE EXCHANGE, Riverside Gardens. Dated 1936; utilitarian rather than the neo-Georgian used earlier for such buildings. Metal windows between brick piers.
WORMWOOD SCRUBS PRISON, Du Cane Road. 1874 by *Sir
Edmund Du Cane*. Built by convicts. Tall rectangular blocks with
quite lively roof-lines, placed in line (not radially, as was the
fashion earlier). Gatehouse with Romanesque details, and busts
of Elizabeth Fry and Sir Edmund Du Cane. (Good CHAPEL.)

STAMFORD HOUSE, N of Goldhawk Road. Remand home and assessment centre by *Yorke, Rosenberg & Mardall*, 1964. Brown brick, solid but well detailed. Offices and staff flats with balconies facing the road, the school behind given character by an overhanging upper floor with chamfered edges. Unsympathetic later classrooms.

CARNEGIE CENTRAL LIBRARY, Shepherds Bush Road. 1904–5 by *Henry T. Hare* (of Oxford and Henley Town Halls fame), bulging with much sculpture by *F. E. E. Schenck*, and quite happy of its kind. Ionic colonnade along the first floor, flanked by end pavilions. Statues of Shakespeare and Milton in niches. Big Baroque doorway. Staircase window with stained glass with literary figures; another in the reference library to Dean Colet. The main library and reference library on the first floor have glazed barrel-vaults.

PASSMORE EDWARDS LIBRARY, Uxbridge Road, Shepherds Bush. 1895 by *Maurice B. Adams*. Brick with stone dressings, in a friendly early C 17 classical style. Inside, bronze portrait tablets to Leigh Hunt and Charles Keene by *Frampton*.

WORMHOLT LIBRARY AND INFANT WELFARE CENTRE, Hemlock Road. By *Hampton C. Lucas* of the Borough Engineer's Department, completed by 1930. A small but formal focus in the Wormholt estate, with English Renaissance details and a dome. Internal alterations of the 1980s.

PUBLIC BATHS, Lime Grove. Only the front block remains, converted to flats; brick and stone, with jolly Baroque details, 1907 by *J. Ernest Franck*.

WHITE CITY POOL, Bloemfontein Road. A raw red brick cube concealing one of London's first leisure pools, with beach, waves, and palm trees; 1980 by *Clifford Barnet*, a pioneer of the type (e.g. at Sunderland, 1975).

HAMMERSMITH AND WEST LONDON COLLEGE, Hammersmith Road. By *Bob Giles* of the *G.L.C. Architect's Department, Schools Division* (working for *I.L.E.A.*), planned from 1965, completed 1980. On the site of ST PAUL'S SCHOOL, which moved out in 1969.[*] From the overpowering buildings of 1881–5 by *Waterhouse* there remain only the picturesque High Master's house and a lodge (now council-owned), the pink Mansfield sandstone boundary walls, and a circular garden building. The survivors are in Waterhouse's favourite purple brick and orange terracotta with Gothic detail, which he used also for the main buildings. The materials provided the cue for the new structure, which is faced entirely in hard ruby red brickwork, still a novelty for modern-minded architects at this time, and used here with the exhausting insistence of the newly converted. The brick is relieved by the well-detailed bands of windows, with a strong rhythm of black vertical mullions. A dramatic approach up steps leads to a main entrance facing a formal paved piazza. From this centre each college fans out in an irregular horseshoe, stepping down from seven to four storeys, looking out to gardens to E and W In practice this is more confusing than it looks on a plan. As

---

[*]The school is now at Barnes (Ri), along with the appealing COLET MONUMENT by *Thornycroft*, 1902.

a further complexity, two paths run through the buildings, in an effort to provide some urban continuity between the college and the housing which occupies the N part of the old school site. The college is one of the most ambitious of the I.L.E.A. enterprises bringing together the West London College and the Hammersmith College of Further Education (the Hammersmith College of Building was originally intended to join them as well), and catering for 3,000 students on site. In the grounds, 'London West', a sculpture by *Anthony Caro*, 1980.

HAMMERSMITH SCHOOL OF BUILDING, Lime Grove. 1907 by the L.C.C. Architect's Department under *W. E. Riley*, dark brick in a quiet Tudor, a good composition of gables, mullioned windows, and steep pitched roofs. Additions of 1928 and 1950. The N parts are now used by Chelsea College of Art.

BURLINGTON DANES, Wood Lane. Built as Burlington School for Girls by *Sir John Burnet, Tait & Lorne*, 1936, a pioneer of the style widely adopted for schools of the later 1930s by progressive county architects. In the Dudok manner, like the same firm's Masonic Hospital at Hammersmith (q.v., below). The reinforced concrete frame is faced with carefully laid yellow brick with brown brick for the bell-pier and trimmings; large, plain steel-framed windows. The narrow site dictated a departure from the conventional courtyard plan: streamlined classrooms stretch out in a long block behind, shielded from the noisy street by the assembly hall, with the external stairs rising at its side to the entrance hall and rounded stair-tower – a well contrived, asymmetrical cubic composition.

HAMMERSMITH SCHOOL, Erica Street. Built in 1954–8 by the *L.C.C.* (architect in charge *Edward Hollamby*) as boys' and girls' secondaries with shared facilities. The brick buildings are grouped informally around two courtyards, on a N axis from Wormholt Park. The centrepiece of the main courtyard is the music and assembly hall, with a strong pattern of louvred windows between sturdy mullions running up to a shallow gable. Shortage of building materials inspired an inventive use of traditional brick and timber, which produces plenty of visual interest: the structural brick piers support ingenious shallow pitched roofs with trusses of mahogany laminated and combined with stressed steel, and there are timber barrel-vaults over the gymnasia and curved hinged walls of laminated wood around the drama hall. Decorative features – characteristic of the L.C.C.'s concern at this time with visual education – included patterned wall tiles (designed by *Hollamby*), *William Morris* wallpapers (an early and influential example of their revival), and tapestry curtains in the drama hall by *Gerald Holtom* (the stage curtains showing Morris flanked by Burne-Jones and Rossetti, the foyer ones with Wren's spires of London). Only the tiles remain.

LATYMER UPPER SCHOOL, King Street. A Gothic arcade of 1930 by *J. M. Kellett* separates the forecourt from the street. The main buildings are of 1895 by *G. Saunders*. The street front is like a church gable, the whole brick Gothic. Gymnasium 1951–4 by *Chesterton*; new buildings 1966–71 by *Barron & Smith*; swimming pool 1975 by *Seifert*; sports hall 1979–80.

St Paul's Girls School, Brook Green. Established in 1904 by the John Colet Foundation responsible for St Paul's Boys School. Main buildings of 1904–7 by *Gerald Horsley,* music 70 block and High Mistress's house 1910–13 (Gustav Holst was the school's first director of music). One of the best Edwardian school buildings in London, a friendly free classical composition of orange brick and stone, symmetrical, amply proportioned, with big segmental pediments and generous and original use of sculpture: tendrils of flowers around the stone panel with the main doorway, large low-relief figures in the gables of the wings. The plan is formal, with a groin-vaulted spine corridor at right angles to the entrance hall and a glazed dome over the junction. Broad, barrel-vaulted assembly hall with a gallery, clerestory lunettes, and an organ in a handsome case against the end wall. Woodwork and fittings of high quality. Library in the w wing with coved ceiling and Palladian window. The music block to the w has an upper singing room with circular windows high up set in deep recesses cut through the coved ceiling. Attached behind is the High Mistress's house (No. 48 Rowan Road), a busy domestic Queen Anne front (rather in the manner of Ernest Newton's small houses), with two central bay-windows with slate-hanging and five pedimented dormers squeezed between two tall stacks. Behind the main school building the former SWIMMING POOL by *Horsley,* 1909, utilitarian (converted to engineering workshops 1984), and the dull neo-Georgian science block (1933, modernized in 1978 by *Jane Drew).* Other extensions and alterations 1970–4 by *Robert Matthews, Johnson-Marshall & Partners,* including an extra floor of glass-roofed classrooms tactfully added on either side of the hall. To the e the CELIA JOHNSON THEATRE BUILDING, 1983–4 by *Fitzroy Robinson Partnership.* Further w along Brook Green, SWIMMING POOL by *Robert Matthew, Johnson-Marshall & Partners,* 1971–4, orange brick with Y-shaped supports visible behind the sloping glazed clerestory.

PRIMARY SCHOOLS. St Peter's School, St Peter's Road, is a typical modest mid C19 church school, 1849 with additions; two storeys, gabled wings. Another mid C19 former school in Down Place, s of King Street: a formal front of two storeys, with a little pediment, dated 1855; gabled extensions in Macbeth Street 1896. PADDENSWICK ROAD SCHOOLS, founded and endowed by John Betts and built in 1868 by *G. A. Burn,* are more ambitious, with a tall gabled centre between wings; covered entrance arcade on fat black columns. Surviving early Board Schools are taller, in response to the challenge of growing numbers. VICTORIA, Becklow Road, is of 1856, with many additions, the original part with residual Gothic touches. LATIMER ROAD EDUCATION CENTRE, Freston Road (formerly Latimer Road School), is a classic *Robson* design of 1879–80, three-storeyed, symmetrical, with small shaped gables, the central hall flanked by staircase blocks and classrooms. KENMONT, Valliere Road, is of 1883–4, later work by *Robson,* a romantically asymmetrical three-storey composition with battlements and turret. (*See also* Fulham.)

POST WAR PRIMARY SCHOOLS. The most interesting is WEST-
VILLE ROAD, designed by *E. Goldfinger,* 1950–3, in conscious
reaction to the earlier generation's dominating monoliths (cf.
Lasdun's Hallfield School, Paddington, Wm outer). Low and
informally grouped buildings with curved brick links, the airy
classrooms looking out on to a generous playground. Given presence by the tough exposed concrete framework, and by a rectangular brick tower close to the entrance. Mural by *Gordon
Cullen* in the entrance hall. CANBERRA INFANTS AND
JUNIORS, Australia Road, is a good but more conventional
example of *L.C.C.* work of the 1950s, brick, with one wing on
blue-tiled columns, and the hall projecting to the road with an
external sculpture. ST MARY'S R.C. PRIMARY, Masbro Road,
1977–8 by *P.J. Mabley,* has the semi-open plan introduced from
the late 1960s.

VANESSA NURSERY SCHOOL, Cathnor Road. 1974 by *Fitch &
Co.* A curious coloured plastic plaything peeping up above a
wooden fence. Rounded bays inside, which appear externally like
ships' sirens; indoor swimming pool.

CONVENT OF THE SACRED HEART, Hammersmith Road. By
J.F. Bentley, his first major commission. Planned for St Thomas's Seminary in 1868 but not begun until 1876. Main buildings
completed 1881, chapel 1884. Well renovated in 1990. One of
Bentley's major works in London, early and still far from the
broad, masterful treatment of his Westminster Cathedral. Brick
with stone dressings. The chapel faces the street with a large
Perp window. By its side is the cloister; this, and even more the
garden front, is in a strong, masculine, not at all easy-going style.
The row of chimneys on the S and E ranges of the cloister,
corbelled out from the second floor, are specially characteristic.
The N range has instead double-height bay-windows. The cloister is surrounded by long barrel-vaulted walks with mullion-and-
transom windows and WALL PAINTINGS by *Mother Maycock,*
1902–4. In the N range the bishop's parlour, with heavy beams,
dado panelling, and a large fireplace with dying arches. In the
CHAPEL Bentley's details are in a refined and restrained late
Gothic: shallow arches with dying mouldings; ceiled wagon roof
with crenellated wall-plate. The original orientation has been
reversed. Reredos with open tracery. The convent which took
over in 1893 established a girls' school in the buildings. Extensions: day school to the N, 1902 by *J.A. Marshall*; gymnasium,
1935–9 by *Wallace Gregory*; E classroom block, 1957 by *Nicholas
& Dixon Spain.* Science wing planned to the S in 1991 by
Farrington Dennys Fisher, on the site of the junior school of
1893–4 by *J.H. Pollen.*

101 ROYAL MASONIC HOSPITAL, Ravenscourt Park. 1931 by *Sir
John Burnet, Tait & Lorne.* Large and of great variety in the
grouping of blocks which are nevertheless symmetrical in themselves. Brick with raked joints, treated with much appreciation
of the material. Metal windows (renewed 1990). Closely dependent on the Dutch style of W.M. Dudok, one of the first examples
of this type of modern architecture in London. Formal front to
the park with sculpture, and another one to the garden to the S,
with far-projecting wings with curving metal balconies swooping

around the ends, rather nautical. Later extensions by the same firm: Wakefield wing 1958, surgical block and Frank Douglas Court 1973. Long sloping roofs to the N, with a neatly continued corner on piers linking old and new buildings, tactfully low when seen from the park.

QUEEN CHARLOTTE'S HOSPITAL, Goldhawk Road. The core is a house called OAKBURN, stuccoed, neo-Gothic, with a rather charming r. part which looks early C19 and still rather Strawberry-Hillish, and a bigger and heftier l. part by *Brandon*, 1878, with buttresses, oriel, and heavy roof with crenellations and pinnacles. The hospital was established in 1929. Additions from 1939. Outpatients' department, day nursery, and boiler house 1976–7 by *GMWP*.

HAMMERSMITH HOSPITAL, Du Cane Road. The main entrance is now through the MEDICAL SCHOOL, a handsome brick and stone composition of 1904 by *Giles Gough & Trollope* in Queen Anne style, with canted corner bays, pedimented windows to ground and first floors, and raised centre with tall clock-turret. At the back is the WOLFSON INSTITUTE (postgraduate medical school) by *Lyons Israel & Ellis*, *c*. 1961, reinforced concrete, in the well-handled brutalist style typical of this firm. It is dominated by a pile of three windowless lecture theatres, and attached by a bridge to the ten-storey COMMONWEALTH BUILDING by the same firm, of 1966. Further E a more recent addition, large and sleek, red brick with cheerful yellow and green trimmings, 1985–7 by *Llewelyn-Davies, Weeks & Partners*, the first phase of a major redevelopment. In the outpatients' department on the ground floor, mural by *Susan Tebby*: Riverside. Top floor with two wards overlooking a small courtyard with fountain by *William Pye*.

RAVENSCOURT PARK. The grounds of Palingswick Manor were acquired for a public park in 1887. The flat site is made interesting by winding paths and a curved lake. According to Faulkner, George Scott, the last private owner, who bought the estate in 1812, consulted *Repton*, although there is no other known proof of this. From the early C18 there remain the straight avenue leading from King Street to the site of the house (destroyed in 1941), and the brick STABLES, now refreshment rooms, a single range with central pediment and cupola. The C18 iron gates with overthrow at the entrance to the flower garden to the NE bear the cypher of Thomas Corbell, Secretary to the Admiralty, who bought the estate in 1741 and renamed it Ravenscourt in allusion to his name (corbeau-corbell). Stuccoed and pilastered C19 LODGE in Paddenswick Road. The Sir William Bull Memorial Gates in King Street are of 1933.

QUEENS PARK RANGERS FOOTBALL STADIUM, Loftus Road and South Africa Road. Rebuilt in stages from 1968 (N stand). S, E, and W stands 1969–72 by *Quine & Newberry*. Blue-trimmed, steel-framed grandstands and terraces, providing 16,500 seats and 8,500 standing spaces.

OLYMPIA, Hammersmith Road. *See* Perambulation 4.

PUMPING STATION, Great West Road. Grand classical of 1908 for the Metropolitan Water Board. Red brick with stone dressings; pedimented entrance.

UNDERGROUND STATIONS. The Metropolitan line extension
reached HAMMERSMITH in 1864. Dignified street front with
curved gable and ball finial, a small shopping arcade on the
awkward triangular site behind. The future of WHITE CITY, of
1947, is uncertain. It has a long street front of brick, asymmetrical, with curved N end stepping up to an airy foyer; the clarity
of the pre-war station style giving way to Festival picturesque.
HAMMERSMITH FLYOVER. 1962 by the L.C.C. (chief engineer
B. Rawlinson). A notable achievement at the time: half a mile of
pre-stressed concrete, elegantly cantilevered from central supports – a solution possible only for a four-lane width, and so not
repeated for later, larger roads.
HAMMERSMITH BRIDGE. See Perambulation 1.

PERAMBULATIONS

1. The Broadway and the riverside

HAMMERSMITH BROADWAY, the second busiest traffic junction
in London, resembles the centre of a minor town, not a suburb.
It developed in the later C 19 around its two stations when nobody
yet bothered about planning, and the traffic became the main
force in tying together what was otherwise senseless. This was
the challenge that faced the planners. In the 1960s an attempt to
rationalize the muddle was made with the construction across
Queen Caroline Street of the GREAT WEST ROAD FLYOVER
(q.v. Public Buildings, above). However, the flyover is hardly an
undiluted blessing; the desolate surroundings are still full of
ground-level traffic, and the setting of St Paul's church has been
ruined. In the 1970s–80s several controversial schemes were put
forward for the large area between the Broadway and the flyover,
traversed from the 1860s by the District Railway.* Finally in
1988 *Elsom Pack & Roberts's* revised plans were adopted after
ministerial intervention, and almost the whole area was flattened.
The new development covers the railway with a deck for a bus
station, and rings the whole with a continuous series of formally
composed commercial buildings of six to ten storeys, designed
with the striped cladding and occasional curved excrescences
which suddenly became so popular in the late 1980s.
In QUEEN CAROLINE STREET, near the SW corner the plan
includes new buildings lower than the rest, which step back to
give minimal breathing space to the one survival, the façade of
BRADMORE HOUSE, re-erected here in 1913 as part of a bus
garage, incorporated in the new scheme as the front of a separate
office block. The façade, formerly a garden front facing E, with
its main rooms on the first floor, was once the N part of a larger
mansion called Butterwick House, the rest of which had been
demolished in 1836. When rebuilt in 1913 it was raised up on a

---

*Foster Associates' daringly high tech proposals were abandoned in 1979 in favour
of a more banal speculative office scheme for Bredero by *Elsom Pack & Roberts*. An
alternative by the *Terry Farrell Partnership* (1983), preserving more buildings, was
also rejected.

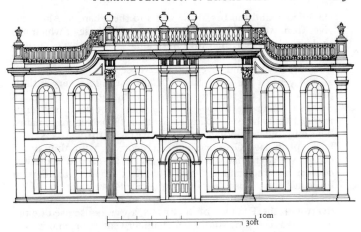

Hammersmith, Bradmore House,
elevation before reconstruction of garden front

plinth and reduced slightly in width. Nevertheless it remains a
remarkable brick front of *c.* 1700, bold and Baroque, in a style
strongly reminiscent of *Archer* (cf. the house on the N side of
Covent Garden). It is worthy of a less cramped setting. Two
storeys, seven bays, the middle three raised with an up-curving
of the top cornice. The centre is flanked by long thin composite
pilasters, the outer angles by equally long and thin Tuscan pilasters. Red brick with rubbers, and stone for the pilasters and
balustrade. All windows and the door are round-headed.

s of the flyover, at the corner of Queen Caroline Street, the large
ODEON (formerly Gaumont Palace), 1932 by *Robert Cromie*, a
rather weak curved front, classical going art deco, hiding an
impressively huge, little altered auditorium seating 3,560, with
organ (surviving below extended stage), cantilevered balcony
with deeply coved ceiling, and murals by *Newberry A. Trent*.
Further E in this desolate area, the HAMMERSMITH
LANDMARK, begun in 1990, an office block of a highly original
design by *Ralph Erskine*, for two Swedish companies. It
resembles a great glass moored liner, an enclosed world insulated
from its drab and noisy urban setting – a curious blend of space-
ship imagery with expressionist allusions. The curved outline
is conditioned by the flyover, which wraps around the N side of
the site. Nine storeys above basement parking, the bellying-
out copper-banded upper floors anchored by roughly textured
tapering brick piers. An interesting roofscape, with clerestory
lighting for the atrium set back from the outer walls, below a
curved copper roof which extends over terraces stepping down
on the side away from the flyover. The roof excrescences also
look rather nautical. They include a viewing tower reached by a
lift through the atrium. On the s side a low building for the
borough (archives, training centre, and local studies centre) has
been included as part of the same scheme.

The interruption of flyover and Great West Road makes it difficult
to appreciate that in the C18 and C19 the village of Hammersmith

extended round the Broadway and s to the Thames. Along the river front were the best houses, presumably those of which it is said already in 1697 that they were inhabited by 'divers citizens of the City of London who reside in ... Hamersmith ... onely in summertyme, and divers others whose constant residence is all the year in the said place'. Of all that only a very little is preserved. The old route to the river is along QUEEN CAROLINE STREET. Here the *Survey of London* in 1915 could still enumerate twenty houses of dates earlier than 1800. Not one remains. The only older building left is TEMPLE LODGE, No. 51, set back, plain late Georgian, with a doorway with thin fluted columns. After that CAROLINE ESTATE, slabs of post-war council housing, and the backs of the Peabody Buildings in Fulham Palace Road (*see* Fulham (HF), Perambulation 3). To the l. CRISP ROAD, in the late C19 an industrial area by the river, with the RIVERSIDE STUDIOS, a warehouse used by the B.B.C. as a recording studio, which underwent an ingenious low-key conversion in 1975 to a successful local arts centre. Ambitious plans for rebuilding were made by *Alsop & Lyall*, but all that materialized was their crisply designed BOOKSHOP of 1980. Next door, CHANCELLORS WHARF, a package in two-tone brick of offices and three rows of fussily decorated town houses, 1986–9 by *D. Y. Davies Associates*.

Now w from Hammersmith Bridge. Just s of the bridge a plain early C19 three-storey yellow brick house overlooking the river. Then the thick forms of the BRIDGE (1883–7 by *Bazalgette*),[*] and QUEEN'S MANSIONS, late Victorian flats with a corner dome and elaborate iron balconies on the riverside. After that the scale of LOWER MALL comes as a surprise. It is Hammersmith's best street. Nos. 6–9 is a pretty late Georgian group with iron verandas at various heights. No. 10, KENT HOUSE, probably of *c.* 1782, is ambitious and up-to-date, in the Adam style, with two symmetrical canted bay-windows and graceful if restrained decoration of the centre. Good iron railings and gate. Then a happy mixture of new and renewed buildings, boathouses and pubs, with nothing out of scale. Nos. 11–12 are humble cottages, early C17 altered (upper-floor windows with sliding sashes). The grander WESTCOTT LODGE, set further back, has a mid C18 five-bay centre, a later Adamish doorway to the l., a matching C20 addition to the r., and an early C19 back with windows recessed in arches. (Good C18 staircase.) FURNIVALL GARDENS links Lower and Upper Mall. It was laid out in 1951 on the site of Hammersmith Creek, a once picturesque area badly damaged in the war.

The beginning of UPPER MALL is marked by SUSSEX HOUSE, built (as two houses) *c.* 1726. It has a characteristic early C18 doorway with Roman Doric pilasters and a segmental pediment; straight-headed windows, three storeys, five bays; stock brick and red brick dressings. Opposite is a row of cottages, starting with Nos. 13–15, the former DOVES BINDERY where the Doves Press operated and Cobden Sanderson lived. Then the river is reached, and the first noteworthy house facing the water is

*For details on the Thames crossings, *see London 2: South.*

KELMSCOTT HOUSE, a plain, five-bay, three-storey house of the 1780s, with a bowed back addition of *c*. 1800. William Morris, who lived here between 1878 and his death in 1896, named the house after Kelmscott Manor, his country retreat in Oxfordshire. The basement is now the offices of the William Morris Society and a small museum. Morris used the coach house for meetings, had a tapestry loom installed in his bedroom, and started printing the books of the Kelmscott Press in the cottage No. 14 Upper Mall. Interior with some later plasterwork added by *G. P. Bankart, c.* 1910; other alterations, including a rear addition, by *Philip E. Pilditch,* 1916.

The RIVER WALL in this area has bastions dating from *c*. 1680, the time when the dowager Queen Catherine lived in Upper Mall. Farther E Upper Mall is somewhat disappointing, with nothing like the sustained charm of Chiswick Mall. There are only two older houses worth singling out. RIVERCOURT HOUSE, No. 36, of 1808, has a handsome doorway with Ionic columns and pediment and a three-storey projecting wing on the l. LINDEN HOUSE (Corinthian Sailing Club) is of nine bays, *c*. 1733, with a pediment over the central five. Tripartite centrepiece with Ionic columns and pilasters (a comparison with the later Rivercourt House is instructive). The stretch of the river walk here was created in the 1960s and is especially happy in its variety. A neat WATCH OFFICE on a pole, near the sailing club (1964). Buildings are pleasantly grouped and not too crowded. The maisonettes above garages (MYLNE CLOSE) are by the *Borough Architect's Department,* 1962; the converted buildings in OIL MILL LANE, and the new flats overlooking the river, by *Chapman Taylor Partners, c.* 1971. The river walk passes picturesquely through an arcade and then past upper-level private gardens to the OLD SHIP INN and an open space in front of the waterworks. At the back of the inn the remains of an interesting entrance, brick, C 17, and probably rather early than late. What can it have been, with its brick pilasters with heavy intermittent rustication which originally carried a pediment? Old views show it attached to a rambling gabled house, of the time of Charles I according to Faulkner.

A little further on HAMMERSMITH TERRACE begins, sixteen identical houses, plain brick, three-storeyed in the E half, four-storeyed in the W. The whole block was built *c*. 1750, its main fronts facing gardens which originally ran down to a private promenade above the river. There is no public road between them and the water. Architecturally they are plain and entirely urban (a surprising fact if one remembers that they stood right in the country). Their backsides to the road (except for Nos. 1 and 2 facing down SOUTH BLACK LION LANE) have an odd jerky fenestration joining up in a diagonal rhythm, explained by the position of the staircases. Among distinguished residents were Edward Johnston, the calligrapher (No. 3), and Loutherbourg, the painter (Nos. 7 and 8, which were later occupied by Emery Walker, the engraver and friend of William Morris, and May Morris; *Morris* furnishings and decoration in No. 7). Just beyond, on the Chiswick boundary, ST PETER'S WHARF, a simple, dark brick group of studio flats, staggered to the road, with a private courtyard by the river. By *M. Pattrick, c.* 1975. Then CHISWICK MALL begins modestly with MALL COTTAGE (Victorian Tudor detail) and EYOT COTTAGE, a pretty group right on the river. For the continuation *see* Chiswick (Ho).

2. *King Street and streets to its* N *and* S

At the NE corner of KING STREET is the only building that puts up a decent show to the Broadway, the SWAN HOTEL of 1900–2 by *F. Miller,* with mosaic decoration, a swan in a gable, and good fittings inside. King Street starts quite well, with the ornate Victorian HOP POLES (pretty coloured tile decoration to a front of 1860–1) and its neighbour on the W side, but quickly degenerates into the muddle of C20 rebuilding common in suburban shopping streets. Most prominent is KING'S MALL on the N side, a lumpy 1970s package by *R. Seifert & Partners,* with covered shopping centre below car park, offices, and over 200 local authority flats, their roof-top setting left bleak and uninviting. The only exceptional upper building, completed in 1979, is the LYRIC THEATRE, formerly at the back of the Broadway, where its demolition in 1971 was permitted on condition that *Frank Matcham*'s auditorium of 1895 was reconstructed within the new development – a landmark in the revival of appreciation of such interiors. A mean approach leads to a spacious, if austere, informal foyer through which stairs rise to circle and gallery, a neutral prelude to the delectable exuberance of Matcham's lofty yet intimate auditorium. 450 seats; curvaceous balconies with well integrated boxes, all with rich and confident Rococo plasterwork. Pretty cusped arch to the proscenium (tactfully made slightly wider than the original). Small modern studio theatre below.

S of King Street BRIDGE AVENUE entices by a mid C19 terrace of some character – close set arched windows and roof balustrade – but further S the townscape disintegrates in the neighbourhood of the Great West Road and flyover approach. The clumsy office blocks of the UNITED DISTILLERS, refaced in the 1980s, were originally a slab of *c.* 1962 (for British Oxygen) with a polygonal extension of the 1970s.

So back to KING STREET, where a few inter-war shops once made quite an elegant show: Nos. 111–115, in streamlined black and cream faience, were built as the British Home Stores in 1937 by *Albert L. Forman,* a model modern store in its day; opposite, at the corner of Leamore Street, is another with white art deco trim. The CANNON CINEMA, near the Town Hall, is of 1936 by *W. R. Glen,* much altered. The most interesting accents are the numerous pubs typical of an old thoroughfare, such as the decent Victorian HAMPSHIRE HOG and the more eccentric Edwardian SALUTATION INN by *A. P. Killick,* 1910, with its extraordinarily lurid blue and mauve tiles. In front of the mid C20 RAVENSCOURT ARMS, the stone figure of a lively black bull, brought from the Holborn Inn demolished in 1904. Further on a few older houses: Nos. 200–224 of 1761–4, a humble terrace with mansard roofs, is the most obvious group. On the s side, set back, No. 241, PALINGSWICK HOUSE, grand, rather dour late Victorian Italianate. On the N, No. 246, POLISH CULTURAL CENTRE, 1971 by *M. F. Grzesik,* a perversely ugly design, with heavy concrete piers tapering up and down from the first floor, and a yawning recessed entrance.

Several of the streets leading N from King Street still have a pleasing variety of mid C19 terraces and villas. In CAMBRIDGE GROVE an attractive mixture of mid C19 houses; in DALLING ROAD a few plainer brick early C19 villas. The grander stucco-trimmed paired villa of the early to mid C19 is a speciality of the streets built up around the grounds of Ravenscourt Manor (q.v. Public Buildings, Ravenscourt Park); see especially PADDENSWICK ROAD (with new arrivals in keeping) and RAVENSCOURT ROAD, where there is also a stately terrace with giant rusticated pilasters. W of the park, close to the backs of the two hospitals, RAVENSCOURT SQUARE, where No. 17 sports a belvedere tower, and RAVENSCOURT GARDENS, with a very complete set of villas. No. 1 RAVENSCOURT PARK is the former stained glass studio of Christopher and Veronica Whall, converted for this use in 1907 by *Charles Spooner* (PC).

s of King Street is the neighbourhood in Hammersmith which is most consistently attractive as a piece of planning: ST PETER'S SQUARE with St Peter's church nearby (q.v.), developed from *c.* 1825 on land belonging to George Scott of Ravenscourt Park. The square has the flavour of a suburban Belgravia, with tall stuccoed three-storeyed houses in groups of three on s, E, and W sides of the communal gardens. The two end houses of each group project, and have pediments. Ionic porches in set-back end bays, and an Ionic loggia in the centre for the middle house, disguising its front door, the one piece of asymmetry in each group. The groups were originally connected by low walls to hide the service entrances. The arrangement survives on the W side: thick scrolls on top; the volutes of the columns are thick too, and pineapples and eagles adorn the walls. Such was the designer's taste. His identity remains uncertain, although *J. C. Loudon* (to whom Faulkner attributes the design of the gardens) is a tempting possibility (cf. his own pair of villas in Porchester Terrace of 1823–5 (*see* Paddington, Wm outer, Perambulation 1b); another is *Edward Lapidge,* the architect of St Peter's church. The gardens, threatened by building in 1912, were acquired by the borough, redesigned, and opened to the public in 1915. In the centre a bronze Greek Runner by *Sir William Richmond,* erected 1926. The streets around, with terraces of cottages, are on a smaller scale but evidently part of the same scheme, see e.g. to the E BLACK LION LANE, with small paired villas and short terraces of cottages, the low Tudor ST PETER'S SCHOOL (q.v.), and the well preserved contemporary buildings of CHAPMANS, builders and decorators. Even simpler houses in ST PETER'S GROVE. In ST PETER'S ROAD, No. 83 is an early example of a substantial mass concrete house, 1883 by *W. H. Henley* of the Patent Concrete Building Co. Traditional rendered exterior. Further W BRITISH GROVE runs along the parish boundary.

3. N and NW; Brook Green to Shepherds Bush and Goldhawk Road

A mixed bag of C19 and C20 buildings links the Broadway to the older centres to the N, Brook Green and Shepherds Bush Green. In SHEPHERDS BUSH ROAD, near the corner with the Broadway, No. 10, offices by *Percy Thomas Partnership*, 1989–90, typical of their date in the use of classically inspired details. Quite pleasingly proportioned, a big roof lunette echoing a large central arch. Further on it is mainly the public buildings that are of note (Library, Police Station, Fire Station, qq.v.). W of Brook Green were the former OSRAM WORKS which manufactured electric light bulb filaments, developed from 1893, much extended later, but mostly demolished in 1988. The main survivor is the factory range of 1915–16 by *Charles Heathcote & Sons*, built as a Ford service depot and showroom), which presents a handsome front to the green; nine bays with large windows between pilasters, two colours of brick enlivened by stone cartouches. Three storeys, originally intended to be five, of reinforced concrete construction (exposed on the S flank). To its N is the landmark of the seven-storey OSRAM TOWER, its pinched classical detail topped by an octagon with a little copper dome; by *John S. Quilter & Son*, 1920–1. At the N corner the BROOK GREEN HOTEL, a confident late C19 corner pub with turret.

BROOK GREEN opens to the E, a pleasant wedge-shaped space with large trees. On the S side, MERCERS PLACE, by *John Melvin & Partners*, 1982–3, a design intended to respond to traditional London housing (cf. the firm's earlier infill housing in Penton Street, Islington, Is). Red brick and grey slate in sympathy with the area, although the style is Palladian rather than Victorian in inspiration. Formally composed three-storey block of flats with strongly articulated verticals met by very deep eaves, and a central entrance up semicircular steps answered by the curve of a lunette-shaped dormer. The terrace of houses forming a backdrop was part of the scheme (but was not completed to the design of the original architects). After the obtrusive swimming pool of St Paul's Girls School (q.v.), the QUEEN'S HEAD and a few small early C19 paired cottages round the corner in ROWAN ROAD are a reminder of the old scale of the hamlet. Nos. 26–39 Brook Green form a grander High Victorian balanced terrace, with the surprisingly conservative motif of arched windows with fan decoration. After more stucco-trimmed terraces, Holy Trinity R.C. church (q.v.) and, beyond, ST JOSEPH'S ALMSHOUSES, of which only one range remains of the once picturesque composition of 1851 (probably by *Wardell*). Ragstone, with two storeys of pretty square-headed traceried windows.

Back from E to W on the N side of Brook Green, first WINDSOR WAY, a hard, very urban development, all brick-faced, of expensive flats and houses on part of the Lyons site (*see* Hammersmith Road, Perambulation 4), 1984–9 by *David Landaw & Partners*. The houses, arranged in small closes, have big arched upper windows as their main feature, an idea perhaps cribbed from the Talgarth Road studios (*see* Fulham (HF), Perambulation 4). A pleasant C19 miscellany follows, although little of special note. The best building is No. 59, the tall ÉCOLE

FRANÇAISE, in Queen Anne style. No. 84, where the Silver Design Studio was set up in 1884, has a touch of the artistic spirit; roughcast top floor and mullioned windows with leaded lights. N of Brook Green, a network of small mid C19 streets which grew piecemeal, a happy mixture of minor Victorian houses of every type. The awkward cuckoo in the nest, SPRING VALE TERRACE in MASBRO ROAD, in obtrusively dour dark brick, was one of the borough's early attempts at an alternative urban recipe for high-rise flats: terraces of one and four storeys, by *Renton Howard Wood Associates*, 1967–70.

At the N end of SHEPHERDS BUSH ROAD, THE GRAMPIANS, quite a stylish block of flats, with curving shops flanking the entrance, 1935 by *Collcutt & Hamp*. Nearby, behind the Baptist church (q.v.), a curious little nook of 1980s offices apparently composed chiefly of architectural salvage. Quirky little bell-turret at one end. All certainly more appealing than the combination on the S side of SHEPHERDS BUSH GREEN, a shopping centre (depressingly battered and shabby by the late 1980s) with car park and four massive blocks of flats above (*Sidney Kaye*, 1971). The green is a triangle of former common land which was drained in 1871; at its E apex, Winged Victory, a WAR MEMORIAL of 1922 by *H. C. Fehr*. In front, decorative railings to the former underground lavatory (now a snooker hall). The other surroundings of the green are mostly early C20, although to the N, behind the underground station, there is still a small mid C19 cottage terrace in SHEPHERDS BUSH PLACE. Nearby, in STERNE STREET, a rare late work by the designer *George Walton*, 1922–3, a modest row of two-storey houses (No. 53 for himself). Admirably simple, almost a factory aesthetic, with rendered upper floor and metal casements. Round the corner, Nos. 28–30 is also by him, a more consciously picturesque pair, with its brick and tiled ground floor, and little window high up in the central gable. Other windows horribly altered.

On the W side of SHEPHERDS BUSH GREEN a more urban scale was introduced already in 1903 with the EMPIRE (now B.B.C. television theatre) by *Frank Matcham*, one of his few surviving suburban London variety theatres. Unusually for him, it has an exterior in a free and inventive Arts and Crafts style, roughcast combined with terracotta and brick. Playful corner tower with cupola. (Good foyer. The auditorium, built to seat 1,600, retains much of its rich plaster decoration.) The ODEON, formerly the Pavilion, is by *Frank Verity*, 1923, the building which made his reputation. One of the first cinemas in England to be treated as serious architecture. Large and chaste, with carefully crafted expanses of brick below a strong stone cornice, with barrel roof rising above. Corner tower with arched window, a little classical detail elsewhere. Interior simplified after war damage and subdivided since. Originally it seated 3,000.

GOLDHAWK ROAD, the main road leading SW from Shepherds Bush, begins with stucco-trimmed terraces with shops. To the S HAMMERSMITH GROVE with stately later C19 houses. Further W, one still has the sense of leaving town, as the scale of building along Goldhawk Road decreases to lower, more suburban mid C19 villas. A good group is in the neighbourhood of STARCH

GREEN, N of Ravenscourt Park (*see* Public Buildings). Others further W in STAMFORD BROOK ROAD (Nos. 5, 9–11, 17–23). The characteristic type here is a stuccoed pair, with shallow arches framing the ground-floor windows. No. 15 is a curious flint-decorated exception in *cottage orné* style. Nos. 187–193 Gold-hawk Road are two cheerful striped brick blocks of old people's housing, 1986–9 by *Pollard Thomas Edwards & Associates*, for the Notting Hill Housing Trust. Other villas, larger and grander, in the part of the road which turns SW past Queen Charlotte's Hospital (q.v.), on the fringes of the area around Ravenscourt Park (*see* Perambulation 2).

In UXBRIDGE ROAD, the main road towards Acton, very scattered points of interest: CLIFTON HOUSE, at the corner of Hetley Road, a grand debased Italianate palazzo of *c.* 1870; and Nos. 159–167, a decent brick and stucco terrace. Opposite, the QUEEN ADELAIDE at the corner of Adelaide Grove is a jolly pub of *c.* 1900, green tiles, moulded brick band, and a turret, its half-timbered gable echoed by a contemporary shopping parade.

4. Hammersmith Broadway to West Kensington

In HAMMERSMITH ROAD the most important building is the Sacred Heart Convent on the N side (*see* above, Public Buildings). On the S side, the convent of NAZARETH HOUSE with its chapel hides behind high walls. Main wing 1857 and chapel 1866 by *Gilbert Blount*; additions with rendered top floor 1885 and 1889 by *Leonard Stokes*; children's wing 1908 by *Pugin & Pugin*. At the corner of SHORTLANDS, offices making some effort to be stylish, by *Malcolm Hecks Associates, c.* 1984; gables with circular windows. The site of St Paul's School is still marked by its original perimeter walls (q.v. Hammersmith and West London College) and by the former High Master's house, a picturesque Gothic composition by *Waterhouse* of 1881–5, with plenty of terracotta, and a lively skyline with tall chimneys. COLET COURT opposite, the former junior school, converted to offices in 1990, is of 1890 by *W. H. Spaull*; also terracotta Gothic, but dour in comparison. Past Brook Green (*see* Perambulation 3) the N side becomes exceedingly inhuman. Lyons' vast offices and factories, which set a new scale for the street, were replaced in the 1980s by an incoherent series of forbidding offices by *Scott, Brownrigg & Turner*; faceless mirror-glazed frontages whose scale makes nonsense of the surviving C19 buildings opposite and in the little roads to the S (e.g. MUNDEN STREET, with its mixture of low terraces and C20 infilling). Further E was a vast area of Victorian warehouses and laundries developed beside the railway for William Whiteley's store in Bayswater (*see* Pad-dington (outer Wm), Perambulation 1b), chiefly of 1892–1901 by *Alfred Ridge*. Much was converted to housing in 1990–1.

N of Hammersmith Road, the exhibition halls of OLYMPIA. The part along Hammersmith Road was refaced and extended in a grim and sensational modernistic style in 1929–30 by *Joseph Emberton*. The monumental front looks uncompromisingly con-crete, but is of steel and brick, rendered. Details are borrowed from progressive continental buildings such as the Einstein tower (see the corner windows). At the back, towards SINCLAIR ROAD, a quieter, well-proportioned addition of 1936, with new entrance hall and booking office, also by *Emberton*. His OLYMPIC GARAGE of 1936 in MACLISE ROAD, for 1,200 cars, was claimed to be the largest in Europe when built. Ten half-storey-height floors, exposed shuttered concrete inside, brick-faced outside, with long window bands – a remarkable foretaste of both building type and style of thirty years later. Behind Emberton's façade remain the large and small glazed barrel-vaulted exhibition halls dating from 1885, built as a National Agricultural Hall by *Henry E. Coe*, co-architect of the earlier Agricultural Hall at Islington. The large hall, 145 metres long, has an iron roof of 52 metre span with braced lattice ribs (engineers *Walmesley & Am Ende,* ironwork by *Handyside* of Derby). Coe's main front faces Olympia Way alongside the railway line (the explanation for the siting of the building); quite handsome screen walls of brick with stone dressings, with carving over the entrance (obscured by an ugly C20 porch).

In this curiously muddled area intruding into decent streets of West Kensington stucco (Sinclair Road, Hazlitt Road) the other major landmark is the former POST OFFICE SAVINGS BANK in BLYTHE ROAD (now a museums depository), its vast bulk not very convincingly dressed up with Wrenaissance trimmings (striped quoins, little turrets). It is of 1899–1903 by *Sir Henry Tanner* of the Office of Works, the main block planned for 4,000 workers. E wing added *c.* 1920. In front of this, a small, more playful corner POST OFFICE and POSTMAN'S OFFICE (1903–4), much more successful in their free use of classical detail.

For the area S of Hammersmith Road, *see* Fulham (HF), Perambulation 4.

5. N *of Uxbridge Road*

The N part of the borough was little built up until the early C20, when its open land began to be used for council housing. A tour from W to E must largely be devoted to a chronological conspectus of the type over seventy years. Much of it is a sad story of declining standards as quality was sacrificed to quantity. A precursor is provided by a small group of C19 planned cottages built by the railway in OLD OAK COMMON LANE. Much more extensive is the OLD OAK ESTATE of 1911 onwards, a snug L.C.C. development of small two-storeyed red brick houses, especially skilfully grouped in the streets around East Acton station, the first part to be built (over 300 houses and flats by 1914). *A. S. Soutar* was responsible for some of the most picturesque parts, for example the groups of cottages at the corner of FITZNEAL STREET and DU CANE ROAD. Other architects involved were *F. J. Lucas* and *J. M. Corment*. The lay-out was clearly influenced by Hampstead Garden Suburb. Some of the front gardens still have their little privet hedges, but the general effect is now marred by too many unsuitable window replacements. The parts NE of the railway date from 1919–21. S of

Westway the WORMHOLT ESTATE, planned from 1919, follows similar garden city principles with more generously designed houses. Built for Hammersmith by *H. T. Hare* with *J. E. Franck*, *M. J. Dawson*, and *P. Streatfield* (each architect responsible for one section), and intended to relieve the crowded slums of the Hammersmith riverside (considered 'as bad as Poplar' according to comments in 1923). By 1926 600 houses existed on the 50 acres between Old Oak Common Lane, Steventon Road, and Bloemfontein Road. This portion still gives a good idea of the high quality of design and materials employed in the 'homes fit for heroes' campaign. The houses are mostly of brick with pan-tiled roofs and are set back attractively around little greens, see e.g. VIOLA SQUARE, for which *H. T. Hare* and *B. Lisle* were responsible. On the N fringe, off Primula Street, now sandwiched between Westway and the railway, a delightful addition, ROSE-WOOD SQUARE, sheltered housing for old people, 1984 by *I. Orr*, *T. Ryland*, and *M. Lister* of the Borough's Architecture and Building Department. Two-storey terraces around a little square, lovingly designed with pretty trellis balconies, tile decoration, and other playful details. In the centre a gazebo-cum-laundry with tiled roof, set lozenge-wise on an octagonal plinth. Further E, Hammersmith School (q.v.) and WORMHOLT PARK, made in 1909–11.

The informality of the Wormholt estate contrasts strongly with the Peabody CLEVERLEY ESTATE just to the S. This is of 1928, with blocks only three storeys high along SAWLEY ROAD (i.e. lower than Peabody estates in the centre of London), but formally laid out, and with unusually lavish trimmings in Hampton Court Wrenaissance (circular windows and grand tripartite archways). No such luxuries grace the *L.C.C.*'s WHITE CITY ESTATE, begun in 1938–9 and completed after the war on part of the derelict 200-acre site used for the Franco-British Exhibition and the Olympic Games in 1908 and subsequently for other exhibitions. It was the largest L.C.C. estate of its time, its blocks of flats spreading over 52 acres. The flats were of an up-to-date design of 1934–6, much praised at the time for their variety of size and for their separate bathrooms and kitchens. But they are contained within dismally monotonous five-storey balcony-access brick blocks, laid out in a dull regular grid. Spaces were left along the main E–W route, COMMONWEALTH AVENUE, for churches and public buildings, but they are too insignificant to provide focal points. A welcome respite is provided by MALABAR COURT at the corner of India Way, housing for old people arranged as a pile of ascending hexagons, by *Neil Moffett & Partners*, completed 1966. In NEW ZEALAND WAY, small community buildings by the borough, 1989–90. At the E end, HAMMERSMITH PARK, laid out in 1952, opened 1955.

s of South Africa Road the return to a more humane townscape after the excesses of the 1960s (*see* below) is illustrated by quiet brown brick terraces by *Darbourne & Darke*, 1975–8, in the tradition of their work in Westminster (Lillington Gardens) and Islington. Four storeys, with much attention devoted to private access and spaces, and to the landscaping of the pedestrian ways. The other buildings to note in this area are in WOOD LANE, chief among them the B.B.C. TELEVISION CENTRE, also built on part of the White City exhibition site. An ambitious concept, the first purpose-built television studios in England, planned from 1950 by *Norman & Dawbarn*, continued into the 1960s following the same master plan. A circle of offices around a courtyard, surrounded by a lower outer ring of projecting studios linked by a runway to a scenery store. To the outsider it all looks a huge muddle, apart from the entrance, which has a little period flavour, with a covered approach set against a plain brick wall studded with discs, typical patterning of the 1950s. The ingenious concentric plan is only apparent from the inner court, unfortunately dominated by an obelisk with a silly gilded figure by *Huxley-Jones*. Extensions to the N completed 1989, by the *B.B.C. Architectural and Civil Engineering Department*. Further N, on the site of the White City Stadium, the vast area of the B.B.C. CORPORATE HEADQUARTERS, the move here determined after rejection of Foster's scheme for rebuilding on the Langham site in Portland Place (*see* St Marylebone (Wm outer), Streets 1). By *Scott, Brownrigg & Turner*, 1989–90. Later phases designed by *Renton Howard Wood Levin* (1989–90): W side (phase two) for News and Current Affairs, with a tower at the W corner, E side (phase 3).

Between Wood Lane and the M41, an industrial area, also once part of the White City Exhibition, much rebuilt in the 1980s, with further major redevelopment planned for the 1990s. The one older building of interest is near the S end, DIMCO MACHINE TOOLS, 1898–9, a large single-storey shed with semicircular openings with small glass panes which began life as the first known electricity generating station built for the London underground. To be incorporated in a shopping scheme by *Balfour Beattie*. Immediately S of Westway, a commercial scheme by *CZWG* called RADIO CITY was planned in 1990.

Some way N of Westway and the railway lines, COLLEGE PARK, a small, isolated pocket of late Victorian streets just S of Harrow Road, on the borders of Harlesden and Kensal Green (q.v. Brent).

6. *The NE corner of the borough*

This is a narrow strip, cut off by the M41, merging at the S end into the smart fringe of the Norland estate, and at the N into working-class Notting Dale (*see* Kensington, KC, Perambulation 2a, i). It comprises a mixture of small industries and housing, the latter now mostly of the later C20, a telling mixture of traditional local authority effort and community architecture. From S to N: E of Norland Road two- and three-storey housing for the Notting Hill Housing Trust by *Pollard Thomas Edwards & Associates*. Despite a tight budget, a brave, relatively early effort to provide visually interesting detail. The group pivots on an unusual mid C19 stone-faced terrace, reconstructed in 1977–9 on a new site after it had been truncated by the motorway; it has curiously elaborate details, pedimented doorways, central gable, windows and cornice with paired brackets. The new build-

ings (1977–83) are of brick, somewhat self-consciously combining arched openings and Diocletian windows with more
mundane features. One pair with split pediment and mosaic
tympanum over the doorways (an odd mixture) faces down
Queensdale Road. Immediately to the N the borough's high-rise
flats of the 1960s: the EDWARD WOODS ESTATE (*Hammersmith
Borough Architect's Department*, 1964), four twenty-one-storey
towers surrounded by lower maisonettes, some on stilts. The
estate was the last large one in the borough for which houses were
demolished. To the w, in OLAF STREET, a tobacco warehouse of
c. 1910, converted to studio and offices by *Troughton McAslan*,
1985, with a large glazed atrium inserted in the centre.

Further N, around FRESTON ROAD, small-scale rebuilding and
rehabilitation of the 1980s, again by *Pollard Thomas Edwards &
Associates*. The cheerful brick patterning goes well with the
cleaned-up red brick PEOPLE'S HALL of 1901. Phase 1 (1983–
9) was designed for (and with much participation by) the Bramley
Housing Co-op; forty low houses and flats backing on to a
communal garden, the terrace along Freston Road with ingeniously angled inset doorways. Phase 2 (1985–9) includes sheltered
housing as well; the larger blocks are given identity by rather
wilful corner porches strutted with steel poles. In contrast, the
Victorian BRAMLEY ARMS deftly turns the corner of Bramley
Road with a curving balustrade with a proud array of urns.

Further N in Freston Road, the HARROW CLUB, a picturesque
group which originated as a mission church, whose great E
window is now prominent from the raised slip road from the
M40. Mission room 1883–4, the former Holy Trinity church,
Latimer Road, 1887–9, clergy house and clubroom 1896–7, all
by *Norman Shaw*. The church was converted to a youth club in
1967 by *A. G. Savill*. It is of brick (the only example among
Shaw's later churches), with a broad E front with window with
reticulated Dec tracery divided by very pronounced mullions, a
seminal design for Sedding and other church architects of the
1890s. Inside, raised up above basement vestries, there was just
a large hall with a ceiled wagon roof with wrought-iron principals
stabilized by three massive tie-beams encasing iron girders – a
much simplified version of Shaw's first design with vaulted
double nave and passage aisle. No aisles, transepts, chancel arch,
or side windows. The furnishings (probably largely by Shaw's
pupil *Lethaby*) were removed (the pews to St Helen, North
Kensington (KC), q.v.) to create a games hall, with the floor
raised to accommodate club rooms below.

FULHAM

INTRODUCTION

Fulham lies within a great loop of the Thames. Within this fertile low-lying area there was until the mid C19 only a cluster of settlements given over largely to market gardening, and a few larger riverside houses in their grounds. After 1850 the rural peace was broken, for from then until *c.* 1910, to house the workers in the industries that were springing up along the river and elsewhere, small streets proliferated, covering much of the area with modest terraces of no special aesthetic pretensions. Fulham's transformation into a smart suburban annexe to Chelsea began only in the 1960s, and the riverside, for long relatively remote and inaccessible, was exploited for expensive housing only from the late 1970s.

The tight grid of small late C19 streets does not entirely obscure the pattern of winding roads that linked the older village and hamlets: Fulham proper around the parish church at Putney Bridge, and Parsons Green along the New Kings Road, both still with some C18 buildings; Walham Green to the NE, reached via Fulham Road, where already in the C19 buildings extended as far E as the creek between Fulham and Chelsea, and where the main civic centre developed at Fulham Broadway; and to the N North End, on the West Kensington border. Hammersmith, the most important subsidiary settlement in the old parish, is dealt with separately.

In the C18 the riverside was fringed with great houses set in their own grounds. The major survival is Fulham Palace, the former country seat of the Bishops of London, a courtyard house of medieval origin, standing in its park to the W of the parish church. Also remaining are the C18 Hurlingham House, now a club, and, in more cramped surroundings near the Chelsea boundary, the smaller mid C17 Sandford Manor. Many others have disappeared, including Craven Cottage, N of Fulham Palace, quite a famous *cottage orné*, built in 1780 for Lord Craven, enlarged *c.* 1805 (with Egyptian interiors) by *Thomas Hopper* for the picture dealer Walsh Porter, and burnt down in 1888; its name became attached to the later football ground on the site. Other major houses lost without trace include Lord Cholmondeley's estate and Brandenburgh House, also on the river, inhabited from 1792 onwards by the Margrave and Margravine of Brandenburg-Bayreuth and later by Queen Caroline.* The site of Peterborough House at Parsons Green, the home of the Mordaunt family, is marked by a homogeneous set of late C19 streets just S of New Kings Road.

*Two staircases from Brandenburgh House are now in Warkworth House Hotel, and in Coquet House, Warkworth, Northumberland.

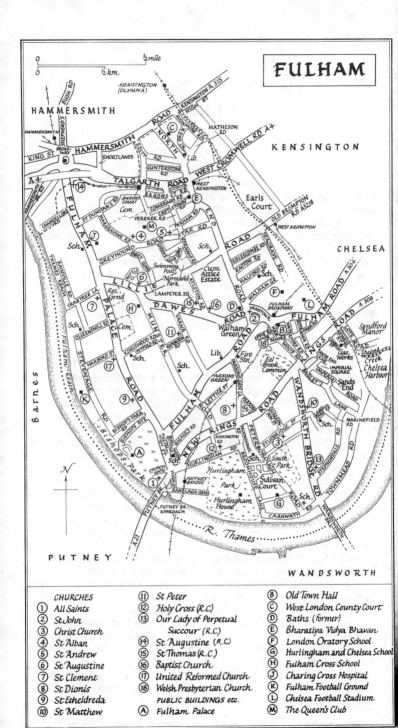

FULHAM

½ mile
½ km

HAMMERSMITH

KENSINGTON

CHELSEA

Barnes

PUTNEY

R. Thames

WANDSWORTH

CHURCHES		
① All Saints	⑪ St Peter	Ⓑ Old Town Hall
② St John	⑫ Holy Cross (R.C.)	Ⓒ West London County Court
③ Christ Church	⑬ Our Lady of Perpetual	Ⓓ Baths (former)
④ St Alban	Succour (R.C.)	Ⓔ Bharatiya Vidya Bhavan
⑤ St Andrew	⑭ St Augustine (R.C.)	Ⓕ London Oratory School
⑥ St Augustine	⑮ St Thomas (R.C.)	Ⓖ Hurlingham and Chelsea School
⑦ St Clement	⑯ Baptist Church	Ⓗ Fulham Cross School
⑧ St Dionis	⑰ United Reformed Church	Ⓙ Charing Cross Hospital
⑨ St Etheldreda	⑱ Welsh Presbyterian Church	Ⓚ Fulham Football Ground
⑩ St Matthew	PUBLIC BUILDINGS etc.	Ⓛ Chelsea Football Stadium
	Ⓐ Fulham Palace	Ⓜ The Queen's Club

Up to the middle of the C19, the chief business of Fulham was to supply Londoners with vegetables. Faulkner calls it 'the great fruit and kitchen garden north of the Thames'. Of early industries the most important was pottery-making: a C19 kiln marks the site of John Dwight's pottery, established in 1672 just N of New Kings Road; William de Morgan also started workshops at Fulham (in Sands End) when he left Chelsea. Fulham's popularity with artists in the later C19 is attested by several remaining studios, and in the early C20 it was an important centre for the production of stained glass (see Lettice Street, Perambulation 4). More intensive late C19 industry developed along the river – a dismal barrier largely replaced from the 1970s onwards by a river walk alongside new housing. The flamboyance of the 1980s ranges from *Richard Rogers*'s elegant flats near the N end of Fulham Reach, to the brash groups of Chelsea Harbour created around the dock of the old Kensington Canal. Elsewhere, the C19 streets are disrupted by patches of more mundane rebuilding of the middle third of the C20, and the old shopping centres by the inevitable large retail developments. Nevertheless Fulham still retains an overall flavour of respectable minor Victoriana, reflecting the years of its greatest population expansion. The population was *c.* 600 in 1634, *c.* 3,500 in 1793, and *c.* 12,000 in 1851. By 1871 it had risen to over 23,000, by 1881 to over 42,000, by 1891 to over 91,000, by 1901 to 137,000. The 1931 figure was 151,000, the 1951 figure 122,000; by 1981 it had fallen to 75,251.

CHURCHES

The old parish church, All Saints, marks the site of the riverside village; a chapel for the hamlet of North End was provided in 1814, a Commissioners' church at Walham Green in 1828. A dozen rather undistinguished churches accompanied the suburban expansion of the last quarter of the C19, of which two have disappeared,[*] and several others have been rebuilt. However many are worth visiting for their contents, particularly the stained glass of the Arts and Crafts period, much of it emanating from the local workshops in Lettice Street.

ALL SAINTS, Church Gate. The sturdy late medieval w tower is 10 prominent at the end of Putney Bridge. It is a good example of the favourite Thames valley type: ragstone, of four storeys, with diagonal buttresses, SW turret, and a three-light belfry window. Work on the tower was in progress in 1440 under the masons *Richard Garald* and *Piers Chapell*, when stone was being brought from Kent. The large ground-floor w window was reconstructed when the tower was opened up in 1840–1, probably by *Edward*

*ST JAMES, Moore Park Road, demolished in 1980, was of 1867 by *H. A. Darbishire* (whose patron, Miss Burdett Coutts, had in 1865 given an iron room for a temporary church). It was of stock brick with red banding; original interior slender wooden nave arches on stone columns, low aisles, and dormer windows. Polygonal chancel by *Christian*, 1877. w windows by *Pepper & Co.*, *c.* 1878. ST OSWALD, Anselm Road, 1898–9 by *A. J. Hopkins* and *W. V. Aspen*, demolished in 1977, was aisled, Perp, and with nave and chancel in one.

Lapidge, responsible for alterations to the church at this time. Refacing, and removal of the wooden spire, took place in 1845 under *George Godwin.* The rest of the church was rebuilt by *Sir Arthur Blomfield* in 1880–1, ragstone with Bath dressings, a faithful if dull imitation of a generously scaled late Perp church: five-bay nave, tall clerestory, S chapel opening to the chancel by a lofty two-bay arcade. Only the N organ chamber is more overtly Victorian, divided off by a S arch with black marble column. – REREDOS. Painted panels with figures against gold brocade. By *Heaton, Butler & Bayne,* 1885. – FONTS. One battered medieval bowl with Victorian cover, one of 1622, very small, but otherwise still entirely Gothic, octagonal and panelled. – SCREEN. Low, with lively ironwork. – COMMUNION RAILS. Good late C17, twisted balusters, carved standards. – ORGAN CASE incorporating parts from a former late C17 pulpit, etc. – In the tower is a PAINTING of John Hudnett, beadle and sexton, in red coat with quart pot and churchwarden's pipe, dated 1690. – STAINED GLASS. In the SE chapel S window, Evangelists by *Wailes,* 1840, from the E window of the old church. Bright, hard colours, progressive for its time. – W window with C17 heraldic glass. – Nearly all the rest with glass of the 1880s by *Heaton, Butler & Bayne,* well drawn pictorial scenes against pale backgrounds. – S chapel E *c.* 1938 by *M. E. Aldrich Rope,* still in the late Arts and Crafts tradition; soft blues against white.

MONUMENTS. A very rich collection. Margaret Hornebolt, wife of the painter Gerard Hornebolt, brass, *c.* 1529, probably Flemish, an unusual lozenge shape, with inscription tablet held by angels, and above it a demi-figure in a shroud (S aisle E). – William Plumbe † 1593. A restrained wall-monument in coloured marbles with Corinthian columns (tower). – Lady Margaret Legh † 1603, an unusual and moving effigy. She sits strictly frontal in a flat niche between columns, upright and quiet, in the stiff robes and the widow's hood of the day, one hand on her breast, the other holding a baby stiff as a mummy. Another stands to her right, equally tightly swaddled and even more like a mummy. Southwark school ribbon ornament on the upper part (chancel). – Katharine Hart † 1605. A small wall-tablet with kneeling mother and four children beneath an arch, well carved (organ chamber). – Thomas Smith † 1609 and his wife Jane † 1610, without effigies, yet ambitious in size, with a large inscription plate between columns; the strapwork not very imaginative. Open pediment with arms and obelisks (chancel). – William Payne † 1626, again kneelers, this time facing each other (S chapel). – John Mordaunt, Viscount Mordaunt, † 1675, by *John Bushnell,* a design meant to be of the most swaggering Italian Baroque, yet curiously dry and bare sculpturally as well as architecturally. The figure with baton and grandly draped toga stands in a commanding posture; the pedestal has four bleak, hard, bulging corner balusters, each as broad as the figure and more than half as high. We know from the Old Bailey and from Ashburnham church in Sussex how much better Bushnell could do (tower).* – Thomas Winter

---

*The *Gentleman's Magazine* of 1818 attributes this monument to both *Bushnell* and *Bird*; Bowack refers to work in two parts, with Bushnell responsible for the figure (which Fèret attributes to Bird).

† 1681. Altar with urn, and inscription on feigned drapery against grey marble back. Possibly by *Edward Pierce* (GF). – Elizabeth Limpany † 1694. Cartouche against a large wooden 'reredos', carved with fruit and putti in the *Gibbons* style (N porch). – Dorothy Clarke † 1695 and her second husband Samuel Barrow † 1682, by *Gibbons*, with a large draped urn on a bulging sarcophagus. – Thomas Kinsey † 1696. Small tablet with two cherubs' heads (S aisle). – Anthony Nours and wife † 1704. Possibly by *Robert Easton* (GF). Good Baroque cartouche with drapery and cherubs' heads (N aisle). – Bishop Edmund Gibson † 1748. Elegant wall-tablet of coloured marbles with nicely carved volutes; relief with book, palm, and crozier (N aisle). – Caroline, Viscountess Ranelagh, † 1804, a Grecian tablet (S aisle). – Elizabeth Hatsell † 1805, signed by *P. M. Vangelder,* but very plain, with fluted urn decoration. – Sir John Beckett †1847 by *Bedford,* with little urn and little palm-tree and weeping willow. – Good tombs in the CHURCHYARD: to the E of the church a number of heavy sarcophagi of the late C18 and early C19, including a fine sequence to the Bishops of London. The large scrolly one below the E window, to Bishop Sherlock † 1761, is signed by *John Vardy.*

CHRIST CHURCH, Studdridge Street. 1902–3 by *J. E. K. & J. P. Cutts,* and a predictable Cutts design: long red brick clerestoried nave, no tower, Perp W window facing down Quarrendon Street. Reordered in 1989–90 by *Mark & Hawkins*; altar brought forward, rood screen moved back behind it with vestries beyond, the W bays of the nave divided off as hall and upper room. The above-average fittings remain. – Small late C17 FONT COVER from St Benet Gracechurch Street. – Of the same period, from St George Botolph Lane, the carved octagonal PULPIT and the handsome ALTAR RAILS with spiral balusters and carved rail (future uncertain). – Good STAINED GLASS: *Burne-Jones* designs made by *Morris & Co.* Five apse windows, 1909–12, with Christ and the evangelists against backgrounds of flowers and fruit. The evangelists are from *Burne-Jones*'s popular designs originally made *c.* 1873 for Jesus College Cambridge. – Lady Chapel E 1911, Faith, Hope, and Charity (designs of *c.* 1871). – N aisle NE 1932–3: St Christopher and the Virgin against landscapes (also earlier designs re-used, 1867 and 1874). – The three war memorial W windows are by *Karl Parsons,* 1922, much influenced by the rich colours and fine draughtsmanship of the Morris tradition.

ST ALBAN, Margravine Road. 1895–7 by *Aston Webb & E. Ingress Bell.* Red brick; Perp W front, transepts with large windows with reticulated tracery, the intended polygonal chancel and Lady Chapel never built. Light interior of red and yellow brick, with low polygonal piers, original capitals, and clerestory windows of two lights behind free-standing wooden columns. – STAINED GLASS. In the W porch, two lights of 1902 by *Jones & Willis.* – Heraldic window in the S aisle by *C. Townshend* and *J. Howson,* 1931. – Flanking the church, and by the same architects, polygonal CHURCH HALL of 1913, and the VICARAGE, neo-Georgian, with irregular canted bays to fit the angular site.

ST ANDREW, Greyhound Road, West Kensington. 1873–4 by

Newman & Billing; enlarged 1894–6 by *Aston Webb* (vestry converted to chapel, additional w bay); w end subdivided in 1972–4 by *J. A. Lewis* and *Maxwell, New, Haile & Holland*. Tough, big-boned French Gothic, rather Teulonesque. Stock brick with red bands and stone dressings. Above the s porch a sturdy tower with corner turret and spire. Lush crocket capitals inside. – Colourful but bitty SANCTUARY FITTINGS of 1898–1901, designed by *Aston Webb* in the mixture of materials typical of the time – stencilling, alabaster, and mosaic – around an ornately carved REREDOS by *H. Hems & Sons*. Further mosaics added to the E wall in 1902, designed by *Forrester* and made by *Powells*. – Timber ROOD SCREEN also by *Webb*, 1897, on stone angel corbels. – STAINED GLASS. The window worth noting is the SE chapel E: three lights, restrained original Arts and Crafts work of 1902 by *Paul Woodroffe*, medallions with angular figures (Christ in Majesty, Annunciation, Nativity) with much white and blue, set in stylized trellis work.

ST AUGUSTINE, Lillie Road. Brick mission-church-cum-hall with cusped Tudor windows by the *Cutts*, 1891–2 (the church of 1899 was destroyed in the war).

ST CLEMENT, Fulham Palace Road. The church of 1885–6 by *Arthur Blomfield* was replaced in 1969 by a package of flats and CHURCH CENTRE, 1975–6 by *Michael Biscoe*. Small top-lit chancel with blank dark brick wall with curved corners; hall behind.*

ST DIONIS, Parsons Green. 1884–5 by *Ewan Christian*. A good composition, brick and stone, Perp, with a NE tower with pinnacles and short pyramidal top, completed in 1896. Plain interior, red brick on stone arcades; timber barrel-vault. – The FONT of 1684, a cup on baluster, comes from *Wren*'s St Dionis Backchurch; so does the PULPIT with a stair whose finely twisted balusters look a little later. Large, curious FONT COVER, inspired by the tower of the City church, by *Martin Travers*, who also in 1932–3 designed the ROOD SCREEN and ROOD, an English altar of which only the simple REREDOS remains (chancel s wall) and the painted wooden MEMORIAL with relief of St Denis to the Rev. J. S. Sinclair († 1919). Two other wooden tablets of 1935, no doubt also by *Travers*, to S. H. Gardiner and the local benefactor Charlotte Sulivan († 1911). – STAINED GLASS. Weak post-war E window, 1951 by *Christopher Webb*. – Some older glass in the s aisle: at the w end, Christ as Shepherd, 1898, between two landscapes with sheep, *c*. 1903 by *H. A. Hymers*. – Across the road the handsome brick and stone PARISH HALL, a former mission church of 1876 by *A. Billing*.

ST ETHELDREDA, Fulham Palace Road. 1955–8 by *Guy Biscoe*, replacing a church of 1896–7 by *A. H. Skipworth*. Straightforward concrete portal frame with plain brick walls, not in a revival style. NE tower with slatted belfry, a well-placed landmark at a curve in the long dull road. Tall rectangular windows to the s; the N nave wall to the road punctuated only by a pattern of small cross-shaped openings. Side-lit chancel. – Inside, the blank

---

*The FONT from St Clement, with its beautiful carved cover, originally in Wren's City church of St Matthew Friday Street, is now at St Andrew by the Wardrobe (City of London).

E wall has a large wooden CRUCIFIX by *Rita Ling*. – Semicircular
w baptistery with copper FONT and mosaic glass by *W. C. Carter
Shapland*. – To the N, modest brick Arts and Crafts VICARAGE.

ST JOHN, North End Road, Walham Green. By *J. H. Taylor*,
1827–8; white brick, Commissioners' lancet style. Tall thin
battlemented w tower, its belfry also with lancets. Interior
remodelled in 1893 by *E. P. Warren* (side galleries removed) and
more radically transformed in 1985–9 by *Broadbent, Hastings,
Reid & New*. The w bays were divided off by a glazed screen
and floored to provide a spacious upper hall. The three E bays
remain; a simple, light interior, piers without capitals, pointed
arches and clerestory, and a fine traceried timber roof. Unified
by new furnishings: fan-shaped seating, polished granite altar
and font, and no longer 'wholly without mystery' as Pevsner
found it in 1952. – STAINED GLASS. In the E window a Crucifixion of 1881. – In the NW sanctuary chapel TABERNACLE with
sunburst design in steel, brass, silver, and copper, by *Richard
Greening*, 1979, made for Nashdom Abbey, Bucks.

ST MARY, Hammersmith Road. Modest rebuilding by *Seely &
Paget*, 1960–1, of a chapel of 1814 by *Richard Hunt* which had
been enlarged in 1883–4 by *E. P. Loftus Brock*.

ST MATTHEW, Wandsworth Bridge Road and Rosebery Road.
1893–5; another of the churches in the area by *A. W. Blomfield
& Sons*, big and unattractive. Red brick, lancet style with thin
flèche. – (STAINED GLASS by *Clayton & Bell*, 1866–86, brought
from St Mary, Westminster, where it was given by Sir James
Knowles in memory of his wife.) – Future uncertain.

ST PETER, Varna Road and Reporton Road. 1882–3 by *Arthur
Billing*. One of the many brick lancet-style churches of the later
C19, this one with a vaulted apsidal chancel with stone ribs. A
tower was intended over the SE porch. Interior subdivided to
make a hall, 1978 by *Biscoe & Stanton*. – C19 FONT from St
James, East Hanney, Oxon (formerly Berks), presumably by
Street.*

HOLY CROSS (R.C.), Ashington Road. 1924 by *Scott & Williamson*. A plain red brick building with nave and aisles of equal
height, extended w in 1955–6 by *T. B. Scott* with a rather etio-
lated Italian w front with small pediment raised high above the
roof-line. – Adjacent SCHOOL 1884 by *F. W. Tasker*.

OUR LADY OF PERPETUAL SUCCOUR (R.C.), Stephendale
Road. 1922 by *Scott & Williamson*, grey brick, simple Romanesque, with tower. Interior also of the hall type, with square piers
and carved capitals.

ST AUGUSTINE (R.C.), Fulham Palace Road. 1915–16 by *R. L.
Curtis*, extended in 1960 by *D. Plaskett Marshall & Partners*.
Rudimentary Romanesque w front.

ST THOMAS OF CANTERBURY (R.C.), Rylston Road. 1847–8
by *A. W. Pugin*. London has not many churches by Pugin, and
altogether Pugin is far better known by his writings and engravings than by his actual buildings. This was one of only three
major commissions he received after 1846, and remains his only

---

*The fine late C17 PULPIT, brought from St Matthew Friday Street in the City,
was moved to St Andrew by the Wardrobe in 1965.

complete parish church in London. So it is well worth studying, with its original fittings and the attached presbytery. In the original illustration the group of church and presbytery looks picturesque enough: in reality, the neighbourhood makes it difficult to evoke this original charm. It has all gone very grey and shabby, the stock brick of the presbytery as well as the Kentish rag and stone of the church. The presbytery has Gothic detail in Caen stone, and, inside, some simple Gothic fireplaces. The nucleus of the adjacent schools is also by Pugin. The architectural detail of the church is not specially inspired. It is in the Dec style. The E end with three gables faces the street, the N W tower and pinnacled steeple the churchyard. Simple interior: plain circular columns, four bays to the nave, two to the chancel, no chancel arch. Open nave roof, boarded chancel ceiling, decorated in 1980 with large floriated crosses derived from Pugin's *Glossary of Foliated Ornament*. It does a little to compensate for the earlier whitewashing of the walls. The alterations of 1969 (by *Bartlett & Purnell*) fortunately retained Pugin's fittings. They are of Caen stone and, in contrast to the plainness of the building, are adorned with figures and C14 foliage. – In the N aisle the former REREDOS and HIGH ALTAR FRONTAL (now combined) carved with the eagle of St John. – S aisle: Lady Chapel REREDOS and ALTAR FRONTAL, with well carved Coronation of the Virgin. Attractive PULPIT with ogee arches and angels; AUMBRY (W end of S aisle); FONT with evangelist symbols at the base (now covered in shiny white paint). Pugin was not permitted to erect a screen. The ORGAN LOFT SCREEN has pretty openwork quatrefoil panelling. – STAINED GLASS. Three E windows and SE window designed by *Powell*, made by *Hardmans* (main light of the central window 1947 by *Goddard & Gibbs*, a feeble renewal after war damage). – W window: Assumption of the Virgin, 1896 by *N. Westlake*. – Many eminent people are buried in the CHURCHYARD, including the architects Joseph Hansom † 1882 and Herbert Gribble † 1894. – The Laughnan monument of the 1850s was brought over, it is said, from Boulogne; it is like a monastic well, with a timber canopy and a little statue of the Madonna. – Tomb 37, a flat upright slab with floriated cross and good lettering, is by *Philip Webb* for A. Warrington Taylor, William Morris's devoted business manager, who died young, of consumption, in 1870. – Helen Tasker † 1888. An elaborate carved cross on a pink marble base.

NONCONFORMIST CHURCHES were once numerous in Fulham. Among the survivors the remains of *Cubitt*'s fine WEST KENSINGTON CONGREGATIONAL CHURCH are now an Indian Cultural Institute (*see* Public Buildings); the UNITED METHODIST FREE CHURCH in Walham Grove, of 1865–6, brick Gothic with stone dressings, provides a smart front for the Kensington College of Business; and the METHODIST NEW CONNEXION, North End Road, a tall debased Gothic church of 1887–8 by *A. H. Goodall*, is a scruffier furniture store.

BAPTIST CHURCH, Dawes Road. 1889 by *Charles Bell*; extensions at the rear, including a large church room, by *P. Morley Horder*, 1906. Red brick with yellow brick dressings. Busy debased classical front with pediment and round-headed windows flanked by two incipient towers. Interior floored at gallery level, 1977; further alterations 1989.

HUNGARIAN REFORMED CHURCH, St Dunstan's Road. *See* Perambulation 4.

UNITED REFORMED CHURCH, Fulham Palace Road and Harbord Street. Simple brick church with large foyer in front, and housing behind, replacing the CONGREGATIONAL CHURCH AND SCHOOL by *Cooper & Williams* (hall 1904–5, church 1908).

WELSH PRESBYTERIAN CHURCH, Effie Road. 1900–1 by *Edward Avern*. Tall ragstone front over basement; polygonal porch with pretty free Gothic detail.

FULHAM CEMETERY, Fulham Palace Road. 1865. LODGES and CHAPEL, thickset Victorian Gothic with bellcote, by *J. G. Hall*.

PUBLIC BUILDINGS

FULHAM PALACE, Bishops Avenue. One of the best medieval domestic sites in London, close to the Thames, in spacious grounds extending from the parish church of All Saints to Bishops Avenue. The palace is of far greater interest than might be expected from its undemonstrative exterior. The E parts of the irregular cluster of two-storey brick buildings are in their present form very plain C18 and early C19, the W parts are earlier, with a S feature of three pretty asymmetrical C16 bargeboarded gables close to the projecting C19 chapel.

The Bishops of London held the manor from 704, when the Bishop of the East Saxons bought the estate of Fulhanham from the Bishop of Hereford. The mile-long moat around the grounds (filled up in 1921–4) may be even older, as excavations have indicated it may have had its origin in pre-Saxon defences. The palace of the first Bishops may have been in the SW corner of the grounds, where there were complex ditches and earthworks. During the Middle Ages Fulham Palace was one of several country seats of the Bishops of London. It became their main residence in the C18 and remained so until 1973, although from 1956 parts were used for other purposes. A period of deplorable neglect and unsympathetic alterations followed, and new uses are still under discussion at the time of writing. The following account owes much to the investigations by Warwick Rodwell in 1987–8; repairs and conversion are likely to reveal much more.

The buildings are grouped round two courtyards, with the late C15 great hall between. The E court was the medieval core of the palace, and must have been the first part to be reached by the main approach from the river. We know little of its original appearance except that the medieval chapel lay on the E side and the Bishop's private rooms were to the N, as is made clear by the Parliamentary Survey of 1647 and by a survey plan of 1764. These buildings were replaced by the existing suites of reception rooms on N, E, and S sides for the wealthy prelates of the later C18 and early C19. The W court is still largely of the early C16, 16 built with lodgings in the ranges flanking the hall and with an

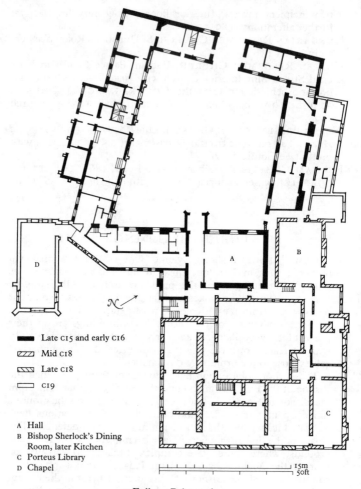

Late C15 and early C16
Mid C18
Late C18
C19

A Hall
B Bishop Sherlock's Dining
   Room, later Kitchen
C Porteus Library
D Chapel

15m
50ft

Fulham Palace, plan

entrance on the w side. Another entrance, much altered since, on the s side of the w court is marked by the projection with three uneven gables. These appear to belong to a remodelling of a more regular entrance block added possibly by Bishop Fitzjames (1506–22), whose arms are set above the doorway.

The early C16 w courtyard has an unassuming domestic atmosphere. It is entered from the w by a large but plain four-centred brick archway with a pair of oak gates whose construction suggests re-used medieval work. The brick ranges on w, e, and n sides of the courtyard have a diaper pattern of vitrified headers. The windows are all much altered, and the s range was rebuilt in 1853 by Bishop Blomfield, with painted diapering to the walls. However, in the n range, despite c 20 alterations, there is still much early C16 joinery, with moulded and stopped beams hidden above ceilings of 1818 (rooms 108–12 on the first floor), as well as two large Tudor chimneystacks on the outer wall. Some of the other internal features are due to antiquarianizing bishops: stone doorways in the s range, a re-used(?) four-centred wooden archway and the arms of Bishop Laud in the s projection, and the 'armoury' in the porter's lodge in the w range with reset C17 overmantel and C18 stone arms of Bishop Robinson.

The E range with the hall lies at an odd angle, suggesting that it is not of the same date as the rest of the court. The fabric, including the roof, appears to date from *c.* 1480, although the three-storey porch with vault with bosses and pretty (reconstructed) cupola is an early C16 addition (the diapering of the hall wall runs behind). The hall has been remodelled several times. It appears originally to have been a ground-floor hall with great chamber above – a progressive piece of planning for the late C15. The upper floor was destroyed in 1750 when the hall became Bishop Sherlock's drawing room: a tall room with a coved ceiling and with long Georgian sash-windows replaced in the 1780s under the antiquarian-minded Bishop Porteous by the present windows in C17 style. The sombre post-Restoration air of the interior is attributable chiefly to the monumental wooden panelling and screen brought in the C19 from Doctors' Commons on the edge of the City. The fine open pediment and brackets and the large bolection-moulded panels were installed by *Butterfield* in 1867, when the hall was refurbished after a period of use as a chapel. There is also some reset C18 dado panelling and other woodwork brought from the chapel in the Bishops' City mansion (a pedimented wooden reredos with big volutes). The balustrade on top of the screen may be the former communion rails. Below the reredos, in the centre of the dais end, Butterfieldian tiles conceal an original fireplace (another fireplace in the same stack served the original upper floor). The crown-post roof hidden above the ceiling is of five bays, with chamfered arch braces and two tiers of wind-braces, much repaired and strengthened.

When Bishop Sherlock converted the hall to a drawing room, he created a dining room to the N, on the site of the medieval solar block. Although horribly disguised and subdivided, this once elegant room still preserves its excellent Rococo plasterwork of 1750 above a C20 inserted ceiling. The three N-facing windows remain, the central one with an arch. They formerly had lower sills.

Most of the rebuilding of the E court was carried out by Bishop Terrick (1764–87). His architect was *Stiff Leadbetter*. Along the s front of the E court is a series of reception rooms: drawing room with overdoor, door with enriched panelling, an Adamish ceiling, and a later fireplace in dark marble. On the first floor above this suite are several bedrooms with good C18 fireplaces. The SE corner rooms were in a tower which was matched by a similar tower to the NE. The double-height library created by Leadbetter in the E range between them was swept away in the extensive and rather dull alterations carried out for Bishop Howley by *S.P. Cockerell* in 1813, when Leadbetter's picturesque Gothic crenellations were removed, the E range was rebuilt as reception rooms with bedrooms above, and the building line was brought forward

to that of the corner towers. In the central drawing room of the
E range a good coloured marble fireplace of c. 1750 attributed to
Vangelder, brought from Appuldurcombe House, Isle of Wight.
At the NE end, the C18 chapel which had been constructed over
medieval cellars was converted to the Porteous Library. It still
has its mahogany bookcases and a handsome coved ceiling.

At the service end of the hall the screens passage leads E into
a later vestibule at the corner of the inner court. On the r. the
early C18 staircase with ramped handrail and finely carved tread
ends comes from Peckham House, Fulham. The passage s from
the screens passage still reflects the route to the medieval kitchen
and service rooms which stood at the SE corner of the W court.
On their site the CHAPEL now stands, 1866–7 by *Butterfield* for
Bishop Tait. Exterior with diapering, W wall with trefoil lancets
and a quatrefoil. The interior was emasculated by alterations
after war damage: the polychrome brick walls were concealed by
cream paint, with pale murals by *Brian Thomas,* 1953. Sugar-
icing frills of plaster coving were put in below the inserted ceiling.
The reredos (not *in situ*) has mosaics designed by *Butterfield* and
made by *Salviati*. Stained glass in the W windows 1868 by *Clayton
& Bell*; the E window 1953 by *Sir Ninian Comper*.

The GROUNDS of Fulham Palace were from the C16 among
the most important botanical gardens in London, embellished in
the late C17 at the time of Bishop Compton with many exotic
species. They included tulip trees, walnuts, maples, and a cork
oak. The tradition was continued in the C19 by Bishops Porteous,
Blomfield, and Tait. Rocque's map of 1741–5 still shows the
palace surrounded by formal gardens; they were replaced from
c. 1770 by landscaped grounds. E of the palace there remains a
stretch of late medieval brick garden wall with bee boles, and a
gateway with the arms of Bishop Fitzjames, leading now to a
herb garden beside the derelict early C19 vineries. At the entrance
from Bishops Avenue, sturdy C19 Gothic gatepiers, and a picturesque early C19 bargeboarded LODGE with colossal twisted
chimneys and circular turret. A C17 barn survived nearby until
the 1950s.

At the W end of the grounds an ADVENTURE PLAY CENTRE
for handicapped children, a pioneer of its type; 1976 by *Stephen
Gardiner*. E of the palace the demesne meadows along the Thames
were embanked and opened to the public as BISHOP'S PARK in
1893 and extended in 1900 and 1903. At the Putney Bridge end,
PRYORS BANK, a picturesque park lodge of 1900, half-timbered
and roughcast. Small adjoining formal garden laid out in 1953
with stone figure SCULPTURE: Adoration, Protection, Grief, and
Leda, presented by the sculptor, *J. Wedgwood*; Affection, a tender
Mother and Child by *Hermon Cawthra*, was added in 1963.

OLD TOWN HALL, Fulham Road. 1888–90 by *G. Edwards*. Florid
Renaissance stone front to Fulham Road, with raised centre with
oval below a pediment. Extended to the l. in 1934 by *Walter
Cave*. Round the corner in Harwood Road large addition with
concert hall, 1904–5 by *Francis Wood*. Sumptuous interiors; in
the main building, first-floor hall with curved end and ceiling
with three domes. On the staircase landing, large pictorial stained
glass window depicting Erconald, Bishop of London at 'the dawn

of the history of Fulham', 1931 by *Francis Spear*, made by *Lowndes & Drury*.

WEST LONDON COUNTY COURT, North End Road. 1907–8 by *H. N. Hanks* in the English Baroque favoured for such buildings. Central pediment, rusticated brick quoins; large segmental pediment over the entrance.

FIRE STATION, Fulham Road. 1895–6 by *Robert Pearsall* under *T. Blashill* of the L.C.C., i.e. still in a Gothic and romantic vein rather than in the classical used later by the Fire Brigade Branch. A handsome pile, with asymmetrical corner turrets and lantern, well preserved with its original lettering. Practice tower behind.

PUBLIC LIBRARY, Fulham Road. 1909 by *Hare*, brick with stone 68 dressings, one-storeyed, but impressively monumental, with heavy stone aedicules to three of the five bays (cf. Hare's similar design for Islington Library, Holloway Road, Is).

BARONS COURT LIBRARY, Edith Road. A neat octagonal structure cantilevered from a central base; by the borough architect, *E. G. Sames* (job architect *R. F. Guilford*), 1964–5.

PUBLIC BATHS, North End Road. By *E. Deighton Pearson*, 1902. Only the entrance block remains, unusually jolly, with squat intermittently rusticated columns at the entrance, two carved relief figures above, and monstrously fat little columns in the gable.

FULHAM LEISURE POOLS, Lillie Road. 1979–82 by *Techno Leisure Ltd*. The new type of informal pools with beach, wave machine, etc., behind reticent brick gabled walls on the edge of Normand Park.

BHARATIYA VIDYA BHAVAN (Institute of Indian Culture), Castletown Road. A noble fragment: the two w bays of a cruciform church with central tower, all that survived the war of the West Kensington Congregational Church built in 1882–5 by *James Cubitt* (architect of the Union Chapel Islington, Is). Gabled brick front with three grouped lancets under an arch; flank walls with flying buttresses.

LONDON ORATORY SCHOOL, Seagrave Road. by *David Stokes & Partners*, completed 1970. An ingeniously compact group on a tight site hidden away s of Lillie Road. Planned as a six-form-entry comprehensive. Impressive, well proportioned four-square main block, with three floors on projecting concrete uprights, and a top floor of brick, windowless to the outside. At each corner glazed staircase towers, flush with the rest. The building is a hollow cube containing classrooms, library, art rooms, science laboratories, etc., arranged around a one-storey top-lit hall and gymnasium (the dull view of their flat roofs from the upper floors is a disappointment). Linked to the cube by glazed bridges is a three-storey house-room block, with dining halls over kitchens; other links to lower offices, swimming pool, and workshops. Within the main block the CHAPEL, a plain white flat-ceilinged room given distinction by *Patrick Reyntiens*'s stained glass: two sanctuary windows (set back too far to be easily visible) and w clerestory in pale colours with a motif of pink and gold clouds. Simple wooden fittings by *Stokes*.

LADY MARGARET SCHOOL, Parsons Green. *See* Perambulation 2.

HURLINGHAM AND CHELSEA SCHOOL, Peterborough Road. Built as Hurlingham School for Girls, 1956 by *Sheppard Robson & Partners* for the L.C.C. A formal plan on a confined site. Ranges around two courtyards, with the entrance through an open ground floor below a lively patterned tiled façade; a good period piece.

FULHAM CROSS SCHOOL (formerly Fulham Gilliatt), Munster Road. 1908 by *T. J. Bailey* for the L.C.C., built as Fulham County School, a secondary school for girls. Developed from the standard Board School type (*see* below). Impressive free Renaissance composition: arched hall windows, lunettes above, under gables; end pavilions with shaped gables.

BOARD SCHOOLS. Fulham has one of the best collections of Board Schools in London, built for the rapidly expanding population of the late C19. The HARWOOD ROAD SCHOOL of 1873 by *Basil Champneys* (demolished in 1928) was an early and influential demonstration of the use of the Queen Anne style for this type of building. But the London School Board was busiest in Fulham from the 1890s; its characteristic production was the stately three-decker of the era of *T. J. Bailey* (superintending architect from 1884 to 1910). His schools have superimposed central halls flanked symmetrically by a romantic silhouette of stair-turrets and gabled wings, especially effective among Fulham's low terraces. A large number survive. Good examples are HALFORD ROAD (1889–91), LANGFORD ROAD (1890, 1893), and MUNSTER ROAD (1892–3, 1895), the last two of the same basic design, an especially satisfactory composition with a tall centre articulated by buttresses with urns, stepping down to wings with boldly scrolled Dutch gables. LILLIE ROAD (Sir John Lillie, 1893, 1895) is very similar, enlivened by red and yellow brick. KINGWOOD ROAD (Henry Compton), 1898, has especially elaborate turrets to the stair-towers, and PETERBOROUGH SCHOOL, Clancarty Road, and FULHAM PALACE ROAD SCHOOLS, 1901 and 1902, demonstrate the popularity of buff terracotta trimmings at this time. QUEENSMILL ROAD, 1904, marks the turn to English Renaissance detail, with large arched hall windows.

ALL SAINTS C. OF E. PRIMARY SCHOOL, Fulham High Street. Founded in 1861. The present street frontage, probably of 1906, is enlivened by shaped gables and the buff terracotta much favoured in Fulham.

ST JOHN'S SCHOOL, Dawes Road, 1894 by *A. J. Pilkington,* with an entrance gatehouse. Flemish Gothic detail in terracotta.

POST WAR PRIMARY SCHOOLS. SULIVAN, Peterborough Road. A typical low group of 1951, contemporary with the neighbouring council flats. Concrete clad, built on the Hills 8′ 3″ system borrowed from Hertfordshire. NORMAND PARK of 1959 is of one and two storeys with some purple brick end walls and black and white cladding, typical of the bolder materials used from the late 1950s.

CHARING CROSS HOSPITAL, Fulham Palace Road. Not a welcome addition to the riverside skyline. Its protracted planning history is typical of London hospitals. The decision to move from the original cramped central London location was taken in 1936, but the Fulham site agreed on only in 1957. *Ralph Tubbs* was appointed architect in 1959. Final plans were approved in 1966, and the first phase, the massive curtain-walled seventeen-storey tower on a cross-shaped plan (for 630 beds), was built in 1969–73. Its plan allows for more windows than could be achieved with a rectangle, with natural light even for the operating theatres (sited on the fourteenth floor). But however humane the intentions, building on this scale intimidates, although the lattice of cantilevered metal balconies does a little to alleviate the bulk. The surrounding lower buildings were added according to the original plan in 1975–84, bringing the total number of beds to 790. Two-storey entrance block, with outpatients' department on the first floor; three residential tower blocks to the s. At the back a small CHAPEL, polygonal, top-lit, with raking roof struts. Four notable panels of stained glass. Flanking the altar, Earthly Life and Everlasting Life by *Alfred Fisher*, angular forms, good colours, but lacking the lively sparkle of the two near the entrance by *John Piper* and *Patrick Reyntiens*, River of Life, 1978, and Tree of Life, 1981, the last especially delightful in its flowing forms and naive Chagall-like detail. The hospital occupies the site of the Fulham Union Workhouse (1849 by *A. Gilbert*, infirmary 1883 by *Giles & Gough*, additions 1889 by *Saxon Snell*, chapel by *Blomfield*, 1889).

FULHAM FOOTBALL GROUND, Craven Cottage, Stevenage Road. (Future uncertain.) Grandstand and offices of 1905 by *Archibald Leitch*, a rare survival of an early example by the Glasgow engineer who specialized in these structures. Utilitarian iron-framed stand; exterior of brick with stone dressings, with shaped gables to the centre bays. The offices are housed in a domestic-looking building angled across the SE corner, known as Craven Cottage in allusion to the *cottage orné* previously on the site (*see* Fulham Introduction).

CHELSEA FOOTBALL STADIUM, Stamford Bridge, Fulham Road. An impressive cantilevered steel-framed E stand with three very steeply raked tiers of seats for 1,150; 1972–4 by *Darbourne & Darke*.

FULHAM POWER STATION, Townmead Road. Fulham was a pioneer in the early use of electricity; lighting order 1897, first supplies 1901. Only a range along Townmead Road remains; 1934–6 for the borough, consulting engineers *J. H. Rider* and *A. J. Fuller,* masonry by *G. E. Baker*. The row of four chimneys has been demolished. When built it was the largest municipally owned generating station in the country.

GASWORKS, Sands End Lane. The Imperial Gasworks established itself here, close to Chelsea Creek, in 1824. Gasholder No. 2, of *c.* 1830, is reputed to be the oldest in the world (a single-lift water-sealed holder in a subterranean brick tank, 30 metres in diameter). Little to see except for the attractive cast-iron stanchions. The C19 buildings were by the Company's architect, *Francis Edwards* (*see also* Perambulation 2, Imperial Square). The mid C20 buildings added for North Thames Gas are of above average quality (*see also* Perambulation 1, Peterborough Road). Neat four-storey LABORATORIES, 1966–7 by *Mayorcas & Guest*, faced with unbonded tiles; exposed concrete porches.

LONDON TRANSPORT STATIONS. PUTNEY BRIDGE is of 1880, cream brick, with a giant arch with big keystone. WEST KENSINGTON, opened in 1874, was refronted in the 1930s. BARONS COURT, 1905, has an attractive classical front in glazed brown terracotta; FULHAM BROADWAY is similar.

PERAMBULATIONS

Fulham's more interesting buildings are scattered amidst long dull stretches. The most enjoyable areas for walking are along the riverside.

1. Between New Kings Road and the river

The old centre of the riverside village is marked by All Saints' church (q.v.) in its green setting of the old churchyard on the edge of Bishops Park. To the N in CHURCH GATE the POWELL ALMSHOUSES, 1869 by *J. P. Seddon,* a perfect repository of the endearing forms of 1870. One-storeyed, with high pitched roof and eleven dormer windows. L-shaped plan. Towards the churchyard a turret with an outer staircase, picturesque and heavy-handed. Sentimental little figures of Faith, Hope, and Charity, and also Miriam, Anna, Deborah, Dorcas, Ruth, and St Mary. In the garden opposite, WAR MEMORIAL of 1921 by *Alfred Turner,* with bronze figures of Peace and a kneeling cherub. The low terrace continuing into STEEPLE CLOSE is of c. 1965 by *J. de Segrais,* unusually tactful for its date; discreetly neo-Georgian apart from obtrusive garage doors. Nos. 5 and 6 are a genuine early C18 pair, No. 6 with good iron gate. At the corner with FULHAM HIGH STREET, TEMPERANCE BILLIARD HALL, 1909, with a large barrel roof, art nouveau glass in its shallow bow-windows, and a corner entrance with dome and glazed tiles, not tall, but with enough presence to confront the KINGS ARMS opposite of 1888, with its busy pedimented windows on the curve of the junction with NEW KINGS ROAD. Lavish glazed terracotta-trimmed one-storey extension.

To the S Putney Bridge Approach is the main traffic route, and the HIGH STREET has become a drab back lane between clumsily sited slab-and-podium offices of the 1960s–70s. Among them one unusual C18 survivor: FULHAM HOUSE, whose dignified front was revealed only after its restoration in 1987–9 by *Stroud Nullis & Partners* for the Territorial Army. Five-bay yellow brick front, austere but lively, somewhat in the manner of Vanbrugh. Rate books suggest a date in the 1730s. The centre steps forward, the end bays step back; decoration is confined to moulded bands and to large stone keystones to the centre windows. Fine stone staircase with S-shaped iron balusters at the NW corner of the house, probably moved, perhaps in the 1860s, when a large reception room was added at the back; several good fireplaces. Large rear addition of 1987–9, in brick, nicely detailed, but unfortunately close to the house. The pedimented gateway to the forecourt is a reconstruction based on old photographs. Next door the EIGHT BELLS, with a modest early C 19 front. By the river the new housing keeps in scale: SWANBANK COURT, Willow Bank, plain vernacular massing in brown brick, provides sheltered housing for the borough, 1981 by *Green, Lloyd & Adams*; CARRARA WHARF is a larger private scheme (by *Higgs & Hill Architects Department, 1987–9*) with pleasant staggered layout, and the more cheerful and self-confident detail of the late 1980s. Blue metal balconies and yellow roughcast gables are the main motifs.

Further E, the streets S of New Kings Road are predominantly late Victorian and Edwardian, with a few scattered stuccoed villas of the early C 19 (BROOMHOUSE ROAD, HURLINGHAM ROAD). One older house in Hurlingham Road: No. 76, THE VINEYARD, with a rendered three-storey three-bay front, but the early C 17 date revealed by the L-shaped lower back, and the end stacks with diagonally set chimneys.

HURLINGHAM HOUSE, Ranelagh Gardens. Since 1869 the Hurlingham Club (founded initially for pigeon shooting but later famous for polo); the only survival among the Georgian mansions which once fringed this part of the river, insulated from a later world by its grounds, still spacious though less extensive than before the Second World War. The former No. 1 polo ground is now HURLINGHAM PARK, the second polo ground is covered by the Sulivan estate. *Repton* worked on the grounds (mentioned in his *Theory* of 1803). The plain three-bay, three-storey house of brown brick built by Dr William Cadogan in 1760 is still recognizable from the N, flanked by the additions made by *George Byfield* in 1797–8 for John Ellis: lower two-bay extensions and long two-storey wings (formerly service wing and stables), forming the sides of what is now the entrance courtyard. The two porches in the re-entrant angles, with paired Doric columns and ogee lead domes capped by urns, must belong to an early C 20 remodelling and may be part of the work carried out for the club by *Lutyens* c. 1906–12: the pair of pavilions on this side, each with a deep brick niche with pediment above, are very similar to Lutyens's niched garden temple at Nashdom, Taplow, Bucks.* *Byfield*'s more spectacular achievement was the transformation of the river frontage into a white stucco-faced mansion in Nash's grand manner. He created a suite of ample reception rooms by adding two slightly projecting three-bay wings (drawing room and dining room) linked by an oval anteroom which projects into the central bow retained from the earlier house. In front of this he added a giant pedimented Corinthian portico; giant Corinthian pilasters continue along the wings. Good interiors of Byfield's time: dining and drawing room each have crisp, delicately detailed neo-classical cornices, and the drawing-room fireplace has matching arabesques. Carved dado rails and door surrounds; wall panels with colourful painted *grottesche* (repainted after the Second World War). In the oval anteroom two niches and a cornice of upright leaves. Parallel to these rooms, a tripartite long gallery, formed in the early C 20 (possibly part of the work by

*I owe this comparison to Peter Gotlop.

Lutyens) from the space formerly occupied by the main staircase, a back staircase, and another room. The niched entrance hall to the W, with staircase leading off it, must also be of this date. Good cornice of *c.* 1760 in the central first-floor room facing the river. On the E side many low additions for the club. The conservatory to the W was demolished after war damage. Pretty tilehung and half timbered LODGE by Broomhouse Lane.

CASTLE CLUB, Broomhouse Lane. Built as a school by *Horace Francis*, 1854–5, quite a pretty symmetrical Tudor brick and stone composition with two stepped gables, a hefty central tower, and picturesquely grouped chimneys.

SULIVAN COURT, between Broomhouse Lane and Peterborough Road, on the former No. 2 polo ground of the Hurlingham Club. An extensive, progressively designed council estate of 432 flats, 1949–56 by the Borough Housing Department under *J. Pritchard Lovell,* mostly three- to five-storey L-shaped blocks with staircase access, informally grouped; one taller block with curved front.

BRITISH GAS OFFICES AND LABORATORIES, S end of Peterborough Road. 1961–3 by *E. R. Collister & Partners,* an enterprising effort to brighten an indifferent industrial area. Six-storey curtain-walled slab with blue spandrels, with low projecting exhibition wing on stilts, faced with a cheerful coloured abstract relief in polyester resin and glass, designed by *John Piper* and made by *Gillespie & Manzerolli Associates.*

Between Hurlingham Park and Chelsea Creek the solid wedge of riverside industry fringed by late C19 working-class terraces was all in the throes of transformation by 1990. At the time of writing TOWNMEAD ROAD was a curious medley of down-at-heel depots and derelict utilities, building sites for smart new flats, and strings of little two-storey Victorian houses barely touched by gentrification. Amidst the relics of Fulham power station, once one of the borough's proudest monuments, a spreading SAINSBURY'S hogs a prime riverside site; further E, at SANDS WHARF, a vast development of Bovis flats masquerades as minimal Hanseatic warehouses. Inland it is worth exploring up BAGLEYS LANE, past the former TOWNMEAD ROAD SCHOOLS (now part of Chelsea School of Art), low, well detailed Edwardian Board Schools with dentilled gables. Beyond them, STANFORD COURT, two-storeyed sheltered housing by the borough, *c.* 1986, with triple entrances grouped under quasi-broken pediments – classical allusions invading the neo-vernacular. More relaxed at the back, where timber balconies overlook a moated garden. Beyond is an imaginatively landscaped small PARK, also a creation of the 1980s, with a circular green buffered by enclosed sitting and play areas, one with an octagonal children's centre. More infilling further W: a steep-roofed neo-Victorian terrace in STEPHENDALE ROAD, and in MARINE-FIELD ROAD, ELIZABETH BARNES COURT, sheltered housing, a friendly sequence of broad tile-hung gables with inset balconies. For the area to the N around the Imperial Gas Works, *see* Perambulation 2, Sands End.

CHELSEA HARBOUR, Lots Road. Now the E focus of Townmead Road. An instant riverside town for the rich; hotel and housing (*c.* 500 dwellings) with attendant amenities for 4,000 people, built in 1986–9 on derelict railway land at Chelsea Basin. The marina which forms the focus of the development originated as a dock for the Kensington Canal. Initial ideas for the area formulated in 1981 by *Ray Moxley* and *Peter Bedford* envisaged a wider social mix than was in the end achieved. The final scheme was carried out by *Peter Bedford* together with the *Moxley Jenner Partnership* and *Chamberlin, Powell, Bon & Woods*. A cheerfully 'inclusivist' mixture of eclectic styles provides a stage set around the marina, with one twenty-storey tower, THE BELVEDERE, as a landmark. Its profile is a faint echo of the campanile of St Mark's in Venice, with the additional spectacle of a golden ball on its summit intended to rise and fall with the tide. The other prominent roof-line is that of the complex called CHELSEA GARDEN MARKET, where three glazed domes cover the atria of a covered mall with shops, offices, and workshops. HARBOUR YARD, another complex with restaurants, offices, and workshops, has a façade to the marina with an unhappy mixture of classical elements: columns rising between two tiers of balustraded balconies – an overblown effect which competes for attention with the undulating balconies of the rather better composed CONRAD HOTEL by *Triad Architects*, seven storeys above a striped granite two-storey plinth. The housing ranges from versions of neo-Georgian terraces over garages, tightly packed and cheaply detailed, to sleek modernist flats in a crescent overlooking the river.

2. *New Kings Road, Parsons Green, Sands End*

NEW KINGS ROAD originated in the later C17 as the royal route from Westminster to Hampton Court; it became an official public road only in 1830. Near the w end, FULHAM POTTERY, for which John Dwight was granted a patent in 1672. It was owned by his descendants until 1859; a C19 BOTTLE KILN is preserved in a horribly cramped setting by an office block of 1979–80 called KILN HOUSE. N of the pottery, No. 38 BURLINGTON ROAD, a Georgian three-bay, two-storey villa. To the e, in RIGAULT ROAD, studios created in the 1980s from the laundry block of a women's prison, built in 1853 as a training centre for women prisoners and closed in 1888.

New Kings Road attracted spasmodic ribbon development between Chelsea and Fulham from the early C18. No. 190 is another late Georgian detached villa, with pretty enriched cornice and doorcase. Nos. 146–154, originally part of a terrace of twelve houses, has a date plaque 'Elysium Row 1738'; not as blatantly euphemistic as it sounds now, for at that time it stood alone among the market gardens that were Fulham's main industry. Of the early C18 are No. 136, red and yellow brick, with doorcase with fluted pilasters, and No. 134 (heightened and altered, but with good staircase and interior).

PARSONS GREEN, a former hamlet inhabited in the early C18 (according to Bowack) 'mostly by Gentry and Persons of Quality', preserves another concentration of older houses. The green remains as a pleasant wedge-shaped space opening off New Kings

Road to the N. On the S side No. 247, three storeys and basement
with a later top storey and lower wings; good fanlight. Nos. 237–
245, a terrace of three-bay houses dated 1795, is unusual in
having centrally placed doorways. On the E side the best houses
are part of LADY MARGARET SCHOOL, a girls' school established in 1917. BELFIELD HOUSE has an early C18 front of five
bays, with the two outer windows in slightly projecting wings.
Handsomely detailed, with red brick used for quoins and window
heads, and stone keystones. Restored by the artist Theodore
Roussel in 1890. Interior much altered (fine staircase and fireplaces removed when converted for the school in 1917). ELM
HOUSE adjoining to the N, of c. 1800, recorded as a school already
in 1803, became part of the present one in 1937. Five bays, with
recessed windows with mask keystones, and tripartite doorway
in rusticated surround. Entrance hall with simple cantilevered
stair curving up over the doorway; the room behind on a generous
scale, with bow-window to the garden. The room above, also
with a bow, is now the CHAPEL; central window with painted
glass by *Sasha Ward*, 1987: Tree of Life, birds in a trellis pattern.
Good original cornices in both rooms and in the SW room. To
the N, HENNIKER HOUSE, plain Italianate of c. 1841, much
altered. Back wings for the school, plain well-detailed brick
ranges, from 1962 (hall completed 1965), by *Seely & Paget*.

Near the apex of the green the late C19 WHITE HORSE, red
terracotta with tall gable with horse under a canopy. On the w
side St Dionis (q.v.), with the CHURCH HALL (1876 by *Arthur
Billing*) and RECTORY with Gothic doorway and a little tilehanging. Humble cottagey terraces of c. 1840 (much gentrified)
lead away W.

S of New Kings Road was Peterborough House, a major C17
mansion rebuilt in the late C18 and demolished c. 1900. On the
PETERBOROUGH ESTATE a remarkably coherent grid of streets
was developed from the 1890s by the local builder *J. Nichols*
(between Peterborough Road, Wandsworth Bridge Road, and
Studdridge Street). Much terracotta trim (originally buff, but
mostly now painted white). The shared gables decorated with
heraldic lions are the distinctive signature. In New Kings Road,
the Peterborough Hotel of 1892 (now the SOUTHERN CROSS)
is grander, but in the same style. Further E along New Kings
Road, EEL BROOK COMMON, with a few more late Georgian
pairs and terraces (Nos. 113–121, 99–107, and 71–77).

SANDS END, where New Kings Road becomes Kings Road, is
Chelsea-over-the-border, with a surfeit of antique shops. To the
S, much rebuilding of the 1980s in a welter of ill-digested styles.
The confident Victorian Italianate of the IMPERIAL ARMS
(corner of Cambria Street) comes as welcome relief. So does
IMPERIAL SQUARE, a delightful enclave of simple C19 cottage
terraces with generous front gardens, built for workers in the
Imperial Gas Company nearby (*see* Public Buildings). The hard
landscaping and the appropriate reproduction gaslamps date
from the 1980s. The poorly detailed low-rent housing of the
1980s to the N is in sad contrast; MAYNARD CLOSE off Kings
Road E of Cambria Street, by *Robert Patterson* (of *Romulus
Construction*), is perhaps better than the rest.

SANDFORD MANOR, Rewell Street. Hidden amidst the 1980s closes, the one older survival. Despite its C19 roughcast and parapet, essentially a mid C17 house, a rare survival in the inner suburbs. After long neglect, restored and converted to offices in 1987–9 by *Romulus Construction Ltd*. It is a lesser version of the new type of progressive, compact brick mansion built at this time in the countryside around London (cf. Kew Palace, Ri, Boston Manor, Ho). Until the 1840s, when it was divided into two dwellings for gas employees, it had a front with three shaped gables. 2–1–2 windows, their heavy brick mid C17 surrounds still evident beneath the render, as is the moulded brick string course. Flank walls with three plain gables. The plan is now a roughly rectangular double pile; there was originally a back courtyard between two wings (filled in in the C19). The wings are at different levels (because of a cellar below the NW room). Front range with central entrance hall flanked by a larger room on each side, each with a hefty chimneystack also serving the room behind. The hall – an entrance hall only, not a hall of the old type – also contains the staircase; a typical mid C17 example, with small well, closed string, turned balusters, and newels with simple balls and pendants. It continues up to the attic floor. Restored with honey-coloured paint and graining; the hall panelling treated likewise (that on the l. side a facsimile). In the NW wing, first-floor room with restored panelling (medium-size panels); in the room above, remains of C17 black and red painting of a vase of flowers in the fireplace reveal. The restoration is a good example of the 'conserve as found' philosophy of the 1980s, i.e. the later phases of the building's history have not been removed.

3. Between Fulham High Street and Hammersmith Bridge

In the HIGH STREET the dominant building is the KINGS HEAD, a lively asymmetrical composition; conical turret with romantic steep cap, and plenty of the buff terracotta so popular in Fulham at the turn of the century. The long stretch of FULHAM PALACE ROAD leading to Hammersmith was built up *c.* 1900 with low, quite genteel residential terraces on the W side, a mixture of houses and two-storey flats, likewise in the streets running towards the river. The E side is more varied. FULHAM WASTE-LANDS AND LYGON ALMSHOUSES are replacements of C19 almshouses, 1980 by *Trenwith, Wills & Wills* with *Alan Mitchell & Partners*, low buildings pleasantly grouped around an L-shaped court. Then the well-treed cemetery (q.v.) and recreation ground, and at the corner of Lillie Road, the jolly OLD CON-VENIENCES of 1894, with dentilled gable above big bold central archway, glazed in when converted to architect's offices by *Paul Brooks Associates* in 1986. The approach to Hammersmith is heralded by the larger scale of the neatly ranked blocks of the GUINNESS TRUST ESTATE (1901), a major slum clearance effort, and the PEABODY ESTATE of 1914–26, built on the site of the Good Shepherd Convent.

W of Fulham Palace Road FULHAM REACH remained rural until

the later C19, when the market gardens and the few country houses were replaced by industry (the first and largest concerns were Hammersmith Distillery, 1857, on the site of Brandenburgh House, and the Manbre sugar refinery, opened in 1876). Now hardly anything remains of this era. From the 1970s the borough encouraged a shift to residential development, and, in an enlightened way, ensured that a riverside walk was gained at the same time. Near the Hammersmith end the walk makes a splendidly stylish start with THAMES REACH in RAINVILLE ROAD, three groups of flats by *Richard Rogers & Partners*, 1985–8, five storeys of clean-cut curtain-walling to the river, with lively articulation provided by jutting white tubular steel balconies. This nautical imagery contrasts with the overpoweringly solid back elevations, with brick staircase drums and perversely stepped bedroom windows. Nearby a group of offices in crisply refurbished industrial buildings, originally part of Duckham's oil refinery, unified by the use of blue-painted windows. The largest has been converted by *Lifschutz Davidson* for Rogers's own offices. They are grouped round a well landscaped open space. For the adjoining site to the NW, development according to a master plan by *Foster Associates* was agreed in 1990: housing by *David Landaw & Partners*, and two five-storey office blocks by *Foster Associates*. To the SE there is nothing as exciting. The riverside walk skirts borough housing of the late 1970s: unexceptional low brick terraces with raised private patios. Pleasantly landscaped, especially at BLAKES WHARF at the end of QUEENSMILL ROAD, where a small park provides a river vista for the school beyond. The bases of former silos have been incorporated into play areas. Further S RIVER GARDENS, one of the first sites to be redeveloped, a forceful if rather dour dark brick polygonal cluster of 1974–7 by *Ted Levy Benjamin & Partners*, surrounding private gardens open to the river – an early trendsetter for luxury riverside flats. Raked-back profiles and strong horizontal balcony bands. The Fulham football ground at Craven Cottage follows (*see* Public Buildings). Immediately S Bishops Park (*see* Fulham Palace) continues the walk to Putney Bridge.

4. *Walham Green, North End, and the rest of Fulham*

The Victorian centre of Fulham developed at WALHAM GREEN, once a hamlet around a green on the Fulham Road $1\frac{1}{2}$m. NE of the old village. St John's church (q.v.) was built here in 1828; WALHAM GROVE to its E is an attractively complete street of 1862, with stuccoed terraces facing trim paired villas with side entrances, and a former Nonconformist church (q.v.) of the same period. The S side of the green became FULHAM BROADWAY, but there is little to commend in the C19 and C20 medley, apart from the Town Hall of 1888 and some public buildings along North End Road (qq.v.), the grand Italianate mid C19 GEORGE and its neighbour at the corner of Fulham Road, and the JOLLY MALTSTER, a perkier gabled pub of 1900 by *Nowell Parr & Kates* tucked away in VANSTON PLACE. The spiky SCULPTURE in the Broadway, by *Philip King*, 1981, is hardly a visual asset. A more dignified addition to the townscape is the shopping development near the George; 1987 by *Renton Howard Wood Levin*, in a vaguely Venetian palazzo style, yellow brick with red trimmings.

FULHAM ROAD winds E towards Chelsea with a few genteel mid C19 terraces. The main intrusion on the N side is the long undistinguished Baroque frontage of the SIR OSWALD STOLL FOUNDATION, 1917–23 by *Inigo R. Tasker*, with housing behind for disabled ex-servicemen. Further E, behind Nos. 410–416 is hidden the so-called 'Italian Village', picturesque low pantiled buildings created around his workshops in the 1920s by the sculptor *Mario Manenti*. To the S, pleasant minor mid Victorian streets (BRITANNIA ROAD, WATERFORD ROAD, etc.), with stucco-trimmed terraces. In MOORE PARK ROAD a Mark II version (*c.* 1970) of the borough's experimental deck-access housing by *Higgins, Ney & Partners* (*see* Reporton Road, below), starker and more cost-conscious than its prototype. Opposite, LORD ROBERTS MEWS, private housing with the artful arched features and fancy brickwork favoured a decade later (*Michael Brown Associates*, 1983). CLARE MEWS, off Waterford Road, is another small infill of the 1980s.

FULHAM ROAD W of the Broadway has little character until one reaches the consistently Victorian stretch of *c.* 1880 between Parsons Green Lane and Munster Road; shopping parades with upper floors with lavish brickwork and iron cresting, built to serve the neighbouring small streets built up in the last quarter of the C19. A diversion S can take in No. 11 LETTICE STREET, the GLASS HOUSE, built in 1906 to specifications by *Christopher Whall* and *Alfred Drury* as the premises of the stained-glass workers Lowndes & Drury. Studios on the upper floor were rented out to independent glass workers. It became the centre for most of the major stained-glass artists of the early C20. Two-storeyed, symmetrical, functional front with central entrance, and four gables above large upper windows.

N of Fulham Road only the towering Board Schools and the occasional unambitious church break the skyline of a dense minor Victorian landscape of prim bay-windowed terraces. Among the relatively few later intrusions, ST PETER'S TERRACE in REPORTON ROAD, public housing built on a bomb-damaged site by *Higgins & Ney*, 1966–8. This was an early commission by the new borough (although initiated already by Fulham in 1964) and is historically of some interest. It was intended (although not proceeded with) as a prototype for a new type of high-density urban housing which could provide a low-rise alternative to the tower block. At that time Fulham's not-yet-fashionable Victorian and Edwardian terraces were still considered expendable in the interests of higher density and tidy garaging. Flats are arranged around and over a garage area and service road; those on the upper floors are approached from the deck above, intended as a new version of a traditional street. The solution is a modest version of megablocks such as Brunswick Square Camden. Brown brick and staggered frontages produce quite a homely effect here (a foretaste of things to come) in contrast to the gloomy corridors to the lower flats, and the yawning garage entrance.

LILLIE ROAD provides some more contrasts in public housing. The area N of Fulham Cross was acquire by the G.L.C. *c.* 1965 but rebuilt slowly and only after many setbacks. On the N side, brown brick low-rise terraces around CREFELD CLOSE (completed *c.* 1981) contrast with the bleaker LAMPETER SQUARE (1972), where slabs of flats build up to a ten-storey ziggurat on one side. The area further N was completed only in 1985 by a housing association; attractive small-scale groups along pedestrian ways, ending in ABBEY GARDENS with friendly brown brick houses with pantiled roofs. Further E along Lillie Road, the CLEM ATTLEE ESTATE, Fulham's post-war showpiece begun in 1955 (*J. Pritchard Lovell*), three Y-shaped point blocks overlooking Normand Park across the road (a bombed area transformed into a park in 1951–2) – a typically Corbusian conjunction. The towers were the highest in Fulham when built. Equally typical of the large estate of this date are the jaunty caps to the water tanks, and the contrast with the dull lower terraces behind in a poorly landscaped setting, where two taller towers have been crammed in later. LIBRARY in the ground floor of the E point block. E of North End Road, the N side of Lillie Road has two stately pairs of stuccoed villas of *c.* 1840 (one with a plaque with the incongruous name Hermitage Cottages) before the streetline disintegrates into ill-thought-out wasteland around the EMPRESS STATE BUILDING. This is by *Stone, Toms & Partners*, completed in 1962 for the Admiralty, and was one of the first London office towers on a massive scale, 320 ft high, Y-shaped, with concave sides. The S side of Lillie Road is equally disparate; the bulky concrete RAMADA INN, and the Peabody FULHAM ESTATE of *c.* 1900, five-storey blocks, ultra-plain apart from terracotta doorways. To their S a more appealing group of streets (Sedlescombe Road, Racton Road, etc.) developed *c.* 1900–4 with model housing for the Gunter estate (*see* also Kensington (KC), Perambulation 4), by the estate's surveyor, *Walter Cave:* low terraces and cottage flats in a simple Arts and Crafts style: striped quoins, casement windows. Also by *Cave*, the picturesque ST OSWALD'S STUDIOS and No. 40 RACTON ROAD, formerly the vicarage for the demolished St Oswald's, with narrow sash-windows in the manner of Philip Webb.

NORTH END ROAD runs from Walham Green to Hammersmith Road, passing until the late C19 through market gardens. The S part was much rebuilt when quantity not quality was the aim in public housing. On the E side the terraces and towers of the WEST KENSINGTON ESTATE, begun in 1970 by *Gleeson Industrialised Building Ltd* (the borough's first Design and Build project), the towers brick clad in response to the Ronan Point disaster, but nonetheless uninviting. Off to the W in STAR ROAD housing begun in 1971; by then nothing over four storeys was acceptable, although CHEESEMAN'S TERRACE still has the awkward linked upper-level walkways so popular in ambitious high-rise schemes of the 1960s. Further N the BARONS COURT area remains largely C19, with classy terraces of Kensington grandeur in Castletown Road, Comeragh Road, etc., developed by W. H. Gibbs & Co.

(later Gibbs & Flew), one of the major developers of West Kensington. At first they produced a final flourish of the stucco tradition, but the style is abandoned w of Vereker Road, where it is replaced by plainer red brick terraces. Further s, off Normand Road, QUEEN'S CLUB GARDENS, a pleasantly secluded enclave of red brick mansion flats with shaped gables of 1894, also laid out by W. H. Gibbs, around generous communal gardens. The QUEEN'S CLUB itself lies to the N off Field Road, an athletics and sports club which opened in 1887 with a range of facilities including covered tennis courts, billiard rooms, and an ice rink. Many of its original buildings remain, rather gaunt brick sheds by *William Marshall*, as unconcerned with aesthetics as most sports centres today.

N of Talgarth Road (now part of a busy bypass around Hammersmith Broadway), alternative High Victorian fashion of the 1880s (stock brick, gabled dormers, Gothic trim) can be studied in the stately terraces of the area around Gunterstone Road and Edith Road, with THE FOX in North End Crescent as the culmination.

A few exceptional individual houses need a special note, reminders of a time when, hard though that may be to visualize, this part of London was still attractive enough to appeal to the artistic community. In the later C19 Burne-Jones lived in North End Road, Onslow Ford in Matheson Road. Nearby in AVONMORE ROAD No. 122 is by *James MacLaren*, 1888–9, a studio house built for the society portrait sculptor H. R. Pinker, an original design, very free for its date. Brick with pronounced stone bands. Three storeys, an asymmetrical composition, with large functional studio doors on the l., a stubby octagonal lantern over a stair-tower as the central feature, and the living quarters set back on the r. with a porch with short bulgy columns. In TALGARTH ROAD, the picturesque buff-terracotta-trimmed Nos. 135–149, 63 a prominent sight s of the flyover approach, were built as ST PAUL'S STUDIOS in 1891 by *Frederick Wheeler*, designed for 'bachelor artists', each with a large N-facing arched studio window on the first floor, and housekeeper's apartment in the basement. They adjoin the earlier No. 151, built in 1885 for Sir Coutts Lindsay, founder of the Grosvenor Gallery. A final excursion s to ST DUNSTAN'S ROAD, to another studio, No. 17 (altered in 1958 for the HUNGARIAN REFORMED CHURCH), built in 1891 on a rural spot on the edge of Hammersmith Cemetery by *C. F. A. Voysey* for the decorative painter W. E. F. Britten. It is an appealingly humble cottage with studio behind, deceptively simple, but designed with Voysey's characteristic attention to detail. Roughcast walls, battered chimney, delectably inventive iron railings. Broad central door with canopy suspended from iron brackets. To its l. the timber window of the former kitchen, and another window, formerly a large studio door. To the r. the more formal stone-mullioned corner window of the well-lit small entrance hall. The staircase formerly rose within the hall. The studio had a gallery above a deep fireplace recess, now partitioned off. The exterior was originally quite colourful; the woodwork painted green, with green-glazed brick sills to the large segmental-arched studio windows.

HARROW

INTRODUCTION

Harrow has the most distinctive natural landmark of all the w
London boroughs, a 200 ft hill rising suddenly and steeply above
the surrounding plains of suburbia. The hilltop town now dominated by the school grew around the substantial church on the
summit. The church – perhaps the successor to a pagan religious
centre – was a possession in the Middle Ages of the Archbishops
of Canterbury and extended its authority over a wide area, including
Wembley and Sudbury to e and s (Brent), and Pinner to the w.
Pinner early on developed into a centre with its own church. Its
attractive village High Street still preserves echoes of its prosperous
pre-suburban past. Rocque's map of the mid c18 shows in the rest
of the w part of the present borough only the hamlets of Roxeth,
Greenhill, Wealdstone and Hatch End, the Archbishops' moated
manor house standing on its own at Headstone, and scattered

settlements on the wooded uplands of Harrow Weald to the N. Further E the pattern of fields was interrupted by the formal avenues of the Duke of Chandos's early C18 estate at Canons, Little Stanmore, between the village of Great Stanmore and the Edgware Road.

Remarkably, the manor house at Headstone still survives with part of its C14 hall, as do parts of Chandos's park, although his great mansion was short-lived. Traces of the old hamlets can still be distinguished, and parts of Harrow Weald are still countryside, with Grimsdyke, a possibly Saxon earthwork, still visible along parts of the northern boundary.*

The heavy overlay of C19 and C20 development is in general less oppressive than elsewhere in outer London. During the C19 the pleasant undulating woodland of Harrow Weald and Stanmore Common became increasingly popular for large houses in their own grounds. Outstanding among the few survivors are Bentley Priory, with additions by *Soane* and flamboyant mid Victorian extensions, and *Norman Shaw*'s Grim's Dyke, Harrow Weald. The railway, the main agent for change, arrived in 1837 at what is now Harrow and Wealdstone station, and industry developed in the neighbourhood. Houses for commuters started a little later; some tentative development at Hatch End followed the station opened in 1844, but the most vigorous activity came after the construction of the Metropolitan line, which arrived at Harrow in 1880 and at Pinner in 1885. The population of the town of Harrow, which had doubled between 1851 and 1881, trebled between 1881 and 1911 to reach 312,217. Much of the development of that time was still on a generous scale: large houses along winding roads on the slopes of the hill, in styles ranging from romantic High Victorian Gothic to gentler Arts and Crafts interpretations of the Queen Anne tradition by the turn of the century. The most accomplished architects of the later phase were *E. S. Prior* and *Arnold Mitchell*, both Harrow residents. Meanwhile the forceful new buildings for Harrow School by *Scott* and *Burges* became the focal points of the town, but the school playing fields ensured that much of the immediate surroundings remained open land.

The flatter farmland between the older hamlets was built up rapidly in the 1920s and 30s, the more imaginative developments making some effort to be in sympathy with the rural image promoted as the Metroland ideal; the fringes of Pinner have some of the more picturesque, if sometimes self-conscious, results. Daring, forward-looking design (as in Kerry Avenue Great Stanmore) was rare. Churches, schools, and the other service buildings which were needed for these fast-expanding communities were sometimes more innovative.

Since 1950 the picture has not altered radically. The post-war pockets of council or low-rent housing at Edgware and South Harrow in blocks of flats or later neat neo-vernacular terraces remain the exception in this land of the semi-detached owner-

*A slight scatter of prehistoric remains is to be found in the borough, particularly on the higher ground, and w of Brockley Hill is a possible Bronze Age barrow. The most important Roman site was near the Roman Watling Street at Brockley Hill (Bn), and at Edgware there were Roman tileworks.

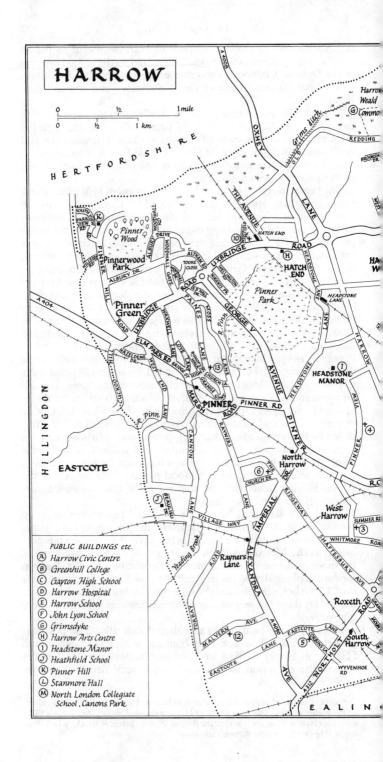

HARROW

0   ½   1 mile

0   ½   1 km

HERTFORDSHIRE

Harrow
Weald
G Common

REDDING

BROOKSH
DR.

Pinner
Wood

SOUTH
PARK
VIEW
RD K

WOODHALL

ALBURY
DRIVE

HILLSIDE
RD

Pinnerwood
Park

ALBURY DR.

Pinner
Green

UXBRIDGE
ROAD

HILL

HAZELDENE
DR.

ELM PARK RD

WEST
END

MARSH

CANNON
LANE

BEAULIEU
DR. J

OXHEY
LANE

Grims
Ditch
Old

THE AVENUE

HATCH END

UXBRIDGE
ROAD

WELLINGTON
RD

TOOKE
CLOSE
ALTHAM

BYRON HILL ROAD

LANE
PAINES

LOVE DRANE

GRANGE
RD

ROAD

PINNER

PINNER RD

RAYNERS

HIGH
ST

BRIDGE ST

CHURCH LA

GRANGE
GDNS

LANE

10

HATCH
END

H

HEADSTONE
LANE

Pinner
Park

R.
Pinn

GEORGE V

AVENUE

HEADSTONE
MANOR

HEADSTONE

AVENUE

PINNER

WEST
HA
W

HA
W

HEADSTONE
LANE

HARROW

PINNER
VIEW

1

4

RC

A 404

A 404

HILLINGDON

EASTCOTE

r. Pinn

13

PINNER

VILLAGE WAY

THE
RIDGEWAY

CHURCH DR.

North
Harrow

6

IMPERIAL

West
Harrow

SUMNER RD

3

WHITMORE ROA

RAYNERS

Yeading Brook

ALEXANDRA

Rayners
Lane

AVENUE

MALVERN
AVE

A 4090

12

EASTCOTE
LANE

SHAFTESBURY AVE

ROXETH

ROAD

GREENHILL
LANE

EASTCOTE LANE
A 312

NORTHOLT

WYVENHOE
RD

Roxeth

South
Harrow

5

AVE

EALING

PUBLIC BUILDINGS etc.

- Ⓐ Harrow Civic Centre
- Ⓑ Greenhill College
- Ⓒ Gayton High School
- Ⓓ Harrow Hospital
- Ⓔ Harrow School
- Ⓕ John Lyon School
- Ⓖ Grimsdyke
- Ⓗ Harrow Arts Centre
- Ⓘ Headstone Manor
- Ⓙ Heathfield School
- Ⓚ Pinner Hill
- Ⓛ Stanmore Hall
- Ⓜ North London Collegiate
  School, Canons Park

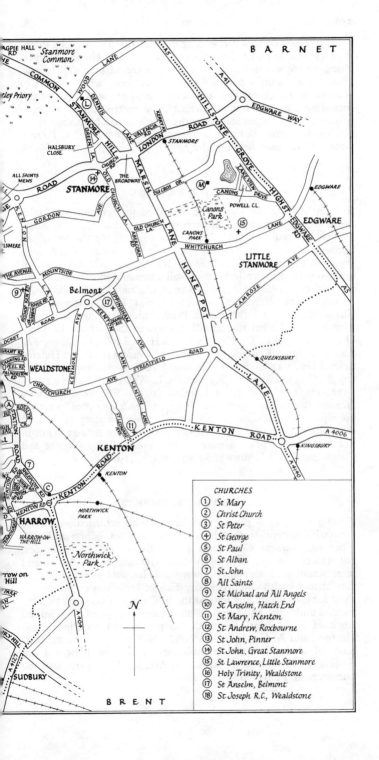

CHURCHES
1. St Mary
2. Christ Church
3. St Peter
4. St George
5. St Paul
6. St Alban
7. St John
8. All Saints
9. St Michael and All Angels
10. St Anselm, Hatch End
11. St Mary, Kenton
12. St Andrew, Roxbourne
13. St John, Pinner
14. St John, Great Stanmore
15. St Lawrence, Little Stanmore
16. Holy Trinity, Wealdstone
17. St Anselm, Belmont
18. St Joseph R.C., Wealdstone

occupier. However, as everywhere in outer London, larger gardens
are increasingly under threat from the developer. The most radical
changes have occurred in the area between Wealdstone and Harrow,
transformed from a poor relation of the more affluent parts of
Harrow to an expanding commercial district, with new offices,
including the large but indifferent civic centre, and a shopping
precinct near Harrow station in the typically brash manner of the
retail-crazy 1980s. Borough architects from 1965: *Geoffrey Foxley;
Stuart J. Murphy; Brian Mills; John H. C. Lamb; Anthony Smith.*

FURTHER READING

Robbins's *Middlesex* should be consulted for references to older
literature. The borough has been well researched recently. Stanmore is covered by V.C.H. *Middlesex*, vol. v (1976), the rest of the
borough by vol. IV (1971). The DoE *List* dates from 1983. Among
the most useful recent publications for the architectural historian
are two fascinating collections of well annotated illustrations, both
assembled by Alan C. Ball: *Paintings, Prints and Drawings of
Harrow on the Hill 1562–1899* (1978) and *The Countryside Lies
Sleeping, 1685–1950* (Paintings, Prints, and Drawings of Pinner,
Stanmore, and other former villages now in the London Borough
of Harrow) (1981). On Canons see C. H. and M. I. C. Baker, *The
Life of . . . James Brydges, First Duke of Chandos* (1949). On Harrow
School see E. D. Laborde, *Harrow School Yesterday and Today*
(1948). On the work of E. S. Prior, see L. Walker, *E. S. Prior 1852–
1932*, Ph.D. University of London (1978). Elizabeth Cooper's
Harrow Walkabout (1973) and *Harrow Strolls and Ambles* (1983)
are well informed short guides; they include the story of the C20
development of the borough, which is covered in greater depth in
her pioneering *Pinner Streets Yesterday and Today* (Pinner and
Hatch End Local Historical Society, vol. v) (1976).

ACKNOWLEDGEMENTS

Among many local people who helped with information we are
especially grateful to the Harrow Local History Librarian R. W.
Thomson, who provided most informative notes and references,
particularly on the work of Arnold Mitchell. R. D. Abbot and
members of the Stanmore, Edgware and Harrow Historical Society
furnished us with comprehensive lists of buildings of interest in
their area. Malcom Airs and Anthony Quiney advised on timber-
framed buildings, and Lynne Walker kindly supplied notes on the
work of E. S. Prior. Elizabeth Cooper helped on Pinner and
Harrow, and A. Goedicke and NADFAS recorders on the contents of churches. On the buildings of Harrow School I am
especially indebted to the archivist, Alasdair Hawkyard, and the
bursar, S. G. Patterson.

BENTLEY PRIORY

BENTLEY PRIORY (R.A.F.), The Common, lies in open country
between Stanmore and Harrow Weald. Inside this picturesque,
externally Victorian mansion (whose name derives from a small
Augustinian priory probably founded in the early c13) are quite
substantial remains of late c18 work by *Soane*. The house built
here by James Duberly, an army contractor who owned the estate
from 1755, was acquired in 1788 by John James Hamilton, first
Marquess of Abercorn, for whom between 1788 and 1798 *Soane*
prepared numerous schemes,* eventually remodelling and
extending the existing house and providing a lavish new reception
wing. A later resident, Queen Adelaide, died here in 1849. Heavy
victorianization after 1852 for Sir John Kelk, the railway engineer
who paid for the Albert Memorial, was followed in 1885 by
conversion to a hotel for Frederick Gordon. From 1902 the
Priory was used by a school, and in 1926 it was acquired by the
R.A.F. (during the Battle of Britain it was the headquarters for
Fighter Command). Much of the interior was restored in virtual
facsimile after a severe fire in 1979.

The swagger Victorian exterior quite successfully unites the
disparate parts: on the r. a tall mid c19 campanile with emphatic
projecting eaves, in the centre the remains of the c18 house, and
on the l. the tallest range, *Soane*'s extension much remodelled.
This is now a substantial nine-bay, three-storey Italianate affair
on a high basement, cement-rendered, with rusticated quoins
and balustraded parapet. The recessed three-bay wings are
Soane's, but the centre was remodelled by Kelk after Soane's
single-storey projecting music room had been removed. Through
an open upper colonnade with pierced screens one can see the
roof of Soane's chief feature, the central rotunda, around which
he grouped main reception rooms of different shapes and sizes.
On the garden side the rotunda is hidden by Soane's drawing
room, against which Kelk built a portico in place of the original
simpler veranda. To the w of this is the lower three-storey range
of the mid c18 house, which has on the garden side giant pilasters
with idosyncratic palmette capitals, perhaps additions by Soane;
on the entrance side it is masked by Soane's projecting hall and
porte-cochère and by a c19 curved screen wall which sweeps
round from the porch, hiding miscellaneous excrescences to the
w (now much rebuilt). A sketch plan of 1827 by C. R. Cockerell
shows a projecting wing of offices here, balancing Soane's music
room, probably part of additions of 1810–18 by *Sir Robert
Smirke*. The bold stencilling on the vault was uncovered in 1991.

The shallow vault of Soane's sober entrance hall springs from 44
eight Greek Doric columns with upper fluting, originally
marbled, now painted white. Apsed niches on either side of the
front door, the one on the r. containing a door now leading to a
corridor to the later additions. One of the two Corinthian aedicules in the inner hall leads to a room on the garden front (inter-

*Drawings survive in the Soane Museum.

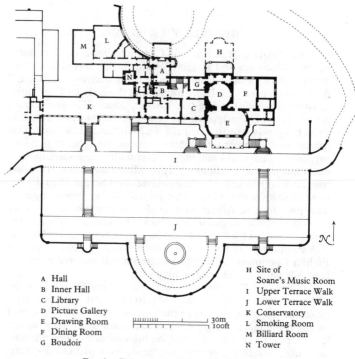

A Hall
B Inner Hall
C Library
D Picture Gallery
E Drawing Room
F Dining Room
G Boudoir

H Site of
   Soane's Music Room
I Upper Terrace Walk
J Lower Terrace Walk
K Conservatory
L Smoking Room
M Billiard Room
N Tower

30m
100ft

Bentley Priory in the later nineteenth century

ior redone after the fire of 1979). Off to the r. an elegant minor
staircase with curved end; to the l., Ionic columns at the entrance
to the staircase hall. All this is by Soane (again, restored after the
fire). His main staircase to the E was enlarged in Victorian times.
It now consists of a sumptuous neo-Renaissance extravaganza of
three stone cantilevered flights leading to an arcaded landing
with a pretty corbelled-out balcony; corpulent carved newels
(originally with lamp standards), and gilded inset panels (originally of cast iron). Soane's again is the vaulted corridor leading
to his tribune, the large central rotunda with partly glazed dome,
designed for the display of pictures and objects of virtu. Simple
wall niches, very tall doorcases, and a marble fireplace. The
cornice decoration looks later. To the s the rotunda opens into a
large drawing room with shallow apses at each end; to the N there
is a delightful Soanic sequence of little lobbies, the corner ones
with two steep domes. The thought devoted to the compact
combination of rooms of different shapes and to the ingenious
lighting of small circulation areas is typical of Soane (cf. Pitshanger Manor Ealing, Ea). The central lobby originally led into
the music room; the others connect with the former dining room
to the E, which has another marble fireplace, and the smaller
room to the w, known as Queen Adelaide's Room, which has an
excellent early Victorian decorated ceiling in Renaissance style
with painted lunettes with scenes of the months.

The large conservatories to the W of the house were replaced by utilitarian post-war blocks for the R.A.F. Of the famous C 19 GARDENS the Victorian terraces to the S remain, with urns and a circular pond with a fountain. Close to the house is a small neo-classical MONUMENT to John James Hamilton † 1808 aged eight. Large parts of the grounds, which formerly extended much further S and include a lake, were acquired by the county council as part of the green belt, and so happily remain open land.

EDGWARE

Edgware was a main-road settlement along Watling Street, the W boundary of the parish of Little Stanmore. The parish church on the E side is outside the borough (*see* Barnet). Road widening has left little of the old village apart from a short stretch on the W side of the HIGH STREET which recalls the pre-C 19 scale of such places. The uneven roof-lines of the row of COTTAGES N of the Whitchurch Lane crossroads suggest a C 17 or earlier date, although the buildings are now much disguised, apart from the exposed timber-framed gable of No. 97. S of Whitchurch Lane, Nos. 65–67 is a low timber-framed former hall house. The main range is probably early C 16 (smoke-blackened roof with lower kingstruts and clasped purlins); there are besides a N cross-wing, a rebuilt S wing, and two low rear extensions. Outliers among the dismal wasteland further S are the WHITE HART, with a battered early C 18 front and timber-framed back wing, and a much altered and restored C 18 brick house within the office development at the N corner of Camrose Avenue.

For Canons Drive and Canons *see* The Stanmores (Hw).

HARROW-ON-THE-HILL

INTRODUCTION

The old hilltop settlement enjoys all the advantages of its situation on a sudden eminence. The High Street runs N up the gentlest ascent to come close to the church, whose spire is as prominent here above the tree-tops as it is from the surrounding country. School and town are inextricable: whereas at Dulwich (Sk) in south London the school, established at much the same time as Harrow, remains quite distinct from the village, here the ambitious C 19 buildings dominate the old centre, still investing it (as Pevsner found in 1952) with a formidably mid-Victorian character of hearty and confident gloom. The school, moreover, has taken over many buildings which once had other uses, so that much of the old town is subservient to it. But at least this has led to the survival – albeit with a hint of nostalgic artifice – of the agreeable country-town character of the High Street and the narrow streets leading off it, with their small shops and pubs; indeed, fate has dealt more kindly with hilltop Harrow than with most of its London cousins, for the old landmarks remain unobscured by large-scale later C20 development. Insulated by playing-fields and other open land acquired by the school, and by spacious late Victorian and Edwardian mansions hidden on the leafy slopes, it is a world away both from the modern shopping centre downhill to the N around the station and from the surrounding sea of Metroland suburbia.

CHURCHES

CHRIST CHURCH, Roxeth Hill. 1862 by *G. G. Scott*; N aisle *c.* 1870. The first new church in the old parish, and still very much a church for a country hamlet rather than a suburb. Prettily set into the slope of the hill away from the road, it is small and flint-faced, with a tiny bell-turret and plate tracery. Separated by a glazed link, a w extension of 1979 by *K. C. White & Partners*, large, yet not obtrusive from the road, is faced with flint edged with white brick above white breeze blocks – a surprisingly successful mixture. Inside, Scott's church has low brick arcades on stone octagonal piers, made to look even lower by the raised floor of the reordering of 1979. Substantial chancel in the correct ecclesiological manner.

ST ALBAN, Church Drive, North Harrow. 1936–7 by *A. W. Kenyon*. Much praised at the time as a bold departure from Gothic traditions. Brown brick, with a fine square NW tower, slightly Swedish in feeling and one of the best of its style in England. The rest of the composition has Early Christian reminiscences: simple white interior with concrete tunnel-vault and narrow aisles. Oddly shaped stepped window-heads. Little altered inside, apart from the removal of the modernistic light fittings. – Two curved AMBONES – an interesting idea.* – Opposite the entrance, STATUE of St Alban by *J. C. Blair*. – CHURCH HALL. 1989 by *Peter Blanfield & Partners*.

ST GEORGE, Pinner View, Headstone. 1911 by *Alder, Turrill & Davies*. Brick with stone dressings. Perp detail. – REREDOS by *J. Crawford*, 1949. – STAINED GLASS. E window by *M. Travers*.

ST JOHN, Sheepcote Road, Greenhill. Begun in 1904 by *J. S. Alder*, replacing a church of 1866. Tall clerestoried nave of stone, in the thin conservative Dec often favoured by this architect. Extended E in 1925 by *Alder & Turrill*; completed in 1938 by a lower chancel and chapel. The intended tower and spire not built. The chancel and its FURNISHINGS and STAINED GLASS are by *Martin Travers*.

ST MARY, Church Hill. Externally the best thing is the general view with the roughcast C12 tower and its tall, handsomely scaled octagonal lead spire. In medieval times the church was one of the most important in Middlesex, a peculiar of the Archbishop of Canterbury. The chancel, and perhaps the nave also, was rebuilt in the C13, when the rector was *Elias de Dereham*, the canon of Salisbury who was deeply involved in some of the most

---

*Much cheapened since (wrote Pevsner in 1952) by the frequent adoption of the same curved effect for shop counters and bars.

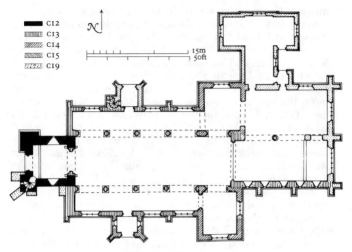

■■■	C12
▨▨▨	C13
▨▨▨	C14
▨▨▨	C15
▨▨▨	C19

Harrow-on-the-Hill, St Mary, plan

remarkable buildings of the time. Timbers for the roof were acquired in 1242. Perp refashioning (windows, clerestory, roof, and upper part of the tower) took place under John Byrkhed, rector from 1437 to 1468. But all this was heavily restored, and the chancel rebuilt, in *G. G. Scott*'s campaign of 1846–9. At the same time a N chapel was added, the N porch rebuilt, and the upper part of the S porch reconstructed. The exterior, apart from the tower, is now uniformly flint-faced. The Norman date of the tower is declared by the small N and S windows with enormous splays inside, and the W doorway with ornament of *c.* 1140: two orders, the inner columns supporting a very slightly segmental lintel decorated with chevron on two faces, with a tympanum now faced with flint. The nave is of four bays plus transept arches; the irregular N transept arch suggests a later rebuilding. Plain double-chamfered pointed arcades on low round piers. Scott's chancel has lancet windows. C15 nave roof, flat-pitched, with cambered tie-beams on curved braces which spring from wall-posts carved with figures of apostles under canopies. The wall-posts in their turn rest on coarse grimacing head-corbels.

FONT. Late C12 Purbeck marble round bowl with ornament developed from scalloped Norman capitals, the shaft with spiral fluting. – PULPIT. Handsome oak of *c.* 1675 (though given to the church in 1708), supported on six scrolled brackets like the legs of contemporary tables. – ORGAN CASE (chancel). 1913 by *Aston Webb.* – STAINED GLASS. In the chancel, lancet windows by *Kempe Studios*, 1901; in the E window, 1908 by *Comper*, individual figures, hardly any red, chiefly white and blue, in contrast to the bold red of the side windows by *Powell, c.* 1850. – Chancel S, 1907 and 1909, and tower, 1908, by *Kempe & Co.* – BRASSES. An excellent series in the chancel floor, especially a small knight in armour of *c.* 1370 (E. Flambard?); John Flambard, late C14, also in armour; John Byrkhed † 1468, priest with saints on the orphreys, the head and most of the architectural canopy

missing; George Aynsworth † 1488, with three wives and fourteen children. – Dorothy Frankishe † 1574. Inscription with palimpsest with head and canopy-work from Flemish brasses of *c*.
1360–70. – The small brass of John Lyon, founder of Harrow
School, † 1592, and his wife, is against a pier of the N arcade. –
MONUMENTS. Directly above the Lyon brass is *Flaxman*'s memorial to Lyon of 1815. The theme is that of the teacher instructing
boys, the interpretation tender and intimate, as in Flaxman's
more famous Warton monument in Winchester Cathedral. The
Lyon monument has a gothicizing top and the gentle classicist
relief goes well with its soft curves (as well as classicism and
romanticism go in Blake's drawings). – Sir Edward Waldo † 1707.
Architectural, with two mourning putti. – Thomas Graham
† 1733. Sarcophagus on brackets against obelisk, by *T. Scheemakers*. – James Edwards, collector and bookseller, † 1816 ('to
his skilful research and liberal spirit of enterprise his country is
indebted for the rarest specimens biblical and classical of the
typographic arts'). Relief above inscription with portrait
medallion, Capo di Monte vase, and books; by *Turnerelli*.
Edwards owned the Bedford Missal. In his will he stipulated that
his coffin should be made out of his library shelves. – J. H. North
† 1831. With allegorical figures weeping over a very odd urn (note
the inscription); by *Hopper*. – Joseph Drury † 1835, 'ludo-
magister' of Harrow School, with two boys standing respectfully
by his bust; by the younger *Westmacott*. – Rev. Henry King
† 1832. Gothic arch with naturalistic foliage. – No older monuments of importance; one to two William Gerards († 1584 and
† 1609), with two figures kneeling opposite each other in profile,
survives in fragments in the N transept. – Picturesque hilltop
CHURCHYARD with a plentiful variety of tombs. – N of the
church, matching flint-faced C19 VESTRIES, and a plain brick
HALL of 1960.

ST PAUL, Corbins Lane, South Harrow. 1937–8 by *N. F.
Cachemaille-Day*. One of his more daring modernist buildings.
The austere tower-cum-chancel sailing above the surburban
roofscape is an arresting sight from the railway. Rendered
exterior, now sadly drab. The blocky shapes, very elongated E
lancets, and rounded turret recall fortress-like Mediterranean
Gothic churches such as Albi, but also the Early Modern
fascination with uncluttered geometric forms. Former main
entrance in the E wall next to the tower, opening into the N aisle
with its plain Gothic arcade – no capitals. Original grid ceiling
over the E end; the coffered nave ceiling was concealed in a
refurbishment of 1964 when the fittings were given cosier
boarded surfaces. – STAINED GLASS (E, N chapel, W baptistery)
in abstract, fairly hard colours, by *Christopher Webb*.

ST PETER, Sumner Road, West Harrow. Now St Peter's Christian
Centre. 1911–13 by *G. H. Fellowes Prynne*. Ragstone, the long
rectangle of nave and chancel given some interest by double-
gabled transepts and buttresses linked by shallow arches above
the Dec windows. A tower was intended. Originally with a fine,
lofty interior. A floor was inserted in all except the W end in the
conversion by *Ian Goldsmid*, 1988–9. The arcade arches die into
hexagonal piers striped in two shades of brown stone; their

bases are panelled. Timber vault over the nave; the aisles with transverse stone arches. Gallery over the N chancel aisle, Lady Chapel beyond, apsed W baptistery. – *Fellowes Prynne* FUR-NISHINGS included the Perp woodwork in the chancel, the STAINED GLASS in Lady Chapel and baptistery (the other windows have plain coloured glass with pretty Arts and Crafts leading), and the Lady Chapel REREDOS of *opus sectile*, made in 1920.

OUR LADY AND ST THOMAS OF CANTERBURY (R.C.), Rox-borough Park. 1894 by *Arthur Young*. Simple roughcast Perp; timber barrel-vault. – STAINED GLASS by *J. E. Nuttgens*.

ST JOHN FISHER (R.C.), Imperial Drive, North Harrow. Mean Romanesque of 1939, in mottled brick. Plain brick arcades; top-lit altar.

BAPTIST CHURCH (former), Byron Hill Road. *See* Perambulation 1.

PUBLIC BUILDINGS

HARROW CIVIC CENTRE. *See* Wealdstone (Hw).

POLICE STATION, West Street. *See* Perambulation 1.

LIBRARY, Gayton Road. 1965 by *Sobielski* of *Middlesex County Council*; a glazed box with free-standing concrete stanchions.

HARROW SCHOOL AND JOHN LYON SCHOOL. *See* Per-ambulation 1.

HARROW COLLEGE OF TECHNOLOGY, Northwick Park. *See* Kenton (Br).

ST DOMINIC'S COLLEGE, Mount Park Avenue. Successor (from 1979) to a convent and school on the same site, founded in 1878, which had occupied Mount Lodge and Bydell House (*see* Perambulation 2). School buildings of 1928 by *Wallace J. Gregory*, extended 1937, and of 1978–80 by *Boris Kaye*, the latter with a forceful grid of timber mullions set in brick walls. Stone CHAPEL by *Arthur Young* of *Young & Reid*, 1921, conservative Perp, with a turret between nave and transept. Reredos flanked by carved panels. The stained glass in the E window is by *Wilfred Hill*. In the grounds a battlemented circular tower with Gothic windows survived until the 1960s.

PURCELL MUSIC SCHOOL, Mount Park Road. *See* Per-ambulation 2.

ORLEY FARM SCHOOL, South Hill Avenue. By *Arnold Mitchell*, 1902, a picturesque combination of favourite Mitchell features: dentilled gables, semicircular window, and a little turret. Exten-sions by *Sheppard Robson & Partners*, 1974.

GREENHILL COLLEGE, Lowlands Road. The centre is a much altered early C19 stuccoed *villa rustica* with a three-storey tower on the garden side, broad bracketed eaves, and tall inset panels as corner decoration. To the w, *M.C.C.* buildings of 1913 for Harrow County Girls' School in a minimal Queen Anne style. To the E, large additions in striped orange and red brick by the *Borough of Harrow*, Controller of Architecture *J. H. C. Lamb*, 1988.

GAYTON HIGH SCHOOL, Gayton Road and Sheepcote Road.

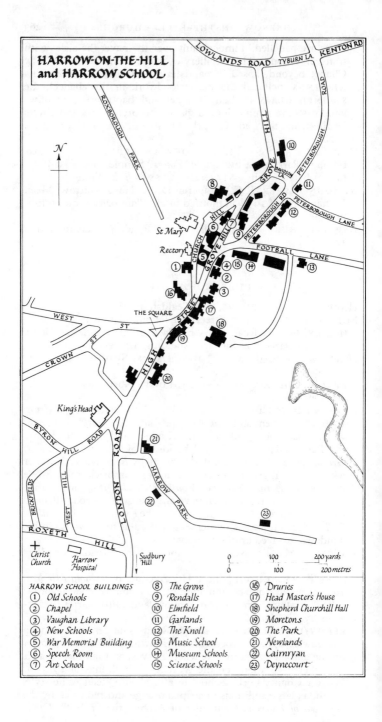

HARROW-ON-THE-HILL
and HARROW SCHOOL

N

LOWLANDS ROAD
TYBURN LA.
KENTON RD
ROXBOROUGH PARK
GROVE HILL
PETERBOROUGH ROAD
DAVIDSON LA.
⑩
⑪
⑧
PETERBOROUGH LANE
St Mary
⑥
⑦
⑫
Rectory
⑨
PETERBOROUGH RD
⑤
FOOTBALL LANE
CHURCH HILL
①
④ ⑮ ⑭
⑬
GROVE HILL
②
⑯
③
WEST ST
THE SQUARE
⑰
⑱
HIGH STREET
⑲
CROWN ST
⑳
King's Head
BYRON HILL ROAD
㉑
LONDON ROAD
WEST HILL
BRUXFIELDS
㉒
HARROW PARK
㉓
ROXETH HILL
✝ Christ Church
Harrow Hospital
Sudbury Hill

| 0 | 100 | 200 yards |
| 0 | 100 | 200 metres |

HARROW SCHOOL BUILDINGS
① Old Schools
② Chapel
③ Vaughan Library
④ New Schools
⑤ War Memorial Building
⑥ Speech Room
⑦ Art School
⑧ The Grove
⑨ Rendalls
⑩ Elmfield
⑪ Garlands
⑫ The Knoll
⑬ Music School
⑭ Museum Schools
⑮ Science Schools
⑯ Druries
⑰ Head Master's House
⑱ Shepherd Churchill Hall
⑲ Moretons
⑳ The Park
㉑ Newlands
㉒ Cairnryan
㉓ Deynecourt

Built by *H. G. Crothall* of the *M.C.C.* as the County Boys' School, 1910. Mannered Baroque in two colours of brick, the grand corner entrance with a semicircular porch with blocked Ionic columns between two turrets. Angled wings with curved dormers between stone pilasters. s extension of the 1930s.

ROXETH FIRST AND MIDDLE SCHOOLS, Roxeth Hill. A pretty Gothic group built for the National Society by *Habershon* in 1851 and 1854. Steep patterned-tile roof, bell-turret beside a gable, fancy cusped tracery.

WELLDON PARK SCHOOLS, Wyvenhoe Road. FIRST SCHOOL by *Stillman & Eastwick-Field* and the *Borough of Harrow*, 1976. Pale brick with pitched roofs. Two-storeyed centre with lower wings projecting from the hall; open-plan teaching areas. MIDDLE SCHOOL of 1911.

HARROW HOSPITAL, Roxeth Hill. 1905–6 by *Arnold Mitchell*, a lively design in a homely free Baroque, just right for a cottage hospital. Striped quoins of red and yellow stone, the rest purple brick. Baroque doorway; inset bowed windows to the ground floor. Later additions behind.

CLEMENTINE CHURCHILL HOSPITAL, Sudbury Hill. A sleek, low private hospital in part of the grounds of a former convent (*see* Perambulation 2). 1987–8 by *A.M.I.* Two storeys. Streamlined clinical exterior; white bands on a brick base.

HARROW-ON-THE-HILL STATION. A Metropolitan line station rebuilt in 1938–43 in plain brick.

SOUTH HARROW STATION. Opened for the Metropolitan District line in 1903. The present station for the Piccadilly line, 1935 by *Stanley A. Heaps* with *Charles Holden*, is a little more mannered than some of the earlier Piccadilly line stations.

BUS STATION, College Road. By *A. R. Clayton Welch*, 1975, well organized, with glazed doors opening to recessed bus bays, and cheerful red-painted fittings.

PERAMBULATIONS

1. Harrow School and the old town centre

HARROW SCHOOL. John Lyon's foundation charter dates from 1572. He died in 1592, leaving money for a building that was finally erected in 1608–15 and is now the w part of the Old Schools on the slope above Church Hill. By the time of the Restoration the headmaster no longer lived in the school, and during the late C17 and C18 boarding houses were established in the town. No additional premises went up until 1819–21, when *C. R. Cockerell* doubled the size of John Lyon's building, going on in 1838–9 to add a chapel (boys and masters had hitherto worshipped in the parish church). This chapel made way in 1854–7 for a grander building by *G. G. Scott*, for by then, under the headship of Dr Charles Vaughan (1844–59), the school's numbers had swelled from less than a hundred to 466. At the same time, in 1855, the New Schools went up, to the design of *F. Barnes*. H. M. Butler, as headmaster from 1860 to 1885, oversaw the building of the Vaughan Library (1861–3 by *Scott*), the Speech Room (1874–7 by *Burges*), and the Science Schools (1874). All this time boarding houses were being built. Later, a wider curriculum called for the Butler Museum and Museum Schools (1886 by *Champneys*), the new Music Schools (1891 by *E. S. Prior*, to replace the old Music School of 1873), and the Art School (1895 by *W. C. Marshall*). The major buildings are on both sides of the High Street, around the junction with Church Hill and Grove Hill. In the early C20 the character of the group was altered by the War Memorial Building of 1921–6 by *Sir Herbert Baker* and the steps and terraces of 1929 which provide a formal approach to Old Schools. Recent additions include the dining hall by *Dennis Lennon & Partners*, discreetly tucked away downhill to the sw, and the craft design and technology buildings some way N in Grove Hill.

OLD SCHOOLS. A picturesque little building to the w of the High Street, with its two projecting s-facing wings with tall Tudor oriels and crowstepped gables, a triple arch lying far back between them, and a small cupola on top. All the exterior features (except on the w side) date from 1819–21, when *Cockerell* enlarged and embellished the original school of 1608–15. It formerly faced E towards Church Hill, a plain, compact brick block with straight gables, two and a half storeys high and five bays wide, with the conservative Tudor details typical of schools of this date. The single schoolroom lay below rooms for master, usher, and governors.* The schoolroom (later the fourth form room), 18 by 7 metres, is still mid C17 inside, with the headmaster's hooded throne at the N end, and the boys' low narrow forms lining the long sides of the room. Heavily inscribed fielded panelling on the lower walls; large fireplace of the 1730s with voluted brackets. The governors' room above has panelling of 1661–2. *Cockerell*'s wing provided a library, together with a speech room (now the Old Speech Room Gallery) which has a neatly inserted mezzanine and plain glass balcony by *Alan Irvine*, 1976. Sculptures include Spencer Perceval by *J. Nollekens*, 1813; R. B. Sheridan, attributed to *Nollekens*; Byron by *E. H. Baily*, 1826; and Cardinal Manning by *B. Gotto*, 1928.

CHAPEL, across the road from the Old Schools. 1854–7 by *Scott*, the gift of Dr Vaughan, and the school's first uncompromisingly Gothic building. Flint with stone dressings: large and serious, and somewhat reminiscent of Scott's contemporary chapel for Exeter College Oxford. w front with two different gables; apsidal E end; spirelet added in 1865. Inside, the nave has a wide s (Crimea War Memorial) aisle and a narrower N aisle, circular piers, and an open timber roof. The transepts were added in 1902–3 by *Sir Aston Webb*. Around most walls run thick blank E.E. arcades of polished marble, with memorial tablets, added in 1868. – REREDOS and wall panels of *opus sectile* in alabaster frames by *Sir Arthur Blomfield*, 1899, with memorial tablet to Dr Vaughan by *E. Onslow Ford*. – STALL CANOPIES. 1882 by *J. O. Scott*. – Marble PAVING of 1903–20 and ORGAN CASE of 1921, both by *Sir Charles Nicholson*. – Much STAINED GLASS.

*An alternative but rejected plan drawn by 'Old' *Sly*, 'the Surveyor' shows a different arrangement, with a schoolroom projecting between master's and usher's rooms.

Chancel 1857–61, small scenes, by *Wailes*, 'bleached' by *A. K. Nicholson*, who was also responsible for the w windows, except for the one over the inner entrance, which is by *Hardman*, 1858 (behind the organ). – N aisle windows later c 19 by *Clayton & Bell*: large figures of educational founders, ending with John Lyon and his wife; charming vignettes of their foundations below. – s aisle by *A. Lusson* of Paris. – MONUMENTS. In the N aisle, Christopher Wordsworth by *Alfred Gilbert*, 1890–1. – In the N and s transepts, South African War Memorial, two tablets flanked by bronze figures by *Alfred Drury*.★ – The CRYPT was converted to a memorial chapel in 1918 by *Sir Charles Nicholson*.

VAUGHAN LIBRARY, s of the chapel. 1861–3 by *Scott*. A symmetrical Ruskinian Gothic design. Red brick, with those patterns of vitrified blue and yellow brick which were to become so typical of Victorian Harrow, and seem here to appear for the first time. Patterned roof as well. A path paved with encaustic tiles leads to a centrally placed entrance in a deep porch with polished pink and grey marble columns and naturalistically carved capitals. Inside is a bay-window (with a splendid view) in line with the entrance. Stained glass by *J. Bell*, 1883, 1885.

NEW SCHOOLS, N of the chapel. 1855 by *Frederick Barnes* of Ipswich. Built as six form-rooms on three floors; gabled Tudor. N wing 1924.

WAR MEMORIAL BUILDING. By *Sir Herbert Baker*, begun in 1921. Much smoother and more civilized than the Victorian buildings, it takes its style from its surroundings, leaving out all the trimmings, and adding some Baroque detail. The once-controversial terrace with its spectacular stairs is now one of the key effects of the town. Inside, all is bare stone domes and distinguished-looking dark woodwork, the very style which would appeal to wealth and nobility about 1930. The Alexander Fitch Room has Elizabethan fittings from Brooke House, Hackney. Fluted pilasters with panels between paired arches, bracketed cornice. Stone fireplace with four-centred arch; busts below capitals, strapwork and arms. Much sculpture in the Glyptotheca; among numerous busts, Sidney Herbert by *Foley*, 1865; Lord Palmerston by *R. Jackson*, 1870; Bishop Perry by *G. Summers*, 1876; Winston Churchill, a very large bronze head, by *Clare Sheridan*, 1942. On the staircase Sir Robert Peel by *M. Noble*, 1850. In the central hall the 4th Earl of Aberdeen by *W. Theed*, and Stanley Baldwin and Archbishop Davidson, two bronze busts by *Newberry A. Trent*, given in 1927.

SPEECH ROOM. *William Burges* was almost certainly recommended as architect for this ambitious tercentenary project by his friend and patron, the 3rd Marquess of Bute, an ex-pupil at the school. Executed in 1874–7, it follows only partially the original published design of 1872 in Sicilian Gothic; the two forceful corner towers were omitted, and instead the dominating feature was a flat front with polychromatic arcades on ground and first floor, and plate tracery windows elsewhere. The asymmetrical tower at the N end was finally added in 1919 by *Sir*

★Richard Dorment suggests that the figures of St George and St Michael are rejected designs by *Gilbert* from the Duke of Clarence's tomb in the Albert Memorial Chapel, Windsor Castle.

Charles Nicholson, faithfully realizing Burges's intentions. The s one was designed by *Sir Herbert Baker* in 1926 to complement the War Memorial Building; against it, a statue of Queen Elizabeth by *Sir Richard Westmacott*, brought from Ashridge Park in Hertfordshire and given in 1925. The back of the building is semicircular (in the manner of the Sheldonian Theatre at Oxford). The classical tradition of the plan mixes oddly with the Gothic detail. Burges died before he could formulate his lavish scheme of interior decoration, with Moorish ceiling and painted walls somewhat in the manner of Cardiff Castle; instead there is only the strangely jarring contrast of the thin paired columns of the hemicycle, and the thicker columns of the proscenium (the stained glass behind it is by *J. C. Bell*). The decoration of the proscenium vault is by *Sir Charles Nicholson*, 1926.

ART SCHOOLS, N of the Speech Room. The older part is by *W. C. Marshall*, 1891, the mezzanine floor of 1987. Low extension by *S. Pointon Taylor*, 1913; in the E wall stone medallions of Hogarth and Reynolds, 1919.

Nearby are some of the earliest BOARDING HOUSES. At first the school took over existing houses, such as THE GROVE, formerly the rectory and manor house, between the church and GROVE HILL. It is of the C18, much rebuilt after a fire in 1830 and altered since. Seven-bay rendered front with projecting centre; much added to behind. The LEAF SCHOOLS closer to the road, of 1936 by *A. L. N. Russell*, re-use some old brickwork from the stables of The Grove. The first floor was added in the early 1960s. To the E, opposite the Art Schools, RENDALLS of 1853 was the first purpose-built boarding house, an honest utilitarian structure by *Barnes*, red brick, with straight-headed windows with hoodmoulds. Refurbished, with top-floor addition and new roof, in 1989. THE FOSS of 1854 and GROVE HILL of 1859 by *E. Habershon* are still quite plain, brick with Tudor diaper and stepped gables. Further N is ELMFIELD, an earlier C19 house taken over by the school, whose taller addition of 1893 introduces us to the late Victorian Harrow style of Norman Shaw derivation. Down Davidson Lane to PETERBOROUGH ROAD, where GARLANDS of 1863 and THE KNOLL (now No. 35) of 1867, both by *C. F. Hayward*, brother of a housemaster, show the overwhelmingly assertive public school style of the mid Victorian years at its most concentrated: the houses are characterized not only by their towering height, quite out of keeping with the tradition of the town, but by their decoration of purple brick with bands or diapers in vitrified blue brick or yellow brick. Garlands has some stone E.E. detail and glazed tiles, No. 35 a more playful timber porch and little stair-turret. They form picturesque asymmetrical compositions. Garlands no longer belongs to the school, and was converted in 1987 to flats, with extensive but not too unsympathetic tall gabled additions stepping down the slope. No. 35 has later parts connecting it with HILLSIDE of 1870.

CHURCHILL SCHOOLS, Station Road. 1987 by *Kenneth W. Reed & Associates*. Craft, design, and technology workshops neatly tucked into the slope of the hill, a crisp design with roof-lights and glazed corners.

Further s, at the corner with FOOTBALL LANE, the OLD MUSIC SCHOOL of 1873 (now Resources Centre), as small as a wayside chapel. Nearby THE KNOLL, a new boarding house by *Dennis Lennon & Partners*, 1980. At the foot of the lane is the NEW MUSIC SCHOOL of 1890–1 by *E. S. Prior*, a remarkable contrast in style to its predecessor, illustrating the growth of the school within one generation. The best frontage faces E, a large canted bay with Venetian windows. The double-height barrel-vaulted hall is boldly expressed at the W end by a shallow gable (considered ugly by contemporaries). It is flanked by two towers at the end of the corridors separating the hall from the practice rooms at the sides. The plain SWIMMING POOL and SPORTS HALL are of 1984 by *J. T. Design Build*. Then from E to W the unassuming MATHEMATICS AND PHYSICS SCHOOLS, one and two storeys, with slated pyramid roofs, 1971, and the tall MUSEUM SCHOOLS, 1884–6 by *Basil Champneys*, in a spirited 71 Shavian style, the first of the Harrow school buildings to depart from the seriousness of High Victorian Gothic. The Butler Museum (now careers centre) on the top floor enjoys magnificent views from its balcony and little corbelled-out oriels; it is approached by a French-château-like open staircase on the s side. With the low SCIENCE SCHOOLS by *Hayward*, 1874, extended 1913, 1930–1, one returns to the main buildings.

Now to the s. On the w side of the HIGH STREET is DRURIES, 1864 by *Hayward*, again in his characteristic robust style: purple brick with blue headers, and a composition as if it were a spa hotel at Harrogate or some such place. Opposite is the HEAD-MASTER'S HOUSE, 1840 by *Decimus Burton*, enlarged by him in 1845–6; quite plain, with lighter brickwork and straight-headed windows with hoodmoulds, but also a stucco porch and Jacobean gables. It replaced a house destroyed by fire in 1838. Attached to it is another Harrovian Gothic turreted structure of Hayward style, dated 1866. These buildings flank the start of the High Street and the town proper, where other buildings intermingle with those used by the school. Behind those on the E side, down a slope, is the SHEPHERD CHURCHILL DINING HALL, by *Dennis Lennon & Partners*, 1976, approached formally by a flight of steps flanked by small lodges, leading down to a garden with pool and pergolas. Discreetly traditional brick exterior, with a big pitched roof with central clock-turret. Separate masters' and boys' dining areas, the latter made more interesting by being split up by brick piers into house units. The masters' room was extended in 1989 after a fire. Balconies and a big canted bay overlook the garden; the services are tucked in neatly beneath. Further down the slope, PEEL HOUSE, 1981 by *Edginton Spink & Hyne*, reticent, with hipped roof.

The houses of the High Street are delightfully various: Nos. 3–7 cool elegant Regency, then projecting tile-hung gables, then plain C18 brick. More boarding houses follow: THE MORETONS, Georgian private houses mainly rebuilt in 1828, with additions of after 1870 and 1881, then FLAMBARDS, late C18. The name Flambards previously belonged to the predecessor to THE PARK, a more substantial house, set back from the road, which was formerly approached from the E by a long drive from

Sudbury Hill. The grounds were landscaped in 1768–71 by *Capability Brown* for Francis Herne. The house was remodelled in 1797–8 by *John Nash* for Richard Page, a school governor; unfinished at his death in 1803, further work was carried out by *John Shaw* for Lord Northwick in 1806–7. It was used as a school boarding house from 1831. The late C18 stuccoed E front with Diocletian window between two full-height canted bays is still recognizable, although much enlarged by N and S wings. The *Coade* stone lion in low relief now on the S wing dates from the 1806–7 campaign. It was formerly above the E doorway. S entrance hall with four Greek Doric columns. On the W side of the High Street, BRADBYS, another boarding house, of 1848, enlarged in 1853, 1901, and 1986; brick, of five bays, with a Tuscan porch.

THE SQUARE at the top of the hill (in reality an irregular triangle) is disappointing. On the W side the KING'S HEAD, established in 1533, but in appearance indifferent late Georgian and Victorian stuccoed. At the S corner the modest former council offices of 1913 by *H. Price*, in a dignified late C17 style, flanked by a Jacobean bank of 1883 and former fire station of 1888. N and W from here one can still follow the net of streets of old Harrow, with small straight or curved lanes leading downhill to Crown Street and West Street, with their humble cottages, small shops, and C19 amenities for the local populace. In WEST STREET the former PARISH MISSION ROOM, 1884–5 by *E. S. Prior*, with shaped gable and terracotta trim (now SRM PLASTICS); also the OLD PIE HOUSE, a C15 timber structure faced with red brick, and the POLICE STATION of 1873 by *F. Caiger*.* CROWN STREET leads S to MIDDLE ROAD; here JOHN LYON SCHOOL dominates. It was established to serve the local needs no longer fulfilled by the older foundation. On the N side the original building of 1876 by *H. M. Burton*, plain brick and stone Tudor of 1876. Inter-war additions, slightly neo-Georgian; later, plainer buildings in dark brick by *Sheppard Robson & Partners*, 1973, 1981, 1989. The school also occupies the RED HOUSE opposite. Its substantial back addition is of 1883–5 by *E. S. Prior* for his brother John T. Prior. Half-timbered gable, a big chimneystack, and Ipswich windows, in contrast to the regular Georgian three-bay front. Further on the delightful Nos. 60–66 of 1887, also by *Prior*, a family venture in speculative building, a row of highly picturesque cottages with quirky porches and tilehanging alternating with roughcast. The plain earlier C19 cottages and villas further down the hill underline how much this vernacular revival was a conscious reaction against the immediate past. Back E towards the High Street up BYRON HILL ROAD past No. 40, a pleasant, plain, three-bay Regency villa, and the former BAPTIST CHURCH, plain stock brick Gothic of 1862 and 1872. Opposite, BYRON HILL HOUSE, with a tall S-facing Georgian front. The *Prior* extensions of 1887 (for J. T. Prior) have been truncated and are now surrounded by new development.

---

*At the time of writing, Harrow School has proposals for a development behind West Street, with a theatre and twenty houses, by *Kenneth W. Reed & Associates*.

2. To S and E

Along London Road and Sudbury Hill, the continuation of the High Street, a nicely varied miscellany of Victorian villas. The best group in LONDON ROAD starts with the low Gothick TOLLGATE COTTAGE. Then THE GERARDS, early Victorian crowstep-gabled Tudor villas, LINCOLN HOUSE, Italianate, and HIGHLANDS, mid C19, with a central Doric porch and bracketed eaves. Further on, after a stuccoed group close to the road, the low LITTLE HOUSE and THE HERMITAGE, gabled, with decorative bargeboards. SUDBURY HILL continues with more Victorian houses, starting with MARSTON LODGE with its curious half-domed porch with fanlight. On the w side buildings are more scattered: MOUNT LODGE, diapered with decorative bargeboards, at the start of Mount Park Avenue (*see* below); BYDELL HOUSE, large and Italianate early C19 with later top storey; ARMSTRONGS, a former coach house; then, further down at the bend in the road, THE ORCHARD, inscribed 'domus Mitchellorum aedificat AD MDCCCC Arnoldus'. This was the second home *Arnold Mitchell* built for himself in Harrow (cf. Grove Hill, Perambulation 3) and it displays to the full his skill in creating a snug Arts and Crafts house on a tight site. Large roof tiles sweeping down to broad projecting eaves, red chimneys, buff tilehanging. The house is L-shaped on the road side, hugging two sides of a tiny courtyard entered through a lunette-archway. Stone-mullioned bowed window beside the doorway, larger square bays on the garden side. Ironwork by the *Bromsgrove Guild* (the gate a copy of the original, moved by Mitchell to Lyme Regis when he retired). A little further on a tall Victorian pair, KINGSGATE and QUEENSGATE, by *Carpenter & Ingelow*, 1886. The low WHITE COTTAGE follows, built for a musician, Arnold Bussweiler, in 1908 by *Baillie Scott* in his typical roughcast vernacular manner, with asymmetrically grouped gables.

Across the road to the E, set back in the grounds of the former convent of the Little Company of Mary, is a former CHAPEL of 1905–6 by *Giles Gilbert Scott*, incorporating details (roofs, doorways, and windows) from its predecessor of 1901–2 by *Thomas Garner*. Late Gothic detail; red brick striped with stone. The main elevation is to the s, an unusual and striking composition, with windows high up between buttresses with stone-capped set-offs, and a low projection with s-facing gable balancing the gabled w bell-turret. E gable with Crucifixion. The older convent buildings attached have been replaced by CHASE-WOOD PARK, a large, free-standing block of flats, flamboyantly designed in a post-modern idiom, with shallow pitched roofs and plenty of balconies to break up the six-storey elevation. 1987–8 by *Phippen, Randall & Parkes*.

E and W of Sudbury Hill, off secluded lanes, are the wealthier C19 and early C20 houses. Taking them clockwise, the start is HARROW PARK to the E, where a few large houses appear between the shrubberies. First NEWLANDS, built as a boarding house for Harrow School in 1889 by *W. C. Marshall*, brother of a housemaster, tall and gaunt; then CAIRNRYAN, 1883 by *J. T.*

Walford for David Brown, in a curiously exotic Swiss-chalet style
(although less elaborate than its original design illustrated in the
Builder). DEYNECOURT of 1870 is a spare but stately Italianate
palazzo in hard red brick with terracotta trim. Triple-arched
porte-cochère, shallow bow, and pretty balcony to catch the
distant views N. Opposite, among trees, the ruinous remains of
a Gothick FOLLY which stood in the grounds of the Park (q.v.,
above). Further S, opposite The Orchard, the leafy JULIAN
HILL leads to the house of the same name built for Anthony
Trollope's father in 1817: two storeys, stock brick, with two bow-
windows to the S; lower entrance wing of 1910. Further on,
JULIAN WAY (formerly Julian Cottage) of *c*. 1905 by *Arnold
Mitchell*, with his characteristically picturesque details: tilehung
gables glimpsed through a semicircular entrance archway.

W of Sudbury Hill there was more consistent development, with
two select estates laid out from the later C19. SOUTH HILL
AVENUE starts with GOODEN COTTAGE, a lodge of 1883 by
Higgs & Rudkin, red brick with tilehanging. Further on are
semi-detached pairs of the 1880s, the style changing with the
bargeboarded RED LODGE and WESTLANDS of 1896, and the
half-timbered SOUTH HILL LODGE of 1903. Some way on,
near Orley Farm School (*see* Public Buildings), is the part of the
estate developed in the early C20. It was planned on garden
suburb principles by *S. Pointon-Taylor* in consultation with
Raymond Unwin, preserving plenty of old trees and setting to
work a variety of architects. LEAFLANDS and COLLINGWOOD
are two detached houses by *Ferdinand Good*, 1911. Smaller
houses of the 1920s follow, among them DUNSMORE by *A. P.
Starkey* for himself, 1928; POPLAR COTTAGE by *Pointon-
Taylor*, 1928; and MEADOWSIDE and ROSEMEAD, a pair
prettily decorated with pargetting. Near the end several houses
of 1911 by *Pointon-Taylor*, including HERON'S GHYLL and THE
COTTAGE, 1911, close to the tollgate which still marks the
boundary of the estate.

Further up the hill (reached from beyond the gate by Mount Park
Road, or from Sudbury Hill by Mount Park Avenue) is the
MOUNT PARK ESTATE, where 'sites for residences that cannot
be surpassed in any of the southern counties' were being advertised already in 1879. The best group is in MOUNT PARK ROAD.
From W to E, first OAKHURST (Purcell School), in large grounds,
with additions by *A. Mitchell* of 1895 (plans for additions by
Edward Cullinan & Partners under discussion in 1990). Then
the arresting former billiard room added to BERMUDA HOUSE
in 1889 by *E. S. Prior*. It was converted to a separate house in
1985, with new front door on the E side. It is on a shallow Greek
cross plan with an extraordinary faceted tiled roof of twelve sides
with tall polygonal lantern. The two projecting N and S arms each
have a single large window with small panes of glass. The roof
covers a Byzantine-inspired dome on pendentives. Prior also
designed the built-in furniture. The house itself has been
replaced by flats. Then CARLYON, 1884, and opposite ST MAR-
GARET'S, 1895 by *Arnold Mitchell* for Andrew Devitt, a relation
of Mitchell's wife, a substantial house, charmingly detailed, with
tilehanging, canted bays, and gabled wings. (Well preserved

interior with good woodwork.) Chunky dovecote-cum-cupola above an outbuilding. THE OAKS is by *Robert A. Briggs*, 1893, eclectic Old English, with Renaissance stone porch. EGERTON opposite, by *Higgs & Rudkin*, is dated 1884, with a huge, rather French-looking wooden gable, and half-timbering and tall brick chimneys in a Shavian manner. Further N St Dominic's College (*see* Public Buildings). Along MOUNT PARK AVENUE were Harrovian Gothic houses of the 1870s; the only survivors are BELMONT (emasculated by whitewash) and the still very atmospheric THORNLEA, 1871 by *Hayward*, tall, with much diapering. Elsewhere the pines now shelter prim neo-Georgian villas of the 1970s-80s.

ROXETH, W of London Road, began as a separate hamlet, for which a church and school were supplied in the mid C19 in ROXETH HILL (*see* Christ Church and Public Buildings). The former vicarage, now a nurses' home and much altered, is by *George & Peto*, 1884-6. The remains of the older settlement along NORTHOLT ROAD have been replaced by a scrappy muddle of offices as one approaches South Harrow station. The only older building of note is the BRITISH LEGION HEADQUARTERS, 1928 by *S. Pointon Taylor*, with shaped gable to the road. Much housing by *Harrow Architect's Department*: on the w side, GRANGE FARM, completed 1968, built on an industrialized system; three-storey cream-painted flats, with some landscape interest provided by low brick screen walls. On the E side more miscellaneous development replacing C19 artisan housing, the later parts to the N with the hard brick surfaces of 1970s neo-vernacular. Hidden within this, in HORNBUCKLE CLOSE off Grange Road, is *E. S. Prior*'s admirable building for the former HARROW SCHOOL LAUNDRY, 1887-8, the superintendent's house with workers' dining hall below. The N front is most inventive: a large mansard roof, corbelled-out dormers, and tall chimneys in between. If only it could have inspired the pathetically crude detail of the surrounding buildings. Further N in BESSBOROUGH ROAD, on the edge of playing fields and so still with a rural air, is ROXETH FARMHOUSE, an appealing early C18 front, weatherboarded, with five sash-windows; one later bay to the S.

3. *The northern slopes*

On the northern slopes of Harrow Hill, in Grove Hill and Peterborough Road, is an interesting group built after the w part of the Northwick estate was sold in 1889. If the earlier perambulations have been followed, *Arnold Mitchell*'s distinctive 'artistic' style will by now be easily recognized. Here he demonstrates how small, carefully planned houses can appear highly picturesque through the skilful use of varied materials and textures inspired by the vernacular tradition of the home counties – a warm red brick mixed with tilehanging, roughcast, and half-timbering or weatherboarding. The first house to be built, and also the first house that Mitchell built for himself in Harrow, was WHITE TOPS in GROVE HILL (formerly Grove Hill Cottage),

1891–3, still attractive, although altered: the s wing is an addition, the white boarded gables were formerly half-timbered, and the strikingly placed chimney over the porch has gone. To its N THE GABLES, 1892 for the artistic Kirkpatrick family, roughcast over brick, with two half-timbered gables. (Good original features inside.) Set back, added as a studio for them in 1895, GROVE HILL COTTAGE, not by Mitchell but by *R. A. Briggs*. The rest are all by *Mitchell*. THE HAVEN, 1894, has roughcast gables and mullioned Ipswich windows, irregularly set. At the corner, GROVE END, with a steep dentilled double gable, also 1894, with additions of 1919, when Mitchell lived there. He added the smaller GROVE END COTTAGE in 1920. The close-set brick group in PETERBOROUGH ROAD is more urban, and reads happily as a single informal composition of the type that grows by chance in an older town. CHALGROVE of 1893, and FAR-THINGS, also of 1893, enlarged in 1914, both have inventively varied fenestration; HEATHFIELD (formerly ST KEVERNE), 1892, enlarged in 1987, has pretty tilehanging over a round-arched entrance.

4. Central Harrow

The commercial centre lies N of the hill and directly N of the station, in the area known as GREENHILL. The only notable older build-ing is the NATIONAL WESTMINSTER BANK by *Banister Flet-cher*, 1915, at the corner of STATION ROAD and St Ann's Road, a confident classical display, entirely in brick, including even the blocked three-quarter columns. Further E, in SHEEPCOTE ROAD, the CANNON CINEMA (former Granada), 1937 by *J. Owen Bond*, with an interesting interior by *T. Komisarjevsky* in classical vein, very complete, a curious contrast to his Gothic frivolities at Tooting (Ww) and Woolwich (Gr). The first large post-war buildings loom up further E in LYON ROAD, part of the 1960s drive for out-of-town offices: three blocks of seven and five storeys, on stilts, all with the same drab grey bands and slate-coloured spandrels. 1965 by *Morgan & Branch*.

The consumer-boom developments of the 1970s–80s lie further W, on both sides of the pedestrianized ST ANN'S ROAD, displaying colourful frontages with plenty of tricky post-modern brick detailing. The most spectacular is ST ANN'S, 1986–7 by *Bernard Engle & Partners*, with a covered shopping mall by *David Davies Associates*. The mall leads to a pleasantly light and airy central atrium. The grander front of this development lies to the s, where the central entrance and stair-tower, with emphatic blue frames to the glazing, are flanked by tall, symmetrically composed ranges of brick with stone trimmings. That they contain car parks is less than usually obvious by virtue of the variation in size of the openings. Further W the slightly earlier QUEENS HOUSE, an eight-storey curtain-walled slab, also incorporates car parks, but with less panache.

N of Queens Road FIRST NATIONAL HOUSE, 1978–81 by *G.M.W. Partnership*, five storeys over a podium with shops along a covered way to the station. Polygonal, faced with orange brick, with long recessed window bands turning the corners. Further w, in BESSBOROUGH ROAD, the less obtrusive CUNNINGHAM HOUSE, 1975 by *Green, Lloyd & Adams* for the Harrow Building Society, two storeys, dark brick. s of the railway, in LOWLANDS ROAD, SHERIDAN HOUSE, 1989 by *G.M.W. Partnership*, offices with crisp glazing and polychrome brickwork.

HARROW WEALD

The old hamlets of the Harrow Weald are recalled today only by a few farmhouses and cottages. Of its woods considerable tracts survive in the form of the grounds of the large private houses mostly built after 1850 and themselves sadly depleted over the last thirty years:* Grim's Dyke is their most important survivor.

ALL SAINTS, Uxbridge Road. Mostly by *William Butterfield*, who in 1845 added nave and aisles to a simple stone chancel of 1842 by *J. T. Harrison*, and then in 1889–92 widened the N aisle and built the SW tower. Stone exterior, the tower with tiled, half-hipped roof – a form Butterfield used more often for his secular buildings. Inside, the plain nave walls, of brick roughcast, contrast with the decoration added in the 1890s: lively foliage scrolls on the nave roof, and around the chancel arch mosaic patterning in the pale colours typical of Butterfield's late style. The widened N aisle is roofed transversely. – Butterfield's FURNISHINGS include the FONT of the 1840s and, of the 1890s, the PULPIT and COMMUNION RAILS, of wood, and the chancel TILES. – The WEST GALLERY dates from the 1960s. – Much STAINED GLASS. Chancel S: two lancets by *Kempe*, 1900. – N aisle E: good C19 glass in the Clayton & Bell tradition. – N aisle: by *Heaton, Butler & Bayne*, c. 1890, in pale colours matching Butterfield's decoration. – The outstanding window is in the S aisle: three lights by *Morris & Co.*, 1883, with pale, delicately drawn figures of Faith and Hope (designed by *Dearle*) and Charity (designed by *Burman*), with a flowery background (by *Stokes*). – S aisle w: 1961 by *Whitefriars Studios*, in deep, rather strident colours. – MONUMENT. W. S. Gilbert † 1911 by *B. Mackenna*. Two mourning figures; gilded reliefs and profile. – In the churchyard an elaborate LYCHGATE and two typically Victorian TOMBS to the Cross and Blackwell families (1862 and 1870 etc.), the first like a fragment of a church roof, the second with a glossy sarcophagus.

ST MICHAEL AND ALL ANGELS, Bishop Ken Road. The long, meanly detailed neo-Romanesque hall of 1935 is off-putting, the church attached at the s end, 1958 by *Thomas F. Ford*, more interesting. Vigorously carved figure of St Michael over the entrance by *David Paul Konigsburger*. Spacious interior in an odd eclectic neo-Regency: twin columns with palm-leaf capitals; internal transepts marked by shallow lunette windows; gently apsed E end. – Large, bold apse PAINTING of St Michael and

*Demolished since the first edition of this book: Woodlands, Clamp Hill; The Hall, Brookshill; Harrow Weald Park, Brookshill; Hanworth House and The Cedars, Uxbridge Road.

angels and painted lunettes of the evangelists on either side by *Hans Feibusch*.

PERAMBULATION. Close to All Saints church, ALL SAINTS MEWS, a well grouped cluster of houses by *Melvin Lansley & Mark*, 1987. In UXBRIDGE ROAD the best house is No. 92, HARROW WEALD HOUSE, just W of the church. C18: five-bay centre with eaves cornice; a pediment over the projecting three-bay centre. Later C18 two-bay additions on either side, each with a ground-floor window recessed in a brick arch. Later bay-windows. S of Uxbridge Road only one important survival, HARROW WEALD FARMHOUSE, a surprise in the otherwise suburban ELMS ROAD (No. 40). A picturesque composition of timber, tile, and brick, partly the result of alterations by *Guy Church* in the 1930s, using old materials. The oldest part is a four-bay timber-framed wing with arch-braced tie-beams, collar and through purlin construction, probably of *c.* 1600. At the W end a later two-bay timber-framed addition; to the SW a C19 brick extension. S of Elms Road off WILSMERE DRIVE the former HARROW WEALD HOUSE, early C19, stock brick, nine-bay front with small pediment, later extensions on both sides. Little else to the S apart from the ALMA in the High Road, a simple early C19 pub, altered; in KENTON LANE, various cottages, and (of the C17 onwards) the SEVEN BALLS and the HERMITAGE; and round the corner in MOUNTSIDE, BELMONT COTTAGES, a pretty row probably of the C18. For Kenton Lane Farm further S *see* Wealdstone (Hw).

N of Uxbridge Road buildings are too scattered to make up a perambulation. They are described roughly from S to N.

UXBRIDGE ROAD (E–W). Only a few reminders of the past. At the corner with Brookshill C19 gatepiers remain from Harrow Weald Park.* A half-timbered late C19 LODGE, the former mid C19 STABLES, a U-shaped block with clock turret, and other service buildings lie at the far end of WEST DRIVE, and PINNER LODGE, also late C19, further along Uxbridge Road. At the E end of Uxbridge Road an excellent curved entrance with ornamental iron railings and Gothic stone piers, all that remains of The Cedars, the house which belonged to the Blackwell family. Beyond the roundabout one of the estates built by the British Iron and Steel Federation in the late 1940s, with two-storey prefabricated houses designed by *Sir Frederick Gibberd*, an example of how aesthetically good emergency construction could be when texture, colour, and those details unaffected by shortage of materials were handled with taste. The upper floor is faced with corrugated-steel sheets, originally painted in dark colours. The graceful porch has slim tubular steel shafts. The houses have survived well beyond their intended life span.

CLAMP HILL (S–N). At the SE corner was Woodlands, an C18 house now demolished, of which the LODGE dated 1882 survives in Uxbridge Road. Further on, HERMITAGE GATE, a romantic composition with octagonal tower, belonged to another lost house. PRIORY HOUSE is a secluded timber-framed farmhouse,

*Harrow Weald Park was an ambitious and extensive house of 1870 with battlements and pinnacles, all of stone.

A Studio
B Bedrooms
C Hall
D Dining Room   F Breakfast Room
E Drawing Room   G Kitchen

FIRST FLOOR

GROUND FLOOR

YARD

Harrow Weald, Grim's Dyke, plans of first and ground floors

much altered (C16, said to re-use materials from the medieval
Bentley Priory).

BROOKSHILL (S–N). NORTH LODGE (to Harrow Weald Park) is
of the later C19, castellated Gothic. Further N is HILLSIDE, by
Roumieu, later C19, built in the gloomy dark diapered brick style
of Victorian Gothic (cf. Harrow School buildings). At the corner
of Old Redding THE HARE, a pleasant stuccoed C18 pub.
COPSE FARM, Brookshill Drive, is a rural corner with a farmhouse of the C17–18 (timber-framing cased in red brick), a weatherboarded BARN with undulating tiled roof, and some lumpily
detailed cottages of the late C19, still in the *cottage orné* tradition.

OLD REDDING (E–W). THE CASE IS ALTERED is a country inn
of *c.* 1800. Farther on, THE CITY COTTAGES, the last remnants
of a red brick group built for C17 kiln-workers (cf. Common
Road, below). Then the LODGE of 1871 to Grim's Dyke.

GRIM'S DYKE itself, 1870–2 by *Norman Shaw*, is a gem of the 60
'Old English' version of the Domestic Revival style of the late
C19, that is a style which is a free adaptation of Tudor forms
with picturesque many-gabled compositions and the warm and
rich effects of much ornamental tilehanging and half-timbering.
It had enormous influence, and there are plenty of derivatives to

be seen in the Harrow area. The 'Old English' style evolved during the 1860s, when Shaw and his early partner Nesfield studied the Surrey vernacular in company with a group of artists who included the future patron of Grim's Dyke, Frederick Goodall, a popular R.A. genre painter. Grim's Dyke was designed both as an artist's studio house and for entertaining – too ambitiously, as it turned out, for Goodall had to sell it in 1882. A later owner added a billiard room (*c.* 1885 by *Arthur Cawston*) and further additions and alterations were made by *Ernest George & Peto c.* 1890–1, when the house was owned by W. S. Gilbert (of Gilbert and Sullivan). (George also designed Gilbert's town house in Harrington Gardens, South Kensington (KC), q.v.) The entrance front has a large timber-framed gable over an off-centre Gothic porch and a large mullioned hall window. To the l. a wing at an angle, with kitchen etc. below, studio above. The angled wing became one of Shaw's favourite devices for increasing the picturesque irregularity of his country houses; here, however, there was a genuine need for N–S studio lighting. The later extensions lie E of the studio. The planning is more straightforward than the exterior suggests. The porch leads into the hall, with living rooms on two sides, the dining room facing the garden with a large inglenook fireplace. From a corner of the hall the staircase proceeds in leisurely fashion, with generous landings; there is a branch up to the bedrooms over the living rooms, and another towards the studio (now hotel dining room), a sumptuous room modelled on a medieval hall, with an open timber roof and an oriel window on the side in addition to the mullioned windows at either end. The spectacular carved alabaster chimneypiece in mannerist style was added, to designs by a French sculptor, by *George & Peto* for W. S. Gilbert. In the garden a fountain with river gods by *Cibber*, 1681, originally erected in Soho Square.

OXHEY LANE FARMHOUSE. Stuccoed brick, with an C18 pedimented doorcase in a later segment-arched porch. Later extensions.

COMMON ROAD (S–N). On the W side THE KILN, with a red brick C18 exterior (timber-framed inside). In its grounds, remains of an C18 BRICK KILN and DRYING SHEDS. On the E side the OLD BARN, a brick and timber sham made up in 1902–6 from materials from a house near Worcester. The half-timbered GATE LODGE is of *c.* 1890 by *Waterhouse*. The house (now Newlands, part of an old people's home) combines tilehanging and timbering with the more urbane Queen Anne feature of a shell-hooded porch. TANGLEWOOD and its lodge are also later C19.

BUSHEY HEATH. First in this cluster of roads on the Hertfordshire border KESTREL GROVE, Hive Road, 1910 by *Harold Goslett*, on a butterfly plan of the type made popular by Prior in the 1890s. An angled wing flanks the central entrance with its semicircular Doric porch and Venetian window and bell-turret over. In the HIGH ROAD some cottages and THE WINDMILL, *c.* 1800. COUNTY END in Magpie Hall Road is white stuccoed, with an C18 core, C19 pedimented wings, and a pretty trellised and tented veranda.

BENTLEY PRIORY, The Common. *See* above under its own entry.

HATCH END

A hamlet to the N of Pinner which began to expand after the arrival
of the railway station in 1844.

St Anselm, Westfield Park, N of Uxbridge Road. 1895 by *F. E.
Jones*: N aisle 1906. Flint with brick bands, free Gothic tracery,
no tower. Simple, broad interior with octagonal columns, dominated by a lofty traceried ROOD SCREEN with carved spandrels
and rood figures, 1901 by *Charles Spooner*. – REREDOS. 1921,
also by *Spooner*. – STAINED GLASS. E window of 1903, sensitive
if slightly sentimental work by the Arts and Crafts designer *Louis
Davis* – a well composed Nativity, angels, and small scenes against
white grounds. Also by *Davis* S aisle easternmost (with small
panel of St Anselm), *c.* 1905, N chapel windows, 1910, N aisle
(Christ and St Mary Magdalene), 1932, S aisle W, 1915 (incorporating a medieval fragment from Ypres Cathedral), and baptistery, 1927. – W window with a stiff Epiphany, 1915 by *Selwyn
Image* (PC).

Harrow Arts Centre, Uxbridge Road. Opened in 1988 in part
of the celebrated Royal Commercial Travellers' School which
was founded for orphans in 1845 at Wanstead and moved here
in 1855. Most of the buildings were demolished in 1968 after the
school closed.* The chief survivor is ELLIOT HALL, 1904 by
H. O. Cresswell, large and handsome institutional Perp, brick
with stone dressings, the W end with an external balcony between
two little turrets. Fine open timber roof. War memorial stained
glass. Other buildings to the W are now part of St Teresa's
R.C. School.

Post Office, Uxbridge Road. Pleasant early C20 free style.

Hatch End Station, Uxbridge Road. Rebuilt in 1911 by
Gerald Horsley, a charming Wrenish pavilion with steep roof and
clock turret.

Grimsdyke. The possibly Saxon earthwork which runs along
part of the N borough boundary is visible at Hatch End golf
course. *See also* Pinner.

The Railway, a tall stuccoed pub on the S side of Uxbridge
Road, belongs with the mid C19 beginnings of the suburb, but
little else of this date remains. The first commuters' housing was
to the W of the station: the Woodridings estate S of Uxbridge
Road, large semi-detached villas advertised by *Richard Field*,
surveyor, in 1855. One pair remains in Wellington Road
(Nos. 40–42), plain stucco, with triple windows to the top floor.
In Nugents Park further W Four Oaks and Tall Trees
are a neo-Georgian house of 1902, 3-2-3 bays, by *Harrison &
Ward*. To the N, in Altham Road, Altham House, a well
preserved early modern house, 1934 by *W. J. Flower*, rendered
and flat-roofed, with a curved corner. E of the station, pleasant
tree-lined Edwardian streets of large houses around The
Avenue.

---

*The original main buildings were by *Lane & Ordish* with wings of 1868 by
Knightley.

HEADSTONE MANOR

At first acquaintance, it is difficult to appreciate the full significance
of Headstone Manor House.* Picturesquely sited on a moated
island in the middle of a municipal park between Pinner and Wealdstone, it seems nothing more than the modest and neglected house
of some C18 farmer. Yet behind its unassuming exterior lies the
earliest timber-framed house known to have survived in Middlesex,
built shortly after 1344 as the principal residence in the county of
the Archbishop of Canterbury. Part of its original open hall
remains, together with a two-storeyed cross-wing at the service
end. The hall is at the S corner of the present building, and the
truncated gable end of the cross-wing is visible on the SW front.
The cross-wing is quite plain, with arch-braced wall framing and
a simple undecorated crown-post roof.

The hall is one of the most important medieval domestic rooms
in Greater London. Only one bay remains out of two or possibly
three. The closed truss, next to the screens passage which was
situated within the cross-wing, is of conventional aisled construction, but the surviving open truss which now marks the truncated SE
end of the building dispenses with the aisle-posts in an intriguingly
experimental way. It seems to have framed two opposing bay-
windows which were roofed at right angles to the remainder of the
hall, so that the wall-posts rise to the full height of the tie-beam,
whose exceptional span was supported by a pair of massive arch-
braces springing from the inner face of each wall-post. A similar
arrangement has recently been revealed at Upton Court, Slough,
Bucks, of c. 1330. This tantalizing truss was closed by a brick wall
in 1772 and the braces were removed, but it retains its magnificent
decorated crown-post with three of its four upward braces still in
position and heavily encrusted with soot. Indeed, despite successive
remodellings, the hall has always remained undivided by an inserted
floor.

In the 1630s the building was remodelled for Simon Rewse,
Receiver-General to Lord North. The outer walls of the hall were
raised, and a long mullioned and high-transomed SW window was
inserted. Much of the panelling in the hall, together with the
decorative brackets to the aisle-plates and the panelled bench
against the NE wall, date from this time, as do the entrance porch
with wooden doorcase and little window to its side at the N end of
the screens passage, and the adjacent tall two-storeyed timber-
framed and rendered block erected in the angle between the hall
and the cross-wing. Twenty years later the house was further
enlarged by the addition of another timber-framed range parallel
to the cross-wing which incorporates a massive chimneystack with
diamond-shaped shafts and an elegant staircase. The present
appearance of the house was largely accomplished in 1772, when
the entrance front was extended and faced in fashionable brick
(there is a dated brick in the W wall) and the hall was reduced in

*This account was contributed by Malcolm Airs.

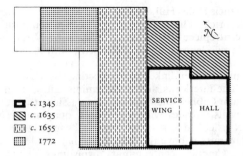

Headstone Manor, schematic plan to show phases of development

length. Another wing was added at the rear at right angles to the range of the 1650s and here, out of public view, the timber-framed tradition lingered on a little longer.

The whole complex of rambling house glimpsed through trees across a moat possesses great charm. It is further enhanced by the GREAT BARN, one of the best of surviving Middlesex barns, strategically placed a few yards w of the bridge leading over the moat. Formerly it was one of at least four barns surrounding a farmyard beyond the moat. Built in 1506 by *Richard Boughton*, carpenter, it is ten bays in length and of exceptional width for an unaisled structure. It has the earliest datable queen-strut roof in Middlesex, with arch-braced tie-beams and a double row of butt-purlins. Two wagon porches project on the s side and are flanked by later lean-tos. Before the Dissolution the porch and the three bays at the s w end were partitioned off from the rest of the barn and were reserved for the Archbishop's produce, the remaining seven bays served by the NE porch being let to the tenant farmer. The barn was carefully restored in 1973 by the present owners, the London Borough of Harrow, under the meticulous supervision of *Michael Thorne*. Although the waney-edged cladding is a poor substitute for the previous weatherboarding, the restoration reflects great credit on a responsible civic attitude towards conservation. Such an attitude has yet to be extended to the manor house, and to the smaller, later barn to the s. This is of six bays with queen-strut roof. It was gutted by fire in 1979, and still awaits attention at the time of writing.

KENTON

The s part of Kenton is in Brent (q.v.). Amorphous 1930s suburbia extends on either side of Kenton Road; for the few older buildings to the N in Kenton Lane, *see* Wealdstone and Harrow Weald (both Hw).

ST MARY, Kenton Road and St Leonard's Avenue. 1936 by *J. H. Gibbons*. A fine, if late, example in the early C20 tradition of free Gothic (instead of the Romanesque which Gibbons used earlier at St Francis Dollis Hill, Br (q.v.), and St Francis Bournemouth). Of pale brick. The w front is an effective composition with a stone centrepiece incorporating a standing Virgin and Child between two lancets, above a stepped plinth flanking a pointed arch with recessed entrance. The door has pretty ironwork with two lions. SE tower, linked to a projecting church hall (completed 1959). The interior is somewhat reminiscent of Temple Moore (for whom Gibbons had worked as an assistant), with buff rendered walls, arcades without capitals, quadrant arches to the wider N aisle, and as its chief surprise a vaulted E chapel behind the altar, raised above the vestries so that it is level with the w gallery. – Complete contemporary furnishings. – BALDACCHINO with cusped and filigree decoration. – Multifoil marble FONT with handsome hanging cover. – Set in the wall nearby, small medieval angel from the font of St Giles Cripplegate. – CALVARY at the w end by *A. Toft*. – Fragments of medieval heraldic STAINED GLASS from All Saints York. – Italian glass by the font.

KENTON FREE CHURCH, Streatfield Road. 1939; hall 1965.

LIBRARY, Kenton Lane. 1938 by *Curtis* and *Burchett*. Simple L-shaped building, carefully detailed, typical of the M.C.C. just before the war.

PINNER

INTRODUCTION

Pinner has two images. The first is of a carefully cherished old centre, somewhere between a village and a country town. There was a market and fair here already in the C14, and the pre-suburban era is recalled by a well placed medieval church and an exceptionally large number (for outer London) of attractive timber-framed buildings, both in the High Street and in what were once outlying hamlets. Pinner's second image is of quintessential Metroland, of the suburbia which rapidly swallowed up the countryside, especially to the s, in the first half of the C20. The earliest railway station (1844), on the London to Birmingham line, some way N at Hatch End (q.v.), barely affected the old village. In 1885, however, a station was built at Pinner for the Metropolitan line from Harrow, and another opened at Rayners Lane in 1906. The Metropolitan set up companies to exploit its surplus land, and local builder-developers soon joined the fray (*Cutler, Garnett, T. F. Nash*, and *E. S. Reid* were among the most active).* In the streets s of the old village, the ubiquitous semi-detached house can be studied in all its variations. The most attractive areas of between the wars are the Metropolitan Company's Harrow Garden Village N of Rayners Lane, and further N Pinnerwood Park estate built by the Artizans and General Dwellings Company, both described in Perambulation 4.

---

*For details see *Pinner Streets Yesterday and Today* (Pinner and Hatch End Local Archaeol. Soc., v, 1976).

CHURCHES

St Alban, The Ridgeway. *See* Harrow-on-the-Hill (Hw).

St Andrew Roxbourne, Malvern Avenue. 1956 by *Farey & Adams*. Well massed, although crude in detail. Pale brick with a polygonal apse and a bold porch-tower with a helm spire. Box-framed windows, triangular and segment-headed. Exposed portal frame inside. The remarkable feature is a complete set of forty-nine STAINED GLASS windows by the Dutch artist *Max Nauta* (paid for by war damage money from a church in Poplar), far superior to average English post-war glass. Stylized figures, broadly Romanesque in inspiration, people an unconventional combination of Old and New Testament scenes. The S aisle includes the prodigal son and Jacob's dream, the N aisle (devoted to women and children) the births of Christ and Moses, Jesus in the Temple, St Veronica, and Florence Nightingale. In the clerestory emblems of the creation, evangelists, saints, etc., against pebble coloured patterns. ,

St John the Baptist, High Street. A chapel of Harrow until 1766, although clearly a significant church already by the C14. The battlemented W tower of flint with Reigate stone dressings, and the Perp W doorway with quatrefoils in the spandrels, are typical late medieval Middlesex features, but there was a consecration in 1321, and the cruciform plan and the lower parts of the NE wall may be C13. Aisle walls of flint, the narrow transepts distinguished by quoins of dark local ferruginous conglomerate or 'ferricrete', hard enough in this corner of Middlesex to be used as dressed stone. Windows all renewed in Bath stone in *Pearson*'s restoration of 1879–80, paid for by W.A. Tooke of Pinner Hill (*see* Perambulation 4). Also by Pearson the roofs, excellent inside as well as out, with gabled dormers (replacing C18 attic windows). Long chancel, lower than the nave. Perp four-bay nave arcade with low octagonal piers of Reigate stone with plain double-chamfered pointed arches. The same double-chamfering appears in the chancel arch. The medieval windows are lancets, plain or, in the aisles, with pointed cinquefoiled heads. C15 five-light E window. S chapel of 1859, lengthened in 1880. Vestry by *Temple Moore*, 1911. – FONT. C15, octagonal, with quatrefoils. – Three-tier FONT COVER of 1909. – ALTAR RAILS. Plain C17, alternately plain and twisted balusters. – SCREEN at the W end by *Charles Spooner*, 1914, with decorative glazing by *Christopher Whall*, 1900 (PC). – STAINED GLASS. A varied collection. E window by *Heaton, Butler & Bayne*, c. 1861, large figures in bright colours, rather crude and old-fashioned for its date. – N transept 1872, early work by *James Powell & Sons*; scenes from the life of John the Baptist. – W wall, N and S aisles, by the same firm, 1915: Zachary and Elizabeth. – In the N aisle two pairs of saints by *N. Comper*, 1906 and 1907, in his usual pale colours. – In the S aisle two interesting Arts and Crafts works: to the E of the door figures with landscapes by *Clement Skilbeck*, c. 1900, to the W two bold impressionistic pre-Raphaelite figures of Faith and Hope, c. 1914 by *Louis Davis*. – S chapel E 1980 by *Alfred Fisher*, painted by *Peter Archer*. Annunciation, including a quotation from the Chartres Belle Verrière; subtle

blues flowing across four lights. – MONUMENTS. Small chrisom
brass to Anne Bedingfeld † 1580, a palimpsest with Flemish
inscription on the back. – John Day † 1622. A small marble tablet
with an engraved kneeling figure with book and scroll inscribed
'Theres my treasure'. – Sir Christopher Clitherow, who lived in
a 'corrupt, seditious, wicked age' and died in 1685. By *William
Stanton* (design in the Victoria and Albert Museum). Black and
white marble portrait. The central motif, an urn with festoons
hanging down, stands on a sarcophagus flanked by Ionic columns
with a pediment and putti (an early occurrence of the urn as
monument so popular *c.* 1800). – Edward Auberry † 1767, a
discreet pedimented tablet by *Sir Robert Taylor*, and Mary
Aubery † 1813, a matching tablet by *J. Tomkinson*. – In the
churchyard several good LEDGER STONES. – S of the church
the eccentric monument erected by *John Claudius Loudon*, the
encyclopedist and garden writer, to his parents William and
Agnes († 1809 and 1831). It is a tall tapering mass of masonry
with an arch cut into the foot on each side; higher up, two ends
of a sarcophagus stick out incongruously.

ST LUKE (R.C.), Love Lane. 1957 by *F. X. Velarde*, in the neo-
Romanesque tradition he introduced at Bootle in 1936. Twin w
towers. Large aisle windows of opaque glass in alternately square
and arched panes. Arcades opening to passage aisles. On the w
front low-relief figure of St Luke as an artist portraying the
Virgin. – CHURCH HALL. 1965 by *Grima*, with a sharply angled
roof, like a paper dart on a shoebox.

METHODIST CHURCH, Love Lane. 1937 by *Smee & Houchin*. As
elsewhere in Metroland, the Methodists acquired a good corner
site. Brick with cusped stone windows and a steep w gable.
Inside, minimally but carefully detailed, with low, trabeated
passage aisles and a pointed plastered barrel-vault.

QUAKER MEETING HOUSE, Rayners Lane. 1935. Domestic brick.

UNITED FREE CHURCH, Paines Lane. Formerly Baptist. 1908–9
by *Spalding, Spalding & Myers*. Cheerful Free Gothic, with
small asymmetrical tower. Interior with big timber roof; no side
galleries.

CEMETERY, Pinner Road. 1933 by *S. W. Richardson*. Stone lodge
and chapel in a dry Tudor, approached through grand iron gates.

PUBLIC BUILDINGS

The schools provided between the wars for the new suburbs furnish
good illustrations of the County Council's changing tastes. A selection follows in chronological order.

NOWER HILL HIGH SCHOOL, Pinner Road and George V
Avenue. 1929 onwards, still in the *M.C.C.*'s pre-modern phase;
gabled red brick. Indifferent post-war additions of brick, exposed
concrete, and curtain-walling.

ROOKS HEATH HIGH SCHOOL, Eastcote Lane. Built as Roxeth
Manor Secondary School, 1932 by the *M.C.C.*, in a more distinguished 1700 revival style. Symmetrical front with the quoins
picked out by tiles, steep hipped roofs, the centre a little taller

and crowned by a chimney. The adjoining ROXETH MANOR
FIRST AND MIDDLE SCHOOLS of 1933 are similar but simpler.
PINNER PARK SCHOOLS, Headstone Lane. 1935 by *W. T. Curtis*
and *H. W. Burchett* of the *M.C.C.*, an early example of the plainer
'factory aesthetic'. Two-storey classroom block, a stair-tower
with zigzag glazing providing relief. Low brick INFANTS'
SCHOOL by *Mayorcas, Guest & Partners*, 1970s.
ROXBOURNE FIRST AND MIDDLE SCHOOLS, Torbay Road.
1937 by *W. T. Curtis* and *H. W. Burchett*. Simple elements composed with some care: an asymmetrically grouped central composition with tall l. turret and curved wall on the side of the main
entrance.
HEATHFIELD SCHOOL FOR GIRLS, Beaulieu Drive, off Cannon
Lane. Built as Pinner County Grammar School, 1937 by *W. T.
Curtis* and *H. W. Burchett*. On a quadrangular plan, with one of
the best of their formal fronts in the modern manner inspired by
W. M. Dudok. It steps up from one-storey wings by two and
three storeys to a central four-storey library tower over the
entrance. Continuous stone sills produce horizontal articulation;
discreet brick fins add vertical interest on the tower and upper
walls.
HATCH END HIGH SCHOOL, Headstone Lane. An early post-
war comprehensive by the *M.C.C.*, 1948, on a vast finger plan.
Assembly hall by *J. & E. Eastwick-Field*, 1953.
TELEPHONE EXCHANGE, Marsh Road. A tall, good-looking brick
building in the style of 1700 by *Christopher Bristow* of the Office
of Works, 1928. Segment-headed windows.
RAYNERS LANE STATION. Rebuilt in 1938 by *Charles Holden* in
association with *R. H. Uren*. Tall rectangular booking hall, as at
Sudbury Hill (Br); the interior distinguished by the use of black
glazed bricks for the lower walls.
GRIMSDYKE. The possibly Saxon earthwork running along part
of the N borough boundary is visible at Pinner Green, N of the
Montesole Playing Fields. *See also* Hatch End.
CHALK MINES, Uxbridge Road. Chalk was worked here at least
from the C17; about 600 metres of galleries survive, the oldest
from the C18. No. 2 shaft was dug in 1840, No. 3 in 1850,
remaining in use until 1887.

PERAMBULATIONS

1. The High Street area

In the HIGH STREET, as one approaches the church, a pretty
mixture of timber-framed and brick buildings, much altered, but
essentially of the C15–18 – an intimate vista conscientiously
protected from C20 intrusion (a large store to the N is totally
invisible up a discreet alleyway, BISHOP'S WALK). Notable
among the older buildings are THE SHIP at the W end, jettied,
though much altered and adorned with a modern date; Nos. 9
and 11 opposite, timber-framed; and Nos. 25–27 (which, behind
later fronts, preserve a C15 crown-post roof to a former two-bay
open hall (floored in the C16), a blocked six-light window at the

dais end, and a three-light window to the first-floor solar). The
QUEEN'S HEAD has genuine C16 parts behind its fake half-
timbered front. No. 35 is a substantial house with two cross-
wings, No. 34 has a single wing and a good clustered diagonal
brick stack. A converted barn behind. Near the church the little
HILLTOP WINE BAR is C17 beneath its later trappings. The
best of the C18 houses is No. 32, three bays with recessed entrance and central pediment. Immediately NW of the church
HAYWOOD HOUSE, plain Georgian brick, with an addition
made by *Sir Ernest George* in 1878, when it was the temperance
COCOA TREE TAVERN; characteristic tilehanging and a strikingly picturesque tall chimney.

CHURCH FARM, at the beginning of Paines Lane, is screened by a
green with horse-chestnut trees. Its long, low, irregular rendered
front conceals a medieval timber-framed building of unusual
form. The exceptionally long main range of five bays may once
have extended still further E. Substantial well preserved timber-
framing with close-studded walls and collar and tie-beam trusses.
The extreme W bay was originally heated by an open hearth,
but the hall in the centre two bays was apparently unheated,
suggesting that it had some public function; it may have been
the Church House known from documents to have survived into
the C17. At the E end a later, narrower two-bay wing with a lower
king-strut roof (a type not later than the early C16) projects at
right angles. Other alterations include the added floors, and
chimneystacks in both hall and smoke bay.*

s of the High Street GRANGE GARDENS starts with GRANGE
COURT, a presumptuous mock-Tudor cornerpiece of 1933–4,
with shops and the offices of Cutler's, the local builders, pro-
claiming that this is the start of a C20 development close to the
railway line (by the Metropolitan Railway Surplus Lands Co.).
The 1920s commuters' houses here (several by the company's
architect, *L. W. Clark*) are not yet of a standardized design; they
were described as 'exceptionally artistic detached residences'.

2. Church Lane and East End

CHURCH LANE meanders leafily away from the church. Older
survivors amid the suburban newcomers include No. 59, earlier
C19, and CHESTNUT COTTAGE, an irregular C18 front, rendered. PINNER HOUSE, dated 1721, is a larger mansion, a five-
window brick front with giant pilasters, but a timber-framed
tilehung side. Behind, extensions of *c.* 1980 in matching
materials. From the green with the DRINKING FOUNTAIN (1886
to W. A. Tooke) MOSS LANE leads N. The first house to note is
THE FIVES COURT, 1900–8 by *Cecil Brewer* for the son of
Ambrose Heal.‡ White rendered, with very simple details, a
gable at one end, and tall chimneys – a little in the manner of
Voysey. s additions of 1906–13. Good original interiors.

*This account is based on a survey kindly made available by Mrs Charmian Baker.
‡Ambrose Heal's own house nearby, Nower Hill House, enlarged for him by *Brewer*
in 1895, was demolished *c.* 1960. Smith and Brewer were later to be the architects of
Heal's department store in Tottenham Court Road.

At a bend further N a specially pretty group survives from the old
hamlet of East End. EAST END HOUSE has a four-bay brick c18
front to the garden. TUDOR COTTAGE is mostly a picturesque
pastiche of old pieces, but the attractive timber-framed EAST
END FARM COTTAGE is a genuine medieval survival, one of the
best in Greater London, a textbook case in the way it preserves
remarkably complete evidence of each stage of its gradual transformation from a c15 open hall with central hearth to a c17 two-
storeyed house with fireplaces. The story is worth telling in
detail.

The house in its present form consists of the former two-bay hall
and a third, storeyed bay to its E, in the traditional position of a
service end, divided into two ground-floor rooms and an upper
room rising into the roof space. The framing suggests that there
was once also a W bay extending beyond the high end of the hall.
The hall has been subdivided, but the original open roof remains,
with a hollow-chamfered, arch-braced tie-beam and a crown-
post with four-way struts. All this is likely to belong to the c15.
Probably towards the end of the c16 the W bay of the hall was
floored over, leaving the E one as a smoke bay above the hearth,
at first extending across the whole width of the house, as the
smoke blackening in the roof shows. Screens were put in to form
a cross-passage between the entrances, and perhaps early in the
c17 the pretty S porch with cusped bargeboards was added. At
the same time the W bay may have been demolished and the E
bay improved; while the hall retained its open hearth, the upstairs
room to its E was modernized with a fireplace, its stack rising,
smoke-blackened, up the side of the smoke bay. An ovolo-
moulded window, which still has its leaded casements, was added
in the E gable. The square upper newel of the staircase and the
rough lattice balustrade must date from the same phase. The
front service room below now became a living room, with a new
fireplace with a stack attached at the gable end. The inner wall
was painted from floor to ceiling, covering plaster panels and
timber-framing alike, with a fine hunting scene. A hound, the
underside and legs of a bleeding stag(?), and a hilly landscape in
grey and red remain as the sole representatives of such a mural
in Greater London. When the open hearth in the hall was finally
replaced by a fireplace, the smoke bay survived upstairs, containing the new flue rising at a crazy diagonal towards the older
stack. The hall was now completely floored over, the smoke bay
reduced in size to allow upstairs access from one end of the house
to the other, and three dormers were provided to light the upper
rooms. To the E of the house BARNS remain around the former
farmyard.

N of this hamlet the suburban development is agreeably interspersed with greenery, with nothing of note until the corner
of PAINES LANE, where MOSS COTTAGE has an irregular
weatherboarded front, some Jacobean details inside, and enlargements of 1887.

3. W of the High Street

First the older buildings. In WAXWELL LANE a few timber-framed survivals on the W side: ORCHARD COTTAGE, with an attractive exterior, and No. 23, plastered, with chimney-stack, probably C17. MANOR COTTAGE opposite, disguised by an ugly C20 extension and bogus half-timbering, is in origin a medieval hall house, with remains of a smoke bay. Much further N, No. 125, a large, rambling group, the E parts perhaps of the C17. In WEST END LANE the best house is SWEETMANS HALL (No. 90), an attractive, long C17 storeyed range with a lower wing at the end. Further S, by Pinner Memorial Gardens, the remains of WEST HOUSE, the late Georgian yellow brick service wings of the former manor house.

The other buildings that strike the visitor belong to Pinner's sub-urban phase. In ELM PARK ROAD is TUDOR COTTAGE, 1920 by *Ernest Trobridge*, a twin-gabled house with his unmistakable eccentric details (cf. Kingsbury, Br). Further W ELM PARK COURT, 1936 by *H. F. Webb*, a stunningly lavish layout of flats, admirably maintained; green-tiled roofs, white walls, plenty of period detail, approached through a large semicircular archway. (In HAZELDENE DRIVE, Nos. 1 and 22–24 are by *R. J. Lindsay*, 1937.)

4. The outlying areas

To the N, on PINNER HILL, the presiding genius is that of the eccentric C19 landowner A. W. Tooke. Of his follies the only survivor is the surprisingly grandiose clock tower of 1862 at PINNER HILL FARM, its narrow arched windows with elaborate brickwork formerly crowned by a steeply pitched roof with iron cresting. Is it by *J. P. Seddon*, who built cottages on Tooke's estates in the 1850s (see his drawings in the Victoria and Albert Museum)? The farmhouse itself (with barns behind) is simple early C19 red brick. Tooke lived further up at PINNER HILL (now a golf clubhouse), which his father acquired in 1845. The owners of a house that stood here from the C17 included the Clitherow family (*see* Pinner church). The present harmless brick garden front, three bays with pediment, probably dates from the time of Lady Jane Brydges, who lived here from 1755. The entrance side was embellished by Tooke in 1867 in a forceful and eclectic Gothic-cum-Italianate, in banded brown and cream brick. Octagonal kitchen. C18 and C19 outbuildings, including an ICE HOUSE to the NE.

Most of the wooded slopes of Pinner Hill are now covered by private estates of discreetly affluent inter-war houses, of the type extolled in 1929 in P. A. Barron's *The House Desirable*. In HILLSIDE ROAD to the W is an early example, MONK'S REST, a 1924 Ideal Home showhouse by *Blunden Shadbolt*, who specialized in picturesque creations made up from old buildings, in this case from Old Friar's House, Horley, Surrey. POND COTTAGE, Pinner Hill, is also by Shadbolt, 1925. In SOUTH VIEW ROAD, OAKWOOD is of 1927 by *L. G. Williams*, in PARK

VIEW ROAD, NASEBY of the same date is by *J. Eustace Salisbury*. Further down the hill is the largest area of Harrow Council housing of between the wars (285 houses), and to the E bald 1960s development around ALBURY DRIVE, but N of this a rural strip remains, introduced by a little C19 lodge at the end of WOODHALL ROAD. Beyond lies PINNER WOOD HOUSE, a main range with a truncated cross-wing; the C17 timber frame is visible in the W gable end. Nearby, PINNER WOOD COTTAGE, with pretty C19 bargeboards, the date 1867, and A. W. Tooke's initials. Further on, PINNER WOOD FARM, another Tooke property, with quite an elaborate C19 brick farmhouse with decorative central gable flanked by dormers, and a low veranda on either side of the entrance.

s from here was the WOODHALL ESTATE, which also belonged to Tooke; here from 1864 onwards he built his exotic Woodhall Towers (replaced in 1965 by Tooke Close). The surrounding area was built up in 1931–9 as the PINNERWOOD PARK ESTATE of the Artizans and General Dwellings Company (427 houses by 1939). It was intended for middle-class tenants who could afford the rail fare – a departure from the policy of the Artizans' earlier London estates. The layout is exceptionally attractive, in the Parker & Unwin garden suburb tradition, with a varied range of single and semi-detached houses, much less pretentious than those of Pinner Hill. Mostly of brick with a little tilehanging; front gardens with rustic fences. The two main roads, WOODHALL DRIVE and WOODHALL GATE, curve round to meet by a little green, with small closes opening off. At the corner of Uxbridge Road the prominently sited estate office. In Woodhall Drive is one older survivor: WOODHALL FARM, of interest for its association with the young J. C. Loudon, the Scots C19 encyclopedist and garden writer. Loudon, then at the beginning of his career, was keen to demonstrate to feckless Middlesex farmers how their land could be cultivated more profitably and their buildings better planned (*see also* Kenton Lane Farm, Wealdstone, Hw). The neat s range, stuccoed, with hoodmoulded windows, dates from *c.* 1808, when an older farmhouse was enlarged to designs by *Robert Abraham* during the occupancy of Loudon's father, who died in 1809 (*see* Pinner churchyard). The E wing was altered later, in a similar style. Loudon proposed large model farm buildings further N (illustrated in his *Observations on Laying Out Farms in the Scotch Style Adapted to England*, 1812). Further E, to the s of Uxbridge Road, lay Pinner Hall, demolished in 1956, from which a C19 lodge remains in OLD HALL DRIVE.

E of the centre of Pinner, Headstone Manor and its park (q.v.) are marooned in a sea of inter-war development that merges into Harrow. In PINNER ROAD, flanking the cemetery entrance, PINNER COURT, 1935 by *H.J. Mark*, luxury flats with the flamboyant green-tiled roofs so popular at the time. E of George V Avenue, PINNER PARK FARM, with C18 and C19 buildings, survives in a pocket of unbuilt open country.

To the s, focusing on Rayners Lane Station (*see* Public Buildings), the most interesting Metroland development is the anomalously named HARROW GARDEN VILLAGE, planned by the Metropolitan Railway from 1926 and built up largely between 1930 and 1934. It is bounded by Village Way on the s, the Yeading Brook on the w. The most attractive features of the layout are the widened areas along RAYNERS LANE, forming little greens, with plenty of trees. s of the station, in ALEXANDRA AVENUE, the former GROSVENOR CINEMA (now a wine bar), 1936 by *F. E. Bromige,* an amazing modern-Baroque concave front with one huge volute in the centre, an elephant's trunk which originally supported a revolving triangular sign. Well preserved interiors: oval foyer, with coved plaster ceiling to a sunken tea-room. Auditorium with deep coved ribs; proscenium arch flanked by fluted columns.

THE STANMORES

INTRODUCTION

The old parishes of Great and Little Stanmore in the NE corner of the borough, bounded to the E by the line of the Roman Watling Street (the modern Edgware Road), are completely outer suburban to the s, but still quite rural to the N. Before the C20, Little Stanmore, or Whitchurch, was a tiny place with hardly more than St Lawrence's church at the s approach to Canons Park. The great house, the famous Canons, rebuilt by the Duke of Chandos from 1713, was replaced after the sale of 1749 by a more modest villa, now the core of the North London Collegiate School. But Chandos's church and its fittings survive, the most complete Baroque ensemble of its kind in outer London, and, despite suburban encroachment, the C18 layout of the park can still be recognized in the school grounds to the E and in the public park to the w. Great Stanmore was a larger village, its centre extending from the present St John's church E along the Broadway. One substantial timber-framed building is a lonely reminder of earlier days; the rest has succumbed to C20 commercialism. To the N, the slopes of Stanmore Hill are more attractive, still with a few dignified C18 and early C19 houses amidst the affluent arrivals of the C20. Extensive wooded stretches still remain on the high ground of Stanmore Common where, as at Harrow Weald, the Victorians built themselves lavish houses, of which Stanmore Hall is the most ambitious survivor. The railway station (now closed) built in 1890 in Gordon Avenue to the s of Great Stanmore village brought commuter houses in its wake, and denser suburban growth spread N between the wars, especially after the opening of another line with stations at Canons Park and London Road. Some of the houses of these years present curious contrasts – extremes of Tudor make-believe in Old Church Lane and Canons Drive, progressive modernism around Kerry Avenue.

GREAT STANMORE

ST JOHN THE EVANGELIST, Church Road and Uxbridge Road. Two churches in one churchyard. The medieval church stood further s. It was rebuilt closer to the village centre by Sir John Wolstenholme, a wealthy and influential merchant adventurer, and consecrated in 1632 by Archbishop Laud. His building remains as a ruin. Apart from its battlemented tower, it must have been every inch as rational and matter-of-fact as what the Victorians called the 'red brick boxes' of the c 18; now, overgrown and open to the sky, it is truly picturesque, and one of the best ruins in London. Nave and chancel in one, with a Venetian e window, a very up-to-date motif (cf. Inigo Jones's chapel at St James's Palace, Westminster) perhaps ascribable to the involvement of *Nicholas Stone*, who was paid £30 for the s doorway of Portland stone.

The present church was begun in 1849 to the design of *Henry Clutton*.* It is of irregularly coursed Kentish rag with Bath stone dressings, with a battlemented tower over the N porch, and Dec detail; 'extraordinarily good and solid for its date ... better than Scott' (Goodhart-Rendel). Half the cost was borne by the first rector and his father the Earl of Aberdeen. The interior, whitewashed in the 1960s, when the chancel floor was lowered and some furnishings removed, is now rather dull. Carved chancel arch responds, some diapering of Westminster Abbey type on the E wall, and the PULPIT of 1873 with alabaster reliefs remain from the c 19. The N chapel was converted from vestries by *E. B. Glanfield* in 1955. – STAINED GLASS. e window remade in 1950, incorporating a central light by *Willement*. – s aisle central window by *Morris & Co.*, 1877 (designers *Bowman* and *Dearle*). Four minstrel angels. The surrounding wall with stencilled decoration. – From the c 17 church the delicate FONT made by *Nicholas Stone*, a small octagonal marble bowl with the Wolstenholme crest, on a baluster. Contemporary wooden cover. – Also many MONUMENTS moved from the old church, beginning with John Burnell † 1605 and family, the usual type with the two principal figures kneeling opposite each other and the children kneeling small, in relief, below. Flanking columns and a top with two obelisks and a crest with strapwork. – Sir John Wolstenholme † 1639. An excellent bearded marble figure, asleep: a typical 24 work by *Nicholas Stone*, set up in 1641, his last recorded effigy. Originally part of a four-poster composition which cost £200. – John Wolstenholme † 1669, tucked away awkwardly beneath the N tower. A stout four-poster with substantial drapery and columns with capitals as elementary as if they were of the c 10, all of stone. John Wolstenholme, recumbent, is observed pensively by his semi-reclining wife. A babe and a little girl lie rather incongruously behind her back: surely a case of wrong reassembly. However that may be, the whole monument is a belated follower of the type of the Countess of Derby at Harefield (Hi). – Elizabeth Colins † 1670 and daughters. Architectural wall-tablet of alabaster and black marble. – John Dalton by *Bacon*, 1791, a good if conservative work with a life-sized mourning woman bending over an urn with a portrait medallion: no trace yet of the 'Grecian' taste. – 1st Earl of Aberdeen † 1860 by

*Of Hartswood, Surrey, not to be confused with the Henry Clutton who worked for the Duke of Bedford.

Boehm, 1875, recumbent. – Plenty of minor c 18 and c 19 tablets in the tower.

ST WILLIAM OF YORK (R.C.), Du Cros Drive. 1960 by *H. O. Corfiato*, in response to a request for Romanesque. Plain brick tower.

STANBURN SCHOOL, Abercorn Road. One of the many put up in the 1930s in a modern idiom by *Curtis* and *Burchett* for the county council. The long plain brick ranges of two storeys are broken by the favourite device of an arresting curved stair-tower and by a less usual entrance arch with catenary curve.

STANMORE STATION, London Road. 1930–2 by *C. W. Clark* for the Metropolitan line's extension (q.v., Baker Street, St Marylebone, Wm outer). In a traditional manner, for an area still rural, with steep tiled roof and dormers.

OLD CHURCH LANE leads s from the church. The picturesque groups on each side are largely a creation of 1930–5 out of old outbuildings and cottages. On the w side they incorporate a barn (with beams of the c 15 but much rebuilt in 1730). Opposite, standing back in its own grounds, is the so-called MANOR HOUSE, and close to the road its appendages, both of 1930: first the CHURCH HOUSE (built as a 'banqueting house') with flamboyant twisted Tudor chimneys and a loggia to the garden behind, then an elaborate brick and timber LODGE. The manor house itself, which began as an unexciting late Victorian mansion of 1901 called The Croft, was transformed between 1930 and 1933 (when the owner, Samuel Wallrock, ran out of money) into a rambling old-world composition incorporating old timbers and roofing tiles, an oak porch with four-centred arch, heraldic glass, etc. The grounds, planted by Wallrock with mature trees (a novelty at the time), have been partly filled with houses, but the E parts remain as a public park.

In CHURCH ROAD, E of the church, there is only one good house, No. 21, sweetly out of place among the recent commercial development. An c 18 front with a doorcase with open pediment was added to a c 15 timber-framed building with crown-post roof – see the irregular hipped roof with dormers and the weatherboarded flank wall. The front to Church Road was formerly jettied. Good c 18 rear staircase. In THE BROADWAY the only interesting relic of the old village is Nos. 37–65, an exceptionally long row of jettied houses, eight bays (with a further bay to the w until 1865), probably of the c 16 or early c 17. There were originally individual front entrances but possibly a common stair (in the central back projection) to upstairs lodgings. One original chimneystack with clustered shafts at the E end. (In No. 59 an overmantel with fluted pilasters and another upstairs with arcaded panels, probably brought in.) The small ERNEST BERNAYS MEMORIAL INSTITUTE, 1870, dressed up in brick stripes and lettered tiles, is quite lovable compared to the mid c 20 buildings that have swamped the rest of the Broadway with their clumsy, excessively restless façades. BROADWAY HOUSE (No. 82), a supermarket and offices at the E end at the corner of Dennis Lane, although bulky, demonstrates the more carefully detailed traditionalist garb of the eighties: red brick, upper floors stepped back below emphatic pitched roofs with jutting eaves. By *Gollins, Melvin, Ward & Partners*, 1982–3.

STANMORE HILL presents a good varied sequence, climbing up from the Broadway. On the W, No. 17, ELM HOUSE, early C18 with additions; Nos. 19–21, gabled Victorian; and No. 23, on a C19 scale with neo-Tudor windows but an C18 doorcase. On the E side No. 44, formerly Ravensdene, quite a large late Georgian neo-classical mansion (now divided). Stucco, three-bay centre, arched ground-floor windows. Balustraded parapet. S front with Greek Doric porch between two full-height bows. On the W, in HALSBURY CLOSE, No. 1 is of 1938 by *Rudolf Frankel*, a brick cube, its most progressive feature (a cut-away corner on the garden side) screened by a garage wing. No. 2 is by the same architect for himself. The outstanding house is halfway up Stanmore Hill on the W side: No. 73, ROBIN HILL (formerly LUSCOMBE LODGE), a small but excellently detailed house of the second quarter of the C18. Only three bays, of brick with stone cornice, string course, and windowsill brackets. Doorcase with columns and pediment. Venetian window in the S wall. On the E side the ABERCORN ARMS, set back from the road, quite a grand late Georgian inn, brick, three storeys with pediment, large Edwardian additions. Lesser cottages continue to the junction with Green Lane, ending with Nos. 113–115, weatherboarded, with some Gothick windows. Back to the church down GREEN LANE, past more cottages: PYNNACLES PLACE, 1822, and others; PARK PLACE, *c.* 1800, three storeys. Near the foot of the hill OLDE COTTAGE, weatherboarded, possibly originally a barn, and RYLANDS, *c.* 1880, with timber-framed three-bay back part made from a former barn, probably C17. Gatepiers with balls. Some of the back garden wall belonged to PINNACLES HOUSE, a larger mansion demolished in the 1930s. Close to the church the picturesquely spiky CHURCH LODGE (No. 1 UXBRIDGE ROAD), red brick with terracotta infilling between half-timbering; 1881 by *Brightwen Binyon* in memory of Robert Hollond of Stanmore Hall.

At the top of Stanmore Hill is THE COMMON. On the W side several good houses. First HILL HOUSE, an austere C18 parapeted centre with pedimented wings. Built before 1771, when it was used as a school in rivalry to Harrow. THE ROOKERY, No. 101, is an irregular C18 composition, altered and added to. Nine-window early C18 front with eaves cornice; pedimented porch. Later C18 canted bay to the garden (drawing room with good chimneypiece and doorcases). STABLES with pretty weatherboarded clock turret. Then OLD BREWERY HOUSE, C18 with C19 additions, formerly adjoining the premises of Clutterbuck's Brewery (replaced by housing in 1988). Further on, hidden down a drive, HERIOTS, a good substantial house of 1925 by *Frank Pearson*, still in a free Arts and Crafts style; plain white rendered entrance front, with small windows below the eaves, battered chimneys and shallow bowed porch. On the E side THE VINE, an inn with a simple three-bay Regency front on the fringe of LITTLE COMMON, a charmingly informal area irregularly scattered with small buildings of all dates. The centrepiece is a C19 group of former STABLES and outbuildings (presumably

once serving Stanmore Hall), replete with decorative bargeboards, cresting, and shaped gables. Among the earlier buildings
are No. 3, timber-framed, and Nos. 5 and 13, early C18. Nearby,
Nos. 44 and 45, with bold but well grouped monopitch roofs, are
by *J. Redman*, 1970.

STANMORE HALL is approached past a ragstone Gothic LODGE
in Wood Lane. The house, in the same style and materials, with
irregular gabled front and picturesque turreted and castellated
skyline, was sympathetically repaired after a fire in 1979 but is
now sadly compromised in views from the Common by a large,
lumpily roofed office addition extending forward on the NE side.
The original house was built in 1847 for John Rhodes by *John
Macduff Derick*. Later owners were John Forbes, Robert
Hollond, and W. Knox D'Arcy, a wealthy oil magnate, for whom
Brightwen Binyon made additions in 1888–91, including a new
dining room and billiard room. The most important element of
this work – the lavish interior decoration, particularly the hall
and staircase, carried out for D'Arcy by *Morris & Co.* – has alas
disappeared. It was their most important commission in Morris's
lifetime – although Morris himself had by then little enthusiasm
for this kind of patron. Designs for stone chimneypieces, a marquetry staircase, and furniture were supplied by *W. R. Lethaby*,
but only a floral mosaic floor in the hall survives as a reminder
of all the richly patterned surfaces.* About 1850, during the
ownership of James Forbes of the East India Company, the
grounds were adorned with Hindu sculpture, said to be the
earliest of such displays in England.

SPRINGBOK HOUSE (now an Islamic Centre), formerly Warren
House, further E along Wood Lane, is austere Jacobean revival
in yellow brick around an earlier core. The later, more ornate
porte-cochère was probably added by the Keysers (owners up to
1890); Sir John Keyser was the influential chairman of the Colne
Valley Water Company. A previous owner was the architect
Robert Smirke, known to have made alterations c. 1824.

Finally, the housing areas which grew up by the stations of which
the first, opened in 1890 s of the church, survives, much altered
on conversion to a house. It is at the SE corner of GORDON
AVENUE, which was created around it. Most of the substantial
turn-of-the-century villas have been crowded out by denser later
development. Survivors include HERONDALE on the N side,
by *Waterhouse*, 1891–2, red brick with tilehanging and a half-
timbered gable, in the Shaw manner which Waterhouse used for
his later houses. No. 63, CHEYNE COTTAGE, is of 1910 by
Clough Williams-Ellis and *Scott*. Rendered brick, with odd top-
heavy mansard with cupola; a Venetian window in the gable.
Further W, a few early C19 cottages with Tudor detail (Nos.
124–130), and some C19 gatepiers that belonged to STANMORE
PARK. This was a Palladian mansion built by *Vardy* in 1763,
altered by *Holland* in 1786 for the Drummonds, bankers, and
demolished in 1938. Parts of the grounds remain: N of Gordon
Avenue is a lake, to the S a golf course with BELLMOUNT, a

---

*The notable series of tapestry panels of the Holy Grail, designed for the dining
room by *Burne-Jones* and woven by *J. H. Dearle* in 1890–4, were sold in 1920. Later
versions of five of the six panels are in Birmingham Museum and Art Gallery.

mound erected as a *point de vue* from Canons by the Duke of
Chandos.

Two areas of C20 commuters' houses can be recommended. N of
London Road and the terminus of the Metropolitan line extension of 1932 is an unusually daring thirties enclave, part of the
development on the S end of the Warren House estate. Nos. 1,
3, and 6 KERRY AVENUE are by *Gerald Lacoste*; Nos. 2–10
VALENCIA ROAD, with curved glazed staircases as their main
front feature, by *Douglas J. Wood*, 1933–4. At the end of Valencia
Road are two contemporary blocks of flats (WARREN FIELDS),
c. 1937 by *Sir Owen Williams*, since made more demure by
tilehanging. One back wall still reveals a ruthlessly plain concrete
grid. The best building is near the N end of Kerry Avenue: No.
14, *R. H. Uren*'s own house, 1937, pale brick, with the well
proportioned cubist massing one would expect from the architect
of Hornsey Town Hall (Hy). Two storeys on a tall plinth, one
side set slightly forward, a taller belvedere at the back to make
the most of the enviable views. Its neighbour, No. 16, is of the
1970s, purple brick, with three floors stepping back, monopitch
roofs, and a large window in the top floor. In total contrast is the
well manicured Tudor nostalgia of CANONS DRIVE to the SE,
developed from 1926, with detached half-timbered or tiled
houses by *A. J. Butcher*. The first and most varied stretch lies
between Lake View and Powell Close overlooking the basin
remaining from the C18 Canons Park (*see* below).

LITTLE STANMORE

ST LAWRENCE, Whitchurch Lane, at the S end of the former S
avenue to Canons. Of the medieval church only the W tower
remains, the usual Middlesex C14 and C15 type with diagonal W
buttresses and a projecting NE turret. An appealing multi-
coloured mixture of flint, dark local ferricrete, and Reigate stone,
speckled with later brick repairs. C18 W door and window. The
rest of the church was rebuilt by *John James* for Chandos in 1715,
very much in the style of a private chapel, and dedicated in 1720.
It has a restrained exterior, typical of James, of brick with heavy
stone dressings, with undecorated arched windows and broad
Tuscan corner pilasters. The S side of the nave projects at either
end; the chancel has a pedimented E wall. The interior is all the
more surprising: unaisled and with a chancel, or rather retro- 34
choir, appearing stage-fashion behind a segmental pediment supported by fluted Corinthian columns and pilasters of dark wood,
and above a low wooden reredos. The splendid carved decoration
is attributed to *Gibbons*. Behind this is the organ, originally by
Gerald Smith, but much enlarged. The church is painted from
vaulted top to bottom with virtues, evangelists, biblical scenes,
and figured architecture. The artists responsible were *Laguerre*
for the vault, with scenes of the miracles, mostly in sepia and
grey, with gilding, and probably *Sleter* for the nave walls, which
have monochrome figures of the cardinal virtues and the evangelists (the N side painted after 1736, when the windows were
blocked by the new mausoleum). At the E and W ends are large,

more colourful paintings attributed to *Bellucci*. In the semi-dome over the Duke's box in the w gallery, an excellent copy of Raphael's Transfiguration. Flanking the altar the Nativity and the Pietà, and beyond, on either side of the organ in the retro-choir, Moses with the Tablets of the Law, and the Sermon on the Mount. – The fine contemporary furnishings include the FONT, an octagonal marble bowl on a baluster; the PULPIT, altered from a three-decker in 1854; excellent wrought-iron COMMUNION RAILS and GATES; STALLS with uniform fronts; and BOX PEWS, some still with chains for prayerbooks.

The E end, with the vista through the columns, is highly effective in the international Baroque sense. Originally the retro-choir was given radiance by concealed lighting from the side. This was obscured when the enlarged organ and its flanking paintings were brought forward. However the C18 aesthetic intentions can be better appreciated now that the Victorian screen and stained glass* have been removed and the paintings thoroughly and painstakingly cleaned and conserved (1973–83 by the *Eve Baker Trust* and later under *Dr H. D. Ingenhoff* of Tübingen). Yet despite these improvements, Pevsner's verdict of 1952 holds good. The church is Baroque only in its intentions. The glow which one would expect from such lavish decoration is absent. The climate is English and moderate. So long as this country remained faithful to its own Baroque, the Baroque of Greenwich and Blenheim, success was assured. Where it strove to emulate the Berninis and Asams it failed.

Attached to the church on the N is a contemporary room intended as the Chandos Mausoleum but now merely the anteroom to the larger mausoleum erected in 1735–6 to house the grand monument to the Duke and his two wives. *Gibbs*'s square space is splendidly and completely painted by *Sleter* and *G. Brunetti* with fictive architecture and with a dome with an oculus showing the sky – a Pantheon-like setting for the monument against the w wall, which is impressive, though sculpturally by no means up to the standard of Rysbrack and Roubiliac. *Grinling Gibbons* was paid for it in 1718, although Chandos objected to the price. The Duke stands in the middle, in Roman costume and bewigged; to l. and r. his two wives kneel like virtues, 'veiled and devout' (Mrs Esdaile). Plain pilasters separate the three figures. They carry urns, and between the urns is a kind of canopy in relief, the whole of a grand and noble restraint. Against the S wall are two more monuments to members of the family: Mary, wife of the first Marquess of Carnarvon, 1738 by *Henry Cheere*, no figures, but a black sarcophagus against a pyramid in relief in an Ionic aedicule; and Margaret, Marchioness of Carnarvon, *c.* 1760 († 1768), a colossal plain classical sarcophagus with S-curved fluting at the ends. In the anteroom, minor family wall-tablets to Francis Brydges † 1714, a cartouche with cherubs attributed to *Andrew Carpenter* (GF); Henry Brydges † 1728, coloured marbles, with pediment; and John Marquess of Caernarvon † 1727. – In the CHURCHYARD a fine Rococo headstone to Thomas Waterfall † 1747.

*A window by *W. de Morgan* of *c.* 1870 is now in the stained glass museum at Ely.

CANONS

CANONS derived its name from its medieval owners, the priory of St Bartholomew the Great. In 1709 the estate was acquired by James Brydges, who between 1713 and c. 1720 created an exceedingly lavish mansion. It lasted less than forty years, but its existence conditioned the whole development of the area, and as one of the most ambitious houses near London it deserves some account here. Brydges was the son of the eighth Baron Chandos of Sudeley. He became Earl of Caernarvon in 1714, and Duke of Chandos in 1719, after he had amassed a fabulous fortune as Marlborough's Paymaster-General of Forces abroad from 1707 to 1712. Pope's neat comments on Timon's Villa in his Epistle to Lord Burlington were no doubt suggested by Chandos, even if not meant to be applied only to him. Pope's doubts proved justified. The estate was broken up almost immediately after the princely owner's death. A sale took place in 1747, when much was salvaged from the house and grounds for use elsewhere, and the house was demolished by 1753, although the private chapel attached to the NE corner survived as a ruin as late as 1821.

The estate had belonged from 1604 to Sir Thomas Lake, James I's Secretary of State. Plans by the surveyor *John Thorpe* entitled 'My Lady Lake's house', probably made after 1630, show a large courtyard house with a symmetrical bowed and bayed frontage (cf. Holland Park, Kensington, KC), which probably survived as the core of the C18 house. Brydges began to make plans for improvements in 1713, the year he married into the Lake family. He was not an easy client, and ran through several architects. *William Talman* was the first, responsible for offices for the old house in 1713–14, and for an unexecuted project for the new one; then came *John James*, who rebuilt St Lawrence's church (*see* above) in 1714–16, and was probably responsible for remodelling the N front of the old house, introducing the giant pilasters which conditioned the elevation of the rest. The credit for the completed design, with its two festive eleven-bay fronts to S and E, is due to *James Gibbs*, employed from 1716 to 1719, although the work was completed under *John Price*, whose name appeared on engravings of the elevations. *Vanbrugh* and *Robert Benson* were also consulted. The main fronts were of stone, two-storeyed, with a lower attic storey above the cornice, and statues on the parapet. The S front had a giant attached Ionic portico. It was 'the most magnificent house in England,' said Defoe, with *Bellucci* paintings on the ceilings of hall and staircase, plasterwork by *Bagutti*, and grates and firebacks of silver. *Gibbs*'s private chapel, where Handel was Kapellmeister from 1717 to 1719, had especially splendid fittings. The park included an equestrian statue of George I and a standing figure of George II.

After the sale the staircase was incorporated into *Ware*'s Chesterfield House in Mayfair, later moved to the Odeon cinema Broadstairs, and destroyed in the Second World War. Altar, pulpit, and font from the private chapel are at Fawley church, Oxfordshire (formerly Bucks); the organ is at Holy Trinity, Gosport, Hampshire; paintings by *Bellucci* and *Joshua Price*'s

painted glass windows from the chapel were bought by Lord
Foley and installed for him by *Gibbs* in Great Witley parish
church, Worcestershire. From the park, wrought-iron gates and
railings went to St John, Hampstead (Ca), a gate to Durdans,
Epsom, Surrey, and the equestrian George II to Golden Square
(Wm).

CANONS PARK. The successor to the short-lived early C18
mansion of James Brydges has since 1929 formed part of the
North London Collegiate School (*see* below), but substantial
areas of Brydges' park are still recognizable. It was laid out by
A. Blackwell, with six radiating avenues; the landscaping was
later modified by *Repton*. Within the school grounds to the E
there is a lake. To the W the public park includes the site of the
W avenue up to Marsh Lane and the S avenue leading from the
parish church. Between them, close to a lawn with cedars, is a
TEMPLE: four Ionic columns and pediment to the N, two
columns, perhaps re-set, on the other side. S of this are the tall
C18 red brick walls of the kitchen garden, now sheltering the
GEORGE V MEMORIAL GARDENS, with a formal layout of 1938.
The main approach to the house was from the SW, along Canons
Drive, providing an impressive simultaneous view of both S and
E fronts, as Defoe records. Here trees and a basin survive amid
select Tudor suburbia (*see* above), and a pair of gatepiers at the
entrance from Edgware High Street.

NORTH LONDON COLLEGIATE SCHOOL. Soon after the sale of
Chandos's palace in 1747, William Hallett, a worthy cabinet-
maker, built for himself in its place, and partly from its material,
a compact two-storeyed villa of the type that was becoming
popular from the mid C18 in the countryside around London: it
had a broad, three-bay S front and E and W fronts with central
bows, and survives today as the core of the school, enlarged,
embellished, and heightened in 1910 by *C. E. Mallows* for Sir
Arthur Du Cros, founder of the Dunlop Rubber Company. He
added a new entrance courtyard to the E, and a large N wing with
Corinthian pilasters above the channelled ground floor. On the
W front the resulting lopsided elevation is balanced by an open
screen of similar pilasters linking the house to a terraced garden
with a bold pergola of brick and stone bands. The paved gardens
to the N were covered in 1939–40 by *Sir Albert Richardson*'s
additions for the school, of buff brick, in a neutral style, with
set-back rendered top floor. Separate hall, with tall rectangular
windows and shallow pitched roof. Further N a drawing school,
also by *Richardson*, was added in 1957. The music school of
1971, brick and glass, and the headmistress's house of 1977, a
simple detached neo-Georgian building at the end of Canons
Drive, are both by *John O'Neilly*, a pupil of Richardson.

WEALDSTONE

The only industrial centre in the borough, developed in the later
C19 around the railway line, with some good minor Edwardiana
along the main street. The uneventful suburbs merge imperceptibly

into the surrounding areas, with one surprising reminder of the pre-war countryside: the buildings of an early C19 model farm in Kenton Lane.

HOLY TRINITY, Tudor Road. By *Roumieu & Aitchison*, 1881. Dull, coarse exterior of Kentish rag with Bath stone plate tracery to the aisles and circular clerestory windows. Polygonal apse, no tower; the two w bays built only in 1904. Finished off in 1967 by *James E. Ralph* with a w lobby which also leads to a hall above a range of shops. Ingeniously reordered in 1977 by *A. J. Watkins*, who converted the chancel to an informal sitting area, divided from the nave by folding doors, and with its own access through the former organ chamber and new SE porch. Watkins also reorientated the nave, so that one now looks S between the heavy stone columns to the altar placed against the S wall, with the original pews rearranged fanwise. – STAINED GLASS. Chancel lancets late C19: Crucifixion and evangelist symbols. – S aisle central window 1917, the angel appearing to Isaiah (a portrait of the vicar's son, H. J. C. Chapman) – a forceful design in Arts and Crafts greens and purples.

ST ANSELM, Uppingham Avenue, Belmont. A large brick basilica, 1938–41 by *N. H. Cachemaille-Day*, surprisingly grand for its date. One of several suburban churches built in place of central London churches demolished at the same time (cf. St Andrew Kingsbury, Br), re-using old materials and furnishings. Here they came from St Anselm, Davies Street, Mayfair, an interesting neo-Byzantine church of 1891 by *Balfour & Turner*. Its fine stone columns, originally set in pairs, were re-used for simpler arcades below plain brick walls with small clerestory windows. w gallery; apsed E end. The large traceried w window, and the side windows set within internal stone arcading, and with thick-paned 'Prior' glass, also come from Davies Street. In the apse a new BALDACCHINO, incorporating a PAINTING of saints around the cross attributed to *Giovanni Caroto*, and surrounded by handsome marble paving; the Virgin and Child in the Lady Chapel, below a *Comper*-like tester, is attributed to the studio of *Luca Giordano*. Both paintings came to the Mayfair church from the Hanover Chapel, Regent Street.

ST JOSEPH (R.C.), High Street. 1931 by *Adrian G. Scott*. A notable, though still medievalizing exterior of warm coloured stone. w tower with entrance recessed within a tall arch; two large dormer windows in the low steep-pitched roof. Inside, a fine and unusual effect is created by the use of stone for the chief structural elements and whitewash otherwise, and by the introduction of two transepts in the second and fourth bay of five in all. The dormer windows correspond to them. In the other bays small clerestory windows. Aisles with open lean-to roofs (these and the dormers derive from Lutyens's St Jude Hampstead Garden Suburb, Ca). Very low outer aisles. There are no capitals or bases to the piers throughout. – Figure SCULPTURE on the w front by *Peter Watts*, 1952.

BAPTIST CHURCH, High Street. 1905 by *John Wills & Sons* of Derby. Bright red terracotta, Perp tracery. The thin NW tower with the curious feature of green glass in the belfry windows is a distinctive landmark. Halls of 1930.

METHODIST CHURCH, Locket Road. 1904. A sturdy red brick building with a large Perp w window with thick mullions running down as buttresses to flank the w door.

HARROW CIVIC CENTRE, Milton Road and Station Road. 1972 by *Eric Broughton* in association with the *Borough Architect*. Six storeys around a courtyard, where the planting is more appealing than the architecture. Heavy-handed contrasting vertical and horizontal rhythms, the former achieved on the upper storeys by clumsy projecting stone panels. Separate council chamber linked by a glazed bridge.

HARROW ARTS CENTRE. *See* under Schools, below.

COURT HOUSE, Rosslyn Crescent. Demure one-storeyed neo-Georgian front range; balustraded centre with cupola; two clerestory-lit courtrooms behind. Pantiled roofs. 1931–4 by the *M.C.C.* Architect's Department under *W. T. Curtis* (an interesting contrast to its progressive modern school designs of the later 1930s – *see* below).

POLICE STATION, High Street. 1905. Handsome free Tudor front with central archway flanked by two canted stone mullioned bays, and a doorway with the mannered elongated consoles typical of *J. Dixon Butler*'s Metropolitan Police buildings of this period.

LIBRARY, Grant Road. By the *M.C.C.*, *c.* 1960, a simple two-storeyed building of mottled brick.

SALVATORIAN COLLEGE, High Street, next to St Joseph. A well organized approach, with the plain rendered assembly hall of *c.* 1962, on mosaic-clad columns, by *John A. Strubbe*, screening the older buildings (1931 onwards) from the street, with a line of trees in front and behind.

SCHOOLS. Representatives of all periods. The earliest is in Grant Road (now YOUTH AND COMMUNITY CENTRE), C19, still on a village scale; red brick with a little Gothic detail and tilehung gables. The HARROW ARTS CENTRE, Wealdstone High Road, was formerly *Ernest George & Peto*'s last school for the Harrow School Board, 1886. Tile-hung master's house in front; nicely proportioned school block behind. WHITEFRIARS FIRST AND MIDDLE SCHOOLS, Whitefriars Avenue, 1910, is an early effort by the *Middlesex County Council* (*H. G. Crothall*), still the London Board School type, with an imposing two-storey centre and gabled wings. The 1930s examples demonstrate how variety of massing of simple forms was used to give individuality. The former BELMONT SECONDARY SCHOOL, Fisher Road, of 1935 (disused at the time of writing), is one of the first of the progressive designs of the 1930s by *Curtis* and *Burchett*. Asymmetrical brick front with entrance tower; hall range decorated by white stone fins running through the windows. Plain courtyard layout behind. Adjoining this site to the SW, BELMONT FIRST AND MIDDLE SCHOOLS, Hibbert Road, 1938, an austere, formal composition with central tower flanked by angled wings. The school of 1936 in Kenton Lane has a long range which builds up to a three-storey centre, the staircase tower accentuated by a little turret for the water tower.

BELMONT HEALTH CENTRE, Locket Road. Neat dark brick; *c.* 1980.

HARROW LEISURE CENTRE, Christchurch Avenue. 1975 by the *London Borough of Harrow Architect's Department*. Indoor swimming pool and games courts within the usual large brick cubes, but with the entrance side successfully broken up by projecting glazed areas. A well-lit foyer, more generous than average.

HARROW AND WEALDSTONE STATION. Opened as Harrow Station in 1837, the London and Birmingham Railway's first stop after Euston. Pretty, haphazard buildings of 1875 for the London and North Western Railway Co., w of the tracks, in a rustic Italianate with deep eaves; on the E side, facing the High Street, an original asymmetrical composition of 1911 by *Gerald Horsley*, fitted on to a tight site, and so not quite as successful as his contemporary station at Hatch End (Hw) (q.v.). Orange brick with stone dressings. Gabled end with Venetian window and cartouche; lower booking hall with canted entrance. A striped clock tower rises behind. Good platform buildings and canopies of both dates.

PERAMBULATION. The station lies at the s end of the main road of the C19 hamlet. The HIGH STREET has become the usual miscellaneous shopping street; apart from the churches and public buildings the best building is LLOYDS BANK (No. 36) by *Horace Field & Simmons*, 1907, an accomplished brick Baroque front, quite narrow, with pilasters, pediment, and bowed ground-floor window still with its good original lettering. To the E, the Harrow Park estate, laid out from 1854 around CANNING ROAD, PALMERSTON ROAD, and PEEL ROAD, was built up slowly with very minor villas and terraces.

w of the High Street, the industrial sites close to the railway for long included the Whitefriars glass works (E) and the Stationery Office works (W). The only old giant left today is KODAK (Headstone Drive and Harrow View), established here in 1891 and with buildings of every period since. The SOCIAL CENTRE of 1939 is by *F. J. Wills*. In WHITEFRIARS AVENUE, WINSOR & NEWTON (now part of a larger concern), with quite a handsome post-war main office building, an austere but careful design in brick with plain boxed windows and a stone cornice with the firm's logo as carved centrepiece.

To the s, one relic of the rural past: in HIGH MEAD, off Station Road, a weatherboarded BARN from Greenhill Farm.

BELMONT, E of Wealdstone, is almost entirely inter-war suburbia, traversed from s to N by the older KENTON LANE running gently uphill from the former hamlet of Kenton (q.v.) towards Harrow Weald. Opposite Grange Avenue one remarkable survival: KENTON LANE FARM, an early C19 model farm to the designs of *Robert Abraham* for William Loudon, the father of J. C. Loudon (*see also* Pinner, Perambulation 4), who illustrated it in his early work, *Observations on Laying Out Farms in the Scotch Style Adapted to England* (1812). His plan shows a regular farmyard with buildings on three sides, the central one a barn for straw and corn, with roundhouse behind, flanked by lower cowsheds and stables, and a detached farmhouse facing the yard on the fourth side. The roundhouse has gone, but the simple brick and timber farm buildings (now used for milk bottling) are still recognizable. The shelter shed on the s side was originally open-sided. The farmhouse is in a plain Regency style, now of red brick, but formerly plastered. Two storeys with shallow hipped roof; ground-floor windows within blind arches. The E entrance on the garden side, away from the farm buildings, is later, and so is the upper storey of the fourth bay to the N.

HILLINGDON

INTRODUCTION

Hillingdon, on the fringe of the built-up area of London, is one of the largest of the outer London boroughs and has some of the most extreme architectural contrasts to be found anywhere in England. It stretches N for about seven miles from a flat, noisy plain dominated by motorways and airport, through the respectable, monotonous suburbia of the parish which gives the borough its name, to undulating green-belt countryside around Northwood and Harefield, the only sizeable area where something remains of rural Middlesex. In the southern parts much evidence of prehistoric settlement has been found, although nothing of this is now visible.*

*At Harmondsworth was an important multi-period occupation site, ranging from the Mesolithic to the Saxon periods, with considerable Neolithic, Bronze Age, and Iron Age occupation, a sub-oval Romano-British enclosure with field system, and a Middle Saxon hut in an enclosure. Part of a major monument, a Neolithic cursus – a long ditched avenue 21 metres wide – ran approximately N–S from Stanwell (Surrey) to an apparent terminal at Bigley Ditch. It is crossed by a second fragmentary cursus at Heathrow, where there are traces of a Neolithic hengiform monument and a probable mortuary enclosure; Heathrow also had settlements from the Late Bronze Age to the Roman period. Evidence for early occupation has been found in most of the other southern parishes; at Stockley Park there was an Iron Age settlement with four huts, granaries(?), and evidence for metal-working. Further N, Palaeolithic material has been found at Uxbridge, Harefield Moor is rich in Mesolithic and Neolithic finds, and there is a probable Roman site at Ruislip.

In the northern parts, scattered among their C20 imitations, there are still timber-framed farmhouses, remodelled or rebuilt in the C16 and C17, sprouting the characteristically showy brick chimneystacks of that period. Few farm buildings are still in agricultural use, but the mighty early C15 barn at Harmondsworth is one of the best in the country and the great barn at Ruislip Manor is probably even older, although more altered. Despite suburban expansion, many of the old village centres, bypassed by the major roads slicing through the neighbourhood, have preserved enough of their old character to be enjoyable. Miraculously, this is true even of some of those at the s end of the borough; West Drayton, surrounded by indifferent suburbia, still has a pleasant green; Harmondsworth and Longford are still small, friendly oases even though they are so close to Heathrow.

The medieval churches include some of the most interesting in the outer London area, relatively unaltered by Victorian restoration. The C12 work ranges from tiny, unassuming Cowley to the elaborately carved doorways of Harmondsworth and Hillingdon; Harmondsworth has a C12 arcade as well. Ruislip, Hillingdon, and Hayes all illustrate the substantial enlargements common in the C13 and C14. Many churches have the typical, rather squat late medieval tower common in the area around London, with a little turret rising above the battlements, or sometimes with a later small cupola, as at Harlington and Uxbridge. Some of these churches – especially Cranford, Hillingdon, and Harefield – will be visited less for their architecture than for their rich collections of monuments of the C16–18; many are outstanding on a national level, a reflection of the closeness of this area to metropolitan workshops.

What is missing is nearly all the large houses of the patrons of these monuments – the Newdigates at Harefield, the Astons and Berkeleys at Cranford – so one's picture of the spread of architectural fashion in secular buildings is much less complete here than for example in Hounslow. From the C16 and early C17 the main survivals are confined to the gatehouse alone of the grand Tudor establishment of the Pagets at West Drayton and a fragment of Treaty House at Uxbridge. The one important surviving house of the C17 is Swakeleys, a fascinating reflection of the meeting of City artisan mannerist traditions and the court style in the 1630s. The compact gentleman's house of the late C17 onwards also has few surviving representatives – the best was the short-lived Dawley

---

CHURCHES and PUBLIC BUILDINGS etc

① St Lawrence, Cowley	⑭ St Martin, West Drayton
② St Dunstan, Cranford	⑮ St Matthew, Yiewsley
③ St Mary, Harefield	Ⓐ Harefield Hospital
④ St Peter and Paul, Harlington	Ⓑ Breakspears, Harefield
⑤ St Jerome, Dawley	Ⓒ Manor Farm, Harmondsworth
⑥ St Mary, Harmondsworth	Ⓓ Hillingdon Court, Hillingdon
⑦ St Mary, Hayes	Ⓔ Bishopshalt School, Hillingdon
⑧ St John Baptist, Hillingdon	Ⓕ Hillingdon Hospital
⑨ St Giles, Ickenham	Ⓖ Ickenham Manor
⑩ Holy Trinity, Northwood	Ⓗ Manor Farm, Ruislip
⑪ St Martin, Ruislip	Ⓘ Hillingdon Civic Centre, Uxbridge
⑫ St Margaret, Uxbridge	Ⓙ Mount Vernon Hospital, Northwood
⑬ St Andrew, Uxbridge	Ⓚ Brunel University

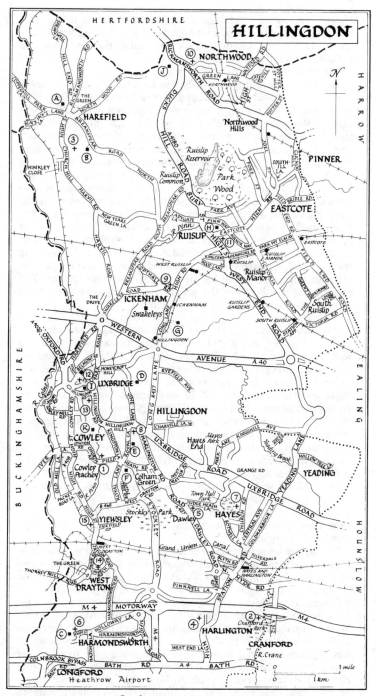

HILLINGDON

See also maps on pp. 341, 345, 347.

House, Harlington – although lesser buildings remain to illustrate
the changing tastes of the C 17–18 (Cedar House, Hillingdon; Breakspears, Harefield). Among C 19 country houses the best preserved
is *Hardwick*'s Hillingdon Court.

The rural nature of the area, in which the only exception was the
town of Uxbridge, long established as the main market centre for
NW Middlesex, was first disturbed around 1800 by the building of
the Grand Union Canal, running S of Hayes W towards Yiewsley,
then N along the river valley up to Uxbridge. Some attractive
stretches of canalscape remain, with locks, bridges, and keepers'
cottages, e.g. at Cowley. Elsewhere, more intensive industry
developed along the canal banks, and working-class housing sprang
up to serve it. The main railway line running through Hayes and
Yiewsley encouraged further indiscriminate expansion, and it is no
coincidence that these areas are now the least appealing in the
borough. On the higher ground further N, suburban expansion was
more carefully planned, for the rural character of the area was the
main appeal for the residents of the new 'Metroland', dependent
on the Metropolitan Railway which arrived in the 1880s. Among
the first places to grow was Northwood, with an ample quota of
superior houses, followed by the more middle-class Ruislip. The
rapid expansion between the wars, here and around other older
centres, was generally less distinguished.

The new borough of Hillingdon, created in 1965 from the local
authorities of Uxbridge, Ruislip, Northwood, Hayes and Harlington, and Yiewsley and West Drayton, made its mark architecturally
in the 1970s, both with its civic centre by *RMJM* forcefully
declaring its allegiance to the suburban spirit and with an inventive
range of council housing provided by the borough architect's
department under *Thurston Williams* (borough architect 1965–77).
In reaction against earlier council housing, low-rise buildings with
pitched roofs and entrances at ground level became basic requirements, but they did not lead to uniformity. The experimental
types built at this time included accommodation for single people
(Whitehall Road Uxbridge), expandable houses (Harefield), and a
community house (Hayes). It was declared council policy to scatter
such buildings widely over the borough; Highgrove, Eastcote (by
Edward Cullinan & Partners), is the most daring response to the
challenge to fit tactfully into the select northern fringe of Metroland. Later borough architects: *Paul Ferrari* (from 1977); *Mervyn
Oakley* (from 1990).

The major agent for change since the second world war has been
Heathrow Airport. Although conceived in the 1940s, its wider
impact has been gradual. Tall, alien-looking hotels around the
fringe of the site began to arrive in the 1970s; the growth of major
business centres came only in the 1980s, most notably at Stockley
Park near Yiewsley, an imaginative creation on waste land, where
both architecture and landscaping are of a high order. The increasingly commercial nature of the area is reflected by the way in which
larger surviving older houses have been given over to office use
(Swakeleys is the most notable conversion). Likewise, existing
centres have been transformed. At Uxbridge, glassy office towers
of the 1980s now loom over the small-scale buildings remaining
from an older era.

The population of Hillingdon has remained nearly static since 1961. In 1981 it was 229,913.

FURTHER READING

The area is covered by the *Middlesex V.C.H.* vol. 4 (1971); the DoE list dates from 1974. The Ruislip, Northwood and Eastcote Local History Society produces both a Journal and occasional publications, among them D. Tottman, *Ruislip-Northwood, an early example of town planning*, no. 2 (1982). Older works still of value include vol. VI of the *St Paul's Ecclesiological Transactions* on the monuments of St Dunstan Cranford, H. Wilson, *800 Years of Harlington Church* (1926), and W. Goatman, *Harefield and her Church* (1947). On Swakeleys there is a Survey of London Monograph (1934), and a summary of new discoveries by Neil Burton in an English Heritage Report (typescript, E.H. London Division).

More recent general histories: E. Bowlt, *The Goodliest Place in Middlesex* (a history of Ruislip) (1989); A. H. Cox, *West Drayton and Yiewsley through the Centuries*, and *St Martin's Church, West Drayton's Heritage* (1975); D. Rust, *Parish Church of Harmondsworth* (1966); M. Evans, *Harefield's Old Buildings* (1982); C. Hearmon, *Uxbridge, A Concise History* (1982); M. V. Hughes, *The Story of Ickenham* (1983); S. A. J. MacVeigh, *Drayton of the Pagets* (1970).

ACKNOWLEDGEMENTS

Many local experts gave me the benefit of their knowledge of their areas; I am especially grateful to Eileen Bowlt, who introduced me to much in Ruislip, Eastcote, and Northwood, to Carolyn Cotton (Uxbridge), A. H. Cox (West Drayton), Elona Cuthbertson (Harefield), K. H. Pearce and members of the Uxbridge Local History Society, Douglas Rust (Harmondsworth), and B. T. White of Hayes and Harlington Local History Society. Among many others who helped on particular subjects I must thank in particular the Rev. R. D. Fenwick (Ruislip), the Rev. S. Beebee (Cranford), Anthony Quiney (timber-framed buildings), Elain Harwood (Breakspears), R. S. Adlington and I. Hamilton-Penney (Brunel University), Peter Eley (borough architecture of the 1970s), and the staff of Hillingdon Borough Council.

BRUNEL UNIVERSITY

Between Kingston Lane and Cleveland Road, s of Uxbridge: a purposeful, no-nonsense group of buildings, as befits a university which concentrates on technical training, and a little forbidding because of the prevalence of purple brick and concrete, those favourite materials of the mid 1960s. The university began life as the College of Advanced Technology at Acton. Plans were already afoot to move the college to a site near Uxbridge when the Robbins

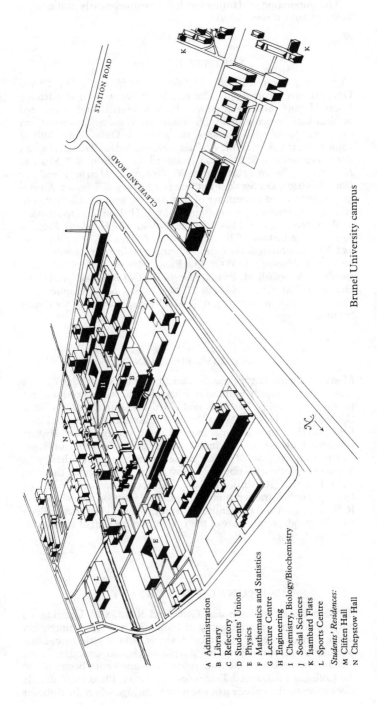

STATION ROAD

CLEVELAND ROAD

Brunel University campus

A Administration
B Library
C Refectory
D Students' Union
E Physics
F Mathematics and Statistics
G Lecture Centre
H Engineering
I Chemistry, Biology/Biochemistry
J Social Sciences
K Isambard Flats
L Sports Centre

Students' Residences:
M Cliffen Hall
N Chepstow Hall

report of 1963 recommended upgrading. The master plan for a new
university for 5,000 students was drawn up by *Richard Sheppard*
in 1965; the main buildings were complete by 1971. Communal
buildings, library, lecture centre, and residences are by *Sheppard
Robson & Partners*; laboratories and technical buildings by *Stillman
& Eastwick-Field*.

Despite the deliberately limited architectural vocabulary, the
different buildings have distinctive characters – an asset on such a
large, flat site with no special physical characteristics. A central
pedestrian spine route runs from W to E, from the plain administrative building (1966) next to the formal pool which defines the
edge of the campus, past library and refectory, to the focal point of
the LECTURE CENTRE (1966–8), the building with the most rugged
individuality. It has a rounded staircase at either end, and on the
N side a monumental entrance beneath two levels of jutting-out
lecture theatres. This entrance front forms the tallest and grandest
side of a paved sunken square, suggestive of a formal amphitheatre,
although, disappointingly, the buildings on the other sides are
irregular, and mostly turn their backs on this square. The area
would no doubt have been livelier had the students' union been
built on the W side, as had originally been intended. Instead,
there is PHYSICS (1969–71), a long block with bays articulated by
projecting uprights, and on the E side MATHEMATICAL SCIENCES
(1966–8). Further W later technical buildings (BIOLOGY, CHEM-
ISTRY, BIOCHEMISTRY). To the S is a more informal grassy area,
surrounded by the crisp brutalist group of *Stillman & Eastwick-
Field*'s ENGINEERING BUILDINGS (1965–7). When planned, these 107
were one of the largest centres of their kind in Europe. They form
an imposingly massive square with projecting upper floors, partly
open on the ground floor to a central courtyard. Around this is an
L-shaped group with four towers cantilevered out over lower link
buildings. Expanses of shuttered concrete are relieved by the glazed
links with a repeating pattern of corner beams cutting into the
window areas. W of the centre is *Sheppard*'s LIBRARY, a serious
building, simply arranged. Four floors, with broad horizontal concrete panels, a central approach up to the first floor. In contrast,
the REFECTORY opposite is low and unassuming, a deliberate
expression of the democratic approach of a new university (compare
Sheppard's monumental dining hall at Churchill College, Cambridge). On the E fringe of the campus a typically bleak red brick
SPORTS CENTRE and students' residences of the 1960s, also of
red brick, blocks of irregular outline, three and four storeys tall,
containing rooms off staircases. W of the main entrance, SOCIAL
SCIENCES, 1985 by *Stillman & Eastwick-Field*, red brick in the
manner of Hillingdon Civic Centre, Uxbridge (a palpable failure
of nerve). Further W in ISEMBARD CLOSE, students' flats of 1975–
7, designed by the university; standard components arranged in the
suburban image of groups of two- to four-storey houses with hipped
roofs and pebbledashed walls.

INTERIORS. In the LECTURE CENTRE, between the projecting
theatres and the sixteen inner ones in the core of the building, a
generous roof-lit upper foyer. Large geometric mural. The
LIBRARY also has a roof-lit inner space, over the librarians' desks
on the first floor, which rises as a curved concrete funnel through

the upper floors. On the staircase landings three RELIEFS by *Joe Tilson*, wooden panels with the themes of ladders, pyramid, and circle. In the pool by the w entrance perspex shapes chamfered to reflect the colours of the rainbow, by *Trevor Long*.

COWLEY

A small rural parish until the C19. A few old houses remain along the unpleasantly busy main street, amongst the indifferent C20 buildings that extend from Uxbridge to Yiewsley. The church, no doubt representing an older settlement, is some distance to the E; to the w is the quiet retreat of the canal with its inn and locks, and the river beyond, right on the edge of the Greater London boundary.

ST LAWRENCE, Church Road. An unenlarged early medieval church, a remarkable survival. The small C12 rubble building of flint and local ferricrete has a C13 chancel and a timber bellcote rebuilt in 1780. Restored in 1897. Inside, a white-ceiled late medieval roof with crown-posts. No chancel arch, but above the site of the rood screen a simple arrangement of six openwork arches resting on the tie-beam. In the chancel three E lancets and a C13 N door. Among the varied nave windows one on the s side has typically early C14 tracery: two ogee-headed lights and a quatrefoil. Two-storeyed w gallery, quite picturesque, created when the bellcote was rebuilt. – Medieval woodwork: PEWS in the chancel, and tracery heads from a SCREEN incorporated in later work. – BRASS. Walter Pope † 1505 and wives (one missing) (N wall of chancel).

In CHURCH ROAD No. 27 is the former rectory, a pleasant villa built in 1807–11. Central door with fanlight flanked by blank bays. N wing added after 1825.

In the HIGH STREET the best houses are N of Station Road: THE OLD HOUSE, close to the road, a three-window front with a pretty C18 pedimented doorcase; THE CROWN, a low timber-framed inn, much altered; and THE BEECHES, much restored C18, five windows wide with red brick dressings. POPLAR COTTAGE, a yeoman farmer's house of *c.* 1710 (dated brick) consisting of a simple brick front of three bays, is brutally separated by ugly offices from OLD VINE COTTAGE, a picturesque mixture which has developed from a main N–S range of *c.* 1600 with cross-wing; C18 brown brick front. COWLEY HOUSE, set back behind high walls, is substantial: five bays wide, three storeys high, called newly built in 1738, but probably recased in the late C18. It was altered by *Sir Reginald Blomfield* in 1896 (when a N extension was added), gutted by fire in 1929, and converted to flats *c.* 1980, with new flats added in the grounds.

COWLEY PEACHEY was a separate settlement further S along the HIGH ROAD, marked now by THE OLD COTTAGE, a late medieval Wealden-type hall house, an unusual survivor in this area. Exposed timber-framing, the centre with a later jettied floor inserted; half-hipped roof. Opposite, BARNACRE is C17 with

square framing; MAYGOODS FARM is a much altered c 17 lobby-
entry house. Also on the main road, four modest brick cottages
of 1947, well detailed, with the typical slight roof pitch of the
1940s. By *F. R. S. Yorke* of *Yorke, Rosenberg & Mardall.*
The GRAND UNION CANAL, built in 1791–1805, runs to the w
of the main road. Off PACKET BOAT LANE, Cowley Peachey,
is the Packet Boat Dock, built for the passenger- and parcel-
carrying 'fly' boats from Paddington, early c 19. Humped brick
arch over the entrance, cottages grouped on the opposite side of
the canal. Further w, OLD MILL LANE, still rural, winds
between two branches of the river Frays. The OLD MILL
HOUSE, with a fine red brick mid c 18 front, is alas a burnt-out
shell. Further n, at IVER LANE, some attractive canalscape by
the bridge (1794) at COWLEY LOCK with the SHOVEL INN, a
two-storey TOLL HOUSE, and the LOCK-KEEPER'S COTTAGE.
The locks were largely reconstructed in the late c 19. The river
Frays passes in a brick aqueduct under the canal. To the e,
CURRAN CLOSE, yellow brick houses of *c.* 1980, with red brick
and dark timber trimmings, an early example of a favourite type
of the 1980s.

CRANFORD

Until the Second World War Cranford consisted of that common
English rural combination of a great house in its park with the
parish church close by, and a village some way off. The estate was
given to Lord Windsor after the Dissolution, later belonged to Sir
Roger Aston, and in 1618 was bought by the Berkeleys. The park
remains as a golf course; the mansion was demolished in 1939. Only
the early c 18 STABLES built by the third Earl of Berkeley survive,
grazed by the motorway to the n, from which one glimpses an
intriguing back view of the red brick range with two-storey ends
and shaped central pediment. The front of the building has arches
with stone keystones, facing a cobbled yard. The approach to stables
and church by a drive over a humped bridge still has much charm,
despite the roar of the traffic. For the village brutally cut off from
this oasis by the new roads, *see* Hounslow.

ST DUNSTAN. The church, like its approach, has great charm; an
aisleless little building of an all-over length of only about 20
metres. It has a c 15 w tower with sw polygonal stair-turret of
flint rubble, but the top storey of the tower is later, of brick. The
nave also is brick, rebuilt after a fire in 1710 by Elizabeth,
Dowager Countess of Berkeley. It has angle pilasters and a
doorway with an intermittent ashlar surround and a big, heavy
keystone. The chancel, now pebbledashed, is older, with a
blocked lancet, a straight-headed s window of three lights, and a
small Tudor brick n doorway. The e window dates from the
restoration of 1895 by *J. L. Pearson.* A later restoration by *Martin
Travers,* 1935–6, removed Pearson's interior decoration and
added the unusual ALTAR CANOPY, FRONTAL, and REREDOS,
of wood simulating draped tapestry, all by *Travers,* and the
SANCTUARY LAMP by *Omar Ramsden.* – FONT. 1710. White

marble bowl on a black baluster. – WALL PAINTING, on the upper part of the E wall. Fragmentary remains of C15 ashlar patterning and crowned Ms. – Among the VESTMENTS of the church, a C17 chasuble and a C17 cope with thick floral embroidery. – STAINED GLASS. E window with Crucifixion by *Kempe*, 1895. – BRASS (nave W wall). Nicholas Bownell † 1581; a C15 palimpsest.

The chief fame of the church is its remarkable collection of MONUMENTS, so many as to dominate the interior completely. – In the chancel Sir Roger Aston and wife, 1611–13 by *William*
21 *Cure II*, Master Mason to the King, one of his few documented works. Standing wall-monument, tripartite on the Venetian-window scheme, as used earlier for the tombs of Elizabeth I and Mary Queen of Scots in Westminster Abbey. Reconstructed in 1936; it originally projected 60 cm. further into the chancel. Under the coffered arch in the centre kneels Sir Roger (who was Keeper of the King's Wardrobe) and opposite him are his two wives. Two daughters kneel in each of the outer compartments, and a fifth lies in front of her father. The monument is of 'alabaster, tuche, rance, and white and black marble', as stated in the agreement. Well carved figures, repainted (alas) in the 1950s. – Against the other chancel wall is the restrained but accomplished tomb of Elizabeth, widow of Sir Thomas Berkeley, † 1635, by *Nicholas Stone*: the contract of 1635–6 survives. The three pietra dura escutcheons on the tomb-chest were inlaid in Rome by a *Signor Domenico* and dispatched to England by Nicholas Stone Junior in 1639.* The effigy is in white marble, in quite low relief, in a shroud, in front of a tablet with floral volutes and open segmental pediment. – Also in the chancel: Thomas Fuller † 1661 (author of *The Worthies of England*), rector of Cranford, attributed to *Thomas Burman* (GF); a curly cartouche. His remains lie beneath a small stone inscribed 'Fuller's Earth'. – Sir Charles Scarborough † 1693/4, white marble, with two putti supporting drapery. – George Earl of Berkeley † 1698 and George Lord Berkeley † 1658, two matching architectural tablets, presumably erected together, with black tablets in white marble eared surrounds with pilasters and pediments. – In the nave against the N wall William Smythe † 1720, who married a Berkeley. Large monument with a somewhat pedestrian portrait medallion with two seated cherubs at the foot of a large grey marble inscription plate. Flanked by pilasters and with a shell top (cf. Bishop Fowler, Hendon, Bn). – Opposite, an equally large monument consisting of two superimposed tablets, with volutes delicately decorated with oak leaves and other foliage, in the tradition of *Cheere*, to Pelsant Reeve and his wife † 1727 and 1729.

EASTCOTE

Eastcote used to be within the parish of Ruislip, and so has no old church. First impressions are entirely C20 suburban, but a surprising number of minor Middlesex vernacular farmhouses

*Information from Adam White.

remain, quite close together, embedded among their later cottagey imitations; nothing spectacular, but much that is attractive. The two largest mansions were both demolished in the 1960s: their grounds remain as public parks, but their absence leaves the village centre without a focus. They stood close to the crossing of Eastcote High Road and Field End Road. Eastcote House was the home of the Hawtreys (*see* St Martin Ruislip, Hi); Haydon Hall was rebuilt by the Countess of Derby in the early C17 (*see* Harefield, Hi) and *c.* 1700 by Sir Thomas Franklin. For a plan. *See* Ruislip, p. 345.

ST LAWRENCE, Bridle Road. 1932–3 by *Sir Charles Nicholson*. Brick, with short SE gabled tower. A pleasant interior with Tuscan columns, round arches, and a wagon roof. – Chancel gallery with painted wooden SCREEN of 1935.

ST THOMAS MORE (R.C.), Field End Road. 1976 by *John Newton* of *Burles, Newton & Partners*. Plain brick, outside and in. Informally planned. A boarded ceiling, broken by clerestory lighting above the altar. The old church hall of 1937 by *L. Shattock* is incorporated.

FIELD END SCHOOL, Field End Road. Typical asymmetrical *M.C.C.* grouping of the 1930s; of brick, with flat roofs, and a clock tower to add interest.

GRANGEWOOD SCHOOL. Equally typical of the vernacular revival of the late 1970s: a group of barn-like shapes on the edge of Park Wood.

PERAMBULATION. An excursion can start from EASTCOTE STATION, opened in 1906, rebuilt in 1938–9 (*Adams, Holden & Pearson*). Booking hall flanked elegantly by two little circular kiosks; good platform furniture, all in concrete. Now N past the suburban trappings of an inter-war shopping parade to explore the rural survivals along FIELD END ROAD. BARN HOUSE is a poor office conversion of a barn with a queen-strut roof once belonging to FIELD END FARM. The farmhouse has a C16–17 timber frame behind its whitewashed brick. TUDOR LODGE HOTEL (Field End Lodge) is another former farmhouse, also timber-framed, with later additions. The frame is visible at the E end; the centre is clad in brick. Good timber details exposed inside. RETREAT COTTAGE is another converted barn with queen-strut roof. PARK FARM has brick and timber-framed parts. After some C19 villas, EASTCOTE COTTAGE, also timber-framed, with gables, much added to.

From the crossroads EASTCOTE HIGH ROAD runs E–W. On the E side of Field End Road the park remains from Eastcote House; to the N was Haydon Hall. A LODGE to its grounds remains: 1880 by *George & Peto*, in George's typically picturesque brick and half-timbered Tudor, with carved pillar figures in the porch, all so much more elaborate than the indigenous timber-framed tradition. Now to the E. The older houses are mostly rather prettified. EASTCOTE GRANGE, C16 and C17, is an attractive group of converted farm buildings with gabled and weather-boarded farmhouse, a long range with clustered stacks. THE OLD SHOOTING BOX is C16, refaced in the C18; RAMIN has a gable to the road, jettied over a brick-faced ground floor. Back to the crossroads and to the W: OLD BARN HOUSE, with a timber-framed gable to the road, is not a barn but a late medieval hall house of three bays, with inserted floor and later additions. The OLD COACH HOUSE, a converted C 17 timber-framed outbuilding, with adjacent garden walls and DOVECOTE, are remnants from Eastcote House. Then the BLACK HORSE, rebuilt in the early C 19, and further on FLAG COTTAGE, C 18, with pretty four-bay front and a neo-Georgian doorcase brought from Eastcote Lodge in 1968. The prettily half-timbered NEW COTTAGE of 1879 was built as three houses for the Haydon Hall estate, probably by *George & Peto* (likewise FINDEN in Southill Lane, also formerly three cottages).

Further E along the High Road one reaches HIGHGROVE, a set of low-cost terraces by *Edward Cullinan*, 1974–7, for Hillingdon Borough Council. A startling example of the borough's enterprising search at this time for new and acceptable images of public architecture. Unlike the contemporary civic centre at Uxbridge, here it is not achieved by the use of local materials or a traditional suburban idiom. The shrieking blue pitched roofs above rendered walls are a decidedly wayward (but not unsuccessful) means of creating a sense of identity. (The idea was borrowed from Erskine's Byker housing at Newcastle.) In other respects also the terraces are unconventional, yet they fit very happily into the landscape: low, wide-frontage houses nestling behind little garden hedges, grouped together in back-to-back clusters divided by narrow paths. They are built in the grounds of HIGHGROVE HOUSE, which survives up a drive to the S, converted to council accommodation *c.* 1982. The house was rebuilt *c.* 1881 by *Edward Prior* (q.v., Harrow-on-the-Hill, Hw), although it is not one of this architect's most individual works. Brick, L-shaped, with picturesquely irregular entrance front with porch at an angle against one corner. Long S-facing garden front. An attractive roof composition with heavy cornice, dormers, and tall stacks. The interiors were gutted after a fire in 1978.

N of the High Road a series of old lanes run N into what were once the wooded slopes of the common (cleared 1607, enclosed 1814). From W to E: JOEL STREET starts with the SHIP (called the Sun in 1747), popular with C 19 London day-trippers. Further on, JOEL STREET FARM, with a three-bay red brick C 18 exterior, and some C 19 farm cottages of the Haydon Hall estate (No. 29, Cowman's Cottage, and Nos. 124–126, with pretty patterned glazing). In WILTSHIRE LANE, which branches off to the l., IVY FARM and CHERRY COTTAGE, an L-shaped, timber-framed early C 16 former hall house with extensions (the hall has a side-purlin roof of late type, but with smoke-blackening). In SOUTHILL LANE, another inn, the CASE IS ALTERED (repaired after a fire in 1891), and SOUTHILL FARM, a very attractive early C 18 three-bay house of chequered brick with with hipped roof. In CATLINS LANE, ST CATHERINE'S FARM, much altered outside but with good interior features (chamfered beams, exposed timber partitions, C 16 panelling; one downstairs room with four-centred fireplace arch). In CUCKOO HILL, MISTLETOE FARMHOUSE, the front two l. bays C 16, the r. bay C 17; timber-frameed, the two parts divided by a brick chimney. C 18 and late C 19 additions. CUCKOO FARMHOUSE is also chiefly C16 (with a side purlin roof with thick wind-braces) but much altered and with later roughcast. The central jettied bay rests on a moulded beam.

C20 Eastcote grew first in the neighbourhood of the station. In HAWTHORNE AVENUE and LIME GROVE to the W, developed piecemeal from 1909 by the British Freehold Syndicate, a few of the modest bungalows remain which spurred the local council to take planning seriously (*see* Ruislip, Hi). In contrast, MORFORD WAY has a series of small, carefully designed houses of the 1920s by *Telling Brothers*, with a variety of Regency trimmings, uncommon at this time. Further S, on the W side of Field End Road, the CAVENDISH PAVILION, built as a staff recreation centre for Debenhams *c.* 1914, when this area was still open country, a very lavish affair, symmetrical, the entrance side with a half-timbered centrepiece, the back with a brick centre with covered verandas between half-timbered gables.

HAREFIELD

The NE tip of Greater London, but within the green belt, and still rural, with plenty of timber-framed buildings which go back at least to the C16, several C18 and C19 mansions, and a church with a collection of monuments unrivalled in Middlesex. The church lies S of the village, near the site of the main manor house, which no longer exists. It was the seat of the Newdigates from the C14, then from 1585 owned by Alice Countess of Derby and her descendants. The Newdigate family regained possession in 1675, but the house was demolished in 1814 after Sir Roger Newdigate built a new mansion further S (*see* Ickenham, Hi). A second major house, Breakspears, which belonged to the Ashbys, still survives to the E of the village. A third was Moor Hall, which was a cell of the Knights Hospitallers of Clerkenwell. Here until 1922 there was a timber-framed house which was an altered medieval hall, and until 1960 a much rarer survival (scandalously demolished by the local authority), a stone two-storey building of *c.* 1220 with two chambers over an undercroft.

ST MARY, Church Hill. Right in the fields, at the foot of the hill which the village climbs up – an irregular, picturesque little building with aisles the same height as the nave and three distinct roofs. The N aisle and the low NW tower are battlemented. The building material is mainly flint rubble with stone dressings, but part of the tower is refaced with brick, and the s aisle has delightful flint and stone chequerwork. The interior is a pleasant mixture of many periods, despite an extensive restoration of 1841, when the windows were renewed and the s aisle was extended w by two bays. The C14 dominates, with the typical quatrefoil s nave pier with four slim intermediate shafts, the pointed arches with S-shaped chamfers, and the curvilinear tracery of the s aisle windows. In the s aisle a C14 PISCINA. But the w wall of the nave is supposed to incorporate Norman masonry, and the chancel dates back to the C13: see a blocked lancet window in

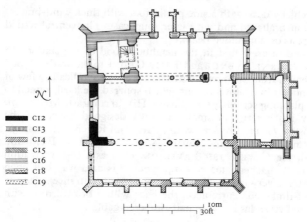

CI2
CI3
CI4
CI5
CI6
CI8
CI9

N

10m
30ft

Harefield, St Mary, plan

the N wall. The tower, N aisle of two bays with octagonal column and responds, and N chancel chapel are early C16 (bequests recorded in 1500 and 1545). The nave roof (restored in 1705–6) is barrel-shaped and plastered; so is the chancel roof, but with pretty Early Gothic Revival panelling. The detail of the chancel arch shows that it belongs to the same period. The alterations were made in 1768 by *Henry Keene* for Sir Roger Newdigate (Keene was also responsible for the Gothic Revival work at Arbury, the Newdigate seat in Warwickshire).

The prevailing impression inside the church is one of happy crowding: tall PEWS, a Gothic Revival GALLERY in the W part of the N aisle, a SCREEN of *c.* 1500 (much restored) separating N aisle from N chancel chapel, plenty of other furnishings, and more funeral monuments than any other church of similar size anywhere near London. The chancel especially is as cram-full of curious objects as the rooms of the Soane Museum. The REREDOS, with sumptuous acanthus scroll and ribbonwork carving and two elegant kneeling angels on top looking up towards two COMMANDMENT BOARDS of frosted glass, the equally sumptuous late C17 ALTAR RAILS, and the CHAIRS are said to come from a Flemish monastery. They were installed in 1841. In style they are as close to French work as they are alien in England. – The Georgian PULPIT is an intricately combined affair with reading desk and pew for the parish clerk; four little cages of different size, shape, and height. – In the vestry, a good late C17 CHEST of hutch type. – Of ancient GLASS there are only a few C16 pieces of little importance in the E window of the N aisle.

MONUMENTS. They must be taken topographically. They are chiefly to the Newdigate family, who held the main manor from the C15 to 1586, and then again from 1675, and to the Ashbys of Breakspears. Two large monuments jog against the reredos, four-square and solid in comparison with its courtly grandeur. On the r. is the most stately of all the Harefield monuments, that of Alice Spencer, Countess of Derby, who acquired the manor of

20

Harefield in 1601. She died in 1637. Her tomb is a four-poster, old-fashioned for its date, with the Countess lying on a tomb-chest in whose w wall three kneeling daughters are set up in niches. The four columns with thick looped-up curtains of stone support a baldacchino with crests at the corners. The colouring has been carefully renewed. The whole is of a robust naivety. The second husband of the Countess was Lord Chancellor Egerton, whose daughter was the mother of Lady Julian Newdigate. – A famous carver of a later generation, *Grinling Gibbons,* showed his more up-to-date version of the Countess of Derby motif in his monument to the l. of the altar to Mary Newdigate † 1692 and her husband Sir Richard. Here again a reclining figure and a canopy with curtains, but now all is white, and the lady lies in a comfortable position, half sitting up; she displays a simple loose Roman robe and no emotion whatever. – The s wall of the chancel has a small canopied tomb-chest of *c.* 1500 of a common Purbeck marble type. Against the back of the niche the original brasses have been replaced by little kneeling brass effigies of John New-digate † 1545 and his wife with thirteen children. – Above this in the wall are three large identical niches with three white urns of very similar shape. The middle one is to Elizabeth, the mother of Sir Roger Newdigate (founder of the Newdigate Prize), † 1765, signed R.H. (*Richard Hayward:* his bill is dated 1776); the urn on the l. is to Sophia, his first wife, † 1774, evidently by the same hand, the one to the r. to Hester, his second wife, † 1800 (by *J. Bacon Jun.*). The l. urn has a reclining allegorical figure and the genius of death on top, and says: 'Fungar Inani Munere' (let me perform this empty duty) from *Aeneid* VI. The middle one has Faith, Hope, and Charity, and Religion on top and says: ΤΩΝ ΑΓΑΘΩΝ Η ΜΝΗΜΗ ΑΕΙΘΑΛΗΣ (the remembrance of the righteous is everlasting: Psalm 112, 9). The r. one has Religion kneeling and an angel above and says: ΜΑΚΑΡΙΟΙ ΟΙ ΠΕΝΘΟΥΝΤΕΣ (blessed are they that mourn: Matthew 5, 6). The slender dark niches, the chaste whiteness of the urns, and the classical imagery are in the strangest contrast to the massiveness of the preceding monuments of the Baroque. – Above the niches mostly restored pieces of C15 to C17 armour. – Against the N wall of the chancel several individually less import-ant wall-monuments, for example Sarah Newdigate † 1695, with two seated cherubs l. and r. of an urn (in spite of its indifferent quality, by *Grinling Gibbons*), Richard Newdigate † 1727, with a bust by *Rysbrack* on top, Edward Newdigate † 1734, with a profile portrait in relief in an oval medallion (Mrs Esdaile: *Rys-brack?*), and Charles Parker † 1795 (son-in-law of Newdigate), with an allegorical scene by *J. Bacon Jun.*

In the N (Breakspear) chapel monuments to the Ashbys of Breakspears, after the Newdigates the chief landowners in and around Harefield. The earliest are brasses: George Ashby and his wife Margaret † 1474 (inscription); and George Ashby † 1514 and his wife Rose, probably made at the same time as the brasses to William Ashby and his wife Jane † 1537. They are all pal-impsests. – A tablet shows reproductions of the fragments of late C14 and C15 figures on their backs. – Sir Robert and Sir Francis Ashby † 1617 and † 1623 is the usual affair with the principal figures kneeling opposite each other, their children in relief below, and with columns with looped-up curtains to l. and r.

In the nave, against a spandrel on the N side, William Ashby † 1769, an excellent portrait bust above a grey oval inscription tablet with white ash branches around, ascribed by Mrs Esdaile to *Sir Robert Taylor,* the architect-sculptor. – On the s side, John Pritchett † 1680, cartouche with masks, cherubs, and arms. – In the s aisle against the s wall the small brass to Editha, wife of William Newdigate, † 1444, the earliest Newdigate effigy and the earliest monument in the church altogether. – Also a tomb-chest of *c.* 1500 similar to the one in the chancel. – Yet another with brasses of John Newdigate † 1528, his wife † 1544, and seventeen children, against the E wall. – In the SE corner, Sir John New-digate † 1610 and his wife, the same usual type as the Ashby monument in the N chapel, but a little earlier in style in that it has pilasters instead of columns and a round-headed niche instead of the curtain arrangement and the out-curving entablature of the other. By *W. White.* – In the NE corner, Sir Richard New-digate † 1678 and his wife Juliana † 1685, signed by (*William*) *Stanton.* – Against the w wall a pretty if somewhat sentimental urn carved with a broken lily; it is the monument to Diana Ball † 1765. – In the N aisle many architectural wall-monuments to Newdigates. (They retained the aisle for burial after they had exchanged the manor for Arbury in 1586.) – On the w wall John Newdigate † 1642, with inscriptions between curtains below a broken pediment, and Robert Newdigate † 1695, black and white marble. – On the floor several black marble slabs, for example to Abraham and John Stanyon, by *William Stanton.* – Against the outer N wall the tablet to Robert Mossendew, gamekeeper to the Ashby family, † 1744, with a primitive relief and the following inscription:

> In frost and snow thro' Hail & rain
> He scour'd the woods & Trudg'd the plain
> The steady pointer, Leads the way,
> Stands at the scent then springs the prey
> The timorous birds from stubble rise
> With pinions stretch'd divide the skys
> The scatter'd lead pursues the sight
> And death in thunder stops their flight.
> His spaniel of true English kind
> Who's gratitude reflam'd his mind
> This servant in an honest way
> In all his actions copy'd Tray.

In the CHURCHYARD an unusual number of wooden 'bedhead' tombstones and several larger monuments, among them John Truesdale of Harefield Place † 1780, square with an urn, and William Spedding † 1826, also with an urn, slightly Grecian. – In the Australian cemetery to soldiers who died at Harefield Hospital, an obelisk and arch, erected 1921 and 1924.

UNION CHAPEL (Baptist), Rickmansworth Road. Stuccoed front dated 1834. Two pedimented windows and central arched doorway.

HAREFIELD HOSPITAL, W of the Green. Built as a county sanatorium in 1933–7 in the grounds of Harefield Park. Hospital
buildings by *W. T. Curtis* of the *M.C.C.* Progressively plain (cf.
Mount Vernon, Northwood (Hi), of thirty years earlier), with
gently curving three-storey ward blocks of brick with long
balconies, symmetrically arranged. Administrative offices in the
centre of the main building, with a big bow-window to the
committee room. Lower children's ward to the S, also curved. A
curved one-storey paediatric surgical unit was added in 1989–90
by *Harris Stow Partnership*. Adjoining it a play area in a glazed
pyramid. To the E the mansion called HAREFIELD PARK, formerly known as Belhammonds, survives as a staff centre. Built
by Sir George Cooke (rainwater heads 1710, 1718), but much
altered. On either side, flanking the approach, detached one-
storey stable blocks, now rendered, but formerly of exposed brick
(see the sides). Their fronts have windows with segmental arches
with large keystones. The W block retains its cupola with the
date '48. So presumably these were mid C18 additions to the
earlier house. The house itself now looks early C19, with a
stuccoed seven-window entrance front of three storeys, plain
apart from an eared window-surround to the central first-floor
window. On the N side tall arched windows lighting a first-floor
ballroom, also probably early C19, but the windows below with
thick glazing-bars must be early C18. In the hall Corinthian
pilasters at the foot of the stairs; in the ballroom grained panelling; other C18 woodwork elsewhere.
HEALTH CENTRE, by the entrance to the hospital. Low and
domestic-looking, with pantiled roofs. Built *c.* 1986.
COUNTESS OF DERBY'S ALMSHOUSES, Church Hill, close to the 19
church. Built after the Countess's death in 1637. A compact H-
shaped group of brick. Originally eight two-storey dwellings,
four on each side of a central passage. Windows with brick
hoodmoulds, straight gables, stately clusters of tall, diagonally
set chimneystacks.
CHURCH HILL leads uphill to the HIGH STREET and the village
centre. On the W side the WHITE HORSE, low painted brick, of
C16 origin, and the VICARAGE, grossly picturesque Gothic of *c.*
1860. The rest is suburban until one reaches the village. Here
there is plenty of C17 and C18 origin: little that is out of scale,
but little to single out. On the E side MANOR COURT, C16 and
C17 with C19 additions, and, set back, HAREFIELD HOUSE
(now Ministry of Defence), quite a grand C17 house (staircase
through three floors), disguised by a plain early C19 stuccoed
front with Tuscan porch. Five windows wide, the two r. bays
blind, the l. bay set back. In the 1920s owned by the country
house historian *Avray Tipping*, who laid out the gardens and
built some houses in its grounds (*see* Breakspear Road North,
below). At the SW corner of the extensive GREEN, the KINGS
ARMS, large, timber-framed, but much altered. Prominent on
the opposite side of the Green two early Victorian villas with
ornamental bargeboards and some tactful infilling of 1982.
Outside the village centre the countryside still has a mixture of brick
and timber farmhouses and barns, and a few larger mansions –
one of the few areas where one can still glimpse the old unostenta-

tious character of rural Middlesex. Noteworthy buildings are described clockwise, starting from the N.

HILL END ROAD leads to SPRINGWELL LANE, a winding country road. Here, at CRIPPS FARM, a long rendered front with late Georgian windows conceals an older house. Attractive timber-framed BARN, weatherboarded on a brick plinth, with half-hipped eaves; C16 queenpost roof with wind-braces; the r. part later. NE up RICKMANSWORTH ROAD one reaches the drive to HAREFIELD GROVE, hidden away in its own park, restored and converted to offices for Initial Services in 1984–5 by *Graham Moss Associates*. It is a sizeable three-storey house of five plus two bays, probably C18 in origin (see the low ceiling heights of the ground floor), stuccoed later, and given an early C19 pedimented porch. Much altered inside in the early C20 and again in 1984. On the garden side, to the E, a grand early C19 two-storeyed bow, a pure neo-classical piece with giant Ionic columns. On the ground floor it lights two intercommunicating rooms with handsome honeysuckle decoration below the cornice. At the opposite end was a one-storey bow (now removed) on the entrance side. The curved porch to the N dates from 1987. Most of the service wing to the S has been replaced by quite tactful offices consisting of three brick ranges flanking a courtyard entered through the former stable block. This is of brick, with round-headed windows on two floors and a pretty little Italianate clock-tower at one end. Apart from the tower, rebuilt rather than restored, the proportions and details all slightly wrong. A covered way leads to a glazed greenhouse entrance in the main offices, with an open top-lit stair leading off the foyer. Delightful grounds with a series of small lakes. THE LODGE, further S, is a long, low, pretty house of two builds, the older (S) part a two-bay early C19 villa with doorway with radial fanlight and a Doric porch.

To the ENE, off Northwood Road, SHEPHERDS HILL HOUSE (residential study centre), a five-bay Regency stuccoed front with a pretty iron veranda; two shallow bay-windows behind it.

BREAKSPEAR ROAD NORTH leads SE from the village centre. Near the pond, in the grounds of Harefield House (*see* above), three simple, well designed brick houses of *c.* 1934 by *Avray Tipping*, APPLE TREES and PEAR TREES with steep gables, LITTLE HAMMONDS larger, with hipped roof and pilasters. A similar larger house, Walnut Trees, was replaced by POND CLOSE. Further S on the E side, the OLD WORKHOUSE, dated 1782 on a brick over the centre. The design is identical to the Ruislip workhouse (q.v.), but less altered. Half-H plan with rear wings and a very simple old-fashioned front of pleasantly mottled brick, with five casement windows.

W of the road is BREAKSPEARS, a medieval sub-manor and the seat of the Ashbys in the C17. It is a substantial house in its own grounds, much extended in several phases in the C19, but with recognizable C17 parts. Owned by Alfred H. Tarleton from 1887; used as an old people's home from 1956 to 1987. C18 drawings show two show fronts. The main range, since entirely rebuilt, faced E. The entrance front is now in the long N range, approached down a drive made in 1903–4. This range consists of a handsome late C17 centre of six bays (with a seventh on the l. masked by a later bay-window), distinguished by red brick with blue headers. Central entrance, formerly with a shell hood; tall casement windows on two floors, divided by a plat band. To the E a two-bay set-back links up with the E range. To the W six further bays were added in the later C19 in tactful late C17 style. The sympathetically designed eaves cornice, roof, and dormers are likewise C19 reconstruction. The garden front to the S has one small section opposite the late C17 N range where the low floor-levels and rough brickwork in English bond (disturbed by a later Venetian window) look early C17; to its W is a long addition with late Georgian sashes. The E range with its taller rooms is all C19, with an E extension for enlarged drawing room and smoking room added in 1899 by *C. H. Mileham*. The interiors were all much reworked in the C19. In the N entrance hall a (re-set?) early C17 chimneypiece and panelling with small squares. The adjoining 'oak room' to the W, which extends into the C19 addition, has another re-set C17 chimneypiece boldly decorated with the Ashby rebus and motto, and panelling with Ionic pilasters. In the centre, between N, S, and E ranges, is the stair hall; its lantern is C19, but the sturdy well stair with closed string and thick spiral balusters looks late C17. Early C19 cornice in the entrance passage of the S range. In the E wing are the main C19 reception rooms: the drawing room has a pretty plaster ceiling, the billiard room enriched wall panels. Older than the surviving parts of the house, and indeed more enjoyable, is the DOVECOTE [17] to the W, a rare survival in the London area. A fine example of early C16 Tudor brickwork, square, with a cupola. Moulded brick jetty, small Tudor archways, and battered angle-buttresses. LODGE of 1904 by *Ernest Walker*.

S of the village the suburban fringe has grown around CHURCH HILL. IN HINKLEY CLOSE well grouped one- and two-storey houses of different heights in a simple vernacular mode (white walls, pantiled roofs); one of the experimental designs of the *Borough of Hillingdon* during its energetic 1970s building period. Of 1972–6 (job architect *Brian Wood*). Intended to be expandable by extra rooms in the roof. Further S there is still open country. HIGHWAYS HOUSE FARM, close to the road, is a good example of a neat C18 brick front added to an earlier timber-framed building. A big early chimneystack at the rear. Large eight-bay queen-strut BARN of typical C17 type. Another farmhouse in NEWYEARS GREEN LANE to the SE: ST LEONARD'S, a brick-cased timber-frame on a T-plan, memorable for its hefty five-flue stack at the junction of the two ranges. (Ground-floor room with good chamfered ceiling beams and joists.)

Finally W towards river and canal. Off Park Lane, BLACK JACK'S LANE leads to a charming spot where a Victorian water mill (now restaurant) and an earlier fishing lodge stand on an island between two waterways, reached by a nice curved canal bridge. The lock is dated 1870. E of the canal a small thatched cottage with yet another example of a prestigious early brick chim-neystack (three flues) bursting through the roof. At the W end of Park Lane, COPPERMILL LANE leads to a group of mill build-ings. Paper mills here were converted and extended as copper mills after the site had been leased to the Mines Royal Company in 1781. A two-storey range faces the water, unusually stylish, with its Gothic glazing-bars in round-arched windows. Contemporary two-storey manager's house close by, much altered. To the s, by the canal (just over the Hertfordshire boundary), the FISHERMAN'S INN. To the N, an early LOCK HOUSE and a row of pre-1812 millworkers' cottages. Opposite, a group of buildings associated with old limeworks. Dwarfing these modest survivals from an earlier industrial era is SALAMANDER QUAY, s of the road, an extensive business development of 1986–8 by *Michael Aukett Associates*.

HARLINGTON

The s end of the parish borders on Heathrow (Hi, q.v.) and is dominated by the string of monster hotels along the Bath Road. To the N is the railway and much earlier C20 housing. In the centre, just s of the M4, the medieval church still stands in a patch of countryside.

ST PETER AND ST PAUL, St Peters Way. Flint rubble with some russet ferricrete at the E end, a fine colour harmony, especially as seen with the old yew tree to the s. w tower of *c.* 1500 (see the w door and tower arch). Battlemented parapet and cupola on the corner turret (cf. Harmondsworth, Hi). Pretty s porch, early C16, reconstructed, with open timber arches (cf. Hayes, Hi; Heston, Ho). C12 nave (aisleless until the C19), with the best Norman doorway in outer London. Four orders, under a hoodmould decorated with linked roundels. The outer order has a battlement motif on both voussoirs and jambs, the second and third shafts have chevron ornament divided by bands, and voluted capitals, some with foliage. The second arch is decorated with cats' heads with tongues curling over a spirally decorated roll – an unusual variant of beakhead which can be paralleled most closely by the doorways of the 1140s on the w front of Lincoln Cathedral (where the battlement motif also occurs). The third arch has chevron on two faces; the inmost order is plain. Much of the carved stone (where not repaired) is Reigate, the usual stone used for medieval carving in Middlesex churches, although the jambs of the doorway are partly of an oolitic limestone, probably Barnack. Chancel rebuilt in the C14, much restored; two large Dec s windows. E window 1893, replacing C17 brick tracery. N arcade added 1880 by *J. Oldrid Scott*; rather harsh stilted arches on octagonal columns. The single-framed trussed rafter roof of the nave may be as early as the C14. – FONT. C12, Purbeck marble; square bowl with round-headed blank arcades on five shafts. – STAINED GLASS. E window 1873 by *Kempe Studios*: Crucifixion against golden quarries. – Chancel s: busy scene of the Ascension, 1889 by *A. L. Moore*. – N aisle and nave: several of the 1950s, one designed by *Francis Stephens* and signed by *John Hayward*. – Tower s: 1908 by *Kempe & Co.*

MONUMENTS. Brass to John Monemouthe † 1419, rector, a demi-figure (cf. Greenford, Ea; Harrow, Hw; Hayes, Hi;

Stanwell, Surrey). – Gregory Lovell † 1545 and wife (now against
the s wall of the chancel). Small brass figures, shields and inscription plate, all palimpsests (inscription on the back to George
Barlee † 1513). – The Lovell brasses were before the 1880 restoration set in the table top of the puzzling monument on the N
side of the chancel which has generally been identified as an
EASTER SEPULCHRE. It has a narrow four-centred arch below a
band of quatrefoils, and a well carved vine-scroll and cresting
with fleur-de-lys and ihs monogram. The detail is close to earlier
C16 London monuments (cf. St Mary Lambeth, La). Beneath
the arch is a small recess with its own moulded four-centred arch
(no sign of a door), a feature not found in other Easter sepulchres
of this date. It is possible that the masonry, like the brasses, was
re-used from elsewhere for the Lovell tomb. – In the nave, Sir
John Benett Lord Ossulstone, dated 1686 although he died in
1695, and his two wives, with three outstandingly good portrait
busts, standing on a gadrooned tablet flanked by well carved
putti-heads and flowers. Attributed to *John Nost* (GF). – In low
niches (medieval, though restored) in N and s chancel walls the
recumbent effigies on tomb-chests of Henrietta Fane, Countess
de Salis, † 1865, and of the Count de Salis † 1836, by *R. C. Lucas*
(whose fame is connected with the dispute over the so-called
Leonardo da Vinci Flora at the Berlin Museum, restored or made
by Lucas). – In the churchyard a splendid High Victorian tomb to
William Brookes † 1869, in the form of a Gothic shrine: crocketed
gabled end, the sides studded with coloured stones.

ST JEROME, Dawley Road and Judge Heath Lane. 1933 by *J. H.
Gibbons*. Brick, in a quiet domestic style, but quite large. w tower,
transepts, and apse; steeply pitched roofs.

HARLINGTON SECONDARY SCHOOL, Pinkwell Lane. Dull
MACE school brightened up in 1978 by daring use of colour by
Gollins, Melvin, Ward & Partners.

s of the old church is the main village street, the HIGH STREET,
bittily rebuilt. Two modest pubs (White Hart, Red Lion) contrast with a tall stuccoed Italianate BAPTIST CHAPEL (1879 by
W. Ranger) facing a little green with a row of C19 cottages.
Opposite the chapel is its C18 predecessor (now a church hall),
with two storeys of round-arched windows. Further s No. 393,
the DOWER HOUSE, L-shaped, with irregular C18 brick four-
bay front and earlier timber-framed parts behind. Down WEST
END LANE, past the early C19 PHEASANT and a frolicsome
steakhouse, a few more rural buildings remain among later
rebuilding. The best is ELDER FARMHOUSE, a two-window
C18 brick front concealing timber-framing (ground-floor room
with chamfered beams and joists).

DAWLEY was a small hamlet to the N of the railway. Its most
notable building was Dawley House, rebuilt for the Earl of
Tankerville *c.* 1720, probably by *Nicholas Dubois*, remodelled
and enlarged for Viscount Bolingbroke by *James Gibbs* (*see*
p. 36), and demolished *c.* 1770. Some C18 garden walls remain
in DAWLEY ROAD, and estate walls stretch for over a mile to
the N up JUDGE HEATH LANE.

HARMONDSWORTH

The village is relatively undisturbed, despite the Bath Road and
Heathrow to the s and the M4 to the n. Its first claim to remembrance is its great medieval barn, but the c12 doorway of the church
also ranks among the chief monuments of Middlesex. w of the
village one still has an all-too-rare glimpse of the quiet, uneventful
Middlesex countryside, with barn and church rising above flat
willow-lined water meadows.

ST MARY. One of the few churches in outer London whose historical complexity has not been smoothed out by c19 restorations
and additions. The distinguishing feature is the little open c18
cupola (a popular Middlesex feature, cf. Harlington, Hi) on top
of the sw tower, whose battlements and upper two storeys are of
c16 brick. Ground storey, of flint with lumps of local ferricrete
and quartzite, at least partly medieval, and moreover oddly placed
in relation to the s aisle, as the tower is twice as wide and projects
6　　s. This aisle has a c12 arcade which, it has been suggested, was
originally a n arcade added to an aisleless church which stood
directly in line with the tower. If so, the mid c12 s doorway,
next to Harlington (Hi) the most elaborate piece of Norman
decoration in the county, must have been re-set when the church
was given its late medieval form. The doorway is of oolitic
limestone (Barnack?), of three orders, the inner with rosettes and
knots of square shapes running uninterrupted through jambs
and voussoirs, the middle one with plain shafts and primitive
beakheads in the voussoirs, and the outer again with uninterrupted zigzag. Probably of similar date is the scratch dial re-
set in the s wall. The walls otherwise mostly flint, the window
tracery originally of Reigate stone, but much renewed. Inside,
the two columns of the s arcade rest on high plinths (evidence of
an earlier outer wall). Bases with spurs, shallow scalloped
capitals, the e respond with the little rolls beneath the scallops
characteristic of the mid c12. The pointed arches with hood-

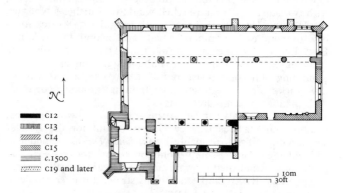

Harmondsworth, St Mary, plan

moulds must be an early C 13 reconstruction. The N arcade also
C 13, with more widely spaced piers, moulded capitals, and hoodmoulds similar to those at nearby Stanwell (now over the county
boundary in Surrey). The chancel was rebuilt in 1396–8 by
Winchester College, patron of the church. John Harvey attributes
the work to *William Wynford* on the basis of the similarity of the
Perp E window to the side windows of Winchester College chapel.
The interior is made still more irregular by the N chapel, probably 6
added in the C 14 (see the small trefoil-headed lancet in the N
wall) but remodelled *c.* 1500, with low late Perp three-light
windows and octagonal piers with flattened four-centred arches,
thickly wave-moulded, which run abruptly into the N arcade (the
start of an unfinished building campaign?). In the chancel Perp
PISCINA and SEDILIA: cinquefoiled arches in square heads.
Notable medieval roofs: in the nave (preserved above the ceiling
removed in 1862) tie-beams with (renewed) crown-posts with
four-way struts; in the N chapel a mini-hammerbeam roof of
c. 1500 with lower S-shaped braces. – FONT. Unadorned Purbeck
marble, octagonal on circular shafts, *c.* 1200. – PEWS. A large
number, of *c.* 1500, with slender stepped buttresses. – STAINED
GLASS of the 1860s onwards. – Minor MONUMENTS: architectural tablets of veined grey marble to Anne Banks † 1734,
Richard Banks † 1750, John Bush and family *c.* 1762, the last
with broken pediment and arms. – In the CHURCHYARD some
prettily carved C 18 to early C 19 tombstones.

MANOR FARM BARN, E of the church. One of the largest and 13
finest aisled timber-framed barns in the country. Dendrochronology has confirmed that it dates from the early C 15,
when the manor was owned by Winchester College; it can almost
certainly be identified with the barn mentioned in the Winchester
muniments as under construction in the 1420s. In 1423–4
William Kipping was paid for a journey to view the timber at
Kingston in Surrey for a new barn at Harmondsworth, which was
built in 1427. The barn is nearly 60 metres long, an impressive
unbroken roof-line with half-hipped ends above black weatherboarded walls. Three wagon doors on the E side only. Inside,
the massive main posts are carried on square Reigate stone blocks
on chamfered bases, linked by low sleeper walls; the end walls
rest on stone foundations consisting of very large blocks of the
local pebbly ferricrete, an unusually late date for the use of the
material; all the rest is of timber. The roof construction is
unusual. Unlike most medieval barns of the south-east, it is
double-framed, i.e. with purlins to provide lateral strengthening.
The main trusses have a single central post between tie-beam
and collar. The purlins at collar level have curved wind-braces.
The lower purlins in the aisles are unbraced, but strutted to
braced aisle-ties at wall-plate level. Other farm buildings were
converted to offices in 1990–1.

To the S, MANOR FARMHOUSE, a pleasant early C 19 three-bay
front with widely spaced windows beneath deep eaves.

The village green remains a peaceful oasis, although suburbanized
by rose-bushes. At the E end of the HIGH STREET the FIVE
BELLS, with an old tiled roof hiding behind simple C 19 brick

frontages. Near the church SUN HOUSE, the former Sun Inn, C16, timber-framed with a brick front, then the VICARAGE, stock brick, rebuilt in 1845, but still in the late Georgian tradition, with the addition of a later C19 tower with a big window with crude tracery.

On the S side, down Summerhouse Lane, HARMONDSWORTH HALL on the r., with C18 brick fronts, but incorporating an earlier house with a C17 chimney. Opposite, THE GRANGE, now offices, dated 1675 over the doorway. L-shaped, with characteristic late C17 hipped roof and modillioned cornice; five-bay fronts to N and W, the W windows unevenly spaced. Staircase with heavy turned symmetrical balusters, much restored; one C18 marble fireplace. Conservatory to the S. E of the green first ACACIA HOUSE with early C19 front, five bays of yellow and red brick, then at the corner of Harmondsworth Lane THE LODGE, an elegant early C19 villa: doorway flanked by sidelights, all under a big segmental arch. Shallow bow on the E side. In SIPSON ROAD the WILLIAM IV pub, with exposed timbers at side and rear. Although disguised by refronting, this is a Wealden-type medieval hall house with typically hipped roof; much of the framing survives inside.

S of the village the BATH ROAD is an uninviting mixture of industry and airport hotels. Commercial development began after the building of the Colnbrook Bypass in 1929. At the corner of Hatch Lane, SUMMIT CENTRE, by *Michael Lyell Associates, 1985–7*, attempts to bring some post-modern jollity to warehouse design (coloured window-frames and angled doors). Further E, PENGUIN BOOKS, established here from 1938. Large warehouses discreetly screened by good planting. The earliest buildings, by *Ralph Tubbs*, have been replaced; his post-war additions (warehouses of 1954–62, now offices, and offices of the mid 1960s) remain, grouped around imaginatively planted small courtyards. They are concealed by a later one-storey concrete and glass extension with pronounced eaves and prominent beam ends, 1971–2 by *Arup Associates*; a forceful but elegant version of 60s brutalism. Behind, the main warehouse, for 37 million books, also by *Arup Associates, 1968*, designed around the dimensions of forklift trucks, and an even larger warehouse further W, of 1984–5.

See also Longford (Hi) *and* Heathrow (Hi).

HAYES

One of the least attractive parts of Hillingdon. Industry developed early in the neighbourhood of canal and railway, and monotonous inter-war housing followed, almost entirely obscuring the earlier history of this large parish. Before the C19 the small village of Hayes was surrounded by scattered hamlets – principally Botwell, Hayes End, Wood End, and Yeading. Now, except for Yeading (q.v.), all have run together. Botwell, on the road to Harlington, because of its position near the station has become the main commercial centre. A few tall slabs arrived with the office boom of the

1960s, but new development has been too scattered and piecemeal
to create a thoroughly urban centre. Neither have the assets of older
buildings and open spaces been sufficiently cherished.

St Anselm, Station Road. 1926–8 by *Hubert C. Corlette*. Aisled
nave, chancel, bell-turret. Yellow brick with red brick dressings.

St Mary, Church Road. The medieval parish church, like Harrow
(Hw), was a 'peculiar' of the Archbishop of Canterbury. It has
much that is unusual. Externally it is a flint rubble building with
a late C13 chancel with lancet windows in the N and S walls, a
C15 N aisle and W tower, and an early C16 S aisle and picturesque 7
open timber S porch. In the chancel the C13 SEDILIA, with
moulded capitals, and PISCINA are preserved. The lancet
windows have moulded rere-arches on corbels carved with
figures. The N arcade of the nave has low octagonal piers and
simple double-chamfered arches, the S arcade octagonal piers
and arches of typical early C16 form. There is no clerestory or
chancel arch. The roofs all survived the restoration by *Sir G. G.
Scott* in 1873. The chancel roof, perhaps C14 or early C15,
wagon-shaped with close-set rafters, extends into the first two
bays of the nave, where it is supported on the N side on three
odd irregular depressed arches (apparently added to align the
nave and chancel walls). The other roofs late medieval: in the
nave boarded and panelled with small bosses with heraldry and
emblems of the Passion, in the aisles flat-pitched with chamfered
tie-beams and curved braces. – FONT. Round bowl of *c.* 1200
with very coarse lobed leaves along simple scrolls. – WALL
PAINTING. Large, against the N wall: St Christopher carrying
the Christ Child as he wades through a stream swarming with
serpents and monstrous fishes (with a mermaid of the type usual
among misericords among them). On the bank sits a little boy
angling. The banks extend upwards along the painting as though
perspective were still an unknown science. Yet the painting can
hardly be earlier than *c.* 1500. – MONUMENTS. Robert Levee, *c.*
1370, brass, a small demi-figure of a priest, the earliest brass in
the former county of Middlesex (the same type was repeated later
at Stanwell (now Surrey), and Harlington, Hi). – Walter Grene
† 1456. Tomb-chest with traceried panels and brass effigy in
armour on the lid. – Thomas and Elizabeth Higate † 1576. Tomb-
chest with brasses on the lid: two effigies, two groups of
children. – Sir Edward Fenner † 1612. A grand wall-monument;
a London design also used elsewhere (e.g. for the Bluett monument of 1614 at Holcombe Rogus, Devon). Sir Edward lies stiffly
on his side, his head propped up on his elbow. The effigy is
placed between columns, and at the top are two small (much
better) allegorical figures flanking a large arch. In the tympanum
an inscription in a broad scrolled strapwork cartouche. – Edward
Fenner † 1615. Simple wall-monument with frontal demi-figure
in shell niche between pilasters. The gentleman in armour lays
a long hand with long fingers on his helmet which lies in front
of him. Very noble, very self-conscious, and very typical of the
ideals of Mannerism. – Charles Manning † 1799. Plain tablet
with bust above. – In the CHURCHYARD a good collection of
tombs and an attractive LYCHGATE.

IMMACULATE HEART OF MARY (R.C.) (Claretian Fathers),
Botwell Lane. 1961 by *Burles, Newton & Partners*. Plain brick
exterior, with a tall campanile. Statue of the Virgin by *Michael
Clark* against the W window. A generous, light interior with
ambitious modern furnishings. Long aisled basilica, segmental
arches between piers clad in green mosaic. Above the arches,
STATIONS OF THE CROSS, carved perspex, gold on black, by *A.
Fleischmann*. – PAINTINGS. Over the high altar, Virgin and
Child by *Pietro Annigoni*, 1962, very large and heavily symbolic. –
Above other altars, Crucifixion by *Roy de Maistre*; St Anthony
Mary Claret by *William Redgrave*; St Jude by *Daniel O'Connell*. –
Effective STAINED GLASS, both abstract and figurative, by
Goddard & Gibbs.

METHODIST CHURCH, Station Road. *See* Perambulation.

COUNCIL OFFICES, Botwell Lane, on the edge of the park. 1872,
Jacobean, with shaped gables; now painted white.

ALFRED BECK LEISURE CENTRE, Grange Road. In the park
between the old church and Uxbridge Road. 1972–7 by the
Borough Architect's Department. Like the civic centre at Uxbridge
(Hi), a deliberate effort to evoke a homely image by the use of
sweeping roofs and picturesque irregularity. The broken outline
of slate roofs conceals a regular plan: the main space is a hexagonal
multi-purpose hall with projecting stage. Top-lit foyer opening
on to an outdoor terrace.

ST CHRISTOPHER'S COMMUNITY HOME, Uxbridge Road and
Coldharbour Lane. The first example of a community home built
under the 1969 Children and Young Persons Act. Linked two-
storey houses of yellow brick with attractively grouped monopitch roofs, creating a deliberately non-institutional image. 1970–
3 by the Borough Architect's Department (*Thurston Williams*).

The old village centre around the church is pleasantly green, with
a park between the church and the former town hall, and more
open space to the N stretching up to the Uxbridge Road. The
old buildings which once complemented this have been sadly
diminished in the last thirty years. In CHURCH ROAD a few C18
and early C19 houses remain, much altered; also the so-called
MANOR HOUSE, now a community building amid sheltered
housing of 1980 by the *Borough Architect's Department*. Probably
only part of a larger house. Timber-framing with brick infilling
visible on the N side; the rest cased in later brick. The former
STABLES, a long brick range hard by the road, are C18, but an
office conversion has whittled away their character. Across the
park CHURCH WALK is still quite a rural cul-de-sac, with the
quaintly named PROVIDENCE, EBENEZER, and SURPRISING
VILLAS, 1881. The nearby Charity School of 1861 has been
demolished, as has Hayes Court, S of the church, which was
owned by the Minet family up to 1967. It was replaced by low
housing of 1974 (*Shankland Cox Partnership*). The area E of
Church Road was developed between the wars with private
housing; the layout around the formal axis of CENTRAL AVENUE
looks ambitious on the map, but the architecture is indifferent.

To the s in BOTWELL LANE, by Compton Road, WHITEHALL,
a tall early C18 house of two bays with a lower wing. Further
on the group of R.C. church (q.v., above), social centre, and

BOTWELL HOUSE, early C19, three bays and three storeys, the first-floor windows within brick arches.

Nearer the station in STATION ROAD all is C20 and singularly uninspiring. Humble shops for early C20 commuters are dwarfed by two curtain-walled slabs by the bridge: the gimmicky TELECOM HOUSE (1973 by *PSA* with *Gray Associates*), and the duller and earlier BRIDGE HOUSE (1963 by *David Stern*). Some community benefit has been squeezed into the 1970s commercial packages – a COOP with METHODIST CHURCH above, with jazzy zigzag front, and a design-conscious SAINSBURY'S with CIVIC HALL attached: a red brick front with corbelled-out windows. The most powerful of the larger buildings lies further N: COLMAN HOUSE, a concrete slab with the brutalist detail characteristic of *Owen Luder*'s numerous out-of-town offices of the late 1960s.

W of Station Road the industrial area which grew up around the canal has been swamped by the vast premises of EMI. This began with a new factory in 1908 for the Gramophone Company. When this merged in 1931 with Columbia to form Electrical and Musical Industries (His Master's Voice), extensive buildings were erected by *Wallis, Gilbert & Partners*: frankly colossal multi-storey concrete-framed blocks with long bands of windows (mostly modernized *c.* 1970). On the N side of BLYTH ROAD the later C20 EMI RESEARCH LABORATORIES adopt a different approach, their huge bulk primly disguised at one corner by a cluster of glazed polygonal porches (1985 by *Fitzroy Robinson*).

E of the station in SILVERDALE ROAD is a former PIANO FACTORY (now BENBOW WORKS), the only survival from the large Aeolian Works. By *Walter Cave,* 1909, extended 1912. Noted at the time for its frame of reinforced concrete by *E.P. Wells.* It is clad in brick, its elevation enlivened by Diocletian windows to the top floor within full-height arches.

Finally HAYES END, away to the NW along the UXBRIDGE ROAD. From the old hamlet, a small group of early C19 cottages and villas remain near the corner of West Drayton Road (Nos. 891–901). In WEST DRAYTON ROAD, THE ROSERY, an altered late C17 house with hipped roof and weatherboarded outbuildings. So far Uxbridge Road has attracted few C20 offices: the brutalist brave new world is represented by POINT WEST; THE GRANGE opposite, low and pitched-roofed (*Cecil Denny Highton & Partners,* 1984), proclaims the good manners of the neovernacular mode. More interesting than these is HAYES PARK, to the N off Park Lane. Here a Victorian mansion standing in its own park was replaced by offices, administration, and research centre for HEINZ, from 1961, by *Gordon Bunshaft* of the American firm *Skidmore Owings & Merrill,* together with *Matthews Ryan & Simpson.* Two buildings, each of three storeys, the lowest sunk as a semi-basement. Strongly expressed aggregate-faced concrete frame with tapering uprights (the kind of detail imitated badly by so many later English office buildings). Here the elevation is given repose by the deeply recessed windows, and by the typical SOM wide grid. The finishes and landscaping are of an American standard, i.e. of a far higher quality than English prestige offices of this date. The administration building

has a courtyard in the centre with a pool. Near the back entrance
in HAYES END ROAD, in poignant contrast, the remnants of
the hamlet of Hayes End, a straggle of C19 cottages and villas,
and HOME FARM, with C19 farmhouse and derelict C18 outbuildings.

HEATHROW

The airport takes its name from a small hamlet, now entirely
obliterated, in the parish of Harmondsworth, on the edge of the
flat W part of Hounslow Heath (for its prehistory *see* p. 303).

HEATHROW AIRPORT, with its attendant roads, hotels, and warehouses, has radically altered this part of Middlesex since the
Second World War. The first runway opened in 1945. The first
permanent buildings for passenger traffic, approached from the
N by a tunnel from Bath Road, were completed in 1955. They
consisted of the control tower, Queen's Building (offices, restaurant, etc.), and a terminal for short-haul traffic (now Terminal
2), all by *Frederick Gibberd & Partners*. They rapidly proved
inadequate. Between 1953 and 1955 passengers rose from one to
three million p.a.; twenty years later the figure was over twenty
million. Expansion was decided upon in 1957, and there have
been alterations and additions ever since, so that no description of
the buildings can hope to be definitive. Externally, the confused
jumble of terminals and car parks on the original site has little
to recommend it. Fortunately today's passenger can be carried
smoothly along broad underground passages right into the terminals. Heathrow Central station dates from 1977 (*London
Transport's Architect's Department*). Above ground there is one
cheery focus on a friendly scale, the crisply detailed BUS
STATION of 1979 by *Darbourne & Darke:* curved plastic roofs
over red brick walls. The earliest buildings can also be recognized
by their use of red brick. They have the more delicate detailing
characteristic of the fifties, now much obscured by later
104 additions. The CONTROL TOWER has canted-out windows, as
has the cafeteria of the QUEEN'S BUILDING, although here the
panoramic views are blocked by later finger piers. To view the
aircraft one has to visit the roof gardens, planned, one must
remember, when passenger planes were still something of a
novelty, and when aircraft noise was less continuous. The
gardens, or rather patios, are on several levels with vistas through
columns, all rather in the spirit of the modern movement as
presented at the time of the Festival of Britain.

The group of three terminals is cluttered by ugly multi-storey
car parks added from 1963 (Nos. 5–6 of 1966, with 2,129 spaces,
was the largest of its time in Europe). The straightforward brick
and glass elevation of TERMINAL 2 is marred on the entrance
side by the bulgy white snakes of the later ramps from the
underground. The interiors were remodelled in 1975–9 by
Pascall & Watson (with *Murdoch Design Associates*) in the high
tech taste of the time. Shiny, curved, colour-coded surfaces:

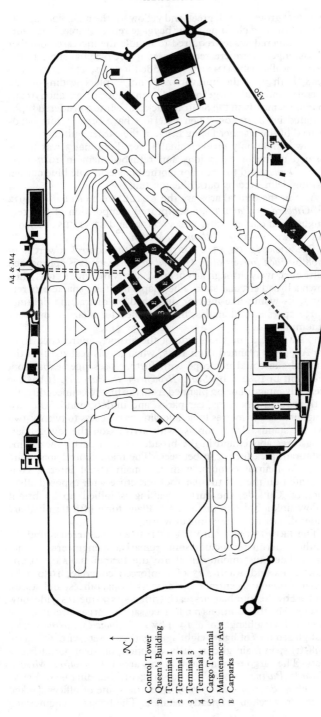

Heathrow Airport, plan

A Control Tower
B Queen's Building
1 Terminal 1
2 Terminal 2
3 Terminal 3
4 Terminal 4
C Cargo Terminal
D Maintenance Area
E Carparks

orange at ground level, green and yellow for the main floor above, blue corrugated cladding in the baggage retrieval area. The wide, unencumbered spaces required to handle the increased number of passengers were created by moving the original stairs to the outside walls. TERMINAL 3 was added in 1961, TERMINAL 1 in 1968, both with the innovation of finger piers leading to the aircraft, and with large open-plan interiors of an anonymous character, mostly in the neutral black and white considered sophisticated in the 1960s. Their exteriors have broad white bands instead of the warmer facing brick of the earlier buildings. This is now visible only on Terminal 1, for Terminal 3 was transformed by major extensions and refurbishment in 1987–8 by *D. Y. Davies*, and the exterior clothed in sleek, pale blue curtain walling delineated by dark blue jointing.

Also in the central area are the CHILLING STATION of 1972 (*F. Gibberd & Partners*), a sculptured composition of two rectangles with curved water tanks on top, and STATUES of Alcock and Brown, 1954 by *William McMillan*.

The CHAPEL OF ST GEORGE, near the control tower, is of 1968 by *Jack Forrest* of *F. Gibberd & Partners*. It is approached quite effectively through an enclosed courtyard with a cross, then down a broad circular stair. The chapel itself is a sparse concrete crypt, its womb-like interior disturbed by distracting lighting. Three apses at odd angles, first intended for altars of different denominations.

TERMINAL 4, on the S side of the airport, approached from the A30, was planned from 1975, when it was realized that the original site could not cope with further passenger expansion, and built in 1982–6 by *Scott, Brownrigg & Partners*. It has the great advantage of being planned from the first to connect directly with covered bus stops, car parks, and underground. The vast concourse is 650 metres long, allowing easy access to twenty-two aircraft stands. Two storeys, with arrivals on the lower floor, departures above, and in the broader central part a mezzanine restaurant area tucked in between. The main central spaces are lofty, in neutral colours, with the main visual interest concentrated on the red tubular roof structure with exposed silver ducting. Outside, the curtain-walling is jollied up by bright yellow link lobbies to the aircraft. Plans for a fifth terminal are under discussion at the time of writing.

The FREIGHT and SERVICE BUILDINGS scattered round the southern perimeter include some remarkable engineering structures. The most monumental are the former B.O.A.C. HEADQUARTERS and HANGARS of reinforced concrete, 1950–4 by *Owen Williams*: a central cross of workshops, offices, and stores, abutted by the four hangars, each with doors 90 metres wide (now obscured by the additions made necessary by larger aircraft). The extended wing hangar of *c.* 1964 by *F. J. Snow & Partners* has a vast glazed roof of lightweight aggregate concrete with 60-metre (198-ft) span main girders of box section, on steel portal-frame piers. The cargo terminal also in this area is by *Gollins, Melvin, Ward & Partners*, 1968. The cargo agents' building is by *Yorke, Rosenberg & Mardall*, 1967–9, a central spine of offices flanked by lower warehouses, neatly detailed. The hangars, engineering buildings, and offices for the former B.E.A., of 1962 onwards, are by *Murray, Ward & Partners*; engineers *Scott Wilson Kirkpatrick & Partners*. The Boeing hangar for jumbo jets, of *c.* 1970, had the largest diagonal steel grid in the world when built. It is by *Norman Royce Tipping Harley & Stewart* (architects) and *Z. S. Makowski & Associates* (engineers).

Along the busy BATH ROAD N of the airport the main landmarks are a disparate string of large, undistinguished airport hotels. It is not an easy setting in which to create a welcoming image. They start by Harlington High Street with one of the earliest, and still the most attractive: the ARIEL HOTEL, quite modest in scale, smooth, white, and circular, with an inner courtyard. 1962 by *Russell Diplock & Associates*. The later hotels exploit the contrast between a luxurious inner world and a tough, rugged exterior. Behind the dour russet concrete of the SHERATON SKYLINE, by *Kenzie Lovell Partnership*, 1970, is a spectacular glazed palm court with swimming pool. On the S side, HEATHROW HOTEL, *c.* 1973 by *R. Seifert & Partners*, has one of the most emphatic profiles: a forceful inverted ziggurat. The POLICE AND CUSTOMS OFFICES flanking the airport approach are low, severe boxes of dark brick with crenellated roof-lines, 1966 by *Manning & Clamp*. Nearby, left over from another age, the THREE MAGPIES, a country pub with a canted bay-window. At the junction with the M 4 slip road the EXCELSIOR, 1964 by *M. Lyell Associates*, and further N, on its own in Sipson Road, the tall POST HOUSE by *Nelson Foley*.

S of the airport, the STERLING HOTEL, 1988–90 by *Manser Associates* with *YRM Anthony Hunt Associates* as structural engineers. Connected to Terminal 4 by a bridge and to the surrounding car parks by an elevated road, the first of the Heathrow hotels to be so conveniently and logically sited. A vast lozenge-shaped shed, with two five-storey banks of bedrooms, and a huge atrium in between for reception and restaurants. A neat white-clad envelope, the end walls given interest by the inset double-glazed ends of the atrium, flanked by the curves of the emergency stairs. *See also* Harmondsworth (Hi) *and* Longford (Hi).

HILLINGDON

INTRODUCTION

Hillingdon was a large medieval parish, with its centre around St John's church on the Uxbridge Road. West Hillingdon developed further W along the main road. Uxbridge originally was also within the parish, but early on became a town in its own right. Colham Green was a hamlet to the S. Several larger mansions survive in institutional use, but the area N of the Uxbridge Road has nearly all been covered by indifferent C20 suburbia. Private housing expanded rapidly in the 1930s around Long Lane, followed by council housing after the Second World War. The most notable post-war arrival was Brunel University (Hi, q.v.) at West Hillingdon.

CHURCHES

ALL SAINTS, Long Lane and Ryefield Avenue. 1932 by *Sir Charles Nicholson*. Simple, of brick, with minimally Perp windows, but round-arched arcades inside. – STAINED GLASS. E window with older glass re-set. Given by the Worsley family; from a chapel at Evelyns School, Colham Green (a preparatory school closed in 1931). Delicate small scenes by *Kempe*, 1891.

ST ANDREW, West Hillingdon. *See* Uxbridge (Hi).

ST JOHN THE BAPTIST, Uxbridge Road. Of flint, and surprisingly of a piece in its appearance, considering that nave and aisles are C14 and the W tower was rebuilt in 1629 – a good example of the faithful continuation of Gothic traditions. In 1847–8 *Sir G. G. Scott* restored the church and added transepts and E parts (not very effectively) in place of a small medieval chancel with reticulated E window. NE vestry 1964, neatly done by *H. Norman Haines*. Inside the church there is one remarkable fragment older than the rest: the C13 chancel arch with stiff-leaf capitals (the best of their date in Middlesex) on short shafts which in their turn rest on head-corbels. The N one is original: a grimacing face with tongue sticking out. The nave receives much light from the large W window in the tower, and also from the typically Middlesex feature of dormers (restored, but shown on a print of 1807). Three-bay nave with octagonal piers with capitals and arch mouldings (sunk chamfers with scrolled stops) typical of their C14 date. C15 N aisle roof with main timbers supported by corbels with stone busts (cf. Stanwell, Surrey). – Few furnishings of note apart from the traditional well carved WAR MEMORIAL ALTAR (N chapel), with reredos, frontal, and riddel posts, executed by *T. Bavois* to designs by *Caröe & Passmore*, 1922, and the STAINED GLASS of chancel E, N, and S and N chapel E, post-war replacements by *Alfred E. Buss* of *Goddard & Gibbs*, 1955: figures against a clear background, the designs not outstanding, but the quality of the handmade glass above average for its date.

The special feature of the church is several remarkable monuments. First the BRASSES. The large brass to Lord Strange (N aisle), erected 1509, is the most ambitious of the Middle Ages to survive in Greater London. Lord and Lady Strange and a small daughter between them are represented under tall gables with incurving sides. – Henry Stanley † 1528 (chancel). Small military figure, inscription lost. – Anne Wilson † 1569. Acrostic inscription. – William Gomershall † 1597. Inscription and shield. – John Atlee † 1599 (N aisle). Small figure. – The best MONUMENTS are in the chancel: Sir Edward Carr † 1636 and Henry Pagett, Earl of Uxbridge, † 1743. The Carr monument is an up-to-date variation of the old-established theme of the kneelers facing each other. Not only are the costumes later than one usually finds on tombs of this type, but this idea of having the children stand in front of the prayer desk between the parents, ready to walk out of the monument towards us, heralds the conception of a new age. The perversely steep broken gable on top against which two allegorical figures can sit as on stiff chairs also shows a spirit of innovation not quite certain yet of where to turn. – The Uxbridge

monument opposite is infinitely more accomplished, and consequently less gritty. The effigy in Roman garb is semi-reclining 33
on a tomb-chest, head and hands splendidly modelled. The altar
background has urns standing in front of the flanking columns,
a straight pediment on top, and the customary grey pyramid in
relief rising behind the figure and between the columns. – In the
nave Thomas Lane († 1795 'having acquired a fortune by constant application') by *John Bacon*, a seated woman holding a
medallion with profile portrait. – Many lesser c 17 and later wall-
monuments. Mary Walker † 1685, flowery cartouche. – John
Walker † 1715, with bold swan-necked open pediment. – John
Mist † 1737 (paviour and scavenger to the royal palace), small
veined marble tablet with scrolled segmented pediment on
volutes. – Several more sober Doric tablets, among them two
connections of the Newdigates (cf. Harefield, Hi): Robert Beale
† 1711 and Samuel Nicoll † 1758. – Also John and Julian Nicoll
† 1723 and † 1724, with a very elegant Latin inscription, on a
cartouche with putti heads, and Jenkyn Newdigate † 1740, with
an urn against marble background. – CHURCHYARD with many
fine tombs.

ST BERNADETTE (R.C.), Long Lane. 1960–1 by *T. G. B. Scott*.
Feeble Romanesque. – SCULPTURE by *Michael Clark* (St Bernadette, Stations of the Cross, Crucifixion).

HILLINGDON AND UXBRIDGE CEMETERIES, Hillingdon Hill.
Gothic entrance lodge with gateway and chapels by *B. Ferrey*.

PUBLIC BUILDINGS

OAK FARM LIBRARY, Long Lane. A one-storey box with canted
clerestory and red-painted space-frame roof. 1976 by *Douglas
Stephen & Partners*.

BISHOPSHALT SCHOOL, Royal Lane. A substantial Victorian
villa on the site of a medieval rectory held by the Bishop of
Worcester. A school since 1925. Built in 1858 by John Jackson,
from the the the firm of plasterworkers in Rathbone Place, Marylebone, and later owned by Stephen Martin of Day and Martin's
blacking factory. Many-gabled red brick front, balcony with
stone strapwork, cupola. Inside, heavy neo-Jacobean ceilings, a
speciality of *Jackson's* firm. The entrance hall extends right
through the house to the pretty conservatory between the two
garden wings. It has a bowed front and a curved roof, with
delicate ironwork supported on thin columns. Large *M.C.C.*
school additions of 1957–61 (hall, library, classrooms) and of the
later 1970s by the *Borough of Hillingdon*.

HILLINGDON COURT, Vine Lane. American Community School
since 1978. 1854–8 by *P. C. Hardwick* for the banker Charles
Mills, later Lord Hillingdon, founder of Glyn Mills & Co. The
most impressive of Hillingdon's surviving major houses, somewhat French classical, in white brick with stone dressings. Dignified N entrance front of two tall storeys and five bays, the end
bays projecting slightly and emphasized by heavy pediments with
carving. Triple-arched porte-cochère with later glazing. The S
front is more demure, with a central loggia between the square

bay-windows of the main reception rooms. To the w is the typical Victorian feature of service and guest wings much bigger than the main house: on the N side three storeys above basements, on the s side lower and less intrusive. Lavish interiors: large entrance hall with ornately carved grand staircase; on the garden side a central anteroom flanked by reception rooms, all sumptuously decorated in French late C18 style with enriched doors and panelling, heavy gilded cornices, and ceilings with painted roun- dels. The grounds now much reduced, but a formal garden remains to the E, and an open prospect beyond (now a public park). To the w are additions for the school by *Porter Wright*: sensitively designed SPORTS HALL in cream brick with stone cornice, 1985–7; classroom wings to N and w of the C19 service wing planned in 1989. C19 LODGE by the road.

HILLINGDON HOSPITAL, Pield Heath Road. The site is the incoherent muddle typical of most large hospitals. It was expanded from the C18 workhouse on the N side of the road. To the s, rising above a sprawl of car parks and temporary structures, new buildings of 1966 onwards by *Gollins, Melvin, Ward & Partners*. Planned for 700 beds. Low buildings round courtyards, crisply designed, and one tall white ten-storey ward block, in two sections, with a projecting top floor. Windows recessed behind exposed concrete frames. Internal planning progressive for its date, with beds arranged in small groups within each ward. The CHAPEL, depressingly tucked away in a low basement, is redeemed by interesting stained glass by *Jane Gray*, 1965; rectangular panels 1.20 metres high, with angular symbolic forms in strong colours. To the E, HILLINGDON HOUSE, now School of Nursing, a two-storey C19 mansion covered in gloomy grey roughcast, built shortly after 1878 for Count Peter de Salis.

MOORCROFT, Harlington Road. Rambling and cluttered up, but with some good features. Used as a private mental home from 1798, later as an old people's home and social services depart- ment. Overlooking the garden to the s, amidst the extensions on either side, is a handsome C18 brick range of three storeys and seven bays. The core may be older (Tudor fireplace on the ground floor). Early C19 NW wing; later C19 SE wing with a series of canted bay-windows. To the N a separate five-bay two-storey house with Doric porch.

HILLINGDON HOUSE, Hillingdon Road. The manor house of West Hillingdon, in large grounds still stretching N to Vine Lane. The house rebuilt in 1717 by the Duke of Schomberg was destroyed by fire in 1844. Its plain replacement, much altered, is now the officers' mess of the R.A.F., which bought the estate in 1915. In the grounds a serpentine lake.

HILLINGDON STATION, Long Lane. A new building by *Cassidy Taggart Partnership* (planned 1987), with ticket hall on a bridge over the platforms, linked to covered walkways over the rerouted Western Avenue.

PERAMBULATION

Despite the busy main road, there is still a recognizable old village
centre at the corner of ROYAL LANE opposite the church. On
the brow of the hill, overlooking the descent towards Uxbridge,
is a little green with the RED LION INN, which has a C16 core
(chamfered beams and some re-used panelling inside), and some
other low gabled houses. The oldest is the COTTAGE HOTEL,
C16, timber-framed, with three gables and a fourth on the projecting porch, but with its exterior surfaces depressingly of the
C20.

On the N side of the main road (UXBRIDGE ROAD) the best of
Hillingdon's older houses, CEDAR HOUSE. Hiding behind the
cedar tree (a replacement of the one planted in 1742) is a handsome brick building chiefly of the C17, restored and converted
by *Peter Bond & Partners* for the civil engineers Shephard Hill
& Co. Symmetrical front with two straight gables and a central
three-storey projecting porch with a smaller gable. Quite plain,
apart from a pediment over the doorway, and moulded strings
between the storeys, i.e. pre-dating the elaborate artisan brickwork of the second third of the C17 (cf. Swakeleys, Hi). The
front all with Georgian sashes except for wooden mullioned-and-
transomed windows in the gables. A larger gable in the E flank,
lopsided, because the roof has been extended back over later
additions. The front part of the original roof (a simple A-frame)
is visible in the drawing office now occupying the attics. A (recast)
rainwater head with the date 1680 at the back suggests a date for
the alterations. The interior has plenty of interesting woodwork,
but much is not *in situ* and appears to be the result of C19 and
C20 Jacobeanizing efforts. Hall to the E of the porch; to the w a
big chimneystack with a delightful piece of medieval carving
(Tudor rose and two leopards) obviously brought in. Ceiling
with simple geometric pattern. Simple Jacobean staircase off the
E end of the hall, C17 panelling in the NE room, on the first floor
later C17 panelling, and in the SE room a Jacobean chimneypiece
(another re-used in a later NE wing). To the w a showy half-
timbered C19 wing with C20 additions made for Sir Howard
Button; brought-in and replica panelling inside. Tactful extensions of 1973. Red brick garden walls in English bond. Good
C18 S gate.

Further E an C18 to early C19 group hidden behind trees: GLEN-
THORNE, three bays, C18, with an early C19 oriel; PERRYFIELD,
C18, with pedimented doorcase with shell; some smaller houses;
and MAGNOLIA HOUSE, three good late C18 bays with
additions and a pilastered doorcase with sidelights and fanlight.
On the S side, at the corner of Harlington Road, the PRINCE OF
WALES, by *Nowell Parr, c.* 1922. E of Long Lane, in CHARVILLE
LANE WEST, PARKFIELD HOUSE, sadly hemmed in by later
C20 development. C18 white stucco, five bays and three storeys;
porch with paired Roman Doric columns; canted bays to E and
W.

WEST HILLINGDON, an old settlement on the way to Uxbridge,
is marked by a group of early C19 cottages and villas on the w
side of the main road, built after the Enclosure Act of 1812,

e.g. PLEASANT PLACE, dated 1826, and the OLD SCHOOL in clumsy early C 19 Gothic. They face the grounds of the former Hillingdon House, now R.A.F. (*see* above).

At COLHAM GREEN, which was a small hamlet to the S, MOOR-CROFT (*see* Public Buildings, above). In MOORCROFT LANE the surprise of some open countryside, with the early C 19 MOORCROFT FARMHOUSE and a few cottages. In WEST DRAYTON ROAD a late C16 weatherboarded BARN, five bays with E aisle, queen-strut roof.

ICKENHAM

The old village centre with its medieval church and green makes a pleasant break in the genteel C 20 suburbia that between the wars ate into the grounds of the older houses but did not destroy all of them. The most notable survivals are C 17 Swakeleys (*see* separate entry) and the partly late medieval Ickenham Manor.

ST GILES, High Road and Swakeleys Road. A small, aisleless C 14 Middlesex church (cf. Perivale and Greenford, both Ea), of flint rubble, partly rendered, with a tactful W extension of 1958 by *E. C. Butler*, its windows based on the simple two-light early Perp windows of the chancel. The most attractive features of the exterior are the rustic timber-framed porch (of *c.* 1500, much restored) and the pretty little shingled bell-turret. To the N a broad aisle of brick was added by William Say *c.* 1575–80, with a re-used E window; other window surrounds are of brick plastered to look like stone (cf. Swakeleys). This N aisle has to its W a most unusual little mortuary chapel, added *c.* 1640–50, probably by the Harringtons of Swakeleys. Inside, a series of niches (for upright coffins, removed 1914). Small oval windows in the N wall; some strapwork decoration on the end piers. The interior of the rest of the church is homely but incoherent because of the untidy junction of cross-gabled N aisle and nave, now divided by a C 19 arcade. Good late medieval roof: chancel with trussed rafters, nave with crown-posts with two-way struts. – FONT. C 17; a good oak-carved octagonal piece. – Jacobean COM-MUNION TABLE and BENCHES, now in the mortuary chapel. – Other WOODWORK by *C. R. Davie*, 1926–8. – SCULPTURE. Bust of the Earl of Essex, formerly on the C 17 screen at Swakeleys. – STAINED GLASS. Chancel windows of 1895 and 1898, in the *Kempe* manner. – Two good windows in the W extension, 1965 and 1971 by *Alan Younger*, the first with Virgin and Child, the second a more abstract pattern of dove shapes; excellent colours. – COFFIN LID. Of tapering shape, with foliated cross; late C 14, discovered in 1962. – BRASSES. Civilian, *c.* 1545. – William Say † 1582 and family. – Another of the late C 16 to the Shoreditches of Ickenham Manor. – MONUMENTS. Robert Clayton † 1665. A recumbent marble infant in swaddling clothes, found in the churchyard in 1921, now on a windowsill in the chancel, and in its accidental loneliness all the more pathetic. The baby is commemorated by a similar sculpture on *Crutcher*'s grand monu-

ment to his parents at Bletchingley, Surrey. – In the mortuary
chapel minor tablets to the Harringtons. – In the N aisle others
to the later owners of Swakeleys, the Clarkes, among them two
by *Thomas Banks*: the Rev. T. Clarke † 1796, and J. G. Clarke
† 1800, aged twenty-four, with a fine relief of the youth sitting
reading. – In the CHURCHYARD some good C18 table-tombs.

UNITED REFORMED CHURCH, Swakeleys Road. Formerly Congregational. 1936 by *Percy W. Meredith*. Gothic central window,
slightly 'moderne' details.

ICKENHAM CENTRE, Glebe Avenue. Low, with spreading pitched
roofs. By the *Borough Architect's Department*, 1979.

DOUAY MARTYRS R.C. SECONDARY SCHOOL, Edinburgh
Drive and Long Lane. 1962. Large, but quite humane; yellow
and red brick, with monopitch roofs.

BREAKSPEAR JUNIOR AND INFANTS SCHOOL, Bushey Road.
1937, one of the progressive pre-war designs of the *M.C.C.*

ICKENHAM STATION. 1923 by *C. W. Clark* for the Metropolitan
Railway.

The character of the former village has been diminished by the
1930s shopping parade on the W side and by the traffic rushing
down Long Lane, but the old centre, at the junction with Swakeleys Road, is still marked by a little GREEN with a pond, and a
pump with a charming iron-and-timber octagonal Gothic canopy
erected in 1866. To the S an appropriately modest 1970s
LIBRARY with glazed gable to the road. Opposite the church,
HOME FARMHOUSE, High Road, with late medieval jettied
gable-end and red brick early C18 extension, and a weatherboarded BARN. Down SWAKELEYS ROAD, the former Back
Lane, GELLS ALMSHOUSES, a pretty group with three gables
in flint and red brick, dated 1857, endowed by Charlotte Gell,
who also paid for the pump canopy.

The houses further afield are listed here roughly clockwise.

ICKENHAM HALL, Glebe Avenue, to the E. Mid to late C18 red
brick front of five bays with stone parapet.

ICKENHAM MANOR, E of Long Lane, to the SE. The manor house
which until the early C19 belonged to the Shoreditch family
survives in a surprisingly rural setting in this suburban neighbourhood, approached by a rutted track, even with some farmland to the S. The house, L-shaped with additions, is exceedingly 15
picturesque, an irregular composition of brick, exposed timbering, and tiled roofs. The well preserved interior features give an
unusually complete impression of the architectural standard of
the smaller Middlesex manor house in the C16. The earliest part
is the late medieval two-bay W wing, possibly once longer, which
has a crown-post roof with a smoke-blackened W bay. The floor
with moulded beams may have been inserted in the C16, the date
of the two-storeyed E range with its large ground-floor hall with
moulded beams and opposing four-centred timber doorways. A
similar doorway at the N end and two simpler blocked ones led
to the service rooms, now a single large space, though two original
arched mullioned windows of four lights remain in the E and W
walls, as well as a patch of old herringbone brick floor. The N
wall has a jettied upper storey resting on a moulded beam. In
the chamber over the hall a stone Tudor-arched fireplace. The

present staircase is a later addition, somewhat altered, sited in a timber-framed tower in the angle between the two ranges. C17 turned balusters on the landing; a narrow upper flight with solid treads rises to the attics. The C18 improvements are very modest: two little rooms in small symmetrical brick wings projecting E from the main range. The s one, a parlour opening from the hall, is panelled and has an arched recess. Traces of a moat remain around the house.

HAREFIELD PLACE, The Drive, off the road to Harefield, to the w. Built as Harefield Lodge in 1786 by *Henry Couchman* for Sir Roger Newdigate of Harefield, Hi (q.v.), as a modest replacement to the old manor house near Harefield church. Much altered since: used as a convalescent home and hospital after purchase by Middlesex County Council in 1934; refurbished as offices *c.* 1983–5. A long, low, stuccoed building with Doric porch on the E side. Pilastered garden front of seven bays with stepped wings of two and three bays. Large curved office wing added to the N in the 1980s. The grounds were sold up in the 1930s and the drive is sprinkled with lush suburban houses of that date. At the N end, in Harvil Road, the NORTH LODGE remains, a sweet Reptonian design with thatched roof, diamond-leaded windows, and semi-octagonal bay.

BRACKENBURY, Breakspear Road, to the NW. Now two houses. On a moated site, owned by the Newdigates from the C15. The house is chiefly C16–17, with a low early part towards the road, of brick; big chimneystack (inglenook fireplace inside), with crowstepped top and diagonal shafts. Attached to this part is a substantial timber-framed house, now pebbledashed, of two storeys and attics. (Good staircase with turned balusters.) Later used as the Newdigate bailiff's house.

CROWSNEST FARMHOUSE, Breakspear Road, to the NW. A good mid C16 L-shaped house, timber-framed, faced in brick in the C18.

COPTHALL FARM, Copthall Road, to the NW. A small C16 timber-framed building (framing exposed at the rear), with a later brick front and C19 SE wing.

LONGFORD

A small settlement along the old Bath Road, within the parish of Harmondsworth. Although so close to Heathrow, it has miraculously preserved its village character, helped by the diversion of through traffic to the Colnbrook Bypass opened in 1929.

The E end starts unpromisingly with an airport hotel on the s side, and a half-timbered mock Tudor group on the N (Tudor House, Phoenix House, The Stables). Opposite this, set back from the road, No. 493, a genuine late C17 timber-framed building. In the centre of the village is the WHITE HORSE, a simple two-storey pub of whitened brick at an angle to the road, with a row of rendered cottages of 1739 beyond. YEOMANS opposite is a good C16 timber-framed house with two cross-wings, the jetties

underbuilt later. Exposed close studding throughout; several
mullioned windows preserved. Further w No. 583, a substantial
brick house, late C 17. Main front, much altered, at right angles
to the road; the end wall with two floors of three segment-headed
windows, and two more windows in the broad gable. Big weatherboarded barn behind. Opposite, No. 550, a more usual three-
bay C 18 brick front. At the w end of the village a little BRIDGE
with cast-iron parapet over the Colne with the royal cipher WR
and the date 1834.

NORTHWOOD

Northwood, the hilly N part of the medieval parish of Ruislip, in
the C 18 consisted of only a few cottages along the Rickmansworth
Road and some outlying farms. The major mansion, Moor Park, is
just over the Hertfordshire boundary. Development came after a
station opened in 1887 on the Metropolitan line in Green Lane,
and the elevated area, with its fine views S, became popular for
superior late Victorian and Edwardian houses, like Harrow Weald
(Hw) further E. Many have been replaced by flats, but enough
remain to convey the flavour of the social hierarchies of the turn of
the century. Among the architects active here at this time both
Frank Elgood (chairman of the Ruislip–Northwood planning committee from 1910 to 1915) and *Charles Harrison Townsend* were
Northwood residents. To the SE less ambitious suburban development followed the opening of Northwood Hills station in 1933.

EMMANUEL, High Street. 1903 by *Frank Elgood,* repaired in 1948
after war damage. Free Perp; red brick. The usual dull, towerless
composition of cheaper churches of this period, but cheered by
stone chequerwork around the broad clerestory windows, and by

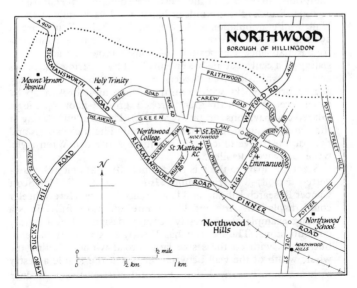

stripy W corners (now partly hidden by a boxy brick W extension of 1982 by *Riley & Glanfield*). Long nave with moulded brick arches on stone piers; windows with art nouveau leading; the chancel cants in slightly to the straight-ended sanctuary.

HOLY TRINITY, Rickmansworth Road. By *S. S. Teulon*, 1854, in his least ostentatious mood; flint-faced, with a NE tower and Dec windows. Rather a spreading composition, because of the N aisle added in 1894 by *Cutts*, and the S aisle and W baptistery added by *W. C. Waymouth* in 1927. – STALLS with low-relief carving by *Alan Durst*, 1960s. – SE (Lady) chapel refurnished by *Cecil Brown*, 1967. – Some notable STAINED GLASS. In the N aisle several original windows with small scenes in medallions; also a striking later one († 1915) by *Leonard Walker*, deep colours, with a star reflected on water. – In the Lady Chapel the Grosvenor memorial window with two trumpeting angels by *Morris & Co.*, 1887. – Baptistery window by *Comper*, 1930, traditional. – In the churchyard several large MONUMENTS, among them family tombs of the Grosvenors of Moor Park (just over the Hertfordshire border), including a bronze plaque of 1898, and the grave of Sir Robert Morier † 1893, Russian ambassador, with a large jasper cross given by the Czar.

ST MATTHEW (R.C.), Hallowell Road. 1924. Ultra-plain neo-Romanesque.

ST JOHN'S PRESBYTERIAN CHURCH, Hallowell Road. By *Frederick Rowntree*, 1914. A large, carefully detailed brick building in the tradition of Lutyens's free classical, steeply roofed churches at Hampstead Garden Suburb (Bn). W gable with Venetian window; a shallow curved porch with stumpy stone columns and eccentric composite capitals. Cruciform plan with apse. – Immediately to the E the CHURCH HALL, with another steep tiled roof.

MOUNT VERNON HOSPITAL. Originally a hospital for consumption and diseases of the chest, moved here from Hampstead in 1904. Built in the grounds of Northwood Park (now Denville Hall, *see* Perambulation). The original hospital buildings are of 1902–4 by *F. L. Wheeler*. The wards face S over open country: a free Renaissance composition of considerable character consisting of a central stone tower enlivened by tapering buttresses and some whimsical free classical ornament, flanked by two long angled brick blocks with continuous balconies, broken up by stone-faced bays with round-arched ground-floor openings. Glazed end pavilions (originally solaria). The window-glazing of the wards has unfortunately been altered. The N elevations and the administrative offices are in a more sober neo-Wren style, but equally well detailed.

Standing apart to the E is the former CHAPEL, tactfully converted in 1987–8 by *Bill Miller Associates* as the Fowler Scott Cancer Research Library and Conference Centre. Here Wheeler could display his Arts and Crafts interests more fully. It is a striking example of progressive church design, all in a crisply cut buff stone. The exterior has Voysey's excessively battered buttresses, with on the S side large broad windows filling the whole width of the wall between them. On the N side a vestry with ingeniously turned stair. Forceful little W tower. W door with excellent metalwork, framed by low-relief sculpture. All the details, and also the woodwork inside, of frank art nouveau licence. The low stone SCREEN has widely set tapering posts linked by sinuous trails. Sanctuary floor of small mosaic tiles in muted colours, E wall with a Last Supper in mosaic, and a tiled frieze.

Recent hospital additions by *David Baker Architects:* imaging department 1984–5; children's ward 1985–6; prefabricated medical ward blocks 1987; linear accelerator 1988.

POLICE STATION, Murray Road. 1910 by *J. D. Butler*. A prominent corner building with deliberately domestic half-timbered frontages in keeping with its suburban neighbours.

LONDON BIBLE COLLEGE, Green Lane. Built for the London College of Divinity, which moved here from Highbury. Extensive buildings of 1955 onwards, in indifferent red brick.

NORTHWOOD SCHOOL, Potter Street, Northwood Hills. Several phases: 1930s, 1950s, and 1970s. The last is the most prominent: crisp curtain-walled classrooms, with boarded panels, articulated by yellow brick staircase drums.

NORTHWOOD COLLEGE, Maxwell Road. Large, purpose-built girls' school of 1891 in the tilehung style of Shaw or George. Attached to the l. a more eccentric wing, possibly built as a separate house, in the style of R. A. Briggs (cf. Murray Road in the Perambulation, below).

ST JOHN'S SCHOOL, Potter Street Hill. Built as Potter Hill House, 1924. Spectacularly sited on a ridge looking s. Garden side of 1–3–1 bays, decent neo-Georgian, with Ionic colonnade between two projecting wings; neo-classical detail inside.

The most interesting of the few older buildings in the centre of Northwood is THE GRANGE in RICKMANSWORTH ROAD. A confusing brick-faced exterior conceals a C15 range with crown-post roof and a cross-wing of the same date. Inside, much brought-in woodwork from the time of Dr Llewelyn Nash, *c.* 1890. Adjoining to the w (now a separate house) is another range with a roof of *c.* 1600. On the s side of the road, THE GATE is a low C17 timber-framed inn. further w, KILN FARM has a timber-framed core concealed by roughcast and tilehanging. N of the High Street in GATEHILL ROAD, hemmed in by suburban houses, GATEHILL FARMHOUSE, with a Georgian three-bay brick front and older projecting back wings; some timber-framing visible.

The suburban development of Northwood took off in 1887 when Frank Murray Maxwell Hallowell Carew bought up the land around the new railway station and sold it off in building plots, as the names of the new streets testify. The hub is the area around the station in GREEN LANE, with a tall pilastered BARCLAYS BANK providing some urbanity. s of Green Lane the railway marks a clear social division: the smaller houses are to the E, graduating downward along HALLOWELL ROAD to the very modest HIGH STREET, although even here the shopping parades are smartened by a little decorative plasterwork.

The wealthier houses (many now replaced by flats) begin in the roads to the w: Maxwell Road and Murray Road. Further afield are even larger houses, for example in Dene Road and The

Avenue, and also in CAREW ROAD further E. Among those
worth a special look are the house in MURRAY ROAD with two
eccentric cranked gables and a rounded turret by the entrance,
1889 by *R. A. Briggs,* and two (of after 1889) in MAXWELL
ROAD, next to Northwood College (q.v.), eclectic and rather
unusual: No. 30 has high-relief stucco garlands in C17 style; No.
32 has more delicate Adamish swags combined with mullion-
and-cross windows. (The same design as No. 30 recurs at Manor
Lodge, Rickmansworth Road.) In DENE ROAD, No. 7, dated
1904, quite small, an appealing, understated Arts and Crafts
composition with tilehung upper floor and casement windows,
may be by *Harrison Townsend,* as it was built on the land of
GREENHILL FARM (now GREENEND, No. 17), just round the
corner, which Townsend altered for C. E. Masterman after 1893.
This is a C17 timber-framed house with an attractive irregular
gabled front, tilehung above roughcast, with a battered buttress
and thin iron supports to the porch as *Townsend*'s signature.
Further on Dene Road has a few big turn-of-the-century houses
in large grounds: TORMEAD, quite grand neo-English Baroque,
with a curved porch and a steep dentilled pediment, and BROAD
OAK (now Sunshine Homes), substantial and half-timbered.
Of Tower Dene, the most fanciful of *Briggs*'s houses, only the
gatepiers remain. In THE AVENUE, s of Rickmansworth Road,
THE VANE, built for West, the artist, a neat, symmetrical plan
with a tall tilehung gable on each side, and an arched chimneystack. (Close to Mount Vernon Hospital, in Rickmansworth
Road, a group of houses by *Hazan Smith & Partners,* 1989–90;
clustered pitched roofs, semicircular dormers.)

DUCKS HILL ROAD leads s to Ruislip Common. From N to S,
first a mid C19 flint-faced former LODGE to Northwood Park,
part of whose grounds are occupied by Mount Vernon Hospital
(q.v.); then the mansion itself, now called DENVILLE HALL,
rebuilt *c.* 1840 for the Norton family, in stock brick with gables
and heavy pierced strapwork balustrading. Close to the road a
little flint gazebo or FOLLY, a drum tower with pointed arches.
Then several more large turn-of-the-century houses, mixed with
suburban encroachment of the 1980s, before one reaches open
country and a few scattered rural survivals. The attractive
YOUNGWOOD FARMHOUSE, cream-rendered, has one range
with a queen-strut roof (see the framing visible in one gable-end,
with a brick stack built against it). DUCKSHILL FARMHOUSE
is rendered brick of 1783. In JACKETS LANE to the w a much
altered timber-framed house of C16 origin with a big brick
chimney at one end.

To the SE NORTHWOOD HILLS grew after the station was built
in 1933. Around here one can find a few half-hearted efforts at a
flat-roofed modern style: Nos. 153–163 NORTHWOOD WAY by
Morgan & Edwards, 1934, and Nos. 156–186 JOEL STREET
(now mostly disguised by later roofs and windows), 1934 by
Robert de Burgh; likewise Nos. 1–39 NORWICH ROAD.

Finally, NE along WATFORD ROAD, on the ridge around the
boundary with Hertfordshire, are several especially grand
houses. The best (just over the border) is ADMIRALTY HOUSE
(formerly Frithwood House) by *Mervyn Macartney,* 1900, in

an accomplished late C17 style; elaborate red brickwork with mullion-and-transom windows, a hipped roof with deep eaves, and tall chimneys.

RUISLIP

INTRODUCTION

Ruislip was the second largest medieval parish in Middlesex, including Eastcote and Northwood to the E and NE (qq.v.). C20 development has been extensive, but better planned than in many areas. The village character of the old centre around the church and Manor Farm, cherished by the new residents, is still recognizable, and an unusually large number of old farmhouses remain to the N (albeit mostly suburbanized), on the open land of Ruislip Common between the village and Northwood. The railway arrived at Ruislip in 1904, some way to the S of the village, and the first suburban expansion began in the following year along a new road linking the station to the old hamlet of Kingsend, on land belonging to the chief landowner since the C15, King's College Cambridge. Further haphazard development followed after the opening of Northolt Junction (later South Ruislip) in 1908, and a year later came a more ambitious scheme by *A. & J. Soutar* for a garden suburb for the King's College land to the E of the village. This was incorporated into a progressive plan of 1914 by the Ruislip–Northwood U.D.C., but not entirely carried out. Building took

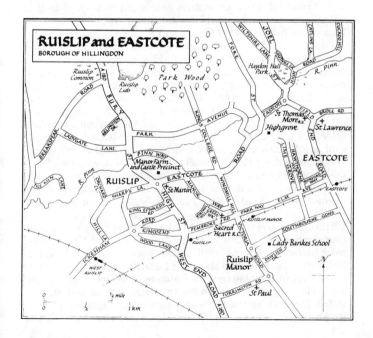

place briskly between the wars to E, W, and S of the village, but Park Wood to the N, originally designated for superior detached houses, was preserved as open space.

CHURCHES

St Martin, High Street. A sizeable building, over 30 metres long, of flint rubble with stone dressings: a C13 aisled church much remodelled and extended. All the exterior stonework was heavily renewed during restorations by *Christian* (chancel, 1869) and *Scott* (nave, 1886), and again from 1910 and 1970. Parapeted C15 SW tower; of the same date the battlemented S aisle wall with blocked S doorway, extended *c.* 1500 by a S chapel. Chancel also rebuilt in the C15; its flint walls are attractively speckled with other stones (greenish Reigate, dark local ferricrete). The N aisle is a late Perp rebuilding, a handsome composition with four windows in deep soffits and a central Tudor doorway with carved spandrels under a straight head. The W walls were dressed up in the C19 by two statues, one over the porch of 1896, one on a N buttress. Inside, C13 arcades with alternating circular and octagonal piers, the S side with one square and one chamfered order, the N side with double-chamfered arches, and so a little later. Chancel arch also C13. Fine Perp carpentry: arch-braced and wind-braced roof in the chancel; both aisles with low-pitched roofs with carved bosses and decorated spandrels to the tie-beams (the N aisle especially good). Nave roof with a six-sided ceiling above older tie-beams, and carved bosses (many renewed). – Also late Perp are the DOORS in the N aisle, chancel N, and rood-loft entrance on the N aisle, a few PEWS in the S aisle with buttressed ends (cf. Harmondsworth, Hi), and two oak-bound hutch-type CHESTS (nave and N aisle).

FONT. C12. Flat, square Purbeck marble bowl with foliage in the spandrels on top. – PULPIT. Hexagonal, Jacobean, with restrained, chiefly abstract ornamentation: studding, faceted blocks, etc. – BREAD CUPBOARD, N aisle. 1697, with four shelves, decorated pilasters and bracket, and segmental pediment: a handsome piece. – WALL PAINTINGS. Traces of *c.* 1500: on the N side the Seven Deadly Sins; on the S side (barely visible) the Acts of Mercy; above the rood-loft entrance St Michael weighing a soul and St Lawrence; in the S aisle St Christopher and others yet uncovered. – TILES (chancel). Late medieval, with leaf, fleur-de-lys, and heraldic designs, of the type made at Penn, Bucks. – HATCHMENTS. An unusually large collection, mostly displayed in the tower. – STAINED GLASS. Chancel N: life of St Martin, two delicately detailed windows by *C. E. Kempe, c.* 1900. – Chancel NE, 1953 (by *CSL?*), St Martin, good colours. – S aisle: four windows of 1870 with scenes from the life of Christ, good work by *Lavers, Barraud & Westlake*. – MONUMENTS. Roger de Sothcote, C14. Inscribed slab with Lombard lettering. – Several memorials to the Hawtreys of Eastcote. Two late C16 brasses: John Hawtrey † 1593 and wife, two large figures and shields; Ralph Hawtrey and wife † 1574, figures on engraved plate. – Ralph Hawtrey † 1638 and Mary Hawtrey † 1647 by *John and*

Matthias Christmas. Wall-monument with two busts in oval niches, not yet with any sign of Carolean courtly ease and self-conscious elegance (cf. the Barkham monument at Tottenham (Hy) of 1644 for an example of progressive work of this time). – Jane Clitherow † 1659, attributed to *Joshua Marshall* (GF). Flat marble scrolled cartouche. – Lady Mary Bankes † 1661. Pedimented, with putti. – Thomas Bright † 1673, with mourning putti to l. and r. of a marble aedicule. – John Reading † 1705. Small cartouche. – Christopher Musgrave, C18, coloured marbles. – Many good LEDGER STONES in the chancel.

ST MARY, The Fairway, South Ruislip. 1958–9 by *Laurence King*. Simple exterior, a concrete portal frame with yellow brick infilling, relieved by a clerestory with shallow gables, a short W steeple, and a large Crucifixion against the W window by *Brian Asquith*. Polygonal E end with abstract STAINED GLASS in deep colours by *Keith New*. The W front is flanked by vicarage and church hall.

ST PAUL, Tiverton Road, Ruislip Gardens. 1936 by *N. F. Cachemaille-Day*; S aisle 1952. Traditional in plan but not in detail. Brick, with a simple interior with lozenge-shaped piers, intended to be painted white and gold. In St Jude's Chapel a window from St Jude, Grays Inn Road, an art nouveau figure of St Agatha.

SACRED HEART (R.C.), Pembroke Road, Ruislip Manor. 1939 by *George Drysdale*, a large brick Early Christian basilica. Lady Chapel with decoration and several statues by *Siegfried Pietzch*. Two ANGELS carrying candlesticks, possibly formerly on riddle-posts, by *Pugin*, brought from the diocese of Leeds. Arcade linking church and hall, 1984.

ST GREGORY THE GREAT (R.C.), Victoria Road, South Ruislip. By *Gerard Goalen*, 1966–7, an ingenious combination of an oval plan with a visibly rectangular framework. The roof-beams project above the clerestory and are supported inside by shuttered concrete columns forming an ambulatory round the W end. Polygonal baptistery with open bell-cage above. – FURNISHINGS of unusually high quality, all of 1967: SCULPTURE of the Virgin and Child and St Gregory by *Willi Soukup*; LETTERING in stone by *Ralph Beyer*; lintel over the main door by *Stephen Sykes*; also by him the enamelled CROSS over the altar. The oval STAINED GLASS window above and the baptistery windows are by *Patrick Reyntiens*. The nine windows of slab-in-resin glass by *Charles Norris* were added in 1987–9.

BAPTIST CHURCH, West Way, Ruislip Manor. 1963–4 by *J. Ainsworth*. Polygonal, roof-lit; a compact plan with steeply raked seats, with spacious corridor and rooms off tucked in underneath.

PUBLIC BUILDINGS

MANOR FARM, Bury Street. A group of former farm buildings near the centre of the village, now in public use. The farm stands in the precinct of the motte-and-bailey castle held in the late C11 by Ernulf de Hesdin; the site was still moated in the C18. The dominant buildings are two BARNS. The smaller was converted to a LIBRARY by the *M.C.C.* (*W. T. Curtis* and *H. W. Burchett*) in 1937, when it was extended and given new foundations, windows, and cladding. Outside not much looks old, but inside the roof is visible, a good example of the characteristic c 16–17 type, with arch-braced tie-beams, queen-struts, and wind-braces. Extended in 1963. The older GREAT BARN, with its mighty sweeping tiled roof and weatherboarded walls, has been much rebuilt but remains uncluttered by any conversion. Enough original framing remains to indicate its type of construction, although only one truss survives to demonstrate it fully. Arcade posts, tie-beams, and aisle-ties were connected by passing-braces that terminated at now removed aisle-posts, a form characteristic of the c 13 and c 14. Also archaic are the straight braces between arcade posts and plates with various types of medieval scarf-joint (presumably much replaced). The roof and aisle walls are later. The group is completed by the COW BYRE, rebuilt in 1981 after a fire in a straightforward vernacular but not old-world style (*Peter Schembri*, Borough of Hillingdon), an object lesson to the lumpish WINSTON CHURCHILL HALL behind. The MANOR FARM HOUSE (now used for public purposes, restored in 1958) is only a fragment: one range and the beginning of another which may have extended w; close-studded timber-framing and early c 19 windows. About 1087 Ernulf gave the manor to the abbey of Bec in Normandy; it later became a cell of Ogbourne Priory in Wiltshire, a dependency of Bec, and from 1451 belonged to King's College Cambridge. To the N, across the river Pinn, remains of EARTHWORKS enclosing a former park of 350 acres.

LIBRARY, South Ruislip. 1971 by *Douglas Stephen & Partners*, a transparent steel-framed box.

RUISLIP LIDO, Reservoir Road. The grounds were laid out in 1934–6 by *T. H. Mawson* for the Grand Union Canal Company as the prototype for a series of what one would now call leisure centres. The central building by *George W. Smith*, progressively 'moderne' in appearance, housed a restaurant and dance floor.

LADY BANKES JUNIOR AND INFANT SCHOOLS, Dawlish Drive, Ruislip Manor. 1936–7 by *W. T. Curtis* and *H. W. Burchett*, one of the best and least altered examples of progressive Middlesex schools of the thirties. The frontage, given interest by two colours of brick, has a curved staircase tower as the main feature. Future uncertain at the time of writing.

SOUTHBOURNE SCHOOL, Southbourne Gardens, Ruislip Manor. A secondary school for the M.C.C. by *H. V. Lobb*, 1946–7 and characteristic of the date. Disused at the time of writing.

QUEENSMEAD SCHOOL, Long Drive, South Ruislip. Built as a secondary modern in 1968 by *Yorke, Rosenberg & Mardall*. Set amidst generous playing fields, unike the earlier schools. The hall and administration around a courtyard, but classrooms, gym, workshops, etc., in separate blocks. Crisply designed, the classrooms in a long range with boarded upper floor on free-standing columns. Close by is the DEANSFIELD PRIMARY SCHOOL and a SPORTS CENTRE, both with neat dark cladding.

WHITEHEATH JUNIOR SCHOOL, Ladygate Lane. By the *Borough Architect's Department*, 1978.

STATIONS. RUISLIP of 1904, dignified brick, is one of the few

remaining original stations on the Metropolitan line. RUISLIP
MANOR is of 1938 by *Holden*. SOUTH RUISLIP on the Central
line was opened in 1948. Cantilevered concrete platform
canopies. Polygonal entrance hall with opaque clerestory, 1963
by *F. F. Curtis*; inside is a cast concrete abstract frieze.

POLISH WAR MEMORIAL, Western Avenue. 1948 by *Miecystam
Lubelski*. Plain stone with bronze lettering, an eagle above.

PERAMBULATION

A tour should start in the churchyard. On the N side a two-storey
timber-framed house with a well documented history: built *c.*
1570, converted in 1616 to back-to-back cottages (five on each
side), in the C18 used to house the poor. The framing of the
upper floor has curved braces; the former jetty was underbuilt
in brick on the S side in 1616. Opposite, at the entrance to Manor
Farm (*see* Public Buildings), a small square former LODGE. In
BURY STREET, facing S down the High Street, the VILLAGE
TEA AND SWEET SHOP, an attractive low C17 exterior of brick,
with two slightly projecting wings. An older timber-framed
interior, altered but visible in the l. half of the house. The
fireplace to the l. of the central chimneystack has a moulded
beam. In the HIGH STREET a picturesquely informal group of
timber-framed buildings hugs the churchyard, with a tactful
LYCHGATE of 1902 attached. In the house to its N a fireplace
with carved lintel and trefoil-headed brick niches above. To the
S is a long range, plainly rendered on the High Street side, but
facing the churchyard with C16 close studding above a moulded
jetty.

On the W side of the High Street, PARK HOUSE of *c.* 1827, much
altered and once with large grounds. To the road, a stuccoed end
wall above shops; longer S frontage with shallow bow. The rest
of the High Street is fairly genteel early C20, with little that is
out of scale until one reaches the station, marked by the seven-
storey TIMES HOUSE, a characteristically tactless sixties office
block (*c.* 1965 by *Frank Rutter*). S of the station the BARN
HOTEL, a small C16–17 L-shaped timber-framed farmhouse of
good quality – see the richly moulded beam in the S ground-floor
room of the main range. Queenpost roof of very solid timbers,
with lower wind-braces, and curved braces to the tie-beams.
Converted timber-framed barn and stables nearby.

E from the High Street KINGSEND, laid out in 1905, the first of
the King's College developments, starting with Nos. 13–15 by
Mansford; a pair intended to impress as a single house, white
rendered with brick trim. Further on, at the junction with Wood
Lane and Sharps Lane, the remnants of the old hamlet of Kings-
end. ORCHARD COTTAGE is sweetly weatherboarded over a
C16 timber-framed core; tactful C20 additions. The WHITE
BEAR opposite is early C19. N from here the grounds of Park
House (*see* above), built up slowly from 1906 (DULCE DOMUM
in King Edward's Road is among the earliest houses).

For the best of the rural timber-framed survivals one should explore
N along BURY STREET, from the Manor Farm towards Ruislip

Common. On the w side the OLD HOUSE, C16–17 with early
C19 stucco, and the MILL HOUSE by the Pinn, L-shaped, the
wing projecting to the road once a barn. Good brick chimney to
the main range. The brick exterior of BURY FARM (Nos. 1–3
Bury Street), with bricks dated 1776 and 1786, conceals a C17
lobby-entry house (with a smoking-chamber preserved in the
central stack) remodelled from a medieval hall house whose
central hearth was found during repairs. Further on a little group
of which the PLOUGH INN is the centre: timber-framed, altered,
but essentially of *c.* 1500 or earlier. The attractive WOODMANS
FARMHOUSE on the E side is a C17 lobby-entry house with
exposed framing and a big compound brick stack in the centre.
The curious little timber-framed turret opening off the r. hand
room at the back corner was perhaps for a closet or garderobe.
In ARLINGTON DRIVE, LITTLE MANOR, timber-framed with
gabled cross-wings, the front refaced in C18 brick. On the r.
CANNONS BRIDGE FARM, a small C19 brick farmhouse with
weatherboarded barn. At the beginning of BREAKSPEAR ROAD
another old group, spoilt by a garage. The best house here is
BRILL COTTAGE, with a good medieval wind-braced roof of
three and a half bays (smoke-blackened at the w end) and a later
chimney at the E end.

To the w are some more isolated houses. HILL FARMHOUSE
in ORCHARD CLOSE, now rather hemmed in, is nevertheless
interesting for its several building phases. The low back wing
with a crownpost roof is medieval; the two-storey timber-framed
front range with brick infilling dates from *c.* 1700. Central chimneystack. In one gable a window with diamond-set mullions.
(Inside, stone fireplaces and a stair with turned balusters.) Later
C18 additions. Further w still in TILE KILN LANE, in a quite
rural setting, OLD CLACK FARMHOUSE, C16 or earlier, with
exposed square framing, and a small weatherboarded BARN.
Further N, at the beginning of DUCKS HILL ROAD leading
across Ruislip Common, the brick SIX BELLS INN of 1806 on
the w side, and on the E THE OLD WORKHOUSE, dated 1789,
a replica of the Harefield workhouse of 1782. Red brick with
dentil cornice, two rear wings; the w wing was added when it
was restored *c.* 1922.

To the E of the village part of the Manor Farm land was developed
by Ruislip Manor Cottage Society with low-rental housing for
artisans, intended to serve the needs of the garden suburb
planned for Ruislip–Northwood, all very much in the spirit of
Hampstead Garden Suburb. The houses are mostly scattered
along Manor Way and Windmill Way. The earliest are in
MANOR WAY (1911–12), a tilehung pair by *Michael Bunney*,
and a larger composition of simple brick cottages in groups
of four, set back from the road behind a green. The central
group is by *C. M. Crickmer*, the two flanking ones by *A. & J.
Soutar*, the smaller end groups, set a little forward, by *H. A.
Welch*. MANOR CLOSE carried on the tradition after 1914. At
the entrance to WINDMILL WAY a nice tiled pair, and further
along another composition on three sides of a green, by *Cecil
Hignett*, more fancifully detailed, with patterned brickwork.
Along GREEN WALK pairs with steep pantiled roofs, rather

East Anglian in feeling, designed before 1914, built after the war.

The Soutar plan for a garden suburb included larger houses in the wooded area to the N (only three to an acre). They were never built, and KINGS COLLEGE ROAD, the main N–S axis, peters out at the beginning of Park Wood. The existing houses are of moderate size and mostly of no special distinction – a disapointment after the Cottage Society housing; two hundred had been built by 1914, more followed in the 1920s. Amid the rural idyll of brick and half-timbering one outré group stands out: Nos. 97–101 PARK AVENUE, a pair and a single house, by the 98 pioneer modernists *Connell, Ward & Lucas*, 1936. No. 99 is the least altered. White stucco, flat roofs. The façades play a game with L-shapes on different planes, with linking balconies and long horizontal windows. Projecting garage and inset door further stress the movement through three dimensions. In EASTCOTE ROAD, No. 152, a quieter house in the modern idiom, 1952 by *Dex Harrison*, a rarity at this time. Brick-faced with monopitch roof. A neat L-shape, with upper floor extending on slender columns over a car port, and a garden wing with a double-height living room.

The area now called RUISLIP MANOR, s of the railway, which had been scheduled for twelve houses to the acre, was mostly built up only in 1933–9 with speculative housing (George Ball's Manor Homes). SOUTH RUISLIP also dates largely from between the wars. Its centre, at the junction of Victoria Road and Long Drive, is marked by a large SAINSBURYS with a series of jutting pantiled roofs (1987 by *Sainsbury Architectural Practice*), a deliberately friendly vernacular image replacing the short-lived brutalist office tower built for B.E.A. in 1964 by *Murray, Ward & Partners*. In STATION APPROACH, SOUTH RUISLIP DAY NURSERY by the *Borough Architect's Department*, 1978–80; a large playroom under a broad-eaved tiled roof. s of Long Drive are schools (q.v.) and playing fields. Between Victoria Road and the railway a small industrial estate developed from the 1930s; the GOLDSCHMIDT factory is a good example of the streamlined type of brick front with ribbon windows and rounded entrance tower.

GLEBE FARM, near the junction of West End Road and Western Approach, was built by Charles Mills of Hillingdon Court (q.v.) in 1882. Quite fanciful, with patterned tilehanging, shouldered-headed windows, and coloured brick bands. For the nearby Polish War Memorial *see* above.

STOCKLEY PARK

An internationally orientated business park E of Yiewsley, con- 116 veniently close to Heathrow, designed to employ *c.* 5,000 people when complete. Laid out from 1985 to a master plan by *Arup Associates* and one of the most ambitious and imaginative examples of its date in England of landscaping on a grand scale. It is the third major business park in the country (its predecessors

are the Cambridge Science Park of the 1970s, and Aztec West
outside Bristol, begun in 1980), although small compared with
similar parks in France and the United States. Of 350 flat and
featureless acres of green-belt land formerly used for gravel-
extracting and rubbish-dumping, 250 acres remain open space,
remodelled by a hefty quantity of earth-moving as a public park
and ample golf course. The business area occupies 100 acres at
the s end, the elegant white pavilions of phase 1 in the centre
approached along a winding route beside a necklace of informal
lakes and semi-mature trees, with car-parking screened by formal
hedges. In contrast to the reticent palette of the buildings, there is
plenty of colourful planting (with good winter as well as summer
colour): informally grouped shrubs around the lakes, firm lines
of evergreens defining the main approaches. The textures of the
hard surfaces are equally satisying and varied; brick, gravel, and
wood are used throughout instead of tarmac and concrete.

The ARENA building (by *Arup Associates*, completed 1988),
with sports club, restaurant, management offices, and conference
centre, provides a long, low focus between park and business
area. Unlike the pavilions, it is faced in coursed buff reconstituted
stone, the neat precision of the detail contrasting with the fluid
shape of the building as a whole – an aesthetic effect similar to
the tension between the formal and free-flowing shapes in the
surrounding landscape. At the w end is a polygonal conservatory
for the restaurant; at the e end the ground slopes up to the large
windows of the swimming pool. The hub of the building is a
curious circular piazza, small but monumental, whose rigorous
geometry recalls Arup's Broadgate Centre in the City, with
fainter echoes of Stirling's gallery at Stuttgart. It has shops on
the ground floor, a set-back first-floor balcony with views cut
through the wall, and a distinctive roof-line of open squares
stepping down to the car park to the NW. In the lake in front,
quirky SCULPTURE of formation swimmers by *Kevin Atherton*.

The eight pavilions of 1985–7 by *Arup Associates* that line
LONGWALK ROAD, running s, established the site's initial
pattern of neat isolated buildings orthogonally set in a well controlled landscape. They are similar but not identical, two-
storeyed, with shallow hipped roofs and white cladding, of basic
components that can be grouped in different ways with custom-
ized accessories such as glazed stair-towers and porches. In Pavilion A 1.2 a stained-glass stairwell window by *Alex Beleschenko*,
1986. By the canal at the s boundary this pattern is broken by
three larger buildings of 1987–90. These are downright indi-
vidualists. The first is by *Foster Associates*, supremely grand, yet
elegantly minimal. It consists of three staggered blocks of three
storeys, with sheer glass walls suspended from lofty Y-frames.
The glazing of the central block is set back, so that the end frame
forms a porte-cochère in front of a full-height atrium. Beyond
this are airy top-lit staircase halls between each of the three
sections. On the long walls the immaculate glazing varies between
opaque and white spotted glass panes, imparting to the whole a
mysteriously poetic shimmer, especially effective when seen from
across the lake to the E. On the other side of the lake, the next
building, by *Geoffrey Darke Associates*, also of three storeys, is

less ethereal. It has a hipped roof like the Arup pavilions, but is distinguished by its stone cladding with patterns of square panels for canopy brackets. The third building, further W, by *Ian Ritchie Architects*, with neat curtain-walling with pale green bands, departs from the restrained grey and white predominant elsewhere, although the colour is muted by the enclosing steel framework of solar shades. Returning N up ROUNDWOOD AVENUE, the first block to the E is by *Troughton McAslan*, 1988, two floors of offices arranged around an internal 'street', contained in a trim box with projecting upper floor, enlivened on the S side by a fringe of tensile sun blinds. Then, set back beyond a formal approach and circular pool, an imposing, all-white building by *Arup Associates*, 1989–90, with a flamboyant entrance emphasized by two towers flanked by curved projecting screens. Further N a double pavilion also by *Arup Associates*.

Phase 2, to the E, offers further variety, with *Eric Parry Associates*' elegant glass-block-walled building (1990–1), and more to come by *Peter Foggo* (barrel-vaulted roof) and *Richard Rogers*. W of Stockley Road three large blocks by *SOM* for Glaxo, in progress in 1990; beyond is a further development site (phase 3).

SWAKELEYS
Ickenham

Swakeleys House was built by Sir Edward Wright, a London alderman who was Lord Mayor in 1640–1. He acquired the estate in 1629–30; a completion date is provided by the rainwater heads dated 1638. The house comes as a surprise after the drive fringed by select suburban villas of the 1930s and the office buildings that helped to finance restoration and conversion in 1981–5.

The main front faces W, two storeys and an attic, with pedimented gables appearing not only on the W-facing walls, but also on the return sides of the projecting wings. The roof-line is further enlivened by clustered stacks, and may have had a central cupola. Pediments also adorn the windows of the main range, sitting rather oddly above a cornice which is continued as a double string course all round the building. Like its contemporaries of the 1630s, Kew Palace and Cromwell House Highgate, Swakeleys is a revealing demonstration of the mixture of traditional and up-to-date influences at work at this time. The lively massing with projecting wings is still in the Jacobean tradition. The flamboyant pedimented gables with concave sides springing from curly volutes are an obvious borrowing from Netherlandish classicism. They recall the first known example of this feature in London, the gabled house in Holborn drawn by John Smithson in 1619. Swakeleys can indeed be seen as an example of city taste in the country, its swanky exterior quite different in spirit from the sophisticated Italian classicism of Inigo Jones's court style.

The house is of red brick, but with contrasting mullioned and transomed windows, pediments, and other details. Most are of brick plastered and painted to look like stone, although more costly genuine black marble was used for the main doorways and

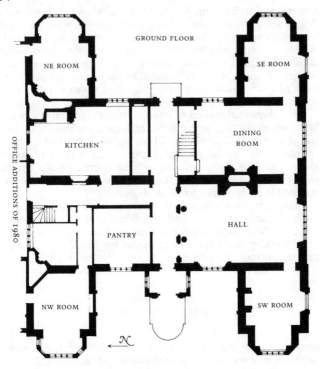

Swakeleys, plans of ground and first floors

the windows of the show rooms. To the s there is a long flat front
with two main windows each of six plus six lights. The smaller
windows that flank them were altered in the c18. The breaks in
the brick plinth show that they were intended to incorporate
doorways; blocked slots in the brickwork suggest there may have
been early balconies above. The E front also has projecting wings,
but a flat centre whose busy arrangement of stepped windows
with central oval reflects the position of the staircase; compositions of this kind with small windows of different shapes, an
idea derived from Serlio, appear in drawings of several lost
London houses of this time. Here the pattern is emphasized by
bold plaster strapwork around the openings. The finely detailed
rubbed red brick surround to the doorway is probably an addition
of *c.* 1700. The N side facing the service yard also has small
central windows which light the back staircase. The ground floor
here is concealed by discreet additions made when the house was
converted to offices in 1981–5 by *Kirby Adair Newson*: low brick
pavilions and top-lit one-storey entrance hall.

The c20 approach on the N side has the advantage of leaving
the original w entrance undisturbed. Through the porch one
reaches a ground-floor hall in the traditional position, entered at
the screens passage end. The screen is a splendid showpiece
(attributed by Mrs Esdaile to *John Colt*), of wood painted to look
like stone, with marbled columns and a central arch with broken

FIRST FLOOR

GREAT CHAMBER

15m
50ft

segmental pediment surmounted by lions awkwardly squeezed in below the ceiling. According to Pepys, who visited the house in 1665, soon after it had been bought by the wealthy goldsmith Sir Robert Vyner, the screen was an addition by the previous owner, the Parliamentarian Sir James Harrington, Wright's son-in-law, who inherited the house in 1649. In Pepys's time the screen had busts of Charles I, Fairfax, and Essex on the hall side, and on the other side 'the parson of the parish, the Lord of the Manor and his sisters' – a curious mixture. The bust of Essex is now in the church; Fairfax is on the opposite side of the screen; two other male busts, presumably Harrington and the parson, are now on the chimneypiece, probably an addition of the later C17, as may be the black and white chequer floor. The fielded panelling of the hall looks C18.

While the position of the hall is old-fashioned, the plan of the house as a whole is progressive, with its compact double-pile central range, with dining room directly behind the hall. This has panelling of early C17 type, as does the small parlour in the NW wing, opening off the pantry. Both the NW parlour and the NE room opening off the former kitchen have corner fireplaces, early examples of a feature which became common in later C17 town houses. The main staircase on axis with the entrance has been rebuilt. From the original one only two newel posts with crude strapwork remain. The present stair is in C18 style, with

carved tread-ends and fluted balusters, but may be a C 19 reconstruction. The wall and ceiling paintings with scenes of Dido and
Aeneas are probably C 18.

On the first floor the great chamber occupies the whole of the
front of the central range. This is the grandest room in the house,
its importance emphasized by its up-to-date plaster ceiling. Like
the great chamber ceiling of Cromwell House, it is an early
imitation of the sober classical style of interior decoration introduced by Jones. The ceiling is divided into a grid of fifteen
compartments, with a central circle and beams enriched by classical mouldings. On the S side of the house there was originally a
long gallery, partitioned later, and much altered; in other rooms
plain C 17 fireplaces and panelling, not all *in situ*. The attic floor,
now opened up and stripped out, originally consisted of small
rooms, two of them with surprisingly smart marble fireplaces.

In the grounds a C 17 DOVECOTE with ice house on the ground
floor.

UXBRIDGE

INTRODUCTION

Uxbridge grew up at the crossing over the river Colne at the
boundary between Middlesex and Buckinghamshire, on the edge
of the parish of Hillingdon. The town appears to have been established in the C 12, when it had its own market and chapel (although
the chapel did not achieve independence until 1827). The still
recognizable narrow burgage plots along the High Street may have
been laid out on the curving strips of one of Hillingdon's open
fields. By the C 16 Uxbridge had become one of the most important
market towns in Middlesex, close enough to serve the city and too
far to be swallowed by it. It flourished in the C 18 as the first
stopping-place for stage coaches from London to Oxford. Industry
came in the C 19, chiefly to Uxbridge Moor to the W, taking advantage of the transport provided by the Grand Junction Canal. In
1846 the Great Western Railway built a branch line from Cowley
(now defunct); the extension of the Piccadilly line in 1933 brought
Uxbridge within the orbit of Metroland. The town was an urban
district from 1894, a borough from 1955, and in 1965 became the
main focus of the new London borough of Hillingdon.

Until the 1960s the pre-industrial market town was still recognizable, with a centre marked by the modest group of C 18 market
house and medieval church, and a winding main street with plenty
of inns and handsome Georgian frontages surviving from its coaching past. Much disappeared with the construction of a brutally
destructive ring road and a ruthlessly new shopping area in the NW
central quarter. The SW corner was filled in the 1970s by the new
civic centre, which made amends for its bulk by adopting a homelier
vernacular imagery. An even faster pace of change since, influenced
by the proximity of motorways and airport, turned Uxbridge into
the Croydon of the 1980s, producing poignant contrasts between

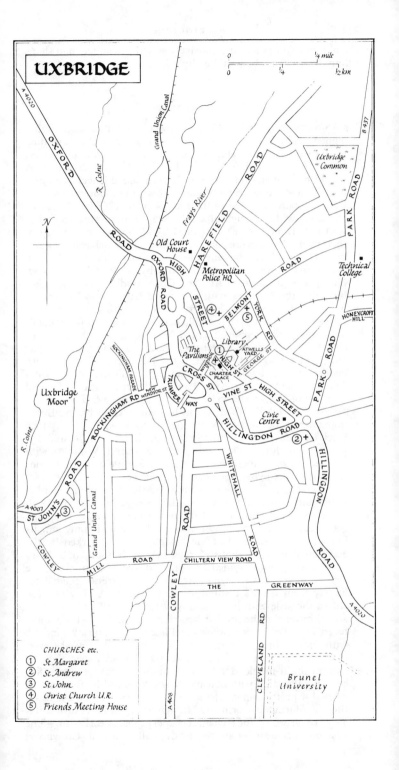

UXBRIDGE

0 .... ¼ mile
0 ......¼...... ½ km

A 4020
OXFORD ROAD
R. Colne
Grand Union Canal
Frays River
N
B 437
Uxbridge Common
PARK ROAD
HAREFIELD ROAD
Old Court House
OXFORD ROAD
HIGH STREET
Metropolitan Police HQ
ROAD
Technical College
④ ✕ BELMONT
⑤ YORK RD
HONEYCROFT HILL
Library
The Pavilions
① HIGH ST
ATWELLS YARD
WINDSOR ST
GEORGE ST
CHARTER PLACE
Uxbridge Moor
ROCKINGHAM PARADE
CROSS ST
TRUMPER
WAY
NEW WINDSOR ST
VINE ST
HIGH STREET
PARK ROAD
ROCKINGHAM RD
HILLINGDON ROAD
Civic Centre ■
② ✕
R. Colne
ST JOHN'S ROAD
A 4007
③ ✕
Grand Union Canal
WHITEHALL ROAD
HILLINGDON ROAD
COWLEY MILL ROAD
ROAD
CHILTERN VIEW ROAD
COWLEY
THE
GREENWAY
A 4020
CLEVELAND RD
A 408
Brunel University

CHURCHES etc.
① St Margaret
② St Andrew
③ St John
④ Christ Church U.R.
⑤ Friends Meeting House

the older buildings and the massively scaled new offices and shops filling the backland behind the High Street.

CHURCHES

ST ANDREW, Hillingdon Road. NE tower with tall broached spire, a good landmark at the S end of Uxbridge where the expanding town merges into the older settlement of West Hillingdon. 1865 by *G. G. Scott*, red and yellow brick with stone dressings. A decent but not lavish interior: nave with paired lancets, columns of brick and stone, and a wagon roof with two dormer lights. – Carved stone REREDOS of the Last Supper, 1868 by *Farmer & Brindley*, within a high altar of 1892, with painted frontal. – WALL PAINTINGS in the chancel by *Hemmings*, c. 1891–1913, their painted frames creamed over since. – Low alabaster SCREEN by *J. O. Scott*, now bearing the most remarkable furnishing in the church, a timber superstructure by *W. R. Lethaby*, 1927. Non-period detail in an Arts and Crafts tradition gone angular; high up, three arches with geometric lattice-work instead of pierced tracery as a backing to the rood, with two formalized angels. The screen itself has solid ogee shapes with flowery finials along the parapet, above painted relief scenes. – S aisle ALTAR (Lady Chapel), with riddel-posts and angels in Sarum style, 1924; N aisle ALTAR (Chapel of the Resurrection), 1954, with classical reredos by *Bagen Beagle* and figure of Christ by *Beauford Lindley*. – STAINED GLASS. Good small scenes with the life and ministry of Christ (chancel E, nave S) by *Clayton & Bell*.

ST JOHN, St John's Road, Uxbridge Moor, close by the Buckinghamshire border. 1838 by *Henry Atkinson*, the E.E. stock brick Commissioners' type. Shallow pitched roof with stuccoed parapet, porch to match, and a little bell-turret. Windows with Y-tracery. Later sanctuary, with lancets. Simple unspoilt interior with rustic poppyhead pews and a W gallery.

ST MARGARET. The parish church nestles behind the market house and forms with it an irregular triangle between the High Street, Windsor Street, and the new Charter Place. Although the church was until 1827 a chapel of ease to Hillingdon, its importance by the end of the Middle Ages is marked by the addition of an incongruously large S aisle by the Guild of St Mary and St Margaret, founded in 1443. Looked at from the S, the aisle appears nearly as high as the tower. The exterior detail dates largely from *Scott*'s restoration of c. 1882–5. A view of 1809 shows the aisle with just one tiny W lancet (a relic of an earlier aisle?) instead of the present large Perp W window set in a flint-faced wall. The S windows were all like the existing SW window, with simple three-light tracery. The plain unbuttressed tower, in an odd position N of the N aisle, may be older than the C15 (see the multi-moulded N doorway) but was much rebuilt in 1820 and smartened up with new belfry windows and battlements. It carried a pretty cupola already in 1809 (restored in 1988); cf. those at Harmondsworth and Hillingdon (both Hi). Nave and N aisle are early C15, the N chancel chapel probably early C16. – The best internal features are the ROOFS: all medieval. Crownpost construction over nave and chancel; a hammerbeam roof (much repaired and reconstructed) over the s aisle, a rarity in a Middlesex church (but cf. Harmondsworth). After reordering by *Michael Reardon Associates* in 1985–8 the s aisle became the main church (as it was in the c17 and c18), but with the old orientation reversed. The nave and N aisle are divided off by well detailed timber and glass partitions, with an upper floor inserted. The E end has been left open as a chapel, with extra lighting from a lantern ingeniously contrived within the roof. Few old furnishings. – FONT. Late c15, with quatrefoiled panels (cf. Brentford, Ho). – Of MONUMENTS the most remarkable by far is that to Leonora Bennet + 1638, an altar-tomb with the effigy stiffly semi-reclining on the tomb-chest and in the middle of the chest a round recess with prison bars behind which the artist has displayed a generous charnel-house still-life. One bony hand grips the bars. Attributed to *John & Matthias Christmas*.

CHRIST CHURCH (United Reformed), N off Belmont Road. 1972 by *Beard Bennett Wilkins & Partners*, replacing the Old Meeting House N of the High Street (*see* Perambulation 1: Watts Hall). A big slated pyramid roof over the meeting room as a distinguishing landmark.

FRIENDS' MEETING HOUSE, Belmont Road. 1817–18, superseding meeting houses of 1755 and 1692. In a little garden, an oasis among the surrounding offices. A plain, honest London stock brick rectangle with arched windows. Originally two rooms divided by a cross-passage with sliding shutters. The smaller room has been subdivided; the large meeting room preserves its lofty coved ceiling but, alas, lost its original panelling and stand in a fire in 1987.

Little else remains to show that Uxbridge was an important early centre of Nonconformity (seven conventicles in 1669). In New Windsor Street a former METHODIST CHURCH of 1847 survives, originally of the Commissioners' type (not a usual model for the Methodists) but drastically Georgianized for the Freemasons in the 1950s.

PUBLIC BUILDINGS

HILLINGDON CIVIC CENTRE. Planned from 1970; built in 1973– 110 8 by *Robert Matthew, Johnson Marshall & Partners* (architect in a,b charge: *Sir Andrew Derbyshire*). The civic centre cannot be missed. It occupies the whole of the area between the s end of the High Street and the ring road. It marked a turning-point in the c20 approach to civic buildings, acknowledging the traditional desire to express the identity of a newly formed authority while rejecting the language previously used by such buildings. The plans put forward in 1971 by the architects (hitherto well known for their work in the modern tradition) together with the borough of Hillingdon proposed 'familiar and friendly materials' and 'a formal vocabulary well known to the public'. The result is superficially reminiscent of a formalized hill-village of suburban brick houses clustering around an outsize barn; quintessential Metroland imagery. The first impression is of spaciousness.

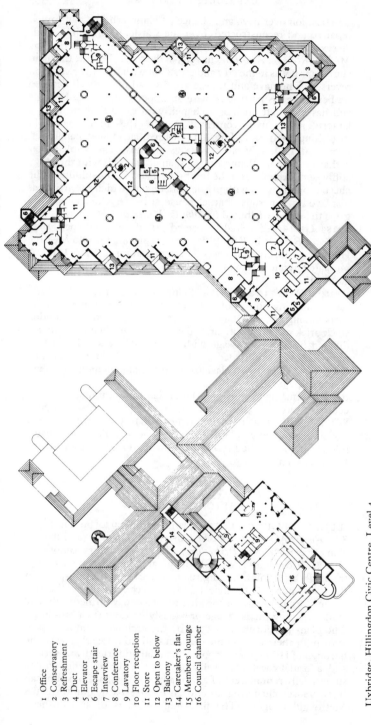

1 Office
2 Conservatory
3 Refreshment
4 Duct
5 Elevator
6 Escape stair
7 Interview
8 Conference
9 Lavatory
10 Floor reception
11 Store
12 Open to below
13 Balcony
14 Caretaker's flat
15 Members' lounge
16 Council chamber

Uxbridge, Hillingdon Civic Centre, Level 4

Adjoining the High Street is a generous plaza, with buildings on two sides, landscaped by *Maurice Lee*. The council chamber is within the projecting wing, covered by tall sweeping tiled roofs, crowned by a spindly cupola re-used from the old civic hall. The second impression is of the relentlessly repetitive brick detail of the zigzagging façades, full of forty-five-degree angles, broken up by a series of receding hipped roofs. The pattern is at its most emphatic on the sides facing the ring road. The motif used throughout is a square window divided in four like a child's drawing, with moulded concrete lintel and surrounding brick frame. Recesses detailed in the same way recur around the open cloisters which connect the different parts of the building, and even on bits of blank wall.

The abundance of surface detail and the various projecting staircases obscure what is basically a straightforward plan: the council chamber and public rooms are attached by a wing with members' and committee rooms, etc., to a large square office building set lozenge-wise to the High Street. The offices, open-plan and air-conditioned, for a staff of 1200, are divided into four triangles on different levels around a central service core. The split-level planning allows for views up and down as well as through the building. The breaking up of a very large building into parts which should be comprehensible and so not intimidating was one of the architects' laudable intentions. The best interior space is the uncluttered curving staircase up to the council chamber. In the stairwell, a hanging wooden sculpture by *John Phillips* called 'Life Continues'. In the entrance wing leading to the council chamber stained glass by *Jane Gray* on the theme of town twinning. The council chamber is octagonal, with a flat ceiling with a few recessed triangles – a disappointment after the promise of the soaring roof. Throughout, the exterior is indeed only a surface skin, and is unrelated to what one finds inside.

OLD COURT HOUSE, Harefield Road. 1906–7 by the county architect, *H. T. Wakelam*, a jolly building, brick with stone dressings. Edwardian free classical: two entrances with octagonal turrets above, flanking a three-bay court room with arched windows; gabled wings with Venetian windows. There is a second, larger court behind (subdivided 1959–60, when other interiors were also altered).

METROPOLITAN POLICE HEADQUARTERS, Harefield Road. 1987–8 by *Jeff Rutt* of the *Metropolitan Police Architect's Department*. Stylistically, one move further on from the civic centre. The large brick bulk is not only tempered by pitched roofs, but livened up by white surfaces, green paintwork, and triangular windows. A cheerfully jazzy post-modern entrance, with a mannered gable canting forward on red trusses. What image of the police is this intended to suggest?

POLICE STATION, Windsor Street. *See* Perambulation 4.

LIBRARY, High Street. 1985–7 by *Frederick Gibberd, Coombes & Partners* (project architect *Christopher Darling*). A deceptively unassuming gabled frontage of dark brick, distinguished from the neighbouring shops by oddly shaped windows. Inside, an interesting sequence of spaces: a two-storey foyer, a low book-issue area, then an airy atrium overlooked by the upper floors: free-flowing spaces with the back and front parts at different levels. Designed together with Charter Place (*see* Perambulation 4).

BRUNEL UNIVERSITY. *See* under its own entry.

TECHNICAL COLLEGE, Park Road. 1963–8 by the *Borough of Hillingdon Architect's Department* (*Thurston Williams, Ernest Seal,* and *S. F. Smith*) in succession to the M.C.C. The usual college type of the time; three-storey curtain-walled main block.

MARKET HOUSE, High Street. *See* Perambulation, first paragraph.

UXBRIDGE STATION. The terminal station of the Piccadilly line, 1938 by *Adams, Holden & Pearson* with *L. H. Bucknall.* Unlike the simple suburban stations further down the line, the exterior is a slightly pompous, consciously urban composition opposite the market hall in the town centre. Brick with marble trimmings. A crescent of shops flanks the entrance; the parapet above is adorned with winged wheels (the sculpture by *Joseph Armitage*). Civic pride is further emphasized inside by the clerestory window with heraldic stained glass by *Erwin Bossanyi.* Otherwise all is satisfyingly rational and functional. Cruciform plan, with spacious hall leading directly to platforms on the same level. Crossing with circular roof-lights. All under concrete portal frames (cf. Cockfosters, Bn) with exposed shuttering. Well preserved integrated fittings (seats, signs, etc.) in the Piccadilly line tradition.

PERAMBULATIONS

The perambulation starts in the centre and proceeds clockwise. From the station (q.v.) one emerges straight into the HIGH STREET and the middle of the historic town centre. Opposite is the MARKET HOUSE, 1788 by *Thomas Niell,* a stately composition. Eleven bays, the centre taller, with a pediment and clock-turret behind; three arched windows to the brick upper floor. The ground floor now has shops which since a restoration of 1986 have been tactfully recessed behind the original wooden Tuscan columns. When built, the ground floor was entirely open (as open as any Le Corbusier design); it was used for pitching corn. The upper floor served as a grain store and as premises for a charity school.

1. To the N

The first excursion to the N leads abruptly into the later C20. On the E side of the HIGH STREET shops of the 1970s, then BARCLAYS BANK, with a busy late C19 stucco façade preserved in 1975 as an envelope to new buildings – an indication of how the approach to urban design was changing at this time. Opposite is the cause for the reaction: most of the NW quarter of the town was flattened in 1963–75 for an unfeelingly out-of-scale package of shops, offices, and flats (by *Turner Lansdowne Holt & Partners*). The original plan of the shopping areas was an uninspired

example of the common 1960s type pioneered in England by
Stevenage – open pedestrian squares linked by partly covered
shopping parades – but in 1985–8 the whole complex was transformed by *Fitch Bendy* and renamed THE PAVILIONS: the
towers of offices were re-clad, the two squares became glazed
atria, and the malls between them were decked out with classical
trimmings. In the first square this window-dressing even
includes an operatic piece of whimsy in place of the original
central pub: a mock-Italian classical belvedere, complete with
simulated cracked stucco.

Further N along the High Street some examples remain of the
dignified C18 frontages characteristic of the main street of a
prosperous small town. First No. 134, C18, three storeys and
five bays, with rubbed brick window-heads and central wooden
canted oriel. Then a pleasant mixture of more altered houses on
a smaller scale (provided one ignores the intrusive MacDonald's):
No. 122, four bays, with C18 brick cornice; Nos. 120–121, a late
C18 pair with stone central keystones to the windows; and No.
119, a brick front with bowed window, but probably timber-
framed behind. No. 118 is a more solid C18 house of five bays,
with a good doorcase, and a parapet concealing a steep hipped
roof. On the W side only two houses of note: No. 64, OLD BANK
HOUSE, of three storeys with a rusticated stucco ground floor,
five windows wide, with an extra two bays added on the r.; and
No. 66, THE CEDARS, an especially handsome tall C18 house,
with another good doorcase with fanlight, curly brick lintels to
the second-floor windows, and shaped gables to the flank walls.
The rest of the High Street is broken up by roads, and by
the unsatisfactory COURT HOUSE and INLAND REVENUE
OFFICES, bitty 1970s affairs in red brick, just where a solid street
front is needed to lead the eye downhill. Opposite, their setting
much improved by the demolition in 1986 of the vast Odeon,
Nos. 74–75, the late Georgian terrace type, with very pretty
fanlights and the first-floor windows recessed in blind arches.
Then FOUNTAINS MILL, formerly a water mill by the river
Frays. One three-storey yellow brick building and a tall chimney
remain next to the inner ring road.

Beyond, in OXFORD ROAD, right at the end of the town by the
canal and river, is the CROWN AND TREATY, an inn since *c.*
1802, when it was converted by James Spiller, with *Soane* as
consultant, after the canal company had acquired the grounds
for building a wharf. The name commemorates the meeting held
here in 1644 between Charles I and the Parliamentarians. The
present building consists of one wing of the formerly half-H-
shaped Treaty House, otherwise known as The Place, which
belonged to the Bennet family in the early C17; the rest was
demolished in the 1750s, and the road was later diverted across
the forecourt. To the street is a curved gable, probably Jacobean.
On the S side two bay-windows with shaped brick mullions and
transoms. The porch is pastiche C18. The N side is the most
picturesque, and suggests that the core of the building is C16:
straight gables, three clusters of hexagonal chimneystacks, and
an octagonal turret. Inside, a ground-floor fireplace (re-set) with
carved scrollwork on the lintel; upstairs, the so-called Treaty

Room, with C16 panelling with Corinthian pilasters and an elaborate strapwork overmantel, and another room with C17 panelling. The woodwork, removed in 1922 to New York to decorate
the Empire State Building, was returned in the 1950s. Nearby,
the two BRIDGES (rebuilt 1938) over the canal and the river
Colne (the boundary with Buckinghamshire), with a low group
of canalside houses between them.

2. *To the* NE *and* E

An excursion NE up HAREFIELD ROAD can take in the Old Court
House and the new police headquarters (*see* Public Buildings)
and return past the latter via a back route to WATTS HALL,
restored in 1982 as the focus of a little alley off the High Street.
The hall began life as the Old Meeting House, the only substantial Nonconformist chapel to be built in Middlesex in the
earlier C18. An agreement made in 1716 with the builder, *William
Thurbin*, survives. The N wall, with its simple round-headed
windows, is still of this date. The entrance was originally on this
side. The roof, W front, and stocky brick tower containing the
gallery stair date from a remodelling in 1883 by *J. Sulman*. Back
to the High Street and E down BELMONT ROAD. The early C20
half-timbered WHITE HORSE TAVERN and, further on, the
lowly Friends' Meeting House (*see* Churches) recall the scale of
old Uxbridge, but all around are overweening offices of the 1980s.
Nos. 59–65, of 1988 by *Ketley Goold Associates,* has arched
conservatory-inspired staircase halls as its distinguishing feature.
Further on, YORK HOUSE, 1986–7 by *Michael Lyell Associates*,
tries harder to fit in, with pitched roofs at different levels. Down
YORK ROAD, the blocks N and S of the railway line are more
uncompromising. HARMON HOUSE, with its ramped entrance
between huge splayed wings building up to a central tower, is
the most ruthless in its sleek anonymity and ambiguous scale.
1984, again by *Ketley Goold Associates*: a skin of silver-glazed
rectangular panels, without any articulation, not even any indication of floor levels. Back by ATWELLS YARD and GEORGE
STREET, suddenly low and C19 again, into the High Street.

3. *To the* S

The W side of the HIGH STREET still has a pleasantly pre-C20
scale and variety of detail into which the deceptively demure
front of the new library (q.v.) fits tactfully. At first the C19 sets
the scale, with No. 28, a stuccoed bank, and Nos. 25–27, four
storeys with pediment, brick with stucco trim. Nos. 20 and 24
are former inns, the Three Tuns and the King's Arms, both low
C16 timber-framed buildings, much altered. The King's Arms
has three gables and oriels, and a coachway to a back yard (its
old character lost, alas, since rebuilding in 1986 by *Ketley Goold
Associates*). Further on, the ROYAL BANK OF SCOTLAND
(1987) turns the corner to Vine Street with clumsy post-modern
panache: triple gables and porthole windows. A glimpse down

VINE STREET can take in RANDALLS, a department store which
originated in the 1890s, rebuilt in 1937–8 by *W. L. Eves*, a period
piece in streamlined cream faience, with a vertical feature with
flagstaff, and elegant original lettering.

The E side of the High Street survived redevelopment until 1990,
when a massive shopping scheme by *Leslie Jones Architects* was
put forward for the scruffy backland behind the old frontages.
Incorporated within this, No. 222, THE SHRUBBERY, a good
three-storey, five-bay brick house, built in 1832–3 for the adju-
tant of the Royal West Middlesex Militia. Further on, the
REGAL, a former cinema, 1932 by *E. Norman Bailey* (now a 100
night club). Quite modest in size, with an appealingly lively art
deco faience front with touches of colour, not a standard cinema
chain design. (Lavish interior with Chinese allusions: a fancifully
curved proscenium arch, and doorways with pierced chinoiserie
detail.)

4. To the W

Behind and at a picturesque angle to the market house, St Margaret's church (q.v.) stands at the head of WINDSOR STREET,
now the only consistent remnant of the old town, a short but
almost complete sequence of low timber-framed or brick houses.
The early C19 QUEEN'S HEAD and its C17 timber-framed
neighbour make a good group near the church. Then the small
Victorian POLICE STATION, 1871, brick with arched windows
with pronounced keystones, and a low C18 front of 2–3–2 bays
with end pilasters. On the other side, MILLERS is similar, with
the addition of a central pediment. Nos. 39–40 is clearly older,
perhaps C16, the ground floor gutted, but still with mullioned
timber windows to the upper floor, and a steep, uneven roof. At
the end, where the ring road cuts across, is the former post office,
with Edwardian Baroque corner entrance, and, beyond the road,
the OLD BURIAL GROUND, with a gateway with the dates 1777
and 1855 (when it was turned into a park).

CHARTER PLACE, between Windsor Street and the ring road, an
elegant high tech creation by *Frederick Gibberd, Coombes &
Partners*, 1985–8, is the most distinguished of the town's rash of
1980s buildings. It was undertaken together with the new library
(*see* Public Buildings) on the adjacent site. A symmetrical composition on a raised podium, with five storeys of offices, shops,
and leisure centre, around a landscaped central court. Two glazed
staircase towers. The blue-tinted glass walls are broken up by
quite delicate horizontal white aluminium sun canopies. The
formal approach from Windsor Street is flanked by two little
brick pavilions serving as transition between the old Uxbridge
and the new.

5. Outliers

To the E: THE CHESTNUTS, Honeycroft Hill, has an attractive
frontage of *c.* 1700, two storeys and five bays, modillioned cornice

and steep hipped roof; the rest entirely rebuilt and extended in
1978.

To the s: s of the ring road St Andrew's church (q.v.) with the
former early C19 rectory behind; further along the main road
some traces of the old settlement of West Hillingdon (*see* Hillingdon, Hi). w towards Cowley Road, minor streets with a
mixture of mid C19 artisan housing (pleasant small villas in
CHILTERN VIEW ROAD) interspersed with reticent *Borough of
Hillingdon* vernacular infilling, among them COLLEY HOUSE,
No. 9 WHITEHALL ROAD, of 1977, an early public response to
the need for housing for young single people; three storeys, with
pitched roof, and friendly low pantiled entrance porch.

To the w: the C19 artisan settlement of UXBRIDGE MOOR
developed around river and canal. NEW WINDSOR STREET was
made only in the mid C19. On the N side brick cottages and
a former Methodist church (q.v.). The older route w was by
Rockingham Road, curving round from Lynch Green (now lost
beneath the ring road) to ROCKINGHAM BRIDGE over the
Frays. The bridge dates from 1809; three brick arches, the centre
one on the N side with a carved keystone. Facing the water on
the E side, near the entrance to Fassnidge Park, UNION VILLAS
(Nos. 15–16 ROCKINGHAM PARADE), dated 1846, a two-storey
group, the unaltered part with quite fancy giant pilasters. Further
w is the CANAL with its wharves. On its w bank the GENERAL
ELLIOT, a late Georgian canalside inn with two canted bays; on
the E side UXBRIDGE BOAT CENTRE, formerly Fellows,
Morton & Clayton, canal carriers, with dry dock and an open-
sided boat-building shed, perhaps of the 1880s, with iron-trussed
timber roof-beams of a full 80 ft (24 metre) span, allowing narrow
boats to be launched sideways into the canal. Still further w, C19
cottages, St John's church (q.v.), and the former NATIONAL
SCHOOLS, 1846, enlarged in 1889 by *George Eves,* quite picturesque yellow and red brick, with pierced bargeboards and
roofs of variegated tiles. Now offices, with glazed porte-cochère
added at the side.

The industrial structures that grew up around the canal from
the early C19 have been largely rebuilt. The most interesting
contribution of the C20 is IMHOF's factory in COWLEY MILL
ROAD, 1961 by *Tayler & Green,* a low group with pitched roofs
with deep eaves above brick walls; a sensitive and elegant effort
to escape from traditional factory design. The planning also
broke new ground, with works and office entrances sited side by
side.

To the N, on high ground at UXBRIDGE COMMON, the landmark
of a sturdy square battlemented former WATER TOWER of *c.* 1900
for the Rickmansworth and Uxbridge Valley Water Company.

WEST DRAYTON

Two old centres redeem the indifferent C20 sprawl. The older is
the group of the church with the remains of the manor house close
by, the brick of the gatehouse and the varied textures of the flint

of the church tower forming an exceedingly fine picture. Further
w is the spacious green, with several good houses in its vicinity. To
the s council estates extend to the M4, to the N suburban development stretches from the station at Yiewsley, Hi (q.v.).

ST MARTIN, Church Road. The flint-work, apart from the w
tower, dates from the restoration of 1850–2 by *Charles Innes*, as
does the s porch. The tower has a Perp w doorway, but its
unbuttressed corners, thick walls, and simple set-backs suggest
an older structure remodelled. It is the only Middlesex example
with a polygonal stair-turret in the centre of the N side instead
of in the more usual corner position. Many tiles used as quoins,
probably dating from later repairs. Unusually long C13 chancel
(lancet windows were found in the N wall in 1930–1). It now
serves, somewhat disconcertingly, as the main entrance, as the
radical reordering by *Norman Haines Associates* in 1974–5
reversed the orientation and placed the altar at the w end of the
nave. E.E. PISCINA, a fine though very restored piece with multi-
moulded arches on bell-shaped capitals. The nave was rebuilt in
the C15, with N and s arcades on three relatively tall octagonal
piers. Contemporary low-pitched roofs, those of the aisles on
corbels with heads. Chancel arch similar to the nave arcades.
Beneath the chancel remains were found in 1974 of a C13 CRYPT
which had been remodelled in the mid C17 as a burial vault for
the Pagets, with arcaded niches for upright coffins (cf. Ickenham,
Hi). COFFIN PLATES from the vault are displayed on the chancel
walls. – FONT. The most elaborate in Middlesex. C15, an octagonal bowl on a nine-stemmed foot. The bowl has eight figured
panels, five with figures of angels, one with a man with hood and
dagger, one with a Pietà (of the Bohemian type of *c.* 1400), and
one with a Crucifixion with the Virgin and St John. – CLOCK.
The works, with angle-standards as Gothic buttresses, are
ascribed to the early C16. – STAINED GLASS. N window to the
Mercer family, 1925–6 by *Morris & Co.*, a *Burne-Jones* design.
Four figures, angels in the tracery. – BRASSES. In the chancel:
civilian of *c.* 1520; James Good † 1581 and wife, partly a palimpsest. – In the s aisle: Margaret Burnell † 1529, and an exceptionally fine engraved frame of early Renaissance character
(Venetian segmental top) to John Burnell † 1551. –
MONUMENTS. Rupert Billingsley of H.M. Ship the Royal
George, † 1720, with a lively relief of a ship, a three-master, at the
foot (cf. the ships on such monuments as Gibbons's Cloudesley
Shovell at Westminster Abbey, 1703). – Fysh de Burgh † 1793
by *Bacon*. Fine and delicate, with an urn on a pedestal with a
seated allegory, the whole against the usual grey marble obelisk. –
Fysh de Burgh, heretofore Coppinger, father of the former,
† 1800, also by *Bacon*; similar but simpler. – Catharine de Burgh
† 1809 by *Bacon Jun.*, with a heavy Grecian Fides in a clumsy
arcade. – General Arabin † 1828 by *T. Denman*.
ST CATHERINE (R.C.), The Green. Built for Irish immigrants,
1869 by *Wilson & Nicholl*, surprisingly ambitious. Brick, with
Dec tracery. w tower completed in 1985, but without the spire
originally intended. At the E end a rose window high up. –
The large REREDOS and stone screens between side chapels and

sanctuary all have elaborately carved Dec detail. – FONT by
S.J. Nicholl. – STAINED GLASS. Baptistery windows by *Lavers,
Barraud & Westlake.*

The gatehouse and extensive Tudor brick walls along Church Road
are all that remains of the MANOR HOUSE of the Pagets, built
by the statesman Sir William Paget, who was granted the estate
in 1547. The house must once have been a spectacular monument
to Tudor splendour. An inventory of 1556 mentions over fifty
private chambers. The brick GATEHOUSE with two polygonal
turrets is still in the early Tudor tradition of Richmond or
Hampton Court. It has been reduced to two storeys and much
restored but is still impressive; the windows are C19, but the
excellent doors and the moulded brickwork of the jambs and
voussoirs of the four-centred central archway are original. The
mansion was demolished *c.* 1750. An C18 survey and C20 excavations showed that it lay immediately w of the church, encroaching on the medieval churchyard.

DRAYTON HALL, Church Road. The house of the Fysh de
Burghs, standing in a small public park: an uneventful stuccoed
late Georgian exterior with later additions. E side with two
rounded ground-floor bows with Doric pilasters and balconies
above; N front with tripartite round-headed windows flanking a
pedimented centre window above a Doric porch. (Entrance hall
with two Doric columns.) Derelict at the time of writing.

THE GREEN. West Drayton is lucky in possessing a large green
still with a good deal of character, in spite of DAISY VILLAS,
1896, making up half of the E side. The best houses are at
and beyond the s end. Across a sub-green at the SE corner,
SOUTHLANDS, now an arts centre, a stately five-bay early C18
front of red brick, built by a farmer, George Cowdery († 1747),
as a genteel addition to an earlier house since replaced by the
present rear wing of 1864. Basement, two storeys, and parapet;
windows with rubbed brick heads. Well preserved interior: a
panelled room on each side of the entrance hall, the r. one with
a niche with still-life painting in the arch, and a staircase with
turned balusters. Small C17 weatherboarded BARN. Nearby,
AVENUE HOUSE, with a similar history, and also with a BARN
(three bays, queen-strut roof). Here the house preserves a low
C16 timber-framed part as a wing to the r. of the C18 five-bay
addition. At the corner of the Green proper is BEECHWOOD,
early C19, two bays, and next door THE OLD HOUSE, with an
early C18 three-bay brick front. After Daisy Villas, the low
Nos. 33–33a also has an C18 brick front, four bays, with two
pedimented doorcases (one a copy), but is clearly an older house
disguised. Then No. 31, a taller, more self-assured Regency
house in pale brick, with an Ionic porch flanked by ground-floor
windows recessed in shallow arches. It stands by the entrance
to the former BRITANNIA BREWERY, established in 1806. A
picturesque assemblage of industrial buildings rises up at the
back of the yard, behind a row of timber-framed gabled houses
facing the Green, which formerly included two pubs.

The w side of the Green is of less consistent interest, but includes
No. 24, five bays, with rubbed brick window-heads with stone
keystones, set back in a garden with rusticated gatepiers, and the

OLD COTTAGE, timber-framed behind a later brick front. The N side is satisfyingly closed by a row of cottages formerly used as a workhouse. One modest C19 shopfront; good continuous tiled roof. The taller house at the E end is a tactful addition of the 1950s.

Near the Green some good individual houses survive. To the N in SWAN ROAD, No. 1, modest Georgian, C18 and early C19. W of the Green in MONEY LANE a former BAPTIST CHAPEL (now three dwellings), dated 1827, with two round-headed windows flanking the entrance. At the end, sadly hemmed in by FRAYS CLOSE, THE FRAYS, a C16 timber-framed house cased in brick. Hall range and a slightly later bargeboarded cross wing; rear wing added c. 1700. S of MILL ROAD, another substantial house of similar date: ST GEORGE'S MEADOWS (formerly Woodpecker Farm), the first floor with exposed timber-framing with curved braces. A later bay on the r. side. Further W in THORNEY MILL ROAD, by the river, the attractive OLD MILL HOUSE and FRAYS COTTAGE, late C18, three storeys, with a Venetian window to the first floor (oval top-lit stairwell). The mill itself has gone, but the MILLWHEEL remains.

YEADING

The NE corner of the old parish of Hayes, now mostly mid C20 housing estates.

ST EDMUND OF CANTERBURY, Yeading Lane. 1961 by *Anthony Lewis*: dull brick exterior, but with SCULPTURE and good jewel-like STAINED GLASS by *Lawrence Lee* in the Lady Chapel.

ST NICHOLAS, Raynton Drive. Also 1961 by *Anthony Lewis*.

ST RAPHAEL (R.C.), Ayles Road. 1961 by *Justin H. Alleyn*. More daring than its Anglican contemporaries. Yellow brick, hexagonal clerestory windows, aisles with concrete columns. Open-cage bell-tower. – Coloured GLASS in the aisle windows by *Pierre Fourmaintreaux*. – STATUE of St Raphael by *Hugh Powell*.

E of Yeading Lane, off Willow Tree Lane, much new housing; also the LONDON POSTAL REGION MOTOR TRANSPORT WORKSHOP, smart hangars of 1980 with glazed ends; an old pub called the WILLOW TREE; and a new park made in the 1980s from derelict land on the Ealing border, around the Paddington branch of the Grand Union Canal. Around HOBART ROAD the borough's deliberate avoidance of municipal and institutional imagery is demonstrated by friendly brick one- to three-storey terraces in a series of closes, built as a mixture of council and private housing. Among them, TASMAN HOUSE, a well integrated hostel for the mentally handicapped. All by *Shankland Cox*, 1978–80.

YIEWSLEY

Once the s part of the large parish of Hillingdon, but since the arrival of the railway an unappealing N suburb of West Drayton.

St Matthew, High Street. Of two dates. The present N aisle began as a small church of 1858–9 by *G. G. Scott,* an unusually bold design for him, in a Butterfieldian spirit (cf. his churches at Crewe Green Cheshire and St Andrew Leicester*). Yellow brick diapered with red, plate-tracery windows below gables, and an apsed chancel with bellcote over the chancel arch. The larger additions (nave, chancel, s aisle) are by *Nicholson & Corlette,* 1898. Exterior with more muted polychromy: yellow and blue brick, in deference to Scott. Pleasant interior with low Gothic piers without capitals and a pretty pointed wagon roof.

To the w the Church School, mid C 19 Gothic with many additions.

Evelyns School, Apple Tree Avenue. Built as a county secondary, by *W. T. Curtis* and *H. W. Burchett* of the *M.C.C.,* 1936, one of the best of the progressive, economically built Middlesex schools of the 1930s. Simply detailed, of mottled brick with bands of tiles. The original layout quite formal – a main range flanked by projecting wings, with a taller stair-tower as the main accent – but compromised by deliberately off-centre post-war additions, with a porch on stilts.

West Drayton Station. Of *c.* 1878, a good example of the G.W.R. style of the period. Cream brick with red bands, tall chimneys, a crown of spiky ironwork on the booking-office roof, and valancing in sweeping curves on the island platform ends.

The High Street is a mess. No. 106, with an angled entrance at the corner of Fairfield Road, is the former Town Hall, very modest neo-Georgian of 1930 by *A. S. Soutar.* The De Burgh Arms by the railway has a C 17 core, but this is difficult to guess. More attractive is the Railway Arms to the s, C 19 brick, with a pretty balcony. Further N along the main road a few older buildings remain among scrappy later C 20 development. Next to Barn House (barn-shaped offices of the 1980s on the site of Phillpotts Farm) a weatherboarded three-storey C 16 or C 17 barn also converted to offices, its queen-strut roof exposed in the e wall. Further on, Yiewsley Grange, quite a complicated story, with a C 16 timber-framed core. What one sees is chiefly C 18 and early C 19. Early C 18 red brick front (with contemporary staircase inside). The N end is embellished with later C 18 battlements and a little turret, much rebuilt when the house was converted to offices in the early 1980s. Another converted barn nearby, with large additions behind.

Grand Union Canal. From Yiewsley to Rickmansworth the canal runs beside the river Colne, attracting industry along its route. Many pleasant brick arched bridges and lock-keepers'

*I owe these comparisons to Geoffrey Brandwood.

cottages. Traces of canal branches serving old brickfields remain, notably the five-mile-long SLOUGH ARM of 1879–82, one of the last English canals to be built. *See also* Cowley (Hi), Hanwell and Southall (Ea), and Brentford (Ho).

STOCKLEY PARK. *See* under its own entry.

HOUNSLOW

INTRODUCTION

Long and flat, the borough of Hounslow – an area of London Clay overlaid by gravels and brickearth, with some remains of heathland around the river Crane at Hounslow* – runs W from the banks of the Thames at Chiswick. The ancient settlement pattern is indicated by

---

*PREHISTORIC AND ROMAN REMAINS include a scatter of Palaeolithic finds across the N of the borough. There was a Neolithic settlement at Brentford. At Bedfont traces were found of a Neolithic hengiform monument; excavation of a possible causewayed camp revealed a double-ditched enclosure of probable Late Bronze Age date. There was late prehistoric occupation at Chiswick. In the Bedfont area, notably at East Bedfont, there was an Iron Age/Romano-British settlement, and at Brentford, on the Silchester road, a substantial Roman one.

the survival of parish churches of early medieval origin at riverside Chiswick and Isleworth, and at rural Hanworth, Heston, East Bedfont, and Feltham further w, but has been overlaid by the development generated by three major routes out of London. The oldest, beginning at the E end as Chiswick High Road, runs through Turnham Green some way N of the old riverside village of Chiswick. Maps show it fringed by houses already around 1800. It continues through the riverside town of Brentford, historically Middlesex's most important urban centre, whose main street, once of much interest and character, was ruined by post-war road widening and indifferent rebuilding. Across the river Brent the road pushes w through Hounslow (which developed from a scrappy roadside hamlet) to emerge on Hounslow Heath, notoriously dangerous wasteland in the c 18, now diminished by Heathrow Airport (Hi) and tamed by dull suburban housing of the c 20. The Great West Road, the first attempt to bypass the old Brentford bottleneck, driven through the open country to the N in the 1920s, soon spawned a 'golden mile' of factories whose qualities as a period piece were appreciated too late to save it in anything like its full show. When this road too filled up, the M4 was laid out further N, slicing in the 1960s across the remaining unbuilt areas of Osterley and Cranford Parks. So far preserved, these open spaces surprise the outward-bound motorway traveller with fragmentary glimpses of countryside long before the edges of Greater London are reached. In this flat landscape, the utilities provided for expanding London are the outstanding landmarks: the waterworks of the c 19 at Kew Bridge (Brentford), impressive, with a tall tower, and at the other end of the borough the early c 20 engine houses for yet more waterworks at Kempton Park (Hanworth). In between, in prominent view from the M4, is the bold refuse transfer station of the 1970s at Brentford.

Hounslow's architectural riches are less apparent to the through traveller. Yet there is much to see. The parks enfold mansions of national repute: Chiswick House, Gunnersbury, Osterley, Boston Manor Brentford, and Syon. Away from the main roads are the picturesque riverside stretches of Chiswick and the less familiar interesting houses hidden away at Isleworth, another riverside village favoured in the c 18 and c 19 by rich Londoners for their country houses (and rediscovered as a developer's paradise in the 1980s). At Brentford there is another surprise, for behind the unprepossessing High Street is The Butts, an exceptionally attractive and unspoilt group of houses of c. 1700. The Victorian suburbs that developed in the grounds of older houses are appealingly varied, from the relics of the grand villas of Grove Park Chiswick and Spring Grove Isleworth to the pretty winding roads of St Margarets Isleworth and the cosier and consciously artistic Bedford Park, between Chiswick and Acton. Further w there is less of note. Feltham expanded indifferently with the c 19 railway, but East Bedfont still preserves a feeling of rural Middlesex, with timber-framed houses and a c 12 church. The church at Heston has a good medieval tower and some fine monuments, and at Hanworth there are a few worthwhile houses, but this sw part of the borough is in general a medley of c 20 buildings, sadly undistinguished apart from an interesting church of the 1950s at Hanworth, and a handful

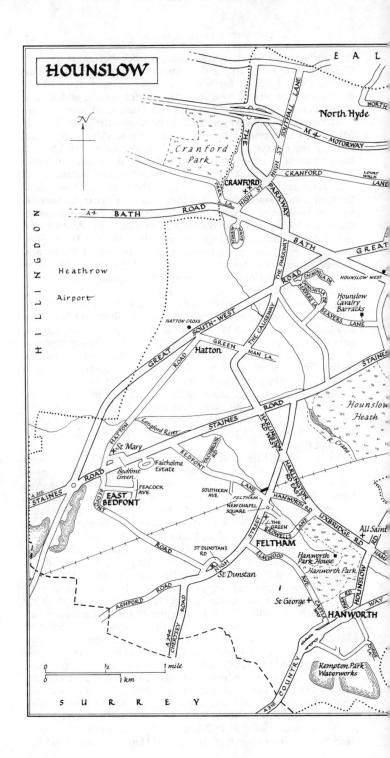

HOUNSLOW

N

EAL

North Hyde

M 4 — MOTORWAY

SOUTHALL LANE

THE HIGH ST

Cranford Park

CRANFORD

CRANFORD

LOVAT WALK

LANE

PARK LA.

HIGH ST

PARKWAY

A4 BATH ROAD

BATH ROAD

GREAT

HILLINGDON

Heathrow

Airport

CHINCHILLA DR.

HOUNSLOW WEST

Hounslow Cavalry Barracks

BEAVERS LA.

BEAVERS LANE

THE PARKWAY

THE CAUSEWAY

SOUTH-WEST

Hatton Cross

GREEN

MAN LA.

GREAT ROAD

Hatton

STAINES

STAINES ROAD

Hounslow Heath

R. Crane

HATTON ROAD

Longford River

BEDFONT

HATCHBROOK

HARLINGTON

HARLINGTON RD WEST

St Mary

Fairholme Estate

Bedfont Green

BEDFONT ROAD

PEACOCK AVE.

A 315 STAINES

EAST BEDFONT

SOUTHERN AVE.

LANE

FELTHAM

NEW CHAPEL SQUARE

HANWORTH RD.

HARLINGTON RD EAST

UXBRIDGE RD.

All Saint

RD

HAM

STREET

THE GREEN

THE BROWELLS

FELTHAM

LANE

ST DUNSTAN'S RD

HIGH

ELMWOOD

AVE.

Hanworth Park House

Hanworth Park

PARK RD

HOUNSLOW

WAY

St Dunstan

ASHFORD ROAD

ROAD

St George +

CASTLE

HANWORTH

CHERTSEY ROAD

A 244

Kempton Park Waterworks

CLARE

COUNTRY

A 316

0   ½   1 mile

0   1 km

SURREY

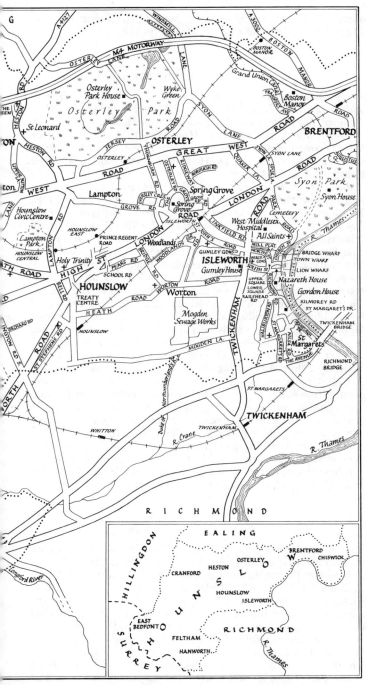

For a map of Brentford and Chiswick see pp. 390–1

of schools. Borough architects from 1965: *G. A. Trevett* (to 1979–80); *Brian Noble* (to 1983); *Peter McKay* (to 1991).

FURTHER READING

Among older books, especially useful are T. Faulkner, *History and Antiquities of Brentford, Ealing and Chiswick* (1845), and G. J. Aungier, *The History and Antiquities of Syon Monastery, the Parish of Isleworth and the Chapelry of Hounslow* (1840). The Middlesex V.C.H. covers Hounslow and Isleworth in vol. III, Chiswick in vol. VII. The DoE *List* for Hounslow dates from 1973. Local histories of individual places include F. Turner, *History and Antiquities of Brentford* (1922), W. Draper, *Chiswick* (1923, reprinted 1973), H. Arthure, *Life and Work in Old Chiswick* (1982), K. Judges, *Strand on the Green*, A. Cameron, *The History of the Royal Manor of Hanworth* (1979), and the Bedfont Research Group (Hounslow and District Local History Society), *Bedfont* (1987). The Brentford and Chiswick Local History Society produces its own *Journal*. Richard Hewlings' excellent English Heritage Guidebook, *Chiswick House and Gardens* (1989), sums up the latest research on these subjects. On the grounds see also J. Dixon Hunt, *Garden & Grove* (1986). Enlightening studies on the architectural history of other individual buildings are A. Oswald, 'Boston Manor House', *Country Life* (18 March 1965), C. Brooke Coles, *A Guide to Chiswick Parish Church*, R. White, 'Gunnersbury Park', *Country Life* (11 November 1982), Osterley Park Guide (1985), J. Yorke, 'Osterley before Adam', *Country Life* (14 September 1989), and A. C. B. Urwin, *Railshead, a History of Gordon, Lacy and St Margaret's Houses* (Isleworth). On suburbs, the authority on Bedford Park is T. Affleck Greeves, *Bedford Park, the First Garden Suburb* (1975) (also in *Country Life*, 7 and 14 December 1967, 27 November 1975), and on Chiswick James Wisdom, 'The Making of a West London Suburb: Housing in Chiswick 1861–1914' (Leicester University M.A. thesis, 1975–6). On the Great West Road factories, J. J. Snowdon and R. W. Platts in *Architectural Review* (July 1974) and Helen Baws (Open University thesis, 1975).

ACKNOWLEDGEMENTS

For reading and commenting on draft entries we owe especial thanks to His Grace the Duke of Northumberland (Syon House), to Maurice Tomlin and James Yorke of the Victoria and Albert Museum (Osterley Park), H. Arthure and Jeremy Benson (Chiswick), and K. Judges (Strand on the Green). T. A. Greeves was of especial help over Bedford Park, providing information from his own research. Among many others who helped over particular subjects we are grateful to Helen Baws for details about the Great West Road, Roger Sattin and R. H. Allen for much assistance with The Butts, Brentford, James Wisdom, who filled in details on Grove Park Chiswick and many other subjects, and the staff of Hounslow Planning Department, who were informative over new developments. We are particularly indebted to the local history librarian, Andrea Cameron, who not only provided answers to numerous queries, but checked the text for the whole of the borough.

BRENTFORD

INTRODUCTION

The landmark of c 19 Brentford, the minaret-like standpipe of the waterworks near Kew Bridge, is now rivalled by the cluster of tower blocks of the Haverfield Estate and by yet more recent commercial buildings near the Great West Road. But Brentford has a much older history. Like Uxbridge (Hi), the town developed along a main road out of London. New Brentford, to the w, derived its importance from its command of a ford over the Thames and a crossing over the Brent. A bridge over the Brent existed in 1280 and was rebuilt in stone in the c 15. There was a chapel and a hospital nearby already in the c 12 and a market in the c 14, although the area did not become a separate parish until the c 18. Old Brentford, nearer Kew Bridge, remained in the parish of Ealing until the c 19. From 1701 New Brentford became famous as the site of the notoriously riotous Middlesex elections and approached the status of a county town, although the county administration and the county court remained in London. In the c 19 industry expanded both along the Grand Union Canal (which here followed the line of the river Brent) and along the Thames between Old and New Brentford, but Faulkner in 1845 could still describe picturesque Elizabethan and Jacobean town houses in the centre, their gabled and pargetted fronts contrasting with the 'stiffness of modern brick buildings'. One would hardly guess this today, for although there are some good buildings to discover, the later c 20 has destroyed most of Brentford's historic townscape.

The one exception is the area of The Butts, tucked away to the N of the former market place, still with a delightful assortment of friendly late c 17 and early c 18 brick houses. Further N, in their own grounds, two major country mansions remain – Boston Manor and Gunnersbury (q.v.) – severed, alas, from the town in 1925 by the Great West Road and in 1974 by the M4. Much undistinguished rebuilding elsewhere included the widening of the narrow High Street in the 1960s, losing in the process nearly all the houses of the c 18 and earlier.* Little has been made of the splendid riverside sites: in the 1970s and 1980s the sprawling c 19 gasworks and breweries which dominated the area between Old and New Brentford were replaced by unimaginative warehouses and offices, with a mean riverside path angling awkwardly around them. In the other direction the lumpish Tiber Estate spreads over the remains of the docks. Even the pre-war factories developed with such panache along the Great West Road are fast disappearing.

---

*The late Georgian shopfront of Nos. 288–289 (Rattenbury's) is now in the Museum of London.

CHURCHES

St Faith, Windmill Road, in the N suburbs, cut off from the
town by the Great West Road. 1906–7 by *Bodley & Hare*. Red
brick, no tower, only a bell-turret springing from the S side of
the E gable. Simple Dec tracery; tall clerestory windows. The
carefully proportioned interior has the austerity of a friars'
church: long nave, straight-ended chancel, piers without capitals,
pointed arches, all thoughtfully and feelingly detailed. Ceiled
wagon roof with tie-beams resting on shafts continuing up from
the piers. Carved shields in the spandrels as minimal decoration. –
FONT. Octagonal, Perp type, with well carved angels and evangelist symbols around the base, raised up on a remarkably tall
cross-shaped plinth. – ALTAR. In the S chapel a C19 carved
wooden frontal from St James's Palace chapel. – STAINED
GLASS. In the E window Christ in majesty and angels under
elaborate canopies with much purple glass, in the NW window
Suffer Little Children, both perhaps by *Burlison & Grylls*, who
were often employed by Bodley. – In the S chapel E, the Virgin,
St Alban, and St Martin, pale figures by *J. N. Comper*, in the
style of Kempe.

St George, High Street. 1887 by *A. Blomfield* (octagonal tower
of 1913), replacing the chapel built at Old Brentford in 1762 by
J. J. Kirby. Closed in 1959 and used as a MUSICAL MUSEUM.

St Lawrence, High Street. The chapel existing at New Brentford by the C12 became independent of Hanwell only in 1749.
The existing building, disused and vandalized, is at the time of
writing in a pathetic condition. It consists of a C15 W tower, low,
embattled, of Kentish rag, with diagonal buttresses and NE stair-
turret, and a plain brick box built by *Thomas Hardwick* (who
lived locally) in 1764. Giant arches enclosing two storeys of
windows. The interior was remodelled by *B. & E. B. Ferrey*
in 1875, when the galleries were removed and deplorably tall
octagonal E.E. timber piers put in. – The plain C15 FONT and
some of the MONUMENTS have been destroyed; others are in
store.* Still *in situ* is a wall-monument to Thomas Hardwick
† 1829, a neo-Greek tablet with very elongated urns on the short
flanking pilasters.

St Paul, St Paul's Road. An ambitious remodelling, planned
1987, begun 1990, of a church of 1868–9 by *F. & H. Francis*.
From the C19 remains the SW tower with broach-spire, a prominent landmark, of the usual Kentish rag with Dec detail. The
C19 church had brick walls (whitewashed later), arcades with
typically gross naturalistic foliage (cf. St Mary Acton, Ea), and
a large raised chancel in the correct ecclesiological manner. The
new building, by *Michael Blee Design*, incorporates the chancel
walls and the S wall and columns of the nave, extending N from
the old nave into a polygonal clerestory-lit space with three E
chapels, covered by sweeping slate roofs. The chancel remains
as a side chapel (cf. St Mary Barnes, Ri). – PAINTING. The Last

---

*In store: a damaged miniature brass to H. Redman † 1528, kneeling in profile,
formerly with the Trinity higher up in the centre (Redman was Chief Mason of the
King's Works); John Middleton and wife † 1628, a wall-monument with figures kneeling opposite each other; and W. H. Ewin † 1804, by *Flaxman*.

Supper by *Zoffany* (who lived in Strand on the Green). Intended
for but rejected by St Anne Kew (Ri), and given to St George
Brentford. A large but rather weak and woolly picture. The
disciples are said to be modelled from Thames fishermen. –
STAINED GLASS. E window 1882, five lights with the Crucifixion
and the life of Christ. Pale colours, quite lively drawing. –
Chancel S (*c.* 1906) and two S aisle windows (1884, 1901) by
Heaton, Butler & Bayne. – MONUMENTS. Boer War Memorial
by *F. Wheeler*. – J. Macallan Swan † 1910. Bronze tablet with
portrait medallion by *Frampton*.

ST JOHN (R.C.), Boston Park Road. 1866 by *Jackman*. – (ALTAR
and SCREEN by *Bentley*.)

PARK BAPTIST CHAPEL, Boston Manor Road. The church of
1865 by *C. B. Searle* (Commissioners' type, brick, Dec) was
replaced in 1987–8 by an office block and church by *Scott, Brownrigg & Partners*.

UNITED REFORMED CHURCH, Boston Manor Road. Built for
the Whitakers in 1782; reduced to a single storey in 1955 after
war damage. Pedimented front behind a very grand entrance
gateway with wrought-iron gate and piers with pineapples.

PUBLIC BUILDINGS

MAGISTRATES COURT, High Street. On the site of the market
house. The stone Beaux-Arts front with paired pilasters and a
steep roof dates from 1929. The stock brick and stucco part
behind was built in 1850 by *F. Byass* as Brentford Town Hall
and Police Court; a second court was added in 1891 by *F. H.
Pownall*.

POLICE STATION, High Street. *See* Perambulation.

LIBRARY, Windmill Road. By *Nowell Parr*, surveyor to the
council, 1903, a bold and jolly free Renaissance composition
typical of this architect, and one of his few surviving municipal
works.* Much red terracotta, bold lettering, emphatic cornices.
Large entrance hall with staircase on two sides leading to the
former reference library and lecture room. The BATHS behind
in Clifden Road, 1895–6, were Parr's first job for Brentford,
before he took up terracotta. Two stone-faced gables filled by
Venetian windows.

WATERMANS ARTS CENTRE, High Street. 1982–4. The community share of the commercial package designed by *O. Garry
& Partners* to fill some of the site of the gasworks. Disappointingly dull exterior: of red brick with some brown brick
trim; roof terraces overlooking the river. Inside is a long multi-
purpose foyer, also with river views, with high tech trimmings:
stridently painted walls and exposed pipework. Opening off it a
120-seat cinema and a 239-seat theatre.

BRENTFORD FOUNTAINS LEISURE CENTRE, Chiswick High
Road. On the site of *Nowell Parr*'s Brentford market. Swimming
baths and sports centre, glossily packaged, by the *Borough Architect's Department*, 1987.

*His vestry hall of 1898 in Half Acre and the extensions to Brentford Market of 1905
have been demolished, as have his civic buildings for Hounslow.

St Lawrence with St Paul C. of E. Primary School, St Paul's Road. Older parts with large plate-tracery windows boldly edged in red and black brick. 1873, extended 1883 and 1898.

Health Centre, High Street. Low, brick, in the Dudok manner popular in the 1930s for progressive social buildings by the *Middlesex County Council*.

Waterworks Pumping Station, Kew Bridge. The Grand Junction Waterworks Company moved here in 1835–8 from a polluted site by the mouth of the Ranelagh sewer in Chelsea, but the water was still drawn from the tidal Thames. From 1855, as the result of the 1852 Metropolis Water Act, water was piped from Hampton and filtered at Kew Bridge – a filter bed of 1845 remains, an early survivor. When the Metropolitan Water Board phased out its older steam engines in 1944, five classic engines at Kew Bridge were selected for preservation.

The sober sub-Georgian western engine house is of 1837 by *William Anderson*, two storeys of stock brick, the string courses, cornice, and imposing entrance of granite. The house was built for four engines in two rooms separated by the entrance lobby – the layout is almost that of a respectable middle-class residence. The Boulton & Watt beam engine of 1820 (brought from the Chelsea site) deserves architectural mention for the quality of its detail. The turned baluster-shaped links in the parallel-motion gear (below the beam) look almost the work of a cabinet-maker in another material. The framework supporting the beam is in an engineer's much watered-down and attenuated Doric. The Maudslay engine of 1837 is more solid and workaday. The E half of its beam is a replacement of 1889. This house also contains one of the world's last surviving Bull engines, 1855 by Harvey's of Hayle. The steam cylinder is mounted vertically above the pump, with a noticeable saving of space. The hipped roof has closely spaced trusses of wrought iron, mainly flat bars, i.e. an early type, now rare. Iron battens support the slates, so the building has very few inflammable components. The boiler house roofs are of generally similar construction.

The eastern engine house is three storeys high, vigorous Victorian Italianate with round-headed windows and a prominent cornice. One bay wide when built in 1845, it was doubled in size for a second engine in 1869, as can be deduced from the splayed openings (formerly windows) in the dividing wall inside. The scale of the engines and the space around them is truly vast. Each stands on four Greek Doric columns in cast iron, repeated in miniature to support the valve gear. The 90 in.* engine on the W is of 1845, built by the Copperhouse Foundry of Hayle to the design of *Thomas Wicksteed*. This was one of the earliest Cornish-type‡ beam engines specifically designed for waterworks use, and the largest waterworks engine at the time. The 100 in. engine on the E, added in 1869 by Harvey's of Hayle, is the world's largest surviving beam engine. It deliberately adheres to the archi-

*The size is the diameter of the steam cylinder.

‡The Cornish system improves on that of James Watt by using high-pressure steam in the downward stroke. The earlier engines in the Western House were converted to the Cornish system and otherwise modified c. 1848 by Wicksteed.

tectural style of the earlier engine, but the details of the mechanical parts are coarsened, giving an appearance of absolute strength. The beam in fact broke in 1879; all beams here were strengthened in the C19 by heavy wrought-iron straps, trussed over saddles.

The manometer or STANDPIPE TOWER of 1867 by *Alexander Fraser* dominates the district. It is over 60 metres high, topped by a cupola.* A chimney between the engine houses was demolished in 1958.

The gentle sound of the preserved beam engines contrasts with the roar and stench of a vintage Allen diesel engine housed in a 'temporary' asbestos-clad shed of 1934 which provides an instructive comparison with its neighbours. Water is still pumped to the district from a 1980s pump house in the filter beds.

REFUSE TRANSFER STATION, Transport Avenue. By the *General Works Department* of the *G.L.C. Department of Architecture* (*Jake Brown, Clive Crawford, Alex Stok, Stephen Taylor*), 1978. A notable landmark from the M4, cheerful and practical. Huge tipping-hall of dark blue brick and orange-painted steel on a concrete podium which houses the compaction machinery. The refuse is taken away by rail.

KEW BRIDGE STATION, Kew Bridge Road. 1849 by *Tite*, a good late classical design (cf. Chiswick, Ho).

BOSTON MANOR STATION, Boston Manor Road. 1934, one of *Charles Holden*'s stations on the Piccadilly line extension. Low entrance block with a distinctive squat tower with vertical finial, inspired by his visit to Holland.

GRAND UNION CANAL. Until 1929 called the Grand Junction Canal. Broad, with locks a little over 4 metres wide, it is the direct line from London to the Midlands, joining the earlier Oxford Canal at Braunston in Warwickshire and the Thames at Brentford, with a branch to Paddington (*see* outer Wm). It was designed by *William Jessop,* with *James Barnes* as resident engineer, in accordance with an Act obtained in 1793. The section from Brentford to Uxbridge (Hi) opened in 1794, and to Kings Langley, Hertfordshire, in 1797. Through traffic started in 1800, and the canal was complete throughout its length in 1805. Through Brentford, the canal follows the course of the river Brent. There is a modernized DEPOT for barge traffic from the Thames, thronged until the 1960s with narrow boats transshipping cargoes. Below the high railway bridge carrying the Piccadilly line is GALLOWS BRIDGE, a cast-iron roving bridge of about 23 metres' span by the *Horseley Iron Works,* 1820: two arch ribs in a sweeping curve, with diamond-ribbed spandrels. Above the motorway bridge at Osterley Lock was an attractive single-storey COTTAGE with an arcade of elliptical relieving arches and the characteristic shallow hipped roof with central chimney.

---

*Until recent restoration of the dome on the cupola, it looked rather like a minaret.

PERAMBULATIONS

1. Central Brentford: The Butts

THE BUTTS is the most rewarding part of Brentford. It consists of a broad street parallel to the High Street, ending in a large, comfortably informal square immediately behind the former town hall. The space was used for a market from the later C17, and in the C18 the Middlesex elections were held here. The square now serves as a car park – an unworthy setting for some of the most appealing groups of houses in west London. Dating from the late C17 to the early C18, they are a most interesting illustration of the adaptation of the type of compact brick house that had evolved in court circles for relatively modest buildings in a town just outside London. The developer appears to have been William Parish, landlord of the Red Lion Inn, who acquired the land in 1663 from John Goldsmith of Boston Manor. Plots were let in the 1680s and building was taking place in the 1690s; it probably continued into the early C18. As so often with specu-lative developments, the larger houses appear to be the earlier ones. The houses are of two storeys over basements and vary in detail, although a uniform impression is created by their building materials: local reddish-brown brick, with brighter red brick sometimes used for window dressings, white wooden modillion cornices, and steep hipped and tiled roofs. Some are detached, some in pairs, others in short terraces, mostly set back behind front gardens, so that the mood is not overridingly urban.

35   Starting in the square, the dominant building is Nos. 24–26 on the NE corner, two houses giving the appearance of one. It is the most elegant and probably the latest of the group, with to each side a five-bay front with a central door; the E side has an extra bay on the r. of a former coach house. Handsome elevation with narrow eight-pane segment-headed windows with the thick glaz-ing-bars of the early C18. Brick keystones and brick aprons below, all tied together by the vertical brick lacing becoming fashionable *c*. 1715. As in many of the Butts houses, both have good panelled rooms and staircases (not identical, although both stairs have closed strings and twisted balusters). To the E, Nos. 20 and 22 are a pair of smaller houses one room wide and two rooms deep, with hall and stairs to one side; a closet is fitted in behind the stairs. Urn-shaped balusters. Then ST MARY'S CONVENT, C18 but much added to; three storeys, doorway with Gibbs surround. Opposite, Nos. 15–17 are another pair, lower and broader in their proportions, each of four bays, with straight-headed windows, the heads of rubbed brick, and a brick floor band in the C17 tradition. To No. 17 was added a pretty late C18 doorcase with carved frieze and fanlight, and a wrought-iron gate with overthrow. The distinctive L-shaped original plan of these two houses, which is shared by several of their neighbours (e.g. No. 1 Upper Butts and No. 17 Somerset Road), demonstrates that the newfangled double-pile layout had not yet been fully assimilated. The broad frontage (a rural rather than an urban type) consists of two front rooms divided by a central passage leading to a dog-leg stair; behind one is a kitchen (with a large

chimneystack shared with the room in front), behind the other only a small closet.

Along UPPER BUTTS to No. 1 at the far end, an especially attractive five-bay front with segment-headed windows. Staircase with simple turned balusters continuing to attic level; good panelling throughout. In the garden a summer house with three ogee Gothic windows brought from a shop in Brentford High Street. No. 17 SOMERSET ROAD, facing down Upper Butts, now disguised by the lowered upper windows of *c.* 1800 and by a Victorian top floor and porch, was once similar to No. 1 Upper Butts, although the elevation is more sophisticated (the three central bays break forward). THE CEDARS further N, with a later stucco front, marks the limit of the C18 development.

Back now to the square and to a continuous but irregular group of houses on the N side. No. 19, one of the larger ones, has a four-bay front and a long back wing; Nos. 21–23 are a smaller pair (the staircase balusters to No. 21 suggest a date after *c.* 1720). On the S side, encroaching into the square, No. 40, a formal C18 urban three-storey parapeted house with central arched windows over a doorway with Corinthian pilasters, and the more modest and earlier group that includes No. 42, with the narrow windows of the early C18, and No. 46, a little later, with quite an elaborate staircase. On the W side, enjoyably incongruous, the early C20 CANAL BOATMEN'S INSTITUTE by *Nowell Parr*, backing on to the canal: slightly Arts and Crafts, with its roughcast upper floor and battered buttresses. Then back to the High Street past the WHITE HORSE and a few minor C18 buildings.

2. The High Street and the areas to N and W

After The Butts, the rest of Brentford is an anticlimax. First to the E. In the HIGH STREET, the main E–W thoroughfare, C20 road widening has ensured that there is remarkably little to see. The only notable landmark is THE BEEHIVE at the corner of Half Acre, a small but confident corner pub of much character by the local architects *Nowell Parr* and *A. E. Kates*, 1907. Beehive-shaped turret, art nouveau glass, and Parr's typical shiny tiles, in green and an unusual mottled slate blue. Further E No. 60, early C18, of three bays, altered (but with original staircase and panelling). No. 80, late C18, has seven windows, a projecting central bay, and an Adamish porch with delicate capitals and entablature with urns and garlands. Opposite, the big pitched roof of a supermarket of the 1980s fortunately partly conceals the ugly tower of flats over the POLICE STATION behind (1963 by *J. Innes-Elliot*). Towards Old Brentford little remains of the narrow bottleneck that was notorious among travellers from the C18 onwards. On the S side glossy offices of the 1980s, but also the former FIRE STATION (now offices) by *Nowell Parr*, 1897, boldly detailed in bright red terracotta, the gables with 'ornamented Patra bricks'. In FERRY LANE, down towards the river, the blue-tiled WATERMANS ARMS must be another of *Parr's* jobs. Further S, PEERLESS PUMPS occupy an altered and extended C18 house (see the side to the river with six windows

with rubbed brick straight-headed arches). Nearby a MONU-
MENT to Brentford's historical events, a granite cylinder erected
by the local council in 1909 (when wooden palisades were discovered here, supposed to mark the ancient ford over the
Thames). Opposite Ferry Lane ALBANY PARADE, a draughty
L-shaped shopping precinct with flats above, built by Brentford
and Chiswick Council (*J. Wolton*) *c.* 1961. Behind, around
ALBANY ROAD, a few working-class terraces of the 1880s that
escaped the wholesale post-war clearance. Further E only street
and pub names – Distillery Walk, Pottery Road, and the
POTTERY ARMS in Clayponds Lane (1922 by *Nowell Parr*) –
recall the industries that dominated this part of Old Brentford
until the 1960s. The only older survivals are St George (q.v.)
and the little church school by the High Street where Sarah
Trimmer taught, a plain rectangle dated 1786 'for religious
Instruction and Industry'. Around it the HAVERFIELD ESTATE,
one of Hounslow's most ambitious and depressing enterprises
(borough architect *G. A. Trevett*). Over half of its population live
in the six twenty-three-storey towers (completed 1971). Seen
from afar at night they are a striking, even quite elegant group,
an impression not sustained at close quarters. E of Ealing Road
the later phases consist of messily grouped houses and low flats
(completed 1974 and 1979).

Along the river, nearly all is of the 1980s: landscaped areas alternating with indifferent warehouses, offices, and arts centre (q.v.)
which replace the gasworks demolished in 1965. Around the
approach to KEW BRIDGE several inns, a reminder of the former
importance of the road, notably the STAR AND GARTER, tall
with stucco trim, and a cluster of offices. PARSONS HOUSE, a
slab with blue spandrel panels, is characteristic of those bright,
no-nonsense out-of-town office blocks of 1960 (*H. C. Duncan &
Partners*). KEW CAMPUS represents the more image-conscious
approach of a quarter of a century later (1984–7 by *Eric Askew
& Partners*; *M. Howlett* and *M. Everson*), a cluster of five brick
offices in a crisply picturesque neo-brewery style, cleverly
grouped around a raised walk towards a river terrace. Lift-towers
with little hipped roofs; well contrived car parking. Nearby the
smaller AUTOBAR HOUSE, set back towards the river, with
trickily composed staircase tower and car-park mural (by *Lister
Drew & Associates*, completed 1974), represents the awkward
transition from earlier straightforward modernism.

HALF ACRE leads N from the centre of Brentford. The best houses
here have been demolished.* To its E, St Paul's church and the
C19 church schools (qq.v.), and beyond them a RECREATION
GROUND, the gift marked by a red marble Jubilee OBELISK of
1887. N of Half Acre BOSTON MANOR ROAD starts with the
boldly labelled BUTTS ESTATE (semi-detached houses of the
1870s). On the E side, between a recent office block and the library
(q.v.), INVERNESS LODGE, with an irregular mid C19 stucco
front of six bays (earlier behind?) and two large bay-windows at
the back. In WINDMILL ROAD, near the station, three pairs of

*They were New Grove Mansions, neo-Grecian with Doric porch; and Clifden
House of the second quarter of the C18, large, with seven bays, pediment, and a little
Ionic porch connected into one composition with the window above.

1. *West London urban townscape:* Kensington (KC, 2b,ii), Trellick Tower,
by Ernö Goldfinger & Partners, completed 1972, from Golborne Road

2. *West London riverside:* Chiswick (Ho), Chiswick Mall
3. *West London suburbs:* Pinner (Hw), Moss Lane
4. *West London industrial building:* Paddington Station (Wm),
   by I. K. Brunel, 1850-4

5. Harlington (Hi), St Peter and St Paul, detail of south doorway, twelfth century
6. Harmondsworth (Hi), St Mary, south arcade twelfth century, chancel 1396-8, north chapel *c.* 1500
7. Hayes (Hi), St Mary, tower and south porch, late medieval
8. Greenford (Ea), Holy Cross, old church, chancel, late medieval

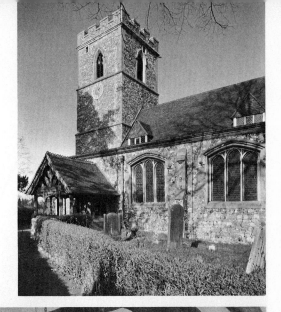

9. Northolt (Ea), St Mary, *c.* 1300
10. Fulham (HF), All Saints, west tower, fifteenth century
11. East Bedfont (Ho), St Mary, wall painting, thirteenth century
12. Chelsea (KC), All Saints, south chapel, capital, 1528

<table>
<tr><td>9</td><td>11</td></tr>
<tr><td>10</td><td>12</td></tr>
</table>

13. Harmondsworth (Hi), Manor Farm Barn, probably 1427
14. Pinner (Hw), East End Farm Cottage, fifteenth century and later
15. Ickenham (Hi), Ickenham Manor, fifteenth-eighteenth centuries

16. Fulham (HF), Fulham Palace, hall range from the west courtyard,
    c. 1480 and early sixteenth century
17. Harefield (Hi), Breakspears, dovecote, early sixteenth century
18. Harrow-on-the-Hill (Hw), Harrow School, Old Schools, 1608-15
19. Harefield (Hi), Countess of Derby's Almshouses, after 1637

20. Harefield (Hi), St Mary, monument to Alice Spencer,
 Countess of Derby, † 1637
21. Cranford (Hi), St Dunstan, monument to Sir Roger Aston,
 by William Cure II, 1611-13
22. Hillingdon (Hi), St John the Baptist, monument to Sir Edward Carr † 1636
23. Ickenham (Hi), St Giles, monument to Robert Clayton † 1665

20 | 22
21 | 23

24. The Stanmores (Hw), St John the Evangelist, Great Stanmore,
    monument to Sir John Wolstenholme † 1639, by Nicholas Stone,
    set up in 1641
25. Chiswick (Ho), Chiswick House, gateway from Beaufort House,
    Chelsea, by Inigo Jones, 1621
26. Swakeleys (Hi), 1638, from the east
27. Brentford (Ho), Boston Manor, ceiling of great chamber, 1623

24	26
25	27

28. Chelsea (KC), Royal Hospital, by Sir Christopher Wren, 1682-91
29. Chelsea (KC), Royal Hospital, by Sir Christopher Wren, 1682-91,
    council chamber with carving by William Emmett
30. Kensington (KC), Kensington Palace, orangery, probably by
    Nicholas Hawksmoor, 1704
31. Chiswick (Ho), Chiswick House, by the third Earl of Burlington,
    1727-9, from the south-east

28 | 30
29 | 31

32. The Stanmores (Hw), St Lawrence, Little Stanmore, Chandos Mausoleum, by James Gibbs, 1735-6, painted by Sleter and Brunetti, with
monument to the first Duke of Chandos by Grinling Gibbons, 1718
33. Hillingdon (Hi), St John the Baptist, monument to Henry Pagett, Earl
of Uxbridge, † 1743
34. The Stanmores (Hw), St Lawrence, Little Stanmore, by John James,
1715, with paintings by Bellucci, Sleter, and Laguerre

39. Syon House (Ho), anteroom, by Robert Adam, after 1761
40. Osterley House (Ho), portico by Robert Adam, 1763
41. St Marylebone (Wm), Home House, No. 20 Portman Square,
    by Robert Adam, 1773-6, staircase

42. Ealing (Ea), Pitshanger Manor, by Sir John Soane, 1801-3, entrance
43. Ealing (Ea), Pitshanger Manor, by Sir John Soane, 1801-3, breakfast room
44. Bentley Priory (Hw), entrance hall, by Sir John Soane, 1788-98
45. Hanwell (Ea), The Hermitage, Church Road, early nineteenth century

42 | 44
43 | 45

46. Paddington (Wm), St Mary, by John Plaw, 1788-91
47. St Marylebone (Wm), Wyndham Place, former school, probably
    by Edward Tilbury, 1824
48. Acton (Ea), Goldsmiths' Almshouses, East Churchfield Road,
    by Charles Beazley, 1811
49. Kensington (KC, 3b), former Western Grammar School, No. 7 North
    Terrace, by W. F. Pocock, 1835

50. St Marylebone (Wm), Regents Park, Cumberland Terrace,
    planned by John Nash from 1811, executed by James Thomson, 1826
51. Kensington (KC, 3b), Pelham Crescent, by George Basevi, 1833
52. St Marylebone (Wm), Nos. 62-64 Clifton Hill, St John's Wood,
    c. 1840-50
53. Paddington (Wm), Nos. 3-5 Porchester Terrace, by J. C. Loudon,
    1823-5

54. Kensington (KC, 2a,ii), Stanley Gardens, and St Peter, Kensington
    Park Road, by Thomas Allom, 1852
55. Kensington (KC, 4b), The Boltons, by George Godwin Jun., 1851-60
56. Kensington (KC, 1b,iii), Cornwall Gardens, north side, 1866-79
57. Kensington (KC, 3c), Ensor Mews, Cranley Gardens, 1873-5

54 | 56
55 | 57

58. Chelsea (KC), Cadogan Square, Nos. 68 and 72 by Norman Shaw, 1877-9, No. 70 by A. J. Adams
59. Chelsea (KC), No. 35 Glebe Place, by Philip Webb, 1868-71
60. Harrow Weald (Hw), Grim's Dyke, by Norman Shaw, 1870-2

61. Kensington (KC), Leighton House, Holland Park Road,
   by George Aitchison, Arab Hall, 1877-9
62. Kensington (KC, 1a,iv), Tower House, No. 29 Melbury Road,
   by William Burges, 1876-8
63. Fulham (HF), St Paul's Studios, Talgarth Road,
   by Frederick Wheeler, 1891

61 | 62
   | 63

64. Kensington (KC), Albert Memorial, by G. G. Scott, 1863-72, Asia, sculptural group by J. H. Foley
65. Kensington (KC), Victoria and Albert Museum, Henry Cole wing (former School of Naval Architects), by H. Y. D. Scott, 1868-73
66. Kensington (KC), Albert Hall, by Francis Fowke and H. Y. D. Scott, 1867-71
67. Kensington (KC), Natural History Museum, by Alfred Waterhouse, begun 1872

| 64 | 66 |
| 65 | 67 |

68. Fulham (HF), Public Library, Fulham Road, by Henry Hare, 1909
69. St Marylebone (Wm), Fire Station, Chiltern Street, by Robert Pearsall (L.C.C.), 1889
70. Hammersmith (HF), St Paul's Girls' School, by Gerald Horsley, 1904-7
71. Harrow-on-the-Hill (Hw), Harrow School, Museum Schools, by Basil Champneys, 1884-6

72. Chelsea (KC), Nos. 38-39 Cheyne Walk, by C. R. Ashbee, 1898-9
73. Chiswick (Ho), The Tabard Inn, Bedford Park, by Norman Shaw, 1880
74. Ealing (Ea), Brentham Garden Estate, laid out by Parker & Unwin from
    1907, Meadvale Road by F. Cavendish Pearson, with Institute, 1911

75. Chiswick (Ho), Voysey House (formerly Sanderson's factory),
Barley Mow Passage, by C. F. A. Voysey, 1902
76. Kensington (KC, 1a,iv), No. 8 Addison Road, by Halsey Ricardo, 1905
77. St Marylebone (Wm), No. 37 Harley Street, by Beresford Pite,
1899-1900

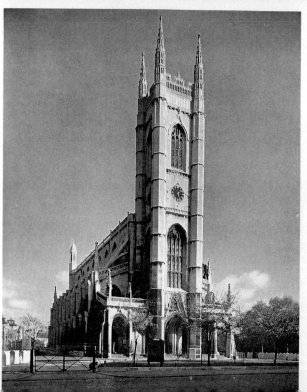

78. St Marylebone (Wm), St Mary, Marylebone Road,
by Thomas Hardwick, 1813-17
79. Chelsea (KC), St Luke, by James Savage, 1820-4
80. Kensington (KC), Kensal Green Cemetery, laid out 1833
81. Paddington (Wm), St Augustine, Kilburn, by J. L. Pearson, 1870-7,
spire completed 1898

82 and 83. St Marylebone (Wm), All Saints Margaret Street,
  by William Butterfield, 1849-59
84. Kensington (KC), Oratory of St Philip Neri (R.C.), by Herbert
  Gribble, 1878, dome by George Sherrin, 1896
85. Kensington (KC), Oratory of St Philip Neri (R.C.), by Herbert
  Gribble, 1878, south side of nave, looking into the chapel of St Mary
  Magdalene; nave plasterwork by C. T. G. Formilli, 1927-32,
  statues of the apostles by G. Mazzuoli, c. 1680-5

82 | 84
83 | 85

86. Kingsbury (Br), St Andrew, pulpit and chancel screen (from
St Andrew Wells Street, St Marylebone), by G. E. Street, after 1862
87. Ealing (Ea), St Mary, remodelled by S. S. Teulon, 1866-74
88. Harlesden (Br), All Souls, by E. J. Tarver, 1875-6
89. Chelsea (KC), Holy Trinity, Sloane Street, by J. D. Sedding, 1888-90,
chapel grille by Henry Wilson, *c.* 1892

90. Paddington (Wm), St Mary Magdalene, Woodchester Square,
Chapel of St Sepulchre, by J. N. Comper, 1895
91. Cricklewood (Br), Baptist Chapel, by Arthur Keen, 1907-8
92. Paddington (Wm), New West End Synagogue, St Petersburgh Place,
by Audsley & Joseph, 1877-9

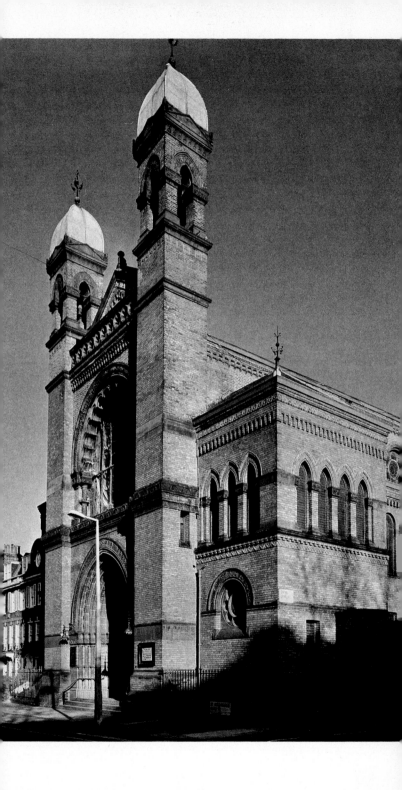

93. Chelsea (KC), Michelin Building, Fulham Road,
    by François Espinasse, 1909-11
94. Perivale (Ea), Hoover factory, by Wallis, Gilbert & Partners
    (F. Button), 1931-5
95. Chelsea (KC), Peter Jones, Sloane Square, by Slater & Moberly
    and William Crabtree, 1935-7
96. Kensington (KC, 1a,i), Barkers, Kensington High Street,
    by Bernard George, 1933

97. Ealing (Ea), Hanger Hill Garden Estate, by Douglas Smith & Barley, 1928-36
98. Ruislip (Hi), Nos. 97-101 Park Avenue, by Connell, Ward & Lucas, 1936
99. Sudbury (Br), Sudbury Town Station, by Charles Holden, 1930-1, ticket hall
100. Uxbridge (Hi), Regal Cinema (former), High Street, by E. Norman Bailey, 1932

101. Hammersmith (HF), Royal Masonic Hospital, by Sir John Burnet,
Tait & Lorne, 1931
102. St Marylebone (Wm), Regents Park, Zoological Gardens,
Penguin Pool, by Tecton, completed 1934
103. St Marylebone (Wm), No. 66 Portland Place (Royal Institute
of British Architects), by Grey Wornum, 1932-4

104. Heathrow Airport (Hi), control tower, by Frederick Gibberd & Partners, 1955
105. Paddington (Wm), Hallfield Estate, Hallfield School, Bishop's Bridge Road, by Denys Lasdun, completed 1955
106. Kensington (KC), Commonwealth Institute, by Robert Matthew, Johnson-Marshall & Partners, 1960-2
107. Brunel University (Hi), engineering buildings, by Stillman & Eastwick-Field, 1965-7

108. Kensington (KC), Imperial College, student lodgings,
Princes Gardens, by Sheppard Robson & Partners, 1960-3
109. Paddington (Wm), Maintenance Depot, by Bicknell & Hamilton,
1968
110a and b. Uxbridge (Hi), Hillingdon Civic Centre, by Robert Matthew,
Johnson-Marshall & Partners, 1973-8
111. St Marylebone (Wm), Regents Park, Royal College of Physicians,
by Sir Denys Lasdun, 1961-4

112. Chelsea (KC), World's End Estate, by Eric Lyons, Cadbury-Brown, Metcalfe & Cunningham, 1967-77
113. Kensington (KC, 2b,ii), St Mark's Road, housing by Jeremy Dixon, 1976-80
114. Greenford (Ea), IBM warehouse and distribution centre, Rockware Avenue, by Norman Foster Associates, 1978-9
115. Kensington (KC, 2b,ii), McKay Trading Estate, Kensal Road, by John Outram, 1981

116. Stockley Park (Hi), phase 1, by Arup Associates, planned 1985
117. St Marylebone (Wm), Lord's Cricket Ground, Mound Stand,
by Michael Hopkins, 1985-7

presentable mid C19 stucco villas; in ORCHARD ROAD, on the other side of the tracks, modest terraces of similar date (the railway came in 1849). Beyond the junction with the GREAT WEST ROAD, marked by two unappealing slabs of offices of 1960–4 and overshadowed by the M4 viaduct, a little more of the C18 is to be found: No. 67 (Prospect House), five windows, three storeys, restored; and No. 69, a tall pair and a lower house converted as one office with a new basement. Further N, BOSTON MANOR is reached (*see* below).

The W end of the HIGH STREET has nothing of interest except for St Lawrence's church (q.v.), close to the Ham, the area near the Brent crossing which was the oldest part of New Brentford (as has been confirmed by excavations). In the Middle Ages there was a small hospital here. To the S Augustus Close leads to the TIBER ESTATE (1970–9), on the site of the railway and docks built under *Brunel* from 1859 to provide a link for the G.W.R. with the port of London. The peninsula between canal and Thames is now filled up with banal brown brick maisonettes up to six storeys high (built by the G.L.C. as local authority housing, but sold off on completion). Only the lower curved group at the mouth of the canal, and the stretches around the dock itself, which rest on the original brick retaining arches, respond a little to the *genus loci*. The landscaping (by *Peter Barefoot*) should help in time. The dock itself has been preserved.

3. The Great West Road and Boston Manor

THE GREAT WEST ROAD was the chief showplace in outer London for the airy and hygienic factories of the light industries developed between the wars. When the road was constructed in 1920–5 to provide an alternative to the congested Brentford High Street, the area was still rural. Ten years later, a 'golden mile' of factories stretched W from the Chiswick roundabout, many of them producing motor accessories. The favourite composition was a formal, symmetrical office frontage, neatly railed off from the road and concealing the workshops behind, with a central tower to provide an eyecatcher for neon advertising. The most successful architects were the firm of *Wallis, Gilbert & Partners*. Façade styles varied from vestigial classicism to American-inspired modernism, jazzed up by trimmings ranging from Egyptian to aeronautical. They survived little altered until the late seventies, but since then change has been rapid. The remaining pre-war buildings, in their time considered garishly vulgar, now appear demure in comparison with the flashy glazing and strident detail of their bulkier successors. The ragbag of indiscriminately sited speculative offices and warehouses is relieved only by one forthright purpose-built retail store at the W end.

The E end of the road is now overshadowed by the M4 flyover. On the N side much was demolished in 1987–8. The first landmark is VANTAGE WEST, a 1960s tower of offices, transformed by showy blue glass cladding of 1990, when it was refurbished by *Covell Matthews Wheatley*. Then a survivor, a flat thrusting finger clock, all that remains from a Henley's garage of 1937 by

Wallis, Gilbert & Partners, now an adjunct to offices of 1988–9. Further w on the s side, a dominating brick-faced eleven-storey slab, BEECHAMS since 1955, but built for Simmonds Aerocessories. It forms the centre of a composition of which the l. wing dates from 1936 by *George Warren;* the matching r. wing and the tower – on an exceptional scale for its date – were added by *Wallis, Gilbert & Partners* in 1938–42. The wings have ribbon windows ending in rounded corners. Winged SA emblems on the railings.

After the flyover veers N, the corner with Boston Manor Road has on the N side RANK AUDIOVISUAL, built in 1932 by *F.E. Simpkins* for the toothpaste company, Macleans, a low, rather fussy rendered façade with stepped art deco pavilions and parapets. It is overshadowed by a tall slab glossily refurbished in 1985 as prestige headquarters for WANG computers by *Fairhursts*. Then the original premises of TRICO, makers of windscreen wipers, a low range of 1931 with Egyptianizing door surrounds. Their later buildings to the w, set back at an angle, began as premises for Thompson & Norris (corrugated cases), with plain rendered frontages of 1932–7 added by *Robert Sharp*. Opposite, a late 1980s stretch of speculative offices by *Laing Property*, 1988: MERCURY COMMUNICATIONS occupies buildings with domestic pitched pantiled roofs above blue-trimmed glazing; LINOTYPE is in low pavilions away from the road. BMW (Cooper), also on the s side, was built as prestige offices and warehouses for Curry's electrical shops by *F.E. Simpkins*, 1935, a modernist composition of cubes and rectangles, the central tower slightly recessed, windows with curved sides to the lower wings. Then one of the most ambitious factories, now WESTLINK HOUSE, built in 1930 for PYRENE (fire extinguishers and car accessories), by *Wallis, Gilbert & Partners*. It has a grand two-storey frontage of offices, and a central tower approached up a ceremonial flight of steps. The details have alas been simplified and the windows reglazed. Strips of coloured tiles remain in a band above the windows, and around the central doorway. Opposite were the equally imposing premises of the Firestone Tyre and Rubber Company, also by *Wallis, Gilbert & Partners*, of 1928–9, scandalously demolished in 1980 on the eve of their statutory listing. The entrance lodge and boundary fences with tapering Egyptian stone piers are all that remain, reminders of the care that was taken over the perimeter detail of these early factories. The impersonal speculator's showmanship behind dates from 1983, by *Eric Askew & Partners*, a series of mirror-glazed buildings grouped asymmetrically around WESTCROSS HOUSE, a taller office block with free-standing uprights to give it added consequence.

On the s side the GATE CENTRE, 1980s hangars with ribbed cladding, next to the reconditioned No. 941, the former premises of COTY (now Softsel Computers Products). This is of 1932 by *Wallis, Gilbert & Partners*, an unusually restrained white façade with recessed entrance distinguished by curved abstract sculptural motifs. On the N side FOUNTAINS OFFICE PARK, 1990–1, developed by *Markheath Securities*, a group of large buildings of yellow brick with a plethora of post-modern trappings. The s side ends at Syon Lane with by far the most interesting of the newcomers, SAINSBURY'S HOMEBASE, 1987–8 by *Nicholas Grimshaw*, a cousin of his Sainsbury's at Camden Town. It is a forcefully explicit structure: a vast shed without internal supports, roofed by seven gently curving spans playfully reminiscent of aeroplane wings. They project as deep curved eaves and are anchored in biplane fashion by free-standing angled braces, painted bright green, which create a lively pattern along the ribbed flank walls. In front, a slim openwork tower supports the tension rods bracing the mid-point of the central roof beam. It doubles effectively as an advertisement for the store. On the N side the small NATIONAL WESTMINSTER BANK, by *W. F. C. Holden,* quiet and well detailed 1930s modern, with bowed brick front. Then GILLETTE's, a colossus with a frontage of nearly 150 metres and an enormous central tower, 1937 by *Sir Banister Fletcher.* Of a very incongruous, timidly modernistic grandeur. The *Architect and Building News* commented that its 'restrained qualities and dignity have particular point in a bypass noted for garish features'. Dudok-influenced brickwork, stone portico, large cast-iron windows, each with two gently canted panes. The factory is on the ground floor, with offices above.

BOSTON MANOR, Boston Manor Road. Still in its own grounds, although divided into flats in 1963. It is one of a small group of substantial brick houses built in the London neighbourhood in the first half of the C17 that are notable for their early use of a compact double-pile plan. The exterior is attractive, but not in its original state. It is of six by four bays, three storeys high, with a lower service wing to the N. The gables and wide-jointed red brickwork of English bond are of the early C17, but the heavily modelled classical window surrounds and bold dentilled cornice of stone between second and third floors are additions, probably of the later C17, in a not entirely satisfactory effort to bring the house up to date with the style of Jones and Webb. The rainwater heads indeed bear two dates, 1622 and 1670. The house belonged

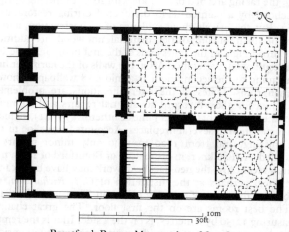

Brentford, Boston Manor, plan of first floor

to Mary, Lady Reade, widow of a stepson of Sir Thomas Gresham, who had owned Boston Manor together with Osterley Park. Lady Reade's initials and the date 1623 also appear on the great chamber ceiling. In 1670 the estate was bought by James Clitherow, an East India merchant. His account book records that the purchase price was £5,336, and that in 1671 he spent £1,439 on the house. This implies quite substantial alterations, which may include the cornice and window surrounds. On the s side remains of a small blocked circular window imply different earlier fenestration; on the N side there are suggestive remnants of a brick plat band which, if carried round, would occupy the space now taken by the ground-floor pediments, which are triangular on front and back of the house, segmental on the s. The windows above have no pediments, but heavy triple keystones. The top-floor windows are simply linked in pairs by a moulded band. In each gable is a round-headed niche. The entrance is on the E side, by a porch which is an obvious C19 Jacobean pastiche. The side windows of a former tripartite entrance (presumably C18) remain. (It is shown on a view of 1794.) The doorway surround was added in 1963, when the house was restored by *Donald Insall & Partners*. The w side is more irregular: the windows of the two centre bays reflect the staircase, and there is no second-floor cornice. On this side there is no break with the service wing, which, although much altered, may be of the same date as the house. It was extended E after 1840.

The original plan of the house can only partly be understood. The N part, with the service end, has been much altered, and the centre too, with entrance hall leading to the staircase, may not be in its original form. s of this are the main rooms, facing s and E, divided by a massive spine wall with chimneystacks. The entrance hall, with its coarsely scaled screen and plasterwork, is, like the porch, C19 Jacobean revival; it may originally have been part of the larger room to the s. In the sw room, formerly the library, is a C19 painted ceiling with tentative strapwork and fictive grained beams. The staircase is partly authentic earlier C17; the raking arcaded balustrade with square tapering uprights is echoed by a painted dado discovered during restoration in 1963. But the newels show evidence of reconstruction, and the lions on them (of composition material, not wood) are additions. The broad flight of the stairs ends at the first floor (again perhaps as a result of later alterations). On the walls of the narrower flight continuing to the second floor is a mid C18 wallpaper showing Roman ruins. Dates of the later alterations are problematic. Accounts for 1805–8 record substantial repairs and alterations after the accession of Colonel James Clitherow († 1841), including the installation of several fireplaces. Accounts from 1809 to 1820 are missing, and from 1820 to 1840 only minor repairs are recorded. As Faulkner, in his history of Brentford of 1845, mentions a recent fire, the neo-Jacobean work may have been carried out later, perhaps at the instigation of *C. J. Richardson*, who published drawings of the 1623 ceiling in *The Builder* in 1844.

The best rooms are on the first floor. The great chamber, measuring 12.50 by 6 metres, is on the E side. In it is the remarkable plaster ceiling of 1623, with an intricate pattern of enriched

27

double ribs with strapwork in lower relief, and an exceptional number of emblematic reliefs in roundels, including the five senses, the four elements (from designs by *Gheeraerts*), Faith, Hope, and Charity, War and Peace, and Peace and Plenty. On the chimneypiece a plaster overmantel with lovely strapwork and arabesques based on an engraving of 1584 by *Abraham de Bruyn*. In the centre an oval with the sacrifice of Isaac and the inscription 'In the Mount of the Lord it shall be seene' (discovered during restoration beneath the Clitherow motto). The plaster panel is flanked by ferns; the gadrooned shelf below, and the carved panel with festoons of fruit and a head, are in a more Jonesian spirit, quite different from the old-fashioned Netherlandish ornament of the rest. In the smaller state bedchamber to the s w is another strapwork ceiling with a single medallion of Hope, a strapwork frieze (uncovered during restorations), and a later c 17 fireplace surround with marble bolection-moulding. Between this room and the staircase a plain anteroom with a marble fireplace of c 18 type.

In the grounds, brick STABLES, and a square PIGEON HOUSE.

CHISWICK

INTRODUCTION

The parish of Chiswick had 3,235 inhabitants in 1801, 6,303 in 1851, 15,975 in 1881, and 29,801 in 1901. It is a development typical of the areas just outside the old L.C.C. boundaries; the change from village to suburb belongs to the second half of the c 19. What distinguishes Chiswick from nearby Ealing or Acton is that of its existence independent of London much more survives, and what survives is of a high quality, aesthetically, historically, and picturesquely. The old centre lay around the village church of St Nicholas close to the river. From it, Georgian and earlier houses still extend N W for some 150 yards and N E along the river for half a mile to join up with the Hammersmith Mall. A similar but more modest ribbon, Strand on the Green, starts from Kew Bridge and runs S E along the river. Between these two extended the grounds of a few large houses (Grove House, Sutton Court, etc.) of which only Chiswick House remains. Along the N edge of the parish ran the main road out of London, past Chiswick Common and Turnham Green, now the main shopping area. It was fringed by houses by the early c 19; fragments of the pre-Victorian era are still just recognizable amidst much rebuilding. Christ Church on Turnham Green dates from 1841–3, and here and along the High Road the main Victorian public buildings accumulated: town hall, fire station and police station (all extant but in different uses). They have considerably more charm than their bleak c 20 successors. The first suburbs to spread over the former market gardens were Gunnersbury to the W, in the 1860s; the more distinguished Bedford Park to the N, laid out from 1870; and Grove Park, down by the river, developed from c. 1867. By the c 20 little open land remained, apart from Chiswick Park and the low-lying water

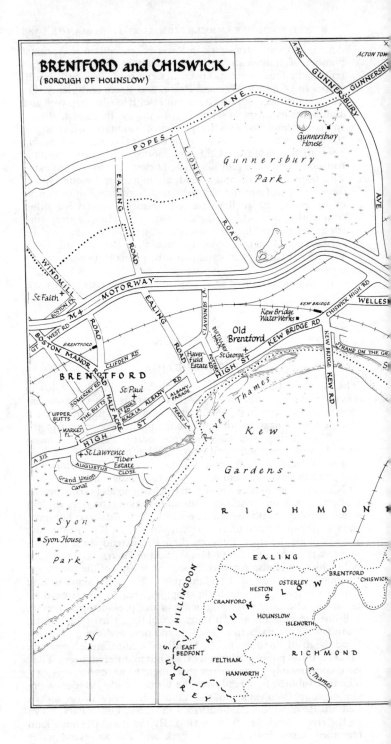

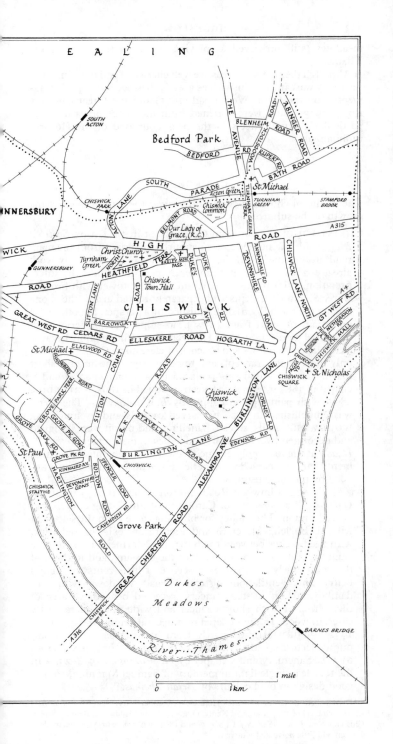

E A L I N G

SOUTH ACTON

Bedford Park

BEDFORD

THE AVENUE

BLENHEIM ROAD

WOODSTOCK ROAD

RUPERT RD

ABINGER ROAD

BATH ROAD

SOUTH   PARADE

Acton Green

St.Michael

INNERSBURY

CHISWICK PARK

ACTON LANE

TURNHAM GREEN TERR.

TURNHAM GREEN

STAMFORD BROOK

Chiswick Common

BELMONT ROAD

Our Lady of Grace (R.C.)

ROAD   A 315

WICK

HIGH

Christ Church

NORTH

Turnham Green

HEATHFIELD TERR.

BARLEY MOW PASS.

DUKES

DUKE

DEVONSHIRE RD

ANNANDALE RD

CHISWICK LANE NORTH

GUNNERSBURY

ROAD

SUTTON LANE

ROAD

Chiswick Town Hall

CHISWICK

GT WEST RD

A4

GREAT WEST RD

CEDARS RD

BARROWGATE   ROAD

ROAD

DUKES AVE

CHISWICK LANE NORTH

NETHERAVON

St.Michael

ELMWOOD RD

ELLESMERE   ROAD

HOGARTH LA.

CHISWICK MALL

AYLMER RD

ASHBURN

PARK   ROAD

SUTTON COURT

CHURCH ST

PAGES

St Nicholas

CHISWICK SQUARE

ROAD

Chiswick House

BURLINGTON LANE

CORNEY RD

GROVE PARK TERR.

GROVE

PARK RD

GROVE PK GDNS

STAVELEY   ROAD

St Paul

GROVE PK RD

KINNAIRD AV

HARTINGTON

DEVONSHIRE GDNS

BOLTON   ROAD

SPENCER   ROAD

BURLINGTON   LANE

CHISWICK

ALEXANDRA   AVE

EDENSOR   RD

ROAD

CHISWICK STAITHE

CAVENDISH RD

Grove Park

GREAT   CHERTSEY   ROAD

Dukes

Meadows

A 316

CHISWICK BR

River   Thames

BARNES BRIDGE

0   1 mile

0   1 km

meadows (still preserved as playing fields) in the bend of the Thames.

Although the riverside areas are well cherished and have survived relatively unscathed, Chiswick as a whole has been unhappily fragmented by the Great West Road (1925) and the Great Chertsey Road (1933). Both were widened from the 1950s onwards, with particularly brutal effects in the neighbourhood of the Hogarth roundabout.

CHURCHES

The medieval church is close to the river; the C19 ones chart the growth of the suburbs.*

CHRIST CHURCH, Turnham Green. Built in 1841–3 by *Scott & Moffatt* for the new Victorian suburb expanding from the main road around the green. Scott proves himself in this early work already a competent if uninspired performer in E.E. interpretation. Flint with stone dressings; tall w tower with broach-spire. Shallow transepts and separately roofed aisles, the N one (facing the High Road) distinguished by a parapet, but otherwise no ornament apart from a few head-stops. Lofty interior with octagonal piers (cf. St Mary Hanwell, Ea), rather gloomy because of the lancet windows and absence of clerestory. Of the galleries, only those in the transepts and tower remain. The original short half-hexagonal E end was replaced by a longer chancel and N chapel in 1887 by *Brooks*; SE vestries added in 1895. – REREDOS. 1894, with paintings on copper by *E. W. Alleyn*. – The E end was embellished in 1906 by carved capitals and by much oak WOODWORK: stalls, screen, panelling, and pulpit were designed and decorated by a group of local ladies trained under *Arthur T. Heady* at the local polytechnic. Flowers, foliage, musical instruments, etc., are carved with meticulous realism. – FONT COVER. 1908 by the same team.

ST MICHAEL, Elmwood Road, Sutton Court. 1908–9 by *W. D. Caröe & Passmore*, one of Caröe's most interesting churches in outer London. The money for building came from the sale of St Michael Burleigh Street, Strand. Picturesque exterior; red brick, with tiled arches between the buttresses, dormers to the nave, a shingled and tile-hung turret over the crossing, and to the N of this a curiously domestic excrescence of little roofs (housing a belfry and ventilation system). Broad windows with free flamboyant Gothic stone tracery, recessed beneath an arch of tiles. Interior with short chancel and wide nave, piers partly cased in wood. In the s chapel roof decoration by *Antony Lloyd*, 1932. – FURNISHINGS partly from St Michael Strand (font, pulpit, lectern). – CHOIR STALLS by *Caröe*, 1911. – STAINED GLASS. Sanctuary and s chapel by *H. Wilkinson*, 1914–25. – In the N aisle a single light in memory of Samuel Manning, 1961, a good design in bold colours by *Brian Thomas*.

*Demolished: St James, Chiswick High Road, Gunnersbury. 1887 by *T. Chatfeild Clarke;* chancel of 1897. Large, of Kentish rag – St Mary Magdalene, Bennett Street, Chiswick New Town. 1848 by *J. C. Sharpe* and 1894 by *Newman & Newman*, modest, with an odd little polygonal N turret.

ST MICHAEL AND ALL ANGELS, Bedford Park. *See* Perambulation 3.

ST NICHOLAS, Church Street. A church is mentioned in 1181. A lost brass recorded that the present W tower was begun when William Bordall was vicar (1416–35). Ragstone, three stages, with diagonal W buttresses, a SW stair-turret, battlements, and square-headed belfry windows. The Perp window below on the W side was renewed when the rest of the church was rebuilt by *J. L. Pearson* in 1882–4. He incorporated into his chancel three windows made for *William Burges*'s intended rebuilding, begun in 1861 but never completed. Their robust geometric tracery contrasts with Pearson's sensitive and competent neo-Perp. Pearson's E window is a tactful compromise. Comfortably broad battlemented aisles, of rough brown ragstone, nearly as wide and nearly as high as the nave. S porch with panelled barrel-vault, N porch open on three sides, with a fan-vault. The roofs inside also interestingly varied: the nave with moulded tie-beams and crownposts, the aisles with wooden tracery above the tie-beams, a wagon roof in the chancel. Quatrefoil piers, no clerestory, as in the late medieval churches of Devon and Cornwall. – REREDOS. By *Pearson*. Alabaster, with carved figures in cusped niches. – CHOIR STALLS, and SCREEN with much delicate cusping, coving, and cresting in the West Country manner, all of the 1880s. – REREDOS in the S chapel of painted wood, the Last Supper below elaborate Gothic tabernacle work, 1909 by *W. D. Caröe*. – Chapel SCREENS of the same date also by *Caröe*. – STAINED GLASS. E window 1882–3 by *Clayton & Bell*; not their best work. Given by Henry Smith of the local brewery, who paid for most of the rebuilding. – Similar, and of the same date, the S chapel E and easternmost on the chancel N. – The much livelier and more vividly coloured second chancel N window is of 1867, given by the hymn-writer J. E. Neale in memory of his brother; probably designed by *Burges*. – S chapel S, the E window of the old church, installed *c.* 1838 in memory of members of the Sharpe family. Voluminously draped figures of Christ, St James, and St John, with large flat areas of colour. – Tower window 1877, decidedly better than the later aisle windows (S side 1880s by *Powell* of Whitefriars, N side 1890s by *Clayton & Bell* and 1884 by *Shrigley & Hunt*).

MONUMENTS. The most interesting is in the S chapel: Sir Thomas Challoner † 1615, Chamberlain to Prince Henry. Alabaster, with Sir Thomas and his wife kneeling and facing each other across a prayer desk. Above them is a projecting semicircular Doric canopy with curtains held back by two bearded armed servants. Pyramidal top with small standing allegorical figure. – Most of the other monuments are in the tower. – James Howard † 1669. Inscription on a carved tablet flanked by columns. – Richard Taylor † 1698. Two coarse jolly cherubs and two cherubs' heads peer around fringed drapery. – Sir Richard Taylor † 1716. A much more elegant architectural tablet, with two mourning putti outside a Corinthian aedicule in veined marble. On the segmental pediment an achievement flanked by Father Time and a skull. – Thomas Plunkenett † 1721 and wife † 1738. Broken pediment and putti heads. – Sir John Taylor

† 1729. Pedimented architectural frame. – Charles Holland, the actor, † 1769, *W. Tyler*. Pyramidal wall-tablet with bust; epitaph by Garrick. – Thomas Bentley † 1780 (above the s door), by *T. Scheemakers Jun*. Casket-shaped, with portrait head and cherubs with inverted torches l. and r. – Tabitha Dickonson † 1786 (above the N door). Small, with an angel reclining by an urn. – Thomas Tomkins † 1816, with portrait medallion, signed by *Chantrey*. – Many good monuments in the large CHURCHYARD, s of the church, including an urn on a tall pedestal for William Hogarth † 1764, with epitaph by Garrick, and to the w a little mausoleum by *Soane* for P. L. de Loutherbourg, the painter, designer of moving scenery and panoramas, and faith healer, † 1812. To the sw, chest-tomb to Ugo Foscolo († 1827), erected 1871, probably by *Marochetti*. Among other eminent people buried here were Lord Burlington and William Kent (*see* Chiswick House). *Kent* may have designed the elaborately carved table-tomb to Richard Wright, Lord Burlington's bricklayer, † 1734.

ST PAUL, Grove Park Road. 1872 by *H. Currey;* faced with irregular uncoursed stone. Dec. Apsed E end, no tower. Paid for by the Duke of Devonshire, for the new Grove Park estate.

OUR LADY OF GRACE AND ST EDWARD (R.C.), Chiswick High Road and Duke's Avenue. 1904 by *Kelly & Birchall*. Dignified red brick front in the Roman C17 manner. The rubbed brick capitals carved by *Joseph Cribb*. NE tower added by *Sir Giles G. Scott*, 1930; open belfry with pyramid roof. Interior with Corinthian columns carrying a flat entablature. Remodelled in 1953 by *D. Plaskett Marshall* after war damage.

BAPTIST CHURCH, Annandale Road. Red brick; 1897 by *John Wills* of Derby. A tightly planned, irregular composition: rooms and stairs facing the road, the church lying behind; one turret.

METHODIST CHURCH, Barrowgate Road. 1987–8 by *David Rogers,* replacing a free Perp building of 1907 by *Withers & Meredith,* and a Gothic hall of 1880.

PUBLIC BUILDINGS

TOWN HALL, Turnham Green. 1876 by *W.J. Trehearne,* symmetrical, Italianate, with a big porte-cochère; three-bay E and one-bay w extensions of 1900 in matching style by *A. Ramsden*. Well preserved interiors: main hall and imperial stair with cast-iron balustrade in the older part; in the extension, a lavish marble stair to the council chamber and committee room.

POST OFFICE, Church Street. *See* Perambulation 1.

CAVENDISH SCHOOL, Edensor Road. A good example of a post-war primary by the *Middlesex County Council* (*C. G. Stillman*), 1950–1.

ST MARY'S CONVENT AND ST JOSEPH'S HOSPITAL, Burlington Lane. 1896 by *Charles Ford Whitcombe*. Picturesque chapel with a small tower, in a free Arts and Crafts Gothic. Classical reredos. Ceiling paintings by *George Ostrehan*; tapestry panel by *Morris & Co*.

CHISWICK STATION, Burlington Lane. By *Tite*, 1849, a typical late classical plain and decent station building with a Tuscan porch (cf. Kew Bridge Station, Brentford, Ho).

GUNNERSBURY STATION. Rebuilt with tall office block and car park in 1966 by *Raymond Spratley & Partners*.

CHISWICK PARK UNDERGROUND STATION. *See* Acton (Ea).

For former public buildings (fire station, police station, tramways power station) *see* Perambulations.

CHISWICK HOUSE, Burlington Lane. The most famous English 31 C18 Palladian villa, a small but splendid recreation of the antique spirit. The formal cube, with its smooth, sparkling walls, crisply carved detail, and distinctive shallow dome and obelisk chimneys, now stands in jewel-like isolation. This is misleading, for the villa built in 1727–9 by *Richard Boyle, third Earl of Burlington,* was planned as an adjunct to a Jacobean house which stood immediately to the E and was linked to it after 1732. In 1788 the fifth Duke of Devonshire and his wife Georgiana, the friend of Charles Fox, demolished the old house and added wings to the villa, to designs by *John White*. The wings were demolished, in ill-advised compliment to the purity of Burlington's original design, after the house, by then very dilapidated, passed to the Ministry of Works in 1952. But the villa does not stand quite on its own because Burlington's small link building which had connected it to the older house, and his adjoining summer parlour were both preserved. The house remained in the family, although let to aristocratic tenants, until 1892, when most of the contents were removed to Chatsworth. It was meticulously restored under *Patrick Faulkner* in 1956–7, when its NW garden staircase and NE and SW outer walls were reinstated according to Burlington's original designs. The villa is now the property of English Heritage; the grounds are a public park.

Chiswick became well known through its publication in Kent's *Designs of Inigo Jones* (1727) and its details were imitated throughout the C18. However, it was too idiosyncratic and personal a creation to become as influential a Palladian prototype as Campbell's Mereworth and Stourhead, or Morris's Marble Hill. Its creator, Richard Boyle, third Earl of Burlington, born in 1694, in 1704 inherited the Chiswick estate acquired by the first Earl in 1682. He visited Italy for the first time in 1715, and again in 1719, after his interest in architecture had been kindled by Leoni's translation of Palladio and Campbell's *Vitruvius Britannicus*. Annotations made during his travels in his copy of Palladio suggest he may already have conceived the intention of building a villa on a Palladian model. He returned home accompanied by William Kent, a young history painter who was to become his chief protégé, and with a collection of architectural drawings made by Palladio of the Roman baths, which were to prove especially influential. Designs for the villa were in progress in 1726–7, and building took place probably in 1727–9. By 1728 the old house had been given a partial Palladian refacing (shown in a view by P. A. Rysbrack of this date); the link building connecting it to the villa was added in 1732–3, it seems as an afterthought.

Burlington employed draughtsmen, but was himself responsible for the design of the house. It is loosely inspired by Pal-

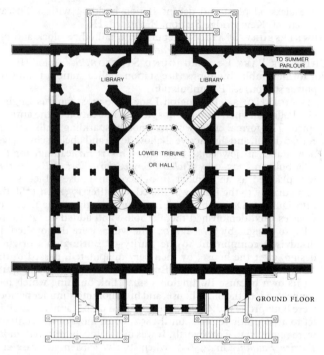

Chiswick House, plans of ground and first floors

ladio's Villa Rotonda but is not a direct copy of it, as Campbell's slightly earlier Mereworth was, and the varied shapes of the main rooms, raised above a basement and grouped round a central hall, owe more to the planning of Roman baths than to Palladio's precise symmetry. Scamozzi's Villa Pisani was also an important inspiration, especially for the general massing. The eclectic details derive from both antique and c16 Italian sources, for Palladio was only a means to Burlington's chief end, the revival of the architectural traditions of the classical world. Thus the shallow stepping of the dome is borrowed from the Pantheon, the lunette windows of the lantern from the baths of Diocletian, and the richly modelled entrance portico on the SE side, with its six Corinthian columns, takes its cornice and capitals from Roman temples. But the relationship of the basement to the portico comes from Palladio's Villa Foscari, and its boldly textured rustication in imitation of tufa from his Palazzo Thiene. Burlington's originality lies in his deployment of such classical and c16 Italian borrowings side by side with features more in tune with the Baroque spirit of his age, of which the most remarkable is the double staircase leading up to the portico, a design far more spectacular and complex than Palladio would have tolerated. The balusters however are not of the Baroque urn type but symmetrical, a Jonesian motif, as is the row of ball-shaped finials along the low screen walls extending beyond the entrance front.

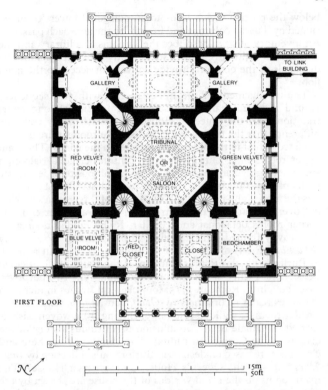

FIRST FLOOR

On either side of the portico are statues by *Rysbrack* of Burlington's mentors, Palladio and Jones, highly melodramatic in attitude and drapery. Burlington paid further homage to Jones by re-erecting in the grounds his gateway from Beaufort House Chelsea (*see* below).

The other fronts of the house, instead of striving for the four-square symmetry of the Villa Rotonda, adopt the popular C16 Italian feature of the tripartite or Venetian window as their principal motif. On NE and SW sides there is one large central window austerely isolated in much blank wall, on the NW side a more festive arrangement of three Venetian windows, each framed by an outer arch (a type that inspired many C18 copies). The centre opening forms a door to the garden staircase. This façade is based on an unpublished Palladio drawing in Burlington's possession.

INTERIOR. The sumptous and colourful main reception rooms come as a surprise after the chaste exterior, in a manner that would have been approved by Inigo Jones. Much of the *piano nobile* was devoted to reception rooms for the display of Burlington's collections. This floor could be approached ceremonially by the portico, or more formally by the link building. Alternatively one can go in by the lower floor and relish the dramatic contrast between its intimate low-ceilinged rooms and the state rooms above. The lower floor is entered by a passage below the portico which leads to an octagonal lower 'tribune', ringed by Tuscan columns and lit only by the approach passages. An inventory of 1770 describes the N rooms as a library and the W rooms as bedrooms. Newel stairs neatly concealed behind the diagonals of the octagon provide convenient access to the main floor.

The arrangement of the upper rooms, with two sequences around a central hall, owes something to English C17 court traditions (cf. the Queen's House Greenwich, Gr), with the difference that the dining room and service rooms were accommodated at first in the old house and later in the wings. The main upper rooms interconnect with the central octagonal saloon, a space both grave and splendid, with its composite order, dome with antique coffering, and brackets with classical busts. To the N is the more light-hearted gallery, a suite of three spaces looking out over the gardens, the centre room apsed at either end, the corner rooms octagonal and circular. Richly gilded doorcases, the heavily framed central ceiling with a painting (possibly by *Sebastiano Ricci*) of the Relief of Smyrna, perhaps in allusion to Burlington's position as Captain of the Band of Gentlemen Pensioners. Plenty of decoration in antique style: two porphyry vases bought in Rome in 1715; four classical statues in niches in the apses (casts of originals by *Guelfi* and *Scheemakers*). In the smaller rooms are gilded festoons springing from woven baskets carried on female heads, an allusion to Vitruvius's story of the origins of the Corinthian capital. The chimneypieces here and elsewhere are based on designs in Burlington's collection by *Inigo Jones* (e.g. for the Queen's House and Somerset House). The main rooms on the E and W sides of the house are shown by the 1770 inventory to have been picture galleries – hence the blank walls outside. On the W side the Red Velvet Room has a painted panelled ceiling, probably by *Kent*, with an allegory of the arts in which Painting is represented by a portrait of Kent, Sculpture by a fallen bust of Jones. The overmantels are by *Ricci* (possibly painted for Burlington House Piccadilly when the artist visited England in 1711–16). The adjoining SW room, the Blue Velvet Room, was Burlington's study, where he may have shown his architectural drawings – a holy of holies whose effect is heightened by an exotically rich ceiling with emphatic paired brackets which may derive from a ceiling design in Burlington's possession and attributed to Cherubino Alberti. It is of the type used in the *studiolo* of the duke of Mantua. The central painting, of Architecture surrounded by boys with drawing instruments, is probably by *Kent*. The small Red Closet beyond must have been the repository for precious smaller objects. It had thirty-six paintings. On the E side the Green Velvet Room was also a picture gallery, with overmantels again by *Ricci*, and the NE room was the state bedchamber, where Lady Burlington died in 1758. A small closet adjoins, as on the other side.

The upper and lower rooms of the link building are divided by screens of columns (Composite and Tuscan, in accordance with their levels). The summer parlour or garden room beyond, probably built in the 1730s, was described by Horace Walpole in 1760 as Lady Burlington's dressing room. The elaborate ceiling decorated with grotesque work can be ascribed to *Kent* (cf. his work at Kensington Palace, KC). The owls are the badge of the Saviles, Lady Burlington's family. The chimneypiece may have come from one of the 1788 wings by *John White*.

GROUNDS. The complicated development of the grounds of Chiswick encapsulates the whole history of garden design in the first half of the C18: the transition from the tradition of precise geometric layouts to a conscious effort to recreate antique gardens in which judiciously placed buildings play an important role, and thence to a new interest in less formal picturesque effects. The story is recorded in several series of C18 views, and the various stages can still be appreciated in different parts of the gardens. The main surviving features of the grounds are described here roughly chronologically, beginning with the N part around the villa, and proceeding to the W and E extensions.

The sole survivor of the formal gardens and enclosures which had been laid out around the Jacobean house, shown by Kip in a view of 1707, is the line of the northern avenue aligned on the SW terrace in front of the old house. Some time after 1707, and certainly before he began the villa, Burlington used this as the central avenue of a *patte d'oie*, with new, lesser avenues leading to small buildings as *points de vue*. The northern avenue (to the immediate r. of the main axis) survived later alterations, as did its terminal building, the RUSTIC HOUSE, at the far end of the gardens, an arched alcove of rusticated stone. The other avenues were swept away in the later C18, together with their buildings (a Casina and a pagan temple), but re-formed in the 1950s. The idea of using buildings as terminal points to such avenues was a novel one, perhaps inspired by theatrical designs (Burlington had visited the Teatro Olimpico at Vicenza in 1715 and was a keen patron of Italian opera in England). On the site of the temple at the end of the main avenue there is now a fragment of wall with a Venetian window, from one of the demolished wings from the house. To the E of the avenue to the Rustic House, lesser avenues once converged on the DORIC COLUMN on which formerly a statue of the Venus de' Medici stood. Further E, a DEER HOUSE remains from a deer paddock which existed until *c.* 1727. It is a simple rectangular building with two stone arches and a pantiled roof. A second deer house was replaced by the Inigo Jones gateway (*see* below). W of the *patte d'oie* a grass amphitheatre was excavated, around a pool with an OBELISK. Overlooking this charming spot, embellished in summer with orange trees in pots according to the C18 custom, is a small domed IONIC TEMPLE, circular, with a four-column portico, inspired by the Pantheon. It is illustrated (without its rear porch, added before 1736), and attributed to *Burlington*, in Kent's *Designs of Inigo Jones* (1727). The formal basins to N and S, the N one with a small classical pavilion, disappeared in later alterations.

With the building of the villa on the former lawn SW of the old house, Burlington began to transform the surrounding gardens. To the SW a lawn and a short-lived maze were laid out. To the NE the thick grove of trees around the main N avenue was gradually cleared so as to open out the view. The present broad lawn on the axis of the villa, ending in a semicircular EXEDRA of

Roman type, was created between 1733 and 1736, and by 1742
linked to the house by rows of stone urns and sphinxes. Around
the exedra are pieces of stone SCULPTURE (in place by 1753)
including urns, lions, and termini, and three antique statues said
to come from Hadrian's villa at Tivoli, formerly in one of the
temples. *Kent* may have had something to do with the idea for
the exedra, for a rejected design of his shows a curved masonry
structure with niches similar to his later Temple of British Worthies at Stowe. E of the villa is the GATEWAY designed by *Inigo
Jones* for Sir Lionel Cranfield's Beaufort House Chelsea in 1621,
acquired by Burlington from Sir Hans Sloane when he demolished the house, and erected here in 1738. It is of the greatest
interest as one of the few extant structures by Jones, a sober
Doric design, with an archway flanked by plain slender columns
against vermiculated rustication, an entablature with unusually

A The Villa
B Link building
C Summer parlour
D Inigo Jones gateway
E Site of Orangery
F Italian garden
G Conservatory
H Deer house
I Doric column
J Rustic house
K Exedra
L Amphitheatre
M Temple
N Classic bridge
O Obelisk
P Terrace
Q Cascade
R Corney Road lodge

Chiswick House, plan of the grounds

broad triglyphs, and a shallow pediment. At the back there are pilasters instead of columns.

In front of the villa the drive was shorter than at present, as until 1818 the road ran much closer to the house. The forecourt is lined with two rows of TERMINI, restored to their original position in the 1950s. The GATEPIERS, re-erected in their old position, formerly bore sphinxes, as can be seen in Rigaud's view of 1733.

Around the same time, after he acquired the Sutton Court estate in 1727, Burlington was able to enlarge the grounds W of the old boundary formed by the Bollo brook. They were laid out as a WILDERNESS GARDEN, originally traversed by a typically earlier C18 mixture of winding paths and straight avenues. The wilderness is approached from the villa by a raised TERRACE along the S edge, built up to capture the views S towards the Thames. The terrace continues to a W gate and OBELISK nearby, whose base incorporates an antique sculpture (now replaced with a replica) from the Arundel collection given to Burlington in 1712. The avenues diverged in a *patte d'oie* based on the obelisk, leading back towards the Bollo brook, irregularly enlarged at this time to form a sizeable 'river'. The new grounds were skilfully integrated with the old: a bridge was built to link the N avenue with the Casina, and the Ionic temple on the E side of the water was given a new porch aligned with the central avenue.

The most novel creation of these years was the transformation of the Bollo brook into a large informal stretch of water, the focus of the lawn to the W of the villa (enlarged by the removal of the maze), integrating house and landscape in a way that presaged the Picturesque movement of the later C18. The extent of *Kent*'s involvement in all this is unclear, but we do have a series of alternative designs of his for another innovation, the CASCADE or GROTTO built of cyclopean masonry at the S end of the enlarged river, designed by *c.* 1736 but not completed for several years and altered in the early C19. The handsome BRIDGE at the N end of the river, with a bold segmental arch, decorated with urns and *Coade* reliefs, is a rebuilding of 1774, possibly by *James Wyatt*. From 1784 *Samuel Lapidge* re-landscaped the wilderness in an informal manner and replaced the N avenue with a serpentine drive leading to the new bridge.

In 1812 the sixth Duke of Devonshire extended the grounds to the E by acquiring the neighbouring estate with the late C17 Moreton House, built for Sir Stephen Fox by *Hugh May*, which the duke demolished. In the next year, further N, but on the same axis, *Samuel Ware* added the CONSERVATORY, a long glass-roofed range set against a brick wall, with an innovative central dome with cast-iron ribs carried on cast-iron columns (considerably earlier than, for example, the domed conservatory at Syon House, or Paxton's work at Chatsworth). It was criticized as 'gloomy' by Loudon in 1824, and the details were modified in 1855 (larger panes of glass) and in 1933 (central rotunda reconstructed as a sixteen-sided pavilion). To its S an ITALIAN GARDEN was laid out by *Lewis Kennedy*. The two large urns are by *Coade & Sealy*. The sixth Duke was also responsible for moving Burlington Lane further S, and for the CORNEY ROAD

LODGE, by *Decimus Burton*, 1835. The C19 gates and gatepiers on the main axis of the villa, re-erected here in 1934, come from Grosvenor House, Park Lane.

PERAMBULATIONS

1. The riverside village

2 CHISWICK MALL. The impression is still almost wholly that of the riverside village for wealthy landowners. Coming from Hammersmith, the boundary is marked by a brown brick terrace of the 1970s, with staggered frontage to the road, the only later C20 building here which dares to eschew a period style. After that the houses are on the N side. The river is unembanked: hence the small front gardens between street and water. MILLER'S COURT is a tactful neo-Georgian prelude of 1971 by *Chapman & Taylor*. The older buildings begin with CEDAR HOUSE and SWAN HOUSE, a late C18 three-storey pair of red brick, with a bow-window on the W side. ISLAND HOUSE and NORFOLK HOUSE are another pair, early C19, stuccoed, taller than the others and more pretentious. Then ST JOHN'S HOUSE, similar but plainer. After the former Chiswick Maternity Hospital (1912), THE OSIERS, with a stucco front on an older house, is followed by the splendid group of C18 façades: Morton House, Strawberry House, and Walpole House. MORTON HOUSE has a front of brown brick with red dressings, the urban type of three storeys and basement, three bays wide. The rate-books suggest a date of *c.* 1726. STRAWBERRY HOUSE is long and low, a brown brick front of *c.* 1735 added to an earlier house. Pretty late C18 porch on the slenderest of columns with delicate balcony above. (Interior: drawing-room ceiling and mantelpiece in the Adam style.)

WALPOLE HOUSE is the largest and most complex of the houses in the Mall. Behind the delightful irregular front, with its early C18 brickwork and modillioned eaves to the main projecting parts, lies a substantial house of Tudor origin. The three bays to the l. of the front door belong to a large ground-floor reception room. Above this is an even larger chamber, extending over the passage hall. This upper room had until the 1920s a fireplace with a four-centred arch. The C16 chimneystack, corbelled out twice and carrying a row of diagonal stacks, is visible from the garden. The second floor was heightened later. The E part of the house is an early C18 extension and remodelling of an older core. The porch, set within the projecting E wing, has a doorcase with fluted Corinthian pilasters. To the garden this wing has a handsome five-bay, three-storey frontage, the windows with fine flat arches of rubbed brick, their centres extended upwards as keystones. Aprons below the first-floor windows, and a moulded cornice below the parapet. Throughout there are good interior fittings of the early C18 (as well as some displaced C16 panelling). Fielded panelling in the two main rooms, the lower one with Corinthian pilasters framing the fireplace, and a small oriel room projecting towards the river. At the back of the house some original thick-barred sash-windows with only one movable frame. The outstanding feature is the main staircase (corresponding to two bays of the C18 garden front), virtuoso craftsmanship of c. 1720; two fluted and one spiral baluster to each tread, fluted newels, carved tread-ends, and a low ramped handrail which breaks forward in a little curve as it reaches the landing. A good back staircase as well, fitted between the front and back rooms of the wing, extending from cellar to second floor. It still has the more old-fashioned closed string. The rooms on either side have typically early C18 corner fireplaces.

The Mall continues with ORFORD HOUSE and THE TIDES, 1886 by *John Belcher*, with one tile-hung and one timber-framed gable. Then CYGNET HOUSE and RIVERSIDE, early C19; OAK COTTAGE, small and stuccoed; and MAGNOLIA and THAMESCOTE, a tall C18 pair. GREENASH (despite its whitewash and paintwork) is the most interesting later house. It was built in 1882 by *Belcher* for Sir John Thornycroft (whose famous wharf lay just W of the church) in a wildly Shavian manner, its high double gable breaking all Georgian good manners concerning the skyline. Converted to flats by *E. Musman* in 1934. After this, indifferent houses of c. 1875 on the site of the old prebendal manor house which stood at the corner of Chiswick Lane.*

CHISWICK LANE SOUTH is a short lane leading N from the river, now cut off from its continuation towards Chiswick High Road (Perambulation 2) by the noisy line of the Great Chertsey Road and the widened Burlington Lane. At the S end the GRIFFIN BREWERY (from 1845 Fuller Smith & Turner). The central part, now offices, is late C18, built as the owner's residence. (Interior: C18 staircase, ground-floor board room.) The brewery buildings were largely rebuilt in 1979–81 but some picturesque parts remain. N of this MAWSON ROW, a terrace of plain three-storey early C18 houses. Back by the river CHISWICK MALL continues W with more old houses between Chiswick Lane and the church. RED LION HOUSE, five windows wide, is early C18, but with unattractive later rendering. (Good staircase.) Some cottages at right angles to the road, then THAMES VIEW and LINGARD HOUSE, three-storeyed with later C18 doorcases (the l. one with a good fanlight); SAID HOUSE, Victorian, georgianized c. 1935 by *Darcy Braddell* with an over-large bow-window with painful expanse of glass; and EYNHAM HOUSE and BEDFORD HOUSE, originally one, an C18 front with four-bay pediment, and additions of the mid C18 and later, although the house goes back at least to the time of Edward Russell † 1665, second son of the fourth Duke of Bedford. In the grounds of Bedford House a mid C18 Gothic GAZEBO. WOODROFFE HOUSE, early C18 (third storey added later), is forbiddingly severe. The neo-Georgian vicarage of 1973 follows, in the grounds of the OLD VICARAGE, rebuilt in 1657–8 and in the later C18 given a stuccoed front with bow-window to the Mall. The back extension (the Chapter House) is of 1890.

*In NETHERAVON ROAD the tall late C17 brick wall at the back of the gardens of the Chiswick Mall houses is part of the old boundary wall of this house, which was used as a rural retreat by the scholars of Westminster School after 1571. During demolition of the house in 1875 'Norman mouldings' were said to have been discovered.

CHURCH STREET, from the Old Vicarage up to the bypass along Burlington Lane, is similarly rewarding. On the E side VINE HOUSE, late C18, brown brick, with good railings and gate, is followed by the picturesque contrast of Nos. 1–2 (the Old Burlington, a former inn), C16 with overhanging upper floor with exposed timber-framing, and by LAMB COTTAGE, with weatherboarded parts in front of the former late C19 brewery building (red brick with louvred lantern). Then a few more C18 brick houses (BRAMPTON HOUSE with weatherboarded S oriel, FERRY HOUSE, seven bays with Venetian window, WISTERIA, and the POST OFFICE). On the W side LATIMER HOUSE and HOLLY HOUSE, formerly one C18 house, with projecting lower wing on the r. and a fine wrought-iron gate. Off on the W PAGES YARD, a restored group of C17 cottages. The intimacy is rudely shattered by the widened main road (for which other old houses were demolished in the 1960s), but a little way W along BUR-LINGTON LANE, CHISWICK SQUARE remains, a group with houses of c. 1680 on two sides forming a kind of forecourt to BOSTON HOUSE, a composition like the Albany or Stratford Place, London. Boston House itself was refronted c. 1740, three storeys, brown brick with red dressings, five windows wide (inside a room with plasterwork and a ceiling in the Adam style). Good bracketed doorcase to No. 7, one of the side houses. Facing this was the site of the Chiswick Polish Company (Cherry Blossom Boot Polish), rebuilt as FLEMMING HOUSE by *Covell Matthews Wheatley* in 1983–5, large sleek offices with tinted glass panels. Further buildings by the same firm for the adjacent BUSINESS PARK, 1985 onwards.

To the N, in HOGARTH LANE, cruelly brushed by the busy road, is HOGARTH HOUSE, Hogarth's home from 1749 to 1764, now a museum. Well restored by *J. Macgregor* after war damage. A tall, simple brick house of three storeys, five windows wide, with a central wooden oriel window overlooking the garden.

2. *Chiswick High Road and Turnham Green*

Chiswick High Road and Turnham Green constitute the main shopping area of Chiswick. Few older houses of any note survive, but there is plenty of minor evidence for the growth of the area in the C18 and C19, together with numerous pubs, successors to the coaching inns. At the E end the HIGH ROAD starts with Nos. 1–21, of c. 1830–40. Behind one-storeyed additions, a unified composition with giant pilasters at the ends and in the centre, a total of nineteen bays, the l. end the better preserved. Also on the S side occasional smaller Georgian houses: Nos. 111–113 and their more altered neighbours; the former Fire Station of 1891, probably by *Arthur Ramsden*, surveyor to the local board, with a clock tower (an early example of a hose tower), and helmets carved above the windows; and the PACK HORSE AND TALBOT, a substantial pub of the C20 reformed type: tile-hung gables, roughcast dormers. A diversion S down DEVONSHIRE ROAD, past late C19 artisan terraces, can take in two further pubs on a more modest scale, both by *Nowell Parr* (*see* Brentford):

the DUKE OF YORK (1926) and the MANOR TAVERN (1924), rebuildings in the area once known as Chiswick New Town. This began as an isolated pocket of early C19 working-class terraces just N of Hogarth Lane which gradually expanded N to the High Road. (The earliest houses have all been replaced by council housing.)

Back now to the N side of the High Road. By far the most exciting building here is No. 70, THE POWER HOUSE, built as a power station for the London United Electrical Tramway Company in 1899–1901. The engineer was *Parshall*, the architect *W. Curtis Green* (also responsible for a classical power station for Bristol Tramways). The Chiswick building is the best surviving example in London from the early, heroic era of generating stations whose bulky intrusion in residential areas was tempered by thoughtful architectural treatment. It is a monumental free Baroque brick and stone composition, three by five bays, with a big bracketed cornice above huge arches with elongated stone voussoirs. Aedicules between the arches and a tall striped attic with circular openings. Above the entrance, carved figures of Electricity and Locomotion. Converted in 1985 by *David Clarke Associates*, with flats ingeniously tucked into the roof. The vast lower spaces have been imaginatively converted to recording studios by *Powell-Tuck Connor & Orefelt*, 1989. At the N end part of an elaborate original iron staircase has been incorporated.

Further W the assortment of buildings on the N side includes CHISWICK EYOT (formerly the Roebuck), a stately stuccoed pub of *c.* 1895, with reliefs of stags on pediments to S and E; Nos. 62–64, a pair of *c.* 1800, three storeys with entrance in lower side wings (nice fanlight to No. 62); and, further on, No. 210, 1874, a former police station, small but dignified, stone-faced, with a large coat of arms over the entrance. A few older houses on the S side; Nos. 147–149, next to the R.C. church, terrace houses of *c.* 1800 with *Coade* keystones; and No. 183 with a Georgian shop-window. The more interesting buildings lie behind, along a small lane which diverges from the High Road on the S side, marking the original extent of the green. First, just off Duke's Avenue, AFTON HOUSE, an example of the wealthier houses of *c.* 1800, of which there were once many along the High Road. Five bays wide, stucco ground floor, semicircular porch with fluted columns; good fanlight. Intermittent roof balustrade. A little further W, where the lane becomes BARLEY MOW PASSAGE, is VOYSEY HOUSE, built in 1902 as an extension to 75 SANDERSON'S WALLPAPER FACTORY opposite. By *C. F. A. Voysey*; his only factory building, and a clean and charming design. White glazed brick with ground floor and dressings in Staffordshire blue brick (now painted black). Three floors of large horizontal segment-headed windows and a fourth with small circular windows. Buttresses (housing ventilation shafts) ending with flat 'mortarboard' projections like wooden bedsteads in the Arts and Crafts taste. A tall parapet curves gracefully between them. The interiors are equally satisfactory; well lit, and given character by shallow concrete barrel-vaults above corrugated iron shuttering. The supporting iron columns are progressively slenderer on each floor. Well restored from 1989 by

Lawrence & Wrightson (with a roof-top flat tactfully added behind the parapet).

After this comes the pleasantly open stretch of TURNHAM GREEN, with Christ Church as its centrepiece (q.v.). Facing N across the green, first No. 2a, a two-storey Georgian cottage. It is dwarfed by the Army and Navy Repository close by, on the site of C19 barracks, converted to flats in 1988. Then Nos. 10–13, a C19 brick and stucco terrace. After the town hall (q.v.) HEATHFIELD TERRACE with Nos. 16–19, an early Victorian stucco group with corner pilasters and recessed entrance wings, and Nos. 20–26, a taller continuous terrace in the same style, symmetrical, with larger central house. Paired Ionic porches, pretty balconies. At the SW corner (some way from the church, as there were objections to buildings on the green), the CHURCH HALL of 1913, red brick, with Arts and Crafts details. The W side of the green is mostly late C19, but tucked away behind is ARLINGTON COTTAGES, a rare older survival, a low rendered former farmhouse of three bays with a two-bay r. extension. Early C19 windows, but the fabric probably older. In front of it ARLINGTON PARK HOUSE, a small mid Victorian villa, and the more dominant ARLINGTON PARK MANSIONS, in the coarsely robust Baroque of c. 1900. At the NW corner the OLD PACK HORSE, with plenty of jolly terracotta detail and bowed ground-floor windows, 1910 by *Nowell Parr*. To its E, the CHISWICK CENTRE (No. 414) by *Carl Fisher*, an obtrusive tower of 1959 sleekly reclad since with tinted glass. Further W larger office blocks (e.g. ENTERPRISE HOUSE by *Halpern Partnership*, 1983–4) have sprouted up haphazardly since the 1960s among the tall stuccoed mid C19 villas of Gunnersbury.

In contrast to these, CHISWICK BUSINESS PARK, further along the High Road, was designed to a coherent plan by Stanhope Trafalgar in 1990–1, on the site of a bus station, an urban counterpart to Stockley Park (Hi). The master plan by *Terry Farrell & Co.* proposed a lavishly landscaped central piazza, designed to show off buildings by a galaxy of famous names: *Foster Associates*, *Peter Foggo*, and *Terry Farrell & Co.* around the main square; *Richard Rogers* and *ABK* around a lesser square on a different axis. Between the two a low amenity building by *Eric Parry*.

3. Bedford Park

Bedford Park,* begun in 1875, is probably the best known later Victorian suburb in outer London, owing its fame both to its contemporary eulogists and to an energetic and successful preservation campaign of the 1960s, when its survival was threatened.‡ Its reputation as the earliest garden suburb needs some qualification. Trees and green spaces (both communal and private) are

---

*Partly in the borough of Ealing, but treated as a whole here.

‡The Bedford Park Society was founded in 1963. In 1967 the government agreed to list 356 houses, an unprecedented preservation measure, necessary as at that time Conservation Areas did not yet exist. Conservation Area status followed in 1969 and 1970.

found in many earlier suburbs; the novelty of Bedford Park is their combination with 'artistically designed' houses of moderate size, inspired not by classical or Gothic pattern books but by the red brick and tiled idiom derived chiefly from the home counties vernacular of the C17 and C18. Elements of the style had been used earlier (for example in rural estate housing by George Devey), and the concept of the picturesque village is older still (Nash's Blaise Hamlet near Bristol, Paxton's Edensor, Derbyshire). But Bedford Park was the first example where the relaxed, informal mood of a market town or village was adopted for a complete speculatively built suburb.

The story begins with Jonathan T. Carr (1845–1915), a cloth merchant and property speculator, who bought 24 acres N of Turnham Green in 1875. The layout is not especially inspired: three straight main roads (Bath Road, Woodstock Road, The Avenue) converging in traditional manner on the new church and inn, sited a little to the N of Turnham Green station. What is of more interest is the treatment of the minor roads, with their odd bends taking account of existing groups of trees, and the siting of individual houses, often placed quite close to the pavements; detached houses are rare, so that the buildings make a direct impact on the street scene. Specially picturesque effects are achieved at the angular road junctions by the irregular grouping of roofs, tall chimneys, and white-painted bay-windows. Carefully designed front garden walls and fences also play a crucial part in the composition.

Carr's first architect was *E.W. Godwin*, with *Coe & Robinson* in the first two years, but none of their designs was considered satisfactory. From 1877 to 1886 *Norman Shaw* was employed first as estate architect until his resignation in 1880, then as consultant,

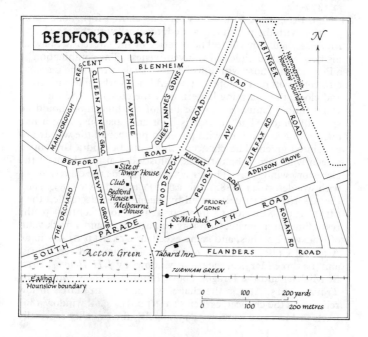

and it is his style that dominates, a scaled-down, countrified version of the 'Queen Anne' idiom he was using during the same years for his larger houses in Chelsea and Kensington. He was succeeded by *E. J. May*, who lived in Bedford Park, as did *Maurice Adams*, who was also involved.

The planning of the smaller houses attracted attention as well as their picturesque exteriors. Around thirty prototype designs were used. Relatively modest in scale, they yet included generous front doors and entrance halls, some with well staircases, instead of the customary narrow passages and dog-leg flight of the Georgian terrace tradition. There were no basements, and tall overshadowing rear extensions were avoided. The suburb rapidly became a show-piece: it was visited by the Architectural Association in 1877, its houses were illustrated in *The Building News*, and it was praised by William Morris in 1880 for its 'quaint and pretty architecture' and for its preservation of trees. The *St James' Gazette* (17 December 1881) was less complimentary, its 'Ballad of Bedford Park' lampooning the new village of 'Biled lobster 'ouses ... where men may lead a chaste correct aesthetical existence'. There was no doubt a certain self-consciousness about the early population: G. K. Chesterton evoked its arty character in *The Man Who Was Thursday*. The development was indeed intended to attract artists, and includes over twenty studios (some incorporated within the houses). By 1883 the estate covered 113 acres with 490 houses, and a club and school of art (destroyed in the war) supplemented the church and pub.

A tour of Bedford Park should begin with its chief focus, the group of St Michael's church and the Tabard Inn, designed by *Shaw* in 1879–80.

St Michael and All Angels. The church forms one composition with the parish hall added, together with the N aisle, by *Maurice Adams* in 1887. The exterior of the church is Shaw at his best, inexhaustible in his inventiveness. The combination of a Perp ground floor with upper features taken from the C17 and C18 comes off most happily. The red brickwork gable with cross and clock, the charming lantern over the crossing, and the bold white timber balustrade at the foot of the high roof should be specially noted. The interior is light and spacious, with a fine open roof and columns with panelled plinths; all the woodwork is painted green. The chancel is high up, beyond a large open screen with turned balustrades; balustrades also in front of the clerestory windows. – The pews are by *Shaw*; the carved font with wooden cover (1884), the pulpit in C17 style (1894), and the bishop's throne are all by *Adams*, who also added the S chapel of all souls in 1909. It is in total contrast to the rest, dim and intimate, with tiny passage aisles and a brick vault of transverse arches, and some excellent stained glass in an Arts and Crafts style with much purple, blue, and red; Christ and the three Marys in the two E windows by *J. H. Bonnor*, 1912, St Michael and the Dragon above London in the S window by *Travers*, 1915. Also in the chapel is a painted reredos in low relief. – In the chancel, earlier stained glass: N window 1890 (Acts of Mercy), S window 1895 (angels), their quality especially apparent when contrasted with the lifeless E window of 1952. – The elaborate marble SANCTUARY PAVING dates from 1887.

The TABARD INN of 1880, at the corner of Bath Road and Acton Green, opposite the church, is especially attractive, with tile-hung gables and very original shallow-curved, completely glazed bay-windows. The public bar has *de Morgan* tiles on the upper walls, the saloon bar an original narrow fireplace with tiles above. Adjoining is the former BEDFORD PARK STORES, with large bay-windows and jettied, roughcast upper floors with Shaw's favourite 'Ipswich window' motif.

E of the church up PRIORY GARDENS, all of 1880 by *May*. On the l. the VICARAGE, with a big hipped roof and staircase windows expressed, and on the r. a picturesque three-storey red brick terrace with shaped gables and small hooded porches. At the end PRIORY HOUSE, a detached house built for Dr Hogg (planned with central heating and air conditioning). Then around the church and up WOODSTOCK ROAD. Here *Shaw*'s range of designs of 1878–9 can be studied. On the E side, semi-detached houses with generous bay-windows and wooden balconies (now somewhat spoilt). Further on, detached houses with pretty tile-hanging at the corner of Rupert Road, then Nos. 24–34, Shaw's first terrace design (1878), taller, with more obvious borrowing of C17 urban forms than his other houses. Big roughcast over-hanging gabled bay-windows to the two upper floors, tiny dormers in between, doorways with segmental hoods. Now along Bedford Road to THE AVENUE, which has the very first houses of the estate, the detached Nos. 1 and 2, 1876 by *Godwin* (tile-hung gable over the bay-window) and by *Coe & Robinson* (paired gables). The change in spirit after Godwin's resignation is marked by *Shaw*'s first semi-detached design (Nos. 20–22); note the deliberately picturesque sunflower panel and corbelled bay, details which were simplified on later houses.

In BLENHEIM ROAD to the E, No. 36 (opposite intrusive flats of *c.* 1938) is the studio of Joseph Nash, attached to a tile-hung *Shaw* corner house dated 1879 (plastered vaulted ceiling inside). Nos. 2–10 are by *Wilson*, some of his few known designs. Probably also by him are No. 9 QUEEN ANNE'S GARDENS, dated 1880, hidden in a large garden (a rarity), and No. 7, built in 1878 for the artist T. M. Rooke, which in contrast to its neighbours stands close to the road.

W along MARLBOROUGH CRESCENT, which has smaller cottages and (round the corner) a *May* terrace with shaped gables. This and the other nicely varied streets in the NW part of the suburb date largely from 1880–6. Back along Bedford Road to THE ORCHARD, mostly by *May*, apart from No. 1, with crowstepped gables, possibly by *Shaw*, and to QUEEN ANNE'S GROVE, which has a terrace of *Shaw* houses of the later type (Nos. 15–25). S down NEWTON GROVE: on the w side Nos. 12–14, an impressive group of 1880 by *Adams* for the artist J. C. Dollman, containing a large first-floor studio now obscured from the road by a later extension. The entrance was formerly at the side. Nos. 3 and 1 opposite are larger detached houses (No. 1 by *May*, with well preserved interiors).

Back to THE AVENUE. On the w side is the BEDFORD PARK

CLUB (now mutilated), designed in 1878 by *Shaw*, executed by *May*; the main social centre of the suburb. Close by are the remains of BEDFORD HOUSE, the late c18 house which gave the suburb its name. The courtyard was filled with shops in 1924. Half of the main s front is visible behind, the centre with a pediment enclosing a shallow lunette; ground-floor windows in recessed arches. To the w, MELBOURNE HOUSE, plain, three storeys, late Georgian. Jonathan Carr's own house, Tower House, large, with spacious grounds, designed by *Shaw* in 1878, stood to the n; it was replaced by dismal flats in the 1930s. This w part of the suburb was the most fashionable in the late c19, but is the least well preserved, for its larger houses with big gardens were an obvious prey to developers.

In SOUTH PARADE it is the later intruders that catch the eye. First No. 2 by *F. Ruhemann* and *M. Dugdale*, a modern newcomer of 1938–9, brick and concrete ground floor, with open-plan interior with fitted furniture; large first-floor terrace with curved sun roof and a porch roof to match. Then No. 14 of 1891 by *C. F. A. Voysey* for the artist J. W. Forster, a tower house, with the large studio occupying the whole of the top floor in the tradition of urban studio houses (cf. Tite Street Chelsea, KC). It was one of Voysey's first houses, designed evidently in conscious opposition to the red brick cosiness of the suburb. It is roughcast and shows proudly its bare grey walls and the robust (originally unpainted) stone dressings around the metal frames of the horizontal windows. The far-projecting eaves are carried on elegant thin iron brackets. Voysey added the lower side wing in 1894.

4. Grove Park

The area around Chiswick Station (1849) belonged to the Duke of Devonshire's Grove Park estate. It makes a telling contrast to Bedford Park. It was developed slowly from 1867, with very large upper-class mansions and ample recreational areas, in the grounds of Grove Park, an c18 house altered by *Decimus Burton*. The original character is still recognizable, even though (as so often in grandly conceived Victorian suburbs) diluted by diverse less ambitious later replacements and additions. Development began near the station with the GROVE PARK HOTEL, 1867, with spare Gothic detail originally enlivened by balconies. Here the three main roads with the earliest houses converge: Bolton Road, Spencer Road, and Grove Park Road. They have a mixture of huge Italianate villas (cf. Cubitt's Clapham Park, La) and more individual designs of which the best are in GROVE PARK ROAD, where St Paul's church (paid for by the Duke of Devonshire) was built opposite the old mansion. (This survived until 1928, when it was replaced by KINNAIRD AVENUE, laid out, together with DEVONSHIRE GARDENS, with modest semi-detached houses by *L. H. Harrington* for the Kinnaird Park Estate Company.) In Grove Park Road THAMES BANK, much extended for the Redcliffe Missionary Training College, has a symmetrical Tudor front to the river. Nos. 70–74, a jolly composition with turrets and crowstepped gables, are a speculation

of 1871 by a local architect, *D. S. Sergeant*. Further N, GROVE
PARK TERRACE. Here, Nos. 1–9 form a more urban mid Victorian terrace; Nos. 52–70 are a charming modest late Georgian
group which preceded the development of the estate; and
Nos. 80–94 (N of the railway) are four tall pairs of 1888, by this
time with fancifully Shavian detail *à la* Bedford Park. GROVE
PARK GARDENS, running back to the Grove Park Hotel, is
mostly of the 1890s, with BELFAIRS, 1898 by *W. Hearne*, brick
with half-timbering, as its centrepiece.

Back near the river in HARTINGTON ROAD some later contributions. The UNIVERSITY OF LONDON BOATHOUSE, 1936
by *Thompson & Walford*, is crisply modern in blue and white.
Further E is CHISWICK STAITHE by *Green, Lloyd & Son*,
1964–5, terraces alongside and near the Thames: gabled fronts,
a few bay-windows, and a little tile-hanging add a variety unusual
at this date. Just beyond is the POLYTECHNIC GRANDSTAND,
1936 by *Joseph Addison*, with concrete cantilevers and corner
windows, looking more dated now than the University Boathouse.

N of the railway line SUTTON COURT ROAD recalls the hamlet
around Sutton Court, with SUTTON COURT MANSIONS, 1906,
on the site of the old manor house. The C16 LITTLE SUTTON
COTTAGE in CEDARS ROAD is the only survival.* In BAR-
ROWGATE ROAD suburban housing of the 1880s onwards with
one grander house in the middle, GARTHOWEN, by *E. Monson*,
1900. The house opposite is by *Wimperis & East*, also 1900.
No. 114 is an early infill job by *R. Seifert*, 1946.‡

5. Strand on the Green

Between Grove Park and Kew Bridge is STRAND ON THE GREEN,
a riverside ribbon of the same period as Chiswick Mall, more
intimate because instead of a road there is only a pathway between
the houses and the water. It began as a fishing settlement, to
which some more elegant houses were added in the later C18.
The houses are on the whole more modest than those in the Mall,
chiefly cottages resolutely prettified. The area is still exceptionally attractive and admirably well cared for. From E to W,
No. 1, STRAND ON THE GREEN HOUSE, is one of the grander
houses, rebuilt in 1788, five windows wide, with central polygonal
bay of two storeys over a porch with Tuscan columns. Then
mostly cottages, including low almshouses (carefully rebuilt in
1933, restored in 1974), until No. 23 is reached, a refreshingly
bold and totally modern interloper of shuttered concrete and
glass, excellently detailed, by *Timothy Rendle*, 1966. Open-plan
interior with spiral concrete staircase. MAGNOLIA WHARF
(completed 1963), which follows, tries harder to be tactful. Then
Nos. 52–55, a tall, self-possessed early C19 group with pediment.
No. 62 etc. with shaped gables, of old brick, is a cosily picturesque

---

*The almshouses nearby were demolished in 1957.

‡I am indebted to James Wisdom for information on the suburban development of
Chiswick (see his Leicester M.A. Dissertation: 'The Making of a West London
Suburb: Housing in Chiswick 1861–1914' (1975–6) for further details.

contribution of 1930. The best group is Nos. 64–68: No. 64 is
early C 19 with two-storey upper windows; No. 65, ZOFFANY
HOUSE (the home of the painter from 1790 to 1810), is c. 1700
(segment-headed windows); and Nos. 68–69 (with later stucco)
are also early C 18. The fat E.E. railway bridge cuts oddly across
the lane and its houses.

CRANFORD

Cranford has been fragmented by new roads and consists of several
separate parts: the end of the High Street near the Bath Road,
the bleak area extending E of The Parkway towards Heston, and
the old church to the W in Cranford Park, which is within the
borough of Hillingdon (q.v.). The M4 passes over The Parkway
on a reinforced concrete viaduct of 1964 (*Sir Alexander Gibb &
Partners*).

The S end of the HIGH STREET is a straggling lane with little of
interest remaining apart from a small circular LOCK UP with
conical roof, an isolated reminder of village days, and one good
C 18 house set back from the road: No. 42. Two-storey centre of
five bays; lower wings. Red brick with yellow brick dressings.
Nice gatepiers with urns. Two indifferent recent churches cheek
by jowl:

HOLY ANGELS. 1970–1 by *Norman Haines Design Partnership*.
Brick with slit windows.

ST CHRISTOPHER (R.C.). 1969–71 by *Gerard Goalen*, a little
more enterprising. White brick with exposed concrete inside.
Polygonal worship area with adjoining hall separated by screens.

On the BATH ROAD the BERKELEY ARMS HOTEL, 1932 by *E. B.
Musman*, modest Scottish Baronial, with crowstepped gable and
turrets. Also (near WAYE AVENUE) offices by *Malcolm Hecks
Associates*, 1977, brick-faced, with a display of semicircular
windows on the upper floor.

E of The Parkway almost all is C 20. Facing one of Hounslow's large
estates of industrialized housing (1966–8), CRANFORD COM-
MUNITY SCHOOL by the *Borough Architect's Department* (*G. A.
Trevett*), 1972–6, an enterprising effort to provide some life for
this area, with its combination of school (for 1,440 pupils) with
public library, sports hall, pub, concert hall, etc. – one of the
first examples of its kind in Greater London. But, alas, it is all
packaged without imagination in two ultra-plain parallel ranges.
Small double-glazed windows (to cut out the horrific aircraft
noise). In CRANFORD LANE (towards Heston) the one bright
spot is LOVAT WALK, a charming almshouse group on three
sides round a courtyard, 1977 by *Edward Jones*. White façades
with echoes of the 1920s. Portholes, built-in window boxes, and
a continuous pergola for creepers are the memorable touches. In
CHURCH ROAD, now truncated by the motorway junction, one
old house, much altered.

WESTERN INTERNATIONAL MARKET in Southall Lane, 1970–4
by *W. & C. French (Construction) Ltd*, is a fruit and flower
market replacing Brentford Market. Two very long steel-framed

sheds with central link provide 170,000 sq. ft for sales and storage. Crisply detailed shallow-pitched roofs with deep overhanging eaves – a trim, functional vernacular, with a welcome lack of self-consciousness.

EAST BEDFONT

East Bedfont, although on the main London–Staines road, has been lucky in escaping the complete destruction of its former character. The road only skirts the spacious green, and the small church lies comfortably back from the traffic, screened by plenty of trees and partly hidden by two ancient yews. Old views show that these once formed part of a perfectly crazy outsized display of topiary (trimmed into large peacocks, with initials, and the date 1704).

ST MARY. Chiefly of the local orange-brown speckly gravelstone or ferricrete, with Reigate stone dressings (partly replaced by Bath stone in the C19). Evidence for an aisleless C12 building remains. In the N chancel and S nave walls Norman windows with deep internal splays. Norman S doorway of two continuous orders of chevron, the outer chevron at right angles to the wall, and combined with simple leaf decoration. The chancel was extended in the C15 (see the former gravelstone quoins on the N side) and a shapeless N transept of brick added in 1829. In 1865 a W extension to the nave, and a S porch with a pretty tower adjoining, replaced the former free-standing S tower. The upper part of the tower is recessed and of timber; the lower storey and the W extension are of gravelstone (presumably re-used), blending well with the rest of the building. Inside, several remarkable features. The chancel arch is mid C12 (the only surviving example in the former county of Middlesex): chevron on both arch and jamb, imposts but no capitals. To its N a remarkable pair of C13 recesses, with pointed arches, uncovered in 1865, one in the N wall of the nave, one around the corner in the E wall. In the recesses are two WALL PAINTINGS of the mid C13, representing the Last Judgement (Christ in Glory surrounded by angels, in a quatrefoil frame, the Resurrection of the Dead below) and the Crucifixion. Both paintings are in red line on red background. There is nothing else in Middlesex to emulate them – they are no doubt Westminster work. Both nave and chancel roofs are C15, crown-posts with four-way struts in the chancel, two-way struts in the nave. The N transept was given Victorian propriety by a N arcade but still has its pre-ecclesiological gallery painted with texts of the Ten Commandments. – Small Flemish wooden RELIEF of the Crucifixion, c. 1530. – STAINED GLASS. Chancel N: later C15 flowered quarries. – W window: roundels with the Works of Mercy, 1893, good. – MONUMENTS. An unusual one in the chancel (W wall): a wooden panel darkly painted with a coat of arms to record W. Weldish † 1640. – Brass to Matthew Page † 1631. Two figures. – Jane Smith † 1806. Marble on coloured background, by *Tomlinson* of Uxbridge. – MEETING HALL of 1954 attached to the N transept.

In the neighbourhood of the church are a few older buildings, although much has been demolished.* BURLINGTON HOUSE, facing the green to the E of the church, is a handsome brick house built in 1791 for William Reed. Five bays and two storeys with mansarded roof of old tiles.

In BEDFONT ROAD, DAVID HENRY WARING COURT (old people's home), a plain C19 house standing in its own grounds, remarkable for its charming Edwardian one-storey library extensions of 1905 by *Edward Paine* for D. H. Rheinerwaring. Barge-boarded veranda around a polygonal bay-window with art nouveau leaded glass. Interior with barrel-vaulted ceiling and original bookcases. Opposite, bleakly surrounded by housing of the 1980s, FAWNS MANOR. An unappealing exterior, doused in cream paint, hides remnants of a C15–16 timber-framed main range and cross-wing. The old work was much disguised by alterations in 1889 by an eccentric owner, *William Sherborn*, a surveyor who was in partnership with *Joseph Tall*. His additions include a S entrance wing which contains a vault of Tall's patent concrete. In the main range the hall has quarter-round chamfered beams. Now divided into flats.

PATES, Hatton Road. A well preserved timber-framed building with many features of high quality uncovered in 1964–6. They suggest that this small house enjoyed considerable status from the C15 to the C17. The manor belonged to Christ's Hospital from 1623, but the house was leased to tenant farmers. The house consists of a hall facing W, and a S wing; a N service wing may have disappeared. The two-bay hall is perhaps of *c.* 1500, later subdivided. Its exposed N gable has a pretty arrangement of curved braces, lower and upper king-struts and queen-struts – a pattern imitated in the prominent jettied gable to the S wing. Below this, two posts frame the space for a former bay-window. The flank wall of the S wing has a high brick plinth and a handsome stack, suggesting an early C16 date for this part. But the lower back of the S wing may have started life as a free-standing storeyed building. Later alterations to the hall range include the prominent front brick stack, and the position of the entrance, probably originally further N. Inside the hall, massive slots for braces, window mullions, and internal sliding shutters confirm that the S wall of the hall was once external. The roof has wind-braces supporting the purlins; the lack of smoke-blackening implies that the chimney on the back wall was original. On the first floor at the NW end two small blocked two-light ovolo-moulded windows, dating from the flooring over of the hall. In the S wing a stone fireplace with four-centred arch on each floor, the upper room or great chamber with late C16 panelling, the lower room plain. Ovolo-moulded window next to the fireplace. The E end of this room is divided off for a later staircase hall; the staircase itself is within a truncated bay of the earlier back part of the S range (see the cut-off purlins). The roof over this is similar to the hall roof. In the S wall of the upper room a small

*Among the lost buildings are Bedfont Lodge, built in imitation of Asgill House, Richmond (Ri), by the miniature painter George Enghelheart (demolished 1961), and the White House, late C18 (demolished *c.* 1957).

but elaborate inserted c 17 transomed oriel with tiny side-lights, resting on scrolly brackets.

BENNETTS FARM (No. 735 Staines Road) demonstrates the abandonment of the Middlesex timber-framed tradition. It is of brick, built in 1700 as a farmhouse for the Hatchett family, as is known from a series of dated and initialled bricks. Transitional plan: facing the farmyard at the side, two rooms with lobby entrance in between; facing the road, the main entrance leading into a hall between one of these rooms and a further room, making the plan a primitive kind of double pile (cf. the houses of The Butts, Brentford, Ho).

FAIRHOLME ESTATE in Staines Road was built in 1934 by *T. Cecil Howitt* as low-rental housing from a bequest by Elizabeth Jones, a Fulham resident. A formal layout around a large quadrangle: seventy-two one- and two-storeyed brick houses with an attractive variety of Dutch gables and tile-hung walls. The houses are in groups; in the linking ranges are large semicircular arches which function as porches and provide access to the gardens. At the corners are angled groups, in the manner of Parker & Unwin. Opposite the entrance a community hall with colonnaded centre and clock tower; panelled hall, with decorative plaster barrel-vault in early c 17 style. The Arts and Crafts tradition is evident also in the pretty half-timbered shelter with carved bargeboards that forms the centrepiece of the quadrangle. Carved sundial at the entrance. All in immaculate condition.

FAIRHOLME JUNIOR AND INFANT SCHOOLS, Peacock Avenue, s of Staines Road. 1952 by the *Middlesex County Council* (*C. G. Stillman*), a good example of how the best post-war primary schools were handled with sensitivity and originality compared with the routine productions of the 1930s. This effort of the Festival period has a rectangular hall for the juniors and a circular hall for the infants, both with shallow curved copper roofs with knobs. By the junior hall a wall of patterned concrete blocks.

BEDFONT LAKES, Bedfont Road. A business park developed from 1990, to an interesting master plan by *Michael Hopkins Associates*. Phase one, NEW SQUARE, is a formal layout around a double square with concentric circles of parking, the steel and glass buildings around the s part by *Hopkins* for IBM, the N ones a speculative group designed by *Edward Cullinan* in a contrasting idiom, with white cladding above brick, and shallow pitched roofs.

HATTON was a hamlet to the N of East Bedfont. It is now a miserably noisy wasteland on the borders of Heathrow.

ST MARY, Hatton Road. A timber-framed building converted to a mission church. Three bays of a typical c 17 Middlesex roof visible: queen-struts, straight wind-braces to one tier of clasped purlins. Lower walls encased in red brick; c 19 w additions.

HATTON CROSS STATION. 1975 by the *L.T. Architect's Department*. Glass box with roof-lit foyer and pretentious but apparently purposeless porte cochère.

In HATTON ROAD a few c 18 or earlier cottages. GREVILLE HOUSE, further s, is the former national school and school-teacher's house, 1847, a pretty Tudor design in diapered brick with a large three-light window in the r. gable. Tactful office extensions behind of 1985. Nearby, BEDFONT COMMUNITY CENTRE in a former pebbledashed school building of 1906. In GREEN MAN LANE, the GREEN MAN, a country inn from the late c 18.

N of Staines Road, in a wood on the W bank of the river Crane, were the BEDFONT POWDER MILLS, active from the C 17, closed in 1926. A network of leats and waterwheel pits remains, together with edge-runners, millstones, and machine foundations.

FELTHAM

Feltham – the dull SW part of the borough, beyond Hounslow Heath, S of the Staines Road – consists of Upper and Lower Feltham, with the High Street running between the two. Upper Feltham, which developed around the railway (1848), is now almost entirely later c 20. Lower Feltham, further S, has the old parish church and a few remnants of the old village. Beyond, the suburbs peter out among scruffy fields and gravel workings.

ST DUNSTAN, Lower Feltham. The medieval church was rebuilt in 1802 by *William Walker*. Brick with round-headed windows and deep eaves, and a low battlemented tower with later shingled spire. Aisles were added and the windows normanized in 1855–6. Inside, original pleasant wooden W gallery on Roman Doric columns with elaborate commemorative inscriptions, all in a handsome flowing script. The box pews of 1802, panelling, and reredos were removed in the 1950s (destroyed by rot and deathwatch beetle). The ceiling is flat, the E end has a Venetian window. – STAINED GLASS. C 19. The E window and the S aisle E are the most notable. – Churchyard with high brick walls.

ST LAWRENCE (R.C.), The Green. Pinched brick Romanesque of 1933–4 by *T.H.B. Scott*, extended with transept in 1936–40, reordered in 1972 (baptistery converted to Lady Chapel) by *Broadbent, Hastings, Reid & Todd*. – (STAINED GLASS by *John Trinick*, SCULPTURE by *P. Lindsey Clark*.)

FELTHAM COMMUNITY SCHOOL, Browells Lane. The recent parts of 1984 by the *London Borough of Hounslow* are a good example of the more appealing image adopted for large schools in the 1980s. Well detailed ranges of red brick; pantiled roofs with deep eaves. The library, projecting to the l. of the entrance, is distinguished by large semicircular-headed dormers.

YOUTH CUSTODY CENTRE, Bedfont Road. On the site of the Middlesex Industrial Schools of 1857–9 by *Banks & Barry*, of which nothing remains but the plinth walls of the cruciform chapel, incorporated in the garden landscaping. The new buildings are by *Brewer, Smith & Brewer*, 1976–88. The informal design, intended to reflect a progressive programme of custodial treatment, consists of triangular-shaped house blocks for a population of c. 850, with classrooms, sports halls, etc. Brick walls, shingled roofs. Of the STAINED GLASS from the former chapel the S transept window of five lights (Prodigal Son and Acts of

Mercy), 1873 by *O'Connor*, is now partly at St Mary Dundee
and partly at the Stained Glass Museum in Ely. Some of the
other windows (which included two with St Peter and St Paul,
also by *O'Connor*, and six windows by *Mayer* of Munich, 1857–
91) have been re-used in the new buildings.

LONGFORD SCHOOL, Tachbrook Road. 1936 by *Curtis* and *Burchett* of the *M.C.C.*, a secondary school on a courtyard plan with
tower facing the approach road.

At Lower Feltham the best building is the VICARAGE next to the
church, C 17, with a late C 18 four-window front. To the N, along
the curve of ST DUNSTAN'S ROAD, traces of the old village:
a timber-framed building, No. 8 with an early C 19 pilastered
doorcase, and a few cottages, indifferently treated. Up the HIGH
STREET little to note until No. 51, offices by *Malcolm Hecks
Associates*, 1978, red brick, with the eye-catching motif of neatly
turned inverted arches. Then THE GREEN, with the RED LION
INN at the corner, C 18 brick with additions, and on the far side,
overlooking the pond, a row of low early C 19 houses and a
glimpse of Feltham House (*see* below) from Browells Lane.

After this C 20 Feltham begins in earnest with PHILIP MORRIS
HOUSE, 1980–2 by *Trehearne & Norman, Preston & Partners*,
bulky dark brick, made a little less abrupt in typical later C 20
manner by a slightly mansarded top storey and splayed plinth.
Then NEW CHAPEL SQUARE, 1976 by *Manning Clamp &
Partners*, a compact group of flats in a hot red brick, somewhat
in the Darbourne & Darke Lillington Gardens tradition. Four
to five storeys around a raised pedestrian square. Opposite, a
SHOPPING PRECINCT and curtain-walled slab of offices of
earlier vintage, 1961–4 by *R. Seifert & Partners*, the entrance to
the precinct marked by the familiar Seifert mannerism of angled
piloti. At the corner of Hanworth Road the one notable landmark,
ST CATHERINE'S; the tower of the C 19 church of St Catherine,
incorporated into offices by *Biscoe & Stanton*, 1979–81. The
church was of 1878–80 by *Carpenter & Ingelow*. The tower,
added in 1898, has a spire which rises rather fussily from an
octagonal drum, behind corner pinnacles. On the S side the
transition from the stone-faced tower to the modern materials
behind is handled quite skilfully by a series of stepped-out projections; the aluminium windows inserted in the W entrance are
less happy. To the E in HANWORTH ROAD former SCHOOLS,
low and gabled; opposite, a pleasant open area with a pond.
Beyond are GOVERNMENT OFFICES, a quiet two-storeyed
building of the 1970s in re-used stock brick, the windows recessed
in arches, which has the merit of partially masking the mediocre
slab-and-podium block of ASTRONAUT HOUSE beyond the
railway line. NW up BEDFONT LANE, the usual contrasts in
council housing: HIGHFIELDS, uninspired slabs of the 1960s,
and less demonstratively municipal yellow brick terraces of the
1970s around SOUTHERN AVENUE.

At NORTH FELTHAM, in HARLINGTON ROAD WEST, STABLES
to Feltham Lodge, *c.* 1800; five bays with central pediment.
Between STAINES ROAD and the Duke of Northumberland's
River, a few villas remain from a mid Victorian suburb. Further
N the NATIONAL MARITIME INSTITUTE, which includes a

ship-towing tank (No. 3) 400 metres long, of reinforced concrete, built in 1959. Boiler house chimney cum water-tower in sculptured reinforced concrete with observation gallery.

FELTHAM HOUSE, approached from Elmwood Avenue, s of Lower Feltham, is an interesting although horribly mutilated building, probably of the mid c 18, when it was owned by the Villebois family. In the mid c 19 it was a private school run by A. F. Westmacott, a son of the sculptor Richard Westmacott; since 1914 it has been an army depot. Red brick; three storeys above basements. w entrance front of 2–3–2 bays, the centre a full-height central bay. The garden front, partly obscured by additions, has two projecting wings with Venetian windows. The central room on this side is divided by Corinthian columns and has two mid c 18 carved wooden chimneypieces; good modillioned cornice and Vitruvian-scroll chair rail. The s wing is now a kitchen and of no interest, but the tall NE room has late c 18 cornices and a plaster wall medallion with a classical figure, somewhat in the manner of Wyatt. The marble fireplace below it has been removed. On the w side of the house a handsome staircase with wrought-iron balustrade curving round an apse; plaster frieze with lyres and rams' heads.

GUNNERSBURY PARK

The park lies between Brentford and Ealing. The vanished mansion built *c.* 1658–63 for Sir John Maynard by *John Webb* lay between the two present houses (*see* p. 33). It was one of the very few c 17 examples of a compact Palladian villa with a pedimented first-floor loggia, a design reminiscent of Jones's Prince's Lodging at Newmarket. From 1762 to 1786 it was the summer residence of Princess Amelia, George III's aunt, who improved the grounds and added many ornamental garden buildings. When the house was demolished in 1800 and the estate sold for building, most of the land was bought by *Alexander Copland*, a partner in Henry Holland's building firm. By 1802 he had built for himself, probably to his own design, a house (now incorporated in the present 'Large Mansion', i.e. Gunnersbury Park) which was bought in 1835 by Nathan Mayer Rothschild († 1836) and substantially remodelled and extended for him by *Sydney Smirke*. The smaller house to the E (Gunnersbury House, now called the 'Small Mansion') was completed by 1805 on a separate building plot and occupied from 1807 to 1828 by Major Alexander Morison, a retired East India Company officer, and from 1828 to 1889 by the Farmer family, for whom additions were made *c.* 1837–44 by *W. F. Pocock* and in the 1850s by *W. W. Pocock*. In 1889 the house was sold to the Rothschilds, who used it for their guests. After 1917 the estate was split up; the houses and 186 acres were acquired by the local authorities (boroughs of Acton, Ealing, and later Brentford and Chiswick; now Ealing and Hounslow) and the grounds were opened as a public park in 1926.

The LARGE MANSION, now partly used as a local museum, is

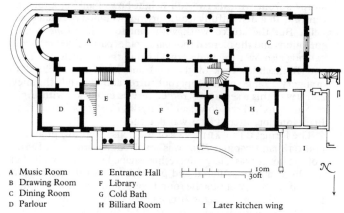

A Music Room   E Entrance Hall
B Drawing Room   F Library
C Dining Room   G Cold Bath
D Parlour   H Billiard Room   I Later kitchen wing

Gunnersbury Park, Large Mansion
as altered by Sydney Smirke in 1835, plan

essentially *Sydney Smirke*'s creation of 1835. Copland's house
probably occupied the SE part of the present building. Smirke
added a NE parlour and a SW dining room (cellars with cast-iron
columns) and encased all in a handsome and regular stucco
exterior. The garden front has a three-storey centre with tall
arched first-floor windows above a ground-floor Doric loggia.
To the E is a bow-window surrounded by a conservatory. The
entrance front has a porch with paired Doric columns, all very
restrained. But the interiors are an early essay in the heavy
and sumptuous French-inspired neo-classical style that Smirke
developed for his later London clubs. On the N side a large
staircase hall, the stair with gilded balustrade rising from behind
two stone pillars. Lavish cornice below a coved ceiling. The
main reception rooms form an impressive suite on the S side,
approached awkwardly through a roof-lit corridor with balustraded gallery (the odd plan must reflect the legacy of
Copland's house). The music room and drawing room, separated
by a little lobby, with dining room further E, are all embellished
in an ornate neo-classical style, with scagliola columns and rich
door surrounds and cornices. The hefty carved fireplace in the
music room, with iron and glass inner fire surround, must be a
late Victorian addition; the lushly naturalistic ceiling rinceaux in
music room and dining room are also perhaps later enrichments.
The central drawing room has a ceiling lower than the end
rooms, prettily decorated with a trellis pattern and an oval ceiling
painting of c. 1836 by *E. T. Parris*. W of the entrance hall the
former library, now plain apart from an eccentric fireplace with
early C19 tapering claw-footed columns. The adjoining rooms,
according to the plan with 'cold bath' and billiard room, have
been altered. Further W, Smirke's service wing, extended in the
later C19; well preserved late Victorian kitchen.

The SMALL MANSION has been much extended from its original state. To the N, the curved porch with half-fluted Doric
columns is perhaps of 1806, as is the main part of the low two-

storey s front with its two full-height bows flanking a four-bay centre with a delightfully exotic oriental veranda decorated with bells. But the stucco work with fanciful *dixhuitième* window surrounds and the pierced roof balustrade (partly filled in), which extends also over the orangery added to the w, must be Farmer and Rothschild work of the mid and later C19. Behind the orangery a range with pepperpot turret and very tall chimneys, and N w of this a separately roofed service extension with triplets of round arched windows, added by *W. F. Pocock* in the 1850s. Plain interior, altered after war damage.

The formal C17 GARDENS s of the house were swept away by mid C18 landscaping. *Kent* was involved, according to Lysons. s of the house was a large horseshoe-shaped pond (now filled in). To the w a large coffered and pedimented ARCHWAY remains, perhaps C18. N w of this the round pond, and beside it a TEMPLE from the time of Princess Amelia, probably built in the 1760s. Red brick, with wooden pedimented front with four Doric columns and frieze with bucrania. Three classical reliefs inside. The interior formerly of two storeys, altered in the early C19. By the site of the horseshoe pond is *Smirke*'s lofty ORANGERY (repaired after long neglect in 1989), with a glazed roof, and front with a central bow with engaged columns. Further E, close to Gunnersbury Avenue, *Smirke*'s STABLES, two ranges at right angles, the E one a formal composition with channelled stucco ground floor, lunette windows, and the Rothschild arms grandly set over central archway, the N one, with coach house and bell-turret, an earlier building encased and enlarged. Nearby, remains of JAPANESE GARDENS made by the Rothschilds *c.* 1900, and relics of picturesque Roman-cemented Gothic ruins erected by *W. F.* and *W. W. Pocock* to screen the Rothschild stables from the Small Mansion. Closer to the latter, another C19 Gothic complex which encases a rubble flint structure containing a sunken BATH (probably of the early C19). In the sw corner of the park the POTOMAC LAKE created from a flooded claypit by Lionel Rothschild *c.* 1861, with Gothic folly-boathouse, an octagonal Gothic tower probably converted from a pottery kiln.

LODGES. E lodge with Greek Doric portico (a derelict shell); N lodge, also with Doric portico by *Smirke*, next to impressive iron gates.

HANWORTH

Hanworth has lost its old centre. Its few good buildings are scattered around the edge of Hanworth Park, a reminder of the hunting lodge frequented by Henry VIII.

ALL SAINTS, Uxbridge Road. By *N. F. Cachemaille-Day*, planned in 1951, built in two stages. An unusual design for its date. Austere blocky exterior of pale brick: a long, low forechurch with Lady Chapel and baptistery (1951–2), a circular lantern rising above the taller cube of the main building (1957). Corner porches and vestries around a very shallow Greek cross, with a broad apse instead of an E arm. No historicist details, but the rectangles

softened by the generous semicircle of the apse, echoed by the N
and S arches, and by the dominating free-standing concrete arcs
which intersect below the lantern and carry the post which supports the external cross. Walls of exposed brick, apart from the
apse, which has a flickering repeated pattern of angels' heads on
gold leaf (from a design by *Christopher Webb*). The choir stalls,
at first planned for the W end, were later set in a sunken area
further E (now filled in), to avoid impeding the view of the altar. –
ALTAR on four plain concrete columns. – FONT also of concrete,
but more conventionally decorated with reliefs of the Seven
Sacraments, to designs by *Cachemaille-Day*. – FONT COVER.
Blue-edged openwork canopy around a painted wooden kneeling
figure of the Virgin, which is Italian of *c.* 1500. – STAINED GLASS
in the Lady Chapel with sand-blasted backgrounds; figural
designs by *Goddard & Gibbs*. – SCULPTURE. Lamb of God over
the W door by *Bainbridge Copnall*.

ST GEORGE, Castle Way. Attractively sited on the SW side of the
park. The medieval church was replaced in 1812 by a small
building by *James Wyatt* of which only N and S walls remain,
overlaid by a rebuilding of 1865 by *S. S. Teulon*, paid for by
Algernon Perkins of Hanworth Park House. Teulon added the
apsidal chancel and sturdy NE tower with broached spire. Only
a few of his roguish touches are evident: the polygonal vestry
cutting into the tower buttressing, the NE pinnacle, and the
Gothic canopy to the clock face. Inside, a hammerbeam roof and
a Teulon reredos. – STAINED GLASS, N transept. Two late C13
angels surrounded by early C17 quarries with flowers.

ST RICHARD OF CHICHESTER, Forge Lane, S of the motorway.
1964–5 by *Leslie Channing*. Prominent gables and central spire. –
One STAINED GLASS window with the life of St Richard by *A.
Stafford*.

HANWORTH HOUSE, Castle Way. Immediately S of the medieval
church was the hunting lodge acquired by Henry VII, which
Camden described as Henry VIII's 'chief place of pleasure'.
Henry gave it to Anne Boleyn and then to Katharine Parr. It
later passed through a series of aristocratic owners – the widow
of the Protector Somerset, Sir William Killigrew, Sir Francis
Cottingham, Sir Thomas Chambers, and finally Aubrey Vere
Beauclerk, second Baron Hanworth – before being destroyed by
fire in 1797. A new house built *c.* 1800 was demolished after a
sale in 1873. The indifferent late C19 TUDOR HOUSE built on
part of the site was converted into flats in the 1920s. Close to the
road TUDOR COURT, the former stables, which survived the
fire of 1797. Designed *c.* 1750 for Aubrey Vere Beauclerk by
Sanderson Miller, they consist of a two-storey L-shaped brick
block of symmetrical design, with battlemented corner towers
and Gothic windows. They too were converted to flats *c.* 1924.
Behind is a weatherboarded granary on staddle stones. In the
gardens remains of large Tudor walls and fireplaces, probably
the royal kitchens. Red brick walls in English bond near the
church are the only other relics of the Tudor hunting lodge,
which C18 drawings show to have been a rambling group of
buildings with a long timber-framed wing. Of the Tudor period,
although not original to Hanworth, are the two terracotta

MEDALLIONS with heads, comparable to those at Hampton Court, re-erected on later C19 garden buildings at the entrance to the drive to Tudor House. Acquired by Aubrey Vere Beauclerk in 1759, they are supposed to come from the Holbein Gate, Whitehall, and were perhaps intended to match other Tudor decoration recorded in the accounts of 1529–38 which refer to the 'new painting and gilding of certain antique heads brought from Greenwich to Hanworth'.

HANWORTH PARK HOUSE (old people's home), in the middle of the park. An odd but very attractive house, probably built soon after 1828, when the estate was acquired by Henry Perkins, a brewer. A shallow E-plan with a long frontage of 2–2–3–2–2 bays, stock brick, two storeys above a tall basement. Portico with four Greek Doric columns approached up a grand flight of steps. Along the whole of the front, and continuing above the portico, two-storey cast-iron verandas of graceful form have been added. The centre pediment to the house has incongruous (and perhaps later) decorative bargeboards; the end bays have hipped roofs. Later extensions behind, those on the w side added c. 1860 for the Perkins family, a white brick block with groups of narrow arched windows, ending in a campanile cum clock-tower with aediculed belfry windows. Much altered inside. Toplit staircase behind the entrance hall, with cast-iron balustrades. Remains of some good earlier C19 cornices in the upstairs rooms; a lofty ballroom with elaborate plasterwork in the 1860 addition. Some of the interiors may date from 1935, when the house was used as a club for the London Air Park, which was in existence from 1929 to the Second World War, the successor to J. A. Whitehead's private aerodrome opened in 1917. The grounds and former aerodrome were bought by the U.D.C in 1956 and opened as a public park in 1959.

There is little else earlier than the C20 to see in Hanworth, as the centre of the old village to the s of Hanworth Park was bulldozed in 1973 for the feeder road to the M3. To the E of the park, down a drive off PARK ROAD, the former RECTORY, 1808 by *James Wyatt*, altered by *Teulon* in 1865. Five windows wide, with Greek Doric porch. Off Hampton Road West, BUTTS COTTAGES remain from the Hanworth Farms and Factories, an extensive enterprise begun in 1891 by William Whiteley to provide fresh produce for his Bayswater store. They consist of a symmetrical terrace of small but superior dwellings (bay-windows and coloured bricks). At the end a former chapel. There were also dormitories and messrooms for fruit pickers, and other dwellings (the population was over 400). Much of the farmland was built over after 1933 by New Ideal Homesteads; the farm buildings were replaced from 1976 by lumpy corrugated-clad factories.

KEMPTON PARK WATERWORKS, Country Way (A316). Begun by the New River Company (Act of 1897) and opened by the Metropolitan Water Board in 1908 to supply the expanding northern suburbs (via a trunk route to Cricklewood and Fortis Green). Fed by an open channel from an intake and reservoir at Staines. The *pièces de résistance* are the two 1008 h.p. triple-expansion steam engines by *Worthington Simpson Ltd*, in an engine house of 1925–9. They are among the world's largest, standing 19 metres (62 ft) high from the bases of the pumps to the tops of the cylinders. Adjacent is the single-storey engine house of 1905 by *W. B. Bryan*, the round-arched waterworks style acquiring Baroque appendages. Matched pair of chimneys, of 1905 and 1929. PRIMARY FILTER HOUSE of 1929 by *H. E. Stilgoe*, of reinforced concrete, with a plain, elegantly proportioned tower.

HESTON

ST LEONARD, Heston Road. The pivoting LYCHGATE and charming timber W porch (reconstructed from old materials), with four-centred arches, carved wooden spandrels, and wavy bargeboards, complement a handsome late Perp W tower, one of the best of the Middlesex type. SE turret, diagonal buttresses, and small trefoiled windows. Tall belfry windows with transoms (cf. Isleworth, Ho). The W door is also genuine late medieval, with a moulded and crenellated centre rail, within a Perp doorway with a square label. To the side of this a recess for a stoup with its own small matching label, a delightful and unusual detail. Alas, despite protests, the rest of the medieval church was entirely rebuilt in 1863–6 by *T. Bellamy* ('such an act of vandalism as our age has seldom seen'; *Ecclesiologist*, 1865).* Bellamy's three E gables with Dec windows make a striking group, but his interior is disappointingly mechanical. Bath stone, alternating piers, no clerestory, outer N aisle. E end reordered 1969, with simple slatted wood pulpit and reading desk. – FONT COVER. A gem of *c*. 1500, repaired in 1908 (when *William Weir* was involved in restoration work). Octagonal, oak, of cupola shape, with a finial; flowing blind tracery in the panels. Formerly taller. – STAINED GLASS. Much C19 and C20 work. Especially good of their type: S chapel S, Nativity by *Kempe*, 1899, and Marys at the Sepulchre, 1894 by *Heaton, Butler & Bayne*, a lively rendering. – In the N aisle, two by *Rosemary K. Smith Marriot*, 1938 and 1940, in vivid colours, heavily leaded. – Several others by *R. J. Newbery*, of 1892 etc. – BRASS. M. Bownall † 1581 and wife, with a woman in bed, an angel, and a figure of Christ above. – MONUMENTS. A large collection. Henry Collins † 1765. Tablet with well carved putto heads, skull and cartouche. – Anne Lovibond † 1710. Cartouche with putto heads. – William James † 1727. Very large, with open pediment, Corinthian pilasters, and gadrooned base. – Samuel Child † 1752. Large, obelisks and urns. – Walter Cary † 1752, signed by *William Atkinson*. Boldly handled, with cartouche, wreath, and large lettering. – Lord George Bentinck † 1759. Restrained architectural composition of coloured marbles with trophies below. – Robert Child (q.v., Osterley Park, Ho) † 1782. An excellent composition signed by *Robert Adam* and *P. M. van Gelder* (the two also worked together at Warkton, Northants). Above a very Grecian sarcophagus in relief stands a chaste urn against the usual pyramid or obelisk. Two woeful

*The old church had aisles of the C13 and C14, probably added to an older building.

putti are draping the urn; further out are two exquisitely designed candelabra. – John Hudeeston Watson, drowned aged sixteen in 1827. His sorrowing parents by an urn, on a Grecian stele, with a quotation from Lycidas. Signed by *Thomas Denman*, who completed this unfinished work by his brother-in-law, *Flaxman*. – CHURCHYARD. Extensive; several early C19 tomb-chests.

OUR LADY QUEEN OF THE APOSTLES (R.C.), The Green, Heston Road. 1964 by *Burles, Newton & Partners*. Modernized Early Christian. Brick with a campanile with a spike, and a plain W front with recessed narthex. The interior more interesting: the aisles with shallow transverse barrel-vaults on columns; restrained lighting. Polygonal Lady Chapel with coloured abstract glass.

INFANTS' SCHOOL, Heston Road. 1861. Quite picturesque poly-chrome brick, Gothic, with lancets in triples, a projecting wing with tracery, and a little bell-turret.

Heston, familiar to most travellers only as a service station on the M4, began as a hamlet within the parish of Isleworth; by the C16 it had developed into a large parish including Sutton, Lampton (*see* Hounslow, Ho), Wyke, and Osterley Park (q.v.). The old centre, between the M4 and the Great West Road, is now nondescript, much rebuilt and expanded between the wars, with a few older buildings near the church: CHURCH HALL of 1880 with neat extensions of the 1970s; VICARAGE (No. 147) of 1780 with early C19 additions: a nice tented porch and a bow-window to the garden. In UPPER SUTTON LANE the one reminder of the old hamlet is No. 17, L-shaped, roughcast and thatched, with an early C19 cottage orné N front of three bays with ogee-headed upper windows.

At NORTH HYDE a settlement developed around the Grand Junction Canal, where the old powder magazine and docks have been filled in. Now all is council housing of pre- and post-war date, and fragmented by the motorway.

HESTON AIR PARK existed from 1929 to 1947 to the N of Cranford Lane. Of the original buildings, some of the earliest of their kind, only one large curved reinforced concrete hangar remains, designed and constructed in 1929 by *Jackson & Son* of Slough. It was used for private planes. A single broad sliding door on the end. The clubhouse and control tower of 1929 by *L. M. Austin* and *H. F. Murrell* were demolished in 1978. On part of the site, BRITISH EUROPEAN AIRWAYS TRAINING CENTRE, 1961 by *R. S. Harvey* (staff architect), a progressive design for its date, especially the well detailed teaching block, with three-storey curtain-walled upper part poised on columns.

HOUNSLOW

INTRODUCTION

Nobody can say that the High Street of Hounslow possesses much character. The straggly shopping street, with rebuilding of the

1960s onwards at either end, originated as a humble settlement along the road out of London, the last stop for coaches before the main roads to the s w and w (Staines Road and Bath Road) diverged across the desolate Hounslow Heath. Hounslow lay on the edges of Heston and Isleworth parishes (cf. Brentford); the church in the High Street became parochial only from 1856. It is the successor to a Commissioners' building of 1828 (by *H. Mawley*) which replaced the chapel of a medieval Trinitarian friary founded in the early c 13. Lampton was an early hamlet to the N; Victorian suburbs with their own churches developed w along the Bath Road and s w along Hanworth Road.

CHURCHES

HOLY TRINITY, High Street. 1961 by *W. E. Cross*. The previous church was destroyed by arson in 1943 (cf. Isleworth, Ho). The replacement is a depressing affair externally, approached beneath a gaunt free-standing concrete tower in the shape of an obelisk. Foyer with folding doors to the church. Long, cool, subaqueous interior, with pale blue glass in slit windows and crisscrossing concrete ribs. Lady Chapel and crypts beneath. – SCULPTURE of the Holy Trinity by *Wilfred Dudeny*, fibreglass. – Engraved glass SCREEN in the Lady Chapel, by *Anna Zinkeisen*. – The surviving MONUMENTS from the previous church are tucked away. Beside the stairs to the crypt, Whitelocke Bulstrode (owner of the house on the site of the medieval friary) † 1724. Bust with weeping putti. – In the crypt, the Windsor monument: two small kneeling figures of a man in armour and his wife, opposite each other in a moulded frame, with broken pediment. Possibly only part of one of the monuments ordered in the will of Andrew Lord Windsor in 1543. The date is early for this type of monument, which became so popular later. The quality is remarkably good.

ST PAUL, Bath Road. 1873–4 by *Habershon & Pite*. Given some character by a s w tower and spire. Large Dec windows to nave, transept, and chancel; clerestory with trefoils and quatrefoils. – (Much STAINED GLASS, including two in the N aisle by *Alan Younger*, 1967 (Christ the Carpenter) and 1971 (Harvest), in a semi-abstract style.)

ST STEPHEN, St Stephen's Road. 1875–6 by *Ewan Christian*, a substantial red brick building in the manner of Brooks, with lancet windows, and apses to chancel, vestry, and w baptistery. s w tower added by *N. F. Cachemaille-Day*, 1935, all of brick, an austere and powerful design relieved only by a row of lancet belfry windows and a multi-ordered, sharply pointed s doorway. – (Mosaic REREDOS. – FONT of alabaster and coloured marbles, c. 1914.)

ST MICHAEL AND ST MARTIN (R.C.), Bath Road. 1928–9; neo-Romanesque.

EVANGELICAL CHURCH, Hanworth Road. 1985 by *Brian Hubble & Partners*. A polygonal plan for an awkward island site. Of brick, with sweeping angular roofs and recessed windows.

METHODIST CHURCH, Bell Road. 1879. A busy stuccoed front

with channelled pilasters and pediment. Well preserved galleried interior with original fittings.

UNITED REFORMED CHURCH (formerly Congregational), Hanworth Road. 1835, enlarged in 1865. Pedimented box with projecting flat bays with triple windows. Manse attached at the E end. Schoolrooms replaced by meeting rooms, 1987.

PUBLIC BUILDINGS

CIVIC CENTRE, Lampton Road. By *G. A. Trevett*, borough architect, planned in 1965, completed in 1975. On the edge of Lampton Park, with a carefully planned approach between a Victorian mansion and a delightful Regency house, The Lawn (*see* Perambulation). Large but neatly detailed red brick car park in the foreground. The main building, also long and low, is faced with red brick and vertical stone panels. The central reception area, with split-level interior, links four pavilions, one housing the council chamber, which is expressed externally by a brick drum rising through the roof. A few drum staircases are the only other adornments. The straightforward modern style, achieved here with an elegance lacking in some of Hounslow's cheaper developments, is characteristic of the work of the first decade of the borough's architect's department.

HEATHLANDS SCHOOL, Wellington Road South. 1972 by the *Borough of Hounslow Architect's Department* (*G. A. Trevett*), a compact fortress for 1,440 pupils. Prominent staircase towers with angled roofs. The central four-storey core has the hall with library, year bases, and specialist departments above; linked to this are three single-storey wings arranged around internal courtyards.

HOUNSLOW MANOR SCHOOL, Prince Regent Road. Large additions in exposed concrete of 1975 by *Scherrer & Hicks*.

GIRLS' SCHOOL, School Road. *See* Perambulation.

HOUNSLOW WEST STATION, Bath Road. 1931, one of the earlier Piccadilly line extension stations built under *Charles Holden*. Stone-faced, with polygonal entrance hall.

PERAMBULATION

The perambulation runs roughly anticlockwise from the SW, starting at the junction at the W end of the High Street, the nearest approach to a town centre, where NEAL'S CORNER, 1902 by *W. A. Davies*, tall, terracotta-trimmed, with an onion-dome turret, bravely holds its own against the faceless later C20 office blocks spreading down Staines Road to the SW and Lampton Road to the N. In STAINES ROAD the most prominent is TRINITY SQUARE on the N side, 1987–8 by *Renton, Howard, Wood, Levin Partnership* – two white slabs sliced by a greenhouse roof over entrance and staircases. E along the narrow HIGH STREET plain later C19 terraces remain, with the church set back on the N side. To the S, mostly concealed behind C19 frontages, is the vast TREATY CENTRE, 1984–7 by *Fitzroy Robinson Part-*

nership, for Hounslow and Taylor Woodrow Properties: a package of shopping, library, and advice centre. The covered shopping precinct is approached down a mall filling up the former Treaty Road. In the centre a galleried atrium with elaborately trussed glazed roof. At the back, the exterior is of red brick with set-back pitched roofs. A covered arcade and some blank arches on this side provide a little relief, but there is no attempt at the visual interest of the contemporary centre at Ealing (Ea). The result is the sadder because this great hulk replaced a distinguished group of civic buildings in Treaty Road: the council house, public library, and baths, all of 1904–5, the *chef d'œuvre* of the local architect *Nowell Parr*. They were adorned by his favourite colourful glazed tiles both inside and out. Fragments of the rich decoration have been preserved. Terracotta figures of Justice and Wisdom from the council house are meaninglessly set up on a plinth on the s side. Four panels of art nouveau glass from the library are reassembled to create a feature on the E side of the atrium, the glass dome from the stairs to the council room is now in the library, and some terracotta is re-used over the entrance from the High Street. In HANWORTH ROAD, leading s from here, a few earlier C19 houses near the United Reformed Church, and, some way s, remains of a mid C19 suburb around St Stephen's church.

Off the High Street further E, in SCHOOL ROAD, assorted C19 and C20 school buildings, most notably the GIRLS' SCHOOL, a low range with elaborate chimneys and little dormers. At the E end of PEARS ROAD No. 103, built as barracks in 1854 by *F. H. Pownall* and in 1978–9 admirably converted and extended as sheltered housing by the *Borough Architect's Department* (*G. A. Trevett*). Dignified pedimented centre of three bays, with brick quoins and keystones; lower pavilions with lunettes. At the back the tiny courtyard has been preserved, with its covered walks and iron columns, and a glazed link added to connect with the new flats on a staggered plan.

N of the High Street, the better detailed among the recent buildings include PHARMACIA, Prince Regent Road, 1977 by *G.M.A. International*. Down LAMPTON ROAD, after the commercial buildings, NANTLEY HOUSE is a pleasant, modest one-storey day nursery on a hexagonal cluster plan, in yellow brick with garden walls to match (*Borough Architect's Department*, 1969). Further on, THE LAWN, a Regency house excellently restored by *Haslemere Estates* in 1975. It stands at right angles to the road in counterpoint to the unadorned red brick civic centre car park behind. Three-bay front with two shallow bows; upper windows and ground-floor verandas with elegant fringed ogee hoods of cast iron.

HOUNSLOW HEATH once stretched w from the junction of the Bath and Staines Road to what is now Heathrow Airport. In this dull flat area a sprinkling of early and mid C19 villas remains from the suburb which developed along the BATH ROAD. Hounslow West Station (q.v.) marks the extent of suburban expansion by the 1920s. Further s, apart from the cavalry barracks (*see* below), there was little building until after the Second World War. The most prominent development is at the N end of BEAVERS LANE:

a group of office towers, shopping centre, and G.L.C. estate of *c*. 1969–70 (consultant architect *Clifford Culpin & Partners*), with two-to-four-storey concrete slabs in CHINCHILLA DRIVE and other incongruously furry roads.

CAVALRY BARRACKS, Beavers Lane. Begun in 1793, under *James Johnson*, the first of forty barracks built during the Napoleonic wars; added to in the mid C19, major extensions under *L. B. Ewart*, 1876. The main buildings, formally arranged on three sides of a large parade ground, still reflect the orderly layout of the late C18. Central block of *c*. 1793, but refronted and heightened to three storeys in 1876. Fifteen bays, with a pediment over the central five; lower flanking ranges each of fourteen bays, all in yellow stock brick with paler gault brick bands and window surrounds. At right angles to these, long plain two-storey blocks, much altered, built as stables with dormitories above, an arrangement declared unhealthy by the 1861 Report of the Commission for Improving the Sanitary Conditions of Barracks and Hospitals. The two-storey verandas were added to the centres in 1861 by *Lothian Nicholson*. Also of *c*. 1793 three (originally four) one-storey buildings at the ends of the barrack blocks, built as coach houses and stores. The NW one preserves its cast-iron window frames.

Later additions are neatly ranged around the periphery. Opposite the main buildings, close to the entrance, the former CHAPEL (later subdivided) of *c*. 1840, very utilitarian; stock brick, with a continuous clerestory like a workshop, and some simple wooden tracery at the E end. Close to the gates the former CANTEEN, of the same period, still in the late Georgian style, of two storeys with recessed panels and large sash-windows.

The 1876 buildings are a little more flamboyant, recognizable by their use of stock brick with gault bands. The most imposing is the KEEP, near the entrance, at an angle to the parade ground, with two massive corner staircase towers and a third tower at the back. Nearby, facing the road, the OLD FUSILIERS BLOCK, built as quartermaster's quarters and offices; thirteen bays with projecting wings, a little decorative brickwork to gables and eaves. To the E of the parade ground the former MARRIED QUARTERS, probably by *Nicholson*, 1860, and an early example of its type. Only one room deep (to provide cross-ventilation), and planned with only one room for each family. Entrances from lobbies off iron verandas on the W side (the veranda posts now cased in concrete). Facing this the OLD HOSPITAL, 1861, attractively faced in cream terracotta (an early use of the material) and trimmed with red brick. The plan follows the recommendations of the 1861 report; long one-storey ward blocks attached to the two-storey centre. This and the end pavilions are distinguished by round-headed windows. To the N the monotony of the large blocks is broken by a group of terraced houses with nicely varied gables, *c*. 1910. Nearby the OLD SERGEANTS' MESS (later first hospital), late C18, very plain, heightened later, and a former RIDING SCHOOL, much altered. To the NW the INSTITUTE, *c*. 1876, two storeys, with decorative brickwork and a clock turret, and on the W side large later barrack blocks, three storeys, with big gables over recessed arches framing the staircase windows.

ISLEWORTH

INTRODUCTION

Despite much late C 20 building, the shape of the old village is still recognizable: a compact settlement close to the Thames, with the parish church of All Saints away to the N, on the fringe of Syon Park. Nearby are the great houses of Syon and Osterley (qq.v.), and from the C 17 to the early C 19 the area enjoyed an esteem comparable to neighbouring Twickenham, with many large mansions in their own grounds. A surprising number remain, buried in C 19 and C 20 suburbia and converted to offices or institutions (*see* Public Buildings). Market gardens survived in between until the suburbs began to expand. The first date from the 1850s: the grandiose Spring Grove and the more modest Woodlands, both near the new station and with churches to match; and the more varied and better preserved St Margarets, further s, close to the river. The village centre quietly declined in the C 20, suffering from unsympathetic piecemeal rebuilding, until rediscovered by developers in the 1980s and largely rebuilt for affluent commuters.

CHURCHES

ALL SAINTS, Church Street. Like the parish church at Hounslow (Ho), All Saints was destroyed by fire in 1943. The decision to rebuild rather than to restore took some time to reach: *Michael Blee* was appointed architect in 1963, and building took place in 1967–70. The idyllic setting by the river might have dictated an inoffensively traditional reconstruction. Instead, the architect grafted on the old tower and nave walls a building not afraid to make an uncompromisingly original C 20 statement. The contrast between the red brick of the 1960s and the older parts is abrupt, but no more so than the previous contrasts between the C 19 chancel, *John Price*'s nave of 1706, and the C 15 tower, which is of Kentish rag with diagonal buttresses, crenellated top, and a lower stair-turret. Transomed E belfry window with square head (cf. Heston, Ho). The shell of the C 18 nave forms the outer walls of two ranges of rooms around a secluded courtyard in front of the entrance to the church (cf. the post war remodelling of St George in the East, Tower Hamlets). The flat roofs project emphatically through the old windows, like an interlocking puzzle. The square church has narrow vertical windows between buttresses and rather mannered projecting horizontal fins of triangular section. They form roof-lights inside. A stream flows into the courtyard as if from the font visible through the glazed w wall. The interior is calm and restrained, with muted light from the narrow windows and opaque roof strips, and plain, quite brusque surfaces and details. The roof consists of four structurally independent inverted triangles resting on supports, the w ones rather clumsily related to the w gallery. To the s up some steps the projecting JOSHUA CHAPEL, a tiny octagonal

space with a window framing a tranquil view of trees and river. –
Movable FURNISHINGS of wood and steel. – STAINED GLASS.
Central E window with good abstract glass by *Keith New*. –
BRASSES (beneath the W gallery) of a C15 knight and a C16
civilian. – MONUMENTS. Two important survivals, well displayed in niches in the W gallery. Sir Orlando Gee † 1705 by
Francis Bird. Frontal demi-figure with elaborate wig, holding a
scroll and addressing us as from a pulpit; flanking columns with
twisted lower part. – Mrs Ann Dash † 1750 by *William
Halfpenny*. Bust on a decorated sarcophagus of coloured marbles.
Portrait medallions above of her benefactors, Caleb and Susan-
nah Cotesworth † 1741. Interesting inscription. – Many good
sarcophagi and tombstones in the churchyard.

ALL SOULS, Haliburton Road. 1896–8 by *E. Monson*. Red brick,
on a cramped site.

ST JOHN, St John's Road. 1855–6 by *James Deason*. Near the new
suburb of Woodlands. The site and £2,000 were given by the
Duke of Northumberland. A sturdy ragstone composition with
NW battlemented tower with a corner turret in the Middlesex
tradition, a two-storey porch, and Perp windows. (Inside, stone
arches and some contemporary stained glass.) Nearby a characteristic, attractive mid-Victorian group, all paid for by John
Farnell, a local brewer: Tudor parsonage house (1856), Gothic
school with gables and turret (1859), and Lady Farnell's Almshouses, two picturesque L-shaped ranges of 1857 around a
garden. (In the former schoolrooms, boarded ceilings decorated
with quatrefoils.)

ST MARY, Osterley Road. By *J. Taylor Jun.*, 1856, and not without
the grit typical of its date. Built for the new Spring Grove estate
(*see* Perambulation) and faced with Taylor's patent Bath stone:
'chaste, substantial and elegant' was the verdict of the *Illustrated
London News*. Tower and spire over the S porch; tall nave with
octagonal columns; aisles with somewhat clumsy Dec windows
on two levels to allow for galleries. S chapel neatly divided off by
wood and glass screens in 1976 by *Anthony Elliott* of *Norman
Haines Partnership*. – Some excellent STAINED GLASS: chancel
E, S chapel E, W window, and porch windows, all in the lively and
colourful style of *Robert T. Bayne*, *c*. 1866. – Two nave windows
by *Veronica Whall*, N aisle 1948, S aisle 1949.

ST MARY, Worton Road. 1952–4, a late work by *H. Goodhart
Rendel*, Gothic, of brick. Plain exterior, but the interior somewhat quirky, as one might expect, with large intersecting round-
headed arches at the E end. – (REREDOS of glazed tiles.)

OUR LADY OF SORROWS AND ST BRIDGET (R.C.), Twickenham Road. 1907–9 by *E. Doran Webb*. Clumsy brick and stone
front. NW tower. Renaissance interior with barrel-vaulted nave
and apsidal sanctuary with baldacchino.

CONGREGATIONAL CHURCH, Twickenham Road. 1848, ragstone. Lancets with Gothic glazing-bars.

FRIENDS MEETING HOUSE, Quaker Lane. A modest box dated
1785. Front (NE) wall rebuilt after war damage. (Well preserved
interior: panelled meeting room with original stand at the far
end; gallery with sliding shutters to the main room; a small heated
room below, an attic above).

ISLEWORTH CEMETERY, Park Road. 1859 by *Mr Farnell*. Large, polychrome brick chapels sharing an octagonal spire. – (Granite obelisk to Alice Ayres † 1885, erected by public subscription. – Grand classical monument of granite to the Pears family of Spring Grove, *c*. 1912.)

PUBLIC BUILDINGS

LIBRARY, Twickenham Road. 1936 by *J. J. Carey*. Brick, progressive Scandinavian-modern. Apsed lending library; tall stair-turret with a curved end. BATHS of 1939 adjacent, in a similar style.

WEST LONDON INSTITUTE OF HIGHER EDUCATION. Split between two sites, the Lancaster House Campus and the Gordon House Campus. LANCASTER HOUSE, between Borough Road and the Great West Road, began life as International College, part of an ambitious educational enterprise designed to teach foreign languages. (Similar colleges were to be built in France and Germany.) It is a large, nearly symmetrical Gothic structure in polychrome brick, with projecting wings and a central turreted tower, 1866–7 by *John Norton & P. E. Massey*. On the ground floor a series of portrait medallions whose choice could not be more characteristic: Shakespeare, Montesquieu, Goethe, Dante, Homer, Aristotle, Cicero. From 1890 the building was used by the training college founded by Joseph Lancaster in Borough Road, Southwark (alterations by *James Osborne Smith*). Extensions to the W of 1936 and later.

GORDON HOUSE CAMPUS occupies a long riverside stretch between Railshead Road and St Margaret's Drive. Its history is complex. This part of Twickenham Park, a medieval royal park, was divided up for building in the C17. There was a house on the site of Gordon House by 1607, and the present building was at various times called Railshead, Thistleworth, and Seaton House. Its centre is a substantial two-storey block built *c*. 1718 for Moses Hart, a wealthy London Jew; the S wing was added in 1758–9 by *Robert Adam* for General Bland, a former Governor of Edinburgh Castle; and the extensive enlargements and remodelling from 1868 onwards were made for the 2nd Earl of Kilmorey † 1888, an eccentric Irish peer. Further alterations took place after the building became an industrial school for girls in 1896, and again after the Maria Gray Training College moved here in 1949. The result is a muddle, but with plenty of interest.

The exterior of Gordon House, with its entrance facing the river, is at first sight late C19 and not prepossessing; a long, irregular frontage of red brick with stone dressings with an obtrusive porch and fussy parapet and pediment added by Lord Kilmorey. The five centre bays are essentially Moses Hart's house. The giant Doric corner pilasters of brick, boldly channelled, the stone keystones to the windows, and the stone centre-piece with doorway with Corinthian pilasters (now hidden behind the later porch) appear in C18 views: the building must once have been a notable example of a Baroque villa in the

London countryside. Thomas Archer's work provides the closest parallels. The house appears to have functioned as a virtually square pavilion with reception rooms and grand staircase, added at the end of a building to the N (shown on a view of 1829) roughly on the site of the present C19 service wing. The S side of the C18 pavilion is now concealed by the *Adam* wing added in 1758–9, of yellow stock brick, with three widely spaced pedimented windows and a Greek key frieze. The upper windows were heightened and the parapet made more elaborate in the later C19. N of the centre five bays is a late C19 tower (with a brick pilaster in imitation of the C18 house), and a plain five-bay C19 service wing. The garden front is plainer, regularized in the later C19 around the C18 core, which displays on this side two channelled giant pilasters and a well carved stone two-storey centrepiece. Doorway with fluted pilaster with composite capitals, and carved soffit (apparently with Moses Hart's monogram). This is now in the centre of nine bays flanked by further bays with broad canted bay-windows (the S one possibly a rebuilding of a one-storey extension of the Adam wing).

In the former C18 reception room on the garden side (now subdivided) remains of cornice and panelling. Behind, the staircase hall occupies three bays of the entrance front. The stair is an excellent piece of C18 joinery, rising against W and N walls with landings along E and S walls. Two Corinthian-column balusters to each tread (a treatment usually reserved for newels), panelled soffits, marquetry below the second landing, pilastered dado panelling. The room to the S of the stair-hall was linked to it by *Adam* with two columns and now forms an anteroom leading into his new drawing room, a fine lofty room with a coved ceiling. The original doorcases and overmantel have gone, but the marble fireplace with panel of trophies and the plaster ceiling survive, Adam's first work after his return from Italy. The ceiling has quite florid plasterwork around the centre oval, with arabesques and medallions with winged figures and putti on the cove. Adam wrote to his brother: 'The stucco work pleases them much and I am convinced will please generally, although *entre nous*, it is not executed in the antique taste, as it is impossible to get English workmen who will leave their angly stiff sharp manner'. NE of the house the present dining hall, previously a chapel, but possibly built by Kilmorey as a conservatory: free Renaissance interior with Corinthian columns on high plinths.

Close to this, and at an angle to the house, the former STABLES, with Kilmorey's initials, a single range of red brick, grandly conceived. Giant arches frame segmental windows with circular windows above; rusticated quoins and recessed entrance. Late C19 LODGE in St Margaret's Drive.

Around the campus nondescript college buildings of the 1950s onwards, of which the most attractive is the students' union (1970). The campus includes part of the grounds formerly attached to the neighbouring house. Known as St Margaret's and earlier as Lacy House, it was rebuilt for Kilmorey by *Lewis Vulliamy* in 1856, damaged in the Second World War, and demolished in 1945. The separate CHAPEL added *c.* 1870 remains as LACY SCHOOL, a part of the college. Brick and stone striped, with a w gable and a wheel window.

The most remarkable survival of Kilmorey's time, hidden behind a high wall next to the later suburban development along St Margaret's Road, is the MAUSOLEUM he erected in the grounds of Gordon House. Designed by *Kendall*, it is a massive Egyptian temple of grey and red granite, windowless, with battered walls and doorway carved with Egyptian motifs. Inside is the marble MONUMENT, carved in Rome, to Priscilla Hoste, Kilmorey's mistress, † 1854. She lies on her deathbed, attended by the Earl and their young son. The mausoleum has a strange history: it was erected in Brompton Cemetery in 1854, moved in 1862 to Woburn Park Chertsey, where Kilmorey lived until 1868, and finally brought to Isleworth. He was buried here in 1880.

HOUNSLOW BOROUGH COLLEGE, Spring Grove Road. The site of Spring Grove, a mid C18 brick house built for Elisa Biscoe and from 1780 to 1820 the home of Sir Joseph Banks, botanist and explorer. Most of the grounds were developed from 1850 (*see* Perambulation). The house itself was altered and extended *c.* 1840–3 by *Henry Pownall* and in 1886–93 expensively remodelled for Andrew Pears, grandson of the founder of the nearby soap factory on the London Road. Now visibly all of the late C19, red brick above a stone basement, although the plain seven-bay s range may incorporate the older building. The C19 entrance is on the E front, with a large Greek Doric porch. The w front, opening on to a curved terrace, is a straggling late C19 composition of bow-windows, mansarded projection, and a massive conservatory with circular windows and double-curved roof. Generously scaled staircase hall with much debased Jacobean woodwork and a decorative plaster ceiling; two rooms with Adamish plasterwork. The house is wrapped around by college extensions on three sides (*Hounslow Borough Architect's Department*, completed 1969): they provide a deliberately contrasting foil of sleek white pre-cast panels and narrow horizontal windows. The N block is the most elegant, with exposed columns on the ground floor. To the w a late C19 SUMMER HOUSE with prettily finicky white woodwork.

ISLEWORTH AND SYON BOYS' SCHOOL, Ridgeway Road. Formerly Isleworth County School, in St John's Road from 1897, rebuilt in 1936–8 by the *Middlesex County Council*. A formal front with the slightly pretentious detail (stone mullions and transomed windows) typical of inter-war grammar schools. One- and two-storey ranges dominated by a powerful tower with a more progressive tall curved staircase window. Extensive additions behind of after 1979, when the school became comprehensive.

GUMLEY HOUSE CONVENT SCHOOL, Twickenham Road. Set back behind big gatepiers. The centre is an excellent house built *c.* 1700 for John Gumley († 1729), the eminent cabinet- and mirror-maker. Five-bay brick front with segment-headed window, two storeys with cornice, and a big hipped roof broken by a three-bay pedimented attic storey above the cornice (an original feature, as old views show). The wings, formerly one-storeyed at the front, two-storeyed on the garden side, were heightened after the convent took over the house in 1841, and now unfortunately dwarf the centre. Colonnades on either side of the front courtyard (incomplete on the w side). On the garden side a further extension on the s (the White Parlour) which, with the colonnades, could be the additions which *James Gibbs* is known to have made for Gumley. All five bays of the front of the house are occupied by the hall and staircase, an exceptionally lavish piece with three balusters (fluted between twisted) to each step, carved tread-ends, moulded and carved soffits to the steps, and marquetry below the landing. Black and white marble paving; wall panelling with Corinthian pilasters. The staircase walls and coved ceiling had paintings until the early c19. Simple c18 fireplaces in the reception rooms on the garden side and in the small room l. of the staircase. To the s, down the road, the former coach entrance with gatepiers with pineapples.

NAZARETH HOUSE (convent of the Sisters of Nazareth and old people's home), Richmond Road. Formerly Isleworth House. Lavishly rebuilt in 1832 by *Edward Blore* for George III's chaplain, Sir William Cooper, who had married into the Anglo-Jewish Franks family, the c18 owners of the estate. A tall white mansion (channelled stucco ground floor, upper parts now roughcast) in the neo-classical cum Italianate made popular by Nash, an uncommon choice for Blore. Entrance front, perhaps incorporating the old house, of five bays, with a later two-bay w addition. Pediments to the first-floor windows; balustraded parapet. Garden front to the river with Italian campanile to the E, and a handsome pair of two-storey balustraded bows, their French windows complete with curved glazing and blind boxes. The bows light two ground-floor reception rooms with exceptionally rich cornices, as in the sumptuous stair-hall. Two grey scagliola Ionic columns at the foot of a grand imperial stair with stone treads and cast-iron banisters. There were further reception rooms on the first floor. A service stair behind now leads via an extension to the first-floor L-shaped CHAPEL added for the convent after 1893. Red brick with stone dressings, a canted apse, and a distinctive free Gothic w window, circular with vertical mullions. Early c19 stuccoed outbuildings, gatepiers, and one-storey LODGE by the road, which was diverted by Sir William Cooper so as not to divide the house from the river. Near the lodge, plain red brick neo-Georgian former industrial school by *Leonard Stokes*, 1901, all windows renewed.

GROVE ROAD PRIMARY SCHOOL. Victorian buildings ingeniously adapted and extended in 1988–9 by *Plancke Leaman & Browning*: staffrooms and administration in the old buildings; semi-circular additions with covered play area, library, and a fan of classrooms, each with its own entrance through a garden.

WEST MIDDLESEX HOSPITAL, Twickenham Road. An ill-planned muddle: developed from 1896, much added to in the c20, rebuilding planned 1984. The starting point, as with so many hospitals, was a workhouse infirmary.* The buildings

*Nothing now remains of *Lewis Vulliamy*'s distinguished neo-Tudor workhouse buildings for the Brentford Union. They dated from 1838 and were intended to avoid the 'prison-like associations found in buildings of this description' (Aungier, 1840).

include (at the time of writing) the MATERNITY UNIT near the entrance, 1932, extended 1970, and the MEDICAL DEPART-MENT, a six-storey ward block with concrete bands at the back of the site (*RMJM*, 1967) with MEDICAL CENTRE added behind (*Andrew Sherlock & Partners*). Near the entrance the more recent sleek OUTPATIENTS DEPARTMENT: white slabs and mirror glass. In the centre a late C19 block remains; attached to it is a rather spartan small polygonal top-lit CHAPEL, of breeze blocks, brick-lined inside, 1970 by *RMJM*.

MOGDEN SEWAGE WORKS, Mogden Lane. 1931–4, the largest and most advanced of its time, serving 171 square miles of west Middlesex. The treatment beds are sunk below ground level, and the excavated earth forms a high peripheral mound, planted with trees. The Duke of Northumberland's River runs axially through the middle. Handsome Georgian-modern power house with special thin red bricks. It runs on methane gas.

PERAMBULATION

The prettiest view of the village is from the river, with the trees by Syon House on the r., the rebuilt church and the trees of the churchyard, and a ribbon of houses to the l., overlooking the water. Facing them, directly on the riverside, is the LONDON APPRENTICE, an early C18 pub (much extended). The nicely varied houses at the beginning of CHURCH STREET start with BUTTERFIELD HOUSE, two cottages transformed into immaculate Strawberry Hill Gothic in 1971 by *Howard V. Lobb & Partners*. No. 61 is early C19 stucco with Soanian pilasters to the top floor and a tented balcony; No. 59, with a two-bay brick front of *c.* 1825–30, is a remodelling of an older house; and Nos. 55–57, *c.* 1870, are of red brick, with angular Gothic doorways. Then three earlier C19 brick terrace houses, and RICHARD REYNOLD'S HOUSE, two storeys, detached, a three-bay Georgian house with continuous balcony. On the other side lesser cottages, some Georgian (Nos. 50–42), some later, continue up to the bridge over the DUKE OF NORTHUMBERLAND'S RIVER, created in the mid C16 to improve the flow of water to mills by the Thames. No mills remain, but along MILL PLAT by the canal are the delightful INGRAM ALMSHOUSES, 1664, a simple row of six dwellings, one-storeyed and, with their big pediments, rather Dutch-looking.

The centre of the village, with its two squares, was until the 1980s a muddle of decaying riverside industry, with gaps caused by war damage and slum clearances. Between these, PERCY GARDENS, a totally inappropriate 1960s tower of flats, glowered over a few older buildings, until in 1986–8 an instant townscape arose, terrace houses, offices, and riverside pub, all developed by Speyhawk, in the stagey picturesque mode used also for much Docklands housing: terraces with fancy wooden balconies, brick-work in several colours, even decorative terracotta. The new buildings start by the canal with BRIDGE WHARF (*Edgington Spink & Hyne*, 1981) and continue around TOWN WHARF (a large pub with terraces to the river by *Hunt Thompson Associates*,

1986) to LION WHARF (more overtly post-modern, by *Broad-way Malyon*, 1987). Along this route several older buildings have been incorporated including HOLLAND HOUSE, late C18 with a front of *c*. 1840, simple Italianate stucco with Roman Doric porch, and No. 11 (John Day House), a polite stone front with pilasters above rustication (entirely resurfaced during restoration). Opposite is the former Northumberland Arms, plain stuccoed C18. Adjoining, LAWRENCE PARADE, shops, flats, and offices overlooking Lower Square, of 1988 by *Broadway Malyon*. The dominant centrepiece is still the OLD BLUE SCHOOL, a commodious free-standing building rather like a market house, 1841–2 by *C. F. Maltby*, built of an unusual pale yellow and greenish gault brick; Tudor Gothic, originally with open ground-floor arcades and a little turret with a clock. The school was first endowed in 1630 and refounded in 1715.

s of the village were large mansions overlooking the river. For the two survivors *see* Public Buildings: West London Institute of Education and Nazareth House. Further s, beyond these, is ST MARGARETS ESTATE, laid out in 1854 on part of the grounds of St Margaret's, a house whose site lay within the campus of the West London Institute of Education (q.v.). Built up slowly, by the Conservative Land Society (architect and surveyor *George Morgan*). The plan is enterprising, with curving roads and with parts of the old grounds preserved as romantic pleasure gardens. In those by Ailsa Road, two iron bridges with segmental arches. The houses vary in style and size (the more modest were designed for the forty shilling freeholder eligible to vote after the Reform Bill). The earliest are in THE AVENUE. Elsewhere there were still only a few by 1865. Earlier examples have stucco trim and gables, later ones colourful decorative brickwork. There is one older house in KILMOREY ROAD, CLIFTON LODGE (Gordon House Department of Social Studies), a seven-bay front with oddly huge trellis porch, and one modernistic intruder in AILSA ROAD, No. 46, 1935 by *Couch & Coupland* of Richmond.

In TWICKENHAM ROAD, running parallel to the river, first on the edge of Syon Park BUSH HOUSE, small, two-storeyed, late C18, with blind fanlights over ground-floor windows. School buildings in the grounds behind by *Scherrer & Hicks*, 1976. On the w side, opposite the straggling hospital buildings, a few Georgian houses: Nos. 99–107 and 173, C18, and Nos. 185–187, early C19. By North Street, SARAH SERMON'S ALMSHOUSES built in 1849, six one-storey dwellings, polychrome brick Gothic. Opposite, the best surviving C18 house in this area, Gumley House (*see* Public Buildings). Further s one notices the GEORGE at the corner of South Street, with a good C18 brick front of four bays and a cornice below gables, and s again, past neo-Georgian flats (replacing an C18 terrace), Nos. 158–160, another substantial house of *c*. 1700, a fine example of its date, five bays, three storeys, straight-headed windows with rubbed brick surrounds. Van Gogh taught here in a prep school in 1876.

Connecting Twickenham Road towards its N end with London Road, LINKFIELD ROAD, with cottages of the early to mid C19 (some dated 1842); also RAYBELL COURT by *Manning & Clamp*, 1976, a traditional almshouse composition in brown brick with steeply pitched roofs. Parallel and further S ST JOHN'S ROAD, leading off towards the station (1849), is at first largely industrial, with the dinosaur humps of WATNEY'S BREWERY rising behind Gumley Gardens. The buildings by *S. Hutchings* of Watney Mann include two with Silberkuhl roofs (no internal columns), the single-storey beer warehouse of 1964–5 (120 by 45 metres), and a two-storey building of 1967–70 with bottling and canning hall (70 by 60 metres) on the upper floor. Further N, after St John's church, WOODLANDS ROAD and WOODLANDS GROVE, a mid C19 commuters' suburb of modest stucco-trimmed villas near the railway.

A little further W, to the N of LONDON ROAD, are the remains of the grander Victorian suburb of SPRING GROVE which grew up on the edge of a former hamlet called Smallberry Green. It was developed around Sir Joseph Banks's former house (whose successor is now Hounslow Borough College, *see* Public Buildings) by *John Taylor Jun.*, for H. D. Davies, who bought the Spring Grove estate in 1850 and further land to the N a few years later. Osterley Road, Thornbury Road, and Eversley Crescent were laid out by 1855, and nearly a hundred houses were up by 1887. Only a few remain, notably in THE GROVE and OSTER-LEY ROAD, tall gaunt classical villas in spacious gardens, faced with Taylor's own patent stone which he used also for the estate church of St Mary (q.v.). In THORNBURY ROAD, CAMPION HOUSE, a grander Italianate stuccoed mansion of 1860, much added to, was Davies's own house. On the gardens which once extended between this and the church, some quirky Arts and Crafts semi-detached infilling of 1913–14, roughcast and tile-hung, with prominent front chimneystacks hugging canted bays. Also in Thornbury Road the former HONNOR ALMSHOUSES, (now Osterley Mansions), built by the Saddlers' Company in 1860.

WORTON, now submerged in C20 suburbia, was another hamlet away to the SW. The one survival is WORTON HALL in HEATH ROAD, a late C18 house (now offices) in its own grounds, owned and perhaps built by the Devall family, master masons (*John Devall Sen.* † 1771, *John Devall Jun.* † 1794). Three-storey, five-bay centre with ground-floor windows in arched recesses; semi-circular porch with fluted columns; lower wings, their upper parts probably added by *William Jackson*, a Kensington specu-lative builder who lived here from 1850 to 1860. The stucco is also probably C19.

Back along LONDON ROAD. A few older buildings alongside Syon Park: a handsome Georgian group consisting of the COACH AND HORSES, PARK COTTAGES (of 1728–32), and SYON LODGE, with delicate C18 detail (brought, it is said, from Foley House in Marylebone) and a good iron gate. On the N side, No. 280, PINE HOUSE, in the grounds of Marlborough Training Centre, formerly the house of the steward of the Syon Hill estate; an elegantly restrained design of c. 1760 (date from rate books). Three bays with deep eaves.

WYKE GREEN. *See* Osterley, below.

OSTERLEY

ST FRANCIS, Great West Road. 1933–5 by *E. C. Shearman*, with
its apse to the main road. A large brick structure without steeple.
An impressive interior: very tall, with passage aisle, the arcades
with the simplest dying mouldings, and a large clerestory with
paired trefoiled lancets under a segmental arch. The whole pulled
together by wooden transverse arches across the nave, their spandrels filled with bold mullions.

OSTERLEY PARK STATION. Similar to Boston Manor (*see* Brentford, Ho). 1934 by *Charles Holden*, with a tower.

Osterley, part of the parish of Heston, did not become a suburb
until after the building of the Great West Road. Around the edge
of Osterley Park, a few rural buildings remain. In Osterley Lane
to the N of the park, just S of the motorway in a forgotten fragment
of countryside, OSTERLEY PARK FARM, an C18 brick house
with two-storey bow; high brick garden walls. To the S, in Jersey
Road, Nos. 133–135, ROSE FARM, with C18 barn and older
farmhouse. To the SE, WYKE GREEN, by Syon Lane, was a
former hamlet. Its most interesting house, WYKE HOUSE (C18,
with an addition probably by *Adam*) was demolished in 1978,
but its home farm, WYKE FARM, preserves its farmhouse, barn,
and outbuildings of *c.* 1790. In WYKE GARDENS a small C18
cottage.

OSTERLEY PARK. The house stands in serene splendour in its
park between the roaring traffic on the M4 and the Great West
Road. It was given to the National Trust in 1949. Built by Sir
Thomas Gresham *c.* 1575, it was completely transformed in the
C17 and C18, and the present regular exterior, in its final form
the result of *Robert Adam*'s alterations of the 1760s–70s, gives
no hint of its complex earlier history.* Blocked doorways in an
early brick wall survive in the basement of the W range. From
1683 to 1698 a later owner, the property speculator Nicholas
Barbon, made substantial alterations involving partial demolition, to the extent that in 1689–90 the house was described
as uninhabitable. It was acquired in 1711 by the banker Francis
Child († 1713), and further remodelling took place under his
sons Robert † 1721, Francis † 1740, and Samuel † 1752, and his
grandson Francis † 1763. Few details are known: a puzzling
undated plan at Osterley, entitled 'Plan for the Alterations of Mr
Child's House at Osterley', may represent an unexecuted mid
C18 scheme, for it bears no relation to the present house. Carpenters' bills for 1759 indicate that extensive repairs and alterations were then in progress, including the completion of the
long gallery. The name of the architect *Boulton Mainwaring*
appears on these bills. Adam's work of after 1761 may have been
but the completion of all this activity.

The existing house consists of red brick wings of three storeys
around a raised courtyard, with a taller tower with stone quoins

---

*Documentation is inadequate and confusing. This account owes much to research
by Maurice Tomlin and James Yorke of the Victoria and Albert Museum, and by
Frank Kelsall. The full history of the pre-Adam house has yet to be elucidated.

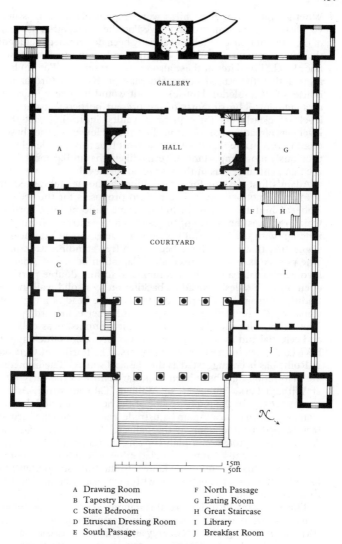

GALLERY

HALL

A   G

B   E   F   H

COURTYARD

C

I

D

J

15m
50ft

A Drawing Room   F North Passage
B Tapestry Room   G Eating Room
C State Bedroom   H Great Staircase
D Etruscan Dressing Room   I Library
E South Passage   J Breakfast Room

Osterley House,
first floor, plan

and ogee cap projecting at each outer corner. The courtyard is
entered through a grand portico on the E side. The state rooms
are all on the level of the courtyard, i.e. on the first floor. The
superficial similarity of the exterior to Elizabethan and Jacobean
houses with corner turrets, such as Syon House, Ho (q.v.) or
Blickling, Norfolk, is deceptive. Although the four ranges may
to some extent reflect the basic form of the Elizabethan house,
the present turrets are not Gresham's but later antiquarian
creations no doubt intended to allude to Gresham's ownership.

Whether Barbon or the Childs were responsible for this is not
yet clear.* By the time Adam arrived on the scene, other aspects
of the present house which had already been determined included
the raised courtyard and the entrance and state rooms at first-
floor level. The dates of these also are uncertain. Mr Tomlin has
argued that the raised courtyard may go back to Gresham's
house (cf. Wimbledon House); if so it would be a very unusual
arrangement. The supports of the present portico at basement
level are clearly cut through brick vaults, indicating that this
level was already a basement in the 1760s. However other basement rooms in the N and S wings suggest that this floor level was
previously more important. It seems likely that in Barbon's time
the main entrance was in the S wing, at this level.

Adam's first designs for remodelling the house, submitted in
1761, were not accepted. The revised proposals for the second
Robert Child, from 1763, included the magnificent Ionic portico
which replaces the centre of the range on the entrance front. Its
junction with the brick walls on either side is somewhat uneasy,
suggesting that it may have begun as a free-standing structure.
The portico is a highly successful adaptation of one of Adam's
favourite motifs: a screen of columns to form a double portico,
open on both sides, instead of backing on to a solid wall in the
traditional manner. The portico stands at the head of a flight of
steps boldly connecting outer space and inner courtyard space.
The effect, with the slim unfluted Ionic columns, is as delicate
and celestial and as chastely theatrical as any opera Gluck might
have composed in these very same years. The Portico of Octavia
in Rome has been suggested as the classical source. The immediate inspiration may have been a similar feature of the early C18
at Witham Park, Somerset, by William Talman, which Adam
saw in 1762.‡ On the opposite side of the house, a curved double
staircase with a typical Adam balustrade leads down to the garden
from a pedimented door in the gallery. Beneath the staircase
Adam built a grotto on a plan copying in miniature that of the
interior of the mausoleum of Diocletian's palace at Spalato, which
he had investigated and made known to the English dilettanti in
his folio of 1763. It is octagonal with niches, and painted in the
Etruscan fashion.

The rooms at Osterley are throughout lower than at Syon.
This comparative lowness is especially marked in the ENTRANCE
HALL in the E wing, of c. 1766, grey and white, with two segment-
headed coffered apses, trophies in panels, and a general scheme
of decoration still markedly more structural and less filigree than
in the later rooms. Yet the use of the more elegant segmental
arch of the Burlingtonians is already clear indication of Adam's
new *finesse*. The LONG GALLERY behind seems to have been
virtually left alone by Adam (apart from the suppression of
Venetian windows in the end walls). It was completed in 1759.
The two marble chimneypieces with terms have convincingly

---

*The only known view of Gresham's house is the small sketch on Moses Glover's
plan of 1635 at Syon House. It shows what seems to be a courtyard house with internal
turrets. Rocque's plan (1741–5) shows a house with two external turrets only.

‡J. Harris, 'The Transparent Portico', *Architectural Review*, CXIII (1958), pp. 108–
9.

been shown to be close to drawings by *Sir William Chambers*, who may have been responsible for other work here. Classical doorcase with fluted pilasters, but frieze with some Rococo detail – a typical mixture of the 1750s. The EATING ROOM in the s wing is remarkable chiefly for its exquisite furniture designed by *Adam* in 1767, now rearranged in its original position against the walls. The large landscapes are by *Zucchi*, the painting over the fireplace is by *Cipriani*. The stucco ornament is white on green and pink, and the grapes and ribbons of the ceiling are unusually Rococo and not typical of Adam's work.* The STAIRCASE has the original lamps and iron balustrade. The ceiling painting is a copy of the original destroyed by fire in 1949 after removal by the previous owner. It was an Apotheosis of the Duke of Buckingham by *Rubens* made originally for York House, London, and acquired by Sir Francis Child *c.* 1697. A corridor along the wing leads to the LIBRARY of 1766–73, with architectural bookcases (Ionic order and pediments), still in Adam's earlier and more structural manner. The colourful ceiling decoration, redone in the early 1970s according to the original colour scheme, is of the same refined delicacy as found in the entrance hall.‡ At the w end of the s wing, the BREAKFAST ROOM is pre-Adam, with a fireplace attributed to *Chambers*. The walls were redecorated in blue and yellow in the 1970s from descriptions and evidence of the original colours. The ceiling is white, with a rather wild Rococo pattern.

The DRAWING ROOM in the N wing belongs to *Adam*'s first phase at Osterley. It is warmer in tone than the hall and the library and still has its original Adam carpet, which echoes the design of the richly moulded coffered ceiling in pink and pale green (inspired by Wood's *Ruins of Palmyra*, published in 1753). The next three rooms are later, 1775–7, and at once recognizable as such by their excessive thinness of decorative motifs. The first is the TAPESTRY ROOM or antechamber, with furniture and carpet designed by *Adam*. The tapestries and chair covers *en suite* are French, dated 1775, with scenes of the Elements designed by *Boucher* and woven by *Neilson* at the Gobelins works in Paris. They give a luxuriance to this room quite different from the daintiness of Adam's ceiling ornament, with its small painted medallions and delicate garlands. The STATE BEDCHAMBER which follows has a spectacular domed state bed designed by *Adam*, and a ceiling with central medallion inspired by a painting by *Angelica Kauffmann*. The ETRUSCAN DRESSING ROOM, adorned with motifs painted by *P. M. Borgnis*, is in a flat style inspired by, though not very similar to, Greek vases (then thought to be Etruscan). Adam designed several Etruscan rooms, but only this one and the one in Home House, Portman Square (Wm outer), survive. Horace Walpole, who did not approve of Adam's late style, wrote that this room was like 'going out of a palace into a potter's field'.

On the second floor of the N wing are the Child family rooms. They belong to the mid c 18, pre-Adam scheme of decoration.

---

*Mr Tomlin suggests that it may date from before Adam's time.

‡In a passage leading from the library to the sw turret a grand set of bookcases with columns, perhaps part of earlier, pre-Adam c 18 fittings.

MRS CHILD'S DRESSING ROOM has a particularly elaborate
Rococo chimneypiece by *John Linnell*, *c.* 1764, incorporating a
pastel portrait above a mirror. THE BEDCHAMBER, MR CHILD'S
DRESSING ROOM, and the TAFFETA BEDCHAMBER have simple
marble chimneypieces close to drawings by *Chambers*. The bed
in the TAFFETA BEDCHAMBER is by *Adam*.

In the basement below the S wing is a sequence of late C18
servants' rooms: the KITCHEN, with scullery in the SE turret
room, the FOOTMEN'S BEDCHAMBER, MRS BUNCE'S ROOM,
and the STEWARD'S ROOM, the last two with heavy bolection-
moulded panelling of *c.* 1700 which must date from Barbon's
time, when they would have been ground-floor rooms, Mrs
Bunce's room forming the entrance hall. The design of the panelling in the steward's room, with its thin corner strips, is very
close to that in Barbon's houses in Essex Street off the Strand.
The staircase in the SW turret, with newels and twisted balusters
of *c.* 1700, was made from old material in 1756–9. The basement
of the N wing (not shown to the public) includes a room with
Tuscan columns also perhaps once more important.

GROUNDS. The brick U-shaped STABLE BLOCK, NE of the
house, still looks largely Elizabethan despite later alterations to
doors and windows and the addition of a cupola, with a clock
supplied in 1714. The W wing may well have been the original
manor house that existed before Gresham's house. Polygonal
stair-turret in the NE angle. NW of the stable block lies *Adam*'s
GARDEN HOUSE, designed about 1780, with a semicircular front
of five linked Venetian windows. W of this, the DORIC TEMPLE
of Pan, with a low Tuscan portico with eight columns. Probably
by *Chambers*, it has mid C18 interior plasterwork with Rococo
flourishes and medallions of Colen Campbell and Sir Isaac
Newton. The series of serpentine lakes to the S and E of the house
were formed by the damming of a stream. The CHINESE TEMPLE
in the lake nearest the house dates from 1987. Nearby is the
mound of the former icehouse.

Further up the stream, cut off from the park by the motorway,
a splendid BRIDGE designed by *Adam*, now in a ruinous state,
which suits its Piranesian cyclopic rustication. One large segmental arch, the central keystones with carved heads; flanking
pairs of blocked columns. The C18 approach to the house was
from Wyke Green, for which Adam designed ENTRANCE
LODGES in 1775.

SYON

SYON HOUSE. The Duke of Northumberland's seat is the only
major mansion in the London area still in private ownership.
The approach through the park, so close to the busy London
Road, yet preserves the illusion of the countryside. The house
stands aloof behind a lawn and two small lodges, away from the
bustle around its converted outbuildings, a large, rather dull
four-square battlemented building with regular Georgian fenestration. It gives little indication either of its rich *Adam* interiors

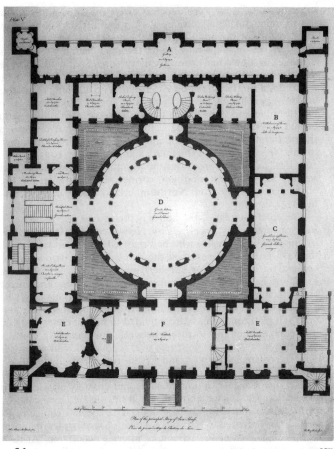

A Gallery
B Drawing room
C Dining room
D Rotunda (not executed)
E Anterooms
F Hall

Syon House, Adam's proposed plan

or of its early origins. The stone facing, probably by *Thomas Cundy I*, dates from 1819–26, but the massing goes back to the Duke of Somerset (1547–52) and the Duke of Northumberland who succeeded him. The little projecting corner towers, their brick construction now concealed, are characteristic of that date. The plan, with its central courtyard, is older still, from the time of the first owners, the Bridgettine nuns whose convent, founded by Henry V in 1415 at Twickenham, was moved here in 1431. Their cloister is the present courtyard: two undercrofts with plain C15 vaulting on octagonal columns survive in the s parts

of the w range. Late Perp doorways were recorded in the N part
of this range during alterations in 1823, but little is known of the
early history of the other parts of the house. In the late C16 the
great hall was in the w range, with the great chamber to its S; the
E range, as now, had a long gallery (presumably the former
dormitory). The present building is of three storeys, with the
main rooms on the first floor. At ground level all along the W front
a plain open loggia, probably of the time of the 10th Earl of
Northumberland † 1668. The Percys, Earls of Northumberland,
owned the house from 1604. Little other evidence remains of
their C17 improvements, although the 9th Earl († 1632) is known
to have spent £9,000 on the house and grounds by 1613. For the
10th Earl *John Webb* produced, among other work, an unexecuted
scheme in 1656 for a modillion cornice. The LION on the roof
of the E range came from Northumberland House in the Strand
in 1874.

The chief interest of the house is the spectacular sequence of
interiors created by *Robert Adam*. He was commissioned in 1761
by Sir Hugh Smithson, who had married the granddaughter of
the 11th Earl. Smithson took the name of Percy, and was later
created 1st Duke of Northumberland by George III. Adam in
his *Works* calls him 'a person of extensive knowledge and correct
taste'. Adam's plans were at first much more ambitious than what
was ultimately executed. In addition to a suite of reception rooms
occupying all four ranges, he intended to fill the courtyard with
a circular saloon and to insert between this and the E front an
oval two-arm staircase with two oval rooms to l. and r. As it is,
only the rooms in the w, s, and E ranges were remodelled.

The Adam rooms start with the ENTRANCE HALL in the centre
of the w side, nearly a double cube, and chastely classical in its
decoration. Ceiling with bold diagonal ribs, echoed by the pattern
of the black and white marble floor. The special feature of the
hall, unprecedented in Europe, is Adam's use of copies of antique
sculpture as part of the scheme of interior decoration. At the N
end, within a coffered apse, a copy of the Apollo Belvedere, the
idol of C18 artists and dilettanti; at the s end a bronze copy by
Valadier, made in 1773, of the similarly highly esteemed Dying
Gaul. On either side of this, curved steps (disguising a change in
levels) lead up under a tunnel-vaulted recess to the neighbouring
room. The recess is separated from the hall by a screen consisting
of two Roman Doric columns supporting a thin entablature.
There is no wall above it, so that hall and recess are, in a manner
eminently characteristic of Adam, divided and yet one. The Doric
entablature continues all round the walls of the hall, breaking
forward as part of the aedicules which frame the large doorways.
The windows have smaller aedicules with late Roman spiral
fluting of the kind Adam had met in Italy and Spalato. In between
are copies of classical statues on high plinths.

39   After the whiteness of the hall the rich colours of the ANTE-
ROOM to the s give a luxurious, even heavy impression. The floor
is of polished scagliola, and twelve columns of *verde antico*,
brought from Italy in 1765, with gilded Ionic capitals and gold
and blue entablatures over each, jut forward from the walls to
support small gilded copies of antique statuary. The columns are

cleverly placed so as to convert the rectangular room into a square. The chief sculptures are two more bronze copies: Silenus and the infant Bacchus, and the Belvedere Antinous. On the wall large panels with gilded trophies (plasterwork, as elsewhere at Syon, by *Joseph Rose*); mahogany doors with gilded beading. As is typical of Adam, the sources of the classical details are an eclectic mixture: the Ionic capitals for example are a combination of Greek and Roman sources (Erechtheion and Roman baths), and the panels derive from Piranesi's illustrations on the trophies of Octavius Augustus in the Campidoglio.

The DINING ROOM follows to the E, the first of the new rooms to be completed (1763). It is long and somewhat narrow, with an apse to E and W screened off by columns without entablatures. Tripartite ceiling with a vigorous pattern of fans and palmettes. Exceedingly rich chimneypiece with a relief of the Three Graces. On either side three niches for Roman figures; above, grisaille panels by *Andrea Casali*. After the white and gold of this room the large WITHDRAWING ROOM is strong in colour again, a warm red, with Spitalfields silk wall-hangings, a coved ceiling with medallions painted by *Cipriani* with small figures, and a glorious carpet designed by *Adam* and dated 1769 on the border. Doorcases with pilasters inlaid with ivory and decorated with Quattrocento motifs in gilded lead. Marble chimneypiece with ormolu enrichment by *Matthew Boulton*. The door at the E end opens into the library or GREAT GALLERY, 41 metres long all along the E front and only 4.25 metres wide. Adam overcame these difficult proportions by keeping the room low, subdividing the walls into many parts by groups of flat pilasters (painted by *Pergolesi*), and by decoration of 'great variety and amusement', as he says of it. The colour scheme is predominantly mauve and pale green. From the point of view of correct classical revival the detail is most objectionable, but it has much charm and lightness. Motifs of Roman 'grottesche' and of Spalato, but also of the Renaissance, are used with Rococo freedom. In the NE and SE turrets tiny round and square BOUDOIRS (not shown to the public). From the centre of the round one hangs a gilt birdcage with a clock. The square one has painted panels with trees and birds in imitation of Chinese silks.

The N range of the house was remodelled only in the C19. The PRINT ROOM adjoining the gallery dates from 1864. Simple geometric ceiling from a design by *Monteroli*, executed by *Charles Smith*; fireplace with terms. In the NORTH CORRIDOR reset early C16 wooden panelling with Percy badges. In the NW corner of the house, in place of the oval antechamber shown on Adam's plan, the STAIRCASE HALL, dating from the 1820s, large but quite plain; stone steps, enriched iron balusters.

OUTBUILDINGS. The two little LODGES in front of the house, early C17 in origin, have been refaced with aediculed windows over rusticated basements. STABLES to the N, castellated, by *James Wyatt*, 1789–90. Domed Ionic BOATHOUSE by the river, by *Robert Mylne*, 1803.

CONSERVATORY. 1827–30 for the 3rd Duke by *Charles Fowler*, the first of his iron and glass buildings. The domed centre is linked to end pavilions by curving glazed wings. A transitional

type: the Bath stone pilasters and pediments of centre and pavilions are still in the tradition of the c 18 orangery, but the curved
surfaces of the tall dome (designed for direct transmission of the
sun's rays) demonstrate the new theories of J. C. Loudon. The
dome is supported on a ring of cast-iron columns. The ribs are
not of cast iron but of gunmetal, a more malleable alloy (wrought
iron was not used for such structures until the 1840s, see the
Palm House, Kew, Ri). The small overlapping panes of glass are
still characteristic of early c 19 construction. Elegantly curved
triangular areas of glass fill the corners of the roof. The wings,
with glazed roofs of shallow pitch, have a single row of slender
columns.

The GARDENS were famous from the time of the Duke of
Somerset, to whom William Turner dedicated his *Names of
Herbs*, written at Syon. The formal gardens laid out around the
house in the mid c 16 were replaced by *Capability Brown*'s open
landscaping for the 1st Duke of Northumberland, which included
the lakes N and W of the house and a lawn around a statue of
Flora on a Doric column. Across one of the lakes a wrought-iron
arched BRIDGE of 1790. In the early c 19 the 3rd Duke added a
formal garden in front of his new conservatory, with a basin with
a copy of *Giovanni da Bologna*'s Mercury. He opened the gardens
to the public in 1837. The GARDEN CENTRE in the former stables
and riding school was established by the 10th Duke in 1968,
followed by the motor museum in 1980, the butterfly house in
1981, and the art centre in 1982. The early c 19 RIDING SCHOOL
is notable for its iron roof.

The SCREEN along the London Road, with the former entrance
archway, is by *Adam*. On the archway is a Northumberland lion
outlined against the sky; on either side, five bays with lower
columns and straight entablature. It is a most delicate, spirited
composition, the apogee of Adam's taste in transparency, of a
'filigree' character which Horace Walpole saw clearly enough
when he passed the gateway while it was being built in 1773, but
which he strangely disliked. Repaired with *Coade* stone before
1799 and in 1814.

KENSINGTON AND CHELSEA

The Royal Borough of Kensington and Chelsea was created in 1965. It is the smallest of the London boroughs, but still the most densely populated, although its 1981 total (138,759; 116 persons per hectare) is a substantial decline from 1961 (218,528). In 1881 the combined total for Kensington and Chelsea was over 251,000. As the dual name suggests, each of the two ancient constituent boroughs cherishes a strong sense of its own identity. They are treated separately here, with Chelsea beginning on p. 551.

KENSINGTON

The general plan *overleaf* is supplemented by detailed plans on pp. 500, 513, 522, 530, 534, 545.

INTRODUCTION

The Kensington of today is the Kensington created by the building
explosion of the C19. The dominant impression is of repetitive
streets of respectable stuccoed terraces filling almost every space
between the main roads running W from London. A leap of the
imagination is needed to picture the village as it was on maps of
c. 1800, surrounded by farms and grand houses, with Kensington
Church Street climbing N from the church and village by the High
Street towards pastures and meadows on the uplands of Notting
Hill, and Brompton and Old Brompton Roads still rural lanes
winding between prosperous market gardens in the flat land to the
s. Even by 1837, outside the village centre there was little more
than sporadic development along the three main highways running
from E to W through the parish to Fulham, Hammersmith, and
Uxbridge.

The architectural history of Kensington begins for us with the
series of compact show houses in the London countryside, so
popular with Elizabethan and Jacobean courtiers and merchants.
Only a fragment of one remains in its early C17 state: a wing of
Holland House, part of an elaborate, fanciful building designed
from c. 1605 onwards for Sir Walter Cope. Further E Campden
House, built by the City merchant Sir Baptist Hicks, Lord
Campden († 1629), and later the home of the young son of the
future Queen Anne, survived until c. 1890. It was conveniently
close to another early C17 house that since 1689 had become still
more illustrious through its acquisition by King William and Queen
Mary. Enlarged to become their rural retreat outside London,
Kensington Palace (as it became known under the Georges) gave
Kensington a social cachet which it has retained ever since.

Urban development, however, came only slowly. It began on the
edge of the village a few years before the arrival of the court, when
in 1685 Thomas Young, an eminent London woodcarver, laid out
Kensington Square among fields, introducing the new type of red
brick terrace house developed after the Great Fire. Other houses
of C18 date remain tucked away in Holland Street N of the High
Street, and scattered here and there along Church Street, but
systematic development of Kensington estates did not start until
the early C19. Then, in 1811, Lord Kensington began to grant
building leases for his land further W, s of the High Street, and
the pace quickened in the 1820s as prosperity increased after the
Napoleonic wars. Pembroke Square followed to the SE of Edwardes
Square; around the same time modest streets began to be laid out
w of Church Street extending towards Campden Hill, where the
ambitious Campden Hill Square was begun in 1827.

Meanwhile, to the s, Brompton developed as an appendage to
Knightsbridge, where Henry Holland had already laid out Hans
Town in the later C18 (see Chelsea, KC, Perambulation 3). It is
here that one begins to find echoes of Nash, stucco, and the first
whispers of Italianate influence. Kensington has some of the most
exquisite domestic architecture in London from this transitional
phase between the prim Georgian and the bold High Victorian.
Especially accomplished is the work of *George Basevi* on the Smith's

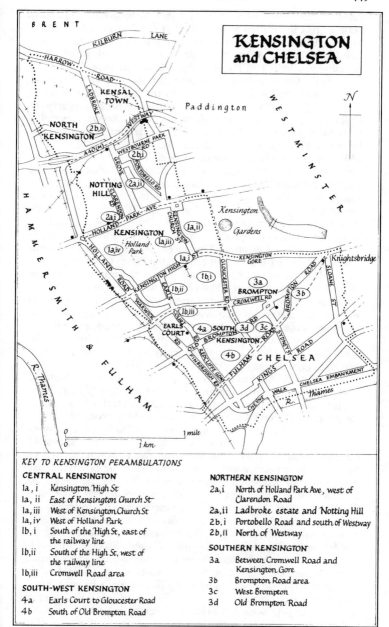

KENSINGTON and CHELSEA

KEY TO KENSINGTON PERAMBULATIONS

CENTRAL KENSINGTON

1a, i	Kensington High St
1a, ii	East of Kensington Church St
1a, iii	West of Kensington Church St
1a, iv	West of Holland Park
1b, i	South of the High St, east of the railway line
1b, ii	South of the High St, west of the railway line
1b, iii	Cromwell Road area

SOUTH-WEST KENSINGTON

4a	Earls Court to Gloucester Road
4b	South of Old Brompton Road

NORTHERN KENSINGTON

2a, i	North of Holland Park Ave, west of Clarendon Road
2a, ii	Ladbroke estate and Notting Hill
2b, i	Portobello Road and south of Westway
2b, ii	North of Westway

SOUTHERN KENSINGTON

3a	Between Cromwell Road and Kensington Gore
3b	Brompton Road area
3c	West Brompton
3d	Old Brompton Road

Charity estate; Pelham Crescent of 1833 and Egerton Crescent and Terrace of the 1840s. *John Blore*'s contribution is more severe but no less elegant: Brompton Square 1834–5, Hereford Square 1845, Drayton Gardens 1846.

The urbanity of terraces in squares and crescents could be tem-

pered by the inclusion of villas in leafier surroundings. This was
Nash's great innovation at Regents Park (*see* Westminster (outer),
St Marylebone), and its reverberations echoed throughout the
London suburbs. A group of detached villas (of which little
remains) was built E of Holland Park already in 1814. Hyde Park
Gate, to the S of Kensington Gardens, was laid out with a mixture
of villas and terraces in the 1830s. On the less expensive sites of
northern Kensington this trend is especially pronounced. N of
Holland Park Road, on the Norlands estate, *Robert Cantwell*'s
formal composition of Royal Crescent is surrounded by streets of
Gothic and Italianate villas and semi-detached houses of the 1840s,
while on the spacious concentric layout of the Ladbroke estate
(built up largely in the 1840s and 50s, although planned earlier) the
sumptuously stuccoed houses and terraces by *William Reynolds*
and *Thomas Allom* are separated by generous communal gardens (a
device developed earlier in Tyburnia (*see* Westminster (outer),
Paddington, Perambulation 1a). In the 1850s a similar mixture of
house types is found in and around The Boltons, the *chef d'œuvre*
of *George Godwin Jun.* on the Gunter estate in SW Kensington, but
grandest of all are the houses of Kensington Palace Gardens, *palazzi*
rather than villas, of 1845 onwards, by such eminent figures as
Owen Jones, Sydney Smirke, and Charles Barry's pupil *R. R. Banks*.

The population of Kensington was 8,556 in 1801; by 1841 it was
26,834, then in the next ten years it shot up to 44,053. From the
1850s the success of this western suburb was assured, and with the
rapid expansion of building activity that followed, by 1881 the
population was 163,151. By then nearly all the parish was built
over, and growth was less rapid.

It was the Great Exhibition of 1851, and the ensuing development
of the museums and academic area, that elevated 'South Kensington' to a social level hitherto reserved for Mayfair. The grand
boulevard of Queen's Gate and the surrounding streets were built
up from 1855 with very tall stucco terraces of impressive richness
and invention (*T. Cundy III* and *C. J. Richardson* were responsible
for some of the best). This free Italianate manner was imitated over
the next twenty years, generally with less skill, to an extent that has
made much of Kensington drearily repetitive. As the *Survey of
London*'s painstaking research has shown, such houses were built
speculatively, often to builders' specifications and not to architects'
designs – although sometimes the roles were one and the same (as
in the case of *Cundy*, and also of the most eminent of the Kensington
builder-developers, *Sir Charles James Freake*). So one turns with
relief to the style which broke the mould: the red brick and vigorous
Dutch Renaissance detail of *Norman Shaw* and his followers. It
was heralded already in 1869 by *Philip Webb*'s No. 1 Palace Green,
but made its chief impact with *Shaw*'s Lowther Lodge, Kensington
Gore, of 1873–5. Soon red brick was making inroads in Queen's
Gate, and was adopted with special enthusiasm by the successful
artists and architects (among them *William Burges*) who settled in
Melbury Road on the W fringe of Holland Park. At first favoured
only by individual clients, during the 1880s 'Queen Anne' was
adopted by developers eager to be up-to-date (see *George & Peto*'s
Harrington and Collingham Gardens, *J. J. Stevenson*'s Kensington
Court).

By the 1870s Kensington was well supplied with underground stations, and with easier access to central London, the demand for high-density housing grew as that for stabling declined (although many mews cottages survived to become superior C20 accommodation). Artists' studios, or at least artistically conceived small dwellings, became a popular way of filling small plots (see e.g. around Stratford Road in central Kensington). But it was blocks of flats which provided the most promising outlet for the Kensington developer. It was again *Norman Shaw* who showed the way, with Albert Hall Mansions of 1879. Throughout the last decades of the C19 Kensington filled up with ponderously picturesque blocks of flats, giving way in the early C20 to more widely spaced compositions in a less jolly and more genteel semi-Georgian and semi-modernistic style. Kensington High Street and its hinterland demonstrates the progression. Among them stand out a few more inventive buildings of the turn of the century, when the influence of the Arts and Crafts movement had an effect even on this staid and respectable borough: *F. S. Chesterton*'s Sundial House in the High Street and his terrace in Hornton Street, *Harold Cooper*'s No. 1A Palace Gate, and above all *Halsey Ricardo*'s highly individual, colourfully tiled No. 8 Addison Road of 1908. The early modern movement had less success: its main representatives are flats by *Wells Coates* in Palace Gate, and by *Maxwell Fry* in Ladbroke Grove.

Apart from the museums and academic area of South Kensington, which is a story of its own (*see* Public Buildings 2), there are few outstanding C19 and early C20 public buildings. The most interesting aspect is the popularity in the mid C19, in complete contrast to most of the housing, of a Tudor or Jacobean style, perhaps influenced by the genuine local examples of Holland House and Campden House (Brompton Hospital 1844–6, St Mary Abbots Workhouse 1848, former Vestry Hall in the High Street 1851). Unlike other parts of London, Kensington did not make a show of civic pride; its most enterprising public work was the Silchester Road Baths of 1886–8 (now replaced). The vestry commissioned only one new library, a pretty building of 1891–4 in Ladbroke Grove, while the newly constituted borough of 1901 was content to keep as its Town Hall an undistinguished building of 1878 (also now demolished).

What of Kensington in the later C20? Since the Second World War the centre of the borough has acquired some prominent public buildings ranging in mood from the post-war idealism of the government's Commonwealth Institute and the L.C.C.'s Holland Park School to the pedestrian solidity of the borough's own main Library and Civic Centre, respectively neo-Georgian and modern movement, but neither of them in the vanguard of style. In the museums area of South Kensington the principal change has been the expansion of Imperial College – an uninspiring use of a prime site, apart from the student lodgings in Princes Gardens. However, Kensington's predominant character is still that of a rich residential area. Compared with the diverse achievements of the later C19, when the domestic buildings of the borough were in the forefront of architectural fashion, the bulk of the C20 contribution is disappointing: the best positions along the main roads have been monopolized by ungainly hotels and unremarkable blocks of flats for the well-to-do, and many of the mews have been rebuilt as pretentious small town houses. The few exceptions to the low architectural level of recent times include *Fry, Drew & Partners'* imaginatively laid out private housing in Woodsford Square, and some individual houses in Cathcart Road and Lansdowne Crescent. Fortunately, however, stringent conservation measures have ensured that, away from the main roads, the later c 20 has made relatively little impact. Kensington is still full of elegant stuccoed terraces and charming villas basking in well cossetted affluence, with alterations (sometimes radical, as in Lansdowne Walk) discreetly confined to interior or rear.

The northern part of the borough is a different story. In the area from Notting Hill to Kensal Green the post-war planners faced a century of poverty, overcrowding, and neglect. Reconstruction, begun in the notorious Potteries area already in the late c 19, continued there and in the rest of North Kensington for the next hundred years, complicated by the disruption caused by the arrival of Westway in the 1960s. Here one can trace the whole story of changing fashions in urban improvement, from the piecemeal philanthropy of the late c 19, through the radical slum clearance schemes, planned in the 1930s but not carried out until the 1950s and later, of which *Goldfinger*'s Trellick Tower is the most prominent monument, to the reaction from the 1970s onwards in favour of rehabilitation and more homely contextual infilling (the Swinbrook area and St Mark's Road).

The economic background to the working-class character of northern Kensington was the c 19 development of industry and warehousing along the Grand Union Canal and the Great Western Railway; a similar pattern is to be found along the w border, beside the site of the Kensington Canal later used by the railway line that runs past Olympia. The industrial character of both these areas is fast disappearing as, with the decline of London manufacturing, long-derelict sites are replaced by housing, offices, and warehouses in the variegated styles of the late c 20.

FURTHER READING

The following account is heavily indebted to the quartet of meticulously researched volumes published by the Survey of London, vols. 37, *Northern Kensington* (1973), 38, *South Kensington, the Museums Area* (1975), 41, *Southern Kensington and Brompton* (1983), *Southern Kensington*, and 42, *Southern Kensington: Kensington Square to Earls Court* (1986), which trace in great detail the story of the suburban building booms of the c 19. The well illustrated *Policy Statements* on individual conservation areas, published by the borough in the 1980s, include useful succinct historical appraisals, which cover more recent c 20 development. For Kensington before its c 19 expansion: T. Faulkner, *History and Antiquities of Kensington* (1920), and W. J. Loftie, *Kensington Picturesque and Historical* (1888). A good recent general account is A. Walker with P. Jackson, *Kensington and Chelsea* (1987). For Kensington Palace see G. H. Chettle and P. A. Faulkner, 'Kensington Palace and Sir Christopher Wren: a Vindication', *J. Brit. Archaeol. Assoc.*, 3rd series, XIV (1951), pp. 1–10, and *History of the King's Works*, vols. V (1976), VI (1973); for the South Kensington Museums (in addition to the Survey volumes) J. Physick, *The Victoria and Albert Museum, The History of its Building* (1982), and M. Girouard, *Alfred Waterhouse and the Natural History Museum* (1981). *The London Oratory*, ed. M. Napier and A. Laing (1984), has essays on the main R. C. church and its contents. On parts of South Kensington: Dorothy Stroud, *Henry Smith's Charity Estate, Its History and Development* (1975). Of special relevance to Kensington architecture of the 1870s onwards are M. Girouard, *Sweetness and Light* (1977), and A. Saint, *Richard Norman Shaw* (1976).

ACKNOWLEDGEMENTS

The preparation, organization, and much of the writing of the Kensington perambulations were carried out by Tye Blackshaw. We are grateful to the staff of the Survey of London for help on miscellaneous problems, particularly to John Greenacombe, who supplied many unpublished details, and to Victor Belcher and Andrew Saint, former members of the Survey team, who also read and commented on the Kensington text. Alan Sanders, former principal planning officer of the borough, gave us much information on C20 developments, especially in North Kensington. On Kensington Palace both Juliet West and Richard Hewlings made helpful comments; the geological remarks on Kensal Green cemetery owe much to Eric Robinson.

CHURCHES AND OTHER PLACES OF WORSHIP

Anglican expansion began in the 1820s when the old parish church of St Mary Abbots was supplemented by two Commissioners' churches of the usual type, Holy Trinity Brompton and St Barnabas Addison Road. The main growth came after 1842, when John Sinclair became vicar of St Mary Abbots and proceeded to establish a total of fourteen new parishes. By 1872 no less than fifty-three churches and chapels were recorded by the *Church Index*, fifteen of them opened within the previous five years. The new Anglican churches ranged from safe 'low church' buildings designed to provide a focus on large new estates (for example the three churches by the *Godwins* in South Kensington of 1849 onwards, and *Vulliamy*'s St James Norlands of 1844–5) to the charming Lombardic Romanesque of All Saints Ennismore Gardens (now Russian Orthodox), 1848–9, also by *Vulliamy*, and the rogue Gothic experiments of *Bassett Keeling* (St George Aubrey Walk, 1864). In addition there were more controversial centres of Anglo-Catholicism, often paid for privately by High Church enthusiasts and embellished by their congregations with lavish furnishings at a slightly later date. To list the most interesting examples is to provide a roll call of major Victorian church architects: *White*'s determinedly original All Saints Talbot Road of 1852–61, *Scott*'s stately rebuilding of St Mary Abbots of 1868–79, with its fine spire, *Butterfield*'s wayward St Augustine Queen's Gate, 1870–7, and *Brooks*'s noble and lofty St John the Baptist Holland Road of 1872–89. In the 1870s the intention to make Kensington the main Roman Catholic centre in London led to a flurry of building, notably the *Hansoms*' Our Lady of Dolours Fulham Road and *Gribble*'s flamboyantly Roman Baroque Brompton Oratory. Other congregations have made some interesting C20 contributions, ranging from the tiny, exquisite Armenian church of St Sarkis (1922–3 by *Mewès & Davis*) to the lavish Ismaili Centre of 1978–83 by *Casson, Conder & Partners*.

The numbers and letters that follow addresses refer to the Perambulations.

1. *Church of England*

ALL SAINTS, Talbot Road (2b,i). 1852–61 by *William White*. Damaged in the Second World War, its spire now sadly truncated, although the octagonal top of the tall, slim W tower is still a striking landmark, much improved by cleaning in the 1980s. The church was part of an idealistic project by the Rev. Samuel Edward Walker of St Columb Major, Cornwall. Between 1852 and 1855 he acquired *c.* 90 acres in North Kensington for a new town of which All Saints and its intended college of priests was to be the focus. But his speculations collapsed, and the church was left as a shell; it was completed only in 1859–61, not by White but by a civil engineer (said to have been the brother of the incumbent). The general proportions of the tower are modelled closely on St Bavo, Ghent, although the detail is early rather than late Gothic. The tower is clasped by prominent buttresses rising to corner pinnacles and has no less than five stages, the two upper ones with tall two-light windows. The top stage not only turns octagonal but is enriched by bands of coloured stone and marble shafts. White's interest in polychromy is further displayed by the coloured tiles and gilding under the eaves which enliven the Bath stone of the body of the church. The equally original interior was praised by the *Ecclesiologist*, but its richness and colour were all but extinguished first by the 1930s whitewashing which concealed the tile and mosaic decoration, and then by war damage. Repairs by *Milner & Craze* were completed in 1951; the nave roof is simpler than White's original design. The broad arches of the wide nave, on red Devonshire marble clustered piers, continue across the shallow transept. Exceptionally large bold plate-tracery clerestory windows. The C19 fittings have all been replaced. – REREDOS. 1933 by *Cecil Hare*, Flemish Gothic. – REREDOS and ALTAR in the S transept, by *M. Travers*, from St Columb, Lancaster Road. – Chancel PAINTING by *Sir Ninian Comper*. – Post-war STAINED GLASS by *Gerald E. R. Smith* and by *Comper* (Lady Chapel, 1955).

CHRIST CHURCH, Victoria Road (1b,i). Built in 1850–1 by *B. Ferrey* as a chapel-of-ease to St Mary Abbots. Plain Gothic, before the wealthy began to be attracted to the district. Kentish rag and Bath stone, in approved Middle Pointed, with NE tower with broach-spire. Dormers were added to the nave in 1881. The w gallery was removed by *E. B. Ferrey* in 1896–7, when the w porch and the FONT were installed. – Chancel furnishings of 1914: REREDOS by *Powell & Sons*, SCREEN and STALLS by *Heaton, Butler & Bayne*, ALTAR RAILS and MOSAIC PAVE-MENT by *J. Arthur Reeve*. – CROSS and CANDLESTICKS. 1923–4 by *Omar Ramsden*. – MONUMENTS. Charlotte Athanass † 1860 by *Manning*, with deathbed relief. – Archdeacon Sinclair † 1875. Bust by *John Bell*.

HARROW MISSION, Latimer Road. *See* Hammersmith and Fulham, p. 226.

HOLY TRINITY, Prince Consort Road (3a). 1901–6 by *G. F. Bodley*, an exceptionally sensitive interpretation of a C14 hall church, making the most of a confined site; one of Bodley's last works before his death in 1907. Externally all of stone, with elaborate, finely drawn Perp tracery. Interior with broad nave, aisles, and outer aisle to the l. Tall slender shafts, wagon-roofed nave, no clerestory, lean-to aisles with transverse arches. – *Bodley* designed most of the fittings (carved by *Laurence A. Turner*), including the ALTAR, STALLS, FONT, and PULPIT. – Also his is the splendid REREDOS, executed only in 1911–12, a large late Gothic triptych with carved figures under elaborate canopies, with the Crucifixion as centrepiece. – ORGAN CASE by *C. G. Hare*. The present organ was brought from St Mark North Audley Street in 1950 (the future of its organ case, still in St Mark, was under discussion at the time of writing). – STAINED GLASS by *Burlison & Grylls*. – The MONUMENT to Bodley was designed by his pupil *E. P. Warren* in 1910, in Jacobean style – a surprising choice. Alabaster and marble with a bust.

HOLY TRINITY, Brompton Road (3b). 1826–9 by *T. L. Donald-son*, a Commissioners' church built on the site of a burial place of St George's Hospital. Set back from the road down an avenue planted in 1831, and somewhat overshadowed by the Oratory, it is the usual tight composition, of Suffolk brick with a thin w tower, originally with a s porch symmetrically set in the centre of the s aisle, and on the N side a corresponding entrance to the burial vaults. Ecclesiologically improved in 1843, when tracery was added to the windows by *Blore* and the s entrance removed, and more radically in 1879–82 by *Blomfield*, who added a new raised chancel in coloured brick. Later additions include the wooden vaulted nave roof of 1882, the sw porch by *R. W. Knightley Goddard*, 1913, and the N chapel and NW porch, 1920–4 by *A. Blomfield Jun*. Despite all this, inside, the original thin piers and galleries (front altered 1882) still convey something of the flavour of the original building. Many later Victorian embellishments. – REREDOS. Large, of gold mosaic, by *Clayton & Bell*, 1885. – FONT. By *E. C. Hakewill*, 1863, with carved reliefs on stumpy columns. – Low chancel SCREENS of marble, 1914. – Plaster RELIEF above sedilia, designed by *Henry Wilson*, executed by *E. Lanteri*, 1906. – STAINED GLASS. s aisle by *Warrington*, 1863. – Chancel and w windows of the 1880s by *Heaton, Butler & Bayne*. – In the NW corner of the churchyard, CHURCH HOUSE by *Laurence King*, 1965.

ST AUGUSTINE, Queen's Gate (3a). The first High Church enterprise in the new Kensington suburbs, established by the church musician R. R. Chope and built in 1870–7 by *Butterfield*, his last major church in London. The way his tall, gaunt stock brick façade, with its stone and blue and red brick bands and its w bellcote, placed at a jarring angle, breaks into the continuity of the well-mannered stucco façades of the surrounding houses is very typical of his style. The interior, wide rather than long, was also designed with a lively polychrome pattern of coloured brick (including Pether's buff patent bricks with moulded fleur-de-lys), with tiles on the aisle walls. All whitewashed in the 1920s, although in 1975 an attempt was made to return to Butterfield's original colour scheme, painting over the white distemper where it could not be removed. The HOLY SOULS CHAPEL is by *Nicholson*, 1923. – FONT, PULPIT (carved by *Earp*), and BRASS LECTERN are original. – The wildly southern Baroque REREDOS is by *Martin Travers*, 1928. – Also by him the STATIONS OF THE CROSS and aisle ALTAR. – STAINED GLASS by *Butterfield* and *A. Gibbs*.

ST BARNABAS, Addison Road (1a,iv). Designed in 1825 by *Lewis Vulliamy*, built in 1827–9 to slightly simplified plans. A Commissioners' church of the King's College chapel type so popular at the time: a rectangle in white Suffolk brick, with four corner turrets of stone. Perp tracery, projecting tripartite w porch (original pinnacles replaced in 1957–8). The side walls, now with late C19 battlements, were originally more delicately decorated with pinnacles and pierced parapets. Broad nave with flat ceiling; galleries on three sides on iron columns. An upper gallery for the organ was removed *c.* 1878. The wide chancel arch, flanked by remarkable two-tier Perp openwork tracery, dates from 1860–1, when a chancel was added by *T. Johnson*. The present larger chancel is of 1909 by *J. Arthur Reeve*. No original furnishings: the interior was redecorated and reseated in 1885–7 by *A. Baker*, in sympathetic Tudor Gothic. – Low SCREEN, with marble angels, and openwork Perp PULPIT added in 1895. – STAINED GLASS. E window by *Clayton & Bell*, 1883, w window by *O'Connor*, 1851 (the two transposed in 1895, and the E window reconstructed in 1910). – N aisle, beneath the w gallery, 1902 by *J. Byam Shaw*: St Cecilia and St Margaret, an Arts and Crafts design in rich golden colours. – Chancel N: war memorial window by *Christopher Webb*, 1922. – MONUMENTS. George Shaw † 1901, by *Gerald Moira* and *Derwent Wood*. Severe aedicule with twin arches on Doric columns housing a recumbent effigy with a startling figure of the risen Christ against the back wall. – John Byam Shaw † 1919. A pretty painted wooden Gothic wall-monument incorporating a painting in Flemish style, attributed to *Gilbert Pownall* (Survey of London).

ST CLEMENT, Treadgold Street (2a,i). 1867–9 by *St Aubyn*. A modest church for the poor quarter of Notting Dale. Yellow brick with red bands, plate tracery, a small shingled spirelet. Iron columns inside; double transepts. s chancel aisle rebuilt as a chapel in 1908. Interior whitened. – REREDOS. 1896. – Some *Kempe & Co.* STAINED GLASS in s aisle and chapel.

ST CUTHBERT, Philbeach Gardens (4a). 1884–8 by *H. Roumieu Gough*, E. E., with an exterior of red and black brick and a lofty interior with polished Devonshire marble piers and clerestory. No chancel arch or tower, and no E window; instead a blank area with external niches for statues. W bellcote removed in 1946–8, when the church was re-roofed in copper. Remarkable chiefly for the lavish embellishments carried out from 1887 to 1914 under the notoriously Anglo-Catholic vicar Henry Westall. Enormous, overwhelming carved REREDOS made in 1913–14, largely by *Gilbert Boulton* to a design of 1899 of Hispanic inspiration by the Rev. *Ernest Geldart*. Much excellent work by the Arts and Crafts designer *Bainbridge Reynolds*, who was a member of the congregation. By him the bizarre LECTERN, almost entirely of wrought iron and repoussé copper, 1897 (additions 1910–11), the light fittings of 1887, the royal arms, silver-panelled high-altar frontal (1910), communion rails, Paschal candlestick, altar rails of the Lady Chapel, chapel and organ screens, and clock. Some of his work, especially in metal, has a charm almost art nouveau, much more playful than most Arts and Crafts work. Other decoration, e.g. the diapering of the walls, was carried out by the Guilds of St Peter and St Joseph, groups of lay men and women, who also executed vestments and frontals designed by *Geldart*. In addition there are *Gough*'s original fittings (PULPIT, SEDILIA, and PISCINA, carved by *Felix de Sziemanowisz*, 1887–8, and ROOD SCREEN, 1893); STATIONS OF THE CROSS, paintings by *Franz Vinck* of Antwerp, 1888; and the Lady Chapel REREDOS, 1908, and PULPIT CANOPY, 1907, by *J. Harold Gibbons*, who also did the CALVARY outside. Baptistery STAINED GLASS 1888 by *C. E. Kempe*. On the E wall outside, STATUE of St Gregory by *Gilbert Boulton*, 1908. – The CLERGY HOUSE (No. 50) is of brick, with trefoil-headed windows. – PHILBEACH HALL, with library, gymnasium, and curate's flats, is of 1894 by *Gough*, N end rebuilt 1956–7.

ST GEORGE, Aubrey Walk (1a,iii). 1864 by *Bassett Keeling*. Quirky rogue-architect front (Pevsner called it atrocious), with open narthex on short columns, multi-coloured. The tower with stairs to the gallery, formerly with a spire, now with a short post-war cap by *Milner & Craze*. The interior has been considerably altered (apse demolished, walls whitewashed, columns cased). It was originally exceedingly patterned, with red and black brick arches on iron columns, small circular clerestory windows, and a restless criss-cross of timbers in the roof – STAINED GLASS. Clerestory windows and S aisle window with St George by *Hugh Arnold*, 1906. – Three S aisle windows by *C. Townshend* (PC).

ST HELEN, St Helen's Gardens (2b,ii). A mild late Gothic group of church, hall, and vicarage in pale brick, 1954–6 by *J. B. S. Comper*, replacing a church of 1884 by *Currey* destroyed in the war. Whitewashed, rather Netherlandish interior, dominated by a fine large ORGAN CASE by *Ninian Comper*. – Brass LECTERN from the previous church. – PEWS by *Norman Shaw*, from the Harrow Mission church, Holy Trinity Latimer Road (HF). – STAINED GLASS also by *Ninian Comper*.

ST JAMES NORLANDS, St James's Gardens (2a,i). 1844–5 by *Lewis Vulliamy*, white brick, with geometric tracery. The square tower with spiky pinnacles is placed in the centre of the S side so as to make a good vista down Addison Avenue. It was to have had a stone broach-spire. Interior with tall, very wide arcades on quatrefoil iron piers. The galleries added in 1850 have been removed. Tiny pushed-up clerestory. Chancel, with E.E. stepped lancets, by *R.J. Withers*, 1876. Much polychrome interior decoration was removed in 1950. – REREDOS. 1880. The Last Supper, in carved and painted wood. – FONT. Stone and green marble with mosaic bands; 1872. – STAINED GLASS. Small scenes in the chancel S aisle E. – W rose window with Christ in Majesty and angels.

ST JOHN THE BAPTIST, Holland Road (1a,iv). The angular W porches with their fussy turrets, added in 1909–11 by *J.S. Adkins*, disguise the noble simplicity of *James Brooks*'s soaring church of 1872–89, early French Gothic in its inspiration – see the cluster of rounded, steep-roofed apses, the semicircular flying buttresses to N and S, and the W wheel window with its plate tracery. The original plan included a flèche above a crossing-lantern, and a large W tower. Within the later W end are three deep porches of the Chartres transepts type, intended to be external (the N one now a memorial chapel, the S one within a coffee room). The central portal has accomplished figures of the wise and foolish virgins on the jambs, added in 1909–11, but according to Brooks's intentions (except for the missing trumeau figure). The carving is by *J.E. Taylerson*. The interior, like the exterior, is all of stone, tall, cool, and vaulted, like a fragment of a cathedral. Nave with clustered piers, lancet clerestory windows, banded shafts for the vault. Lady Chapel, apsed, with sexpartite vault. Impressively tall arches to the shallow transepts. The spaciousness is somewhat cluttered by the later very elaborate furnishings. – Triple-arched stone SCREEN, 1895, with much sculpture on the upper parts added later. – PARCLOSE SCREENS. – REREDOS. 1892, embellished and enlarged by *Adkins* in 1909. – Lady Chapel REREDOS also carved and coloured by *Adkins*. – Much coloured marble was used, e.g. for the two low AMBONES, the PULPIT with tabernacled canopy, the PASCHAL CANDLESTICK, and the elaborate FONT in the baptistery erected by *Adkins*. – Good STAINED GLASS; by *Clayton & Bell*, apart from one S aisle window by *Kempe*, 1895.

ST JOHN THE EVANGELIST, Ladbroke Grove (2a,ii). 1844 by *J.H. Stevens & G. Alexander*. The pivot in the great Ladbroke estate planning scheme, at the top of Notting Hill, on the site of the grandstand of the short-lived hippodrome (*see* Perambulation 2a,ii). Architecturally undistinguished, although far more archaeologically correct (that is, at the time, 'modern') than for example St James Norlands. E.E., cruciform, with central tower and spire, and a spacious interior (redecorated in 1955 by *Milner & Craze*). – (REREDOS by *Aston Webb*, 1890. – STAINED GLASS in the E window by *Kempe*.)

ST JUDE, Courtfield Gardens (4a). 1867–70 by *George & Henry Godwin*. Kentish rag exterior with central gables with three Dec windows. To the S a more interesting random composition, with gables, chimney, two-storey porch, and a good solid tower with tall belfry windows and spire (built in 1879). Spacious interior with a low church flavour: a hall church, galleries throughout, with banded columns of iron in the manner of Bassett Keeling, originally painted buff to match the brick walls. The capitals in transitional style are of sheet copper. Galleries discreetly placed in the transversely-vaulted outer aisle. – The FURNISHINGS are mostly of 1879–81: REREDOS of alabaster with *Salviati* mosaics, marble and alabaster PULPIT, brass LECTERN, all by *Edward Frampton*. Low chancel SCREEN added in 1895. The brick walls of the chancel retain some stencilling, the nave walls were white-washed after post-war restoration by *Travers*, 1947. W end rearranged by *Romilly Craze*, 1969–70. – MONUMENTS. An unusual display of small matching plaques by *Powell*'s, starting in the 1890s. – VICARAGE to the N, 1874, also by the *Godwins*.

ST LUKE, Redcliffe Square (4b). 1872–3, the last and grandest of the three Kensington churches by the *Godwins*; grandly sited too, near the centre of the square. Apsed E end, NE tower and spire, all Kentish rag. Architecturally more conventional inside than their other churches, with a long nave with stone columns and brick walls. Remarkable chiefly for the quantity of sculptural embellishment. The sanctuary celebrates Pslam 150, with corbels on musical angels; the chancel-arch responds are each supported by no less than three three-quarter-length angels. The statues in the nave of martyrs and Protestant reformers (including St Sebastian, Huss, Tyndale, and Cranmer) were added in 1889 at the expense of the Rev. W. Handcock. The carving is all by *Richard Boulton* of Cheltenham, who also supplied the REREDOS and PULPIT (1874–6) and READING DESK, all of alabaster with coloured marble shafts and elaborate figure work. – Alabaster FONT, a copy of *Thorvaldsen*'s Angel of Baptism in Copenhagen. – ORGAN CASE. Large and elaborate Gothic, by *W. Aumonier*, 1920. – STAINED GLASS. W windows by *Ward & Hughes*.

ST MARY ABBOTS, Kensington High Street (1a,i). *Sir G. G. Scott*'s proud and lofty building of 1868–72 stands on the site of the original parish church of Kensington. Its name derives from its medieval ownership by Abingdon Abbey. The old church was rebuilt in 1683–96, its tower in 1772. The most remarkable features of its replacement are the commanding NE tower and spire built in 1872–9, over 60 metres high, inspired by St Mary Redcliffe, Bristol, and the winding and rising vaulted cloistral approach to the S door, added by *J. Oldrid Scott* in 1889–93, with its good iron gates and screens. W front with three tall two-light windows above a crisply carved doorway (cf. Dunblane Cathedral). The interior, not specially original but a spacious and dignified essay in Second Pointed, still gives a satisfactorily complete impression of the rich fittings to be expected in a wealthy Victorian parish. Six-bay nave, with slim octagonal and quatrefoil piers and paired clerestory windows, all faced with Bath stone. Plain barrel-vaulted ceiling of 1955 by *Romilly Craze*, replacing the wooden rib-vault destroyed in the Second World War. Double-aisled transepts; S chancel chapel remodelled as a war memorial chapel in 1920–1 by *Giles Gilbert Scott*. The chancel enriched by marble paving, banded marble shafts, and stiff-leaf carving e.g. around the trefoiled rere-arches of the clerestory. The sanctuary projects slightly, with elaborately canopied sedilia on the S, tall two-light windows on either side, and a proud geometric E window, all filled with excellent STAINED GLASS by *Clayton & Bell* in gloriously glowing colours. The glass elsewhere is largely also by them (exceptions: s chapel E rose by *Powell*; N aisle w, 1966, designed by *Alfred Fisher* made by *Whitefriars*), but borders and background of aisle and clerestory windows were regrettably removed after the Second World War. – REREDOS. Arcaded, with marble columns, by *Clayton & Bell*; mosaic panels with the evangelists completed 1879. Flanking mosaics of angels 1882 by *Salviati*. – Brass eagle LECTERN, 1873. – FONT by *Farmer & Brindley*, a large marble bowl with figures of the rivers of Paradise. Tall openwork cover of wrought iron added in 1881. – PULPIT. 1697 from the old church, hexagonal, with inlaid panels. – STALLS and PEWS. Completed under *J. Oldrid Scott* after his father's death in 1878. Handsome work, with the ungothic motif of curvaceous top scrolls. Iron screenwork above the back stalls.

MONUMENTS. Many minor works removed from the old church. The most ambitious is in the s transept, Edward, Earl of Warwick and Holland, Addison's stepson, † 1721. Seated figure in Roman costume on base, elbow on urn; made in 1730 by *Guelfi*. – Among the others: Aaron Mico † 1658, attributed to *Joshua Marshall*, a sober architectural frame although with a touch of mid C17 mannerism in its multi-layered pediment. – T. Courten † 1702, by *Grinling Gibbons*. Only one panel with cherubs' heads survives (N porch). – T. Henshaw † 1700. An unusual and well carved version of a cartouche with cornucopias against drapery. – The cartouches to C. Campbell † 1708 and Philip and Elizabeth Colby, erected 1727, have the more common cherubs' heads or garlands. – Francis Colman † 1771 by *W. Tyler*. Urn and shields. – Richard Warren † 1797, a very restrained classical urn. – General Fanning † 1818 by *Bacon Jun.* Mourning figure by a broken column. – Maria Mackennon † 1833, a similar theme but with an altar, by *Paten Marble Works*. – Colonel Hutchins † 1823 by *Chantrey*, a neo-classical altar draped with a flag. – Rev. T. Rennell † 1824. A bust, also by *Chantrey*; the matching bust is to Archdeacon Sinclair † 1875, rebuilder of St Mary Abbots and the inspiration behind many of the parish's new churches. – Richard Westmacott R.A. † 1872 and wife † 1898, with a relief of a pilgrim (signed RW). – Kneeling angel commemorating Alfred Duke of Edinburgh † 1900 and Leopold Duke of Albany † 1884. – In the CHURCHYARD several sarcophagi. The one to the w of the church with S-shaped fluting, to Elizabeth Johnstone, was part of a monument designed by *Soane* in 1784 and carved by *John Hinchcliffe Sen.* Nearby a tomb of severe Grecian design to William Townsend † 1823, and s of the church those of Frances Harper † 1794 and the Blewitt family, 1830s.

ST MARY, The Boltons (4b). 1849–50 by *George Godwin*, his first church in the district he laid out on the Gunter estate (*see* Perambulation 4b), bolder and more eccentric than his later Kensington churches. Financed largely by the first incumbent, the Rev. Hogarth Swale. Aisleless cruciform plan, an unusual choice. The crossing tower is decorated with large angels at the corners of the pierced parapet, and above this rise an octagonal lantern and short spire (completed 1856). Dec detail, with hefty crossing arches with foliage capitals. The *Ecclesiologist* strongly disapproved of the low church manner in which the stone pulpit under the open lantern provided the main focus. Arrangements were modified by *Joseph Peacock* in 1870–2, when the crossing was ceiled with a wooden groin-vault, diagonal arches were cut through to the transepts, and the organ was moved to the N vestry. The present austere whitewashed character dates from *Romilly Craze*'s post-war refurbishing of 1952, when the altar was moved forward, a Lady Chapel was created in the chancel, and most of the Victorian fittings were removed. Only the finely carved nodding arched SEDILIA and the FONT remain from Godwin's furnishings. – A new ORGAN was installed in the W gallery in 1956–60, when the site of the old organ was converted to a N chapel by *David Nye & Partners*. – STAINED GLASS. E window by *Margaret Kaye*, 1955, a brave effort for its date; a Nativity with bold, almost grotesque figures in deep colours. – W window 1964 by *Harper & Hendra*, abstract mosaic. – Two-storey neo-Tudor CHURCH HALL attached to the SE, 1965–6.

ST MICHAEL, Ladbroke Grove (2b,ii). 1870–1 by *James Edmeston Jun.* and his son *J. S. Edmeston*, in a Rhineland Romanesque, with elaborately moulded brickwork. Apsed sanctuary, S transept, and W baptistery. SW tower never completed; N transept added 1882. Simple unaisled interior. – Baroque REREDOS with a copy of a Veronese Virgin and Child.

ST PAUL, Onslow Square (3c). 1859–60 by *James Edmeston* for the developer C. J. Freake, who developed the neighbourhood (*see* Perambulation 3c). Kentish rag. Tower and spire at the E end facing the square; chancel to the W. Perp, with galleries on cast-iron columns, a preaching box of the Commissioners' type, by then very out of date. Sanctuary extended 1888–9 by *Wallace*. – REREDOS, tall marble PULPIT, and the excellent STAINED GLASS of the E window (probably by *Clayton & Bell*) all of *c.* 1890. The nave S, first from E, is by *Arild Rosencrantz*, 1930; figures in striking colours. – MONUMENTS. Sir Charles James Freake † 1884. Alabaster Gothic canopy on the W wall. – Anne and John King, erected *c.* 1900, with cherubs' heads in C 17 style. – Prebendary H. Webb-Peploe † 1919. Marble tablet in Italian style.

ST PETER, Kensington Park Road (2a,ii). The only classical C 19 54 church in the whole district – a style out of date for churches by the time Kensington developed. The architect is *T. Allom*, surveyor to the Ladbroke estate, the date is 1852, though the architecture looks earlier: façade with forward-curving front with attached giant portico carrying the usual W tower of square and then circular stages and crowned by a cupola. Interior with giant Corinthian columns, tucked-in galleries, flat ceiling (renewed 1951), and a chancel added in an Italian High Renaissance style by *Barry* and *James Edmeston Jun.* in 1879. White and gold colouring. Much enrichment of the 1880s onwards: alabaster chancel mosaic 1880, alabaster PULPIT 1888, baptistery with iron grille.

ST PHILIP, Earls Court Road (1b,ii). 1857–8 by *T. Johnson* of Lichfield (father-in-law of the first vicar). Brick with stone dressings. Dec w window; NW turret with spire. Enlarged in 1863 (s aisle widened, s transept added). The interior was radically refurbished in 1978–82, when much seating was removed and the walls were painted deep red, the octagonal columns and arcades white. – Painted REREDOS designed by *Walter Tapper*, 1912–13. – SEDILIA and sanctuary blank arcading with marble shafts (carved by *Farmer*) by *Johnson*, 1863. – PULPIT. 1889 by *Arthur Baker*. – SE Lady Chapel by *Francis Bacon*, 1919. – W gallery extended for a new ORGAN by *Noel Mander*, 1962. – STAINED GLASS. E window 1966 by *Alfred Fisher* of *White-friars*. – To the E, PARISH ROOMS by *A. Baker*, 1887–8.

ST STEPHEN, Gloucester Road (1b,iii). 1866–7 by *Joseph Peacock*. Coursed stone exterior, well buttressed, with unusually large transepts. The intended tower was not built. Peacock's interior had polychrome decoration (since painted over), with clustered marble columns, but his work has been overwhelmed by lavish later High Church furnishings (reredos and sanctuary fittings 1903 by *Bodley*, rood 1908 by *Walter Tapper*). NE vestry and chapel added by *Gough*, 1887. – STAINED GLASS. E window by *John Hayward*, 1962.

ST THOMAS, Kensal Road (2b,ii). 1967 by *Romilly Craze*, replacing a church by *Romaine & Brierley* of 1889, destroyed in the war. A dull rectangle, brick-faced, with windows high up. Fibreglass figure of St Thomas by *A. W. Banks*; another inside, of Christ in Majesty.

2. Roman Catholic

ASSUMPTION, Kensington Square (1b,i). 1870–5 by *George Goldie*. Exterior of banded brick; Gothic detail. Remarkable chancel arch on giant columns of Aberdeen marble, with flanking arches. Further columns around the high altar were removed after a fire in 1957, when the nave roof was rebuilt in concrete by *Bartlett & Purnell*. – Also by *Goldie* ST ANDREW'S HALL (former school). Brick Gothic, 1873–4, and the SECONDARY SCHOOL, in a more elaborate institutional Gothic, 1875–88. – Post-Second-World-War additions for a teacher training college and convent buildings from 1959 onwards, all by *C. Lovett Gill*.

84 ORATORY OF ST PHILIP NERI, Brompton Road (3b). London's most thoroughgoing C19 import of the Italian style: a group consisting of the large Roman Baroque church at the r.; the Italian-Renaissance-looking house of the Oratorians at the back, stock brick and very restrained, 1853 by *J. J. Scoles*; and St Wilfrid's Hall by *L. Stokes*, 1910, on the l. In front of this the MONUMENT to Cardinal Newman by *Bodley & Garner*, 1896, sharply detailed, and in Newman's own Italian taste. The church is the result of an important competition, won in 1878 by *Herbert Gribble*, a pupil of J. A. Hansom. It is designed to create an atmosphere of Italian devotion and Italian fervour, and succeeds

85 in it. The spacious interior is composed on the Gesù scheme of the Italian Baroque: nave with side chapels instead of aisles, and a dominant crossing with dome and drum. The only distinctly modern and northern idea in the interior is the covering of the

nave by concrete vaults pierced by domes with glazed centres. The steel-framed main dome, taller than Gribble's original design, was built only after his death, in 1896 by *George Sherrin* and his assistant *E. A. Rickards*. The W front was completed in 1893 (apart from the two campanili, which were never built). It has a narthex, its most original feature, and behind it coupled pilasters, a pediment, and statuary along the skyline. The rest of the church was opened in 1884. – Much of the FURNISHINGS is by Italians. Interior decoration of the nave by *C. T. G. Formilli*, 1927–32, with many stucco reliefs, yellow Siena marble and pilasters, Venetian mosaics below the dome. – The most important SCULPTURES are the gigantic marble statues of the Apostles by *G. Mazzuoli*, *c.* 1680–5, on corbels between the chapels. They stood originally in Siena Cathedral. – Sanctuary with marble walls by *I. Cosgreave*, 1888–90. – HIGH ALTAR with large painting of St Philip in Ecstasy, and the side walls of the chancel with scenes of St Philip Neri, founder of the Oratorians, by *B. Pozzi*, 1924–7. – Seven-branch CANDLEHOLDERS by *William Burges*, given by the Marquess of Bute in 1878. – CHAPELS, clockwise from the NW. – SACRED HEART. Decoration by *Geoffrey Webb*, *c.* 1935. – ST JOSEPH. Altar and reredos by *Scoles*, 1861, from the old church. Statue of St Joseph, Belgian, 1884. – SEVEN DOLOURS. Altarpiece painted in Rome by *Ferenc Szoldatits*, a Nazarene follower, *c.* 1859. – ST PHILIP. Altar and baldacchino by *Gribble*, with tympanum in Italian cement by *G. Moneta*, 1890. Wall reliefs by *L. Bradshaw*, *c.* 1927; apse 1901–3. – ST WILFRED. Altar and baldacchino originally from St Servatius Maestricht, *c.* 1710. – ENGLISH MARTYRS. Two altars by *David Stokes*, 1936–8. Bas-relief on St Theresa altar by *A. Pollen*; triptych over English Martyrs altar by *Rex Whistler*. – LADY CHAPEL. Altar and reredos from the Chapel of the Rosary in San Domenico, Brescia, 1693, richly inlaid with semi-precious stones, made and probably designed by *F. Corbarelli & Sons*. Statues of St Rose of Lima and St Pius by *O. Marinali*, *c.* 1690–2. Other figures by *Thomas Ruer* († 1696). – In the ORGAN GALLERY, one of the two angels is signed by *Calegari*, early C18. – ST MARY MAGDALENE. Mosaics flanking the altar by *A. Capello*, 1883–4. Altar and reredos by *Gribble*; decorations by *Cosgreave*; bronze gates by *Starkie Gardner*. – ST PATRICK. Altar from Naples with reredos by *Gribble*; altar paintings by *P. Pezzati*; paintings on wooden panels possibly by *F. Floris*. War memorial 1918–21 by *L. Berra*, with an Italian Pietà. – BAPTISTERY. Red breccia marble basin on alabaster, with eight Carrara lions, 1891. Bronze cover by *Starkie Gardner*.

OUR LADY OF DOLOURS, Fulham Road (4b). Built for St Mary's Priory of Servite Friars, 1874–6 by *J. A. Hansom*. The brick exterior is entirely hidden from the road by the entrance (1880, simplified 1962) and long E. E. passage whose climax is a low vaulted narthex with quatrefoil piers and shouldered transverse arches, added in 1894 by *C. F. Hansom*. The church beyond is on an impressive scale, of stone, with E. E. detail: six-bay nave with granite columns with polished marble shafts, the colours alternating. Disappointing spindly roofs; sanctuary with canted apse, lavish fittings. The interior decoration is mostly by *Thomas*

Orr & Co. – HIGH ALTAR, with tall, pinnacled REREDOS, 1882–3 by *J. S. Hansom*, carving by *Richard Boulton*. The altar was reduced in size in 1974. – Many SIDE ALTARS off the aisles, in the Italian manner, and with furnishings to match (cf. Brompton Oratory, above). Among them, SEVEN HOLY FOUNDERS, with Trecento-style panels by Father *Piriteo Simoni*, 1875 (now Chapel of Our Lady). – ST JOSEPH, with painted panels by *L. Galli* of Florence, and statute by *Mayer* of Munich. – The N chapel (now BLESSED SACRAMENT CHAPEL), reconstructed as a Lady Chapel in 1890 by *J. S. Hansom*, is a tiny Gothic space thickly encrusted with stone-carving and with a double layer of arcading. – BAPTISTERY, W of the narthex. 1925, free Byzantine, with rather eerie green marble walls and floor. Bronze octagonal FONT with low reliefs. – STAINED GLASS. E windows by *Clayton & Bell*. – MONUMENT. Prior Appolloni † 1900, with a marble Pietà by *J. W. Swynnerton* against the S wall.

OUR LADY OF THE HOLY SOULS, Bosworth Road, Kensal Town (2b,ii). 1882 by *J. F. Bentley*; fairly modest, red brick, Gothic.

OUR LADY OF MOUNT CARMEL, Kensington Church Street (1a,ii). 1954–9 by *Sir Giles Scott*, one of his last works. Slightly modernistic late Gothic, brick with stone dressings, replacing a building by *E. W. Pugin* of 1866, destroyed in the Second World War. A very lofty aisleless nave with pointed concrete transverse arches carrying a continuous clerestory, with flat ceiling above. Small openings in the bases of the arches: a relic of the passage-aisle tradition.

OUR LADY OF VICTORIES, Kensington High Street (1a,i). A post-war replacement of 1955–8 by *Adrian Scott* of a church of 1867–9 by *Goldie*. Unenterprising and austere brick Gothic, less interesting than the first designs. Interior with passage aisles. NE chapel 1971 by *Archard & Partners*. – STAINED GLASS by *C. F. Blakeman*.

ST FRANCIS, Pottery Lane (2a,i). A small site tightly packed with schools, church, and presbytery, built by the oblates of St Charles, founded by Manning, to serve the Notting Dale slums. The church, quite small, in minimal French Gothic, stock brick banded with black, with a polygonal apse, was built in 1859–60 by *Henry Clutton*. It is famous chiefly for the first work by Clutton's pupil *J. F. Bentley*, who added the ingenious Lady Chapel curving around the apse, the NW porch, and the baptistery (1861–3), and supervised the interior decoration and fittings. (He was also the first person to be baptized in the church, after his conversion in 1862.) Both chancel and baptistery are vaulted. Apart from wall painting which disappeared in redecorations of 1926 and 1960, the rich and colourful furnishings remain remarkably complete. – HIGH ALTAR. 1863, with marble and glass inlay and painted REREDOS. – LADY CHAPEL ALTAR. Also of 1863, with paintings by *Westlake* (Seven Dolours of Our Lady). – ALTAR OF ST JOHN. 1861, also with *Westlake* painting, in Quattrocento style. – STATIONS OF THE CROSS along the NE wall by *Westlake*, 1865–70. – FONT. 1861–2, red granite, with green columns; wooden cover 1865. – Excellent iron baptistery SCREENS by *Osmond Bentley*, 1907; gallery above of 1882. – SCULPTURE. Crucifix (W end) and Virgin and Child in a C14 style, with elaborate canopy, both by *T. Phyffers*, 1870. – STAINED GLASS. The E windows designed by *Bentley & Westlake*, made by *Lavers & Barraud*. – Much other work also by *Bentley* (candlesticks, vestments, splendid jewelled monstrance (1864), etc.).

ST PIUS X, St Charles Square (2b,ii). The former chapel of St Charles College, 1908 by *P. A. Lamb & R. O'B. North*. Classical brick exterior. Barrel-vaulted nave; coffered chancel arch. – Large REREDOS and domed TABERNACLE in Italian baroque style. – STAINED GLASS. Eleven tall round-headed clerestory windows by *Trinick*, post-1945 (DE). – The college (replaced by secondary schools after 1945) had been founded by Manning in 1863, moved to this site in 1874, and was taken over by the nuns of the Sacred Heart as a training college from 1905.

3. Nonconformist and other places of worship
(arranged alphabetically by name)

ASSUMPTION AND ALL SAINTS (Russian Orthodox), Ennismore Gardens (3a). Built as All Saints C. of E., 1848–9 by *L. Vulliamy*, tower added 1870. Lombardic Romanesque façade and campanile, stone with some red brick banding. Impressive interior: a basilica with very tall Corinthian columns of iron, small clerestory, and galleries on three sides. The Early-Christian/Italian-Romanesque style was a speciality of the 1840s: cf. Wilton, Wiltshire, and Christ Church Streatham (La). The polychrome decoration of the apse by *Owen Jones* (cf. Christ Church) was replaced in 1911 by tiled panels and coffering by *Derwent Wood*. The other decoration is of the 1890s, an interesting example of the Italian trend in the Arts and Crafts movement: sgraffito by *Heywood Sumner* on the upper nave walls and above the chancel arch; the clerestory STAINED GLASS of the type with tree decoration more usual in houses than in churches. The W end was decorated by *Harrison Townsend* in 1892.

BETHESDA CHAPEL, Kensington Place, Campden Hill (1a,iii). A modest stuccoed building of 1824.

DEUTSCHE EVANGELISCHE CHRISTUSKIRCHE, Montpelier Place (3b). 1904 by *Charles Rees*. Small and rather pretty, with two fanciful Gothic stair-turrets flanking a large geometric W window. Given by Baron J. Henry Schroder. The congregation was first established in the city in 1669 and from the early C18 had occupied the Royal Chapel at St James's Palace. – FONT, C17, wooden base and cover – STAINED GLASS: some by *F. X. Zettler*.

ISMAILI CENTRE, Cromwell Road and Thurloe Square (3b). A religious and cultural centre built to celebrate twenty-five years of leadership by the Aga Khan. 1978–83 by *Casson, Conder & Partners*. Sleek exterior with a skin of polished pale grey Sardinian granite. Narrow windows to the prayer hall on the second floor. The main visual interest is provided lower down, by the series of recessed, jewel-like lower bay-windows to S, E, and W, with small panes of bevelled glass and brass-inlaid glazing-bars. The interiors are very pure and chaste in their ornament, very rich in their materials; chiefly white with touches of blue and grey. Irregular spaces, because of the awkward site, cleverly handled. Polygonal foyer with five piers (the five pillars of the Koran), and a pool, floor tiles, and ceiling pattern all based on heptagons (the seven prophets of Islam). Wedge-shaped inner hall and staircase – a leisurely ascent, with ingeniously lit upper vistas at the half-landing, leading to a conference hall at first-floor level which is lit by the bay-windows on two sides. Decorative calligraphic wall panel by *Gulgee*. Another stair to the prayer hall above, a low-ceilinged rectangle, where exterior light is diffused through formalized calligraphic tracery. Islamic-inspired fittings throughout the building by *Karl Schlaminger*, including the teak doors with a distinctive pattern of close-set mullions, and the staircase chandelier, a cluster of little glass goblets on gold chains. On the top floor a library and a roof garden with evergreens and five fountains by *Saski Associates*.

KENSINGTON TEMPLE (Elim Pentecostal Church), formerly HORBURY CONGREGATIONAL CHAPEL, Kensington Park Road (2a,ii). 1848–9 by *John Tarring*. Prominently sited. Kentish rag, Dec detail; cruciform with two towers. Galleries on cast-iron columns. An early example of Nonconformist Gothic.

KENSINGTON UNITED REFORMED CHURCH, Allen Street (1b,ii). 1854–5 by *A. Trimen*. Built as a Congregational chapel when the street was developed. Stone classical front with giant portico of Bath stone with two pairs of Corinthian columns and pediment.

MORMON CHURCH, Exhibition Road (3a). 1961 by *T. P. Bennett & Son*, in a straightforward contemporary style with pronounced vertical emphasis. N tower with a spike; beneath it a STAINED GLASS window by *P. Fourmaintreaux*. Double-height hall and chapel, with two storeys of classrooms above.

NOTTING HILL METHODIST CHURCH, Lancaster Road (2b,i). 1879 by *Alexander Lauder* of Barnstaple. One of the few older landmarks left in this area. White brick with stone dressings, the front asymmetrical, with an elaborate Geometric Gothic window embellished by a stone angel. Rounded stair-turret and spirelet on the r. Tall gabled flank walls, with basement below.

ST MARK (Coptic Orthodox Patriarchate), Allen Street and Scarsdale Villas (1b,ii). Ragstone, mostly Dec detail, with a tower at a street corner, turning octagonal at the top with a quirky angled corner turret. Built in 1863 by *J. M. McCulloch* for the Scottish Presbyterians. Chancel arch inserted into the barn-like interior by *J. Theodore Barker* in 1876–80, when galleries were also added. Further alterations of 1884–8 by *J. M. MacLaren* (nave roof opened up).

ST PETER (Armenian since 1975), Cranley Gardens (3c). 1866–7, from the office of the developer of the neighbourhood, *C. J. Freake*. Kentish rag, Dec, a little spindly in its detail. NW porch with broach-spire; large galleried transepts. Alterations by *W. D. Caröe*, 1907–9, paid for by Percy Morris of Elm Park Gardens, Chelsea: stone W gallery, organ cases, vestries, and vaulted N chapel with much carving by *N. Hitch* and *H. Whitaker*. Apsidal chancel embellished and given dormer windows in 1922 by *Caröe & Passmore*. Arcades on clustered columns; walls originally of polychrome brick, whitewashed in the 1930s. – STAINED GLASS.

Clerestory windows by *Mary Lowndes*, 1904–6. – Other glass by *Ward & Hughes*, *Clayton & Bell*, and *Heaton, Butler & Bayne*. – MONUMENTS. Frank Macrae † 1915, with painting of St George, by *Jesse Bayes*. – WAR MEMORIAL by *Caröe*.

ST SARKIS (Armenian), Iverna Court (1b,ii). Small and exotic. Purpose-built in 1922–3 by *Mewès & Davis*, largely financed by Calouste Gulbenkian. The exterior is a faithful copy of the C13 bell tower of the monastery at Haghpat, Armenia. It is faced with large, immaculately dressed blocks of Portland stone. Greek-cross plan. Seven-sided open belfry with round arches below shallow gables, over an octagonal crossing supported on concave exterior corbelling. Apsidal baptistery 1937, SE sacristy 1950, by the same firm and in the same style. (Inside, a saucer dome on shallow arches, the walls plastered and lined to look like ashlar.) – Rich BALDACCHINO and ALTAR of alabaster, marble, onyx, and lapiz lazuli, with capitals of gilded metal, by the *Bromsgrove Guild*. – Seven-sided ELECTROLIER by *Baguès*. – VICARAGE. 1922, also by *Mewès & Davis*, brick with hipped roof, very simple.

ST SAVA (Serbian), Lancaster Road (2b,i). Built as St Columb (C. of E.) by *C. Hodgson Fowler*, 1900–1, a brick basilica in the Romanesque style. Plain W front with Lombard hanging arches and a circular window. – (BALDACCHINO. 1907. – STAINED GLASS. Three-light windows in the baptistery by *M. Travers*, 1915.) – The SERBIAN CHURCH CENTRE, on the site of the 1889 mission church, is of 1970 by *Scott, Brownrigg & Turner*, rather dour, four storeys faced with unbonded brown tiles.

SECOND CHURCH OF CHRIST SCIENTIST, Palace Gardens Terrace (1a,ii). 1926 by *T. S. Tait* of *Sir John Burnet, Tait & Son*. Neo-Early-Christian brick building with attached house and garden. Plain square interior with raked seats.

SIKH TEMPLE, Norland Road (2a,i). Built *c.* 1965. Simple cubic brick exterior.

SPANISH AND PORTUGESE SYNAGOGUE, St James's Gardens (2a,i). 1928. Brick, slightly Moorish-Romanesque in style. Arched narthex surmounted by a large Diocletian window and flanked by two squat towers.

TABERNACLE COMMUNITY CENTRE (former TALBOT TAB-ERNACLE), Talbot Road (2b,i). 1887 by *Habershon & Fawkner*, Waterhousian Romanesque, in bright orange terracotta with much diapering. Recessed, with gardens to the street.

UNITARIAN CHURCH, Nos. 112–114 Palace Gardens Terrace (1a,ii). 1976–7 by *Morgan & Branch*, replacing a red brick building of 1886–7 by *T. Chatfeild Clarke & Son* (known as the Essex Church from the old Essex Street Chapel near the Strand, whose sale financed the building). A satisfactory design, of yellow brick with rounded corners, with a gatehouse feature and bridge to the first floor. Circular roof-light to the foyer. – CARVING. A pair of angel's wings from the old church. Other furnishings from the old building were dispersed

WESLEYAN CHAPEL, Westbourne Grove (2a,1). 1858 by *W. W. Pocock*. Classical. Large arched upper windows between Ionic columns; big pediment.

4. Cemeteries

KENSAL GREEN CEMETERY OF ALL SOULS, Harrow Road
(2b,ii). Opened in 1833, the first of the eight new cemeteries
started on a commercial scale, and with standards of mortuary
hygiene in contrast to the horrid conditions then general in inner
London graveyards. Kensal Green is the largest of them and the
one favoured by the most generous patrons. Also it contains, in
recognition of its social purpose, two royal entombments: the
Duke of Sussex † 1843 and the Princess Sophia † 1848 (son and
daughter of George III).

The layout of the cemetery consists of a formal tree-lined
avenue leading to the Anglican chapel near the W end, and paths
that wind around the site. The design, executed by *J. W. Griffith*,
may owe something to schemes by *H. E. Kendall*, and by a Mr
Liddell, who had worked with Nash. There is much charm about
the shady mature trees, the formal and informal vistas, and the
haphazardly grouped tombs with their evocative array of famous
Victorian names, in styles ranging from pompous classical mausolea along the main avenue to the unostentatious dissenters'
memorials at the E end. Unfortunately the character has in too
many places been flagrantly eroded by the most insensitive siting
of recent graves, crammed along the walks and even intruding
into the pathways. The buildings are all to the design of *J. W.
Griffith*, the protégé of the chairman of the company, Sir John
D. Paul, who favoured the neo-Grecian. By 1834 Griffith had
completed the E lodge, the main W entrance, with a Doric semicircle and triumphal arch of exceptionally large blocks of Portland stone, and the Nonconformist chapel, an Ionic temple (now
derelict, its curving colonnades demolished). The competition
for the Anglican chapel had been won already in 1831 by *H. E.
Kendall* but, to his annoyance, his Gothic design was set aside,
and in 1836 *Griffith* provided instead a prostyle Greek Doric
temple with lower colonnades to the l. and r., enclosing open
courtyards behind. Further W the WEST LONDON CREMA-
TORIUM was added in 1939 by *G. Berkeley Willis*, cream brick,
in a classical idiom, with fountain court and garden by *Edward
White*.

MONUMENTS. Many of the earliest are simple slabs of white
Portland stone or yellow Midland sandstone, materials easily
accessible by canal to the local monumental masons. Traditional
graveyard types – urns, obelisks and sarcophagi – are legion;
sculpture is less plentiful, and what there is, often in Carrara
marble (introduced from the 1840s), has suffered from pollution
from the neighbouring gasworks. Visually, there is a telling contrast between the weathered textures of the vulnerable limestone
and sandstones, and the immaculate surfaces of the granites that
became available from the mid C19, when the railways could
provide access to more distant quarries. Red Peterhead and dark
grey Rubislaw granite from Aberdeenshire, often highly
polished, were the most popular.

The earliest of the grander monuments are Greek or Greco-
Egyptian mausolea. Near the N wall, James Morison the Hygeist
† 1840, plain Grecian without openings. The others are grouped

80

near the main avenue. Among the most fanciful is the mausoleum dated 1837, 'erected by genius for the reception of its remains', for Andrew Ducrow † 1842, equestrian and circus owner, a wildly Egyptian affair of painted Portland stone with artificial stone sphinxes. It cost £3,000. – Nearby, John St John Long † 1834, a quack; a chaste Ionic aedicule with four pediments, by *Sievier*. – Aikman family, 1844. Greek, with front with four Doric columns *in antis*. – The family of George Birkbeck † 1841, founder of the Mechanics' Institutes. Mausoleum of granite and Portland stone. – Major-General Sir William Casement † 1844. Of artificial stone, Greco-Egyptian of four-poster type, with four life-size be-turbaned carytids, by *F. M. Lander*; cannons as iron railings. – 2nd Viscount Strangford † 1857. An open Italian Gothic canopy with an end panel of two angels in Carrara marble. – Commander C. S. Ricketts † 1867 by *William Burges*. A gorgeously rich Gothic shrine. Shafts of red Peterhead granite and green serpentine from Cornwall. Capitals of Portland stone, carved in one with the tomb-chest, which is decorated with applied stencilling. The roof is lavishly furnished with gargoyles and crockets. – Opposite, *H. E. Kendall's* family tomb, a gross Gothic cross. – William Mulready, the painter, † 1863 by *G. Sykes* (cf. Victoria and Albert Museum, Public Buildings 2), a charming Lombard Renaissance four-poster, mostly of artificial stone, with effigy and incised stories on the base. – Molyneux family, 1866 by *John Gibson*. High Victorian Gothic, in Peterhead granite and Carrara marble, polygonal, formerly with spire. – *John Gibson* himself † 1892, also polychrome and Gothic, but of Portland and very worn sandstone. – Mary Eleanor Gibson † 1872. Carrara marble, with twelve fluted columns around the tomb-chest; large and lively angels above. – Richard Mayne † 1868, a huge Peterhead granite obelisk, all in one piece. – Holland family, 1856. A well carved chest with figures, swags, and upturned torches between roundels, standing on griffins. – The fashion for carved chests was set no doubt by the tomb of the Princess Sophia † 1848, in the place of honour close to the Anglican chapel: a Quattrocento Carrara marble sarcophagus on a tall pedestal, designed by Professor *L. Grüner*, Prince Albert's artistic adviser, and carved by Signori *Bardi*. – The Duke of Sussex † 1843, across the avenue, has only the plainest of low tomb-slabs. – At the end of the s wing behind the chapel the Sievier family, showing a man reclining on a couch and a mourning woman kneeling beside him, by *R. W. Sievier* († 1868), who was a director of the General Cemetery Company. – Opposite, Georgina Clementson † 1868, a reclining effigy, by her father, *J. G. Lough*.

Along the lesser avenues, smaller monuments. Among the famous names: to the s, Bazalgette, a large tapering chest of Portland; the Brunel family, simple Carrara block on a granite base; and the Chartist Feargus O'Connor † 1855, hexagonal, of Portland stone, with a spire and a Carrara tablet. To the N, Sir Robert Smirke † 1845, simple, with portrait medallion, and Mme Elizabeth Soyer † 1842 with large standing figure on a painted Portland base with her portrait in Carrara marble showing her as a prettily dressed young girl, with two large cherubs above and a palette below. Her real palette used to be under glass at the back. Among the few other examples of serious sculpture are the monuments to James Ward the painter † 1859 by *Foley*, with a standing figure of the muse of painting, and Ninon Michaelis † 1895, a stele with a well carved low relief of a mourning female figure.

In the dissenters' burial area, among the much more modest tombs, an early example of a Gothic tomb-chest (unusually of slate), to James Prowle † 1843, and a memorable pair of granite obelisks, both erected by Joseph Corfield, one of 1879 to Robert Owen, pink and grey polished granite with bronze portrait profile, the other commemorating 'the Reformers' with an idiosyncratic list of 'Those who have given their time to improve the conditions and enlarge the happiness of all classes of society.'

ST MARY'S R.C. CEMETERY, Harrow Road. *See* Hammersmith (HF).

BROMPTON CEMETERY, between Old Brompton Road and Fulham Road (4b). Founded as the West of London and Westminster Cemetery in 1837, consecrated in 1840. Like the earlier Kensal Green (*see* above), an example of the large, non-committal, hygienic cemeteries by which the age of early humanitarian reforms overcame the horrors of the overcrowded churchyards of London. The first architect appointed was *Stephen Geary*, but the buildings were designed by *Benjamin Baud*, winner of a competition in 1838. The N entrance screen of stock brick looks cheap and somewhat debased, but the main architectural feature is an impressive composition: an octagonal Anglican chapel to the S of a circular enclosure approached from the N by extensive colonnades designed with catacombs below (their construction was expensive, however, and they were not popular). The intended R.C. and Nonconformist chapels were not built, and the company sold out to the government in 1852.

The layout is not specially inspired: rectangular plots divided by paths, with circular breaks at intervals for larger mausolea. The landscape gardener was *J. Finnemore*; *J.C. Loudon* was consulted on the planting. The formality of the arrangement around the great circle is now compromised by too many later tombs. The monuments in total are less remarkable than at Kensal Green. The exceptions among the repetitively standard types range from quaintly literal-minded memorials to a scatter of excellent mausolea in styles extending from late classical and Egyptian to Gothic and art nouveau. Many later well-lettered headstones.*

The most notable tombs flank the main path (sections numbered from the N). Only a selection to indicate the variety can be included here. – Thomas Cundy II, the architect, † 1867 (E, near the entrance). A Gothic ledger stone with Gothic rails. – Emmeline Pankhurst † 1928. Celtic cross with draped figure in the manner of Eric Gill. – McDonald Mausoleum (1W), 1902, a small chapel in flamboyant Gothic. – Courtoy, 1850–2 (circle 3, E). A dour grey granite Egyptian revival mausoleum, perhaps by *Avis* of Putney. – Meyrick, 1855 (section N, W of 3W). A fine neo-

*This account owes much to the survey made by Professor James Stevens Curl for English Heritage in 1988–9.

classical mausoleum in Portland stone, with good railings. –
Valentine Prinsep † 1904, the Pre-Raphaelite artist (4w). Fine
pink and white marble tomb-chest with weepers under ogee
arches. – Nearby is the most remarkable tomb in the cemetery,
to Frederick Leyland † 1892, shipowner and artistic patron,
designed by *Burne-Jones* – an exquisite Romanesque marble
shrine inlaid with bronze floral scrolls, standing on short
columns, with pitched copper roof, and surrounded by art
nouveau iron railings. – George Godwin † 1888, the architect
(4E), with portrait and reliefs of architectural instruments on the
pedestal. – Sangiorgi, 1893–4 (4E). A lavish Italian *fin-de-siècle*
sarcophagus with mourning youth. – John Jackson the boxer,
known as Gentleman Jackson, † 1845 (near the E terrace). By
E. H. Baily; a large lion on a tall base with Jackson's portrait in
medallion (cf. the monument to the boxer Thomas Cribb at St
Mary Magdalene, Woolwich, Gr). – Borthwick mausoleum (E
terrace). A classical sarcophagus with weepers by *A. Ashpitel*, *c.*
1867. – Godfrey Sykes, the artist who did so much work in the
South Kensington Museums (q.v., Victoria and Albert Museum,
Public Buildings 2), † 1865 (section U , W of 5E) – appropriately
in terracotta, with tiled roof and relief carvings. – Near the S
entrance Robert Coombes † 1860, champion rower on the
Thames for seven years, with an upturned skiff on top.

KENSINGTON PALACE

Kensington Palace dates chiefly from the time of William and Mary.
Never did a powerful monarch of the age of Louis XIV build a less
ostentatious residence. But Kensington was conceived more as a
private royal house than as a palace, and so is in a different category
from Versailles or Schönbrunn. The closest parallel to its restrained
brick elevations is William's own country retreat in Holland, Het
Loo.

The palace has its origin in a small country house – one of the
many that had begun to spring up w of London – built *c.* 1605 for
Sir George Coppin. *John Thorpe* may have been responsible for its
progressive plan, with symmetrically disposed central hall, as it is
included in his collection. Nothing of it remains visible, although
its site and floor levels dictated the development of the additions
around it. The estate was acquired in 1619 by Sir Heneage Finch,
from whose descendant, the second Earl of Nottingham, it was
bought in 1689 by King William III and Queen Mary, who were
anxious to find a London base away from the unhealthy atmosphere
of Whitehall. Their first additions were modest (the building did
not become known as Kensington Palace until the C 18). As enlarged
by William and Mary, and then by George I, the house consisted
of an irregular group of buildings around three courtyards. The
royal apartments in the SE corner, where the early C 17 house stood
(the C 18 Cupola Room is on its site), are the only compositions of
any ambition, although the attached lower ranges deprive the S and
E elevations of total symmetry.

Today's piecemeal effect is the result of a series of changes of

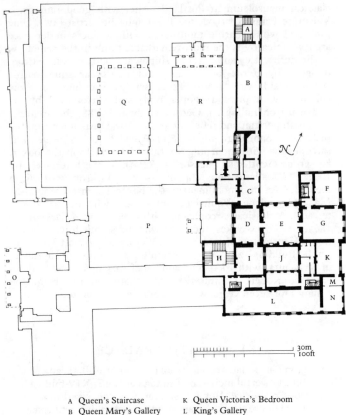

A Queen's Staircase   K Queen Victoria's Bedroom
B Queen Mary's Gallery   L King's Gallery
C Queen's Drawing Room   M Anteroom
D Privy Chamber   N Duchess of Kent's
E Cupola Room   Dressing Room
F Council Chamber   O Portico
G King's Drawing Room   P Clock Court
H King's Staircase   Q Prince of Wales's
I Presence Chamber   Court
J White Court   R Princesses' Court

Kensington Palace, first floor, plan

plan. The first proposals by the Office of Works under *Wren* in
1689 provided for ingenious symmetrical enlargements by pavilions
attached to each corner of the old house, for main staircase and
chapel (SW), king's apartments (SE), council chamber (NE), and
queen's apartments (NW). Lower wings extended W to form a new
entrance court (Clock Court), with a service wing in its N range
and a ground-floor gallery in its S range providing the approach to
the main house. N of this court were service buildings surviving
from the older house. This work was completed rapidly, but in 1690
the queen determined on extensions, and her suite was enlarged by
a long gallery extending N, approached by a staircase at the far end.
In 1691–2 a formal two-storey entrance portico was added to the

w of the house, facing into Clock Court, providing a link between the queen's apartments and the main staircase. After Queen Mary's death in 1694, when work on the new buildings at Hampton Court was suspended, William made Kensington his chief seat. The s range with the king's gallery, intended primarily for his fine picture collection and already proposed on a plan of c. 1690, was added to the old house in 1695, and at the same time the main staircase was rebuilt on a grander scale, with an enlarged guard room to its w. The gallery gave the palace its first grand exterior façade, looking out on the formal gardens to the s, beyond which an avenue was intended to lead all the way to Chelsea Hospital (see Chelsea, Public Buildings). The second front, to the E, was created by the alterations carried out for George I, which involved the rebuilding of what remained of the early C17 house together with the late C17 w entrance portico, to provide a suite of three new state rooms. There were no further grand additions. George II was the last monarch to live at Kensington, and from the later C18 the palace was occupied by members of the royal family; subsequent alterations reflect the haphazard improvements that were made for their accommodation.

EXTERIOR. The palace is entirely of brick with rubbed brick dressings, except for the portico at the w end of Clock Court. The s front, of 1689–c. 1695, consists of two quite distinct parts, both with hipped roofs: the unassuming two-storey range on the s side of Clock Court of c. 1690, and the taller eleven-bay wing of 1695 containing the king's gallery, raised up above a basement. Its end and centre three bays are emphasized by giant Doric pilasters in rubbed red brick. Above the centre is a tall blind attic with stone bases carved by *Cibber*. These features, and the brackets of the top cornice (originally enriched in paint), are virtually the only decoration. *Wren* was in overall charge of the Royal Works at this time, and the unadorned domestic style of the modest first additions at Kensington has a family resemblance to his earlier work in brick, such as Chelsea Hospital. However, the more monumental king's gallery is in a different spirit; Hawksmoor, then working as Wren's assistant, has been suggested as the architect, but the restrained style, with its flat brick elevation, minimal pilasters, and central blind attic, relates the design most closely to contemporary Dutch architecture of the 1690s, especially the work of Jacob Roman, who had been appointed architect to William in Holland in 1689, and who was in the early 1690s busy with extensions to William's country seat of Het Loo.

To the E the main elevation is twelve bays long, of which three are the return side of the king's gallery. The remaining part forms a composition of nine bays, the taller pedimented centrepiece with Venetian window dating from the rebuilding of 1718–26. It marks the shift in the Royal Works under *Benson*, who replaced Wren as Surveyor in 1718, towards the Palladian principles of *Colen Campbell* (who was perhaps involved in the design). The three plain bays on each side of this centre consist of the pavilions added in 1689. Set back to the s is the queen's gallery, only two storeys high and as humble as if it were almshouses. The upper windows retain their sashes with thick glazing-bars. The only elaborate individual features are the contemporary doorway at the far NE end by the queen's staircase, with monogram in a decorative cartouche under a segmental pediment, and a Georgian porch around the corner.

The courtyards are not shown to the public. The Prince of Wales's Court, rebuilt under *Henry Joynes*, the resident Clerk of Works, in 1724–6, has simple cloister walks on three sides; the kitchens were on the W side, and on the N was a self-contained house fitted up by *Kent*, possibly used as lodgings by the Duchess of Kendal and also by Frederick Prince of Wales (staircase and four rooms, much restored, remain). Other buildings visible from the N and W sides were added for later members of the royal family: the SW wing in the later C18 for the Duke of Sussex, who occupied the S range of Clock Court; the much altered former stables N of Prince of Wales Court in 1740 for the Duke of Cumberland, who had a separate house further N, since demolished. Along the N edge of the group, discreetly in keeping, a range of houses with a clock turret, 1989 by the *Property Services Agency*. One-storeyed N lodge, 1845 by *Wyatt & Brandon*; classical SW lodge and railings, 1990.

At the S end of Palace Green, overshadowed by the hotel immediately behind, former barracks and stables of *c.* 1700, much altered for domestic use, of thirteen bays with timber cross-windows to the ground floor, the projecting end bays with hipped roofs. At the entrance to Palace Green gatepiers with *Coade* stone lion and unicorn.

INTERIOR. Only the state apartments are open to the public. The queen's apartments preserve much of their fittings of 1689–91; the interiors of the king's principal apartments have paintings by *Kent* of 1723–7, his first major commission for interior decoration. The earlier work is architecturally very simple; the Kent work grander but not very skilful. The state apartments were first opened to the public in 1899. Major renovation, partly to repair bomb damage, and refurnishing with appropriate pictures and furniture from the royal collections took place under the Department of the Environment in 1972–5.

From the NE corner the visitor starts with the sequence of the QUEEN'S STATE ROOMS. Their fittings are plain but handsome: simple marble fireplaces, walls mostly covered with bolection-moulded panelling (in the queen's gallery painted white by Kent, but since restored to its original appearance). The QUEEN'S STAIR-CASE, with turned wooden balusters, still quite sturdy, but displaying the new type of open string construction, leads to the QUEEN'S GALLERY, 26 metres long, with delicately carved cornice; the sumptuous gilt mirror frames were carved by *Grinling Gibbons*, the Vauxhall plate glass was supplied by *Gerrit Jensen* (1689–91). The mirrors over the doors are restorations of 1979. Three smaller, more intimate rooms follow, a CLOSET and DINING ROOM, and the QUEEN'S DRAWING ROOM, with cornice enriched with crowned monograms in foliage. The QUEEN'S BEDCHAMBER lies to the W (restored in 1975, now with the state bed of James II's wife, Mary Beatrice of Modena). The late C17 mood is then interrupted by the C18 remodelling. The next room is the KING'S PRIVY CHAMBER, looking out over the Clock Court. It has an oval ceiling painting by *Kent*, showing Mars (with the Order of the Garter in allusion to the king) and Minerva surrounded by the arts. The adjacent KING'S PRESENCE CHAMBER in the SW pavilion of 1689 has an overmantel by *Grinling Gibbons* (originally in the king's gallery), but the ceiling with its startlingly bold reds and blues on white, in the Etruscan-Pompeian taste, was added by *Kent* in 1724, perhaps the earliest example in England of a fashion which was to become so general under Robert Adam fifty years later.

This room opens on to the landing of the KING'S STAIRCASE, rebuilt on a larger scale in 1696, with minor alterations of the 1720s (landing enlarged and windows altered) to accommodate *Kent's* painted decoration. The stairs are a splendid affair, with marble steps and iron balustrade by *Tijou*. The wall and ceiling paintings added by Kent were evidently influenced both by Veronese at the Villa Barbaro, Maser, and by Lebrun at the Escalier des Ambassadeurs at Versailles. The walls have *trompe l'œil* sculpture in grisaille, but on the N and E walls a more colourful arcaded loggia with portraits of members of the court. Other figures look down over the balustrade of an illusory open dome on the ceiling. The idea was earlier used by Verrio. The stairs no longer fulfil their original function as part of the main approach to the state rooms because the stone gallery in the W wing and the grand guard room on the ground floor adjoining the stairs were subdivided in the early C19, as part of a suite for the Duke of Sussex. The chapel of 1690 E of the stairs retained its fittings until 1833, when an intermediate floor was inserted.

The KING'S GALLERY along the S front is of the magnificent length of nearly 30 metres (subdivided in the early C19, but restored by 1899). It retains an evocative reminder of William's concerns: an overmantel with windvane set against a map of northern Europe painted by *Robert Norden*. Its setting and the fireplace below date from Kent's redecoration, of which the main feature is a painted ceiling with scenes on canvas of the adventures of Ulysses. The surrounding ornament was painted by *F. de Valentia*. The small rooms at the E end, and the former STATE BEDCHAMBER in the SW pavilion of 1689, are now displayed in early C19 form, in recollection of their use by the future Queen Victoria. Their restoration was undertaken by Queen Mary in 1932. The KING'S DRAWING ROOM, the easternmost of the C18 rooms, has the E-facing Venetian window overlooking the park. Of its decoration it retains only a stately marble fireplace with terms in profile, made by *James Richards* (the top part reconstructed in the 1970s), and *Kent's* ceiling of 1722–3, an impressive Baroque creation with its oval centrepiece of Jupiter and Semele set in a deep oval frame. The room to the N was King William's COUNCIL CHAMBER, also redecorated by Kent, but altered since. The square CUPOLA ROOM, rebuilt by George I as the principal reception room of the palace, was the first of *Kent's* works at Kensington, its ceiling painted in 1722 as soon as the rebuilding had been completed. According to Vertue, Kent was selected instead of Thornhill, the Sergeant Painter, because his estimate was considerably lower, but Kent's sympathy for the new Palladian movement may also have been part of the story. The inspiration here is antique Rome. The coved ceiling has a splendidly lavish, if not entirely convincing, display of feigned coffering in blue and gold, with the Garter star in the centre. The walls, painted in 1725, are equally busy, although the disparate materials do not blend very successfully; feigned monochrome trophies crowd between giant Ionic pilasters and svelte marble niches holding gilt Italian statues (these are earlier than the decorations). Above are casts of bronze busts by *Le Sueur* of Greek poets and philosophers. The doors are surrounded by marble aedicules with Ionic columns, likewise the fireplace, which has as its overmantel *Rysbrack's* excellent carving in antique style of a Roman Marriage.

The floors below the state apartments (now largely used for a display of court dress) have simple fittings, mostly of *c.* 1804–12, the time when these rooms were converted by *James Wyatt* as apartments for the Duke of Kent. They were later used (until 1837) by the Duchess and the young Princess Victoria. The entrance hall with porte-cochère and double staircase with neo-classical balustrade is the grandest surviving feature. The columns supporting the Cupola Room probably date from 1833.

KENSINGTON GARDENS. The combination of Hyde Park with the grounds of Kensington House created a park two miles in extent – an unrivalled asset for west London which, because of its royal status, remained almost immune to development in the C 19. Enviably sited adjoining the royal hunting enclosure of Hyde Park, the gardens were famous already before they became a royal possession. The area s of the house now covered in plain lawns was laid out for William and Mary by *London & Wise* in four square plots with different formal patterns, which were redesigned to a more unified plan under Queen Anne. A summer house built at this time at the s end is now near Marlborough Gate (*see* below). The small alcove seat with decorative plastered panels above the entablature in the manner of Talman, now near the w gate, may date from William's time. In front of the king's gallery, fine late C 17 iron GATES, installed in 1910 (reset in an exedra in 1990). Behind them, a florid bronze statue of William III by *H. Baucke*, presented by Kaiser Wilhelm II, on a pedestal by *Aston Webb*. Between the E front and the Round Pond, a seated stone statue of a youthful Queen Victoria by her daughter *Princess Louise*, 1893.

Queen Anne's most ambitious contribution was the ORANGERY N of the palace, built by the Office of Works in 1704 to a Baroque design far livelier and bolder than any of the additions to the house. It is probably due to *Hawksmoor* as Clerk of the Works under Wren, with some revisions recorded by *Vanbrugh*. The orange brickwork is exceptionally fine. The windows of the end bays are set in large channelled niches, flanked by smaller niches; the centre has banded columns between banded pillars and a raised attic with broken segmental pediment. The interior is equally impressive: all painted white, a long central room with Corinthian columns flanking niches opposite the doorways; at both ends arches with carving above, possibly by *Gibbons*, leading into circular rooms with niches. In these rooms a pair of large late C 17 vases carved by *Cibber* and *Pierce* (originally designed for the gardens at Hampton Court). w of the orangery two massive brick gatepiers with urns mark the N boundary of the late C 17 gardens. The area to the N was laid out with elaborate formal plots and wilderness under Queen Anne (shown on Rocque's plan of 1736), later replaced by kitchen gardens, and given

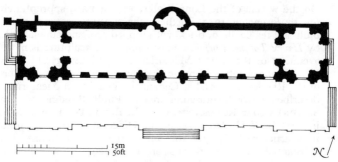

15m
50ft

Kensington Palace Orangery, plan

up in 1841, when the NW part was built over (*see* Perambulation
1a,ii, Kensington Palace Gardens).

The surviving royal landscape begun under George I by *Henry
Wise* and *Charles Bridgeman* lies E of the palace. Its broad scope
can be appreciated admirably from the king's drawing room: the
BROAD WALK, the oval GREAT BASIN (known as the ROUND
POND) made by *Charles Withers* in 1726–8, and the three main
avenues which diverge from it to lead towards Hyde Park through
wooded areas. These were originally more dense than today, and
broken up by winding paths. The boundary with Hyde Park was
defined by a ha-ha E of the LONG WATER which, with the
SERPENTINE, was created in 1731 by linking up a series of pools
formed by the Westbourne Brook. It is a very early example of
a picturesquely irregular water feature on a grand scale, and like
the winding paths was due, it seems, to the involvement of *Kent*
(busy at the same time with similar projects on a much smaller
scale in the grounds of Chiswick House, Ho). Kent also designed
buildings in the grounds, of which one remains, to the W of the
Serpentine: the QUEEN'S TEMPLE, later converted to a park
keeper's house, restored to its original form in 1976. It is a small
stone building with three boldly vermiculated arches, a taller
octagonal centre with hipped roof behind a parapet, and niches
to the side compartments projecting as apses on the flank walls.
At Marlborough Gate is QUEEN ANNE'S ALCOVE of 1706–7,
moved here in 1868. It formerly stood at the S end of the gardens
S of the palace. Its scale is a match for the orangery: a large,
stone-fronted structure with four engaged Corinthian columns
and a tall central alcove under an open pediment, flanked by
shell-headed niches with carved festoons above.

Also at Marlborough Gate are the ITALIAN WATER GARDENS
(intended to provide filter beds for the Serpentine), built in 1861,
the only example in a London park of the mid C19 taste for
formal gardens of this kind. One-storey Italianate shelter cum
pumping-house by *Banks & Barry* with an ornate central
chimney rising from its pantiled roof. It overlooks four pools
with fountains and elaborate urns; on their S side, stone balustrades with carved roundels flank water nymphs attending the
cascade down to the Long Water, all by *John Thomas*. On the E
side bronze seated statue of Jenner, by *W. Calder Marshall*, 1858.

On the W side of the Long Water, PETER PAN, appropriately fey, by *Frampton*, 1912. Further S the SERPENTINE GALLERY, built as a tea pavilion, brick, with hipped roof and cupola, 1934 by *Henry Tanner Jun.* The most impressive sculpture is in the avenue N of the Albert Memorial: Physical Energy, by *G. F. Watts*, 1907, a colossal bronze rider based on the central feature of the Rhodes memorial at Capetown. The Albert Memorial is described under the museums area (*see* Public Buildings 2). The BANDSTAND in Regency style S of the Round Pond was erected in 1931 by *J. H. Markham* of the Office of Works, a delicate iron structure with ogee roof on eight slender columns. The substantial cast-iron GATES on Kensington Road opposite Queen's Gate were made by the *Coalbrookdale Company* for the Great Exhibition.

PUBLIC BUILDINGS

1. Excluding the museums area

CIVIC CENTRE, Phillimore Walk (1a,iii). The combined identity of the boroughs of Kensington and Chelsea is expressed by a great red whale of a building uneasily constrained within the tight grid of residential streets N of the High Street. The bulk is softened a little by the trees along the perimeter and in the courtyard. The design was sketched out for the brand new borough in 1965 by *Sir Basil Spence* and executed in 1972–6 by his former partner *John S. Bonnington* of the *John S. Bonnington Partnership.* The building defers to its immediate neighbour, the library, only in its use of red brick (the detail should be compared). Two massive wings jut out aggressively in studied asymmetry: the ruthlessly plain windowless public halls, rising from a splayed plinth; and the polygonal council chamber, supported on stilts. Chamfering of windows is used (like classical mouldings) to emphasize the significant centres of power. In the centre is the mayoral suite, above a dramatically cavernous entrance-passage lit by a pretty scatter of ceiling lights. Around the courtyard beyond are stepped-back offices, landscaped and open-plan inside, a progressive idea at the time. They were intended to house the entire council staff (up to 1,250), a reflection of the bureaucratic aggrandisement that was so often a source of pride in the 1960s. Council chamber with lavishly sleek panelling; public halls more austere, the larger one with a raised brick pattern on the end wall, and quite a striking diagrid ceiling.

FIRE STATION, Old Court Place, N of Kensington High Street (1a,ii). 1905, one of the inventive compositions from the golden age of the *L.C.C. Architect's Department, Fire Brigade Branch.* Boldly rusticated garages of stone, with two-storeyed centre, prancing forward from the taller domestic red brick block behind.

AMBULANCE STATION, Ladbroke Grove. *See* Perambulation 2b,ii.

CENTRAL LIBRARY, Phillimore Walk (1a,iii). By *E. Vincent Harris*, 1955–60. Directly S of the Civic Centre, built on part of the bombed site acquired by the council in 1946. A safe classical composition in the ponderous Kensington tradition established in the earlier C 20. Handsome traditional details: red bricks of a

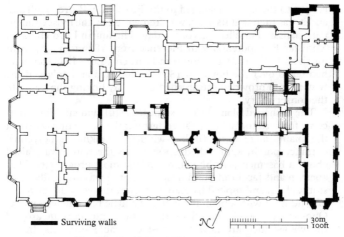

Surviving walls $\mathcal{N}$ 30m
                                                 100ft

Kensington, Holland House, plan as in 1925

special size, pedimented Portland stone surrounds to the main
windows. Five bays and two main storeys, with projecting end
pavilions with very tall arched porches. Over the main doors
busts of Caxton and Chaucer by *William McMillan*. The impressively spacious reference library occupies the whole of the first
floor.

PUBLIC LIBRARY, Ladbroke Grove, Notting Hill (2a,ii). 1891–4
by *Henry Wilson* with *T. Phillips Figgis*. Kensington's first purpose-built library. A charming building in a free neo-Tudor,
brick with stone stripes, small corner turrets, and much fanciful
detail simplified, alas, from the original art nouveau scheme.

HOLLAND HOUSE, Holland Park (1a,iii). Only fragments remain
of the elaborate and romantic Jacobean composition which
existed until the Second World War. The L.C.C. took over the
park and its buildings in 1952. The house, seriously damaged in
1941, was largely demolished in 1955–7, leaving only the shell of
the ground floor as a backdrop for an open-air theatre, together
with the three-storey E wing, which was restored and converted
as a youth hostel, supplemented by new buildings to its E. To
the W are extensive remains of stables and outbuildings.

This house was first called Cope House or Cope Castle, after
Sir Walter Cope, Chamberlain of the Exchequer in 1609, Keeper
of Hyde Park in 1610, and Master of the Court of Wards and
Liveries in 1612. He had patiently and relentlessly built up
for himself a large estate by assembling scattered Kensington
properties: West Town (the site of his house) in 1591, the Kensington manor of St Mary Abbots in 1599, Earls Court in 1610.
He began building *c.* 1605; the central block was completed by
1607, the wings, it seems, added soon after. *John Thorpe* made a
design for them before Cope's death in 1614. The house was
renamed Holland House after it had passed to Cope's son-in-
law, Sir Henry Rich, who became first Earl of Holland in 1629.
He added a W wing after 1639 (demolished 1704), and an
especially extravagant range of stables. From the later C 18 to the

early C 19 the house belonged to the Fox family, Lords Holland, and it was then that its salon was frequented by the most eminent patricians and intellectuals of the day. The fourth Lord Holland, Minister Plenipotentiary in Florence from 1839 to 1846, spent much on Italianizing the house and gardens; Lord Ilchester, who had taken over the house in 1890, remodelled and enlarged the W wing and provided the arcaded causeway linking the house to the conservatory.

The E-shaped plan of Cope's house is still evident. The wings come forward to enclose a raised terrace; the projecting centre of the main range has two bay-windows flanking a polygonal entrance porch, approached up steps, as the house was raised above a basement, in the manner of the most progressive Elizabethan and Jacobean buildings. The porch was originally three storeys high and topped by an ogee turret; it now ends above the ground floor with a plain parapet and a little bit of new cresting. One-storey stone loggias flank this centre and continue around the wings; they are now the most enjoyable survivals, busily decorated, with pilasters with a restless diamond rustication and bold fleur-de-lys cresting. They appear to be an afterthought, perhaps added at the same time as the wings. Such loggias were especially fashionable in the first years of the C 17 (cf. Nevile's Court at Trinity College Cambridge, and the loggia at Hatfield House, Hertfordshire, of 1611). Above and behind the E loggia are the brick shaped gables of the surviving E wing and the ogee-roofed stair-turret between wing and main range – sole reminders of the picturesque roof-line that complemented the projecting and receding wall planes of the front of the house (*see* p. 31).

The surviving E side of the SE wing is quieter, its three storeys articulated by three orders of enriched superimposed pilasters with shaped gables above. The ground floor has round-headed arches, formerly open, with jewelled keystones. This side now overlooks a formal pool, together with the buildings for the YOUTH HOSTEL added by the *L.C.C.* in 1955–7. Apart from the use of brick for the low N wing, the new buildings make no historic concessions, firmly expressing the post-war spirit which transformed this aristocratic enclave into a people's park. The main block is of four storeys with exposed concrete frame. Extension by *Louis Hawkins*, 1990–1.

The innovative interior of Cope's house can now only be appreciated from plans. The central range was an early example of a compact house with double-pile plan, a type popular in the London neighbourhood from the late C 16 onwards. The hall was entered in the centre of its long side, a grand principal staircase on the r. leading to the main reception rooms on the first floor. The corner staircase towers may have been built with the original house, although they do not appear on Thorpe's plan, which differs also by showing wings projecting N as well as S.

S of the house the GATEPIERS are in complete contrast to the fussier taste of the Jacobean age. They are of 1629, by *Nicholas Stone*, after a design by *Inigo Jones*: a restrained classical composition, on both back and front a niche between two banded pilasters and a pediment with supporter on top.

The remains of the OUTBUILDINGS frame a series of formal

gardens. To the SW the arcaded CAUSEWAY of 1890, decorated rather oddly with panels of tiles, runs in a dog-leg from house to stables. The STABLES with cupola and coach house facing an enclosed yard date from the early C19. To their N the CON-SERVATORY, a long N–S range with large arches on the W side. This is the S part of the stables and coach house of 1638–40, a monumental creation originally 73 metres long, formerly with an attic storey with dormers, and with elaborately decorated stalls, as the accounts make clear. Much was demolished after 1796; the remainder, reduced in width and lengthened to the S, became conservatory and orangery. It was converted in the mid C19 by the estate architect *J. H. Browne* to a ballroom, finished off at the N end by an extravagantly neo-Jacobean belvedere. Further N some picturesque arches erected from old material. E of the conservatory the IRIS GARDEN formed in 1812, with on the E side a circular tiled ICE HOUSE, restored in 1975 as an exhibition centre, with a stair added to link up with the causeway. The formal DUTCH GARDEN, its walls partly C17, was originally laid out in 1812 as a Portuguese garden by *Buonauiti*, Lord Holland's librarian. Female STATUE by *Eric Gill*. S of the house, seated bronze of the third Lord Holland † 1840, designed by *Watts* and *Boehm*. Near the restaurant, Boy with Bear Cubs by *J. MacAllen Swan*, 1902.

Much of the existing park (reduced in size in the C19) is woodland. Charles Hamilton of Painshill advised on tree-planting in the mid C18.

LEIGHTON HOUSE, No. 12 Holland Park Road (1a,iv). Now a museum, but designed as a house in 1866 for the artist Frederic Leighton by his friend *George Aitchison*. The reticent exterior conceals the most sumptuous and colourful C19 artist's house in London, testimony to the influence of Middle Eastern art in the later C19. At first only three bays wide to the street, classical trim, brick with stone dressings. The studio faced the garden, a very long upper room with big central window. To its E a winter studio was added in 1889, supported on iron columns now concealed by the PERRIN GALLERY, added in 1929 by *Halsey Ricardo* after the house had been acquired by the borough. To the W, extensions of 1877–9, notably Leighton's ARAB HALL, a 61 small domed area on a cruciform plan approached through a long central inner hall. Its purpose was to house Leighton's Eastern collections, principally his glorious collection of Middle Eastern tiles of the C13–17 which cover the walls inside. The tightly meshed grids in the windows are *musharabiyeh* work from Cairo; the coloured glass in the dome incorporates pieces from Damascus. All this blends most happily with the contributions by Leighton's contemporaries: the mosaic in the Persian manner by *Walter Crane*, the copper corona by *Aitchison*, and the alabaster capitals carved by *Boehm* with birds designed by *R. Caldecott*. The lusciously exotic atmosphere is enhanced by the central pool with a jet of water springing from a black marble octagon.

The rest of the house is boldly coloured, with black lacquered inlaid woodwork. The staircase, divided from the entrance hall by two sturdy columns, also has a mixture of tiles, some Eastern, some by *de Morgan*. In the drawing room an elegant marble fireplace with brass inlay, ingeniously set below a window with sliding mirrored shutters. The 18 metre studio above is not decorated with tiles but with a cast from the Parthenon frieze. It possesses that necessary adjunct for a successful Victorian artist, the separate back stairs (for models and dealers); also a tall door next to the E apse, for lowering large pictures.

SOUTH KENSINGTON MUSEUMS. *See* Public Buildings 2.

EARLS COURT EXHIBITION CENTRE, Warwick Road (4a). The first permanent centre in London for commercial exhibitions (nearly 140,000 square metres). 1936–7 by *C. Howard Crane* of Chicago, with *Gordon Jeeves*. Large, utilitarian and heavy-handed. Reinforced-concrete frame, one of the most ambitious of its date, with 30 metre beams spanning the District line beneath. The façade awkwardly grafts vertical display panels of cinema derivation on to a curved foyer a little reminiscent of Charles Holden's booking halls. Behind, a vast new hall by *RMJM*, 1989–91, with barrel-vaulted roof on seventeen steel trusses spanning 84 metres.

KENSINGTON POOLS AND LEISURE CENTRE, Silchester Road (2a,i). The pools are by *Slater & Hodnett*, 1971–4 – a drab, uninspiring concrete-panelled exterior in a drab world of tower blocks. The sports halls to the w by *Darbourne & Darke*, 1982–4, with trim walls of striped brick, try harder to be a visual asset in this desolate area. They replaced, alas, the admirable Silchester Baths of 1886–8 by *T. Verity*, Kensington's most lavish C19 public works.

COMMONWEALTH INSTITUTE, Holland Park (1a,iii). Planned from 1958, built in 1960–2 by *Robert Matthew, Johnson-Marshall & Partners*, with *A. J. & J. D. Harris* as engineers, *James Gardner* as exhibition designer, and *Sylvia Crowe* as landscape architect. London's first major public building after the Festival Hall, informal and inexpensive, and full of post-war optimism – the antithesis to its predecessor, Collcutt's Imperial Institute in South Kensington (*see* Public Buildings 2). The building is set back from the High Street within the park, with a pedestrian approach past a pool and trees to the exhibition hall, which is placed lozenge-wise to the street, and is roofed by a dramatic hyperbolic-paraboloid canopy, its tent-like allusions confirmed by the angular supports at two corners. The form reflects the search at the time for alternatives to the rectangularity of the modern tradition, influenced especially by Candela's experiments with parabolic roofs in Mexico and by Hugh Stubbins's Kongresshalle in Berlin, but externally it lacks their confidence, and is not helped by the indifferent opaque patent glazing used for the walls. Inside, the roof comes into its own, spanning 56 square metres, the centre consisting of a thin prestressed concrete shell, with light radial ribs to the outer sections. It covers impressive if confusing free-flowing spaces and galleries at different levels, still somewhat in the spirit of the Festival Hall. Attached on the w side is a three-storeyed curtain-walled administration block, with art gallery on the top floor. Alterations and extensions by *Alï Sanei* under discussion in 1990–1.

QUEEN ELIZABETH COLLEGE, Campden Hill (1a,iii). The Ladies' Department of King's College was founded in Kensington Square in 1885. The Household and Social Science Departments, established on this site in 1915, became an independent college in 1928 but were reamalgamated in 1985. Buildings by *Percy Adams* and *Charles Holden* of 1913–15. Two fivestorey blocks of brick with canted bays and sparse Wrenaissance trim, linked by a one-storey refectory with steep roof rising behind balustraded parapet with urns. E end completed only in the 1930s. Later additions behind: N block with laboratories, 1959 by *K. H. Urquardt*; physics and physiology block added *c.* 1970 in the main quadrangle.

ROYAL COLLEGE OF ART, Kensington Gore. *See* Public Buildings 2.

IMPERIAL COLLEGE OF SCIENCE AND TECHNOLOGY. *See* Public Buildings 2.

INSTITUT FRANÇAIS AND LYCÉE FRANÇAIS (3c). A French enclave bounded by Cromwell Road, Harrington Road, and Queensberry Place. Institut of 1939 by *Patrice Bonnet*, a determined survival of expressionism tinged with art deco, rather Dutch than Parisian, with wild angular brick patterns, wildly patterned glazing bars, and stepped-back upper storeys. Plainer grey brick neo-Georgian school buildings behind of the same date by *A. J. Thomas*, extended to the N by a long dull range of the 1950s by *Jacques Laurent* (filling a gap in the Cromwell Road terraces caused by bomb damage). Along Harrington Road, a tall, cheerfully eclectic classroom range of 1982–4 by *Reoven Vardi*, dark red brick relieved by panels of white tiles and glazed barrel-vaults to the staircase towers. A more brutalist concrete staircase on the playground side. On the roof, pergolas and play areas for the infants' school.

HOLLAND PARK SCHOOL, Airlie Gardens (1a,iii). The first large post-war comprehensive in west London, 1956–8 by the *L.C.C. Architect's Department Schools Board* (architect-in-charge *D. Rogers Stark*). An enviable site on the edge of Holland Park in the mature grounds of large houses built by the Phillimore estate in 1807–17. Planned for over 2,000 pupils; a compact layout, not yet broken down into the smaller units favoured later on, but with nothing over four storeys (to pacify local residents, who had successfully resisted an earlier scheme for council flats). Two long parallel classroom ranges, buff and dark brick, articulated by projecting glazed stair towers, slightly angled – a typical fifties mannerism. Corridors on alternate floors only. Large glazed entrance foyer in the E block, looking out towards the hall in the centre. The hall originally had a formal glazed S front, with ground-floor columns in the Festival Hall style, but stolider extensions for library and teaching areas, completed in 1973, have diminished the transparency. At first there were only light, almost flimsy covered ways connecting hall and classrooms. Clerestory-lit hall, quite lavishly panelled, with movable partitions to side halls so the whole school can be accommodated. Technical block to the N, gyms and swimming pools to the S, across a bridge over a road which had to be preserved. Near this, GATE COTTAGE, a single-storey lodge from the early C19 layout.

THORPE LODGE (Sixth Form Centre), by the entrance from Airlie Gardens. Another survival: a small early C19 house with bow-windowed studio added to the w by *J. L. Pearson* for the artist H. T. Wells, totally transformed inside in 1904–13 in the most lavish turn-of-the-century artistic taste, by and for *Montagu Norman* (later a Governor of the Bank of England but also a member of the Art Workers Guild). His sketches were carried out chiefly by *A. J. Shirley* (metalwork and light fittings, now alas mostly gone) and *J. H. Wakelin* (furniture and joinery, of which much survives). The architect *W. K. Shirley* (Lord Ferrers) also assisted. Rich colours and precious materials typical of the period: hall walls shimmering with mother-of-pearl-like tiles (in fact industrial silicone), fireplaces with *De Morgan* tiles, much excellent simple panelling in a Gimson manner in a great variety of exotic woods. Huge Japanese peacock embroidery in the drawing room, another in the back hall. The studio was transformed into a groin-vaulted music room, dominated by a large C 17 stone Italian fireplace with the Medici arms. Barrel-vaulted dining room with vine-scroll plaster frieze. Remnants of a carefully contrived small garden, with pergola, pool, and pleached avenue.

CARDINAL VAUGHAN R. C. SCHOOL, Addison Road (1a,iv). 1961–3 by *David Stokes & Partners*. A well-proportioned three-storey cube; red brick above glazing with sturdy mullions.

ST MARY ABBOTS C. OF E. PRIMARY SCHOOL, on a narrow site facing the churchyard of St Mary Abbots (1a,i). Girls' school 1861 by *G. M. Hills*; boys' school 1875, tall asymmetrical Gothic, brick with stone dressings. Two charity statues, from the previous school by *Hawksmoor*, set high up on a battlemented tower with corbelled-out stair-turret.

COLVILLE SCHOOL, Lonsdale Road (2b,i). 1879, a classic *Robson* design for the London School Board, similar to Park Walk Chelsea, KC (q.v.), with gabled classroom range to the road.

OUR LADY OF VICTORIES R. C. PRIMARY SCHOOL, Clareville Street. A former London Board School (Gloucester Grove East) of 1881, an unusual design on a narrow back site, with covered arcades on upper floors.

BOUSFIELD PRIMARY SCHOOL, South Bolton Gardens (4a). 1954–6 by *Chamberlin Powell & Bon* for the L.C.C., a notable example of the low, colourful, child-scaled school built after the war in reaction against the old inner London three-deckers. Much thought given to the landscaped setting, which provides play space at different levels, including an amphitheatre (converted from a war-time water tank). The use of a variety of colours for the curtain walling was equally innovative. The buildings are light and transparent, planned on a 40 inch module. A compact arrangement: one-storey infant and two-storey junior classrooms around their own courtyards, with the two assembly halls and staffrooms in the centre. One of the courtyards was covered in in 1971.

ST CLEMENT AND ST JAMES SCHOOL, Penzance Place (2a,i). 1986 by *Green Lloyd Adams*. A welcome change from the pre-fabricated schools of the sixties and seventies. Low, attractive buildings of one and two storeys with a lively pattern of small-paned windows below shallow-pitched roofs with deep eaves.

BROMPTON HOSPITAL, Fulham Road (3c). The first consumption hospital. The earliest part is to the N of Fulham Road, 1844–6 by *F. J. Francis*, rather like a large Tudor almshouse, in red brick with black diaper, with offices on the low ground floor and two storeys of wards above. Symmetrical, apart from the accent of a corner turret to the central battlemented tower. The E wing along Sumner Place, added in 1851–5, has a grander gatehouse feature as its centre, and a tower behind for a ventilating shaft, by *Francis* together with *E. B. Lamb*.

The CHAPEL OF ST LUKE is of 1849–50 by *E. B. Lamb*, who was selected by the chapel's benefactor, the Rev. Sir Henry Foulis, a Yorkshire landowner. Although the building was enlarged and given a N aisle in 1890–1 by *William White* (the chancel is mostly his), Lamb's distinctive style is still recognizable in the intricate tracery (apart from the simplified E window) and in the characteristically complicated timberwork which dominates the interior. Notable collection of *Lamb* fittings: stone cusped and crocketed sedilia and aumbry, much pierced and varnished woodwork (made by *Samuel Pratt*), and stained glass in deep colours with much black paint, mostly designed by Lamb, although the N transept window with St Cecilia is probably by *Lady Frankland Russell*, who had worked with Lamb in Yorkshire. It has largely grisaille figures set against diagonal bands of texts. N aisle W by *A. L. Moore*, 1892, pictorial. The FONT with painted ceramic panels is of 1875 by *J. Rochefort*.

S of Fulham Road (i.e. in Chelsea), taller and more forbidding additions to the hospital, begun in 1879 by *T. H. Wyatt*, completed by *Matthew Wyatt* in 1892. Cliff-like proportions relieved by shaped gables and some bands of orange terracotta. Much added to: 1920s–30s infilling between the wings, by *A. Saxon Snell & Phillips*; five-storey extension to the W by *Adams, Holden & Pearson*, 1964. Facing Chelsea Square a jollier gabled wing of 1892, and a long NURSES HOME of 1898 by *E. T. Hall*, in a pleasant free classical style.

ST CHARLES HOSPITAL, Barlby Road (2b,ii). One of the chief landmarks of North Kensington, a fortress-like pile with corbelled parapet to the prominent tower containing water tanks and chimney. The detail debased pointed; the material yellow stock brick. Built as a Poor Law infirmary by the St Marylebone Union, 1879–81 by *Saxon Snell*, with later additions. Planned on the pavilion principle advocated by Florence Nightingale.

ST MARY ABBOTS HOSPITAL, Marloes Road. *See* Perambulation 1b,ii.

CROMWELL HOSPITAL, Cromwell Road (1b,iii). A private hospital by the *Building Design Partnership*, 1978–81. Smooth, secretive frontage of Sicilian granite with blue-tinted window bands; entrance at the back in an octagonal extension. Rear additions by *Holder & Mathias Partnership*.

PRINCESS BEATRICE HOSPITAL, Old Brompton Road. *See* Perambulation 3d.

KENSINGTON GARDENS. *See* Kensington Palace, above.

PUMPING STATION, Aubrey Walk. *See* Perambulation 1a,iii.

KENSINGTON CENTRAL DEPOT, Warwick Road (1b,ii). The NEW DEPOT is by *Arup Associates*, 1970–6. Its special feature is that it supports housing and planting high up at roof level (*see*

Perambulation 1b,ii). Below, the S block houses a monumental transport workshop, with a massive central concrete column with radiating beams. Long, quite decorative brick curtain walls along Warwick Road.

UNDERGROUND STATIONS. There is a wide range of early examples. The District line station at EARLS COURT (4a) was rebuilt on a new site in 1876–8 by *John Wolfe Barry*, with an elegantly light-weight roof of shallow pitch and 29 metre span (unusually wide for the underground). The Earls Court Road frontage was rebuilt in pale faience in 1915 by *H. W. Ford*; the Warwick Road approach, with circular entrance, is of 1936–7, contemporary with the Exhibition Centre opposite. At GLOUCES-TER ROAD (1b,iii) the handsome District line station of 1868, two-storeyed with arched windows, is a rare survival of its date. It was enlarged in 1907 and restored and slightly altered in 1988–9 when the mammoth shopping and office development behind (by *John R. Harris*) was built over the tracks. HOLLAND PARK (2a,ii) is of 1900 by *H. B. Measures*. HIGH STREET KEN-SINGTON (1a,i), of 1865–7, was reconstructed in 1903–6 by *George Sherrin* with a four-storey block to the High Street and a top-lit shopping arcade leading to an octagonal foyer. Booking hall to the S rebuilt in 1937–8. SOUTH KENSINGTON (3b) was rebuilt in 1906–7, the S side with oxblood terracotta entrance by *Leslie Green* for the District line, the Metropolitan section, together with the glazed arcade with pretty ironwork between the entrance columns, by *George Sherrin* (future uncertain).

PORTOBELLO DOCK, Kensal Road. *See* Perambulation 2b,ii.

2. Museums area and academic centre*

An accumulation of cultural institutions as compact and varied as exists in the sixth of a square mile between the Albert Memorial and the Victoria and Albert Museum is probably unparalleled anywhere, and certainly was unparalleled when the buildings were first planned. This cultural centre may be said to represent the climax of that faith in the propagation of intellectual achievement which characterized the middle classes of the C19, and was also the faith of Prince Albert and Queen Victoria. The C19, it must be remembered, saw the first public museums at its beginning and innumerable new universities, schools, technical colleges, research institutes and so forth as it went on.

Prince Albert himself laid special emphasis on the practical advantages of housing educational institutions and illustrative collections close to each other. This approach was shared by the key figure in the development of South Kensington, Sir Henry Cole, committee member of the 1851 exhibition, then Secretary of the Department of Practical Art, later Science and Art, set up under the Board of Trade under the influence of Prince Albert, and Superintendent of the new Kensington museums.

The site between Kensington Gardens and Cromwell Road was purchased for educational uses out of the proceeds of the 1851

*The buildings are in the area covered by Perambulation 3. For a map see p. 534.

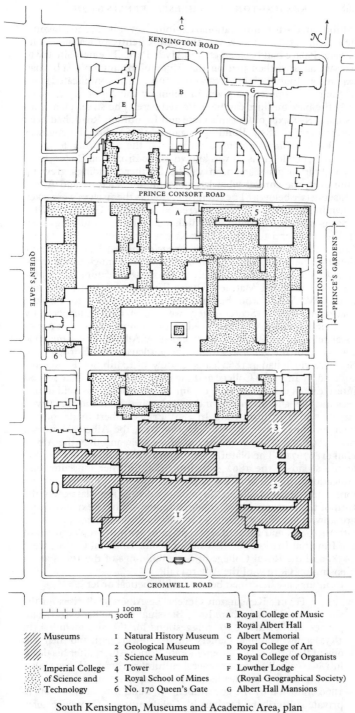

KENSINGTON ROAD

PRINCE CONSORT ROAD

QUEEN'S GATE

EXHIBITION ROAD

PRINCE'S GARDENS

CROMWELL ROAD

100m
300ft

///// Museums

::::: Imperial College
::::: of Science and
::::: Technology

1 Natural History Museum
2 Geological Museum
3 Science Museum
4 Tower
5 Royal School of Mines
6 No. 170 Queen's Gate

A Royal College of Music
B Royal Albert Hall
C Albert Memorial
D Royal College of Art
E Royal College of Organists
F Lowther Lodge
  (Royal Geographical Society)
G Albert Hall Mansions

South Kensington, Museums and Academic Area, plan

exhibition, the first international exhibition ever held, and a favourite scheme of Albert's, as was this future centre of learning. The
Crystal Palace had been erected in Hyde Park. The new site lay to
its sw, an area then just on the fringe of Brompton's suburban
expansion. Eighty-eight acres were secured. The complicated story
of their development is given in detail by the *Survey of London*;
only the bare outlines can be indicated here. The street plan, with
its main N–S axes of Queen's Gate and Exhibition Road, had been
determined by 1853. Building began in 1856, when the engineer
Sir William Cubitt put up a building at the SE corner to house
various art collections. It was known as the Brompton Boilers from
its utilitarian glass and iron vaults. Further buildings grew up
around it, the core of what later became the Victoria and Albert
Museum (*see* below). (The Brompton Boilers themselves were taken
down in the 1860s and parts re-erected at Bethnal Green (TH) for
what is now the Museum of Childhood.) The new buildings were
in the brick and terracotta Renaissance style favoured by Henry
Cole and his architect, Captain *Francis Fowke*. The ornamental
detail of the South Kensington museums owes much to the influence of the artistic circle involved in the 1851 exhibition, whose
members included Matthew Digby Wyatt and Owen Jones, and
also J.W. Wild, who became the chief assistant to Fowke's
successor, Henry Scott. They were probably influenced by
Gottfried Semper, who had lived in London in 1849–53 as a political refugee, and was much esteemed by Albert. The same style
was used for the galleries around the gardens of the Horticultural
Society, which had in 1860 leased a site W of Exhibition Road (now
covered by Imperial College and the museums to its S). The second
international exhibition to be organized in London was held in this
area in 1862, and the layout of this period is reflected in the curved
streets S of the Albert Hall. In 1861 Prince Albert died, and the
next buildings arose to commemorate him, the Albert Memorial
first (1863–72) at the N end of the whole area, and then the Albert
Hall (1867–71). The Natural History Museum followed (1872–81)
at the S end of the 1862 exhibition site. Further museums and
educational institutions flocked to fill the remaining spaces, no
longer in terracotta, but in the more ponderous free classical of the
turn of the century. Most remain, although all have expanded and
are now cramped for space. The most radical C20 changes to the
late Victorian and Edwardian scene came with the replacement of
the Imperial Institute by new buildings for Imperial College from
1958, and the Royal College of Art's buildings of the 1960s along
Kensington Gore W of the Albert Hall.

Buildings are described below in alphabetical order.

66 ALBERT HALL, Kensington Gore. The Albert Hall rises on the
site of Gore House, where Lady Blessington held her extravagant
parties in the early C19. Suggestions for the site included (in
1852) a new National Gallery, then a concert hall, and then – as
one of the projects to commemorate Prince Albert after his death
in 1861 – a hall for more general cultural purposes. Henry Cole's
enthusiasm for the idea led him in 1864 to set up a scheme (by
1866 endorsed by the government) to build it by selling seats to
private subscribers. Designs by Cole's protégé, Captain *Francis
Fowke*, were preferred to earlier ones by *G. G. Scott* and were

carried out after Fowke's death in 1867 by Major-General
H. Y. D. Scott. The hall was opened in 1871.

In contrast to the verbosity of the Albert Memorial opposite,
the hall, a vast oval building seating 8,000 within its circumference of 224 metres, is of a clean, convincing simplicity: a
domed brick cylinder with four porches and very little decoration
in terracotta and mosaic. The style is no doubt influenced by
Gottfried Semper and his first Dresden Opera of 1837–41. The
details correspond to those of Fowke's earlier buildings on the
Brompton site. The boldest external features, additions by Scott
to Fowke's design, run all round: a projecting balcony, and above
it a terracotta mosaic frieze of the Triumph of Art and Letters
which – although on a much larger scale – is closely related to
the work on the South Kensington Museums (*see* Victoria and
Albert Museum, below). The committee of designers included
Pickersgill, Marks and *Yeames*, later joined by *Armitage,
Armstead, Horsley*, and *Poynter*, each responsible for a section;
the mosaic panels were made up by the ladies of the South
Kensington museum mosaic class.

The hall has three tiers of boxes plus the balcony and above it
the gallery. The dome is of glass with wrought-iron trusses made
by the Fairbairn Engineering Co., designed by *Scott* with advice
from the engineers *John Hawkshaw, John Fowler*, and *J. W.
Glover*. Fowke had originally suggested a flat ceiling. Acoustically
the interior was problematic until the addition of suspended
glass-fibre diffusers in 1968–9. The Albert Hall was called by
M. D. Conway in 1882 'a pile worthy of Rome in its palmiest
days', by Loftie in 1888 'on the familiar curves of the common
bandstand'.

ALBERT MEMORIAL, Kensington Gardens. 1863–72 by *Sir
George Gilbert Scott.* This 'memorial of our blameless Prince'
(*Builder,* 1863, p. 361) is the epitome in many ways of High
Victorian ideals and High Victorian style, rich, solid, a little
pompous, a little vulgar, but full of faith and self-confidence. It
is 53 metres high and has more than 175 life-size or more-than-
life-size figures. It has costly marble, plenty of granite, bronze,
and mosaics, and around £150,000 was expended on it. Scott's
idea was noble: 'to erect a kind of ciborium ... on the principle
of the ancient shrines ... to protect a statue of the Prince ...
These shrines were models of imaginary buildings, and my idea
was to realize one of these imaginary structures with its precious
metals, its inlaying, its enamels, etc.' Scott regarded the memorial
as his 'most prominent work', the outcome of his 'highest and
most enthusiastic efforts'. The memorial consists of a canopy
constructed around an iron frame, raised on twenty-four steps.
The columns are Ross of Mull granite, the top parts of Portland
stone (instead of the marble Scott at first proposed), abundantly
adorned with Salviati glass mosaic designed by *Clayton & Bell.*
The terracotta so characteristic of South Kensington is absent.
Beneath the canopy is the seated bronze statue of Prince Albert,
4.20 metres high, by *J. H. Foley*, completed in 1876. It was
originally gilded. The base of the canopy carries a marble frieze
with the figures of painters (E), poets and composers (S), architects
(N), and sculptors (W). The sculptors and architects are by *J. B.*

Philip, the others by *H. H. Armstead*. The corners project and carry four marble groups: Agriculture by *Marshall*, Manufacture by *Weekes*, Commerce by *Thornycroft*, Engineering by *Lawlor*. At the outer corners of the whole memorial four more groups, their compositions devised by Scott: Asia by *Foley*, Europe by *Macdowell*, Africa by *Theed*, and America by *John Bell*. There are plenty of smaller bronze figures on the pillars and canopy (by *Armstead* and *Philip*) and on the spire (Christian and moral virtues by *Redfern*). The architectural stone carving is by *William Brindley*. M. D. Conway called it 'beyond question the finest monumental structure in Europe', Loftie in 1888 'an uncomfortable feat of engineering'. So quickly had the younger generation moved away from Albert's ideals to those of the late Victorian decades.

CITY AND GUILDS INSTITUTE, Exhibition Road. 1881–5 by *Waterhouse*; demolished for Imperial College (*see* below).

GEOLOGICAL MUSEUM, Exhibition Road. Designed in 1914 by *Sir Richard Allison* of the Office of Works; the E part, with a Classical Re-Revival stone front, completed only in 1933–5 under *J. H. Markham*.

IMPERIAL COLLEGE OF SCIENCE AND TECHNOLOGY. The present form of the college, chiefly concentrated on the island site bounded by Prince Consort Road, Exhibition Road, Imperial Institute Road, and Queen's Gate, dates from 1953 onwards, when the decision was made to almost double the number of students to 3,000 p.a.; by 1964 the aim was 4,700. Before 1953 the college consisted of the Royal College of Science (established at South Kensington in 1890), the Royal School of Mines (founded 1851, moved from Jermyn Street to South Kensington from *c.* 1872), and the City and Guilds College (established at South Kensington from 1880). The three all had their own purpose-built premises but had been united as a single college within the University of London since 1910. The post-1953 expansion involved the demolition of most of the older college buildings, with the exception of what is now the Henry Cole wing of the Victoria and Albert Museum (q.v.) and several buildings along Prince Consort Road (*see* below).

The bulk of Imperial College's island block is taken up by the buildings of the 1950s onwards. For these the controversial decision was taken to demolish *Collcutt*'s splendid Imperial Institute of 1887–93, although by a late reprieve its central tower was saved. Revised plans to a slightly less dense design than first proposed were agreed in 1958, and a programme set in hand that continued for nearly twenty years. The island site buildings are by *Norman & Dawbarn*; the consultants were *Sir Hubert Worthington* († 1963) followed by *Lord Holford*. The main entrance is from Exhibition Road beneath a broad canopy projecting in front of MECHANICAL ENGINEERING (1957–65). From here a pedestrian walkway threads through the site, forming an E–W spine elevated above the vehicle access roads and parking spaces entered from N and S – a straightforward, comprehensible plan, unlike some of the over-complex multi-level arrangements so characteristic of the period. The buildings disposed around this informal grid are mostly of a reticent curtain-walled nature, and of no special distinction, although mildly varied in their heights and cladding materials. ELECTRICAL AND CIVIL ENGINEERING is of 1960–3; then comes COLLEGE BLOCK, with great hall and libraries, 1966–9. In this area the walkway runs beside refectories and shops, but it is all a little too mean to be a convincingly Corbusian 'street in the air'. To the s the hard urban mood is tempered by two lawns, the larger one providing the setting for the TOWER, incongruously flamboyant in isolation from the rest of *Collcutt*'s demolished Imperial Institute. The walkway ends within MATHEMATICS (Huxley Building) facing Queen's Gate, its later date (*c.* 1971) indicated by its harsher, and uglier, concrete-panelled facing – a blot on the Victorian sequences of Queen's Gate (*see* Perambulation 3a, also for *Shaw*'s No. 170, now the residence of the Rector of the College).

s of Imperial Institute Road, on the site of Aston Webb's buildings for the Royal College of Science of 1900–6, BIOCHEMISTRY (1962–5) and CHEMISTRY (1968–70), both by the *Architects Co-partnership*, the latter with the type of Louis-Kahn-inspired crenellated roof-line so often used *c.* 1970 to give a more forceful image to the flat roofs of the 1960s.

Along Prince Consort Road on the s side, from w to e, PHYSICS (*c.* 1957–9, with a design of incised diagrams over the entrance by *John Skeaping*) and AERONAUTICS and CHEMICAL TECHNOLOGY (Roderick Hill Building), planned in 1949 by *Worthington* before the expansion of the college, held up through lack of steel, and completed to revised designs by *Norman & Dawbarn* in 1954–7. Stolider than the later buildings, with green spandrels and stone-clad mullions enclosed within a stone frame. In the entrance hall, a decorative wall with the college arms in Copeland bone china, designed by *R. W. Baker*.

Opposite, on the N side of Prince Consort Road, IMPERIAL COLLEGE UNION BUILDING, the back neo-Tudor brick, 1910–12 (enlarged 1955–7) by *Sir Aston Webb*; likewise the E side (BOTANY), 1912–14, and the w side (BIOCHEMISTRY), 1921–3. The front (BEIT BUILDING), built after Webb's death by his son *Maurice Webb*, 1929, is in the terrible style of the reactionaries of the 1920s, that is, plain brick, with occasional outbursts of pilasters and columns and pediments.

Further E on the s side, after the Royal School of Music (q.v.), the ROYAL SCHOOL OF MINES, 1909–13 by *Sir Aston Webb*, whose effusive Edwardian Classical Re-Revival transformed the district so much in the early C20. Note the giant niche of the entrance flanked by giant pilasters, and the giant sculpture (by *P. R. Montford*, 1916–20), with busts of Beit and Wernher above allegorical figures. Adjoining to the E is the Goldsmiths Extension of the City and Guilds College, 1913, in a similar spirit.

E of Exhibition Road, Princes Gardens has been taken over for STUDENT LODGINGS by *Sheppard Robson & Partners*. The 108 dominant building is on the s side, an impressive, well-proportioned Corbusian slab of 1960–3. The students' rooms, arranged in clusters of eight, occupy six storeys, divided into two groups of three by an upper level 'street', above a podium of common rooms and refectories. The shuttered concrete surfaces of the box-frame construction are left exposed both outside and in the communal areas, tempered by timber window-frames and ceilings. Weeks Hall, at the NE corner of the square, dates from 1957–9; the other lodgings and the sports hall on the N side are of the later 1960s.

IMPERIAL INSTITUTE. Only the central tower remains (*see* Imperial College, above). The Institute, founded as an outcome of the Colonial Exhibition of 1886, was built in 1887–93 by *T. E. Collcutt*. It formed a stately, symmetrical pile with Renaissance detail, all of stone, with three copper-roofed towers.

67 NATURAL HISTORY MUSEUM, Cromwell Road. The decision to move the Natural History section of the British Museum to Kensington was taken in 1860; the site was acquired in 1864, and a competition held which was won by *Francis Fowke*. On his death *Waterhouse* was commissioned instead. His plans were submitted in 1868 and simplified in 1870–1. Building began in 1872; the first three departments were opened in 1881. The building is in the Romanesque style, the detail inspired chiefly by late Romanesque monuments in southern Germany – an unusual source, but well suited to the elaborate architectural ornament introduced at the suggestion of the superintendent, Sir Richard Owen. The building is totally symmetrical and on axis with the newly completed Albert Hall. In contrast to the V. and A., it benefits by being set back from Cromwell Road, with its main floor raised up above basement workshops. Its chief feature is a pair of tall towers, 58 metres high, flanking a large entrance with multiple orders of arches. The iron frame is covered all over with Waterhouse's favourite terracotta slabs (a material which had already been proposed in Fowke's plans), the supply of which caused considerable delay in the building work. Their surprisingly delicate shades of buff and grey-blue were revealed during cleaning in the 1970s, and transformed the general impression previously given by the exterior (Pevsner in 1952 referred unflatteringly to the 'soapy hardness' of the terracotta). The elevations are relieved by a prodigious quantity of ornament methodically related to the subject matter of the museum (E wing with extinct, W wing with living species, reflecting the geological and zoological collections). The modelling was carried out by *Dujardin* of *Farmer & Brindley*.

In contrast to the undisciplined expansion of the South Kensington museums, the interior planning of the Natural History Museum was rigorously organized in relation to the collections. The broad lines of the plan had been put forward by Owen already in 1859. The main hall was intended as an index museum, flanked by the specialized collections; in the N part of the site the public galleries alternated with narrow reference galleries for students (an arrangement soon given up as the former required more space). C20 museum display has made nonsense of this logical plan, although wholescale rebuilding of the parts NE of the central hall, proposed in 1978, was resisted, and in this area something of the original arrangement still survives.

The entrance leads into a huge hall with a bold glass and iron roof (probably painted by *Best & Lea* of Manchester) and a monumental staircase at its far end leading to the first floor. From

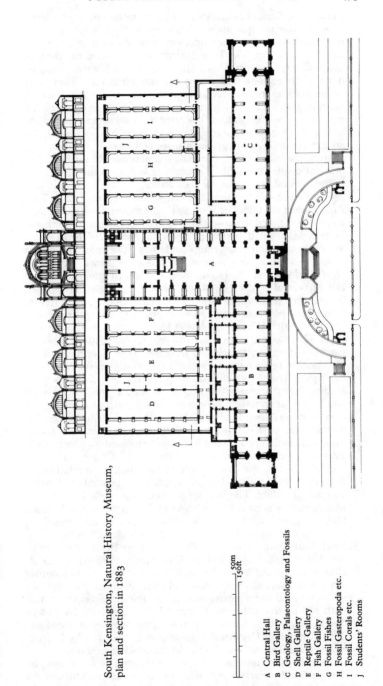

South Kensington, Natural History Museum,
plan and section in 1883

50m
150ft

A Central Hall
B Bird Gallery
C Geology, Palaeontology and Fossils
D Shell Gallery
E Reptile Gallery
F Fish Gallery
G Fossil Fishes
H Fossil Gasteropoda etc.
I Fossil Corals etc.
J Students' Rooms

the upper galleries one can look down on the hall through a series of large Romanesque arches. The second floor is reached by a bridge across the entrance side, sweeping up without any intermediate supports. The long exhibition halls along the front of the building to w and e of the entrance hall were originally devoted to geology and fossils (e) and birds (w). They have ceilings of iron and concrete, with iron supports clad in terracotta, charmingly decorated with appropriate subject matter. The w gallery on the ground floor has later mezzanines inserted in the aisles; the e one was transformed in 1990 by *Ian Ritchie* for an exhibition on ecology, in a manner blatantly at odds with Waterhouse's measured, rational, and naturally lit interior. The original display can still be appreciated (at the time of writing) in the mineral gallery on the floor above.

Later additions: to the N, the vast whale hall, 1929–32 by *J. H. Markham* of the Office of Works. To the w, entomological block, 1935–8, extended 1949–52; the N extension, linking with the Science Museum, dates from 1955–8 (*W. Kendall* of the Ministry of Works), second stage completed 1973. The most prominent addition is the e wing with stores and laboratories, 1971–5 by *G. A. H. Pearce* of the Department of the Environment, a bold but successful contrast to Waterhouse: bronze glazing recessed behind prominent white concrete vertical supports, and a lecture theatre in a polygonal pavilion with corona marking the corner.

ROYAL ALBERT HALL. *See* Albert Hall.

ROYAL COLLEGE OF ART, Kensington Gore. 1959–64 by *H. T. Cadbury-Brown* in association with *Sir Hugh Casson* and *R. Y. Goodden*, to replace the art schools previously on the V. and A. site (q.v.). The tall slab block of workshops with large roof-top studios facing the park, austerely detailed in dark brick with bands of aggregate-faced concrete, is a gaunt foil to the ample curves of the Albert Hall next door. Behind, ingeniously angled to make the best of the tiny site, library and common rooms pleasantly looking out over a little courtyard with two trees, their interiors given some character by their lack of right angles. On the fourth side, the lower Gulbenkian Hall, a double-height, flexibly planned galleried space; simple white painted brick walls, suspended ceiling. The interior has been remodelled; the Henry Moore gallery is by *R.C.A. Project Office*, 1986, the Gulbenkian Hall 1989 by *Colquhoun, Miller & Partners*. By the same firm, extensions incorporating houses in Queen's Gate, 1988–91.

ROYAL COLLEGE OF MUSIC, Prince Consort Road, on axis with the Albert Hall, and in red brick to match. 1889–94 by *Sir A. Blomfield*, a grand but rather dull composition with two corner towers, in a sort of French baronial style. Planned with separate wings for men and women students. Double-height entrance hall with red marble columns. Concert hall at the back by *Sidney Smith*, 1899–1901. s extension 1963–4 by *Norman & Dawbarn*. The Museum of Historical Instruments to the SE is by *P. Radinger Associates*, 1968–9. To the s (and looking very odd next to the buildings of Imperial College) the Opera Theatre of 1984 by *Casson Conder Partnership*, with fly tower and auditorium for 400 hiding under Arts and Crafts Revival pitched roofs.

ROYAL COLLEGE OF ORGANISTS, w of the Albert Hall. Built

for the National Training School for Music, and from 1883 (until it moved to larger premises further s) occupied by the Royal College of Music (q.v.). By Henry Cole's son, *H. H. Cole*, 1875–6, with bold and effective sgraffito decoration by *F. W. Moody*. Cole's design is delightfully fresh, with its rigid emphasis on horizontals and verticals and its flat decoration, quite unlike any other public building of its date.

ROYAL SCHOOL OF MINES. *See* Imperial College, above.

ROYAL SCHOOL OF NEEDLEWORK, Exhibition Road. The small and pretty building of 1903 by *Fairfax B. Wade* was demolished for Imperial College (q.v., above).

SCIENCE MUSEUM, Exhibition Road. 1913–28 by *Sir R. Allison* of the Office of Works, the giant columns with the construction (reinforced concrete) showing between. The parts further w are later: central block by *W. Kendall*; lower floors 1949, upper floors 1959–61; other parts still later. The very tall E hall was refurbished by *Gordon Bowyer & Partners*, 1988, with a new high-level walkway, and dramatic hanging banner screens for projection displays.

VICTORIA AND ALBERT MUSEUM, Cromwell Road. Visitors approaching the museum's main entrance from Cromwell Road experience the latest part first. This is by *Aston Webb*, designed for a competition held in 1891, built in its present form in 1899–1909. Compared with the serious and coherent design of the Natural History Museum, it has an almost naughty looseness. It is as scattered in its motifs as the National Gallery was some eighty years before, but the neo-Greek dignity there has given way to a stylistic mixture of Franco–Flemish motifs jostling with Wrenaissance and even Gothic ones. The whole is crowned by a cupola consisting of a classical octagon with columns and a lantern with the open flying buttresses of Edinburgh and New-castle Cathedrals. For the exterior decoration Webb invited con-tributions from the up and coming sculptors of his day, but their work lacks much individual impact. The decoration around the main entrance is by *Alfred Drury*; the portraits of Victoria and Albert probably by *W. S. Frith*; the spandrels by *George Frampton*; the statues of Edward VII and Queen Alexandra by *W. Goscombe John*. Along the front, niches with statues of notable artists, architects, etc. (an entirely English Valhalla), some of them by Professor *Edward Lanteri* and his students from the Royal College of Art, who were also responsible for the figures on the central tower. The exterior was cleaned in 1989–90.

Webb's building provided a fine entrance hall and a series of large, rather austere top-lit galleries opening in long vistas off a central hall – originally a tall space with a glazed barrel-vault, somewhat like the Natural History Museum, but with its gran-deur much reduced after it was floored over to provide library book stacks in 1966–7. The entrance hall was remodelled by *Buzas & Irvine* in 1985, the start of an improvement programme under the direction of *Michael Hopkins & Partners* which has got no further at the time of writing.

Behind Webb's additions lie the confusing mass of older build-ings that grew in piecemeal fashion around the 'Brompton Boilers', the temporary iron and glass exhibition buildings which

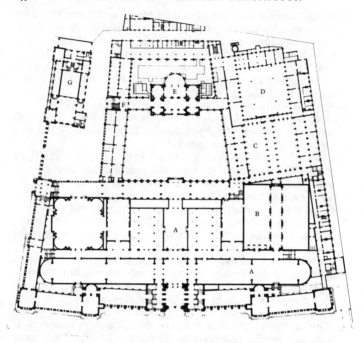

A Aston Webb Wing
   (1899-1909)
B Cast Courts (1868-73)
C South Court (1861-2)

D North Court (1860-2)
E Refreshment Rooms and
   Lecture Theatre range
   (1864-6)

F Ceramic Staircase (1864-6)
G Science Schools
   (former Royal School
   of Mines) (1867-71)

South Kensington, Victoria and Albert Museum,
plan of the ground floor in 1909

existed on the NE part of the site from 1856 to 1867 (*see* introduction to Public Buildings 2). The earlier phases were born of
the energy and enthusiasm of Sir Henry Cole, responsible both
for running the schools and museum and for the building works.
His architect was Captain *Francis Fowke,* succeeded after
Fowke's early death in 1865 by Major *Henry Scott;* their decorators were led by *Godfrey Sykes,* who also died in 1865, aided
principally by *F. W. Moody, Reuben Townroe,* and *James Gamble.*
By the time Cole resigned in 1873, after increasingly bitter dis-
putes between his department and a parsimonious Office of
Works, the museum included the large top-lit N and S courts on
the E side of the central quadrangle (1861-2), and the range
on the N side, intended as the main entrance, with a group on
refreshment rooms with lecture theatre above (1864-9). The
ceramic staircase at the NW corner was added in 1865-71. N of
this is the former School for Naval Architects, now Henry Cole
Wing, added by *Scott* in 1867-72. The pair of lofty cast courts
are an addition of 1870-3; the range to the S of the quadrangle,
with the library on the first floor, was an afterthought of 1877-
83. All these remain, although some interiors have been altered,

and not all are accessible at the time of writing. The s face of the library was left incomplete, for both Fowke and Scott had made plans for extending the museum towards Cromwell Road. The Office of Works, which took over control in 1870, prevaricated until Aston Webb's wings were added at the end of the century.

The style adopted by Cole and Fowke was the pretty Lombardic Renaissance of Como or Pavia which had already been revived in Germany. It had been used for the Horticultural Galleries and was used again later by Scott for the Henry Cole Wing and the Albert Hall. It was an adaptable style that could combine new constructional methods with the revival of the Renaissance ornament in which Sykes was so skilled. Cole and Fowke conceived the buildings as practical examples of experimental decoration and construction: iron, glass, terracotta, ceramics, mosaic, sgraffito and fresco were all explored, often with the aid of the South Kensington art students, although established artists also participated. Externally the results are visible on E, N, and W sides of the main quadrangle (known as the Pirelli Garden since its formal Italian remodelling in 1986–7 by the *Property Services Agency*). The decoration of the N side, intended as the main entrance to the museum, is appropriately rich; it was begun by *Sykes*. The red brick walls are embellished with terracotta columns, made by *Blanchard*, with decorative bands modelled by Sykes on the themes of childhood, manhood, and old age. The mosaic in the pediment is by *Townroe*, the bronze doors (no longer in use) have high-relief panels of eminent figures in the arts and sciences made by *G. Franchi & Son*, all after sketches by Sykes.

Inside, a considerable amount of decoration from this period also remains, although much was destroyed or concealed as a result of later intolerance of Victorian decoration as a background for modern museum display. Anti-clockwise from the entrance hall the main survivals are as follows. The vast CAST COURTS of 1870–3, on a scale suitable for Trajan's Column in two halves, remain much as built, with plain walls (redecorated in deep Victorian colours) relieved only by heftily bracketed balconies. In the corridor between the two courts, mosaic pavements designed by *Moody*, one of many examples of the fine original floors (made by convicts of Woking Prison and termed 'opus criminale'). N of the cast courts, SOUTH COURT, a glass and iron construction of 1861–3, had some of the most lavish and colourful decoration. Much was removed or obscured when divided up after 1949; it deserves to be reinstated. A fragment of *Sykes*'s ironwork with twisted columns, uncovered in the 1970s, demonstrates the richness of what is concealed. The walls had two tiers of arches with mosaics in niches (which included Sykes's first experiment in English ceramic mosaic, a portrait of Prince Albert). At present first-floor level, visible from the corridors at the N and S ends, there survive *Lord Leighton*'s large semicircular paintings carried out in Gambier-Parry's spirit fresco technique: 'The Industrial Arts as applied to War and Peace', designed in 1870–2, 'War', executed in 1878–80, and 'Peace', completed only in 1886. These terminated the easternmost of the two elegant glass and iron barrel-vaults, which still survive above the C20

suspended ceilings. NORTH COURT was created earlier, in 1859–
62, covering an open quadrangle W of older buildings with an
experimental utilitarian cross-shaped glass roof – at first without
any supports. The centre remains open; the sides have inserted
floors. Original decoration also survives on the two STAIRCASES
in this area.

In the NORTH RANGE the galleries were ruthlessly stripped
of their decoration in the early C20, but opening off them on the
ground floor is the suite of REFRESHMENT ROOMS of 1865–9,
restored in the 1970s. The central room, with semicircular bow,
designed by *Sykes*, executed by *Gamble* and *Townroe*, is a ceramic
tour de force, with glossy, highly coloured columns and mirror
surrounds of majolica, and Sykes's decorative alphabet on a frieze
below the cornice. The chimneypiece by *Alfred Stevens*, a major
work of Victorian sculpture, comes from Dorchester House.
The ceiling is of enamelled iron. The golden stained glass in
Renaissance style, with its odd collection of mottoes, which helps
to soften the chilly effect of so many shiny surfaces, was made
by *Powells* to designs by Gamble. The E, or Grill Room, designed
by *Edward Poynter*, is friendlier, with blue Dutch tiles set in
panelling, and larger tiled panels of figures representing the
seasons and the months designed by art school students. The W,
or Green Dining Room, however, was (a very adventurous act
on the part of a national museum) handed over in 1867 to *Morris,
Marshall & Faulkner* to be decorated. It was one of the firm's
first big jobs of secular decoration, and is characteristic enough,
if not as glowing as Morris's work on a more domestic scale.
Philip Webb was responsible for the overall design and much of
the detail; *Burne-Jones* painted the dado panels and designed the
six small figure panels of stained glass. The lower walls are
panelled; the upper parts have low-relief plaster decoration with
boughs and foliage. All is diffused in the dim greenish light
entering through the small circular window panes. At the W end
of the N range is the much gaudier CERAMIC STAIRCASE (1865–
71) designed by *F. W. Moody*. The majolica is *Minton, Hollins
& Co.*'s, the mosaic is *Colin Minton Campbell*'s Keramic Mosaic.
Ceilings and spandrels were painted by Moody in vitrified
ceramic. The stained glass no longer survives. Half way up, a
commemorative mosaic portrait of Henry Cole, in a Renaissance
frame. The former CERAMIC GALLERY on the first floor (i.e.
rooms 65–9) is now plain apart from the pretty ceiling in front
of the stairs up to the LECTURE THEATRE. The stairs have ceiling
paintings by *Moody*; the proposed mosaic decoration of the
theatre itself was never executed.

65   The HENRY COLE WING along Exhibition Road, of 1868–73
by *Henry Scott* in consultation with *Henry Cole* and *Richard
Redgrave*, was originally independent of the museum; it was
occupied by the School of Naval Architects, the Science School,
and then Imperial College before its transformation into new
galleries for the V. and A. in 1978–81 by *David Church*. The
charm of the playful early Renaissance decoration can be enjoyed
on the front to Exhibition Road, which is especially reminiscent
of Semper. There is a piquant contrast between the busy
terracotta and the unrelieved red brickwork. There is a loggia on

the top storey so that students might have access to fresh air whenever needed. The ornaments are in *Minton* majolica. The iron gates in the archway at the N end are by *Starkie Gardner*, 1885. The less visible E side is equally interesting, with Renaissance grotesques by *Moody*, 1871–2, in sgraffito plaster – an experimental technique which had already been tried out in other parts of the museum. The simple grid-pattern iron gates in the low link building to the S of 1978–81 are by *Christopher Hay* and *Douglas Coyne* of the Royal College of Art. Inside the C19 part, a very large staircase takes up much of the interior. Its terracotta balustrade is by *J. W. Wild*.

PERAMBULATIONS

There is so much in Kensington to see and to describe that the Perambulations have been divided and subdivided into relatively small bites. The main divisions are four:

1. Central Kensington
2. Northern Kensington
3. Southern Kensington
4. South-West Kensington

1, Central, falls into two parts.
  (a) Kensington High Street (i) and, working in rectangles from E to W, streets to its N as far as the Holland Park Avenue axis (ii–iv) (map 1a, i–iv).
  (b) streets to the S of the High Street down to Cromwell Road, first E of the railway line (i), then W of it (ii), then W along Cromwell Road itself, starting from Gloucester Road (iii) (map 1b, i–iii).
2, Northern, also falls into two parts.
  (a) Holland Park Avenue and streets to the N of it and S of Westway, first W of Clarendon Road (i), then E of Portland Road, including Notting Hill and the Ladbroke estate (ii) (map 2a, i–ii, 2b, i).
  (b) the areas S and N of Westway, first Portobello Road and the area to its E (i) (map 2a, i–ii, 2b, i), then, N of Westway, the N part of Ladbroke Grove, North Kensington proper, and Kensal Town (ii) (map 2b, ii).
3, Southern, is divided into four.
  (a) the residential section of the museums area – South Kensington 'proper', between Cromwell Road and Kensington Gore.
  (b) East Brompton and Brompton Road. Both (a) and (b) include the strip of the City of Westminster lying to the S of Hyde Park.
  (c) West Brompton.
  (d) Old Brompton Road.
  All are on map 3a–d.
4, South-West, is divided into two.
  (a) N of Old Brompton Road and S of Cromwell Road, starting at Earls Court, continuing E as far as Gloucester Road.

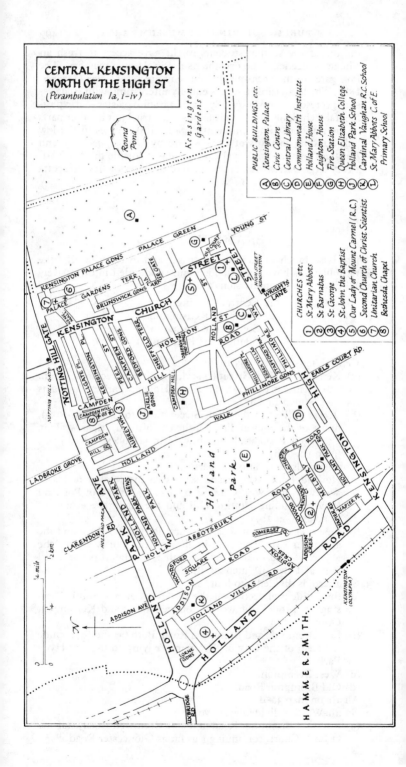

CENTRAL KENSINGTON NORTH OF THE HIGH ST
(Perambulation Ia, i–iv)

PUBLIC BUILDINGS etc.
- (A) Kensington Palace
- (B) Civic Centre
- (C) Central Library
- (D) Commonwealth Institute
- (E) Holland House
- (F) Leighton House
- (G) Fire Station
- (H) Queen Elizabeth College
- (J) Holland Park School
- (K) Cardinal Vaughan R.C. School
- (L) St. Mary Abbots C. of E. Primary School

CHURCHES etc.
- (1) St. Mary Abbots
- (2) St. Barnabas
- (3) St. George
- (4) St. John the Baptist
- (5) Our Lady of Mount Carmel (R.C.)
- (6) Second Church of Christ Scientist
- (7) Unitarian Church
- (8) Bethesda Chapel

Kensington Gardens

Round Pond

KENSINGTON GARDENS TERR.

PALACE GREEN

YOUNG ST

KENSINGTON PALACE GDNS

GARDENS TERR.

BRUNSWICK GDNS

PALACE

CHURCH STREET

HIGH STREET KENSINGTON

WRIGHTS LANE

NOTTING HILL GATE

KENSINGTON CHURCH STREET

HILLGATE PL.

KENSINGTON PL.

PEEL ST.

CAMPDEN ST.

BEDFORD GDNS

SHEFFIELD TERR.

CAMPDEN GDNS

HORNTON ST.

BEDFORD GDNS

GREENWOOD DUCHESS OF BEDFORDS WK.

HOLLAND ST.

HOLLAND RD.

CAMPDEN HILL GS.

CAMPDEN

AIRLIE GDNS

AUBREY WK.

CAMPDEN HILL RD.

DRAYCOTT PL.

ESSEX VILLAS STAFFORDSHIRE

PHILLIMORE GDNS

PHILLIMORE

PHILLIMORE GDNS

CAMPDEN HILL SQ.

HOLLAND PARK

HOLLAND WALK

Holland Park

EARLS COURT RD.

CLARENDON RD.

LADBROKE GROVE

HOLLAND PARK AVE.

HOLLAND PARK MEWS

HOLLAND PARK

HOLLAND PARK

HOLLAND

HOLLAND PARK RD.

ILCHESTER PL.

MELBURY RD.

HOLLAND PARK RD.

ABBOTSBURY ROAD

OAKWOOD CT.

OAKWOOD RD.

NAPIER RD.

NAPIER PL.

SOMERSET SQ.

ADDISON CRES.

WOODSFORD SQ.

ADDISON

ADDISON SQUARE

ADDISON ROAD

ADDISON CRES.

HOLLAND

HOLLAND VILLAS RD.

ADDISON AVE.

LORNE GDNS

HOLLAND

HOLLAND ROAD

KENSINGTON ROAD

KENSINGTON (OLYMPIA)

HAMMERSMITH

UXBRIDGE RD.

¼ mile

½ km

N

(b) s of Old Brompton Road, starting at Redcliffe Gardens and working E to Drayton Gardens and thence to Fulham Road. All are on map 4a–b.

1a,i. Central Kensington: the High Street

KENSINGTON HIGH STREET, a broad and busy thoroughfare lined with large blocks of flats and shops of the later C19 and earlier C20, now has little to show of its long history. The village nucleus lay around the church of St Mary Abbots. Ribbon development along the High Street took place from the later C18 (as it did along other main roads in the parish), but of this date only scattered remnants survive.

Starting from the E, Nos. 1 and 1A on the s side were built in 1884–5 for the London and County Bank by *Alfred Williams*. The style is Gothic – striking Anglo-Flemish of *c.* 1450 – and the fabric Fareham bricks with red Mansfield stone dressings. No. 13 is a smart Arts and Crafts façade by *Frank Sydney Chesterton*. Then from the street's early development Nos. 19–21 of 1690, much altered, and Nos. 23–25 of 1780–2. A random collection of buildings follows, ending with Nos. 55–61, outlandishly striped with terracotta and red brick and also incorporating mosaic and moulded brick panels and an odd, off-centre tower, built speculatively in 1893–4. The N side to this point is less varied and off to an uncomfortable start with the towering slab of the ROYAL GARDEN HOTEL by *Richard Seifert & Partners*, completed in 1965. The approach drive canopy is supported by alarmingly tapered piers. Then Nos. 26–40, 1924 for John Barker and Co. by *Sir Reginald Blomfield* and *H. L. Cabuche*, a domineering stone front with a giant arch crowned by a chunky Renaissance cupola. A series of Queen Anne-cum-Jacobean blocks of *c.* 1902 follows, the best by *Paul Hoffmann*, Nos. 62–70, the gables with large shells sprouting squat obelisks.

We continue on the s side. As the High Street curves gently, it is dominated by the sweeping façade of BARKERS, designed in 96 1933 by *Bernard George* as part of a comprehensive redevelopment which began in 1927 with the rear block and was finished only in 1958. The street front blends the traditional department store formula with some novel features in the spirit of French art deco. Steel frame construction encased in stone piers which alternate with windows set in elaborately decorated bronze frames (as used already in 1908 at Selfridges). Top storeys with triple cornice, accentuating the curving street front, daringly broken by two continuous glazed stairwells (for which George had to negotiate at length with planners) culminating in fully glazed lanterns well above the roof-line. The uncompromising verticality is enhanced by recessed windows and minimal splayed jambs. The interior is now partitioned into a much reduced Barkers and small shopping mall, 1985–8 by *Fitzroy Robinson Partnership*. At the same time the upper floors were converted for ASSOCIATED NEWSPAPERS, incorporating a new atrium rising through seven storeys, and Lord Northcliffe's panelled boardroom, brought from his Tudor Street office near Fleet

Street. Immediately to the w Nos. 101–111 is STOREHOUSE, built in 1929–31 for Derry and Toms, then a Barkers subsidiary. Its dignified, pared-down Beaux-Arts-classical façade (fluted giant pilasters, carved attic frieze), also by *George*, provides an instructive contrast with the flashier Parisian elegance of its neighbour. The flat zodiac reliefs are by *Walter Gilbert*, who also designed the bronze panels over the lifts and on the stairs inside. The *pièce de résistance* of Derry and Toms was its roof garden of 1937–8 (still extant), one of the earliest of its kind in England, incorporating thematic Spanish and English sections.

Beyond Wrights Lane Nos. 129–161 were built in 1893–4 as The Promenade, an ebullient late Queen Anne range by *Boehmer & Gibbs* (cf. Iverna Gardens, Perambulation 1b,ii), decorated with shaped gables and blocked columns. Nos. 173–195 demonstrate the Edwardian shift of taste to Wrenaissance: a powerfully detailed terrace by *Frank Sydney Chesterton*, 1908–9, with a tall central attic *à la* Hawksmoor. To its w the frontages generally degenerate. The plain stuccoed Nos. 197–199, set well back from the road, survive from Allen Terrace of *c.* 1825. Further on, MONARCH HOUSE, 1985 by *Joseph & Partners*, bulky and out of scale in this area, a bald front with curtain-walling between thick cast-stone piers. Further on is the ODEON cinema, built in 1926 by *Julian R. Leathart & W. F. Granger*, one of the foremost cinema design teams of their day. Leathart described his Kensington Kinema as having 'all the paraphernalia of the Neo-Grec, coffers, entablatures, frets, and rondels'. Large advertising panel and zigzag glass-painting crudely mar the elegant and imposing façade of bronze and black granite. The auditorium has been subdivided.

Earl's Terrace, Edwardes Place, and Nos. 343–353 High Street were built in 1820 as part of Lord Kensington's Edwardes Square development (*see* Perambulation 1b,ii). WARWICK CLOSE, by *Robert Angell & Curtis*, 1923, was built in front of Warwick Studios of 1883–4.

Now back to Church Street for the N side of the High Street, again working w. The Tudor building in diapered brick next to the church, with an archway to KENSINGTON CHURCH COURT, was built in 1872–3 as a police station by *F. Caiger*, Surveyor to the Metropolitan Police. The clumsily detailed No. 96, by *Sir Frederick Gibberd & Partners*, 1985, replaced the old Kensington Town Hall (1878 by *R. Walker*). The dormers and grid articulation of the façade in stone and red brick attempt to echo the red brick with Jacobean stone detailing of the eminently more attractive and effective OLD VESTRY HALL immediately w, built in 1851 by *Benjamin Broadbridge*. Between the two a narrow alley leads to secluded gardens around the church, and N to the back streets, where something of the c18 village character still exists (*see* Perambulation 1a,iii). Nos. 98–100 are the sole survivors of LOWER PHILLIMORE PLACE, designed by *William Porden* in 1788 as the first 'ribbon' development along the High Street. Then SUNDIAL HOUSE, Nos. 108–114, an attractive Arts and Crafts block in a late c17 domestic mode, with steep tiled roof and hipped dormers, 1908 by *Frank Sydney Chesterton*. HORNTON COURT is also by *Chesterton*, 1905–7, but in his

Baroque idiom (cf. Nos. 173–195) and much grander; behind the ground floor the main range is set back, with a three-bay stone centrepiece, the middle bay a distinctive ensemble with garlands and shell-hood niche. The frontages further W are given over entirely to a mixed bag of inter-war and post-war blocks, their interest diminishing as the borough boundary is approached.

1a,ii. Central Kensington N of the High Street: Kensington Palace to Kensington Church Street (see plan on p. 500)

Kensington Palace Gardens is a street unique in London, a private road consisting almost entirely of very wealthy private mansions on the site of the kitchen gardens of Kensington Palace. The transformation into what is virtually an ambassadorial precinct hinders observation but has encouraged good maintenance. The street was laid out in 1843 for the Crown Commissioners by *Sir James Pennethorne* and *Thomas Chawner*, the development being undertaken by *J. M. Blashfield* (maker of inlaid pavements, and later terracotta manufacturer). Blashfield had always intended to dispose of some of the sites, but withdrew in 1847, when he went bankrupt. Nevertheless the grand palazzi which he had encouraged (in place of Pennethorne and Chawner's suggested semi-detached villas) set the tone for Kensington development for the next quarter-century.

The S end is called PALACE GREEN, mostly decent, Edwardian houses (Nos. 4–10), but the chief title of fame goes to Nos. 1 and 2. No. 1 is *Philip Webb*'s most important town house, built in 1869 for the artist George Howard, later Earl of Carlisle: a tall urban house with a bold, almost ruthless combination of Queen Anne windows (a very early occurrence, well before Norman Shaw) and pointed arches. Especially odd is the tall pointed niche on the N side, where the staircase goes into the garden – similar to a motif later used by Jackson at No. 2 Kensington Court (*see* Perambulation 1b,i). The front is quite asymmetrical, brick with stone accents unwillingly conceded by Webb to Pennethorne in an effort to bring the house into line with its neighbours. The chief motifs are the porch with its steep gable and the oriel window, both considerably more ornamented than Webb intended, again concessions to Pennethorne. The simplicity of the design has been compromised by several extra windows added on N and E fronts when the house was converted to flats. The *Burne-Jones* interior decoration is now in Birmingham City Art Gallery. No. 2 is neo-Georgian, designed by *Frederick Hering* for and with the help of the novelist *W. M. Thackeray* in 1860–1, when no one was yet dreaming of a Georgian revival. Thackeray was, however, a firm advocate of red brick in the Stuart and early Georgian manner, and his proposals were accepted on the basis that they harmonized with the Palace, e.g. raised brick panels, rusticated brick piers, and very pronounced keystones.* The houses further N, set back behind a fine sequence of stone piers and iron railings, were built in 1903–12. Nos. 4–7 are tall

---

*A preliminary sketch by Thackeray of *c.* 1861 shows the house without pilasters; these were presumably added to satisfy the Crown Commissioners.

and symmetrical (Nos. 4 and 6 by *Read & Macdonald*; No. 5 by
E. P. Warren; No. 7 by *Horace Field* and *C. E. Simmons* with
Amos Faulkner), inspired by the Dutch Baroque style imported
by William III. Nos. 8–10 are more varied, also with a Dutch
flavour: No. 9, with shaped gables, by *J. J. Stevenson* and *H.
Redfern*; No. 10, with idiosyncratic stone dressings and slate-
hung canted gable, by *E. J. May*.

In KENSINGTON PALACE GARDENS proper, the houses were
built from 1844 to *c.* 1865, that is, at a time when Georgian
convention had been withdrawn to the winds by the go-ahead
younger architects. The predominant style is Italianate, ranging
from a pure High Renaissance to more fanciful varieties. Walking
N along this grand tree-lined boulevard some of the most impressive houses are on the E side, where the plots were deeper and the
views to Kensington Gardens an added bonus. No. 15, an elegant
interpretation of the Italian palazzo with astylar rusticated
ground floor and aediculed first-floor windows, was begun in
1854 by *James Knowles Sen.* The house has a fine entrance hall
with top-lit stair rising behind an Ionic colonnade to a spacious
landing with coffered ceiling. Other rooms with much lavish
interior decoration of the 1930s by *Wellesley & Wills*, who also
added the central screen on the garden side, and the windows
below the eaves. Generous STABLES (now a separate house) set
back to the s, also by *Knowles*. The French Renaissance façade
of No. 14 was designed by *White, Allom & Co.* in 1908 and
severely altered the original of 1850 by *T. Cubitt*. On the w side
No. 17, also much altered from the 1844–6 original by *H. E.
Kendall Jun.* – especially by the three-bay extension and by
Charles E. Sayer, 1899–1900. No. 15A is by *David Brandon*,
1852–4, No. 16 by *T. H. Wyatt* and *D. Brandon*, 1846. The semi-
detached Palladian villas Nos. 18–19 are of 1845–7 to designs
emanating from *Charles Barry*'s office. The formal palazzo façade
(cf. Bridgewater House in Cleveland Row, Wm) of five bays, the
recessed central block flanked by two towers, with aediculed and
pedimented windows, cleverly masks an asymmetrical plan. No.
13 on the E side, built in 1851–4, is one of the largest houses in
the road, its odd appearance created by the first owner, *Lord
Harrington*, with the help of his estate surveyor *C. J. Richardson*.
It is of buff brick with Bath stone dressings in a bastardized
Gothic style with heavy drip mouldings, traceried parapet, and
corner buttresses. The most memorable feature is the bastion-
like tower with oriel window. (It was originally topped with a
Gothic belfry, removed in 1924.) No. 12A, a Renaissance mansion
of some dignity, with discreet neo-Georgian ornament, is of 1863–
5 by *James Murray*. Nos. 12 and 20 opposite were built sim-
ultaneously, 1845–6 by *R. R. Banks*, a pupil of Charles Barry.
No. 20, with Vanbrughian giant-order Roman Doric pilasters
and bold corner chimneys, is less elegant than No. 12, an astylar
Italian palazzo in the manner of Barry's Pall Mall clubs, with a
particularly splendid cornice. A 'Moorish' billiard room was
added by *M. D. Wyatt* in 1864. No. 11, 1852–4 by *Sydney Smirke*,
is stucco-faced with refined classical dressings. Its Parisian
appearance derives from the steep hipped roof with tall dormers,
added in 1874 by *E. Tarver* (wrecked by fire, 1990). No. 10 is a

villa of 1846–7 by *Philip Hardwick*, much altered, especially in 1896 by *Leonard Stokes*. No. 9 is another house by *Sydney Smirke*, 1852. On the w side some more Italianate villas: Nos. 21 (1846), 22 (1851), and 23 (1852), then the exotic No. 24, designed by *Owen Jones* in 1845, complete with onion domes peeking from behind the honeycomb parapet. The plethora of Moorish details obscures the essentially Italianate design with symmetrical, fully stuccoed façade, conventional balustrades, bracketed cornice and porch. Jones was Blashfield's original architect, and he designed another Moorish mansion at No. 8, now regrettably replaced by an impersonal 1960s block (*Richard Seifert & Partners*). The serene Italianate villas at Nos. 6–7 were built in 1844, along with the N entrance gates and screen, by *T. H. Wyatt* and *David Brandon*.

Facing Bayswater Road, two houses remain of an original five: Nos. 4–5 of 1842, a semi-detached pair in basic stucco Italianate. At the NW corner No. 26 is the CZECHOSLOVAK EMBASSY by the Prague architects *J. Sramek, J. Bocan & K. Stepanski*, with *Robert Matthew, Johnson-Marshall & Partners*, 1968–9, a forceful, uncompromising design of its time, and a snub to classical good manners: four storeys in aggregate-faced concrete, the large windows deeply recessed, the upper ones with the glass set at an angle to the frame.

Turning w along NOTTING HILL GATE, past the seven-storey CZECHOSLOVAK CENTRE of 1968–9, Nos. 26–55 on the N side are a modest terrace of 1824 now obscured by projecting shopfronts. They were built as workers' housing (cf. Peel Street, Perambulation Ia,iii) when this area was still intensely dug for gravel. KENSINGTON MALL leads SW with BROADWALK COURT, 1934–5, tall flats by *Robert Atkinson*. Then MALL CHAMBERS, a five-storey block of flats in a Venetian Gothic style, built in 1865–8 by *James Murray* as 'model dwellings' for respectable women with small incomes, and considerably more attractive in design than most of its kind.

The Mall opens into KENSINGTON CHURCH STREET, its N end dominated by two of the buildings from the L.C.C. redevelopment scheme of 1962 by *Cotton, Ballard & Blow*. Less of an affront is No. 145 by *Chapman Taylor & Partners*, 1973, dark brown brick punctuated by copper-coloured reflective glass, a reticent composition, if a little lifeless. To the S, a number of miscellaneous Georgian survivals, notably the narrow No. 150 (built between land parcels of different ownership) and Nos. 126–138 on the E side (1736); on the w side, Nos. 103–125 were built as Peel Place in 1823, and Nos. 99–101, rather grander, are of 1826. Nos. 66–104, set back behind stucco garden walls, were built *c.* 1854 along with the attractive stucco terraces behind (BRUNSWICK GARDENS, PALACE GARDENS TERRACE, etc.), laid out in the grounds of Sheffield House. Opposite, on the w side of Church Street near the site of the Jacobean Campden House, CAMPDEN HOUSE TERRACE, 1894, a picturesque group of Queen Anne studio houses with hints of Arts and Crafts: dark red brick with stone dressings, whimsically adorned with shaped gables, oriel windows, and varied entrances. As the road bends E then S into the old village, its frontage is given over to tall blocks reflecting the shifting styles of the 1920s–30s: NEWTON COURT on the W side, traditional brick with stone quoins given interest by some shallow carving, by *Wills & Kaula*, 1926; and WINCHESTER COURT, a more ruthlessly streamlined corner-piece, plain brick above black faience lower floors, by *D. F. Martin-Smith & Beswick*, 1935. It curves round into VICARAGE GATE. At the E end is a tame neo-Georgian parish hall and vicarage by *Antony Lloyd*, 1968. Further s in Church Street, No. 30, YORK HOUSE, a decent, dignified classical palazzo by *H. Austen Hall*, 1926, built as a showpiece for the Gas Light and Coke Company. Brick with stone dressings (the carving by *Aumonier*), large arched ground-floor windows, decorative iron brackets remaining from the original gas lamps. The splendid entrance hall by *Walter Tapper* has been much altered by an inserted mezzanine.

LANCER SQUARE by *BDP*, 1988–9, a mixed development of shops and offices on the site of former barracks, marks the return to the tradition of ornamental frontages. It is of orange and yellow brick with generous cast-stone dressings and ironwork with semi-period motifs, in the manner of BDP's Ealing Broadway Centre (Ea). Even the guttering is imprinted with the date. The Church Street front is of five storeys (uncomfortably tall), with gabled bays, stone-framed ground-floor shops, and intermittent oriels. Behind is a consciously picturesque court with cobbled paving and a restless variety of gable profiles; a sturdy angled clock tower dominates the SE corner. The bulk of the development is disturbing in comparison with the few terraces further s (Nos. 3–7 of 1760 and Nos. 15–17 and 27A of 1724) that remain from Kensington's early C18 heyday (cf. Campden Hill, Perambulation 1a,iii). Most notable among later infill is the PRINCE OF WALES pub, eclectic Gothic dated 1874.

1a,iii. Central Kensington N of the High Street: Kensington Church Street to Holland Park (see plan on p. 500)

The rising ground of Campden Hill includes the area stretching from Kensington Church Street to Holland Park, once distinguished by several large houses in ample grounds and now articulated by a network of narrow streets and mews built up in the C19 to the N of the old village. Vestiges of the C18 village remain in Church Street (*see* Perambulation 1a,ii) and in the narrow HOLLAND STREET, originally a public way from Church Street to Holland House, built up by *John Jones*, a local bricklayer, from the 1720s. Much of the simple red brick terrace on the N side (Nos. 8–12, 18–26) dates from 1724. On the s side the larger No. 13, OLD HOUSE, is of 1760, of four bays with pedimented doorcase and large flat-headed windows. The lanes running s still recall the intricacy of the old village: KENSINGTON CHURCH WALK, although with C19 buildings, existed by the 1720s, leading to the churchyard past Parsonage House, the manor house demolished in the later C18. Near its site, overlooking the N side of the churchyard, is a development in a vaguely Tudor idiom, 1990 by *Andrews Downie & Kelly*.

Further W, along HOLLAND WALK, are modest stucco-fronted

terraces of 1844 by the prolific *Thomas Allason*. A cheerful contrast is the Arts and Crafts Nos. 35–43, a picturesque group of 1903 by *Frank Sydney Chesterton* with steep gables of roughcast over brick. Also his are Nos. 12–54 HORNTON STREET, red brick with stone dressings, distinguished by prominent bays or oriels, appropriately scaled for a side street, in contrast to his grander buildings in the High Street. To the N, No. 60, a tight cubic house in the early modern tradition by *GMW*, 1969.

W past the Library and Civic Centre (*see* Public Buildings 1) one enters a grid of streets with impressive brick villas with rich stucco encrustations (PHILLIMORE GARDENS, STAFFORD TERRACE, ESSEX VILLAS), built in 1858–60, when taste was turning from purer Italianate to more enriched frontages. No. 18 Stafford Terrace (Linley Sambourne House, open to the public as a museum) preserves a characteristically crowded and little altered Victorian interior from the time of the artist Linley Sambourne, who lived here from 1874. Nos. 6–12 PHILLIMORE PLACE provide an interesting alternative: semi-detached Tudor Gothic villas by *Henry Winnock Hayward*, 1857.

By 1837 CAMPDEN HILL ROAD was established as an alternative N–S thoroughfare to Church Street. The earliest surviving buildings, of *c.* 1825, are at the N end (Nos. 108–116, 140–144). But first comes the lengthy terrace of brick and stucco beginning at No. 7, dating from 1857, with Tuscan fenestration at Nos. 15–35. Then CAMPDEN HILL COURT, a large, elaborate block of flats by *E. C. Pilkington*, 1898. Five storeys plus dormers, with a tripartite façade of red brick with stucco and cut brick dressings, lavish portico, double square bays, bow-windows, and a corner turret with cupola. Nearby the opulent OBSERVATORY GARDENS of 1883 provides a French flavour with its thickly applied cement dressings, tall hipped roofs, and striped rustication. The attics have been much altered, although No. 1 still has its original roof-top balustrade and circular dormers.

CAMPDEN HILL to the W was laid out to serve seven detached villas built in 1814 by *John Tasker*. Of these, only THORPE LODGE remains, now the Sixth Form Centre of Holland Park School (*see* Public Buildings 1); the former coach house of AIRLIE LODGE is also part of the school. The picturesque Arts and Crafts villas in Campden Hill were built in 1914–15, No. 1 by *E. P. Warren*, Nos. 2 and 3 by *Arthur G. Leighton* (No. 3 a studio house for Sir William Llewellyn).

Between Campden Hill Road and Church Street are a series of straight roads that map out with text-book clarity the three major C19 building campaigns in Kensington. BEDFORD GARDENS, CAMPDEN STREET, and PEEL STREET have some exquisitely preserved terraces from the 1820s, Nos. 6–53 Campden Street especially appealing, with single-window façades and round-headed doorways. Further N KENSINGTON PLACE and HILLGATE PLACE have densely packed terraces built in 1851–5 to house those employed by wealthy residents nearby. They were in multi-occupation soon after completion, creating one of Kensington's worst slums – a history difficult to recapture from the rainbow-coloured frontages inspired by C20 gentrification. No. 23 Kensington Place, by *Tom Kay*, 1966–7, is a tough interloper of tar-faced blue bricks with a circular stair-turret; inside, a gallery beneath the sloping sunroof overlooks the sitting room. Lastly, among the earlier houses the later Victorian and Edwardian decades have left their mark. In CAMPDEN STREET No. 70, converted to flats in 1989–90, is the former Byam Shaw School of Drawing and Painting, 1910 by *T. Phillips Figgis*; red brick neatly banded with tiles, with a tall studio window rising up into a dentilled semicircular gable. In SHEFFIELD TERRACE, on part of the site of Campden House (cf. Church Street, 1a,ii), is CAMPDEN HOUSE CHAMBERS by *Thackeray Turner* and *Eustace Balfour*, begun in 1894 and highly acclaimed at the time. It is of yellow brick with copious bright orange brick dressings, the main block asymmetrical, with a recessed polygonal entrance bay framed by tall gabled square bays. Glowering from across the street at this cheery version of Queen Anne is the Gothic gloom of No. 38, 1876 by *Alfred Waterhouse* for Edward Conningham Sterling, conspicuously flouting the provision that it be built to match the adjacent houses. Of dark brick with stone dressings, it has three very tall storeys plus an attic with a spacious studio, Gothic upper windows, and much decorative brickwork. On the w side of Campden Hill Road are the very tall gabled houses of AIRLIE GARDENS by *Spencer Chadwick*, 1878, built to exploit the excellent views from the upper storeys. No. 1 has a turreted addition of 1891 in the manner of Norman Shaw's New Scotland Yard, perhaps by *Brydon*. On the E side, THE MOUNT, luxury flats by *Douglas Stephen & Partners*, 1961–4, advanced for its date, with its plain rendered surfaces and stark, somewhat Oud-like play of balconies. Further N No. 118, WEST HOUSE, built in 1876 for George Henry Boughton by *Shaw*. Stock brick with red brick dressings; stone-mullioned bay-window and tilehung upper storeys. The smaller façade gable was once stepped, adding to the asymmetry; the soaring chimney is a Shaw trademark. The s side of NOTTING HILL GATE to the N was comprehensively redeveloped in 1962 for the L.C.C. by *Cotton Ballard & Blow*, with tall concrete slabs punctuating long low ranges with drab and repetitive detail – an unappealingly brutal demonstration of the principles of post-war planning. A lonely survivor among it all is the NOTTING HILL CORONET, opened in 1898 and converted for cinema use in 1916. It was designed by *W. G. R. Sprague* and is one of the few suburban theatres to survive relatively untouched. Exterior with loose classical detail with Baroque swags and pilasters; well preserved interior with excellent plasterwork. AUBREY WALK leads w from Campden Hill Road, past the PUMPING STATION of 1857–8 by *Alexander Fraser* for the Grand Union Junction Water Company, to AUBREY HOUSE. Its site was renowned in the C17 for the medicinal spring known as Kensington Wells. The core of the house probably belongs to one built adjoining the spring *c.* 1698; its present appearance is owed to Sir Edward Lloyd, who added projecting wings to the central block and reconstructed the N façade between 1745 and 1754. Later C18 alterations included a drawing room created by *James Wyatt* in 1774 for Lady Mary Coke. The gauged-arch windows and pediment with acroterial urns are visible from the road; the current doorcase is a reproduction. In Aubrey Walk itself, Nos. 15–17, on the site of former outbuildings, were designed in 1950 for the owners of Aubrey House by the accomplished classicist *Raymond Erith* in a restrained Regency style, unusual for its time. The houses are of stock brick with grey brick dressings, the fronts sparsely fenestrated and some windows ostensibly blocked. The rear façade has two bow-windows flanking a recessed centre. All three houses have stairwells with curved ends and elegant handrails. The modest garages adjoining are also by *Erith* (in place of a grander coach house first proposed). The Erith terrace was intended to recreate the atmosphere of the road's early architecture as illustrated by Nos. 2–6 of *c.* 1826.

CAMPDEN HILL SQUARE, immediately to the N, was the area's major enterprise of the 1820s. It was probably laid out by *Joshua Flesher Hanson*, best known at the time for his promotion of Regency Square, Brighton, begun in 1818: both are three-sided around a large communal garden, with extensions laterally at the closed end. A basic formula is recognizable despite the variety of detail resulting from piecemeal completion over twenty-four years, beginning in 1827: the houses are generally of three storeys, in stock brick with stuccoed ground floors. Nos. 42–47 have stucco architraves with an Italianate flavour; Nos. 4–6 have elegant fanlights. The earliest buildings are near the turnpike road, Nos. 1–5 and 49–53. The double-fronted Nos. 2 and 52 may be by Hanson's surveyor, *George Edward Valentine*. Later alterations include No. 18, dramatically punctuating the summit of the square, rebuilt in 1887–8 in red brick by *J. T. Newman*; Nos. 24–28, rebuilt following damage in the Second World War; and Nos. 29, 30, and 41, C20 additions.

In HOLLAND PARK AVENUE Nos. 13–19 and 21–27 were built with Campden Hill Square as glorified return fronts. Set back in spacious gardens sloping to road level, they preserve a hint of former grandeur despite substantial alterations and, in some cases at the time of writing, a lamentable state of decay.

Further W lies the HOLLAND PARK development, carved from the grounds of Holland House (*see* Public Buildings 1) in 1860–79: ninety identical detached villas of three storeys plus dormers by *Francis Radford*. Above the traditional, sober Italianate ground floors (engaged Doric portico, rusticated quoins) an effervescent gaiety breaks out: the Ionic pilasters with unusually fulsome capitals, lavish flowering urns, and complex dormer profile all illustrate a shift in Victorian taste away from the precise and towards the exuberant. The glass and iron canopies are later additions. DUKE'S LODGE replaced No. 80 in 1939. HOLLAND PARK MEWS, also built in 1860–79, provided sixty-eight stables with accommodation above. The grand entrance gate at the W end and the splendid parapets survive to distinguish these as very ritzy mews.

1a,iv. Central Kensington N of the High Street: W of Holland Park (*see plan on p. 500*)

The entire area was originally part of the grounds of Holland House. It was developed from the 1820s onwards, chiefly with large conventional houses set in spacious gardens, very clearly for the wealthy professional classes. From the 1860s, however, the SE corner attracted leading Victorian artists; it therefore boasts more idiosyncratic mansions of red brick. To all this, C20 metropolitan pressures have added a variety of high-density developments.

The story begins at the S end of ADDISON ROAD, laid out in 1823 with large semi-detached villas, few of which survive. Nos. 36–39 are of 1843–5, two-storey brick houses linked in pairs beneath a pediment, with large back extensions – a typical suburban plan for this era (cf. Addison Avenue, Perambulation 2a,i). Then Nos. 40–47, built as Warwick Villas in 1841–50 in an experimental stuccoed Gothic: buttressed bays with traceried parapets, crock-etted pinnacles (many lost), and crenellation; the original pin-nacled gateway survives at No. 47.

Immediately to the E lies an eminently arty area developed from the mid 1860s on farmland formerly belonging to Little Holland House. No. 14 HOLLAND PARK ROAD was the first to go up (1865), designed by *Philip Webb* for the painter Val Prinsep, a remarkably early example of the revival of red brick for London houses, and also one of the first of the later C19 genre of London 'artist's houses'. The original appearance is completely lost due to Webb's own alterations of 1877 and 1892, when the entire two-bay E wing was added and the original simple profile with two gables obscured. No. 12 is Leighton House, now a museum (*see* Public Buildings 1). Nos. 10–10A, set back from the road, intended as one house for another artist, James Jebusha Shannon, are a complete recasting in orange brick of the former farmhouse (1859) by *W. E. & F. Brown*, 1892–3; the style is a mixture of Jacobean and Dutch Baroque, with a large curly gable. On the S side of Holland Park Road, small-scale neo-Georgian terraces, replacing stabling of c. 1825, by *Stone, Toms & Partners*, c. 1960.

To the E Holland Park Road joins MELBURY ROAD, a street of unique and fascinating variety, with grand red brick houses built from c. 1875 by and for the *crème de la crème* of the Victorian art world. First, however, No. 59, excellent neo-early-Georgian by *Williams & Cox*, 1925. Then Nos. 55–57 (converted to flats in 1950) for the engineer Sir Alexander Rendel by *Halsey Ricardo*, 1894, in his favourite glazed bricks, chosen to repel the adverse effects of age and climate. The detail is very English, with three storeys of sash-windows, a hipped roof above a deep eaves cornice, tall chimneys and prominent dormers. Inside No. 55 survives a lush hall of peacock-blue tiles by *William de Morgan*. Nos. 41–45, by *Martin Richmond*, 1962, are a discreet modern terrace with an imaginative variety of window shapes and place-ments. No. 31, Queen Anne of the utmost precision, by *R. Norman Shaw*, 1876 for the artist Sir Luke Fildes, is a pic-turesque composition in the manner of Lowther Lodge (Per-ambulation 3a), with asymmetrical groupings exploiting its corner site, which for Shaw was 'delicious'. A widow's walk and studio lantern balance the roofscape of tall, slim chimneystacks.

62 TOWER HOUSE, No. 29 Melbury Road, is equally admirable but in a different spirit altogether. It was built for himself by *William Burges* in 1876–8: a French Gothic château reinterpreted in red

brick. Its chief feature is the circular stair-turret with conical top, but the cut-brick chimneystacks, steep gables, decorative ridge tiles, and trefoil-headed lancets also contribute to the medieval effect. Burges had established a reputation for such work at Cardiff Castle in 1865. The sturdy exterior gives little hint of the fantasy he created inside.* The plan is straightforward, an L shape with three main rooms on each floor, the double-height hall in the angle. Burges's lavish carved and painted decoration for each room is a triumphant declaration of his very personal interpretation of medieval tradition (400 drawings survive). Each room has a special theme; the hall was devoted to Time, the drawing room to Love, and the library to the Liberal Arts, with a 'Tower of Babel' chimneypiece with Nimrod and Queen Grammar sending out the parts of speech. The upstairs rooms are still more fantastic. Burges's own room is decorated in deep red, with convex ceiling mirrors to reflect candlelight, and a mermaid chimneypiece in silver and gold. Much of the structural decoration remains, but the furniture has been dispersed.

STAVORDALE LODGE, Nos. 10–12 Melbury Road, 1965–9 by *Messrs Doiling & Partners*, is uncompromisingly modernist, with cold grey and white cubic forms, frankly impertinent in this environment. The other *Norman Shaw* house in the street, No. 8, was built in 1875 for the artist Marcus Stone, with enormous studio oriels (the middle one heightened by *Mervyn Macartney*, *c.* 1881), an almost mannerist attenuation of the ground-floor sash-windows, and a grand cut brick doorcase. Further along, Nos. 2–4 were built in 1876 for the sculptor *Hamo Thornycroft* (cf. Albert Memorial, Public Buildings 2) and designed by him together with *J. Belcher*: a tall asymmetrical pair, with some upper tilehanging as the only ornament. The lower studio block, now MELBURY COTTAGE, was built by *Belcher* in 1892. Turning N into ADDISON ROAD again, traditional middle-class decorum takes over: Nos. 50–59 are a semi-detached pair of 1852, Nos. 64–84 of 1854 are grander and detached, fully stuccoed, with projecting Doric porch and balustraded parapet. On the E side is OAKWOOD COURT, a whole street of rather grim eight-storey blocks, Nos. 1–30 by *William G. Hunt*, 1900, Nos. 31–62 equally tall but in a more rigorous stripped neo-classical by *Richardson & Gill*, 1928–30. Futher E, 1920s development on a more humane scale: OAKWOOD HOUSE in ABBOTSBURY ROAD, pleasant neo-Regency with curved bows, and ILCHESTER PLACE, with two-storey terraces in a precisely detailed neo-Georgian, *c.* 1929 by *Leonard Martin*. It is salutary to contrast these with SOMERSET SQUARE just to the E of Addison Road, 1974 by *Chapman Taylor Partners*, where meagre and superficial Georgian trimmings sit uncomfortably above integral garages.

Nos. 11–17 ADDISON ROAD are the only survivors of the first speculative houses to go up here in 1830–9. Then to the N the showpiece of Addison Road, No. 8, built in 1905 for the store owner Sir Ernest Debenham, and the ultimate expression of *Halsey Ricardo*'s theory of structural polychromy. Above the 76

*For a detailed account see J. M. Crook, *William Burges* (1981).

basement of blue-grey brick rises a Brunelleschi-like framework of variegated Doulton Carrara ware embracing green glazed Burmantofts bricks, all beneath a very deep modillioned cornice. Above this, an attic storey in turquoise glazed bricks and a tiled hipped roof with tall, decorated chimneystacks. The richly coloured tiles of the long entrance corridor are by *William de Morgan*, interspersed with garden vistas through the round glazed windows. The house is planned around a central domed hall with the main rooms looking E over the garden. The decoration is a rare example of Arts and Crafts work on the most lavish scale, the dome and upper walls of the Byzantine hall (inspired by San Vitale, Ravenna) glittering with mosaics designed by Ricardo and executed by *Gaetano Meo*. Elaborate fireplace carved by *George Jack*. First-floor corridors look down through triple arcades with pierced screens. The library in the SW corner has mahogany bookcases intricately inlaid with abalone, and a plaster ceiling by *Ernest Gimson*. Other ceilings also by *Gimson*. Especially appealing are the delightful variety of *de Morgan* tiles, used throughout the house for fireplaces and bathrooms.

WOODSFORD SQUARE, E of Addison Road, offers another version of high-density low-rise development; 1968–74 by *Fry Drew & Partners* for Wates. As one would expect from this firm, the detail is still loyal to the traditions of the modern movement. The layout is intricate, with traffic kept to the perimeter; four-storey brick terraces back on to leafy communal greens somewhat in the manner of Darbourne & Darke's Lillington Gardens Westminster. The blue glazed door jambs add a lively touch.

Addison Road veers l. at ADDISON HALL, a salmon-pink terracotta building of vaguely Flemish Gothic persuasion built as part school, part entertainment hall in 1885 by *Hugh McLachlan*. At the top of the road, facing Holland Park Avenue, is the HILTON INTERNATIONAL KENSINGTON, 1973 by *Triad*, a budget scheme in yellow brick and precast concrete, much too harsh a contrast with Royal Crescent opposite (Perambulation 2a,ii), though stepped down at the back in an attempt to keep in scale with the houses behind. W of this is LORNE GARDENS, a perfectly preserved development of tiny cottages of 1870–4 of an unusual design: they are of brick, without gardens, with only one room to each upper floor, staircases placed against the blind back walls, and unconventional fenestration.

Back E and S into the intensely suburban atmosphere of HOLLAND VILLAS ROAD of 1859, another long, tree-lined street of large, detached brick houses – here with simple stucco bays – barely disturbed by the C20. ADDISON CRESCENT at the S end is the same again. Then into the busier, less select HOLLAND ROAD, mostly built up with large Italianate terraces in the 1850s. Nos. 40–94, begun in 1870, their crisp Lombard detail obviously inspired by Ruskin, form a symmetrical terrace of stock brick, the pairs at each end and in the centre with gabled attic storeys with pinnacles and tiled lunettes. Before reaching the High Street to the S, NAPIER PLACE leads off l., a quiet mews alley of *c.* 1857. GARDEN HOUSE, No. 20, is by *Harry Spencer*, 1963, a three-storey block of flats in brick with timber elements. It is a sound example of the way in which the succinct precision of modernist principles can complement traditional surroundings.

1b,i. Central Kensington s of the High Street and E of the railway line

Tucked in off Young Street behind the bustle of the High Street is KENSINGTON SQUARE, Thomas Young's uniquely early attempt to build a smart residential square on the edge of what was then still a village outside London. Houses were begun in 1685; the N, E, and S sides were largely complete by 1690, the w side not until the 1730s. Alteration – primarily stucco facing – and rebuilding have obscured much of the square's original homogeneity. Nos. 11–12, added c. 1700 at the E end of the S side, have the best preserved exterior, with a hipped roof and dormers above a modillion eaves cornice, and ornate shell door-hoods (No. 12 is a reproduction), vividly recalling the William and Mary period. Also characteristic of this date are the red brick window surrounds still visible behind c19 dressings, the brick bands (now stuccoed) between the storeys, and the projecting closets at the back which are also features of some of the other houses. Nos. 17–19, 25, and 28–29 are all survivors from before 1700. These late c17 houses are not yet to a standard plan; they differ in width, and some (e.g. Nos. 11–12) have staircases between front and back rooms instead of the stair at the side

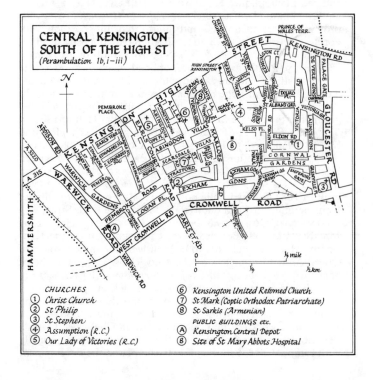

CENTRAL KENSINGTON
SOUTH OF THE HIGH ST
(Perambulation 1b, i–iii)

CHURCHES
① Christ Church
② St Philip
③ St Stephen
④ Assumption (R.C.)
⑤ Our Lady of Victories (R.C.)
⑥ Kensington United Reformed Church
⑦ St Mark (Coptic Orthodox Patriarchate)
⑧ St Sarkis (Armenian)

PUBLIC BUILDINGS etc.
Ⓐ Kensington Central Depot
Ⓑ Site of St Mary Abbots Hospital

common in the C18. No. 17 is the largest, of five bays, with a
grand staircase to the first floor taking up the two l. bays, and a
service stair behind. Nos. 19 and 29 have fine late C18 doorcases
but are earlier inside. Nos. 41–42 were rebuilt in 1804–5; No. 45,
at the corner of Young Street, still only two storeys, as many of
the houses were originally, was adapted by *J. D. Butler* with
details of *c.* 1900. Of the later rebuildings, No. 39 by *G. D.
Martin*, 1900–5, is brazenly tall, though materials and ornament
are relatively sedate. No. 16, of 1876 and by *Goldie & Child*, is
a controlled composition with starkly contrasting areas of painted
brick and red brick dressings. Nos. 5–6, also by *Goldie & Child*,
1876–7, are more ornate Queen Anne. Nos. 2–3, erected as service
buildings with entrance to the stables, are all that remains of
James Knowles Jun.'s gargantuan Kensington House.

YOUNG STREET, laid out in 1685 as the access road to the square,
has suffered considerably in the wake of Barkers' expansion and
post-war redevelopment. No. 16 survives from 1690, but the
double-bow brick façade is of 1804–5. Its distinctive con-
figuration is echoed opposite at No. 9 by *Frank Sydney Chesterton*, 1905, in Arts and Crafts red brick with simple, strong stone
dressings. The very dated car park with heavily perforated
honeycomb façade is by *Roy Chamberlain Associates*, 1968–70.

SE from the square, the haphazard layout reflects C17 lanes to
stabling and a bowling green. No. 10 ANSDELL STREET was
refronted in 1982–3 by *Blissett Macdonald Associates* in an art
deco revival complete with Tuscan portico and abstract blue
and red tile appliqué. RICHMOND COLLEGE, Nos. 7–17, is a
tactfully low modernist exercise by *Riley & Glanfield*, 1976, with
prominent grey-tiled oriels and intermittent hipped roofs with
dormers. Further S, in SOUTH END ROW, opposite a minor
early C19 terrace, ST ALBAN'S STUDIOS, built by *R. Douglas
Wells* in 1911 with gambrel roofs of hand-made tiles and a large
N-facing studio window; plain whitewashed walls conceal the
Tudor details and large oak staircase in an inner courtyard. In
ST ALBAN'S GROVE is Leith's School of Food and Wine,
occupying the former St Mary Abbots Mission Hall of 1894 by
T. Phillips Figgis. The fanciful gable belongs to a 1985 refronting
by *APT Partnership*. KENSINGTON COURT PLACE leads N,
Nos. 6–15 of 1802 unsympathetically dwarfed by the sheer red
brick masses of KENSINGTON COURT GARDENS (1887–9) and
ST ALBAN'S MANSIONS (1894 by *Paul Hoffmann*). No. 35 was
built in 1884 as a hydraulic power station to operate the lifts of
Kensington Court, laid out to the N behind the High Street.

KENSINGTON COURT was begun in 1882, a development by
Jonathan Carr (cf. Bedford Park, Chiswick, Ho) on the Kensington House estate. First to be built were the three terraces of
Queen Anne town houses on the E side (Nos. 3–25) and a block
opposite (Nos. 26–29) all by *J. J. Stevenson*. The terraces are
a handsome group full of original detail: delicately ornamented
terracotta bands between first and second floors, balconies on
projecting brackets below – considerably more festive than
Stevenson's work on the Cadogan estate in Chelsea, KC (q.v.,
Perambulation 3). S of No. 25 the former stables, originally
with ramps. In 1896 blocks of flats completed the development

on the w side, where several different architects worked in a more ponderous and bulky red brick and terracotta Domestic Revival style. Nos. 32–33 are by *Paul Hoffmann*, Nos. 34–35 by *R.J. Worley*. On the footpath leading N to the High Street the Kensington Court Electric Lighting Company built its first substation in 1888: the façade, by *J.A. Slater*, remains in excellent condition. The company was established in 1886 by R.E.B. Crompton, an influential pioneer in the field, to suppy the needs of the wealthy residents of Kensington Court with yet another modern amenity.

The most important houses of Kensington Court – No. 1 by *Stevenson* and No. 2, *T.G. Jackson*'s only London town house – face on to KENSINGTON ROAD; both are of 1883–4. They were joined *c.* 1925 to form the MILESTONE HOTEL, and rehabilitated in 1988–9. The Stevenson house is one of his more ornate, its façade details, in pink brick and buff terracotta, inspired by the rich and complex profiles of late Baroque central Europe. The polygonal tower whose lead cap echoes the curved gables once marked the entrance to mews. Jackson built No. 2 for Athelstan Riley (whose initials are displayed thoughout the terracota dressings) in an enthusiastic Franco-Flemish Gothic, with a tall shaped gable and dramatically soaring pilasters. The cut-brick window tracery is finely wrought in an early Renaissance style. A deeply recessed entrance bay and a remarkably flamboyant ground-floor oriel with lead serpents embracing its roof enliven the return façade. The equally lavish interiors were partially restored in 1989–91.

To the E, in PRINCE OF WALES TERRACE (1865, probably by *Philip Wilkinson*) and DE VERE GARDENS (mostly of 1875–80), are more conservative high Victorian town houses with Italianate detail. DE VERE COTTAGES, with their lattice glazing, rough stucco, wooden entrance gates, and rustic iron hinges, manifest a then-popular rebellion against the traditional image of a 'Kensington' house. They were converted from stabling by *Stanley-Barrett & Driver* in 1918–25.

CANNING PLACE, VICTORIA GROVE, and LAUNCESTON PLACE demarcate John Inderwick's Kensington New Town, efficiently developed from 1837 to 1843 by *Joel Bray*, who was probably the architect. It is a secluded little neighbourhood of the prettiest stucco cottages, in terraces or semi-detached, and with plenty of foliage around. Victorian encroachment on the rural spaces of Kensington continued in the 1840s (Victoria Road, Douro Place) and 1850s (Eldon Road, Stanford Road). In VICTORIA ROAD, amid the orderly suburban stucco, a picturesque roughcast studio was added to No. 25 by *H.G. Ibberson* in 1896. A year later came the substantial Arts and Crafts addition to No. 35 by *Walter Knight Shirley* – an unornamented façade of stock brick with a very broad three-storey bay, long sash-windows, mansard gable, and pointed-arch fanlight. No. 52 is a corner studio-house of 1851–3, Tudor brick, with much dark woodwork inside. In ELDON ROAD, the s terrace varies the usual town-house format by means of projecting quoins and a syncopated rhythm to the first- and second-floor windows. No. 17B is by *W.H. Collbran*, 1882, a rather hefty block with a cheery

contrast of bright orange brick and stone dressings. No. 19 is
an inventive inter-war remodelling now incorporating plaster
sculptures from the D.H. Evans Festival of Britain window
display. In COTTESMORE GARDENS, off Victoria Road, a
Grecian revival house by *Demetri Porphyrios*, 1989 (double-
height entrance hall).

Now w past STANFORD ROAD, with some elegant pairs of houses
with faceted quoins, to KELSO PLACE, intended to link with
development further w but curtailed by the railway. This
destroyed the original houses of 1851, with their unusual arched
ground-floor windows, prominent quoins, and unrendered
façades, except for No. 3. On the w side, Nos. 19–25c, an austere
essay in neo-Georgian, surprisingly by *Owen Luder*, 1960–4.
Plain red brick leavened by curved metal balconies. From here
a return can be made N to Kensington Square and the High
Street.

1b,ii. Central Kensington s *of the High Street and* w *of the railway
line (see plan on p. 513)*

The immediate southern hinterland of the w part of the High Street
is characterized by hefty mansion flats of the 1890s onwards into
which late C20 offices on a similar scale are beginning to intrude.
Further s, more spacious, sedate stucco streets of the mid C19
remain, and, w of Earls Court Road, earlier, simpler terraces built
on the Edwardes estate from 1811.

WRIGHTS LANE runs s from the High Street along the w side of
the railway, with indifferent offices of the 1980s, followed by the
former loading dock for Pontings (a Barkers subsidiary, q.v.
Kensington High Street); 1934–6 by *Bernard George*, in a
restrained 'moderne' style (ground-floor openings filled in in
1953). On the w side, IVERNA COURT and IVERNA GARDENS,
tall mansion flats, the latter of 1894–1903 by *Boehmer & Gibbs*,
an incongruous backdrop to the little Armenian church of St
Sarkis (q.v.) and its vicarage by *Mewès & Davis*, 1912. Further s,
CHENISTON GARDENS, completed in 1881, pale brick terraces
with quite intricate red brick decoration. It was popular on
completion: Sydney Ponting, the High Street draper, lived at
No. 1. No. 46 of 1885 is an obvious afterthought in patternbook
Queen Anne. SCARSDALE PLACE is occupied by two hotels: the
KENSINGTON CLOSE HOTEL by *Charles E. Peczenik*, 1937,
sterile pre-war Georgian disfigured by later windows, and the
LONDON TARA by *Building Design Associates* with *Cassidy Farrington & Dennys*, 1971, a massive, heavily articulated sixteen-
storey slab with projecting black vertical members running across
yellow brick.

s from here the mansion flats give way to leafy residential terraces
built up between 1855 and 1864 for the professional middle
classes, brick with very subdued stucco dressings. In
SCARSDALE VILLAS – the name evokes that sought-after aura of
spaciousness and wealth – the houses at the E end are particularly
elegant, fully stuccoed, with fancier fenestration and arrayed in
pairs. In MARLOES ROAD, laid out *c.* 1850, the w side, Nos.

37–67, dates from 1851, still elegantly reticent, its decoration confined to a guilloche band and a continuous balcony. On the E side was St Mary Abbots Hospital, which grew around the St Mary Abbots workhouse of 1848. The later buildings were replaced by KENSINGTON GREEN, a package of neo-Victorian Italianate terraces, a medical centre, and two nursing homes, 1989–91 by *Norman & Dawbarn*. In the centre, STONE HALL, part of the former male wing of the original workhouse, a handsome Jacobean gabled composition in diapered brick of 1848 by *Thomas Allom*. The original gatepiers in Marloes Road also survive. STRATFORD ROAD is the modest shopping street to this mid Victorian area. Off it, in BLITHFIELD STREET *Thomas Hussey*, on his own initiative, built in 1869 on the site of the pub bowling green a plain three-storey terrace to house the working classes who were then (as he argued before the Vestry) 'being rendered homeless by the improvements ... and demolition for the construction of the Metropolitan Railway'. Elsewhere in the vicinity of STRATFORD ROAD are a variety of artists' studios: STRATFORD STUDIOS, 1878, ALMA STUDIOS at Nos. 32–34, 1902 by *Charles R. Guy Hall*, and SCARSDALE STUDIOS, built in 1890 around a tiny secluded court entered through an archway with a pretty oriel above. Abingdon Road and Allen Street lead back to the High Street. In ALLEN STREET the low BRITANNIA public house (now refronted) is a reminder of the Britannia Brewery of 1834. WYNNSTAY GARDENS, by *Henry S. Copland*, 1883–5, are some of the earliest blocks of really classy flats built in Kensington, of yellow and red brick with enervated Queen Anne cement dressings.

At the N end of ABINGDON ROAD some much altered remnants of the modest terraces developed *c.* 1820 (Nos. 2–14 and 9–15, set back behind later shops, perhaps by *Annesley Voysey*; also Nos. 32–38, nicely preserved, and Nos. 43–51). To the W, the low scale continues in COPE PLACE, with stucco terraces of *c.* 1850 on the S side, facing an eclectically detailed replacement in brick, 1951 by *R. Harold Brine*, with channelled brick pilasters, rendered lunettes to the ground-floor windows, and little gables.

EARLS COURT ROAD, the old lane from the High Street to the manor and farm of Earl's Court, is a mediocre hotchpotch apart from a stucco stretch (Nos. 35–95) belonging with the development of Scarsdale Villas (*see* above). At the N end, the scale of the High Street intrudes with Nos. 1–9, 1987 by *Joseph & Partners*, shops and flats with quite varied frontages of brick and cast stone. Here PEMBROKE PLACE, a small cul-de-sac of workers' cottages of 1868, leads off W. Once a notorious slum with nearly a dozen occupants to each house, it is now smartened up with much bright paintwork and a pleasant tree-lined central square. Nos. 5–13 on the E side are by *Douglas Stephen & Partners*, 1962–3, an attempt to reproduce the original houses of *c.* 1827 (cf. the Edwardes estate, below); No. 19 is by *W. Doddington*, 1933.

W of Earls Court Road lay the Edwardes estate. The second Lord Kensington began to let it for building from 1811. The developer was a Frenchman, *Louis Léon Changeur*, the architect probably *David James Bunning*. Their most ambitious enterprise was

EARLS TERRACE, set back on the s side of the High Street behind small square corner lodges and iron railings: a long, plain, but elegant terrace in the Bloomsbury manner, with stuccoed ground floor, decorative fanlights, and iron balcony. EDWARDES SQUARE was laid out behind with a remarkably large communal garden, its size indicative of the low price of land so far from London. To the E and W are terraces of surprisingly small houses, each only two bays wide, lent a little architectural presence only by the paired and pedimented centre houses. First-floor windows with casements with marginal glazing rather than the usual sashes. The garden was designed by a resident Italian artist, *Agostino Aglio*, 1814–20; the little Tuscan temple was completed in 1821. Along the s side of the square (SOUTH EDWARDES SQUARE) were coach houses and stables, now much rebuilt. PEMBROKE COURT is by *Arthur C. Green*, 1932–3, brown brick, precisely articulated by rendered bays and iron glazing-bars and railings. The studios at Nos. 55–57 are converted stables; No. 59, with an elaborate moulded brick plaque, is by *Charles R. Guy Hall* (cf. Alma Studios, above), 1892.

SE from Edwardes Square is PEMBROKE SQUARE, begun in 1824, an elongated rectangle with N and s terraces of the standard Regency type, with pretty honeysuckle balconies. For the other, less successful enterprise of this time one must return to the High Street and continue w. First a detour into ST MARY ABBOTS PLACE, where there is a good group of Arts and Crafts studio cottages. On the E side, a pleasant irregular roughcast group by *Arthur G. Leighton*, 1910–13. No. 3, the larger brick house at the end, also by *Leighton*, was built for Sir William Llewellyn. On the w side, No. 12 is by *John & Paul Coleridge*, 1922. The broad N end of WARWICK GARDENS, with Nos. 1–9, represents the remains of the unsuccessful 'Warwick Square' laid out and designed by Lord Kensington's surveyor *William Cutbush* in 1824–39, with conspicuous Nash overlay to a basic terrace. The square is now commemorated by the column to Queen Victoria by *H.L. Florence*, re-erected here in 1934. Still further w is WARWICK ROAD, now dominated by the railway works rather than the workers' cottages which once prevailed. At its NW corner, CHARLES HOUSE, by *Arthur S. Ash*, 1948–50, one of the huge office buildings designed for government use under the so-called Lessor scheme, and better than most of them.

Finally the disparate area further s towards West Cromwell Road, built up from *c.* 1860, partly redeveloped after sale to the Prudential Assurance Company in 1903, and much rebuilt since. In PEMBROKE GARDENS, leading off Warwick Gardens, Nos. 31–34, 1927 by *G. A. Coombe* for Prudential, are in a whimsical rural French style with pedimented dormers, mansard roofs, and first-floor shutters. On the N side is a real gem, PEMBROKE STUDIOS, 1890–1, six secluded studios in stock brick with red cut-brick dressings ranged around a charmingly overgrown garden. Around the corner Nos. 13–27 date from 1863, when the street was first built up: large, conventional Italianate houses, most originally semi-detached. The E side was rebuilt after war damage: Nos. 1–7A by *L.H. Nixon*, 1966–8, Nos. 8–12 by *F.F.J.H. Doyle*, 1951, both architects for Prudential Assurance.

Far more flamboyant is the cornerpiece, Nos. 71–73 WARWICK
GARDENS by *Brian Taggart Associates*, begun in 1984, still
under construction in 1990. From the s this appears as a post-
modern version of a neo-classical villa, with sleekly channelled
cream stucco walls, a central bow, and an octagonal tower. But
from the E it is all far too bulky, with an unhappily obtrusive steel-
clad attic rising above the deep eaves. Further s, CROMWELL
CRESCENT, with inter-war cottages (Nos. 10–17) by *Murrell &
Pigott*, 1936–7, with steep, green pantiled roofs. Round the corner
in LOGAN PLACE, No. 1, well hidden, a neo-Georgian house
with a tall pedimented studio wing by *E. W. Marshall* for the
painter Cecil Rea. The w side of Cromwell Crescent is dominated
by WARWICK MANSIONS by *Philip E. Pilditch*, 1903–4, for
John Barker and Co. (their repositories formerly stood behind) –
a competent if eclectic frontage, a mixture of Tudor half-timbering, Queen Anne detail, and Italianate terracotta.

To the w, on the s side of PEMBROKE ROAD, HUNTSMORE
HOUSE by *Norman & Dawbarn*, 1989, a large block of brick-
faced flats whose sharp and angular profiles are broken somewhat
incongruously by a series of tight little bowed balconies. At the
w end, at the junction with Warwick Road, Chesterton Square
and Broadwood Terrace, an ambitious piece of local authority
redevelopment by *Arup Associates*, 1970–6. CHESTERTON
SQUARE, to the s, is skied above the Kensington Central Depot
(q.v., Public Buildings 1) – hence the vast expanses of yellow
brick walling at the lower levels, quite successfully given interest
by panelling with bricks laid in an unusual bond of alternate
courses with pairs of headers. The housing above appears from
the road as four receding tiers, articulated by the white grilles
that divide the continuous balconies. After the mean access, the
generous scale of the airy high-level square comes as a pleasant
surprise, with bushy planting to conceal the vents to floors below.
From within the square the terraces appear as three-storeyed,
minimally detailed, with flat roofs and plain brick walls with two
vertical divisions to distinguish the different units. A transparent
bridge leads to BROADWOOD TERRACE, another roof-top
terrace, sited over a car park, with a triangular planted piazza in
front. This has an alternative access: an amazing piece of abstract
sculpture hidden in a brick-clad drum, a circular white-walled
ramp *à la* Frank Lloyd Wright, around a liftshaft. Open-centred,
and so quite light. At its foot, tucked neatly into an awkward
corner, a DAY NURSERY and PLAY CENTRE with a big, friendly,
deep-eaved barn roof.

Across WARWICK ROAD, industry and warehousing grew up close
to the transport provided first by the Kensington Canal (constructed in 1824–7) and then by the railway which took its place.
Here too is some jokey showmanship, by *Ian Pollard* of *Flaxyard*,
1988–90, for SAINSBURY'S HOMEBASE (toned down from the
original design): neo-Egyptian trimmings in the form of a colonnade with lotus capitals in front of the car park, the same
details emphasizing the entrance to the store, and a big Egyptian
relief to brighten one of its blank walls. This breaks into an
otherwise Stirlingesque wrapping of striped granite with an
undulating window *à la* Stuttgart Gallery. For the site to the s

(known as Rameses II), offices by the same firm were planned in 1990 in the form of a pyramid on a plinth. Further S still a small CANAL-KEEPER'S COTTAGE survives in isolation just N of the West Cromwell Road bridge over the railway.

1b,iii. Central Kensington: Cromwell Road W of Gloucester Road

CROMWELL ROAD was extended W from Gloucester Road to the West London railway extension line in 1869. Only patches of its original high-quality terraces remain among C 20 intrusions. On the S side is the commercial development surrounding the Gloucester Road underground station (*see* Public Buildings 1), by *John R. Harris Architects*. Beyond it looms the LONDON FORUM HOTEL, by *Richard Seifert & Partners*, 1971–2, unnecessarily aggressive with its machicolated wings and menacingly angular roof-line. On the N side is the eighteen-storey tower and smaller main block of the revamped West London Air Terminal, originally by *Sir John Burnet, Tait & Partners*, 1962–3. The conversion, providing around four hundred flats and studios, is by *Michael Baumgarten* with *Rick Mather Architects* and *BOYA Design Group*, 1987–90.

The C 19 character of the area can best be appreciated in the streets to the N: cramped and lofty terraces, the earlier ones still in a genteel Italianate, the later ones more eclectic. First EMPEROR'S GATE, an awkwardly shaped development of 1871–8, where Nos. 26–36 mix lattice bands and fantastic floral tympana; an imaginative handling of the worn-out formula for town houses. Opposite, at No. 17a GRENVILLE PLACE, is a small unassuming house by *Stirling & Gowan*, 1957–9, the channelled concrete blending with adjacent terraces while masking an innovative modern interior. CORNWALL GARDENS, 1866–79, begun under the Broadwood estate surveyor *Thomas Cundy III*, is the classic Kensington High Victorian formula, very tall Italianate terraces facing communal gardens, complete with mews reached through arches at the back. The W end was completed in 1876–8, almost certainly to designs by *Edward Habershon & Brock*, by the builder *William Willett* (development had been delayed by the construction of the Metropolitan and District line). Here two extra blocks have been squeezed in, large and excessively ornate mansions (CORNWALL HOUSE and GARDEN HOUSE) by *James Trant Smith*, 1877–9. They are in a vigorous Second Empire style with mansard roofs, tall pinnacled dormers, continuous balustrades, and lavish, arcaded window surrounds. To the W, LEXHAM WALK, with Voyseyish cottages at Nos. 1–3 by *Stanley-Barrett & Driver*, 1909–10, leads into LEXHAM GARDENS, built gradually from the 1870s. Near the curved S end, Nos. 5–7, the YUGOSLAV EMBASSY, 1972–5 by *Hanna & Manwaring*, in dark brick with projecting concrete balconies.

Now into CROMWELL ROAD, with almost directly opposite on the S side the SWALLOW INTERNATIONAL HOTEL, by *George Beech*, 1968–72, one of the more unforgivable additions to the borough, completed under the auspices of the Development of Tourism Act, 1969. The main façade is clad in unfriendly black granite and a vertical section of angled, corrugated metal panels. The extensions into Knaresborough Place are no better, the primary feature an intrusive and unpleasant footbridge. No. 191, opposite Marloes Road, is by *Dinkha Latchin Associates*, 1989, flats in a post-modern version of C19 Italianate. The real thing is well illustrated by Nos. 188–189 on the N side, where in 1872–6 the builder and probable architect *William Henry Cullingford* erected a series of ostensibly detached villas faced with gault bricks and with cement dressings of a bold, classical character. The interiors were of an exceptionally high calibre: Painswick stone staircases, fireproof flooring of Minton encaustic tiles in the hall, central gas heating and hot water. They were immediately popular. Further on, HUNTINGDON HOUSE, Nos. 200–222, although much altered, is by *Richard Norman Shaw*, very tall red brick with a rhythm of pilasters, the top two storeys rendered and gabled. Next door, MOSCOW MANSIONS, begun in 1892 by *F. E. Williams*, completed in 1900 after a seven-year hiatus by *Everard White* in bright red brick and terracotta. The composition is striking if curiously eclectic, with loggia and open balconies, acroterial urns, and enormous square piers at the entrance. CROMWELL MANSIONS on the s side was built in 1887–9 by *George Hughes* as two red brick blocks of flats, the lively cement dressings and iron-railed balconies in stark contrast to the grave Italianate villas that preceded it.

2a,i. Northern Kensington: Holland Park Avenue and streets to the N, W of Clarendon Road (see plan on p. 522)

Most of the area to the N of HOLLAND PARK AVENUE was farmland until *c.* 1840. During the building boom of the 1820s stuccoed terraces sprang up along the Uxbridge road on the Ladbroke estate, starting with Nos. 8–22 Holland Park Avenue of 1824. The more overtly classical Nos. 2–6 and 24–28 that flank them, their centres with giant Doric columns *in antis*, are of 1826 by *Robert Cantwell*. They foreshadow the Norland estate further W, where the same architect laid out NORLAND SQUARE, ROYAL CRESCENT, and the intersecting roads in 1837. The tall narrow terraces of Cantwell's Royal Crescent, built in 1842–3 – stuccoed, with ground-floor channelling, simple dressings, and regularly spaced Doric porches – belong to the fashion for precise lines and crisply-cut profiles arrayed on a sweeping curve inspired by such groups as Nash's Crescent at Regents Park; moreover, the circular return pavilions recall his West Strand Improvements of 1830–2. The surrounding streets offered the prospective buyer a variety of types and styles of housing (cf. St John's Wood, St Marylebone, outer Wm). Leading from the Crescent, ST ANN'S VILLAS began in 1842 with stucco terraces with whimsical attic balconies and continued in 1845 with more lively and picturesque Jacobean semi-detached villas (Nos. 11–33 and 12–34), red brick with blue brick diapering and Bath stone dressings, their profiles emphasized by gables, porches, towers, and chimneystacks. The architect was possibly *C. J. Richardson*. In QUEENSDALE WALK, tiny stucco mews cottages of 1844,

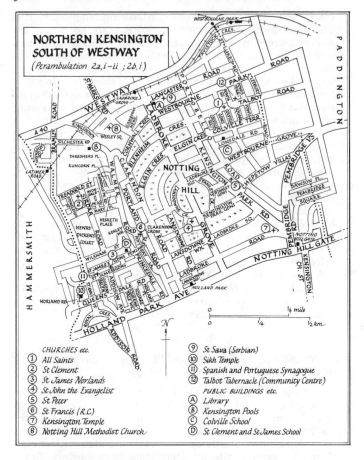

NORTHERN KENSINGTON
SOUTH OF WESTWAY
(Perambulation 2a, i–ii ; 2b, i)

CHURCHES etc.
① All Saints
② St Clement
③ St James Norlands
④ St John the Evangelist
⑤ St Peter
⑥ St Francis (R.C.)
⑦ Kensington Temple
⑧ Notting Hill Methodist Church
⑨ St Sava (Serbian)
⑩ Sikh Temple
⑪ Spanish and Portuguese Synagogue
⑫ Talbot Tabernacle (Community Centre)
PUBLIC BUILDINGS etc.
Ⓐ Library
Ⓑ Kensington Pools
Ⓒ Colville School
Ⓓ St Clement and St James School

also with Jacobean or Tudor details, the double segmental lights
still with their intricate glazing.

An alternative style is provided by the terraces of linked pairs of
villas in the N part of ADDISON AVENUE (Nos. 37–55 of 1843,
Nos. 34–56 of 1850), probably by *F. W. Stent*, classically detailed,
with façades articulated by pilaster strips. Such houses, only two
storeys over basements, might well entice residents to the outer
suburbs by offering more spacious and convenient layouts than
the traditional narrow-fronted tall terrace house. Addison
Avenue provides a vista towards St James's church (q.v.) in the
centre of ST JAMES'S GARDENS, begun in 1847. Nos. 1–24
and 42–45 are by *John Barnett*, broad-fronted three-storey pairs
linked by recessed bays, the stuccoed ground floors with a har-
monious rhythm of arcaded windows.

N of the Norland estate were the infamous Potteries and Piggeries,
hemmed in on the stiff clay ground between Portland Road and
Latimer Road (*see* Kensington Introduction). The access road,
Pottery Lane, drove a wedge between the more prosperous
Norland and Ladbroke estates, evident today in the awkward

connections between Princedale Road and Portland Road. POTTERY LANE is still narrow and winding, and C20 rebuilding (e.g. Nos. 34–42) has respected its old scale, following the tradition of the tiny two-room cottages and sheds of which a few survive (Nos. 29, 35, 43, 67).

This neighbourhood provides an instructive study in varieties of reconstruction. The Piggeries went in the 1870s, but in 1893 the area around Wilsham Street and Sirdar Road was still 'a West End Avernus', one of the poorest and most overcrowded slums in London. Improvements were slow and piecemeal. Octavia Hill was active here by 1900, the year in which the first of several housing organizations in the area, the Improved Tenements Association, was founded. After 1901 the new Kensington Council was empowered to rebuild and renovate, and by 1906 120 tenements had been built in what was by then known as the Notting Dale Special Area, establishing a pattern that was to continue for three quarters of a century. The most humane and appealing recent development, between KENLEY WALK and WILSHAM STREET, is not by the council but by the Octavia Hill and Rowe Housing Trust (successor to the Improved Tenements). It is of 1973–9 by *H. M. Grellier & Son*, a successfully varied mix both of materials (stock brick, tilehanging, rendering) and of housing types, ranging from bedsitters to terraces of family houses (a total of 181 units) arranged in two- to four-storey groups around a tight network of footpaths and small roads. The buildings are unassumingly detailed, but given a sense of identity by decorative blue roundels and by the distinctive stair-towers and rounded brick turrets which provide access to the upper flats. Despite the dense layout there are plenty of small private spaces, and none of the wastelands or graffiti so familiar in large council estates. At the N end of St Ann's Road, Nos. 106–124, for the same Trust, a pleasant terrace completed in 1988.

In SIRDAR ROAD, in complete contrast, HENRY DICKENS COURT, planned by the borough of Kensington in 1939 and built from 1945. Here the former street plan centred on Becher Street was totally obliterated and the small terraces were replaced by grim towers and sterile three-storey ranges. Further N in 1871–84 the landowner James Whitchurch set out to improve the area by laying out STONELEIGH STREET and TREADGOLD STREET around school and church (St Clement, q.v.) with respectable three-storey stock-brick terraces discreetly decorated with bands of moulded bricks. The area W from here is in Hammersmith (q.v., Perambulation 6).

To the N again the street pattern dissolves into a dismally amorphous mixed housing development dominated by an array of unlovable tower blocks. The LANCASTER ROAD WEST ESTATE was planned for the borough council by *Clifford Wearden* in 1964–5, the tower and three-finger block representing Phase 1 of a scheme that was to include a commercial centre and other ambitious housing developments. This plan was given up in favour of more humane domestic developments built in the 1980s; they include CAMBORNE MEWS, off St Mark's Road, a tactful borough housing redevelopment of 1980 by *Robert Martin & Partners*; traditional detail (windows below arched panels, small square metal balconies) with proportions echoing the nearby Victorian terraces. Also from this phase are the borough's KINGSDOWN CLOSE, sheltered housing for old people in pale brick, angled round a garden (with garden rock stones brought from the Marlborough Downs), and WESLEY SQUARE, off Lancaster Road, next to the Methodist church (q.v.), with pleasantly reticent red brick terraces around a communal lawn. For Lancaster Road further E *see* Perambulation 2a,ii. Further W the *G.L.C.*'s SILCHESTER ESTATE, which includes the large WAYNEFLETE SQUARE, the landscaping an improvement of 1987 on 1970s hard surfacing; here also the monotony of the three original four-storey terraces with grey brick bands is broken by the later N side, built on the site of unused garages, with a perky row of two-storey houses in coloured brick, 1985–8 by *Miller McCoy* for the Addison Housing Association. At the NE corner taller flats by *Barratts* with the blocky shape and pitched roofs of later 1980s post modernism.

S from here there is much piecemeal rebuilding of the earlier C20. In WALMER ROAD, NOTTINGWOOD HOUSE is a major Kensington council effort on a brewery site of 1935–9. Five storeys of flats are arranged around a court, their red brick given some character by brick quoins, decorative grilles, curved balconies, and curved arches to the open stair-towers. AVONDALE PARK opposite, created in 1892, was a pioneering amenity for the area. In the streets to the E many small early improvements. AVONDALE PARK ROAD and THRESHERS PLACE (cottage flats with pantiled roofs) were planned in 1918 by *W. H. Raffles* for E. J. Schuster (council-owned by 1935). At No. 4 HESKETH PLACE and in RUNCORN PLACE opposite is some of the first council rebuilding of 1906: one-room tenements in two blocks linked by an inner courtyard, of stock brick with careful red brick dressings. Also by the council, AVONDALE PARK GARDENS, 1919–22, small-scale terraces on a former workhouse site. The MISSION HALL of 1881–6 in MARY PLACE is a somewhat insignificant remnant of the energy pumped into this area by the church.

Further S, a picturesque reminder of the area's past is the TILE KILN rebuilt in 1879 by Charles Adams, now incorporated in the 1970s private housing of HIPPODROME MEWS, by *Michael Brown Associates*, bordering on the Ladbroke estate.

2a,ii. *Northern Kensington: the Ladbroke estate and Notting Hill*

The Ladbroke estate is a coherent layout of crescents and large communal gardens whose main features were first suggested in a plan by *Thomas Allason* of 1823. Building did not take place until the 1840s. It was preceded by the curious episode of the Hippodrome racecourse, which covered an area of *c.* 125 acres between Holland Park Avenue and the present Westway, the crest of Notting Hill providing an ideal vantage point. Opened in 1837, the course was immediately beset with difficulties; its transgression over the public footpath N to Notting Barn Farm resulted in protest marches by local tenants, and it was closed in 1841.

Starting from the w end of the estate, CLARENDON CROSS, one
of the few narrow roads linking Ladbroke land to the w, was
built to provide shops and services. No. 102 is decorated with oil
jars in stucco; Clarendon Works Builders and Contractors, of
some time between 1871 and 1892, and progressively up-to-date
with its terracotta dressings, supplied fittings for redecorations.
Many of the spacious houses in the sw corner of the estate, with
full-height bows and pilaster strips, were designed by *Allason*
and built by *W. Drew* in 1841–5: in CLARENDON ROAD Nos.
12–14 and 23–29; in LADBROKE ROAD Nos. 109–119, Nos. 66–
68, and Nos. 80–86 (with prominently bowed rear façades to
impress the neighbours in Clarendon Road). Still grander are
Nos. 43–45 Clarendon Road by *William Reynolds* (cf. below),
with Corinthian pilasters and pediment. The towering
LANSDOWNE HOUSE, 1904 by *William Flockhart*, is an addition
incongruous both in scale and style; of brick with stone dressings,
with vast, rather institutional-looking studio windows and crowstepped gable. In LANSDOWNE MEWS, GREEN'S COURT by
APT, 1989, preserves a mews character with ground-floor
garages, but the tall, rather stark gables above display disruptive
expanses of glass.

The most interesting later C20 contribution to this area in No. 19
LANSDOWNE WALK, enlarged and transformed in 1978–83 by
and for *Charles Jencks*, working with the *Terry Farrell Partnership*.* The street side is tactfully handled, the lower side extension with a curved roof echoing the fenestration and balcony
patterns of the main house; post-modern features here are confined to details such as the dormers cutting into the cornice, with
the favourite Jencks motif of the curve with staggered base.
These forms are given much fuller rein on the busier garden
front, where the two projecting double-height bays and the two
dormers crowning vertical white rendered strips are intended
to represent the members of the family. The interior, entirely
replanned, is imbued with weightier symbolism, the intense
atmosphere curiously reminiscent of the wilder excesses of
Burges, although the stylistic resonances here are not Gothic but
an eclectic mixture including classical and Egyptian. The main
rooms, representing the seasons, are arranged around the spiral
'sun' staircase, the cosmic theme underlined by such features as
aluminium globes along the rails and, at the base, a Black Hole
mosaic by *Eduardo Paolozzi*. The moon is portrayed on a mirrored semicircular light-well. The iconography was not the start-
ing-point, but emerged during the course of the design. The
winter and spring rooms have bold but restrained fireplaces by
Michael Graves. Opening on to the garden, a jacuzzi with *trompe
l'œil* coffering, a playful contribution by *Piers Gough*; other fittings and furnishings are largely from designs by *Jencks*. The
quantity of detail tends to overwhelm the clarity of the plan,
with its separate but linked rooms around the central stair, with
ingenious vistas cut through both vertically and diagonally.

No. 1 Lansdowne Walk, at the corner of Ladbroke Grove, is an
earlier case of remodelling, by *Aston Webb*, who lived here from

*For discussion of their respective responsibilities see *Architectural Design*, 9/10
(1985).

1890 to 1930; his additions of *c.* 1900 to E and S created a picturesque composition of steep roofs and banded chimneys (not at all in the spirit of his classical public buildings). Interiors with detail of high quality: outer hall with inlaid panelling, inner hall, and staircase with fine plaster ceilings.

The principal architect of Lansdowne Walk, Lansdowne Road, and Lansdowne Crescent was *William Reynolds*, whose work is typified by paired houses, stucco facing, and ornament in a coarse Italianate manner. Nos. 14–32 LANSDOWNE ROAD, with ornate pilasters or heavy quoins, and Nos. 13–16 LANSDOWNE CRESCENT, simply dressed, with squat Lombard towers, exhibit the rich variety of Reynolds's work. The refined stucco terrace at Nos. 19–38 Lansdowne Crescent is by *Henry Wyat*, 1860–2, the centre houses bow-fronted as in Tyburnia (*see* Paddington, Wm (outer), Perambulation 1a). Cleverly sandwiched between two end-terraces is No. 29½ (sic) by *Jeremy Lever* for himself, 1973: proportions and the pale stucco façade help this otherwise pure and stark modernist house to blend amicably with its fancier neighbours. The outer concentric crescents to the N date mostly from the 1860s: ELGIN CRESCENT 1852–62; BLENHEIM CRESCENT 1863–4; CORNWALL CRESCENT 1865.

The central crescents are separated by generous communal gardens (cf. e.g. Princes Square, Paddington) whose ends provide pleasantly leafy interludes to LADBROKE GROVE. This is the spine of the estate, a wide boulevard dominated at the crest of the hill by the spire of St John and the stone Tudor vicarage (No. 63) of 1844. There has been much rebuilding here, and what is left suffers from heavy traffic. The grandest survivals are on the E side: Nos. 36–40 by *Thomas Allom*, and the lofty Nos. 60–68 at the corner of LADBROKE GARDENS. On the W side, the pattern was broken in 1938 by No. 65 by *Maxwell Fry*, a block of flats of an excellent, invigorating rhythm; yellow brick and a greyish-blue paint. Solid on the l., then the main part with loggias, running against the glazed staircase which projects at right angles. From the staircase wing again a porch projects, and here the staircase wall is completely sheer, and does not have any windows.

E of Ladbroke Grove is a spectacular pocket of development, the Stanley Gardens area, where most of the houses were designed in 1852–3 by *Thomas Allom*. The development is denser than in the crescents, with palatial five-storey terraces whose boldly handled bows and towers exploit the picturesque potential of street corners and vistas (e.g. No. 24 KENSINGTON PARK GARDENS, Nos. 10–11 STANLEY CRESCENT. Nos. 1–3 LADBROKE GARDENS). Allom took particular care with interiors and rear façades as well: ornate fireplaces of marble, complex stair balusters, and lavish plaster cornices are features of many houses, and the S terrace of STANLEY GARDENS has particularly splendid garden fronts with balustraded bows, pediments, and Corinthian pilasters. On the S side of Kensington Park Gardens, No. 5 is an interloper of the later C19, very tall, with much terracotta and a corner turret.

To the S, LADBROKE SQUARE of 1843–5 has less ambitious terraces, likewise the neighbouring LADBROKE ROAD. In KEN-

SINGTON PARK ROAD (planned in 1844), Nos. 32–38 were built in 1848; most other terraces are of 1850–60. On the E side, KELVIN COURT, MATLOCK COURT, and BUCKINGHAM COURT (1938) present a distinctively classical balance between stone-faced ground and first floors and red brick above, crowned by a stone parapet, although all have the mildly undulating profiles of residential art deco. The slightly earlier PRINCES COURT (1936) is more angular and more classical.

The area further E around CHEPSTOW VILLAS and PEMBRIDGE VILLAS comprised Ladbroke family and other holdings. It was developed homogeneously with grand detached and paired villas in stucco with Italianate details, ranging from the sedate and dignified DAWSON PLACE (1849–57) to the lavish, albeit standard, *Francis Radford* houses (cf. Holland Park, Perambulation 1a,iii) of PEMBRIDGE SQUARE (1857–64), with their elaborately profiled dormers. Most of the subsequent buildings are of little interest, apart from THORNBURY COURT in CHEPSTOW VILLAS, a hefty red brick block, formerly Our Lady of Sion Convent, 1892–3 by *A. Young*, now converted to flats.

2b. Northern Kensington: from Portobello Road to the E, S of Westway; then N of Westway (see plans on pp. 522, 530)

This is one of the most illuminating areas in London for the study of different types of C20 urban renewal. The farmland immediately N of the Ladbroke estate was built up only gradually from the 1860s, and the district has never been fashionable. Close to the canal on the N boundary the gas works and Kensal Green cemetery were laid out; a workhouse followed to their S. Further E Kensal Town developed as a working-class settlement, expanding from a nucleus of small industries and early Victorian cottages and terraces isolated between the Grand Union Canal and the Great Western Railway line of 1838.

By the 1930s the need to improve housing conditions had prompted the borough to give thought to clearance of particularly bad pockets, to supplement the work already begun by private housing trusts (*see* also Perambulation 2a,i). At Kensal Green, the Gas Light and Coke Company showed the way with *Maxwell Fry*'s progressive Kensal House of 1936. Further activity was interrupted by the war. By 1945 many of the C19 terraces were in multiple occupation, lacking basic amenities, and subject to the evils of poor landlords. Responsibility for the area was divided between the borough and the L.C.C., with the borough giving increasingly greater encouragement to the housing associations, especially the Kensington Housing Trust. Rebuilding began in the 1950s, on the now unacceptably grandiose scale of post-war public housing, notably in the area around Silchester Road (*see* Perambulation 2a,i), around Treverton Street W of Ladbroke Grove, and in Kensal Town. This stage culminated in the *Goldfinger* tower on the Trellick estate, of 1966–72. By that time both public opinion and government policy favoured rehabilitation rather than rebuilding, and new housing, where necessary, that was designed on a more human and homely scale, with emphasis on visual appeal, garden space, and landscaping. So the tall, cramped, multi-occupied terraces around All Saints' church – which in the 1960s constituted some of the worst rented accommodation in London – were converted and rehabilitated, as were the more pleasing Victorian stucco terraces further N in Golborne Road, St Lawrence Terrace, and Ladbroke Grove. Among the older buildings small parks and unassuming low-rise housing were fitted in.

A complication to this overall programme was the arrival in the 1960s of the massive elevated section of Westway alongside the Metropolitan railway line, a visual and aural intrusion imposed with apparently ruthless disregard to its effect on the neighbourhood (albeit preferable to the L.C.C.'s proposal in the 1950s for a surface-level highway running in front of All Saints' church). In the 1970s came efforts to mitigate the worst effects, with 'barrier' housing alongside, and imaginative use of the dead space beneath the road. By the 1980s the programme of housing renewal was complete, and attention began to shift to the growing number of sites close to canal and railway offering scope for redevelopment as a result of the decline of older industries.

2b,i. Northern Kensington: from Portobello Road to the E, S of Westway

PORTOBELLO ROAD, originally a lane leading to Portobello Farm, was built up from *c.* 1864–72 with densely packed terraces. The most interesting individual building is No. 191, the ELECTRIC CINEMA, one of the oldest surviving purpose-built cinemas in Britain, designed by *G. S. Valentin* in 1910–11 and reopened in 1990 after refurbishment (by *Faithful Blyth*, interiors by *Simon Wedgwood*). Classically detailed façade with fluted pilasters, in faience, the asymmetrical roof-line reflecting the barrel-roofed auditorium and domed vestibule. Well preserved interior features: screen around the entrance kiosk; decorative plasterwork in the hall. PORTOBELLO MARKET started up along this route *c.* 1870 – a colourful institution that still dominates the part of the road S of Westway and was largely responsible for the social decline of the district (houses in the Colville Gardens area to the E were subdivided already by 1881).

E of Portobello Road development began in 1852 with Dr Samuel Walker's All Saints Talbot Road (q.v.), but his failing financial circumstances meant that the accompanying housing could not be begun until 1860: the tall, narrow-fronted houses in COLVILLE TERRACE, COLVILLE SQUARE, COLVILLE GARDENS, and POWIS SQUARE are all by *T. S. Tippett*, who worked with G. Wyatt at Princes and Leinster Squares (*see* Paddington (outer Wm), Perambulation 1c). The North Kensington houses range from four to six storeys, fully stuccoed, often with heavy bays and deep porches; some are on a back-to-front plan, albeit with stingier gardens than their prototypes (cf. e.g. Ladbroke Gardens, Perambulation 2a,ii). Rehabilitation from the 1960s has transformed this once down-at-heel area into a quiet and demure neighbourhood. Among the relatively little new building is a four-storey range which replaced a back-to-front terrace in the centre of Powis Square, 1979 by the *Borough Architect's Department*, sparsely detailed, with arched windows to the top floor in deference to the nearby houses, but all in brick – a jarring note among the homogeneous stucco. N of All Saints the first new flats in the area for the Notting Hill Housing Trust, by *Quantic Associates, c.* 1978, alas with an even less appealing exterior; four storeys, the top floor slate-hung. Much more acceptable is TAVISTOCK CRESCENT further N, backing on to the Metropolitan line and Westway, rebuilt in 1977–81 by *H. T. Cadbury-Brown & John Metcalfe* for the borough. It provides a mix of housing types (one to six persons), ingeniously combined – proof that high-density homes need not be overcrowded housing. The elevations should be compared with the broadly similar terrace at the E end of Tavistock Crescent, just over the Westminster border, rebuilt by the *G.L.C.* The Kensington stretch provides a pleasanter streetscape, varied by alternately receding planes of brickwork, and with more generous sunken front gardens. The lighter balconies may be less functional but are certainly less overbearing than the G.L.C.'s jutting profiles.

W of Ladbroke Grove a flashier side of redevelopment is represented by the ROYALTY STUDIOS, No. 105 LANCASTER ROAD, on the site of the former Royalty cinema. Of 1984–6 by *CZWG*, they are an effectively flamboyant yet low-cost group of studios and light industry; a pair of broad frontages in buff brick with blue brick accents, each with a shallow gable broken by a stairtower. Dramatically varied fenestration: oculi and large triple windows with somewhat art-deco glazing patterns. Nos. 111–117, LONDON LIGHTHOUSE, converted to a hospice from an older school building in 1986–8 by *Sproson Barrable*, is more reticent, but uses a similar vocabulary. Curved three-storey red brick front with darker buff brick bands; angular windows behind. Bright blue tubular steel fencing enlivens the forecourt. Imaginative interiors.

2b,ii. Northern Kensington: N *of Westway*

PORTOBELLO GREEN is the name given to a small landscaped area created in the 1970s off Portobello Road immediately N of Westway, and to the ingenious mixed-use development built into the space beneath the road. All by *Franklin Stafford Partnership* with *Buro Happold* engineers, 1979–81, for the North Kensington Amenity Trust (established by the borough in 1970–1 to put the land left over from Westway to community use). A triumphant demonstration that once their functions are clearly defined, such difficult sites need not be disaster areas. On the green a sturdily anchored open tent for a market (planned with a ten-year life). Cheerful, varied frontages beneath Westway, with snug, well-insulated shops and workshops off a central passage; further W, the overhanging roadway has been transformed into a covered arcade, its monumentality counterpointed by the friendly scale and colourful detail of the offices and workshops behind. The bleaker approach of the 1960s is demonstrated by the neat but drab concrete AMBULANCE STATION tucked beneath Westway at the corner of Ladbroke Grove (by the *G.L.C.*, 1968), but further W there is an ingenious addition: the MAXILLA NURSERY CENTRE, with community centre and laundry, 1974–8.

LADBROKE GROVE N of Westway has busy stuccoed terraces, but the streets off – CAMBRIDGE GARDENS, OXFORD GARDENS, and BASSETT ROAD – are more spacious and leafy, still with good sequences of the large detached or paired houses developed by the St Quintin estate in the 1860s–70s for commuters using the Metropolitan line extension opened in 1864. To the W, ST MARK'S ROAD cuts diagonally through this grid of streets towards the site of Notting Barn Farms, the only buildings in this area until the later C19. They stood at the junction with St Quintin Avenue. Today's landmarks are St Helen's church (q.v.) and the terraces at the corner and along St Mark's Road, two striking groups by *Jeremy Dixon* for the Kensington Housing Trust, 1976–80. They mark an influential turning-point in attractive adaptation of the spirit of Victorian suburban housing without recourse to pastiche. The architect's interest in geometrical forms (cf. his early scheme for a pyramidal County Hall for Northamptonshire) is revealed by the details, welded together here in a manner that is satisfyingly humane; a lively roof-line of brick gables edged in white, colourful details provided by a pattern of square wooden-framed panels in the two-storey porch projections, carefully thought out entrances defined by distinctive pyramid-topped gatepiers (a feature rapidly imitated all

113

over London). The s group has a four-storey block of flats, the longer N range houses above basement flats, their narrow fronts disguised by shared gables in a tradition borrowed from earlier C 19 London terraces. Even the backs are unusual, with skewed angles to avoid overlooking.

Much of this area, owned in the C 19 by the St Quintin estate, was built up only in the early C 20 with pleasant two-storey housing quite untypical of Kensington. Amidst it, in WALLINGFORD AVENUE, EVELYN FOX COURT, 1984–5 by *Green Lloyd & Adams*, also for the Kensington Housing Trust, two-storeyed sheltered housing round a cloistered court. Pantiled roofs and white walls, the taller block with communal facilities decorated by a painted tympanum. More sheltered housing for the elderly on the E side of ST MARK'S ROAD, 1987–90 by *Phippen, Randall & Parkes* for Servite Housing. At the N end of St Mark's Road, 202 houses in modest cottage groups built for the borough in 1919–26 by *A. S. Soutar*. Further E, the Y-shaped towers of the TREVERTON STREET flats of the 1950s form more obtrusive landmarks E of the hospital.

Along BARLBY ROAD the two main accents are the PALL MALL DEPOSIT, warehouses of 1911 by *W. G. Hunt*, of reinforced concrete, boldly advertised by large lettering in blue and white mosaic, and the former CLEMENT TALBOT WORKS, the first purpose-built English car factory, 1903–11 by *William T. Walker*. This is also of reinforced concrete (Hennebique system), with the office block disguised by a festive Wrenaissance front; utilitarian one-storey works behind (future uncertain). (Handsome entrance hall with relief decoration.) Other older industries and utilities that grew up beside canal and railway began to give way in the 1980s to a mixture of offices, workshops, and housing, most prominent among them at the time of writing the large SAINSBURYS supermarket of 1989 by the canal. It was the Gas Light and Coke Company that built KENSAL HOUSE, squeezed on to the edge of their site facing Ladbroke Grove, a progressive-minded housing development of 1936–7 (executive architect *Maxwell Fry*, with a committee of *Robert Atkinson, C. H. James, G. Grey Wornum*, and *Elizabeth Denby*). It consists of two tall linked slab blocks of reinforced concrete (sadly shabby at the time of writing), on a curve, with bedrooms mostly on the E side, living rooms on the w. Rendered walls, punctuated on the w by a pattern of impractically tiny pierced drying balconies. The flats were planned to demonstrate the mass provision of fuel and were notable for their up-to-date gas cooking and heating equipment. To the w, the low steel-framed NURSERY SCHOOL built in part of the curve of a demolished gasholder makes an effective contrast.

KENSAL ROAD follows the line of the canal to the E of Ladbroke Grove. On its N side is PORTOBELLO DOCK, built in 1890–1 as a refuse transfer station by Kensington Vestry, a picturesque group evocative of the era of horse-drawn dustcarts. The carts ascended a curved blue brick ramp to a deck above the canal dock to shoot their contents either into barges below or into the low building with arched openings between dock and canal. To the w, offices for VIRGIN, 1988–9 by *Christopher Watts Associates*.

115   Further w the MᴄKᴀʏ Tʀᴀᴅɪɴɢ Eѕᴛᴀᴛᴇ, a smart series of colourful buildings alongside the canal, 1981 by *John Outram* – an eyecatching group that foreshadows his more flamboyant later work. The repeating rhythm of shallow white gables over recessed loading bays with curved brick piers provides a welcome sense of order in this cluttered and incoherent area. Further ᴇ in Kensal Road are the offices of *Arendt Bednarski Roche*, an ingenious conversion of a 1920s warehouse.

The development known in the ᴄ19 as Kᴇɴѕᴀʟ Nᴇᴡ Tᴏᴡɴ began in the 1840s with small cottages in Eᴀѕᴛ Rᴏᴡ, Mɪᴅᴅʟᴇ Rᴏᴡ, and Sᴏᴜᴛʜᴇʀɴ Rᴏᴡ. The street pattern remains, but almost all traces of the modest early buildings have disappeared. The area s of Bᴏѕᴡᴏʀᴛʜ Rᴏᴀᴅ, crammed from the 1860s with small overcrowded houses, has changed even more radically. An early improvement was the Rᴇᴄʀᴇᴀᴛɪᴏɴ Gʀᴏᴜɴᴅ (the Emslie Horniman Pleasance) between East Row and Bosworth Road, presented by Emslie J. Horniman in 1911, with – a great surprise – buildings and garden layout designed by *C. F. A. Voysey*. The rectangular garden is laid out around a formal pool. It is surrounded by roughcast walls, white above a black plinth, pierced by circular openings with iron grilles. At either end are arched shelters, and above the entrance is a well-lettered inscription. The ironwork is by *W. B. Reynolds*.

Slum clearance in this area began in the 1930s and continued on a grander scale after the war, the borough taking responsibility for the area between Bosworth Road and Golborne Road, the county council for the remainder. In the former area the old street pattern is broken up not very happily, following a plan of 1956 by *Sir William Holford & Partners* for the borough of Kensington. The two unattractive fourteen-storey towers are by the same firm, 1959–62. HᴏʟᴍᴇFɪᴇʟᴅ Hᴏᴜѕᴇ, a more satisfactory design, with a long curving frontage along Hᴀᴢʟᴇᴡᴏᴏᴅ Cʀᴇѕ-ᴄᴇɴᴛ and flats around courtyards behind, is by *Julian Keable & Partners*, 1964. Its exterior facelift dates from 1985. The Pʀɪɴᴄᴇ Aʀᴛʜᴜʀ, a token preservation of the ᴄ19, stands in isolation opposite. Much more powerful than all this, however, is the impact of the Cʜᴇʟᴛᴇɴʜᴀᴍ Eѕᴛᴀᴛᴇ to the s (between Golborne Road, Westway, and the canal), commissioned from *Ernö Goldfinger & Partners* by the G.L.C. in 1966, with the unfor-

1   gettable thirty-storey Tʀᴇʟʟɪᴄᴋ Tᴏᴡᴇʀ, completed in 1972. It is one of the last of those rigorously organized mixed housing developments promoted so optimistically by the L. C. C. from the 1950s onwards. The tower contains 217 flats, their arrangement based on Goldfinger's earlier Balfron Tower in Poplar (TH) – that is, with a separate lift and stair-tower with bridges to the main block only at every third storey. The resulting silhouette is highly dramatic, not least when lit up at night. At street level too the group of tower and lower blocks, with their impeccably detailed bush-hammered concrete surfaces, exude a sophisticated urbanity rare in England. But by the 1970s public housing on such a monumental scale was already a dinosaur from another age; however handsome and generously planned (the entrance halls are marble-lined, the balconies are large), family flats in towers were no longer acceptable.

In GOLBORNE ROAD W of the railway are modest stuccoed terraces of small shops, deliberately preserved as an anchor between the reconstructed areas to N and S. To the N, off Wornington Road, the major development is the MURCHISON ESTATE, stretching to Ladbroke Grove, an exceptionally ambitious and forbiddingly large scheme by *Chapman Taylor Partners*, 1974–9, for the Kensington Housing Trust, undertaken at a time of unprecedentedly generous government funding for such enterprises. There are over 500 flats and houses, the flats in five- to six-storey blocks arranged quite pleasantly around leafy pedestrian routes. To the S, immediately N of Westway, is the SWINBROOK area, a forcible demonstration of the strength of popular reaction against high-rise council housing. Care was taken to cause minimum disruption by phasing the rebuilding over ten years – from 1974 to 1984 – and the details and amenities were designed in consultation with local residents. The first building was the *G.L.C.*'s barrier block of 1971, with stepped-out balconies, turning its back on the high-level Westway flyover. It replaced the pathetic terrace in ACKLAM ROAD, left standing with its bedroom windows only 6 metres from the flyover – a haunting indictment of the callous road-building policies of the 1960s. The rebuilding to the N was carried out by Kensington, after the transfer of housing responsibilities from the G.L.C. At the S end is a small park sheltered by the barrier block, and then an unexceptional series of mundane brick pitched-roof terraces by the *Borough of Kensington and Chelsea* (note in the later parts the influence of Dixon's St Mark's Road terrace).

3a. Southern Kensington: the residential development of the museums area

This area, between Cromwell Road and Kensington Gardens, is the heart of High Victorian Kensington, with sumptuous stuccoed terraces on a metropolitan scale lining the grid of streets laid out in the 1850s around the new academic centre. Exhibition Road and Queen's Gate are the two main axes; broad boulevards in the Parisian manner running N from Cromwell Road to the line of Kensington Gore and Kensington Road, where some development facing Kensington Gardens had begun a little earlier. Equally interesting is the challenge – one of the first in London – to the stately regularity of the Italianate terrace by innovative architects of the 1870s onwards. The lively variety of tall red brick houses by Norman Shaw and his followers can be studied especially well in Queen's Gate and Palace Gate. The shift from the individual houses to blocks of flats began around the same time, and gathered momentum by the turn of the century. It is most evident in the extensive C20 rebuilding along Kensington Road, but has produced little outstanding architecture.

The tour is roughly circular: first Cromwell Road, Queen's Gate and streets to the W; then Kensington Gore and Kensington Road and streets off; and finally Exhibition Road and streets to the E.

SOUTHERN KENSINGTON
EAST OF GLOUCESTER RD
(Perambulation 3a–d)

W E S T M I N S T E R

The Serpentine

Kensington
Gardens

Hyde Park

Ⓐ

KENSINGTON RD.   KENSINGTON GORE   KENSINGTON   ROAD   KNIGHTSBRIDGE

PALACE GATE

QUEEN'S

HYDE PARK GATE
SOM PW
KENSINGTON GATE

Ⓑ ALBERT HALL PRINCE'S GATE
ALBERT
MANS
PRINCE'S GATE
COURT

Ⓖ

RUTLAND
GATE

TREVOR
SQUARE

KNIGHTSBRIDGE
TREVOR
SQUARE
MONTPELI
PL
SLOANE
BASIL ST
HANS
CRES.
STREET

①   PRINCE CONSORT ROAD   PRINCE'S
ENNIS
MORE GS   ⑦ MONTPELIER
PL.

EXHIBITION

GLOUCESTER

GATE

QUEEN'S GATE TERR.

Ⓒ

IMPERIAL INSTITUTE RD

GDNS PRINCE'S
⑨ GATE
MEWS
RUTLAND ST
FAIRHOLT ST

②

HANS ROAD

ROAD

BEAUCHAMP PL

PONT ST

Ⓔ   Ⓕ

ROAD   Ⓓ

⑤
+

CROMWELL   ROAD

QUEEN'S

QUEENSBERRY

ⓖ

⑧

THURLOE
PL

SOUTH
THURLOE
SQ

NTH T
ALEX PL
THURLOE
SOUTH ST

BROMPTON

EGERTON GDNS
WALTON ST
WALTON PL

OVINGTON
FIRST
FORMER ROW

BEAUCHAMP PL

PONT ST

A 4
GLOUCESTER
ROAD

HARRINGTON RD

SOUTH KENSINGTON
PELHAM ST

SLOANE AVE

N

STANHOPE GDNS
CLAREVILLE ST
CLAREVILLE
GROVE

③

ONSLOW SQ

SYDNEY ST

PELHAM CR

CHELSEA

OLD

BROMPTON

CLARE
SUMNER PL
ONSLOW
SQUARE

ONSLOW
GARDENS

④

ROLAND

CRANLEY

ROAD

SYDNEY ST

ROLAND GDNS
EVELYN GDNS
⑩
E M T

NEVILLE TERR.
SELWOOD TERR.

EVELYN GDNS   OLD CHURCH ST

LECKY ST

FULHAM

0 ········ ¼ mile
0 ········ ¼ ········ ½ km

CHURCHES etc.
① Holy Trinity
② Holy Trinity Brompton
③ St Augustine
④ St Paul
⑤ Oratory of St Philip Neri (R.C.)
⑥ Assumption and All Saints (Russian Orthodox)
⑦ Deutsche Evangelische Christuskirche
⑧ Ismaili Centre
⑨ Mormon Church
⑩ St Peter (Armenian)

PUBLIC BUILDINGS, etc.
Ⓐ Albert Memorial
Ⓑ Albert Hall
Ⓒ Imperial College
Ⓓ Natural History Museum
Ⓔ Science Museum
Ⓕ Victoria and Albert Museum
Ⓖ Institut Français and
    Lycée Français

The story of CROMWELL ROAD begins in 1857 with the activity of the developer *Sir Charles Freake*. The road itself was laid out by the 1851 Commissioners in 1855, very much in the spirit of the Parisian boulevards of Napoleon III (*see* Public Buildings 2). Opposite the Natural History Museum are Nos. 13–19, built by Freake in 1857–9, followed in 1858–60 by Nos. 21–29, very large double-fronted houses by an unknown architect, with deep Doric porches and balustraded first-floor balconies. Alternating segmental and triangular pediments to the first-floor windows, bold quoins, and a crowning floral frieze. No. 21 was Freake's own house. Then the Lycée Français (Public Buildings 1), an uncompromisingly horizontal interlude, and less distinguished houses of *c.* 1870.

QUEEN'S GATE leads N alongside the academic centres, developed from 1855 to 1870 with expensive town houses with opulent façades. First, a later intruder: BADEN POWELL HOUSE by *Ralph Tubbs*, 1959–61, a first-rate composition with a long, horizontally emphasized front to Cromwell Road and a contrasting entrance block joining it at the corner. Airy, double-height foyer with two columns continuing through an upper loggia to support the three upper floors. The hall behind is reached across an open courtyard. To the N are the lavish terraces built as part of the 1851 Commissioners' vision of South Kensington. The best façades include first Nos. 47–52 by *C.J. Richardson*, 1859–63, with French influence evident in their intricate iron balconies, two-storey porches, and consoles with copious foliage. Nos. 22–24 by *Thomas Cundy III*, 1858–60, are more luxuriant than his usual work, with extraordinarily large brackets to first-floor balconies and prominent aedicules to the central window of the second floor. Nos. 1–19 are again by *Richardson*, the first houses to go up in the street (1855), uniquely adorned with foliate pilasters between each house, and with tripartite windows set between Corinthian columns or pilasters. Finally the mansion at No. 1A with its 30 metre tower, built in 1857–60 by *John Tarring* along with Nos. 1–4 Hyde Park Gate.

Now the E side of Queen's Gate. No. 200 and the corner house, No. 25 Kensington Gore, are by *S.W. Daukes*, 1873. Then Nos. 190–196, in striking contrast to the expositions of grand Italianate directly opposite. No. 196 is by *Norman Shaw* for J.P. Heseltine, 1874, all rubbed bricks with Dutch superimposed pilasters, Shaw's typical Ipswich window motif, and charming early Renaissance decoration. The ground-floor windows are recessed beneath slightly Gothic arches. Shaw's design has unfortunately been tampered with at this level. Thus inspired, Baroque refacing was carried out at Nos. 194 (in buff terracotta by *R.A. Briggs*, 1893), 192, and 190–191 (*F.G. Knight*, 1891–2); original façades of *c.* 1877 by *R.A. Lewcock* at Nos. 193 and 195. Then, after some undisturbed stucco and the C20 buildings of Imperial College (*see* Public Buildings 2), quite suddenly Nos. 170 and 167. No. 170 is by *Shaw*, advised by the client *F.A. White*, 1888–9 – a regular s-facing seven-bay front of brick with stone quoins and doorcases, its conspicuous early C18 historicism requested by White, though features here had been anticipated by Shaw in a house in Ennismore Gardens. Well preserved interiors. No. 167, with its eclectic façade combining a Flemish gable, a double-height Ionic loggia, and a stone mullioned bay-window, is by *Mervyn Macartney*, 1888–9. (Well preserved interior with much panelling and plasterwork; neo-Jacobean staircase; first-floor reception room with marble columns and fireplaces. Good fireplaces also on the upper floors.)

Queen's Gate gives the key to dating the streets to its w, all full of enthusiasm for the lush and grand Italianate house. QUEEN'S GATE TERRACE is the best, the s side, by *William Harris*, 1856–8, characterized by a very rich main frieze and cornice and equally rich patterned railings, the N side mostly by the otherwise unknown *James Matthews*, 1859–60, sporting pedimented dormers and bracketed second-floor balconies. Intruding here at the end are Nos. 56–58 by *Charles Gray*, 1863, Moresque and Venetian Gothic in coloured brick and stone, jauntily competing with the neighbours. Equally jubilant is ST GEORGE'S COURT opposite at Nos. 42–72 GLOUCESTER ROAD, 1907–9 by *Paul Hoffmann*. To the N of this, Nos. 2–34 survive from Inderwick's more modest New Town development (*see* Perambulation 1b,i). They are of 1838–9, and form an oddly low-key termination to the view down Queen's Gate Terrace.

At the junction of Gloucester Road and Palace Gate is KEN-SINGTON GATE, 1850–2 by *Alfred Cubitt Bean* and remarkably homogeneous, with Ionic porches, Italianate façades, and balustrades going Jacobean; No. 1 is detached, with a prominent round tower capped by a small dome. Then into PALACE GATE from the s. No. 10 is the harbinger of the Modern Movement in this area: flats by *Wells Coates*, 1938, of reinforced concrete with artificial stone cladding. An excellent composition; the architect's distinctive 'three-two' system, where three storeys of one section equal two of another, is expressed in the façade fenestration. Glazed stairwells unite the blocks vertically at each angle. The w annexe is more conventionally planned. The pedestrian block opposite at Nos. 33–37, 1989 by *Blampied & Partners*, does not compare favourably. No. 8 is by *J.J. Stevenson*, 1873–4, for H.F. Makins, an artistically minded barrister: a luscious Queen Anne villa – his second in London, with an elevation closely reliant on his 1871 predecessor, the now demolished Red House, Bayswater. No. 2 of the same date is by *P.C. Hardwick* for Sir John Everett Millais, its solid Italianate dressings strikingly conservative against the red brick façade. No. 1A, with its fine Portland stone façade, was reconstructed in 1896–8 by the Arts and Crafts architect *C.J. Harold Cooper*. The front is unmistakably of its era, its tall gable and sheer grey facing relieved by an orderly pattern of verticals and horizontals dictated by the mullioned-and-transomed windows. (Fine interiors by members of the Art Workers Guild.) THORNEY COURT opposite is an overweening mass of red brick flats of the 1980s extending along Kensington Gate, with some salvaged plasterwork displayed in the garage entrance.

HYDE PARK GATE, due E of Palace Gate, a development of the 1830s, owes its complex layout to the late C18 pattern of land ownership; the numbering system allocates to it buildings fronting on to Kensington Road. Very little remains of the original houses apart from STOKE LODGE (No. 45) and CLEEVE LODGE (No. 42; over-restored exterior), overlooking a circular garden. These – the first houses to go up in the layout devised *c.* 1835 for the Campden Charities – are set back from the main road down a short drive. They are of plain stucco with wide over-hanging eaves, their simplicity a hallmark of the mid 1830s. No. 40 is flats of *c.* 1902 by *R. J. Worley*, with terracotta facings supplied by *Doultons*. The large, bland BROADWALK HOUSE facing the park is by *Chapman Taylor Partners*, 1966–9. The long straight road running parallel to the E was largely developed by Joshua Flesher Hanson (cf. Campden Hill Square, Perambulation 1a,iii), beginning in 1835, when a short terrace facing Kensington Road was built. Only No. 36 – the central block – survives, with central pediment (smaller than the original), giant order Ionic columns, and a channelled stucco ground floor in the Nash tradition. The original composition probably resembled Hanson's Holland Park Avenue work, where two plain wings flank a central pedimented section (*see* Perambulation 1a,iii). In the close, Nos. 9–13 are still recognizable (No. 9 originally detached), built in 1846, again fully stuccoed; Nos. 10–11 are the best preserved, with giant Corinthian columns *in antis, œil de bœuf* attic windows, and a boldness reminiscent of Reynolds's work on the Ladbroke estate (Perambulation 2a,ii). Opposite, MONMOUTH HOUSE is part of the addition made in 1928 by *Sir Edwin Lutyens* to what is now No. 29, since subdivided and given a later semicircular porch. No. 30A is a blocky brick cubist composition extending into HYDE PARK GATE MEWS. No. 18 opposite was designed in 1871 by its owner, the painter *E. W. Cooke*, under the supervision of *Norman Shaw* (his first involve-ment in a London house). It is a crisp composition in stock brick with a large gable, Gothic doorway, and tiers of sash-windows in the manner of Philip Webb. The remaining houses to the S, Nos. 19–28, are of 1841–7, much altered. For Nos. 1–4 *see* Queen's Gate, above.

KENSINGTON GORE, which begins E of Queen's Gate, is domi-nated by the Royal College of Art and the Albert Hall (*see* Public Buildings 2). Clustered within this precinct are several red brick blocks of flats of the 1880s and 90s. QUEEN ALEXANDRA HOUSE, built in 1884 by *C. Purdon Clarke* for women college students, is in deep red brick, its tall chimneys cunningly dis-guised within the stepped gables. (Dining room with *Doulton* tile pictures of Music and Pottery.) Then, facing the park, ALBERT HALL MANSIONS, designed by *Norman Shaw* in 1879, the first block of flats in London in the new red brick style which at once had dozens of followers. It is a picturesque design with the two lowest storeys treated as a plinth, the two main storeys distinguished by twice-repeated double arches, a top storey, and then two rows of dormers and tall Dutch gables with Shaw's favourite playful little oriels. Yet its disregard of scale – it dwarfs even the Albert Hall – affords a memorable demonstration of the isolation in which Victorian architects saw their individual creations. Certainly it ruthlessly crushed the happy scale of *Shaw's* own LOWTHER LODGE next door (from 1913 the prem-ises of the Royal Geographical Society). This was planned in

1872 for William Lowther and built in 1873-5, on a larger site
than most Kensington town houses, its forms exhibiting the new
gaiety and liveliness for which Shaw stood: tall, slim Queen Anne
windows combined with Dutch pilasters and gables – and very
tall chimneys, a free and eminently picturesque group. The rendered coved eaves may reflect the influence of W. E. Nesfield. The
interplay between symmetry and asymmetry is worth observing
here and on the garden front. The interior has been little altered.
The projecting entrance hall leads into the inner hall, a noble
space spanned by a stone arch, and lit by five mullioned and
transomed windows. Fireplace with attractive blue and white
heraldic tiles made in 1875 by *Alice Lowther*; lofty beamed
ceiling. At one end broad stairs ascend in leisurely manner to a
generous well-lit landing, from which one can reach a little
mezzanine gallery overlooking the hall, a typical Shaw conceit.
Main rooms to the garden; the boudoir (tea room) and a larger
reception room (map room), both with big canted bays and
decorative plaster friezes, and the dining room (President's
Room). The bedrooms above are now reading room and library,
the latter extending into the w extensions of 1928-30 by *G. L.
Kennedy* and *F. B. Nightingale*. On the ground floor this has a
domed corridor, more Soanic than Shavian, and on the outside,
stiff sculptures of Livingstone (*T. B. Huxley-Jones*, 1953) and
Shackleton (*C. Sargeant Jagger*, 1932) against the blank walls of
the lecture hall. Due s is PRINCES GATE COURT by *T. P.
Bennett & Son*, 1927, conventional formal classical flats. Then
No. 29 EXHIBITION ROAD and No. 1 LOWTHER GARDENS,
1876 by *J. J. Stevenson*, a superb asymmetrical Queen Anne
composition adorned with delicate cut-brick panels, commissioned after the success of No. 8 Palace Gate (*see* above).
Further w in PRINCE CONSORT ROAD is ALBERT COURT,
very tall brick flats with corner tourelles and four-storey loggias.
It is by *R. J. Worley*, 1894-1900, the outcome of what Shaw had
introduced and equally unconcerned with the intended repre-
sentational character of the whole district.

The stretch of KENSINGTON ROAD between Exhibition Road
and Rutland Gate was developed a little earlier than the museums
area. The most extensive survival of the wealthy mid c19 residences facing the park is PRINCES GATE of 1846-53, dull Italianate, five-storeyed and very long, with an attic frieze as the
main embellishment. It is one of the most ambitious enterprises
by the builder-speculator John Elger, loosely based on drawings
provided by the young *Harvey Lonsdale Elmes*. An excursion
further e can take in the area around ENNISMORE GARDENS,
another Elger undertaking. The first phase (Nos. 39-65, e side)
was by *Elger*, possibly with *H. L. Elmes*, but the enterprise was
completed later with taller terraces, stone-faced rather than stuccoed on s, n, and w sides in 1868-71 (builders *P. & A. Thorn*).
These developments took place on the Listowel estate, centring
on the mid c18 KINGSTON HOUSE, whose site is now occupied
by 1930s flats of the same name by *Michael Rosenauer*. Most of
the other frontages to the park are also c20 rebuildings, of which
RUTLAND COURT by *Joseph* represents the still traditional
classical mode of 1920, Nos. 37-39 KNIGHTSBRIDGE by *Mit-*

chell & Bridgwater the style of the 1930s. Nos. 2–8 RUTLAND
GATE are survivals from 1838, possibly by *Sir Matthew Wyatt*,
restored and converted in 1989 by *YRM*. In Rutland Gate, Nos.
9–7 and 10–20 are also of 1838–9. No. 24, now the Italian cultural
centre, and much extended, was built in 1847–8 for the art
collector John Sheepshanks, with a gallery.

Back to EXHIBITION ROAD. For the W side *see* above. The N end
of the E side is a continuation (in both style and numbering) of
Prince's Gate facing the park (*see* above), tall stuccoed frontages
with Doric porches interrupted only by an ugly 1960s interlude
near the corner. For Prince's Gardens to the E *see* Imperial
College. Development further S was continued by Freake, who
laid out PRINCE'S GATE MEWS in 1859 and a terrace to its S
(now reduced to Nos. 69–72) after 1865. The rest of Exhibition
Road is all public buildings (q.v.).

3b. *Southern Kensington: Brompton Road, with streets to its N and S (see plan on p. 534)*

BROMPTON ROAD has been a busy commercial street since the
early C19, when it was the main route between London and the
prolific Brompton nurseries and market gardens. Road-widening
to accommodate increasing traffic began in 1862 and continued
for nearly a century, leaving only a handful of relics from the
first building enterprises of *c.* 1760 among an indifferent muddle
of Queen Anne terraces and taller post-war office blocks.

Beginning at the Knightsbridge end, the N side is dominated first by
PARK MANSIONS (1897–1900) and then by CALTEX HOUSE,
1955–7 by *Stone Toms & Partners*, twelve storeys of glass and
concrete, the upper part rising at an awkward angle from the
two-storey podium along the road. Prominent corner sculpture
by *F. Belsky* of seahorses, made of reinforced concrete covered
in metal. On the S side, an attractive variety of speculative terraces
in Dutch and Flemish styles (Nos. 37–61, *c.* 1900).

Then HARRODS, a majestic and flamboyant parade of the enduring
prosperity that evolved in the later C19 from C.D. Harrod's
grocery shop. Redevelopment began in 1894 under the architect
C.W. Stephens. The main façade (1902–3), encased in pink
Doulton terracotta, rises five storeys above the shop-windows of
the ground floor. The first-floor windows, broader than those
above, have pretty art nouveau glazing under depressed segmental heads. The style otherwise is an eclectic amalgam of
Second Empire and Baroque: the central block projects slightly,
with a grand arcade and a pediment over the three central bays;
above rises the large dome with its cupola. The corner wings,
with mansard roofs and ornate dormers, also project. In HANS
ROAD, entrance No. 1 (1895) was the door to the flats which for
a short time occupied the upper storeys, and is *Stephens* at his
most sensational: a pedimented triple window is set into a broken
pediment above a two-storey arch with faceted voussoirs, set
between paired Corinthian columns. Further down the street,
another lavish entrance dated 1911. Facing BASIL STREET
(which, like Hans Road, is actually in Chelsea) is a splendid

Beaux-Arts block with giant order and heavy cornice, still all in terracotta, by the house architect of Harrods, *Louis D. Blanc*, 1929–30. Inside, the notable survival from the first phase is the tiled MEAT HALL, its exquisite hunting scenes and others by *W. J. Neatby*, executed by *Doultons*.

W of Harrods, little stands out. On the N side, Nos. 106–110 Brompton Road have a pleasant gabled façade of patterned red brick, by *Sheppard Robson & Partners*, 1981–2. Then a stretch of stuccoed houses among which Nos. 128 and 132–136 survive, much altered, from 1766. Nos. 140–148, suitably restrained in their brick facing but rather tall, are by *Duke Simpson & Mac-Donald*, 1980–2. No. 150 plays a different game: an office front given character by bold granite-faced projecting bows, with flats behind in MONTPELIER MEWS, 1983 by *Michael Squire Associates*. On the S side Nos. 179–181 and 185–187 Brompton Road are of 1825 (the latter still with its simple late Georgian windows, a rarity here). Nos. 197–205, a dull block of 1929–30 by *Murrell & Pigott*, unmercifully dwarfs the BUNCH OF GRAPES (No. 207) of 1845, as do the series of five-storey Queen Anne buildings of 1886–9 at Nos. 209–251. The road then hooks sharply S towards Chelsea with, as a disappointing landmark on the corner, the squat dome of EMPIRE HOUSE by *Paul Hoffmann*, 1910–16.

The wedge-shaped area N of Brompton Road*, bounded by Hyde Park to the N, was developed piecemeal from *c.* 1800 in an intricate pattern of small streets and squares. Starting from the W end, BROMPTON SQUARE was laid out in 1821 with conventional narrow-fronted houses by *Robert Darley*. The N crescent is obviously later: it is of 1834–5, probably by *John Blore*, and happily embraces Nash's new Italianate mode, with Doric porches and giant Corinthian pilasters. The intended route N from here towards Hyde Park was blocked by James Elger, the developer of the more exclusive Ennismore Gardens to the N (Perambulation 3a). No. 26 with its jarring gable was rebuilt in 1889–90 by *Frederick Horton*. The narrow streets to the E – CHEVAL PLACE, FAIRHOLT STREET, and RUTLAND STREET – were also laid out in the 1820s. Many of the tiny brick dwellings for the local market garden labourers survive; C20 infilling has been reasonably tactful.

MONTPELIER SQUARE was begun in 1825 but proceeded slowly and was not complete until the 1850s. The S side is grander than the rest, with Ionic pilasters at the ends. In MONTPELIER PLACE a lesser early C19 terrace with stuccoed ground floor. To the NE, TREVOR PLACE, with minor terraces on both sides, and the slightly wider TREVOR SQUARE, laid out in 1818. Of the same period Nos. 235–239 KENSINGTON ROAD, a brick terrace with some later stucco embellishments; bowed fronts towards the park, now dwarfed by the Hyde Park Barracks opposite (*see London 1*).

Now for the streets S of Brompton Road, from E to W. For Hans Road *see* Chelsea (KC), Perambulation 3. OVINGTON GARDENS, with OVINGTON TERRACE on its W side (Nos. 13–14 with Grecian detail), leads to the taller terraces of OVINGTON

*Largely in the City of Westminster.

SQUARE, where the busy Italianate frontages, mostly by *W. W. Pocock*, 1844–51, are broken by Nos. 22–26, a boldly non-traditional post-war replacement by *Walter Segal*, 1957, the cross-walls of loadbearing engineering bricks expressed externally, the façade articulated by a wooden lattice in a manner faintly reminiscent of a Morris Traveller parked among grander saloons. In the mews (SE corner) No. 32A is by *Clough Williams-Ellis*. YEOMAN'S ROW to the W was an old field lane built up on the E side with cottages from 1767. Nos. 9–25 are by *J. J. de Segrais*, 1960, demure neo-Georgian replacements, an unusual effort at the time. Then the originals, Nos. 27–35 of *c.* 1770, stock brick with red brick gauged arches, carved doorcases, and broad ground-floor windows. The C19 working-class pattern was broken in the 1890s by the studios on the W side, asymmetrical compositions with large gables, No. 22 by *Alfred J. Beesley*, Nos. 24–28 by *William Barber*.

The W side of Yeoman's Row, and the Egertons to W and S, are part of the Smith's Charity estate, a substantial Kensington landholding from the time of the bequest of the City merchant Henry Smith († 1628). The first building development, terraces and a crescent begun in 1785 by *Michael Novosielski*, has all been replaced. EGERTON PLACE, horseshoe-shaped, with tall houses, was rebuilt in the 1890s under the supervision of Colonel Harold Malet. Nos. 1–7 are by *Mervyn Macartney*, 1892, very elegant and restrained in their Georgian detail: red brick, with shallow stone bays and doorcases. The less accomplished Nos. 8–14 are by *A. F. Faulkner*, 1894, working for the builder *William Willett* who had taken over the development. The two- and three-storey EGERTON TERRACE and the very attractive EGERTON CRESCENT are of 1843, probably by *George Basevi*, fully stuccoed, with subdued classical details; the main feature of the crescent is a delicate iron balcony. EGERTON GARDENS is in a more standard red brick Flemish gabled style, save for a handful of individual essays: No. 31 by *Thomas Henry Smith*, *c.* 1888, and MORTIMER HOUSE of 1886–8, a picturesque composition in its own large garden, Tudor brick with blue brick diaper, Tudor chimneys with crenellated pots and stone mullions.

Due W of Egerton Gardens the Alexander estate begins with ALEX-ANDER SQUARE, one of the best ensembles of the period in Kensington (houses dated 1827 and 1830). The studded doors of the N group are typical of *George Basevi*, who became surveyor to the estate when the square was under construction. SOUTH and NORTH TERRACES were begun in 1832, following the square's success. No. 7 North Terrace was built by *W. F. Pocock* in 1835 as WESTERN GRAMMAR SCHOOL. Only its façade, 49 perfect Greek Doric, survives, with pedimented centre on four engaged columns; the rest of the building was gutted and rebuilt *c.* 1928 by *Stanley Hall, Easton & Robertson* as No. 17A Thurloe Place. ALEXANDER PLACE, bisecting the square, was begun in 1829 with modest three-storey houses with ground-floor bow-windows (Nos. 1–7 and 4–10); its 1840s continuation is signalled by Doric doorcases and a change in height. A venture into THURLOE CLOSE is rewarding if a bit surprising: an enclave of mock-Tudor dwellings of 1927 by *Francis Gordon Selby*, with such period details as rough stucco, half-timbering, and herring-bone brickwork.

Alexander Place leads into THURLOE SQUARE, begun in 1840 by *Basevi*. Grey gault bricks above channelled stucco ground floors, main cornices below top storeys, and occasionally paired Doric porches firmly announce a new era in Italianate town-house design. Still *au courant* in the 1840s are the gauged brick arches and giant order pilasters. Nos. 1–5 and 52–26 in the SW corner were demolished in 1867 to make way for the underground railway; No. 5, a strange wedge-shaped infill, was rebuilt in 1885–7, possibly by *C. W. Stephenson*, No. 52 in 1888 by *A. Benyon Tinker*.

To the S, PELHAM STREET runs parallel to the railway tracks. Nos. 53–61 survive from 1835, dwarfed by the London Transport offices; Nos. 63–81 are of 1924–5 by *C. Stanley Peach* for the Kensington and Knightsbridge Electric Company, with upper floors added in the 1950s. CROMPTON COURT is also by *Peach*, 1933–5. Opposite, a 1989 office development by *De Brant Joyce & Partners*, of stock brick with arched windows, recreates the appearance of the stabling for PELHAM PLACE and PELHAM CRESCENT, built in 1833 on the Smith's Charity estate. Pre-dating Thurloe Square, these streets by *George Basevi* reveal his more characteristic formula of fully stuccoed terraces with modest dressings and regularly spaced porches. In the crescent, Doric pilasters articulate the end houses, while continuous first-floor iron railings, a plain second-floor band course, and a main bracketed cornice supporting a balustraded parapet unite inter-mediate houses in a single sweep.

3c. Southern Kensington: West Brompton, N and S of Old Brompton Road (see plan on p. 534)

A circular tour starting from South Kensington station. This residential area was developed piecemeal, mostly from the 1840s onwards, but with pockets of the 1820s off Fulham Road and Old Brompton Road. It was on its way to becoming a proper London suburb well before the Great Exhibition of 1851 which led to the creation of the academic centres (*see* Public Buildings 2) and the grand terraces amidst them (*see* Perambulation 3a). To their S *Sir Charles Freake*, builder and developer, was active from 1843. In 1845 he began Nos. 1–7 ONSLOW SQUARE, broadly following designs by *George Basevi*, the fully stuccoed façades with impressive Doric cornices, but Corinthian columns to the porches – a formula that was not continued, for the remaining terraces are of grey brick with stucco dressings. Each range is unified by deep third-floor cornices and regularly spaced Doric porches and given classical emphasis by pedimented first-floor windows on N and S sides; the central porches have continuous colonnades. Freake also built St Paul (q.v.), commanding a respectable position in the SW corner. The vicarage of 1969 is by *Maidment & Brady*. The westerly arm of the square leads directly into ONSLOW GARDENS, an extensive layout built by *Freake* from 1865. These enormous houses realize the aspirations of Onslow Square, the classic High Victorian details of the W terraces including a main cornice now elevated to the top storey, its height accentuated by a balustrade and pedimented dormers. A special feature is the long one-storey back extension into the communal garden (for extra reception or billiard room) with roof terrace above.

S now to Fulham Road by way of NEVILLE TERRACE, 1863, its prominent quoins, balconies, and shaped dormers a lively reply to the flat late Georgian primness of SELWOOD TERRACE opposite of 1824–6. SELWOOD PLACE and ELM PLACE and Nos. 128–132 FULHAM ROAD (remaining from ELM TERRACE) are contemporary. The group is the first systematic development N of Fulham Road, initiated by the estate owner, the architect *Samuel Ware* (cf. Burlington Arcade, Piccadilly), who was perhaps responsible for the design of the double-fronted houses of Elm Place. The taller REGENCY TERRACE (Lecky Street and Nos. 110–126 Fulham Road) is by *Raymond J. Sargent*, 1960–4, in a neo-Georgian idiom attempting to be in keeping. To the W, scale and style change abruptly with Nos. 15–37 CRANLEY GARDENS, rather severe and tall red brick houses of 1884. The Gothic vicarage is by *Alfred Williams*, 1870. Further N, the houses N to Old Brompton Road are contemporary with neighbouring Onslow Gardens, i.e. of 1873–5; likewise ENSOR MEWS, pleasantly secluded behind its original arches. 57 Then EVELYN GARDENS, orange brick of 1886 with elaborate two-storey porch projections, and with some houses of the back-to-front variety. More spirited is ROLAND GARDENS (1871 onwards) to the N and W. The corner house, No. 41, in orange and yellow brick with perfect Shaw asymmetry, was built in 1889 for the founder of Brompton Hospital, Sir Philip Rose. Nos. 43–45 are by *J. A. J. Keynes*, 1891–2, Queen Anne in dark red brick with herringbone tiled panels, intricate iron ties, and miniature pedimented gables above large studio windows. No. 46, more Gothic in spirit, with corner tower and trefoil-headed windows, is of 1883–5 and possibly by *T. Chatfeild Clarke* (cf. Parminter's School, Bethnal Green, TH) Nos. 4–24 and 1–29, built in 1870, vigorously espouse the new fashion for red and yellow brick but with traditional façade elevations enlivened by a deep moulded cornice and a rich frieze.

Just to the NE across Old Brompton Road is a secluded neigh-bourhood of modest houses begun on the compact Lee estate in 1825. Of this period are Nos. 135–137 GLOUCESTER ROAD (No. 133 altered by *E. J. May*, 1834–5) and Nos. 2, 9, and 16–18 CLAREVILLE GROVE, all of only two storeys, set back from the road and once with substantial private gardens. The eclectic neo-Georgian pair Nos. 9C and 11A Clareville Grove are by *Austin Blomfield*, 1929. Nos. 26–36 CLAREVILLE STREET of 1836–9 (Nos. 30–36 much extended) are of brick and semi-detached, their ground-floor windows set into broad segmental arches (cf. Drayton Gardens, Perambulation 4b).

N of here is STANHOPE GARDENS, the W end of the S side by *Thomas Cundy III*, 1871, fully stuccoed and typically reserved in its ornament, each storey clearly marked by a plain band course. The E side and adjoining mews were rebuilt in 1958–60

by *Guy Morgan & Partners*. Stanhope Gardens leads E into
HARRINGTON ROAD, engineered by *John Fowler* in 1867 to
cover the newly laid underground railway tracks. BUTE STREET
leading S is a small shopping street, mostly post-war, built in two
phases, *c.* 1953–4 and *c.* 1965–6. Brick with upper windows
boxed in concrete and ground-floor shops punctuated by fat half-
columns; taller accents at the N corners. Near South Kensington
station is the NORFOLK HOTEL, 1888–9 by *W. H. Scrymgeour*,
with a bold series of Jacobean dormers.

3d. Southern Kensington: Old Brompton Road (see plan on p. 534)

The narrow and gently curving course of OLD BROMPTON ROAD
reflects lost rural southern Kensington. Architecturally, it is of
marginal interest: large, unexceptional blocks of flats scattered
among short terraces mainly built together with the developments on the hinterland estates. Starting from South Kensington
station, MELTON COURT looms up eight storeys on the S side
(by *Trehearne & Norman, Preston & Partners*, 1936–8) followed
by the austere Queen Anne SUSSEX MANSIONS, 1896–1900.
Adjacent, Nos. 87–97, a pretty stucco terrace of *c.* 1848 in the
tradition of Pelham Street (Perambulation 3b). Opposite is a
lively terrace of stock brick and stucco, Nos. 48–60, built in 1875,
with a snappy rhythm of tripartite pediments to the second-floor
windows. Much further along on the N side are Nos. 94–100 of
1823, with plain stucco façades and simple band courses. Then
Nos. 108–110, a delightful pair of Dutch-Baroque-inspired
façades dated 1886 by *William Flockhart*. The windows have
leaded and faceted glass, on the first floor with carved lunettes;
above rise the richly curling profiles of the gables and a tall
central chimneystack.

Returning to the S side, Nos. 135–151 are of 1846 by *John Blore* (cf.
Drayton Gardens, Perambulation 4b), characteristically classical,
with stock brick above channelled stucco ground floors and a
central projecting block with double Doric pilasters supporting
a pedimented attic. In marked contrast to this cool serenity is the
DRAYTON ARMS, No. 153, 1891–2 by *Gordon, Lowther &
Gunton*, in brick and buff terracotta with large oriel windows *à
la* Shaw and very hearty Renaissance decoration. No. 185, heavily
embellished in the spirit of the nearby Boltons, is of *c.* 1875.
Then the rather sprawling COLEHERNE COURT, 1901–4 by
Walter Cave, surveyor to the Gunter estate; purely Edwardian,
that is, with a cheerful mixture of Tudor and Georgian motifs.
Nos. 202–209 opposite are pristine Queen Anne of 1887, probably
by *Cole A. Adams*. Nos. 212–230 of 1876–82 are likely to be by
George & Henry Godwin, part of their Bolton Gardens development for the Gunter estate (Perambulation 4a). Several large
blocks of flats follow on the N side, the best of them REDCLIFFE
CLOSE (1936–7 by *Murrell & Pigott*), succeeded by drab terraces
of 1867–71. On the S side, No. 261, the COLEHERNE ARMS, is
of 1866, also by the *Godwins*, its spirited Lombard stone dressings
resembling their work for the Gunters to the S. No. 281 represents
part of a design by *Aston Webb & Son* for PRINCESS BEATRICE

HOSPITAL, 1930, a stark institutional building of stock and red brick and ashlar.

4a. South-West Kensington: N of Old Brompton Road from Earls Court to Gloucester Road

This large residential area – s of Cromwell Road and West Cromwell Road, w of Gloucester Road, and N of the Old Brompton Road – was built up almost entirely between 1870 and 1890, and consequently demonstrates how Kensington stucco Italianate was given up in favour of red brick Queen Anne. The change took place here *c.* 1880–3, a few years after the introduction of the new style by Norman Shaw at e.g. Lowther Lodge, Kensington, and Cadogan Square, Chelsea, and was achieved as speculative builders began to employ architects adept at the new style. The wealthiest houses are to the SE, where the grids of terraces are broken up by generous communal gardens; to N and W the streets are more cramped, but with houses still on the ambitious scale characteristic of most of Victorian Kensington. In a small area just w of Earls Court Road,

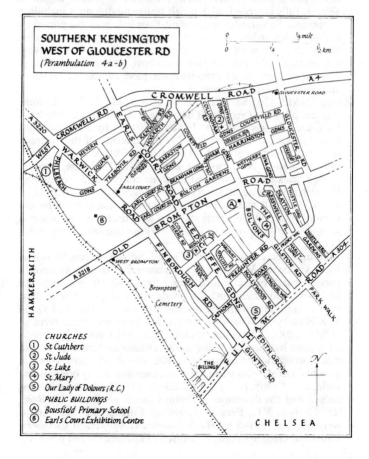

SOUTHERN KENSINGTON
WEST OF GLOUCESTER RD
(Perambulation 4a-b)

CHURCHES
① St Cuthbert
② St Jude
③ St Luke
④ St Mary
⑤ Our Lady of Dolours (R.C.)
PUBLIC BUILDINGS
Ⓐ Bousfield Primary School
Ⓑ Earls Court Exhibition Centre

however, a web of little streets recalls the modest hamlet that existed around Earl's Court Farm; the farmhouse, which stood close to the railway station, was demolished *c.* 1874.

Starting at the E exit of Earl's Court station in WARWICK ROAD, the Earls Court Exhibition Centre (*see* Public Buildings 1) lies like a stranded whale among unkempt terraces of the 1870s and red brick blocks of flats of *c.* 1890. To the NW is PHILBEACH GARDENS, a leafy crescent begun in 1876, with large, mostly four-storeyed houses in a subdued Italianate. The abrupt change to red and yellow brick dates from 1883, with No. 88 as the first, rather unadventurous interloper. Opposite, Nos. 32 onwards are also in red brick although still Italianate in their details. E of Warwick Road the new materials appear a little earlier in NEVERN SQUARE (E side begun 1880, probably by *Walter Graves*); yellow brick with red brick ornament, reticent, but in a wholehearted Queen Anne spirit. The more austere W side, with heavy paired porches, is by *George Whitaker*, 1884. TREBOVIR ROAD to the S, of 1876, is still in the older style, with florid stucco ornament over the windows. The area S of the railway was developed a little earlier: EARLS COURT SQUARE, begun in 1872, is fully stuccoed, with lavish Italianate dressings including continuous balustrades and second-floor balconies supported on a Composite order. The S side is later: Nos. 30–52, a gabled red brick range with various Jacobean motifs, date from 1888. LANGHAM MANSIONS towers above, 1884–6 by *J. A. J. Keynes*, its distinctive terracotta centrepiece combining Jacobean and Second Empire elements.

Along EARLS COURT ROAD from S to N, on the W side some terraces of 1872–3 remain. The E side is dominated by blocks of flats, the ten-storey PARK HOUSE, 1974–5 by *E. F. Starling*, vainly seeking to establish itself as the inheritor of the vigorous red-brick tradition of THE MANSIONS, 1884, or YORK MANSIONS, 1886–7. Nos. 195–201 are by *Horace Cheston*, 1903–4, orange brick severely striated by stone courses and crowned by Flemish gables with delicately curling edges. On the W side, OLD MANOR YARD was laid out in 1874–8 on the site of the old manor house. The original stabling was discreetly redeveloped in 1960–1 by *W. Paton Orr & Partners* as plain two-storey mews houses.

To the immediate E is a group of small, homely streets known as EARLS COURT VILLAGE – a misnomer, as there was never a parish church or communal centre here, only the manor house and farm with their outlying sheds and cottages. The earliest surviving buildings are the humble two-storey terraces of 1819–25 at Nos. 15–33 KENWAY ROAD. The brick and stucco terraces of WALLGRAVE ROAD, now much prettified, were built in 1860–2 for poor labourers working in the vicinity and were quickly in multi-occupation. Further W in Kenway Road, Nos. 35–71, a very plain three-storey brick terrace, each house only one window wide, are of 1807, possibly by *Nicholas Handford*, who was connected with the developer – Thomas Smith – in the King's Road (cf. Chelsea, KC, Perambulation 4). Further on, Nos. 56–70 were built in 1881–2 by *Hugh Roumieu Gough* (cf. St Cuthbert, Philbeach Gardens), crisply dressed in fashionable red brick. By the King's Head, a narrow early C 19 passage, HOGARTH PLACE, leads to HOGARTH ROAD, a solidly middle-class development of 1873–6 with, facing each other, two tall brick terraces with elaborate stucco trim. Near the E end the HOGARTH HOTEL, 1971–3 by *Burton, Truecott & Wall*, bleakly detailed, but respecting the height of the older terraces.

SE from Earls Court Village most of the land belonged in the C 19 to James and Robert Gunter. Development began in 1865 under their surveyors *George & Henry Godwin*, the spacious layout and generous quantity of communal gardens and mews indicating the class of buyer they were aiming to attract. The W end of COURTFIELD GARDENS, comprising Nos. 1–38, was built in 1873–8, contemporary with Earls Court Square, parading the same continuous balustrades and second-floor balconies but with Doric porches instead of Composite. But most Gunter estate houses in this area are somewhat later, early examples of the adoption of red brick for speculative development. BARKSTON GARDENS was begun in 1886, its large gabled houses enriched with cement plaques and intricate diaper work; the leafy BRAMHAM GARDENS to the S, begun in 1883 (Nos. 19–27 by *M. Hulbert*), is in red and yellow brick with deep porches and prominent bays alternately bowed and canted. In BOLTON GARDENS, elaborate roof profiles distinguish Nos. 24–35, built in 1894–6. Nos. 9–23 on the S side are earlier, almost certainly by the *Godwins*, begun in 1865 as the first step in extending the Gunter development already begun S of Old Brompton Road (Perambulation 3d). The very large semi-detached villas are of stock brick with stucco ground floors, shallow but sturdy three-light square bays, and simple window dressings.

Nothing could be more of a contrast than the houses to the E in Collingham Gardens and Harrington Gardens by *Ernest George & Harold Peto*, a mixture of private commissions and speculative work. Their unusually broad frontages offer the maximum variety and surprise: brick is contrasted with terracotta, Franco-Flemish and early Renaissance detail with German Baroque gables. COLLINGHAM GARDENS of 1883–8 is the more cohesive, eloquent evidence of George's passionate espousal of the picturesque Flemish strains of Queen Anne. It consists of two groups of houses facing W and E and backing on to a communal garden. The W side (facing Bramham Gardens) starts at the S end with the reticent Jacobean No. 9 in orange brick and stone, originally occupied by Peto, the modest interior plan enlivened by many enticing fittings of which those that were built-in survive. Nos. 12 and 12A are strikingly faced in yellow and buff terracotta with elaborate gables, a successful foil to the very tall trio of Nos. 14–16 in dark red brick with Renaissance reliefs in panels and lunettes. No. 16 is the most original, with full-height canted façade and angled entrance. Nos. 17 and 18 are quieter. E of the gardens is another inventive sequence. No.7 is faced entirely in buff terracotta, its flat front articulated by large mul-lioned-and-transomed windows and Jacobean banded columns and pilasters. The compact gabled entrance porch is adorned by a slightly mannerist composition of two superimposed Ionic aedicules in relief. No. 6 in deliberate contrast has tall buff pilasters with delicate French Renaissance ornament against red brick, while Nos. 4 and 5, with bolder Gothic blind tracery over the windows, break the street-line with a shared front courtyard. (No. 4 boasted excellent plumbing including a 'shampooing apparatus'.) Nos. 2–3 have chequerwork stone dressing and decorative iron ties.

Further E, HARRINGTON GARDENS, the earlier development. Nos. 20–26 were begun in 1880 in a very sedate Queen Anne, betraying no hint of the exuberance to come with Nos. 35–45, individually commissioned in 1882–5, their broad shaped and crowstepped gables of two and three storeys vying with chimneystacks and arcaded fenestration to provide a lively rhythm. No. 39 for W. S. Gilbert (of Gilbert and Sullivan) has enchanting crowning details of sailing ship and sea monsters which allude not to 'H.M.S. Pinafore' but to Gilbert's descent from an Elizabethan seafarer. The gabled Nos. 1–6 COLBECK MEWS to the NW are also by *George & Peto*, 1883. Back in Harrington Gardens, Nos. 47–75, with odd first-floor arcades bridging deep recesses between houses, are by *Walter Graves*, 1883–5. To the S is WETHERBY GARDENS, another large block of houses in a mixture of styles. *William Willett*, the builder who developed this area, employed *H. B. Measures* as his architect. He designed Nos. 12–19A in 1883–4 with gaily pedimented dormers and deep porches, adapting the conventional materials of yellow brick and stucco to the inventive profiling and grouping of the late Victorian era. The frontages of Nos. 23–24, in eclectically detailed gabled red brick with classical pedimented porches, were designed by *R. W. Edis* to complement No. 25, also by *Edis*, 1883–4. This is yet more elaborate, built for the sculptor Sir Edgar Boehm, with *Boehm*'s own signed Renaissance reliefs on the porch columns. Round the corner in BINA GARDENS, Nos. 16–30 of 1884–6 are again in *Measures*'s red brick with hefty baywindows, deep porches with cut brick festoons, and a variety of gables; a turret at No. 16 introduces the new terrace.

Finally, to the E, set back from Gloucester Road, HEREFORD SQUARE, begun in 1845, is a tidy three-storey composition of stucco terraces on W, N and S sides. *John Blore*'s supremely classical style is best witnessed on the W side, where the nine-bay centrepiece with giant Corinthian paired columns and pilasters attempts to rival the best of Nash's Regent Street. The unity is broken by Nos. 25–26, 1956–8 by *Colin St John Wilson* and *Arthur Baker*, a plain, well-proportioned essay of the Modern Movement, brick with exposed concrete floor bands, and by Nos. 1–5 on the S side, 1953–4 by *Alexander Flinder*. Both blocks replace war-damaged houses.

4b. *South-West Kensington:* S *of Old Brompton Road*

This area is wholly suburban, its network of streets lined with moderately spacious to very large High Victorian villas laid out principally in the 1850s–60s on land owned chiefly by the Gunters. The only older centre was Little Chelsea, a hamlet at the W end of Fulham Road, of which only a little evidence remains. We start from the W, in Redcliffe Gardens, and return W along Fulham Road.

REDCLIFFE GARDENS was the prestigious N–S boulevard of the Gunter estate, begun in 1841 with very large semi-detached houses of stock brick with rich Italianate stucco dressings. It intersects REDCLIFFE SQUARE, a cohesive group of tall, elegantly dressed brick villas designed by the Gunters' prolific surveyors, *George Jun.* and *Henry Godwin*, in 1869–76. These demonstrate the disintegration of the Italianate tradition. Each house boasts an elaborate porch with red granite columns and stiff-leaf capitals. Continuous iron balustrades, keystones, and cornice consoles display an eclectic mixture of Gothic detail, abstract lozenges, and bevelled panels. Variations on the single pedimented dormer also distinguish the roofs of COLEHERNE ROAD (1867–73) to the N, with a fascinating collection of historiated capitals to the bay-windows, and WESTGATE TERRACE (1869–71) to the S, where balustraded parapets accentuate the dormers. HARCOURT TERRACE leads SE from the square, built in 1867–8 of stock brick with regularly spaced Doric porches and an attic storey above the deep modillioned cornice crowning the central sixteen bays: a purely classical design unusual for this date. Most of the original buildings of 1865–70 in REDCLIFFE MEWS were replaced in 1983 by *Bowerbank Brett & Lacey's* very smart range of buff brick mews cottages with gauged arch windows and dentilled cornice intended to evoke C19 authenticity.

TREGUNTER ROAD, which cuts across the bottom of Harcourt Terrace, was named from a Gunter family home in Breconshire. It is lined principally with large semi-detached houses built between 1851 and 1867, mostly by the *Godwin* brothers: brick with straightforward Italianate stucco dressings. The Lombard flavour of the corner houses, Nos. 33–35, testifies to the Godwins' versatility: brick with stucco and red brick dressings, Romanesque capitals on the square tower, and arcaded fenestration. Nos. 20–22 opposite, probably by *J. H. Strudwick*, 1864–6, have Byzantine tiled lunettes and early Renaissance details in polychromatic brick. A short detour S: first into HOLLYWOOD ROAD, with its splendid pub of 1865, THE HOLLYWOOD ARMS, a fanciful Gothic building in the manner of Redcliffe Square, probably by the *Godwins*; then to a tiny enclave of pure modernism near the E end of CATHCART ROAD, where No. 24 is by *Casson Conder Partnership*, 1963, and No. 20 by *C. J. G. Guest*, 1975, clad in reflecting vitreous panels and full of the progressive middle-class urban spirit of Le Corbusier.

The showpiece of the Gunter estate is THE BOLTONS, designed in 1850 and built in 1851–60, an almond-shape spreading N from the top of Tregunter Road. The gentle arc of each crescent is defined by balustraded front garden walls guarding lavish three-storey semi-detached stucco villas by *George Godwin Jun.* The Italianate dressings are heavy – thickset faceted and rusticated quoins, Roman Doric porches, crested window pediments supported on chunky but not clumsy consoles. The mix of traditional and more adventurous elements is a Godwin trademark. GILSTON ROAD leads S, with more *Godwin* semi-detached

houses built in 1850–2, Nos. 24–26 singled out by a tall gabled
bay with a square tower (cf. the corner houses of Tregunter
Road). No. 12 is similar but grander, of the three bays, detached,
and set in ample grounds. No. 4, by *Joseph Peacock*, 1878, was
built as a school in stock brick with red brick and cement dressing
and a stark central gable in the Gothic style. The peaceful enclave
behind Gilston Road to the E is HARLEY GARDENS, begun in
1851, with semi-detached brick houses, their porch capitals with
oddly undulating acanthus leaves. Nos. 9–14 of 1861–3 are
grander: a richly dressed symmetrical terrace with bracketed
main cornice below a parapet punctuated by urns. The short
terrace of pretty stucco houses at Nos. 1–12 PRIORY WALK is
of 1850 by *George Godwin*. Austere and functional, WARNER
HOUSE is by *Austin Blomfield*, 1933–5.

CRESSWELL PLACE was originally a mews; there is converted
stabling of 1885 at Nos. 10–11A and 13–15. No. 25 is of 1970 by
Douglas Norwood & Associates, No. 37 of 1969–70 by *W. R.
Siddons*. Best integrated are Nos. 7–7B by *M. Howard-Radley*,
1969. The 'Surrey-style' tile-hung and weatherboarded cottages
at Nos. 18 and 21–22 were built in 1885–9, probably by *H. Phelps
Drew*, as stables to match Nos. 76–86 DRAYTON GARDENS, to
the E. To the N, *John Blore* designed Nos. 1–47 and 2–56 in 1846:
a formal classical terrace of stock brick with stucco dressings, the
giant order Doric pilasters articulating a twelve-bay centrepiece
on the E side. The extraordinarily varied appearance of the frontages leading S to Fulham Road is largely due to piecemeal par-
titioning into freehold plots which began *c.* 1810. The E side to
Priory Walk is dominated by Queen Anne blocks of flats. On the
W side, Nos. 70–74 are of 1925–6 by *Williams & Cox* in an
excellently precise neo-Georgian (cf. Chelsea, KC, Perambulation 5). No. 100 is more quirky, 1926–7 by *E. Schaufel-
berg*, with a pair of Adamesque garlands, gauged arches in red
tiles, and art deco iron balconies. PRIMROSE COTTAGES, Nos.
93–95, were rebuilt in 1840 by Thomas Johnson, as the wall
plaque indicates. The large front windows set in segmental
recesses and the arched gates lend a degree of dignity not apparent
in the terrace immediately to the E, Nos. 1–9 THISTLE GROVE,
built in 1820 as Robinson Place. These and the original Primrose
Cottages of 1816 formed the E boundary of the old hamlet of
Little Chelsea (q.v. below).

The N side of FULHAM ROAD has a varied appearance. Much of
the early ribbon development has disappeared, and C20 redevelopment has intruded on the *Godwins'* terraces of *c.* 1865. Working
W from Evelyn Gardens, the first striking building is the Cannon
ABC Cinema, 1930 by *J. Stanley Beard & Clare*, with a prominent bowed foyer articulated by giant-order Corinthian columns
and Olympiad bronze torches. The sheer glass office block is a
harsh interruption of 1972–4 by *Turner, Lansdown, Holt &
Partners*. On either side are terraces built in 1847 at the heart of
LITTLE CHELSEA, a tiny settlement on the border of Kensington and Chelsea. Established by 1600, it grew along Fulham
Road close to Stamford Bridge over Counter's Creek. Some of
the best preserved cottages are behind the Fulham Road frontage
in SEYMOUR WALK, built *c.* 1793. Especially elaborate iron

gates at Nos. 2 and 3. Much further along, behind the British Telecom office at No. 234, is a stock brick warehouse of 1880 by *Owen Lewis*. Then BROMPTON COTTAGES, 1971–2 by *Ian Fraser & Associates*, rather stark modernist dwellings over shops. At No. 254 a gateway of *c.* 1793 survives. Then come terraces of 1845 (Nos. 308–356), and behind them a still-secluded development of canalside cottages known as THE BILLINGS, 1846–50, next to the s boundary of Brompton Cemetery (*see* Churches 4). The KENSINGTON CANAL dated from 1828, when Counter's Creek, a former tidal estuary of the Thames, was made navigable. By 1836 it had proved unprofitable and was sold to the Birmingham and Great Western Railways, and in 1859 it was finally filled in to make way for the West London extension line.

For the area s of Fulham Road *see* Chelsea (KC), Perambulation 5.

CHELSEA

INTRODUCTION

Until the late c 18 Chelsea was a riverside village, as much on its own as Teddington or Laleham further upstream. This is how it looks in c 18 views, its c 16 brick church of All Saints lying close to the river at the s end of Old Church Street. Despite the embankment road and the destruction during the Second World War, the old centre is still recognizable, with its narrow streets running back from the river, and its church full of monuments to the eminent and wealthy of Chelsea – a reminder of the exceptional number of grand mansions in their own grounds that once embraced the village. Only three remain: Lindsey House by the river, since subdivided, and Stanley House, preserved among the college buildings N of King's Road, both of the late c 17; and *Leoni*'s Argyll House of 1723, squeezed between later frontages on King's Road. The once fine array along the riverside is recalled now only by street names and the odd garden wall. It started at the w end of the

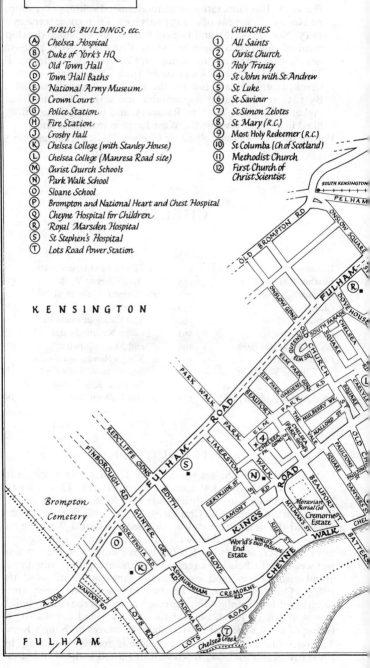

CHELSEA

PUBLIC BUILDINGS, etc.

- Ⓐ Chelsea Hospital
- Ⓑ Duke of York's HQ
- Ⓒ Old Town Hall
- Ⓓ Town Hall Baths
- Ⓔ National Army Museum
- Ⓕ Crown Court
- Ⓖ Police Station
- Ⓗ Fire Station
- Ⓙ Crosby Hall
- Ⓚ Chelsea College (with Stanley House)
- Ⓛ Chelsea College (Manresa Road site)
- Ⓜ Christ Church Schools
- Ⓝ Park Walk School
- Ⓞ Sloane School
- Ⓟ Brompton and National Heart and Chest Hospital
- Ⓠ Cheyne Hospital for Children
- Ⓡ Royal Marsden Hospital
- Ⓢ St Stephen's Hospital
- Ⓣ Lots Road Power Station

CHURCHES

- ① All Saints
- ② Christ Church
- ③ Holy Trinity
- ④ St John with St Andrew
- ⑤ St Luke
- ⑥ St Saviour
- ⑦ St Simon Zelotes
- ⑧ St Mary (R.C.)
- ⑨ Most Holy Redeemer (R.C.)
- ⑩ St Columba (Ch of Scotland)
- ⑪ Methodist Church
- ⑫ First Church of Christ Scientist

KENSINGTON

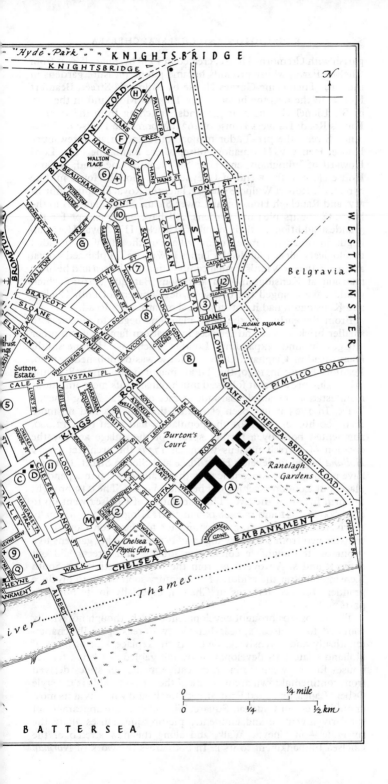

"Hyde Park" KNIGHTSBRIDGE
KNIGHTSBRIDGE

N

BROMPTON ROAD

SLOANE STREET

HANS ROAD

BASIL ST

PAVILION RD

HANS CRES

H

F

WALTON PLACE

6

HANS PLACE

BEAUCHAMP PL

PONT ST

LENNOX GARDENS

PONT STREET

CADOGAN ST

CADOGAN SQUARE

CADOGAN PLACE

CADOGAN LANE

Belgravia

10

OVINGTON SQUARE

TRYON'S ROW

WALTON STREET

G

MILNER ST

MOORE ST

HALSEY ST

7

CADOGAN GDNS

CADOGAN PL.

12

SLOANE TERR.

DRAYCOTT AVENUE

SLOANE AVENUE

LEE ST

CADOGAN ST

3

SLOANE

National Trust Buildings

ELYSTAN ST

8

DRAYCOTT PL.

CLIFFORD GDNS

SLOANE SQUARE

SLOANE SQUARE

WESTMINSTER

Sutton Estate

CALE ST

ST LUKE'S ST

WHITEHEAD'S GRO

ELYSTAN PL.

ANDERSON ST

8

LOWER SLOANE ST

PIMLICO ROAD

5

KINGS ROAD

JUBILEE PL.

WELLINGTON SQUARE

ROYAL AVENUE

SMITH ST

ST LEONARD'S TERR

FRANKLIN'S ROW

CHELSEA BRIDGE ROAD

FRANKLIN ST

MARKHAM ST

SMITH TERR

TEDWORTH SQUARE

WEST ROAD

Ranelagh Gardens

FLOOD ST

C

D

11

CHELSEA MANOR ST

FLOOD ST

CHRISTCHURCH ST

ORMONDE GATE

A

OAKLEY ST

MARGARETTA TERR

M

2

ROYAL HOSPITAL RD

TITE ST

E

Burton's Court

CHEYNE ROW

9

Q

Chelsea Physic Gdn

SWAN WALK

EMBANKMENT GDNS

EMBANKMENT

CHELSEA BR.

CHEYNE WALK

CHELSEA EMBANKMENT

River

ALBERT BR.

Thames

0   ¼   ½ km
0   ¼ mile

BATTERSEA

parish with Cremorne House, created in 1778 by *James Wyatt* from Chelsea Farm, whose grounds became public pleasure gardens in the C 19. Then came Gorges House by Milman's Street; Beaufort House, in the C 16 the home of Sir Thomas More and in the C 17 of Sir Lionel Cranfield, its grounds stretching from the river to King's Road; Danvers House of 1623; Monmouth House by Lawrence Street; the pre-Tudor manor house known as Shrewsbury House; Henry VIII's manor house, where Katharine Parr, Lord Howard of Effingham, and later Sir Hans Sloane lived; Radnor House close to the E end of Cheyne Walk; Gough House in Tite Street; Sir Robert Walpole's house, later the Royal Hospital infirmary; and Ranelagh House near Lower Sloane Street, famous in the late C 18 for its pleasure gardens. All have gone, except for the grandest addition to their number: Charles II's Royal Hospital, begun in 1682 half a mile E of the village on the site of an intended theological college founded by James I. William III planned a royal avenue between Wren's formal composition at Chelsea and his own mansion at Kensington – an ambitious Baroque gesture which would have changed the course of development of both Chelsea and Kensington had it not stopped short at King's Road.

From the early C 18 the large mansions began to give way to smaller brick houses and terraces in a pattern familiar from other villages around expanding London such as Hammersmith, Hampstead or Clapham. Danvers House was demolished *c.* 1720, Beaufort House in 1740, the Tudor manor house in 1758; of the urbanizing growth that followed much remains, its most ambitious manifestation the ample Baroque terrace of *c.* 1720 along Cheyne Walk. In 1705 it has been estimated that Chelsea had no more than 300 houses; by 1801 the population had risen to *c.* 12,000, augmented both by a further spread of the village and by the creation of a fresh nucleus when, in 1777, the architect *Henry Holland* began to develop Hans Place and Sloane Street. Here we have no longer the concentric growth of Chelsea as an independent place, but London reaching out beyond Mayfair. The C 19 brought the firm fusion of the two. The population of Chelsea went up to *c.* 40,000 in 1841 and to *c.* 88,000 in 1881. King's Road (originally a private royal drive from Westminster to Hampton Court) was transformed from a country highway between market gardens to a suburban thoroughfare connecting squares and streets laid out to its N and S. An overflow from the building activity at South Kensington after the middle of the century soon began to produce grander stuccoed terraces in Chelsea, especially in its northern parts.

The 1870s–80s brought developments which, though not wholly confined to Chelsea, appear here in two areas specially characteristically and extensively. One was the replacement of most of Holland's late C 18 development by tall gabled red brick terrace houses for the wealthy, in an evocative medley of styles derived from continental town architecture of the C 15–17. This is the style Osbert Lancaster called Pont Street Dutch, and which is at its most grandiloquent in Cadogan Square. The other is the appearance of similarly inventive and eminently picturesque houses along the riverside – in Cheyne Walk, and along the new stretch of the Chelsea Embankment to its E. In both areas the work of *Norman*

Shaw is pre-eminent. Behind Chelsea Embankment, Tite Street developed in the 1870s as an enclave of rather outré purpose-built artists' houses, acquiring notoriety through its association with Whistler. But Chelsea was already a haven for artists: Rossetti held court in No. 16 Cheyne Walk from 1862; further W Turner in his old age (he died in 1851) had lived incognito in a humble riverside cottage. The artistic element fostered an interest in the picturesque, and in the preservation and indeed re-creation of a somewhat romantically conceived 'Old Chelsea'. *C. R. Ashbee*'s sensitive infill schemes, of which only a pair of very original houses in Cheyne Walk survive, are the most distinguished contribution in this vein; the most dramatic was the removal of the medieval Crosby Hall from the City to the Chelsea riverside in 1908–10. Generally the continuation of this mood into the C20 helped to ensure that at least parts of Chelsea remained on a friendly scale; happy examples are the houses of modest Arts and Crafts character of *c.* 1910 in the area around The Vale, N of King's Road.

Meanwhile, away from the old village, a more urban character took over. The civic consciousness of the late Victorian and Edwardian years was expressed by a distinguished group of public buildings (by *Brydon* and *Stokes*) in King's Road and Manresa Road. The local authority demonstrated its new powers by clearing away the overcrowded cottages of the poor. Their first major target was the neighbourhood of Chelsea Common, E of Sydney Street, which was rebuilt with Edwardian working-class flats. Between the wars larger and less appealing private blocks crowded into the region of Sloane Avenue, a dismal area enlivened only by the exuberant Michelin Building of 1909–11. Since the Second World War the main arena for change has been the west end of Chelsea, where large-scale redevelopment between King's Road and the river was begun by the council in 1949. Its final stage, planned from 1960 but completed only in 1977, was *Eric Lyons*'s cluster of brick towers at World's End, a swan song for high-rise social housing. However, this area is exceptional; what is most noticeable about later C20 Chelsea is the transformation of King's Road into a fashionable shopping street, and the smartening up (sometimes to an unrecognizable extent) of the humble C19 housing in the mews and lanes behind the wealthy streets and squares, so that large tracts are now far more socially homogeneous than when they were first developed.

As for C20 commercial architecture, the outstanding contribution is still the Peter Jones department store in Sloane Square, of 1934–6 by *Slater & Moberly* (with *Crabtree* and *Reilly*), still remarkably undated. The best of more recent contributions are the offices added behind the Michelin Building (*YRM*, 1985–6).

The decline in population triggered already in the early C20 by rebuilding and gentrification has continued: there were *c.* 95,000 inhabitants in 1901, *c.* 59,000 in 1931, and *c.* 47,000 in 1961.

FURTHER READING

There is a vast literature on Chelsea, much of it about people rather than buildings. Especially useful among older books are T.

Faulkner, *An Historical and Topographical Description of Chelsea and its Environs* (1829), and A. Beaver, *Memorials of Old Chelsea* (1892). The early *Survey of London* volumes on Chelsea (1909 and 1913) are useful for buildings up to the early C18. *Images of Chelsea* (1980), by Elizabeth Longford, collects together old views; Thea Holme, *Chelsea* (1972), is a good general survey, as is the relevant section of A. Walker and P. Jackson, *Kensington and Chelsea* (1987). The DOE *List* dates from 1984.

On particular topics: for Crosby Hall, A. W. Clapham and W. H. Godfrey, *Some Famous Buildings and their Story* (1913); on other subjects, P. Kroyer, *The Story of Lindsey House Chelsea* (1956); *Carlyle's House* (National Trust Guide), 1988; R. Pearman, *The Cadogan Estate* (1986), and, on the same topic, J. J. Broome's typescript dissertation of 1980 in Chelsea library; the usefully thorough study by F. H. Spicer, *Holy Trinity Church Upper Chelsea* (1953); and W. Hitchmough, *The Michelin Building* (1987). On Lots Road power station there is an informative typescript account by English Heritage London Division. Specially relevant to late C19 Chelsea are M. Girouard, *Sweetness and Light* (1977), A. Saint, *Richard Norman Shaw* (1976), and A. Crawford, *C. R. Ashbee* (1985).

ACKNOWLEDGEMENTS

Chelsea library's local history collection is an invaluable treasure trove. For help on the area of The Vale I am indebted to Susie Barson; Alan Saunders provided much information on C20 council housing.

CHURCHES

Chelsea has fewer churches than Kensington, but they and their furnishings are among the most rewarding in London. All Saints, the old parish church, still shelters within its much rebuilt walls an unusually rich collection of monuments. The first C19 church, St Luke, built in the 1820s just to the S of what was then Chelsea Common, is an important and precocious example of Gothic revival by *Savage*. Its companion church in Sloane Street, Holy Trinity, serving the smart new suburb of Hans Town, was rebuilt in 1888–90 by *Sedding* and remains an unparalleled treasure house of Arts and Crafts furnishings. Other early C19 churches provided for the fast-growing population have gone (*Basevi*'s St Jude) or been altered (*Basevi*'s St Saviour, *Blore*'s Christ Church), but High Victorian church building is represented by the eccentric St Simon Zelotes by *Peacock*, and by work by the *Pugins* and *Bentley* at the R.C. St Mary Cadogan Street. From the C20 there are *Chisholm*'s novel Edwardian First Church of Christ Scientist, and *Maufe*'s post-war St Columba.

ALL SAINTS (Chelsea Old Church), Cheyne Row. *Walter Godfrey*'s painstaking restoration of 1949–58 after disastrous war damage of 1941 recaptured with remarkable success the atmosphere of the pre-Victorian riverside village church crammed full of worthwhile monuments – the most evocative of such interiors in inner London. The exterior is of brick, dating (where not renewed) from 1667–74, when nave and W tower were rebuilt. The medieval E end is also cased in brick. The chancel is of C13 origin, the chancel chapels C14. The N (Lawrence) chapel, the chapel of the lord of the manor, has a large Gothic arch to the chancel (rebuilt in 1784 and restored to its C14 form after the war). The S one was made into the More Chapel in 1528, when the responds were given new capitals. These lovely pieces of 12 Renaissance carving are among the earliest and the best examples in England of decoration in the new Italian style, and their connection with Sir Thomas More, who lived nearby, is most fitting. They are polygonal (to fit the responds) and are delicately carved with tablets (the E one with the date), symbols of office, and foliage, below rather oddly shaped volutes and heads. The immediate source is the France of Francis I, rather than Italy. The low-pitched roof of the chapel was the only one to survive the war. – FONT. Simple baluster type, 1673, with new font cover based on the original one. – PULPIT. A copy of the original of c. 1680–90 (which had been adapted from a three-decker in 1908), incorporating the original door and carved festoons. – ALTAR RAILS. Late C17, handsomely curved around the altar. – STAINED GLASS. Some C17 Flemish panels in N aisle and N chapel.

MONUMENTS (in chronological order; rearranged when the church was restored). Sir Thomas More † 1535. Erected in 1532, after the death of his first wife, and at the time when he retired from public office. A very simple four-centred arch with carved spandrels, cresting, and panelled recess – standard motifs of C16 Perp work in London (cf. the Easter Sepulchre at Harlington, Hi) – renewed according to the original design c. 1832. Its austerity contrasts with the unusually long biographical inscription on the back panel, an apologia written by More himself and vetted by Erasmus. – Jane Guilford, Duchess of Northumberland, † 1555 (badly damaged). Gothic niche with diapered shafts supporting a flat canopy with fan tracery in the soffit, the

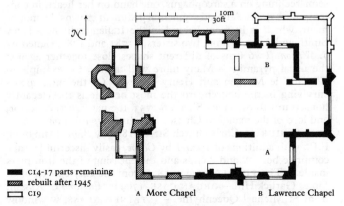

C14-17 parts remaining
rebuilt after 1945
C19

A More Chapel   B Lawrence Chapel

Chelsea, All Saints (Chelsea Old Church), plan

type of Purbeck marble tomb used also for the contemporary
Chaucer monument in Westminster Abbey. Brasses against the
back wall (kneeling figure with daughters, and shields). – Sir
Edmund Bray † 1539. Plain tomb-chest with two lozenge-shaped
panels with shields. – Richard Jervoise † 1563. Free-standing
classical triumphal arch with broad, coarse strapwork decoration
and a heavy fluted attic – a very odd device for a tomb. Under
the arch originally a tomb-chest. The decorative details relate to
the work associated with the French mason Allen Maynard. –
Thomas Hungerford † 1581 and wife, and Thomas Lawrence
† 1593 and wife. The usual type of the period, alabaster, with
small kneeling figures facing each other beneath a classical arch. –
Gregory Fiennes, Lord Dacre, † 1594 and wife † 1595. A much
more ambitious, standing wall-monument with two recumbent
figures on straw mats beneath an arched and coffered niche,
flanked by columns and with the strapwork and ribbonwork at the
back characteristic of the 'Southwark School' of Netherlandish
carvers. Superstructure with tall obelisks and central coat of
arms. – Sir Arthur Gorges † 1625. An engraved brass panel
with small kneeling figures. – Sara Colvile † 1632 (although the
inscription gives 1631), perhaps the most interesting monument
in the church; a demi-figure rising in her shroud, both hands
held up and eyes gazing up to the clouds and the dove carved
beneath the top pediment. The idea was at just that moment
becoming popular in England (and only in England), thanks to
Nicholas Stone's monument to Dr Donne in St Paul's
Cathedral. – Sir Robert Stanley † 1632 and two children, attributed to *Edward Marshall*. Large standing wall-monument with
sarcophagus supporting three pedestals with frontal relief busts
and urns on top. Between the pedestals and urns stand two
angels, rather squeezed in. The portrait of Sir Richard, dead-
frontal, has a very intense ghostly life. – Charles Cheyne,
Viscount Newhaven, and his first wife Jane. Designed in 1672
by *Pietro Bernini*, the great Bernini's less great son, the figure
carved by *Antonio Raggi* from a 'draught of the face' sent him.
Standing wall-monument of reredos type with a curved front.
Tall marble columns flank a niche in which the effigy appears
semi-reclining on a sarcophagus, one hand on her heart, in contemporary dress. A broad segmental pediment crowns the monument, which is lit from behind in the Italian fashion. – Lucy
Smith and Anne Wilton, two sisters, † 1781 and 1787, signed by
J. Wilton. Two urns of different shapes close together against
the usual pyramid. – Many more wall-tablets, for example to
William de Morgan and Henry James. – Of the monuments
surviving in the churchyard the most notable is the elegantly
housed urn to Sir Hans Sloane † 1753, the naturalist, collector,
and lord of the manor of Chelsea. It is by *Joseph Wilton*.

CHRIST CHURCH, Christchurch Street. 1838 by *Blore*, plain brick
E.E., with additions of 1900–1 by *Caröe*, easily discernible: they
comprise both W and E ends and the encasing of the iron piers
inside. – The PULPIT came in 1876 from the City church of St
James Garlick Hill. – ORGAN CASE. 1799 by *England & Russell*,
from St Michael Queenhythe. – (STAINED GLASS. W window
by *A. K. Nicholson*.)

HOLY TRINITY, Sloane Street. 1888–90 by *J. D. Sedding*, replacing a church of 1828–30 by *Savage*. Sedding's last and most
mature work, and the outstanding London example of the Arts
and Crafts movement in the ecclesiastical field. The patron was
the Earl of Cadogan. £22,000 had been spent by 1890. Sedding
wanted churches to be 'by living men for living men', and Holy
Trinity has certainly freshness and daring at a time when Pearson
and the younger Scotts designed in the most accomplished neo-
Gothic idiom. It consists of a nave 12 metres wide and 18 metres
high to the crown of the vault (originally of wood, replaced in
plaster in 1959 by *Michael Farey* after war damage), with narrow
aisles opened in wide arcades. The s aisle is narrower than the
N, but this is concealed outside by the W porch. An outer N aisle
houses a morning chapel, with vestries beyond. The W front is a
free adaptation of the late Gothic type of King's Chapel
Cambridge, with turrets and battlemented parapets. The detail –
with the huge W and E windows with their flowing tracery, the
arches of the arcade sprouting out of the main piers without any
interposed capitals, the abundance of colourful Italian marble
(Ruskin's influence), and the plentiful sculptural decoration – is
all eminently typical of Sedding.

FURNISHINGS. Many of the leading artists of the day contributed to make Holy Trinity a museum of 1890s design. There
is a complete blend between the medievalizing Pre-Raphaelite–
Morris and the Italianizing trends. *Henry Wilson*, Sedding's
pupil and successor, and a first-rate decorative artist, carried on
after Sedding's early death in 1891. He designed the delightful
GRILLE behind the altar in the morning chapel (carried out by
Nelson Dawson), the best piece of ornamental inventiveness in
the church, the ALTAR RAILS, and the RAILINGS outside the
church in Sloane Street, completed in 1903. – MAIN ALTAR with
relief of the Entombment by *Harry Bates*. – REREDOS 1912 by
John Tweedsmuir (in place of a design by Sedding). In the
morning chapel, ALTAR PAINTING of 'the C19 worship of
Christ' by *W. Reynolds-Stephens*. – CHANCEL STALLS and
SCREENS by *F. W. Pomeroy*. – FONT of onyx and marble, cherubs
on shaft, by *F. Boucher* under *Onslow Ford*. – PULPIT also of
coloured marbles with delicate iron balustrade to the stair. –
LECTERNS: in the nave by *Armstead*, in the morning chapel by
J. Williams (1909). – STAINED GLASS. In the huge E windows
forty-eight small panels by *Morris & Co.*, not at all typical of
their work of this date: individual figures of saints by *Burne-
Jones*, the backgrounds by *Morris* himself, 1894–5. Morning
chapel windows by *Powells*, to designs by *Sir William Richmond*,
1904 and 1910. S aisle windows by *C. Whall*, 1900 and 1905.
Six clerestory windows also by *Whall*, 1904–23, the start of an
uncompleted scheme illustrating the angelic hierarchy. Much
more decoration was planned but not executed: a series of apostles carved against the nave piers to designs by *Hamo Thornycroft*, a *Burne-Jones* frieze depicting the life of Christ all
along the zone between arcade and clerestory, and medallions of
prophets by *Armstead* in the spandrels of the nave arcades, of
which only one was carried out. The S chapel was furnished as a
war memorial by *F. C. Eden*, with glass by *Powells*, in 1921.

ST JOHN WITH ST ANDREW, Park Walk. 1912–13 by *Sir A. Blomfield & Son* (replacing a private chapel built in 1718 by Richard Manningham, owner of Chelsea Park, and extended in the C 19). Red brick; S W tower with stone spire. Plain, capacious clerestoried interior, with brick arches on stone octagonal columns.

79 ST LUKE, Sydney Street. By *James Savage*, 1820–4, the earliest of the churches of the new Chelsea of the C 19, followed soon by *Savage*'s first Holy Trinity, Sloane Street, by *Basevi*'s destroyed St Jude and his St Saviour, and by *Blore*'s Christ Church. St Luke is, according to Eastlake's *Gothic Revival*, 'the earliest groined church of the modern revival'. This is indeed important; for however lanky its proportions, however papery some of its detail (in spite of a cost of £40,000), the use of stone vaulting throughout proves earnestness of purpose contrary to the more fanciful and more flippant (and perhaps also more romantic) Gothic of the decades before. The plan is essentially the long narrow rectangle with nave and aisles of the Perp churches and royal chapels, but with wooden galleries between the slender piers. The chancel has a straight E end. Clerestory and triforium are made into one composition, as the later Middle Ages liked it. The vaults are abutted outside by lean flying buttresses. The window tracery is Perp. The W side is different from the normal Church Commissioners' type, which the shape of the church (in spite of a size large enough to seat 2,500) otherwise resembles. Its distinguishing feature is the continuation of a tall W tower in a five-bay open porch across the whole front. A spire was intended. The chilliness of the general impression was very sensitively attributed by Eastlake (in 1872) to such features as the uniformity of the ashlar coursing, the dividing of the buttresses by their set-offs into two equal parts, the dividing of the tower turrets by nine string courses placed at exactly even intervals, etc. Yet its timidity and meagreness have appealing qualities which it is perhaps easier to appreciate now than it was in Eastlake's time. The chancel was redecorated by *Goldie* in 1874, the floor raised and extended W in 1893. – ALTAR with *Northcote*'s Descent from the Cross.* – CARTOON in the N gallery for a *Watts* mosaic. – MONUMENTS. Lt-Col. Henry Cadogan † 1813, in the battle of Vitoria, by *Chantrey*, with two mourning soldiers contemplating a coffin and a portrait medallion. – Luke T. Flood, 1857 by *Pepper* of Brighton, still in the Flaxman–Bacon tradition. Relief with an angel. – STAINED GLASS by *Hugh Easton*, 1959.

ST SAVIOUR, Walton Street. 1840 by *Basevi*, N aisle 1878 by *E. P. Loftus Brock*, chancel, morning chapel, and much else 1890 by the Rev. *Ernest Geldart*. Brick exterior, the three phases easily distinguished: Commissioners' lancet style (W end), standard Dec, and Geldart's more fanciful mixture of flamboyant tracery and diapered brickwork.

ST SIMON ZELOTES, Moore Street. 1858 by *J. Peacock*. A memorable building. The little front overcrowded with gross Gothic motifs in the triumphantly bad taste of the mid Victorian years which is so often a relief after too much pedantic correctness. W

---

*The painting was not visible at the time of writing.

window grouped in a blind arch filled with diaper-work, a little bell-turret above. Earnest, jerky interior, polychrome brick walls, much naturalistic carving, angular stilted arches to the quasi-transepts (which had galleries until 1896). – STAINED GLASS. E window by *Lavers & Barraud*.

ST MARY (R.C.), Cadogan Street. Part of a group with rectory, schools, and almshouses (*see* Perambulation 3). The church is of 1877–8 by *J. F. Bentley* but incorporates as its s chancel chapel *A. W. Pugin*'s mortuary chapel of 1845 for the cemetery belonging to the R.C. chapel built in 1812 for the benefit of Catholic Pensioners of the Royal Hospital. To the w Bentley's church is of brick, nothing special outside, but with a light spacious interior in the idiom of the C14. Nave with hexagonal piers and a narrow blind triforium. Internal tracery to the windows. The N aisle has a series of chapels. In the narrower s aisle is a single larger chapel of 1860 by *E. W. Pugin*, incorporated from the older building; it is vaulted, with carved bosses, and has as part of its original fittings an elaborate carved ALTARPIECE by *J. F. Bentley* with angels crowded round a mandorla. The plainer s chancel chapel of 1845 by *A. W. Pugin* has correct Dec tracery and a simple altar with painted traceried retable. The chancel was re-ordered in 1972. In the N chapel an elaborate Italian Gothic altar of alabaster and mosaic, incorporating a central domed tabernacle. – PULPIT. Marble and mosaic, designed by *Bentley* for the chapel of 1812. – STAINED GLASS. In the s aisle a Magnificat window. – In the s aisle chapel good post-war abstract work.

MOST HOLY REDEEMER AND ST THOMAS MORE (R.C.), Cheyne Row. 1895 by *G. Goldie*, red brick, in an Italian Renaissance style. Broad nave with ribbed and coved ceiling, but without the aisles originally intended.

ST COLUMBA (Church of Scotland), Pont Street. 1950–4 by *E. Maufe*, replacing a church of 1883 destroyed in the Second World War. An effective cornerpiece in gleaming white stone. Scandinavian-modern tower, Georgian windows in moulded surrounds (for the offices in the w part of the building), and some vestigial Byzantine features which do not carry much conviction. A triple entrance in a giant niche, vestibule on two levels with short columns and elementary capitals. The church is upstairs. A long nave, with columns only in the first bay.

METHODIST CHURCH and Pastoral Centre, No. 155a King's Road. Behind the church hall of 1903 along King's Road (*see* Perambulation 4), new buildings of 1984 by *Bernard Lamb* consisting of a simple white plastered narthex, church, chapel (with STAINED GLASS by *Jacques Loire*), and meeting rooms. Sheltered flats above.

FIRST CHURCH OF CHRIST SCIENTIST, Sloane Terrace. Completed in 1908 by *R. F. Chisholm*. A building of originality, if not quite as eccentric as Edgar Wood's slightly earlier Church of Christ Scientist, Manchester, but quite unlike the grand classical Christian Science churches in America, where the sect was founded. The style is a free Byzantine with oriental touches, perhaps because the architect had previously worked in India. Immaculate ashlar exterior; tall bell-tower with concave octagonal cupola set back behind curved, corbelled-out balustrades.

The top of the tower was adapted from Chisholm's rejected first scheme for an extraordinary circular domed church with a row of four domed turrets. The body of the church has on the first floor a row of Byzantine-Romanesque subdivided windows. The sturdy exterior arcade below supports the cantilevered gallery of the first-floor auditorium, an exceptionally wide space, rather like a theatre, with raked seats for 1,300, and no internal columns (except for the E gallery). Trussed steel roof concealed by a shallow barrel-vault, with roof-lights. In the semi-basement a large Sunday school room and generous offices. Lavishly fitted throughout, with high quality woodwork, and windows with handmade opaque glass with coloured interlace patterns.

PUBLIC BUILDINGS

1. Pre-Victorian

28 ROYAL HOSPITAL, between Royal Hospital Road and Chelsea Embankment. 1682–91 by *Sir Christopher Wren*, his first secular commission on a grand scale. England had no standing army before the time of the Commonwealth. Its establishment brought up afresh the problem of how to provide for invalided soldiers and veterans. Poor relief and a few private hospitals or alms-houses were not enough. In 1670 Louis XIV had solved the problem for Paris by founding the Hôtel des Invalides. The London of Charles II and Christopher Wren looked to Paris for guidance on many things. So we find the King buying the land in Chelsea on which James I had begun a theological college in 1609, and laying the foundation stone on 17 February 1682. The moving forces in organizing the building were Sir Stephen Fox, Commissioner of the Treasury, and John Evelyn, who had earlier been involved in the accommodation of sick and wounded during the Dutch war. The original plan was for buildings around a single courtyard; the side courtyards were additions of 1686. In 1689 476 non-commissioned officers and men moved in. The chapel was consecrated in 1692.

The general impression of the hospital is that what it lacks in grandeur it makes up in intimacy and friendliness. Though the idea of the hospital came from France, the spirit is more akin to homely Holland than to pompous Paris. To the N Wren's building exhibits a long straight front with a three-storey centre block of twenty-seven bays, containing chiefly the hall and chapel linked by a central vestibule, and lower side wings connected with the centre by one-storeyed short links. To the s the centre block faces a large courtyard, the FIGURE COURT, closed on the l. and r. by the long wings of the wards, and open towards the river. Lower wings identical with those of the N branch off from the s ends of the ward wings to W and E, thus forming with the N wings two more open courtyards (a complex yet very clear and perfectly symmetrical composition). The buildings are of two colours of brick, with Portland stone chiefly for the quoins and such features as the chief N and s porticoes, the lantern over the vestibule, and the E and W porticoes. These are the main dec-

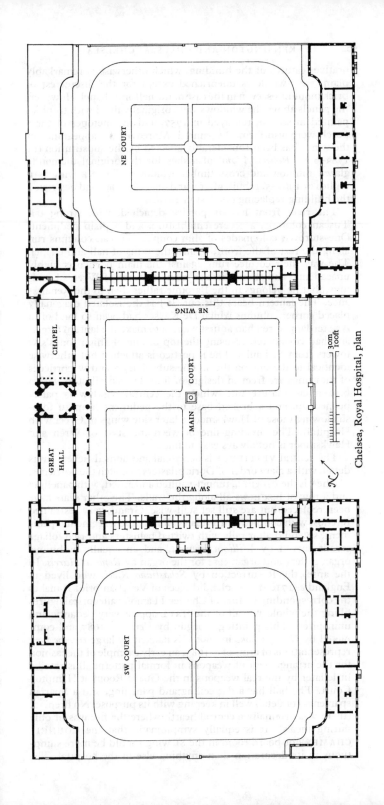

Chelsea, Royal Hospital, plan

orative features of the building, which otherwise is remarkably plain, with windows unenriched except for the discreetest of brick mouldings, even in the case of the hall and chapel. However, the panels above the windows were originally filled with trophies painted in stucco, removed in 1757, and the metopes of the s porch were also formerly painted. Moreover the appearance of the wings has been considerably affected by the substitution (in 1783–6 by *Robert Adam*) of sashes for the original diamond-glazed mullion-and-cross timber windows. The NE wing is a replica of 1964–5, rebuilt after war damage in 1945 had destroyed the building replacing one lost in 1918.

The river front has its portico detached, with strong tall Tuscan columns, a severe entablature, and a plain pediment. One-storeyed colonnades of slim coupled Tuscan columns run along the rest of the front, against the walls of hall and chapel. The way their cornice runs against the main portico is highly unacademic and shows, like so many features of Wren's buildings, that he belongs to the Baroque rather than to the Renaissance. The lantern bears this out. It has the isolated diagonally placed corner columns which De Keyser had been so fond of in Amsterdam. Wren had at first wanted to make the lantern larger, and had considered re-using the top of one of Inigo Jones's w towers from St Paul's. The N portico is attached but otherwise identical to the one on the s. The subsidiary E and W porticoes of the wings are freer in design, of four Tuscan pilasters with a broken entablature into which the central window is partly pushed up, and a broken base to the pediment (a motif foreshadowing those of Hawksmoor's later side wings of Greenwich Hospital). The dividing-line between the style of Wren and Hawksmoor is not always easy to find.

The central VESTIBULE is octagonal and domed, severe in its detail, with a giant order of Doric pilasters to match the porticoes. To the E is the CHAPEL, tunnel-vaulted and apsed, with panelling and a row of box pews all along the walls. The other seats have been replaced but are still set stall-wise. Grand, very restrained reredos, with coupled Corinthian columns and a segmental pediment, splendid altar rails with twisted balusters and rich foliage scrolls carved by *William Emmett*, and an equally ambitious organ gallery and organ case for the organ by *Renatus Harris*. In the apse, the Resurrection by *Sebastiano Ricci*, who lived in England *c*. 1710–15, a splendid piece of Venetian brio. It makes the corresponding picture of Charles I I among allegorical figures filling the whole W wall of the HALL appear very pedantic and uninspired. This painting – begun by *Verrio c*. 1687 and completed by *Henry Cooke* in 1690 – is flanked by large *trompe l'œil* representations of arms of *c*. 1685, an early example of the fashion for the arrangement of weapons in formal patterns illustrated a little later by the real weapons in the Guard Room at Hampton Court. The hall has a flat ceiling and panelling, and a Spartan sparseness of detail well in keeping with its purpose. No fireplace (there was originally a central hearth where the fire was lit only during meals). It is equally symptomatic that the COUNCIL CHAMBER or board room in the SE wing should be more sumptuous in its decoration than anything else in the hospital. The carved trophies above the fireplace are the work of *William* 29 *Emmett*; the plaster ceiling with the Stuart arms and James II's cypher is by *John Grove*. The WARDS on each of the four floors of the E and W wings have been little changed. Each is about 60 metres long, divided by heavy oak panelling into small individual cubicles (tactfully enlarged in the C20). They are set back to back, with a broad corridor along each outer wall – a much airier arrangement than the small courts of the Invalides. The upper floors are reached by sturdy stairs at the ends of each wing; the central area below the pediment was supplied with piped water for the washing facilities. In the FIGURE COURT, fine bronze statue of Charles II in Roman dress, formerly gilded, by *Grinling Gibbons*. Much good ironwork dating from the time when the hospital was built: in the E and W courts two rare, very elaborate wrought-iron lamp standards in the shape of Ionic columns on big bases; richly wrought iron gates at the N entrance; plainer gates to the narrower W entrance.

E and W of the main composition are detached service buildings. Along East Road *Wren*'s small GUARD HOUSE by the burial ground; then the low offices (now secretary's office and museum), 1819 by *Sir John Soane*, where all army pensions were administered until 1955. Along West Road *Soane*'s buildings of 1809–22 start with his remarkable STABLES, its stock brick front the most elegant of minimal designs, just three sets of concentric arches. At the S end, beyond the gatepiers, the present library and R. C. chapel, L-shaped and very plain, were the ORANGERY of *c.* 1725 belonging to Sir Robert Walpole's house, built *c.* 1715 by *Vanbrugh*, converted by *Soane* to the hospital infirmary in 1809, and destroyed in 1941. The new INFIRMARY lies to the E behind the old burial ground, low, but harshly functional in comparison with the old buildings. It is by *Eric Bedford* of the *Ministry of Works*, 1961.

GROUNDS. N of the hospital, BURTON'S COURT, originally a formal parterre, and the short stretch of ROYAL AVENUE, all that was achieved of King William's grand design of 1692–4 of an avenue that was to lead directly to Kensington Palace. The vast sweeps of canals and avenues laid out to the S by *London & Wise*, with summerhouses overlooking the Thames, all disappeared when the embankment was made; the present rather dull EMBANKMENT GARDENS, with lawns divided by a central path, date, like the adjoining Ranelagh Gardens (*see* below), from a remodelling of *c.* 1860 by *John Gibson*. Granite OBELISK by *S. P. Cockerell*, in memory of the victory of Chillianwallah in 1849.

DUKE OF YORK'S HEADQUARTERS (Territorial Army), King's Road. Built in 1801–3 as the Royal Military Asylum, for the children of soldiers' widows, by *John Sanders* (architect of the Royal Military College at Sandhurst). The main block, at right angles to King's Road, has a sturdy Roman Doric four-column portico, impressive if not specially imaginative. The building is of stock brick, very sparing in its mouldings, as is also the chapel at the corner of Cheltenham Terrace, near the entrance. The combination of austerity and dignity is wholly successful. The view from King's Road is obscured by an addition of 1953–4 by *Harold Dicksee*, in stock brick, sympathetically detailed.

CROSBY HALL, Cheyne Walk and Danvers Street. *See* Public Buildings 2.

CHELSEA PHYSICK GARDEN, Swan Walk. The second oldest botanic garden in England, founded by the Society of Apothecaries in 1673 and still flourishing. The first curator, John Watts, surrounded the garden with its high walls, divided it into the existing quarters, and planted four cedars of Lebanon, among the first in the country. One survived until 1904. The garden reached the height of its fame in the C18, when Philip Miller was gardener under the patronage of Sir Hans Sloane, whose statue stands in the centre, a replica of the original of 1737 by *Rysbrack*. The W quarter is still laid out with long, narrow 'systematic order' beds. The rock garden, the first in England, is an addition of 1772; Sir Joseph Banks brought the rocks of basaltic lava from Iceland. The undistinguished offices etc. on the N side replaced the early C18 buildings *c.* 1900.

2. Victorian and later public buildings

The late Victorian and Edwardian public buildings of Chelsea form a stately group around the junction of King's Road and Manresa Road, commendably converted for new public uses after the borough was merged with Kensington.

TOWN HALL (former), King's Road. 1885–7 by *John Brydon*, a very early use of English Baroque for municipal buildings. Brydon's building can be seen from Chelsea Manor Gardens: brick with stone dressings, a pedimented centre for the vestry hall, wings with Venetian windows for council chamber and committee room. The old municipal offices were replaced in 1904–8 by a new front to King's Road by *Leonard Stokes*, in a style remarkably close to Brydon's. Despite the two grand end pavilions with giant columns, the building succeeds, chiefly by renouncing height, in keeping some of the intimate scale of pre–1875 Chelsea. Inside, the old vestry hall is richly decorated with pilasters and circular attic windows with putti and swags, rather oddly detailed Baroque doorcases, and wall paintings by *Mary Sargent* and others. A long passage with saucer domes connects the two parts of the building. (Bust of Leigh Hunt by *Joseph Durham*.) Refurbished by *Roderick Ham & Partners*, 1978, when the Stokes wing was converted to a library. Further interior decoration 1989; not to be missed are the ladies' cloakrooms with faded tawny classical *trompe l'œils* designed by *Rory Ramsden* and painted by *Blaise Designs*.

TOWN HALL BATHS, Chelsea Manor Street. Part of the town hall complex; 1877, rebuilt 1907 by *Wills & Anderson*, with appropriate symmetrical brick and stone Renaissance front. Converted to a sports centre 1978.

CROWN COURT, Hans Crescent. Gabled Edwardian, with angled Jacobean corner pavilions, on a prominent corner site.

POLICE STATION, Walton Street. Mid C19 Italianate stucco-trimmed front with heavy keystones; on the r. an addition with circular oriel, 1895–6 by *R. Norman Shaw*.

FIRE STATION, Basil Street. 1907 by the *L.C.C. Architect's Department, Fire Brigade Branch*, classical, quite staid.

NATIONAL ARMY MUSEUM, Royal Hospital Road. 1968–70 by *W. Holford & Partners*. A strongly articulated exterior, with brick cladding set back from the exposed framework. Large upper storey above two smaller ones, topped by a heavy chamfered cornice.

CHELSEA COLLEGE, between King's Road and Fulham Road. Future uncertain at the time of writing. From 1980 part of King's College. Originally the College of St Mark and St John, established in 1840 by the National Society for the Education of the Poor as one of the first teacher training colleges. This college moved to Plymouth after the site was acquired in the 1960s for (unexecuted) road improvements.

The seven-acre campus was developed in the grounds of STANLEY HOUSE, which remains at the E end of the site facing King's Road, a plain late C17 building of five bays, of brown brick, with red brick raised floor band and end pilasters, hipped roof, and pedimented dormers. It was begun, according to Faulkner, for William Stanley, but remained unfinished at his death in 1691. The windows now have thin late Georgian glazing-bars, perhaps modernized when William Hamilton added the one-bay ballroom to the E. Interior much altered; the main staircase was removed from the three-bay entrance hall in 1923. Between the hall and the drawing room to the N, an elaborate doorway with a coffered soffit below a broken pediment on fluted Ionic columns with garlanded capitals; it looks mid C18. The ballroom, described by Fanny Burney in 1821, was added by William Hamilton. He had been Lord Elgin's secretary; hence the decoration with casts of the Parthenon frieze running around the upper walls, with three metopes over doorways and fireplace.

W of Stanley House, HUDSON and CLARK, two neo-Georgian red brick blocks with steep mansards, by *Beazley & Burrows*, 1910 and 1923. Gabled gymnasium further W. Behind are the more distinguished buildings added for the newly established college by *Edward Blore*. They are of stock brick, 'in a Byzantine style', i.e. an austere Rundbogenstil where the different rhythms of large and small arched windows, determined by the functions of the buildings, provide the sole ornament. The main block, COLERIDGE, somewhat obscured by later additions, is U-shaped, designed with classrooms in the centre, flanked on the E by the assembly hall (now library) with dormitory above, and on the W by a former dining hall (later a theatre, disused at the time of writing). Towards Fulham Road two isolated buildings. The first is the apsed, cruciform neo-Norman CHAPEL with two tiers of windows and, inside, round-arched roof trusses (rebuilt after a fire in 1859). The second is the charming octagon built in 1843 as a training school. The upper floor with galleries was a later addition (remodelled as a library in 1953 by *Seely & Paget*) from which students could observe the classes gathered around the central octagonal chimneystack (complete with fireplace). On the W part of the site student and staff residences, simple domestic blocks of the 1950s.

CHELSEA COLLEGE, Manresa Road. Part of King's College since

1980. On the E side functional *L.C.C.* buildings of the 1960s. In
front of the set-back entrance, sculpture: Two Piece by *Henry
Moore*. On the W side, now also part of the college, the fine
former PUBLIC LIBRARY, 1890 by *Brydon*. Symmetrical brick
and stone front with semicircular Ionic porch; first-floor windows
within round-headed arches; recessed one-bay wings.

CROSBY HALL, Cheyne Walk and Danvers Street. Now International Hostel of the British Federation of University Women.
Collegiate buildings in a Tudor style by *Walter Godfrey*, 1926–
7, incorporating the C15 HALL rescued from the City when
under threat of demolition and re-erected here in 1908–10 under
the supervision of *Godfrey* and *Patrick Geddes*. The hall was built
between 1466 and 1475 in Bishopsgate as part of the grand
courtyard house of a rich wool merchant, Sir John Crosby, and
was described by Stow as 'the highest of that time in London'.
It was used by the Duke of Gloucester in the 1480s and bought
by Sir Thomas More in 1523. The rest of the building was
destroyed in the C17. The hall is invaluable as evidence of how
sumptuously C15 merchants built in London. It is a tall, unbuttressed, stone-faced building, with the hall, of 21 by 8 metres,
raised up above a brick-vaulted undercroft. On the W side, at the
dais end, is a stone-vaulted oriel, five sides of an octagon, with
two-light windows with transoms. The other windows are also
of two lights, set high up, so that their arches are level with the
tops of the oriel windows. The two more closely spaced windows
at the N end lit a gallery over the screens passage. All this is
original, although the walls were rebuilt with a brick instead of
a rubble core, and their facing was replaced in Portland stone,
which contributes to the somewhat over-trim and self-conscious
impression the building makes in its unhistorically exposed riverside setting (the unworthy incomplete S extension of the 1950s
by *Carden, Godfrey & Macfadyen* does not help). Inside, the
lantern, W gallery, entrance doorway, and dormer windows are
new, but the splendid timber roof is original. Its effect is remarkably delicate, quite unlike the contemporary hall roof of Eltham
Palace (Gr); like the stone fan-vaulting of this period, it displays
to the full the late medieval fascination with overlaying a simple
basic structure with complex decoration. The roof has its seven
principals in the form of depressed four-centred arches springing
from stone corbels. Each arch has three octagonal pendants linked
by smaller arches with pierced spandrels. The pendants are
connected longitudinally by little arches too. The areas between
the arches are boarded to form a ceiling. The colouring in red,
green, and gold dates from 1966 (under *Emil Godfrey*). The
louvre opening in the middle was presumably for a central hearth,
although there is also a fireplace.* The pretty lierne-vault of the
oriel has the helm and crest of Sir John Crosby on its central
boss. The doorway beyond the oriel originally led to the great
parlour. In the oriel, stained glass by *Willement* of the early C19.

DIOCESAN TRAINING COLLEGE (R.C.), 28 Beaufort Street.
Built for the convent of the Adoration Reparatrice. CHAPEL by

---

*Another fireplace from Crosby Hall is now at Hamsterley Hall, County Durham.

H. O. Corfiato & Partners, 1959, the w wall entirely filled by a forceful stone gridded window. Plain brick flank walls.

CHRIST CHURCH SCHOOLS, Christchurch Street. Gothic of 1872, three storeys. Lower infants' building of the 1850s.

PARK WALK SCHOOL. An early example of a board school: 1880 by *E. R. Robson*, three storeys of classrooms to the street, with an attractive row of shaped gables decorated with stone plaques. A more haphazard back elevation with hall and projecting stair-turret, not yet with the ordered symmetry of schools of the 1890s.

SLOANE SCHOOL, Hortensia Road. Used for further education at the time of writing. 1908 by *T. J. Bailey* of the *L.C.C.*, one of the first London schools planned entirely for secondary education (510 girls) after the Act of 1904 (cf. the very similar Fulham Cross, HF). It is an adaptation of the standard three-decker elementary school type – an imposing, slightly mannered composition on four floors. Gymnasium on the ground floor, with rusticated openings. Very tall windows to the impressive double-height assembly hall (galleries on bulgy brackets). Art rooms and laboratories above, with music rooms in the wings. The flanking towers have shaped gables. Adjoining to the s the former CARLYLE SCHOOL, with an elegant two-storey block with pedimented wings with Venetian windows, and plainer extensions of 1937.

BROMPTON HOSPITAL, Fulham Road. *See* Kensington (KC), Public Buildings 1.

BROMPTON AND NATIONAL HEART AND CHEST HOSPITAL, Sydney Street. Planned in 1984, first phase built in 1986–9 by *Watkins Gray International*. A long, deadening brick frontage facing St Luke's, quite out of tune with the scale of this part of Chelsea. The tallest parts of five storeys, around three courtyards.

CHEYNE HOSPITAL FOR CHILDREN, Cheyne Walk. 1888 by *Beazley & Burrows*, in an overblown Queen Anne style.

ROYAL MARSDEN HOSPITAL, Fulham Road. Founded in 1852 as the Free Cancer Hospital, opened on this site in 1862; many additions. Forbiddingly tall red brick buildings along the Fulham Road (q.v., Brompton Hospital, Kensington).

ST STEPHEN'S HOSPITAL, Fulham Road. The drab miscellany of buildings developed from the infirmary of St George's Union Workhouse (wards added by *Saxon Snell*, 1882–3) was partly rebuilt from 1958, beginning with an OUTPATIENTS DEPARTMENT of 1966, three storeys, crisply clad in white glass mosaic (*R. Mellor*, architect to the South East Metropolitan Regional Hospital Board). Reconstruction of the rest began in 1989.

RANELAGH GARDENS, Lower Sloane Street. Laid out *c.* 1860 by *John Gibson* on the site of the famous pleasure gardens, a place of resort from 1742 to 1803, in the grounds of the house built *c.* 1690 by the Earl of Ranelagh. The main feature of the C18 gardens was a rotunda bigger than the Pantheon.

ELECTRICITY GENERATING STATION, Flood Street. 1896 and 1901 by *Alfred Roberts* for the Chelsea Electricity Supply Company; a long brick range with faceted buttresses and round-arched windows.

POWER STATION, Lots Road. This monumental Thames-side temple to electricity was built in 1902–4 for the electricification

of the District Railway and the three other lines which formed
the Underground Electric Railway Company controlled by the
American financier Charles Tyson Yerkes. It was then the largest
electric traction station in the world, and the first to be designed
exclusively for steam turbines. Built with American money and
expertise, it was probably designed by the company's chief engineer, *J. R. Chapman*, with *Leslie Green*, architect to the company
from 1903. It is 138 metres (453 ft) long, the steel frame clothed
in brick and terracotta and articulated by a simple series of large
glazed arches. The four 84 metre chimneys were reduced to two
in 1963. The building was originally divided into boiler house
and turbine hall. Coal was brought from barges on the Thames
and conveyed by elevators to the roof of the boiler house where
eighty boilers, arranged in two storeys, supplied steam to the
eight turbo-generators in the adjoining hall. All machinery was
renewed in the 1930s and again in 1963; well preserved 1930s
control room. The future of the building is uncertain.

PERAMBULATIONS

Chelsea does not lend itself to easy perambulation; the three main
thoroughfares, King's Road, Fulham Road, and the Embankment
and Cheyne Walk, all run E–W and are unpleasantly traffic-ridden,
yet the last in particular should not be missed, for the riverside has
some of the most worthwhile buildings in London. Perambulations
1 and 2 start from All Saints' church in the centre of the old village;
1a, 2a, and 2b will be the most rewarding for the c 18 enthusiast;
1b, which continues from 1a, and 3, which starts from Knightsbridge, are predominantly high-quality late Victorian; 4 and 5,
which together make a circular tour down King's Road and back
again to cover the areas to its N, defy simple definition but best
convey the flavour of fashionable Chelsea of the c 20.

1a. *Cheyne Walk* E *of the church*

The remains of the old riverside village around the parish church
were badly damaged in the Second World War. The church has
been faithfully rebuilt, but its surroundings are now more open
than before – not the ideal setting for such a homely building. For
the area to the w see Perambulation 2b.

E of the church is a tame seated figure of Sir Thomas More, 1969
by *L. Cubitt Bevis*, and a spirited Coalbrookdale lamp standard
with boys and cornucopia, commemorating the completion of
the Chelsea Embankment in 1874.

N of the church small streets run back from the river (*see* Perambulation 2a); along the riverside is the famous CHEYNE
WALK, named after the Cheyne family who held the manor
from 1657 to 1712. The traffic pounding along the embankment
deprives this area of the charm still possessed by the c 18 riverside
terraces of Hammersmith or Chiswick, but there is still much to
enjoy both from the c 18 and the later c 19, even though the

part near the church has been sadly depleted. Starting from the church, the first surviving house of the post-Restoration riverside village type is No. 62 (later stucco and pedimented doorcase), once part of a terrace built c. 1686 by Sir Thomas Lawrence. After the Cheyne Hospital (q.v.) and the even grosser CARLYLE MANSIONS of 1886, No. 50, the KINGS HEAD AND EIGHT BELLS, a pleasant, small-scale early C19 inn. Nos. 46–48 are of c. 1711, No. 46 the least altered in front, of brown brick with red brick dressings. The backs have typical early C18 projecting closets. Good wrought-iron railings. The adjoining garden wall to the E is C16, a survival from Shrewsbury House. In the gardens in front, *Boehm*'s MONUMENT to Carlyle, 1882.

Nos. 38 and 39 are survivals from a notable group of three houses, 72 rare examples of the architectural work of the Arts and Crafts designer *C. R. Ashbee*. No. 37, his earlier Magpie and Stump of 1893–4 (built on the site of an inn of that name), was deplorably demolished in 1968 for the lumpish flats stretching far down Oakley Street. The Magpie and Stump, with its projecting oriel, belonged broadly to the Queen Anne tradition of Shaw (cf. Chelsea Embankment, Perambulation 1b); the later houses are a more free and sparing interpretation of the Old English style. The self-effacing No. 39, built as a studio house for Miss C. L. Christian, is of red brick with narrow, evenly spaced Queen Anne windows, the rhythm quickening on the roughcast second floor. At No. 38, in masterly contrast, the windows are spaced more widely, above a bold arched basement entrance, and are crowned by a memorably austere roughcast gable. Excellent, highly original iron railings decorated with gold balls. Ashbee made many other designs for Chelsea houses in a similarly picturesque but restrained idiom, but few were built; the other main group, Nos. 72–75 Cheyne Walk, was destroyed in the Second World War. We have in its stead a demonstration of later C20 aesthetics, with a SCULPTURE in front of the new flats: Boy with a Dolphin, 1975 by *David Wynne*, quite a virtuoso piece of pop art.

OAKLEY STREET was laid out c. 1860 through the grounds of the manor house demolished in 1758 and Winchester House (a C17 addition to the manor house), which was demolished in 1828. On the E side its elegant stucco-trimmed terraces are continued in the same style by Nos. 27–30 Cheyne Walk, a little crescent with a handsome tented balcony. (At the back, some C16 garden walls remain.) Then Nos. 19–26, a terrace built c. 1759–65, soon after the main part of the manor house had been demolished, with several Doric doorcases and nice railings.

Cheyne Walk E of Oakley Street, excepting only a stretch rebuilt fairly unobtrusively in the late C19, nearly all dates from c. 1717–20 – a powerful, stately group with a strong Baroque flavour, thickly overlaid with C19 artistic and literary associations. Nos. 18 and 17 are disguised by later stucco and a tented veranda. No. 16 is the largest in the group, five broad bays, well preserved in its original appearance (with the exception of the painful bay-window), its forceful elevations reminiscent of *Archer*. The builder was *John Witt*. Banded brick pilasters at the corners, windows with arched heads and stone keystones, and a central pediment. The garden side has an even more pronounced rhythm. The plan is unusual: a small hall between two front rooms, a semicircular stair behind one of them, and the dining room at the back with a recess divided off by Roman Doric columns. Plenty of excellent ironwork to the street. The initials R.C. on the house stand for the first owner, an apothecary called Richard Chapman, but the history of the house was mis-interpreted in the C19, when it was assumed to be of royal Tudor origin; hence its name Tudor House. Rossetti lived here from 1862 to nearly the time of his death; he is commemorated in the gardens opposite by *Seddon*'s Rossetti fountain. Other famous residents included Swinburne and Meredith. No. 15 also has a sumptuous iron gate and railings, but is only four bays wide. No. 14 has old ironwork but is a C20 neo-Georgian rebuild; Nos. 12–7 are intruders in the usual Queen Anne style of the 1880s. No. 6 is again early Georgian, five bays wide, three storeys high, with a parapet. Red brick dressings, moulded cornice and bands, otherwise plain. The gate and railings with Chippendale-Chinese fretwork patterns must be later C18, possibly from the time of Dr Bartholme Dominceti (*c.* 1764). Staircase with twisted balusters. The narrower No. 5 is distinguished by boldly chan-nelled quoins at the corners. Its sumptuous iron gate and railings between brick piers with carved urns may come from Lindsey House (*see* Perambulation 2b), perhaps made for Count Zinzen-dorf, i.e. *c.* 1750. No. 4 again has good ironwork and in addition a fine entrance doorway with entablature swinging up in a curved triangle in the centre, a type characteristic of the time of George I. Four bays wide, segment-headed windows with stone keystones, corners with giant Doric pilasters up to the cornice between first and second floors. (The interior is also out of the ordinary: staircase on the l. side; staircase hall painted *c.* 1730 with land-scapes between Corinthian columns; ceiling with gods on clouds. At the back, two projecting closets with angle fireplaces.) George Eliot and the painters Dyce and Maclise all lived at No. 4. No. 3 has a good doorcase with elaborate carved brackets; No. 2 was refronted in 1879 by *S. B. Clark*, but has original interiors. No. 1 is a rebuilding by *F. Hemmings* of 1887, incorporating items from other houses demolished in the area. The doorcase comes from No. 12, likewise woodwork in the library; staircase balusters from No. 8; a chimneypiece with frieze of birds and foliage from Old Radnor House in Paradise Row.

ROYAL HOSPITAL ROAD (formerly known as Paradise Row) continues w. It, too, was built up in the C18 but is now all of the late C19. Off to the s, Nos. 1–4 SWAN WALK are modest C18 outliers facing the Physick Garden (*see* Public Buildings 1). No. 2 has a brought-in doorcase with upswept head of *c.* 1720, and good iron railings with overthrow. For other remains of C18 Chelsea *see* Perambulation 2.

1b. Chelsea Embankment

This is a C19 tour which can be pursued from the E end of Cheyne Walk. CHELSEA EMBANKMENT offers one of the most inter-esting arrays in inner London of grand urban houses in the

Queen Anne style: tall, individualistic designs in red brick, some of the first to challenge the supremacy of the earlier uniform stucco terraces of Belgravia and Kensington. The busy variety of their frontages offers a revealing contrast to the more sober early C18 mood of Cheyne Walk. The Metropolitan Board of Works leased eighteen plots along the embankment after its completion in 1874. They were of a size generous enough to attract wealthy clients interested in employing artistically minded architects.

From W to E, starting at the end of Cheyne Walk, the first house is No. 18, CHEYNE HOUSE, by *Norman Shaw*, 1875–7 for George Matthey, a government assayer, ingeniously turning the corner into Royal Hospital Road with a curved ground floor and canted upper floor with plenty of Queen Anne windows. Converted to flats in 1989. Then the jewel of the group, No. 17, *Shaw's* SWAN HOUSE, 1875–7 for Wickham Flower, a solicitor with artistic interests, who employed *Morris & Co.* for his interiors (their work does not survive). Swan House adopts the 'Old English' device of a jettied first floor, which is handsomely decorated by three of Shaw's favourite oriels, of the type of Sparrowe's house at Ipswich. This floor housed the family rooms; the main reception room, stretching the length of the front, was on the floor above, lit by a charming alternation of three long narrow Queen Anne windows with three equally long slim little oriels. (In using window frames not set back from the wall plane Shaw was deliberately defying London building regulations.) No gables, but a heavy cornice, with small dormers in the roof. The whole design is amazingly original and very graceful. The interior, refurbished by *Aukett Associates* in 1985 as their own office, preserves much of its original detail, which is in an eclectic but successful mixture of styles: early Renaissance for the stone fireplaces, Georgian for the joinery. The large entrance hall with its stone fireplace leads into a generously proportioned stair hall with very tall windows rising up into a pretty stucco frieze of putti. Broad staircase in early C18 style, leading to the two main upper floors. Fine hooded fireplace on the first floor, where the main rooms are embellished with stone columns. The next house, No. 16, by *A. Croft* for A. J. Alt, makes play with curved oriels and recesses, but without Shaw's finesse. No. 15, DELAHAY HOUSE (formerly Farnley House), considerably altered, is again by *Shaw*, 1878–9 for W. J. Armitage. The broad front with its single spreading gable is given interest by a chimneystack (once taller) rising daringly through its centre.

No. 13, GARDEN CORNER, is of *c.* 1878–80 by *I'Anson*, a staid red brick exterior, but refurbished inside in 1906 for Emslie Horniman by *C. F. A. Voysey*, one of his outstanding achievements. His distinctive stamp is immediately apparent at the front door, with its excellent lettering and ironwork. The interior, like Swan House refurbished by *Aukett Associates* in 1980 as their offices, is still very complete, although Voysey's woodwork is now stained darker than originally, and fire regulations alas dictated the loss of some of his original openings and internal glazing (for example the surprising bold oculi lighting the back stairs). There are exposed ceiling beams, much oak panelling of three-quarter height, and typical Voysey fireplaces (the minor ones with birds and foliage on the second floor especially charming). The main stair around a well, with closely set stick balusters, is austerely geometric; the back stair has the tiny playful motif of carved four-way faces on the newels. On the first floor is the former library, with a plaster barrel-vault, and double doors opening to the drawing room. On the second floor, a splendid series of bedroom cupboards.

After this the sequence is broken by the Chelsea Physick Garden (*see* Public Buildings 1). At its E corner No. 12 is by *Hungerford Pollen*, 1877. Nos. 9–11 are again by *Shaw*, a speculative development by his cousin J. W. Temple, 1878–9. The routine design of narrow front with bay-window and gable is varied by the mirror-image plan of the central house. No. 8, CLOCK HOUSE, is a more ambitious *Shaw* design of 1878–80 for Mrs Erskine Wemyss. The broad front, symmetrical apart from the position of the clock, carries many rather arbitrarily disposed little motifs on top of each other. Innovative use of structural ironwork here gave Shaw the freedom to plan remarkably different interiors on each floor. The three Dutch gables that should dominate the design are unhappily compromised by crass additions. No. 7 is by *Phene Spiers*, 1878–9 for Sir Robert Collier, not unlike Nos. 4–6, 1877–8 by *E. W. Godwin*, a speculative development for Gillow & Co., busy elevations with a variety of bay-windows held together by a Doric entablature, but by no means as daring as Godwin's studios in Tite Street (*see* below). No. 3, RIVER HOUSE, is of 1876, a rare secular work by *Bodley & Garner* for the Hon. J. C. Dundas, its substantial, symmetrical seven-bay front with rubbed brick detail and Dutch gables deriving from Kew Palace. Later are No. 2, 1894, and No. 1, 1913 by *E. P. Warren* in quite a festive Wrenaissance style.

TITE STREET, laid out as a new access road to the embankment, was built up from 1877. The smaller, less expensive sites made it a paradise for artists. Studio after studio went up; most survived until the mid C20, although the best have now gone. The *enfant terrible* of the street was Whistler, for whom in 1877 *E. W. Godwin* designed No. 35 on the E side, THE WHITE HOUSE (demolished in the 1960s). The street front (toned down considerably after objections from the M.B.W.) disposed its plain white render and Italian motifs so wilfully and asymmetrically that the total effect was almost art nouveau. The survivors are less daring. On the E side Nos. 33 and 31 are by *R. W. Edis*, 1880 and 1878–9, in two colours of brick, with large arched windows. On the W side (from N to S), the red brick terrace Nos. 28–42 was a speculation by *Butler & Beeston* of 1879–80. No. 44 is of 1878 by *Godwin* for Frank Miles, the friend of Oscar Wilde, with two low floors and a lofty studio window above. The Queen Anne trimmings were added to placate the M.B.W., dissatisfied with Godwin's originally starker design. Inside, a staircase with thin Japanese-style woodwork and, in the studio, a big inglenook fireplace with its own little window. No. 46, THE TOWER HOUSE, also by *Godwin*, c. 1884, has four huge superimposed studio windows with small panes of glass (top altered) abruptly contrasted with eight floors of small windows. The narrower No. 48 is by *C. J. C.*

Pawley, F. S. Waller & Sons for John Collier (whose father built
No. 7 on the Embankment).

2a. The C 18 village: streets N of Cheyne Walk

The streets N of Cheyne Walk in the neighbourhood of the church,
described here from W to E, are a pleasantly small-scale network,
still with a good assortment of c 18 houses. First OLD CHURCH
STREET, with nothing much to single out, but on an agreeably
homely scale; new developments have been tucked in tactfully
behind older frontages (see e.g. Nos. 26–28 by *Francis Bennett
Associates, 1985*). On the E side Nos. 34–38, with remains of a
Georgian shopfront with sliding shutters. On the W side miscellaneous early c 19 houses, and the taller HEREFORD BUILD-
INGS, Gothic working-class flats of 1878 by *Elijah Hoole*, built
for associates of Octavia Hill, a reminder of the poverty and
overcrowding that existed at this time in the centre of old Chelsea.
To the W, in contrast to the intimacy of the old village, a glimpse
down PAULTONS STREET reveals the regular stucco-trimmed
terraces of PAULTONS SQUARE of the 1830s: three balanced
groups with raised centres, the westernmost of the polite suburban squares off King's Road (q.v., Perambulation 4). Further
up Old Church Street on the E side, No. 56, the RECTORY, its
large garden an oasis in this tightly knit area. The house has an
early Georgian core, much added to. A low, spread-out entrance
front with projecting wings of *c*. 1900 in an c 18 spirit (Venetian
windows, and odd pedimental gables pierced by corner piers).
On the garden side a large semicircular bow added in the later
c18.

Now by JUSTICE WALK, past a former Wesleyan chapel of 1841,
a plain pedimented front with three widely spaced windows on
two floors, to LAWRENCE STREET, which led to Lawrence
House, one of the large mansions of Chelsea, demolished in 1835.
Nos. 23–24 (DUKE'S HOUSE, MONMOUTH HOUSE) are an
early Georgian group with segment-headed windows and one
pediment on carved brackets for both the doors together. To its
S a mid Victorian Peabody estate (a tidying-up of the 'garden
surrounded with rather dim houses and questionable miscellanea
among other things clothes drying' described by Carlyle in 1834).
Further N on the W side there is still a terrace of mid c 18 two-
storey mansard-roofed cottages. Chelsea porcelain was manufactured in Lawrence Street from 1745 to 1784, becoming
especially famous under Nicholas Sprimont from 1749 until
1769.

UPPER CHEYNE ROW runs E from Lawrence Street, with Georgian houses of a smaller and cheaper type than those closer to the
river. Nos. 28–24, 22 (the home of Leigh Hunt), and 20 were
built *c*. 1716. No. 16 has a first-floor Venetian window dated
1767. The street runs across the grander CHEYNE ROW, where
the fame of the terrace Nos. 16–34 owes more to its former
inhabitants than to purely architectural qualities. The houses are
much altered; the modillion frieze that would have bound them
all together appears now only on Nos. 16, 18, 26, and 34. They

were begun in 1708 (see the dated tablet on No. 16) and have the same curious rhythm with one narrow blank bay at one side of the house which is found on the contemporary houses of Queen Anne's Gate in Westminster. Fine shell hood to the doorway of No. 32, carved brackets to Nos. 18 and 30. Carlyle lived at No. 24 from 1834 until his death in 1881. As early as 1895 the house was acquired as a museum devoted to his memory, and restored by *C. R. Ashbee*; it passed to the National Trust in 1936. Highly atmospheric Victorian interiors: basement kitchen, ground-floor parlour, Jane Carlyle's drawing room on the first floor, and Carlyle's sparse, roomy attic study made in 1853. Early C18 back closets and staircase (both balusters and newels of spiral form). Nos. 10 and 12 at the S end are also C18, the adjoining houses early C19. At the N end De Morgan had his pottery from 1872 to 1882.

The N end of Cheyne Row becomes GLEBE PLACE, where by far the most interesting house is No. 35, a studio house of 1868–71 by *Philip Webb* for the artist George Boyce, a design both sound and imaginative; a three-bay front with projecting two-storey porch looks down the street, red brick with white sash-windows, one of the earliest occurrences of this symptom of Queen Anne revival, although not as exciting as Webb's earlier work at Red House Bexley (Bx) or in Kensington Palace Gardens (KC), and of course nothing like as entertaining as Shaw's work of the 1870s. The wing on the W side was added by Webb in 1876 and is more obviously picturesque, with two tiny tilehung gablets and a tall chimney. The hall consisted originally of a tall studio with gallery, since floored over. Glebe Place was one of Chelsea's artistic centres. Further E No. 49, *Charles Rennie Mackintosh*'s only London building, a house and studio designed in 1920, late in the architect's life. The distinctive elevation has been emasculated by the upper floor added in 1924, but Mackintosh's austere white plastered ground floor remains, with the quirky feature of a continuous raised band running over the end doors and below the two central windows, between which a chimney-stack originally rose above the low eaves. No. 50, by *Frank Lowe*, with tall, eclectic entrance tower, is of 1985–7.

Now briefly into KING'S ROAD to take in a few buildings on the S side predating the rapid development of this area in the second third of the C19. The most important is No. 211, ARGYLE HOUSE, 1723 by *Leoni* for John Pierene, a severe brick house of two storeys and five bays whose Doric entablature on Tuscan demi-columns is connected with the balcony of the pedimented central upper window. Good iron gate with overthrow; inside, a spacious staircase of three flights around an open well. Nos. 213 and 215 are of 1720, very perfect specimens of their date; windows with straight heads of rubbed brick. The low Nos. 229–231 preserve traces of a Georgian shopfront. Then an irregular mixture, No. 235, C18 above later shopfronts, and the pleasantly haphazard group of Nos. 247–253, before reaching Paultons Square (*see* above), through which one can return towards the river. For the rest of King's Road *see* Perambulation 4.

2b. Cheyne Walk w of the church

w of the church ROPERS GARDENS, a sunken garden opened in
1965 in a bomb-damaged area, with some SCULPTURE: The
Awakening, a bronze figure by *Gilbert Ledward*; and an unfinished stone relief by *Epstein*, in a setting by *Stephen Gardiner*,
commemorating the site of the studios where Epstein worked
from 1909 to 1914. The main landmark further E is the transplanted Crosby Hall (*see* Public Buildings 2), still looking alien
and self-conscious.

Beyond Beaufort Street (laid out in 1766 after Beaufort House had
been demolished), Nos. 91–100 CHEYNE WALK belong to the
best that Chelsea has to offer. They were built after the Moravians
sold off some of the land attached to Lindsey House (*see* below).
No. 91, BELLE VUE LODGE, 1771, has a Venetian window to
Beaufort Street and a glazed veranda to the river (although sadly
no longer with its original iron supports and Gothic glazing).
No. 92, BELLE VUE HOUSE, also of 1771, is unusually large; an
ingenious composition worthy of Adam, with central bay-
window and Venetian windows to its l. and r., above a broad
tripartite doorway under a shallow arched head, matched by a
carriageway on the other side. Nos. 93 and 94 are simpler, of
1777, No. 94 with charming early Victorian balcony carried
round the flank wall. Nos. 95–100 are LINDSEY HOUSE, much
altered, but still recognizable as a single house, the only surviving
example in Chelsea on such a scale. It was originally built (or
more likely remodelled from an older building) *c.* 1674 for Robert
Bertie, third Earl of Lindsey. Drawings show a plain three-
storeyed house of eleven bays with a quoined centre with pediment and two quoined corner pavilions of unequal size. In 1752,
after the house had been acquired by Count Zinzendorf as the
headquarters of the Moravian community in England, major
alterations were made by the Moravian architect *Sigismund von
Gersdorf*. The attic floor was heightened, the mansard roof added,
the l. pavilion enlarged, and the interior much altered. After
Count Zinzendorf's death in 1760, the Moravians fell on hard
times, and the house was sold and divided up in 1775 (although
they retained their burial ground to the N, off Milman's Street, *see*
Perambulation 4). In No. 99 a corner fireplace of 1674 survives;
staircases of 1752 remain in No. 97 and (reset) in No. 100, where
the entrance and bay-window were added by *Devey* in 1890.
Whistler lived in No. 96 from 1866 to 1879; Brunel the great
engineer and John Martin the painter in No. 98. The gardens of
Nos. 99 and 100 were re-done to designs by *Lutyens*.

The glory of Chelsea ends with Lindsey House. Further w is
BRUNEL HOUSE by *Armstrong & MacManus*, *c.* 1950, with
big, rather clumsy inset balcony bays, replacing a war-damaged
patch, but at least respecting the scale of the scatter of minor
Georgian houses and cottages between Nos. 107 and 116. Nos.
118–119 (much rebuilt) has a pretty plaque commemorating the
residence of the painter Turner, who lived here incognito late in
his life.

By the riverside, the end of Cheyne Walk is marked by the new
CREMORNE GARDENS at Chelsea Wharf, created in 1982. Re-

erected here is the fine white-painted wrought-iron gateway with the royal arms that stood at the King's Road end of the original gardens, which belonged to Lord Cremorne's house and were open as a public pleasure ground between 1845 and 1877.

To the N, all is dominated by the brown brickwork of the World's End estate stretching up to King's Road (*see* Perambulation 4), the last phase in the reconstruction of this part of Chelsea. Further W rehabilitation became the policy from 1977: here the low C19 terraces in the shadow of the Lots Road power station (q.v.) belong in character to the artisan stretches of neighbouring Fulham, built up in the hinterland of the formerly industrial riverside. Among them are interspersed tactful new buildings on a sympathetic scale. In TADEMA ROAD the workshops at No. 39, 1985 by *Moxley & Frankl,* introduce a spare post-modern note; orange brick, with deep eaves on thin brackets.

3. The Cadogan estate between Knightsbridge and Sloane Square

The development of the E part of Chelsea began in 1771, when *Henry Holland* took a lease from Lord Cadogan, the lord of the manor, and laid out HANS TOWN. His own house, called Sloane Place or the Pavilion (Holland was the architect of the first Royal Pavilion at Brighton), was built *c.* 1789 to the N of Hans Place. Sloane Street and Sloane Square were laid out further E and named in deference to Sir Hans Sloane, Lord Cadogan's father-in-law. Almost nothing of all this remains. The centre of the estate was developed from the late 1870s, as the Hans Town leases fell in; Cadogan Square was created in the grounds of the Pavilion. The new buildings were in the style dubbed by Osbert Lancaster 'Pont Street Dutch' – tall, sparingly decorated red brick mansions for very wealthy occupants, in the semi-Dutch, semi-Queen-Anne manner of Shaw or George & Peto. The N end of the area was largely rebuilt in more piecemeal fashion *c.* 1900.

Starting from the Knightsbridge end of Sloane Street, one approaches the heart of the area by minor streets rebuilt at the turn of the century. BASIL STREET leads off W, with exuberant 1890s mansion flats sporting flurries of curvaceous bows and balconies. No. 24 is the least altered of a group of three houses by *Arnold Mitchell* (illustrated 1907), an effectively spare design with steep gables and square porch projections. Beyond the back of Harrods (*see* Kensington (KC), Perambulation 3b), in HANS ROAD, is an especially innovative group, Nos. 12–16. Nos. 14–16 are by *Voysey* for Archibald Grove, M.P., 1891 – among his earliest work. The funny little oriel windows are still a sign of dependence on Shaw, but the rhythm of the façades is deliberately different from that prevailing in the neighbourhood: horizontal not vertical, with reduced storey heights, horizontal windows with unmoulded mullions, a curving parapet instead of gables, and the two porches tied together and decorated with a little Arts and Crafts ornament. The doors and surrounds are typical of the architect. (Original panelling inside No. 16.) No. 12 is by *A. Mackmurdo*, 1894, more conventional, although it was Mackmurdo who influenced Voysey in other work. No. 12 takes its ceiling heights and the Shavian oriel from the Voysey houses, although its front demonstrates that its designer always had more sympathy for Italy than did Voysey (see for example the heavy pediment over the door). Hans Road abuts WALTON PLACE, with two formal terraces of c. 1830 by *George Basevi*, marking the E edge of the stuccoland of Kensington (q.v., Perambulation 3b). In WALTON STREET, WALTON HOUSE, 1882–4 by *Shaw*, a tall gabled house and studio for E. S. Kennedy. Hans Road continues into HANS PLACE, a rectangle with bevelled corners, as laid out by *Holland* around a leafy garden, but with only a few houses remaining from the late Georgian period (Nos. 15, 33–34).

The tall red brick gables of the late C19 which dominate the s end of Hans Place belong with Pont Street and Cadogan Square to the s. In few other places in London can the prosperous 1880s be studied more profitably. The houses in this area, a mixture of individual commissions and speculative groups, began to be laid out in the grounds of Holland's Pavilion in the late 1870s by the Cadogan and Hans Place Estate Ltd, established in 1875.

In CADOGAN SQUARE there is plenty that deserves individual study (described here clockwise from the E). The E side, of 1879, is the least interesting, with unadventurous terraces by *G. T. Robinson*. No. 61 is an early example of high-class mansion flats, No. 61a, off the SE corner, a studio house built for F. W. Lawson. The S side is largely by *J. J. Stevenson* (who designed the Cadogan estate chairman's own house in Lowther Gardens, Kensington, Perambulation 3a). Nos. 63–73 date from 1885–6, Nos. 75–79 from 1879–82; their novelty lies in the way their similar plans are concealed behind varied frontages, in reaction against the traditional uniformity of London speculative terraces. This quest for individuality is taken still further on the W side, the showpiece of the square, where generous fronts and expressive gables provide a vision of prosperous burghers of Bruges or Amsterdam. They start with an oddity, No. 84, STUART HOUSE, a substantial house at the S end, adorned with reliefs of the life of Mary Queen of Scots. It was designed c. 1880 and built in 1883–4 for O. L. Stephen, a director of the Great Northern Railway, by *F. G. Knight*, with *Hunt & Steward*. Nos. 76–82 are possibly also by *Knight*, 1885–6. Nos. 68–74 are an effective alternation: 70 and 74 by *A. J. Adams*; 72 and 68 by *Shaw*, 1877–9 and 1878. Shaw's 58 houses are distinguished by their huge, Dutch-looking windows with unusually small panes and by taller, elaborate gables. Their exteriors have been confused by the removal of the porch and doorway to No. 72. No. 68 has an interior characteristic of Shaw's ingenious handling of large and small spaces: a back dining room one and a half storeys high, a small mezzanine, and a first-floor living room the whole depth of the house. The variety of gables is continued by Nos. 64–66. No. 62 is again by *Shaw*, 1881–3, this time with stone mullioned windows. Nos. 54–58 were an undertaking for Lord Cadogan himself, 1877 by *William Young* (who had already designed Lord Cadogan's own house in Cadogan Place, since demolished). Queen Anne detail in the grand manner, with tall Ionic pilasters linking first and second storeys. No. 60, the end house on the l., intended to balance the group, was built to a different design by *Knight* in 1887–8. No. 52, a glorious apotheosis of Flemish Renaissance, is of 1885 for T.A. de la Rue by *Ernest George* of *George & Peto* (cf. his houses in South Kensington). Much riotous decoration in buff and red terracotta. The porch, in a canted bay on the l., leads into an excellent entrance hall with Renaissance overmantel and carved beams and staircase. No. 50, with sober gable in effective contrast, is also by *George*, 1886–7 for Colonel A.W. Thynne. The group of Nos. 28–36, with curly gables and a generous quantity of stone dressings, strikes a different note again: it is by *Devey*, designed *c.* 1886, built in 1888–9 after his death, with some modifications, by his assistant *Isaac Williams*. Nos. 22–26 are by *E.T. Hall*, quite an entertaining mixture of roughcast, tilehanging and half-timbering. Finally the N side, with Nos. 6–18, another terrace by *Robinson*, and No. 4, at the corner, by *Street*, 1879 for the Misses Monk. This (as one might expect from a church architect) is a Gothic intruder, with pretty stone balcony at the side, and Street's characteristically charming and inventive ironwork. No. 2 at the corner of Pont Street, with a little turret and elaborate stone carving, is of 1880–1 for the son of Lord Cranbrook, probably by *David Brandon* (who designed Lord Cranbrook's house in Kent).

PONT STREET is enjoyable in the aggregate, but the houses, nearly all speculative groups, are individually of less interest. On the N side Nos. 26–40, with a mixture of Gothic and Baroque detail, are by *C.W. Stephens*; Nos. 42–58 are by *J.J. Stevenson*, Nos. 60–66 by *W. Niven*. On the S side, after two more terraces by *Robinson* (Nos. 13–39, of *c.* 1876–83), Nos. 47–53, with jolly gables, by *E.T. Hall, c.* 1886; Nos. 55–65 by *E.H. Bouchier*; and No. 67 by *C.W. Stephens*, 1884, enlivened by upper floors with patterned tiles. To the W LENNOX GARDENS, laid out *c.* 1885 on land belonging to Smith's Charity, with more in the same spirit, especially the E curve, where Nos. 17–43 (the last dated 1885) make an enjoyably varied show. On the w side *Harrison Townsend* was responsible for Lord Compton's house (probably No. 54 at the corner), 1883–4, and for four houses for the builder W.H. Willis. The pattern is interrupted further s by quieter early C19 stucco streets: MILNER STREET, MOORE STREET, and HALSEY STREET, the last two leading into CADOGAN STREET. On the s side, near St Mary's church (q.v.), ST JOSEPH'S COTTAGES, slightly Gothic almshouses around a courtyard, largely reconstructed in 1966. The original buildings were by *Pugin, c.* 1850, as was the SCHOOL of 1841, also much rebuilt. The RECTORY, SE of the church, added by *Bentley* in 1877–9, also forms part of the group. Further W towards Draycott Avenue, C20 flats (replacing early workmen's dwellings of the 1890s by the Guinness Trust). The Cadogan Square style reappears to the S and E, with rather less charm, in the more cramped setting of DRAYCOTT PLACE (*c.* 1889 etc.) and in CADOGAN GARDENS. No. 25 Cadogan Gardens, since 1939 part of Peter Jones, is by *A.H. Mackmurdo*, 1893, for the Australian artist Mortimer Mempes, a distinctive elevation with emphatic vertically linked upper windows running up to prominent coved eaves. w from here in CULFORD GARDENS, No. 18, a well designed piece of infilling, 1987.

PETER JONES, still one of London's most likeable modern build- 95 ings, occupies the whole of the w side of SLOANE SQUARE. It was designed from 1932 and built in 1935-7 to designs by *J. A. Slater & A. H. Moberly* and *William Crabtree*, with *C. H. Reilly* as consultant. The first part to be built faced Cadogan Gardens; the later parts incorporate this and the N wing of 1889-95 into a single block. Crabtree and Reilly determined the chief features of the design, the delicate external vertical steel members which articulate the horizontal bands of upright windows, and which are carried right round the curved l. corner into King's Road. It was one of the first examples of the use of the curtain wall in England (preceded only by Owen Williams's Boots factory at Beeston, Notts), and is still one of the most elegant. The parts facing King's Road and Sloane Square are based on 4 ft centres, with mullions clad in manganese bronze (an improvement on the close-set stainless steel mullions of phase one). Only the roof-line is not adequately resolved, because the intended roof-top swimming pool was not built. The extension linking the King's Road section to Cadogan Gardens dates from 1937, enlarged at the back in 1965. Inside, two light-wells, with galleried upper floors. *Franz Singer* advised on aspects of the interior layout.

Sloane Square originated in the late C18 but is now all late C19 and C20. It is enlightening to compare Peter Jones, as the outstanding example of the commercial style of c. 1935, with an example of thirty years earlier: Nos. 34-36 on the S side, a very solid block of shops, offices, and flats for Willetts, the builders, by *Amos F. Faulkner* and *E. W. Mountford*, 1904-11, stone-faced, with rustication and giant columns, and a roof with a busy row of striped chimneys. On the E side the ROYAL COURT THEATRE, 1888 by *Bertie Crewe*. In the centre of the square a FOUNTAIN by *Gilbert Ledward*, installed in 1953. S of Sloane Square LOWER SLOANE STREET and SLOANE GARDENS are Cadogan estate rebuilding of 1887 onwards, undertaken by *William Willett*, with houses designed by *H. B. Measures* (apart from Nos. 2-4 Lower Sloane Street, 1898 by *A. F. Faulkner*).

SLOANE STREET is bitty townscape with a preponderance of C20 flats, but still with one or two reminders of its former Georgian elegance, especially No. 123, with an unusual doorcase, and No. 91, with *Coade* stone voussoirs. The Cadogan Square style reappears, appropriately, with the CADOGAN HOTEL at the S corner of Pont Street, by *H. B. Brace*, 1884, and the block opposite by *H. B. Measures*, c. 1885. Nos. 63-64 are houses of the 1790s, remodelled by *Fairfax Wade*. No. 64 is a narrow but extraordinarily bold Baroque composition of 1895-7, all in black and white, with giant arches on pilasters. Also by *Wade*, No. 3 Hans Street, behind. Of the C20 contributions, by far the most distinguished is No. 55, the DANISH EMBASSY, by *Arne Jacobsen*, completed 1977. It is an immaculate, well articulated design, but uncomfortably impersonal, and with disappointing textures (painted aluminium and concrete were substituted for the intended cladding of bronze and black granite). The street front has a recessed ground floor, with three upper floors with narrow horizontal windows in five bays emphatically defined by curved surrounds. Set back behind is a taller curtain-walled slab; also mews flats in the same idiom. The embassy faces CADOGAN PLACE, a long strip of gardens along Sloane Street (with SCULPTURE of Dancers by *David Wynne*, 1974). On the E side well preserved stretches of early C19 terraces. On the N side the eighteen-storey stone-faced tower of the CARLTON TOWER HOTEL, by *M. Rosenauer*, 1961. Glass murals inside by *F. Topolski*. Next to it, CHELSEA HOUSE, flats by *Thomas Tait* of 1935, on the site of the C19 Cadogan town house by *William Young*. Nos. 190–192 is a sleek curtain-walled block of 1964–5 by *Brett & Pollen*, built for Sekers, resting on four widely spaced columns. Between here and Knightsbridge much indifferent rebuilding of the C20 housing expensive shops with fashionably minimalist interiors of the 1980s.

4. *King's Road from Sloane Square to World's End*

KING'S ROAD began in the late C17 as the King's private royal drive to Hampton Court, and until the early C19 was bordered by market gardens, with a few houses only in the vicinity of Old Church Street (*see* Perambulation 2a). Its transformation into a main artery for genteel suburban expansion took place chiefly *c.* 1830–50. This period can still be appreciated in the neighbouring streets and squares; King's Road itself is mostly overwhelmed by the C20 shops and restaurants which sprang up in response to its reputation from the 1960s onwards as a fashionable parade ground.

Starting from Sloane Square and Peter Jones (*see* Perambulation 3), on the s side first the C20 additions to the Duke of York's Headquarters (*see* Public Buildings 1). Opposite is one of the few remaining coherent stretches of mid C19 stucco development: No. 72, the former Colville Tavern (1843–4), and the terrace up to Anderson Street, quite modest in scale, but articulated by giant pilasters. Nos. 114–116 are earlier, a larger brick pair in the spare, elegant style of *c.* 1800. Behind No. 122, KING'S WALK MALL, a stylish three-level covered shopping area of 1987–9 by *Damond Lock, Grabowski & Partners,* all chrome, glass, and mirrors, with escalators, glass elevators, and even a suspension bridge crammed into its sleek little atrium. To the s, ROYAL AVENUE, a broad gravelled expanse between disappointingly weedy lime trees, laid out in 1692–4 to connect the Royal Hospital (q.v.) with William III's Kensington Palace, a project as bold as the contemporary avenues through Bushey Park to Hampton Court. It got no farther than King's Road. The terrace on its w side dates from the early C19; the E side is a little later, with its N end rebuilt in the mid C20. Overlooking BURTON'S COURT with its plane trees, formerly a parterre in front of the hospital, is ST LEONARD'S TERRACE, pleasant piecemeal development of the later C18 onwards. Five houses at the w end were built by 1795. The older houses are all in brick; good pedimented door-cases to Nos. 27–29. No. 25 was rebuilt in 1968: a tactful brick front by *Sir Hugh Casson* conceals a luxurious interior by *John*

Fowler including a first-floor living room with balcony overlooking the double-height dining room at the back, and a staircase
by *Philip Jebb* with marble treads, glass balusters, and a brass
handrail. Further W TEDWORTH SQUARE, late C 19, the N side
rebuilt in 1978–81 by *Chapman Taylor Partners*; quite a lively
composition in brown brick, with projecting bays and porches.
Back to King's Road up SMITH STREET, with more of the late
C 18 on the W side, early C 19 opposite; some houses with nice
Coade keystones. The small C 19 stuccoed SMITH TERRACE, off
to the W, may be mentioned as an example of the pleasant but
unexceptional minor Chelsea street smartly dolled up in C 20
pastel colours, by now too commonplace to deserve repeated
reference.

The characteristic feature of this part of King's Road is the handsome elongated squares opening up to N and S, interspersed with
lesser service streets and mews alleys. They start on the S (just E
of Smith Street) with WELLINGTON SQUARE, all stuccoed,
built in 1830–52 by *Francis Edwards*, and on the N with
MARKHAM SQUARE, laid out *c.* 1836 (stuccoed ground floors,
good balconies and railings). A little further on, No. 151 King's
Road, THE PHEASANTRY, with a flamboyant Louis XV façade
and a triumphal entrance arch to its front courtyard with caryatids and quadriga. The façade and the odd, extremely heavy
display of Grecian enthusiasm were added to an earlier house in
1881 by the artist and interior decorator Amédée Joubert, who
used the premises as his showroom and workshop before it
became well known as a C 20 club. The name is derived from the
time of an earlier owner, Samuel Baker, a bird dealer, *c.* 1865.
But all except the front and gateway now dates from 1971–81,
together with the bland buildings in Jubilee Place (*Graham James
Associates*). On the S side, at the corner of Chelsea Manor Street,
the pretty group with shops below an upper floor with Gothic
arches was built as a Methodist Sunday school in 1903 (*see*
Churches). Nos. 195–197, the former Six Bells pub, by *C.R.
Crickmay*, 1898, is in a larger-than-life Old English style in the
manner of Shaw or George: two splendidly lavish storeys of
Ipswich windows below three picturesque jettied gables. After
Sydney Street on the N side comes a clutch of public buildings
(q.v.) marking the Edwardian civic centre of Chelsea; also No.
250, the former Poor Law Guardians' offices, 1903 by *Lansdell
& Harrison*, unremarkable free Jacobean. It stands next to
DOVEHOUSE GREEN, a welcome public space, formerly a burial
ground given by Sir Hans Sloane in 1733. An obelisk and a few
tombstones remain. Then, on the site of Chelsea Manor House
and its grounds, OAKLEY STREET, running down to Albert
Bridge, with stately, regular terraces of *c.* 1850–60 on each side
(*see* Perambulation 1a) and MARGARETTA TERRACE off to its
E, a quiet leafy back street, but with a surprisingly grand centrepiece of engaged Corinthian columns. Both streets were
developed by a local notable, Dr J.S. Phené. Back in King's
Road, after a few good C 18 houses (Nos. 211 etc.) near where
Old Church Street leads to the riverside village (*see* Perambulation 2a), the last two squares of the King's Road:
CARLYLE SQUARE to the N, especially generous in scale, with

grand semi-detached houses built after 1862, and the quieter, stuccoed PAULTONS SQUARE to the s of after 1836.

Further w there is a shift in both social pattern and architectural character. A meeting ground for the different orders was provided by No. 350, formerly the CARLYLE GARAGES, of reinforced concrete and steel faced in white faience, built in 1924 by *Robert Sharp* for the Bluebird Motor Company (see the decorative gatepiers). Segregated waiting rooms were provided for chauffeurs, ladies, and owner-drivers. The main building, with workshops and space for 300 cars, has its first floor suspended from the trussed steel roof to avoid the interference of supports in the ground-floor display areas.

BEAUFORT STREET to the s passes the site of Beaufort House, Sir Thomas More's mansion, demolished in the C18. The street's most prominent buildings today are ST THOMAS MORE BUILDINGS on the E side, the first new housing built by the borough, five hefty blocks of flats, 1903–4 by *Joseph & Smithem.* Red brick cheerfully embellished with stone quoins and some carving, and varied gables, although nothing like as picturesque as L.C.C. work of this time. Built to provide 261 self-contained tenements, with eight bathrooms and a drying-room in one of the basements. The contemporary red brick terraces opposite were built for better-off artisans by the Metropolitan Industrial Dwellings Co. An earlier effort at improved working-class housing is illustrated a little further w by THE PORTICOS, on the N side of King's Road, now very select, but originally built in 1885 by *Elijah Hoole* for the Chelsea Park Dwellings Company as sixty labourers' dwellings, complete with central garden, 'in a rural style ... to avoid the barrack-like appearance too common in industrial dwellings' (cf. Hoole's similarly motivated cottages in Southwark). Two three-storey ranges, the one to the street conspicuously picturesque (though hardly rural), with shops below giant red brick Gothic arches, tilehanging and patterned roughcast above.

The bend in King's Road creates quite attractive townscape, spoilt somewhat by the traffic and by No. 355, a custard-coloured tower on the s side (built as council flats by *Chamberlin Powell & Bon,* 1969, revamped by *Fitch & Co.* in 1988 as private flats with new top floor and new cladding to hide the problematic loadbearing brickwork). A glimpse N reveals the spire of St John with St Andrew; No. 400, KINGS HOUSE, of *c.* 1900, looks E with cheerful brick and stone chequer upper floor, while on the s side the WATER RAT, a sweet stuccoed pub, marks the corner of MILMAN'S STREET. The trees behind belong to the former C18 MORAVIAN BURIAL GROUND (now a private garden), established around the former stables of Beaufort House when the Moravians occupied Lindsey House in Cheyne Walk (*see* Perambulation 2b).

The area w of Milman's Street, the poor end of Chelsea village, is now entirely of the C20. First the CREMORNE ESTATE, the borough's major post-war redevelopment. *Armstrong & Mac-Manus* produced a master plan in 1948 for rebuilding the area with 809 dwellings; work began in 1949 with flats in Riley Street (planned already in 1944). The main feature of the estate is a

series of typically neat but uninspiring 1950s slabs ranged behind
a low, austere terrace with shops along the S side of King's Road.
Beyond it, the effervescent WORLD'S END, a pub rebuilt in
1897, has happily survived the road-widening schemes, and steps
out with florid bows and corner turret.

Beyond lies an irregular paved piazza, the prelude to the cluster of
tall chamfered brown brick towers which forms the distinctive
Thames-side landmark of the WORLD'S END ESTATE. This 112
was the later stage of the redevelopment of west Chelsea, carried
out by *Eric Lyons, Cadbury-Brown, Metcalfe & Cunningham*, the
firm which made its reputation from its friendly small-scale Span
estates of the 1950s. Planned from 1961 for the borough of
Chelsea, begun in 1967, and completed ten years later, its laudable intention was to translate the virtues of low-rise housing
into a humane high-rise development on a grand scale (2,500
people). In compensation for the extra-high density (270 p.p.a.
over the whole site, or 350 for the housing area alone), sensitive
landscaping and plenty of local amenities were provided, including a variety of shops, community centre, school, and Methodist
church in the lower buildings which undulate pleasantly around
the paved pedestrian piazza. The use of brick as a facing material
not only for these but for the intricately angled towers as well
(which caused some constructional problems) was an early
example of the reaction against the brutalist aesthetic which had
dominated so much high-rise housing from the later 1950s. The
polygonal module is ingeniously used to create tightly knit, quite
picturesque groups of low and high buildings around two large
courtyards, successfully avoiding the traditional solution of dull
segregated boxes. The individual flats are generously planned,
with large private balconies. Yet the overall impression remains
daunting, a maze both too large and too complicated to inspire
confidence and affection.

The N side of this end of King's Road is still almost completely
residential, the mid C19 terraces broken only by No. 536, a
package of offices with flats behind, 1979 by *Sir John Burnet Tait
& Partners*, built on the site of a brewery. Their plain brick bulk
is uncomfortably at odds with the quite elegantly detailed groups
of C19 stuccoed houses stretching up EDITH GROVE and
GUNTER GROVE, outliers of the classier Gunter estate development around Redcliffe Gardens (q.v. Kensington, Perambulation
4b). Further W, past the large educational campus enfolding
Stanley House (*see* Public Buildings 2, Chelsea College), beyond
the railway line, is WANDON ROAD, with a small pocket of
borough housing built on railway land in 1958–60 by *Bridgwater
& Shepheard*; an eleven-storey tower and lower buildings,
including eight artists' studios.

5. Between King's Road and Fulham Road

This is a bitty area which can be explored as a continuation of
Perambulation 4 (*see* above). It was developed intermittently during
the C19, and patchily rebuilt in the C20 with housing ranging from
cosy Arts and Crafts cottages to some of the most rebarbative blocks
of flats in London.

Starting from opposite World's End, LAMONT ROAD is the main W–E route through a neat grid of stucco terraces extending as far as PARK WALK, where an earlier C19 group remains to the N of St John with St Andrew's church (a replacement of an older chapel). To the NW, in LIMERSTON ROAD, a council development of 1954–8 (*Chelsea Borough Engineer's Department*), intended to be in keeping with Chelsea traditions: mostly flats, including eight studios, but tactfully disguised as semi-detached villas. To the E, CHELSEA PARK GARDENS, a modestly picturesque redevelopment on part of the Sloane Stanley estate (*see* The Vale, below), with groups of small houses in grey and red brick with a variety of gables and tiled mansards, begun in 1913, but mostly built in 1923–8, by *E. F. M. Elms* and *Sydney Jupp*. To the N of this ELM PARK ROAD modulates from low stuccoed villas to more overpowering brick terraces of the later C19 overlooking ELM PARK GARDENS, a communal green space which helps to leaven the tall, somewhat grim surrounding houses of gault brick (complete by 1885). It was laid out by *George Godwin*, and really belongs in character to the parts of Kensington N of Fulham Road (q.v., Perambulation 4b). The central house on Fulham Road and parts of the flanking terraces were rebuilt as flats after the Second World War. Elm Park Gardens occupies the site of a mansion called Chelsea Park, whose grounds were planted with mulberry trees in 1721 in the hope of establishing the silk industry here.

The area to the S, part of the Sloane Stanley estate, remained a secluded spot until the end of the C19, with a few detached houses, popular with artists (William de Morgan and Whistler were among the residents). Its redevelopment began *c.* 1909, when THE VALE was extended N to Elm Park Gardens, and a neo-Georgian block of flats with canted bays (Nos. 2–8) was built by *Elms* and *Jupp* (*see* above) on the E side. The sequence on the W side is mostly in grey and red brick and dates from *c.* 1913; Nos. 9–11 is dated 1912; No. 27 is the most out-of-the-ordinary, with a Venetian window in a jettied timber-framed wing projecting to the street. Development in a low-key 'artistic' manner continued in two new streets to the E, Mulberry Walk and Mallord Street, with small houses in an Arts and Crafts or neo-Georgian idiom by a variety of architects. The street frontages are deliberately varied in their materials, with plentiful use of the projecting bays and wooden doorcases that required special exemption from the London Building Acts. The tone is set by the sequence of 1913 by *Alfred Cox* and *F. E. Williams* on the S side of MULBERRY WALK, where the dominant motifs are again grey and red brick, tiled dormers, and canted bays with sash-windows (see especially Nos. 14–16, 2–4). On the N side No. 3 (1912) was the home of Leonard Stokes, No. 5 (1913) of the Danish designer Arild Rosencrantz, an odd, mannered stripped classical design in brick, with a pair of stone doorcases. In MALLORD STREET No. 28 was built for Augustus John in 1913–14, the studio at the back concealed behind a trim Dutch vernacular front: tall raised main floor with central door, pantiled roof with central chimney, an early work by the Dutch architect *Robert van t'Hoff*. At the W end two taller houses. No. 6, five bays with integral garage, is by *W. D. Caröe*, 1912, for Percy Morris of Elm Park Gardens (a benefactor of St Peter, Cranleigh Gardens, *see* Kensington), intended at first for his coachman. At the NE corner, MALLORD HOUSE is a studio house of 1911 for Cecil Hunt by *Ralph Knott*, the architect of County Hall, a strikingly austere but well detailed version of brick vernacular in the Lutyens tradition; entrance recessed behind a round-headed brick arch with massive keystone, a shallow oriel above, very simple casement windows flush with the wall, clustered brick stacks. The punning cast-iron frieze of a hunting scene between the windows is by *G. P. Bankart.*

Round the corner in OLD CHURCH STREET the variety continues. Nos. 107–111 are dated 1914, an eclectic mixture with Adamish pediment; No. 115 is of 1915, with bow-windows and large tiled roof; No. 117 is by *Halsey Ricardo*, 1914, for another artist, C. Maresco Pearce, tall, with brick pilasters and three gables. Further N on this side the street's older history as a built-up ribbon stretching N from the old village is demonstrated by some informal early C19 terrace houses, low stuccoed studios, and SLOANE HOUSE, a good late C18 house of five bays, with broad arched doorway with two columns, and a decorated upper string course. On the E side are two more exceptional houses, early representatives of the modern movement in England, both of 1935–6. No. 64 is by *Mendelsohn & Chermayeff*, with a long and straight rendered street front of excellent proportions, kept tactfully low. Its upper storey is set back, except at the S end. The two-storeyed garden front is given interest by a curved bow at one end. No. 66 is by *Gropius & Fry*, its main façade towards the garden, and no convincing shape towards the street. The walls are now slate-hung, and only the rounded corner betrays its early modern origin. To appreciate how daring these houses were at the time one should proceed past the neo-Tudor half-timbered QUEENS ELM SQUARE by South Parade to CHELSEA SQUARE, laid out in 1812 as Trafalgar Square and never completed. The S and E sides were entirely rebuilt *c.* 1930, largely in a demure neo-Georgian by *T. A. Darcy Braddell*. At the SW corner a picturesque white stucco interlude in a different spirit: Nos. 40–41 by *Oliver Hill*. No. 40, of 1930, is a pedimented pavilion with long, rather French shuttered windows; No. 41, of 1934, is set back, with a cruciform upper floor with pedimented gables.

The area E of DOVEHOUSE STREET is dominated by hospital buildings (q.v.), the monotonous 1980s extensions along SYDNEY STREET an unworthy counterpart to the E side of the street with St Luke's church, its surrounding gardens, and an early C19 terrace to their S. This area lay on the edge of Chelsea Common, whose southern boundary survives as CALE STREET, running SE from Sydney Street. A few relics survive of the humble C18 and early C19 houses that grew up around the edge of the common close to Fulham Road, e.g. in POND PLACE. In the C19 this area was one of Chelsea's slums, and so became the subject of much improving activity. On the E side of Pond Place, SYDNEY HALL, with broad eaves and off-centre stone doorway, built for the Chelsea Temperance Society in 1908 (a replacement

of an earlier mission hall). Nearby, POND HOUSE by *Joseph &
Smithem*, Chelsea borough flats of 1905–6, an H-shaped block
with quite an ambitious pedimented front and slightly art
nouveau railings. It was built to supplement the neighbouring
Onslow Dwellings, early model tenements built on the site of a
pond in 1862 and replaced by post-war flats of 1950 onwards by
Armstrong & MacManus. The N range has the firm's favourite
portholes lighting the access galleries. To the E the clearance of
c. 1900 resulted in serried ranks of working-class tenements
along IXWORTH STREET. On the N side, large red brick blocks
separated by bleak asphalt courts, built by the Samuel Lewis
Housing Trust, still incomplete in 1914; on the S similar blocks
by *E. C. P. Monson* for the Sutton Trust, completed 1913. The
area further E was redeveloped only in the 1930s, mostly for
wealthier occupants, with a curious mixture of select, consciously
picturesque low housing (e.g. WHITEHEADS GROVE) and
mammoth fortress-like flats. In ELYSTAN STREET, CROWN
LODGE, 1930s neo-Georgian police flats revamped in 1989 as
private apartments, with glass stair-towers and pergolas to titi-
vate the forecourt. Around SLOANE AVENUE even taller and
more forbidding private blocks: the massive red brick neo-
Georgian CRANMER COURT, 1934; NELL GWYNNE HOUSE
and SLOANE AVENUE MANSIONS, with slight art deco touches;
and CHELSEA CLOISTERS, 1937–8, in a more pared-down style,
with canted bays and exposed floor bands.

Between SLOANE AVENUE and DRAYCOTT AVENUE the large
former warehouses for Harrods provide a service interlude before
one encounters the friendly small-scale streets S of Walton Street
(*see* Perambulation 3). But this perambulation must turn N to
end with the *pièce de résistance* at the N corner of Sloane Avenue,
No. 81 FULHAM ROAD, the MICHELIN BUILDING, 1909–11
93 by *François Espinasse* of Clermont-Ferrand, a highly idiosyncratic and colourful three-dimensional advertisement for the
famous tyre company, somewhere between art nouveau and art
deco. The planning is straightforward: two storeys facing Fulham
Road with recessed service bay on the ground floor, and large
arched window to the offices above. The structure is of *Hennebique's* reinforced concrete, an early example in England, but
this is entirely concealed by the exuberant decoration. *Bur-
mantoft's* 'marmo' tiles, chiefly white, are set off by blue, yellow,
and green accents. Tyres and wheels provide the inspiration for
three-dimensional motifs: the glass corner domes, illuminated at
night, simulate a pile of tyres. Bibendum, the tyre-clad Michelin
man, appears in the stained glass of the large upper windows.
There are also panels of bold lettering and no less than thirty-
four charming pictorial tiled panels of famous racing successes
achieved on Michelin tyres. These were designed by a poster
artist, *Ernest Montaut*, and are replicas of a set made for Michelin's Paris headquarters of 1908 by *Gillardoni Fils*. The taller
extensions behind are of 1911–12 and 1922. The present immaculate appearance of the building dates from its painstaking refurbishment by *Conran Roche* and *YRM*, 1985–6 (which included
the reinstatement of the lost glass domes, stained glass, and
wrought-iron gates). The main building is now a restaurant.

Between the two extensions, on the site of the loading bay, is a four-storey block with an elegantly sheer transparent glass wall, housing the Conran shop, with offices above for the Octopus Publishing Company. On the upper floors the space between the glass wall and the original outer wall forms a tall atrium. These interiors are by *YRM*; those of the shop and restaurant (the latter with suitably Michelin-inspired detail) are by the *Conran Design Group*.

The rest of Fulham Road is an unremarkable patchwork of stucco terraces full of smart antique shops, with intermittent taller accents of red brick, mostly provided by the hospitals. For Little Chelsea at the w end *see* Kensington, Perambulation 4b.

WESTMINSTER (OUTER)

In 1965 the City of Westminster was extended to include St Marylebone and Paddington, which existed as separate boroughs within
the London County Council. Their origins and development are
quite distinct, and so are treated separately here with Paddington
beginning on page 667. The rest of the City of Westminster (including Oxford Street) is described in *London 1: The Cities of London
and Westminster*, apart from the small outlying strip s of Hyde Park,
which is included with Kensington.

ACKNOWLEDGEMENTS

We are indebted to the many people who answered inquiries on
this dense but still under-researched area. Especial thanks are due
to the staff of St Marylebone Library, particularly Richard Bowden,
the archivist, and to Westminster Planning Department, above all
to Mike Lowndes and to Graham King, who provided much useful
detail on C20 developments. On Paddington station I am grateful
for help from Robert Thorne, on Lord's Cricket Ground from
Stephen Green.

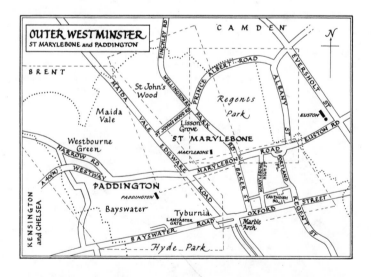

For a detailed plan of Regents Park *see* p. 616; St Marylebone
between Oxford Street and Marylebone Road, pp. 632–3; Lisson
Grove and St John's Wood, p. 661; Paddington, pp. 668–9.

ST MARYLEBONE

INTRODUCTION

On 3 February 1601 the Russian ambassador and other Muscovites rode through the City of London to Marylebone Park and there hunted at their pleasure. After the hunt they were perhaps entertained by the Lord Mayor, who had a banqueting house N of the road to Oxford by the S end of Marylebone Lane. Marylebone Lane still follows its course N in the same leisurely winding way as it did when it was a lane through the fields, although it now passes through an area as densely built up as any part of inner London.

The ancient parish extended N from Oxford Street and NE from Edgware Road to the slopes of Hampstead and Parliament Hill. The village of St Mary-le-Bourne, that is, by the brook, lay N of Oxford Street, along what is now Marylebone High Street, where the site of the old parish church can still be seen near its N end. Today's main E–W artery, Marylebone Road, where the early C20 civic buildings are to be found, was laid out only in 1757, as the New Road intended to provide a route around built-up London.

In the years between 1715 and the end of the C18, as St Marylebone became part of the newly fashionable West End of London, the rural picture changed into a totally urban one. The development started after John Holles, Duke of Newcastle, bought part of the manor of St Marylebone in 1708. In 1717, John Prince, surveyor to the Duke's son-in-law, Edward Harley, laid out a grand open square, Cavendish Square, with surrounding streets. In contrast to Lord Scarborough's Whiggish Hanover Square, Wm (1713), the project was patronized by leading Tory politicians. Building progress was slow; the streets around the square were not yet built up in Rocque's map of 1745. Their names commemorate the Duke's daughter Henrietta and her husband Edward Harley, Earl of Oxford and Mortimer. Their daughter, Lady Margaret Cavendish Harley, married William Bentinck, second Duke of Portland, and the estate remained in the hands of the Portlands until it passed in 1879 to Lord Howard de Walden. Cavendish Square was the centre, and St Peter, Vere Street, built in 1724 and still surviving, was the estate chapel. To the E in Market Place was the Market House (1721), which, like St Peter, was designed by the Tory architect *James Gibbs*. Gibbs himself lived in Henrietta Place and advised on the design of some of the early houses.

N of the square streets grew up only in the later C18, on the site of the 'basin' (filled in in 1764–6) which formed the reservoir of the York Buildings Waterworks which by conduits supplied water to the waterworks at Buckingham Street and the Strand. Further N, Marylebone Gardens survived until 1778. They were the reduced final stage of the career of the building known as Marylebone Palace, the manor house which lay opposite the old church in Marylebone High Street. Opened in 1737, they were on the pattern of Vauxhall, Ranelagh, and so on, providing bowling greens, fireworks, and music ('Some dukes at Marylebone bowl time away,' said Lady Mary Wortley Montagu). A spa was added in 1774, according to the fashion of the day. The palace was pulled down only in 1791. By then the existence of the New Road, that is, the present Marylebone Road and Euston Road, was encouraging the building of houses between it and Cavendish Square. Portland Place, the grandest street of C18 London, was developed by the *Adam* brothers *c.* 1775; at the same time Cavendish Square was itself at last completed, and other streets to the N were built up. Chandos Street, Mansfield Street, Queen Anne Street (with *Adam*'s Chandos House), New Cavendish Street, Devonshire Place, and the N end of Harley Street all retain characteristic buildings of these years.

Further W also new schemes were started. Portman Square was laid out in 1764 on the land of the Portman family. The elegant little enclave of Stratford Place,* on the site of the Lord Mayor's banqueting house N of Oxford Street, was built in 1774, and Manchester Square, with a mansion for the Duke of Manchester, followed in 1776. Baker Street was built up shortly before 1800. The pattern of squares and terraces continued into the C19 with Bryanston and Montagu Squares to the W and Dorset Square N of Marylebone Road, all of the 1820s, so that the built-up area stretched as far as the less respectable developments around the old hamlet of Lisson Green (near the present Edgware Road station).

Soane's Holy Trinity Marylebone Road reflects an equivalent growth further E. Here, Rathbone Place is supposed to have been begun *c.* 1720, but nothing of that date remains. Newman Street and Berners Street (the estate belonged to the Berners family from 1654) followed about 1750–70, and from there development extended N into the neighbouring parish of Camden, where Robert

---

*This is described in *London 1: The Cities of London and Westminster*.

Adam began Fitzroy Square about 1790. On the site of Charlotte Street Nollekens as a little boy could still see, about 1740 or 1745, a pond and a windmill. From Newman Street as late as 1774 one looked N towards a ropewalk and magnificent elm trees.

The most important changes of the earlier c 19 are those for which *John Nash* was responsible. They are of the greatest significance for the history of architecture of London and indeed England. His development of Regent Street and Regents Park, which started with plans of 1812, was carved out from 1817 onwards. Regent Street and Portland Place were united, with All Souls Langham Place at their awkward junction. But the real significance of Nash's scheme lies in the combination of a landscaped park in the picturesque style with classical villas scattered over it and terraces of private houses surrounding it and exhibiting towards it palatial façades on the grandest scale if not of the most solid workmanship. This splendour was achieved by 1827, when St Katharine's Hospital broke into it with its new buildings of 1829 which opposed the Gothic style to Nash's varieties of classical, and brick to Nash's stucco. At the same time Nash himself, in his Park Villages (also on the E side of the park; *see* St Pancras, Ca), introduced detached and semi-detached villas into a neighbourhood so far reserved for the grand manner.

The new style of the bargeboarded villa or the villa with Italian eaves on brackets and an asymmetrical turret became standard when St John's Wood began to grow: the Eyre estate produced a plan for a whole area of such villas as early as 1794. But developments did not really start until the twenties, when both the Eyre estate and Harrow School began to develop their land N of St John's Wood Road. St John's Wood Chapel was built in 1813, St Mark's church farther N in the 1840s, and by 1855 all was built over with stuccoed villas in their 'bosky gardens'.

From then on comes rebuilding rather than expansion. From the High Victorian period most noticeable are the monstrous intrusion of the Langham Hotel in Portland Place, *Butterfield*'s All Saints Margaret Street, and a generous measure of public houses in the less aristocratic quarters. By this time, as fashionable society moved W to Bayswater and Kensington, southern Marylebone had sunk in social esteem, and the small courts and alleys behind the main streets and squares became squalid and overcrowded. From the 1880s onwards there was much piecemeal reconstruction. The shift of taste which Norman Shaw had already initiated in Kensington becomes apparent as the plain Georgian terrace houses S of Marylebone Road begin to be replaced by more boldly modelled frontages with a fanciful variety of doorways, gables, and bay-windows, ranging in style from eclectic Gothic or Queen Anne to the stone-faced Beaux-Arts of the early c 20 (see especially Harley Street, Welbeck Street, and Wimpole Street). The work of *F. M. Elgood*, *W. H. White*, and *R. J. Worley* was especially favoured by the Howard de Walden estate, while *Beresford Pite* was responsible for some of the most original creations of this fertile period (Mortimer Street, Candover Street, Harley Street). These tall, narrow new offices or flats often kept the appearance of houses, while in some of the more spacious streets running E–W (e.g. Devonshire Street) there was a fashion in the early c 20 for lower, domestic-looking buildings fitted into back gardens and mews entrances. This humane scale still survives in many of the smaller streets, although as the parts nearer Oxford Street became commercialized a grander mode took over which paid less regard to the older character of the area. The new scale appears quite decoratively around 1900 in Wigmore Street, more blatantly in the Frenchified rebuilding of parts of Portland Place in the 1920s, and still more ruthlessly in the rebuilding of Baker Street from the 1960s–70s. Meanwhile Marylebone Road was transformed by civic and institutional buildings and mansion flats, and mansion flats went up also in minor streets as the Howard de Walden and Portland estates began to tackle the problems of the slummier corners. One of the most notorious was the disreputable Portland Town, N of Regents Park, reborn around 1900 as the respectable St John's Wood High Street. Further E, a similar transformation was effected somewhat later around Lisson Grove and Church Street, a good area to study the seesaw of fashion between low- and high-rise working-class housing (1880s tenements and cottages near Bell Street, mid C20 flats around Church Street, and along Lisson Grove tall slabs of the 1970s and an interesting variety of lower clusters of the 1980s).

In the wealthier northern parts of St Marylebone the continuing demand for C20 luxury flats has eroded much of the pleasant suburban leafiness of St John's Wood, where only the streets at the N end retain their original character. Regents Park has survived better, its grand frontages immaculately restored after war damage, although the interiors of the terraces have largely been rebuilt or converted to offices.

A few post-war buildings deserve special mention. In the 1950s *Gollins Melvin Ward & Partners* were the pioneers responsible both for London's first slab-and-podium block (Marylebone Road) and some early curtain-walled offices (New Cavendish Street). Among public buildings *Lyons Israel & Ellis's* building for the Polytechnic of Central London is a convincing display of brutalism, while *Denys Lasdun's* subtle Royal College of Physicians in Regents Park remains the outstanding private institution. As for the eclecticism of the 1980s, one can take one's pick between *Terry Farrell's* exuberant art deco extravaganza in Penfold Street and *Quinlan Terry's* demure new villas in Regents Park.

In 1801 the population of St Marylebone was already 64,000. By 1821 it was 96,000, by 1841 138,000, by 1861 162,000. Since then it has decreased (the usual process in the inner suburbs of London): 98,000 in 1931, and in 1961 69,045 – nearly back to the level of 1801.

FURTHER READING

Much has been published on the general development of St Marylebone, and there is yet more unpublished material in the collections of the St Marylebone Library, but there are no Survey of London volumes, and, apart from the DOE *List*, no comprehensive coverage of the very many interesting buildings in the area. J. Smith, *The Parish of St Marylebone* (1833), provides a graphic picture of its burgeoning growth when it was on the fringe of built-up London. Among recent studies, especially illuminating is F. H. W. Sheppard's lucid investigation, *Local Government in St Marylebone 1688–1835* (1958). H. C. Prince paints a broader canvas from a geographer's viewpoint in 'North West London 1814–1863', *Greater London*, ed. J. T. Coppock and H. C. Prince (1964). G. Mackenzie, *Marylebone* (1972), is a useful general historical introduction, J. Whitehead, *The Growth of St Marylebone and Paddington* (1989), a well illustrated assemblage packed with fascinating details. Two picture books published by the borough of Westminster include sections on both St Marylebone and Paddington: *The Living Heritage of Westminster* (1975), with conservation case studies, and *A Prospect of Westminster* (1989), with an excellent text by Tony Aldous.

Detailed investigation has concentrated on the Georgian and Regency periods. Especially relevant for the development of the whole area are the two standard works by John Summerson, *Georgian London* (revised ed.), and *Life and Work of John Nash* (1980). In addition there are studies by E. Bright Ashford: *Lisson Green* (1969), *St John's Wood, the Harrow and Eyre Estates* (1965), and *Tyburn Village and Stratford Place* (1969); and M. Robbins, *Churches and Chapels of St Marylebone* (1970). On Regents Park: Ann Saunders, *Regent's Park* (1969), and *The Regent's Park Villas* (1981); also John Summerson, 'The Beginnings of Regent's Park', *Architectural History*, 20 (1977), 56–62. On St John's Wood: Stella Margetson, *St John's Wood, An Abode of Love and the Arts* (1988). On individual buildings: J. Summerson, 'The Society's House, an architectural study', *Journal of the Royal Society of Arts*, 102 (1954) (on Cavendish Square), and 'Henrietta Place, Marylebone, and its Associations with James Gibbs', *London Topographical Record*, 21 (1958); A. Rowan, 'After the Adelphi, Forgotten Years in the Adam Brothers' Practice', *Journal of the Royal Society of Arts*, 122 (1974); M. Whinney, *Home House, 20 Portman Square* (1969). On later building: Survey of London, *The Langham Hotel* (typescript); J. W. Toovey, '150 Years of Building at London Zoo', *Symp. Zool. Soc. Lond.* (1976), no. 40; M. Robbins, *Baker Street Station* (typescript, 1974), and M. Richardson on the Royal Institute of British Architects in *Archit. Design* (1979), 9–10. For the late Victorian and Edwardian buildings in the southern part of St Marylebone, this account is heavily indebted to the DOE Westminster *List* (published 1987) which incorporates much research carried out by Anne Riches.

ACKNOWLEDGEMENTS

See above, Outer Westminster.

CHURCHES AND OTHER PLACES OF WORSHIP

The oldest place of worship in St Marylebone, and the sole survivor in anything like its original form of the private chapels* built for the growing C18 population, is the former estate chapel of St Peter

*Eight existed by 1800: Oxford Chapel (now St Peter) Vere Street (1721–4), Portland Chapel Portland Street (1766), Bentinck Chapel Chapel Street (1772), Welbeck Chapel

Vere Street, a charming miniature by *Gibbs* of 1721–4. The more
ambitious classical churches which became popular in the early
C 19, and which play such an important role in the townscape, are
better represented: St Marylebone has some of the best examples
in London, ranging from the grand rebuilding of the parish church
of St Mary by *Hardwick* to the elegant Holy Trinity by *Soane*, the
idiosyncratic All Souls by *Nash*, and the demure chapel of St John's
Wood, also by *Hardwick*. The reaction against such buildings is
seen at its most extreme in *Butterfield*'s forceful Gothic creation of
All Saints Margaret Street of 1849–59; the calmer Anglican mood
of the early C 20 is well represented by *Comper*'s St Cyprian and
Tapper's Annunciation. By that time there was a good crop of
buildings for other persuasions, including the R.C. churches of
Our Lady by *Scoles*, an early effort at serious Gothic in the 1830s,
and *Goldie*'s St James, a mature handling of the style fifty years
later; less well known but equally impressive are the synagogues
with rich and original interiors. From the later C 20, apart from a
long list of demolitions* and alterations, there is little to record,
except for the prominent new landmark of *Gibberd*'s mosque at the
edge of Regents Park.

1. Church of England

82 ALL SAINTS, Margaret Street. 1849–59 by *William Butterfield*.
Without doubt the most remarkable and the most important
church in Marylebone. Margaret Chapel, built in 1760, became
in 1839 a centre of Tractarian worship, and the new building was
intended to provide a more fitting setting. It was planned as a

---

Westmoreland Street (1774), Portman Chapel Baker Street (1779), Quebec Chapel
Quebec Street (1788), Brunswick Chapel Upper Berkeley Street (1795), and Margaret
Chapel Margaret Street, built in 1760 for a Deist congregation, which became Anglican
in 1789.

*Demolished churches include the following. ALL SAINTS, Finchley Road. 1845–
6 by *T. Little*. Transepts added and E end enlarged 1854. Tower and spire added by
Christopher & White in 1880–1900, when the galleries were removed. Exterior of
Kentish rag. Stained glass by *Clayton & Bell* (E window 1880, W window and transepts
1892) and by *Bell & Beckman* (aisle windows 1892). – EMANUEL, Northwick Terrace.
1833–4. Stuccoed five-bay front with small square turret. Entrance *in antis*; front
restored and altered in 1890 by *Wallace*. Interior originally with two tiers of galleries
on three sides. – ST ANDREW, Wells Street. 1844–6 by *S. W. Daukes & Hamilton*,
its richly furnished interior a *magnum opus* of the Cambridge Camden ecclesiological
movement. Pulled down and re-erected at Kingsbury (Br) (q.v.) in 1933. – ST BAR-
NABAS, Bell Street. 1875 by *Blomfield*. Yellow brick, red brick, and stone. Starved NE
tower. Cast-iron columns inside. Severely damaged in the Second World War. – ST
JOHN, Charlotte Street. 1845 by *Hugh Smith*. Damaged in the Second World War.
Of that *Rundbogenstil* of the forties rightly described by the *Ecclesiologist* as 'Romanesque, but whether the Anglo, or Lombardo, or German variety, it would probably
puzzle the architect himself ... to determine.' – ST PAUL, Portman Square. A
proprietary chapel of the Portman estate, 1779; altered in 1870, when pilasters were
added to the W front. The interior had a gently curved ceiling, and fluted piers
formerly carrying galleries with thin Tuscan columns. – PADDINGTON CHAPEL
(Congregational), Marylebone Road. 1813. Altered and given a new front in 1899.
Two polygonal turrets. – SYNAGOGUE, Carton Street. Built in 1799 as the Chapel of
St Louis of France, the Chapel Royal of French émigrés. Small, plain, stuccoed three-
bay front. Inside, galleries on cast-iron columns.

model church under the auspices of the Cambridge Camden (later the Ecclesiological) Society, and under the supervision of Sir Stephen Glynne and *Beresford Hope*. Hope took an active part in the design and provided much of the money. The total cost was about £70,000. Butterfield's first plans were made in 1849, but details were changed during the course of the following year. The foundation stone was laid in 1850 by Dr Pusey. The changes to the original plans involved the use of richer materials to achieve 'constructional colour', on principles influenced by Ruskin's *Seven Lamps of Architecture* published in 1849. Modification and embellishment of the original interior designs continued during construction and after completion in 1859, so that the interior and fittings one sees today are a composite creation and, although largely designed by Butterfield, not all of the same date; in some cases they reflect his patrons' rather than his own wishes.

The plan of the church and the massing of the buildings belong to 1849. The site was inconveniently small (*c*. 30 sq. metres) and Hope insisted on the provision of a choir school and clergy house, for the church was to be served by a group of clergy, like a medieval minster. Butterfield's solution was to set the church back from the street behind a narrow courtyard, with clergy house and choir school on either side (linked at basement level). The grouping is not without picturesqueness, although Butterfield's convincedly harsh detail does not make for so playful a quality.

The clergy house (E) and school (W) show façades to the street of great variety. The effect is in fact essentially already the same as Philip Webb was to aim at ten and twenty years later. There are gables of different height and Gothic windows side by side with segment-headed ones. The porch into the church is placed again asymmetrically and squeezed against the house on the l. so that one side of its surround is cut off. The main motif of the part of the church visible from the courtyard is a big buttress with a tall coarse pinnacle over a relief of the Annunciation. This is deliberately not placed centrally. From a distance, however, the church is dominated by a high, slender, sheer brick steeple with a broached slate-covered needle-spire – a decidedly north German effect (cf. the Marienkirche at Lübeck). Butterfield replaced the original grey Welsh slates of the spire by warmer green Westmorland slate in 1893. The church itself, both in its use of brick and in the design of the choir, also draws on German ideas (Freiburg im Breisgau). The building is of dark red brick, with plenty of bands and other patterns in vitrified blackish-blue brick and occasional stone enrichments.

INTERIOR. The church consists of a short nave, only three 83 bays long, with piers with clustered shafts of shiny Aberdeen granite and luxuriant stiff-leaf capitals of alabaster, carved by *Myers*. Clerestory above, with three small windows for each bay, the windows connected into one band by blank arcading. Open timber roof. At the W end the first bay of the S aisle is replaced by the tower, made on the ground floor into a baptistery. The chancel arch is steeply pointed, the two-bay chancel lower than the nave and vaulted with delicate ribs on carved capitals standing on short shafts. The first bay of the chancel opens on to side chapels by means of large tripartite windows with elaborate late geometrical tracery. The second bay is covered on N, S, and E sides by canopy-work. Because of the cramped site there is no E window, and the chancel is lit only at clerestory level. The N aisle also is windowless. This gave plenty of scope for decoration. Butterfield's inspiration here was not north Germany, but the richly coloured interiors of Italian medieval churches, especially the upper church at Assisi. Eastlake says, 'there is evidence that the secret of knowing where to stop in decorative work had still to be acquired'. He then goes on to describe the 'multiplicity of line patterns on the walls, for the most part incised on the ashlar and filled in with coloured mastic', and the frescoes, marbles, carving, mosaics, stained glass, and gilding. The interior is indeed dazzling, though in an eminently High Victorian ostentatiousness of obtrusiveness. It is by no means tasteful and was in fact called ugly, though forceful and powerful, by the very organ of the Cambridge Camden Society, the *Ecclesiologist*. No part of the walls is left undecorated. From everywhere the praise of the Lord is drummed into you. The motifs are without exception big and graceless.

DECORATION AND FITTINGS. WALL DECORATION. In 1854–5 the blank E wall of the SANCTUARY was decorated as a REREDOS by *William Dyce*, who also did the N and S walls and the vault.* The reredos paintings soon deteriorated; restored by *E. Armitage* in 1864, in 1909 they were covered over by panel paintings by *J. N. Comper*, who in 1914 also painted over Dyce's other remaining work. – LADY CHAPEL REREDOS. 1911 by *Comper*. – NAVE. The geometric patterned tiling in green, red, black, and cream over the nave arcades dates from 1853. The N aisle was decorated only in 1876 with large bands of figures designed by *Butterfield* and painted by *Gibbs* on tiles made by *H. Poole & Son*. The W wall, also with figures, dates from 1887, the tower wall from 1891. Butterfield's late colours (maroon and pale green) do not blend happily with the sharper colour contrasts of the earlier nave spandrel panels. The nave roof was repainted in lighter colours at the time of the restoration by *Laurence King* in 1958–60. – SCREENS. Delicate ironwork, made by *Potter* to *Butterfield*'s design, divides off the E chapels. There is no chancel screen, only an unecclesiological low wall of inlaid marble. – In the S aisle a feeble wooden screen added in 1958–60. – FONT. Octagonal, of coloured marbles. – PULPIT. Paul Thompson's description should be quoted: 'Although lumpish in form, a triumphant display of the colour pageantry of rocks and marbles: Derbyshire fossil grey, autumn red Languedoc, warm Siena and cool Irish green, set on brawny pink granite columns, which branch into waving seaweed capitals.' – LECTERN of metalwork, *c.* 1859. – SEATING. Butterfield argued successfully in favour of chairs.‡ – FLOOR TILES. Patterns progress in complexity from

---

*Dyce's vault paintings were removed by Butterfield in 1895 to expose the pink alabaster ribs and grey and white chalk vaulting cells whch he had wanted to leave unpainted originally.

‡To avoid class distinctions (Thompson), or to allow for crinolines (Anson)?

nave to sanctuary. – ALTAR FRONTALS. Green frontal with the Agnus Dei, 1889, and white frontal both designed by *Butterfield*. – PYX. 1930 by *Comper*. A silver turris 3 metres high (containing an electric lift for raising the tabernacle). – STAINED GLASS. Butterfield wanted clear glass in the clerestory to lighten the nave, but was overruled. The geometric patterns in the nave clerestory, 1853, and the S aisle E, with figures, 1857, are by *O'Connor*. – S aisle 1869 by *A. Gibbs*. – W window 1877 by *Gibbs*, replacing an earlier Jesse window of 1849–53 designed by *H. Gerente* and executed by his brother *Alfred*. – In the N aisle W, clear glass with medieval fragments, replacing a window damaged in the Second World War.

ALL SOULS, Langham Place. A Commissioners' church, designed in 1820 and built in 1822–4 by *John Nash* at the junction of Upper Regent Street and Portland Place. Nash solved with the utmost ingenuity the problem of making a positive effect out of the difficulty of the change of direction between the two parts of his *via triumphalis*: he gave the church a circular portico with a giant Ionic order. The capitals (of *Coade* stone) have outsize volutes and cherubs' heads. The circular shape is continued upwards in a curious spire the lower parts of which are surrounded by a ring of free-standing Corinthian columns. By this device the church forms a satisfactory *point-de-vue* both from the S and from the NW. The building was restored by *Goodhart-Rendel* after war damage and converted brilliantly, in 1975–6, by *Brandt Potter Hare & Partners* so that it now doubles as a recording room for the B.B.C. One enters through a circular vestibule (panelled as a war memorial in 1919), then passes through an anteroom where an elegant new double staircase curves down to a CRYPT excavated between Nash's foundations to create both a church hall and a control room for the B.B.C. Nash's inverted foundation arches have ingeniously been left exposed and look curiously like a motif of the 1970s. In the church itself only minor alteration (W gallery enlarged, ground floor slightly raised, E end rearranged) but much cleaning and regilding, considerably lightening the interior. The galleries rest on chamfered piers and carry a coved coffered ceiling by means of Corinthian columns. – MOVABLE FURNISHINGS of cast aluminium by *Geoffrey Clarke*. – PAINTING. Christ shown to the people. – MONUMENTS. William Richard Moore † 1857 by *Gaffin*. Woman mourning by an urn. – In the exterior colonnade a bust of Nash, 1956 by *Cecil Thomas* after one of 1831 by *W. Behnes*.

ANNUNCIATION, Old Quebec Street, SW of Portman Square. 1912–14 by *Sir Walter Tapper*, replacing a church built by *Blomfield* on the site of the Quebec Chapel of 1788. Red brick, with Dec detail in the Bodley tradition. Tall S wall along the street, with powerful buttresses and clerestory windows high up (no S aisle). Very impressive interior, like a fragment of a major medieval church, vaulted throughout. Tall clustered piers and arcade of stone, with triforium above the N aisle. W porch and baptistery also vaulted. – Noble furnishings. The immense REREDOS with painted triptych is by *Bewsey*. – The SCREEN, with curved ROOD BEAM high above, and the ORGAN CASE belong to the original design. – CANDLESTICKS and other fittings in High Church Italian Baroque taste added in the 1920s. – PAINTINGS. Crucifixion by *Calvaert*, c. 1600. – Ecce Homo, Italian early C16. – Full-length BRASS to the Rev. Bernard Shaw, the builder of the church.

CHRIST CHURCH, Cosway Street, off Bell Street. An inexpensive but quite stately Commissioners' church of 1822–4, begun by *Thomas Hardwick*, completed by his son *Philip*. Made redundant in 1978, converted to offices in the 1980s by *Umano Architects*, to a plan by *Rolfe Judd*. A solid rectangle, brick with stone dressings, with an Ionic portico to the E and porches to NE and SE. A broad square tower rises behind the portico, the main stage with detached columns, the top with a polygonal cupola. Interior with three vestibules with domical vaults, and an impressive main space with giant Corinthian columns and clerestory windows cutting with lunettes into the gently curved nave vault, handsomely decorated by plaster ovals. The original galleries were tactfully altered by *Blomfield* in 1885, and the furnishings at the time of redundancy were chiefly of this time. The ALTAR PAINTING of the Transfiguration, by *W. Cave Thomas*, 1887, in early Renaissance style, and the STAINED GLASS – a good pictorial Nativity in the S aisle († 1865) and the N window by *Powell & Sons*, 1875 – were all retained by the tactful conversion, which created a raised foyer in the former sanctuary, and divided up the rest of the area by low, detached partitions that do not interfere unduly with the spatial effect of the interior as a whole.

HOLY TRINITY (now S.P.C.K. offices), Marylebone Road. 1826–8 by *Soane*, the most expensive of his three London churches for the Church Commissioners (it cost £24,708). Soane had made project drawings in 1821–2 in a variety of styles, but the outcome here is classical. The entrance front is to the S, facing Great Portland Street, and the altar at the N end. Ionic four-column portico, no pediment. The tower above with a square main stage, given a Soanic turn by buttress-like columns close to the angles, each with its separated piece of projecting entablature, top stage circular, stone cupola. The long sides with giant Ionic demicolumns, an unusual piece of care for the less important sides. The interior had galleries on short Tuscan columns carrying polygonal piers and arches. Aisles and galleries have now been divided off to form offices for the S.P.C.K. The W end, and since 1977 the nave, are used as bookshops, so that only the chancel (remodelled by *Somers Clarke* in 1876 with much mosaic decoration) remains as a place of worship. The upper part of the W end is a meeting room, with nothing of Soane visible. The conversion, by *Handisyde & Taylor*, 1956, was one of the first efforts to tackle the problem of redundant churches. – Charming MONUMENT by *Sievier* to the Smith family, 1834, now in the chancel. – (Other monuments re-erected in the E crypt.)

ST CYPRIAN, Clarence Gate, Glentworth Street. 1902–3 by *Bucknall & Comper*. Comper's first complete church. Uninteresting towerless exterior, but the interior one of the most completely preserved examples of Comper's early architectural style. The model was the late medieval English parish church. The details were inspired by Attleborough in Norfolk. Tall arcade, low clerestory, no pews at all, chancel kept low so that the altar is at eye level. The altar itself, in the new progressive English mode of the time, has riddel-posts with gilded angels and a low painted dorsal. The light and spacious interior with its white plastered walls sets off to perfection Comper's stunningly lavish gilded and painted furnishings. They were completed only gradually and demonstrate Comper's transition from a refined medievalism to his belief in 'unity by inclusion', that is in design inspired by both classical and Gothic sources. The large openwork ROOD SCREEN dates from 1903, but the painted dado, rood, and side screens were completed only in 1924. LECTERN 1906, PARCLOSE SCREEN to S chapel 1913, PULPIT 1914. The FONT with tall gilt classical FONT COVER dates from 1930–2 (an instance of Comper's interest in Renaissance forms). ORGAN LOFT 1931, Chapel of the Holy Name 1938, CANOPY over the high altar 1948. The STAINED GLASS of the E window was completed gradually around the central figure of the Virgin; S chapel E (Lady Chapel) 1931.

ST JOHN (St John's Wood Chapel), Park Road. The burial ground was bought in 1807, the church, by *Thomas Hardwick*, followed in 1813, intended as a chapel of ease to Marylebone parish church. A very attractive building, close to the corner of Regents Park. Ionic portico; above the pediment a turret with detached coupled Tuscan columns in the diagonals. The front parts stone-faced, the sides exposed brick. Pretty churchyard on the W and N. The ensemble is remarkably reminiscent of New England. Lovely interior with Tuscan columns supporting the galleries. The galleries (glazed after the Second World War) have their own columns, with Tower-of-the-Winds capitals, supporting the slightly curved ceiling. Chancel narrower, lower, and projecting. – BOX PEWS painted white. – Many minor MONUMENTS: for example, Sarah Capel † 1825 by *Chantrey*, a seated figure, very Greek. – Gillespie children † 1832 by *Nixon*, with a pretty group of children. – John Farquhar of Fonthill Abbey † 1826 by *Rouw*, with good profile medallion. – Benjamin Bond † 1834, mourning figure by an urn, by *Physick*. – Many others, e.g. by *Lupton* etc. – To the E of the church excellent, unassertive additions by *Pascall & Watson*, 1977–8. A pleasant paved courtyard is framed by St John's Hall of stock brick, low and polygonal, with narrow concealed windows, and by the curving foyer linking the hall to the church. Well sited statue of St John the Baptist near the entrance. – CHURCHYARD (partly made into a garden in 1886) with many monuments. – (To the E of the church a reclining figure of a woman, a small copy of Maderno's St Cecilia in St Cecilia in Trastevere, Rome.)

ST MARK, Hamilton Terrace, St John's Wood. 1846–7 by *Thomas Cundy II*. Like the now demolished All Saints, Finchley Road, a typical wealthy church for a growing suburb. Kentish rag. Big spire completed in 1864, rebuilt in 1955 after war damage. Inside uninspired; aisleless, 'a large broad Gothic riding-school' (GR). Three-sided gallery on iron columns, a pre-ecclesiological design. Porches, lobbies, and chancel added in 1866–78 by *B*.

Ferrey, the nave roof boarded at the same time. Baptistery 1911 by *C. S. Peach*. – (The fittings are mostly late Victorian. The elaborate decoration of the chancel arch dates from 1886. Rich chancel furnishings: painted roof above the sanctuary, marble floor and panelling, Caen stone REREDOS with paintings by *Armitage*. – Good STAINED GLASS in the chancel (1870s) and first N window of nave (1891), by *Clayton & Bell*. – Two other N windows by *Lavers, Barraud & Westlake*, 1873, 1886, one by *Kempe*, 1896. – N transept E by *Leonard Walker*, 1952. – MONUMENTS. Several mosaic panels of *c.* 1900 onwards. – WAR MEMORIAL (from St Stephen Avenue Road) with painted panels by *Sigismund Goetze*.)

ST MARK, Old Marylebone Road. 1871–2 by *Blomfield*. Brick, of little interest externally. N façade with NE tower with pyramid roof. Inexpensive interior with iron columns, lean-to aisle roofs, low quadruplet clerestory windows, and a plain open timber nave roof. Very tall three-light E window, very pointed chancel arch.

75 ST MARY, Marylebone Road. 1813–17 by *Thomas Hardwick*. The early medieval parish church stood near Oxford Street; it was rebuilt on a site further N, by the present Marylebone High Street, *c.* 1400. The rake's marriage in Hogarth's 'Rake's Progress' shows the interior shortly before it was rebuilt again in 1741–2 to designs by *John Lane*, approved by *Gibbs*. The church survived as a chapel until 1949; its site is now a garden. In 1770 it was agreed that a new, larger building was needed to cope with the vastly augmented population, and in 1771–2 *Sir William Chambers* made plans. However a decision could not be reached on a site, and the matter lapsed. Then, in 1810, ground facing Marylebone Road was given by the Duke of Portland for a chapel, and building was begun in 1813 to *Hardwick*'s design. In 1814, the vestry decided on a fully-fledged parish church, and Hardwick, to give the building more grandeur, altered his original design of a simple four-columned portico (cf. St John's Wood Chapel) to a majestic Corinthian six-columned portico with a tower, to face Marylebone Road. Nash – always quick to seize on a dramatic effect – made his York Gate into Regents Park axial with it. On either side, projecting wings with a further pair of columns against rear end walls. The tower is circular, with free-standing angel-caryatids (probably by *Rossi*) and a stone cupola. The (liturgical) E end is especially interesting, with diagonally projecting wings with giant pilasters flanking the choir; the one on the N, with a broad staircase leading up to the church from Marylebone High Street, was formerly the main entrance. Good iron lampholders flank the steps. The upper parts of the wings functioned as family pews.

Inside there were originally two tiers of galleries on three sides, supported by cast-iron columns (Ionic below, Corinthian above), and a coved ceiling. The E end was filled by the organ case and a large transparency by *Benjamin West* (removed in 1826). In 1883–5 *Thomas Harris* added an apse and chancel arch lavishly faced in different-coloured marbles (by *Burke & Co.*), removed the N and S upper galleries, created the flat ceiling, and cased the columns with wood. – BEADLES' STAVES, with repoussé scenes, of 1764. – Many minor MONUMENTS, e.g. *James Gibbs* † 1754, a small pedimented tablet to his own design. – Sir William Fraser † 1818 by *J. Bacon*. – Edmund Howard † 1827 by *Randall*. Two mourning women by an urn. – Richard Cosway, the painter, † 1821. – Others by *Rouw*, 1811, *Knapp*, 1815. – In the Browning Chapel created in the NW wing relics of Robert Browning including his bronze relief portrait by *G. Natorp*, 1887.

ST MARY, Wyndham Place. 1821–3 by *Sir Robert Smirke*. A Commissioners' church. Large, rectangular, with centrally placed S portico and tower, making a fine vista from Bryanston Square. The tower is circular, rather thin, covered by a stone cupola and surrounded by columns with Tower-of-the-Winds capitals – a very similar design to Smirke's slightly earlier St Anne Wandsworth (Ww). It stands above a semicircular unfluted Ionic portico (as at Archer's St Paul Deptford, Gr). The exterior otherwise of stock brick, with the usual two tiers of windows. At the W end a group of three windows, at the E end a tripartite window. Interior with galleries with tall Roman Doric columns, the piers below cased probably by *A. W. Blomfield*, who lived in the parish and 'improved and adorned' the church in 1875. Gently curved coffered ceiling. – STAINED GLASS. The N aisle window of 1883 from St Paul Portman Square. – S aisle by *A. Gibbs*, 1905.

ST PAUL, Robert Adam Street, NW of Manchester Square. 1970 by *Green Lloyd & Adams*, within the rebuilt block between George Street, Baker Street, and Robert Adam Street; a replacement for St Paul Portman Square.

ST PAUL, Rossmore Road. Very minimal brick Gothic with lancets. 1838 by *J. W. Higgins*. Later church buildings attached.

ST PETER, Vere Street. 1721–4 by *James Gibbs*, built as a chapel to the new estate begun by the laying-out of Cavendish Square. Converted by *Robert Potter* in 1979–80 for the London Institute for Contemporary Christianity. Brick rectangle with a big pediment and a turret of pretty outline on it. One-storeyed Tuscan portico with pediment, not the whole width of the front. Quoins; two tiers of windows along the sides. Venetian E window and large pediment over the whole E side. The historical importance of the interior was first recognized by Sir John Summerson: 'a miniature forecast of St Martin-in-the-Fields, exquisitely carried out'. Giant columns on high pedestals (taking box pews into consideration). Galleries on three sides; curved ceiling with charming, sprightly plasterwork by *Bagutti*. In the chancel, small additional galleries with iron balustrades. Original gallery stairs with urn-shaped balusters. – Pretty twisted ALTAR RAILS. – STAINED GLASS by *Morris & Co.* in *Burne-Jones*'s new pictorial style: E window 1881, three panels in grapevine quarries, S 1883, N 1892. – The tactful C17-style furnishings by *J. G. Colling*, 1882–3, were largely removed for the much less sensitive conversion of a century later which crammed a refectory into the S gallery and a library into the N gallery, where the bookcases are disturbingly intrusive.

2. Roman Catholic

OUR LADY (R.C.), Lisson Grove. 1833–6 by *J. J. Scoles*, one of
the leading C19 R.C. architects, for the Misses Gallini. Stock
brick with stone dressings, lancet windows, a rose at the W end.
The exterior still close to the Commissioners' type; the interior
however gives a surprisingly correct impression of a hall church
of the early C13, with slender piers (of wood and iron) and a
plaster vault with big roof bosses. Restored in 1884 and 1905 by
S. J. Nicholl. The transepts were transformed into chapels in
1937 by *Nicholas & Dixon Spain*, who also rebuilt the sanctuary
in 1956. – Many recent FURNISHINGS: central ALTAR installed
1973; STATUES, STATIONS OF THE CROSS, and other sculpture
by *Michael Clarke*, 1971–6.
OUR LADY OF THE ROSARY (R.C.), Marylebone Road. 1963,
designed by *Goodhart-Rendel*, executed by *F. G. Broadbent &
Partners*, replacing a church of 1870 by *Blount*. Brick exterior
with diapering etc.; white inside (cf. the same architect's Most
Holy Trinity, Bermondsey, Sk). Long nave articulated by large
Gothic transverse arches carrying upper arches. Concrete
vaults. – Sanctuary TILE PICTURES of the Rosary by *T. Ledger*. –
STATUES by *David Wheeler*.
ST CHARLES (R.C.), Ogle Street, off Foley Street. 1862 by *Nicholl*.
Aisled, with plate-tracery clerestory. Vaulted transept chapel. –
LADY ALTAR and large REREDOS by *Bentley*, 1879, similar to
All Saints Margaret Street. – Other ALTARS 1902 and 1905 by
S. J. Nicholl. – In the nave, horrible post-war furnishings in blue
perspex. – PRESBYTERY next door, 1867, Gothic.
ST JAMES (R.C.), Spanish Place, N of Manchester Square. In 1885
Edward Goldie won a competition among Catholic architects for
a church to replace *Bonomi*'s Spanish Embassy chapel of 1793. E
parts completed in 1890, the three W bays, memorial chapel, and
baptistery 1914–18, the intended tower and spire never built.
Large, of rock-faced ashlar, the crisp detail brought out by cleaning in the 1980s. A tall, very serious interior, vaulted throughout. The style is early Gothic, an amalgam of French and English
sources. Apsed E end, W rose window, the elevation that of a
cathedral. Arcade with piers *à la* Westminster Abbey; full-blown
gallery, carried as a bridge across the non-projecting transepts
(cf. Pearson's St Augustine Kilburn, Paddington). Quadripartite
vaults. Sanctuary with carved angels in the gallery spandrels and
foliage bosses (cf. Lincoln Cathedral). The nave has narrow outer
aisles with the confessionals hidden as part of a wall arcade. The
Lady Chapel (N chancel chapel) is lower, the width of both N
aisles. The splendidly lavish interior decoration was begun by
J. F. Bentley in 1891 and continued by *Garner* after 1902.
Bentley's high altar was removed from the sanctuary *c.* 1970
(frontal against the W wall), but his gilded iron COMMUNION
RAILS remain (1892–5, incorporating light fittings), as do the
CHANCEL WALLS lined with *opus sectile* panels (1899), the NE
sacristy grille, and *Garner*'s REREDOS of iron with gilt figures,
CANOPY, CROSS, CANDLESTICK, rock crystal CORONA, and
gilt sanctuary angels. – SEDILIA of wood by *Goodhart-Rendel*. –
PULPIT by *Goldie*, 1894, alabaster, marble, and metal. – The

Lady Chapel and the chapels of St Joseph (1891), the Sacred Heart, and Our Lady of Victories all have *Bentley* furnishings of very rich materials. – BAPTISTERY and WAR MEMORIAL CHAPEL fitted up by *Geoffrey Webb*. – Much SCULPTURE, including a statue of St Anne, C 15 German, and a relief of the Virgin, C 15 Florentine. – STAINED GLASS. By *Bentley* two chancel N clerestory windows; S transept Cardinal Manning memorial window (1896). – BRASS. Canon Barry, builder of the church, † 1900, by *Garner*. – PRESBYTERY, No. 22 George Street. 1889.

3. Other denominations

BAPTIST CHURCH, Abbey Road. Later C 19, in Romanesque style, by *Habershon & Pite*. An apsed front to the road. Partial conversion to flats by *Raymond Hood* proposed 1989.

CHURCH ARMY HEADQUARTERS CHURCH, Upper Berkeley Street. Cheap stuccoed Gothic front with tiny Norman SE turret at the angle of the façade, added by *Hesketh* to the former Brunswick Chapel of 1795.

DANISH CHURCH, Regents Park. *See* Regents Park, Perambulation 1.

ELEVENTH CHURCH OF CHRIST SCIENTIST, Seymour Place. 1926–7 by *O. P. Milne*, a large, dignified brick building with Renaissance and Italian Romanesque detail. Interior with passage aisles, composite columns carrying straight architraves instead of arches; clerestory windows piercing a coved ceiling.

METHODIST CHURCH, Hinde Street. By *Weir*, 1881–7, with a two-turret S front (only one angle-turret executed) and a two-storey portico like St Paul's Cathedral. The W side with two orders of attached columns. – Contemporary CHURCH HOUSE in Thayer Street, Italianate.

SWEDISH CHURCH, Harcourt Street. 1910. The façade was intended to be 'on classical lines', but at the last moment a Gothic design was decided on, based largely on a sketch by the Swedish architect *Axel Haig*, better known as an architectural illustrator of romantic Gothic subjects. *Niven & Wigglesworth* were the executive architects. Broad street front, of stone, the steep gable and spirelet of the church flanked by offices. The church is on the first floor, over a hall; lofty interior with decorated barrel ceiling, shallow chancel with small rose window over an C 18 painted Baroque REREDOS. Fine inlaid PULPIT made in the 1760s. These and the FONT came from the old Swedish church in Princes Square, Ratcliff Highway, Wapping, built in 1728. Two three-tier CANDELABRA, the one dated 1770 also from the old church, the other made in 1911. – STAINED GLASS by *Axel Haig*, 1911. – MONUMENT. Small Gothic tablet, erected 1857, to Emanuel Swedenborg, who died in London in 1772.

WELSH BAPTIST CHAPEL, Eastcastle Street. 1889 by *Owen Lewis*. Free classical, a rather weird but pretty design with a tall three-bay Corinthian colonnade across the whole width of the building, enclosing a double flight of stairs. An intimate, well-preserved interior with original woodwork, an organ facing the entrance, a gallery curving round three sides with decorative iron balustrades, and a coved ceiling.

4. Synagogues

CENTRAL SYNAGOGUE, Great Portland Street. 1956–8 by *Edmund Wilford*, replacing the building of 1870 by *N. S. Joseph* destroyed in 1941. The flank is exposed to the street, an expensively finished exterior of Portland stone, the round-headed gallery windows framed by arches on red granite columns, and the lower walls faced with black granite. – STAINED GLASS showing Jewish festivals by *I. Hillman*.

NEW LONDON SYNAGOGUE, Abbey Road. 1882 by *H. H. Collins*. Lombard Romanesque front; a gable with hanging arches between two incomplete towers. The interior is light and elegant. Classical arch against the E wall; the other sides with paired columns, the lower tier supporting the galleries with their pierced balustrades, the upper tier linked to the roof-beams by filigree brackets.

SYNAGOGUE (Liberal), St John's Wood Road. 1925 by Messrs *Joseph*. Once liberal indeed in scale, but now replaced by an overwhelming pile of flats and a smaller synagogue behind the original Ionic portico (1990 by *Fitzroy Robinson Partnership* and *Preston Rubin Associates*).

UNITED SYNAGOGUE, Grove End Road, St John's Wood. 1958–65 by *T. P. Bennett & Son*. A large but unexciting group: synagogue with curved copper roof, hall, and classrooms on three sides of a courtyard.

WEST LONDON SYNAGOGUE, Upper Berkeley Street. 1870 by *Davis & Emmanuel*, with a giant arched entrance loggia, and all windows in the *Rundbogenstil*. One of the finest of Victorian synagogues. Sumptuous interior with marble columns supporting the gallery, and a central dome on four clustered piers which break into an extraordinary forest of colonnettes below the springing of the arches. The domed Ark stands within pierced grilles. – Good STAINED GLASS. – Administrative building in Seymour Place of 1933–4 by *Mewès & Davis*, extended in 1964, and again in 1973 by *Julian Sofaer*.

5. Mosque

LONDON CENTRAL MOSQUE AND ISLAMIC CULTURAL CENTRE, Hanover Gate, Regents Park. 1972–8 by *Sir Frederick Gibberd & Partners*, built in the grounds of North Villa, one of the Regents Park villas (q.v.), originally of 1821–3 by *C. R. Cockerell* but much altered in the 1920s by *W. E. Lord*. The golden copper dome and minaret rising behind the trees by Hanover Gate make a delightfully exotic contribution to the fringes of Regents Park. But this is a place of worship and study, not another Brighton Pavilion. Perhaps the simplicity of detail was intended to convey seriousness of purpose. However, close up, the mixture of tinted glass and different machine-made off-white textures is disappointingly banal. A bare raised entrance plaza leads to the main foyer, flanked by offices on the l. and a separate residential block on the r. all of the same height. Above the foyer is the library; the mosque lies beyond. Offices and mosque are articulated by giant Moorish arches of precast concrete (Derbyshire span aggregate); the flats have smaller windows and heads of the same shape.

Inside the mosque the arches rise the whole height of the side walls, framing doors leading on to terraces which can be covered over for additional worshippers. The main congregational hall is designed for 1,800. It is architecturally exceedingly plain: a square with four columns, with flat ceilings at the corners, and an internal niche for the mihrab against the solid end wall. The dome, of laminated timber supported by steel trusses, rests on a straight drum decorated with a band of geometric patterns. The dominant colour is pale blue. Furnishings are to be donated by the member countries of the Mosque Trust. The women's gallery, lower hall, and washing-places are all ruthlessly functional. The library is given a little more character by the transverse barrel-vaults which follow the shape of the windows.

PUBLIC BUILDINGS

Town Hall (now Westminster Council House) and Public Library, Marylebone Road. By *Sir Edwin Cooper*, 1912–18 and 1938–9. The difference between the two is eminently characteristic of the reluctant acceptance by an Edwardian architect of the new idiom of the c 20. The older part is massive and effusive, with a big tower in the Wren style, giant fluted columns, heavy cyclopic detail; the newer is essentially the same, but with the Edwardian exuberance knocked out of it. The side has flat giant piers and plain glass and metal between them, the front has unfluted columns and a less boldly projecting cornice, and even the vases on top are plainer and smoother. Both buildings are of good stone throughout. The town hall has a marble-lined entrance hall; a central flight of stairs leads to the council chamber (enlarged in a remodelling of 1967–8 by *T. P. Bennett & Son*, after war damage). The interior of the library was remodelled in 1970.

Magistrates Court, Marylebone Road. The oldest part, the former county court of *c.* 1850 at the corner of Seymour Place, is of brick and stone, in an insignificant Italianate style, but characteristic as illustrating the modest scale of public buildings in the borough at that time. Possibly by *C. Eales*, who was the architect of the public baths and wash houses next door, also of *c.* 1850 (a very early example). These were rebuilt in 1897 by *A. Saxon Snell*, with a taller and busier frontage, and are now part of the magistrates court; likewise the baths extension in Seymour Place.

Police Courts (Inner London Juvenile Courts), Seymour Place. Later c 19, quiet Italianate, stone and white brick, with central pediment.

69 FIRE STATION, Chiltern Street. 1889. The best surviving example of the delightful free Gothic style still used for early L.C.C. fire stations under *Robert Pearsall*. Two bays with a gable on fire-men's head corbels. A crocketed octagonal hose tower at the back. In the yard a little hipped-roofed engine building. Later additions.

WESTERN DISTRICT POST OFFICE, Rathbone Place. 1960 by *A. Dumble* of the Ministry of Public Building and Works; large and plain. For the former post office in Wimpole Street *see* Royal Society of Medicine, below.

TELECOMMUNICATIONS CENTRE, Bell Street, Westway, and Edgware Road. *See* Paddington.

TELEPHONE EXCHANGE, Nottingham Street. 1920s. Very tall, classical, in grey brick, with some Baroque details.

WALLACE COLLECTION (Hertford House), Manchester Square. The five-bay centre is the house built for the Duke of Manchester in 1776. The porch, end bays, and extensions behind around a courtyard date from 1872–82, when the house was enlarged by *Ambler* to provide a home for the art collection of the connoisseur Sir Richard Wallace, the son of the 4th Marquess of Hertford. Brick front with fluted pilasters above a rusticated ground floor; sumptuous interiors in French C18 style. It became a museum in 1900.

ARTS CENTRE, Gateforth Street, NW of Church Street, on the edge of the concrete world of the Lisson Green estate. By *Edward Mendelsohn* of I.L.E.A., 1969–70. The modest exterior is nothing special. But inside is a small square studio with continuous balconies and adaptable seating, built for theatre-in-the-round; the first of its kind in London.

ST MARYLEBONE BATHS, Seymour Place. 1936 by the swimming bath specialist *Kenneth Cross*. Nice long low brick façade in Regency style, with round-headed windows and a lantern on the roof. Planned with two pools, the larger one (132 ft) convertible to a public hall in winter. Effectively lit by stepped clerestories supported by elliptical reinforced concrete arches (as used at the Royal Horticultural Hall in 1927–8).

LORD'S CRICKET GROUND, St John's Wood Road. Lord's settled down on this site in 1814. A jumble without aesthetic aspirations, quite unthinkable in a country like Sweden or Holland, was Pevsner's impression in 1950. Such comment no longer applies to the most spectacular building on the site, the
117 long, gently curving MOUND STAND on the S side, 1985–7 by *Michael Hopkins*. Its dominant feature is its catenary curved tented roof, which so aptly translates the appropriate image of the village marquee into high tech elegance. The translucent fabric and the use of opaque glazing make the top level especially light and airy. The structure is ingenious: both roof and canti-levered stand are supported by six columns, which project as masts between the curving forms of the roof. These upper parts rise above brick arcading with entrance and shops, extended from surviving parts of the earlier stand of 1898–9 by *Frank Verity*, a most successful marriage of old and new. The lower unroofed stands to the E (COMPTON and EDRICH) date from 1990.

The oldest building, the PAVILION on the W side (the third

on its site), is of 1889–90 by *Thomas Verity*, a stately composition in brick and orange terracotta enlivened by corbel-head portraits and much ornamental ironwork. Two balconies (the lower one enlarged, with a new, plainer balustrade). On the ground floor, the LONG ROOM, with handsome plaster ceiling, flanked by Committee Room and Members' Writing Room, all with very large windows overlooking the pitch. None of the other buildings are as successful. The GRANDSTAND on the N side is by *Sir Herbert Baker*, 1925–6, large but low-key, with somewhat oppressive lower parts, and a tiled roof and weathervane with Father Time. To its W the WARNER STAND of 1958 by *Kenneth Peacock* of the *Louis de Soissons Partnership*, all functional and angular, with impressive tapering plate girder cantilevers supported by inclined steel columns. To the SE the TAVERN STAND, similar but less forceful, also by *Kenneth Peacock*, 1968; the TAVERN facing on to St John's Wood Road is of 1967 by *David Hodges* of the same firm, in brutalist purple brick and concrete. Behind this is the Harris Memorial Garden, with gatepiers by *Baker*, 1934, the Royal Tennis Court of 1898–9, and plain buildings of the same date now housing the library and museum (the latter designed by *J. H. Markham*, 1953). The excellent W. G. Grace memorial gates are by *Baker*, 1923. E of the main grounds, the training ground known as the Nursery, former nursery gardens acquired in 1887, still pleasantly surrounded by trees. Indoor cricket school of 1977, a utilitarian shed. On the SE boundary wall a relief sculpture by *Gilbert Bayes*, 1934: 'Play up play up and play the game'.

HEYTHROP COLLEGE. *See* Streets: 1, Cavendish Square.

QUEENS COLLEGE. *See* Streets: 1, Harley Street.

POLYTECHNIC OF CENTRAL LONDON. Founded in 1838 in Upper Regent Street as the Royal Polytechnic Institute for promoting exhibitions and research on the practical sciences, refounded as an educational institution in 1882 by Quintin Hogg, rebuilt from 1911, and much expanded during the 1960s. Now a many-headed monster with over 3,500 full-time students and over 22,000 others on short or part-time courses, occupying eighteen different buildings at the time of writing. Of these the most important are:

CENTRAL ADMINISTRATION BUILDINGS, 309–311 Upper Regent Street. 1911 by *George A. Mitchell* with a street front by *F. T. Verity*. A steel-framed building, stone-faced, with a giant order on Ionic columns, and the top two floors set back in a mansard roof, similar to *Verity*'s design for Nos. 169–201 Regent Street of 1909. The two intended wings were not built. Extended at the back in 1927 by *F. J. Wills*. Nos. 289–293 by *C. T. Armstrong* and No. 295 by *E. Souster* were added *c.* 1935, Nos. 313–319 by *Angell & Curtis* in 1929–35.

SCHOOL OF ENGINEERING AND SCIENCE, 115 New Cavendish Street. By *Tom Ellis* of *Lyons, Israel & Ellis*, 1965–8. In the full-blooded brutalist manner of the 1960s. An impressive formal entrance up a grand flight of steps into a spacious entrance hall. A lecture theatre cantilevered out as a central feature. Along Cleveland Street a broken frontage of concrete towers and curtain walling avoids too monolithic an effect.

SCHOOL OF COMMUNICATION, 18–22 Riding House Street. Also by *Lyons, Israel & Ellis*, a conversion whose main feature is a refreshingly simple glass and concrete tower, a surprise in this narrow street. Facing Little Titchfield Street the original front with fussy Beaux-Arts centrepiece by *F. J. Wills*, 1928–9.

SCHOOL OF ENVIRONMENT, 35 Marylebone Road. Built by the *L.C.C. Architect's Department (Hubert Bennett)* as the College of Architecture and Advanced Building Technology, 1965–9. Contemporary with the School of Engineering (*see* above), and in much the same mode, but far less successful. An overweening street range with heavy projecting top storey; a large entrance beneath, leading up to a disappointing courtyard on the high podium which contains the construction hall and car park. Around the courtyard informally grouped buildings of varied heights, all monotonously faced in Portland stone aggregate. The tower behind is echoed by a tower of council flats beyond.

ROYAL ACADEMY OF MUSIC, Marylebone Road. 1910–11 by *Sir Ernest George & Yeates*. Stately tripartite composition of brick with Baroque stone trimmings, the taller centre – four floors plus attics – with large segmental pediment containing two big reclining figures. A rationally organized interior on a generous scale: entrance hall with shallow barrel-vault; a broad spine corridor on each floor provides access to teaching and practice rooms. Lofty well staircase with iron balustrade containing very pretty panels with musical instruments. In the landing window good stained glass by *Leonard Walker*, 1945, 'Victory arising with the sun of the new era', subtle colours, with much more depth than most post-war glass. First-floor board room with decorative plasterwork. DUKE'S HALL in the E pavilion, with gallery and coved and barrel-vaulted ceiling (remodelled for acoustic reasons by *Bickerdike & Allen*, 1990). Behind, the library created in 1968 in *Nash*'s York Terrace. Squeezed into the middle of the site, a small concert room, and the Sir Jack Lyons Theatre, seating 300, by *Bickerdike & Allen*, 1979. A large collection of busts, including Sullivan by *W. Goscombe John*; Sir Henry Wood by *Donald Gilbert*, 1936; Myra Hess by *Epstein*.

ROYAL COLLEGE OF NURSING AND COWDRAY CLUB, Henrietta Place and Cavendish Square. 1922–6 by *Sir Edwin Cooper*. An ingenious conversion and extension. No. 20 Cavendish Square, the Cowdray Club, a recreational club for nurses established by Lady Cowdray, was given a well proportioned stone front of five storeys, blending well with the Georgian style of the neighbourhood. Behind, Cooper preserved most of the ground and first floors of a five-bay house of 1729. Central entrance; two-bay hall with severe Doric frieze and heavy pedimented doorcases. In the bay to the l. (an unusual position), an impressive stair hall: stone steps, iron balustrade, and bold paintings of *c.* 1730 by *John Devoto*, well known as a theatrical painter, combining grisailles of sculpture in the Bolognese manner with two large landscapes with ruins (cf. No. 76 Dean Street, Westminster), crowned by a feigned cupola supported by caryatids. Good panelling and fireplaces in other rooms, especially the ground-floor back room with giant Ionic pilasters. S of the C18 house, a two-bay extension by *Cooper* of 1933–4 with the Cowdray memorial room, with wood carving by *George Houghton*. This extension abuts the main front of the college, round the corner in Henrietta Street. The centre of this composition has arched openings in its rusticated ground floor. The former entrance leads to the Large Lecture Hall, with demure detail in late C18 style, and stained glass by *Dudley Forsyth*. Adjoining is the more flamboyant dining room, fitted into the garden of the Cavendish Square house, a handsome space, with oak panelling with fluted Ionic pilasters, and a shallow Soanic dome of iron and glass; spandrel reliefs of Lord and Lady Cowdray, Florence Nightingale, and Edith Cavell.

ROYAL SOCIETY OF MEDICINE, Henrietta Place and Wimpole Street. Founded in 1805, expanded in 1907 when it became the umbrella organization for several specialist societies. The building in Henrietta Place is by *Sir John Belcher*, 1910–12, a small but quite monumental front, with recessed giant Roman Doric columns, and a fanciful entrance with blocked fasces below lions' heads, the detail going hard and angular as in all Belcher's late buildings. The decently proportioned zinc-clad attic floor was added in 1953 by Belcher's partner *J.J. Joass*, with *L.K. Watson*; the penthouse dates from 1963. Lecture rooms on either side of the entrance hall, library above. Only the library, occupying the whole front of the building, retains its original rich, restrained decoration. It has an elegant neo-Grec iron gallery balustrade. The main entrance is now round the corner in Wimpole Street in an extension of 1986 by *Elsom Pack & Roberts*, fitted behind part of the flamboyant classical stone frontage of a former post office (1908–9 by *Sir Henry Tanner*). The main post office room remains, the walls with Ionic columns and pilasters. The new parts are surprisingly light and spacious, despite the tight site: inner hall with portrait gallery; restaurant adjoining a planted atrium. On the first floor, by the entrance to the residential part, a fine plaster medallion by *J. Bacon* of Aeneas and his family escaping from Troy, awarded the Royal Academy gold medallion in 1768. It was bought by Chambers for his own house in Berners Street, a former home of the Society.

ROYAL COLLEGE OF PHYSICIANS. *See* Regents Park, Perambulation 1.

LONDON COLLEGE OF FASHION. *See* Streets: 1, Cavendish Square.

TRINITY COLLEGE OF MUSIC, Mandeville Place. Nos. 11–13, in a Cundy-influenced terrace of the 1870s. Prominent Ionic stone screen and internal alterations by *Cheadle & Harding*, 1921–2.

AMERICAN SCHOOL, Loudoun Road, St John's Wood. Planned for 1,500 pupils by the American firm of *Shaver & Co.* in association with *Fitzroy Robinson & Partners* (*L.J. Brockway, K.G.R. Blythe*), 1969–71. A puzzling and not very inviting exterior with its almost windowless brown brick cliffs and inconspicuous entrances. Despite the apparently random grouping of towers, the basic plan is symmetrical; a compact cluster of four three-storey hexagonal classroom blocks surround a central area with theatre, dining area, library, and science and art rooms.

Another hexagon for the elementary school and the large gymnasium to the s give the exterior its irregular outline. The dense use of the site is achieved by air-conditioning – hence the lack of windows. Equally revolutionary in this country was the use of the open-plan system for a secondary school (a principle familiar in British primary schools from the 1960s). The classroom cluster on each floor is divided into five spaces, separated only by a slight lowering of the ceiling for acoustic reasons, and by a central teachers' carrel. The design was later modified to provide separate rooms for the senior classes. The central area was also intended to be almost entirely open-plan, but building regulations stood in the way. Another progressive feature was the built-in audio-visual system connecting library and classrooms. Inside, the atmosphere is less claustrophobic than might be expected. Lack of windows means plenty of pin-up space. Only the low-ceilinged central dining room which doubles as a corridor feels cramped.

FRANCIS HOLLAND SCHOOL, Park Road. 1915 by *H. T. Hare*. A nice, plain, well-proportioned brick building in a late C17 style.

NORTH WESTMINSTER COMMUNITY SCHOOL, Bell Street. By *L. Manasseh & Partners*, 1960–1. Built as Rutherford Secondary School, for 780 boys. A spare, elegant cluster of quite low buildings which has worn well. Memorable for its roof shapes, with faint echoes of Brasilia: a slated pyramid to the hall is echoed by the inverted pyramid of the water tank on the long three-storey teaching block, giving character to an otherwise reticent group. The teaching block is curtain-walled, of concrete construction; the hall and gyms steel-framed (extended at the N end, 1975).

QUINTIN KYNASTON SCHOOL, Finchley Road, St John's Wood. By *Edward D. Mills & Partners*, 1958. Built as two separate schools on one site. Curtain-walled blocks of different heights in a pleasant open setting with trees (landscaping by *Peter Shepheard*), making a welcome break along Finchley Road.

ST MARYLEBONE C. OF E. SECONDARY SCHOOL, Oldbury Place and Marylebone High Street. The older part mid C19 with an E front of five bays; central pediment and double doorways. A voluted chimney-cum-bellcote on the N side facing Oldbury Place. Red-brick Gothic extensions to the High Street dated 1863 and 1894, the latter by *T. Harris*.

ST MARYLEBONE PHILOLOGICAL COLLEGE (later GRAMMAR SCHOOL), Marylebone Road. *See* Streets: 2.

ALL SOULS SCHOOL, Foley Street. 1906–8 by *Beresford Pite*. A simple rectangular building enlivened by Pite's characteristic yellow and purple layered brickwork (cf. Christ Church Brixton Road Lambeth, La). Front to Foley Street with round-arched ground-floor windows and tall blind arcades flanking central quirkily detailed pilasters. The back to Riding House Street is also worth a look: three sets of windows framed by giant arches and a gable end with intersecting arches.

GATEFORTH SCHOOL, Lisson Grove. A good example of the tall 1890s London Board School. BARROW HILL JUNIOR, Barrow Hill Road, 1910 by the *L.C.C.*, is more irregular, given interest by decorative gables and a corbelled-out turret.

St Mary's Church School. *See* Streets: 1, Wyndham Place.

St Edward's R.C. School and Convent, Harewood Avenue. Long ragstone Gothic range of *c.* 1851, attributed to *G. R. Blount*, with picturesque gabled skyline. Later chapel and additions.

Hospital of St John and St Elizabeth, Grove End Road and Circus Road. 1898–1902 by *Edward Goldie* for the Knights of St John of Jerusalem (a rebuilding of their former chapel in Great Ormond Street, of 1864 by *George Goldie*). The plan is a straightforward U facing s, with the chapel (Italian front of Gesù type) in the centre of the connecting range. The chapel has a central dome, carved choir stalls, and a baldacchino over the altar. N of the chapel is an elegant addition by *David Morley*, 1990–1, a white-rendered rectangle with tall windows and glass entrance canopy. Ground floor with open-plan offices; to its w a low hospice extension looks out over gardens.

London Clinic, Devonshire Place. A private hospital of 1932 by *C. H. Biddulph Pinchard*. Large symmetrical front with end pavilions.

London Private Hospital. *See* Streets: 1, Langham Street.

Middlesex Hospital, Mortimer Street. Founded in 1745. The first buildings on the present site, of 1755–78, formed a handsome Palladian composition by *James Paine* facing down Berners Street. Later alterations were made by *James Wyatt* and *Lewis Wyatt* (1823–9). The rebuilding by *A. W. Hall*, 1929–35, with tall gaunt red brick blocks around a *cour d'honneur* no longer on the Berners Street axis, is of no architectural importance. In the entrance hall four large paintings by *Cayley Robinson*, 1916–20. To the w and behind are earlier extensions, the oldest in Nassau Street (1910 and 1897 by *E. T. Hall*). Between these and the w wing of 1930 the chapel, 1890–1 by *J. L. Pearson*. Blunt unadorned brick exterior with early Gothic lancets to the apse and traceried windows to the nave (those on the E side put in by *F. L. Pearson*, after demolition of the old hospital buildings). The w end opens off a hospital corridor with a low triple-arched narthex below the organ gallery. Apsed s transept used as a baptistery; polygonal N transept (added in 1935). The whole interior is sumptuously ornamented in marble and mosaic: decoration continued from 1891 to the 1930s (apse completed 1898). Mosaic-clad groin-vaults on marble shafts, window surrounds with mosaic tiles, lower walls covered in marble slabs. – Furnishings. Mostly early C20 in the medieval Italian tradition. – font. Green marble; 1909. – Marble altar, 1904. – pillar piscina on a Cosmati-type column, 1911. – stained glass. E lancets and N windows by *Clayton & Bell*, good pictorial glass in bold colours of 1900 onwards.

Other buildings include, N of the chapel, the sir jules thorn institute of clinical sciences, 1968 by *T. P. Bennett & Son*, extended to seven storeys in 1974. Facing Riding House Street, the wolfson building (Psychiatry), by *Cusdin, Burden & Howitt*, 1979, four floors with the ground floor recessed. On the w side of Cleveland Street the courtauld institute of biochemistry, 1927 by *A. W. Hall* (tall and dull), and emerson bainbridge house, 1911 (small, free classical with pretty balconies). On the E side the OUTPATIENTS DEPARTMENT, the former Covent Garden workhouse of 1788, three storeys with projecting wings, much altered and with an extension of 1878. Beyond is the obtrusive WINDEYER BUILD-ING (part of the Medical School), by *S. E. T. Cusdin* (then of *Easton Robertson*), 1955–63. Behind in Charlotte Street, ASTOR COLLEGE (students' hostel), by the same firm, completed 1967.*

PRINCESS GRACE HOSPITAL. *See* Streets: 1, Nottingham Place.

ROYAL NATIONAL ORTHOPAEDIC HOSPITAL. *See* Streets: 1, Great Portland Street.

SAMARITAN HOSPITAL FOR WOMEN, Marylebone Road. The older part 1889–90 by *Habershon & Fawkner*. Red brick with terracotta. The centre with pediment and pilasters; lower wings with bow-windows.

WELLINGTON HOSPITAL, Wellington Road, St John's Wood. By *Yorke Rosenberg & Mardall*, 1974–7. On an awkward site over a railway cutting. A sleek concrete ziggurat with two step-ped-back blocks of wards placed back to back, enclosing oper-ating theatres, administration, etc. – a type of design much used for housing in the 1960s–70s, adapted here for a small luxury private hospital with separate rooms with private balconies.

RIDING HOUSE DEPARTMENT OF H.M. ORDNANCE (The King's Troop), Ordnance Hill, St John's Wood. The horses for the Royal Artillery were billeted at St John's Wood Farm from 1804. The oldest building on the site is the RIDING SCHOOL of 1824–5, built by the Royal Engineers, restored in 1972 to its original length (185 by 65 ft). The neo-Georgian officers' mess dates from 1921–2, the more recent buildings from 1969–72 (*Mayorcas & Guest*, *G. Christopher*, and *A. A. R. Scott*).

WESTMINSTER DEPOT, Lisson Grove. By the *City of Westmin-ster's Architect's Department* (*Anthony Salman*), 1975–9, a large, multi-functional building on an awkward site S of the canal, soberly dressed in dark brick with neatly detailed projecting upper floors of metal and tinted glass. Four-storey ranges around a covered service area, accommodating maintenance services, an adult training centre, and an environmental health unit.

MARYLEBONE STATION. The terminus to the extension of the Great Central Railway, the last main line to reach London, completed largely by tunnel in 1897 (engineers: *Sir Douglas & Francis Fox*). It was not a success. Only five tracks were laid, although there was room for a further ten. The passenger station is a modest affair with a pleasantly sleepy atmosphere, hidden in a side street N of the Marylebone Road. The architectural details were designed by *H. W. Braddock* of the engineers' staff. A big iron and glass porte-cochère in front of a low gabled façade with terracotta trim to match the hotel opposite (*see* Streets: 2, Marylebone Road). The Victoria and Albert Bars within the station retain their late Victorian plasterwork and fittings. (N of Rossmore Road an original engine TURNTABLE, over 20 metres in diameter.)

BAKER STREET STATION. Opened in 1863 for the new Metro-

*I am grateful to W. R. Winterton and Mervyn Blatch for details on the hospital buildings.

politan Railway linking Paddington and Farringdon Street, the first station to be built properly underground, with a generous brick vault below Marylebone Road, wide enough to accommodate the broad-gauge engines supplied by the G.W.R. works. Extended for a branch line to Swiss Cottage 1868, and for the Bakerloo line in 1906. The Metropolitan was electrified by 1907; major rebuilding of the station by *C. W. Clark* began in 1911 as part of the campaign to promote this link to the outer suburbs in the face of rival forms of transport. The rebuilding included SELBIE HOUSE, head offices for the company, built out over the tracks, with a front to Allsop Place. Of reinforced concrete faced in white faience, 'treated in a free classic manner suitable to such material', as the *Railway Gazette* reported in 1911. The novel decoration includes wheels, chains, buffers, and other railway motifs, in a cheerful spirit of self-advertisement comparable to the Michelin Building in Fulham. Plans for a hotel were interrupted by the war; instead, a restaurant and the very large block of flats known as Chiltern Court at the corner of Baker Street and Marylebone Road were built in 1927–9, also by *Clark* (*see* below, Streets: 2). The E end was rebuilt in 1960 after war damage. The shopping mall and spacious panelled and tiled halls and corridors still recall the luxurious atmosphere created to entice the Metroland commuter. N of the station entrance in Baker Street, the electricity substation of 1904–5, an elegantly proportioned front in red brick with stone dressings; end bays with pediments and paired Corinthian columns, the centre with stone-mullioned windows in enriched frames.

GREAT PORTLAND STREET L.T. STATION. The distinctive oval booking hall on an island site, faced in cream faience with free classical detail, was built in 1920 by *C. W. Clark* as part of the Metropolitan Railway's scheme of modernization.

ST JOHN'S WOOD L.T. STATION, Finchley Road. By *S. A. Heaps*, 1939, on a corner site (the building above added later). Circular ticket hall with a far-projecting canopy above the entrance. Windows with narrowly set concrete mullions, a motif that distinguishes this and some later stations from the earlier ones by Holden. Until the 1980s it retained its original escalator uplighters, and relief tiles by *Poole* pottery on the platforms.

THE REGENT'S CANAL (cf. Paddington). The canal, which links the Grand Union Canal with the docks, skirts Regents Park in a deep and expensive cutting; 1812–20. The engineer was *James Morgan*, the assistant of *John Nash* the principal promoter. The MACCLESFIELD BRIDGE of 1816 is especially fine: three segmental brick arches with pierced spandrels on Doric cast-iron columns (Coalbrookdale company). It was re-erected after the notorious explosion of a gunpowder boat in 1874. To the W a brick and iron arched FOOTBRIDGE of *c.* 1830. Other cast-iron footbridges through the zoo; Broad Walk footbridge, with a fine cast-iron arch, is of 1864 by *John Fowler*, with ornamental castings by *Henry Grissell*.

REGENTS PARK

Marylebone Park, the later Regents Park, was in the Middle Ages part of the manor of Marylebone, held by the nunnery of Barking. In the C16 it passed to the Crown and was enclosed as a deer park. By the C18 it was farmland leased to the Duke of Portland. When, in 1811, it reverted to the Crown, the area was on the fringe of built-up London, and shortly before that date *John Fordyce*, Surveyor General of H.M. Land Revenue from 1793 until his death in 1809 and *Spiritus Rector* of the enterprise, had caused several development plans to be drawn up for it. Partly owing to the Regent's partiality for *John Nash*, Nash's plan was without hesitation preferred to those of *John White* the Portland estate agent, of *Leverton*, and of *Chawner* – to which it was indeed far superior.

White's plan of 1809, which had proposed a park with a serpentine lake, an outer circular drive fringed by villas, and a grand crescent N of Marylebone Road, may have had some influence on Nash's more elaborate scheme. Nash intended to have far more buildings than were in the end constructed. A circus at the N end of Portland Place at the entrance to the park was to be complemented by a circus in the middle, with houses facing inwards as well as outwards, and by two crescents at the N end. Fifty-six villas

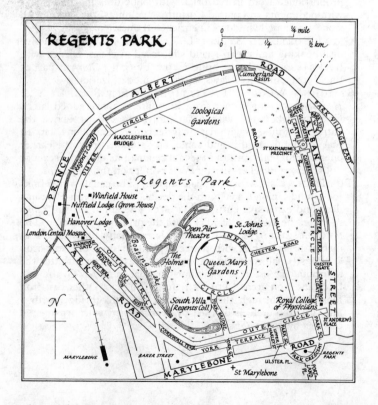

(soon reduced to twenty-six) were to be scattered all over the park, a garden city concept of great daring, possibly influenced by a plan of 1794 for the nearby Eyre estate. There was to be a church in the centre of the s circus, a Valhalla in the centre of the other, and a *guinguette*, or pleasure pavilion for the Regent, to the NE, over-looking a long basin of water. The Regent's Canal, which was another of Nash's favourite ventures, was to run through the park and feed a large serpentine lake. To the N were to be barracks; to the E, off Albany Street, a service area with three markets. The whole development was to be connected with Westminster by a splendid route through the existing Portland Place, and then s by the new Regent Street to the Prince Regent's palace, Carlton House. In the end all that was built in and around the park was half the circus on the s side, the terraces to s, E, and W, the service area to the E, and a handful of villas.

Building began in 1812 with the s half of the circus; by then the drive and plantations were nearly complete. But by 1819 only three sites of villas had been let, the Napoleonic wars were causing financial problems, and the builder of the circus had gone bankrupt. By 1823 the N half of the s circus had been cancelled and replaced by a square, which is indeed a far more satisfactory *ouverture* to the park. Between 1821 and 1826 almost all the terraces were completed or at least put in hand, except for those planned for the N side. As for the inside of the park, it was now felt that too much building would spoil the scenery, and so the villas were further reduced and the central circus given up. Its site became the Inner Circle, leased to the Royal Botanic Society in 1839, and after 1932 used for gardens and an open air theatre. On the N side of the park, on the site planned for the barracks (which were moved to Albany Street), the Zoological Society took up residence in 1826.

Although the Office of Works was responsible for the layout, open spaces, and roads, the buildings themselves were erected by entrepreneurs, chief among them *W. M. Nurse, R. Mott, W. Smith*, and *T. M. Aitkens*, but above all *James Burton*, who built and took leases on several of the terraces and most of the villas, including one for himself. This was designed by his son, the young *Decimus Burton*, who also planned some of the other villas and terraces under Nash's supervision. Other architects similarly involved, although to a lesser extent, were *J. J. Scoles* and *James Thomson*. Nash himself took up the leases of the least popular areas: the Park Villages and the streets E of Albany Street.

Several of the Regents Park buildings were damaged in the Second World War, and – incredible as it may now seem – extensive demolition was seriously contemplated, fuelled by the survival of Victorian prejudice against Nash's grand stucco manner, and by a general belief in the shoddiness of his workmanship. Fortunately, with the exception of the area E of Albany Street, other counsels prevailed, and restoration began in the 1960s, generally of frontages only. The palatial compositions that were originally intended to disguise simple terrace houses are now for the most part façades for offices and institutions. But as a backdrop to the park Nash's grand townscape still reigns supreme, little disturbed by the few newcomers, of which the most notable are *Sir Frederick Gibberd*'s mosque (*see* above, Churches and Other Places of Worship), *Sir*

Denys Lasdun's Royal College of Physicians, and, most recently, *Quinlan Terry*'s villas close to Hanover Lodge.

1. Buildings on the perimeter of Regents Park

This account includes post-Nash as well as Nash buildings. It begins at the SE corner with Park Crescent, continues with the terraces to the W, and ends with those to the E.

PARK CRESCENT (1812–22) is the ideal introduction to the grand display to follow. The gesture of its two wide, embracing, one-storeyed Ionic colonnades is irresistible. The pristine appearance of the crescent's white stucco and elegant Regency glazing dates from the restoration of 1960–3 which reconstructed the original elevations but provided new interiors – a trail-blazer for the policy adopted for many of the other terraces around the park. Near the students' hostel at the W end a BUST of J. F. Kennedy by *Jacques Lipchitz*, 1965; in the gardens, a STATUE of Prince Edward Duke of Kent † 1829.

PARK SQUARE (1823–5) follows, to the N of Marylebone Road, open to S and N, with two identical facing terraces with attached Ionic columns. In the square small Greek LODGES; also an elegant octagonal VENTILATING SHAFT of 1976 for the Fleet line, masquerading as a summer house.

W of Park Square, first comes ULSTER TERRACE (1824), facing the park with symmetrical coupled bow-windows at the ends. An Ionic colonnade runs along the ground floor between. Converted to offices in 1975 by *Green Lloyd & Adams* and *Pentagram Design*, with a large rear extension, visible only from the mews, somewhat roguishly designed: Victorian (or perhaps oriental) in its inspiration, with six tiers of arched windows, building up both from below and from each side into two projecting parts. The detail is handled with unusual care. ULSTER PLACE, facing Marylebone Road, is plain, without columns or pilasters. Between this and Ulster Terrace, UPPER HARLEY STREET, the vast entrance to the park, divided into several blocks, with Ionic pilasters. One stretch was replaced in 1910 by HARLEY HOUSE, by *W. & E. Hunt* (*see* Streets 2: Marylebone Road); the rest, much damaged in the Second World War, has been repaired, apart from the mews behind, which was rebuilt. A Doric villa follows, then YORK TERRACE (1822), about 330 metres long, a bipartite composition framing a further entrance from the outside world axial with the portico of the parish church. Nash had originally intended a continuous terrace, but changed the design to provide a splendid vista for Hardwick's new church. Each block has Ionic giant columns, *in antis* on the end pavilions, and in the centre in the form of a portico carrying a pediment. The unemphasized parts in between have a one-storeyed Greek Doric colonnade. The SW corner of the park is marked by two individual buildings, one repeating the system of Ulster Terrace, the other a four-bay villa with an Ionic portico.

CORNWALL TERRACE (1820–1) to the NW was the first terrace to be built, designed by the young *Decimus Burton* under Nash's supervision. It is all Corinthian, a total length of about 170 metres. The rhythm is complex. Central portico with six free-standing giant columns and pediment; then on each side one recessed bay and one projecting, the latter with attached columns. The end pavilions repeat and vary this motif by giving the main porticoes only four columns. At the w end a handsome bow-window with large caryatids. Restored in 1977 by *Archer, Boxer Partners*; the interiors virtually all new, although with lavish period detail. No. 1 was extensively restored in 1985–9 by *Kerr & Parker*. CLARENCE TERRACE (1823), also by *Burton*, is shorter and also Corinthian. The ends project a good deal – an introduction of depth into the composition which is taken up boldly by the next terrace, Sussex Place.

SUSSEX PLACE (1822) is by *Nash*, again on the grandest scale: seventy-seven bays long (nearly 200 metres), with a forty-seven-bay straight centre, eight-bay curved wings, and seven-bay end pavilions with two polygonal bay-windows each, with a squee-zed-in bay between displaying giant columns *in antis*. The bay-windows carry (the greatest surprise of the terrace) decidedly unclassical steep octagonal domes. These bay-windows and domes are repeated at the ends of the straight part and again to l. and r. of the centre. The centre has Corinthian columns, but these do not represent a special emphasis for they are carried on evenly along all the straight and curved parts of the composition. This replacement of main stresses by an even spreading-out is as unclassical as the domes. Converted in the 1960s for the Graduate School of Business Studies by *B. & N. Westwood, Piet & Partners*.

HANOVER TERRACE (1822–3) is shorter and less capricious. It is forty-one bays long, with the three main accents expressed by giant Roman Doric columns, four on each of the sides, six in the centre; pediments with sculpture; along the ground floor a rusticated segment-headed arcade. Behind, facing Park Road, KENT TERRACE, 1827, relatively plain, with attached Ionic columns marking the chief accents. The builder was *W. Smith*, also responsible for the terrace of houses further along Park Road (Streets: 3a).

ROYAL COLLEGE OF OBSTETRICIANS, set back behind a court-yard facing Park Road. A newcomer; 1960 by *Louis de Soissons, Peacock, Hodges & Robinson*. Plain and discreet, with faint period allusions.

HANOVER GATE, the w lodge, a pretty building, square with chamfered corners, follows after some obtrusive C20 flats. N of this the original villas began. The grounds of the first one are now occupied by the Mosque and Islamic Cultural Centre (*see* Churches and Other Places of Worship).

Starting again from Park Crescent, the terraces to the NE begin with the E side of PARK SQUARE.* No. 18, in the projecting centre, formed the entrance to the DIORAMA, an optical show that was a precursor of the modern cinema, housed in a large polygonal brick building at the back, of which the shell remains. It has an intriguing history. It was constructed in 1823 by *A. C. Pugin* and the engineer *James Morgan*, under the direction of

*The E side of Regents Park is in the borough of Camden but is dealt with here.

James Arrowsmith, the brother-in-law of Daguerre, whose Diorama in Paris had opened to great acclaim the previous year. The English building worked on the principle of a circular auditorium which revolved to give the 200 spectators views of two different painted scenes arranged in the wings behind. These were lit from behind as well as in front to produce realistic atmospheric effects. After the Diorama closed in 1851, *John Thomas*, at the expense of Sir Samuel Morton Peto, converted the building to a Baptist chapel; the machinery was removed, the auditorium divided by a cross wall to form a semicircular vestibule, and the rest of the building thrown into one by means of a new roof supported by a 26 metre iron girder. The large windows which had provided the back lighting were replaced by the present rows of arched windows on the elevation to Peto Place. Inside, the only easily recognizable survival of the original building is one half of the glazed roof of the auditorium, preserved in an attic above the later entrance vestibule. The chapel interior was subdivided after 1922, when the building became the Arthur Stanley Institute of Rheumatic Diseases; the alterations included the provision of a top-lit therapeutic pool. At the time of writing a new use has yet to be found.

ST ANDREW'S TERRACE (1823) is a symmetrical repetition of Ulster Terrace. At its E end ST ANDREW'S PLACE (1823–6) faces N, with two pairs of bow-windows at the ends, and an Ionic portico, a calm foil to the neighbouring Royal College of Physicians.

111 ROYAL COLLEGE OF PHYSICIANS. 1961–4 by *Sir Denys Lasdun*, one of the most distinguished buildings of its decade. It stands on the site of Someries House, a plain villa of 1824, later used as an orphanage and demolished after war damage. The college is the oldest medical society in England, founded in 1518. The present buildings are its fifth home. The first three were in the City. From the third, built by *Robert Hooke* after the Great Fire, some furnishings are preserved. The fourth, of 1825 by *Smirke*, survives as part of Canada House in Trafalgar Square. The new premises still lay plenty of emphasis on the college's ceremonial traditions, but in their form are in no way tied to the past. That is a double achievement, given their setting among Nash's terraces and villas.*

The plan of the building is a T. Along Albany Street is a range of offices with President's flat above; the projecting wing towards Regents Park contains the formal areas – entrance hall with Harveian Library above, a generous staircase hall with Censors' Room off to the S, and a large dining room. Library, staircase hall, and dining room all have galleries. From the entrance hall a staircase leads down to the low lecture theatre on the S. This arrangement is reflected by the exterior, forceful, inventive, and aggressive, with its many hard angles. The entrance façade is all white, the concrete clad entirely in small white mosaic plates (the parts differentiated by two types of pattern). In the middle a triplet of posts, two supporting the projection of the library gallery, the third, central one set back under the lower part of

*The following account is based largely on notes by Sir Nikolaus Pevsner.

the library. A blunt statement and a perfect introduction to the rest of the exterior, although perhaps close up the mosaic is a little too dainty for such a statement. In contrast the lecture theatre, all of blue engineering brick, is a free shape, a kind of mound both angular and curvaceous. Only one window to the W and another to the S. (The W window lights the robing room, approached by a corridor which neatly insulates the lecture theatre from traffic noise.) The lecture block forms the W side of a half-sunken garden which has to its E the office range, also of engineering brick, and to its N the S front of the main building.

This S front is complicated, almost tricky, though nearly all the result of rational thought, or at least not devoid of rational arguments. The staircase hall is expressed by the large glass area. They frame the projecting Censors' Room. Underneath is the Members' Room, brick-faced, with two canted bay-windows recessed behind the cube of the Censors' Room above. The overhanging top floor is all slit windows (a motif fashionable in the sixties), not in a row, nor in any easy rhythm. The arbitrary-seeming singles and groups in fact reflect what goes on behind: from l. to r. gallery of central library, committee rooms, working library (the bookcase area with spare singles). In the office range the top floor also is irregular: the normal windows alternate with a high horizontal strip (for bedrooms and bathrooms). To Albany Street the back of this block has neutral even bands of windows and brick. The N front is the service area, marked as such by one major member of unconcealed concrete: the free-standing staircase. The rest of this side is smoother and more regular.

So the principle is that as often as possible the different functions are distinguished by different materials: concrete plus mosaic for display, brick for more practical everyday elements such as offices and common rooms – although the lecture theatre is an exception to this.

The INTERIOR is entered behind the three posts. The sequence of spaces is impressive, coming as a surprise even after studying the outside. It gives a hint of what the architect was to achieve later in the more complex foyers of the National Theatre. From the entrance hall one can go down on the r. to the lecture theatre, or down to the garden level of the common rooms. By these stairs, armorial glass reset in some slit windows, by *Keith New*. But the climax is the STAIRCASE HALL, reached by a short flight up from the entrance. The hall fills the whole height of the building, with two tiers of galleries and plenty of wall space between the slit windows on the N side for displaying the college's collection of portraits.* In the centre the stair leads up in five leisurely flights to the lower gallery. The spaces are ideal for major functions.

*In addition to the paintings, outside the scope of this book, the college houses some excellent portrait busts: Baldwin Hamey Jun. by *Edward Pearce*, 1680, a good large head with a big hat; William Harvey, a marble bust presented in 1739, small and delicate above a cartouche; Richard Meade, a powerful bust by *Roubiliac* presented in 1756; Thomas Sydenham by *Joseph Wilton*, 1758; Anthony Addington by *Thomas Banks*, 1740–1, with a charming quizzical expression; Matthew Baillie by *Chantrey*, after *Nollekens*; Sir Henry Halford also by *Chantrey*, 1825; William Babington, 1831, and Richard Bright † 1858, both by *Behnes*; Thomas Addington by *Alfred Hone*, 1838; Lord Brain, large bronze bust with hands, by *Epstein*, 1958.

At the bottom of the stairs on the s side the CENSORS' ROOM, approached through a lobby (where the Caduceus, or President's Rod, given by Dr Caius, is displayed). The Censors' Room is a memorial to the past, with old furniture, and panelling with paired Corinthian pilasters from *Robert Hooke*'s building of the 1670s. At the corners four vertical slit windows just to make it clear that this is only a quotation. From the gallery one reaches the HARVEIAN LIBRARY, used chiefly for functions and display, a large galleried rectangular room. At the lower level glimpses of Regents Park appear only through small diagonal corner slits. The OSLER ROOM or dining room on the other side of the staircase hall has galleries on two sides and a lower adjoining area which can be divided off. The upper gallery of the staircase hall, and the committee rooms and working library off it on the s side, are reached by a small staircase next to the library. So the staircase hall functions not only as a grand space, but as the central communicating area for the whole of this wing. Only in the office block at the back are there corridors.

Finally, what is the relationship of the whole building to Nash's Regents Park? It should be remembered that the college is in an area planned not for terraces but for villas, and that Cambridge Gate immediately to the N is of the later C 19, with much variety of surface and detail. The architect has been careful to relate the horizontal levels, the blue bricks, and the angles to the Nash roofs to the s. But if the intention was to be modern and yet in keeping, it has not succeeded. The hardness of all motifs, the blunt surfaces, these are all assertively 1960. Nash was conventional (in his day) not progressive, rhetorical, always of one material (stucco). So the result is that Nash's continuity is broken. But it was already broken here. The intruder is worth having. It makes a more powerful statement on its own terms than Nash's villa.

CAMBRIDGE GATE, 1875 by *Archer & Green*, is faced with Bath stone instead of Nash's stucco – the only terrace in the style of High Victorian prosperity. It occupies the site of the Colosseum, which displayed a famous panorama of London. Then CAMBRIDGE TERRACE by *Nash*, slightly eccentric, with small alternatingly rusticated columns at centre and ends of the ground floor, and otherwise as its decoration only some long vertical incised patterns *à la* Soane. The upper parts of the N end were destroyed in the Second World War and repaired only in the 1980s.

CHESTER TERRACE is the longest unbroken terrace of all, ninety-nine bays (nearly 300 metres) of resplendent cream stucco, elaborately divided up (7–17–5–17–7–17–5–17–7). At the ends, projecting wings are connected to the main façade by paper-thin-looking triumphal arches. Behind the s end, in CHESTER GATE, a two-storey house with Doric detail. The columniation of the accented parts of the terrace is Corinthian. The giant columns rise direct from ground-floor level, three times detached and twice attached (a decidedly bitty effect), with continuous balconies in between, and balconies even running behind the columns. Behind the N end, through an entrance-way with Greek Doric columns and pediment, one reaches CHESTER CLOSE NORTH, a post-war rebuilding by *L. de Soissons*; three-storey terraces in a quiet contemporary idiom, with patterned balconies and a little decorative tilehanging. To the N, CHESTER PLACE, plain, three storeys, with Tuscan pilasters, at a lower level than the terraces facing the park. In front, CUMBERLAND PLACE, four houses but a seven-bay front with Corinthian portico at first-floor level; entrances at the back, facing E.

CUMBERLAND TERRACE (1826). *James Thomson* was the execu- 50 tant architect (also of Cumberland Place, above). The terrace is about 245 metres long, with a projecting centre block displaying ten giant Ionic columns and a pediment full of sculpture – the most flamboyant of all the Regents Park terraces. To l. and r. a pair of identical terraces on each side separated by handsome recessed triumphal arches (a motif much taken up for disguising mews entrances – cf. Bayswater, Paddington, and Kensington). As a composition the terrace is perhaps more successful than any other. Behind the arches lower pairs of houses (pilasters with curious capitals).

N of Cumberland Terrace the style and material change. The DANISH CHURCH was built in 1826 for ST KATHARINE'S HOSPITAL, the royal foundation which was displaced from its original site near the Tower of London by the building of St Katharine's Docks. The buildings are by the young *Ambrose Poynter*, in stock brick, with a central recessed chapel front in the manner of royal chapels. The composition, in spite of the Tudor details, is Palladian: chapel in the centre and curved wings to connect it with the domestic quarters placed as two ranges to the N and S. The CHAPEL was designed to accommodate the medieval stalls from the old hospital.* So the windows are high up; along their sills angel busts with arms of the royal founders. – From the old chapel the Gothic ORGAN CASE by *Green*, 1778; also some good LEDGER STONES of C17 and C18 Masters. – FONT and PULPIT. Danish, C20. – SCULPTURE. Four large wooden figures from the demolished Danish church in Wellclose Square (TH), which was designed by the Danish born sculptor *C. G. Cibber* in 1694–6. Moses and St John the Baptist may be by Cibber himself; St Peter and St Paul, with their especially dynamic Baroque drapery and gestures, are closer to the tradition of the wood sculpture of Antwerp. – STAINED GLASS. E window, 1887; pictorial, strong blues and reds. – Opposite to the W was St Katharine's Lodge, also in the Tudor style, demolished after damage in the Second World War.

This lapse into the medieval taste and display of unplastered brick is followed by one more *Nash* terrace: GLOUCESTER GATE (1827, with additions by *J. J. Scoles*), with giant Ionic pilasters, and columns in the three accented parts. GLOUCESTER LODGE is a nicely symmetrical house with a large central portico of fluted Ionic half-columns and an entrance round the corner in Gloucester Gate. Next to this another house with a small pedimented centrepiece. With these the procession around the park ends. To the E, across Albany Street, Nash added three

*These and other fittings from the old St Katharine's are now at St Katharine's Foundation, Butcher Row, Shadwell (TH); the tomb of Lord Holand is in the chapel of St Peter ad Vincula in the Tower of London.

minor squares (rebuilt since the Second World War) whose
markets were served by a branch of the Regent's Canal (since
filled in), and the two Park Villages. For these *see* Camden
(*London 4*).

2. Buildings within Regents Park

The villas have survived less well than the terraces. Only Nuffield
Lodge (The Grove) remains more or less intact. One has been
replaced by an entirely different building (the Royal College of
Physicians, *see* above); Holford House, *Decimus Burton*'s most elaborate villa, built in 1832 on the N side of the park, was destroyed
in the Second World War; the others have been much added to or
rebuilt. Of these the most interesting are The Holme and St John's
Lodge.

THE HOLME, Inner Circle. Designed in 1816–18 by *Decimus
Burton*, when only eighteen, for his father, the rich and enterprising builder. It is chaste in design, with a four-column Corinthian portico, and columns also to the central bow looking out
on the gardens sloping down to the lake. The wings were added
in 1911 by *Bertie Crewe*. Further alterations were made by *Paul
Phipps* in 1935, when the dome was replaced by a balustrade.
The plan is simple, with a garden front with bowed central
drawing room, flanked by library and billiard room. The central
staircase, removed in the 1930s, was reinstated during a restoration of 1986 by *Donald Insall & Partners*. In the SE corner,
the dining room retains its Empire decoration of 1935 by *M.
Boudin* of Paris. Garden terrace also of the 1930s by *G. A. Jellicoe*.

ST JOHN'S LODGE, Inner Circle. Built in 1817 for Charles Augustus Tulk M.P. by *John Raffield*. Original GATE LODGE to the
Inner Circle with columns *in antis*. The house has a complicated
history. Its present E-shaped entrance front is the result of several
alterations and enlargements, although in the middle there is still
the original small entrance hall, Soanian and tricky. First, in
1831–2, *Decimus Burton* added one-storey wings for Lord Wellesley. Then in 1846–7 *Sir Charles Barry* made additions for
Baron Goldsmid, extending the wings forward to provide library
and ballroom, adding a third storey to the centre, and creating a
new entrance hall and porch with pediment and loggia. In the
ballroom chimneypieces and doors survive from the cinquecento-
style decoration by *Ambrose Poynter*. From 1892 further alterations were made by *Robert Weir Schultz* for the third Earl of
Bute (the eccentric patron of William Burges at Cardiff Castle).
He rearranged the house, inserting a new staircase (brought from
Mount Stewart) to the S of the hall. This staircase was removed
after 1916, and Schultz's other main additions have also gone (an
annexe to the library and a small circular domed chapel of 1892–
6, both demolished in 1959). What remains from this time is
much of the decoration of the central rooms, carried out by *H. W.
Lonsdale* under Schultz's directions: arcane themes of the type
favoured by Lethaby, with much emphasis on heraldic emblems
and astrological symbols. After the Second World War the house
was used for the Institute of Archaeology and then until 1985 by
Bedford College. Proposals to remove the later features were

resisted in 1987–8; refurbishment as a private house began in 1990, by *Purcell Miller Tritton*.* To the E, divided from the house by a new iron screen, are the GARDENS laid out by *Weir Schultz*, approached by a new path from the S. They consist of a series of formal enclosures. In the main circle, a FOUNTAIN with a bronze figure of Hylas, a standing youth with a mermaid, 1894 by *Henry A. Pegram*.

SOUTH VILLA, Inner Circle. Only a little hexagonal LODGE remains as a reminder of the original villa. The main buildings, now called Regent's College, were until 1985 the premises of Bedford College, founded in Bedford Square in 1849. South Villa, probably by *Burton*, *c.* 1818–19, was rebuilt in 1879–83 by *Paull & Bonella*. Bedford College acquired the lease in 1908 and added extensive new buildings by *Basil Champneys*, much enlarged since. Herringham Building, on the site of the villa (which had been replaced in 1930), is of 1950 by *Maxwell Ayrton*, rebuilt after war damage in a neutral stripped classical style with plain brick pilasters, which he also used for his pre-war extensions (Tuke Building, 1927–31). At the back, among undistinguished infilling, Champneys survivals are recognizable by their details in rubbed red brick. The best building is the Tate Library, 1912–13 by Sir Henry Tate's protégé *S. R. J. Smith*; brick with bold stone dressings and large arched windows; entrance with paired columns.

HANOVER LODGE, Outer Circle (W). The villa is probably of *c.* 1827, by *Burton*, for Colonel Sir Robert Arbuthnot. It has a one-storeyed Ionic loggia (now closed) to the park. *Lutyens* added an extra storey and remodelled the interior from 1911. His additions were removed for halls of residence for Bedford College of 1961–6, now replaced by a scheme by *Quinlan Terry* that is more in sympathy with Nash's plans for the park. It consists of six detached villas in different styles. Of the three built in 1989–90, the first is a neat composition of five by five bays, all stucco, with an Ionic portico and – a departure from the Nash idiom – a hipped roof with balustrade and belvedere in late C17 style. The second is of brick; seven bays with a Tuscan order in two storeys. The third is of five bays, with Gothick centrepiece.

WINFIELD HOUSE, Outer Circle (W). Now the residence of the United States Ambassador. Neo-Georgian of 1937, brick with stone dressings, built for Barbara Hutton by *Wimperis, Simpson & Guthrie* on the site of St Dunstan's, *Burton*'s house of 1825 for the third Marquess of Hertford.

NUFFIELD LODGE, Outer Circle (entrance from Prince Albert Road). The headquarters of the Nuffield Foundation since 1953. Built as Grove House in 1822–4 by *Decimus Burton* for G. B. Greenough M.P., founder of the Geographical Society, and an amateur geologist and botanist. It has a portico of fluted Ionic columns, even chaster than at The Holme; it is the purest of the Regents Park villas, and still preserves much of its original interior. The portico leads to a circular hall, then to a rotunda with Corinthian columns beneath a coffered dome. Beyond this

*Plans include reinstatement of Lonsdale's decorations in the entrance hall, and of Poynter's ballroom, the reconstruction of Barry's conservatory adjoining the ballroom, and the restoration of the W gardens with formal allées and small classical buildings.

is the drawing room, with bow-window to the garden. Later
rooms were added at the corners. In the early C20 the artist
Sigismund Goetze converted the drawing room to a music room
(his decorations were painted over in 1954, but his ornament
survives in the entrance hall). The library to the r. of the rotunda
still has Burton's original fittings. The STABLES next to Prince
Albert Road were Goetze's studio. The delicate wrought-iron
CONSERVATORY is contemporary with the house; it is in the
form of a segment of an elliptical sphere, the kind of experimental
curvilinear profile recommended by contemporary theorists such
as Loudon and T. A. Knight.

Within the Inner Circle the OPEN AIR THEATRE, with auditorium of the 1970s by *W. G. Howell*, and QUEEN MARY'S
ROSE GARDEN, laid out in the 1930s, entered by excellent
wrought-iron gates. Fountain sculpture by *William Reid Dick*,
1936; Triton Fountain by *William McMillan*, 1950. The RES-
TAURANT, a low cluster of hexagons, is by *B. & N. Westwood
Piet & Partners*, 1964.

3. The Zoological Gardens

The Zoological Society was founded in 1824, the first such organization to encourage the scientific study of animals. In 1826 it rented
a twenty-acre triangular plot on the N edge of the park which was
laid out in 1827 by *Decimus Burton* and opened to the public the
following year. The example was copied all over the world by the
mid C19. The terrace walk between the Outer Circle and the canal
and the E tunnel below the Outer Circle are part of Burton's original
scheme, although little remains of his modest early structures. The
gardens rapidly grew in popularity, expanding to the N of the canal
and putting up new buildings as more animals were acquired and
as new methods of display were adopted. Appeal had waned by the
later C20; by the 1980s a confusingly crowded precinct, a welter of
signs, and formless expanses of tarmac conspired to distract from
the interest of the individual buildings and their inhabitants. In
1991 the future of the whole of the Zoo was in doubt. Major
structures are discussed here in chronological order.

Burton's S entrance to the EAST TUNNEL (1829) is still in its original
form, a stuccoed front with pediment and balustrade, a miniature
in the spirit of the Regents Park terraces. Also by him are the
CLOCK TOWER, a pretty half-timbered structure originally part
of the camel house, now rather forlornly on its own in the area S
of the tunnel, and the RAVENS' AVIARY on the Fellows' Lawn,
both of 1828. N of the WEST TUNNEL (constructed in 1920),
Burton's GIRAFFE HOUSE, added in 1836–7 on the terrace above
the canal, a handsome brick building in a simple Tuscan *Rundbogenstil*: arched openings and broad eaves. It has been made the
centrepiece of the COTTON TERRACES, with sympathetic low
additions of 1963 by *Peter Shepheard* and *Franz Stengelhofen*.
From the later C19 there remain the plain BIRD HOUSE of 1883
in the SE corner (built as a reptile house, extended 1928), a
functional interior with a wide-span roof on cast-iron columns,
by *C.B. Trollope*. Also by Trollope the STORK AND OSTRICH

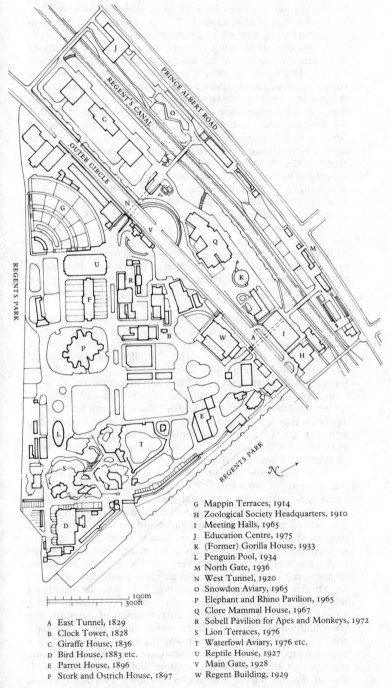

G Mappin Terraces, 1914
H Zoological Society Headquarters, 1910
I Meeting Halls, 1965
J Education Centre, 1975
K (Former) Gorilla House, 1933
L Penguin Pool, 1934
M North Gate, 1936
N West Tunnel, 1920
O Snowdon Aviary, 1965
P Elephant and Rhino Pavilion, 1965
Q Clore Mammal House, 1967
R Sobell Pavilion for Apes and Monkeys, 1972
S Lion Terraces, 1976
T Waterfowl Aviary, 1976 etc.
U Reptile House, 1927
V Main Gate, 1928
W Regent Building, 1929

A East Tunnel, 1829
B Clock Tower, 1828
C Giraffe House, 1836
D Bird House, 1883 etc.
E Parrot House, 1896
F Stork and Ostrich House, 1897

St Marylebone, Regents Park, Zoological Gardens, plan

HOUSE of 1896–7, straightforward domestic brick and roughcast. The PARROT HOUSE of 1898 (*A. Flower*) is in a more ornamental *cottage orné* style, with shaped bargeboards.

The concept of allowing animals some outdoor life received increasing attention from the later C19. An important step was the new lion house of 1874–7 by *A. Salvin Jun.* (demolished 1975), which included outdoor enclosures. The SEALION POND of 1905 was an early attempt at a natural habitat for mammals. But from the point of view of the keeping and showing of animals the most important innovation was the acceptance of the principles of Carl Hagenbeck of Hamburg: no visible cages, a seemingly free existence for the animals, and indeed a much freer existence than before. Hagenbeck's ideas were first implemented in London in *Belcher & Joass*'s MAPPIN TERRACES of 1913–14, whose rugged skyline dominates the W end of the zoo enclosure. The quadrant of artificial hills is supported by a complex hidden structure of reinforced concrete, innovative for its date. The AQUARIUM, by *Joass*, was fitted in beneath in 1925. By the 1980s the terraces and bear pits, pitiably restrictive in comparison with today's safari parks, or even with the zoo's own country establishment at Whipsnade (opened 1932), were no longer considered suitable for their original use; plans (by *Cambridge 7*) for converting them into a Chinese landscape for the giant panda were proposed in 1990.

The early C20 also saw the erection of more organized facilities for the Society and the public. The OFFICES for the Society facing the Inner Circle are of 1910 by *Joass*, in his typically severe and mannered neo-classical style; also, flanking the E tunnel entrance, the Pavilion (now shop) and the pompous Regent Building with restaurant, 1922 and 1929, unsympathetic in scale to the existing animal buildings, and a reaction against the earlier informal planning. They were laid out to accord with a new grand axial plan that came to nothing. Close to the Mappin Terraces the REPTILE HOUSE, with formal pedimented front, was provided in 1927 by *Sir Guy Dawber*, who also built the MAIN GATE with its slightly whimsical Italianate pantiled pavilions.

Then, during the enlightened years when Dr Julian Huxley was secretary of the Society, *Tecton* was called in. Their work is a *tour de force* of the international modern style which derived so much from Le Corbusier, and which formed the origin of that floraison of exhibition displays and stands which characterized English architecture of the 1940s. Tecton were almost as unrestricted in these zoo furnishings as are exhibition architects. In both cases architecture comes very close to abstract art, as can be seen even more strikingly in their more numerous structures for Dudley Zoo. Their first building here was the GORILLA HOUSE of 1933 (later used for other animals), between Outer Circle and canal, a crisp white circular building of concrete. The taller half with clerestory lighting was intended for the animals' winter quarters; the other half was ingeniously intended as a summer cage which could be transformed by means of sliding screens into an indoor winter visitors' hall. Low porches with typical Tecton curves and angles. *Tecton*'s PENGUIN POOL, completed 1934 (executive architects *Lubetkin & Drake*, engin-

102

eers *Ove Arup*), likewise makes play with curvilinear geometry; a lighthearted elliptical enclosure in white rendered reinforced concrete crossed by an interlocking pair of swooping cantilevered spiral ramps. Restored to its pristine appearance in 1986–8 (by *Avanti Architects*, with *Lubetkin* as consultant), with some minor alterations to diving pool and nesting boxes to improve the penguins' quality of life. N of the canal Tecton added the NORTH GATE ENTRANCE OFFICE and KIOSK in 1936 (adapted as a bird incubation area in 1988 by *Colin Wears*) with a characteristic lightweight undulating canopy on thin supports. *Tecton*'s STUDIO OF ANIMAL ART was demolished in 1962; their elephant house planned in 1939 remained unbuilt because of the war.

The post-war structures are much larger than those of the Tecton era, a disparate collection by different architects, built following a development plan drawn up in 1956 by *Casson & Conder*. This reverted to the principle of informal grouping, although the old concept of picturesque buildings in a landscape is not easy to achieve with large enclosures on confined sites. The most successful is the walk-in AVIARY of 1961–5 by *Lord Snowdon* with *Cedric Price* and *Frank Newby*. It straddles the N bank of the canal, an exhilaratingly transparent structure of aluminium mesh supported by tension cables and dramatic raking frames at each end. It is approached by a new bridge over the canal (by *Casson & Conder*, 1962). The prominent ELEPHANT AND RHINO PAVILION (also by *Casson & Conder*, 1962–5) illustrates the search for a new kind of appropriate aesthetic, its engagingly chunky oast-house outline and rough grey concrete textures a deliberate reflection of the nature of its inhabitants. Skilfully lit spacious interior with timber ceiling over the public area, less brutalist than the outside leads one to expect. Less appealing contributions from the same era are the meeting halls and additions to the Society offices (*Llewelyn-Davies & Weeks*, 1965), their shuttered concrete lower walls forming a somewhat grim N extension of the E tunnel. Nearby, N of the canal, is the CLORE MAMMAL HOUSE by *Black, Bayes & Gibson*, 1967–8, dark brick, with rather small glass-walled cages, viewed from roof-lit walks between the different blocks, and a subterranean artifically lit level for nocturnal animals.

The buildings of the 1970s lay greater emphasis on subservience to the natural landscape. The EDUCATION CENTRE at the NW corner, a neat building with split-pitched slated roof, by *Casson & Conder*, 1975–6, is deftly tucked into the slope above the canal. The animal buildings by *J. W. Toovey* are large informally grouped clusters: SOBELL PAVILIONS for apes and monkeys 1972, with covered walks between partly open-air cages; LION TERRACES and WATERFOWL AVIARY 1976, with angular pedestrian walks and attention given to landscaping of more generous animal precincts. The AFRICAN AVIARY is largely by the *John S. Bonnington Partnership* (1990), enclosing *Salvin*'s late C19 EASTERN AVIARY, with a hooped frame covered by an almost transparent net of steel mesh.

STREETS

1. S of Marylebone Road

The tight grid of streets bounded by Oxford Street, Edgware Road, Marylebone Road, and the E borough boundary is so densely packed with worthwhile buildings that it is difficult to devise a satisfactory perambulation. Streets are therefore dealt with alphabetically. The most enjoyable way to sample their variety is to thread one's way through the minor streets from E to W, starting from Cleveland Street: despite some large C20 intrusions, the chief impression is still of a humane and friendly C18 and C19 scale and character. Alternatively, a thematic route might be followed. A GEORGIAN tour, for example, should start with the earliest developments, *Gibbs*'s St Peter Vere Street, and Cavendish Square, around which the Cavendish/Harley (later Portland) estate developed. Chandos Street to the N leads to the later *Adam* work in Queen Anne Street, Mansfield Street, Duchess Street, and Portland Place. Back W along New Cavendish Street, N up Harley Street, and for good quiet later C18 stretches W again to Upper Wimpole Street and Devonshire Place and to the early C19 parish church of St Mary in Marylebone Road. Further W is the Portman estate, developed from the later C18; although only a few original houses remain in Manchester Square, Portman Square, and Baker Street, the long artery of Gloucester Place still shows how uniform (and monotonous) late Georgian streets could be. W again are two elongated early C19 squares, Montagu and Bryanston, still quite complete, with Wyndham Place to the N, a pleasant enclave with contemporary church (St Mary) and school. Between here and Edgware Road, streets of humbler early C19 terraces, a good hunting-ground for original shopfronts.

From the EARLY and MID VICTORIAN periods there is little notable apart from All Saints Margaret Street, the Langham Hotel in Portland Place, and an assortment of pubs (e.g. in Marylebone High Street). The exceptionally rich variety of LATE VICTORIAN and EDWARDIAN street frontages, all endeavouring to show that they could improve on late Georgian restraint, can be studied in many places: affluent houses and flats in the comfortably sedate thoroughfares of the medical neighbourhood of Harley Street (Bentinck Street, Welbeck Street, New Cavendish Street, Harley Street, Devonshire Street, Portland Place, Hallam Street) contrast with the quirkier mixture of commercial and residential buildings in the more congested area further E now dominated by the rag trade and Middlesex Hospital (Great Portland Street, Great Titchfield Street, Little Portland Street, Langham Street, Mortimer Street, Riding House Street, Candover Street, Foley Street, Berners Street).

As for the rest of the TWENTIETH CENTURY, Portland Place has the most presumptuous buildings of between the wars, with Beaux-Arts blocks outfacing Adam's original terraces, and the B.B.C. building overshadowing Nash at the junction with Upper Regent Street. The post-war rebuilding that now dominates some areas (Baker Street, Portman Square) is only occasionally of interest, for example for the borough housing of various types in Clipstone Street, Carburton Street, and Cato Street.

AYBROOK STREET. A messy industrial pocket w of Marylebone High Street, depleted by bomb damage. On the w side, No. 32, a late C19 factory, was converted by *Richard & Su Rogers* in association with *Design Research Unit* as DRU's own offices, 1969–71. Four storeys of open-plan offices with large plain windows and a rooftop extension. High tech expertise (e.g. under-floor services on the top floor) was combined with brilliant colours (since toned down by later owners), a forecast of Rogers's later work.

BAKER STREET, one of the main N–S arteries of the Portman estate, was built *c.* 1790. The best preserved parts are at the N end. On the E side Nos. 100–124 are a single group; tall first-floor windows in blind arches, the N end and Nos. 108–110 in the centre pro-jecting forward. No. 108 has a vermiculated entrance and a pretty string course with masks. Nos. 94–98 were rebuilt in the 1970s with an ingenious near-facsimile front concealing a cinema. Similar but fewer original houses opposite (good door-cases to Nos. 107–109, 115). Further s the architectural standard declines as the scale changes from the four and five storeys of the Georgian terraces to the greedy seven storeys of the C20 offices. The offices start on the E side with Nos. 84–86, 1936 by *Robert Lutyens, W. A. Lewis & Partners*, stone-faced, with residual classical detail. Nos. 72–82, 1904, grand with giant pilasters, were formerly MARKS AND SPENCER'S head offices. Opposite, Nos. 37–67, their present offices, with those of the METAL BOX COMPANY, a podium with four slabs at right angles, fussily detailed, 1958 by *T. P. Bennett & Son*. Nos. 27–35 have relent-lessly smooth projecting balconies; a lower block (1965–6 by *Elsom & Partners*) continues the design along George Street. On the E side ACCURIST HOUSE (No. 38 etc.), a banal façade of dark brown brick with large broad windows, 1968–70 by *Fitzroy Robinson*. Further development by the same estate in 1990 destroyed the last remaining original houses at the s end of Baker Street.

BENTINCK STREET. A small street off the w side of Welbeck Street. On the s side, BENTINCK MANSIONS, 1910 by *William Woodward*, a large block with corbelled-out corner turret. Nos. 17–23, with shaped gables, are of 1909 by *W. H. White*. On the N side, No. 1, early C19; No. 2, 1902, striped quoins and gable. Nos. 3–4 are by *Stanley Hall, Easton & Robertson*, 1937, quite in keeping with the terrace tradition of the neighbourhood, but well detailed in a contemporary idiom. Built as the offices of 'The Practitioner' (see the balcony motifs). Nos. 8 (much restored) and 10 are late C18.

BERNERS STREET. Sir William Chambers built a house for himself in Berners Street, but nothing now is left of the C18. Much rebuilt from the end of the C19 by the Berners estate surveyor, *John Slater*. His most important building is No. 6, the RAMADA, the former Berners Hotel, 1908–10, a rare survival of an Edward-ian private hotel, complete with magnificent plastered ceilings in dining room and entrance hall. Stone and brick exterior with arched ground-floor windows, grand pedimented entrance. On the w side, SANDERSONS, 1957–60 by *R. H. Uren* of *Slater, Moberly Uren*, uncommonly lavish for English shops at the time,

ST MARYLEBONE
BETWEEN OXFORD STREET and MARYLEBONE ROAD

CHURCHES, etc.
1. St Peter
2. St Mary
3. Holy Trinity
4. All Souls
5. All Saints
6. St James (R.C.)
7. Annunciation
8. St Mary
9. St Mark
10. St Charles (R.C.)
11. Our Lady of the Rosary (R.C.)
12. Eleventh Church of Christ Scientist
13. Methodist Church
14. Swedish Church
15. Welsh Baptist Chapel
16. Central Synagogue
17. West London Synagogue

PUBLIC BUILDINGS, etc.

Ⓐ Town Hall, Library
Ⓑ Magistrates Court
Ⓒ Middlesex Hospital
Ⓓ The Polytechnic
Ⓔ Polytechnic of Central London
Ⓕ Polytechnic of Science and Technology
Ⓖ Broadcasting House
Ⓗ Fire Station
Ⓙ Post Office Tower
Ⓚ Wallace Collection
Ⓛ Baths
Ⓜ Royal Academy of Music
Ⓝ Royal College of Nursing
Ⓞ Royal College of Medicine
Ⓟ Samaritan Hospital for Women

enterprisingly incorporating artwork in different media. A long, even, six-storey curtain wall, which continues over the entrance to the customers' car park and courtyard garden (landscaped by *Philip Hicks*). Glass and marble mosaics by *Jupp Dernbach-Mayern*. Over the staircase, large stained-glass window by *Piper & Reyntiens*. Near the NE corner, Nos. 29–33 (COPYRIGHT HOUSE), with a playful undulating pierced roof canopy in the Festival spirit, 1957 by *R. Seifert & Partners*.

BLANDFORD STREET. Parallel, and similar, to George Street (q.v.). Altered C18 terraces at the W end, later ones further E (the S side gutted 1990). (*See also* Manchester Street.)

BOLSOVER STREET, E of and parallel with Great Portland Street. At the N end Nos. 42–44 and 53 of *c*. 1800. For the S end *see* above, Public Buildings: Polytechnic of Central London.

BRENDON STREET. *See* Molyneux Street.

BRYANSTON SQUARE and MONTAGU SQUARE form the chief compositions on the Portman estate between Gloucester Place and Edgware Road. Both were laid out by *Joseph Parkinson*. Bryanston Square was finished by *c*. 1821. Its E and W sides were units, with whole plastered house fronts with attached giant columns as main accents. These survive at the N and S ends of the E side (the N end rebuilt), but no longer in the centre. The centre of the W side has been more drastically altered. At the N end, BRYANSTON PLACE continues W with the same design (doorcases with Greek Doric columns). MONTAGU SQUARE is similar but plainer and more complete. The chief motif of most of the houses is a shallow bow-window, carried up polygonally.

BULSTRODE STREET, W of Welbeck Street. On the S side at the E end Nos. 3–7, late C18, with rusticated stucco ground floors and good staircases. HELEN HALL is of 1905, neo-Georgian, with an elaborate hooded door canopy. On the N side No. 8, 1902 by *F. M. Elgood*. At the W end a nice modest C18 patch, Nos. 18–20 (N) and 15–21 (S), No. 19 with a bowed shopfront with original glazing bars.

CANDOVER STREET, S of Foley Street. This has the most original group in the area of buildings in the Art Nouveau style. On the W side BELMONT HOUSE; opposite, a composition built as flats, which continues round the corner into RIDING HOUSE STREET: TOWER HOUSE, YORK HOUSE (dated 1903), and OAKLEY HOUSE, with bold use of colourful materials (glazed brown brick below, purple and red brick and white stucco above) and charmingly eclectic Arts and Crafts detail (small oriels, mullioned-and-transomed windows, and fanciful gables and parapets; cf. also No. 10 Mortimer Street). On York House big green mosaic panels advertising T. J. Boulting, Sanitary and Hot Water Engineers. The architect was *H. Fuller Clark* (best known for his pub, the Black Friar, in the City of London).

CARBURTON STREET. At the E end on the N side, beyond the unattractive REGENT CREST HOTEL (*Raymond Spratley & Partners*, completed 1972), a substantial four- to six-storey housing redevelopment of 1984 by the *City of Westminster* (*Anthony Selman*), brown brick with red trimmings, its well proportioned elevations with vaguely Georgian window shapes far more of an asset to the neighbourhood than those of the 1960s

Holcroft Court to the s (*see* Clipstone Street). But alas, it replaced a decent terrace of *c*. 1791–1811, one of the last surviving small-scale Georgian groups on the Portland estate.

CATO STREET, parallel with Molyneux Street. A low row of twenty mews flats of brown brick, punctuated by deeply recessed garages, entrances, and balconies. 1972 by Westminster Architect's Department (*M. Stewart*), a successful, fairly early example of the move towards public housing on a small, humane scale.

CAVENDISH PLACE. No. 12 is late c18. Decorated stucco ground floor, a Venetian window over the porch, and another in the centre of the E side, with pediment above, facing a garden (one of the few surviving private gardens in this area). No. 14, at the corner of Chandos Street, is also later c18.

CAVENDISH SQUARE. The development of this part of Marylebone began with the laying out of Cavendish Square in 1717 by Edward Harley's surveyor *John Prince* (*see* St Marylebone Introduction). Building progress was slow. The w side of the square was taken by one big house behind a screen wall, built for Lord Bingley, Chancellor of the Exchequer, later occupied by Lord Harcourt, and known as Harcourt House. It was replaced in 1903 by the present centrepiece of the w side, a symmetrical stone-faced block of flats with domed end pavilions. S of this, No. 20, a discreet front of 1926 by *Sir Edwin Cooper* for the Cowdray Club attached to the Royal College of Nursing in Henrietta Place, but incorporating substantial parts of a house of 1729 (*see* Public Buildings). To the N Nos. 17–18, a dignified pair by *Henry Keene*, 1756, each of three bays, with stuccoed ground floor. No. 18, altered in 1937, retains three chimneypieces by *Carter* and plasterwork by *T. Hayford*. No. 17, altered in 1925, has on the side of the ground floor to Wigmore Street pretty c20 reliefs by *Gilbert Bayes* of musicians and other figures, made when the house was Brinmead's piano showrooms.

The N side was to have had a grand mansion for the Duke of Chandos. An elevation by *John Price* (who worked for Chandos at Canons, Stanmore, Hw (q.v.)), appears in *Vitruvius Britannicus*. But Chandos lost heavily in the South Sea Bubble disaster, and although he bought the freehold of the site in 1724, a much less ambitious plan was adopted. Two quite modest houses were built, one at each corner of the N side, one for his own occupation (No. 16) and one to be sold (No. 9, replaced by flats in 1893). No. 16, at the corner of Harley Street, was built in 1724–31 and inhabited by Chandos from 1735 to 1744. The house was later remodelled by *Adam*, but has been altered since. The ground floor is now a bank. The front is of five bays, the side was originally of seven bays (including Nos. 2–4 Harley Street).

The centre of the N side of the square was still unbuilt on in the 1750s, when Sir Francis Dashwood acquired the site for the Society of Dilettanti, and plans for an Academy were discussed. Nothing came of this, but these schemes may have influenced the design of what is now the most interesting feature of the N side: Nos. 11 and 14 are a pair of grand though small Palladian stone-fronted houses, each with vermiculated rustication to the window surrounds and blocked columns to the doorways. On 36

the upper floor four engaged columns and outer pilasters, with a
central pediment above. They were built in 1769–72 as a speculation by G. F. Tufnell and are in the style of say *Vardy*, although
they have also been associated with *Stuart*. Sir John Summerson
suggested that their unusually elaborate façades might be
explained by Tufnell having to take over cut stone already supplied for the Dilettanti's proposed Academy.* The two houses
are now happily linked by a bridge, stone-faced, with an order
of pilasters echoing that on the houses, by *Louis Osman*, 1953.
It forms the entrance to HEYTHROP COLLEGE (University of
London Faculty of Theology). Over the archway *Epstein*'s Virgin
and Child broods in great stillness. The sculpture, of cast lead,
was commissioned by the Convent of the Holy Child Jesus which
formerly occupied Heythrop College.

The E side of the square was built up in the 1740s. Of this
time, although partly altered, are Nos. 1, 1a (altered 1825 by
Wyatville), 3, 4, and 5, the last three each of four bays (good
interior features). Later intruders: No. 2 by *Robert Angell &
Curtis*, 1934, tactlessly tall; No. 7, 1909, with a mannered aedicule
and set-back attic; and No. 8, restrained 1930s-modern offices
(for Messrs TOOTAL) by *W. A. Lewis* (consultant *L.G. Pearson*).

The S side is all of the C20; the backs of big Oxford Street
stores. JOHN LEWIS is of 1939 by *Slater, Moberly & Uren*, with
F. Singer, stone-fronted with vertical accents, not as uncom-
promisingly modern as the contemporary Peter Jones store in
Sloane Square (KC). Less accommodating is the next block,
No. 33, with a podium with shops and offices (by *T. P. Bennett
& Son*, 1957–62), and on the roof a tower and other buildings
for the LONDON COLLEGE OF FASHION (L.C.C. Architect's
Department, *D. R. Stark*, 1962–3).

The unsympathetically tough railings and walls around the
centre of the square date from 1970, when a car park was constructed beneath and the trees at the corners were destroyed.
The new landscaping is by *Michael Brown*.

CHANDOS STREET, running N from the corner of Cavendish
Square, was laid out after the Marylebone basin was filled in,
and is now overshadowed by the Langham Hotel extensions. On
the r. Nos. 2–6, late C18; on the l. the MEDICAL SOCIETY OF
LONDON occupies the centre of a long, low, stuccoed house
(Nos. 10a–12) only two storeys high. Central feature of five bays,
with Corinthian pilasters from the ground floor, and a bow-
window containing the staircase. Built *c.* 1808, altered (see the
blocked windows) after the Society moved here in 1873. The
meeting room and former library must date from this time. In
the meeting room a delicate *Coade* stone relief of an Egyptian
scene with a sphinx and the figure of Isis, 1787, brought from
the Society's former premises at Bolt Court, Fleet Street, the gift
of Dr Lettsom, who had founded the Society in 1773.‡ The street
has Chandos House as its N termination (*see* Queen Anne Street).

CHARLOTTE PLACE. *See* Rathbone Place.

*See J. Summerson, 'The Society's House', *Journal of the Royal Society of Arts*, LII
(1954).

‡The relief was a copy of one of the many *Coade* stone reliefs designed by *Bacon* for
Lettsom's house in Camberwell (Sk).

CHILTERN STREET. A service street between Baker Street and Manchester Street, much rebuilt in the later C 19. At the N end PORTMAN MANSIONS, *c.* 1890–1900, a romantic composition with Gothic windows and stepped gables; also a Gothic former dispensary (No. 82) and relief office, built for the parish of St Marylebone in 1872 by *H. Saxon Snell*, with additions of 1890. No. 78, former schools of 1859, are in diapered brick, with two Gothic entrances with crisp stiff-leaf decoration in the spandrels. Rear wing with top-floor schoolroom with open timber roof, occupied since 1946 by the Evangelical Library. S of Dorset Street, handsome terracotta-trimmed terraces of flats above shops, with splendidly large gargoyles, of 1891 by *Rowland Plumbe*, built for the Artizans Labourers and General Dwellings Co. (cf. Queens Park, Paddington, Perambulation 2c).

CLEVELAND STREET. A mixed bag on the boundary between St Marylebone and Camden. The E side (in Camden) belongs with Fitzrovia: scruffy late Georgian terraces with small shops at the N end, late C 19 improved dwellings further S. On the W side much is eaten up by the huge bulks of the Middlesex Hospital and the Polytechnic of Central London (qq.v.). Further N a plain row of low shops, part of the redevelopment which includes Holcroft Court in Clipstone Street (q.v.); then mansion flats and a few C 18 houses (Nos. 139–149).

CLIPSTONE STREET, W of Cleveland Street. HOLCROFT COURT, between Clipstone Street and Great Titchfield Street, by *F. MacManus & Partners* for Westminster, 1966–71, is a dense development of six-storey flats (244 dwellings, 342 p.p.a.) looking inward to a small central garden. Neat but dull street elevations (concrete frame with white spandrel panels); forbiddingly impersonal entrances and internal corridors. Beneath the garden is a toddlers' club adjoining a sunken play area – an ingenious idea but chillingly bleak in execution. Refurbished by *Philip Goodhew & Partners*, 1991.

CRAWFORD STREET, like York Street (q.v.), runs E–W across Gloucester Place. Minor early C 19 terraces and shops (No. 105 with good Victorian shopfront) and several pubs, of which the best is the OLIVE BRANCH at the corner of Homer Row, 1882 by *W. E. Williams*.

DEVONSHIRE PLACE. The N continuation of Upper Wimpole 37 Street. Like the N end of Harley Street, to which it runs parallel, an especially complete late C 18 street. Neither the replacements, facsimile (Nos. 3–5, 32) and otherwise (Nos. 26, 32), nor the alterations (see the variety of balconies and attics) disturb the impression of Georgian symmetry. The ends and centre of the E side are emphasized in the discreetest way by slight projections and by windows in blind arches. No. 13 is more elaborately ornamented, with stucco roundels, good fanlight, and ironwork. (For No. 1a, *see* Devonshire Street).

DEVONSHIRE STREET. The northernmost of the streets running E–W across Portland Place, so one does not expect anything very early. E of Portland Place Nos. 13–18, 1914–15 by *A. F. Faulkner*. W of Portland Place: on the S side Nos. 44–47 late C 18, No. 44 with vermiculation round the doorway. No. 43 is also C 18, but lower. Nos. 41–42 are of 1891 by *F. M. Elgood*, a stone-faced

pair with segmental hoodmoulds. No. 39 (round the corner in
Devonshire Close), a small symmetrical office building by *T. S.
Tait*, 1934, is a mixture of the progressive and the conventional
with its mostly horizontal windows, unusual brick bonding, and
classical doorcase. Nearly all the other houses worth noting are
those low, detached C19 or early C20 villas which are also a
speciality of New Cavendish Street. They were built on the
gardens of the terraces running N–S, often in pairs at the entrance
to a mews, and this is reflected in the curious street numbering.
On the S side: No. 40 and No. 112a Harley Street, both Edwardian, the latter of 1909, with brick pilasters and gables. After
Harley Street No. 115a Harley Street, a good symmetrical Queen
Anne villa of 1898, and No. 38. On the N side: No. 12, 1912–14
by *Sydney Tatchell*, with ornate Beaux-Arts stone front, No. 114a
Harley Street, No. 21 (Victorian stucco), and No. 1a Devonshire
Place are all of similar proportions. At the W end of the street a
little of the early C19: Nos. 22 (N) and 32 (S).

DORSET STREET. *See* Manchester Street.

DUCHESS STREET, off Portland Place. The stables of *Adam*'s
Chandos House (*see* Queen Anne Street) front on to Duchess
Street. Altered by *Arthur Bolton*, 1924. An ambitious neo-classi-
cal composition: carriage archway in a raised centre with coupled
pilasters; lower outer bays; end piers with sphinxes. Thomas
Hope's gallery was next door (*see* Mansfield Street).

DUKE STREET. *See* Manchester Square.

EDGWARE ROAD. Along the E side some battered late Georgian
terraces behind shops, and an Edwardian gabled stretch, all
dwarfed by the tower of offices above MARKS AND SPENCER.
This was one of the group of 1960s towers marking the start of
Westway, refurbished by *Fairhurst Architects* in 1990–1.

FOLEY STREET. A broad street with a bend. At the NE corner
with Cleveland Street, opposite All Souls School, the KING
AND QUEEN, a late Victorian pub with Gothic details (unusual
for this area). The tiny cylindrical turret now appears like a
naughty echo of the Telecom Tower beyond. Further W No. 40
with two shaped gables, in a subdued Arts and Crafts style of *c.*
1900 (cf. Candover Street), and some minor survivals of the C18
(Nos. 21a–23, 37, 22, 30).

GARBUTT PLACE. *See* Marylebone High Street.

GEORGE STREET. A long street running W from Marylebone High
Street; terraces mostly with shops, much interrupted by later
developments. At the E end Nos. 2–6, late C18, then, next to the
R.C. church of St James (q.v.), church buildings by *Goldie, Child
& Goldie*, 1889, gabled with mullioned windows. Then more
altered late C18 terraces, notably DURRANTS HOTEL, a hand-
some front with refined details of early C19 type, giant pilasters
and guilloche band. Opposite, an obtrusive block of 1970s flats
over shops, dark brick, which continues back to ROBERT ADAM
STREET and incorporates St Paul's church (q.v.). Scattered early
C19 terraces further W, ending on a very minor scale near
Edgware Road.

GLOUCESTER PLACE. Laid out *c.* 1790, at the same time as Baker
Street, but with less elaborate houses. Unlike Baker Street, the
impression of Georgian frontages is preserved without a break

all the way up to Marylebone Road and beyond, with plenty of good doorways and iron railings. Nos. 24–40 deserve special scrutiny: the impeccable facsimile façades by *Elsom Pack & Roberts*, 1977, conceal new buildings behind.

GOSFIELD STREET, parallel with Great Titchfield Street. A view of Holy Trinity at the N end. Late C18 Nos. 16 (with doorcase), 17, and 27 (four bays, only two storeys, but subdivided and much altered).

GRANVILLE PLACE. *See* Portman Square.

GREAT CASTLE STREET, W of Eastcastle Street. Mostly taken up by the back of Oxford Street shops. Nos. 21–22, Baroque with giant pilasters, is the best among the Edwardian offices.

GREAT CUMBERLAND PLACE. Portman estate development of *c.* 1789–90, running N from Oxford Street to Bryanston Square (q.v.), now much rebuilt. Planned to include a complete circus, of which only the E half was built (Nos. 24–42). Plain houses with stucco ground floors and some good ironwork; the houses on the straight side opposite enriched with groups of thin Ionic pilasters. Possibly by *William Porden*, who had a lease on No. 38. Further N houses of *c.* 1820, contemporary with Bryanston Square.

GREAT PORTLAND STREET. A very mixed bag. The S end near Oxford Street mostly Edwardian, with little of merit. A recurrent motif is the shopfront with large arch embracing big first-floor windows: see Nos. 19–21, 1908 by *F. M. Elgood*, in brick with pilasters above and central pedimented feature; Nos. 14–16, 1914, in stone; No. 50, in faience, heightened in 1928 by *Elgood & Hastie*. Of more interest are the corner buildings: No. 27, THE COCK, terracotta-trimmed, with a pretty frieze, and a corner turret, dated 1897; No. 55, THE GEORGE, later C19 with busy stucco decoration and nice ironwork; and, diagonally opposite, Nos. 54–56, 1890 by *W. J Millar*, a Jacobean bank building. In contrast, No. 73 is a typical corner block of the 1930s, with window bands and rounded corner, quite an anonymous style, 1937 by *Emberton*. On the E side, Nos. 78–80, 1904 by *W. H. White*, with yet another turret, this time of the free Arts and Crafts type. No. 126 is by *Beresford Pite*, 1898, altered later. Built as the Girls and Infants School for All Souls Langham Place. Red brick with oriel windows. No. 128, the HORSE AND GROOM, has a lively mid C19 front, stuccoed quoins and cornice, and an arcaded first floor with blind arches between the windows. Nos. 160–200 (continuing back along Bolsover Street) consist of a vast stone-faced block with elaborate balconies and pavilion roofs, 1904–12 by *Boehmer & Gibbs*. Opposite, Nos. 175–185 by *Robert Angell*, *c.* 1913. Further N on the E side the ROYAL NATIONAL INSTITUTE FOR THE BLIND, a tall stone-faced formal front in the French Beaux-Arts manner, 1909–14 by *Claude Ferrier*, containing Armitage Hall (named after Dr T. R. Armitage, who founded the forerunner to the Institute in 1868). Then the former ROYAL NATIONAL ORTHOPAEDIC HOSPITAL (now AMI Portland Hospital), a very large and busy stone façade dated 1909, by *Rowland Plumbe*.

GREAT TITCHFIELD STREET, from S to N. On the W side, *Beresford Pite's* Y.W.C.A. (*see* Mortimer Street). Nos. 46–54 (BALFOUR HOUSE; built as All Souls Church House) 1891–4 also by *Beresford Pite*. Angels over the doorway. Nos. 85–89 1894 by *A. Whitcombe*. Segmental arches to the ground-floor shops, shallow bows above, the whole tied together by a huge shaped gable. Then in this lively stretch with plenty of small shops, something of the late C18: No. 93 (good fanlight) and Nos. 95–101, a single composition with the end houses given more elaborate first-floor windows (later additions?). No. 101 also has rustication and friezes. The W corners of New Cavendish Street (q.v.) interrupt the mood, but are followed by some jolly turn-of-the-century mansion flats (SELWORTHY, PORLOCK and LYNTON HOUSES). The N end of the street is all new (*see* Clipstone Street, Carburton Street).

GROTTO PASSAGE. *See* Paddington Street.

HALLAM STREET, parallel with Great Portland Street. In the middle of the E side, No. 44, GENERAL MEDICAL COUNCIL, by *Eustace Frere*, 1915–22. A finely detailed stone front: to the r. a shallow bow-window, to the l. also tall windows, but keeping within the flat façade. The tall windows and the bow-window have small caryatids at the top of the mullions. A relief on the lintel of the door. An original, very cultured handwriting. It would be worth while to look for it in other places. (Council chamber with galleries at the E end; its Adamish ceiling is now concealed.) No. 50 was added by *Frere* in the 1930s.

HANSON STREET, parallel with Great Titchfield Street. At the S end some modest houses of the late C18 (Nos. 8, 16–20, 24) and early C19 (Nos. 1–7) between tenements of *c.* 1910.

HARCOURT STREET. *See* York Street.

HARLEY STREET runs N through the Portland estate from the W corner of Cavendish Square all the way to Marylebone Road. It was laid out in the 1720s, but not built up until after 1752, by a variety of different builders. It is a rewarding street to explore, with good C18 stretches complemented by a lively variety of Victorian and Edwardian designs. Almost every house is worth a look. Only the few recent buildings are dull.

W SIDE, from S to N. To begin with the *fin de siècle* dominates. Nos. 1–5, an overpowering terracotta group at the corner of Wigmore Street, 1897, and No. 7, 1900 are all by *R. J. Worley*. No. 9 is of 1891 by *F. M. Elgood*, gabled. No. 11, a little earlier (1886 by *Payne & Elgood*), has a chequered gable and more delicate eclectic detail. Back to the C18 with the modest Nos. 13–21 and 25, not a uniform group. No. 23 is of *c.* 1890, with two shaped gables; No. 27, 1906 by *W. H. White*, has the usual bow-windows and Queen Anne detail, No. 29, 1911–12, *Sydney Tatchell*'s characteristic Beaux-Arts trim (library inside by *C. F. A. Voysey*, 1919). No. 35, a restrained classical stone-faced corner building, 1910 by *W. & E. Hunt*, faces the undoubted gem of the 1900s, No. 37, 1899–1900 by *Beresford Pite*. Stone-faced, with Pite's deft and original handling of exterior decoration. The corner oriel has figures in low relief, and a bolder caryatid higher up, all carefully scaled so as to be easily visible. The top floor, with the architect's typical recessed planes and arches, and the iron railings, are equally worth noting. No. 39, by *F. M. Elgood*, has an extended Venetian window on the first floor; No. 41, 1892 by *C. H. & R. J. Worley*, is stone-fronted, with a canted bay.

Nos. 43–47 (QUEENS COLLEGE) are three plain houses of 1761–5, combined after the foundation of the college as the first women's college in 1848. (Two fine stone staircases with iron balustrades, and a good plaster ceiling.) Rear extensions 1898 and 1924. No. 49 (KYNASTON HOUSE), 1901 by *Elgood*, is another Arts and Crafts corner building (note the big eaves and the bulgy gatepiers). The mixture continues as before with No. 51, 1894 by *Elgood*; Nos. 53–55, *c.* 1910 (putto reliefs); No. 57, 1910 by *Flockhart* (doorway with segmental pediment and shell); No. 59, late C18; and No. 61, 1904 by *R. Hoare & M. Wheeler*. No. 65, 1910 by *Boehmer & Gibbs* (main elevation to New Cavendish Street), is a bold neo-Georgian composition with curved porch and carefully detailed brick and stone dressings. Further N are some of the best C18 survivals, with plenty of *Coade* stone keystones and voussoirs (Nos. 67–71, 75–85, 91–93, 97–99, 107–117), all of the 1770s. Nos. 75–85 have an especially nice variety of Adamish doorcases (cf. Adam's Mansfield Street development just around the corner, although the doors here are not grouped in twos). (Several good interiors.) Fewer later interruptions now, e.g. No. 73, 1905 by *W. H. White*, with a big shaped gable; No. 87, 1911 by *Claude Ferrier*, and No. 89, 1911–12 by *White*, both in the Beaux-Arts manner; No. 90 by *Tatchell* (for No. 90a *see* Weymouth Street). No. 95 by *A. F. Faulkner*, *c.* 1912. No. 101 is of 1901–4 by *White*, with a bow-window. For No. 115a, *see* Devonshire Street. N of Devonshire Street No. 121, with elaborate vermiculated entrance and first-floor windows within blind arches, *c.* 1780. Finally Nos. 127–145, a long terrace of the 1820s, probably by *John White*, the Portland estate agent, built as part of the development of Marylebone Park (*see* Regents Park, above).

The E SIDE, returning S from Marylebone Road, starts with a large and grand Edwardian BANK (National Westminster). Then comes a stretch of the 1820s, as opposite, and further S a good group of the 1770s (Nos. 92–112), with vermiculated entrances in *Coade* stone *à la* Bedford Square. For Nos. 112 and 114a, *see* Devonshire Street. Nos. 97 and 99 are probably by *John White Jun.*, with the plasterer *Thomas Collins*. No. 90, 1912 by *Tatchell*, is stone-faced, with swags over the porch. For No. 90a *see* Weymouth Street. Nos. 88, 86, 82–70, 66, 64 are more well detailed terraces of the 1770s. (No. 88 was leased in 1771 to *John White*. Inside, painted ceiling panels and good plasterwork, possibly by *Papworth Sen.*) The rest can be listed briefly: No. 62, 1934 by *Wimperis Simpson & Guthrie*; Nos. 60 and 58, 1910, probably by *Boehmer & Gibbs*; No. 54, 1904–5 by *Niven & Wigglesworth*, stone-faced; No. 52, similar; Nos. 50–48, late C18 altered; No. 46, 1909 by *Banister Fletcher*, and No. 44, 1907 by *Boehmer & Gibbs*, complementary stone-fronted designs with variations on the bay-window theme; and No. 42, 1892 by *C. H. Worley*, terracotta. Then a boring new section (*see* Queen Anne Street) and finally Nos. 14–6, late C18, and Nos. 4 and 2, much altered, built in 1724–6 as part of Lord Chandos's house, No. 16 Cavendish Square. No. 2 has a fine Adamish ground floor with Roman Doric columns and a first floor with canted tripartite window with pediment and a guilloche band above.

HARROWBY STREET. A humble street near Edgware Road. At the w end a little of the late C 18 or early C 19 (Nos. 42–44 with small keystone heads over the doors), and the DUKE OF YORK, a pub of 1889 by *J. W. Booker* with elaborate debased classical detail.

HENRIETTA PLACE leads w from Cavendish Square, and so is at the heart of the early development of the area, although nothing remains of the original brick houses of *c.* 1730 (which included *James Gibbs*'s own house). The street is now occupied by the back of the Oxford Street stores, a car park, the Royal College of Nursing and the Royal Society of Medicine (*see* Public Buildings), and an office block by *J. B. Gibson, Gordon & Montagu* (1959).

HINDE STREET. Among the few C 18 houses remaining, Nos. 11–12, unusual for their two upper-storey bowed projections.

HOMER STREET. OCTAVIA HOUSE, 1974–5 by *A. & N. Moffet*; old people's flats, discreet elevations of red brick, with timber windows, on the site of Freshwater Place, slum housing bought for Octavia Hill by John Austin in 1866.

LANGHAM PLACE. For All Souls, *see* Churches; for the Langham Hotel, *see* Portland Place.

LANGHAM STREET. The prize goes to No. 35, built as the Howard de Walden Nurses' Home, now the LONDON PRIVATE HOSPITAL. A neo-Gothic hygienic aberration, seven bays, four storeys, all in a Romanesque variety, but of glazed white brick with black brick decoration. 1901 by *Arthur E. Thompson*. Opposite a modest group: Nos. 42 and 48, late C 18, and No. 46, the YORKSHIRE GREY, a pub of *c.* 1860 at the corner of MIDDLETON BUILDINGS, which leads to RIDING HOUSE STREET, a pedestrian alley with humble late C 18 terraces (the only 'third-rate' houses on the Portland estate to survive).

LITTLE PORTLAND STREET, s of Mortimer Street, No. 21 is worth a special look: a warehouse by *Beresford Pite, c.* 1910, with a narrow four-storey front, windows with Byzantine allusions, each floor different.

LUXBOROUGH STREET. The traditional street pattern is broken here by the tower block of council flats behind the Polytechnic building facing Marylebone Road. The flats are on the site of Luxborough Lodge (demolished in 1965), the old workhouse of 1775, itself a successor of Marylebone manor house (*see* Introduction to St Marylebone).

MANCHESTER SQUARE. Laid out in 1776. Its N side is Hertford House, built for the Duke of Manchester and completely altered from 1872 by Sir Richard Wallace for the Wallace Collection (*see* Public Buildings). The NW corner of the square is C 20. No. 18 has offices for E.M.I. and for themselves by *Gollins Melvin Ward & Partners*, 1960, an elegant solution: two ranges of different heights and different, but even, fenestration, linked by a transparent staircase block in the angle. No. 15 is by the same firm (1953, refurbished 1979). The rest of the square dates from *c.* 1776–88, although some of the terraces have been heightened later. Good doorcases to a standard pattern (a frame with half-pilasters). To the s DUKE STREET leads off with some C 18 houses on both sides (varied doorcases); to the N, SPANISH PLACE, with a more modest terrace on the E side, and Manchester Street (q.v.).

MANCHESTER STREET. The s end has been spoilt by rebuilding, but N of George Street are complete late C18 terraces on both sides. Doorways with small *Coade* stone heads. Mid C20 flats in DORSET STREET make a feeble end-piece. At the corner of Blandford Street an early generating station of 1889–90, extended by an Edwardian brick and stone façade of 1901–2 by *W. H. White*.

MANSFIELD STREET. The street was intended as a prelude to a house for the Duke of Portland; it leads instead to a handsome pair in New Cavendish Street (q.v.). At the s end, Nos. 2–4, a massive Beaux-Arts creation by *Wills & Kaula*, 1923, with end pavilions and columned centrepiece, occupies the site of the house in Duchess Street built in 1768 by *Adam* for General Clerk and altered by Thomas Hope, the connoisseur and prophet of the French Empire style. No. 3, opposite, 1914 by *A. F. Faulkner*, is a stone-faced two-storey building (cf. the low early C20 houses in New Cavendish Street) with a screen of Ionic columns linking it to No. 8 Queen Anne Street. But the N end of the street is a genuine *Adam* speculation of c. 1770–5, i.e. contemporary with Chandos House round the corner, and with Portland Place. Duchess Mews indeed serves the houses both in Mansfield Street and Portland Place. The doorways of Nos. 5–15 (w), c. 1773 (No. 15 rebuilt in facsimile), are grouped in pairs. Each of the two end houses has excellent fanlights over tripartite entrances. Good interiors: stone staircases with iron balustrades; two *Adam* ceiling designs for No. 13 are in the V and A; the plasterwork in No. 7 is probably by its builder, the plasterer *Joseph Rose* who did so much work for Adam. No. 13 was later the home of both J. L. Pearson, and *Sir Edward Lutyens* (no doubt responsible for the small-paned windows). The houses on the E side are a little more ambitious, each of four bays instead of the usual three, designed as a group with the end houses projecting, but with the varied details typical of individualistic speculative builders. The NE corner house was converted to offices in 1939–40 by *W. Binns* and *Frank Scarlett*, with a new entrance in New Cavendish Street. (Good original entrance hall and central stair-hall with plasterwork.)

MARGARET STREET. At the w end, near Cavendish Square, Nos. 39–40, with broad shallow bow-windows and a Dutch gable, 1891 by *F. L. Pearson*. Next to All Saints (q.v.) Nos. 9–12 (LONDON HOUSE), by *Simpson & M. Ayrton*, 1907, brick and stone, big, with many bay-windows, steep gables, and Tudor windows. On the s side a series of tall five-storey buildings with a variety of gables and dormers, then ALL SAINTS HOUSE (Nos. 82–83), 1913 by *Ernest Willmott*, with triple-gabled front. No. 84, stretching back along MARYLEBONE PASSAGE, is All Saints Church House and School (now INSTITUTE OF CHRISTIAN STUDIES), by *Butterfield*, 1870. Gothic, red brick with vitrified headers, small inner courtyard, some of the windows slim and segment-headed. Opposite, Nos. 2–3, early C19, stucco-trimmed, the only reminder of the domestic past of this street.

MARKET PLACE. Nothing now except the shape remains as a reminder of the site of the 'Oxford Market', planned in 1719 (*see* Introduction to St Marylebone).

MARYLEBONE HIGH STREET. Now almost entirely a shopping street of *c*. 1900, the result of Howard de Walden estate rebuilding, like St John's Wood High Street. Tall, busily detailed gabled terraces on either side. No. 6 at the corner of New Cavendish Street, 1904, is in a jolly bastard Renaissance with ogee-domed corner turret. On the w side several good pubs: the BLACK HORSE, 1892 by *W. Bratford*, ornate Jacobean, with ground-floor openings beneath a large arch; the QUEENS HEAD, 1863 Italianate, with good bold lettering; and THE OLD RISING SUN, 1866, also Italianate. Nos. 36–37 are still terrace houses of *c*. 1800. To the w, off Moxon Street, GARBUTT PLACE, a small cul de sac of early C19 cottages (formerly Paradise Place). They were bought in 1865 by the housing reformer Octavia Hill (who lived nearby in Nottingham Place), the first group of over-crowded working-class properties where her principles of repair and careful management were put into practice (*see also* St Christopher's Place). Further N in the High Street, on either side of Nottingham Street, the opposing turrets of Nos. 72–75, 1910 by *F. M. Elgood*, and the PRINCE REGENT, *c*. 1900, his bust against a faience-faced ground floor. Good early C20 shopfront and bookshop fittings to No. 83. After some more Italianate houses the commercial area peters out. On the r. was the manor house (*see* St Marylebone Introduction), on the l. the old chapel (demolished 1949; *see* St Mary, Marylebone Road). The tiny garden was made by *L. de Soissons*. The foundations of the chapel are outlined in brick. Obelisk to Charles Wesley, erected 1858, and other memorials.

MARYLEBONE LANE. The best feature is the narrow winding shape of the street (*see* St Marylebone Introduction), although at the s end its picturesque character has been destroyed by redevelopment and widening. The jazzy triangular-gridded car park was an early attempt to give visual interest to this type of building (1968–9 by *Michael Blampied*). The most presumptuous intruder is No. 9, ROSEHAUGH, a glossy cliff of striped black and brown marble with projecting upper bays, 1988–9 by *D.E.G.W.*, quite an elegant street front, but an unwelcome backdrop to the C18 Stratford Place off Oxford Street. N of Wigmore Street there are some houses still on a Georgian scale: Nos. 33–35 (later stucco fronts), No. 39, plain C18, with a simple shopfront, and No. 94 opposite. At the corner of Bentinck Street the COACHMAKERS ARMS, Jacobean of 1901. Further N the pleasant mid C19 stucco-trimmed façade of the PRINCE ALFRED looks down the street.

MARYLEBONE PASSAGE. *See* Margaret Street.

MARYLEBONE MEWS. *See* Welbeck Street, footnote.

MOLYNEUX STREET, E side, and SHOULDHAM STREET, w side. The most complete minor early C19 terraces in the much rebuilt area between Seymour Place and Edgware Road, each house of two bays only. The w side of Molyneux Street is also late Georgian, but less unified. Some more in BRENDON STREET to the w.

MONTAGU SQUARE. *See* Bryanston Square.

MORTIMER STREET. The E end starts on the N side with the Middlesex Hospital (*see* Public Buildings) and continues with an interesting mixture of styles of *c*. 1900. No. 10 (formerly Bratt Colbran) now belongs to the hospital as well. Possibly by *W. T.*

Walker, 1898, in a charming subdued Arts and Crafts style. Nice ironwork and a big mullioned-and-transomed window (cf. the groups in Candover Street). No. 16 is by *Lush & Lester*, 1972, in carefully detailed purple brick with projecting bays. No. 28, Arts and Crafts with Gothic trim, is by *Augustus E. Hughes & Son*, 1914–15. Nos. 34–38 have striking turquoise-tiled upper floors (influenced by Halsey Ricardo?) and an open balcony along the top storey. 1915 by *F. L. Pither and F. M. Elgood*. Nos. 42–44, designed as a hostel for the Y.W.C.A. in 1903, a large but restrained work by *Beresford Pite*. Banded red and purple brick, the flank to Great Titchfield Street given much interest by gables, tall chimneys, and windows recessed within arches on different planes. No. 46 is probably C 18. No. 82, by *Beresford Pite* again, is of 1896, a small building, but with the central first- and second-floor windows connected by over-lifesize atlantes (by *Thomas Tyrell*). Pite, no doubt impressed by Alfred Stevens, was fond of prominent sculpture in his façades.

Less on the S side: the most elaborate Nos. 27–35, 1899 by *Alfred J. Hopkins* in Free Renaissance, the first-floor bowed windows with friezes. No. 49 is plain late C 18, No. 93 of 1909 by *W. & E. Hunt*, Greek Revival, with giant Ionic columns, stone-faced, serious and tall.

NASSAU STREET leads N off Mortimer Street. The E side all Middlesex Hospital (*see* Public Buildings). Opposite, Nos. 15–16, tenements of *c.* 1890, yellow and red brick (typical Howard de Walden), then a little of the C 18: Nos. 20, 23 (good doorcase), and 26.

NEW CAVENDISH STREET. At the W end a good group with Art Nouveau leanings: Nos. 4–12 and 18–24, flats with shops built by the Howard de Walden estate, 1902. In between Nos. 14–16 (formerly a dairy, B. Davies & Son), of 1901 by *Saul & Hardy* (S. Gray), especially attractive with its flat stylized carvings of trees and birds over the curved shop-window. Further on, the S side dates largely from *c.* 1890–1900: tall narrow houses given a Dutch flavour by their variety of gables and oriels (see e.g. No. 42), in the manner of Shaw and his followers in Chelsea (q.v.), one of the best sequences in the area to show how the late C 19 was trying to escape from the monotony of the Georgian frontage (*see* also Nos. 58–59 Wimpole Street). On the N side No. 45, early C 19, shopfront with Ionic columns. Then grander cornerpieces of 1910 (*see* No. 65 Harley Street). No. 76a has a porch with urns, shell-hood, and a scrolly plaque. Further E are several low houses of the early C 20 which tried to restore a domestic character to an area which had gone too professional (cf. also Weymouth Street, Devonshire Street): No. 76, two storeys, seven bays, with stone centrepiece; No. 55, two storeys with shaped gables; No. 59, with central porch and blocked columns.

Facing down Mansfield Street are Nos. 61–63, the best remaining late C 18 houses. The site had been intended in the 1770s for a grand house for the Duke of Portland. Instead, a pair was built by *John Johnson* in 1776–7, seven bays wide, treated as a single 38 composition with two arched doors and an arched window between, all faced with the kind of *Coade* stone surrounds familiar from Bedford Square. Pretty covered balconies, added later.

(Both houses have good interiors. No. 61, built for William
Udney, has a vestibule leading to a curved staircase with
wrought-iron balustrade and oval lantern. Oval room on the
ground floor with pilasters and grisailles. First-floor reception
room with original ceilings in the Adam style, the front one with
painted panels, the back one coved, with Etruscan decoration. No. 63, built for Sir Charles Bampfylde, was altered by
Soane in 1782–4 for the Hon. P. Yorke. Two rooms with ceiling
paintings assigned by Croft-Murray to *P. M. Borgnis*, of before
1795.)

E of Portland Place: No. 73, mid C19 stucco, two storeys only.
At the W corners of Great Titchfield Street, two office blocks by
GMW Partnership. The S one (Nos. 118–126) dates from 1991,
replacing one of 1957 by the same firm. The N one (Nos. 93–97),
originally of 1955, was refurbished in 1976–80, when it was
entirely transformed by dark brown cladding. The original buildings were among the first curtain-walled office blocks in London,
with very minimal fifties detail and pale spandrel panels. Further
E, lesser C18 remains (Nos. 150–154), a nice C19 Italianate pub
(THE SHIP), and then the Polytechnic and All Souls School (*see*
Public Buildings).

NEW QUEBEC STREET. A pleasant, modest later C18 street W of
Portman Square, complete except for later shopfronts and minor
alterations.

NEWMAN STREET. Built up from the 1750s, but of the later C18
nothing remains except a few houses towards the N end: No. 73,
and on the E Nos. 26–29 and 33 (29 and 33 with Tuscan doorcases). Nos. 36–39 are Edwardian flats with segmental hooded
gables and a little Art Nouveau detail. Nos. 23–24, the brashest of
the recent buildings, has parallel aluminium bands and recessed
tinted glass (1976 by *Michael Newbery*). Under No. 26 an archway
to NEWMAN PASSAGE, perhaps the most attractive of the many
little alleyways remaining in this area. It leads to Rathbone Street
(q.v.).

NOTTINGHAM PLACE. At the S end Nos. 1–3, turn-of-the-century
mansion flats with exuberantly exaggerated Baroque detail,
opposite a mid C19 Italianate terrace (Nos. 6–14). At the N end
uniform terraces of C18 character, embellished in 1891 with bay-
windows, gables, and red-brick trimmings (cf. Russell Square,
Ca). Near Marylebone Road the PRINCESS GRACE HOSPITAL,
well-mannered brown brick, with projecting bays from the first
floor upwards, 1977 by *R. Seifert & Partners*.

NOTTINGHAM STREET. At the E end some plain C18 houses
(Nos. 2–5, 18) and some more fanciful Italianate examples of the
earlier C19 (Nos. 23–24). Off to the N, OLDBURY PLACE, still
with a mews character.

OSSINGTON BUILDINGS. A cluster of industrial dwellings of
1888, four storeys, not laid out between the usual frigid courtyards, but fitted into an informal network of alleys just to the E
of Paddington recreation ground (*see* Paddington Street).
HOWARD HOUSE, 1988 by *Leslie Jones*, faces down Aybrook
Street with a well proportioned gabled elevation whose eclectic
detail (Georgian windows, timbered bays) blends happily with
the late Victorian character of the area.

OXFORD STREET. *See London 1: The Cities of London and Westminster.*

PADDINGTON STREET. At the E end a mixture of mid C 19 terraces with some C 18 survivals (Nos. 57–58); also the former CHURCH INSTITUTE AND CLUB of 1898, an eccentric Tudor front with terracotta mullioned windows with joggled lintels. Another curiosity further on: GROTTO PASSAGE, a minute alley (The Grotto, established 1846, on the r.) leading to Ossington Buildings (q.v.). Back to Paddington Street and to the former Central Institute for Swedish Gymnastics (Nos. 16–18), 1910 by *Forsyth & Maule*. A broad frontage with stone centrepiece with open pediment with an urn. The agreeably leafy recreation ground to both N and S was previously St George's burial ground. In the S part there is still a large mausoleum to the Fitzpatric family (1777), a square building with an ogee dome, like a conduit. SCULPTURE: Street Orderly Boy, by *D. Barcaglia* of Milan (†1930), presented in 1943. Further W, some early C 19 terraces near Baker Street.

PORTLAND PLACE was started by the *Adam* brothers in 1773 as a speculation as bold and nobly planned as the Adelphi. It was the widest London street of its day, its width conditioned by that of Foley House, which stood on the site of the Langham Hotel (*see* below). Foley House had been built by Lord Foley in 1758, interrupting the street layout planned by the Harley estate. After a long wrangle, an Act of Parliament of 1767 ensured that an unobstructed view N would be preserved.* The Adams first planned the street as an enclave of private palaces. It did not become a thoroughfare until *Nash* incorporated it as part of his *via triumphalis* to the new Regents Park. The houses designed by *James Adam*, the younger brother of Robert, begun in 1776, were not as grand as had been intended, and declined in size as the street progressed N. They were impressive in their compositions, always taking a whole block front between two streets as one unit. London has not behaved better to Portland Place than to the Adelphi. The wilful destruction of this street, which was a monument of European importance, began with the erection of the Langham Hotel at the S end in 1864, and continued when flats began to appear after 1900. The speciality of the N end of the street is the imitation Champs Élysées flats by *Verity* and others. It is a ghastly sight how of the Adam compositions an angle here, a pedimented centre there, remain, and all the rest is replaced. Only between New Cavendish Street and Weymouth Street can the original design still be appreciated.

We begin at the S end. On the W side, after the Langham Hotel (*see* below), No. 5, 1911 by *Percival W. Hawkins*, with Beaux-Arts detail (sculpture at attic level), then No. 9, AMBIKA HOUSE (British Council), a routine 1960s office block, uncomfortably tall. (Multi-purpose hall remodelled in 1978 by *Tim Foster*.) The worthwhile *Adam* survivals start N of Duchess Street at No. 17. No. 21, the former centrepiece, has Ionic pilasters and pediment (top storey later) and good interior features. No. 23 is by *Newberry & Fowler*, 1936, better behaved than most of the other C 20 additions. A tall stone-faced exterior, with some C 18 pieces re-

*The story is told in F. H. W. Sheppard, *Local Government in Marylebone* (1958).

used inside (mantelpieces, ceiling paintings). Nos. 27–47, N of New Cavendish Street, is the best *Adam* group on the W side, complete except for the centre, which was destroyed in the Second World War. (No. 27 has a good interior with a screen of columns between the hall and the stairs with wrought-iron balustrade. Excellent painted ceilings on the first floor (front room original colours). No. 29 also has good plasterwork.) Nos. 49–51, built in 1778, were the northernmost group until 1781 (rebuilt with a facsimile front in 1979, for the CHINESE EMBASSY, by *Stewart & Penn*). Nos. 55–57 by *Beard & Bennett* chop brutally into the pediment and pilasters of Nos. 59–61. Nos. 71–73 are of 1922–5 by *Wills & Kaula*, huge, with a mansard roof. Nos. 75–81 are modest *Adam* work. No. 83, of 1812, is the end of *Nash*'s Park Crescent.

On the E side of Portland Place, from N to S: No. 98 by *Nash*, Nos. 92–96, then an early C20 group: No. 82 by *Wills & Kaula*, 1927, No. 80 by *Boehmer & Gibbs*, Nos. 70–74 by *Verity*. No. 66 is the ROYAL INSTITUTE OF BRITISH ARCHITECTS, 1932–4 by *Grey Wornum*. In contrast to Broadcasting House (*see* below), the scale keeps to that of the C18 Portland Place, or the height is at least no greater than that of the Adam buildings with their later attic storeys. It keeps well below the C20 flats which break the character of the street. The building is a rectangle of Portland stone with a formal front displaying large bronze doors (by *James Woodford*) and an even larger window above. Two odd free-standing pillars to the l. and r. with aspiring but otherwise obscure statues on top (also by *Woodford*). The side towards Weymouth Street has one tier of large windows, small second-floor windows, then a floor, the library floor (without any windows but figures in relief instead representing Christopher Wren, a painter, a sculptor, a craftsman, and a mechanic, by *B. Copnall*), and above these the small windows of the library gallery. The building is decidedly C20, Scandinavian in ancestry, with a flat roof and no superfluous mouldings. The interior is notable for its ingenious handling of spaces of different sizes, and for its high-quality materials: Ashburton marble, veneered wood, ornamented glass. The centre of the building is a vast stair hall surrounded by galleries, with a fine stair leading to the first floor. Halls and meeting rooms open off this space; there are no corridors. Library and Council Room on third and fourth floors are approached by a side stair, with views down to the main stair hall. Much discreet surface decoration related to architectural themes. In the Florence Hall, incised carvings of Man and his buildings through the ages, by *Copnall*; ceiling reliefs of building trades by *Woodford*. Fine engraved glass panels by *Raymond McGrath*, made for the doors to the fourth-floor terrace; other etched glass by *Jan Juta*. The fifth and sixth floors were added in 1957–8 by *Grey Wornum* and *Playne & Lacey*. Additions at the back by *Stanton Williams* were planned in 1990; a sensitive and ingenious scheme allowing for the enlargement of the library by roofing over the back terraces and creating a more spacious library entrance on the fourth floor. Improved public facilities include a restaurant planned on the ground floor in place of the offices on the Weymouth Street side.

s of Weymouth Street on the E side, apart from No. 60 (1927 by *G. Vernon*), No. 54, and No. 24 (1894 by *W. H. White*), two original *Adam* groups remain, with top floors added later. The more elaborate one has as its centrepiece Nos. 46–48. There are decorative panels between the Corinthian pilasters, and the two doorways are recessed at angles within a single broad archway. Good interiors: staircase with oval roof-light, main first-floor room with bowed end and delicate Adam ceiling. Restored, with tactful rear and roof additions, by *Benthall Potter Associates*, 1984. The centre of the second group is No. 28, with the usual pilasters and pediment. Good interiors to Nos. 28 (stone staircase with iron balusters) and 30 (oval first-floor room).

Down the centre of the street three STATUES which belong with the C20 remodelling: Quintin Hogg, 1906 by *Frampton*, a seated bronze figure with two boys; Lister, a colossal bronze bust by *T. Brock*, 1922; and Sir George Stuart White, an equestrian bronze by *J. Tweed*, 1922.

The two ugly ducklings of Portland Place, the B.B.C. and the Langham Hotel, deserve some space to themselves.

THE LANGHAM HOTEL is a High Victorian monster, seven storeys tall above two storeys of basements. Designed in 1863 by *Giles & Murray*, mauled by post-war alterations for the B.B.C. and damaged by fire in 1989, in 1989–90 it was restored to its original splendour by the *Halpern Partnership*. It belongs to the flood of huge Victorian hotels which began in the 1850s with the Great Western, the Westminster Palace, and the Grosvenor, but it is exceptional, like the Westminster Palace, in being built in the centre of an upper-class residential quarter rather than near one of the railway stations. Its scale, it is true, is tactless in a once-C18 neighbourhood, but in itself it is a fine composition whose merits have been revealed by cleaning and restoration. The style is vaguely Trecento, with round-headed windows under pointed relieving arches, but ending at the top with a heavy classical cornice over a carved frieze at the level of the sixth-floor windows, and with French pavilion roofs. The entrance faces N up Portland Place. At the corner where the road curves into Upper Regent Street is a tower (its tall domed top restored in 1990), and on the E side, echoing the curved portico of All Souls opposite, a large two-storey bow-window. On the W side an extension (new in 1884) in the same style as the original building. The hotel was planned with a central entrance hall leading on the l. to the bachelor wing and the public apartments (coffee room occupying the bow-window, ladies' coffee room, reading room, etc.), on the r. to private family suites (including, on the ground floor, an ambassadors' audience room). These separate identities were emphasized by separate staircases, their iron balustrades bearing the Langham monogram. There were also from the beginning both passenger and service lifts, although the present lifts in the stair-wells, with their charming marquetry decoration, appear to be Edwardian. When the hotel opened the *Illustrated London News* mentioned over 600 rooms and apartments, including 30 private suites with their own bathrooms and water closets. (The total of 36 bathrooms, if not generous, was a distinct improvement on the 14 at the Westminster Palace

and the 8 at Charing Cross.) Across the central courtyard, or
winter garden (later covered over), was the huge dining room,
30 metres long, with two rows of columns and a richly panelled
plaster ceiling. The original decoration was said to be by *Owen
Jones*, although by the 1980s no trace remained of the white,
scarlet and gold mentioned in *The Times* account of the opening
by the Prince of Wales in 1865. Among the technical innovations
that attracted attention were the artesian well, the huge service
basement (said to include a swimming bath), and the kitchen
(beneath the coffee room), claimed to be the largest in London,
with twelve tons of highly elaborate iron cooking apparatus. In
a backyard was Ye Fernerie of 1871, a grotto said to have been
constructed by Louis Napoleon while in exile; its scruffy remains
survived into the 1980s.

BROADCASTING HOUSE. 'It seems to me', wrote Uvedale
Price, 'that mere unmixed ugliness does not arise from any
sudden variation, but rather from that want of form, that un-
shapen lumpish appearance, which, perhaps, no one word exactly
expresses.' Broadcasting House is an example of this. It did again
what the Langham Hotel opposite had done sixty-five years
before – it cast a blight on the whole delightful Georgian neighbourhood, and deprives All Souls completely of its subtle siting
value. A specially unfortunate feature is the windows of the
Georgian shape. They make the grimness of the sheer stone walls
twice as painful. Designed by *G. Val Myers*, 1931. Sculpture by
Eric Gill, especially noble the Ariel over the entrance. The
interior plan consists of offices wrapped around an eight-storey
central block of studios. The interior decoration was much more
daring than the exterior, but only the reception area is in anything
like its original state. *Raymond McGrath* was the decorative
consultant (responsible also for the fittings throughout, such as
clocks and door furniture). The most dramatically functional
studios were by *Wells Coates* (news and production). The military
band studio was by *Serge Chermayeff*, the vaudeville studio B by
McGrath. The concert hall by *Myer* and the chapel by *Maufe*
were more traditional.

PORTMAN CLOSE and PORTMAN MEWS. *See* Portman Square.

PORTMAN SQUARE. Laid out by Henry William Portman *c.* 1765:
ruined in the C20. The N side was the last to be built up, and
had the most ambitious houses. At the NW corner an indifferent
hotel has replaced *James Stuart*'s MONTAGU HOUSE of 1777–
82, destroyed in the Second World War.* The two survivors on
the N side, E of Gloucester Place, are Nos. 21 and 20. They form
a single composition, of three and five bays, with *Coade* stone
panels with garlands between guilloche bands below the second-
floor windows, and ground-floor windows set in blind arches.
The attic floors were heightened later; the balconies also are
additions. No. 21, designed *c.* 1772 by *James Adam* for William
Locke, was extensively altered after 1866, when the entrance was
moved to Gloucester Place. The interior was redesigned in 1972
for the HEINZ GALLERY and the R.I.B.A. DRAWINGS COL-

*It was placed diagonally, a disruptive gesture which became more characteristic of
the C19 (cf. Belgrave Square, Wm). The gatepiers from the entrance screen (attributed
to *James Gandon*, Stuart's assistant) are now at Kenwood (Ca).

LECTION by *S. Buzas & A. Irvine*. Good C18 features remain: top-lit stairwell with stone staircase and iron balustrade, good sequence of first-floor rooms, the back drawing room with painted and stucco decoration.

No. 20, HOME HOUSE, *Robert Adam*'s finest surviving town house, was built and furnished in 1773–6 for Elizabeth, Countess of Home, daughter of a Jamaican merchant, and called, according to William Beckford, the Queen of Hell. The restrained frontage with its neat pedimented porch hides an exceptionally elaborate and well preserved interior, unusually well documented by Adam's drawings now in the Soane Museum.* The house was restored for Samuel Courtauld, who occupied it from 1927 to 1932, and used by the Courtauld Institute of Art from 1932 to 1989. The five-bay front makes it possible to have a three-bay front room and a large back room on each of the main floors, and in addition a spacious staircase behind the two-bay entrance hall. The staircase, in its dimensions preceded among London town 41 houses only by Kent's No. 44 Berkeley Square (Wm), is in a circular well, with one straight flight to the first landing, then two curved ones to the first floor. Very elegant balustrades (of iron, brass and lead), in the form of openwork pilasters. The upper floors are reached by the back stairs, but the main stairwell continues to the top of the house and is lit by a circular skylight. The upper walls, unbroken by doors, are given interest by stucco trophies and painted panels with scenes from the *Aeneid*. The two large grisaille figures may be additions made in the 1920s for

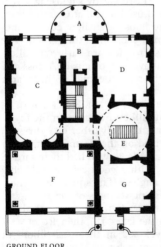

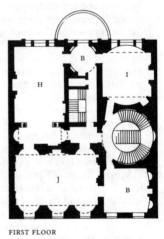

GROUND FLOOR

FIRST FLOOR

A Portico	F Front Parlour
B Anterooms	G Hall
C Back Parlour	H Second Drawing Room
D Library	I Etruscan Room
E Staircase	J Music Room

St Marylebone, Home House, No. 20 Portman Square,
plans of ground and first floors

*For a detailed description see M. Whinney, *Home House* (1969).

Lord Islington by *Philip Tilden*. The planning of both ground and first floors demonstrates Adam's skill in combining rooms of different shapes, a tradition derived from antiquity and used already by the Palladians (*see* Chiswick House, Ho). But in Adam's hands the effects are far lighter and more refined. His use of shallow curves and recesses is especially characteristic, for example in the music room on the first floor, with its three windows set in shallow niches, echoed by the doors in recesses opposite, and in the Etruscan room with its two shallow curved walls with semi-domes. The rooms are exquisitely decorated with stucco of unsurpassed delicacy, small paintings by *Zucchi*, inlaid doors, and elaborate fireplaces. It is all very perfect and very civilized, even if lacking in *brio* and small in scale. The iconography of the painted scenes is idiosyncratic; in contrast to the medallions with well known Virgilian themes (scenes from the *Aeneid* in the front parlour and back drawing room, the Muses in the music room, etc.), the larger library paintings celebrate contemporary English classicism by illustrating two proto-romantic stories published by Addison in the *Spectator* (Vision of a Poet, and the Vision of Mirza); there are also small medallions in grisaille with British poets and philosophers. Most striking is the decoration of the ceiling of the Etruscan room on the first floor, probably used as the Countess's bedroom, its colour scheme of Pompeian red, black and white against a grey ground inspired by Greek vases. The similarly elaborate wall decorations shown in Adam's drawings for this room do not survive. Adam had earlier used such ornament in Lord Derby's house in Grosvenor Square, now destroyed, and used it also at Osterley (Ho) in the 1770s. At the back of the house a shallow curved one-storey portico with Ionic columns opens on to the garden. The first-floor pedimented window surrounds are early C19 alterations, the *Coade* medallions above are original. Across the garden Adam's stable block, with small openings in three large blind arches.

On the W side of the square the CHURCHILL HOTEL of 1970, notable only for the bust of Churchill by *F. Belsky* in the foyer. At the corner of Seymour Street is the only other C18 survival, one of the first houses to be erected on the Portman estate (by the builders *Abraham* and *Samuel Adams*, who had their yard in Portman Street). Upstairs room with a good ceiling, probably late C18 (central octagon and triangles). The square as a whole was first ruined by the big clumsy newcomers of the 1920s and 1930s on the S and E sides: ORCHARD COURT, replacing slums (its site was a rookery already in the late C18), then PORTMAN COURT, their eight storeys developed in the usual idiom of occasional accents by pairs of giant columns (1929 by Messrs *Joseph*). The rest of the S side has been rebuilt to the same height.

There are still some C18 buildings in the mews: in PORTMAN CLOSE, altered stables behind No. 20; in PORTMAN MEWS SOUTH, low houses, a pub, and Nos. 5–6, a thin four-storey house with a plaque to 'Rodney's Patent Concave Shoe', once the home of the Duke of Wellington's farrier. Round the corner in PORTMAN STREET a row of altered C18 houses; in GRANVILLE PLACE an earlier C19 terrace with projecting stuccoed porches.

PORTMAN STREET. *See* Portman Square.

QUEEN ANNE STREET. The most important house is at the E end:
No. 2, CHANDOS HOUSE, built for the third Duke in 1769–
71 by *Robert Adam*, one of his best London town houses. An
unassuming stone front with elegantly carved projecting porch
and nice ironwork. The house is four bays wide (cf. Cavendish
Square E side, Mansfield Street), which allows for a more generous arrangement of the internal space than the average three-
bay house, although it cannot compete with Adam's slightly later
Home House in Portman Square (q.v.). The entrance hall, with
its own window, leads to a rectangular top-lit staircase hall. The
main staircase stops at the first floor, but the upper wall is
enlivened by an open gallery with Ionic columns (approached
from the back stairs). The front room downstairs was the eating
room, with two columns near the door to the back parlour beyond
with its bow-window to the garden. In the back wing the present
dining room was formerly two rooms, possibly with a screen of
columns at the S end. Upstairs, an anteroom over the entrance
hall and two reception rooms. The planning does not yet exploit
the variety of room shapes which Adam had already used in his
country houses (cf. Syon House, Ho) and used later at Home
House and No. 20 St James's Square (Wm), but the decoration
is superb, halfway between Adam's early, more robust style and
the filigree delicacy of his later work. All the main rooms have
excellent ceilings. In the eating room the exquisite doorcases and
matching frieze, the ceiling with bold vine scrolls, and the marble
fireplace with a scene of a sacrifice are especially noteworthy.
The back parlour has a ceiling with flowing scrolls (an early
Adam type) and an unusual coved cornice. In the upstairs rooms
several mirrors, walls with moulded panels, and delicate ceilings
in pale colours, those in the back room with painted medallions
signed by *Angelica Kauffmann*. The COACH HOUSE behind
Chandos House is given a formal front to the back garden with
one of Adam's tripartite openings divided by Ionic pilasters, and
an even more elaborate façade (altered in the C20) to Duchess
Street (q.v.).

Opposite Chandos House, at the corner of Chandos Street and
extending up to Harley Street, flats and offices by *Emberton,
Tardrew & Partners* (job architect *John Tomsett*), 1966–70,
extensive but quite successfully broken up along Queen Anne
Street because Nos. 9–13 of the mid C18 had to be preserved.
The new buildings are of brown brick with obtrusive concrete
projections. At the back a pleasant water garden (ingeniously
contrived over an underground car park) with sculpture by
Lucette Cartwright. The rest of the street is an enjoyable mixture
of the C18 (on the S side Nos. 27–37, No. 29 with a good doorcase,
on the N Nos. 24–28, 34, 38–40) and of *c*. 1900 (e.g. a number of
buildings by *W. H. White*, No. 12, 1911 with Beaux-Arts detail,
Nos. 18–22, 1897, Nos. 30–32 1894, No. 25 1906, with the shallow
bay-window that appears so often in this area). No. 44 is an
unusually detailed corner house of 1890 with shaped gables, bay-
window on a splayed corner, and leaded lights. Nos. 50–60 are
late C18, of different sizes. No. 56 (ROYAL ASIATIC SOCIETY)
is the grandest, larger than the rest, four bays with rusticated

ground floor and doorway with enriched quoins, pediments over
the first-floor windows. (Good interiors.) The s side at this end
is all of *c.* 1900 (except No. 57, late C 18). Worth noting are No. 47
by *E. Carritt*, 1897, with Flemish Gothic detail, and Nos. 59–61
by *H. O. Cresswell*, 1907, with polygonal corner to Welbeck
Street.

RATHBONE PLACE and RATHBONE STREET. A tablet in Oxford
Street reads 'Rathbone Place 1718', but nothing of this date
remains. On the w side a post office (*see* Public Buildings).
RATHBONE STREET to the N, running parallel to Charlotte
Street, with its small shops and restaurants, still has something of
the modest domestic character of the C 18, like the neighbouring
streets w of Tottenham Court Road (Camden). Of the late C 18
Nos. 19–27 with the entry to Newman Passage (*see* Newman
Street), and the DUKE OF YORK at the N end, a stuccoed pub
at the corner of CHARLOTTE PLACE, a pedestrian alley with
C 19 shops.

RIDING HOUSE STREET. *See* Public Buildings: Polytechnic of
Central London; All Souls School. *See also* Candover Street,
Langham Street.

ROBERT ADAM STREET. *See* George Street.

ST CHRISTOPHER'S PLACE, s of Wigmore Street. Formerly Bar-
rett's Court. An alley now lined with smart shops and restaurants,
but in the C 19 one of the many overcrowded slums that festered
behind the respectable main streets of Marylebone. In the houses
bought in 1872 for Octavia Hill (cf. Marylebone High Street:
Garbutt Place) there were forty-five families in forty-nine rooms.
The w side was rebuilt as five-storey model lodgings, Octavia
Hill's first building venture, to designs by *Elijah Hoole*. They are
not yet as deliberately homely as their later efforts (cf. Streets:
3, Ranston Street, Lisson Green): one block with gables, dated
1877, another with Gothic arches embracing ground and first
floor, 1882.

SEYMOUR PLACE. A long street, much rebuilt in the centre. The
s end is pleasantly complete, starting with Nos. 2–10 of the late
C 18. Between Crawford Street and York Street terracotta-
trimmed shopping terraces of 1890 by *Rowland Plumbe* for the
Artizans and General Dwellings Co., the same design as in Chiltern Street. The N end is mid C 19, stucco-trimmed.

SHOULDHAM STREET. *See* Molyneux Street.

SPANISH PLACE. *See* Manchester Square.

STRATFORD PLACE. *See* under Oxford Street, *London 1: The
Cities of London and Westminster*.

THAYER STREET. Some much altered late Georgian terraces of *c.*
1800, and the Church House to the Methodist church, 1881–7
by *James Weir*, Italianate.

UPPER WIMPOLE STREET. Nos. 1–25 are exceptionally complete
late C 18 four-storey terraces, broken only by No. 7, 1896 with
oriel window. No. 26 is a corner house of *c.* 1900, with a hooded
entrance in Weymouth Street (q.v. for No. 1a).

VERE STREET. Nos. 5–6 are of *c.* 1890 with lavish and unusual
detail; elaborate balconies, circular windows.

WELBECK STREET. A similar mixture to Harley Street and
Wimpole Street (qq.v.). E side (S–N). Nos. 7, 8, and 12–14 belong

to the mid to later C18; No. 11a, tall with heavy cornice, and
No. 17, with stucco trim, have been altered in the early C19. In
between No. 10, 1891 by *C. Eales*, and No. 11, 1905 by *F. M.
Elgood*, quite an original corner building with cranked gable and
striped quoins. N of Queen Anne Street a coherent stretch of *c.*
1770 broken only by *C. H. Worley*'s red brick No. 27 of 1893.
Nos. 21–26 and 28–32 all have stucco ground floors but differ in
detail. No. 28 has an especially elaborate doorcase with fluted
columns. No. 29 was the sculptor Thomas Woolner's house.*
No. 32, now the VARIETY CLUB OF GREAT BRITAIN, has a
curious history. From 1813 it was the house of the chaplain
attached to the Russian embassy: the plaster ceiling of the first-
floor front room, including four rustic views of Russian buildings, probably dates from this time. Behind, a chapel (now a
lecture hall) was added in 1864–5 by *James Thomson* in what was
then called the 'Graeco-Russian' style. It has a central dome
(now covered in) constructed of wrought-iron ribs, with arched
lunettes, and walls with blank arcading with very narrow arches –
a motif popular with Thomson.‡

W SIDE (N–S). No. 42, 1907 by *George Sherrin*, has a distinctive
porch on little columns. Then more of the C18: No. 45 with a
similar doorcase to No. 28 opposite, No. 48 with vermiculated
quoins and a good balcony. The S end mostly late Victorian, e.g.
No. 51, 1894, and Nos. 55–56, 1893, all by *C. H. Worley*, and
No. 54, dated 1896, with elaborate Jacobean decoration in pink
terracotta. For Nos. 60–62 *see* Wigmore Street.

WELLS STREET. The pub at No. 13, the CHAMPION, was 're-
victorianized' in 1955 by *John & Sylvia Reid*, with new engraved
glass, bold lettering, and heightening of C19 architectural detail.
It was a landmark in the campaign for the appreciation of Victoriana led by the *Architectural Review* from the 1940s; better
than many of its imitators. Nos. 19–23 (formerly Sanderson's),
1931 by *Richardson & Gill*, is an unusually early example of the
modern office building, with sheer, unmoulded, broad uprights
of stone, and glass and metal between; recessed pavilion roof;
well proportioned. On the W side a very dull MAGISTRATES
COURT has replaced Nurdin & Peacock.§ At the N end I.T.N.
HOUSE, 1966–8 by *William Jack*, with a ten-storey curtain-
walled tower with black spandrel panels, an interloper in these
still quite modest back streets. Opposite is the KINGS ARMS
with quirky Italianate trimmings, stretching round two corners.

WEYMOUTH STREET. First the N SIDE, E–W. E of Portland Place
the only worthwhile older house is No. 12, late C18. W of Portland
Place No. 22, 1936 by *Giles G. Scott*, buff brick with broad
windows and a recessed balcony, is an updated version of those
low Victorian and Edwardian houses popular here and in Devonshire Street and New Cavendish Street. Examples of these are
on either side of Devonshire Mews South. No. 32a Weymouth
Street is by *Davis & Emmanuel*, 1887, with terracotta panels,

*His studio survives behind, at No. 4 MARYLEBONE MEWS. It is of 1861, in a
minimum Venetian Gothic. Open timber roof inside on corbels carved by *James
O'Shea*.

‡See *Building News*, 10 March 1865.

§Big, grim, very restless Gothic of *c.* 1870.

No. 90a Harley Street by *Sydney Tatchell*, 1912. No. 93a Harley Street, also by *Sydney Tatchell*, is of 1910, the end gables with Venetian windows. Then No. 1a Upper Wimpole Street, 1910 by *W. H. White*, a red brick villa with two scrolled end gables and bow-windows. Two shaped gables to No. 34 Weymouth Street, 1908 by *Elgood*. No. 38, early C 19, is similar to the more elaborate No. 40.

Returning along the S SIDE, W–E. Nos. 45–49 simple late C 18; No. 43 earlier C 19, stucco, two storeys only. No. 39, 1936 by *Grey Wornum*, is a simple brick box, two storeys over a basement. No. 31, 1910–13 by *Joass* of *Belcher & Joass*, of ashlar, has a central entrance with thin columns of original design. No. 19 is by *Wills, Anderson & Kaula*, 1916, dull. E of Portland Place, No. 1, WEYMOUTH COURT, by *W. G. Shoebridge*, six storeys, has jolly turrets and shaped gables.

WIGMORE STREET. Not much fun to walk down since the Oxford Street traffic was diverted here. Rebuilding on a large scale took place about 1900.

N SIDE (E–W). Nos. 8–10 are of 1896 by *F. M. Elgood*, an unexpectedly domestic corner building with Venetian window and big hipped roof. Nos. 24 (*see* No. 3 Wimpole Street) and 26, 1891 by *F. L. Pearson*, both have corner turrets (No. 26, alas, painted white all over). Nos. 28–30 are of 1890–2 by *C. H. Worley*. Then Nos. 36–40, a complicated group. No. 40, with a fine terracotta front of 1889–90 by *T. E. Collcutt*, was built as Bechstein's piano showrooms. The ground floor, progressively remodelled by *G. Jellicoe* as showrooms for Gordon Russell in 1935, has since been altered, but some of Collcutt's interiors remain on the upper floors. At the back of No. 36 is the WIGMORE HALL, a handsome small concert hall built as Bechstein Hall by *Collcutt* in 1900, approached by a panelled corridor. The street front to the concert hall was rebuilt by *Walter Cave* in 1904, also of terracotta, to match the Collcutt building, with sumptuous interiors for the Bechstein showrooms in a free English Renaissance style: plasterwork by *Frith*, fire grates by *B. Reynolds*, lavish mahogany panelling. Nos. 42–46 are of 1882–3 by *George & Peto*, with Flemish-style gable. No. 48, 1886 by *J. Norton*, is also terracotta. Then, unmissable, Nos. 50–54 (and Nos. 60–62 Welbeck Street), a stone-faced colossus with corner pavilions, 1906 by *Wallace & Gibson*. Nos. 76–78 by *Treadwell & Martin*, 1906–7, comes as a relief. A tall shaped gable with typical fanciful detail, and a little corner tourelle, although less exuberant than some of their other buildings. No. 84 is again by *C. H. Worley*, 1894, with good terracotta. No. 100 has quite a jolly series of bow-windows. Nos. 122–130 is the only C 18 stretch remaining.

S SIDE (W–E). At the w end *C. H. Elsom & Partners'* huge ten-storey block for I.B.M. (1957 onwards), quite neatly detailed. Then the brasher and later BANK OF CREDIT AND COMMERCE (1972–3 by *Sidney Kaye & Firmin*). No. 71 (PONTEFRACT CASTLE), at the corner of St Christopher's Place (q.v.), is still on a modest mid C 19 scale. Nos. 27–37 is the prize building of the street, formerly Debenham & Freebody (now a variety of shops), by *William Wallace & J. S. Gibson*, 1907–8, with giant recessed columns, three curved pediments, and a turret, the

whole faced with *Doulton*'s white Carrara tiles. (Sir Ernest Debenham had been converted to the use of glazed tiles by Halsey
Ricardo, the architect of his own house in Addison Road Kensington, KC.) The interior was decorated with plasterwork by
Gilbert Seale (ground floor) and *Ernest Gimson* (first and third
floors) and ironwork by the *Birmingham Guild*. Much altered
inside, but some of the ornate plaster ceilings remain, as well as
the marble staircase with bronze balustrade (by *Singer* of Frome)
which winds in two flights up to each floor.

WIMPOLE STREET. Original c18 Portland estate terraces and
later rebuilding, like Harley Street, but not quite as good.

E SIDE (S–N). A monumental Edwardian start with No. 1, an
Edwardian post office façade concealing offices (Kingsley House)
and the Royal Society of Medicine (q.v., Public Buildings). No. 3,
1893 by *C. H. Worley*, is a jolly corner building with fat stripey
turret and gables facing No. 24 Wigmore Street (q.v.), No. 4, by
W. H. White, standard stone-faced Edwardian. Then of the mid
to late c18 Nos. 5, 6, 10, 13–16. In between, No. 7, Edwardian
with much carved decoration. No. 17, also c18, is a little more
special: four bays wide, doorcase with rustication and open pediment. Nos. 18–20 and 23–24, later c18, are interrupted by the
red brick gables of Nos. 21–22, 1893 by *R. W. Edis*. Nos. 28–29a
(WIMPOLE HOUSE), at the corner of New Cavendish Street, is
a somewhat ridiculous pink terracotta pile in a busy late c19
Renaissance. Nos. 30–31, 1912 by *Banister Fletcher*, make a good
contrast with their bold, steep gables. Nos. 33–43, late c18,
irregular and a good deal altered, are broken up by two groups
by *Casson & Conder*, discreet, even façades of the 1960s, but as
usual cramming in extra floors and so breaking up the old horizontal lines of the street, without offering any compensating
detail, as the architects of *c*. 1900 would have done.

W SIDE (N–S). The late c18 still dominates the N end, with
Nos. 44–57 (interrupted by Nos. 49, 50, 52) similar to the houses
opposite. Nos. 58–59 belong with the Dutch-Shavian houses of
New Cavendish Street (q.v.). Nos. 61–71 were also once a coherent c18 group, broken now by Nos. 63–66 (Nos. 69 and 71 have
good interiors). Then comes the usual cocktail of the 1880s
onwards, with nothing special except for two c18 survivals,
Nos. 74 and 79 (both with good interiors). No. 79 has vermiculated bands. Of the rest one might notice Nos. 80 (1885), 81
(1891), and 85 (1913), all by *Elgood*, and No. 84 by *C. H. Worley*.

WYNDHAM PLACE. Enough of the early c19 remains on both
sides to form an appropriate approach from Bryanston Square
to St Mary's church, which faces a little square, paved in the
1980s. To the E of the church, the former SCHOOL, probably by   47
Edward Tilbury, surveyor to Marylebone vestry. Opened in 1824,
for 600 poor children. A bold design of three storeys, end bays
with arched recesses and pediments. The flank wall along York
Street of six bays, rebuilt after war damage. W of the church,
TARRANT PLACE, by *Quinlan Terry*, 1989, pale brick, in a
demure Regency spirit. Central archway with Venetian window
above; mews houses behind.

YORK STREET. Immediately N of Wyndham Place, with the former
school on the corner (*see* above). On the N side YORK STREET

CHAMBERS of 1892 by *Balfour & Turner*, tall neo-Georgian flats in red brick with a cheerful row of pedimented dormers, built as accommodation for professional women, with communal dining hall. Further W pleasant modest early C19 terraces on both sides, the N side with a row of original wooden shopfronts (Nos. 78–94). HARCOURT STREET continues W in similar fashion.

2. Marylebone Road

Marylebone Road is part of the New Road laid out in 1757 to bypass London, which continues E of Regents Park as Euston Road and City Road. It was built up only later in the century, but from this time nothing remains. For the E end *see* Regents Park. The rest is a mixture, with little general appeal, of mansion flats, public buildings, and offices on the grand scale.

From E to W on the N side, replacing a Regents Park terrace, HARLEY HOUSE, huge stone-faced flats in a free Jacobean, 1910 by *W. & E. Hunt*; and the Royal Academy of Music (*see* Public Buildings). Then YORK GATE, the axis between St Marylebone church and Regents Park. Opposite, on either side of the church and school behind (q.v.), and designed so that they do not dominate, two quiet brick-faced office blocks, 1957 by *William Ryder* and *Clifford Culpin & Partners*, followed by the taller METHODIST MISSIONARY SOCIETY, 1939 by *Paul Mauger, A.J. May*, and *L. Sylvester Sullivan*, timidly progressive with its rounded corner entrance and flat relief sculpture above by *David Evans*. For the Polytechnic *see* Public Buildings. On the N side again, MADAME TUSSAUD'S, in its present form externally by *Hunt*, 1884 (long blank wall with pilasters, etc.), internally by *F.E. Jones*. Next door, on the site of Tussaud's cinema, the PLANETARIUM, 1957 by *George Watt*, with a steep dome of concrete covered in copper, springing from low down.

Around Baker Street a variety of mansion flats: the grandest is CHILTERN COURT, the tall, stone-faced block over Baker Street station (q.v.), by *C.W. Clark*, planned as a hotel in 1913–15 in conjunction with the station, but completed as suites and a restaurant only in 1929. A stately classical pile; channelled two-storey plinth with round-headed arches, five plus three storeys above. Beyond Baker Street on the S side BICKENHALL MANSIONS, the somewhat earlier tall many-gabled brick type of flats, 1896 by *W.H. Scrymgeour*. On the N DORSET HOUSE, a lively modernistic block with vertical brick channelling and plenty of balconies with rounded corners, 1935 by *T.P. Bennett & Son*, initially with *Joseph Emberton* as consultant. Garage and shops on the ground floor; the bulk of the nine storeys of flats above effectively broken up by short projecting wings. Entrance in Gloucester Place with carved reliefs by *Eric Gill*, crudely disturbed by a later canopy.

MARATHON HOUSE, opposite the library, 1955–60 by *Gollins Melvin Ward & Partners*, in collaboration with *Casson & Conder*. The earliest London example of the very influential slab-and-podium massing of Lever House, New York. All curtain-walled, the podium with black and white detail, the tower with green spandrel panels, with no visual breaks of any kind, and so optically a little disturbing. Major offices so far from the City represented quite a daring speculation at the time. For the first occupants, Castrol, *Geoffrey Clarke* designed the large semi-abstract relief sculpture in the entrance hall (now partly masked by an inserted floor). Its theme is the development of the oil industry.

HOTEL GREAT CENTRAL, the next big block (No. 222), 1897–9 by *R. W. Edis*, was built in conjunction with Marylebone station behind. Red brick with plenty of Renaissance ornament in buff terracotta, tall with steep gables and a tower *à la* Russell Hotel and Harrods. Originally one drove through the central archway to an inner court. There were 700 bedrooms. The interior, once furnished lavishly with Maple's mahogany (the hotel was one of Sir Blundell Maple's developments), was devised with a series of period rooms. Fine marble staircase; former coffee room with good plasterwork and woodwork. For long maltreated as offices, but in 1989–91 restored and rehabilitated for hotel use by '*S*' *International Architects*.

WOOLWORTH'S is an early work by *R. Seifert & Partners* (1955). In contrast to Castrol's more daring premises (*see* above), its formal stone-faced front is typical of the rather sedate style still generally favoured for head offices in the 1950s (cf. the Shell building on the South Bank).

No. 248, converted to offices in 1989, is the former PHILOLOGICAL COLLEGE (later St Marylebone Grammar School), founded in 1791 in Fitzroy Square, and on this site from 1827. The surviving buildings are of 1856–7 by *W. G. & E. Habershon*, a charming Gothic composition in diapered brick. On the l. a tall gabled part, with an oriel to the former board room; in the centre the Gothic arched entrance leading to a winding staircase; on the r. the former library, an irregular hexagon, originally over an arcaded ground floor, with a delightful interior with open timber roof, lantern, and stained glass (1894, 1901). The other school buildings were replaced by ABBOT HOUSE, 1989–90 by *D. Y. Davies*, which illustrates the brasher picturesque of late C 20 post-modernism. Tapering corner tower; the two lowest floors form a grey granite plinth with striped brick and stone above. The same materials continue along Lisson Grove, where a row of gables with Diocletian windows distracts the eye from the bulk of set-back upper floors of flats.

MANOR HOUSE, close to the flyover, a block of flats by *Gordon & Gunton*, 1907, is an original design, stone-faced, with arcaded top floor and pretty Art Nouveau carving around the bay-windows. On the s side by Old Marylebone Road, No. 199, tall offices by *GMW*, 1986; red metal panels and a thirties-revival glazed turret stair. Brick rear extensions. Opposite the Great Central Hotel, even brasher post modern offices of 1990; blue reflective glazing, a faintly Baroque outline.

3. N of Marylebone Road: The Lisson Grove area

The area between Marylebone Road, Edgware Road, St John's
Wood Road, and Regents Park was filled with three types of early
C 19 development: the terraces and squares at the N ends of Baker
Street and Gloucester Place, continuing the pattern of the Portman
estate work further s; villas around the canal to the N; and scruffier
building to the w, N of the former hamlet of Lisson Green (the
green itself lay just s of the flyover). The respectability of the area
was sadly disturbed in the 1890s, when the Great Central Railway
destroyed the villas and broke into the terraces. The area w of the
railway line is now a medley of every type of urban renewal from
the late C 19 onwards.

3a. E of Lisson Grove

The best pre-Victorian survivals are around DORSET SQUARE, in
   progress in the 1820s and still complete, although with added
   top floors, etc. Tall terraces, with centres and ends projecting,
   the e side the most elaborate: doorways with Ionic columns and
   good fanlights, and pretty covered verandas to Nos. 1, 2 and 8.
   Similar terraces in MELCOMBE STREET, BALCOMBE STREET,
   GLOUCESTER PLACE; lesser ones in IVOR PLACE and
   LINHOPE STREET (with some modish 1970s town houses on
   the e side). e of Dorset Square CHAGFORD STREET, formally
   New Street Mews, where the first Bentley was created in 1909.
   No. 39, CHAGFORD HOUSE, is an exception here: formal Tudor,
   with recessed wings, built c. 1850 as model lodgings.
To the NE PARK ROAD skirts Regents Park. On its w side RUDOLF
   STEINER HOUSE by *Montague Wheeler*, 1926, 1932, and a l.
   extension of 1937, stone-faced, with some of the 'organic' curves
   of Steiner's Goetheanum in Switzerland. (Good staircase.) On
   the e side the tattered row of terrace houses bounding this area
   was reconstituted in 1977–87 by *Westwood, Piet, Poole & Smith*
   by a mixture of repair and rebuilding. The newcomers in the
   middle, Nos. 44–76, have shops behind somewhat clumsy flattened arches. The bowed and battlemented WINDSOR CASTLE
   neatly punctuates the N end. A more distant landmark to the N
   is a lumpy tower with sloping top (No. 125), a block of flats for
   a housing association, cheaply built but with an interesting plan:
   a service core surrounded by flexibly planned rooms. By *Farrell
   & Grimshaw*, 1968–70.
The area w of the railway line, reached via ROSSMORE ROAD, has
   a more diffuse character. To the N stretches the concrete world
   of the Lisson Green estate (*see* below), to the s a more varied
   patchwork of older fragments and C20 rebuilding. In HARE-
   WOOD AVENUE on the w side a stucco-trimmed terrace and St
   Edward's Convent (*see* Public Buildings); to the e, plain low
   yellow brick terraces at right angles to the road (*Westminster
   Architect's Department*, completed 1973), nicely in scale with the
   early C 19 development. Along BROADLEY TERRACE, after the
   austere St Paul's church (q.v.), RED BUS HOUSE, 1887 by *G. H.
   Hubbard*, built as Bryanston Working Men's Club; quite a pretty

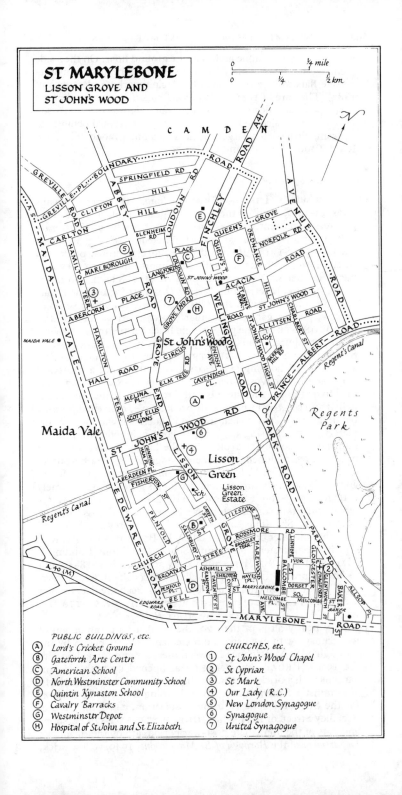

ST MARYLEBONE

LISSON GROVE AND ST JOHN'S WOOD

0 ¼ mile
0 ¼ ½ km

CAMDEN

PUBLIC BUILDINGS, etc.
- (A) Lord's Cricket Ground
- (B) Gateforth Arts Centre
- (C) American School
- (D) North Westminster Community School
- (E) Quintin Kynaston School
- (F) Cavalry Barracks
- (G) Westminster Depot
- (H) Hospital of St John and St Elizabeth

CHURCHES, etc.
- (1) St John's Wood Chapel
- (2) St Cyprian
- (3) St Mark
- (4) Our Lady (R.C.)
- (5) New London Synagogue
- (6) Synagogue
- (7) United Synagogue

design, brick with stone arches to the ground floor. On the s side a change of mood with PORTMAN GATE, the first upmarket private flats to invade the area (replacing working-class flats of 1887). They are of 1986 by *Phippen Randall Parkes*, a piling up of stepped-back, deep-eaved hipped roofs; eight storeys to Lisson Grove, lower balconied ranges around the courtyard behind (cf. the same firm's later, larger blocks in a similar mode in Harrow Road, Paddington, Perambulation 2c).

3b. W *of Lisson Grove*

On the W side of LISSON GROVE a long C19 terrace remains (Nos. 95–127), with at the N end a grander block with Ionic pilasters to its centre (Nos. 129–135). W from here *Westminster City Council*'s restrained low-rise housing of the 1970s in BROADLEY STREET (two and three storeys, brown brick) can be contrasted with the council's later, more adventurous experiments further S. On the S side of ASHMILL STREET an interesting minuscule terrace by *Jeremy Dixon*, 1983; basement flats with maisonettes above, their distinguishing features a series of narrow, perkily gabled triangular staircase oriels. To the S in SHROTON STREET the polychrome brick former mission rooms of Christ Church, dated 1892. Opposite, between DAVENTRY STREET and STALBRIDGE STREET, four-storey ranges of flats and sheltered housing (GLARUS COURT) around a courtyard over garages, for Westminster, by *Lazenby & Smith*, 1987. Like the Dixon terrace, of materials with precedents in the area: channelled stucco ground floor with brick above, enlivened here by banding, curved stucco features, and Diocletian windows. While materials and massing deliberately echo neighbouring pre-war housing, monotony is avoided by the happy intervention of a one-storeyed pedimented warden's lodge and a vista beyond of an enclosed garden. A little further E one can study the different approaches of a century earlier. In RANSTON STREET homely cottage terraces built for Octavia Hill from 1886 (cf. St Marylebone Streets: 1, St Christopher's Place, and Redcross Cottages Southwark, Sk). The earliest are of two storeys, gabled and tilehung, the later ones a little taller. In PENFOLD PLACE, W of North Westminster Community School (*see* Public Buildings), MILES BUILDINGS, less enlightened artisans' flats, 1884, built by the Improved Industrial Dwellings Association, five storeys, with busy classical trimmings, and plainer Peabody flats to their S. An earlier example of planned housing is LISSON COTTAGES, just E of Lisson Grove, 1855 by *Henry Roberts*.

To the N nearly all is of the C20, the result of a combination of war damage with extensive slum clearance efforts begun by the borough of St Marylebone between the wars and carried on into the 1970s. BROADLEY STREET was opened up with pleasant gardens with a brick and timber shelter of 1970, adjoining North Westminster School (q.v.). Much housing by *Louis de Soissons* for the St Marylebone Housing Association, e.g. Lyon House, Broadley Street, of 1934. The CHURCH STREET ESTATE, shops and flats of the immediate post-war period, are by the *Engineer's Department* of the *Borough of St Marylebone*, 1949, yellow brick,

originally flat-roofed (some roofs added *c.* 1989), grouped diagonally to the street in a striving for urban novelty. The characteristic earlier type of balcony-access flats is found in SALIS-
BURY STREET, 1928 for the St Marylebone Housing Association, by *E. W. Barnfield*. Here also the PORTMAN DAY
NURSERY, 1937 by *Howard Robertson*, socially progressive for
its time, with nursery, roof-top playground, laundry, and canteen
for local residents.

In PENFOLD STREET the chief landmark is No. 65, built as a
furniture factory *c.* 1938 by *Wallis, Gilbert & Partners*. Its bold
and colourful neo-art-deco revamping dates from 1985–8, by
Terry Farrell & Co., when it was converted for light industrial
and office units. The two vertical entrance features have been
given new jagged canopies projecting at roof level supported
by a triplet of cone-shaped capitals. The earlier back parts in
HATTON STREET of 1921, which include *Farrell*'s own offices,
are jazzed up as well. The spitfires along the roof and other
playful aeroplane motifs recall the wartime use of the building by
Palmer Aero Products (cf. Farrell's TVAM building at Camden
Town).

Further N the FISHERTON ESTATE (*H. V. Ashley* and *F. Winterton Newman* for the borough, 1924) and the LILESTONE
ESTATE, chiefly the standard type of neo-Georgian blocks of
between the wars, with plainer post-war additions, their setting
improved by 1970s landscaping and playground between
Frampton Street and Orchardson Street by *Trevor Dannatt &
Partners*. Facing Aberdeen Place, a block of 1951 in the austerely
progressive manner of the early post-war years: a six-storey
composition with curved staircase towers and metal windows
(*L.C.C. Valuer's Department*).

The N side of ABERDEEN PLACE is entirely different, the S tip of
the Harrow estate (*see* end of Perambulation 4). A respectable
early C19 terrace remains (Nos. 25–33), attractively detailed, with
honeysuckle balconies, the first-floor windows within shallow
arches. At the E end a lively free classical pub of 1898, now named
CROCKERS after its developer, Frank Crocker, who had hoped
the Great Central terminus would be nearby. More of the earlier
C19 round the corner in CUNNINGHAM PLACE: No. 10a, a
detached villa, one of Landseer's houses, and Nos. 11–18, a
formal terrace, with taller centre and end houses unusually decorated with big paterae. Attached to No. 18, an Arab studio
built for the architect *J. W. Wild*. Opposite, stretching to Lisson
Grove, cul de sacs of two- to four-storey housing of the later
1970s by *Gollins Melvin Ward & Partners* for Westminster, quite
high-density groups (*c.* 185 p.p.a.), their friendly brown brick
and pitched roofs in conscious reaction to the Lisson Green estate
to the E. They replaced the cramped flats of Wharncliffe Gardens,
built by the Great Central Railway for the population displaced
by the line into Marylebone Station.

LISSON GREEN ESTATE, E of Lisson Grove, on the site of Marylebone goods yard, was an ambitious post-war undertaking begun
by the *Borough of St Marylebone* and completed in 1975 by the
City of Westminster, on the scale that was encouraged by the use
of industrialized building techniques. Slab blocks of six to seven

storeys for 50,000 people (1,467 dwellings at 227 p.p.a.). The monotony is somewhat redeemed by good landscaping, and by the open area near the canal at the N end.

4. St John's Wood

St John's Wood, the area N of St John's Wood Road, owes its name to the Knights Hospitallers, who held land here from the C13. From 1732 much of the area belonged to the Eyre family, for whom an ambitious development plan was drawn up in 1794. It was not executed, but its proposed detached and semi-detached villas anticipated, and perhaps influenced, Nash in his slightly later scheme for Regents Park. The buildings that eventually went up in the 1820s and 1830s were a mixture of villas and terraces in generous gardens. There is not much of individual note, but the whole area had until the early C20 a character decidedly of its own, a comfortable, verdant, early Victorian character, never showy and never mean. It was largely destroyed by the incursion of blocks of flats without special local qualities, and the old atmosphere can now best be recaptured N and E of the High Street and in the streets off the N end of Abbey Road; elsewhere there are only isolated pockets.

4a. E of Wellington Road

E of Wellington Road, ST JOHN'S WOOD HIGH STREET was the centre of Portland Town, a disorganized and somewhat slummy development of the early C19 on land belonging to the Portland estate. The area was a much criticized eyesore beside the respectable villas of the Eyre estate until it was entirely rebuilt from the end of the C19. At the S end massive mansion flats overlook the leafy churchyard: NORTHGATE, at the corner by Regents Park, and HANOVER HOUSE, 1903–4 by *E. P. Warren*, striped brick and stone. The shopping parades further N are of the same date and might be in any suburb. The best group is on the E side, Nos. 64–80, 1903, with alternating bowed and square upper bays in a domestic mode reminiscent of Ernest Newton. Further on, at the corner of Allitsen Road, the SIR ISAAC NEWTON, a brick and terracotta-faced pub of 1892; intricate glazing to the ground-floor windows. In ALLITSEN ROAD more improvements: HOWARD DE WALDEN BUILDINGS, built as working-class housing in 1904 for the City and Central Dwellings Co., two parallel blocks three storeys high, the front one with shops below, the back one quite stylish, with elaborate brick arcaded access galleries. No. 90 is in a free Baronial style of *c.* 1900, with a tower over the porch. Round the corner in CHARLBERT STREET the former DE WALDEN ROOMS, 1898–9, probably by *C. H. Worley*, built as assembly rooms. Restrained seven-bay front of yellow brick with a little Queen Anne detail to the red-brick window surrounds. No. 48a next door is a former mid C19 SCHOOL; three-bay, three-storey centre with lower wings. W of Charlbert Street the results of later slum clearance, large and dull post-war flats by the *L.C.C.*, others by *Louis de Soissons* for the St Marylebone Housing Association.

The broad ST JOHN'S WOOD TERRACE was built up in the 1830s. Terraces on both sides, those on the s on a modest scale but with good details (note the doors with a circular motif containing the knocker). Of the same date the former CONNAUGHT CHAPEL (Congregational; now film studios) with four-column Corinthian portico and pediment (a tower over the portico was demolished in the 1930s). The WORONZOW ALMSHOUSES round three sides of a courtyard, originally of 1836 (stuccoed Tudor by *Pink & Erlam*, with central chapel), were rebuilt in 1960 in a neutral buff brick neo-Georgian by *G. B. Drewitt*.

In the streets further N a plentiful mixture of terraces, villas, and detached houses of the 1830s onwards, all stuccoed and in good trim, and in an enjoyable variety of styles from the grandest classical to cottagey Tudor. The later intrusions here, mostly of between the wars, are in brick, but not as out of scale as to the w of Wellington Road. A perambulation could include the following. First ST ANN'S TERRACE, with a grand, not quite symmetrical group with central pediment, giant Corinthian pilasters in the centre and at the N end, and much pretty ironwork. In ACACIA ROAD, villas in all styles, e.g. Nos. 1–5, Tudor Gothic with gables, and Nos. 36–37, tall and stuccoed with Greek-key frieze and pedimented windows. More villas in NORFOLK ROAD, set in generous front gardens, the E end in the *cottage orné* tradition, shallow gables with wavy bargeboards (Nos. 2–4, 17–29). In QUEEN'S GROVE a handsome terrace with giant pilasters (Nos. 2–22) and detached houses with unusual details (No. 27 segmental arches on pilasters and a central recess with brackets, Nos. 30–31 the same motifs in reverse order, dated 1847). Finally, off the SE end of the Grove, at the end of the shopping parade in QUEEN'S TERRACE, the delightful scrolly plaque of the KNIGHTS OF ST JOHN TAVERN should not be missed.

WELLINGTON ROAD once had a similar mixture of styles, but the only villas that remain are a sorry stretch behind high walls at the s end (Nos. 2–26). The rest is nearly all flats. The pattern was set before the Second World War by the monstrous EYRE COURT (*T. P. Bennett & Son*, 1930) and was resumed from the mid 1950s with more up-to-date but equally uninspired designs. Better than the rest is BIRLEY LODGE at the corner of Acacia Road, 1971–5 by *Sanders & Westbrook*, a group of towers with chamfered courses, faced in yellow brick.

4b. W *of Wellington Road*

W of Wellington Road, the area N and s of St John's Wood Road, as old maps show, was originally studded with small villas set in large gardens. Relics of this pattern can still be glimpsed in CIRCUS ROAD and ELM TREE ROAD off it, where some low villas still hide behind high garden walls. CAVENDISH AVENUE and CAVENDISH CLOSE, off Circus Road N of Lord's, represent the grander, more formal mid C19 development that followed: a terrace faced by a regular sequence of large stucco and brick detached mansions with hipped roofs on brackets. A few more villas remain in MELINA PLACE, w of the vast flats in Grove End Road. Elsewhere there is little now to be seen of the late

Victorian tradition of studios and artists' houses and of a 'faint
impropriety' (Elizabeth Bowen), although the atmosphere can
perhaps be sensed by the s end of ABBEY ROAD round the
Onslow Ford monument (obelisk with seated bronze women) by
Sir J. W. Simpson, where Alma Tadema's house survives. This –
Nos. 44 and 44a GROVE END ROAD – has Greco-Egyptian
additions to an older structure. No. 44a was originally the covered
entrance to the house. From the same era, a little further N off
Abbey Road, No. 12 LANGFORD PLACE. With the adjoining
houses, this was the house and studio of *John Adams Acton*,
sculptor († 1910), probably built to his own design, a small spooky
Gothic folly with two steep stone gables and a brick and timber
wing. Behind Nos. 5–7 Langford Place, REGENT MEWS, a small,
tactful piece of infilling by *Barton, Willmore Partnership*, 1983.

Flats invaded the area from the beginning of the C20. At the s end
of Grove End Road, dwarfing Melina Place, SCOTT ELLIS
GARDENS, 1903, built by the Howard de Walden estate to
rehouse tenants from Portland Town. Two symmetrical groups
with oriel windows ending in slated turrets over the entrances.
(Back wings with internal staircases, no access galleries – i.e.
classier than most artisan housing of this date.) More flats followed: GROVE END HOUSE dates from 1913, and N up ABBEY
ROAD there are flats of between the wars up to Abercorn Place,
the most recent the vast block for Rosehaugh by *D. Y. Davies*,
1990. Greed has placed them too tight, and thus this neighbourhood is ruined.

In the more intimate streets crossing Abbey Road from W to E many
complete stretches remain, mostly of the 1840s, with houses
ranging from the two-storeyed classical villa with a low-pitched
hipped roof, the projecting eaves supported by coupled brackets,
to Gothic villas and semi-detached houses with steep gables
and sometimes even with asymmetrically placed towers. Good
examples (from s to N): in ABERCORN PLACE, No. 6, early C19
with Greek Doric porch, older than the rest, and Nos. 8–22,
a grand stuccoed terrace with recessed porches behind Ionic
columns. No. 26 is a late C19 red brick villa, a rarity here, the
home of the artist J. J. O'Connor. MARLBOROUGH PLACE provides a good sample of mid C19 styles: Nos. 24–32, detached
stuccoed Gothic villas, and No. 23, an Italianate composition
with three-storey side bow and a tower. Tudor Gothic again in
LOUDOUN ROAD (Nos. 18–26). In BLENHEIM ROAD Nos. 17–
27, attractive, modest grey brick and stuccoed houses with pediments, late 1840s. The use of Gothic houses to add interest at
strategic points is especially characteristic of these streets (see
e.g. No. 28 Blenheim Road, Nos. 46, 48, 54 Abbey Road, Nos. 30,
42 Carlton Hill, Nos. 62–64, 68 Clifton Hill). The w end of
CARLTON HILL becomes especially ambitious: No. 68 has giant
Ionic pilasters, No. 72 a four-storey Italianate tower, curiously
echoed by a gaunt C19 Romanesque brick version at No. 72a
(formerly a Presbyterian church), while at the top of the hill, at
the corner of GREVILLE ROAD, Nos. 76 and 78 are a picturesque
corner pile of *c.* 1840, gabled and battlemented, more castle than
cottage. Houses of a similar scale continue up to No. 86, which,
with shaped gable and tower with battlemented oriel, stands at

52

the head of Hamilton Terrace (*see* below). Continuing N again, the four corners of Greville Road and Clifton Hill are distinguished by more modest Gothic houses, echoed in miniature by the cottages behind (No. 79 and 36 Greville Road). This area was developed rapidly by one builder, *Francis Armson*, from 1843. CLIFTON HILL retains a specially intact sequence of tall villas and terraces.

The C20 appears along the N edge of the area in different forms: in SPRINGFIELD ROAD genteel neo-Georgian residences of between the wars; in BOUNDARY ROAD (S side) flats by *Armstrong & MacManus* for Marylebone (completed 1956), pale brick on a staggered zigzag plan, with ungimmicky details which have worn well. A pretty landscaped garden behind. For the N side of Boundary Road *see* Camden (*London 4*).

The W strip of St John's Wood, next to Maida Vale, belonged not to the Eyre estate but to Harrow School. Its main thoroughfare is HAMILTON TERRACE, wide and tree-lined, begun in the 1820s at the S end with brick terraces, but continued with a mixture of tall terraces and villas only *c.* 1850 and after, and still largely complete. The only C20 intrusion worth noting is No. 58, by *Tait & Lorne*, 1937; one curved corner, careful brickwork above a stuccoed ground floor (top floor and glazing altered). Returning S by this route one reaches ST JOHN'S WOOD ROAD. Nos. 6–12 at the W end belong with the earlier parts of Hamilton Terrace; otherwise, apart from Lord's and the Synagogue (qq.v.), the most noticeable building is a garage (LEX BROOKLAND) with a pair of unusually elegant sheds with tinted glass end walls of *c.* 1980.

PADDINGTON

INTRODUCTION

Paddington nowadays means a railway station; Paddington until the end of the C18 meant a village W of where the West End of London ended by Tyburn gallows and the road to Edgware. The

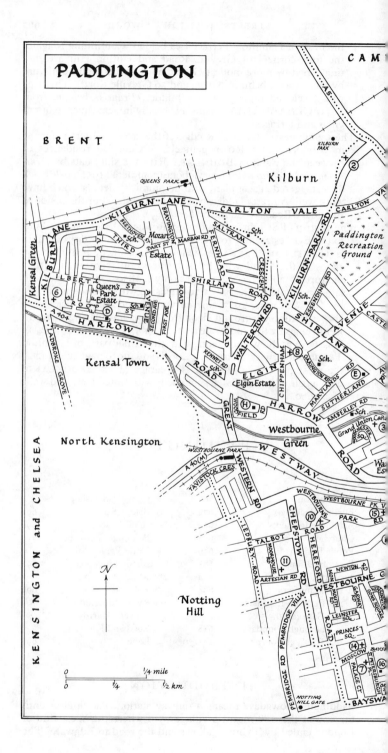

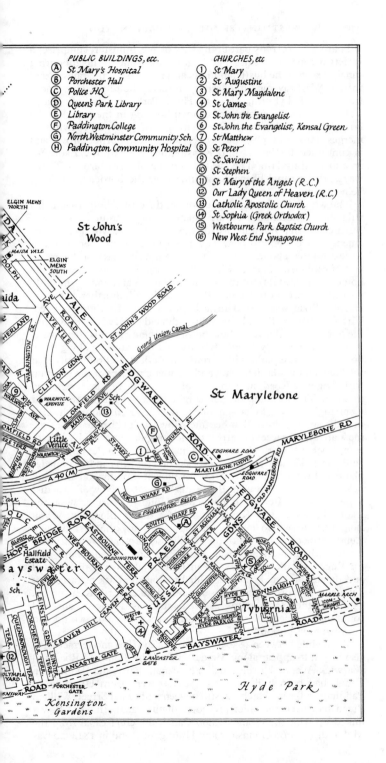

old parish, since 1965 part of the City of Westminster, comprises a variety of separate entities: Paddington Green and the neighbouring canal area with the bustle, muddle, and roar first of the railway and then of Westway superimposed upon them, the respectable stucco frontages of Tyburnia close to Hyde Park, the flats of Maida Vale to the N, the swathes of council housing in the NW. Yet the boundaries are blurred. The character of early C19 Tyburnia merges into mid C19 Bayswater and Westbourne Grove and is continued further W into Kensington (KC) by the Ladbroke area of Notting Hill. The cleared and rebuilt areas around Westway and the canal likewise continue over the border into North Kensington.

The whole district developed only in the C19. About 1820 maps still show Paddington as an isolated village around its green. Further S, near Edgware Road, was a clutter of workmen's tenements called Tomlins New Town; elsewhere, a number of houses were scattered about, such as Paddington Manor, NE of the green, and Westbourne House, where Porchester Hall now stands, the home in the mid C18 of the architect Isaac Ware, and in the early C19 of the architect Samuel Pepys Cockerell. Further N on the Harrow Road was Westbourne Farm, where Mrs Siddons lived. The Westbourne flowed down through fields to Hyde Park to form the Serpentine. Between these houses in their grounds there were, in 1820, no streets yet, only Bayswater Road running along the N boundary of the park, with Orme Square just laid out to its N at the Kensington Gardens end, and Connaught Place at the junction with Edgware Road, near the site of the Tyburn gallows removed in 1783. The building of Connaught Place, begun in 1807, and Connaught Square to its N, heralded the transformation of the area into the smart suburb that became known as Tyburnia, one of the most attractive pieces of early C19 planning in England. Its growth from *Cockerell*'s first plan is traced in more detail in Perambulation 1a. In 1827 Hone's *Table Book* speaks of 'crescents and colonnades planned by the architect of the Bishop of London on the land belonging to the see near Bayswater'. Tomlins New Town disappeared soon after. A similar scheme followed further W on the Ladbroke estate (*see* Kensington, KC). After Bloomsbury and Belgravia these two neighbourhoods show for the first time in London the combination of the English square-and-crescent technique with monumental axes and long vistas. Nash's bold plan for Regents Park must have been influential, as was the palatial and theatrical style he adopted for his Regents Park terraces, but Tyburnia is more consistently urban and, like North Kensington, exhibits other innovations as well, such as service roads and communal gardens not in the middle of squares but behind and between rows of houses.

Meanwhile between 1830 and 1850 stucco villas and terraces had also begun to appear along Maida Vale and in Blomfield Road and Warwick Avenue by the canal. The canal, that is the Paddington Canal, had been built in 1795–1801. It went from Uxbridge to Paddington Basin, which can still be seen N of Praed Street. William Praed had been the chief promoter of the canal. In 1805 it was linked up with the Grand Union Canal, the chief canal from the Midlands (*see also* Hounslow and Hillingdon), and in 1814–20 was extended from Paddington to Regents Park and then to Limehouse and the Thames.

This commercial link was soon followed by another, the opening in 1829 of Mr Shillibeer's omnibus service from Paddington Green to the Bank by the New Road, that is the Marylebone–Euston–Pentonville–City Roads. The fare was one shilling, a newspaper being supplied for the journey. Then in 1832–8 came the Great Western Railway. The choice of a site in Paddington for its terminus brought the area much closer to London. It was no doubt these transport developments that were partly responsible for the rapid growth in the 1840s and 50s. The population figures tell the story: 1,881 in 1801, 4,600 in 1821, 6,500 in 1831, then a hundred-per-cent increase to 14,500 in 1841, by two hundred per cent to 46,000 in 1851, and by sixty per cent to 76,000 in 1861. Soon afterwards the first underground railway, the Metropolitan, opened, providing new fast transport to the City. In 1881 the 100,000 mark was reached and increase slowed down: 1891 118,000, 1901 128,000, 1911 143,000. After that the figure remained more or less stationary until the Second World War. In 1951 it was 125,000.

So much land had been covered by *c*. 1860 that there was little room for later development except on the outer fringes, where the stucco had not yet spread. Maida Vale has an unusual Ruskinian Gothic patch of the 1860s, Harrow Road the humbler Artizans' Queens Park estate of 1875 onwards. The exception further s is Palace Court, built up only in the 1890s, a haven of the Aesthetic Movement, and in its red brick and picturesque roof-lines a remarkable contrast to the rest of Bayswater.

By the early C20 the impractically grand stucco terraces of Tyburnia and Bayswater had already lost their fashionable appeal. The ground landlords (by then the Ecclesiastical Commissioners) permitted piecemeal replacement as leases fell in, but the coherent street layout survived little changed until the late 1950s, when parts of the estate were sold off, and the landlords began to carry out sweeping plans for rebuilding what remained, starting with the area close to Edgware Road. Fortunately other policies prevailed as it became clear that conversion was a viable alternative to towers of flats. The rehabilitation of the run-down area around Porchester Square (where rebuilding had been discussed already in the 1930s by a radical-minded borough council) was at last begun in 1964. It was notable as one of the first major efforts of its kind to be carried out by the newly formed G.L.C. Other restoration work followed (by private as well as public owners), so that many of the remaining terraces of Tyburnia and Bayswater now look, at least on the outside, almost as spick and span as when they were built.

Up to the 1960s – and sometimes after as well – improvement had meant clearance. The borough of Paddington pursued this with especial energy in the years after the Second World War, in order to eradicate the worst slum areas, creating a joint Director of Housing and Borough Architect (until 1958 *R. F. Jensen*). The showpiece in the heart of Paddington is the Hallfield estate in Bishop's Bridge Road, designed by *Tecton* in 1947, bold and imaginative both in its display of progressive aesthetics and in its provision of social amenities. The L.C.C., with rather less coherence, tackled the depressed area around the canal w of Little

Venice. Other ambitious but increasingly unappealing rehousing schemes followed, ranging from the L.C.C.'s sizeable but trim block of flats set down in the leafier outer areas of Maida Vale and Kilburn to the large schemes by the borough of Westminster – the forbidding mammoth linked slabs of the Brunel estate built on derelict railway land at Westbourne Park, and the bewildering Mozart estate at Queens Park. Private enterprise of the 1960s–70s produced much piecemeal rebuilding, including some visually appalling hotels in Bayswater, but nothing of outstanding quality.

The more encouraging achievements of the 1980s are best represented by *Jeremy Dixon*'s group of villas in Lanark Road, Maida Vale, comprising low-rental flats – an exceptionally satisfying and original reworking of traditional forms. Among commercial schemes the most impressive is the renovation-cum-rebuilding of Whiteleys store in Queensway by the *Building Design Partnership*. In the late 1980s developers began to turn their attention to the scruffy but extensive sites close to the canal, forgotten areas occupied by decaying industry or rambling hospital buildings. An ambitious scheme mostly for the luxury end of the housing market by *Phippen Randall Parkes* was begun in 1989 on the Lock Hospital site in Harrow Road. Further major developments are under discussion at the time of writing for the area around Paddington station and St Mary's Hospital.

FURTHER READING

The history of Paddington is traced thoroughly by V.C.H. *Middlesex*, vol. IX (1989). The urban expansion of the area is covered in D. A. Reeder, 'A Theatre of Suburbs, Some Patterns of Development in North West London', *The Study of Urban History*, ed. H. J. Dyos (1966). On Tyburnia, excellent articles by G. Toplis in *Country Life*, 15, 22, 29 November 1973, summarize his detailed research. J. Whitehead, *The Growth of St Marylebone and Paddington* (1989), covers some other topics, as do the general books on Westminster listed under St Marylebone.

ACKNOWLEDGEMENTS

See above, page 590.

CHURCHES

The medieval parish church of St Mary was rebuilt in 1788–91, an original and charmingly restrained building by *John Plaw*, excellently restored in 1972–4. It was supplemented first by the Bayswater Chapel of 1818 in St Petersburgh Place (since rebuilt as St Matthew) and then by large but not very interesting churches strategically sited at focal points in the new wealthy suburbs (no less than seven of these churches were subsidized by the second parliamentary grant for church building). Many of these early to mid c 19 buildings have now gone, although *Fowler*'s St John the Evangelist Hyde Park Crescent (1829–32) and *Kendall*'s St John the Evangelist Kensal Green (1844), Perp and Norman respectively, remain as examples of pre-ecclesiological taste. A more interesting phase comes with the advent of some pioneering Tractarian clergy. Their monuments are *Street*'s intense, ingeniously designed St Mary Magdalene (1865–78) and *Pearson*'s St Augustine Kilburn (1870–7), one of the noblest interpretations of medieval Gothic anywhere in England. His Catholic Apostolic Church of 1891–3 in Maida Vale is in a similar spirit. *Street* was also responsible for the remodelling of St James Sussex Gardens (1881–2). All these churches preserve rich fittings and some outstanding stained glass, and St Mary Magdalene has also one of the high points of late c 19 High Church medievalism: a glittering little Perp crypt chapel of 1895 by *Comper*. As a Roman Catholic counterpart there are *Bentley*'s additions and sumptous furnishings at St Mary of the Angels (1864–87).

Several c 19 churches were lost through war damage, and others have disappeared since then. Of one (Christ Church) only the tower and spire remain; two (St Saviour, St Peter) have been replaced by more compact buildings, and another has been converted to housing (St Simon Saltram Crescent.*

CHRIST CHURCH, Lancaster Gate, of 1854–5 by *F. & H. Francis*, had an asymmetrical façade in the centre of the Lancaster Gate composition.‡ Only the sw tower with its needle spire survives, incorporated in a housing scheme of 1983 (*see* Perambulation 1b).

ST AUGUSTINE, Kilburn Park Road. 1870–7 by *J. L. Pearson* for 81 a high churchman, the Rev. R. C. Kilpatrick. One of the best churches of its date in the whole of England, a proud, honest, upright achievement. The spatial composition is original and wholly successful, both inside and out. The w end is asymmetrical, with the main entrance below the soaring NW Normandy-Gothic steeple (completed only in 1898). The spire reaches the height of 77 metres (254 ft). Inside the tower a generous vaulted entrance lobby with central column. The front of the nave has angle turrets and a large early Gothic rose window in a deep recess somewhat reminiscent of Peterborough. Below the rose window the recession is balanced by a slight projection (for a shallow internal arcade). From the E there is an equally effective grouping of brick masses below the E pinnacles, tower and roofs of different heights (those of the transepts a little lower than the nave and chancel). Very little exterior sculpture (tympanum above the entrance, a little more high up on the E front).

The exterior leads one to expect a lofty but conventional

---

*The following have been demolished since 1950. ALL SAINTS, Norfolk Square. 1895 by *R. Nevill*, replacing a church of 1846–7 by *Clutton*, red brick with terracotta and a timbered gable. – CHAPEL OF THE ASCENSION, Bayswater Road. 1890–3 by *Herbert Horne* (the junior partner of *Mackmurdo*), for Mrs Russell Gurney, chaste Italian Quattrocento. – HOLY TRINITY, Bishop's Bridge Road. 1843–6 by *T. Cundy*. – ST MICHAEL, St Michael's Street. 1861 by *Rhode Hawkins*.

‡There was much stained glass; a window by *Powell*, 1892, is now in the Ely Stained Glass Museum.

cruciform church with low aisles and tall clerestory. The originality of the elevation is only revealed inside. With Pearson's
fanatic consistency, the church is vaulted throughout with brick
vaults on stone ribs (as at his earlier St Peter Vauxhall, Lambeth,
La). The deep buttresses that support the vaults are not visible
externally. The inner aisles – low, narrow spaces – pass through
the bases of the buttresses, the outer aisles lie beyond. The inner
aisles carry a gallery nearly as high as the nave, divided into
tall vaulted compartments connected only by low passageways
through the buttresses. It is an adaptation of the well-known
system of Albi Cathedral in southern France. Pearson, however,
has added projecting transepts of two aisles of equal height, each
with a central pier, and these are not noticeable from the nave
because the buttresses and galleries are carried on uninterrupted
across the transepts as bridges. Square three-bay chancel with
exceedingly narrow and low ambulatory behind (but vaulted all
the same). A similar gangway at the w end with no functional
purpose but to increase the sense of depth. The interior as well
as the exterior frankly exhibit their material, a red brick, dead in
its surface. Inside however this is offset by simple E.E. stone
details (moulded capitals), and by a generous quantity of decoration. Up to the gallery level the wall surfaces are covered with
PAINTINGS (by *Clayton & Bell*), simple ashlar patterning with
foliage in the nave, more ambitious pictorial scenes in the transepts, culminating in the richly ornamented CHAPEL OF ST
MICHAEL E of the s transept, with its apsed sanctuary and gilded
ribs above a spiky Gothic reredos. The intended painting of the
upper walls and vaults of the rest of the church was not carried
out. The chancel is embellished with a profusion of stone sculpture, a piling on of effects that would swamp a lesser church. –
Elaborate REREDOS by *Nicholl* with Crucifixion against mosaic,
flanked by pinnacles and statues. – The stone SCREEN, also
carved by *Nicholl*, was added in 1890. It has five open arches
with much dogtooth, and above them a series of reliefs of the
Passion, continuing also between the N and S chancel arcades.
The sequence is enriched (or confused) by carved stone roundels
and standing figures below trefoiled canopies. – FONT. A sturdy
piece in coloured marbles with baptismal scenes. – PULPIT with
alabaster panels. – LADY CHAPEL (N transept). Furnished after
1930; altar by *Giles Gilbert Scott*, silver lamp by *Omar Ramsden*.*
ST JAMES, Sussex Gardens. Mostly of 1881–2 by *Street*. He used
the chancel of the previous church built by *Goldicutt & Gutch*
in 1841–3, the parish church of the newly completed Sussex
Gardens. It is sited at the w end, a spectacular position. Street
turned the church round, neglected orientation, and made the
chancel his w chapel. His church is flint-faced, Goldicutt's was
yellow brick. His tower had a tall E.E. spire. Good, little altered
interior, in a reticent and dignified C14 style, with clerestory.
Stone transverse arches to the aisles. Wooden ribbed chancel
roof, the nave roof coved and ceiled. Marble-faced dado and
spandrels. – Carved REREDOS by *Forsyth*, against blind tracery

---

*The four notable Italian paintings (by *Crivelli*, *Filippino Lippi*, *Palmezzano*, and
Titian), given to the church by Lord Northcliffe, have been stolen.

filled with pretty floral decoration in inlaid marble by *Blackler*. – Very complete STAINED GLASS, with an instructive contrast between the small, richly coloured scenes of chancel and SE chapel of the 1880s, by *Clayton & Bell*, and the later nave windows by *Heaton, Butler & Bayne*: larger, more turbulent figures of the 1890s in the S aisle; ochre tones of the 1900s in the N aisle. – Sharp, pallid post-war W window by *A. E. Buss* of *Goddard & Gibbs*.

ST JOHN THE EVANGELIST, Hyde Park Crescent. The former Connaught Chapel. Architecturally insignificant, but a necessary accent in the planning scheme for Tyburnia. *S. P. Cockerell* produced an Ionic design for this, but after his death in 1827 the Church Commissioners employed *Charles Fowler*, who built a church in the Perp style (1829–32). Restored and altered in 1888 by *A. W. Blomfield* (new porch, E and W windows). Thin yellow brick chapel front with large Perp window and angle pinnacles. Interior with tall lean-to aisles, thin clustered piers, plaster-vaulted nave, and square chancel. The galleries have been removed. The later work is easily recognizable. – The fittings are largely of the early C20: delicate filigree Gothic SCREEN and PULPIT of 1910; E wall with Perp panelling filled with mosaic; good complete sequence of early C20 pictorial STAINED GLASS in the E window (scenes with the apostles) and in the lower parts of the aisle windows; W window of *c.* 1888; NE chapel windows of 1982.

ST JOHN THE EVANGELIST, Kensal Green, Harrow Road. 1844 by *H. E. Kendall*. An atrocious neo-Norman design with twin-tower façade and central porch with three-order portal. The material is stock brick and flint. The interior barn-like. The chancel, with a wooden vault, was added by *A. Billing* (completed 1903).

ST MARY, Paddington Green. The old parish church was rebuilt in 1788–91 by *John Plaw*, a neo-classical architect interested in neat geometrical design (Belle Isle, Windermere, Cumbria). An unusual and distinguished small building, restored with exquisite 46 sensitivity by *Raymond Erith* and *Quinlan Terry* in 1972–4 (the money came as compensation for the building of Westway, which intrudes so ruthlessly on the green). A restrained exterior of yellow brick, with a white two-stage central cupola with concave lower part. The remarkable feature of the church is the plan, a Greek cross with square centre and lower and narrower arms. The main façade is to the S, but the chancel lies to the E (distinguished by a Venetian window), as it should be. The W side consequently has an entrance portico, but it is kept small so as not to compete with the main, that is S, front. Finely detailed brick niches in the projecting arms. The inside is intimate in scale and out of the ordinary in several ways. In the square centre is a three-sided gallery receding with the arms of the cross in three sides of an octagon. The galleries are carried on columns, those of the main corners of the square being grossly squat to enable them to carry four upper columns on which the shallow pendentives and the shallow dome rest. The arms of the cross also have shallow segmental vaults. This predominance of segmental curves gives an uncommon delicacy to the modest church, brought out well by the new decoration in cream and beige.

FONT. Small marble bowl on a black marble pedestal (new base). Original wooden cover. – PULPIT. Original, but with C17 carvings added in the C19. – BOX PEWS. Original in the gallery; those in the nave of 1972–3. – Also dating from the restoration are the marble floors (two patterns), the fine CHANDELIER, designed by *Erith* in the Dutch tradition, and the ORGAN CASE by *Quinlan Terry* (1978). – COMMUNION RAILS. Iron, very thin, original. – MONUMENTS. Of the unusually fine signed monument to Frances E. Aust by *John Bacon*, dated 1796, only the lower part with a relief medallion remains. – Opposite, on the chancel s wall, General Charles Crosbie † 1807, by *Bacon Junior*. – Higher up on the same wall, Nollekens, the sculptor, † 1823, by *W. Behnes*, with a relief illustrating Nollekens's monument to Mrs Howard at Wetheral, Cumberland. – On the gallery two tablets by *Scheemakers*; also Lieutenant-Colonel Thomas Aubrey † 1814 by *Rouw*, and Charlotte Cumberbatch † 1818, with two ornate figures, by *Cramphorn*. – Memorial tablet to Mrs Siddons. – Eliza Kent † 1810 by *Sealy*, with mourning women and putto by an urn. – Outside, in a niche by the porch, memorial to Joseph Johnson † 1802 with a standing female figure signed *Coade & Sealy*. – In the pleasantly leafy churchyard many good sarcophagi. Buried here also the sculptors Bushnell and Banks, and Benjamin Haydon, who committed suicide at his house in Burwood Place in 1846. – To the w, on part of the site of the former vestry and town hall demolished for Westway, a long, one-storeyed CHURCH HALL in appropriate late Georgian style, by *Terry*, built in 1978–81 (to a smaller plan than had been proposed by Erith). On the outside *trompe l'œil* niches with figures in grisaille.

ST MARY MAGDALENE, Woodchester Square. One of the most remarkable churches in Paddington and one of the most interesting of *G. E. Street*'s London churches. Built for his friend the Rev. Dr Richard Temple West, a former curate of All Saints Margaret Street, as the first centre of High Anglicanism in Paddington. The site, in a poor area close to the canal, was acquired in 1865, and the church was completed by degrees: nave and chancel 1868, s aisle 1870, clerestory and roof 1872, decoration 1878. Since the rebuilding of the neighbourhood in the 1960s the church is much more exposed than formerly, and it is no longer obvious that Street had to cope with a very restricted sloping site filling an acute angle between two roads. The plan, he explained, was not due to the eccentricities of the architect but was the result of 'most prosaic and commonplace compliance with a hard "must" which fortunately the architect of a Gothic building never need object to obey'. Street levelled the sloping site by a concrete vaulted crypt (housing sacristies), and used the narrow s-pointing angle for his E end: a highly effective composition of tall polygonal apsed chancel and a s transept carrying a strikingly slim octagonal belfry of banded brick and stone, with a slender stone spire. The rest of the exterior is of brick, with stone bands used sparingly.

Inside, as there was no room for a full N aisle, Street adopted the curious expedient of two arcades of different rhythms, the S one with conventional clustered piers, the N one in front of a narrow passage, with arches subdivided in two on octagonal piers alternating with slim colonnettes. In the solid spandrels carved medallions with Stations of the Cross (daring at the time). In addition, both arcades are fussily decorated with statues below canopies. A tall clerestory above, with intersecting tracery on the inner plane only, on marble shafts. Walls of striped brick and stone; the cradle roof of the nave painted by *Daniel Bell* with panels of saints etc. but so high up that it is difficult to see. The chancel, as one would expect, more lavishly decorated: walls faced with alabaster, with hexagonal mosaic panels by *Salviati*, some of the first decoration to be completed. – REREDOS with gilded figures carved by *Earp*. – The marble FLOOR and IRON-WORK date from the raising of the chancel in the early 1920s. – Of the same period the LADY CHAPEL ALTAR and the Baroque surround to its altar painting, by *Martin Travers*. The Lady Chapel was originally decorated in 1911 by *Comper* in memory of Dr West. – Excellent STAINED GLASS, all by *Henry Holiday*, made by *Heaton, Butler & Bayne*. Especially good the pictorial scenes of the Passion in the sanctuary (the earliest windows), and the Te Deum in the W window, with unusual tones of green, brown, and purple. The saints in the nave lights dull by comparison, as is the late *Morris & Co.* window (1936) at the E end of the S aisle. – MONUMENTS. Two large medievalizing BRASSES to the first incumbents, with figures below canopies: Dr West † 1893 and the Rev. Bleaden † 1909.

CHAPEL OF ST SEPULCHRE. Formed in the S aisle of the crypt 90 as a memorial to Dr West, and mostly completed by 1895. *J. N. Comper*'s first important work, a lovingly created world of painstakingly accurate Perp detail, strikingly different from the taste of the 1870s. Renovated by *Sebastian Comper* in 1967. Prettily painted ORGAN (1899), with convincingly late medieval figures inside its doors; elaborate wooden SCREENS, STAINED GLASS of 1898 in pale colours, with delicately drawn scenes, one a Last Judgement, another with Dr West as a donor figure with his patron saint, much painting (spangled vault, walls with quotations from the Sarum Missal), and a spectacular ALTAR with a carved, gilded and painted reredos, and projecting panelled canopy above. The centre panel of the reredos was made so that it could conceal the reserved sacrament, as Comper's original proposal for a pyx was considered unacceptable.

ST MATTHEW, St Petersburgh Place. 1881–2 by *J. Johnson* on the site of the Bayswater Chapel of 1818. A large, wealthy E.E. church, with a tall NW (really NE) spire. A very broad interior with shallow aisles and a triple chancel arch. Competent and not without originality, but so totally lacking in inspiration that one finds it hard to do justice to it. – (STAINED GLASS. E and W windows by *Clayton & Bell*.)

ST PETER, Elgin Avenue. 1974–7 by *Biscoe & Stanton*. Church-cum-hall, day centre, sheltered housing, and vicarage packed on to the site of *Newman & Billing*'s church of 1867–70. A similar idea to St Saviour Warwick Avenue, but with the church providing less of a focus. The fine plane tree is more memorable than either the low church or the dull, partly slate-hung old people's flats.

ST SAVIOUR, Warwick Avenue. 1973–6 by *Biscoe & Stanton*, replacing the church of 1855–6 by *Thomas Little* (chancel 1883 by *Fairfax B. Wade*). The needle spire of glass fibre, clasped by clustered brick piers, is a good landmark on the axis of Warwick Avenue, although a more meagre one than its predecessor. The tiny church occupies the tip of the site; the rest has rather too many flats (four to six storeys) around an internal courtyard approached by an ample flight of stairs. Mottled brown brick surfaces and exposed concrete piers and beams, the flats with plenty of angled windows to take advantage of the vistas down the tree-lined streets. The church has a simple brick-faced interior.

ST STEPHEN, Westbourne Park Road. In a good focal position among contemporary stuccoed villas and terraces. Founded by the Rev. H. W. Brooks and built in 1855–6 by *F. & H. Francis*. Standard Kentish rag, Dec. The w tower has lost its spire. Chancel altered 1884, galleries removed 1888. Apses, porch, vestry, etc., added in 1900 by *W. Bassett Smith*; baptistery 1911. – STAINED GLASS by *Gibbs* (s transept) and *Clayton & Bell*. – Future uncertain.

OUR LADY OF LOURDES AND ST VINCENT DE PAUL (R.C.), 337 Harrow Road. 1973–5 by *Clive Broad*. Austere exterior of concrete blockwork housing an interconnecting church and social centre, flexibly planned, with presbytery attached.

OUR LADY QUEEN OF HEAVEN (R.C.), Queensway. 1865, grey brick, with galleried interior. Built for the Methodists; later the home of the Ethical Church; R.C. from 1954.

CHAPEL OF THE TYBURN CONVENT (Shrine of the Sacred Heart and Tyburn Martyrs) (R.C.), Hyde Park Place, Bayswater Road. Rebuilt on the site of a former convent by *F. G. Broadbent*, 1958–62, based on designs by *Goodhart-Rendel*. Wrenian exterior of brick with stone dressings. Calm white-plastered classical interior. T-shaped plan, with apsidal nuns' enclosure. Barrel-vaulted, with an oculus over the altar. Martyr's shields around the cornice. The adjoining CONVENT refronted by *Gerald Murphy, Burles Newton & Partners*, 1990–1.

ST MARY OF THE ANGELS (R.C.), Moorhouse Road. Begun in 1851–2 to designs by *Thomas Meyer*; completed by *Henry Clutton* for Dr Manning in 1857. Additions 1864–87 by *J. F. Bentley*: outer N aisle 1869, outer S aisle and Lady Chapel 1872, roof 1872, Chapel of St Charles 1887, six altars 1872 (St Francis) to 1887 (Holy Ghost), richly adorned with alabaster and mosaic. The exterior of ragstone, with a short tower to one side. Clerestory with a variety of Dec spherical triangle windows. Seven-bay arcades on clustered piers. Presbytery by *Clutton* with an octagonal stair-turret to a third-floor library.

CATHOLIC APOSTOLIC CHURCH, Maida Avenue. 1891–3 by *J. L. Pearson*. Too little known among his works. Large, tall, E.E., with aisles, clerestory, transepts, polygonal apse, and narrow ambulatory; vaulted throughout. The apsed S chapel has its own minute aisles behind slender clustered columns. Exterior of red brick. The front with a lofty niche into which a little apsidal baptistery is fitted. Two small porches l. and r. A SW tower was begun but never completed. (Elaborate altar and sanctuary with tiled floor.)

KINGDOM CHAPEL (Jehovah's Witnesses), Monmouth Road, off Westbourne Grove. Built for French Protestants *c.* 1861–6. Stuccoed chapel with a big pediment and angle pilasters. Handsome lampholders flanking the central stairs.

ST DAVID (Welsh Church), St Mary's Terrace. 1896 by *C. Evans Vaughan* (of Finsbury Town Hall, Is), with Dec w window, approached through a Gothic archway on the street.

ST SOPHIA, Moscow Road. The Greek Orthodox Cathedral of Western Europe since 1932. Built in 1877 by *Oldrid Scott* for the sizeable community of rich Greek merchants who lived in Bayswater. Greek cross shape with a s narthex.* Exterior of striped yellow and red brick. Interior with brick and stone bands, marble and mosaics. Central dome on pendentives. All in the Byzantine tradition, and remarkably restrained and successful. Handsome terracotta walls around the site, with the presbytery (also with some striped brickwork) set on the w side.

UNITED REFORMED CHURCH, Harrow Road, Queens Park. Built as a Congregational church in 1889 by *Rowland Plumbe* for the Queens Park estate (*see* Perambulation 2c). Brick Gothic, rather a gaunt exterior, but an impressive space inside, with galleried aisles, large organ, and well preserved woodwork. Conversion to flats under discussion in 1990–1.

WELSH PRESBYTERIAN CHURCH, Shirland Road. 1874. Debased Italianate front of two storeys; central pediment.

WESTBOURNE PARK BAPTIST CHURCH, Porchester Road. 1961 by *Ansell & Bailey*. Quite daring for its date. Brick with a flèche. Large side windows with rounded corners, the end wall with a solid central fin surrounded by dark mosaic glass. Inside, a bold cantilevered gallery opposite the swooping form of the sounding-board over the pupit.

NEW WEST END SYNAGOGUE, St Petersburgh Place. 1877–9 by   92
Audsley & Joseph. On the grandest scale, closely based on George Audsley's previous synagogue in Liverpool. Harsh red brick with Romanesque (or Byzantine) as well as early Gothic detail. The two front turrets end in a vaguely Moorish way. A big rose window in between. (Interior with tall arcades on octagonal columns with Moorish capitals, a pointed barrel-vault, and domed end. Galleries round three sides. – STAINED GLASS. A window by *Robert Anning Bell*.)

SPANISH AND PORTUGUESE SYNAGOGUE, Lauderdale Road. 1896 by *Davis & Emmanuel*. A Greek plan in the Byzantine manner, with central dome and gabled ends. Polished granite columns inside, with Byzantinesque capitals.

PUBLIC BUILDINGS

There is no civic centre. The old town hall (the former vestry hall), 1853 by *Lockyer*, which stood by Paddington Green, was demolished for Westway.

*In this a stone set into the wall from the earliest Greek Orthodox church in London (1667).

PORCHESTER HALL, Porchester Road. 1925–9 in a flabby Beaux-Arts Baroque by *H. A. Shepherd* and *H. A. Thomerson*. The large stone-faced group incorporates the municipal assembly hall, library, and baths. Round the corner a little one-storey REFERENCE LIBRARY with strip window and porthole window strikes a blow for the modern movement: 1938 by *Thomas Bros*.

POLICE HEADQUARTERS, Harrow Road, near Paddington Green. By *J. Innes-Elliot* of the Metropolitan Police, *c.* 1966–71. Police station, section house, and careers office. One of the group of large buildings planned to punctuate the E end of the elevated Westway. A long abstract relief along the lower part. White seven-storey tower with the favourite 1960s motif of horizontal strip windows.

POLICE STATION, No. 325 Harrow Road. 1912. Early C20 Wrenaissance front with a steep pediment and mannered doorway, in the characteristic style of *J. D. Butler*.

TELECOMMUNICATIONS CENTRE (BURNE HOUSE), Westway, Bell Street, and Edgware Road. 1972–7 by *Charles Pearson Son & Partners*. One of the four landmark towers at the E end of Westway, the position of tower and podium determined by the planners so that the building relates to Westway rather than to Bell Street, where the entrance is to be found. Unappealingly bulky, but well detailed. The tower forms the major element of the vast structure, one of the first three in London to be designed for electro-communications equipment, which occupied 70 per cent of the building when planned and was expected to need more: hence the ingenious detailing of the sleek vitreous enamel skin, whose rectangular glazing panels can easily be changed to allow for internal alterations.

QUEENS PARK LIBRARY, Harrow Road. Well proportioned Queen Anne style with pedimented dormers, a central cupola, and a side doorway with shell hood. 1890 by *Karslake & Mortimer*.

BRANCH LIBRARY, Shirland Road, Maida Vale. A former Methodist church, 1876 by *John K. James,* converted to a library in 1948. Spreading red brick front, pilastered and pedimented.

PADDINGTON COLLEGE, Paddington Green. By the *L.C.C.* for *I.L.E.A.,* 1967 onwards. The use of ingredients similar to those of the North Westminster School on the opposite side of Westway has not guaranteed a similar success, for the college is a lumpy composition of aggregate-faced panels and indecisive fenestration with weak corners. The best part is the glazed recession where the pattern of the staircases gives the exterior some interest.

NORTH WESTMINSTER COMMUNITY SCHOOL (formerly Sarah Siddons), North Wharf Road. 1958–61, one of the *L.C.C*'s large new comprehensives. A satisfying group: an eight-storey and a two-storey block, linked by bridges, and a separate gymnasium with zigzagging roof. The details tough but not over-aggressive, and offset by greenery, especially welcome in this ruthlessly urban area close to Westway. Even, well-proportioned fenestration between aggregate-faced concrete floor bands, dark brick end walls, with just a few touches of colour (red spandrels on the ground floor) and irregularity (top floor windows) to liven things up. Minor alterations by *Cullen & Nightingale,* 1990; major expansion by the same firm planned.

WESTMINSTER SPECIAL SCHOOL, Harrow Road and Kennet Road. Low brick buildings for handicapped children arranged in four inward-looking clusters, with a picturesque variety of monopitched roofs. By the *G.L.C. Architect's Department, Education Section,* 1981.

BOARD SCHOOLS. QUEENS PARK SCHOOL, Droop Street, on the edge of the Artizans' estate (*see* Perambulation 2c), is an early example by *E. R. Robson.* The original part is of 1877, gabled and asymmetrical, with an ogee-roofed lantern. BEETHOVEN STREET SCHOOL is of the early 1880s, PADDINGTON GREEN SCHOOL, off Park Place Villas, of 1900, with curvaceous shaped gables. (Other survivors in Amberley Road, Essendine Road (especially good, of 1900), Oakington Road, and Saltram Crescent.)

HALLFIELD SCHOOL. *See* Perambulation 1c, end.

ST STEPHEN'S SCHOOL (R.C.), Westbourne Park Road. 1897 by *A. T. Bolton.* Brick; Gothic tracery windows.

ST MARY'S HOSPITAL, Praed Street. The original buildings by *Hopper & Wyatt* of 1843–51 face Norfolk Place. Four storeys, with projecting end bays, in rhythm and scale not unlike the nearby Great Western Hotel, but much plainer. Opposite is the medical school, 1933 by *Sir Edwin Cooper,* who also designed the nurses' home (completed 1951). These buildings are of pale brick, in subdued neo-Georgian, but the Clarence wing facing Praed Street displays all the florid glories of late Victorian Baroque (1892 by *W. Emerson*), its stone centrepiece flanked by arcaded balconies. Major development (after abortive plans of the early 1970s) was agreed in 1978, with *Llewelyn-Davies Weeks* as architects. On the tight site between South Wharf Road and the canal, a bulky envelope housing a variety of needs was the only practicable solution. The ten-storey Queen Mother wing of 1980–7 towers above the water with the sleek, overpowering, inward-looking presence of an ocean liner. The lower floors (housing theatres and other services) are crisply faced in yellow brick between continuous window bands in blue, broken on the road side by an effective area of plain wall; the dark brick upper floors, with red windows, which contain the wards and teaching laboratories, are relieved by more broken massing, with recessed centres to the longer sides. Light, airy interiors with a broad central 'street', and much art work: in the entrance hall, tapestries of Earth, Water, and Sky by *Grace Erikson;* in the corridors of the adult wards on the eighth and ninth floors abstract murals by *Bridget Riley;* in the children's department on the seventh floor colourful wall paintings by *Llewelyn-Davies Weeks.* (There are also plans to incorporate some of the decorative tile pictures from the old children's hospital at Paddington Green.) To the w, beyond a raised parking platform leading to a footbridge over the canal, a service block and the five-storey psychiatric hospital, also in yellow brick. A pathology laboratory by the same firm in Praed Street was planned in 1989. Further additions to the N, and demolition of some of the older buildings, under discussion at the time of writing.

PADDINGTON MEDICAL CENTRE. *See* Carlton Gate, Harrow Road, Perambulation 2c.

PADDINGTON CHILDREN'S HOSPITAL (former), Paddington Green. A tall corner building of 1892 by *H.P. Adams* with Flemish gables and much red terracotta. Sculpture over the doorway by *S.W. Elmes & Son.* The interiors were notable for their glazed tile decorations (upper ward with nursery rhymes made by *W.B. Simpson & Sons*, 1895, lower ward with biblical scenes). In the outpatients, landscapes of 1911. Refurbishment as a medical education centre by *Stow Harris Partnership* under discussion 1990; some tile pictures to be transferred to St Mary's Hospital.

109 PADDINGTON MAINTENANCE DEPOT, No. 117 Harrow Road. By *Bicknell & Hamilton*, 1968, a showpiece designed to complement the newly completed Westway, but used only for a short period. Its curved form was a novelty at the time. The streamlined group ingeniously fills the awkward site, its interlocking curved shapes of low tower and three-storey offices composing effectively from different angles as one whizzes past on the flyover. From the canal the low zinc-covered roof of the maintenance shed makes a good contrast with the cream-rendered parts behind. Demolition proposed 1990.

4 PADDINGTON STATION AND THE GREAT WESTERN RAILWAY, Praed Street. Paddington, the London terminus for the Great Western Railway, was begun in 1850 and opened in 1854. The Act for the building of the railway had been passed in 1835, and the line opened as far as Taplow near Maidenhead in 1838, reaching Bristol in 1841. The grandest railway in England, until 1892 the G.W.R. used the 7 ft broad gauge devised by its great engineer, *Isambard Kingdom Brunel.* Brunel was also the designer of the station at Paddington, assisted by *Matthew Digby Wyatt* on the architectural trimmings and *Owen Jones* on the decoration. There were three parallel sheds (the fourth added tactfully in 1913–15), four platforms, and ten tracks. The platforms adjoining the fourth shed were ingeniously inserted in 1913, under the roadway and adjoining Mint Stables (*see* below), using *Hennebique*'s concrete system. The original platforms had to be reached by retractable drawbridges, for there was then no concourse at the s end. The 'transepts' were necessary for traversing frames used instead of turntables. The three long curved roofs (21, 31, and 30 metre spans), their lower parts at first covered with corrugated iron, are of wrought-iron ribs braced by diagonal purlins. The top glazing was originally on the ridge-and-furrow system used by Paxton at the Crystal Palace, a building which had a significant influence on the station, but at Paddington more aesthetic interest was imparted by the tracery patterns on the lower parts of the ribs, the pierced decoration higher up, and, on the end gables, bold swirling patterns of iron straps set against the glazing. The columns, originally of cast iron, were replaced by riveted steel in 1922–4. *Wyatt*'s flanking buildings did not follow any particular period style, although Platform 1, with the Queen's Apartment behind, is in a vague Dixhuitième on the ground floor, and a still vaguer Venetian on the upper (where the oriel was the stationmaster's lookout). The

ornament is mostly pierced or incised, decidedly unbeautiful, but, as Professor Hitchcock has remarked, somehow in harmony with the surrounding ironwork. Redecoration and repair by *Aukett Associates,* begun 1989; remodelling by the same firm of the 'lawn' area E of the main train sheds under discussion 1991. Facing London Street, modernistic offices of 1933 by *P. G. Culverhouse.* In Winsland Street nearby, the former MINT STABLES (now offices) for the G.W.R.'s road delivery department, 1876–83, with concrete ramps and galleries of 1910–11, for 600 horses (future uncertain). In Porchester Road, s of Royal Oak Station, GWR's STATIONERY STORE, 1906–7, an early use of reinforced concrete (Hennebique system); engineer *W. Y. Armstrong.*

GREAT WESTERN HOTEL, Praed Street. Built by directors of the G.W.R., 1851–4. By *P. C. Hardwick,* one of the earliest buildings in England with marked influence from the French Renaissance and Baroque (see the curved roof over the centre and on the taller end pavilions). Central pediment by *John Thomas* illustrating Peace, Plenty, Industry, and Science, a crushingly Victorian programme, in stucco (although stone was intended). Much more ambitious than any previous station hotel, with 115 bedrooms and 15 sitting rooms above the public rooms on the ground floor. All much altered inside, apart from the staircases to the upper three floors, which still have their original decorative iron balusters.

L.T. STATIONS. PADDINGTON STATION is the best preserved of the Metropolitan Railway's standard type: blind arcaded retaining walls, elliptical arched wrought-iron roof. The Metropolitan initially ran from Paddington to Farringdon Street (1859–63, engineer *John Fowler*), the world's first underground railway, mostly constructed in a cut-and-cover tunnel along the line of the New Road. The extension to Hammersmith was completed in 1864; the Circle line to South Kensington dates from 1864–8. MAIDA VALE and KILBURN PARK stations on the District line are of 1915 in the tradition which was established by *Leslie Green.*

POST OFFICE RAILWAY. 1913–27 (engineer *H. H. Dalrympole-Hay*). A tunnel 2.75 metres in diameter, with two 60 centimetre tracks, runs from Paddington to Whitechapel via Mount Pleasant and St Martin le Grand.

CANALS. The earliest is the Paddington arm of the Grand Union Canal (1796–1801) terminating in Paddington Basin between North and South Wharf Roads. Here (in 1990) an early C19 cottage and a slate-roofed transit shed still survived as fragile reminders of the humble scale of early canal-side activity. Redevelopment of the whole area is under discussion at the time of writing (*see* Perambulation 1a). N of this, at the triangular basin at Little Venice, the REGENT'S CANAL (1812–20) (*see* Marylebone) starts on its route to Limehouse, on one level as far as Camden Town. Beside the basin, by Delamere Terrace, the Grand Junction Company's handsome low brick CANAL TOLL OFFICE with broad eaves and gable ends. A good variety of BRIDGES: at Warwick Avenue, 1907, cambered steel beams, ornamental wrought-iron railings; at Westbourne Terrace, 1900, arched steel beams, cast-iron railings; at Harrow Road, *c.* 1860–70, cast-iron arch ribs; at Great Western Road, *c.* 1900, long-span arched steel beams.

PERAMBULATIONS

The first perambulation is of the area s of Westway, the second of the area N of it. Both are divided into three.

1. s of Westway

1a. Tyburnia, from Edgware Road w to Gloucester Terrace

The development of the triangle between Edgware Road and Bayswater Road into a fashionable residential district which the C19 used to call Tyburnia (on the pattern of Belgravia) began after the Grand Junction Canal Company had been given permission to develop part of the Bishop of London's estate for the Paddington Canal Basin in 1795. The first plans for the area to the s were drawn up by *S. P. Cockerell*, surveyor to the Bishop of London's estate, possibly as early as *c.* 1805, although little was built until the 1820s. A plan of Cockerell's dated 1824 shows a design whose principal accents were a main road on the line of the future Sussex Gardens, s of and parallel to the canal, linking Bayswater Road with the bypass round Marylebone to the city. s of this he proposed a polygon and a large crescent facing Bayswater Road, neatly filling the awkward triangle between Bayswater and Edgware Roads. Connaught Street and Connaught Square were begun in the late 1820s. After Cockerell's death in 1827 the plans were modified by his successor, *George Gutch*, so as to produce rather denser development. The crescent was abandoned, and the polygon filled with the smaller Oxford and Cambridge Squares. Nevertheless, the final layout of tree-lined avenues, squares, and crescents which evolved by the late 1830s was more spatially coherent than any known in London until then, and as leafy as the best. The main axis, Sussex Gardens, was designed with service roads to l. and r. with strips of greenery between them, with the church of St James at the w end, where Westbourne Terrace, another tree-lined avenue with service roads, crosses at right angles. N and s of St James symmetrical crescents lead to Gloucester Terrace, another wide avenue parallel with Westbourne Terrace; s of Sussex Gardens is a second nucleus of squares and crescents (Oxford and Cambridge Squares, Hyde Park and Norfolk Crescents). Other squares fill the strategic points in the remaining parts of the triangle.

The earliest houses have their brick walls exposed in the C18 tradition, and stucco only on the ground floor. The later terraces are stucco all over and generally taller (five storeys) with Doric porches, the type that becomes the standard pattern in Bayswater by the 1850s. Around this time one can trace the transition from classical canon to Italianate licence (see Norfolk Square,

Westbourne Terrace). It is not entirely clear who initiated the shift in style to this more grandiose and theatrical street architecture, reminiscent of Nash, used to fill *Gutch*'s terraces, squares, and crescents. Gutch maintained overall control, but plots were let to a number of builders, some of whom may have been their own designers. Architects involved included *Matthew Wyatt,* who lived in the area from 1837, *George Ledwell Taylor,* employed by the estate in 1843–8, who in his autobiography claims credit for parts of Hyde Park Square and the s side of Gloucester Square, and *T. Marsh Nelson,* who worked for the builder William Kingdom, busy in Westbourne Terrace in the 1840s.

By the later 1850s almost the whole area was built up. It remained intact until the early C20, when the frontages facing the park began to attract flat-builders. Between the wars the estate adopted a policy of encouraging the erection of two- and three-storey high-priced terrace houses, mostly in grey brick with mildly neo-Adam detail, as piecemeal replacements to many of the original terraces in the centre of the estate, as leases fell in. From 1957 a much more radical replanning of the edges of the area began, with high-rise luxury flats between Edgware Road and Sussex Gardens, and offices along Eastbourne Terrace opposite Paddington station. More was to have been swept away, but a change of estate policy in 1972 proposed by the planner *Leslie Lane* instead encouraged conservation of what survived. Although the C19 pattern is far from complete, it can still be appreciated, and what remains is now mostly in good order.

For a chronological tour of the best of what survives from the C19 one should start near Marble Arch. The tone is set by CONNAUGHT PLACE, facing the park, for which a building lease was granted in 1807. Tall stucco frontages to the park, but with entrances with large Doric porches on the plainer brick N side; a 'back-to-front' layout that becomes a feature of other parts of Paddington and North Kensington (KC), and which seems to originate with this terrace from the *Cockerell* plan. Refurbished by *B.D.P.* as offices and flats for Cadbury Schweppes, 1972–84, marking the change of policy to conservation. To the N by STANHOPE PLACE to leafy CONNAUGHT SQUARE (1821–30), its four sides still complete. The terraces are in the earlier, more reticent style of much of Marylebone; stucco ground floor, stock brick above, with window heads of rubbed red brick, the centres of each range stepping forward very slightly, but with no other enrichment. Similar houses on a lesser scale can be found along CONNAUGHT STREET, a service street with pleasantly modest shops, and in the turnings off (PORTSEA PLACE, ALBION STREET).

HYDE PARK SQUARE marks the change from the late Georgian style to early Victorian stuccoed grandeur. Only the N side survives complete, four towering storeys above basements, a powerful composition with giant Corinthian columns to the centre, and a continuous stuccoed first-floor balustrade carried round the projecting porches. The NW corner of the square abuts GLOUCESTER SQUARE, on the main SW–NE axis; it is worth studying how the awkward triangular junctions are skilfully handled by means of rounded bows (cf. Nash's West Strand Improvements

of 1832 and Matthew Wyatt's Victoria Square Westminster of
1837). The S side of Gloucester Square, 1844 by *Taylor*, repeats
the Corinthian scheme of Hyde Park Square; of the N side only
Nos. 13–14 and 26–27 are original. STANHOPE TERRACE continues SW, No. 18 with bowed end with pretty ironwork to a two-
tier tented balcony, near the entrance to HYDE PARK GARDENS
MEWS, the most extensive survival of the original service buildings required to support such grand establishments. The formal
entrance is by an archway from Clarendon Place. The tall stuccoed HYDE PARK GARDENS faces the park, but is hidden from it
by a generously leafy private garden. Like the earlier Connaught
Place, it is entered from the back, by large two-storey porches.
John Crake, a pupil of Decimus Burton, exhibited designs for
the terrace in 1836. An extension continues at an angle, with its
back to SUSSEX SQUARE (which is otherwise now of 1933 and
later). From here into WESTBOURNE STREET, which has on the
NE side a series of bow-fronted houses (the windows angled for
a glimpse of the park), a device which first appeared in 1835 in
a terrace in Hyde Park Street (now demolished), and is probably
due to *Matthew Wyatt*, who designed houses for both these
streets.

The opposite side of Westbourne Street is taken up by the ROYAL
LANCASTER HOTEL of 1968, with its dismally mediocre concrete-framed tower overlooking the park, by *R. Seifert & Partners*. (It is poor compensation that more effort was made over the
interiors: reception area by *Gordon Bowyer & Partners*; top-
floor restaurant by *L. Manasseh & Partners*; function rooms by
Margaret Casson, etc.) But to its N stuccoed vistas still lead in
several directions. The dominant one is WESTBOURNE
TERRACE, a broad tree-lined avenue stretching to the horizon,
with stately four-storey terraces set behind private access roads.
It was developed from 1839 and completed only in the late 1850s.
Details vary, but general homogeneity was achieved. On the E
side Nos. 1–31, by the builder *Robert Palmer Browne*, were
complete by 1849, tall but fairly plain, with arched windows to
the first floor. The more elaborate terrace opposite, Nos. 2–30,
was developed by *William King* in the 1840s, a palace front with
raised centre and aediculed first-floor windows. N of Craven
Road two long matching stretches face each other, the work of
William Kingdom, who employed *T. Marsh Nelson* as his architect. They combine pedimented first-floor windows with continuous balconies of cast iron rather than stucco. To the W,
WESTBOURNE CRESCENT, part of *King*'s territory, a confident
composition full of bowed ends, curves off towards the parallel
GLOUCESTER TERRACE, also largely by *King* and *Kingdom*,
where the speciality is terraces with pronounced full-height bow-
windows, some of three storeys, some of two.

NE from St James the major route of SUSSEX GARDENS also
starts with a group of bow-fronted houses, but continues less
ambitiously with stucco-trimmed terraces. Hidden behind these
is a busier, scruffier world of minor streets with shops and pubs in
the neighbourhood of Paddington station and the canal. SPRING
STREET has on the W side a terrace of 1840–5 by *King*, of interest
because its unusual design (arched first-floor windows in square-

headed recesses) is repeated exactly at Nos. 44–50 Canonbury Road Islington (Is), another area of King's activities. The one grander mid C 19 effort here is NORFOLK SQUARE, a cramped pendant to Gloucester Square, now invaded by minor hotels, and with a block of flats replacing a church at the N end.

The line of Spring Street is continued by EASTBOURNE TERRACE alongside Paddington station. Here the w side was entirely rebuilt in 1958–62 by *C. H. Elsom & Partners* with a deadening succession of six-storey office blocks broken by a fourteen-storey tower (replacement of the central block by new offices by *Halpern Partnership* proposed 1990). The station fronts on to the modest terraces of PRAED STREET, named after William Praed, chairman of the company whose canal (q.v., Public Buildings) lies just to the N behind the warehouses in SOUTH WHARF ROAD, an area in the throes of transformation at the time of writing. Up to the later C 20 the immediate neighbourhood of the canal remained a wasteland of lorry parks and declining industry. From here, the glimpse of the parish church of St Mary on Paddington Green beyond Westway provides a poignant reminder of the time when the canal skirted the old village of Paddington before the whole area was overwhelmed by railway lines and suburban growth, and fragmented further by the building of Westway. Along the s bank of the canal there are now the bulky 1980s buildings of St Mary's Hospital (q.v.). In 1990, replacement of the older hospital buildings at the Praed Street end of the site by offices (by *YRM*) was under discussion, as was redevelopment N and E of the canal basin with a package of tall offices, shops, flats, and hotel, by *B.D.P.* At the junction of Praed Street and Edgware Road, large extensions for the METROPOLE HOTEL, by *Igal Yawetz*, 1986–90, adjoining the buildings of 1972 by *R. Seifert & Partners* on HARROW ROAD.

The existence of the canal encouraged early development to its s; much of Praed Street was built up by 1828, as were the better preserved streets to the s: ST MICHAEL'S STREET, STAR STREET, and SALE PLACE. These all retain attractively simple modest terraces. In St Michael's Street they are interrupted by a plain group of artisan houses with minimal brick ornament (Nos. 62–65) of 1878–80, commissioned by the philanthropist William Gibbs from his favourite architect, *William Butterfield*. They adjoined the demolished church of St Michael (of 1860–1 by *Rhode Hawkins*, another Gibbs protégé). In Star Street, next to the church site, a gaunt Gothic SCHOOL.

At the NE end of Sussex Gardens one encounters a drastic change of scale, the result of the radical 1960s reconstruction which followed a master plan drawn up by *Anthony Minoprio* in 1957. Along NORFOLK CRESCENT, THE QUADRANGLE, with tall L-shaped flats and tower; opposite is the WATER GARDENS, 1961–6 by *Trehearne, Norman, Preston & Partners*, developed directly by the Church Commissioners with the intention of setting the required luxury standard. Its tough image and ambitious hard landscaping recall the contemporary Barbican flats in the City. The result here is similarly overpowering, but cruder in its detail. Three assertive towers of flats along the Edgware Road frontage, linked by lower slabs enclosing gardens designed by *Philip Hicks*. Ingenious but contrived planting and formal pools on different levels above the underground car parks; the landscaping still cowed by the hard surfaces, even after twenty years. SW from here the old layout remains, with OXFORD and CAMBRIDGE SQUARES linked by curved crescents at either end, although all the original houses were replaced from 1963 (original plan by *Minoprio & Spenceley* with *P.W. Macfarlane*, detailed design by *C.H. Elsom*, 1965). The low, plain brick terraces broadly continue the pre-war policy (*see* below). Some variety (although not much aesthetic pleasure) is provided by differing treatment of bay-windows and roof-lines. This could not produce the desired density, so alas in addition three domineering towers of flats (completed in 1969) have been squeezed into the squares, painfully overwhelming St John's church in HYDE PARK CRESCENT. To the SW patchy but more spacious 1930s rebuilding around RADNOR PLACE and SOUTHWICK PLACE, low brick houses with dainty neo-Georgian detail, by *Septimus Warwick*, 1939. The best of these inter-war houses is in CLARENDON PLACE (s of Hyde Park Square): CHESTER HOUSE, 1925–6 by *Sir Giles Gilbert Scott* for himself, a restrained villa of seven bays, grey brick, with stone pedimented entrance. The upper storey of the centre, with the main rooms, is set back behind a roof-top terrace sheltered by the projecting wings with hipped roofs. (Elegantly muted neo-classical interiors with black marble skirting and door frames, and a fine roof-lit staircase hall.)

Finally the miscellaneous assortment along BAYSWATER ROAD, from W to E. For Hyde Park Gardens *see* above. ALBION GATE is of 1935 by *S. Warwick*. ST GEORGE'S FIELDS, co-ownership flats in stepped blocks, by *Design 5*, 1973, are set back in gardens on the site of the burial ground of St George Hanover Square, closed in 1854. Earlier flats are represented by Nos. 18–23, neo-Jacobean with Dutch gables, and No. 12, in imitation Parisian style by *Frank Verity*. For Connaught Place at the E end *see* above.

1b. Between Lancaster Gate and the W borough boundary

BAYSWATER ROAD. At LANCASTER GATE the monumentally planned composition dates from 1856–7. Tall well-to-do houses, later than the developments further E, and hence in architectural style more mid C19, with English Baroque details (segmental gables with garlands) and French mannerisms (rusticated bands). Facing the park are long stuccoed terraces by *Sancton Wood*, with two storeys of colonnaded balconies, and at the ends the odd motif of a hollow canted bay-window at third-floor level. All now converted to hotels, but exteriors complete except for No. 100, a post-war insertion, and for the E end of the W terrace, a block of modern flats of 1936 by *O.H. Leicester*. This forms the W return to the square, which had as its centrepiece a Gothic church (*see* Churches: Christ Church). Only tower and spire survive; the rest was replaced in 1983 by SPIRE HOUSE by *Covell Matthews Partnership*, an asymmetrical pile of flats with free-standing uprights supporting concrete flying buttresses in clumsy deference to their predecessor. The tower houses entrance and lifts. In the square a stone MONUMENT to Reginald Brabazon, 12th Earl of March, † 1929. Portrait medallion below a figure of a naked boy. Around the square, terraces by *John Johnson*, 1865. The E terrace of Lancaster Gate (Nos. 1–7) was reconstructed as a hotel with a facsimile façade in 1970. Further W another tall but plainer terrace (now PARK COURT HOTEL), set back behind gardens; a 'back-to-front' plan (cf. Tyburnia above), with a two-storey range and projecting porches to the street behind.

Beyond Leinster Terrace Bayswater Road continues to a different tune. First, Nos. 100–101, the only surviving pair of a group of villas of 1824 by *John Woodward*, a builder who had worked with Nash. No. 100 has a discreet back addition of 1959 by *A. & P. Smithson*, built along the garden wall. These lone reminders of the modest scale of building before the mid C19 are now dwarfed by greedy C20 neighbours: flats stepping up with canted balconies (1980 by *Fitzroy Robinson Miller Bourne & Partners*). Further on is No. 1 PORCHESTER GATE, 1988 by *Green Lloyd & Adams*, whose curved glazed roofs make a striking silhouette when seen from the park. The COBOURG COURT HOTEL, a big, symmetrical brick-and-terracotta affair with Byzantinizing cupolas, is by *Joseph*, c. 1910. ORME COURT is in the same materials, but with a corner turret.

The streets leading N from this stretch of Bayswater Road have a similar mixture of occasional low pre-1850 buildings, tall later Victorian stuccoed terraces, and equally tall or taller late C20 redevelopment often crammed in with scant regard for the character of the area. The outstanding survival in the first category is Nos. 3–5 PORCHESTER TERRACE, *J. C. Loudon*'s 'double detached villa' built for himself and his mother in 1823–5 (and illustrated in his *Suburban Gardener and Villa Companion* of 1838): an original version of the semi-detached villa just then becoming popular in the London suburbs, excellently restored in 1972. It is a plain, square house of brick with stucco quoins, surrounded by an elegant veranda with urns on its roof. Side entrances (originally one-storeyed), and in the centre a domed conservatory, with the steep profile advocated by Loudon for such buildings (cf. the conservatory at Syon House, Ho). It disguises the division between the two houses, and so assists the architect's aim 'to build two small houses which should appear as one, and have some pretensions to architectural design'. The verandas were intended to be specially suitable for invalids; they had capacious service rooms below. The garden was originally larger, with glasshouses to Loudon's experimental designs. On the W side of the street, further N, other quite varied stuccoed villas of the mid C19, and a handsome arch to FULTON MEWS.

In other streets plenty of the more overpowering stuccoed terraces of the mid to later C19, e.g. QUEENSBOROUGH TERRACE, complete apart from its unpleasant corners to Bayswater Road, and INVERNESS TERRACE, with specially elaborate stucco detail (c. 1857). INVERNESS COURT HOTEL (built as a private house) includes an Edwardian theatre by *Mewès & Davis*, c. 1905, now disused. In LEINSTER GARDENS further N a curiosity; Nos.

23–24 are sham fronts built to preserve the respectable monotony of the terrace against the intrusion of the Metropolitan Railway which emerges here. Between here and Eastbourne Terrace, and N as far as the Hallfield estate (for which *see* Perambulation 1c), well preserved stucco streets remain, pleasantly interspersed with greenery. CLEVELAND GARDENS, virtually complete, is another garden square with a stately 'back-to-front' terrace along the N side. In CRAVEN HILL GARDENS the mood is disturbed by COTTINGHAM, a tall eight-story concrete block of private flats, by *Kenneth Frampton* with *Douglas Stephen & Partners*, 1961–2. From here CRAVEN HILL and CRAVEN ROAD picturesquely undulate W–E through the area as the main local thoroughfare, starting with stately stuccoed villas and ending with plenty of small Victorian shops.

QUEENSWAY, the main shopping street further W, starts at the S with a powerful ten-storey tower of flats rising from a lower terrace, 1968–72 by *Owen Luder & Partners*, brick and exposed concrete, quieter than the firm's earlier more overtly brutalist work. To its N the grandly festive C19 stucco frontage of Nos. 36–38, with an archway through to OLYMPIA YARD, a mews crisply refurbished as offices for Chapman Taylor Partners; striped brick with blue window frames. On the W side, further N, WHITELEYS, a shopping precinct created in 1985–9 by the *Building Design Partnership* within the shell of 'the universal provider', the famous store established by William Whiteley, which survived until 1981. Whiteley founded his shop in Westbourne Grove in 1863. Already by 1867 it had expanded to seventeen departments. By 1900 (when he employed a staff of 6,000) there were frontages also to Queensway. Its multifarious enterprises included extensive laundries at Hammersmith (HF) and the growing of produce at Hanworth, Ho (qq.v.). The major rebuilding of 1908–12 by *Belcher & Joass* was intended to be total, although at the N end older buildings remained behind the grand front until the 1980s. Belcher & Joass's store is a metropolitan design never fully assimilated by the neighbourhood. The steel frame is disguised by a stone and granite frontage with two tiers of giant columns binding ground and first floors, and second and third floors. At the SE corner is a generous circular recessed entrance. The reincarnation of the 1980s has incorporated the two original glass-domed and galleried courts, one octagonal, the other circular, as well as the latter's elegant sweeping double staircase. To the N of this the shopping mall continues under a plainer 1980s glazed barrel-vault, successfully blending the luxurious tradition of turn-of-the-century department store with the late C20 fashion for airy atrium buildings. On the top floor, the elaborate plasterwork of the restaurant, added in the 1920s to designs by *Joass*, has also been preserved. A multi-level car park with smart pale blue trimmings is fitted in discreetly behind.

One can return by minor streets W of Queensway to Bayswater Road. In SALEM ROAD, No. 10 is a warehouse transformed into offices and flats by *CZWG*, 1975–6, an early example of postmodern bravado. A cheerfully vulgar exterior of pink-painted brickwork jazzed up by eclectic trimmings (pantiled roofs, curved

ironwork). By Moscow Road to BARK PLACE, with demure mid
C 19 paired villas with arched windows, and so back to Bayswater
Road and ORME SQUARE, which was laid out *c.* 1818, earlier
than anything else in Bayswater. The houses on E and W sides
are still of this date, plain stucco with channelled gound floor. No.
3 has a shallow bow; Nos. 10–11 are narrower, with honeysuckle
balconies. Flanking the square two tripartite compositions with
raised centres, the one on the W the least altered. The purpose
of the MONUMENT with an eagle on a double Tuscan column
has never been elucidated. The square must no doubt be regarded
as a northward feeler of the Kensington Palace purlieus. Further
remnants of modestly scaled early C 19 houses in ST PETERS-
BURGH PLACE (Nos. 17–27); also a later C 19 red brick terrace
in Arts and Crafts style reflecting the mood of Palace Court.

PALACE COURT, the next turning, is the most interesting corner
of Paddington for late Victorian domestic architecture. The street
was a favourite address for aesthetes and collectors *c.* 1890.
The first house to set the tone has alas been demolished: *J. J.
Stevenson*'s Red House of 1871, a precocious example of the
Queen Anne style, already with long segment-headed windows
and Dutch gables. The most notable remaining building is a pair
on the E side, Nos. 10–12, by *J. M. McLaren*, who died young in
1890. It was commissioned by the shipping magnate Sir Donald
Currie for his two married daughters, and appears as a single
house, as the entrance to No. 10 is at the side. It has a wholly
original bow-window with round shafts between the windows,
and friezes of feathery ornament not dissimilar from the work of
H. H. Richardson of Boston. Top floors and chimneys of striped
brick and stone. Both houses had top-lit main stairs (the one in
No. 10 survives, also the main rooms with decorative plaster
ceilings). To its r., No. 2 of 1891, a big, competent, but not
very original job by *Flockhart*, with a corner turret and much
decorative red brick. Facing Bayswater Road is No. 8, the Yellow
House (now Westmorland Hotel and much altered inside), 1892
by *George & Peto* for Percy MacQuoid, the furniture expert and
collector. Terracotta-faced; rather reticent detail. On the W side,
much personality in No. 47 for Wilfred Meynell by *Leonard
Stokes*, 1889; stress on horizontals throughout, red brick and
stone dressings, shallow bay-window on the first floor, firmly
banded in, upper floor quite flat with small windows, gable
absolutely plain except for a few white bands near the top. Most
of the rest are terraces or houses of the 1890s, in the Flemish-
Jacobean spirit, with shaped gables and projecting bays, less
inventive but appropriate in scale.

Ic. The Westbourne Grove and Bishop's Bridge Road area

From Bayswater Road and Palace Court (*see* above) Hereford Road
leads into the stucco world of the mid C 19. PRINCES SQUARE
and LEINSTER SQUARE, the latter attributed by the *Building
News* to *George Wyatt*, are of 1856–9, contemporary with similar
developments in neighbouring North Kensington (Kensington

(K C), Perambulation 2b,i). Terraces of the back-to-front type, as in Tyburnia, opening on to the communal garden. The flanking roads, HEREFORD ROAD and GARWAY ROAD, are distinguished by terraces with undulating bowed fronts, also a Tyburnian device. KENSINGTON GARDENS SQUARE immediately to the E has busier frontages (windows in triplets); it was in progress in 1858.

WESTBOURNE GROVE, running E–W, now an undistinguished shopping street, remained a country lane as late as 1840. Its highlights are No. 26, built as an 'Athenaeum', 1861 by *A. Billing,* stuccoed, with round-headed windows with columns and a good deal of sculpture (musical angels, busts of Milton, Shakespeare, etc.), and Nos. 60–64 (MIDLAND BANK), a grand Edwardian design with three large arches on the upper floor. Opposite, hiding behind old stucco frontages, extensive office and housing redevelopment of 1989 by *Douglas Paskin Associates* (Gable House estates).

N of Westbourne Grove, streets with smaller villas as well as terraces. Among the villas of NEWTON ROAD, No. 32, by *Denys Lasdun,* 1937–8, has quite an original front of painted concrete and russet tiles. Top floor, recessed behind a sun terrace, curved forward in the centre. Living room on the first floor, above garage and service rooms. No one could say the house blends well with its neighbours. However, the radicalism of its architect must have appealed to Paddington Borough Council (*see* below, Hallfield).

Further W the busier CHEPSTOW ROAD leads N with unusually complete stucco terraces, the centres emphasized by giant Corinthian pilasters, and with much pretty ironwork remaining on the E side. In WESTBOURNE PARK ROAD an attractive mixture of villas and terraces around St Stephen's church, a more relaxed layout than in most of Paddington, with picturesque vistas created by the curving streets. The stuccoed idyll is terminated by large borough housing schemes in tough dark brick of which the most ambitious is the BRUNEL ESTATE, close to Westway, begun in the 1960s, completed in 1974, by the *City of Westminster Architect's Department.* A formidable high-density development of 417 dwellings (204 p.p.a.) in huge slabs linked by long ribbon balconies; one tall tower. Like the similar but larger Lisson Green (*see* St Marylebone: Streets 3), built on derelict railway land, with bold landscaping in an effort to mitigate the lumpish forms of the buildings.

Finally, E to the PORCHESTER ROAD area, an interesting study in rehabilitation and renewal. PORCHESTER SQUARE and GLOUCESTER TERRACE, tall stucco terraces, the former of the back-to-front variety (N terrace 1851 by *George Wyatt*), were acquired in a run-down condition from the Church Commissioners in 1955 by the L.C.C. An early, heartening example of successful wholesale rehabilitation instead of the total clearance more common at this time. Gloucester Terrace, the N side of Porchester Square, the Triangle (around a new garden formed above sunken garages, in place of mews alleys), and Gloucester Gardens (also with a new garden behind), were converted to flats by the G.L.C. between 1964 and 1975, with the façades all handsomely restored to their original appearance. The area S of

Porchester Square was given more radical treatment with a lively mixture of buildings by *Farrell & Grimshaw*, 1973–81, proof that the modern package of offices, shops, and housing need be neither ungainly nor inhuman in scale. Half of the s terrace of Porchester Square remains, complemented by an elegantly restrained new terrace in pale brick. The different rhythm of floor levels and windows is tactfully handled. The older part is built out at the back to provide generous s-facing living rooms and patio houses on the roof. A passage leads through to the COLONNADES, a crisply detailed alleyway leading to mews houses faced in yellow and brown tiles, and to a glazed arcade leading to the shops in Porchester Road. The only disappointment is the blank wall along much of Porchester Road. Reticent detailing; the only hint of the two architects' more flamboyant later styles was provided by a temporary building in Bishop's Bridge Road, where a library had been intended: a curvaceous greenhouse using polycarbonate sheeting, for Clifton Nurseries. It was replaced in 1989 by flats by *Percy Thomas Partnership*.

HALLFIELD ESTATE, Paddington's controversial post-war showpiece, extends s from Bishop's Bridge Road. It was designed by *Tecton* in 1947 and executed, after the firm split up the following year, by two of its members, *Drake & Lasdun*. The first phase was completed in 1955. Ten- and six-storey slabs of flats (656 for 2,362 people), forcefully detailed, laid out on a grid at 45 degrees to the surrounding roads, within an informal setting of lawns and trees, deliberately at odds with the stuccoed streetscape of the neighbourhood. The estate was intended as a radical model for the borough of Paddington's post-war rehousing programme. Largely at the insistence of the L.C.C., it was one of the first

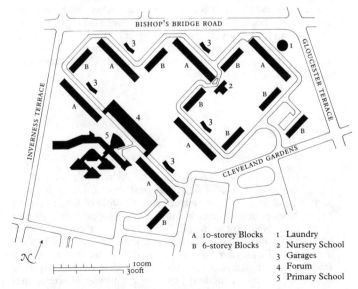

Paddington, Hallfield Estate, plan

post-war estates to include (as in Tecton's work for Finsbury, Is) comprehensive communal amenities such as primary school, shops, laundry, etc., like Tecton's earlier Spa Green, Finsbury (Is). Hallfield also made a determined effort to break with convention in other ways and to show that working-class housing should not be merely utilitarian in appearance – a worthy aim, even if the results are not entirely happy. The aesthetics of the ten- and six-storey slabs are those of abstract art, one of the most confident and rigorous applications of such principles in Britain at the time. Against the ten-storey slabs a powerful grid of rather grim concrete access balconies, artfully composed to minimize the horizontals, and on the other side paired windows set chequerwise (disguising the cross-wall construction, a device which distressed modern movement purists). The patterns are mostly linear, unrelated to interior planning, and underlined by strong colours (cream, maroon, and black). A little contrast is provided on the lower blocks by a few jaunty angled porches and balconies (too few, said those concerned with the comfort of the residents) in the manner that was to be taken up more widely at the time of the Festival of Britain. Despite the untraditional language of the details, the syntax is that of formal planning (as in Tecton's Priory Green estate in Finsbury, Is), subordinating the individual unit to the whole and to some extent sacrificing private convenience to this grand aim. Undeniably, the total design has a visual force and character that distinguish it from much public housing of the 1950s.

105 HALLFIELD SCHOOL. By *Denys Lasdun* of *Drake & Lasdun*, completed 1955. Designed after the first plans for the estate, and deliberately made the hub of the new development, with the assembly hall projecting into the shopping forum. Behind it a long curving spine of two storeys, containing the junior classrooms and the staff rooms and dining rooms of both infant and junior schools. The curved wall with continuous glazing with close-set mullions gives the long low corridors a friendly and intimate character normally lacking in such circulation spaces. Linked to the spine, the lower, more secluded infants' classrooms cluster around little courtyards.

2. N of Westway

2a. Paddington Green, Little Venice, and surrounding area

PADDINGTON GREEN, overwhelmed by the noise of Westway to the s, has no memories of its village past apart from its dignified early C19 church set among trees and a couple of houses on the E side, Nos. 11 and 12, which date back to its wealthier existence in the C18. Next to the hospital (q.v.) at the NE corner a block by *Heery Architects*, 1990. To the w, at the corner of ST MARY'S TERRACE, FLEMING COURT, flats of 1948 by the *Borough of Paddington*, the layout of the better-than-average quality achieved by some of the first post-war rebuilding. Three ranges of varying heights around a grassed court; quite generous balconies. N from here a mixed bag of flats until one reaches the genteel stuccodom of Park Place Villas on the edge of Little Venice.

LITTLE VENICE is given its picturesque character by the meeting of the Paddington Canal and the Regent's Canal (qq.v., Public Buildings). The Regent's Canal, running NE towards the junction of Edgware Road and Maida Vale, is overlooked on either side by MAIDA AVENUE and BLOMFIELD ROAD. Building started here in the 1830s (although the pub, the Hero of Maida, from which the roads take their name, refers to the battle of Maida in Calabria of 1806). Nos. 1–45 Blomfield Road date from 1840–7. The roads form one of the most attractive early Victorian tree-and-stucco landscapes of London. The canal gives it an unusual, somewhat Dutch air. The houses, especially in Blomfield Road, are of no special merit, but the scenic charm is great. The comfortable detached villas were extended S of Maida Avenue along PARK PLACE VILLAS and HOWLEY PLACE in the 1840s. At the W end of Maida Avenue, facing WARWICK AVENUE, was the more ambitious house of the architect *G. L. Taylor* of *c.* 1845–50, now demolished. Its careful antique detailing is echoed on the western houses of Maida Avenue (Nos. 28, 32) and on Nos. 2–16 Warwick Avenue, evidently more expensive houses than those of Blomfield Road. The most elaborate have giant columns *in antis* as their special motif, below a balustraded roof with raised centre. W from here along the N side of the triangular pool the stucco of Blomfield Road continues, but to the S only fragments of the C19 remain. Many of the houses tightly squeezed into the unpropitious area between railway line and canal were swept away from *c.* 1960 in an L.C.C. clearance programme in favour of a mixed policy of restoration and new building. In WARWICK CRESCENT, overlooking the pool, BEAUCHAMP LODGE, a tall mid C19 stuccoed house with Corinthian portico, now a community centre. The rest of the crescent was entirely rebuilt (completed 1966) in an attempt, unusual at the time, to respond to the *genius loci*. The solution adopted was a slightly curved terrace of maisonettes and flats faced in white render (since repainted more colourfully). They have quite a lively rhythm of projecting bay-windows from first-floor level, although the austere details, especially the bleak roof-line, jar sadly in comparison with the C19 neighbours. Nearby, a concrete mural relief by *M. D. Thackwray* recalls Robert Browning, who lived in the area for twenty-five years. Survivors are the beginning of DELAMERE TERRACE, along the S side of the canal, and WESTBOURNE TERRACE ROAD (where the terraces are disguised as separate villas with recessed links), and the E side of BLOMFIELD VILLAS. Further W are the uninspiring four-storey blocks and towers of the *L.C.C.*'s WARWICK and BRINDLEY ESTATES (completed *c.* 1964), scattered around *Street*'s St Mary Magdalene (q.v.), which was preserved as the focus of a new open space called WESTBOURNE GREEN – something of a misconception, as the church was designed to fit into a tight urban setting. The green broadens towards Westway, the opposite, unsatisfactory, approach to the later device of the barrier block shutting off traffic.

N of the canal, the choice from the bridge at Westbourne Green is between the C 19 stucco areas to the E, and the C 20 rebuilding to the W. First the area to the E. Near the W end of BLOMFIELD ROAD, CLIFTON VILLAS leads N. Hidden down a passage, CLIFTON NURSERIES (discerning architectural patrons, cf. Perambulation 1c) boasts a pleasant timber shop by *Jeremy Dixon*, and a hothouse by his former associate *Ken Mackay*, of *Harper Mackay*, 1989. The hothouse is approached by an elegant open butterfly-roofed canopy inspired by Fowler's early C 19 Hungerford Market. Further N, the streets converge on the rebuilt St Saviour's church (q.v.), its austere C 20 brickwork a poignant contrast to the stately stucco villas which were so carefully angled to face its C 19 predecessor. The pair between Clifton Gardens and Warrington Crescent are a tactful rebuilding with replica frontages of 1988 by *David Landaw & Partners*. Between Warrington Crescent and Castellain Road, the COLUMBIA HOTEL, another specially richly decorated pair. Behind this, FORMOSA STREET, a well preserved little service street of shops, and the PRINCE ALFRED, with a sumptuous pub front of *c.* 1900; delicate curved windows, etched glass and tiles, and a good interior. The long tree-lined avenues leading N from here were completed only in the later C 19, when stucco gave way to red brick with stone dressings, and mansion flats replaced houses – see CASTELLAIN ROAD and also further N, in ELGIN AVENUE, BIDDULPH MANSIONS of 1907 and DELAWARE MANSIONS of 1908, both by *Boehmer & Gibbs*. WARRINGTON CRESCENT, dating from *c.* 1865, is still stuccoed; so are CLIFTON GARDENS and the start of RANDOLPH AVENUE further E, which has quite grand terraces (aediculed first-floor windows), restored from 1966, when the Church Commissioners adopted a policy of conversion rather than clearance in this part of their estates. For the area further N *see* Maida Vale, Perambulation 2b.

w of Warwick Avenue, much is of the later C 20. Between the canal and SHIRLAND ROAD, the AMBERLEY ESTATE, begun under the G.L.C., completed by Westminster in 1974–5, long two- and six-storey terraces in pale brick, rather dull, but with plentiful public and private greenery. At the end, an OLD PEOPLE'S HOME, No. 4 Shirland Road, a trim design of concrete blockwork, 1971 by *Renton Howard Wood*. SUTHERLAND AVENUE still has long vistas of busy stuccoed terraces on both sides; the grand EARL OF DERBY near the W end of Amberley Road is of the same vintage. For Harrow Road *see* Perambulation 2c.

2b. Maida Vale and Kilburn

The N tip of Paddington is bounded on the E side by MAIDA VALE, the continuation of Edgware Road. By the mid C 19 it was fringed with the usual paired stucco villas. At the S end its earlier character has been entirely altered by the blocks of flats which began to be built from *c.* 1890, just as in other main roads in well-to-do districts (Kensington High Street, Wellington Road, Finchley Road). The study of London flats can be profitably pursued here from S to N. CUNNINGHAM COURT (1892), ABERDEEN COURT (by *Boehmer & Gibbs*, 1903), CLARENDON COURT (now a hotel), BLOMFIELD COURT (also *Boehmer & Gibbs*, 1903), and ALEXANDRA COURT are all red brick and Edwardian in style, with plenty of terracotta, Baroque doorways, turrets and domes. RODNEY COURT on the E side and the vast CLIVE COURT opposite are similar, even though Clive Court is as late as 1923. CLIFTON COURT (E side), on the other hand, uses sham-Tudor half-timbering ('ill-advised': NP). More modern designs are CROPTHORNE COURT by *Sir Giles Scott,* 1930, with a repeatedly diagonally broken frontage in plain brick above stone and pantile roofs, 1937, and, more in the idiom of the thirties, WELLESLEY COURT by *Frank Scarlett,* 1936. The 1930s designs seem subtle in comparison with the mediocre post-war insertions, the most strident among them the clumsy Y-shaped STUART TOWER, 1964 by *George Wimpey & Co.* for the Church Commissioners.

Further on, one stretch of paired mid C19 villas remains on the E side (Nos. 56–118), facing a long narrow strip redeveloped by the L.C.C.: the MAIDA VALE ESTATE of 1959–64. This is a good example of the characteristic L.C.C. mix of the time: neat six-storey terraces, with lower ranges behind, punctuated at the N end by three eighteen-storey towers set among trees, successfully angled so as to make them appear less bulky. The projecting grid of balconies on alternate floors further reduces the monolithic effect. The towers and lower blocks are separated by an earlier block of flats, HAMILTON COURT, 1937 by *Beresford Marshall.* Nearby, around Maida Vale station in ELGIN AVENUE, an unusual outburst of Ruskinian Gothic polychromy of *c.* 1860–70 in the little shopping parade with corner pub (the LORD ELGIN) and in the entrances to ELGIN MEWS NORTH (rebuilt behind the gateway) and SOUTH. The *pièce de résistance* of this development (begun in 1862 by the builder *Richard Thomas*) is round the corner in RANDOLPH AVENUE, where Nos. 124–164 form a grand symmetrical composition of gault brick embellished with red brick, full of unusual and ornate detail: twisted corner shafts, first-floor windows with terracotta tympana with sculpture and busts in roundels.

Further N in LANARK ROAD are *Jeremy Dixon*'s eight blocks of flats of 1983, an opposite approach in every respect to the L.C.C. towers facing them. They are low-cost private housing (intended for sale to Westminster Council tenants), designed in a villa form derived from the architectural tradition of the locality (cf. his earlier terraces in St Mark's Road, North Kensington, KC). Three storeys above basements, of satisfying proportions, with strongly projecting pediment-shaped gables, and the first- and second-floor windows linked within an arch. Side entrances, with the upper flats reached by external stairs, ingeniously detailed. Finally, an earlier approach to the philanthropic redevelopment of this area – the start of a programme interrupted by the war – is illustrated by DIBDEN HOUSE at the corner of Maida Vale and CARLTON VALE, 1937 by *Caröe & Passmore,* big low-rental brick blocks around a courtyard, plain but formal, built by the Ecclesiastical Commissioners. S of Carlton Vale PADDINGTON RECREATION GROUND, laid out in 1889, imaginatively refurbished in 1987–9 by *Ledward Macdonald.*

KILBURN had in the Middle Ages a priory (of which the only memories are the street names Abbey Road and Priory Road over on the Hampstead side), and in the late C18 one of the innumerable spas that developed on the edge of London; from it remain a prospectus of 1773 of the sulphurous springs of Kilburn, and a commemorative stone at a corner in Station Terrace near Kensal Rise Station (Br). The main landmark now is St Augustine's church (q.v.), surrounded by plentiful grass and trees to N and E, with the surrounding L.C.C. housing of 1960–3 deliberately kept low.

2c. NW Paddington between Harrow Road and Kilburn Lane

HARROW ROAD N of the canal, from E to W, begins on the S side with CARLTON GATE, a vast exclusive precinct, mostly for private flats, built on the large canal-side site released by the demolition of the former Lock Hospital (1841 etc.; later part of St Mary's Hospital Paddington). The first phase, of 1989–90 by *Phippen, Randall Parkes* (SE corner of the site), consists of yellow brick clusters up to nine storeys high in a post-modern idiom, with stepping-back pitched roofs providing the chief visual interest. Also part of this phase are 420 flats for hospital staff, and a MEDICAL CENTRE in Woodfield Road. In total contrast, the area N of Harrow Road around the W end of Elgin Avenue is *G.L.C.* territory, dominated by the two sheer white twenty-two-storey towers of the ELGIN ESTATE – the first ever to have a steel frame clad in lightweight glass-reinforced polyester (1966–9). Further N a few older survivals (WELFORD DAIRIES, at the corner of Shirland Road, c. 1880). E of Fernhead Road is the *G.L.C.*'s LYDFORD ESTATE, low rise of the 1970s, agreeably arranged around squares which are, alas, uncomfortably crammed with railings and parking places. Some of the blocks are of the type with front doors opening on to central decks over garages, here achieved modestly, without any of the grandiose monumentality that such planning sometimes inspired.

On the S side of Harrow Road, KENSAL HOUSE, a handsome stuccoed house set back from the road (first reference 1837); porch with paired columns, heavy cornice on brackets. Extended in 1989 by *Newman Levinson* for Virgin (cf. their offices across the canal at Portobello Dock, North Kensington, KC). Further on, the FLORA HOTEL, C19 polychrome brick, with angular window heads.

The QUEENS PARK ESTATE N of Harrow Road starts at FIRST AVENUE. It is the second of the estates of terraced cottages built by the Artizans, Labourers, and General Dwellings Company (which was also responsible for Shaftesbury Park Battersea, Ww, and Noel Park Wood Green, Hy). The date is 1875 onwards, the developer-builder *Austin*, assisted by *J. G. W. Buckle* and then *Rowland Plumbe*, the size seventy-six acres with more than 2,000 houses. Long terraces with the most minimal of front gardens. Some of the corner houses are emphasized by square turrets with pyramid roofs. The materials are yellow and red brick, the style a minimum Gothic which makes such street names as Fourth

Avenue and Fifth Avenue sound odd. At the corner of First Avenue and Harrow Road the MEETING HALL built by the company, with gabled end and polygonal tower and spire (MURALS inside of Artisans' activities). *Plumbe* also designed the United Reformed Church (q.v.) and an adjoining mission hall (demolished) at the corner of THIRD AVENUE. Further w, the frontages to Harrow Road were replaced in the late 1970s by four-storey terraces by *Yorke Rosenberg & Mardall,* pale brick, with a stepped-back profile. They face a newly opened vista to the canal s of Harrow Road. Further transformations, completed in 1977, have taken place to the N. Behind Second Avenue and Third Avenue, the new QUEENS PARK (the estate, despite its name, was built without any open space). At its E end the somewhat dour red brick JUBILEE SPORTS HALL of 1977. N of this the MOZART ESTATE (*Borough of Westminster,* 1971–7), starting with low red brick terraces matching the scale of the surrounding housing, the s end screened by trees. It is only when one has penetrated further along the pedestrian spine that one realizes the mammoth size of this development, planned with a bewilderingly complicated network of paths and galleries at different levels (734 dwellings at 150 p.p.a., stacked up to eight storeys in the centre). The layout is an extreme example of the over-complex, traffic-segregated system still favoured for large estates at this time, and was judged unsatisfactory as soon as completed. Simple, rather bald elevations, the rectangular outlines broken by a few rounded staircase ends, but softened by plenty of trees. The main path leads to a raised shopping square with a pub, and crosses by a bridge over Dart Street to emerge amid lower blocks in Kilburn Lane. Major remodelling began in 1989 (*Max Lock, Easton, Perlman, King*).

GLOSSARY

Particular types of an architectural element are often defined under the name of the element itself; e.g. for 'dog-leg stair' see STAIR. Literal meanings, where specially relevant, are indicated by the abbreviation *lit.*

For further reference (especially for style terms) the following are a selection of books that can be consulted: *A Dictionary of Architecture* (N. Pevsner, J. Fleming, H. Honour, 1975); *The Illustrated Glossary of Architecture* (J. Harris and J. Lever, 1966); *Recording a Church: An Illustrated Glossary* (T. Cocke, D. Findlay, R. Halsey, E. Williamson, Council of British Archaeology, 1982); *Encyclopedia of Modern Architecture* (edited by Wolfgang Pehnt, 1963); *The Classical Language of Architecture* (J. Summerson, 1964); *The Dictionary of Ornament* (M. Stafford and D. Ware, 1974); *Illustrated Handbook of Vernacular Architecture* (R. W. Brunskill, 1976); *English Brickwork* (A. Clifton Taylor and R. W. Brunskill, 1977); *A Pattern of English Building* (A. Clifton Taylor, 1972).

ABACUS (*lit.* tablet): flat slab forming the top of a capital; *see* Orders (fig. 19).

ABUTMENT: the meeting of an arch or vault with its solid lateral support, or the support itself.

ACANTHUS: formalized leaf ornament with thick veins and frilled edge, e.g. on a Corinthian capital.

ACCUMULATOR TOWER: *see* Hydraulic Power.

ACHIEVEMENT OF ARMS: in heraldry, a complete display of armorial bearings.

ACROTERION (*lit.* peak): plinth for a statue or ornament placed at the apex or ends of a pediment; also, loosely and more usually, both the plinths and what stands on them.

ADDORSED: description of two figures placed symmetrically back to back.

AEDICULE (*lit.* little building): architectural surround, consisting usually of two columns or pilasters supporting a pediment, framing a niche or opening. *See also* Tabernacle.

AFFRONTED: description of two figures placed symmetrically face to face.

AGGER (*lit.* rampart): Latin term for the built-up foundations of Roman roads; also sometimes applied to the ramparts of hillforts or other earthworks.

AGGREGATE: small stones added to a binding material, e.g. in concrete. In modern architecture used alone to describe concrete with an aggregate of stone chippings, e.g. granite, quartz, etc.

AISLE (*lit.* wing): subsidiary space alongside the nave, choir, or transept of a church, or the main body of some other building, separated from it by columns, piers, or posts.

ALTAR: elevated slab consecrated for the celebration of the Eucharist; cf. Communion Table.

ALTARPIECE: *see* Retable.

AMBULATORY (*lit.* walkway): aisle around the sanctuary, sometimes surrounding an apse and therefore semicircular or polygonal in plan.

AMORINI: *see* Putto.

ANGLE ROLL: roll moulding in the angle between two planes, e.g. between the orders of an arch.

ANNULET (*lit*. ring): shaft-ring (*see* Shaft).

ANSE DE PANIER (*lit*. basket handle): basket arch (*see* Arch).

ANTAE: flat pilasters with capitals different from the order they accompany, placed at the ends of the short projecting walls of a portico or of a colonnade which is then called *In Antis*.

ANTEFIXAE: ornaments project-ing at regular intervals above a classical cornice, originally to conceal the ends of roof tiles.

ANTEPENDIUM: *see* Frontal.

ANTHEMION (*lit*. honeysuckle): classical ornament like a honey-suckle flower (*see* fig. 1).

Fig. 1. Anthemion and Palmette Frieze

APRON: raised panel below a win-dow or at the base of a wall monument or tablet, sometimes shaped and decorated.

A.P.S.D.: Architectural Publica-tions Society Dictionary.

APSE: semicircular (i.e. apsidal) extension of an apartment: *see also* Exedra. A term first used of the magistrate's end of a Roman basilica, and thence especially of the vaulted semicircular or polygonal end of a chancel or a chapel.

ARABESQUE: type of painted or carved surface decoration con-sisting of flowing lines and intertwined foliage scrolls etc., generally based on geometrical patterns. Cf. Grotesque.

ARCADE: (1) series of arches sup-ported by piers or columns. *Blind Arcade* or *Arcading*: the same applied to the surface of a wall. *Wall Arcade*: in medieval churches, a blind arcade form-ing a dado below windows. (2) a covered shopping street.

ARCH: for the various forms *see* fig. 2. The term *Basket Arch* re-fers to a basket handle and is sometimes applied to a three-centred or depressed arch as well as to the type with a flat middle. A *Transverse Arch* runs across the main axis of an in-terior space. The term is used especially for the arches be-tween the compartments of tunnel- or groin-vaulting. *Dia-phragm Arch:* transverse arch with solid spandrels spanning an otherwise wooden-roofed in-terior. *Chancel Arch:* w opening from the chancel into the nave. *Nodding Arch:* an ogee arch curving forward from the plane of the wall. *Relieving* (or *Dis-charging*) *Arch:* incorporated in a wall, to carry some of its weight, some way above an opening. *Skew Arch*: spanning responds not diametrically op-posed to one another. *Strainer Arch:* inserted across an open-ing to resist any inward pres-sure of the side members. *See also* Jack Arch; Triumphal Arch.

ARCHITRAVE: (1) formalized lintel, the lowest member of the classical entablature (*see* Orders, fig. 19); (2) moulded frame of a door or window (often borrowing the profile of an architrave in the strict sense). Also *Lugged Architrave*, where the top is prolonged into lugs (*lit*. ears) at the sides; *Shouldered*, where the frame rises vertically at the top angles and returns horizontally at the sides forming shoulders (*see* fig. 3).

ARCHIVOLT: architrave mould-ing when it follows the line of an arch.

ARCUATED: dependent structur-ally on the use of arches or the arch principle; cf. Trabeated.

ARRIS (*lit*. stop): sharp edge where two surfaces meet at an angle.

ASHLAR: masonry of large blocks wrought to even faces and square edges.

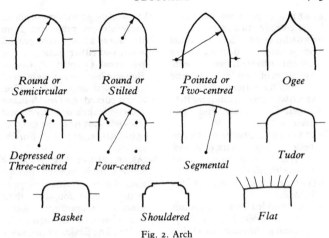

Round or
Semicircular

Round or
Stilted

Pointed or
Two-centred

Ogee

Depressed or
Three-centred

Four-centred

Segmental

Tudor

Basket

Shouldered

Flat

Fig. 2. Arch

Lugged

Shouldered

Fig. 3. Architrave

ASTRAGAL (*lit.* knuckle): moulding of semicircular section often
with bead-and-reel enrichment
(q.v.).

ASTYLAR: term used for an elevation that has no columns or
similar vertical features.

ATLANTES (*lit.* Atlas figures,
from the god Atlas carrying the
globe): male counterparts of
caryatids (q.v.), often in a more
demonstrative attitude of support.

ATRIUM: inner court of a Roman
house; also open court in front
of a church.

ATTACHED COLUMN: *see* Engaged Column.

ATTIC: (1) small top storey, especially within a sloping roof; (2)
in classical architecture, a
storey above the main entablature of the façade, as in a triumphal arch (q.v.).

AUMBRY: recess or cupboard to
hold sacred vessels for the
Mass.

BAILEY: area around the motte or
keep (qq.v.) of a castle, defended by a wall and ditch.

BALANCE BEAM: *see* Canals.

BALDACCHINO: free-standing
canopy, properly of or representing fabric, over an altar
supported by columns. Cf.
Ciborium.

BALLFLOWER: globular flower of
three petals enclosing a small
ball. Typical of the Decorated
style.

BALUSTER (*lit.* pomegranate): a
pillar or pedestal of bellied
form. *Balusters:* vertical supports of this or any other form,
for a handrail or coping, the
whole being called a *Balustrade.*
Blind Balustrade: the same
applied to the surface of a wall.

BARBICAN: outwork defending the entrance to a castle.

BARGEBOARDS: corruption of vergeboards. Boards, often carved or fretted, fixed beneath the eaves of a gable to cover and protect the rafters.

BARROW: burial mound; *see* Bell, Bowl, Disc, Long, and Pond Barrow.

BARTIZAN (*lit.* battlement): corbelled turret, square or round, frequently at a corner, hence *Corner Bartizan.*

BASCULE: hinged part of a lifting bridge.

BASE: moulded foot of a column or other order. For its use in classical architecture *see* Orders (fig. 19).

BASEMENT: lowest, subordinate storey of a building, and hence the lowest part of an elevation, below the main floor.

BASILICA (*lit.* royal building): a Roman public hall; hence an aisled building with a clerestory, most often a church.

BASTION: one of a series of semicircular or polygonal projections from the main wall of a fortress or city, placed at intervals in such a manner as to enable the garrison to cover the intervening stretches of the wall.

BATTER: intentional inward inclination of a wall face.

BATTLEMENT: fortified parapet, indented or crenellated so that archers could shoot through the indentations (crenels or embrasures) between the projecting solid portions (merlons). Also used decoratively.

BAY LEAF: classical ornament of formalized overlapping bay leaves; *see* fig. 4.

Fig. 4. Bay Leaf

BAYS: divisions of an elevation or interior space as defined by any regular vertical features such as arches, columns, windows, etc.

BAY-WINDOW: window of one or more storeys projecting from the face of a building at ground level, and either rectangular or polygonal on plan. A *Canted Bay-window* has a straight front and angled sides. A *Bow Window* is curved. An *Oriel Window* rests on corbels or brackets and does not start from the ground.

BEAD-AND-REEL: *see* Enrichments.

BEAKER FOLK: late Neolithic settlers from western Europe named after a distinctive type of pottery vessel found in their funerary monuments (often round barrows) and their settlements. The Beaker period saw a wider dissemination of metal implements in Britain.

BEAKHEAD: Norman ornamental motif consisting of a row of bird or beast heads with beaks, usually biting into a roll moulding.

BELFRY: (1) bell-turret set on a roof or gable (*see also* Bellcote); (2) chamber or stage in a tower where bells are hung; (3) belltower in a general sense.

BELGAE: Iron Age tribes living in north-eastern Gaul, from which settlers came into Britain between 100 and 55 B.C. and later. These immigrants may not have been numerous, but their impact on material culture in southern Britain was marked.

BELL BARROW: early Bronze Age round barrow in which the mound is separated from its encircling ditch by a flat platform or berm (q.v.).

BELL CAPITAL: *see* fig. 8.

BELLCOTE: belfry as (1) above, usually in the form of a small gabled or roofed housing for the bell(s).

BERM: level area separating ditch from bank on a hill-fort or barrow.

BILLET (*lit.* log or block) FRIEZE: Norman ornament

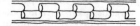

Fig. 5. Billet Frieze

English

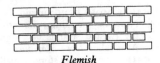

Flemish

Fig. 6. Bond

consisting of small half-cylindrical or rectangular blocks placed at regular intervals (*see* fig. 5).

BIVALLATE: (of a hill-fort) defended by two concentric banks and ditches.

BLIND: *see* Arcade, Balustrade, Portico.

BLOCK CAPITAL: *see* fig. 8.

BLOCKED: term applied to columns etc. that are interrupted by regular projecting blocks, e.g. the sides of a Gibbs surround (*see* fig. 13).

BLOCKING COURSE: plain course of stones, or equivalent, on top of a cornice and crowning the wall.

BOLECTION MOULDING: curved moulding covering the joint between two different planes and overlapping the higher as well as the lower one, used especially in the late C17 and early C18.

BOND: in brickwork, the pattern of long sides (stretchers) and short ends (headers) produced on the face of a wall by laying bricks in a particular way. For the two most common bonds *see* fig. 6.

BOSS: knob or projection usually placed at the intersection of ribs in a vault.

BOW WINDOW: *see* Bay-window.

BOWL BARROW: round barrow surrounded by a quarry ditch. Introduced in late Neolithic times, the form continued until the Saxon period.

BOWSTRING BRIDGE: with arch ribs rising above the roadway, which is suspended from them.

BOX FRAME: (I) timber-framed construction in which vertical and horizontal wall members support the roof. (2) in modern architecture, a box-like form of concrete construction where the loads are taken on cross walls, suitable only for buildings consisting of repetitive small cells. Also called *Crosswall Construction*.

BOX PEW: *see* Pew.

BRACE: subsidiary timber set diagonally to strengthen a timber frame. It can be curved or straight. *See also* Roofs (3) and figs. 24–8.

BRACKET: small supporting piece of stone, etc., to carry a projecting horizontal member. *See also* Console.

BRATTISHING: ornamental cresting on a wall, usually formed of leaves or Tudor flowers or miniature battlements.

BRESSUMER (*lit.* breast-beam): big horizontal beam, usually set forward from the lower part of a building, supporting the wall above.

BROACH: *see* Spire.

BRONZE AGE: in Britain, the period from *c.* 2000 to 600 B.C.

BUCRANIUM: ox skull used decoratively in classical friezes.

BULLSEYE WINDOW: small oval window, set horizontally, cf. Oculus. Also called *Œil de Bœuf*.

BUTTRESS: vertical member projecting from a wall to stabilize it or to resist the lateral thrust of an arch, roof, or vault. For different types used at the corners of a building, especially a tower, *see* fig. 7. A *Flying Buttress* transmits the thrust to a heavy abutment by means of an arch or half-arch.

Fig. 7. Buttresses

CABLE MOULDING: originally a Norman moulding, imitating the twisted strands of a rope. Also called *Rope Moulding*.

CAIRN: a mound of stones usually covering a burial.

CALEFACTORY: room in a monastery where a fire burned for the comfort of the monks. Also called *Warming Room*.

CAMBER: slight rise or upward curve in place of a horizontal line or plane.

CAMES: *see* Quarries.

CAMPANILE: free-standing bell-tower.

CANALS: *Pound Lock*: chamber with gates at each end allowing boats to float from one level to another. *Flash Lock*: removable weir or similar device through which boats pass on a flush of water. Predecessor of the pound lock. *Tidal Gates*: single pair of lock gates allowing vessels to pass when the tide makes a level. *Balance Beam*: beam projecting horizontally for opening and closing lock gates. *Roving Bridge*: carrying a canal towing path from one bank to the other.

CANOPY: projection or hood usually over an altar, pulpit, niche, statue, etc.

CANTED: tilted, generally on a vertical axis to produce an obtuse angle on plan, e.g. of a canted bay-window.

CANTILEVER: horizontal projection (e.g. step, canopy) supported by a downward force behind the fulcrum.

CAPITAL: head or crowning feature of a column or pilaster; for classical types *see* Orders (fig. 19); for medieval types *see* fig. 8.

CARREL: (1) niche in a cloister where a monk could sit to work or read; (2) similar feature in open-plan offices and libraries.

CARTOUCHE: tablet with ornate frame, usually of elliptical shape and bearing a coat of arms or inscription.

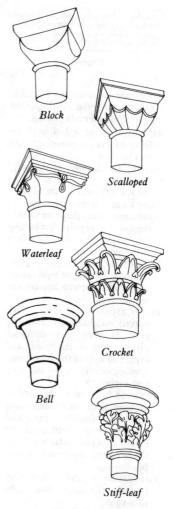

Block

Scalloped

Waterleaf

Crocket

Bell

Stiff-leaf

Fig. 8. Capitals

CARYATIDS (*lit.* daughters of the village of Caryae): female figures supporting an entablature, counterparts of Atlantes (q.v.).

CASEMATE: in military architecture, a vaulted chamber, with embrasures for defence, built into the thickness of the wall of a castle or fortress or projecting from it.

CASEMENT: (1) window hinged at the side; (2) in Gothic architecture, a concave moulding framing a window.

CAST IRON: hard and brittle, cast in a mould to the required shape. *Wrought Iron* is ductile, strong in tension, forged into decorative patterns or forged and rolled into e.g. bars, joists, boiler plates. *Mild Steel* is a modern equivalent, similar but stronger.

CASTELLATED: battlemented.

CAVETTO: concave moulding of quarter-round section.

CELURE OR CEILURE: enriched area of a roof above the rood or the altar.

CENOTAPH (*lit.* empty tomb): funerary monument which is not a burying place.

CENTERING: wooden support for the building of an arch or vault, removed after completion.

CHAMBERED TOMB: Neolithic burial mound with a stone-built chamber and entrance passage covered by an earthen barrow or stone cairn.

CHAMFER (*lit.* corner-break): surface formed by cutting off a square edge, usually at an angle of forty-five degrees. When the plane is concave it is termed a *Hollow Chamfer*. *Double-Chamfer*: applied to each of two recessed arches.

CHANCEL (*lit.* enclosure): E arm or that part of the E end of a church set apart for the use of the officiating clergy, except in cathedrals or monastic churches; cf. Choir.

CHANTRY CHAPEL: chapel, often attached to or inside a church, endowed for the celebration of masses principally for the soul of the founder.

CHEVET (*lit.* head): French term for the E end of a church (chancel and ambulatory with radiating chapels).

CHEVRON: V-shaped motif used in series to decorate a moulding: also (especially when on a single plane) called *Zigzag*.

CHOIR: the part of a church where services are sung. In monastic churches this can occupy the crossing and/or the easternmost bays of the nave.

Also used to describe, more loosely, the E arm of a cruciform church.

CIBORIUM: (1) a fixed canopy of stone or wood over an altar, usually vaulted and supported on four columns, cf. Baldacchino. (2) canopied shrine for the reserved sacrament.

CINQUEFOIL: *see* Foil.

CIST: stone-lined or slab-built grave. If below ground, covered with a protective barrow. It first appears in late Neolithic times and was also used in the Early Christian period in West Britain.

CLADDING: external covering or skin applied to a structure, especially framed buildings (q.v.), for aesthetic or protective purposes.

CLAPPER BRIDGE: bridge made of large slabs of stone, some making rough piers, with longer ones laid on top to make the roadway.

CLASP: *see* Industrialized Building.

CLASSIC: term for the moment of highest achievement of a style.

CLASSICAL: term for Greek and Roman architecture and any subsequent styles derived from it.

CLERESTORY: uppermost storey of the nave walls of a church, pierced by windows. Also applied to high-level windows in domestic architecture.

CLUSTER BLOCK: multi-storey building in which individual blocks of flats cluster round a central service core.

COADE STONE: a ceramic artificial stone made in Lambeth from 1769 to *c.* 1840 by Eleanor Coade († 1821) and her associates.

COB: walling material of clay mixed with straw.

COFFER DAM: a temporary structure to keep out water from an excavation in a river, dock, etc.

COFFERING: arrangement of sunken panels (coffers), square or polygonal, decorating a ceiling, vault, or arch.

COGGING: a decorative course of bricks laid diagonally as an alternative to dentilation (q.v.). Also called *Dogtooth Brickwork*.

COLLAR: *see* Roofs (3) and figs. 25–8.

COLLEGIATE CHURCH: church endowed for the support of a college of priests.

COLONNADE: range of columns supporting an entablature; cf. Arcade.

COLONNETTE: in medieval architecture, a small column or shaft.

COLOSSAL ORDER: *see* Order.

COLUMN: in classical architecture, an upright structural member of round section with a shaft, a capital, and usually a base. *See* Orders (fig. 19).

COLUMN FIGURE: in medieval architecture, carved figure attached to a column or shaft flanking a doorway.

COMMUNION TABLE: unconsecrated table used in Protestant churches in place of an altar (q.v.) for the celebration of Holy Communion.

COMPOSITE: *see* Orders.

COMPOUND PIER: grouped shafts (q.v.), or a solid core surrounded by attached or detached shafts.

CONSOLE: ornamented bracket of compound curved outline (*see* fig. 9).

Fig. 9. Consoles

COPING (*lit.* capping): protective capping course of masonry or brickwork on top of a wall.

CORBEL: projecting block of stone or timber supporting something above. *Corbel Course:* continuous course of projecting stones or bricks

fulfilling the same function. *Corbel Table:* series of corbels to carry a parapet or a wall-plate; for the latter *see* Roofs (3) and figs. 24–7. *Corbelling:* brick or masonry courses built out beyond one another like a series of corbels to support a chimneystack, window, etc.

CORINTHIAN: *see* Orders (fig. 19).

CORNICE: (1) moulded ledge, projecting along the top of a building or feature, especially as the highest member of the classical entablature (*see* Orders, fig. 19); (2) decorative moulding in the angle between wall and ceiling.

CORPS-DE-LOGIS: French term for the main building(s) as distinct from the wings or pavilions.

COTTAGE ORNÉ: an artfully rustic building usually of asymmetrical plan. A product of the late C 18/early C 19 Picturesque.

COUNTERSCARP BANK: small bank on the downhill or outer side of a hill-fort ditch.

COUR D'HONNEUR: entrance court before a house in the French manner, usually with wings enclosing the sides and a screen wall or low range of buildings across the front.

COURSE: continuous layer of stones etc. in a wall.

COVE: a concave moulding on a large scale, e.g. to mask the eaves of a roof or in a *Coved Ceiling*, which has a pronounced cove joining the walls to a flat central panel smaller than the area of the whole ceiling.

CRADLE ROOF: *see* Wagon Roof.

CREDENCE: in a church or chapel, a shelf within or beside a piscina, or for the sacramental elements and vessels.

CRENELLATION: *see* Battlement.

CREST, CRESTING: ornamental finish along the top of a screen, etc.

CRINKLE-CRANKLE WALL: wall undulating in a series of serpentine curves.

CROCKETS (*lit.* hooks), CROCK-
ETING: in Gothic architecture, leafy knobs on the edges
of any sloping feature. *Crocket
Capital: see* Capital (fig. 8).

CROMLECH: word of Celtic origin
still occasionally used of single
free-standing stones ascribed to
the Neolithic or Bronze Age.

CROSSING: in a church, central
space at the junction of the
nave, chancel, and transepts.
Crossing Tower: tower above a
crossing.

CROSS-WINDOWS: windows
with one mullion and one transom (qq.v.).

CROWSTEPS: squared stones set
like steps e.g. on a gable or gateway; *see* Gable (fig. 12).

CRUCKS (*lit.* crooked): pairs of
inclined timbers, usually
curved, which are set at bay-
length intervals in a building
and support the timbers of the
roof (q.v.). The individual
cruck is known as a blade. *Base:*
blades which rise from ground
level to a tie- or collar-beam
upon which the roof truss is carried; in timber buildings they
support the walls. *Full:* blades
rising from ground level to the
apex of a building; they serve as
the main members of a roof
truss and in timber buildings
they support the walls. *Jointed:*
blades formed from more than
one timber; the lower member
normally rises from ground
level and acts as a wall-post; it is
usually elbowed at wall-plate
level and jointed just above.
Middle: blades rising from halfway up the walls to a tie- or
collar-beam upon which the
roof truss is supported. *Raised:*
blades rising from half-way up
the walls to the apex. *Upper:*
blades supported on a tie-beam
and rising to the apex.

CRYPT: underground or half-
underground room usually
below the E end of a church.
Ring Crypt: early medieval
semicircular or polygonal
corridor crypt surrounding the
apse of a church, often associated with chambers for relics.

CUPOLA (*lit.* dome): especially a
small dome on a circular or
polygonal base crowning a
larger dome, roof, or turret.

CURTAIN WALL: (1) connecting
wall between the towers of a
castle; (2) in modern building, a
non-load-bearing external wall
composed of repeating modular
elements applied to a steel-
framed structure.

CURVILINEAR: *see* Tracery.

CUSP: projecting point defining
the foils in Gothic tracery, also
used as a decorative edging to
the soffits of the Gothic arches
of tomb recesses, sedilia, etc.
When used decoratively within
tracery patterns called *Sub-
cusps.*

CYCLOPEAN MASONRY: built
with large irregular polygonal
stones, but smooth and finely
jointed.

CYMA RECTA and CYMA RE-
VERSA: *see* Ogee.

DADO: the finishing of the lower
part of an interior wall (sometimes used to support an
applied order, i.e. a formalized
continuous pedestal). *Dado
Rail:* the moulding along the
top of the dado.

DAGGER: *see* Tracery.

DAIS: raised platform at one end
of a room.

DEC (DECORATED): historical
division of English Gothic
architecture covering the
period from *c.* 1290 to *c.* 1350.
The name is derived from the
type of window tracery used
during the period (*see also*
Tracery).

DEMI-COLUMNS: engaged
columns (q.v.) only half of
whose circumference projects
from the wall. Also called *Half-
Columns.*

DENTIL: small square block used
in series in classical cornices,
rarely in Doric. In brickwork
dentilation is produced by the
projection of alternating head-

ers or blocks along cornices or string courses.

DIAPER (*lit.* figured cloth): repetitive surface decoration of lozenges or squares either flat or in relief. Achieved in brickwork with bricks of two colours.

DIOCLETIAN WINDOW: semicircular window with two mullions, so-called because of its use in the Baths of Diocletian in Rome. Also called a *Thermae Window*.

DISC BARROW: Bronze Age round barrow with an inconspicuous central mound surrounded by a bank and ditch.

DISTYLE: having two columns.

DOGTOOTH: typical E.E. decoration of a moulding, consisting of a series of small pyramids formed by four leaves meeting at a point (*see* fig. 10). *See also* Cogging.

Fig. 10. Dogtooth

DOME: vault of even curvature erected on a circular base. The section can be segmental (e.g. saucer dome), semicircular, pointed, or bulbous (onion dome).

DONJON: *see* Keep.

DORIC: *see* Orders (fig. 19).

DORMER WINDOW: window projecting from the slope of a roof, having a roof of its own and lighting a room within it. *Dormer Head:* gable above this window, often formed as a pediment.

DORTER: dormitory; sleeping quarters of a monastery.

DOUBLE CHAMFER: *see* Chamfer.

DOUBLE PILE: *see* Pile.

DRAGON BEAM: *see* Jetty.

DRESSINGS: the stone or brickwork used about an angle, opening, or other feature worked to a finished face.

DRIPSTONE: moulded stone projecting from a wall to protect the lower parts from water; *see also* Hoodmould.

DRUM: (1) circular or polygonal stage supporting a dome or cupola; (2) one of the stones forming the shaft of a column.

DRYSTONE: stone construction without mortar.

DUTCH GABLE: *see* Gable (fig. 12).

EASTER SEPULCHRE: recess, usually in the N wall of a chancel, with a tomb-chest thought to have been for an effigy of Christ for Easter celebrations.

EAVES: overhanging edge of a roof; hence *Eaves Cornice* in this position.

ECHINUS (*lit.* sea-urchin): ovolo moulding (q.v.) below the abacus of a Greek Doric capital; *see* Orders (fig. 19).

EDGE RAIL: *see* Railways.

E.E. (EARLY ENGLISH): historical division of English Gothic architecture covering the period *c.* 1190–1250.

EGG-AND-DART: *see* Enrichments.

ELEVATION: (1) any side of a building: (2) in a drawing, the same or any part of it, accurately represented in two dimensions.

EMBATTLED: furnished with battlements.

EMBRASURE (*lit.* splay): small splayed opening in the wall or battlement of a fortified building.

ENCAUSTIC TILES: glazed and decorated earthenware tiles used mainly for paving.

EN DELIT (*lit.* in error): term used in Gothic architecture to describe stone shafts whose grain runs vertically instead of horizontally, against normal building practice.

ENGAGED COLUMN: one that is partly merged into a wall or pier. Also called *Attached Column*.

ENGINEERING BRICKS: dense bricks of uniform size, high crushing strength, and low porosity. Originally used mostly for railway viaducts etc.

ENRICHMENTS: in classical architecture, the carved decoration of certain mouldings, e.g. the ovolo (q.v.) with *Egg-and-Dart*, the cyma reversa (q.v.) with *Waterleaf*, the astragal (q.v.) with *Bead-and-Reel*; see fig. 11.

Egg-and-dart

Waterleaf

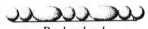

Bead-and-reel

Fig. 11. Enrichments

ENTABLATURE: in classical architecture, collective name for the three horizontal members (architrave, frieze, and cornice) carried by a wall or a column; see Orders (fig. 19).

ENTASIS: very slight convex deviation from a straight line; used on classical columns and sometimes on spires to prevent an optical illusion of concavity.

ENTRESOL: mezzanine storey within or above the ground storey.

EPITAPH (*lit.* on a tomb): inscription in that position.

ESCUTCHEON: shield for armorial bearings.

EXEDRA: apsidal end of an apartment; see Apse.

EXTRADOS: outer curved face of an arch or vault.

EXTRUDED CORNER: right-angled (or circular) projection from the inner angle of a building with advancing wings, usually in C16 or C17 plans.

EYECATCHER: decorative building (often a sham ruin) usually on an eminence to terminate a vista in a park or garden layout.

FASCIA: plain horizontal band, e.g. in an architrave (q.v.) or on a shopfront.

FENESTRATION: the arrangement of windows in a building.

FERETORY: place behind the high altar where the chief shrine of a church is kept.

FESTOON: ornament, usually in relief, in the form of a garland of flowers and/or fruit, suspended from both ends; *see also* Swag.

FIBREGLASS (or glass-reinforced polyester (GRP)): synthetic resin reinforced with glass fibre, formed in moulds, often simulating the appearance of traditional materials. GRC glass-reinforced concrete) is also formed in moulds and used for components (cladding etc.) in industrialized building.

FIELDED: *see* Raised and Fielded.

FILLET: in medieval architecture, a narrow flat band running down a shaft or along a roll moulding. In classical architecture it separates larger curved mouldings in cornices or bases.

FINIAL: decorative topmost feature, e.g. above a gable, spire, or cupola.

FLAMBOYANT: properly the latest phase of French Gothic architecture where the window tracery takes on undulating lines, based on the use of flowing curves.

FLASH LOCK: *see* Canals.

FLÈCHE (*lit.* arrow): slender spire on the centre of a roof. Also called *Spirelet*.

FLEUR-DE-LYS: in heraldry, a formalized lily, as in the royal arms of France.

FLEURON: decorative carved flower or leaf, often rectilinear.

FLOWING: *see* Tracery (Curvilinear).

FLUSHWORK: flint used decoratively in conjunction with dressed stone so as to form patterns: tracery, initials, etc.

FLUTING: series of concave grooves, their common edges sharp (arris) or blunt (fillet).

FOIL (*lit.* leaf): lobe formed by the cusping of a circular or other shape in tracery. *Trefoil* (three), *quatrefoil* (four), *cinquefoil* (five), and *multifoil* express the number of lobes in a shape. *See also* Tracery.

FOLIATE: decorated, especially carved, with leaves.

FORMWORK: commonly called shuttering; the temporary frame of braced timber or metal into which wet concrete is poured. The texture of the framework material depends on the imprint required.

FRAMED BUILDING: where the structure is carried by the framework – e.g. of steel, reinforced concrete, timber – instead of by load-bearing walls.

FRATER: *see* Refectory.

FREESTONE: stone that is cut, or can be cut, in all directions, usually fine-grained sandstone or limestone.

FRESCO: *al fresco:* painting executed on wet plaster. *Fresco secco:* painting executed on dry plaster, more common in Britain.

FRIEZE: (1) the middle member of the classical entablature, sometimes ornamented; *see* Orders (fig. 19). *Pulvinated Frieze* (*lit.* cushioned): frieze of bold convex profile. (2) horizontal band of ornament.

FRONTAL: covering for the front of an altar. When solid called *Antependium*.

FRONTISPIECE: in C16 and C17 buildings the central feature of doorway and windows above it linked in one composition.

GABLE: (1) area of wall, often triangular, at the end of a double-pitch roof; *Dutch Gable*, characteristic of *c.* 1580–1680: *Shaped Gable*, characteristic of *c.* 1620–80 (see fig. 12). *Gablet:* small gable. *See also* Roofs.

GADROONING: ribbed ornament, e.g. on the lid or base of an urn, flowing into a lobed edge.

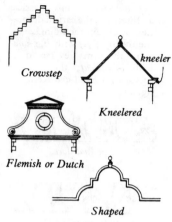

Crowstep

kneeler

Kneelered

Flemish or Dutch

Shaped

Fig. 12. Gables

GALILEE: chapel or vestibule usually at the W end of a church enclosing the main portal(s).

GALLERY: balcony or passage, but with certain special meanings, e.g. (1) upper storey above the aisle of a church, looking through arches to the nave; also called tribune and often erroneously triforium (q.v.); (2) balcony or mezzanine, often with seats, overlooking the main interior space of a building; (3) external walkway, often projecting from a wall.

GALLERY GRAVE: chambered tomb (q.v.) in which there is little or no differentiation between the entrance passage and the actual burial chamber(s).

GALLETING: decorative use of small stones in a mortar course.

GARDEROBE (*lit.* wardrobe): medieval privy.

GARGOYLE: water spout projecting from the parapet of a wall or tower, often carved into human or animal shape.

GAUGED BRICKWORK: soft brick sawn roughly, then rubbed to a smooth, precise (gauged) surface with a stone or another brick. Mostly used for door or window openings. Also called *Rubbed Brickwork*.

GAZEBO (jocular Latin, 'I shall gaze'): lookout tower or raised summer house usually in a park or garden.

GEOMETRIC: historical division of English Gothic architecture covering the period *c.* 1250–90. *See also* Tracery. For another meaning, *see* Stair.

GIANT ORDER: *see* Order.

GIBBS SURROUND: C18 treatment of a door or window surround, seen particularly in the work of James Gibbs (1682–1754) (*see* fig. 13).

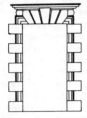

Fig. 13. Gibbs Surround

GIRDER: a large beam. *Box Girder*: of hollow-box section. *Bowed Girder*: with its top rising in a curve. *Plate Girder*: of I-section, made from iron or steel plates. *Lattice Girder*: with braced framework.

GLAZING BARS: wooden or sometimes metal bars separating and supporting window panes.

GOTHIC: the period of medieval architecture characterized by the use of the pointed arch. For its subdivisions *see* E.E., Geometric, Dec, Perp, Flamboyant.

GRANGE (monastic): farm owned and run by members of a religious order.

GRC and GRP: *see* Fibreglass.

GRISAILLE: monochrome painting on walls or glass.

GROIN: sharp edge at the meeting of two cells of a cross-vault; *see* Vault (fig. 35).

GROTESQUE (*lit.* grotto-esque): classical wall decoration in paint or stucco adopted from Roman examples, particularly by Raphael. Its foliage scrolls, unlike arabesque, incorporate ornaments and human figures.

GROTTO: artificial cavern usually decorated with rock- or shell-work, especially popular in the late C17 and C18.

GUILLOCHE: running classical ornament of interlaced bands forming a plait (*see* fig. 14).

Fig. 14. Guilloche

GUNLOOP: opening for a firearm.

GUTTAE: *see* Orders (fig. 19).

HAGIOSCOPE: *see* Squint.

HALF-TIMBERING: archaic term for timber-framing (q.v.). Sometimes used for non-structural decorative timberwork, e.g. in gables etc. of the late C19.

HALL CHURCH: medieval or Gothic Revival church whose nave and aisles are of equal height or approximately so.

HAMMERBEAM: *see* Roofs (fig. 28).

HEADER: *see* Bond.

HENGE: ritual earthwork with a surrounding bank and ditch, the bank being on the outer side.

HERM (*lit.* the god Hermes): male head or bust on a pedestal.

HERRINGBONE WORK: masonry or brickwork in zigzag courses.

HEXASTYLE: *see* Portico.

HILL-FORT: later Bronze Age and Iron Age earthwork enclosed by a ditch and bank system; in the later part of the period the defences multiplied in size and complexity. Varying from about an acre to over fifty acres in area, they are usually built with careful regard to natural elevations or promontories and range in character from powerful strongholds to protected farmsteads.

HIPPED ROOF: *see* Roofs (1) (fig. 23).

HOODMOULD: projecting moulding shown above an arch or lintel to throw off water. When the moulding is horizontal it is often called a *Label. See also* Label Stop.

HUSK GARLAND: festoon of nut-shells diminishing towards the ends.

HYDRAULIC POWER: use of water under high pressure to work machinery. *Accumulator Tower:* to house a hydraulic accumulator which accommodates fluctuations in the flow through hydraulic mains.

HYPOCAUST (*lit.* underburning): Roman underfloor heating system. The floor is supported on pillars and the space thus formed is connected to a flue.

ICONOGRAPHY: interpretation of the subject matter of works of the visual arts.

IMPOST (*lit.* imposition): horizontal moulding at the springing of an arch.

IMPOST BLOCK: block with splayed sides between abacus and capital.

IN ANTIS: *see* Antae.

INDENT: shape chiselled out of a stone to match and receive a brass.

INDUSTRIALIZED BUILDING (system building): the use of a system of manufactured units assembled on site. One of the most popular is the CLASP (Consortium Local Authorities Special Programme) system of light steel framing suitable for schools etc.

INGLENOOK (*lit.* fire-corner): recess for a hearth with provision for seating.

INTARSIA: *see* Marquetry.

INTERCOLUMNIATION: interval between columns.

INTERLACE: decoration in relief simulating woven or entwined stems or bands.

INTRADOS: *see* Soffit.

IONIC: *see* Orders (fig. 19).

IRON AGE: in Britain, the period from *c.* 600 B.C. to the coming of the Romans. The term is also used for those un-Romanized native communities which survived until the Saxon incursions especially beyond the Roman frontiers.

JACK ARCH: shallow segmental vault springing from beams, used for fireproof floors, bridge decks etc.

JAMB (*lit.* leg): one of the vertical sides of an opening.

JETTY: in a timber-framed building, the projection of an upper storey beyond the storey below, made by the beams and joists of the lower storey oversailing the external wall. On their outer ends is placed the sill of the walling for the storey above. Buildings can be jettied on several sides, in which case a *Dragon Beam* is set diagonally at the corner to carry the joists to either side.

JOGGLE: mason's term for joining two stones to prevent them slipping or sliding by means of a notch in one and a corresponding projection in the other.

KEEL MOULDING: moulding whose outline is in section like that of the keel of a ship (fig. 15).

Fig. 15. Keel Moulding

KEEP: principal tower of a castle. Also called *Donjon.*

KENTISH CUSP: *see* Tracery.

KEY PATTERN: *see* fig. 16.

KEYSTONE: central stone in an arch or vault.

Fig. 16. Key Pattern

KINGPOST: *see* Roofs (3) and fig. 24.

KNEELER: horizontal projecting stone at the base of each side of a gable on which the inclined coping stones rest. *See* Gable (fig. 12).

LABEL: *see* Hoodmould.

LACED WINDOWS: windows pulled visually together by strips of brickwork, usually of a different colour, which continue vertically the lines of the vertical parts of the window surround. Typical of *c.* 1720.

LACING COURSE: one or more bricks serving as horizontal reinforcement to flint, cobble, etc., walls.

LADY CHAPEL: chapel dedicated to the Virgin Mary (Our Lady).

LANCET WINDOW: slender single-light pointed-arched window.

LANTERN: (1) circular or polygonal turret with windows all round crowning a roof or a dome. (2) windowed stage of a crossing tower lighting the interior of a church.

LANTERN CROSS: churchyard cross with lantern-shaped top usually with sculptured representations on the sides of the top.

LAVATORIUM: in a monastery, a washing place adjacent to the refectory.

LEAN-TO: *see* Roofs (1).

LESENE (*lit.* a mean thing): pilaster without base or capital. Also called *Pilaster Strip*.

LIERNE: *see* Vault (fig. 36).

LIFT: in a gasholder, one of the telescopic sections.

LIGHT: compartment of a window defined by the mullions.

LINENFOLD: Tudor panelling where each panel is ornamented with a conventional representation of a piece of linen laid in vertical folds.

LINTEL: horizontal beam or stone bridging an opening.

LOGGIA: gallery open along one side of a building, usually arcaded or colonnaded. It may be a separate structure, usually in a garden.

LONG BARROW: unchambered Neolithic communal burial mound, often wedge-shaped in plan, with the burial and occasional other structures massed at the broader end, from which the mound itself tapers in height; quarry ditches flank the mound.

LONG-AND-SHORT WORK: quoins consisting of stones placed with the long side alternately upright and horizontal, especially in Saxon building.

LOUVRE: (1) opening, often with lantern over, in the roof of a building to let the smoke from a central hearth escape; (2) one of a series of overlapping boards or panes of glass placed in an opening to allow ventilation but keep the rain out.

LOWER PALAEOLITHIC: *see* Palaeolithic.

LOWSIDE WINDOW: window set lower than the others in a chancel side wall, usually towards its W end.

LOZENGE: diamond shape.

LUCARNE (*lit.* dormer): small gabled opening in a roof or spire.

LUGGED: *see* Architrave.

LUNETTE (*lit.* half or crescent moon): (1) semicircular window; (2) semicircular or crescent-shaped area of wall.

LYCHGATE (*lit.* corpse-gate): roofed wooden gateway at the entrance to a churchyard for the reception of a coffin.

LYNCHET: long terraced strip of soil accumulating on the downward side of prehistoric and medieval fields due to soil creep from continuous ploughing along the contours.

MACHICOLATIONS (*lit.* mashing devices): in medieval military architecture, a series of openings under a projecting parapet between the corbels that support it, through which missiles can be dropped.

MAJOLICA: ornamented glazed earthenware.

MANOMETER or STANDPIPE TOWER: containing a column of water to regulate pressure in water mains.

MANSARD: *see* Roofs (1) (fig. 23).

MARQUETRY: inlay in various woods. Also called *Intarsia*.

MATHEMATICAL TILES: facing tiles with one face moulded to look like a header or stretcher, most often hung on laths applied to timber-framed walls to make them appear brick-built.

MAUSOLEUM: monumental building or chamber usually intended for the burial of members of one family.

MEGALITHIC (*lit.* of large stones): archaeological term referring to the use of such stones, singly or together.

MEGALITHIC TOMB: massive stone-built Neolithic burial chamber covered by an earth or stone mound.

MERLON: *see* Battlement.

MESOLITHIC: 'Middle Stone' Age; the post-glacial period of hunting and fishing communities dating in Britain from *c.* 8000 B.C. to the arrival of the Neolithic (q.v.) communities, with whom they must have considerably overlapped in many areas.

METOPES: spaces between the triglyphs in a Doric frieze; *see* Orders (fig. 19).

MEZZANINE: (1) low storey between two higher ones; (2) low upper storey within the height of a high one, not extending over its whole area. *See also* Entresol.

MILD STEEL: *see* Cast Iron.

MISERERE: *see* Misericord.

MISERICORD (*lit.* mercy): shelf placed on the underside of a hinged choir stall seat which,

when turned up, supported the occupant during long periods of standing. Also called *Miserere*.

MODILLIONS: small consoles (q.v.) at regular intervals along the underside of the cornice of the Corinthian or Composite orders.

MODULE: in industrialized building (q.v.), a predetermined standard size for co-ordinating the dimensions of components of a building with the spaces into which they have to fit.

MOTTE: steep mound forming the main feature of C11 and C12 castles.

MOTTE-AND-BAILEY: post-Roman and Norman defence system consisting of an earthen mound (motte) topped with a wooden tower within a bailey, with enclosure ditch and palisade, and with the rare addition of an internal bank.

MOUCHETTE: *see* Tracery (fig. 33).

MOULDING: ornament of continuous section; *see* e.g. Cavetto, Ogee, Ovolo, Roll.

MULLION: vertical member between the lights in a window opening.

MULTI-STOREY: modern term denoting five or more storeys. *See* Cluster, Slab, and Point Blocks.

MULTIVALLATE: (of a hill-fort) defended by three or more concentric banks and ditches.

MUNTIN: vertical part in the framing of a door, screen, panelling, etc., butting into or stopped by the horizontal rails.

NAILHEAD MOULDING: E.E. ornamental motif consisting of small pyramids regularly repeated (*see* fig. 17).

NARTHEX: enclosed vestibule or

Fig. 17. Nailhead Moulding

covered porch at the main entrance to a church.

NAVE: the body of a church w of the crossing or chancel which may be flanked by aisles (q.v.).

NECESSARIUM: *see* Reredorter.

NEOLITHIC: term applied to the New Stone Age, dating in Britain from the appearance of the first settled farming communities from the continent *c.* 4000–3500 B.C. until the beginning of the Bronze Age. *See also* Mesolithic.

NEWEL: central post in a circular or winding staircase; also the principal post where a flight of stairs meets a landing. *See* Stair (fig. 30).

NICHE (*lit.* shell): vertical recess in a wall, sometimes for a statue.

NIGHT STAIR: stair by which monks entered the transept of their church from their dormitory to celebrate night services.

NOGGING: *see* Timber-framing.

NOOK-SHAFT: shaft set in the angle of a pier or respond or wall, or the angle of the jamb of a window or doorway.

NORMAN: *see* Romanesque.

NOSING: projection of the tread of a step. A *Bottle Nosing* is half-round in section.

NUTMEG MOULDING: consisting of a chain of tiny triangles placed obliquely.

OBELISK: tapering pillar of square section at the top and ending pyramidally.

OCULUS: circular opening or window in a wall or vault; cf. Bullseye Window.

ŒIL DE BŒUF: *see* Bullseye Window.

OGEE: double curve, bending first one way and then the other. Applied to mouldings, also called *Cyma Recta.* A reverse ogee moulding with a double curve also called *Cyma Reversa* (*see* fig. 18). *Ogee* or *Ogival Arch: see* fig. 2.

ORATORY: (1) small private

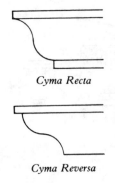

Cyma Recta

Cyma Reversa

Fig. 18. Ogee Mouldings

chapel in a church or a house; (2) church of the Oratorian Order.

ORDER: (1) upright structural member formally related to others, e.g. in classical architecture a column, pilaster, or anta; (2) especially in medieval architecture, one of a series of recessed arches and jambs forming a splayed opening. *Giant* or *Colossal Order:* classical order whose height is that of two or more storeys of a building.

ORDERS: in classical architecture, the differently formalized versions of the basic post-and-lintel (column and entablature) structure, each having its own rules for design and proportion. For examples of the main types *see* fig. 19. In the *Composite*, the capital combines Ionic volutes with Corinthian foliage. *Superimposed Orders:* term for the use of Orders on successive levels, usually in the upward sequence of Tuscan, Doric, Ionic, Corinthian.

ORIEL: *see* Bay-window.

OVERDOOR: *see* Sopraporta.

OVERHANG: *see* Jetty.

OVERSAILING COURSES: *see* Corbel (Corbelling).

OVERTHROW: decorative fixed arch between two gatepiers or above a wrought-iron gate.

OVOLO MOULDING: wide convex moulding.

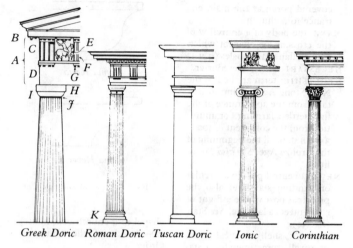

Greek Doric   Roman Doric   Tuscan Doric   Ionic   Corinthian

Fig. 19. Orders: A Entablature; B Cornice; C Frieze; D Architrave; E Metope;
F Triglyph; G Guttae; H Abacus; I Capital; J Echinus; K Base

PALAEOLITHIC: 'Old Stone' Age; the first period of human culture, commencing in the Ice Age and immediately prior to the Mesolithic; the Lower Palaeolithic is the older phase, the Upper Palaeolithic the later.

PALIMPSEST (*lit.* erased work): re-use of a surface. (1) of a brass: where a metal plate has been re-used by turning over and engraving on the back; (2) of a wall painting: where one overlaps and partly obscures an earlier one.

PALLADIAN: architecture following the examples and principles of Andrea Palladio (1508–80).

PALMETTE: classical ornament like a symmetrical palm shoot; for illustration *see* fig. 1.

PANELLING: wooden lining to interior walls, made up of vertical members (muntins q.v.) and horizontals (rails) framing panels (*see* linenfold; raised and fielded). Also called *Wainscot*.

PANTILE: roof tile of curved S-shaped section.

PARAPET: wall for protection at any sudden drop, e.g. on a bridge or at the wall-head of a castle; in the latter case it protects the *Parapet Walk* or wall walk. Also used to conceal a roof.

PARCLOSE: *see* Screen.

PARGETTING (*lit.* plastering): in timber-framed buildings, plasterwork with patterns and ornaments either moulded in relief or incised on it.

PARLOUR: in a monastery, room where monks were permitted to talk to visitors.

PARTERRE: level space in a garden laid out with low, formal beds of plants.

PATERA (*lit.* plate): round or oval ornament in shallow relief, especially in classical architecture.

PAVILION: (1) ornamental building for occasional use in a garden, park, sports ground, etc.; (2) projecting subdivision of some larger building, often at an angle or terminating wings.

PEBBLEDASHING: *see* Rendering.

PEDESTAL: in classical architecture, a tall block carrying an order, statue, vase, etc.

PEDIMENT: in classical architecture, a formalized gable derived from that of a temple, also used over doors, windows, etc. For variations of type *see* fig. 20.

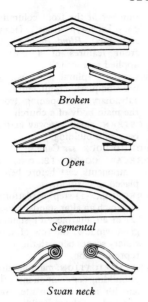

Broken

Open

Segmental

Swan neck

Fig. 20. Pediments

PEEL (*lit.* palisade): stone tower, e.g. near the Scottish–English border.

PENDANT: decorative feature hanging from a vault or ceiling, usually ending in a boss.

PENDENTIVE: spandrel formed as part of a hemisphere between arches meeting at an angle, supporting a drum or dome (*see* fig. 21).

PENTHOUSE: subsidiary structure with a lean-to roof; in modern architecture, a separately roofed structure on top of a multi-storey block.

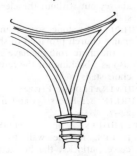

Fig. 21. Pendentive

PERISTYLE: in classical architecture, a range of columns all round a building, e.g. a temple, or an interior space, e.g. a courtyard.

PERP (PERPENDICULAR): historical division of English Gothic architecture covering the period from *c.* 1335–50 to *c.* 1530. The name is derived from the upright tracery panels then used (*see* Tracery).

PERRON: *see* Stair.

PEW: loosely, seating for the laity outside the chancel. Strictly an enclosed seat. *Box Pew*: with equal high sides, entered by a door.

PIANO NOBILE: principal floor, usually with a ground floor or basement underneath and a lesser storey overhead.

PIAZZA: open space surrounded by buildings; in the C17 and C18 used erroneously to mean an arcaded ground floor, especially adjoining or around an open space.

PIER: large masonry or brick support, usually for an arch. *See also* Compound Pier.

PIETRA DURA: ornamental or pictorial inlay by means of thin slabs of stone.

PILASTER: flat representation of a classical column in shallow relief against a wall. *Pilastrade*: series of pilasters, equivalent to a colonnade. *Pilaster Strip*: *see* Lesene.

PILE: row of rooms. The important use of the term is in *Double Pile*, describing a house that is two rows thick.

PILLAR: free-standing upright member of any section, not conforming to one of the Orders.

PILLAR PISCINA: free-standing piscina on a pillar.

PILOTIS: French term used in modern architecture for pillars or stilts that carry a building to first-floor level leaving the ground floor open.

PINNACLE: tapering finial, e.g. on a buttress or the corner of a tower, sometimes decorated with crockets.

PISCINA: basin for washing the communion or mass vessels, provided with a drain; generally set in or against the wall to the S of an altar.

PLAISANCE: summer house, pleasure house near a mansion.

PLATE RAIL: *see* Railways.

PLATEWAY: *see* Railways.

PLINTH: projecting courses at the foot of a wall or column, generally chamfered or moulded at the top.

PODIUM: continuous raised platform supporting a building. In modern architecture often a large block of two or three storeys beneath a multi-storey block covering a smaller area.

POINT BLOCK: high block of housing in which the flats fan out from a central core of lifts, staircases, etc.

POINTING: exposed mortar jointing of masonry or brickwork. The finished form is of various types, e.g. *Flush Pointing, Recessed Pointing*.

POND BARROW: rare Bronze Age barrow type consisting of a circular depression, usually paved, and containing a number of cremation burials.

POPPYHEAD: carved ornament of leaves and flowers, generally in the form of a fleur-de-lys, as a finial for the end of a bench or stall.

PORCH: covered projecting entrance to a building.

PORTAL FRAME: single-storey frame comprising two uprights rigidly connected to a beam or pair of rafters, particularly to support a roof.

PORTCULLIS: gate constructed to rise and fall in vertical grooves at the entry to a castle.

PORTICO: a porch, open on one side at least, and enclosed by a row of columns which also support the roof and frequently a pediment. When the front of it is on the same plane as the front of the building it is described as a *Portico in Antis* (Antae q.v.). Porticoes are described by the number of the front columns, e.g. Tetrastyle (four), Hexastyle (six). *Blind Portico:* the front features of a portico applied to a wall.

PORTICUS (plural porticūs): in pre-Conquest architecture, a subsidiary cell opening from the main body of a church.

POSTERN: small gateway at the back of a building.

POUND LOCK: *see* Canals.

PRECAST CONCRETE: concrete components cast before being placed in position.

PREDELLA: (1) step or platform on which an altar stands; hence (2) in an altarpiece or stained glass window, the row of subsidiary scenes beneath the main representation.

PREFABRICATION: manufacture of buildings or components off-site for assembly on-site. *See also* Industrialized Building.

PRESBYTERY: (1) part of a church lying E of the choir where the main altar is placed; (2) a priest's residence.

PRESTRESSED CONCRETE: *see* Reinforced Concrete.

PRINCIPAL: *see* Roofs (3) and figs. 24, 27.

PRIORY: religious house whose head is a prior or prioress, not an abbot or abbess.

PROSTYLE: with a free-standing row of columns in front.

PULPIT: raised and enclosed platform used for the preaching of sermons. *Three-decker pulpit*: with reading desk below and clerk's desk below the reading desk. *Two-decker pulpit*: as above, but without the clerk's stall.

PULPITUM: stone screen in a major church provided to shut off the choir from the nave and also as a backing for the return choir stalls.

PULVINATED: *see* Frieze.

PURLIN: *see* Roofs (3) and figs. 24–7.

PUTHOLES or PUTLOCK HOLES: in the wall to receive putlocks, the horizontal timbers on which scaffolding boards rest. They are often not filled in after construction is complete.

PUTTO: small naked boy (plural: putti. Also called *Amorini*.)

QUADRANGLE: rectangular inner courtyard in a large building.

QUARRIES (*lit.* squares): (1) square (or diamond-shaped) panes of glass supported by lead strips which are called *Cames*; (2) square floor-slabs or tiles.

QUATREFOIL: *see* Foil.

QUEENPOSTS: *see* Roofs (3) and fig. 26.

QUIRK: sharp groove to one side of a convex moulding, e.g. beside a roll moulding, which is then said to be quirked.

QUOINS: dressed stones at the angles of a building. They may be alternately long and short, especially when rusticated.

RADIATING CHAPELS: chapels projecting radially from an ambulatory or an apse; *see* Chevet.

RAFTER: *see* Roofs (3) and figs. 24–8.

RAGGLE: groove cut in masonry, especially to receive the edge of glass or roof-covering.

RAIL: *see* Muntin.

RAILWAYS: *Edge Rail:* rail on which flanged wheels can run, as in modern railways. *Plate Rail:* L-section rail for plain unflanged wheels, guidance being provided by the upstanding flange on the rail. *Plateway:* early railway using plate rails. *Sleeper Block:* stone block to support rail in lieu of timber sleeper.

RAISED AND FIELDED: of a wooden panel with a raised square or rectangular central area (field) surrounded by a narrow moulding.

RAKE: slope or pitch.

RAMPART: wall of stone or earth surrounding a hill-fort, castle, fortress, or fortified town.

Rampart Walk: path along the inner face of a rampart.

REBATE: rectangular section cut out of a masonry edge to receive a shutter, door, window, etc.

REBUS: a heraldic pun, e.g. a fiery cock as a badge for Cockburn.

REEDING: series of convex mouldings; the reverse of fluting.

REFECTORY: dining hall of a monastery or similar establishment. Also called *Frater*.

REINFORCED CONCRETE: concrete reinforced with steel rods to take the tensile force. A later development is *Prestressed Concrete*, which incorporates artificially-tensioned steel tendons.

RENDERING: the process of covering outside walls with a uniform surface or skin for protection from the weather. *Stucco*, originally a fine lime plaster worked to a smooth surface, is the finest rendered external finish, characteristic of many late C18 and C19 classical buildings. It is usually painted. *Cement Rendering* is a cheaper and more recent substitute for stucco, usually with a grainy texture and often left unpainted. In more simple buildings the wall surface may be roughly *Lime-plastered* (and then whitewashed), or covered with plaster mixed with a coarse aggregate such as gravel. This latter is known as *Roughcast*. A variant, fashionable in the early C20, is *Pebbledashing:* here the stones of the aggregate are kept separate and are thrown at the wet plastered wall to create a textured effect.

REPOUSSÉ: decoration of metalwork by relief designs, formed by beating the metal from the back.

REREDORTER (*lit.* behind the dormitory): medieval euphemism for latrines in a monastery. Also called *Necessarium*.

REREDOS: painted and/or sculptured screen behind and above an altar.

RESPOND: half-pier or half-column bonded into a wall and carrying one end of an arch. It usually terminates an arcade.

RETABLE: a picture or piece of carving standing at the back of an altar, usually attached to it. Also called an *Altarpiece*.

RETROCHOIR: in a major church, the space between the high altar and an E chapel, like a square ambulatory.

REVEAL: the inward plane of a jamb, between the edge of an external wall and the frame of a door or window that is set in it.

RIB-VAULT: *see* Vault.

RINCEAU (*lit.* little branch) or ANTIQUE FOLIAGE: classical ornament, usually on a frieze, of leafy scrolls branching alternately to left and right (*see* fig. 22).

Fig. 22. Rinceau

RISER: vertical face of a step.

ROCK-FACED: term used to describe masonry which is cleft to produce a natural rugged appearance.

ROCOCO (*lit.* rocky): latest phase of the Baroque style, current in most Continental countries between *c.* 1720 and *c.* 1760, and showing itself in Britain mainly in playful, scrolled decoration, especially plasterwork.

ROLL MOULDING: moulding of part-circular section used in medieval architecture.

ROMANESQUE: that style in architecture (in England often called Norman) which was current in the C11 and C12 and preceded the Gothic style. (Some scholars extend the use of the term Romanesque back to the C10 or C9.) *See also* Saxo-Norman.

ROMANO-BRITISH: general term applied to the period and cultural features of Britain affected by the Roman occupation of the C1–5 A.D.

ROOD: cross or crucifix flanked by the Virgin and St John, usually over the entry into the chancel, on a beam (*Rood Beam*) or painted. The *Rood Screen* beneath it may have a *Rood Loft* along the top, reached by a *Rood Stair*.

ROOFS: (1) *Shape:* for the external shapes and terms used to describe them *see* fig. 23. *Helm:* roof with four inclined faces joined at the top, with a gable at the foot of each. *Hipped* (fig. 23): roof with sloped instead of vertical ends. *Lean-to:* roof with one slope only, built against a vertical wall: term also applied to the part of the building such a roof covers. *Mansard* (fig. 23): roof with a double slope, the lower one larger and steeper than the upper. *Saddleback:* the name given to a normal pitched roof when used over a tower. *See also* Wagon Roof.

(2) *Construction:* Roofs are generally called after the principal structural component, e.g. *crown-post, hammerbeam, king-post*, etc. See below under *Elements* and figs. 24–8.

A *single-framed* roof is constructed with no main trusses. The rafters may be fixed to a wall-plate or ridge, or longitudinal timbers may be absent altogether. A *common rafter* roof is one in which pairs of rafters are not connected by a collar-beam. A *coupled rafter* roof is one in which the rafters are connected by collar-beams.

A *double-framed* roof is constructed with longitudinal members such as purlins. Generally there are principals or principal rafters supporting the longitudinal members and dividing the length of the roof into bays.

(3) *Elements: Ashlar piece.* A short vertical timber connecting an inner wall-plate or timber pad to a rafter above.

Braces. Subsidiary timbers set diagonally to strengthen the frame. *Arched braces:* a pair of

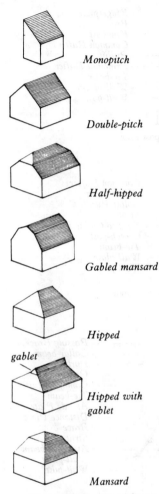

Monopitch

Double-pitch

Half-hipped

Gabled mansard

Hipped

gablet

Hipped with gablet

Mansard

Fig. 23. Roofs: external forms

transverse timber connecting a pair of rafters or principals at a height between the apex and the wall-plate.

Crown-post. A vertical timber standing centrally on a tie-beam and supporting a collar purlin. Longitudinal braces usually rise from the crown-post to the collar purlin. When the truss is open lateral braces generally rise to the collar-beam, and when the truss is closed they go down to the tie-beam.

Hammerbeams. Horizontal brackets projecting at wall-plate level on opposite sides of the wall like a tie-beam with the centre cut away. The inner ends carry vertical timbers called hammerposts and braces to a collar-beam.

Hammerpost. A vertical timber set on the inner end of a hammer-beam to support a purlin; it is braced to a collar-beam above.

Kingpost. A vertical timber standing centrally on a tie- or collar-beam and rising to the apex of the roof where it supports a ridge.

Principals. The pair of inclined lateral timbers of a truss which carry common rafters. Usually they support side purlins and their position corresponds to the main bay division of the space below.

Purlin. A horizontal longitudinal timber. *Collar purlin:* a single central timber which carries collar-beams and is itself supported by crown-posts. *Side purlins:* pairs of timbers occurring some way up the slope of the roof. They carry the common rafters and are supported in a number of ways: *butt purlins* are tenoned into either side of the principals; *clasped purlins* rest on queenposts or are carried in the angles between the principals and the collar; *laid-on purlins* lie on the backs of the principals; *trenched purlins* are trenched into the backs of the principals.

curved braces forming an arch, usually connecting the wall or post below with the tie- or collar-beam above. *Passing braces:* straight braces of considerable length, passing across other members of the truss. *Scissor braces:* a pair of braces which cross diagonally between pairs of rafters or principals. *Wind-braces:* short, usually curved braces connecting side purlins with principals. They are sometimes decorated with cusping.

Collar-beam. A horizontal

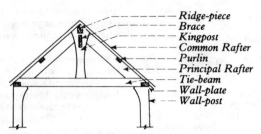

Ridge-piece
Brace
Kingpost
Common Rafter
Purlin
Principal Rafter
Tie-beam
Wall-plate
Wall-post

Fig. 24. Kingpost Roof

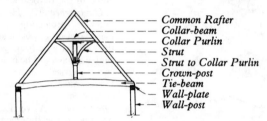

Common Rafter
Collar-beam
Collar Purlin
Strut
Strut to Collar Purlin
Crown-post
Tie-beam
Wall-plate
Wall-post

Fig. 25. Crown-post Roof

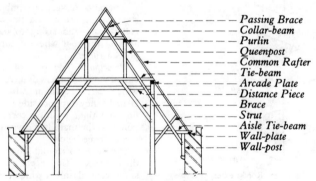

Passing Brace
Collar-beam
Purlin
Queenpost
Common Rafter
Tie-beam
Arcade Plate
Distance Piece
Brace
Strut
Aisle Tie-beam
Wall-plate
Wall-post

Fig. 26. Queenpost Roof

Queenposts. A pair of vertical, or near-vertical, timbers placed symmetrically on a tie-beam and supporting side purlins.

Rafters. Inclined lateral timbers sloping from wall-top to apex and supporting the roof covering. *Common rafters:* rafters of equal scantling found along the length of a roof or sometimes interrupted by main trusses containing principal rafters. *Principal rafters:* rafters which act as principals but also serve as common rafters.

Ridge, ridge-piece. A horizontal, longitudinal timber at the apex of a roof supporting the ends of the rafters.

Sprocket. A short timber placed on the back and at the foot of a rafter to form projecting eaves.

Strut. A vertical or oblique timber which runs between two members of a roof truss but

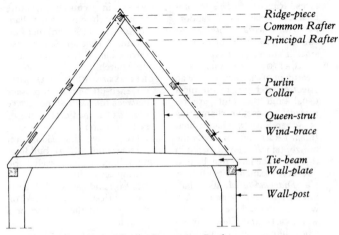

Ridge-piece
Common Rafter
Principal Rafter

Purlin
Collar

Queen-strut
Wind-brace

Tie-beam
Wall-plate

Wall-post

Fig. 27. Queen-strut Roof

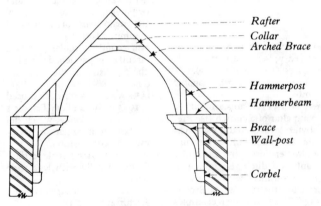

Rafter
Collar
Arched Brace

Hammerpost
Hammerbeam

Brace
Wall-post

Corbel

Fig. 28. Hammerbeam Roof

does not directly support longitudinal timbers.

Tie-beam. The main horizontal, transverse timber which carries the feet of the principals at wall-plate level.

Truss. A rigid framework of timbers which is placed laterally across the building to carry the longitudinal roof timbers which support the common rafters.

Wall-plate. A timber laid longitudinally on the top of a wall to receive the ends of the rafters. In a timber-framed building the posts and studs of the wall below are tenoned into it.

ROPE MOULDING: *see* Cable Moulding.

ROSE WINDOW: circular window with tracery radiating from the centre; cf. Wheel Window.

ROTUNDA: building circular in plan.

ROUGHCAST: *see* Rendering.

ROVING BRIDGE: *see* Canals.

RUBBLE: masonry whose stones are wholly or partly in a rough state. *Coursed Rubble:* of coursed stones with rough

faces. *Random Rubble:* of uncoursed stones in a random
pattern. *Snecked Rubble* has
courses frequently broken by
smaller stones (snecks).

RUSTICATION: exaggerated
treatment of masonry to give an
effect of strength. In the most
usual kind the joints are recessed by V-section chamfering
or square-section channelling.
Banded Rustication has only the
horizontal joints emphasized in
this way. The faces may be flat,
but there are many other forms,
e.g. *Diamond-faced*, like shallow pyramids, *Vermiculated*,
with a stylized texture like
worm-casts, and *Glacial* (frost-
work) like icicles or stalactites.
Rusticated Columns may have
their joints and drums treated
in any of these ways.

SACRISTY: room in a church for
sacred vessels and vestments.

SADDLEBACK: *see* Roofs (1).

SALTIRE CROSS: with diagonal
limbs.

SANCTUARY: (1) area around the
main altar of a church (*see* Presbytery); (2) sacred site consisting of wood or stone up-
rights enclosed by a circular
bank and ditch. Beginning in
the Neolithic, they were elaborated in the succeeding Bronze
Age. The best known examples
are Stonehenge and Avebury.

SARCOPHAGUS (*lit.* flesh-
consuming): coffin of stone or
other durable material.

SAUCER DOME: *see* Dome.

SAXO-NORMAN: transitional
Romanesque style combining
Anglo-Saxon and Norman fea-
tures, current *c.* 1060–1100.

SCAGLIOLA: composition imitating marble.

SCALLOPED CAPITAL: *see* fig. 8.

SCARP: artificial cutting away of
the ground to form a steep
slope.

SCOTIA: a hollow moulding,
especially between tori (q.v.) on
a column base.

SCREEN: in a church, structure
usually at the entry to the chancel; *see* Rood (Screen) *and* Pulpitum. A *Parclose Screen* separates a chapel from the rest of
the church.

SCREENS or SCREENS PASSAGE:
screened-off entrance passage
between the hall and the service
rooms of a medieval, C16, or
early C17 house.

SECTION: two-dimensional representation of a building,
moulding, etc., revealed by
cutting across it.

SEDILIA (singular *sedile*): seats
for the priests (usually three) on
the S side of the chancel of a
church.

SET-OFF: *see* Weathering.

SGRAFFITO: scratched pattern,
often in plaster.

SHAFT: vertical member of round
or polygonal section, especially
the main part of a classical
column. *Shaft-ring:* ring like a
belt round a circular pier or a
circular shaft attached to a pier,
characteristic of the C12 and
C13.

SHARAWAGGI: a term, first used
c. 1685 in Sir William Temple's
Essay on Gardening, which describes an irregular or asymmetrical composition.

SHEILA-NA-GIG: female fertility
figure, usually with legs wide
open.

SHOULDERED: *see* Arch (fig. 2),
Architrave (fig. 3).

SHUTTERED CONCRETE: *see*
Formwork.

SILL: (1) horizontal member at
the bottom of a window- or
door-frame; (2) the horizontal
member at the base of a timber-
framed wall into which the
posts and studs (q.v.) are
tenoned.

SLAB BLOCK: rectangular multi-
storey block of housing or
offices.

SLATE-HANGING: covering of
overlapping slates on a wall,
which is then said to be *slate-
hung. Tile-hanging* is similar.

SLEEPER BLOCK: *see* Railways.

SLYPE: covered way or passage,

especially in a cathedral or monastic church, leading E from the cloisters between transept and chapter house.

SNECKED: see Rubble.

SOFFIT: (*lit.* ceiling): underside of an arch (also called *Intrados*), lintel, etc. *Soffit Roll:* roll moulding on a soffit.

SOLAR (*lit.* sun-room): upper living room or withdrawing room of a medieval house, accessible from the high table end of the hall.

SOPRAPORTA (*lit.* over door): painting or relief above the door of a room, usual in the C17 and C18.

SOUNDING-BOARD: horizontal board or canopy over a pulpit; also called *Tester*.

SOUTERRAIN: underground stone-lined passage and chamber.

S.P.A.B.: Society for the Protection of Ancient Buildings.

SPANDRELS: roughly triangular spaces between an arch and its containing rectangle, or between adjacent arches. In modern architecture the non-structural panels under the windows in a framed building.

SPERE: a fixed structure which serves as a screen at the lower end of an open medieval hall between the hall proper and the screens passage. It has a wide central opening, often with a movable screen, between posts and short screen walls. The top member is often the tie-beam of the roof truss above; screen and truss are then called a *Spere-truss*.

SPIRE: tall pyramidal or conical feature built on a tower or turret. *Broach Spire:* starting from a square base, then carried into an octagonal section by means of triangular faces. The *Splayed-foot Spire* is a variation of the broach form, found principally in the south-eastern counties, in which the four cardinal faces are splayed out near their base, to cover the corners, while oblique (or intermediate)

faces taper away to a point. *Needle Spire:* thin spire rising from the centre of a tower roof, well inside the parapet: when of timber and lead often called a *Spike*.

SPIRELET: see Flèche.

SPLAY: chamfer, usually of a reveal.

SPRING or SPRINGING: level at which an arch or vault rises from its supports. *Springers:* the first stones of an arch or vaulting-rib above the spring.

SQUINCH: arch or series of arches thrown across an angle between two walls to support a superstructure of polygonal or round plan over a rectangular space, e.g. a dome, a spire (*see* fig. 29).

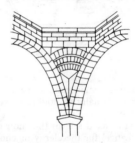

Fig. 29. Squinch

SQUINT: an aperture in a wall or through a pier usually to allow a view of an altar of a church otherwise obscured. Also called *Hagioscope*.

STAIRS: *see* fig. 30. A *Dog-leg Stair* has parallel flights rising alternately in opposite directions, without an open well. *Newel Stair:* ascending round a central supporting newel (q.v.), called a *Spiral Stair* or *Vice* when in a circular shaft. *Well Stair:* term applied to any stair contained in an open well, but generally to one that climbs up three sides of a well with corner landings, e.g. the *timber-framed newel stair*, common from the C17 on. *Flying Stair:* cantilevered from the wall of a stairwell, without newels. *Geometric Stair:* flying stair whose inner edge describes a curve. *Perron (lit.* of stone):

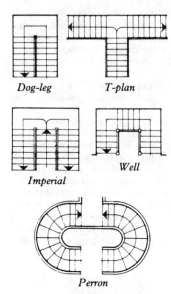

Dog-leg   T-plan

Imperial   Well

Perron

Fig. 30. Stairs

external stair leading to a door-way, usually of double-curved plan.

STALL: fixed seat in the choir or chancel for the clergy or choir (cf. Pew). Usually with arm rests. Often framed together like a bench.

STANCHION: upright structural member, of iron or steel or rein-forced concrete.

STANDPIPE TOWER: see Mano-meter.

STEAM ENGINES: *Atmospheric*: the earliest type, worked by the vacuum created when low pressure steam was condensed in the cylinder, as developed by Thomas Newcomen. *Beam En-gine:* with a large pivoted beam moved in an oscillating fashion by the piston. It may drive a fly wheel or be *Non-rotative*. Differ-ent types are the *Watt* and *Cor-nish* engines (single-cylinder), the *Compound* (two cylinder) or *Triple Expansion* (three cylin-ders). The cylinders may be mounted in various ways.

STEEPLE: tower together with a spire, lantern or belfry.

STIFF-LEAF: type of E.E. foliage decoration. *Stiff-leaf Capital: see* fig. 8.

STOP: plain or decorated blocks terminating mouldings or cham-fers in stone or wood, or at the end of labels, hoodmoulds, or string courses.

STOUP: vessel for the reception of holy water, usually placed near a door.

STRAINER: *see* Arch.

STRAPWORK: late C16 and C17 decoration, resembling strap-like interlaced bands of leather.

STRETCHER: *see* Bond.

STRING COURSE: horizontal stone course or moulding pro-jecting from the surface of a wall.

STRINGS: two sloping members which carry the ends of the treads and risers of a staircase. Closed strings enclose the treads and risers; in the later open string staircase the steps project above the strings.

STUCCO (*lit.* plaster): *see* Render-ing.

STUDS: subsidiary vertical tim-bers of a timber-framed wall or partition.

STYLOBATE: solid platform on which a colonnade stands.

SUSPENSION BRIDGE: bridge suspended from cables or chains draped from towers. *Stay-suspension* or *Stayed-cantilever Bridge*: supported by diagonal stays from towers or pylons.

SWAG (*lit.* bundle): ornament suspended like a festoon (q.v.), but usually representing cloth.

SYSTEM BUILDING: *see* Indus-trialized Building.

TABERNACLE (*lit.* tent): (1) canopied structure, especially on a small scale, to contain the reserved sacrament or a relic; (2) architectural frame, e.g. of a statue on a wall or free-standing, with flanking orders. In classical architecture also cal-led an *Aedicule*.

TABLE TOMB: a memorial slab raised on free-standing legs.

TABLET FLOWER: medieval ornament of a four-leaved flower with a raised or sunk centre.

TAS-DE-CHARGE: the lower courses of a vault or arch laid horizontally.

TERMINAL FIGURE: pedestal or pilaster which tapers towards the bottom, usually with the upper part of a human figure growing out of it. Also called *Term*.

TERRACOTTA: moulded and fired clay ornament or cladding, usually unglazed.

TESSELLATED PAVEMENT: mosaic flooring, particularly Roman, consisting of small *Tesserae*, i.e. cubes of glass, stone, or brick.

TESTER (*lit.* head): flat canopy over a tomb and especially over a pulpit, where it is also called a *Sounding-board*.

TESTER TOMB: C16 or C17 type with effigies on a tomb-chest beneath a tester, either free-standing (tester with four or more columns), or attached to a wall (half tester) with columns on one side only.

TETRASTYLE: see Portico.

THERMAE WINDOW (*lit.* of a Roman bath); see Diocletian Window.

THREE-DECKER PULPIT: see Pulpit.

TIDAL DOORS: see Canals.

TIE-BEAM: see Roofs (3) and figs. 24–7.

TIERCERON: see Vault (fig. 36).

TILE-HANGING: see Slate-hanging.

TIMBER-FRAMING: method of construction where walls are built of interlocking vertical and horizontal timbers. The spaces are filled with non-structural walling of wattle and daub, lath and plaster, brick-work (known as nogging), etc. Sometimes the timber is covered over by plaster, boarding laid horizontally (weather-boarding q.v.), or tiles.

TOMB-CHEST: chest-shaped stone coffin. *See also* Table Tomb, Tester Tomb.

TORUS: large convex moulding usually used on a column base.

TOUCH: soft black marble quarried near Tournai.

TOURELLE: turret corbelled out from the wall.

TOWER HOUSE: compact medieval fortified house with the main hall raised above the ground and at least one more storey above it. The type survives in odd examples into the C16 and C17.

TRABEATED: depends structurally on the use of the post and lintel; cf. Arcuated.

TRACERY: intersecting ribwork in the upper part of a window, or used decoratively in blank arches, on vaults, etc. (1) *Plate tracery: see* fig. 31(*a*). Early form of tracery where decoratively shaped openings are cut through the solid stone infilling in a window head. (2) *Bar tracery:* a form introduced into England *c.* 1250. Intersecting ribwork made up of slender shafts, continuing the lines of the mullions of windows up to a decorative mesh in the head of the win-

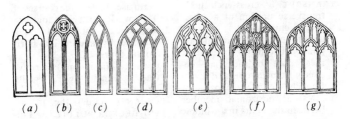

(*a*)   (*b*)   (*c*)   (*d*)   (*e*)   (*f*)   (*g*)

Fig. 31. Tracery

dow. The types of bar tracery are: *Geometrical tracery: see* fig. 31(*b*). Tracery characteristic of *c.* 1250–1310 consisting chiefly of circles or foiled circles. *Y-tracery: see* fig. 31(*c*). Tracery consisting of a mullion which branches into two forming a Y shape; typical of *c.* 1300. *Intersecting tracery: see* fig. 31(*d*). Tracery in which each mullion of a window branches out into two curved bars in such a way that every one of them is drawn with the same radius from a different centre. The result is that every light of the window is a lancet and every two, three, four, etc., lights together form a pointed arch. This also is typical of *c.* 1300. *Reticulated tracery: see* fig. 31(*e*). Tracery typical of the early C 14 consisting entirely of circles drawn at top and bottom into ogee shapes so that a net-like appearance results. *Panel tracery: see* fig. 31 (*f*) and (*g*). Perp tracery, which is formed of upright straight-sided panels above lights of a window. *Dagger:* Dec tracery motif; *see* fig. 32. *Kentish* or *Split Cusp:* cusp split into a fork. *Mouchette:* curved version of the dagger form, especially popular in the early C 14; *see* fig. 33.

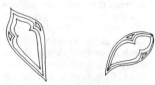

Fig. 32. Dagger Fig. 33. Mouchette

TRANSEPT (*lit.* cross-enclosure): transverse portion of a cross-shaped church.

TRANSITIONAL: transitional phase between two styles, used most often for the phase between Romanesque and Early English (*c.* 1175–*c.* 1200).

TRANSOM: horizontal member between the lights in a window opening.

TREAD: horizontal part of the step of a staircase. The *Tread End* may be carved.

TREFOIL: *see* Foil.

TRIBUNE: *see* Gallery (1).

TRIFORIUM (*lit.* three openings): middle storey of a church treated as an arcaded wall passage or blind arcade, its height corresponding to that of the aisle roof.

TRIGLYPHS (*lit.* three-grooved tablets): stylized beam-ends in the Doric frieze, with metopes between; *see* Orders (fig. 19).

TRIUMPHAL ARCH: type of Imperial Roman monument whose elevation supplied a motif for many later classical compositions (*see* fig. 34).

Fig. 34. Triumphal Arch

TROPHY: sculptured group of arms or armour as a memorial of victory.

TRUMEAU: central stone mullion supporting the tympanum of a wide doorway. *Trumeau Figure:* carved figure attached to a trumeau (cf. Column Figure).

TRUSS: braced framework, spanning between supports. *See also* Roofs.

TUDOR FLOWER: late Gothic ornament of a flower with square flat petals or foliage.

TUMBLING or TUMBLING-IN: term used to describe courses of brickwork laid at right angles to the slope of a gable and forming triangles by tapering into horizontal courses.

TUMULUS (*lit.* mound): barrow.

TURRET: small tower, usually attached to a building.

TUSCAN: *see* Orders (fig. 19).

TWO-DECKER PULPIT: *see* Pulpit.

TYMPANUM (*lit.* drum): as of a drum-skin, the surface between a lintel and the arch above it or within a pediment.

UNDERCROFT: vaulted room, sometimes underground, below the main upper room.

UNIVALLATE: (of a hill-fort) defended by a single bank and ditch.

UPPER PALAEOLITHIC: *see* Palaeolithic.

VAULT: ceiling of stone formed like arches (sometimes imitated in timber or plaster); *see* fig. 35. *Tunnel-* or *Barrel-Vault:* the simplest kind of vault, in effect a continuous semicircular arch. *Groin-Vaults* (which are usually called *Cross-Vaults* in classical architecture) have four curving

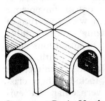

Cross- or Groin-Vault   *Tunnel- or Barrel-Vault*   *Pointed Barrel-Vault*

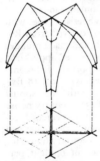
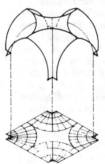

Fig. 35. Vaults

Quadripartite Rib-Vault   *Fan-Vault*

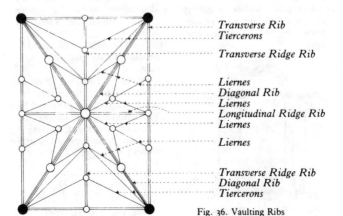

Transverse Rib
Tiercerons
Transverse Ridge Rib

Liernes
Diagonal Rib
Liernes
Longitudinal Ridge Rib
Liernes

Liernes

Transverse Ridge Rib
Diagonal Rib
Tiercerons

Fig. 36. Vaulting Ribs

triangular surfaces produced by the intersection of two tunnel-vaults at right angles. The curved lines at the intersections are called groins. In *Quadripartite Rib-Vaults* the four sections are divided by their arches or ribs springing from the corners of the bay. *Sexpartite Rib-Vaults*, most often used over paired bays, have an extra pair of ribs which spring from between the bays and meet the other four ribs at the crown of the vault. The main types of rib are shown in fig. 36: *transverse ribs, wall ribs, diagonal ribs*, and *ridge ribs*. *Tiercerons* are extra, decorative ribs springing from the corners of a bay. *Liernes* are decorative ribs in the crown of a vault which are not linked to any of the springing points. In a *Stellar Vault* the liernes are arranged in a star formation as in fig. 36. *Fan-Vaults* are peculiar to English Perpendicular architecture in consisting not of ribs and infilling but of halved concave cones with decorative blind tracery carved on their surfaces.

VAULTING-SHAFT: shaft leading up to the springer of a vault.

VENETIAN WINDOW: a form derived from an invention by Serlio, also called a Serlian or Palladian window. The same motif is used for other openings (*see* fig. 37).

VERANDA(H): shelter or gallery against a building, its roof supported by thin vertical members.

VERMICULATION: *see* Rustication.

VERNACULAR ARCHITECTURE: design by one without any training in design, guided by a series of conventions built up in a locality (Brunskill).

VESICA: oval with pointed head and foot, usually of a window or tracery.

VESTIBULE: anteroom or entrance hall.

VICE: *see* Stair.

VILLA: originally (1) a Romano-British farm or country house. The term is one of convenience and covers a wide spectrum of sites, ranging from humble farmsteads to sumptuous mansions associated with large estates. Various architectural traditions, including both classical and vernacular, are evident in villas, but all display some pretension towards fundamental Roman standards. (2) the C16 Venetian type with office wings, derived from Roman models and made grander by Palladio's varied application of a central portico. It became an important type in C18 Britain, often with the special meaning of (3) a country house which is not a principal residence. Gwilt (1842) defined the villa as 'a country house for the residence of opulent persons'. But devaluation had already begun, and the term also implied, as now, (4) a more or less pretentious suburban house.

VITRIFIED: bricks or tiles fired to produce a darkened glassy surface.

VITRUVIAN OPENING: door or window which diminishes towards the top, as advocated by Vitruvius, book IV, chapter VI.

VITRUVIAN SCROLL: classical running ornament of curly waves (*see* fig. 38).

Fig. 37. Venetian Window

Fig. 38. Vitruvian Scroll

VOLUTES: spiral scrolls on the front and back of a Greek Ionic capital, also on the sides of a Roman one. *Angle Volute:* pair of volutes turned outwards to meet at the corner of a capital. Volutes were also used individually as decoration in C17 and C18 architecture.

VOUSSOIRS: wedge-shaped stones forming an arch.

WAGON ROOF: roof in which closely set rafters with arched braces give the appearance of the inside of a canvas tilt over a wagon. Wagon roofs can be panelled or plastered (ceiled) or left uncovered. Also called *Cradle Roof.*

WAINSCOT: *see* Panelling.

WALL MONUMENT: substantial monument attached to the wall and often standing on the floor. *Wall Tablets* are smaller in scale with the inscription as the major element.

WALL-PLATE: *see* Roofs (3) and figs. 24–7.

WARMING ROOM: *see* Calefactory.

WATERHOLDING BASE: type of early Gothic base in which the upper and lower mouldings are separated by a hollow so deep as to be capable of retaining water.

WATERLEAF CAPITAL: *see* fig. 8.

WATER WHEELS: described by the way the water is fed on to the wheel. *Overshot:* over the top. *Pitchback:* on to the top but falling backwards. *Breastshot:* mid-height, falling and passing beneath. An *undershot* wheel is turned by the momentum of the water passing beneath. In a *Water Turbine* water is fed under pressure through a vaned wheel within a casing.

WEALDEN HOUSE: medieval timber-framed house of distinctive form. It has a central open hall flanked by bays of two storeys. The end bays are jettied to the front, but a single roof covers the whole building, thus producing an exceptionally wide overhang to the eaves in front of the hall.

WEATHERBOARDING: overlapping horizontal boards, covering a timber-framed wall, most common after the mid C18.

WEATHERING: inclined, projecting surface to keep water away from wall and joints below. Also called *Set-off.*

WEEPERS: small figures placed in niches along the sides of some medieval tombs. Also called *Mourners.*

WHEEL WINDOW: circular window with radiating shafts like the spokes of a wheel. *See also* Rose Window.

WROUGHT IRON: *see* Cast Iron.

INDEX OF ARTISTS

Architects' practices are indexed under the first surname of their title.
*N.B.: The index groups references under the most recent form of a practice's
title* except where there have been major changes of name.

INDEX OF STREETS AND BUILDINGS

This index has entries for all major buildings mentioned by name in the introduction and gazetteer (all churches and public buildings, and the more important buildings included in the perambulations) and streets mentioned in the gazetteer. For place names see separate index of borough and localities.

References in **bold** type are to the page of the gazetteer on which the street or building receives its principal discussion. References in *italic* type are to buildings which no longer stand. References in roman type within an italic entry are to remaining parts or furnishings of a vanished building.

Broadways, High Roads, and High Streets are indexed together, followed by their individual names. The following types of buildings are indexed under the appropriate main heading: Baptist Chapels and Churches, Baths and Swimming Pools, Cemeteries, Cinemas, Civic Centres, Community Centres, Courts, Fire Stations, Friends' Meeting Houses, Health Centres, Libraries, Manor Houses, Methodist Churches, Municipal Buildings and Council Offices, Police Stations, Post Offices, Power Stations, Presbyterian Churches, Rectories, Synagogues, Telephone Exchanges, Town Halls, United Reformed Churches, Vicarages (major), Water Towers, Waterworks and Pumping Stations, Workhouses.

The following abbreviations are employed for boroughs:

Br	Brent	Ho	Hounslow
Ea	Ealing	Hw	Harrow
HF	Hammersmith and Fulham	KC	Kensington and Chelsea
Hi	Hillingdon	Wm	Westminster (outer)

INDEX OF BOROUGHS AND LOCALITIES

COMPLETE LIST OF TITLES
1991

Bedfordshire and the County of Huntingdon and Peterborough *1st ed. 1968 Nikolaus Pevsner*

Berkshire *1st ed. 1966 Nikolaus Pevsner*

Buckinghamshire *1st ed. 1960 Nikolaus Pevsner, revision in progress*

Cambridgeshire *1st ed. 1954, 2nd ed. 1970, Nikolaus Pevsner*

Cheshire *1st ed. 1971 Nikolaus Pevsner and Edward Hubbard*

Cornwall *1st ed. 1951 Nikolaus Pevsner, 2nd ed. 1970 revised Enid Radcliffe*

Cumberland and Westmorland *1st ed. 1967 Nikolaus Pevsner*

Derbyshire *1st ed. 1953 Nikolaus Pevsner, 2nd ed. 1978 revised Elizabeth Williamson*

Devon *1st ed. in 2 vols. 1952 Nikolaus Pevsner, 2nd ed. 1989 Bridget Cherry and Nikolaus Pevsner*

Dorset *1st ed. 1972 John Newman and Nikolaus Pevsner*

Durham, County *1st ed. 1953 Nikolaus Pevsner, 2nd ed. 1983 revised Elizabeth Williamson*

Essex *1st ed. 1954 Nikolaus Pevsner, 2nd ed. 1965 revised Enid Radcliffe*

Gloucestershire: The Cotswolds *1st ed. 1970, 2nd ed. 1979, David Verey*

Gloucestershire: The Vale and the Forest of Dean *1st ed. 1970, 2nd ed. 1976 reprinted with corrections 1980, David Verey*

Hampshire and the Isle of Wight *1st ed. 1967 Nikolaus Pevsner and David Lloyd, revision in progress*

Herefordshire *1st ed. 1963 Nikolaus Pevsner*

Hertfordshire *1st ed. 1953 Nikolaus Pevsner, 2nd ed. 1977 revised Bridget Cherry*

Kent, North East and East *1st ed. 1969, 3rd ed. 1983, John Newman*

Kent, West, and the Weald *1st ed. 1969, 2nd ed. 1976 reprinted with corrections 1980, John Newman*

Lancashire, North *1st ed. 1969 Nikolaus Pevsner*

Lancashire, South *1st ed. 1969 Nikolaus Pevsner*

Leicestershire and Rutland *1st ed. 1960 Nikolaus Pevsner, 2nd ed. 1984 revised Elizabeth Williamson*

Lincolnshire *1st ed. 1964 Nikolaus Pevsner and John Harris, 2nd ed. 1989 revised Nicholas Antram*

London 1: The Cities of London and Westminster *1st ed. 1957 Nikolaus Pevsner, 3rd ed. 1973 revised Bridget Cherry*

London 2: Except the Cities of London and Westminster *1st ed. 1952 Nikolaus Pevsner, being revised, expanded, and reissued under the following three titles*

London 2: South *1st ed. 1983 Bridget Cherry and Nikolaus Pevsner*

London 3: North West *1st ed. 1991, Bridget Cherry and Nikolaus Pevsner*

London 4: North and North East *1st ed. in progress, Bridget Cherry and Nikolaus Pevsner*

Middlesex *1st ed. 1951 Nikolaus Pevsner, revision in progress for incorporation into the above two titles*

Norfolk, North East, and Norwich *1st ed. 1962 Nikolaus Pevsner, revision in progress*

Norfolk, North West and South *1st ed. 1962 Nikolaus Pevsner, revision in progress*

Northamptonshire *1st ed. 1961 Nikolaus Pevsner, 2nd ed. 1973 revised Bridget Cherry*

Northumberland *1st ed. 1957 Nikolaus Pevsner with Ian A. Richmond, revision in progress*